The Short Story

AN INTRODUCTION

AN INTRODUCTION

Wilfred Stone
Professor of English
Stanford University

Nancy Huddleston Packer
Professor of English
Stanford University

Robert Hoopes
Professor of English
University of Massachusetts

Second Edition

McGraw-Hill Book Company

New York   St. Louis   San Francisco   Auckland   Bogotá
Hamburg   Johannesburg   London   Madrid   Mexico   Montreal   New Delhi
Panama   Paris   São Paulo   Singapore   Sydney   Tokyo   Toronto

This book was set in Times Roman by The Total Book (BCI).
The editor was Phillip A. Butcher;
the production supervisor was Phil Galea.
The cover was designed by Joseph Gillians;
the cover photograph was taken by Al Green.
R. R. Donnelley & Sons Company was printer and binder.

THE SHORT STORY
An Introduction

3 4 5 6 7 8 9 0 DOCDOC 8 9 8 7 6 5

ISBN 0-07-061693-0

See Additional Acknowledgments on pages 609–610.
Copyrights included on this page by reference.

Library of Congress Cataloging in Publication Data
Main entry under title:

The Short story.

    Bibliography: p.
    Includes index.
    1. Short stories. I. Stone, Wilfred Healey,
date   . II. Packer, Nancy Huddleston.
III. Hoopes, Robert.
PN6120.2.S52 1983   808.83′1   82-8925
ISBN 0-07-061693-0   AACR2

Contents

Preface   ix
Introduction   1

PART I. **BEGINNINGS: FORMS OF EARLY STORIES**

Myth and Legend   24
  Myth: *How Things Got Started*   24
  The First Book of Moses, Called Genesis   26
  Kiowa Creation Myth (Trans. Scott Momaday)   29

  Legend: *How Things Went On*   30
  Some Kiowa Legends (Trans. Scott Momaday)   30
  Seneca Myth: "The Origin of Stories," as told to
     Jeremiah Curtin   31
  Arthurian Legend: Sir Thomas Malory's
     The Great Tournament   34

Fable, Parable, Exemplum, and Allegory   38
  Fables: Aesop   39
  Parables: Matthew 25   40
  Exemplum: From St. Gregory the Great, *Dialogues*
     (Trans. Odo John Zimmerman)   41
  Allegory: From John Bunyan (1628–1688), *The Pilgrim's Progress*   42

                                                                             v

A Variety of Secular Tales   43
  Novella: Giovanni Boccaccio (1313–1375), *Decameron*. The Third Day,
    Novell I (Trans. John Florio? 1625)   45
  Fabliau: Geoffrey Chaucer (1340?–1400), *The Miller's Tale*
    (Trans. Nevill Coghill)   52
  Fairy Tale: *The Blue Beard* (Trans. Robert Samber, 1729)   67

PART II. **THE SHORT STORY PROPER:**
            THE FIRST AGE

Nathaniel Hawthorne (1804–1864)   71
  The Minister's Black Veil   72
Nikolai Vassilevitch Gogol (1809–1852)   80
  The Overcoat   81
Edgar Allan Poe (1809–1849)   101
  The Fall of the House of Usher   102
Ivan Turgenev (1818–1883)   113
  Raspberry Spring (Trans. Bernard Guilbert Guerney)   114
Herman Melville (1819–1891)   121
  Bartleby, the Scrivener: A Story of Wall Street   122
Gustave Flaubert (1821–1880)   144
  A Simple Heart (Trans. Robert Baldick)   145
Ambrose Bierce (1842–1914?)   166
  An Occurrence at Owl Creek Bridge   167
Henry James (1843–1916)   173
  The Beast in the Jungle   174
Guy de Maupassant (1850–1893)   200
  A Country Outing (Trans. Andrew R. MacAndrew)   201
  The Avenger (Trans. Andrew R. MacAndrew)   209
Anton Chekhov (1860–1904)   212
  Ninochka: A Love Story (Trans. Ann Dunnigan)   213
  Heartache (Trans. Avrahm Yarmolinsky)   216
  The Lady with the Pet Dog (Trans. Robert Payne)   220
Edith Wharton (1862–1937)   230
  Roman Fever   231
Stephen Crane (1871–1900)   239
  The Open Boat   240

PART III. **THE GOLDEN AGE**

Thomas Mann (1875–1955)   256
  Mario and the Magician (Trans. H. T. Lowe-Porter)   257
Sherwood Anderson (1876–1941)   283
  I Want to Know Why   284
E. M. Forster (1879–1970)   289
  Dr Woolacott   290
James Joyce (1882–1941)   298
  A Painful Case   300

Virginia Woolf (1882–1941) 305
The Mark on the Wall 306
Franz Kafka (1883–1924) 310
A Hunger Artist (Trans. Willa and Edwin Muir) 312
D. H. Lawrence (1885–1930) 317
The Horse Dealer's Daughter 318
Tickets, Please 329
Katherine Mansfield (1888–1923) 337
The Garden-Party 338
Conrad Aiken (1889–1973) 347
Silent Snow, Secret Snow 348
Katherine Anne Porter (1890–1980) 359
The Grave 360
Isaac Babel (1894–1941) 364
My First Goose (Trans. Walter Morison) 365
The Sin of Jesus (Trans. Walter Morison) 367
F. Scott Fitzgerald (1896–1940) 370
Babylon Revisited 371
William Faulkner (1897–1962) 383
That Evening Sun 384
Ernest Hemingway (1899–1961) 395
Hills Like White Elephants 396
Richard Wright (1908–1960) 399
The Man Who Was Almost a Man 400

PART IV. THE CONTEMPORARY SCENE: THE ONGOING TRADITION

Eudora Welty (1909–   ) 409
A Worn Path 410
John Cheever (1912–1982) 415
The Country Husband 417
Bernard Malamud (1914–   ) 432
The Magic Barrel 433
Carson McCullers (1917–1967) 443
*A Tree * A Rock * A Cloud* 444
Aleksandr Isayevich Solzhenitsyn (1918–   ) 449
The Right Hand (Trans. Michael Glenny) 451
Richard Wilbur (1921–   ) 457
A Game of Catch 458
Grace Paley (1922–   ) 461
Friends 462
Flannery O'Connor (1925–1964) 469
Revelation 470
Yukio Mishima (1925–1964) 483
Patriotism (Trans. Geoffrey W. Sargent) 484
Cynthia Ozick (1928–   ) 498
The Shawl 499

John Updike (1932–   )   502
  Leaves   503
Raymond Carver (1938–   )   506
  Neighbors   507
Joyce Carol Oates (1938–   )   510
  Where Are You Going, Where Have You Been?   511
Toni Cade Bambara (1939–   )   522
  Raymond's Run   523

PART V. THE CONTEMPORARY SCENE:
BREAK WITH TRADITION

Jorge Luis Borges (1899–   )   529
  The Waiting (Trans. James E. Irby)   530
  Borges and I (Trans. James E. Irby)   533
  Everything and Nothing (Trans. James E. Irby)   533
Samuel Beckett (1906–   )   534
  The End (Trans. Richard Seaver and Samuel Beckett)   535
Tommaso Landolfi (1908–   )   546
  Gogol's Wife (Trans. Wayland Young)   547
Fredric Brown (1906–1972)   554
  Solipsist   555
Delmore Schwartz (1913–1966)   556
  In Dreams Begin Responsibilities   557
Julio Cortázar (1914–   )   562
  Axolōtl (Trans. Paul Blackburn)   563
Heinrich Böll (1917–   )   566
  Like a Bad Dream (Trans. Leila Vennewitz)   567
Alain Robbe-Grillet (1922–   )   571
  The Shore (Trans. Bruce Morrissette)   572
Gabriel García Márquez (1928–   )   575
  Balthazar's Marvelous Afternoon (Trans. J. S. Bernstein)   576
John Barth (1930–   )   580
  Petition   581
Donald Barthelme (1933–   )   588
  At the End of the Mechanical Age   589

Alternative Tables of Contents: Theme and Subject   594
Brief Glossary of Terms   602
List of Useful Books   606
Additional Acknowledgments   609
Index   611

Preface

We had two objectives in mind in making this book. First, we aimed to gather a collection of stories richly representative of the short story genre; second, we aimed to make a book that would be, owing to its critical and introductory material, as useful to the beginning writer as to the critical reader and teacher.

Any gathering that covers so many years (roughly from 1800 to the present—with bows to a farther past) represents some painful compromises and omissions. We have steadfastly tried to adhere to the following two tests for inclusion: Is the story good in and of itself, that is, is it an outstanding achievement as a work of art? And is it representative, that is, does it in its writing, technique, or theme represent an important event in the historical development of the short story? We believe that, in the main, our goals have been achieved.

We have prefaced the book with a fairly long introduction which provides, among other things, most of the information about technique that the reader (or writer) needs to know. The work of each writer is preceded by a short introduction which provides biographical information together with enough critical discussion about the particular story to get the student-critic on his way. At the end of the book is a Thematic Table of Contents—which will assist the reader who wants an entry into the range of human experiences the stories deal with—a Brief Glossary of Terms, and a List of Useful Books. Finally, we have tried to make our Index genuinely valuable by listing there all critical terms or other matters from the introductions that we thought would be useful. We have avoided the detailed questions and other apparatus that can make a book like this look more like an instrument of pedagogy than a book of wonderful readings. When the life of the reader intersects with the life of the story—that is when criticism ought to begin. In designing our critical aids, we have attempted to enhance rather than to stifle that moment.

We think it is worth mentioning that the editors of this volume include a short story writer as well as two persons with more usual academic credentials and experience. We hope that the crossing of the critical and creative strains has brought a useful focus to what we have selected and to what we have written. In the short introductions no attempt has been made to "homogenize" the writing styles of the three editors.

Many people have helped us, in large and small ways. We hope that a mere listing of their names will signal our genuine gratitude: Barbara Baer, Nancy Bazin, Betty Brereton, George Brown, Christine Gwynn, John Felstiner, Şuzanne Ferguson, Guelfo Frulla, Roger Harm, Arturo Islas, Dana Levitt, Eric Lindquist, Dagmar Logie, Tom Moser, Emily Olmstead, Thomas G. Parker, Lawrence Ryan, Scott Turow, and Stephanie Vaughn.

Wilfred Stone
Nancy Huddleston Packer
Robert Hoopes

AN INTRODUCTION

Introduction

1

Storytelling is as old as campfires. The need for human beings to cast their experience in narrative form is probably as old as consciousness itself. Gathered about the tribal fire, bonded by their common struggle for survival, our early ancestors gave voice in story form to their fears and beliefs—and thus helped make for themselves a magic defense against the trials of life. The earliest stories, traveling from campfire to campfire, across seas and down the generations, registered humanity's slow emergence from animal status. The forms of these stories, like the forms of other rituals, were the structures of each teller's history and identity—part of the creative impulse that made men and women consciously human.

All "primitive" cultures have their myths and legends—narratives of how things began, how the humans came, how the tribe survived, how the gods were dealt with, how the heroes fought. Though these tales are sometimes funny, their purpose is intensely serious. For the tribe that related them, they were part of the sacred word— matter not of make-believe but of belief itself. Since we no longer see the world as primitive storytellers did (though the word "primitive" is less and less a pejorative term), a lot of this folklore can seem naive and strange, a matter of superstition. But increasingly, as the "modern" continues to sweep over us, we read such lore with nostalgia, and are moved by a sense of things we have lost—our kinship with nature, a sense of community, the certainty of belief.

Many of our earliest written narratives—the Gilgamesh epic, the Old Testament

1

stories, the Greek and Roman myths, Beowulf—borrow heavily from such prehistoric lore. They are in great part the forms of such stories that have been developed, sophisticated, and written down.

But "modern" fiction has come a long way from those early beginnings (though it often reshapes those ancient forms to new uses). One cannot read a modern novel or story after an ancient myth without realizing that it exists in a vastly different world of value. Myths, as Frank Kermode points out, are for explaining things "as they are and were," whereas fictions "are for finding things out." "Myths are the agents of stability, fictions the agents of change. Myths call for absolute, fictions for conditional assent." Today in the West we accept no one or no "correct" way to view truth or reality. Our culture for the past three hundred years has been one of fantastic change and instability. The forces of science, industry, capitalism, and democracy that swept away the feudal order (along with many of its injustices) also swept away many of the traditional grounds for human confidence. Centuries-old beliefs were challenged, institutions radically altered or destroyed, and the Christian myths that supported the old order lost much of their power to explain and comfort. The new age became as much an age of anxiety as of optimism, and in this century it has seemed to many like an age of despair. It is the age of fiction.

The impulses that make the modern fiction writer are probably, at heart, no different from those of the "primitive" storyteller. He too would like to be a myth maker, and often is, but his problem is vastly complicated. Early stories were vehicles of assertion. Modern fiction is one of search. Early stories spoke for a whole community, modern fiction is the work of individuals called "authors." Myths record a completed vision of something true; fiction often represents, for writer and for reader, a crisis of belief and a groping for certainty. The modern writer does not receive his worldview, he discovers it. He does not, like the ancient myth maker, inherit his rituals, he invents them. But— and this is the vital point—though he may not give voice to universal truths, he is nevertheless making a statement about values. "Our whole age," said the poet Mallarmé, "is seeking to bring forth a sacred book."

Gogol's "The Overcoat" may not, like the myth of Adam and Eve in the Garden, identify the source of original sin, but it unforgettably reminds us of the perversity that prevents people from being their brother's keepers. Babel's "The Sin of Jesus" betrays a ragged sense of Christian ethics, yet it expresses a passionate longing for human justice. Beckett's "The End" offers no hint that life has meaning or that afterlife has either existence or consolation, but these negations cry out for some denial from the reader. Though the human sacrifice in Mishima's "Patriotism" is a traditional samurai ritual, it has lost its redemptive power and seems absurd in its anachronistic modern setting. Finally, Heinrich Böll's "Like a Bad Dream" shows an evil act reduced to the banality of business-as-usual, but the evildoer does not get off scot-free: he experiences something "like a bad dream," which we might, at a stretch, call his conscience.

Stories are not sermons. They tend to present rather than to preach; their values are more often implicit than explicit. Yet no matter how objective a writer is, no matter how given to *showing* over telling, his values seep into his story—into his subject matter, his style, his characterization, his plots, his very tone of voice. The careful reader will learn to read these signs.

When Guy de Maupassant writes that the mother in "A Country Outing" uncovered "a leg whose erstwhile slenderness was vanishing under the invasion of flesh coming down from her thighs," but writes that the daughter was "one of those women who, met in the street, fill a man with a sudden, whipping desire and leave that vague disturbance and agitation of the senses with him until he goes to sleep," he tells us what he valued, giving voice to the unrefined sexual code of what the French call *l'homme moyen sensuel*.

When Updike in "Leaves" appeases his guilt by contemplating nonhuman things—the birds and leaves he sees out the window—he is making of them emblems (see p. 8) of value, holy signs through which he tries to gain a degree of redemption.

As the stories of this volume progress toward the present day, the values they express become more difficult to decipher. A story like "Gogol's Wife" may seem no more than a gag, a *jeu d'esprit*. Delmore Schwartz's "In Dreams Begin Responsibilities" may seem, in its semicomic and multimirrored surrealism, absurdly Freudian. And Barth's "Petition," which violates all normal expectations for character and theme sequence, may seem only the game playing of some clever wordsmith.

Certainly in such works there is a radical turning away from "realism," from the "manners and morals" that Lionel Trilling called the proper subject for fiction, toward fantasy, absurdity, and far-out invention. Many of these writers—especially American writers of the last two decades—are responding to their sense of cultural break-up, and to a sense that the old fictional conventions are inadequate for expressing it. Writers like Barthelme are especially sensitive to what they feel to be the corruption of language by the mass media, government, and advertising; to that world of Doublespeak where peace is war, the lie merely something "inoperative," aggression against the enemy a "protective reaction strike," and official illegalities merely "inappropriate." To such writers the modern "wasteland" is a waste of words, a flood of *dreck* in Barthelme's terms, and they have sought their artistic integrity partly through opposing that flood: by eliminating plot, fracturing syntax, and in every way imaginable and unimaginable defying the lexical and fictional patterns that were conventional in earlier decades. They are responding not only to the corruption of language, but to its shrinkage. As George Steiner says:

> Large areas of meaning and praxis now belong to such non-verbal languages as mathematics, symbolic logic, and formulas of chemical or electronic relation. Other areas belong to the sublanguages or antilanguages of nonobjective art and *musique concrète*. The world of words has shrunk.

All the arts have reflected these trends, and the short story is no exception.

But it would be a mistake to suppose that these writers have abandoned values. To say that they have atomized the conventional short story is not to say that they have made nihilism or pointlessness or craziness their new creed. They are, it is true, deeply aware of what T. S. Eliot has called "the immense panorama of futility and anarchy which is contemporary history," and, ironically, their reaction has been largely apolitical and personal rather than polemical and engaged. Yet they are making their positive comment, though making it in surprising, and sometimes shocking, new ways.

Barthelme's "At the End of the Mechanical Age," for example, shows a couple who come together without courtship and part without pain, as emotionless, even in their "clinging and clutching," as a computer. They are the robots of a mechanical age, and their joining is that of socket and plug. Yet we laugh, as Henri Bergson said we should, at this sight of the mechanical being encrusted on the living—and that laughter is the assertion of a protest and a counter-value. In "The Shore," Alain Robbe-Grillet gives us a story from which he has removed any human observer, a fitting device for depicting a depersonalized culture. And John Barth's "Petition" shows human beings in a state of grotesque humiliation, yet Barth tells his story in language that we can't help but laugh at.

In all these tales there is the implicit wish that *things were not this way*. "I want to go to some other country . . . I want to go somewhere where everything is different," says a character in one of Barthelme's early stories, and that unspoken desire almost defines these modernist writers, and perhaps tells us why they have gone in for fantasy.

These experimental writers deserve our careful attention, whether or not they express experiences the reader can easily share. For the form of fiction as well as the content, the technique as well as the subject matter, are vital indicators of what is happening to us—and vital purveyors of value. In his important anthology *Anti-Story,* Philip Stevick has rightfully classified these antitraditional tendencies as a series of negations:

"Against Mimesis"   or dismissal of the traditional goal of imitating "real life." (Compare Melville's "Bartleby, the Scrivener" with Landolfi's "Gogol's Wife.")

"Against Reality"   or the indulgence in fantasy and dreams. (See Schwartz's "In Dreams Begin Responsibilities" or Borges's "Everything and Nothing.")

"Against Event"   or a tendency in the direction of plotless stories. (See Paley's "Friends" or Updike's "Leaves.")

"Against Subject"   or fiction in search of something to say. (See Barthelme's "At the End of the Mechanical Age.")

"Against the Middle Range of Experience"   or new forms of extremity. (See Beckett's "The End" or Barth's "Petition" or Ozick's "The Shawl.")

"Against Analysis"   or the objective depiction of the phenomenal world. (See Robbe-Grillet's "The Shore.")

"Against Meaning"   or forms of the absurd. (See Cortázar's "Axolōtl" or Landolfi's "Gogol's Wife.")

"Against Scale"   or the minimal story, the epigram. (See Brown's "Solipsist" or consider the entire "minimal" story that follows; it is "Taboo" by Enrique Anderson Imbert:)

> His guardian angle whispered to Fabián, behind his shoulder:
>   "Careful, Fabián! It is decreed that you will die the minute you pronounce the word *doyen*."
>   "Doyen?" asks Fabián, intrigued.
>   And he dies.

Negation—even perverse negation—is a sign that the moral sense is not dead. It is too early to say whether these experimental stories are classics or these trends permanent. It is enough to say that they represent something undeniably present in our culture: a sense of despair, break-up, horror, absurdity, violence, and often as well a saving humor. But not all contemporary writers are working with these "against" techniques, for the good reason that they do not all share this kind of vision. Traditional techniques and traditional attitudes toward the human condition seem to go hand in hand. The contemporaries using more traditional techniques—Welty, Malamud, Cheever, O'Connor, Updike—seem less concerned with the forces breaking up our culture than with the forces holding it together.

Flannery O'Connor wrote: "People without hope not only don't write novels, but what is more to the point, they don't read them." The act of writing is in itself a kind of act of faith. The search for redemption, if we look deeply and tolerantly enough, can be found in all the stories in this book.

2

What is the short story? Is it only a truncated and incomplete version of the novel? Or is it a genre, a category of art with a distinctive content, form, and style? This question has preoccupied a great many thoughtful practitioners of the form, Frank O'Connor, Sean O'Faolain, H. E. Bates eminent among them. Generally speaking these writer-critics do not think of a story as merely a work that happens to be short, but as a unique literary form, with techniques and effects that cannot be achieved through another medium. What are those effects, those techniques?

One of the most useful answers came from Edgar Allan Poe in 1842 when the short story was in its infancy. He believed that the prose tale stood just below the lyric poem in the hierarchy of literary art. For Poe, the "unity of effect or impression" was of prime importance, but, he felt, this unity could be obtained only in works that could be read "at one sitting." For Poe, the novel does not have this unity, cannot achieve the "immense force derivable from *totality*." Poe believed the short story is different from the novel, and superior to it. Not shortness, but intensity of impact was what Poe the romantic valued most highly.

Although Poe's concern with effect, particularly the effects he chiefly sought—terror, passion, horror—has had little influence on important writers of the short story, his views on singleness and unity are widely shared. Elizabeth Bowen wrote in *Collected Impressions:*

> The story should have the valid central emotion and inner spontaneity of the lyric.
> . . . It must have tautness and clearness. . . . Poetic tautness and clarity are so
> essential to it that it may be said to stand at the edge of prose.

While this analogy with lyric poetry is a tricky one, it is also illuminating, and a great many writers have suggested it. Faulkner, no doubt only half in earnest, said in his *Paris Review* interview (1956):

> Maybe every novelist wants to write poetry first, finds he can't, and then tries the
> short story, which is the most demanding form after poetry. And, failing at that,
> only then does he take up novel writing.

Like a fine lyric poem, the short story requires the reader's utmost attention, a focusing of the mind on each detail in order to realize the final fullness of effect. The short story depends on concreteness, on sensual impressions that deliver their meaning without waste. Like the lyric, it is a lean form; it can tolerate little if any digression, and it stays within the world it creates. The action of a conventional short story is compressed within a short (usually continuous) time frame and space. The characters, few in number, are revealed, not developed. The background and setting are implied, not rendered. Like most drama, the short story's action begins *in medias res*. The story gets going as quickly as possible: "Once upon a time in a distant land there lived a princess . . ." and the story is off and running. ("Beginners," said Chekhov, "often have to . . . fold in two and tear up the first half. . . . The first half is superfluous.") The effects are, as Poe said, intense and total.

Consider Chekhov's brilliant "Ninochka." In fewer than 2,000 words we are given an ironic minidrama—a love triangle in which the cuckolded husband, miserable over his wife's infidelity with his best "friend," goes helplessly to that friend for advice.

("Tell me, what is Ninochka supposed to do now? Should she go on living with me, or do you think it would be better if she moved in with you?") The solution is given without emotion, the writer carefully repressing his pity so the reader can provide it himself:

> Having deliberated briefly, we left it at this: Ninochka would continue to live at Vikhlyenev's; I would go to see her whenever I liked, and he would take the corner room, which formerly had been the storeroom, for himself. This room was rather dark and damp, and the entrance to it was through the kitchen, but, on the other hand, he could perfectly well shut himself up in it and not be a nuisance to anyone.

If a writer attempted that kind of concentration of energy for, say, 300 pages, he would surely exhaust the reader, and would not in any case be able to maintain such emotional tension. The pace of a novel can be leisurely, its settings, characters, and events slowly developed until fully rendered.[1] The novelist—at least the conventional novelist—can tolerate subplots and digressions from the main thrust of his story; he can even desire them in order to achieve changes in pace and intensity. But that kind of pacing and development is not appropriate to the short story, and it is revealing that great novelists like Henry James, Joseph Conrad, and Thomas Mann found the short-story form troublesome. They were sticklers for fullness of presentation, for the richly rendered context, and for the slow unfolding. The James and Mann stories in this volume will indicate how difficult it was for these authors to squeeze into the short-story form, to sacrifice expansiveness to compression.

There are in the main three qualities that mark the short story as clearly different from other forms of prose fiction, that make it a "genre." The first quality is of course brevity. The second is its power of compensating for the consequences of shortness. And the third is the interaction of one and two.

How does the story manage to tell it all in such a brief space? Such a fine story as Gogol's "The Overcoat" seems quaintly old-fashioned today: the lengthy biography of the main character, the thorough development of each scene, the slow pacing of the action. Even Chekhov, that master of the form, was sometimes unwilling to sacrifice such embellishments for tautness.

But the development of the form has been toward greater and greater compression. A comparison of "The Lady with the Pet Dog" by Chekhov and "Hills Like White Elephants" by Hemingway will suggest just how far compression has gone. Chekhov's story starts far back, when Gurov and Anna first meet at Yalta. Through four chapters, we watch their relationship develop from idle seduction to the mature, though heart-breaking, love they come to recognize. Along the way Chekhov has described three different physical settings and a variety of characters. He tells us a good deal about the lives of both Gurov and Anna. Along the way he describes several settings in each of three different towns, and he introduces a number of characters. Hemingway's story takes place in a few minutes at one crossroads community and between two characters. We don't know the characters' names or their history—we can't be sure they are married. There is no buildup to the drama and no explanation. We know the characters

---

[1] There is a fictional form called the "lyrical novel" which includes such books as Virginia Woolf's *The Waves,* Herman Hesse's *Demian,* and André Gide's *Les Faux-Monnayeurs,* and there are modern novelists like John Hawkes who would like to eliminate "plot, theme, character, and structure," thus carrying fictional compression almost to the point, if such wishes could be fulfilled, of nihilism. But these facts do not, we believe, contradict seriously the above generalizations.

and the situation not because we are told—as Chekhov told us—but because we over-hear them when they speak revealing words and we see them perform revealing acts. The man in the story repeats the word "perfectly"—and we realize he is a hypocrite. He stops to have a drink alone—and we understand that in an important way he is divorcing himself from the woman. A very little—a word, a gesture, a description—stands for so much. Hemingway has followed Chekhov's advice to "fold in two and tear up the first half." His story begins in the middle—the struggle between the man and the woman is in progress—and the rising action is uninterrupted until the drama is complete.

How to choose between the Chekhov style and the Hemingway style? One cannot, of course. Both are brilliant examples of the art. Yet in the hands of a lesser writer than Hemingway, the cost of compression can be high. Elizabeth Bowen says that the short story's disadvantage is an "emotional narrowness." Compression can distort human experience and undercut the richness, ambivalence, complexity of human beings.

Writing in 1917, Herbert Ellsworth Cory said, "The very technique of the short-story is pathological, and titillates our nerves in our pathological moments. The short-story is the blood kinsman of the quick-lunch, the vaudeville, and the joy-ride." No doubt the short story is one manifestation of the modern speedup, though Cory's rather shuddering vision of a world full of "pathological moments" is one that even Kafka might reject. However, he does touch on the short-story writer's chief difficulty: how to be succinct without being shallow, how to create a single effect without creating a merely transitory one.

How does the short story achieve depth, or the feeling of depth? As we have noted, the short-story writer cannot, like certain novelists, stop his narrative while his characters' psyches are analyzed or their portraits painted. He cannot take time out to draw a scene. The story writer must intimate the setting, imply the complexity, insinuate the character, and the reader must infer the rest. When a story writer violates these practices—as when Melville in "Bartleby, the Scrivener" stops the story to summarize background—the result seems awkward and static, inimical to the spirit of the short story (however fitting to that of the novella). There are ways of avoiding such summarization, and they are all encompassed in one vital word: *suggestion*. The story reveals the "tip of the iceberg" in Hemingway's phrase: the rest of the iceberg is *suggested*. Consider that haunting dialogue between the old man and the boy in McCullers' "A Tree * A Rock * A Cloud" in which the old man, battered by life, tells the boy about love, and about the "science of love" he found could heal the hurt of being abandoned by the one woman he ever loved. His whole life is encompassed in those five pages, yet we learn only a few facts. When he tells the boy that, in trying to love a woman, he had begun at "the wrong end" of love, at the "climax," and that love should be begun with "A tree. A rock. A cloud." we are by these few words taken into the very center of his life and into the heartbreak that defined it. His "science" is the last desperate resource of an alienated man:

> Son, I can love anything. . . . I see a street full of people and a beautiful light comes in me. I watch a bird in the sky. Or I meet a traveller on the road. Everything, Son. And anybody. All stranger and all loved! Do you realize what a science like mine can mean?

Was he drunk? Was he a dope fiend? the boy wanted to know. Was he crazy? Leo, the stingy café owner, answered no to the first two questions, but was silent as to the third, though he felt himself to be an expert on craziness. But the reader must answer, for the tale lives by its suggestions and is incomplete on the printed page; it is completed in the imagination of the reader.

Sometimes a single detail will stand for a wealth of meaning—for a whole social class or a character's background or, as in the case of Updike's "Leaves," an emotional state. Such an "emblem"—less than a symbol yet more than a thing—is a potent means of suggestion. The milkman's cart in Maupassant's "A Country Outing" identifies the family as lower middle class, of modest means, just as the higher status of the young oarsman becomes clear from the description of "two splendid skiffs, fine and worked like costly pieces of furniture." The drink of Anis del Toro in Hemingway's "Hills Like White Elephants" tells us that these are sophisticated and worldly people. In the same story the repetition of the word "perfectly"—perfectly natural, perfectly simple—pegs the speaker as disingenuous, a manipulator, not to be trusted.

In a letter to his brother, an aspiring writer, Chekhov wrote:

> In my opinion, descriptions of nature should be extremely brief and offered by the way, as it were . . . you will evoke a moonlit night by writing that on the mill dam the glass fragments of a broken bottle flashed like a bright little star, and that the black shadow of a dog or a wolf rolled along like a ball, and so on.

And to Maxim Gorki he wrote:

> It is intelligible when I write, "The man sat down on the grass"; it is intelligible because it is clear and does not impede the reader's attention. Conversely, it will be unintelligible and tax the reader's brain if I write: "The tall, narrow-chested man of average build, who had a short, red beard, sat down on the green grass, already trampled by passers-by; sat down noiselessly, timidly and fearfully glancing around him." One's brain cannot grasp this at once, yet fiction must be grasped at once—on the spot.

Sometimes the setting is an emblem (the star-point on the neck of the broken bottle), sometimes it is not; but it is in the short story always abbreviated, caught out of the corner of the eye, in passing, as other things get done.

Compression and suggestion working together create what Sean O'Faolain calls "the point of illumination," and that in a nutshell is what the short story is all about. "Every short story," O'Faolain writes, "has some bright destination and . . . every step into the story must imperceptibly lead toward its point of illumination." He continues:

> I believe the whole craft of the short story is summed up in those last half-dozen words—"that it must lead imperceptibly toward its point of illumination," with the maximum of emphasis on the word "imperceptibly." The main fun of writing short stories and part of the fun of reading them, consists in being led onward, of leading the reader onward to the moment of surprised pleasure when the story behind the story, the meaning behind the Yarn, the interior significance of the event, makes us utter a delighted "Ah!"—as when a train comes around a headland and there, in front of us, is the place to which we have been travelling on a Mystery Tour the destination of which until that moment we did not realize.

The point of illumination is the essential unifying element in the story. It is the light at the end of the tunnel, the target all the story elements are deployed to reach. At that moment the plot has come to its climax, the characters have been revealed, the relationship between character and environment has achieved at least a tentative equilibrium. The human significance of the story is manifest. Thereafter, there is a unity of feeling and of understanding. Such an "exaltation of the soul" cannot, as Poe said of the poem, "be long sustained," but what a moving experience it can be! As V. S. Pritchett says, "Every short story is a drama, but every writer of short stories has his own idea of what is dramatic. A story moves towards a disclosure and that may be an event, a complete revelation of character, the close of a mood, the changing of an emotion, the clinching of an idea, the statement of a situation now completed." The beauty of the short story is that all its elements can be drawn to a single point that shines with such brightness that all the past moments of the tale are bathed in light—seen as a whole, as a radiance.

For this experience James Joyce used the word *epiphany,* a term borrowed from Christian thought and signifying the manifestation of God in the world. In *Stephen Hero* Joyce said:

> First we recognize that the object is *one* integral thing, then we recognize that it is an organized composite structure, a *thing* in fact: finally, when the relation of the parts is exquisite, when the parts are adjusted to the special point, we recognize that it is that *thing* which it is. Its soul, its whatness, leaps to us from the vestment of its appearance.

In Joyce's story "A Painful Case" there are several small epiphanies all building towards a final, transforming one. Mr. Duffy, the bank cashier who "abhorred anything which betokened physical or mental disorder," meets Mrs. Sinico. Gradually they begin to share more than ideas; gradually they let the darkness as well as the light in:

> Many times she allowed the dark to fall upon them, refraining from lighting the lamp. The dark discreet room, their isolation, the music that still vibrated in their ears united them. This union exalted him, wore away the rough edges of his character, emotionalized his mental life.

But when she "caught up his hand passionately and pressed it to her cheek," he is shocked. His response is disillusionment and withdrawal—back to sexlessness and his sterile "order"—while she, rejected, departs sorrowing. It is a turning point in the story—it *is* the story, in fact—for it is Duffy's shrunken nature and blindness that prepare us for the final illumination—or epiphany. Two years later Mrs. Sinico is killed at a railroad crossing; the coroner called it "a most painful case" (since it appeared that she had been drinking) but asserted that "no blame is attached to anyone." The irony is obvious, for we know that much blame attaches to Duffy. His first reaction to the newspaper account is violently defensive: "Not merely had she degraded herself; she had degraded him." But then begins a movement, via a series of minor epiphanies, toward the major one. "As the light failed and his memory began to wander, he thought her hand touched his." Ironically, he goes to a public house for a drink, and he realizes how lonely she was and that his life would be lonely too. He walks to the park and down the "bleak alleys" where they had walked, and he feels his "moral nature falling to pieces." He sees lovers in the shadow of the wall. "One human being had seemed to love him and he had denied her life and happiness." He knows that the lovers wish him gone and he recognizes that he is "an outcast from life's feast." Each of the details functions as an epiphany for Mr. Duffy, leading him deeper and deeper into himself. At the end, he sees "winding through the darkness" a train reminding him and us of the train that killed her—reiterating her name as it takes the memory of her from him. After that, he "could not feel her near him in the darkness or hear her voice touch his ear. . . . He felt that he was alone." The really painful case is, of course, Mr. Duffy, not Mrs. Sinico. That irony is the final epiphany conveyed by the story.

Similarly in Isaac Babel's brilliant tale "My First Goose." From the narrator's first fearful, admiring glance at the Commander (". . . and I wondered at the beauty of his giant's body. . . . His long legs were like girls sheathed to the neck in shining riding boots") to his rejection by the Cossacks (when the steam from the cook-pot was "like the far-off smoke of home in the village") to the killing of the goose, the cruel act that gained him acceptance ("the moon hung . . . like a cheap earring"), we are fascinated by the progression of events. But though the events are consecutive, causative, they seem to have no special meaning. Then in the last two lines, that master Babel provides the point of illumination: "I dreamed, and in my dreams saw women, but my heart, stained with bloodshed, grated and brimmed over."

Is such a story the blood kin of the quick lunch? Is it just a fragment of a novel or a digest of what would be superior if it were fleshed out? Has compression impaired the possibilities of depth and meaning? We think not. We think the short story at its best is an art form responsive to the highest reaches of the human imagination.

But *epiphany* is a word with echoes from an age of faith, and many contemporary writers react to our age as one of doubt and despair. As Philip Stevick says in *Anti-Story,* speaking of the work of certain avant-garde writers:

> Characters . . . do not learn. There are no insights. Relationships are not grasped in an instant. Structurally, the stories are flat, or circular, or cyclic, or mosaic constructions, or finally indeterminate or incomprehensible in their shape—they are not climactic. What we start with is pretty much what we have at the end. No epiphanies.

Illumination is not "in" these days. To point the way, to shine the light, implies that one knows—or has some idea—where one is going. The idea of where one is going used to be called a *plot*. The idea of what one means used to be called a *theme*. The idea of what a person is used to be called a *character*. Many modernist storytellers are in flight from these assertions, and their chapters of the "sacred book" open more often into absurdity than into transcendence, into the wilderness than into any promised land. Only time will tell whether they represent a new tradition or a dead end.

3

Henry James said, "Nothing . . . will ever take the place of the good old fashion of 'liking' a work of art or not liking it!" Literature begins where the life of the story intersects with the life of the reader. And it is this fresh, unmeditated, immediate response that the reader should treasure above all else.

But criticism is important as well. The pale cast of afterthought can yield rich rewards. What caused the immediate response? Why was I so torn between love and hate for a character? Why did the plot disappear—or never emerge? Why did that technical trick bother me? By analyzing the parts of a story and seeing how they work together, we can enlarge the impact of the work upon us—and enlarge our understanding of literature and how it is made.

The creative life of a writer is a mystery. He makes many decisions unconsciously; his choices in matters of tone or point of view are not usually the result of critical analysis. The old adage, "How do I know what I think until I see what I say?" applies frequently to writers. Writing is a process of *discovering* the story and its meaning. Faulkner said, "With me, a story usually begins with a single idea or memory or mental picture. The writing . . . is simply a matter of working up to that moment, to explain why it happened or what it caused to follow."

This process of *discovering* can be a disaster for the would-be writer who has no control of techniques; without craft, he can discover very little, for himself or for the reader. Yet with most writers, technique is not a matter of first priority. Sean O'Faolain writes:

> I do not deny that there are some technical tricks to be learned, and quickly forgotten, having become second nature. . . . The things I like in a story are punch and poetry . . . "technique" is the least part of the business.

But making something "second nature" is usually the result of a long, dedicated apprenticeship. "Art is the habit of the artist," writes Flannery O'Connor; "and habits have to be rooted deep in the whole personality." For her,

> The only way, I think, to learn to write short stories is to write them, and then to try to discover what you have done. The time to think of technique is when you've actually got the story in front of you.

In the following pages we discuss, in reference to the stories in this volume, such elements as point of view, tone, characterization, dialogue, setting, symbol, and theme. A story is a whole greater than the sum of its parts, but seeing how those parts work is often to see into the heart of the whole.

Point of View

Some writers believe that the second most important decision they make, after selecting that "idea or memory or mental picture" Faulkner identified as the source of a story, is point of view. Point of view is a term of art which refers to the relationships between the storyteller, the story, and the reader. What vantage point has the writer selected from which to relate his story? Does the story come directly as a happening to the reader, or is it filtered through another mind or personality? Through what window is the reader permitted to see the characters and actions?

Every story has a storyteller. He may announce his role or he may conceal himself. In Eudora Welty's "A Worn Path," the storyteller seems to be a kind of disembodied spirit hovering near the old woman—all-knowing, yet invisible. In Gogol's "The Overcoat," the narrator calls attention to himself in the first sentence and reappears frequently, always as a narrator outside the story, not as a character. The storyteller *is* the character in Solzhenitsyn's "The Right Hand." And sometimes there is hardly a trace of him anywhere, as in Flaubert's "A Simple Heart." It was Joyce's theory and practice that the writer, "like the God of Creation, remains within or behind or beyond or above his handiwork, invisible, refined out of existence, indifferent, paring his fingernails."

But invisible or not, unobtrusive or participating, he is always there, controlling the story. His tone and his subject matter govern the reader's responses; it is his plot that will carry the meaning. Above all, it is he who determines the window through which the reader views the story.

There are many possible windows on a story. If the window is remote from the characters, the view will be long and very likely wide. If the reader is close up, he will feel the intimacy, but he may find it difficult to see around the character's biases to the truth. With one view, the reader may be privy to mental states; with another, he may be limited to what can be seen or heard. These are just some of the possibilities. Each window, each point of view has opportunities and limitations. In the four points of view discussed below, we get some idea of their range.

Omniscient point of view   "None of them knew the color of the sky" is the opening sentence of Stephen Crane's "The Open Boat," and it tells the reader that the storyteller is omniscient. There will be no limitation on the storyteller's knowledge, his power to range widely wherever he chooses. The storyteller knows what the men know, and more. He knows they believe they are near a lifesaving station, and he knows they are wrong. He knows the color of the sky, and the ache in the muscles of the oarsmen. He can be two places at once, in many minds, enjoying many perspectives. And he shares his freedom and knowledge, so that the reader as well can take a broad overview.

Omniscience also permits philosophic depth. Crane's storyteller, for instance, comments not alone on these shipwrecked men but on all men lost at sea ("When it occurs to a man that nature does not regard him as important. . . ." "A high cold wind on a winter's night is the word he feels she says to him"). The omniscient narrator is free to bring his own views into the story.

Omniscience has limitations. Crane's wide angle requires distance, making close identification with characters difficult. Our experience therefore tends not to be intimate or intense. Crane attempts to overcome this limitation by frequently restricting his focus to the mind of the correspondent. But—and this is the problem—he still maintains his detached, mildly ironic and philosophic tone:

> The correspondent wondered ingenuously how in the name of all that was sane could there be people who thought it amusing to row a boat. It was not an amusement; it was a diabolical punishment.

This from a man who is struggling for his life against a raging sea! It is all right for gods to be omniscient, but when writers play that game, they can sometimes seem to know too much—and thereby to impair the reader's sense of participation and discovery as he reads the story.

A more successful use of omniscience, though not for that a better story, is Mishima's "Patriotism." This chronicle of a ritual suicide moves from a broad view of a culture to a most intimate view of two lovers. "Their lives were lived beneath the solemn protection of the gods and were filled with an intense happiness which set every fiber in their bodies trembling." The tone remains the same throughout, reverential and mystical. Though the narrator is omniscient, he has little emotional distance from the two. As their relationship is profoundly sensual, yet ritualized, so is his attitude. He is at one with the values of what he narrates. He offers no ironic perspective: as they view themselves so their creator views them. Thus, Mishima knows what only an omniscient narrator can know, but he presents it from the point of view of a participant.

Direct observer Almost the exact opposite of the omniscient is the direct observer. As the omniscient storyteller goes everywhere, knows everything, and comments when he chooses, the direct observer has no memory of the past, no understanding of the present; he is little more than a fly on the wall, recording the scene. This kind of story approaches pure drama: all action, dialogue, setting, stage directions. The audience does the rest.

But a short story, even one with this point of view, is not a play, as a look at Hemingway's "Hills Like White Elephants" shows. About seven-eighths of the story is enclosed within quotation marks, but in that little which is not dialogue is the difference between a story and a play. The story opens with a paragraph of description which concludes: "It was very hot and the express from Barcelona would come in forty minutes. It stopped at this junction for two minutes and went on to Madrid." This passage sets the physical and psychological stage for the story. The time interval and the place are established; the barren quality of the crossroads is a comment on the lives of two characters. Each detail counts, laden with meaning. The reader's eyes and imagination are insistently led to those elements the storyteller wishes him to notice. Although the two characters are discussing abortion, the subject is not named. Finally the man carries out their bags:

> Coming back, he walked through the barroom, where people waiting for the train were drinking. He drank an Anis at the bar and looked at the people. They were all waiting reasonably for the train.

Notice how smoothly and quickly the reader is taken through time and space, avoiding the irrelevant. A crowd of people is suggested in a line; minutes pass in a phrase. Although quick cutting to condense time is possible in a movie, and a play can suggest a setting without filling in details, neither can create a dense and rapid scene with quite such quick brushstrokes. The direct observer moves rapidly through time and space; his eye is always on the story's center. Of all points of view, the direct observer provides the greatest dramatic intensity and compactness. No storyteller stands between the reader and the scene. The storyteller focuses our senses on the relevant details. We are there.

The disadvantages of this method are obvious. Limited as he is to speech, gesture, action, and setting, the direct observer will find it difficult to render subtly shifting psychological states or to provide a wide range of understanding and feeling. Complexity and subtlety can only be suggested. The drama must speak for itself.

First-person narration First-person narration can avoid the sprawling quality of omniscience and the narrowness of direct observer. But it has other limitations.

With this point of view, the reader is told what he knows by a "person" who speaks in his own voice. The reader knows only what that person knows and when he knows it and tells it. The reader cannot witness scenes the narrator has not witnessed, nor witness them from angles the narrator does not provide. He cannot be taken into other minds. But first person has a special authenticity and a special vibrancy. The reader feels in touch with a real person who cares about what he is telling. In Maupassant's "A Country Outing"—told by an omniscient narrator—the reader never for a moment believes the teller is involved in his story. But in first person, the words come to us with the force of the narrator's commitment.

The narrator need not be the main character in the story, as he is not in Schwartz's "In Dreams Begin Responsibilities," but typically is an active participant, as in Updike's "Leaves." To compare these two stories and two narrators is to glimpse the great flexibility of first-person strategy.

"Leaves" is narrated in the first person and present tense, which greatly increases the reader's sense of authenticity and immediacy. The reader identifies closely with the narrator, who sees, remembers, tells—inevitably in a light favorable to himself. The story of this divorce would probably be quite different if told by the wife. The narrator's tone creates a touch of suspicion (surely the wife was angrier than this?) and the resultant tension is never fully resolved. Updike takes full advantage of the ironies thus created: by the end of the story the reader's sympathies have shifted several times toward and away from the narrator.

Schwartz's narrator looks back at his parents' lives from a perspective of many years. Indeed, rather than relying solely on memory, he imagined what occurred even before he was born. Sufficient time has elapsed for his early confusions and misunderstandings to give way to a mature understanding. He knows what he thinks of the characters and has weighed them on an ultimate scale. He firmly guides the reader to the appropriate conclusions. But the reader does not feel distanced from the events or the people. The characters and actions are so minutely observed and the language is so laden with emotion—the emotion the child has carried into his adulthood—that the reader feels right at the heart of the action. The intimacy and excitement of first person have not been sacrificed.

Generally speaking, the closer the narrator is in time and space and the more self-interest is involved, the less reliable he or she is as an interpreter to the reader. The point of view of an "unreliable witness" can be very useful to a writer. The reader slowly comes to recognize the discontinuity between usually accepted norms and perceptions and those of the narrator. In Chekhov's "Ninochka," the reader moves from belief in the narrator to doubt, from a beginning assumption of his decency to a final realization of his nastiness. As the reader's sympathy is destroyed, something important is gained: an ironic insight into the self-serving venality of which human beings are capable, and the common fault of judging by appearances.

Third-person intimate   Third-person intimate provides a double vision. The reader not only observes the main character, but also is intimately involved with the character's feelings and thoughts. This point of view creates tension between what the storyteller and the reader understand and what the character knows, between external action and internal reaction, between the grossness of gesture and the refinement of thought, between what really is and what the character thinks. Third-person intimate can be flexibly adapted to a writer's intentions. At one end of the spectrum is "The Beast in the Jungle" by Henry James; at the other end is "The Grave" by Katherine Anne Porter.

Henry James made many contributions to the craft of fiction, and two of them converge here. In his maturity, James came to believe that the writer should *show* rather than *tell* the reader, that everything should be "rendered," dramatized. He also believed that the most effective point of view for a story was to submerge the storyteller into a character he called the "central intelligence." As the character sees, the reader sees; as he knows, the reader knows. The scenes in "The Beast in the Jungle" come to us through the consciousness of John Marcher, but it is a consciousness rendered in the language of Henry James. Thus we understand more than Marcher does. We can "see" the drama of his shifting mental states, and his blindness. Despite our intimate contact with his mind, we can judge him and his experience from the distance of our own moral perspective, and James's.

"The Grave" illustrates a different use of third-person intimate. Its anonymous storyteller directs the reader's attention to setting, characters, situation. Then she steps offstage and turns the reader loose to share the thoughts and feelings of the main character, Miranda. The storyteller remains in the wings, however, occasionally calling out directions for the next scene, dropping comments to help the reader understand Miranda. Thus, we see Miranda from the outside, in a context of action which is presented objectively, and we understand her from the inside. Under Porter's skillful direction we feel no disruption in the shift, no cracking of the "single effect."

Between these two uses are any number of possibilities. This volume contains numerous examples. Perhaps the most striking is that mixed approach in Delmore Schwartz's "In Dreams Begin Responsibilities." The first-person narrator *imagines* a film about his parents in their youth. The film, however, is described in third-person intimate and is believable in its own right; it is believable also as a projection of the narrator's subjectivity. This fictionalized "memory" provides the reader with a multidimensional psychological experience, an experience made possible by the rich artistic resources of point of view.

Tone

The tone of a story is the "voice" in which it is conveyed and the attitude that voice expresses. Even when there is no obvious storyteller or "I," a story has a voice, a style, a special signature that conveys the author's conscious or unconscious intentions.

Part of the meaning of sentences is carried by pitch, cadence, tempo, rhythm, and syntactical arrangement. Together with the subject matter, these create the personality of a story. Imagine a Chekhov story told by Hemingway, a Mann story in the tone of Robbe-Grillet. The results would probably be grotesque; they would certainly be different. Tone is the load of meaning that cannot be paraphrased but that nonetheless shapes the reader's responses. Even before he makes the plot apparent, the writer begins to create the universe of feeling in which the story takes place. Here is the beginning of Poe's "The Fall of the House of Usher":

> During the whole of a dull, dark, and soundless day in the autumn of the year, when the clouds hung oppressively low in the heavens, I had been passing alone, on horseback, through a singularly dreary tract of country; and at length found myself, as the shades of the evening drew on, within view of the melancholy House of Usher.

Here is a paraphrase: "I arrived at the House of Usher in the late afternoon of a cloudy autumn day." The difference is immense and the difference is of course the tone. The paraphrase is a barren statement of fact and lacks complexity and intensity of feeling. The reader has no idea where the story is headed or what kind of story it will be. The original prepares the reader and sets up the atmosphere of the story. It foreshadows disaster and horror to come. The inversions, slow cadence, archaic literary expression, even particular words like "soundless" and "oppressively" are used not only to convey information but to stimulate a Gothic mood of mystery, unreality, fear.

The range of possible tones is as wide as the range of human attitudes. But one tone needs special notice: irony. Some people confuse irony with sarcasm or even invective, but it is a much subtler tone. Irony occurs when there is a difference between what is stated and what is implied, between appearance and reality, between the ideal and the real, between what people believe and what is true. Bernard Malamud's "The Magic Barrel" begins ironically. As soon as we are told that Leo Finkle, the rabbinical student, thinks he "might find it easier to win . . . a congregation if . . . married," we recognize the irony: ideally one marries for love, not for expediency. Of course, the final irony of the story is that he does marry for love—and marries a prostitute at that. Irony can be extremely funny, as it is in Barth's "Petition" when the Siamese twin inveighs against his brother's lust, in part because he is precluded from exercising his own. Irony can also be serious, indeed heartbreaking, as it is in Chekhov's "The Lady with the Pet Dog" when what started as frivolous flirtation becomes the most important thing in the protagonist's life. More often, it is somewhere in between, as it is in Landolfi's "Gogol's Wife" in which a man tries to shape reality to his ideal by taking a rubber doll as his wife. Sometimes the ironies of a story are so subtle that they give up their meanings only to careful, intelligent readers who read between the lines.

In addition to being a tone, irony may also be a mode of organization, for conflict between the expected and the actual or between the assumed and the true can be registered in the plot as well as in the voice of a story. Wharton's "Roman Fever" is an excellent example. Through her bullying, Mrs. Slade brings on a series of disclosures that leave her reeling. When we enjoy that, we are enjoying the irony of the situation.

Plot

In *Aspects of the Novel*, E. M. Forster distinguishes the simple story from the more complex plot: " 'The king died and then the queen died' is a story. 'The king died and then the queen died of grief' is a plot. The story, with its "then . . . and then," is only, writes Forster, "the chopped-off length of the tape-worm of time," and satisfies nothing more than mindless, time-killing curiosity. But over the plot "will hover the memory of the reader (that dull glow of the mind of which intelligence is the bright advancing edge)." The intelligent reader wants to know not only what happened, but why, and what it means. The acts are not merely consecutive, as in the simple "story," they are consequential. Implicit in the idea of plots is the belief that human beings shape their lives and are shaped by their experiences. "What is character," asks Henry James, "but the determination of incident? What is incident but the illustration of character?"

The James dictum and the Forster distinction between story and plot would rule out the "surprise ending" story. Life is in some measure unpredictable, flowerpots do fall fourteen floors and land on innocent heads, people do behave in ways even their analysts find strange. But if the ending of a story is an accident or a coincidence, or if the characters act "out of character" in capricious ways, the reader will be unprepared for the ending, and the body of the story will seem literally of no consequence.

Plot is not life; a plot is a writer's arrangement of events that will express his attitude toward the human condition. Most of the stories in this volume have conventional plots. Indeed, the reader might diagram the plots of stories like Gogol's "The Overcoat," or Lawrence's "The Horse Dealer's Daughter," or O'Connor's "Revelation" and discover that they follow quite nicely the classic contours of situation, complication, rising action, climax, falling action, and dénouement. Consider this diagram of "The Overcoat":

1 Akakii is content in his dull civil service job.   SITUATION
2 His overcoat is in rags, and he must have a new one. He has no money.
                                                                        COMPLICATION
3 By dint of scrimping and saving, he finally gets the coat. It transforms him. He begins to come out of his shell.   RISING ACTION
4 The overcoat is stolen.   CRISIS
5 Akakii seeks justice but encounters only bureaucratic indifference and delay.
                                                                        FALLING ACTION
6 He sickens and dies; but his ghost haunts all the city's petty bureaucrats and busies itself snatching off their overcoats.   DÉNOUEMENT (POETIC JUSTICE)

Not all stories are so strong in plots as the three mentioned; indeed, Chekhov, the master himself, was noted for the slightness of his plots. Somerset Maugham once said, "If you try to tell one of [Chekhov's] stories, you will find there is nothing to tell. The anecdote, stripped of its trimmings, is insignificant and often inane."

Stories may promise movement, change, development without relying upon external action. The opposing force the hero is up against may be the elements, the universe, other people, the social system, or it may be his own inner need, ambition, sensitivity. When the real battlefield of a story is inside a character, rather than between him and external forces, then the movement of plot from situation through complication to resolution is most likely to be interior also. In Carson McCullers' delicate story, "A Tree * A Rock * A Cloud," there is almost no action at all, yet some profound movements of mood and insight occur. In Bernard Malamud's "The Magic Barrel," things happen, but the drama lies in the psychic change.

It has become commonplace today to deny the necessity of plot. Many avant-garde writers no longer see events as connected or sequential, but rather as products of chance, randomness, coincidence. Thus does art reflect, perhaps unconsciously, such commonplaces of modern science as Werner Heisenberg's "Principle of Uncertainty"—which says that "no events, not even atomic events, can be described with certainty." Orderly plots with beginnings, middles, and ends do not express the way things seem to these writers. Plots imply that human actions make sense and have predictable consequences, but this is not the view expressed in Robbe-Grillet's "The Shore" or Borges's "Borges and I." As Philip Stevick says in *Anti-Story,* when a writer finds that "the universe is absurd . . . then the only possible story expresses without blinking a vision of that absurdity." The fiction writer may then become a camera's eye, as does Robbe-Grillet, who refuses to draw from or impose meaning on the scene he depicts; or he may become an essayist of fantasy, as does Borges. Many modernists agree in greater or lesser degree with Ronald Sukenick:

> God was the omniscient author, but he died; now no one knows the plot, and since our reality lacks the sanction of a creator, there's no guarantee as to the authenticity of the received version. Time is reduced to presence, the content of a series of discontinuous moments. Time is no longer purposive, and so there is no destiny, only chance.

Yet, from another point of view, these stories and others written from a similar perspective can be seen as subtle and oblique narratives of event. Each story comprises a journey, through space, or time, or an individual psyche; each promises revelation or exposure of important and connected acts or thoughts; each gives an impression at its end of closure.

Setting and Dialogue

"Nothing," says Elizabeth Bowen, "can happen nowhere." The place where the action happens can powerfully focus the reader's expectations. Without place there would be vagueness, uncertainty.

Early short stories generally began with a lengthy description of the setting and the historical or personal background of the characters. Gogol's "The Overcoat" has no forward motion or conflict until we encounter, some five pages into the story, the paragraph that begins, "For some time Akakii Akakiievich had begun to notice the cold. . . ." And Turgenev's "Raspberry Spring" has several pages of physical description before the characters are introduced. Even Maupassant and Chekhov took a little time to place their stories before they started the action.

The development of the short story has been toward more compression of description. Most writers try to render the setting swiftly, sparsely, or impressionistically. As the narrative progresses, they slip in representative concrete details of the setting and the backgrounds of the characters. Thus Eudora Welty gives us the setting of "A Worn Path" not before the story begins but while it is moving:

> It was December—a bright frozen day in the early morning. Far out in the country there was an old Negro woman with her head tied in a red rag, coming along a path through the pinewoods. Her name was Phoenix Jackson. She was very old and small and she walked slowly in the dark pine shadows, moving a little from side to side in her steps; with the balanced heaviness and lightness of a pendulum in a grandfather clock.

Phoenix Jackson is going somewhere, and the pinewoods, the frozen day, her oldness and smallness are all relevant to that fact and to her purpose for making the journey. The setting is not window-dressing—it helps to bring about the events and to establish their meaning.

Dialogue appears in almost all stories. Few writers are willing to sacrifice the talk of characters. Talk creates a sense of verisimilitude and immediacy. They speak, therefore they are; we overhear, therefore we believe. Nothing defines characters and relationships more quickly than speech. Consider this exchange in O'Connor's "Revelation":

> "They ought to send all them niggers back to Africa," the white-trash woman said. "That's wher they come from in the first place."
> "Oh, I couldn't do without my good colored friends," the pleasant lady said.
> "There's a heap of things worse than a nigger," Mrs. Turpin agreed.

From this exchange, we glimpse the fear and ignorance of one woman, the patronizing superiority of the second, and the self-satisfied bigotry of the third. O'Connor allows the reader to experience these women and indeed a whole society.

Generally, dialogue is not used as a vehicle for exposition. Although frequently a character will by his words drop important information, conveying facts is not a primary function of dialogue. Its primary function is human interaction. Effective dialogue sounds the way people talk, but few writers attempt a phonographic representation of speech—partly because much day-to-day speech (Pass the butter. May I have the car?) is nonfunctional in a short story. Dialogue is interaction, and interaction pushes the story toward its conclusion. For instance, after the dialogue quoted above, and because of it, the young woman throws a book at Mrs. Turpin and assaults her, and from that the rest of the story grows.

Of course, monologue, reverie, letters, confession—as in Landolfi's "Gogol's Wife" and Barth's "Petition"—are variations on dialogue that can have similar effects. Occasionally a writer will forego the benefits of dialogue (Cortázar does not use any speech in "Axolōtl"), but nothing quite takes the place of letting the reader overhear significant exchanges.

Character

All of us engage in characterization almost every day of our lives. We tell our family or friends what happened at work or school, who said what, who did what, maybe why. Perhaps we mimic a voice or a gesture; we may even invent mannerisms to convey what we felt about a person. Yet common as characterization is, it is one of the mysteries of tale-telling. T. S. Eliot said:

> A "living character" is not necessarily "true to life." It is a person whom we can see and hear, whether he be true or false to human nature as we know it. What the creator of character needs is not so much knowledge of motives as keen sensibility; the dramatist need not understand people, but he must be exceptionally aware of them.

What goes into a living character? How does a writer create the breath of life on a page with mere words? Perhaps a few notions will cast a little light on the mystery. All that we have said about point of view touches on character, for the way we see the character determines the character we see. If the omniscient narrator of Maupassant's "A Country Outing" had been inside the ridiculed mother's mind, the reader might, instead of despising her as a foolish woman, have shared her hope for pleasure, her fear of ridicule, her sense of isolation from an indifferent husband. Third-person intimate or first person would have changed the character—and our attitude.

Tone also creates character. If the author's tone is contemptuous or humorous, the reader will likely see the character as contemptible or funny. Imagine the difference had Joyce Carol Oates in "Where Are You Going, Where Have You Been?" treated the overheated young girl humorously, or if Barth's tone in "Petition" had been honestly solemn and pathetic instead of mock-solemn and humorous. Our understanding of the characters would have been radically different.

Everything about a character defines him and contributes to the impact on us: looks, gestures, attire, social class, words spoken, views held, motives revealed, deeds done or not done. Discussing how these qualities are conveyed brings us again to *showing* versus *telling*. Some writers prefer to tell about their characters. The lawyer in "Bartleby, the Scrivener" simply informs the reader about his work, personal qualities, values. In "The Open Boat," Crane goes so far in telling as to summarize not only a character's emotional state but also to compare it to that of leaders in other situations:

> The injured captain, lying in the bow, was at this time buried in that profound dejection and indifference which comes, temporarily at least, to even the bravest and most enduring when, willy nilly, the firm fails, the army loses, the ship goes down.

And he even explains why:

> The mind of the master of a vessel is rooted deep in the timbers of her, though he command for a day or a decade, and this captain had on him the stern impression of a scene in the greys of dawn of seven turned faces, and later a stump of a top-

mast with a white ball on it that slashed to and fro at the waves, went low and lower, and down.

In cases like these two, telling provides a richness of background difficult to achieve by showing.

But Henry James believed that if details were rendered sharply enough, the reader would be able to infer character. In *Collected Impressions,* Elizabeth Bowen says,

> Characters must *materialize*—that is, must have a palpable physical reality. They must be not only see-able (visualizable): they must be able to be felt. . . . Physical personality belongs to action. . . . Pictures must be in movement. Eyes, hands, stature, etc. must appear, and only appear, in play.

In "A Simple Heart," Flaubert introduces Félicité's only lover: "a smart young fellow, who had been leaning on the shaft of a cart, came up and asked her to dance." And the seducer takes shape before our eyes.

In first-person and third-person-intimate point of view, there is often a simultaneous characterization of two characters. In Babel's "My First Goose," the narrator, upon seeing the commanding officer,

> wondered at the beauty of his giant's body. He rose, the purple of his riding breeches and the crimson of his little tilted cap and the decorations stuck on his chest cleaving the hut as a standard cleaves the sky.

A character can be revealed in the way others see him and in his view of others.

There are, as E. M. Forster says, flat characters and round characters. Flat characters do not change or develop, and though usually humorous, they are apt to be less interesting than round ones. Yet they must be given life adequate to their function in the story. Sometimes simple naming assists this function, as Dickens brilliantly shows with his Gradgrinds and Pecksniffs. (Although Akakii Akakiievich in Gogol's "The Overcoat" is not really flat, his name, which in Russian refers to feces or defecation, fixes him as one of the offal of human society.) Sometimes a flat character is pinpointed by a physical characteristic, like the after-lunch anger of the clerk Turkey in "Bartleby, the Scrivener." Sometimes a flat character can be identified by an emblem: the blaring transistor radio of the friend in "Where Are You Going, Where Have You Been?"

Flat characters are often types and easily tagged: the "artist" and the "capitalist pig" in "Balthazar's Marvelous Afternoon," the "overbearing wife" in "The Lady with the Pet Dog," the "jealous lover" in "The Avenger." Yet even as we laugh at characters whose souls have been solidified by early rigor mortis or who are beset by an *idée fixe,* we may catch a glimpse of the tragedy as well as the comedy of life.

Though a round character may be no more difficult to create than a flat one, he is almost by definition more complex. Each appearance of a round character adds to our understanding of him *and* is consistent, of a piece, with what we already know. Each gesture, each word spoken opens a door to the whole person, seems to imply a wholeness of personality. In "The Magic Barrel" we are introduced to Leo Finkle as a rabbinical student who seeks a wife in order to obtain a congregation. Thus far, he is flat and somewhat laughable. Then Malamud tells us that the look of sadness in the marriage broker's eyes "put Leo a little at ease although the situation, for him, was inherently tense." Leo is thus rounded, and the rest of the story is further evidence of his complex, touching humanity.

Sometimes stories seem not to be concerned with character at all. In "Axolōtl," Cortázar substitutes sensibility and obsessiveness for characterization. Sometimes when the main purpose of a story is its theme or moral, as in Aesop's *Fables,* or Bunyan's *The Pilgrim's Progress,* or modern counterparts like Brown's "Solipsist," the characters are only ends toward means.

People, ideally, are ends in themselves, not means to ends. But artists are creators and, for the sake of their compositions, often treat their people with the freedom a musician takes with his notes: manipulating, foreshortening, flattening, rounding. For the characters in a story are only part of a whole; it is within the whole context that we finally read the story.

Symbolism

A symbol is a sign standing for a meaning. It can be a *stipulated* meaning—as, for example, when a new nation "decides" on the symbolic colors for its new flag—but usually it is a *derived* meaning, one born from the history and experience of a culture, as the blindfolds on our statues of Justice stand for that impartiality of the law which is rooted in our Western tradition. Broadly speaking, all words are symbols (since they are signs standing for meanings); but in literature we limit the term to those words which have, in the context of the work, collected unto themselves—like iron filings unto a magnet—something of the story's essential point or meaning. Such a sign can light up a single character, an event, a scene, a whole story—can be, in fact, inseparable from its point of illumination. Indeed, the very titles of some stories in this volume name the symbols that unite them: "The Overcoat," "The Fall of the House of Usher," "Axolōtl," "A Worn Path." Unlike traditional symbols—the Cross of Christianity, the Star of David, the dove of peace—the symbols in these stories are not inherited but created by the writers, shaped by the pressures of their narratives. We no longer live, as Joseph Campbell has reminded us, in a "mythologically instructed community" that comes fully equipped with the traditional symbols embodying the traditional values and beliefs of that community. Instead, we are symbol-poor; as Carl Jung has said, "only an unparalleled impoverishment of symbolism could enable us to rediscover the gods as psychic features . . . as archetypes of the unconscious." But the need persists, in literature and in life, to focus our feelings and beliefs—or, more likely, our longing for belief and our groping for assurance. Writers, in their explorations of human experience, in their pursuit of the art (in Kermode's words) of "finding things out," are in some measure supplying those needs. Not all writers are clearly symbolists, and not all symbols in stories are big flags waving in our eyes; symbols can be quite unpretentious and, often, are no more than simple *things* or *acts* around which the meaning of the story clusters.

Thus that simple path in Welty's "A Worn Path" is a symbol. It is the *way* of Old Phoenix's suffering just as the stations of the Cross have, in Christian tradition, become ritualized as the *way* of Christ's suffering.

"Leaves" is much more self-conscious and complex in its symbolism. The story can be considered a meditation on the way we use symbolism in everyday life. Each description—from the grape leaves to the spider—tells us about the narrator's state of mind. Sometimes the referent is explicit: "The shadows these leaves cast upon each other . . . [contain] innumerable barbaric suggestions of scimitars, flanged spears, prongs, and menacing helmets." At the end, the narrator recognizes that nature cannot effectively symbolize and therefore cannot rid us of pain and responsibility: "The spider and I inhabit contiguous but incompatible cosmoses."

Less portentously, the "magic barrel" in Malamud's story symbolizes the unknown future of the rabbinical student, and at the end provides him with the fulfillment of both his hopes and his worst fears. In Babel's "My First Goose," the killing of the goose symbolizes for the Cossacks the narrator's manliness—but for the narrator his own cruelty.

Emblems are symbols of limited scope, and are sometimes mere impressionistic details—like Chekhov's bit of bottle shining in the starlight (see p. 8). In Babel's story, the Cossacks' shaving each other is an emblem of the camaraderie the narrator kills the goose to achieve. In McCullers's "A Tree * A Rock * A Cloud," we recognize the brightly lighted cafe as a haven for the lonely on a dark, rainy morning.

Are the details of the following passage from Wright's "The Man Who Was Almost a Man" emblems or just details?

> [Dave] came in sight of Joe's store. A yellow lantern glowed on the front porch. He mounted steps and went through the screen door, hearing it bang behind him. There was a strong smell of coal oil and mackerel fish.

The central symbol of that story is the gun—the symbol of Dave's rage and frustrated manhood—but these details spell his poverty, the condition that subsidizes, so to speak, the meaning of that gun. Emblems or details? The question is academic; the important thing is that we recognize how the particulars of a story can have profound and wide-ranging reverberations.

In the hands of a clumsy writer, a symbol may seem pasted onto a story, as if the writer were saying, "This way to the meaning." To be effective, a symbol will emerge from the story's own life, and help the reader back into the story. The snow in Aiken's story is such a symbol, and we must read its meaning in order to understand the trouble of the boy. Unfortunately, however, symbol hunting has become an overindulged indoor sport with some readers. Such readers should be reminded that Freud himself said that sometimes a cigar is only a cigar.

Theme

As we pointed out in Part I of this introduction, a story expresses the values of a writer and his conception of the human condition. In that sense, the whole story embodies his theme.

But the thoughts and feelings that a writer embodies in a story are seldom very simple. Most stories cannot be reduced, like Aesop's *Fables,* to a simple moral. A modern short story is not fertile soil in which to plant a sermon. Chekhov wrote to his editor:

> You upbraid me about objectivity, styling it indifference to good and evil, absence of ideals and ideas, etc. You would have me say, in depicting horse thieves, that stealing horses is an evil. But then, that has been known a long while, even without me. Let jurors judge them, for my business is only to show them as they are. . . . Of course, it would be gratifying to couple art with sermonizing, but, personally, I find this exceedingly difficult and, because of conditions imposed by technique, all but impossible.

Nor can a story be translated into a philosophic treatise or a sociological tract. Weighty ideas need systematic presentation as free as possible from the mess that is human beings. Organized knowledge by its very nature deals in generalities, but fiction deals with the specific person in the specific situation. And sometimes characters can take on a life of their own—almost in defiance of their creator's intention.

Still and all, as Chekhov well knew, serious readers demand more than an accounting of events; they demand that these events in some way illumine their own lives—that events be shaped into a meaning. After the pleasure or pain, excitement or perplexity caused by the story has receded, the reader is left with a residue, a distillation that we call its *theme*. After we lay aside Anderson's "I Want to Know Why," we can abstract its point: the intertwining of good and evil in people might be one way of putting it. When we have recovered from the shock of the cruelty in Lawrence's "Tickets, Please," we understand that Lawrence is saying something unusual about physical violence as a form of possession.

The reader should be cautioned against overemphasizing theme. Writers seldom set out to imbed an idea in a story. More likely, the theme emerges in the act of writing. If you had asked William Faulkner what "That Evening Sun" was about, he might have stated the subject, but he probably would not have wanted to abstract the meaning. If you asked the authors of "Like a Bad Dream" or "The Shawl" what their theme was, they would probably refer you back to their stories. For, just as the light at the end of the tunnel is inconceivable without the tunnel and inseparable from it, so the theme is inseparable from the totality of the story.

Part One

Beginnings: Forms of Early Stories

Myth and Legend

Myth: HOW THINGS GOT STARTED

How and where to draw the line between myth and legend is a vexed question with anthropologists and folklorists. It is usually said that a legend is the story of some wonderful or miraculous human event, or saint's life, which is believed to have a historical (though unverifiable) basis; whereas a myth more often deals with divinities and heroes and with ultimate natural events like the origin of man, or of the customs, rites, and institutions of a people. Of course, in their native milieus myths are held to be historically true, just as some Christians hold the Genesis story to be a literal account of the Creation. But myths normally deal with matters antecedent even to vestigial human memory, whereas legends approach historical time. To complicate things, there is also that generic term "folktale," which is almost synonymous with "legend," but not quite. Here is how Géza Róheim, a great pioneer in cultural anthropology and psychoanalysis, makes the distinction:

> In a myth the actors are mostly divine and sometimes human. In a folktale the *dramatis personae* are mostly human and especially the hero is human, frequently with supernatural beings as his opponents. In a myth we have definite locality; in a folktale the actors are nameless, the scene is just anywhere. A myth is part of a creed; it is believed by the narrator. The folktale is purely fiction, and not intended to be anything else.

The Genesis myth begins, "In the beginning God created the heaven and the earth"; the creation myth of the Native American Kiowa tribe begins, "You know, everything had to begin, and this is how it was. . . ." In the one the actors are both human and divine, in the other only human; the "definite locality" in the one is the Garden of Eden, in the other a "hollow log." But they are both parts of creeds and are both, in their living cultural contexts, believed to be true.

The Senecan Indian myth about the origin of stories is only another kind of creation myth, for the lore describing first things is inseparable from the sacred events themselves. That magic rock, which gives voice to "what happened a long time ago" in return for a gift of birds, might seem to take us across the divide from prehistory to history, and hence into legend. But legend occurs when the telling of stories is already a familiar act; here we are at the beginning of things, and are relearning what all primitive peoples know instinctively—that storytelling is a sacred act, arising out of man's earliest negotiations with the gods for survival and prosperity.

If that is how things began, the other Kiowa stories from N. Scott Momaday's beautiful collection are about how things went on as the tribe accumulated its history and values. The first two (about the talking dog and the girl who married the sun) are doubtless "folktales" in Róheim's sense; the third (an exploit against a Kiowa enemy) is unquestionably a legend, since it reflects an honorific memory of real events by real people.

In Sir Thomas Malory's great retelling of the stories of King Arthur and the round table, called *The Morte d'Arthur,* we get a similar mix of the miraculous and the historical. Merlin and his magic, Galahad's finding of the Holy Grail, exist side by side with more realistic tales of King Arthur and his attempts to bring some political and moral order to a barbarous land. Whether we call these stories "legends" or "folktales" (real events or fictions) depends on how much we want to suspend our disbelief. The particular story here, "The Great Tournament," is doubtless most appropriately called a legend.

But whatever we call them, these stories out of a believing past have increasing charm for modern readers. Perhaps, as Philip Rahv says, "The craze for myth is the fear of history." "To some people," he writes, "it appears as though the past, all of it together with its gods and sacred books, were being ground to pieces in the powerhouse of change, senselessly used up in the fabrication of an unthinkable future." But mythic time and—to a lesser extent—legendary time, have the advantage of "confounding past, present, and future in an undifferentiated unity," thus giving us timeless events "endlessly present," rather than historical events that occur "once only." To say this is to say in a particular way that myths and legends are part of sacred lore, whereas the genre of the short story is secular. Perhaps Saul Bellow has put it best in saying: "Myth, rising from the unconscious, is superior to mere 'story,' but myth will not come near while ordinary trivial ideas of self remain. The powers of myth can be raised up only when the well-known pretensions of selfhood are surrendered. Therefore consciousness must abase itself, and every hidden thing must be exhumed."

Yet one of the paradoxes of this collection is that, as we approach the present, those stories which ostensibly record despair, absurdity, and cultural breakup are, at the same time, those stories most close to myth and legend. The events of Samuel Beckett's "The End" or Heinrich Böll's "Like a Bad Dream" hardly seem events that occur "once only"—like the events in Thomas Mann's "Mario and the Magician" or Katherine Mansfield's "The Garden-Party." Rather they seem like timeless events, "endlessly present"—and such effects suggest that the search for final value via fiction may also be endless.

The First Book of Moses, called Genesis

CHAPTER 1

1   In the beginning God created the heaven and the earth.

2   And the earth was without form, and void; and darkness *was*[1] upon the face of the deep. And the Spirit of God moved upon the face of the waters.

3   And God said, Let there be light: and there was light.

4   And God saw the light, that *it was* good: and God divided the light from the darkness.

5   And God called the light Day, and the darkness he called Night. And the evening and the morning were the first day.

6   ¶ And God said, Let there be a firmament in the midst of the waters, and let it divide the waters from the waters.

7   And God made the firmament, and divided the waters which *were* under the firmament from the waters which *were* above the firmament: and it was so.

8   And God called the firmament Heaven. And the evening and the morning were the second day.

9   ¶ And God said, Let the waters under the heaven be gathered together unto one place, and let the dry *land* appear: and it was so.

10   And God called the dry *land* Earth; and the gathering together of the waters called he Seas: and God saw that *it was* good.

11   And God said, Let the earth bring forth grass, the herb yielding seed, *and* the fruit tree yielding fruit after his kind, whose seed *is* in itself, upon the earth: and it was so.

12   And the earth brought forth grass, *and* herb yielding seed after his kind, and the tree yielding fruit, whose seed *was* in itself, after his kind: and God saw that *it was* good.

13   And the evening and the morning were the third day.

14   ¶ And God said, Let there be lights in the firmament of the heaven to divide the day from the night; and let them be for signs, and for seasons, and for days, and years:

15   And let them be for lights in the firmament of the heaven to give light upon the earth: and it was so.

16   And God made two great lights; the greater light to rule the day, and the lesser light to rule the night: *he made* the stars also.

17   And God set them in the firmament of the heaven to give light upon the earth,

18   And to rule over the day and over the night, and to divide the light from the darkness: and God saw that *it was* good.

19   And the evening and the morning were the fourth day.

20   And God said, Let the waters bring forth abundantly the moving creature that hath life, and fowl *that* may fly above the earth in the open firmament of heaven.

21   And God created great whales, and every living creature that moveth, which the waters brought forth abundantly, after their kind, and every winged fowl after his kind: and God saw that *it was* good.

---

[1] Italics indicate words inserted by the original translators to make better English sense.

22 And God blessed them, saying, Be fruitful, and multiply, and fill the waters in the seas, and let fowl multiply in the earth.

23 And the evening and the morning were the fifth day.

24 ¶ And God said, Let the earth bring forth the living creature after his kind, cattle, and creeping thing, and beast of the earth after his kind: and it was so.

25 And God made the beast of the earth after his kind, and cattle after their kind, and every thing that creepeth upon the earth after his kind: and God saw that *it was* good.

26 ¶ And God said, Let us make man in our image, after our likeness: and let them have dominion over the fish of the sea, and over the fowl of the air, and over the cattle, and over all the earth, and over every creeping thing that creepeth upon the earth.

27 So God created man in his *own* image, in the image of God created he him; male and female created he them.

28 And God blessed them, and God said unto them, Be fruitful, and multiply, and replenish the earth, and subdue it: and have dominion over the fish of the sea, and over the fowl of the air, and over every living thing that moveth upon the earth.

29 ¶ And God said, Behold, I have given you every herb bearing seed, which *is* upon the face of all the earth, and every tree, in the which *is* the fruit of a tree yielding seed; to you it shall be for meat.

30 And to every beast of the earth, and to every fowl of the air, and to every thing that creepeth upon the earth, wherein *there is* life, *I have given* every green herb for meat: and it was so.

31 And God saw every thing that he had made, and, behold, *it was* very good. And the evening and the morning were the sixth day.

CHAPTER 2

1 Thus the heavens and the earth were finished, and all the host of them.

2 And on the seventh day God ended his work which he had made; and he rested on the seventh day from all his work which he had made.

3 And God blessed the seventh day, and sanctified it: because that in it he had rested from all his work which God created and made.

4 ¶ These *are* the generations of the heavens and of the earth when they were created, in the day that the LORD God made the earth and the heavens,

5 And every plant of the field before it was in the earth, and every herb of the field before it grew: for the LORD God had not caused it to rain upon the earth, and *there was* not a man to till the ground.

6 But there went up a mist from the earth, and watered the whole face of the ground.

7 And the LORD God formed man *of* the dust of the ground, and breathed into his nostrils the breath of life; and man became a living soul.

8 ¶ And the LORD God planted a garden eastward in Ē'-děn; and there he put the man whom he had formed.

9 And out of the ground made the LORD God to grow every tree that is pleasant to the sight, and good for food; the tree of life also in the midst of the garden, and the tree of knowledge of good and evil.

10 And a river went out of Ē'-děn to water the garden; and from thence it was parted, and became into four heads.

11 The name of the first *is* Pī'-sŏn: that *is* it which compasseth the whole land of Hăv'-i-läh, where *there* is gold;

12   And the gold of that land *is* good: there *is* bdellium and the onyx stone.

13   And the name of the second river *is* Gī'-hŏn: the same *is* it that compasseth the whole land of Ē-thī-ō'-pī-ă.

14   And the name of the third river *is* Hĭd'-dĕ-kĕl: that *is* it which goeth toward the east of Ăs-sўr'-ĭ-ă. And the fourth river *is* Êu-phrā'-tēs̀.

15   And the LORD God took the man, and put him into the garden of Ē'-dĕn to dress it and to keep it.

16   And the LORD God commanded the man, saying, Of every tree of the garden thou mayest freely eat:

17   But of the tree of the knowledge of good and evil, thou shalt not eat of it: for in the day that thou eatest thereof thou shalt surely die.

18   ¶ And the LORD God said, *It is* not good that the man should be alone; I will make him an help meet for him.

19   And out of the ground the LORD God formed every beast of the field, and every fowl of the air; and brought *them* unto Ăd'-ăm to see what he would call them: and whatsoever Ăd'-ăm called every living creature, that *was* the name thereof.

20   And Ăd'-ăm gave names to all cattle, and to the fowl of the air, and to every beast of the field; but for Ăd'-ăm there was not found an help meet for him.

21   And the LORD God caused a deep sleep to fall upon Ăd'-ăm, and he slept: and he took one of his ribs, and closed up the flesh instead thereof;

22   And the rib, which the LORD God had taken from man, made he a woman, and brought her unto the man.

23   And Ăd'-ăm said, This *is* now bone of my bones, and flesh of my flesh: she shall be called Woman, because she was taken out of Man.

24   Therefore shall a man leave his father and his mother, and shall cleave unto his wife: and they shall be one flesh.

25   And they were both naked, the man and his wife, and were not ashamed.

CHAPTER 3

1   Now the serpent was more subtil than any beast of the field which the LORD God had made. And he said unto the woman, Yea, hath God said, Ye shall not eat of every tree of the garden?

2   And the woman said unto the serpent, We may eat of the fruit of the trees of the garden:

3   But of the fruit of the tree which *is* in the midst of the garden, God hath said, Ye shall not eat of it, neither shall ye touch it, lest ye die.

4   And the serpent said unto the woman, Ye shall not surely die:

5   For God doth know that in the day ye eat thereof, then your eyes shall be opened, and ye shall be as gods, knowing good and evil.

6   And when the woman saw that the tree *was* good for food, and that is *was* pleasant to the eyes, and a tree to be desired to make *one* wise, she took of the fruit thereof, and did eat, and gave also unto her husband with her; and he did eat.

7   And the eyes of them both were opened, and they knew that they *were* naked; and they sewed fig leaves together, and made themselves aprons.

8   And they heard the voice of the LORD God walking in the garden in the cool of the day: and Ăd'-ăm and his wife hid themselves from the presence of the LORD God amongst the trees of the garden.

9   And the LORD God called unto Ăd'-ăm, and said unto him, Where *art* thou?

10   And he said, I heard thy voice in the garden, and I was afraid, because I *was* naked; and I hid myself.

11   And he said, Who told thee that thou *wast* naked? Hast thou eaten of the tree, whereof I commanded thee that thou shouldest not eat?

12   And the man said, The woman whom thou gavest *to be* with me, she gave me of the tree, and I did eat.

13   And the LORD God said unto the woman, What *is* this *that* thou hast done? And the woman said, The serpent beguiled me, and I did eat.

14   And the LORD God said unto the serpent, Because thou hast done this, thou *art* cursed above all cattle, and above every beast of the field; upon thy belly shalt thou go, and dust shalt thou eat all the days of thy life:

15   And I will put enmity between thee and the woman, and between thy seed and her seed; it shall bruise thy head, and thou shalt bruise his heel.

16   Unto the woman he said, I will greatly multiply thy sorrow and thy conception, in sorrow thou shalt bring forth children; and thy desire *shall be* to thy husband, and he shall rule over thee.

17   And unto Ăd'-ăm he said, Because thou has hearkened unto the voice of thy wife, and hast eaten of the tree, of which I commanded thee, saying, Thou shalt not eat of it: cursed *is* the ground for thy sake; in sorrow shalt thou eat *of* it all the days of thy life;

18   Thorns also and thistles shall it bring forth to thee; and thou shalt eat the herb of the field;

19   In the sweat of thy face shalt thou eat bread, till thou return unto the ground; for out of it wast thou taken: for dust thou *art,* and unto dust shalt thou return.

20   And Ăd'-ăm called his wife's name Ēve; because she was the mother of all living.

21   Unto Ăd'-ăm also and to his wife did the LORD God make coats of skins, and clothed them.

22   ¶ And the LORD God said, Behold, the man is become as one of us, to know good and evil: and now, lest he put forth his hand, and take also of the tree of life, and eat and live for ever:

23   Therefore the LORD God sent him forth from the garden of Ē'-dēn, to till the ground from whence he was taken.

24   So he drove out the man; and he placed at the east of the garden of Ē'-dēn Chĕr'-ū-bims, and a flaming sword which turned every way, to keep the way of the tree of life.

Kiowa Creation Myth

I

You know, everything had to begin, and this is how it was: the Kiowas came one by one into the world through a hollow log. They were many more than now, but not all of them got out. There was a woman whose body was swollen up with child, and she got stuck in the log. After that, no one could get through, and that is why the Kiowas are a small tribe in number. They looked all around and saw the world. It made them glad to see so many things. They called themselves *Kwuda,* "coming out."

From *The Way to Rainy Mountain* by N. Scott Momaday, pp. 16, 20, 22, 46. Copyright 1969 by The University of New Mexico Press. Reprinted by permission.

Legend: HOW THINGS WENT ON

Kiowa Legends

II

Before there were horses the Kiowas had need of dogs. That was a long time ago, when dogs could talk. There was a man who lived alone; he had been thrown away, and he made his camp here and there on the high ground. Now it was dangerous to be alone, for there were enemies all around. The man spent his arrows hunting food. He had one arrow left, and he shot a bear; but the bear was only wounded and it ran away. The man wondered what to do. Then a dog came up to him and said that many enemies were coming; they were close by and all around. The man could think of no way to save himself. But the dog said: "You know, I have puppies. They are young and weak and they have nothing to eat. If you will take care of my puppies, I will show you how to get away." The dog led the man here and there, around, and around, and they came to safety.

III

They lived at first in the mountains. They did not yet know of Tai-me, but this is what they knew: There was a man and his wife. They had a beautiful child, a little girl whom they would not allow to go out of their sight. But one day a friend of the family came and asked if she might take the child outside to play. The mother guessed that would be all right, but she told the friend to leave the child in its cradle and to place the cradle in a tree. While the child was in the tree, a redbird came among the branches. It was not like any bird that you have seen; it was very beautiful, and it did not fly away. It kept still upon a limb, close to the child. After a while the child got out of its cradle and began to climb after the redbird. And at the same time the tree began to grow taller, and the child was borne up into the sky. She was then a woman, and she found herself in a strange place. Instead of a redbird, there was a young man standing before her. The man spoke to her and said: "I have been watching you for a long time, and I knew that I would find a way to bring you here. I have brought you here to be my wife." The woman looked all around; she saw that he was the only living man there. She saw that he was the sun.

IV

If an arrow is well made, it will have tooth marks upon it. That is how you know. The Kiowas made fine arrows and straightened them in their teeth. Then they drew them to the bow to see if they were straight. Once there was a man and his wife. They were alone at night in their tipi. By the light of the fire the man was making arrows. After a while he caught sight of something. There was a small opening in the tipi where two hides were sewn together. Someone was there on the outside, looking in. The man went on with his work, but he said to his wife: "Someone is standing outside. Do not be afraid. Let us talk easily, as of ordinary things." He took up an arrow and straightened it in his teeth; then, as it was right for him to do, he drew it to the bow and took aim, first in this direction and then in that. And all the while he was talking, as if to his wife. But this is how he spoke: "I know that you are there on the outside, for I can feel your eyes upon me. If you are a Kiowa, you will understand what I am saying, and you will speak your name." But there was no answer, and the man went on in the same way, pointing the arrow all around. At last his aim fell upon the place where his enemy stood, and he let go of the string. The arrow went straight to the enemy's heart.

Seneca Legend: The Origin of Stories

[Told by Henry Jacob to Jeremiah Curtin]

"This happened long ago, in the time of our forefathers."

In a Seneca village lived a boy whose father and mother died when he was only a few weeks old. The little boy was cared for by a woman, who had known his parents. She gave him the name of POYESHAO^n (Orphan).

The boy grew to be a healthy, active little fellow. When he was old enough, his foster mother gave him a bow and arrows, and said, "It is time for you to learn to hunt. To-morrow morning go to the woods and kill all the birds you can find."

Taking cobs of dry corn the woman shelled off the kernels and parched them in hot ashes; and the next morning she gave the boy some of the corn for his breakfast and rolled up some in a piece of buckskin and told him to take it with him, for he would be gone all day and would get hungry.

POYESHAO^n started off and was very successful. At noon he sat down and rested and ate some of the parched corn, then he hunted till the middle of the afternoon. When he began to work toward home he had a good string of birds.

The next morning POYESHAO^n's foster mother gave him parched corn for breakfast and while he was eating she told him that he must do his best when hunting, for if he became a good hunter he would always be prosperous.

The boy took his bow and arrows and little bundle of parched corn and went to the woods; again he found plenty of birds. At midday he ate his corn and thought over what his foster mother had told him. In his mind he said, "I'll do just as my mother tells me, then some time I'll be able to hunt big game."

POYESHAO^n hunted till toward evening, then went home with a larger string of birds than he had the previous day. His foster mother thanked him, and said, "Now you have begun to help me get food."

Early the next morning the boy's breakfast was ready and as soon as he had eaten it he took his little bundle of parched corn and started off. He went farther into the woods and at night came home with a larger string of birds than he had the second day. His foster mother praised and thanked him.

Each day the boy brought home more birds than the previous day. On the ninth day he killed so many that he brought them home on his back. His foster mother tied the birds in little bundles of three or four and distributed them among her neighbors.

The tenth day the boy started off, as usual, and, as each day he had gone farther for game than on the preceding day, so now he went deeper into the woods than ever. About midday the sinew that held the feathers to his arrow loosened. Looking around for a place where he could sit down while he took the sinew off and wound it on again, he saw a small opening and near the center of the opening a high, smooth, flat-topped, round stone. He went to the stone, sprang up on to it and sat down. He unwound the sinew and put it in his mouth to soften, then he arranged the arrow feathers and was about to fasten them to the arrow when a voice, right there near him, asked, "Shall I tell you stories?"

POYESHAO^n looked up expecting to see a man, not seeing any one he looked behind the stone and around it, then he again began to tie the feathers to his arrow.

"Shall I tell you stories?" asked a voice right there by him.

The boy looked in every direction, but saw no one. Then he made up his mind to watch and find out who was trying to fool him. He stopped work and listened and when the voice again asked, "Shall I tell you stories?" he found that it came from the stone, then he asked, "What is that? What does it mean to tell stories?"

"It is telling what happened a long time ago. If you will give me your birds, I'll tell you stories."

"You may have the birds."

As soon as the boy promised to give the birds, the stone began telling what happened long ago. When one story was told, another was begun. The boy sat, with his head down, and listened. Toward night the stone said, "We will rest now. Come again to-morrow. If anyone asks about your birds, say that you have killed so many that they are getting scarce and you have to go a long way to find one."

While going home the boy killed five or six birds. When his foster mother asked why he had so few birds, he said that they were scarce; that he had to go far for them.

The next morning POYESHAO^n started off with his bow and arrows and little bundle of parched corn, but he forgot to hunt for birds, he was thinking of the stories the stone had told him. When a bird lighted near him he shot it, but he kept straight on toward the opening in the woods. When he got there he put his birds on the stone, and called out, "I've come! Here are birds. Now tell me stories."

The stone told story after story. Toward night it said, "Now we must rest till to-morrow."

On the way home the boy looked for birds, but it was late and he found only a few.

That night the foster mother told her neighbors that when POYESHAO^n first began to hunt he had brought home a great many birds, but now he brought only four or five after being in the woods from morning till night. She said there was something strange about it, either he threw the birds away or gave them to some animal, or maybe he idled time away, didn't hunt. She hired a boy to follow POYESHAO^n and find out what he was doing.

The next morning the boy took his bow and arrows and followed POYESHAO^n, keeping out of his sight and sometimes shooting a bird. POYESHAO^n killed a good many birds; then, about the middle of the forenoon, he suddenly started off toward the East, running as fast as he could. The boy followed till he came to an opening in the woods and saw POYESHAO^n climb up and sit down on a large round stone; he crept nearer and heard talking. When he couldn't see the person to whom POYESHAO^n was talking he went up to the boy, and asked, "What are you doing here?"

"Hearing stories."

"What are stories?"

"Telling about things that happened long ago. Put your birds on this stone, and say, 'I've come to hear stories.'"

The boy did as told and straightway the stone began. The boys listened till the sun went down, then the stone said, "We will rest now. Come again to-morrow."

On the way home POYESHAO^n killed three or four birds.

When the woman asked the boy she had sent why POYESHAO^n killed so few birds, he said, "I followed him for a while, then I spoke to him, and after that we hunted together till it was time to come home. We couldn't find many birds."

The next morning the elder boy said, "I'm going with POYESHAO^n to hunt, it's sport." The two started off together. By the middle of the forenoon each boy had a long string of birds. They hurried to the opening, put the birds on the stone, and said, "We have come. Here are the birds! Tell us stories."

They sat on the stone and listened to stories till late in the afternoon, then the stone said, "We'll rest now till to-morrow."

On the way home the boys shot every bird they could find, but it was late and they didn't find many.

Several days went by in this way, then the foster mother said, "Those boys kill more birds than they bring home," and she hired two men to follow them.

The next morning, when POYESHAO^n and his friend started for the woods the two men followed. When the boys had a large number of birds they stopped hunting and hurried to the opening. The men followed and, hiding behind trees, saw them put the birds on a large round stone, then jump up and sit there, with their heads down, listening to a man's voice; every little while they said, "Û^n!"

"Let's go there and find out who is talking to those boys," said one man to the other. They walked quickly to the stone, and asked, "What are you doing, boys?"

The boys were startled, but POYESHAO^n said, "You must promise not to tell anyone."

They promised, then POYESHAO^n said, "Jump up and sit on the stone."

The men seated themselves on the stone, then the boy said, "Go on with the story, we are listening."

The four sat with their heads down and the stone began to tell stories. When it was almost night the stone said, "To-morrow all the people in your village must come and listen to my stories. Tell the chief to send every man, and have each man bring something to eat. You must clean the brush away so the people can sit on the ground near me."

That night POYESHAO^n told the chief about the storytelling stone, and gave him the stone's message. The chief sent a runner to give the message to each family in the village.

Early the next morning every one in the village was ready to start. POYESHAO^n went ahead and the crowd followed. When they came to the opening each man put what he had brought, meat or bread, on the stone; the brush was cleared away, and every one sat down.

When all was quiet the stone said, "Now I will tell you stories of what happened long ago. There was a world before this. The things that I am going to tell about happened in that world. Some of you will remember every word that I say, some will remember a part of the words, and some will forget them all—I think this will be the way, but each man must do the best he can. Hereafter you must tell these stories to one another—Now listen."

Each man bent his head and listened to every word the stone said. Once in a while the boys said "Û^n!" When the sun was almost down the stone said, "We'll rest now. Come to-morrow and bring meat and bread."

The next morning when the people gathered around the stone they found that the meat and bread they had left there the day before was gone. They put the food they had brought on the stone, then sat in a circle and waited. When all was quiet the stone began. Again it told stories till the sun was almost down, then it said, "Come to-morrow. To-morrow I will finish the stories of what happened long ago."

Early in the morning the people of the village gathered around the stone and, when all was quiet, the stone began to tell stories, and it told till late in the afternoon, then it said, "I have finished! You must keep these stories as long as the world lasts; tell them to your children and grandchildren generation after generation. One person will remember them better than another. When you go to a man or a woman to ask for one of these stories carry something to pay for it, bread or meat, or whatever you have. I know all that happened in the world before this; I have told it to you. When you visit one another, you must tell these things, and keep them up always. I have finished."

And so it has been. From the Stone came all the knowledge the Senecas have of the world before this.

Arthurian Legend: Sir Thomas Malory's
The Great Tournament

(*Caxton XVIII, 21–4*)

So at after Christmas king Arthur let call unto him many knights, and there they advised togethers to make a party and a great tournament and jousts. And the king of North Wales said to king Arthur he would have on his party king Anguish of Ireland and the King with the Hundred Knights and the king of Northumberland and sir Galahalt the Haut Prince. So these four kings and this mighty duke took party against king Arthur and the knights of the Round Table.

And the cry was made that the day of jousts should be besides Westminster, upon Candlemas day, whereof many knights were glad and made them ready to be at that jousts in the freshest manner.

Then queen Guenevere sent for sir Lancelot and said thus: 'I warn you that ye ride no more in no jousts nor tournaments but that your kinsmen may know you. And at this jousts that shall be ye shall have of me a sleeve of gold, and I pray you for my sake to force yourself there, that men may speak of you worship. But I charge you, as ye will have my love, that ye warn your kinsmen that ye will bear that day the sleeve of gold upon your helmet.' 'Madam,' said sir Lancelot, 'it shall be done.' And other made great joy of other.

And when sir Lancelot saw his time he told sir Bors that he would depart, and no mo with him but sir Lavain, unto the good hermit that dwelled in the forest of Windsor, whose name was sir Brastias. And there he thought to repose him and to take all the rest that he might, because he would be fresh at that day of jousts. So sir Lancelot and sir Lavain departed, that no creature wist where he was become but the noble men of his blood. And when he was come to the hermitage, wit you well he had great cheer.

And so daily sir Lancelot used to go to a well fast by the hermitage, and there he would lie down and see the well spring and burble, and some time he slept there. So at that time there was a lady that dwelled in that forest, and she was a great huntress, and daily she used to hunt. And ever she bore her bow with her, and no men went never with her, but always women, and they were all shooters and could well kill a deer at the stalk and at the tryst. And they daily bore bows, arrows, horns and wood-knives, and many good dogs they had, both for the string and for a bait.

So it happed the lady, the huntress, had abated her dog for the bow at a barren hind, and so this barren hind took the flight over heaths and woods. And ever this lady and part of her women coasted the hind, and checked it by the noise of the hound to have met with the hind at some water. And so it happened that that hind came to the same well thereas sir Lancelot was sleeping and slumbering.

And so the hind, when she came to the well, for heat she went to soil, and there she lay a great while. And the dog came after and umbecast about, for she had lost the very perfect fewte of the hind. Right so came that lady, the huntress, that knew by her dog that the hind was at the soil by that well, and thither she came straight and found the hind. And anon as she had spied her she put a broad arrow in her bow, and shot at the hind, and so she overshot the hind, and so by misfortune the arrow smote sir Lancelot in the thick of the buttock over the barbs.

When sir Lancelot felt him so hurt, he whirled up woodly, and saw the lady that had smitten him. And when he knew she was a woman he said thus: 'Lady, or damsel, whatsomever ye be, in an evil time bore ye this bow. The devil made you a shooter!'

'Now mercy, fair sir!' said the lady, 'I am a gentlewoman that useth here in this forest hunting, and God knoweth I saw you not, but as here was a barren hind at the soil in this well. And I went I had done well, but my hand swerved.'

'Alas,' said sir Lancelot 'ye have mischieved me!'

And so the lady departed. And sir Lancelot, as he might, pulled out the arrow and left the head still in his buttock, and so he went weakly unto the hermitage, evermore bleeding as he went. And when sir Lavain and the hermit espied that sir Lancelot was so sore hurt, wit you well they were passing heavy. But sir Lavain wist not how that he was hurt nother by whom. And then were they wroth out of measure. And so with great pain the hermit got out the arrow head out of sir Lancelot's buttock, and much of his blood he shed. And the wound was passing sore and unhappily smitten, for it was on such a place that he might not sit in no saddle.

'Ah, mercy Jesu!' said sir Lancelot, 'I may call myself the most unhappy man that liveth, for ever when I would have fainest worship there befalleth me ever some unhappy thing. Now, so Jesu me help,' said sir Lancelot, 'and if no man would but God, I shall be in the field on Candlemas day at the jousts, whatsomever fall of it.'

So all that might be gotten to heal sir Lancelot was had. So when the day was come sir Lancelot let devise that he was arrayed, and sir Lavain and he and their horses, as they had been Saracens. And so they departed and came nigh to the field.

So the king of North Wales he had a hundred knights with him, and the king of Northumberland brought with him an hundred good knights, and king Anguish of Ireland brought with him an hundred good knights ready to joust. And sir Galahalt the Haut Prince brought with him an hundred good knights, and the King with the Hundred Knights brought with him as many, and all these were proved good knights.

Then came in king Arthur's party, and in came with him the king of Scots, and an hundred knights with him, and king Uriens of Goore brought with him an hundred knights, and king Howell of Brittany he brought with him an hundred knights, and duke Chalence of Clarence brought with him an hundred knights. And king Arthur himself came into the field with two hundred knights, and the most party were knights of the Round Table that were all proved noble men. And there were old knights set on scaffolds for to judge with the queen who did best.

Then they blew unto the field. And there the king of North Wales encountered with the king of Scots, and there the king of Scots had a fall. And the king of Ireland smote down king Uriens, and the king of Northumberland smote down king Howell of Brittany, and sir Galahalt the Haut Prince smote down duke Chalence of Clarence. And then king Arthur was wood wroth, and ran to the King with the Hundred Knights, and so king Arthur smote him down. And after with that same spear he smote down other three knights—and then his spear broke—and did passingly well.

So therewith came in sir Gawain and sir Gaheris, sir Agravain and sir Mordred, and there every of them smote down a knight and sir Gawain smote down four knights. And then there began a great medley, for then came in the knights of sir Lancelot's blood and sir Gareth and sir Palomides with them, and many knights of the Round Table. And they began to hold the four kings and the mighty duke so hard that were nigh discomfit. But this sir Galahalt the Haut Prince was a noble knight, and by his mighty prowess of arms he held the knights of the Round Table strait.

So all this doing saw sir Lancelot, and then he came into the field with sir Lavain with him, as it had been thunder. And then anon sir Bors and the knights of his blood espied sir Lancelot anon and said unto them all, "I warn you, beware of him with the sleeve of gold upon his head, for he is himself my lord sir Lancelot.' And for great goodness sir Bors warned sir Gareth. 'Sir, I am well paid,' said sir Gareth, 'that I may know him.' 'But who is he,' said they all, 'that rideth with him in the same array?' 'Sir, that is the good and gentle knight sir Lavain,' said sir Bors.

So sir Lancelot encountered with sir Gawain, and there by force sir Lancelot smote down sir Gawain and his horse to the earth. And so he smote down sir Agravain and sir Gaheris, and also he smote down sir Mordred, and all this was with one spear. Then sir Lavain met with sir Palomides, and either met other so hard and so fiercely that both their horses fell to the earth. And then were they horsed again. And then met sir Lancelot with sir Palomides, and there sir Palomides had a fall.

And so sir Lancelot, or ever he stint, and as fast as he might get spears, he smote down thirty knights, and the most party were knights of the Round Table. And ever the knights of his blood withdrew them, and made them ado in other places where sir Lancelot came not.

And then king Arthur was wroth when he saw sir Lancelot do such deeds, and then the king called unto him sir Gawain, sir Gaheris, sir Agravain, sir Mordred, sir Kay, sir Grifflet, sir Lucan de Butler, sir Bedivere, sir Palomides and sir Saphir, his brother. And so the king with these nine knights made them ready to set upon sir Lancelot and upon sir Lavain.

And all this espied sir Bors and sir Gareth. 'Now I dread me sore,' said sir Bors, 'that my lord sir Lancelot will be hard matched.' 'Now by my head,' said sir Gareth, 'I will ride unto my lord sir Lancelot for to help him whatsomever me betide. For he is the same man that made me knight.' 'Sir, ye shall not do so,' said sir Bors, 'by my counsel, unless that ye were disguised.' 'Sir, ye shall see me soon disguised,' said sir Gareth.

And therwithal he had espied a Welsh knight where he was to repose him, for he was sore hurt before of sir Gawain. And unto him sir Gareth rode, and prayed him of his knighthood to lend him his shield for his. 'I will well,' said the Welsh knight.

And when sir Gareth had his shield—the book saith it was green with a maiden which seemed in it—then sir Gareth came driving unto sir Lancelot all that ever he might, and said,

'Sir knight, take keep to thyself, for yonder cometh king Arthur with nine noble knights with him, to put you to a rebuke. And so I am come to bear you fellowship for the old love ye have shewed unto me.' 'Grauntmercy,' said sir Lancelot. 'But, sir,' said sir Gareth, 'encounter ye with sir Gawain, and I shall encounter with sir Palomides, and let sir Lavain match with the noble king Arthur. And when we have delivered them let us three hold us sadly togethers.'

So then came in king Arthur with his nine knights with him, and sir Lancelot encountered with sir Gawain and gave him such a buffet that the arson of his saddle burst, and sir Gawain fell to the earth. Then sir Gareth encountered with sir Palomides, and he gave him such a buffet that both his horse and he dashed to the earth. Then encountered king Arthur with sir Lavain, and there either of them smote other to the earth, horse and all, that they lay both a great while.

Then sir Lancelot smote down sir Agravain and sir Gaheris and sir Mordred, and sir Gareth smote down sir Kay, sir Saphir and sir Grifflet. And then sir Lavain was horsed again, and he smote down sir Lucan de Butler and sir Bedivere, and then there began great throng of good knights. Then sir Lancelot hurled here and there, and raced and pulled off helms, that at that time there might none sit him a buffet with spear neither with sword. And sir Gareth did such deeds of arms that all men marvelled what knight he was with the green shield, for he smote down that day and pulled down mo than thirty knights. And, as the French book saith, sir Lancelot marvelled, when he beheld sir Gareth do such deeds, what knight he might be. And sir Lavain smote and pulled down mo than twenty knights. And yet, for all this, sir Lancelot knew not sir Gareth; for and sir Tristam de Lyonesse other sir Lamorak de Wales had been on live, sir Lancelot would have deemed he had been one of them twain.

So ever as sir Lancelot, sir Gareth and sir Lavain fought on the tone side, sir Bors, sir Ector de Maris, sir Lionel, sir Bleoberis, sir Galihud, sir Galihodin and sir Pelleas and many mo other of king Banis blood fought upon another party and held the King with the Hundred Knights and the king of Northumberland right strait.

So this tournament and jousts dured long till it was near night, for the knights of the Round Table relieved ever unto king Arthur; for the king was wroth out of measure that he and his knights might not prevail that day. Then said sir Gawain to the king,

'Sir, I marvel where are all this day sir Bors de Ganis and his fellowship of sir Lancelot's blood, that of all this day they be not about you. And therefore I deem it is for some cause,' said sir Gawain.

'By my head,' said sir Kay, 'sir Bors is yonder all this day upon the right hand of this field, and there he and his blood doth more worshipfully than we do.'

'It may well be,' said sir Gawain, 'but I dread me ever of guile. For on pain of my life, that same knight with the red sleeve of gold is himself sir Lancelot, for I see well by his riding and by his great strokes. And the other knight in the same colours is the good young knight sir Lavain, and that knight with the green shield is my brother sir Gareth, and yet he hath disguised himself, for no man shall make him be against sir Lancelot, because he made him knight.'

'By my head,' said king Arthur, 'nephew, I believe you. And therefore now tell me what is your best counsel.'

'Sir,' said Gawain, 'my counsel is to blow unto lodging. For and he be sir Lancelot du Lake and my brother sir Gareth with him, with the help of that good young knight, sir Lavain, trust me truly, it will be no boot to strive with them but if we should fall ten or twelve upon one knight, and that were no worship, but shame.'

'Ye say truth,' said the king, 'it were shame for us, so many as we be, to set upon them any more. For wit you well,' said king Arthur, 'they be three good knights, and namely that knight with the sleeve of gold.'

And anon they blew unto lodging, but forthwithal king Arthur let send unto the four kings and to the mighty duke and prayed them that the knight with the sleeve of gold depart not from them 'but that the king may speak with him.' Then forthwithal king Arthur alight and unarmed him and took a little hackney and rode after sir Lancelot, for ever he had a spy upon him. And so he found him among the four kings and the duke, and there the king prayed them all unto supper, and they said they would with good will. And when they were unarmed king Arthur knew sir Lancelot, sir Gareth and sir Lavain. 'Ah, sir Lancelot,' said king Arthur, 'this day ye have heated me and my knights!'

And so they yode unto king Arthur's lodging all together, and there was a great feast and great revel. And the prize was given unto sir Lancelot, for by heralds they named him that he had smitten down fifty knights, and sir Gareth five-and-thirty knights, and sir Lavain four-and-twenty.

Then sir Lancelot told the king and the queen how the lady huntress shot him in the forest of Windsor in the buttock with a broad arrow, and how the wound was at that time six inches deep and inlike long.

Also king Arthur blamed sir Gareth because he left his fellowship and held with sir Lancelot. 'My lord,' said sir Gareth, 'he made me knight, and when I saw him so hard bestead, methought it was my worship to help him. For I saw him do so much deeds of arms, and so many noble knights against him, that when I understood that he was sir Lancelot du Lake I shamed to see so many good knights against him alone.'

'Now, truly,' said king Arthur unto sir Gareth, 'ye say well, and worshipfully have ye done, and to yourself great worship. And all the days of my life,' said king Arthur unto sir Gareth, 'wit you well I shall love you and trust you the more better. For ever it is,' said king Arthur, 'a worshipful knight's deed to help and succour another worshipful knight when he seeth him in danger. For ever a worshipful man will be loth to see a worshipful man shamed, and he that is of no worship and meddleth with cowardice never shall he shew gentleness nor no manner of goodness where he seeth a man in danger, for then will a coward never shew mercy. And always a good man will do ever to another man as he would be done to himself.'

So then there were made great feasts unto kings and dukes, and revel, game and play, and all manner of noblesse was used. And he that was courteous, true and faithful to his friend was that time cherished.

Fable, Parable, Exemplum, and Allegory

The earliest fables were beast fables, stories about animals who behave like humans and convey a moral lesson. The Greek slave Aesop (ca. 620–560 B.C.) is, of course, the great exemplar here. Through his dogs and crows, foxes and lions, he speaks cautionary wisdom that is still taken to heart. And lest we miss the point, the moral is explicitly stated at the end ("familiarity breeds contempt" or "little by little does the trick")—a device that satirical fabulists like George Ade and James Thurber have used with delightful effect. A fable need not have animals as actors, but it must always have a moral, implied or explicit: that is its chief identifying characteristic. The stories by Hawthorne, Updike, Wilbur, Brown, and Barthelme in this volume can all, with more or less accuracy, be called fables.

Teaching moral lessons via fiction is an ancient custom, and one specialized way of doing this is with the *exemplum* ("example"), a story used to spice up a sermon. One of the great exempla in our literature is Chaucer's *The Pardoner's Tale,* in which a priestly con man fleeces his congregation with the help of a tale containing the moral: *radix malorum est cupiditas* ("greed is the root of all evil"). In a more serious vein, St. Gregory's sermon about Adam's sin is brought to life by the story of the woman who gives birth to a babe in a dungeon. How can the mother ever describe to her boy what the sun, moon, and stars are like? How can we, born in the darkness of Adam's sin, ever know the glory of the unfallen state? The point is clear: the reaches of the unknown or the unimaginable are brought home by a simple illustration.

A parable is like an exemplum except that it is shorter and pithier and has a more or less clear-cut allegorical twist. The New Testament is full of parables, like that of the talents and of the five wise and foolish virgins; and the sermons of Jesus are continually spiced with these homely illustrations that made clear to an unlettered audience the meaning of his words ("Ye are the salt of the earth: but if the salt have lost his savour, wherewith shall it be salted?" [Matt. 5:13]). A parable is perhaps best defined as a short fable; excellent modern examples are Hawthorne's "The Minister's Black Veil" and Borges's "Everything and Nothing" and "Borges and I."

Allegory is more complex, and the interested student would do well to consult Angus Fletcher's *Allegory: The Theory of a Symbolic Mode* (1964). In an allegory the characters are not individuals but personified abstractions, and the happenings are purely symbolic. Like the above forms, allegories are designed to teach something—an idea, a moral lesson—but they sometimes have a wayward habit of lapsing into fictions pure and simple. As Fletcher says, allegory embraces "a quite extraordinary variety of literary kinds." One of the purest examples of the mode is John Bunyan's *The Pilgrim's Progress* (1675), which had a prodigious popularity with Puritan readers who scorned other kinds of fiction as snares of the Devil. Bunyan is a born storyteller, and a particularly memorable part of his tale is the experience of Christian and Faithful in the town of Vanity, with its famous Fair, where everything is for sale from titles to bawds to souls. In an allegory like this, everything stands for something else, everything is symbolic (see Symbolism, pp. 21–22), so the reader is inevitably involved in a process of discovery and interpretation. It is a clever device, since it relieves the reader of the feeling that he is being preached at; instead he is participating in the story, in a sense *creating* it. Strangely enough, allegory, though it is an ancient form, seems to have a renewed appeal for certain modernist story writers like Kafka, Updike, and Böll. The stories of these writers are mixed modes, but they all show an allegorical bent toward the symbolic—where character and event mean more than themselves and suggest the timeless.

Fables: Aesop

THE FOX AND THE CROW

A Fox once saw a Crow fly off with a piece of cheese in its beak and settle on a branch of a tree. "That's for me, as I am a Fox," said Master Reynard, and he walked up to the foot of the tree. "Good-day, Mistress Crow," he cried. "How well you are looking today: how glossy your feathers; how bright your eye. I feel sure your voice must surpass that of other birds, just as your figure does; let me hear but one song from you that I may greet you as the Queen of Birds." The Crow lifted up her head and began to caw her best, but the moment she opened her mouth the piece of cheese fell to the ground, only to be snapped up by Master Fox. "That will do," said he. "That was all I wanted. In exchange for your cheese I will give you a piece of advice for the future—

Do not trust flatterers."

The Flatterer doth rob by stealth,
His victim, both of Wit and Wealth.

THE DOG IN THE MANGER

A Dog looking out for its afternoon nap jumped into the Manger of an Ox and lay there cosily upon the straw. But soon the Ox, returning from its afternoon work, came up to the Manger and wanted to eat some of the straw. The Dog in a rage, being awakened from its slumber, stood up and barked at the Ox, and whenever it came near attempted to bite it. At last the Ox had to give up the hope of getting at the straw, and went away muttering:

"Ah, people often grudge others what they cannot enjoy themselves."

Parables: Matthew 25

Then shall the kingdom of heaven be likened unto ten virgins, which took their lamps, and went forth to meet the bridegroom.

2 And five of them were wise, and five *were* foolish.

3 They that *were* foolish took their lamps, and took no oil with them:

4 But the wise took oil in their vessels with their lamps.

5 While the bridegroom tarried, they all slumbered and slept.

6 And at midnight there was a cry made, Behold, the bridegroom cometh; go ye out to meet him.

7 Then all those virgins arose, and trimmed their lamps.

8 And the foolish said unto the wise, Give us of your oil, for our lamps are gone out.

9 But the wise answered, saying, *Not so;* lest there be not enough for us and you: but go ye rather to them that sell, and buy for yourselves.

10 And while they went to buy, the bridegroom came; and they that were ready went in with him to the marriage: and the door was shut.

11 Afterward came also the other virgins, saying, Lord, Lord, open to us.

12 But he answered and said, Verily I say unto you, I know you not.

13 Watch therefore, for ye know neither the day nor the hour wherein the Son of man cometh.

14 ¶ For *the kingdom of heaven is* as a man traveling into a far country, *who* called his own servants, and delivered unto them his goods.

15 And unto one he gave five talents, to another two, and to another one; to every man according to his several ability; and straightway took his journey.

16 Then he that had received the five talents went and traded with the same, and made *them* other five talents.

17 And likewise he that *had received* two, he also gained other two.

18 But he that had received one went and digged in the earth, and hid his lord's money.

19 After a long time the lord of those servants cometh, and reckoneth with them.

20 And so he that had received five talents came and brought other five talents, saying, Lord, thou deliveredst unto me five talents; behold, I have gained beside them five talents more.

21 His lord said unto him, Well done, *thou* good and faithful servant: thou hast been faithful over a few things, I will make thee ruler over many things: enter thou into the joy of thy lord.

22 He also that had received two talents came and said, Lord, thou deliveredst unto me two talents: behold, I have gained two other talents beside them.

23 His lord said unto him, Well done, good and faithful servant; thou hast been faithful over a few things, I will make thee ruler over many things: enter thou into the joy of thy lord.

24 Then he which had received the one talent came and said, Lord, I knew thee that thou art an hard man, reaping where thou hast not sown, and gathering where thou hast not strawed:

25 And I was afraid, and went and hid thy talent in the earth: lo, *there* thou hast *that is* thine.

26 His lord answered and said unto him, *Thou* wicked and slothful servant, thou knewest that I reap where I sowed not, and gather where I have not strawed:

27 Thou oughtest therefore to have put my money to the exchangers, and *then* at my coming I should have received mine own with usury.

28 Take therefore the talent from him, and give *it* unto him which hath ten talents.

29 For unto every one that hath shall be given, and he shall have abundance: but from him that hath not shall be taken away even that which he hath.

Exemplum: From St. Gregory The Great, *Dialogues*

After Adam, the father of the human race, was driven from the joys of paradise as a result of sin, he entered upon the distress of this dark exile we are now suffering. Driven outside of himself by his sinful act, he was no longer able to perceive the joys of heaven which had been the object of his contemplation before. In paradise he habitually enjoyed converse with God and in purity of heart and loftiness of vision mingled with holy, angelic spirits. After falling from that noble state he also lost the inner light which enlightened his mind. Born as we are of his flesh into the darkness of this exile, we hear, of course, that there is a heavenly country, that angels are its citizens, and that the spirits of the just live in company with them; but being carnal men without any experimental knowledge of the invisible, we wonder about the existence of anything we cannot see with our bodily eyes. Adam could not possibly have entertained such doubts, for, although he was excluded from the happiness of paradise, he remembered what he had lost, because he had once known it. Carnal men, on the other hand, cannot remember or appreciate these joys when they hear about them, because, unlike him, they have no past experience to fall back on.

Take the case of an expectant mother cast into a dungeon where she gives birth to a son. He stays there with her and grows up in the darkness. Suppose this boy's mother described to him the sun, the moon, and the stars, the mountains and fields, birds flying in the air and horses running in the fields. Born and raised in the dungeon, knowing only the perpetual darkness around him, he would doubt whether the things he heard his mother describe actually existed, since he had no experience of them. So it is with men born into the darkness of this earthly exile. They hear about lofty and invisible things, but hesitate to believe in them, because they know only the lowly, visible things of earth

From St. Gregory The Great, *Dialogues*. Translated by Odo John Zimmerman, O.S.B. New York: Fathers of The Church, Inc., 1959.

into which they were born. It was for this reason that the Creator of the visible and invisible worlds came as the Only-begotten of the Father to redeem the human race and to send the Holy Spirit into our hearts. From Him we were to receive new life in order to believe those truths of which we as yet had no knowledge through experience. All of us, therefore, who have received this Spirit as the pledge of our inheritance are no longer in doubt about the existence of invisible beings. On the other hand, anyone who is not yet solidly grounded in this faith ought to accept what his elders say, putting his trust in them, since they have experimental knowledge of the invisible world through the Holy Spirit. In our story, too, it would have been foolish for the little boy to think his mother was telling him lies about the light, merely because he himself knew nothing but the darkness of the dungeon.

Allegory: Bunyan's *The Pilgrim's Progress*

Evang. My Sons, you have heard in the words of the truth of the Gospel, that you must through many tribulations enter into the Kingdom of Heaven. And again, that in every City, bonds and afflictions abide in you; and therefore you cannot expect that you should go long on your Pilgrimage without them, in some sort or other. You have found something of the truth of these testimonies upon you already, and more will immediately follow: for now, as you see, you are almost out of this Wilderness, and therefore you will soon come into a Town that you will by and by see before you: and in that Town you will be hardly beset with enemies, who will strain hard but they will kill you: and be you sure that one or both of you must seal the testimony which you hold, with blood: but be you faithful unto death, and the King will give you a Crown of life. He that shall die there, although his death will be unnatural, and his pain perhaps great, he will yet have the better of his fellow; not only because he will be arrived at the Cœlestial City soonest, but because he will escape many miseries that the other will meet with in the rest of his Journey. But when you are come to the Town, and shall find fulfilled what I have here related, then remember your friend, and quit your selves like men; and commit the keeping of your souls to your God in well-doing, as unto a faithful Creator.

Then I saw in my Dream, that when they were got out of the Wilderness, they presently saw a Town before them, and the name of that Town is *Vanity;* and at the town there is a *Fair* kept, called *Vanity-Fair.* It is kept all the Year long: it beareth the name of *Vanity-Fair,* because the Town where 'tis kept, *is lighter than* Vanity; and also, because all that is there sold, or that cometh thither, is *Vanity.* As is the saying of the wise, *All that cometh is Vanity.*

This Fair is no new erected business, but a thing of ancient standing; I will shew you the original of it.

Almost five thousand years agone, there were Pilgrims walking to the Cœlestial City, as these two honest persons are; and *Beelzebub, Apollyon,* and *Legion,* with their Companions, perceiving by the path that the Pilgrims made, that their way to the City lay through *this Town of Vanity,* they contrived here to set up a Fair[1]; a Fair wherein

---

[1] Behold Vanity Fair! the Pilgrims there
     Are chain'd and stand beside:
     Even so it was our Lord pass'd here,
     And on Mount *Calvary* dy'd.

From John Bunyan, *The Pilgrim's Progress.* Reprinted by permission of Oxford University Press.

should be sold of *all sorts of Vanity,* and that it should last all the year long. Therefore at *this Fair* are all such Merchandize sold, as Houses, Lands, Trades, Places, Honors, Preferments, Titles, Countries, Kingdoms, Lusts, Pleasures and Delights of all sorts, as Whores, Bawds, Wives, Husbands, Children, Masters, Servants, Lives, Blood, Bodies, Souls, Silver, Gold, Pearls, Precious Stones, and what not.

And moreover, at this Fair there is at all times to be seen Jugglings, Cheats, Games, Plays, Fools, Apes, Knaves, and Rogues, and that of every kind.

Here are to be seen too, and that for nothing, Thefts, Murders, Adulteries, False-swearers, and that of a blood-red colour.

And as in other fairs of less moment, there are the several Rows and Streets, under their proper names, where such and such Wares are vended: So here likewise, you have the proper Places, Rows, Streets, (*viz.* Countreys and Kingdoms,) where the Wares of this Fair are soonest to be found: Here is the *Britain* Row, the *French* Row, the *Italian* Row, the *Spanish* Row, the *German* Row, where several sorts of Vanities are to be sold. But as in other *fairs,* some one Commodity is as the chief of all the *fair,* so the Ware of *Rome* and her Merchandize is greatly promoted in *this fair:* Only our *English* Nation, with some others, have taken a dislike thereat.

Now, as I said, the way to the Cœlestial City lies just through *this Town,* where this lusty Fair is kept; and he that will go to the City, and yet not go through this Town, *must* needs *go out of the World.* The Prince of Princes himself, when here, went through *this Town* to his own Country, and that upon a *Fair-day too:* Yea, and as I think, it was *Beelzebub* the chief Lord of this *Fair,* that invited him to buy of his Vanities; yea, would have made him Lord of the *Fair,* would he but have done him Reverence as he went through the *Town.* Yea, because he was such a person of Honour, *Beelzebub* had him from *Street* to *Street,* and shewed him all the Kingdoms of the World in a little time, that he might, if possible, allure that Blessed One, to *cheapen* and *buy* some of his *Vanities.* But he had no mind to the Merchandize, and therefore left the *Town,* without laying out so much as one Farthing upon these *Vanities.* This *Fair* therefore is an Ancient thing, of long standing, and a very great *Fair.*

A Variety Of Secular Tales

In the centuries before the rise of the short story, the Western world saw a great variety of secular tales, in prose and verse. Preeminent among them were the short prose tales of Giovanni Boccaccio (1313–1375) called *novelle* (sing. *novella*). Unlike *romances* (idealized, poetic, and often improbable tales of chivalry and love) the novella dealt with the actual cause-and-effect world of imperfect men and women. The very word *novella* suggests their secular nature; they are something new (fr. Italian *novello*), not the retelling of the traditional and the sacred, and it is appropriate that from *novella* came the modern word *novel. The Decameron,* Boccaccio's most famous work, is a series of 100 tales told by seven ladies and three men who have fled the plague that visited Florence in 1348. They visit neighboring villas between Settingnano and Fiesole, agreeing to spend part of each of ten days (hence the title) telling stories, each giving one story per day. This "frame" for a series of tales became a familiar medieval device and was used by Chaucer in *The Canterbury Tales.* But with Chaucer the storytellers of the frame are as lively as the stories; with Boccaccio the storytellers remain "flat" while the tales take on all the life. In either case they are secular tales: they deal with earthly, not heavenly, love and are often deliberately bawdy, scandalous, and irreverent. Though the *novella* has a reputation for "epigrammatic terseness," it is, like the age of its origin, a leisurely form compared to what we know as the short story. If the following tale by Philostratus seems to betray some male chauvinism, be assured that in others the ladies get some of their own back.

The Miller's Tale is a *fabliau,* a humorous tale of French origin that had wide popularity in the twelfth and thirteenth centuries. Normally in verse (octosyllabic couplets), it was a favorite of the medieval *jongleurs,* or minstrels, who spread them throughout France. They were full of bawdy humor and irreverent practical jokes, and favorite butts of their satire were the clergy and women as the daughters of Eve. In the Prologue to *The Canterbury Tales,* Chaucer describes the Miller as stocky, fat-faced, and red-bearded, with a wart atop his flat nose—all characteristics that Chaucer's contemporaries (ca. 1340–1400) would have associated with a "choleric" man: quarrelsome, hot-tempered, loudmouthed, and lecherous. The fabliau is his perfect métier: its lusty vulgarity fits his character perfectly.

Although *fabliau* means "little fable," the form has little in common with fables: its characters are always human and its "moral"—when it exists—is not meant for the ears of puritans.

As we near the nineteenth century, many new story forms emerge—satires, picaresque (or rogue) tales, gothic tales, oriental tales, didactic tales, and many others. The form represented here is one we all know, the "fairytale." The fairytale has its roots deep in folklore and the oral tradition, and many scholars, beginning with Charles Perrault (*Contes,* 1697) and continuing notably with Jacob and Wilhelm Grimm (*Grimm's Fairy Tales,* 1812, 1815), have discovered and "revived" the old originals. Collections now exist from virtually every ancient culture on earth—including the Japanese—but Europe has perhaps yielded the richest treasure trove. Familiar tales like "Hansel and Gretel," "Cinderella," and "The Sleeping Beauty" were all collected (and edited) by the Brothers Grimm, who saw in fairytales, as Max Lüthi says, "remnants of ancient myths, playful descendants of an ancient intuitive vision of life and the world." But other familiar tales, like "The Three Bears," are not ancient at all, but the creations of modern writers (in this case Robert Southey, writing in the early 19th century) who, in imitating and embellishing the old forms, found a wonderful way to enter the world of childhood. Other examples are Sir James Barrie's *Peter Pan* (1904), L. Frank Baum's *The Wizard of Oz* (1903), and Kenneth Grahame's *The Wind in the Willows* (1908), to name but a few. So the fairytale as we know it is a modern as well as ancient form, and reminds us that the childhood of the race and our individual childhoods have much in common. The story reproduced here, "The Blue Beard" was first revived by Charles Perrault in 1697, and translated into English—along with many other tales—by Robert Samber in 1729. These tales were all given "morals"; the lesson to be derived from "The Blue Beard" was revealed in the phrase: "curiosity, thou mortal bane." Present readers, especially women, will no doubt derive a more apt moral from this tale of sadism and male chauvinism.

Novella: Boccaccio's *The Decameron*[1]

THE THIRD DAY

Upon which Day, all matters to be discoursed on, doe passe under the regiment of Madam Neiphila: concerning such persons as (by their wit and industry) have attained to their long wished desires, or recovered something, supposed to be lost.

The Induction to the Ensuing Discourses

The morning put on a vermillion countenance and made the Sunne to rise blushing red, when the Queene (and all the faire company) were come abroad forth of their Chambers; the Seneshall or great Master of the Houshold, having (long before) sent all things necessary to the place of their next intended meeting. And the people which prepared there every needfull matter, suddainely when they saw the Queene was setting forward, charged all the rest of their followers, as if it had beene preparation for a Campe; to make hast away with the carriages, the rest of the Familie remaining behind, to attend upon the Ladies and Gentlemen.

With a milde, majesticke, and gentle pace, the Queene rode on, being followed by the other Ladies, and the three young Gentlemen, taking their way towards the West; conducted by the musicall notes of sweete singing Nightingales, and infinite other pretty Birds beside, riding in a tract not much frequented, but richly abounding with faire hearbes and flowres, which by reason of the Sunnes high mounting, beganne to open their bosome, and fill the fresh Ayre with their odorifferous perfumes. Before they had travelled two small miles distance, all of them pleasantly conversing together; they arrived at another goodly Pallace, which being somewhat mounted above the plaine, was seated on the side of a little rising hill.

When they were entred thereinto, and had seene the great Hall, the Parlors, and beautifull Chambers, every one so stupendiously furnished, withall convenient commodities to them belonging, and nothing wanting, that could be desired; they highly commended it, reputing the Lord thereof for a most worthy man, that had adorned it in such Princely manner. Afterward, being descended lower, and noting the most spacious and pleasant Court, the Sellars stored with the choysest Wines, and delicate Springs of waters every where running, their prayses then exceeded more and more.

And being weary with beholding such variety of pleasures, they sate downe in a faire Gallery, which tooke the view of the whole Court, it being round engirt with trees and flowres, whereof the season then yeelded great plenty. And then came the discreete Master of the Houshold, with divers servants attending on him, presenting them with Comfits, and other Banquetting, as also very singular Wines, to serve in stead of a breakefast.

Having thus reposed themselves a while, a Garden gate was set open to them, coasting on one side of the Pallace, and round enclosed with high mounted walles. Whereinto when they were entred, they found it to be a most beautifull Garden, stored with all varieties that possibly could be devised; and therefore they observed it the more respectively. The walkes and allyes were long and spacious, yet directly straite as an arrow, environed with spreading vines, whereon the grapes hung in copious clusters; which being come to their full ripenesse, gave so rare a smel throughout the Garden, with other sweete savours intermixed among, that they supposed to feele the fresh spiceries of the East.

[1] From the English edition of 1625.

It would require large length of time, to describe all the rarities of this place, deserving much more to be commended, then my best faculties will affoord me. In the middest of the Garden, was a square plot, after the resemblance of a Meadow, flourishing with high grasse, hearbes, and plants, beside a thousand diversities of flowres, even as if by the Art of painting they had beene there deputed. Round was it circled with very verdant Orenge and Cedar Trees, their branches plentiously stored with fruit both old and new, as also the flowres growing freshly among them, yeelding not onely a rare aspect to the eye, but also a delicate savour to the smell.

In the middest of this Meadow, stood a Fountaine of white Marble, whereon was engraven most admirable workemanship, and within it (I know not whether it were by a naturall veine, or artificiall) flowing from a figure, standing on a Collumne in the midst of the Fountaine, such aboundance of water, and so mounting up towards the Skies, that it was a wonder to behold. For after the high ascent, it fell downe againe into the wombe of the Fountaine, with such a noyse and pleasing murmure, as the streame that glideth from a mill. When the receptacle of the Fountaine did over-flow the bounds, it streamed along the Meadow, by secret passages and chanels, very faire and artificially made, returning againe into every part of the Meadow, by the like wayes of cunning conveighance, which allowed it full course into the Garden, running swiftly thence down towards the plaine; but before it came thether, the very swift current of the streame, did drive two goodly Milles, which brought in great benefit to the Lord of the soile.

The sight of this Garden, the goodly grafts, plants, trees, hearbes, frutages, and flowres, the Springs, Fountaines, and pretty rivolets streaming from it, so highly pleased the Ladies and Gentlemen, that among other infinite commendations, they spared not to say: if any Paradise remayned on the earth to be seene, it could not possibly be in any other place, but onely was contained within the compasse of this Garden. With no meane pleasure and delight they walked round about it, making Chaplets of flowers, and other faire branches of the trees, continually hearing the Birds in melodious notes, ecchoing and warbling one to another, even as if they envied each others felicities.

But yet another beauty (which before had not presented it selfe to them) on a sodaine they perceyved; namely divers pretty creatures in many parts of the Gardens. In one place Conies[2] tripping about; in another place Hares; in a third part Goats browsing on the hearbes, and little yong Hindes feeding every where: yet without strife or warring together, but rather living in such a Domesticke and pleasing kinde of company, even as if they were appointed to enstruct the most noble of all creatures, to imitate their sociable conversation.

When their senses had sufficiently banquetted on those severall beauties, the tables were sodainly prepared about the Fountaine; where first they sung six Canzonets[3] and having paced two or three dances, they sate downe to dinner, according as the Queene ordained, being served in very sumptuous manner, with all kinde of costly and delicate viands, yet not any babling noise among them. The Tables being withdrawne, they played againe upon their instruments, singing and dancing gracefully together: till, in regard of the extreame heate, the Queene commanded to give over, and permitted such as were so pleased, to take their ease and rest. But some, as not satisfied with the places pleasures, gave themselves to walking: others fell to reading the lives of the Romanes; some to the Chesse, and the rest to other recreations.

But, after the dayes warmth was more mildely qualified, and every one had made benefit of their best content: they went (by order sent from the Queene) into the

---

[2] Rabbits
[3] Short, lighthearted songs, or airs.

Meadow where the Fountaine stood, and being set about it, as they used to do in telling their Tales (the argument appointed by the Queene being propounded) the first that had the charge imposed, was Philostratus, who began in this manner.

Massetto di Lamporechio, by counterfetting himselfe to be dumbe, became a Gardiner in a Monastery of Nunnes, where he had familiar conversation with them all.

THE FIRST NOVELL

Wherein is declared, that Virginity is very hardly to be kept in all places.

Most worthy Ladies, there wants no store of men and women, that are so simple, as to credit for a certainty, that so soon as a yong virgin hath the veile put on hir head, and the black Cowle given to cover her withall, she is no longer a woman, nor more sensible of feminine affections, then as if in turning Nun, shee became converted to a stone. And if (perchance) they heard some matters, contrary to their former perswasion; then they grow so furiously offended, as if one had committed a most foule and enormous sinne, directly against the course of Nature. And the torrent of this opinion hurries them on so violently, that they will admit no leisure to consider, how (in such a scope of liberty) they have power to doe what they list, yea beyond all meanes of sufficient satisfying, never remembring how potent the priviledge of idlenes is, especially when it is backt by solitude. In like manner, there are other people now, who verily beleeve, that the Spade and Pickaxe, grosse feeding and labour, do quench al sensual and fleshly concupiscence, yea in such as till and husband the ground, by making them dull, blockish, and (almost) meere senslesse of understanding. But I will approve (according as the Queene hath commanded me, and within the compasse of her direction) by a short and pleasant Tale; how greatly they are abused by errour, that build upon so weake a foundation.

Not farre from Alexandria, there was a great and goodly Monasterie, belonging to the Lord of those parts, who is termed the Admirall. And therein, under the care and trust of one woman, divers virgins were kept as recluses, or Nuns, vowed to chastity of life; out of whose number, the Soldan[4] of Babylon (under whom they lived in subjection) at every three yeers end, had usually three of these virgins sent him. At the time wherof I am now to speake, there remained in the Monastery, no more but eight religious Sisters only, beside the Lady Abbesse, and an honest poor man, who was a Gardiner, and kept the Garden in commendable order.

His wages being small, and he not well contented therewith, would serve there no longer: but making his accounts even, with the Factotum or Bayliffe belonging to the house, returned thence to the village of Lamporechio, being a native of the place. Among many other that gave him welcom home, was a yong Hebrew pezant of the country, sturdy, strong and yet comely of person, being named Masset. But because he was born not farre off from Lamporechio, and had there bin brought up all his yonger dayes, his name of Masset (according to their vulgar speech) was turned to Massetto, and therefore he was usually called and knowne by the name of Massetto of Lamporechio.

Massetto, falling in talke with the honest poore man, whose name was Lurco, demanded of him what services hee had done in the Monasterie, having continued there so long a time? Quoth Lurco, I laboured in the Garden, which is very faire and great; then I went to the Forest to fetch home wood, and cleft it for their Chamber fuell, drawing up all theyr water beside, with many other toilsome services else: but the

---

allowance of my wages was so little, as it would not pay for the shoes I wore. And that which was worst of all, they being all yong women, I thinke the divel dwels among them, for a man cannot doe any thing to please them. When I have bene busie at my worke in the garden, one would come and say, Put this heere, put that there; and others would take the dibble[5] out of my hand, telling me, that I did not performe any thing well, making me so weary of their continuall trifling, as I have lefte all busines, given over the Garden, and what for one mollestation, as also many other; I intended to tarry no longer there, but came away, as thou seest. And yet the Factotum desired me at my departing, that if I knew any one who would undertake the aforesaid labours, I should send him thither, as (indeed) I promised to do: but let mee fall sicke and dye, before I helpe to send them any.

When Massetto had heard the words of Lurco, hee was so desirous to dwell among the Nunnes, that nothing else now hammered in his head: for he meant more subtilly than poore Lurco did, and made no doubt to please them sufficiently. Then considering with himselfe, how best he might bring his intent to effect; which appeared not easily to bee done. He could question no further therein with Lurco, but onely demaunded other matter of him, saying: Introth thou didst well Lurco, to come away from so tedious a dwelling, had he not need to be more then a man that is to live with such women? It were better for him to dwell among so many divels, because they understand not the tenth part that womens wily wits can dive into.

After their conference was ended, Massetto began to beate his braines how he might compasse to dwell among them, and knowing that he could wel enough performe all the labours whereof Lurco had made mention, he cared not for any losse he should sustaine thereby, but onely stood in doubt of his entertainment, because he was too yong and sprightly. Having pondered on many imaginations, he said to himselfe. The place is farre enough distant hence, and none there can take knowledge of mee; if I have wit sufficient, cleanely to make them beleeve that I am dumbe, then (questionles) I shal be received. And resolving to prosecute this determination, he tooke a Spade on his shoulder, and without revealing to any body whether hee went, in the disguise of a poore labouring Countryman, he travelled to the Monastery.

When he was there arrived, he found the great gate open, and entering in boldly, it was his good hap to espy the Factotum in the court, according as Lurco had given description of him. Making signes before him, as if he were both dumbe and deafe; he manifested, that he craved an Almes for Gods sake, making shewes beside, that if need required, he could cleave wood, or doe any reasonable kinde of service. The Factotum gladly gave him food and afterward shewed him divers knotty logs of wood, which the weake strength of Lurco had left uncloven; but this fellow being more active and lusty, quickly rent them all to pieces. Now it so fell out, that the Factotum must needs go to the Forrest, and tooke Massetto along with him thither: where causing him to fell divers Trees, by signes he bad him to lade the two Asses therewith, which commonly carried home all the wood, and so drive them to the Monasterie before him, which Massetto knew well enough how to do, and performed it very effectually.

Many other servile Offices were there to bee done, which caused the Factotum to make use of his paines divers other dayes beside; in which time, the Lady Abbesse chancing to see him, demanded of the Factotum what he was? Madam (quoth hee) a poore labouring man, who is both deafe and dumbe, hither he came to crave an almes the other day, the which in charity I could do no lesse but give him; for which, hee hath done many honest services about the house. It seemes beside, that hee hath pretty skill

---

[5] A gardening tool for making holes in the ground for bulbs or seedlings.

in Gardening, so that if I can perswade him to continue here, I make no question of his able services: for the old silly man is gon, and we have need of such a stout fellow, to do the busines belonging to the Monastery, and one fitter for the turne, comes sildome hither. Moreover, in regard of his double imperfections, the Sisters can sustaine no impeachment by him. Whereto the Abbesse answered, saying; By the faith of my body, you speake but the truth: understand then, if hee have any knowledge in Gardening, and whether hee will dwell heere, or no: which compasse so kindly as you can. Let him have a new paire of shoes, fill his belly daily full of meate, flatter, and make much of him, for wee shall finde him worke enough to do. All which, the Factotum promised to fulfill sufficiently.

Massetto, who was not far off from them all this while, but seemed seriously busied about sweeping and making cleane the Court, heard all these speeches; and being not a little joyful of them; said to himselfe. If once I come to worke in your Garden, let the proofe yeeld praise of my skill and knowledge. When the Factotum perceived, that he knew perfectly how to undergo his businesse, and had questioned him by signes, concerning his willingnesse to serve there still, and received the like answere also, of his dutifull readinesse thereto; he gave him order to worke in the Garden, because the season did now require it; and to leave all other affayres for the Monastery, attending now onely the Gardens preparation.

As Massetto was thus about his Garden emploiment, the Nunnes began to resort thither, and thinking the man to be dumbe and deafe indeede, were the more lavish of their language, mocking and flowting him very immodestly, as being perswaded, that he heard them not. And the Lady Abbesse, thinking he might as well be an Eunuch, as deprived both of hearing and speaking, stood the lesse in feare of the Sisters walkes, but referred them to their owne care and providence. On a day, Massetto having laboured somewhat extraordinarily, lay downe to rest himselfe awhile under the trees, and two delicate yong Nunnes, walking there to take the aire, drew neere to the place where he dissembled sleeping; and both of them observing his comelinesse of person, began to pitty the poverty of his condition; but much more the misery of his great defectes. Then one of them, who had a little livelier spirit then the other, thinking Massetto to be fast asleepe, began in this manner.

Sister (quoth she) if I were faithfully assured of thy secrecie, I would tell thee a thing which I have often thought on, and it may (perhaps) redound to thy profit. Sister, replyed the other Nun, speake your minde boldly, and beleeve it (on my Maiden-head) that I will never reveale it to any creature living. Encouraged by this solemne answere, the first Nun thus prosecuted her former purpose, saying. I know not Sister, whether it hath entred into thine understanding or no, how strictly we are here kept and attended, never any man daring to adventure among us, except our good and honest Factotum, who is very aged; and this dumbe fellow, maimed, and made imperfect by nature, and therefore not worthy the title of a man. Ah Sister, it hath oftentimes bin told me, by Gentlewomen comming hither to visite us, that all other sweetes in the world, are mockeries, to the incomparable pleasures of man and woman, of which we are barred by our unkind parents, binding us to perpetuall chastity, which they were never able to observe themselves.

A Sister of this house once told me, that before her turne came to be sent to the Soldane,[6] she fell in frailty with a man that was both lame and blinde, and discovering

---

[6] Literally "sultan." This usage represents an attempt by an early editor to remove the scene of Massetto's rise and fall from a Christian to a pagan environment. The present translator had evidently consulted the version of Lionardo Salviati which read as follows:

the same to her Ghostly Father in confession; he absolved her of that sinne; affirming, that she had not transgressed with a man, because he wanted his rationall and understanding parts. Behold Sister, heere lyes a creature, almost formed in the self-same mold, dumbe and deafe, which are two the most rationall and understanding parts that do belong to any man, and therefore no Man, wanting them. If folly and frailty would be committed with him (as many times since hee came hither it hath run in my minde) hee is by Nature, sworne to such secrecie, that he cannot (if he would) be a blabbe thereof. Beside, the Laws and constitution of our Religion doth teach us, that a sinne so assuredly concealed, is more than halfe absolved.

Ave Maria Sister (saide the other Nun) what kinde of words are these you utter? Doe not you know, that we have promised our virginity to God? Oh Sister (answered the other) how many things are promised to him every day, and not one of a thousand kept or performed? If wee have made him such a promise, and some of our weaker-witted sisters do performe it for us, no doubt but he will accept it in part of payment. Yea but Sister, replied the second Nun againe, there is another danger lying in the way: If we prove to be with childe, how shall we doe then? Sister (quoth our couragious wench) thou art affraide of harme before it happen: if it come so to passe, let us consider on it then: thou art but a Novice in matters of such moment, we are provided of a thousand meanes, whereby to prevent conception. Or, if they should faile, we are so surely fitted, that the world shall never know it. Let it suffice, our lives must not be by any so much as suspected, our Monastery questioned, or our Religion rashly scandalized. Thus shee schooled her younger Sister in wit, albeit as forward as shee in will, and longed as desirouslie, to know what kinde of creature man was.

After some other questions, how this intention of theirs might bee safely brought to full effect: the sprightly Nun that had wit at will, thus answered. You see Sister (quoth she) it is now the houre of midday, when all the rest of our sisterhood are quiet in their Chambers, because we are then allowed to sleep, for our earlier rising to morning Mattins. Here are none in the Garden now but our selves, and while I awake him, bee you the watch, and afterward follow mee in my fortune, for I will valiantly leade you the way. Massetto immitating a Dogges sleepe, heard all this conspiracie intended against him, and longed as earnestly till shee came to awake him. Which being done, he seeming very simple and sottish, and she chearing him with flattering behaviour: into the close Arbour they went, which the Sunnes bright eye could not pierce into, and there I leave it to the Nunnes owne approbation, whether Massetto was a man rationall, or no. Ill deeds require longer time to contrive, then act: and both the Nuns having bene with Massetto at this new forme of confession, were enjoyned (by him) such an easie and silent penance, as brought them the oftner to shrift, and made him to proove a very perfect Confessour.

Desires obtayned, but not fully satisfied, doe commonly urge more frequent accesse, then wisedome thinkes expedient, or can continue without discovery. Our two joviall Nunnes, not a little proud of their private stolne pleasures, so long resorted to the close Arbour, till another Sister, who had often observed their haunt thither, by meanes

---

"Not far from *Alexandria,* there was (and yet is) a great & goodly Monastery, belonging to the Lord of those parts, who is termed the Admiral. And therein, vnder the care and trust of one woman, diuers virgins were kept as recluses or Nunnes, vowed to chastity of life; out of whose number, the Soldan of *Babylon* (vnder whom they liued in subiection) at euery three yeares end, had vsually three of these virgins sent him."

[Quoted in Herbert G. Wright, *The First English Translation of the "Decameron"* (1620). Uppsala: A. B. Lundequistska Bokhandeln, 1953, p. 162.]

of a little hole in her Window; that shee began to suspect them with Massetto, and imparted the same to two other Sisters, all three concluding, to accuse them before the Lady Abbesse. But upon a further conference had with the Offenders, they changed opinion, tooke the same oath as the forewomen had done; and because they would be free from any taxation at all: they revealed their adventures to the other three ignorants, and so fell all eight into one formall confederacie, but by good and warie observation, least the Abbesse her selfe should descry them; finding poore Massetto such plenty of Garden-worke, as made him verie doubtfull in pleasing them all.

It came to passe in the end, that the Lady Abbesse who all this while imagined no such matter, walking all alone in the garden on a day, found Massetto sleeping under an Almond tree, having then very little businesse to doe, because he had wrought hard all the night before. She observed him to be an hansome man, young, lusty, well-limbde and proportioned, having a mercifull commisseration of his dumbenesse and deafenes, being perswaded also in like manner, that if hee were an Eunuch too, hee deserved a thousand times the more to be pittied. The season was exceeding hot, and he lay downe so carelesly to sleepe, that somthing was noted, wherein shee intended to be better resolved, almost falling sicke of the other Nunnes disease. Having awaked him, she commanded him by signes that he should follow her to her chamber, where he was kept close so long, that the Nunnes grew offended, because the Gardiner came not to his daily labour.

Well may you imagine that Massetto was no misse-proud man now, to be thus advanced from the Garden to the Chamber, and by no worse woman then the Lady Abbesse her selfe: what signes, shews, or what language he speaks there, I am not able to expresse; onely it appeared, that his behaviour pleased her so well, as it procured his daily repairing thether; and acquainted her with such familiar conversation, as she would have condemned in the Nunnes her daughters, but that they were wise enough to keep it from her. Now began Massetto to consider, that hee had undertaken a taske belonging to great Hercules, in giving content to so many, and by continuing dumbe in this manner, it would redound to his no meane detriment. Whereupon, as he was one night sitting by the Abbesse, the string that retained his tongue from speech, brake on a sodaine, and thus he spake.

Madam, I have often heard it said, that one Cocke may doe service to ten several Hennes, but ten men can very hardly even with all their best endeavour, give full satisfaction every way to one woman; and yet I am tied to content nine, which is farre beyond the compasse of my power to do. Already have I performed so much Garden and Chamber-work, that I confesse my selfe starke tired, and can travaile no further, and therefore let me entreate you to lycense my departure hence, or finde some meanes for my better ease. The Abbesse hearing him speake, who had so long bene there dumbe, being stricken into admiration, and accounting it almost a miracle, said. How commeth this to passe? I verily beleeved thee to be dumbe. Madam (quoth Massetto) so I was indeed, but not by Nature; onely I had a long lingering sicknes which bereft me of speech, and which I have not onely recovered againe this night, but shal ever remaine thankfull to you for it.

The Abbesse verily credited his answer, demanding what he meant in saying, that he did service to nine? Madam, quoth he, this were a dangerous question, and not easily answered before all the eight Sisters. Upon this reply, the Abbesse plainely perceived, that not onely she had fallen into folly, but all the Nunnes likewise cried guilty too: wherfore being a woman of sound discretion, she would not grant that Massetto should depart, but to keepe him still about the Nunnes businesse, because the Monastery should not be scandalized by him. And the Factotum being dead a little before, his strange recovery of speech revealed, and some things else more neerely concerning them: by generall consent, and with the good liking of Massetto, he was created the Factotum of the Monasterie.

All the neighboring people dwelling thereabout, who knew Massetto to be dumbe, by fetching home wood daily from the Forest, and divers employments in other places, were made to beleeve, that by the Nunnes devout prayers and discipline, as also the merite of the Saint, in whose honour the Monastery was built and erected, Massetto had his long restrained speech restored, and was now become their sole Factotum, having power now to employ others in drudgeries, and ease himselfe of all such labours. And albeit he made the Nunnes to be fruitfull, by encreasing some store of yonger sisters, yet all matters were so close and cleanly carried, as it was never talkt of, till after the death of the Ladie Abbesse, when Massetto beganne to grow in good yeeres, and desired to returne home to his native abiding, which (within a while after) was granted him.

Thus Massetto being rich and olde, returned home like a wealthy father, taking no care for the nursing of his children, but bequeathed them to the place where they were bred and borne, having (by his wit and ingenious apprehension) made such a benefit of his youthfull yeeres, that now he meerily tooke ease in his age.

Fabliau: Chaucer's *The Miller's Tale*

WORDS BETWEEN THE HOST AND THE MILLER

When we had heard the tale the Knight had told,
Not one among the pilgrims, young or old,
But said it was indeed a noble story
Worthy to be remembered for its glory,
And it especially pleased the gentlefolk.
Our Host began to laugh and swore in joke:
'It's going well, we've opened up the bale;
Now, let me see. Who'll tell another tale?
Upon my soul the game was well begun!
Come on, Sir Monk, and show what can be done;
Repay the Knight a little for his tale!'
    The Miller, very drunk and rather pale,
Was straddled on his horse half-on half-off
And in no mood for manners or to doff
His hood or hat, or wait on any man,
But in a voice like Pilate's he began
To huff and swear. 'By blood and bones and belly,
I've got a noble story I can tell 'ee,
I'll pay the Knight his wages, not the Monk.'
    Our Host perceived at once that he was drunk
And said, 'Now hold on, Robin, dear old brother;
We'll get some better man to tell another;

From *Chaucer: The Canterbury Tales,* trans. Nevill Coghill (Penguin Classics, Revised Edition, 1977), pp. 102–122. Copyright 1951 by Nevill Coghill; Copyright © the Estate of Nevill Coghill, 1958, 1960, 1975, 1977. Reprinted by permission of Penguin Books Ltd.

You wait a bit. Let's have some common sense.'
'God's soul, I won't!' said he. 'At all events
I mean to talk, or else I'll go my way.'
Our Host replied, 'Well, blast you then, you may.
You're just a fool; your wits are overcome.'
   'Now listen,' said the Miller, 'all and some,
To what I have to say. But first I'm bound
To say I'm drunk, I know it by my sound.
And if the words get muddled in my tale
Just put it down to too much Southwark ale.
I mean to tell a legend and a life
Of an old carpenter and of his wife,
And how a student came and set his cap . . .'
   The Reeve looked up and shouted, 'Shut your trap!
Give over with your drunken harlotry.
It is a sin and foolishness,' said he,
'To slander any man or bring a scandal
On wives in general. Why can't you handle
Some other tale? There's other things beside.'
   To this the drunken Miller then replied,
'My dear old brother Oswald, such is life.
A man's no cuckold if he has no wife.
For all that, I'm not saying you are one;
There's many virtuous wives, all said and done,
Ever a thousand good for one that's bad,
As well you know yourself, unless you're mad.
What's biting you? Can't I tell stories too?
I've got a wife, Lord knows, as well as you,
Yet for the oxen in my plough, indeed,
I wouldn't take it on me, more than need,
To think myself a cuckold, just because.
I'm pretty sure I'm not, and never was.
One shouldn't be too inquisitive in life
Either about God's secrets or one's wife.
You'll find God's plenty all you could desire;
Of the remainder, better not enquire.'
   What can I add? The Miller had begun,
He would not hold his peace for anyone,
But told his churl's tale his own way, I fear.
And I regret I must repeat it here,
And so I beg of all who are refined
For God's love not to think me ill-inclined
Or evil in my purpose. I rehearse
Their tales as told, for better or for worse,
For else I should be false to what occurred.
So if this tale had better not be heard,
Just turn the page and choose another sort;
You'll find them here in plenty, long and short;
Many historical, that will profess
Morality, good breeding, saintliness.

Do not blame me if you should choose amiss.
The Miller was a churl, I've told you this,
So was the Reeve, and other some as well,
And harlotry was all they had to tell.
Consider then and hold me free of blame;
And why be serious about a game?

THE MILLER'S TALE

Some time ago there was a rich old codger
Who lived in Oxford and who took a lodger.
The fellow was a carpenter by trade,
His lodger a poor student who had made
Some studies in the arts, but all his fancy
Turned to astrology and geomancy,
And he could deal with certain propositions
And make a forecast under some conditions
About the likelihood of drought or showers
For those who asked at favourable hours,
Or put a question how their luck would fall
In this or that, I can't describe them all.
  This lad was known as Nicholas the Gallant,
And making love in secret was his talent,
For he was very close and sly, and took
Advantage of his meek and girlish look.
He rented a small chamber in the kip
All by himself without companionship.
He decked it charmingly with herbs and fruit
And he himself was sweeter than the root
Of liquorice, or any fragrant herb.
His astronomic text-books were superb,
He had an astrolabe to match his art
And calculating counters laid apart
On handy shelves that stood above his bed.
His press was curtained coarsely and in red;
Above there lay a gallant harp in sight
On which he played melodiously at night
With such a touch that all the chamber rang;
It was *The Virgin's Angelus* he sang,
And after that he sang *King William's Note,*
And people often blessed his merry throat.
And that was how this charming scholar spent
His time and money, which his friends had sent.
  This carpenter had married a young wife
Not long before, and loved her more than life.
She was a girl of eighteen years of age.
Jealous he was and kept her in the cage,
For he was old and she was wild and young;
He thought himself quite likely to be stung.
  He might have known, were Cato on his shelf,

A man should marry someone like himself;
A man should pick an equal for his mate.
Youth and old age are often in debate.
His wits were dull, he'd fallen in the snare
And had to bear his cross as others bear.
   She was a pretty creature, fair and tender,
And had a weasel's body, softly slender.
She used to wear a girdle of striped silk,
Her apron was as white as morning milk
To deck her loins, all gusseted and pleated.
Her smock was white; embroidery repeated
Its pattern on the collar front and back,
Inside and out; it was of silk, and black.
And all the ribbons on her milky mutch
Were made to match her collar, even such.
She wore a broad silk fillet rather high,
And certainly she had a lecherous eye.
And she had plucked her eyebrows into bows,
Slenderly arched they were, and black as sloes.
And a more truly blissful sight to see
She was than blossom on a cherry-tree,
And softer than the wool upon a wether.
And by her girdle hung a purse of leather,
Tasselled in silk, with metal droplets, pearled.
If you went seeking up and down the world
The wisest man you met would have to wrench
His fancy to imagine such a wench.
She had a shining colour, gaily tinted,
And brighter than a florin newly minted,
And when she sang it was as loud and quick
As any swallow perched above a rick.
And she would skip or play some game or other
Like any kid or calf behind its mother.
Her mouth was sweet as mead or honey—say
A hoard of apples lying in the hay.
Skittish she was, and jolly as a colt,
Tall as a mast and upright as a bolt
Out of a bow. Her collaret revealed
A brooch as big as boss upon a shield.
High shoes she wore, and laced them to the top.
She was a daisy, O a lollypop
For any nobleman to take to bed
Or some good man of yeoman stock to wed.
   Now, gentlemen, this Gallant Nicholas
Began to romp about and make a pass
At this young woman, happening on her one day,
Her husband being out, down Osney way.
Students are sly, and giving way to whim,
He made a grab and caught her by the quim
And said, 'O God, I love you! Can't you see

If I don't have you it's the end of me?'
Then held her haunches hard and gave a cry
'O love-me-all-at-once or I shall die!'
She gave a spring, just like a skittish colt
Boxed in a frame for shoeing, and with a jolt
Managed in time to wrench her head away,
And said, 'Give over, Nicholas, I say!
No, I won't kiss you! Stop it! Let me go
Or I shall scream! I'll let the neighbours know!
Where are your manners? Take away your paws!'
    Then Nicholas began to plead his cause
And spoke so fair in proffering what he could
That in the end she promised him she would,
Swearing she'd love him, with a solemn promise
To be at his disposal, by St Thomas,
When she could spy an opportunity.
'My husband is so full of jealousy,
Unless you watch your step and hold your breath
I know for certain it will be my death,'
She said, 'So keep it well under your hat.'
'Oh, never mind about a thing like that,'
Said he; 'A scholar doesn't have to stir
His wits so much to trick a carpenter.'
    And so they both agreed to it, and swore
To watch their chance, as I have said before.
When things were settled thus as they thought fit,
And Nicholas had stroked her loins a bit
And kissed her sweetly, he took down his harp
And played away, a merry tune and sharp.
    It happened later she went off to church,
This worthy wife, one holiday, to search
Her conscience and to do the works of Christ.
She put her work aside and she enticed
The colour to her face to make her mark;
Her forehead shone. There was a parish clerk
Serving the church, whose name was Absalon.
His hair was all in golden curls and shone;
Just like a fan it strutted outwards, starting
To left and right from an accomplished parting.
Ruddy his face, his eyes as grey as goose,
His shoes cut out in tracery, as in use
In old St Paul's. The hose upon his feet
Showed scarlet through, and all his clothes were neat
And proper. In a jacket of light blue,
Flounced at the waist and tagged with laces too,
He went, and wore a surplice just as gay
And white as any blossom on the spray.
God bless my soul, he was a merry knave!
He knew how to let blood, cut hair and shave,
And draw up legal deeds; at other whiles

He used to dance in twenty different styles
(After the current school at Oxford though,
Casting his legs about him to and fro).
He played a two-stringed fiddle, did it proud,
And sang a high falsetto rather loud;
And he was just as good on the guitar.
There was no public-house in town or bar
He didn't visit with his merry face
If there were saucy barmaids round the place.
He was a little squeamish in the matter
Of farting, and satirical in chatter.
This Absalon, so jolly in his ways,
Would bear the censer round on holy days
And cense the parish women. He would cast
Many a love-lorn look before he passed,
Especially at this carpenter's young wife;
Looking at her would make a happy life
He thought, so neat, so sweet, so lecherous.
And I dare say if she had been a mouse
And he a cat, she'd have been pounced upon.
   In taking the collection Absalon
Would find his heart was set in such a whirl
Of love, he would take nothing from a girl,
For courtesy, he said, it wasn't right.
   That evening, when the moon was shining bright
He ups with his guitar and off he tours
On the look out for any paramours.
Larky and amorous, away he strode
Until he reached the carpenter's abode
A little after cock-crow, took his stand
Beside the casement window close at hand
(It was set low upon the cottage-face)
And started singing softly and with grace,
   'Now dearest lady, if thy pleasure be
   In thoughts of love, think tenderly of me!'
On his guitar he plucked a tuneful string.
   This carpenter awoke and heard him sing
And turning to his wife said, 'Alison!
Wife! Do you hear him? There goes Absalon
Chanting away under our chamber wall.'
And she replied, 'Yes, John, I hear it all.'
If she thought more of it she didn't tell.
   So things went on. What's better than 'All's well'?
From day to day this jolly Absalon,
Wooing away, became quite woe-begone;
He lay awake all night, and all the day
Combed his thick locks and tried to pass for gay,
Wooed her by go-between and wooed by proxy,
Swore to be page and servant to his doxy,
Thrilled and rouladed like a nightingale,

Sent her sweet wine and mead and spicy ale,
And wafers piping hot and jars of honey,
And, as she lived in town, he offered money.
For there are some a money-bag provokes
And some are won by kindness, some by strokes.
   Once, in the hope his talent might engage,
He played the part of Herod on the stage.
What was the good? Were he as bold as brass,
She was in love with gallant Nicholas;
However Absalon might blow his horn
His labour won him nothing but her scorn.
She looked upon him as her private ape
And held his earnest wooing all a jape.
There is a proverb—and it is no lie—
You'll often hear repeated: *'Nigh-and-Sly*
Wins against Fair-and-Square who isn't there.'
For much as Absalon might tear his hair
And rage at being seldom in her sight,
Nicholas, nigh and sly, stood in his light.
Now, show your paces, Nicholas you spark!
And leave lamenting to the parish clerk.
   And so it happened that one Saturday,
When the old carpenter was safe away
At Osney, Nicholas and Alison
Agreed at last in what was to be done.
Nicholas was to exercise his wits
On her suspicious husband's foolish fits,
And, if so be the trick worked out all right,
She then would sleep with Nicholas all night,
For such was his desire and hers as well;
And even quicker than it takes to tell,
Young Nicholas, who simply couldn't wait,
Went to his room on tip-toe with a plate
Of food and drink, enough to last a day
Or two, and Alison was told to say,
In case her husband asked for Nicholas,
That she had no idea where he was,
And that she hadn't set eyes on him all day
And thought he must be ill, she couldn't say;
And more than once the maid had given a call
And shouted but no answer came at all.
   So things went on the whole of Saturday
Without a sound from Nicholas, who lay
Upstairs, and ate or slept as pleased him best
Till Sunday when the sun went down to rest.
   This foolish carpenter was lost in wonder
At Nicholas; what could have got him under?
He said, 'I can't help thinking, by the Mass,
Things can't be going right with Nicholas.
What if he took and died? God guard his ways!

A ticklish place the world is, nowadays.
I saw a corpse this morning borne to kirk
That only Monday last I saw at work.
Run up,' he told the serving-lad, 'be quick,
Shout at his door, or knock it with a brick.
Take a good look and tell me how he fares.'
   The serving-boy went sturdily upstairs,
Stopped at the door and, standing there, the lad
Shouted away and, hammering like mad,
Cried, 'Ho! What's up? Hi! Master Nicholay!
How can you lie up there asleep all day?'
   But all for nought, he didn't hear a soul.
He found a broken panel with a hole
Right at the bottom, useful to the cat
For creeping in; he took a look through that,
And so at last by peering through the crack
He saw this scholar gaping on his back
As if he caught a glimpse of the new moon.
Down went the boy and told his master soon
About the state in which he found the man.
   On hearing this the carpenter began
To cross himself and said, 'St Frideswide bless us!
We little know what's coming to distress us.
The man has fallen, with this here astromy,
Into a fit, or lunacy maybe.
I always thought that was how it would go.
God has some secrets that we shouldn't know.
How blessed are the simple, aye, indeed,
That only know enough to say their creed!
Happened just so with such another student
Of astromy and he was so imprudent
As to stare upwards while he crossed a field,
Busy foreseeing what the stars revealed;
And what should happen but he fell down flat
Into a marl-pit. He didn't foresee that!
But by the Saints we've reached a sorry pass;
I can't help worrying for Nicholas.
He shall be scolded for his studying
If I know how to scold, by Christ the King!
Get me a staff to prise against the floor.
Robin, you put your shoulder to the door.
We'll shake the study out of him, I guess!'
   The pair of them began to heave and press
Against the door. Happened the lad was strong
And so it didn't take them very long
To heave it off its hinges; down it came.
Still as a stone lay Nicholas, with the same
Expression, gaping upwards into air.
The carpenter supposed it was despair
And shook him by the shoulders with a stout

And purposeful attack, and gave a shout:
'What, Nicholas! Hey! Look down! Is that a fashion
To act? Wake up and think upon Christ's passion.
I sign you with the cross from elves and sprites!'
And he began the spell for use at nights
In all four corners of the room and out
Across the threshold too and round about:
    Jesu Christ and Benedict Sainted
    Bless this house from creature tainted,
    Drive away night-hags, white Pater-noster,
    Where did you go St Peter's soster?
    And in the end the dandy Nicholas
Began to sigh, 'And must it come to pass?'
He said, 'Must all the world be cast away?'
The carpenter replied, 'What's that you say?
Put trust in God as we do, working men.'
Nicholas answered, 'Fetch some liquor then,
And afterwards, in strictest secrecy,
I'll speak of something touching you and me,
But not another soul must know, that's plain.'
    This carpenter went down and came again
Bringing some powerful ale—a largeish quart.
When each had had his share of this support
Young Nicholas got up and shut the door
And, sitting down beside him on the floor,
Said to the carpenter, 'Now, John, my dear,
My excellent host, swear on your honour here
Not to repeat a syllable I say,
For here are Christ's intentions, to betray
Which to a soul puts you among the lost,
And vengeance for it at a bitter cost
Shall fall upon you. You'll be driven mad!'
'Christ and His holy blood forbid it, lad!'
The silly fellow answered. 'I'm no blab,
Though I should say it. I'm not given to gab.
Say what you like, for I shall never tell
Man, woman or child by Him that harrowed Hell!'
    'Now, John,' said Nicholas, 'believe you me,
I have found out by my astrology,
And looking at the moon when it was bright,
That Monday next, a quarter way through night,
Rain is to fall in torrents, such a scud
It will be twice as bad as Noah's Flood.
This world,' he said, 'in just about an hour,
Shall all be drowned, it's such a hideous shower,
And all mankind, with total loss of life.'
    The carpenter exclaimed, 'Alas, my wife!
My little Alison! Is she to drown?'
And in his grief he very near fell down.
'Is there no remedy,' he said, 'for this?'

'Thanks be to God,' said Nicholas, 'there is,
If you will do exactly what I say
And don't start thinking up some other way.
In wise old Solomon you'll find the verse
"Who takes advice shall never fare the worse,"
And so if good advice is to prevail
I undertake with neither mast nor sail
To save her yet, and save myself and you.
Haven't you heard how Noah was saved too
When God Forewarned him and his sons and daughters
That all the world should sink beneath the waters?'
'Yes,' said the carpenter, 'a long time back.'
'Haven't you heard,' said Nicholas, 'what a black
Business it was, when Noah tried to whip
His wife (who wouldn't come) on board the ship?
He'd have been better pleased, I'll undertake,
With all that weather just about to break,
If she had had a vessel of her own.
Now, what are we to do? We can't postpone
The thing; it's coming soon, as I was saying,
It calls for haste, not preaching or delaying.
  'I want you, now, at once, to hurry off
And fetch a shallow tub or kneading-trough
For each of us, but see that they are large
And such as we can float in, like a barge.
And have them loaded with sufficient victual
To last a day—we only need a little.
The waters will abate and flow away
Round nine o'clock upon the following day.
Robin the lad mayn't know of this, poor knave,
Nor Jill the maid, those two I cannot save.
Don't ask me why; and even if you do
I can't disclose God's secret thoughts to you.
You should be satisfied, unless you're mad,
To find as great a grace as Noah had.
And I shall save your wife, you needn't doubt it,
Now off you go, and hurry up about it.
  'And when the tubs have been collected, three,
That's one for her and for yourself and me,
Then hang them in the roof below the thatching
That no one may discover what we're hatching.
When you have finished doing what I said
And stowed the victuals in them overhead,
Also an axe to hack the ropes apart,
So, when the water rises, we can start,
And, lastly, when you've broken out the gable,
The garden one that's just above the stable,
So that we may cast free without delay
After the mighty shower has gone away,
You'll float as merrily, I undertake,

As any lily-white duck, behind her drake.
And I'll call out, "Hey, Alison! Hey, John!
Cheer yourselves up! The flood will soon be gone."
And you'll shout back, "Hail, Master Nicholay!
Good morning! I can see you well. It's day!"
We shall be lords for all the rest of life
Of all the world, like Noah and his wife.
  'One thing I warn you of; it's only right.
We must be very careful on the night,
Once we have safely managed to embark,
To hold our tongues, to utter no remark,
No cry or call, for we must fall to prayer.
This is the Lord's dear will, so have a care.
  'Your wife and you must hang some way apart,
For there must be no sin before we start,
No more in longing looks than in the deed.
Those are your orders. Off with you! God speed!
To-morrow night when everyone's asleep
We'll all go quietly upstairs and creep
Into our tubs, awaiting Heaven's grace.
And now be off. No time to put the case
At greater length, no time to sermonize;
The proverb says, "Say nothing, send the wise."
You're wise enough, I do not have to teach you.
Go, save our lives for us, as I beseech you.'
  This silly carpenter then went his way
Muttering to himself, 'Alas the day!'
And told his wife in strictest secrecy.
She was aware, far more indeed than he,
What this quaint stratagem might have in sight,
But she pretended to be dead with fright.
'Alas!' she said. 'Whatever it may cost,
Hurry and help, or we shall all be lost.
I am your honest, true and wedded wife,
Go, dearest husband, help to save my life!"
  How fancy throws us into perturbation!
People can die of mere imagination,
So deep is the impression one can take.
This silly carpenter began to quake,
Before his eyes there verily seemed to be
The floods of Noah, wallowing like the sea
And drowning Alison his honey-pet.
He wept and wailed, his features were all set
In grief, he sighed with many a doleful grunt.
He went and got a tub, began to hunt
For kneading-troughs, found two, and had them sent
Home to his house in secret; then he went
And, unbeknowns, he hung them from a rafter.
With his own hands he made three ladders after,
Uprights and rungs, to help them in their scheme

Of climbing where they hung upon the beam.
He victualled tub and trough, and made all snug
With bread and cheese, and ale in a large jug,
Enough for three of them to last the day,
And, just before completing this array,
Packed off the maid and his apprentice too
To London on a job they had to do.
And on the Monday when it drew to night
He shut his door and dowsed the candle-light
And made quite sure all was as it should be.
And shortly, up they clambered, all the three,
Silent and separate. They began to pray
And '*Pater Noster* mum', said Nicholay,
And 'mum' said John, and 'mum' said Alison.
The carpenter's devotions being done,
He sat quite still, then fell to prayer again
And waited anxiously to hear the rain.

  The carpenter, with all the work he'd seen,
Fell dead asleep—round curfew, must have been.
Maybe a little later on the whole.
He groaned in sleep for travail of his soul
And snored because his head was turned awry.

  Down by their ladders, stalking from on high
Came Nicholas and Alison, and sped
Softly downstairs, without a word, to bed,
And where this carpenter was wont to be
The revels started and the melody.
And thus lay Nicholas and Alison
At busy play in eager quest of fun,
Until the bell for lauds had started ringing
And in the chancel Friars began their singing.

  This parish clerk, this amorous Absalon,
Love-stricken still and very woe-begone,
Upon the Monday was in company
At Osney with his friends for jollity,
And chanced to ask a resident cloisterer
What had become of John the carpenter.
The fellow drew him out of church to say,
'Don't know; not been at work since Saturday.
I can't say where he is; I think he went
To fetch the Abbot timber. He is sent
Often enough for timber, has to go
Out to the Grange and stop a day or so;
If not, he's certainly at home to-day,
But where he is I can't exactly say.'

  Absalon was a jolly lad and light
Of heart; he thought, 'I'll stay awake to-night;
I'm certain that I haven't seen him stirring
About his door since dawn; it's safe inferring
That he's away. As I'm alive I'll go

And tap his window softly at the crow
Of cock—the sill is low-set on the wall.
I shall see Alison and tell her all
My love-longing, and I can hardly miss
Some favour from her, at the least a kiss.
I'll get some satisfaction anyway;
There's been an itching in my mouth all day
And that's a sign of kissing at the least.
And all last night I dreamt about a feast.
I think I'll go and sleep an hour or two,
Then wake and have some fun, that's what I'll do.'
   The first cock crew at last, and thereupon
Up rose this jolly lover Absalon
In gayest clothes, garnished with that and this;
But first he chewed a grain of liquorice
To charm his breath before he combed his hair.
Under his tongue the comfit nestling there
Would make him gracious. He began to roam
To where old John and Alison kept home
And by the casement window took his stand.
Breast-high it stood, no higher than his hand.
He gave a cough, no more than half a sound:
'Alison, honey-comb, are you around?
Sweet cinnamon, my little pretty bird,
Sweetheart, wake up and say a little word!
You seldom think of me in all my woe,
I sweat for love of you wherever I go!
No wonder if I do, I pine and bleat
As any lambkin hungering for the teat,
Believe me, darling, I'm so deep in love
I croon with longing like a turtle-dove,
I eat as little as a girl at school.'
'You go away,' she answered, 'you Tom-fool!
There's no come-up-and-kiss-me here for you.
I love another and why shouldn't I too?
Better than you, by Jesu, Absalon!
Take yourself off or I shall throw a stone.
I want to get some sleep. You go to Hell!'
'Alas!' said Absalon. 'I knew it well;
True love is always mocked and girded at;
So kiss me, if you can't do more than that,
For Jesu's love and for the love of me!'
'And if I do, will you be off?' said she.
'Promise you, darling,' answered Absalon.
'Get ready then; wait, I'll put something on,'
She said and then she added under breath
To Nicholas, 'Hush . . . we shall laugh to death!'
   This Absalon went down upon his knees;
'I am a lord!' he thought, 'And by degrees
There may be more to come; the plot may thicken.'

'Mercy, my love!' he said, 'Your mouth, my chicken!'
   She flung the window open then in haste
And said, 'Have done, come on, no time to waste,
The neighbours here are always on the spy.'
   Absalon started wiping his mouth dry.
Dark was the night as pitch, as black as coal,
And at the window out she put her hole,
And Absalon, so fortune framed the farce,
Put up his mouth and kissed her naked arse
Most savorously before he knew of this.
   And back he started. Something was amiss;
He knew quite well a woman has no beard,
Yet something rough and hairy had appeared.
'What have I done?' he said. 'Can that be you?'
'Teehee!' she cried and clapped the window to.
Off went poor Absalon sadly through the dark.
'A beard! a beard!' cried Nicholas the Spark.
'God's body, that was something like a joke!'
And Absalon, overhearing what he spoke.
Bit on his lips and nearly threw a fit
In rage and thought, 'I'll pay you back for it!''
   Who's busy rubbing, scraping at his lips
With dust, with sand, with straw, with cloth, with chips,
But Absalon? He thought, 'I'll bring him down!
I wouldn't let this go for all the town.
I'd take my soul and sell it to the Devil
To be revenged upon him! I'll get level.
O God, why did I let myself be fooled?''
   The fiery heat of love by now had cooled,
For from the time he kissed her hinder parts
He didn't give a tinker's curse for tarts;
His malady was cured by this endeavour
And he defied all paramours whatever.
   So, weeping like a child that has been whipped,
He turned away; across the road he slipped
And called on Gervase. Gervase was a smith;
His forge was full of things for ploughing with
And he was busy sharpening a share.
   Absalon knocked, and with an easy air
Called, 'Gervase! Open up the door, come on!'
'What's that? Who's there?' 'It's me, it's Absalon.'
'What, Absalon? By Jesu's blessed tree
You're early up! Hey, *benedicite*,
What's wrong? Some jolly girl as like as not
Has coaxed you out and set you on the trot.
Blessed St. Neot! You know the thing I mean.
   But Absalon, who didn't give a bean
For all his joking, offered no debate.
He had a good deal more upon his plate
Than Gervase knew and said, 'Would it be fair

To borrow that coulter in the chimney there,
The hot one, see it? I've a job to do;
It won't take long. I'll bring it back to you.'
Gervase replied, 'Why, if you asked for gold,
A bag of sovereigns or for wealth untold,
It should be yours, as I'm an honest smith.
But Christ, why borrow that to do it with?'
'Let that,' said Absalon, 'be as it may;
You'll hear about it all some other day.'
    He caught the coulter up—the haft was cool—
And left the smithy softly with the tool,
Crept to the little window in the wall
And coughed. He knocked and gave a little call
Under the window as he had before.
    Alison said, 'There's someone at the door.
Who's knocking there? I'll warrant it's a thief.'
'Why, no,' said he, 'my little flower-leaf,
It's your own Absalon, my sweety-thing!
Look what I've brought you—it's a golden ring
My mother gave me, as I may be saved.
It's very fine, and prettily engraved;
I'll give it to you, darling, for a kiss.'
    Now Nicholas had risen for a piss,
And thought he could improve upon the jape
And make him kiss his arse ere he escape,
And opening the window with a jerk,
Struck out his arse, a handsome piece of work,
Buttocks and all, as far as to the haunch.
    Said Absalon, all set to make a launch.
'Speak, pretty bird, I know not where thou art!'
This Nicholas at once let fly a fart
As loud as if it were a thunder-clap.
He was near blinded by the blast, poor chap,
But his hot iron was ready; with a thump
He smote him in the middle of the rump.
    Off went the skin a hand's breadth round about.
Where the hot coulter struck and burnt it out.
Such was the pain, he thought he must be dying
And, mad with agony, he started crying,
'Help! Water! Water! Help! For Heaven's love!'
    The carpenter, startled from sleep above,
And hearing shouts for water and a thud,
Thought, 'Heaven help us! Here comes Nowel's Flood!'
And up he sat and with no more ado
He took his axe and smote the ropes in two
And down went everything. He didn't stop
To sell his bread and ale, but came down flop
Upon the floor and fainted right away.
    Up started Alison and Nicholay
And shouted, 'Help!' and 'Murder!' in the street.

The neighbours all came running up in heat
And stood there staring at the wretched man.
He lay there fainting, pale beneath his tan;
His arm in falling had been broken double.
But still he was obliged to face his trouble,
For when he spoke he was at once borne down
By Nicholas and his wife. They told the town
That he was mad, there'd got into his blood
Some sort of nonsense about 'Nowel's Flood',
That vain imaginings and fantasy
Had made him buy the kneading-tubs, that he
Had hung them in the rafters up above
And that he'd begged them both for heaven's love
To sit up in the roof for company.
    All started laughing at this lunacy
And streamed upstairs to gape and pry and poke,
And treated all his sufferings as a joke.
No matter what the carpenter asserted
It went for nothing, no one was converted;
With powerful oaths they swore the fellow down
And he was held for mad by all the town;
Even the learned said to one another,
'The fellow must be crazy, my dear brother.'
So to a general laughter he succumbed.
    That's how the carpenter's young wife was plumbed
For all the tricks his jealousy could try,
And Absalon has kissed her nether eye
And Nicholas is branded on the bum.
And God bring all of us to Kingdom Come.

The Blue Beard

There was once upon a time a man who had several fine houses both in town and country, a good deal of silver and gold plate, embroider'd furniture, and coaches gilt all over with gold. But this same man had the misfortune to have a *Blue Beard*, which made him so frightfully ugly that all the women and girls ran away from him.

One of his neighbours, a lady of quality, had two daughters who were perfect beauties. He desired of her one of them in marriage, leaving to her the choice of which of them she would bestow upon him. They would neither of them have him, and sent him backwards and forwards from one another, being resolved never to marry a man that had a *Blue Beard*. That which moreover gave them the greater disgust and aversion, was that he had already been marry'd to several wives, and no body ever knew what were become of them.

The *Blue Beard*, to engage their affection, took them with my lady their mother, and three or four other ladies of their acquaintance, and some young people of the neighbourhood, to one of his country seats, where they staid full eight days. There was

"The Blue Beard" by Robert Samber. Reprinted from *The Classic Fairy Tales*, edited by Iona and Peter Opie, by permission of Oxford University Press.

nothing now to be seen but parties of pleasure, hunting of all kinds, fishing, dancing, feasts and collations. No body went to bed, they past the night in rallying and playing upon one another: In short, every thing so well succeeded, that the youngest daughter began to think, that the master of the house had not a *Beard* so very *Blue*, and that he was a very civil gentleman.

As soon as they returned home the marriage was concluded. About a month afterwards the *Blue Beard* told his wife, that he was obliged to take a journey into a distant country for six weeks at least, about an affair of very great consequence, desiring her to divert herself in his absence, send for her friends and acquaintance, carry them into the country, if she pleased, and make good cheer wherever she was: Here, said he, are the keys of the two great rooms that hold my best and richest furniture; these are of my silver and gold plate, which is not to be made use of every day; these open my strong-boxes, which hold my gold and silver money; these my casket of jewels; and this is the master-key that opens all my apartments: But for this little one here, it is the key of the closet at the end of the great gallery on the ground floor. Open them all, go into all and every one except that little closet, which I forbid you, and forbid you in such a manner, that if you happen to open it, there is nothing but what you may expect from my just anger and resentment. She promised to observe every thing he order'd her, who, after having embraced her, got into his coach and proceeded on his journey.

Her neighbours and good friends did not stay to be sent for by the new married lady, so great was their impatience to see all the rich furniture of her house, not daring to come while the husband was there, because of his *Blue Beard* which frighten'd them. They ran through all the rooms, closets, wardrobes, which were all so rich and fine that they seemed to surpass one another. After that, they went up into the two great rooms where were the best and richest furniture; they could not sufficiently admire the number and beauty of the tapestry, beds, couches, cabinets, stands, tables and looking-glasses, in which you might see yourself from head to foot; some of them were framed with glass, others with silver and silver gilt, the finest and most magnificent as ever were seen: They never ceased to extol and envy the happiness of their friend, who in the mean time no ways diverted herself in looking upon all these rich things, because of the impatience she had to go and open the closet of the ground floor. She was so much pressed by her curiosity, that without considering that it was very uncivil to leave her company, she went down a back pair of stairs, and with such an excessive haste, that she had like to have broken her neck two or three times.

Being come to the closet door, she stopt for some time, thinking upon her husband's orders, and considering what unhappiness might attend her were she disobedient; but the temptation was so strong she could not overcome it: She took then the little key and opened it in a very great trembling. But she could see nothing distinctly, because the windows were shut; after some moments she began to observe that the floor was all covered over with clotted blood, on which lay the bodies of several dead women ranged against the walls. (These were all the wives that the *Blue Beard* had married and murder'd one after another.) She thought that she should have died for fear, and the key that she pulled out of the lock fell out of her hand: After having somewhat recover'd her surprise, she took up the key, locked the door and went up stairs into her chamber to recover herself, but she could not, so much was she frightened. Having observed that the key of the closet was stain'd with blood, she tried two or three times to wipe it off, but the blood would not come out; in vain did she wash it and even rub it with soap and sand, the blood still remained, for the key was a Fairy, and she could never quite make it clean; when the blood was gone off from one side, it came again on the other.

The *Blue Beard* returned from his journey the same evening, and said he had received letters upon the road, informing him that the affair he went about was finished to his advantage. His wife did all she could to convince him she was extremely glad of his speedy return. The next morning he asked for the keys, which she returned, but with such a trembling hand, that he easily guess'd what had happen'd. What is the matter, said he, that the key of the closet is not amongst the rest? I must certainly, said she, have left it above upon the table. Do not fail, said the *Blue Beard*, of giving it to me presently: After several goings backwards and forwards she was forced to bring him the key. The *Blue Beard* having very attentively consider'd it, said to his Wife, how comes this blood upon the key? I don't know, said the poor Woman paler than death. You don't know, replied the *Blue Beard*, I know very well, you were resolv'd to go into the closet, were you not? Very well, Madam, you shall go in, and take your place amongst the ladies you saw there.

Upon this she threw herself at her husband's feet, and begged his pardon with all the signs of a true repentance, and that she would never more be disobedient. She would have melted a rock, so beautiful and sorrowful was she; but the *Blue Beard* had a heart harder than the hardest rock! You must die, Madam, said he, and that presently. Since I must die, said she, looking upon him with her eyes all bathed in tears, give me some little time to say my prayers. I give you, said the *Blue Beard*, a quarter of an hour, but not one moment more.

When she was alone, she called out to her sister, and said to her, Sister *Anne,* for that was her name, go up, I desire thee, upon the top of the tower, and see if my brothers are not coming, they promised me that they would come to day, and if thou seest them, give them a sign to make haste. Her sister *Anne* went up upon the top of the tower, and the poor afflicted lady cried out from time to time, *Anne, sister Anne, dost thou see nothing coming?* And sister *Anne* said, *I see nothing but the sun that makes a dust, and the grass that grows green.* In the mean while the *Blue Beard*, holding a great cutlass in his hand, cried out as loud as he could to his wife, Come down, presently, or I'll come up to you. One moment longer, if you please, said his wife, and immediately she cried out very softly. *Anne, sister Anne, dost thou see nothing coming?* And sister *Anne* said, *I see nothing but the sun that makes a dust, and the grass that grows green.* Come down quickly, cried the *Blue Beard*, or I'll come up to you. I am coming, answer'd his wife, and then she cried, *Anne, sister Anne, dost thou see nothing coming?* I see, replied sister *Anne,*a great dust that comes on this side here. *Are they my brothers?* Alas! no, my dear sister, I see a flock of sheep. Will you not come down? cried the *Blue Beard*. One moment longer, said his wife, and then she cried out, *Anne, sister Anne, dost thou see nothing coming?* I see, said she, two horsemen coming, but they are yet a great way off. God be praised, said she immediately after, they are my brothers; I have made them a sign as well as I can to make haste. The *Blue Beard* cried out now so loud, that he made the whole house tremble.

The poor Lady came down and threw herself at his feet all in tears with her hair about her shoulders: This signifies nothing, says the *Blue Beard,* you must die; then taking hold of her hair with one hand, and holding up the cutlass with the other, he was going to cut off her head. The poor lady turning about to him, and looking at him with dying eyes, desired him to afford her one little moment to recollect herself: No, no, said he, recommend thy self to God: for at this very instant there was such a loud knocking at the gate, that the *Blue Beard* stopt short of a sudden: They open'd the gate, and immediately enter'd two horsemen, who drawing their swords, ran directly to the *Blue Beard*. He knew them to be his wife's brothers, one a dragoon, the other a musqueteer, so that he ran away immediately to save himself: but the two brothers pursued him so close, that they overtook him before he could get to the steps of the porch, when they ran their swords through his body and left him dead.

The poor lady was almost as dead as her husband, and had not strength enough to rise and embrace her brothers. The *Blue Beard* had no heirs, and so his wife became mistress of all his estate. She made use of one part of it to marry her sister *Anne* to a young gentleman who had loved her a long while, another part to buy captains commissions for her brothers, and the rest to marry herself to a very honest gentleman, who made her forget the ill time she had pass'd with the *Blue Beard*.

Part Two

The Short Story Proper: The First Age

Nathaniel Hawthorne (1804–1864)

Hawthorne was born in Salem, Massachusetts, into a family which numbered among its ancestors one of the judges at the infamous witchcraft trials in 1692. The family's Puritan roots were deep, and perhaps no other American writer of the nineteenth century reflects the mood and cultural heritage of colonial New England as does Hawthorne. Lamed at the age of seven, he spent his youth with books, developing a profound interest in early American history and in the works of Spenser, Bunyan, and Milton. After graduation from Bowdoin College in 1825, he returned to Salem to write. A little over a decade was to pass before he won approval with the publication in 1837 of *Twice-Told Tales.* Hawthorne joined the Brook Farm experiment, a socialistic cooperative, in 1841, but left when he found that his writing was suffering. For the next seven or eight years he worked as a customs official and befriended other New England writers, among them Melville, who dedicated *Moby Dick* to him. Hawthorne's fame was established in 1850 with the publication of his masterpiece, *The Scarlet Letter,* our literature's first—and by many still regarded as greatest—symbolic novel. Thereafter Hawthorne wrote *The House of the Seven Gables* (1851), *The Blithedale Romance* (1852), and *The Marble Faun* (1860).

Like Poe, Hawthorne read Gothic novels, and worked as assiduously as Poe in

evoking a dominant *atmosphere.* Unlike Poe, however, he did not concentrate on
the single, startling, or sensational, at times almost convulsive, *effect.* Most of his
stories in fact developed from anecdotes he picked up, from places he visited, or
from incidents he had read or heard about. Indeed, nothing more distinguishes
Hawthorne as literary artist than his capacity to transform utterly unexceptional
events into brooding and compelling fiction.

In the story that follows, we get almost an inversion of the preceding statement, for there is surely nothing ordinary about a minister who, at age thirty, dons
a black veil, which conceals his features from forehead to just above the mouth,
and which he wears through the rest of his long life. Yet Hawthorne domesticates
the act by telling the reader in a footnote about another and historical New England clergyman, the Reverend Joseph Moody, who once "made himself remarkable by the same eccentricity." The footnote goes on to say that the veil is a
symbol; but we are told that with Mr. Hooper "the symbol had a different import,"
which is to say that the wearing of a crepe veil did not mean for the Reverend
Hooper a symbolic confession of some specific, earlier trespass or sin, as it did for
the historical Moody.

The veil is both metaphor and symbol (see Introduction, pp. 21–22) as well as
a physical reality. In the story our attention tends to concentrate more on the veil
itself, and the effects of the veil on the citizens of Milford, than on Reverend
Hooper. Our feelings about him may finally be mixed. Some may like him for his
regular smile, others dislike him for his seeming hypocrisy. For many readers
Hawthorne's final meaning is to be found in the penultimate paragraph, which
seems to allow Hooper to say, finally, what he had been able only to intimate
through his long life, namely that human beings are united only in what divides
them. As Roy R. Male puts it, according to the Reverend—now Father—Hooper,
"the one universal bond of humanity" consists in "the very sins and aberrations
that separate" individuals from one another. The veil is there, so to speak, to
remind us that each one of us also wears a veil.

The Minister's Black Veil

A Parable

THE sexton stood in the porch of Milford meeting-house, pulling busily at the bell-rope.
The old people of the village came stooping along the street. Children, with bright faces,
tripped merrily beside their parents, or mimicked a graver gait, in the conscious dignity
of their Sunday clothes. Spruce bachelors looked sidelong at the pretty maidens, and
fancied that the Sabbath sunshine made them prettier than on week days. When the
throng had mostly streamed into the porch, the sexton began to toll the bell, keeping his
eye on the Reverend Mr. Hooper's door. The first glimpse of the clergyman's figure was
the signal for the bell to cease its summons.

"But what has good Parson Hooper got upon his face?" cried the sexton in astonishment.

All within hearing immediately turned about, and beheld the semblance of Mr.

Hooper, pacing slowly his meditative way towards the meeting-house. With one accord they started, expressing more wonder than if some strange minister were coming to dust the cushions of Mr. Hooper's pulpit.

"Are you sure it is our parson?" inquired Goodman Gray of the sexton.

"Of a certainty it is good Mr. Hooper," replied the sexton. "He was to have exchanged pulpits with Parson Shute, of Westbury; but Parson Shute sent to excuse himself yesterday, being to preach a funeral sermon."

The cause of so much amazement may appear sufficiently slight. Mr. Hooper, a gentlemanly person, of about thirty, though still a bachelor, was dressed with due clerical neatness, as if a careful wife had starched his band, and brushed the weekly dust from his Sunday's garb. There was but one thing remarkable in his appearance. Swathed about his forehead, and hanging down over his face, so low as to be shaken by his breath, Mr. Hooper had on a black veil. On a nearer view it seemed to consist of two folds of crape, which entirely concealed his features, except the mouth and chin, but probably did not intercept his sight, further than to give a darkened aspect to all living and inanimate things. With this gloomy shade before him, good Mr. Hooper walked onward, at a slow and quiet pace, stooping somewhat, and looking on the ground, as is customary with abstracted men, yet nodding kindly to those of his parishioners who still waited on the meeting-house steps. But so wonder-struck were they that his greeting hardly met with a return.

"I can't really feel as if good Mr. Hooper's face was behind that piece of crape," said the sexton.

"I don't like it," muttered an old woman, as she hobbled into the meeting-house. "He has changed himself into something awful, only by hiding his face."

"Our parson has gone mad!" cried Goodman Gray, following him across the threshold.

A rumor of some unaccountable phenomenon had preceded Mr. Hooper into the meeting-house, and set all the congregation astir. Few could refrain from twisting their heads towards the door; many stood upright, and turned directly about; while several little boys clambered upon the seats, and came down again with a terrible racket. There was a general bustle, a rustling of the women's gowns and shuffling of the men's feet, greatly at variance with that hushed repose which should attend the entrance of the minister. But Mr. Hooper appeared not to notice the perturbation of his people. He entered with an almost noiseless step, bent his head mildly to the pews on each side, and bowed as he passed his oldest parishioner, a white-haired great-grandsire, who occupied an arm-chair in the centre of the aisle. It was strange to observe how slowly this venerable man became conscious of something singular in the appearance of his pastor. He seemed not fully to partake of the prevailing wonder, till Mr. Hooper had ascended the stairs, and showed himself in the pulpit, face to face with his congregation, except for the black veil. That mysterious emblem was never once withdrawn. It shook with his measured breath, as he gave out the psalm; it threw its obscurity between him and the holy page, as he read the Scriptures; and while he prayed, the veil lay heavily on his uplifted countenance. Did he seek to hide it from the dread Being whom he was addressing?

Such was the effect of this simple piece of crape, that more than one woman of delicate nerves was forced to leave the meeting-house. Yet perhaps the pale-faced congregation was almost as fearful a sight to the minister, as his black veil to them.

Mr. Hooper had the reputation of a good preacher, but not an energetic one: he strove to win his people heavenward by mild, persuasive influences, rather than to drive them thither by the thunders of the Word. The sermon which he now delivered was marked by the same characteristics of style and manner as the general series of his pulpit oratory. But there was something, either in the sentiment of the discourse itself, or in the imagination of the auditors, which made it greatly the most powerful effort that they had ever heard from their pastor's lips. It was tinged, rather more darkly than usual, with the gentle gloom of Mr. Hooper's temperament. The subject had reference to secret sin, and those sad mysteries which we hide from our nearest and dearest, and would fain conceal from our own consciousness, even forgetting that the Omniscient can detect them. A subtle power was breathed into his words. Each member of the congregation, the most innocent girl, and the man of hardened breast, felt as if the preacher had crept upon them, behind his awful veil, and discovered their hoarded iniquity of deed or thought. Many spread their clasped hands on their bosoms. There was nothing terrible in what Mr. Hooper said, at least, no violence; and yet, with every tremor of his melancholy voice, the hearers quaked. An unsought pathos came hand in hand with awe. So sensible were the audience of some unwonted attribute in their minister, that they longed for a breath of wind to blow aside the veil, almost believing that a stranger's visage would be discovered, though the form, gesture, and voice were those of Mr. Hooper.

At the close of the services, the people hurried out with indecorous confusion, eager to communicate their pent-up amazement, and conscious of lighter spirits the moment they lost sight of the black veil. Some gathered in little circles, huddled closely together, with their mouths all whispering in the centre; some went homeward alone, wrapt in silent meditation; some talked loudly, and profaned the Sabbath day with ostentatious laughter. A few shook their sagacious heads, intimating that they could penetrate the mystery; while one or two affirmed that there was no mystery at all, but only that Mr. Hooper's eyes were so weakened by the midnight lamp, as to require a shade. After a brief interval, forth came good Mr. Hooper also, in the rear of his flock. Turning his veiled face from one group to another, he paid due reverence to the hoary heads, saluted the middle aged with kind dignity as their friend and spiritual guide, greeted the young with mingled authority and love, and laid his hands on the little children's heads to bless them. Such was always his custom on the Sabbath day. Strange and bewildered looks repaid him for his courtesy. None, as on former occasions, aspired to the honor of walking by their pastor's side. Old Squire Saunders, doubtless by an accidental lapse of memory, neglected to invite Mr. Hooper to his table, where the good clergyman had been wont to bless the food, almost every Sunday since his settlement. He returned, therefore, to the parsonage, and, at the moment of closing the door, was observed to look back upon the people, all of whom had their eyes fixed upon the minister. A sad smile gleamed faintly from beneath the black veil, and flickered about his mouth, glimmering as he disappeared.

"How strange," said a lady, "that a simple black veil, such as any woman might wear on her bonnet should become such a terrible thing on Mr. Hooper's face!"

"Something must surely be amiss with Mr. Hooper's intellects," observed her husband, the physician of the village. "But the strangest part of the affair is the effect of this vagary, even on a sober-minded man like myself. The black veil, though it covers only our pastor's face, throws its influence over his whole person, and makes him ghostlike from head to foot. Do you not feel it so?"

"Truly do I," replied the lady; "and I would not be alone with him for the world. I wonder he is not afraid to be alone with himself!"

"Men sometimes are so," said her husband.

The afternoon service was attended with similar circumstances. At its conclusion, the bell tolled for the funeral of a young lady. The relatives and friends were assembled in the house, and the more distant acquaintances stood about the door, speaking of the good qualities of the deceased, when their talk was interrupted by the appearance of Mr. Hooper, still covered with his black veil. It was now an appropriate emblem. The clergyman stepped into the room where the corpse was laid, and bent over the coffin, to take a last farewell of his deceased parishioner. As he stooped, the veil hung straight down from his forehead, so that, if her eyelids had not been closed forever, the dead maiden might have seen his face. Could Mr. Hooper be fearful of her glance, that he so hastily caught back the black veil? A person who watched the interview between the dead and living, scrupled not to affirm, that, at the instant when the clergyman's features were disclosed, the corpse had slightly shuddered, rustling the shroud and muslin cap, though the countenance retained the composure of death. A superstitious old woman was the only witness of this prodigy. From the coffin Mr. Hooper passed into the chamber of the mourners, and thence to the head of the staircase, to make the funeral prayer. It was a tender and heart-dissolving prayer, full of sorrow, yet so imbued with celestial hopes, that the music of a heavenly harp, swept by the fingers of the dead, seemed faintly to be heard among the saddest accents of the minister. The people trembled, though they but darkly understood him when he prayed that they, and himself, and all of mortal race, might be ready, as he trusted this young maiden had been, for the dreadful hour that should snatch the veil from their faces. The bearers went heavily forth, and the mourners followed, saddening all the street, with the dead before them, and Mr. Hooper in his black veil behind.

"Why do you look back?" said one in the procession to his partner.

"I had a fancy," replied she, "that the minister and the maiden's spirit were walking hand in hand."

"And so had I, at the same moment," said the other.

That night, the handsomest couple in Milford village were to be joined in wedlock. Though reckoned a melancholy man, Mr. Hooper had a placid cheerfulness for such occasions, which often excited a sympathetic smile where livelier merriment would have been thrown away. There was no quality of his disposition which made him more beloved than this. The company at the wedding awaited his arrival with impatience, trusting that the strange awe, which had gathered over him throughout the day, would now be dispelled. But such was not the result. When Mr. Hooper came, the first thing that their eyes rested on was the same horrible black veil, which had added deeper gloom to the funeral, and could portend nothing but evil to the wedding. Such was its immediate effect on the guests that a cloud seemed to have rolled duskily from beneath the black crape, and dimmed the light of the candles. The bridal pair stood up before the minister. But the bride's cold fingers quivered in the tremulous hand of the bridegroom, and her deathlike paleness caused a whisper that the maiden who had been buried a few hours before was come from her grave to be married. If ever another wedding were so dismal, it was that famous one where they tolled the wedding knell. After performing the ceremony, Mr. Hooper raised a glass of wine to his lips, wishing happiness to the new-married couple in a strain of mild pleasantry that ought to have brightened the features of the guests, like a cheerful gleam from the hearth. At that instant, catching a glimpse of his figure in the looking-glass, the black veil involved his own spirit in the horror with which it overwhelmed all others. His frame shuddered, his lips grew white, he spilt the untasted wine upon the carpet, and rushed forth into the darkness. For the Earth, too, had on her Black Veil.

The next day, the whole village of Milford talked of little else than Parson Hooper's black veil. That, and the mystery concealed behind it, supplied a topic for discussion between acquaintances meeting in the street, and good women gossiping at their open windows. It was the first item of news that the tavern-keeper told to his guests. The children babbled of it on their way to school. One imitative little imp covered his face with an old black handkerchief, thereby so affrighting his playmates that the panic seized himself, and he well-nigh lost his wits by his own waggery.

It was remarkable that of all the busybodies and impertinent people in the parish, not one ventured to put the plain question to Mr. Hooper, wherefore he did this thing. Hitherto, whenever there appeared the slightest call for such interference, he had never lacked advisers, nor shown himself averse to be guided by their judgment. If he erred at all, it was by so painful a degree of self-distrust, that even the mildest censure would lead him to consider an indifferent action as a crime. Yet, though so well acquainted with this amiable weakness, no individual among his parishioners chose to make the black veil a subject of friendly remonstrance. There was a feeling of dread, neither plainly confessed nor carefully concealed, which caused each to shift the responsibility upon another, till at length it was found expedient to send a deputation of the church, in order to deal with Mr. Hooper about the mystery, before it should grow into a scandal. Never did an embassy so ill discharge its duties. The minister received them with friendly courtesy, but became silent, after they were seated, leaving to his visitors the whole burden of introducing their important business. The topic, it might be supposed, was obvious enough. There was the black veil swathed round Mr. Hooper's forehead, and concealing every feature above his placid mouth, on which, at times, they could perceive the glimmering of a melancholy smile. But that piece of crape, to their imagination, seemed to hang down before his heart, the symbol of a fearful secret between him and them. Were the veil but cast aside, they might speak freely of it, but not till then. Thus they sat a considerable time, speechless, confused, and shrinking uneasily from Mr. Hooper's eye, which they felt to be fixed upon them with an invisible glance. Finally, the deputies returned abashed to the constituents, pronouncing the matter too weighty to be handled, except by a council of the churches, if, indeed, it might not require a general synod.

But there was one person in the village unappalled by the awe with which the black veil had impressed all beside herself. When the deputies returned without an explanation, or even venturing to demand one, she, with the calm energy of her character, determined to chase away the strange cloud that appeared to be settling round Mr. Hooper, every moment more darkly than before. As his plighted wife, it should be her privilege to know what the black veil concealed. At the minister's first visit, therefore, she entered upon the subject with a direct simplicity, which made the task easier both for him and her. After he had seated himself, she fixed her eyes steadfastly upon the veil, but could discern nothing of the dreadful gloom that had so overawed the multitude: it was but a double fold of crape, hanging down from his forehead to his mouth, and slightly stirring with his breath.

"No," said she aloud, and smiling, "there is nothing terrible in this piece of crape, except that it hides a face which I am always glad to look upon. Come, good sir, let the sun shine from behind the cloud. First lay aside your black veil: then tell me why you put it on."

Mr. Hooper's smile glimmered faintly.

"There is an hour to come," said he, "when all of us shall cast aside our veils. Take it not amiss, beloved friend, if I wear this piece of crape till then."

"Your words are a mystery, too," returned the young lady. "Take away the veil from them, at least."

"Elizabeth, I will," said he, "so far as my vow may suffer me. Know, then, this veil is a type and a symbol, and I am bound to wear it ever, both in light and darkness, in solitude and before the gaze of multitudes, and as with strangers, so with my familiar friends. No mortal eye will see it withdrawn. This dismal shade must separate me from the world: even you, Elizabeth, can never come behind it!"

"What grievous affliction hath befallen you," she earnestly inquired, "that you should thus darken your eyes forever?"

"If it be a sign of mourning," replied Mr. Hooper, "I, perhaps, like most other mortals, have sorrows dark enough to be typified by a black veil."

"But what if the world will not believe that it is the type of an innocent sorrow?" urged Elizabeth. "Beloved and respected as you are, there may be whispers that you hide your face under the consciousness of secret sin. For the sake of your holy office, do away this scandal!"

The color rose into her cheeks as she intimated the nature of the rumors that were already abroad in the village. But Mr. Hooper's mildness did not forsake him. He even smiled again—that same sad smile, which always appeared like a faint glimmering of light, proceeding from the obscurity beneath the veil.

"If I hide my face for sorrow, there is cause enough," he merely replied; "and if I cover it for secret sin, what mortal might not do the same?"

And with this gentle, but unconquerable obstinacy did he resist all her entreaties. At length Elizabeth sat silent. For a few moments she appeared lost in thought, considering, probably, what new methods might be tried to withdraw her lover from so dark a fantasy, which, if it had no other meaning, was perhaps a symptom of mental disease. Though of a firmer character than his own, the tears rolled down her cheeks. But, in an instant, as it were, a new feeling took the place of sorrow: her eyes were fixed insensibly on the black veil, when, like a sudden twilight in the air, its terrors fell around her. She arose, and stood trembling before him.

"And do you feel it then, at last?" said he mournfully.

She made no reply, but covered her eyes with her hand, and turned to leave the room. He rushed forward and caught her arm.

"Have patience with me, Elizabeth!" cried he, passionately. "Do not desert me, though this veil must be between us here on earth. Be mine, and hereafter there shall be no veil over my face, no darkness between our souls! It is but a mortal veil—it is not for eternity! O! you know not how lonely I am, and how frightened, to be alone behind my black veil. Do not leave me in this miserable obscurity forever!"

"Lift the veil but once, and look me in the face," said she.

"Never! It cannot be!" replied Mr. Hooper.

"Then farewell!" said Elizabeth.

She withdrew her arm from his grasp, and slowly departed, pausing at the door, to give one long shuddering gaze, that seemed almost to penetrate the mystery of the black veil. But, even amid his grief, Mr. Hooper smiled to think that only a material emblem had separated him from happiness, though the horrors, which it shadowed forth, must be drawn darkly between the fondest of lovers.

From that time no attempts were made to remove Mr. Hooper's black veil, or, by a direct appeal, to discover the secret which it was supposed to hide. By persons who claimed a superiority to popular prejudice, it was reckoned merely an eccentric whim, such as often mingles with the sober actions of men otherwise rational, and tinges them all with its own semblance of insanity. But with the multitude, good Mr. Hooper was irreparably a bugbear. He could not walk the street with any peace of mind, so conscious was he that the gentle and timid would turn aside to avoid him, and that others would make it a point of hardihood to throw themselves in his way. The impertinence of the latter class compelled him to give up his customary walk at sunset to the burial ground; for when he leaned pensively over the gate, there would always be faces behind the gravestones, peeping at his black veil. A fable went the rounds that the stare of the dead people drove him thence. It grieved him, to the very depth of his kind heart, to observe how the children fled from his approach, breaking up their merriest sports, while his melancholy figure was yet afar off. Their instinctive dread caused him to feel more strongly than aught else, that a preternatural horror was interwoven with the threads of the black crape. In truth, his own antipathy to the veil was known to be so great, that he never willingly passed before a mirror, nor stooped to drink at a still fountain, lest, in its peaceful bosom, he should be affrighted by himself. This was what gave plausibility to the whispers, that Mr. Hooper's conscience tortured him for some great crime too horrible to be entirely concealed, or otherwise than so obscurely intimated. Thus, from beneath the black veil, there rolled a cloud into the sunshine, an ambiguity of sin or sorrow, which enveloped the poor minister, so that love or sympathy could never reach him. It was said that ghost and fiend consorted with him there. With self-shudderings and outward terrors, he walked continually in its shadow, groping darkly within his own soul, or gazing through a medium that saddened the whole world. Even the lawless wind, it was believed, respected his dreadful secret, and never blew aside the veil. But still good Mr. Hooper sadly smiled at the pale visages of the worldly throng as he passed by.

Among all its bad influences, the black veil had the one desirable effect, of making its wearer a very efficient clergyman. By the aid of his mysterious emblem—for there was no other apparent cause—he became a man of awful power over souls that were in agony for sin. His converts always regarded him with a dread peculiar to themselves, affirming, though but figuratively, that, before he brought them to celestial light, they had been with him behind the black veil. Its gloom, indeed, enabled him to sympathize with all dark affections. Dying sinners cried aloud for Mr. Hooper, and would not yield their breath till he appeared; though ever, as he stooped to whisper consolation, they shuddered at the veiled face so near their own. Such were the terrors of the black veil, even when Death had bared his visage! Strangers came long distances to attend service at his church, with the mere idle purpose of gazing at his figure, because it was forbidden them to behold his face. But many were made to quake ere they departed! Once, during Governor Belcher's administration, Mr. Hooper was appointed to preach the election sermon. Covered with his black veil, he stood before the chief magistrate, the council, and the representatives, and wrought so deep an impression, that the legislative measures of that year were characterized by all the gloom and piety of our earliest ancestral sway.

In this manner Mr. Hooper spent a long life, irreproachable in outward act, yet shrouded in dismal suspicions; kind and loving, though unloved, and dimly feared; a man apart from men, shunned in their health and joy, but ever summoned to their aid in mortal anguish. As years wore on, shedding their snows above his sable veil, he acquired a name throughout the New England churches, and they called him Father Hooper. Nearly all his parishioners, who were of mature age when he was settled, had been borne away by many a funeral: he had one congregation in the church, and a more crowded one in the churchyard; and having wrought so late into the evening, and done his work so well, it was now good Father Hooper's turn to rest.

Several persons were visible by the shaded candlelight, in the death chamber of the old clergyman. Natural connections he had none. But there was the decorously grave, though unmoved physician, seeking only to mitigate the last pangs of the patient whom he could not save. There were the deacons, and other eminently pious members of his church. There, also, was the Reverend Mr. Clark, of Westbury, a young and zealous divine, who had ridden in haste to pray by the bedside of the expiring minister. There was the nurse, no hired handmaiden of death, but one whose calm affection had endured thus long in secrecy, in solitude, amid the chill of age, and would not perish, even at the dying hour. Who, but Elizabeth! And there lay the hoary head of good Father Hooper upon the death pillow, with the black veil still swathed about his brow, and reaching down over his face, so that each more difficult gasp of his faint breath caused it to stir. All through life that piece of crape had hung between him and the world: it had separated him from cheerful brotherhood and woman's love, and kept him in that saddest of all prisons, his own heart; and still it lay upon his face, as if to deepen the gloom of his darksome chamber, and shade him from the sunshine of eternity.

For some time previous, his mind had been confused, wavering doubtfully between the past and the present, and hovering forward, as it were, at intervals, into the indistinctness of the world to come. There had been feverish turns, which tossed him from side to side, and wore away what little strength he had. But in his most convulsive struggles, and in the wildest vagaries of his intellect, when no other thought retained its sober influence, he still showed an awful solicitude lest the black veil should slip aside. Even if his bewildered soul could have forgotten, there was a faithful woman at his pillow, who, with averted eyes, would have covered that aged face, which she had last beheld in the comeliness of manhood. At length the death-stricken old man lay quietly in the torpor of mental and bodily exhaustion, with an imperceptible pulse, and breath that grew fainter and fainter, except when a long, deep, and irregular inspiration seemed to prelude the flight of his spirit.

The minister of Westbury approached the bedside.

"Venerable Father Hooper," said he, "the moment of your release is at hand. Are you ready for the lifting of the veil that shuts in time from eternity?"

Father Hooper at first replied merely by a feeble motion of his head; then, apprehensive, perhaps, that his meaning might be doubtful, he exerted himself to speak.

"Yea," said he, in faint accents, "my soul hath a patient weariness until that veil be lifted."

"And is it fitting," resumed the Reverend Mr. Clark, "that a man so given to prayer, of such a blameless example, holy in deed and thought, so far as mortal judgment may pronounce; is it fitting that a father in the church should leave a shadow on his memory, that may seem to blacken a life so pure? I pray you, my venerable brother, let not this thing be! Suffer us to be gladdened by your triumphant aspect as you go to your reward. Before the veil of eternity be lifted, let me cast aside this black veil from your face!"

And thus speaking, the Reverend Mr. Clark bent forward to reveal the mystery of so many years. But, exerting a sudden energy, that made all the beholders stand aghast, Father Hooper snatched both his hands from beneath the bedclothes, and pressed them strongly on the black veil, resolute to struggle, if the minister of Westbury would contend with a dying man.

"Never!" cried the veiled clergyman. "On earth, never!"

"Dark old man!" exclaimed the affrighted minister, "with what horrible crime upon your soul are you now passing to the judgment?"

Father Hooper's breath heaved; it rattled in his throat; but, with a mighty effort, grasping forward with his hands, he caught hold of life, and held it back till he should speak. He even raised himself in bed; and there he sat, shivering with the arms of death around him, while the black veil hung down, awful, at that last moment, in the gathered terrors of a lifetime. And yet the faint, sad smile, so often there, now seemed to glimmer from its obscurity, and linger on Father Hooper's lips.

"Why do you tremble at me alone?" cried he, turning his veiled face round the circle of pale spectators. "Tremble also at each other! Have men avoided me, and women shown no pity, and children screamed and fled, only for my black veil? What, but the mystery which it obscurely typifies, has made this piece of crape so awful? When the friend shows his inmost heart to his friend; the lover to his best beloved; when man does not vainly shrink from the eye of his Creator, loathsomely treasuring up the secret of his sin; then deem me a monster, for the symbol beneath which I have lived, and die! I look around me, and, lo! on every visage a Black Veil!"

While his auditors shrank from one another, in mutual affright, Father Hooper fell back upon his pillow, a veiled corpse, with a faint smile lingering on the lips. Still veiled, they laid him in his coffin, and a veiled corpse they bore him to the grave. The grass of many years has sprung up and withered on that grave, the burial stone is moss-grown, and good Mr. Hooper's face is dust; but awful is still the thought that it mouldered beneath the Black Veil!

Nikolai Gogol (1809-1852)

Nikolai Gogol is considered the father of realism in Russian Literature, yet he has been called a romantic and even, by Vladimir Nabokov, a "fantast." These apparently disparate qualities converged to create one of the most influential short stories ever written. "The Overcoat," along with the work of Edgar Allan Poe, Nathaniel Hawthorne, and a few other writers of the age, stands as the bridge between the tale, that simple recital of happenings, and the modern short story, with its moral view and social commentary and complex psychology.

Frank O'Connor said that an alternate title for his fine study of the short story, "The Lonely Voice," might have been a line from "The Overcoat": "I am your brother." These words—uttered by the harassed and ridiculed little clerk—so moved one of his colleagues, who here represents the narrator, that "many a time in his life thereafter did he shudder, seeing how much inhumanity there is in man." O'Connor points out that in this story is "the first appearance in fiction of the Little Man. . . . Everything about Akakii Akakiievich, from his absurd name to his absurd job, is on the same level of mediocrity, and yet his absurdity is somehow transfigured by Gogol."

Though obviously not every story is set in a city, in a way the modern short story is an expression of the life led in the modern city, with its estrangement and anonymity and its special awareness. Gogol spends a good deal of time describing St. Petersburg, especially life among the bureaucrats. "The Overcoat" is as much a story of that society as it is of the Little Man we laugh at and are moved by. A decent coat is hardly his only deprivation. The "formidable foe" against which even "Titular Councilors are sometimes utterly defenseless" is as much the isolation and loneliness of the city as it is the northern frost. To make this point and paint this picture, Gogol brilliantly uses techniques of realism, romanticism, and fantasy.

"We all came out from under Gogol's 'Overcoat' " is a remark variously attributed to Dostoevsky and Turgenev. That either or both might have said it is a sign of the story's wide significance.

Gogol, whose name translates as "wild duck," was born in 1809 in the Ukraine, but before he was twenty went seeking literary fame and fortune in St. Petersburg, which was the artistic capital of czarist Russia. In 1836 his satirical play *The Inspector General* caused such a storm of criticism that he was forced into an exile that lasted twelve years. *Dead Souls,* his satirical novel, was published in 1837 and *Taras Bulba,* a novel which deals with the Cossack struggles in the sixteenth century, in 1842. Gogol died, quite mad, in 1852.

The Overcoat

In the Bureau of . . . but it might be better not to mention the Bureau by its precise name. There is nothing more touchy than all these Bureaus, Regiments, Chancelleries of every sort, and, in a word, every sort of person belonging to the administrative classes. Nowadays every civilian, even, considers all of society insulted in his own person. Quite recently, so they say, a petition came through from a certain Captain of Rural Police in some town or other (I can't recall its name), in which he explained clearly that the whole social structure was headed for ruin and that his sacred name was actually being taken entirely in vain, and, in proof, he documented his petition with the enormous tome of some romantic work or other wherein, every ten pages or so, a Captain of Rural Police appeared—in some passages even in an out-and-out drunken state. And so, to avoid any and all unpleasantnesses, we'd better call the Bureau in question *a certain Bureau*. And so, in *a certain Bureau* there served *a certain clerk*—a clerk whom one could hardly style very remarkable: quite low of stature, somewhat pockmarked, somewhat rusty-hued of hair, even somewhat purblind, at first glance; rather bald at the temples, with wrinkles along both cheeks, and his face of that complexion which is usually called hemorrhoidal. Well, what would you? It's the Petersburg climate that's to blame. As far as his rank is concerned (for among us the rank must be made known first of all), why, he was what they call a Perpetual Titular Councilor[1] a rank which, as everybody knows, various writers who have a praiseworthy wont of throwing their weight about among those who are in no position to hit back, have twitted and exercised their keen wits against often and long. This clerk's family name was Bashmachkin. It's quite evident, by the very name, that it sprang from *bashmak* or shoe, but at what time, just when and how it sprang from a shoe—of that nothing is known. For not only this clerk's father but his grandfather and even his brother-in-law, and absolutely all the Bashmachkins, walked about in boots, merely resoling them three times a year.

His name and patronymic were Akakii Akakiievich. It may, perhaps, strike the reader as somewhat odd and out of the way, but the reader may rest assured that the

---

[1] A relatively low-level civil servant.

author has not gone out of his way at all to find it, but that certain circumstances had come about of themselves in such fashion that there was absolutely no way of giving him any other name. And the precise way this came about was as follows. Akakii Akakiievich was born—unless my memory plays me false—on the night of the twenty-third of March. His late mother, a government clerk's wife, and a very good woman, was all set to christen her child, all fit and proper. She was still lying in bed, facing the door, while on her right stood the godfather, a most excellent man by the name of Ivan Ivanovich Eroshkin, who had charge of some Department or other in a certain Administrative Office, and the godmother, the wife of the precinct police officer, a woman of rare virtues, by the name of Arina Semenovna Byelobrushkina. The mother was offered the choice of any one of three names: Mokii, Sossii—or the child could even be given the name of that great martyr, Hozdavat. "No," the late lamented had reflected, "what sort of names are these?" In order to please her they opened the calendar at another place—and the result was again three names: Triphilii, Dula, and Varahasii. "What a visitation!" said the elderly woman. "What names all these be! To tell you the truth, I've never even heard the likes of them. If it were at least Baradat or Baruch, but why do Triphilii and Varahasii have to turn up?" They turned over another page—and came up with Pavsikahii and Vahtissii. "Well, I can see now," said the mother, "that such is evidently his fate. In that case it would be better if he were called after his father. His father was an Akakii—let the son be an Akakii also." And that's how Akakii Akakiievich came to be Akakii Akakiievich.

The child was baptized, during which rite he began to bawl and made terrible faces as if anticipating that it would be his lot to become a Perpetual Titular Councilor. And so that's the way it had all come about. We have brought the matter up so that the reader might see for himself that all this had come about through sheer inevitability and it had been utterly impossible to bestow any other name upon Akakii Akakiievich.

When, at precisely what time, he entered the Bureau, and who gave him the berth, were things which no one could recall. No matter how many Directors and his superiors of one sort or another came and went, he was always to be seen in the one and the same spot, in the same posture, in the very same post, always the same Clerk of Correspondence, so that subsequently people became convinced that he evidently had come into the world just the way he was, all done and set, in a uniform frock and bald at the temples. No respect whatsoever was shown him in the Bureau. The porters not only didn't jump up from their places whenever he happened to pass by, but didn't even as much as glance at him, as if nothing more than a common housefly had passed through the reception hall. His superiors treated him with a certain chill despotism. Some assistant or other of some Head of a Department would simply shove papers under his nose, without as much as saying "Transcribe these," or "Here's a rather pretty, interesting little case," or any of those small pleasantries that are current in well-conducted administrative institutions. And he would take the work, merely glancing at the paper, without looking up to see who had put it down before him and whether that person had the right to do so; he took it and right then and there went to work on it. The young clerks made fun of him and sharpened their wits at his expense, to whatever extent their quill-driving wittiness sufficed, retailing in his very presence the various stories made up about him; they said of his landlady, a crone of seventy, that she beat him, and asked him when their wedding would take place, they scattered torn paper over his head, maintaining it was snow.

But not a word did Akakii Akakiievich say in answer to all this, as if there were actually nobody before him. It did not even affect his work: in the midst of all these annoyances he did not make a single clerical error. Only when the jest was past all bearing, when they jostled his arm, hindering him from doing his work, would he say: "Leave me alone! Why do you pick on me?" And there was something odd about his words and in the voice with which he uttered them. In that voice could be heard something that moved one to pity—so much so that one young man, a recent entrant, who, following the example of the others, had permitted himself to make fun of Akakii Akakiievich, stopped suddenly, as if pierced to the quick, and from that time on everything seemed to change in his eyes and appeared in a different light. Some sort of preternatural force seemed to repel him from the companions he had made, having taken them for decent, sociable people. And for a long time afterward, in the very midst of his most cheerful moments, the little squat clerk would appear before him, with the small bald patches on each side of his forehead, and he would hear his heart-piercing words "Leave me alone! Why do you pick on me?" And in these heart-piercing words he caught the ringing sound of others: "I am your brother." And the poor young man would cover his eyes with his hand, and many a time in his life thereafter did he shudder, seeing how much inhumanity there is in man, how much hidden ferocious coarseness lurks in refined, cultured worldliness and, O God! even in that very man whom the world holds to be noble and honorable. . . .

It is doubtful if you could find anywhere a man whose life lay so much in his work. It would hardly do to say that he worked with zeal; no, it was a labor of love. Thus, in this transcription of his, he visioned some sort of diversified and pleasant world all its own. His face expressed delight; certain letters were favorites of his and whenever he came across them he would be beside himself with rapture: he'd chuckle, and wink, and help things along by working his lips, so that it seemed as if one could read on his face every letter his quill was outlining. If rewards had been meted out to him commensurately with his zeal, he might have, to his astonishment, actually found himself among the State Councilors; but, as none other than those wits, his own co-workers, expressed it, all he'd worked himself up to was a button in a buttonhole too wide, and piles in his backside.

However, it would not be quite correct to say that absolutely no attention was paid him. One Director, being a kindly man and wishing to reward him for his long service, gave orders that some work of a more important nature than the usual transcription be assigned to him; to be precise, he was told to make a certain referral to another Administrative Department out of a docket already prepared; the matter consisted, all in all, of changing the main title as well as some pronouns here and there from the first person singular to the third person singular. This made so much work for him that he was all of a sweat, kept mopping his forehead, and finally said: "No, better let me transcribe something." Thenceforth they left him to his transcription for all time. Outside of this transcription, it seemed, nothing existed for him.

He gave no thought whatsoever to his dress; the uniform frock coat on him wasn't the prescribed green at all, but rather of some rusty-flour hue. His collar was very tight and very low, so that his neck, even though it wasn't a long one, seemed extraordinarily long emerging therefrom, like those gypsum kittens with nodding heads which certain outlanders balance by the dozen atop their heads and peddle throughout Russia. And, always, something was bound to stick to his coat: a wisp of hay or some bit of thread; in addition to that, he had a peculiar knack whenever he walked through the streets of getting under some window at the precise moment when garbage of every sort was being thrown out of it, and for that reason always bore off on his hat watermelon and cantaloupe rinds and other such trifles. Not once in all his life had he ever turned his attention to the everyday things and doings out in the street—something, as everybody knows, that is always watched with eager interest by Akakii Akakiievich's confrère, the young government clerk, the penetration of whose lively gaze is so extensive that he will even take in somebody on the opposite sidewalk who has ripped loose his trouser strap—a thing that never fails to evoke a sly smile on the young clerk's face. But even if Akakii Akakiievich did look at anything, he saw thereon nothing but his own neatly, evenly penned lines of script, and only when some horse's nose, bobbing up from no one knew where, would be placed on his shoulder and let a whole gust of wind in his face through its nostrils, would he notice that he was not in the middle of a line of script but, rather, in the middle of the roadway.

On coming home he would immediately sit down at the table, gulp down his cabbage soup and bolt a piece of veal with onions, without noticing in the least the taste of either, eating everything together with the flies and whatever else God may have sent at that particular time of the year. On perceiving that his belly was beginning to swell out, he'd get up from the table, take out a small bottle of ink, and transcribe the papers he had brought home. If there were no homework, he would deliberately, for his own edification, make a copy of some paper for himself, especially if the document were remarkable not for its beauty of style but merely addressed to some new or important person.

Even at those hours when the gray sky of Petersburg became entirely extinguished and all the pettifogging tribe has eaten its fill and finished dinner, each as best he could, in accordance with the salary he receives and his own bent, when everybody has already rested up after the scraping of quills in various departments, the running around, the unavoidable cares about their own affairs and the affairs of others, and all that which restless man sets himself as a task voluntarily and to an even greater extent than necessary—at a time when the petty bureaucrats hasten to devote whatever time remained to enjoyment: he who is of the more lively sort hastening to the theater; another for a saunter through the streets, devoting the time to an inspection of certain pretty little hats; still another to some evening party, to spend that time in paying compliments to some comely young lady, the star of a small bureaucratic circle; a fourth (and this happened most frequently of all) would simply go for a call on a confrère in a flat up three or four flights of stairs, consisting of two small rooms with an entry and a kitchen and one or two attempts at the latest improvements—a kerosene lamp instead of candles, or some other elegant little thing that had cost many sacrifices, such as going without dinners or good times—in short, even at the time when all the pretty bureaucrats scatter through the small apartments of their friends for a session of dummy whist, sipping tea out of tumblers and nibbling at cheap zweiback, drawing deep at their pipes, the stems thereof as long as walking sticks, retailing, during the shuffling and dealing, some bit of gossip or other from high society that had reached them at long last (something which no Russian, under any circumstances, and of whatever estate he be, can ever deny himself), or even, when there was nothing whatsoever to talk about, retelling the eternal chestnut of the commandant to whom people came to say that the tail of the horse on the Falconetti monument had been docked—in short, even at the time when every soul yearns to be diverted, Akakii Akakiievich did not give himself up to any diversion. No man could claim having ever seen him at any evening gathering. Having had his sweet fill of quill-driving, he would lie down to sleep, smiling at the thought of the next day: just what would God send him on the morrow?

Such was the peaceful course of life of a man who, with a yearly salary of four hundred, knew how to be content with his lot, and that course might even have continued to a ripe old age had it not been for sundry calamities, such as are stewn along the path of life, not only of Titular, but even Privy, Actual, Court, and all other sorts of Councilors, even those who never give any counsel to anybody nor ever accept any counsel from others for themselves.

There is, in Petersburg, a formidable foe of all those whose salary runs to four hundred a year or thereabouts. This foe is none other than our Northern frost—even though, by the bye, they do say that it's the most healthful thing for you. At nine in the morning, precisely at that hour when the streets are thronged with those on their way to sundry bureaus, it begins dealing out such powerful and penetrating fillips to all noses, without any discrimination, that the poor bureaucrats absolutely do not know how to hide them. At this time, when even those who fill the higher posts feel their foreheads aching because of the frost and the tears come to their eyes, the poor Titular Councilors are sometimes utterly defenseless. The sole salvation, if one's overcoat is of the thinnest, lies in dashing, as quickly as possible, through five or six blocks and then stamping one's feet plenty in the porter's room, until the faculties and gifts for administrative duties, which have been frozen on the way, are thus thawed out at last.

For some time Akakii Akakiievich had begun to notice that the cold was somehow penetrating his back and shoulders with especial ferocity, despite the fact that he tried to run the required distance as quickly as possible. It occurred to him, at last, that there might be some defects about this overcoat. After looking it over rather thoroughly at home he discovered that in two or three places—in the back and at the shoulders, to be exact—it had become no better than the coarsest of sacking; the cloth was rubbed to such an extent that one could see through it, and the lining had crept apart. The reader must be informed that Akakii Akakiievich's overcoat, too, was a butt for the jokes of the petty bureaucrats; it had been deprived of the honorable name of an overcoat, even, and dubbed a *negligée*. And, really, it was of a rather queer cut; its collar grew smaller with every year, inasmuch as it was utilized to supplement the other parts of the garment. This supplementing was not at all a compliment to the skill of the tailor, and the effect really was baggy and unsightly.

Perceiving what the matter was, Akakii Akakiievich decided that the overcoat would have to go to Petrovich the tailor, who lived somewhere up four flights of backstairs and who, despite a squint-eye and pockmarks all over his face, did quite well at repairing bureaucratic as well as all other trousers and coats—of course, be it understood, when he was in a sober state and not hatching some nonsartorial scheme in his head. One shouldn't, really, mention this tailor at great length, but since there is already a precedent for each character in a tale being clearly defined, there's no help for it, and so let's trot out Petrovich as well. In the beginning he had been called simply Gregory and had been the serf of some squire or other; he had begun calling himself Petrovich only after obtaining his freedom papers and taking to drinking rather hard on any and every holiday—at first on the red-letter ones and then, without any discrimination, on all those designated by the church: wherever there was a little cross marking the day on the calendar. In this respect he was loyal to the customs of our grandsires, and, when bickering with his wife, would call her a worldly woman and a German frau. And, since we've already been inadvertent enough to mention his wife, it will be necessary to say a word or two about her as well; but, regrettably, little was known about her—unless, perhaps, the fact that Petrovich had a wife, or that she even wore a house-cap and not a kerchief; but as for beauty, it appears that she could hardly boast of any; at least the soldiers in the Guards were the only ones with hardihood enough to bend down for a peep under her cap, twitching their mustache as they did so and emitting a certain peculiar sound.

As he clambered up the staircase that led to Petrovich—the staircase, to render it its just due, was dripping all over from water and slops and thoroughly permeated with that alcoholic odor which makes the eyes smart and is, as everybody knows, unfailingly present on all the backstairs of all the houses in Petersburg—as he clambered up this staircase Akakii Akakiievich was already conjecturing how stiff Petrovich's asking-price would be and mentally determined not to give him more than two rubles. The door was open, because the mistress of the place, being busy preparing some fish, had filled the kitchen with so much smoke that one actually couldn't see the very cockroaches for it. Akakii Akakiievich made his way through the kitchen, unperceived even by the mistress herself, and at last entered the room wherein he beheld Petrovich, sitting on a wide table of unpainted deal with his feet tucked in under him like a Turkish Pasha. His feet, as is the wont of tailors seated at their work, were bare, and the first thing that struck one's eyes was the big toe of one, very familiar to Akakii Akakiievich, with some sort of deformed nail, as thick and strong as a turtle's shell. About Petrovich's neck were loops of silk and cotton thread, while some sort of ragged garment was lying on his knees. For the last three minutes he had been trying to put a thread through the eye of a needle, couldn't hit the mark, and because of that was very wroth against the darkness of the room and even the thread itself, grumbling under his breath: "She won't go through, the heathen! You've spoiled my heart's blood, you damned good-for-nothing!"

Akakii Akakiievich felt upset because he had come at just the moment when Petrovich was very angry; he liked to give in his work when the latter was already under the influence or, as his wife put it, "He's already full of rot-gut, the one-eyed devil." In such a state Petrovich usually gave in willingly and agreed to everything; he even bowed and was grateful every time. Afterward, true enough, his wife would come around and complain weepily that, now, her husband had been drunk and for that reason had taken on the work too cheaply; but all you had to do was to tack on another ten kopecks—and the thing was in the bag. But now, it seemed, Petrovich was in a sober state, and for that reason on his high horse, hard to win over, and bent on boosting his prices to the devil knows what heights. Akakii Akakiievich surmised this and, as the saying goes, was all set to make back tracks, but the deal had already been started. Petrovich puckered up his one good eye against him very fixedly and Akakii Akakiievich involuntarily said, "Greetings, Petrovich!" "Greetings to you, Sir," said Petrovich and looked askance at Akakii Akakiievich's hands, wishing to see what sort of booty the other bore.

"Well, now, I've come to see you, now, Petrovich!"

Akakii Akakiievich, the reader must be informed, explained himself for the most part in prepositions, adverbs, and such verbal oddments as have absolutely no significance. But if the matter was exceedingly difficult, he actually had a way of not finishing his phrase at all, so that, quite frequently, beginning his speech with such words as "This, really, is perfectly, you know—" he would have nothing at all to follow up with, and he himself would be likely to forget the matter, thinking that he had already said everything in full.

"Well, just what is it?" asked Petrovich, and at the same time, with his one good eye, surveyed the entire garment, beginning with the collar and going on to the sleeves, the back, the coat-skirts, and the buttonholes, for it was all very familiar to him, inasmuch as it was all his own handiwork. That's a way all tailors have; it's the first thing a tailor will do on meeting you.

"Why, what I'm after, now, Petrovich . . . the overcoat, now, the cloth . . . there, you see, in all the other places it's strong as can be . . . . it's gotten a trifle dusty and only seems to be old, but it's really new, there's only one spot . . . a little sort of . . . in the back . . . and also one shoulder, a trifle rubbed through—and this shoulder, too, a trifle—do you see? Not a lot of work, really—"

Petrovich took up the *negligée,* spread it out over the table as a preliminary, examined it for a long time, shook his head, and then groped with his hand on the window sill for a round snuffbox with the portrait of some general or other on its lid— just which one nobody could tell, inasmuch as the place occupied by the face had been holed through with a finger and then pasted over with a small square of paper. After duly taking tobacco, Petrovich held the *negligée* taut in his hands and scrutinized it against the light, and again shook his head; after this he turned it with the lining up and again shook his head, again took off the lid with the general's face pasted over with paper and, having fully loaded both nostrils with snuff, covered the snuffbox, put it away, and at long last, gave his verdict:

"No, there's no fixin' this thing: your wardrobe's in a bad way!"

Akakii Akakiievich's heart skipped a beat at these words.

"But why not, Petrovich?" he asked, almost in the imploring voice of a child. "All that ails it, now . . . it's rubbed through at the shoulders. Surely you must have some small scraps of cloth or other—"

"Why, yes, one could find the scraps—the scraps will turn up," said Petrovich. "Only there's no sewing them on: the whole thing's all rotten: touch a needle to it—and it just crawls apart on you."

"Well, let it crawl—and you just slap a patch right on to it."

"Yes, but there's nothing to slap them little patches on to; there ain't nothing for the patch to take hold on—there's been far too much wear. It's cloth in name only, but if a gust of wind was to blow on it it would scatter."

"Well, now, you just fix it up. That, really, now . . . how can it be?"

"No," said Petrovich decisively, "there ain't a thing to be done. The whole thing's in a bad way. You'd better, when the cold winter spell comes, make footcloths out of it, because stockings ain't so warm. It's them Germans that invented them stockings, so's to rake in more money for themselves. [Petrovich loved to needle the Germans whenever the chance turned up.] But as for that there overcoat, it looks like you'll have to make yourself a new one."

At the word *new* a mist swam before Akakii Akakiievich's eyes and everything in the room became a hotchpotch. All he could see clearly was the general on the lid of Petrovich's snuffbox, his face pasted over with a piece of paper.

"A new one? But how?" he asked, still as if he were in a dream. "Why, I have no money for that."

"Yes, a new one," said Petrovich with a heathenish imperturbability.

"Well, if there's no getting out of it, how much, now—"

"You mean, how much it would cost?"

"Yes."

"Why, you'd have to cough up three fifties and a bit over," pronounced Petrovich and significantly pursed up his lips at this. He was very fond of strong effects, was fond of somehow nonplusing somebody, utterly and suddenly, and then eyeing his victim sidelong, to see what sort of wry face the nonplusee would pull after his words.

"A hundred and fifty for an overcoat!" poor Akakii Akakiievich cried out—cried out perhaps for the first time since he was born, for he was always distinguished for his low voice.

"Yes, Sir!" said Petrovich. "And what an overcoat, at that! If you put a marten collar on it and add a silk-lined hood it might stand you even two hundred."

"Petrovich, please!" Akakii Akakiievich was saying in an imploring voice, without grasping and without even trying to grasp the words uttered by Petrovich and all his effects. "Fix it somehow or other, now, so's it may do a little longer, at least—"

"Why, no, that'll be only having the work go to waste and spending your money for nothing," said Petrovich, and after these words Akakii Akakiievich walked out annihilated. But Petrovich, after his departure, remained as he was for a long time, with meaningfully pursed lips and without resuming his work, satisfied with neither having lowered himself nor having betrayed the satorial art.

Out in the street, Akakii Akakiievich walked along like a somnambulist. "What a business, now, what a business," he kept saying to himself. "Really, I never even thought that it, now . . . would turn out like that. . . ." And then, after a pause, added: "So that's it! That's how it's turned out after all. Really, now, I couldn't even suppose that it . . . like that, now—" This was followed by another long pause, after which he uttered aloud: "So that's how it is! This, really, now, is something that's beyond all, now, expectation . . . well, I never! What a fix, now!"

Having said this, instead of heading for home, he started off in an entirely different direction without himself suspecting it. On the way a chimney sweep caught him square with his whole sooty side and covered his whole shoulder with soot; enough quicklime to cover his whole hat tumbled down on him from the top of a building under construction. He noticed nothing of all this and only later, when he ran up against a policeman near his sentry box (who, having placed his halberd near him, was shaking some tobacco out of a paper cornucopia on to his calloused palm), did Akakii Akakiievich come a little to himself, and that only because the policeman said: "What's the idea of shoving your face right into mine? Ain't the sidewalk big enough for you?" This made him look about him and turn homeward.

Only here did he begin to pull his wits together; he perceived his situation in its clear and real light; he started talking to himself no longer in snatches but reasoningly and frankly, as with a judicious friend with whom one might discuss a matter most heartfelt and intimate. "Well, no," said Akakii Akakiievich, "there's no use reasoning with Petrovich now; he's, now, that way. . . . His wife had a chance to give him a drubbing, it looks like. No, it'll be better if I come to him on a Sunday morning; after Saturday night's good time he'll be squinting his eye and very sleepy, so he'll have to have a hair of the dog that bit him, but his wife won't give him any money, now, and just then I'll up with ten kopecks or so and into his hand with it—so he'll be more reasonable to talk with, like, and the overcoat will then be sort of. . . ."

That was the way Akakii Akakiievich reasoned things out to himself, bolstering up his spirits. And, having bided his time till the next Sunday and spied from afar that Petrovich's wife was going off somewhere out of the house, he went straight up to him. Petrovich, sure enough, was squinting his eye hard after the Saturday night before, kept his head bowed down to the floor, and was no end sleepy; but, for all that, as soon as he learned what was up, it was as though the Devil himself nudged him.

"Can't be done," said he. "You'll have to order a new overcoat."

Akakii Akakiievich thrust a ten-kopeck coin on him right then and there.

"I'm grateful to you, Sir; I'll have a little something to get me strength back and will drink to your health," said Petrovich, "but as for your overcoat, please don't fret about it; it's of no earthly use any more. As for a new overcoat, I'll tailor a glorious one for you; I'll see to that."

Just the same, Akakii Akakiievich started babbling again about fixing the old one, but Petrovich simply would not listen to him and said: "Yes, I'll tailor a new one for you without fail; you may rely on that, I'll try my very best. We might even do it the way it's all the fashion now—the collar will button with silver catches under appliqué."

It was then that Akakii Akakiievich perceived that there was no doing without a new overcoat, and his spirits sank utterly. Really, now, with what means, with what money would he make this overcoat? Of course he could rely, in part, on the coming holiday bonus, but this money had been apportioned and budgeted ahead long ago. There was an imperative need of outfitting himself with new trousers, paying the shoemaker an old debt for a new pair of vamps to an old pair of bootlegs, and he had to order from a sempstress three shirts and two pair of those nethergarments which it is impolite to mention in print; in short, all the money was bound to be expended entirely, and even if the Director was so gracious as to decide on giving him five and forty, or even fifty rubles as a bonus, instead of forty, why, even then only the veriest trifle would be left over, which, in the capital sum required for the overcoat, would be as a drop in a bucket. Even though Akakii Akakiievich was, of course, aware of Petrovich's maggot of popping out with the devil knows how inordinate an asking price, so that even his wife herself could not restrain herself on occasion from crying out: ''What, are you going out of your mind, fool that you are! There's times when he won't take on work for anything, but the Foul One has egged him on to ask a bigger price than all of him is worth''—even though he knew, of course, that Petrovich would probably undertake the work for eighty rubles, nevertheless and notwithstanding where was he to get those eighty rubles? Half of that sum might, perhaps, be found: half of it could have been found, maybe even a little more—but where was he going to get the other half?

But first the reader must be informed where the first half was to come from. Akakii Akakiievich had a custom of putting away a copper or so from every ruble he expended, into a little box under lock and key, with a small opening cut through the lid for dropping money therein. At the expiration of every half-year he made an accounting of the entire sum accumulated in coppers and changed it into small silver. He had kept this up a long time, and in this manner, during the course of several years, the accumulated sum turned out to be more than forty rubles. And so he had half the sum for the overcoat on hand; but where was he to get the other half? Where was he to get the other forty rubles? Akakii Akakiievich mulled the matter over and over and decided that it would be necessary to curtail his ordinary expenses, for the duration of a year at the very least; banish the indulgence in tea of evenings; also, of evenings, to do without lighting candles, but, if there should be need of doing something, to go to his landlady's room and work by her candle; when walking along the streets he would set his foot as lightly and carefully as possible on the cobbles and flagstones, walking almost on tiptoes, and thus avoid wearing out his soles prematurely; his linen would have to be given as infrequently as possible to the laundress and, in order that it might not become too soiled, every time he came home all of it must be taken off, the wearer having to remain only in his jean bathrobe, a most ancient garment and spared even by time itself.

It was, the truth must be told, most difficult for him in the beginning to get habituated to such limitations, but later it did turn into a matter of habit, somehow, and everything went well; he even became perfectly trained to going hungry of evenings; on the other hand, however, he had spiritual sustenance, always carrying about in his thoughts the eternal idea of the new overcoat. From this time forth it seemed as if his very existence had become somehow fuller, as though he had taken unto himself a wife, as though another person was always present with him, as though he were not alone but as if an amiable feminine helpmate had consented to traverse the path of life side by side with him—and this feminine helpmate was none other than this very same overcoat, with a thick quilting of cotton wool, with a strong lining that would never wear out.

He became more animated, somehow, even firmer of character, like a man who has already defined and set a goal for himself. Doubt, indecision—in a word, all vacillating and indeterminate traits—vanished of themselves from his face and actions. At times a sparkle appeared in his eyes; the boldest and most daring of thoughts actually flashed through his head: Shouldn't he, after all, put marten on the collar? Meditations on this subject almost caused him to make absent-minded blunders. And on one occasion, as he was transcribing a paper, he all but made an error, so that he emitted an almost audible ''Ugh,'' and made the sign of the cross.

During the course of each month he would make at least one call on Petrovich, to discuss the overcoat: Where would it be best to buy the cloth, and of what color and at what price—and even though somewhat preoccupied he always came home satisfied, thinking that the time would come, at last, when all the necessary things would be bought and the overcoat made.

The matter went even more quickly than he had expected. Contrary to all his anticipations, the Director designated a bonus not of forty or forty-five rubles for Akakii Akakiievich, but all of sixty. Whether he had a premonition that Akakii Akakiievich needed a new overcoat, or whether this had come about of its own self, the fact nevertheless remained: Akakii Akakiievich thus found himself the possessor of an extra twenty rubles. This circumstance hastened the course of things. Some two or three months more of slight starvation—and lo! Akakii Akakiievich had accumulated around eighty rubles. His heart, in general quite calm, began to palpitate. On the very first day possible he set out with Petrovich to the shops. The cloth they bought was very good, and no great wonder, since they had been thinking over its purchase as much as half a year before and hardly a month had gone by without their making a round of shops to compare prices; but then, Petrovich himself said that there couldn't be better cloth than that. For lining they chose calico, but of such good quality and so closely woven that, to quote Petrovich's words, it was still better than silk and, to look at, even more showy and glossy. Marten they did not buy, for, to be sure, it was expensive, but instead they picked out the best catskin the shop boasted—catskin that could, at a great enough distance, be taken for marten.

Petrovich spent only a fortnight in fussing about with the making of the overcoat, for there was a great deal of stitching to it, and if it hadn't been for that it would have been ready considerably earlier. For his work Petrovich took twelve rubles—he couldn't have taken any less; everything was positively sewn with silk thread, with a small double stitch, and after the stitching Petrovich went over every seam with his own teeth, pressing out various figures with them.

It was on . . . it would be hard to say on precisely what day, but it was, most probably, the most triumphant day in Akakii Akakiievich's life when Petrovich, at last, brought the overcoat. He brought it in the morning, just before Akakii Akakiievich had to set out for his Bureau. Never, at any other time, would the overcoat have come in so handy, because rather hard frosts were already setting in and, apparently, were threatening to become still more severe. Petrovich's entrance with the overcoat was one befitting a good tailor. Such a portentous expression appeared on his face as Akakii Akakiievich had never yet beheld. Petrovich felt to the fullest, it seemed, that he had performed no petty labor and that he had suddenly evinced in himself that abyss which lies between those tailors who merely put in linings and alter and fix garments and those who create new ones.

He extracted the overcoat from the bandanna in which he had brought it. (The bandanna was fresh from the laundress; it was only later on that he thrust it in his pocket for practical use.) Having drawn out the overcoat, he looked at it quite proudly and, holding it in both hands, threw it deftly over the shoulders of Akakii Akakiievich, pulled it and smoothed it down the back with his hand, then draped it on Akakii Akakiievich somewhat loosely. Akakiievich, as a man along in his years, wanted to try it on with his arms through the sleeves. Petrovich helped him on with it: it turned out to be fine, even with his arms through the sleeves. In a word, the overcoat proved to be perfect and had come in the very nick of time. Petrovich did not let slip the opportunity of saying that he had done the work so cheaply only because he lived in a place without a sign, on a side street, and, besides, had known Akakii Akakiievich for a long time; *but* on the Nevski Prospect they would have taken seventy-five rubles from him for the labor alone. Akakii

Akakiievich did not feel like arguing the matter with Petrovich and, besides, he had a
dread of all the fancy sums with which Petrovich liked to throw dust in people's eyes.
He paid the tailor off, thanked him, and walked right out in the new overcoat on his way
to the Bureau. Petrovich walked out at his heels and, staying behind on the street, for a
long while kept looking after the overcoat from afar, and then deliberately went out of
his way so that, after cutting across a crooked lane, he might run out again into the
street and have another glance at his overcoat from a different angle—that is, full front.

In the meantime Akakii Akakiievich walked along feeling in the most festive of
moods. He was conscious every second of every minute that he had a new overcoat on
his shoulders, and several times even smiled slightly because of his inward pleasure. In
reality he was a gainer on two points: for one, the overcoat was warm, for the other, it
was a fine thing. He did not notice the walk at all and suddenly found himself at the
Bureau; in the porter's room he took off his overcoat, looked it all over, and entrusted it
to the particular care of the doorman. None knows in what manner everybody in the
Bureau suddenly learned that Akakii Akakiievich had a new overcoat, and that the
negligée was no longer in existence. They all immediately ran out into the vestibule to
inspect Akakii Akakiievich's new overcoat. They fell to congratulating him, to saying
agreeable things to him, so that at first he could merely smile, and in a short time became
actually embarrassed. And when all of them, having besieged him, began telling him that
the new overcoat ought to be baptized and that he ought, at the least, to get up an
evening party for them, Akakii Akakiievich was utterly at a loss, not knowing what to
do with himself, what answers to make, nor how to get out of inviting them. It was only
a few minutes later that he began assuring them, quite simpleheartedly, that it wasn't a
new overcoat at all, that it was just an ordinary overcoat, that in fact it was an old
overcoat. Finally one of the bureaucrats—some sort of an Assistant to a Head of a
Department, actually—probably in order to show that he was not at all a proud stick and
willing to mingle even with those beneath him, said: "So be it, then; I'm giving a party
this evening and ask all of you to have tea with me; today, appropriately enough,
happens to be my birthday."

The clerks, naturally, at once thanked the Assistant to a Head of a Department and
accepted the invitation with enthusiasm. Akakii Akakiievich attempted to excuse himself at first, but all began saying that it would show disrespect to decline, that it would be
simply a shame and a disgrace, and after that there was absolutely no way for him to
back out. However, when it was all over, he felt a pleasant glow as he reminded himself
that this would give him a chance to take a walk in his new overcoat even in the evening.
The whole day was for Akakii Akakiievich something in the nature of the greatest and
most triumphant of holidays.

Akakii Akakiievich returned home in the happiest mood, took off the overcoat, and
hung it carefully on the wall, once more getting his fill of admiring the cloth and the
lining, and then purposely dragged out, for comparison, his former *negligée,* which by
now had practically disintegrated. He glanced at it and he himself had to laugh, so great
was the difference! And for a long while thereafter, as he ate dinner, he kept on smiling
slightly whenever the present state of the *negligée* came to his mind. He dined gaily, and
after dinner did not write a single stroke; there were no papers of any kind, for that
matter; he just simply played the sybarite a little, lounging on his bed, until it became
dark. Then, without putting matters off any longer, he dressed, threw the overcoat over
his shoulders, and walked out into the street.

We are, to our regret, unable to say just where the official who had extended the
invitation lived; our memory is beginning to play us false—very much so—and everything in Petersburg, no matter what, including all its streets and houses, has become so

muddled in our mind that it's quite hard to get anything out therefrom in any sort of decent shape. But wherever it may have been, at least this much is certain: that official lived in the best part of town; consequently a very long way from Akakii Akakiievich's quarters. First of all Akakii Akakiievich had to traverse certain deserted streets with but scant illumination; however, in keeping with his progress toward the official's domicile, the streets became more animated; the pedestrians flitted by more and more often; he began meeting even ladies, handsomely dressed; the men he came upon had beaver collars on their overcoats; more and more rarely did he encounter jehus with latticed wooden sleighs, studded over with gilt nails—on the contrary, he kept coming across first-class drivers in caps of raspberry-hued velvet, their sleighs lacquered and with bearskin robes, while the carriages had decorated seats for the drivers and raced down the roadway, their wheels screeching over the snow.

Akakii Akakiievich eyed all this as a novelty—it was several years by now since he had set foot out of his house in the evening. He stopped with curiosity before the illuminated window of a shop to look at a picture, depicting some handsome woman or other, who was taking off her shoe, thus revealing her whole leg (very far from ill-formed), while behind her back some gentleman or other, sporting side whiskers and a handsome goatee, was poking his head out of the door of an adjoining room. Akakii Akakiievich shook his head and smiled, after which he went on his way. Why had he smiled? Was it because he had encountered something utterly unfamiliar, yet about which, nevertheless, everyone preserves a certain instinct? Or did he think, like so many other petty clerks, "My, the French they are a funny race! No use talking! If there's anything they get a notion of, then, sure enough, there it is!" And yet, perhaps, he did not think even that; after all, there's no way of insinuating one's self into a man's soul, of finding out all that he might be thinking about.

At last he reached the house in which the Assistant to a Head of a Department lived. The Assistant to a Head of a Department lived on a grand footing; there was a lantern on the staircase; his apartment was only one flight up. On entering the foyer of the apartment Akakii Akakiievich beheld row after row of galoshes. In this midst, in the center of the room, stood a samovar, noisy and emitting clouds of steam. The walls were covered with hanging overcoats and capes, among which were even such as had beaver collars or lapels of velvet. On the other side of the wall he could hear much noise and talk, which suddenly became distinct and resounding when the door opened and a flunky came out with a tray full of empty tumblers, a cream pitcher, and a basket of biscuits. It was evident that the bureaucrats had gathered long since and had already had their first glasses of tea.

Akakii Akakiievich, hanging up his overcoat himself, entered the room and simultaneously all the candles, bureaucrats, tobacco-pipes and card tables flickered before him, and the continuous conversation and the scraping of moving chairs, coming from all sides, struck dully on his ears. He halted quite awkwardly in the center of the room, at a loss and trying to think what he ought to do. But he had already been noticed, was received with much shouting, and everyone immediately went to the foyer and again inspected his overcoat. Akakii Akakiievich, even though he was somewhat embarrassed, still could not but rejoice on seeing them all bestow such praises on his overcoat, since he was a man with an honest heart. Then, of course, they all dropped him and his overcoat and, as is usual, directed their attention to the whist tables.

All this—the din, the talk, and the throng of people—all this was somehow a matter of wonder to Akakii Akakiievich. He simply did not know what to do, how to dispose of his hands, his feet, and his whole body; finally he sat down near the card-players, watched their cards, looked now at the face of this man, now of that, and after some time began to feel bored, to yawn—all the more so since his usual bedtime had long since passed. He wanted to say good-by to his host but they wouldn't let him, saying that they absolutely must toast his new acquisition in a goblet of champagne. An hour later supper was served, consisting of mixed salad, cold veal, meat pie, patties from a pastry cook's, and champagne. They forced Akakii Akakiievich to empty two goblets, after which he felt that the room had become ever so much more cheerful. However, he absolutely could not forget that it was already twelve o'clock and that it was long since time for him to go home. So that his host might not somehow get the idea of detaining him, he crept out of the room, managed to find his overcoat—which, not without regret, he saw lying on the floor; then, shaking the overcoat and taking every bit of fluff off it, he threw it over his shoulders and made his way down the stairs and out of the house.

It was still dusk out in the street. Here and there small general stores, those round-the-clock clubs for domestics and all other servants, were still open; other shops, which were closed, nevertheless showed, by a long streak of light along the crack either at the outer edge or the bottom, that they were not yet without social life and that, probably, the serving wenches and lads were still winding up their discussions and conversations, thus throwing their masters into utter bewilderment as to their whereabouts. Akakii Akakiievich walked along in gay spirits; he even actually made a sudden dash, for some unknown reason, after some lady or other, who had passed by him like a flash of lightning, and every part of whose body was filled with buoyancy. However, he stopped right then and there and resumed his former exceedingly gentle pace, actually wondering himself at the sprightliness that had come upon him from none knows where.

Soon he again was passing stretch after stretch of those desolate streets which are never too gay even in the daytime, but are even less so in the evening. Now they had become still more deserted and lonely; he came upon glimmering street lamps more and more infrequently—the allotment of oil was now evidently decreasing; there was a succession of wooden houses and fences, with never another soul about; the snow alone glittered on the street, and the squat hovels, with their shutters closed in sleep, showed like depressing dark blotches. He approached a spot where the street was cut in two by an unending square, with the houses on the other side of it barely visible—a square that loomed ahead like an awesome desert.

Far in the distance, God knows where, a little light flickered in a policeman's sentry box that seemed to stand at the end of the world. Akakii Akakiievich's gay mood somehow diminished considerably at this point. He set foot in the square, not without a premonition of something evil. He looked back and on each side of him—it was as though he were in the midst of a sea. "No, it's better even not to look," he reflected and went on with his eyes shut. And when he did open them to see if the end of the square were near, he suddenly saw standing before him, almost at his very nose, two strangers with mustaches—just what sort of men they were was something he couldn't even make out. A mist arose before his eyes and his heart began to pound.

"Why, that there overcoat is mine!" said one of the men in a thunderous voice, grabbing him by the collar. Akakii Akakiievich was just about to yell "Police!" when the other put a fist right up to his mouth, a fist as big as any government clerk's head, adding: "There, you just let one peep out of you!"

All that Akakii Akakiievich felt was that they had taken the overcoat off him, given him a kick in the back with the knee, and that he had fallen flat on his back in the snow, after which he felt nothing more. In a few minutes he came to and got up on his feet, but there was no longer anybody around. He felt that it was cold out in that open space and that he no longer had the overcoat, and began to yell; but his voice, it seemed, had no intention whatsoever of reaching the other end of the square. Desperate, without ceasing to yell, he started off at a run across the square directly toward the sentry box near which the policeman was standing and, leaning on his halberd, was watching the running man, apparently with curiosity, as if he wished to know why the devil anybody should be running toward him from afar and yelling. Akakii Akakiievich, having run up to him, began to shout in a stifling voice that he, the policeman, had been asleep, that he was not watching and couldn't see that a man was being robbed. The policeman answered that he hadn't seen anything, that he had seen two men of some sort stop him in the middle of the square, but he had thought they were friends of Akakii Akakiievich's, and that instead of cursing him out for nothing he'd better go on the morrow to the Inspector, and the Inspector would find out who had taken his overcoat.

Akakii Akakiievich ran home in utter disorder; whatever little hair still lingered on his temples and the nape of his neck was all disheveled; his side and his breast and his trousers were all wet with snow. The old woman, his landlady, hearing the dreadful racket at the door, hurriedly jumped out of bed, and, with a shoe on only one foot, ran down to open the door, modestly holding the shift at her breast with one hand; but, on opening the door and seeing Akakii Akakiievich in such a state, she staggered back. When he had told her what the matter was, however, she wrung her hands and said that he ought to go directly to the Justice of the Peace; the District Officer of Police would take him in, would make promises to him and then lead him about by the nose; yes, it would be best of all to go straight to the Justice. Why, she was even acquainted with him, seeing as how Anna, the Finnish woman who had formerly been her cook, had now gotten a place as a nurse at the Justice's; that she, the landlady herself, sees the Justice often when he drives past her house, and also that he went to church every Sunday, praying, yet at the same time looking so cheerfully at all the folks, and that consequently, as one could see by all the signs, he was a kindhearted man. Having heard this solution of his troubles through to the end, the saddened Akakii Akakiievich shuffled off to his room, and how he passed the night there may be left to the discernment of him who can in any degree imagine the situation of another.

Early in the morning he set out for the Justice's, but was told there that he was sleeping; he came at ten o'clock, and was told again, "He's sleeping." He came at eleven; they told him, "Why, His Honor's not at home." He tried at lunchtime, but the clerks in the reception room would not let him through to the presence under any circumstances and absolutely had to know what business he had come on and what had occurred, so that, at last, Akakii Akakiievich for once in his life wanted to evince firmness of character and said sharply and categorically that he had to see the Justice personally, that they dared not keep him out, that he had come from his own Bureau on a Government matter, and that now, when he'd lodge a complaint against them, why, they would see, then. The clerks dared not say anything in answer to this and one of them went to call out the Justice of the Peace.

The Justice's reaction to Akakii Akakiievich's story of how he had been robbed of his overcoat was somehow exceedingly odd. Instead of turning his attention to the main point of the matter, he began interrogating Akakii Akakiievich: Just why had he been coming home at so late an hour? Had he, perhaps, looked in at, or hadn't he actually visited, some disorderly house? Akakii Akakiievich became utterly confused and walked out of the office without himself knowing whether the investigation about the overcoat would be instituted or not.

This whole day he stayed away from his Bureau (the only time in his life he had done so). On the following day he put in an appearance, all pale and in his old *negligée*, which had become more woebegone than ever. The recital of the robbery of the overcoat, despite the fact that there proved to be certain ones among his co-workers who did not let pass even this opportunity to make fun of Akakii Akakiievich, nevertheless touched many. They decided on the spot to make up a collection for him, but they collected the utmost trifle, inasmuch as the petty officials had spent a lot even without this, having subscribed for a portrait of the Director and for some book or other, at the invitation of the Chief of the Department, who was a friend of the writer's; and so the sum proved to be most trifling. One of them, moved by compassion, decided, at the least, to aid Akakii Akakiievich with good advice telling him that he oughtn't to go to the precinct officer of the police, because, even though it might come about that the precinct officer, wishing to merit the approval of his superiors, might locate the overcoat in some way, the overcoat would in the end remain with the police, if Akakii Akakiievich could not present legal proofs that it belonged to him; but that the best thing of all would be to turn to a *certain important person;* that this important person, after conferring and corresponding with the proper people in the proper quarters, could speed things up.

There was no help for it; Akakii Akakiievich summoned up his courage to go to the important person. Precisely what the important person's post was and what the work of that post consisted of, has remained unknown up to now. It is necessary to know that the certain important person had only recently become an Important Person, but, up to then, had been an unimportant person. However, his post was not considered an important one even now in comparison with more important ones. But there will always be found a circle of people who perceive the importance of that which is unimportant in the eyes of others. However, he tried to augment his importance by many other means, to wit: he inaugurated the custom of having the subordinate clerks meet him while he was still on the staircase when he arrived at his office; another, of no one coming directly into his presence, but having everything follow the most rigorous precedence: a Collegiate Registrar was to report to the Provincial Secretary, the Provincial Secretary to a Titular one, or whomever else it was necessary to report to, and only thus was any matter to come to him. For it is thus in our Holy Russia that everything is infected with imitativeness; everyone apes his superior and postures like him. They even say that a certain Titular Councilor, when they put him at the helm of some small individual chancellery, immediately had a separate room for himself partitioned off, dubbing it the Reception Center, and had placed at the door some doormen or other with red collars and gold braid, who turned the doorknob and opened the door for every visitor, even though there was hardly room in the Reception Center to hold even an ordinary desk.

The manners and ways of the important person were imposing and majestic, but not at all complex. The chief basis of his system was strictness. "Strictness, strictness, and—strictness," he was wont to say, and when uttering the last word he usually looked very significantly into the face of the person to whom he was speaking, even though, by the way, there was no reason for all this, inasmuch as the half-score of clerks constituting the whole administrative mechanism of his chancellery was under the proper state of fear and trembling even as it was: catching sight of him from afar the staff would at once drop whatever it was doing and wait, at attention, until the Chief had passed through the room. His ordinary speech with his subordinates reeked of strictness and consisted almost entirely of three phrases: "How dare you? Do you know whom you're talking to? Do you realize in whose presence you are?" However, at soul he was a kindly man, treated his friends well, and was obliging; but the rank of General had knocked him completely off his base. Having received a General's rank he had somehow become muddled, had lost his sense of direction, and did not know how to act. If he happened to be with his equals he was still as human as need be, a most decent man, in many respects—even a man not at all foolish; but whenever he happened to be in a group where there were people even one rank below him, why, there was no holding him; he was taciturn, and his situation aroused pity, all the more since he himself felt that he could have passed the time infinitely more pleasantly. In his eyes one could at times see a strong desire to join in some circle and its interesting conversation, but he was stopped by the thought: Wouldn't this be too much unbending on his part, wouldn't it be a familiar action, and wouldn't he lower his importance thereby? And as a consequence of such considerations he remained forever aloof in that invariably taciturn state, only uttering some monosyllabic sounds at rare intervals, and had thus acquired the reputation of a most boring individual.

It was before such an *important person* that our Akakii Akakiievich appeared, and he appeared at a most inauspicious moment, quite inopportune for himself—although, by the bye, most opportune for the important person. The important person was seated in his private office and had gotten into very, very jolly talk with a certain recently arrived old friend and childhood companion whom he had not seen for several years. It was at this point that they announced to the important person that some Bashmachkin or other had come to see him. He asked abruptly, "Who is he?" and was told, "Some petty clerk or other." "Ah. He can wait; this isn't the right time for him to come," said the important man.

At this point it must be said that the important man had fibbed a little: he had the time; he and his old friend had long since talked over everything and had been long eking out their conversation with protracted silences, merely patting each other lightly on the thigh from time to time and adding, "That's how it is, Ivan Abramovich!" and "That's just how it is, Stepan Varlaamovich!" But for all that he gave orders for the petty clerk to wait a while just the same, in order to show his friend, a man who had been long out of the Civil Service and rusticating in his village, how long petty clerks had to cool their heels in his anteroom.

Finally, having had his fill of talk, yet having had a still greater fill of silences, and after each had smoked a cigar to the end in a quite restful armchair with an adjustable back, he at last appeared to recall the matter and said to his secretary, who had halted in the doorway with some papers for a report, "Why, I think there's a clerk waiting out there. Tell him he may come in."

On beholding the meek appearance of Akakii Akakiievich and his rather old, skimpy frock coat, he suddenly turned to him and asked, "What is it you wish?"—in a voice abrupt and firm, which he had purposely rehearsed beforehand in his room at home in solitude and before a mirror, actually a week before he had received his present post and his rank of General.

Akakii Akakiievich already had plenty of time to experience the requisite awe, was somewhat abashed, and, as best he could, in so far as his poor freedom of tongue would allow him, explained, adding even more *now's* than he would have at another time, that his overcoat had been perfectly new, and that, now, he had been robbed of it in a perfectly inhuman fashion, and that he was turning to him, now, so that he might interest himself through his . . . now . . . might correspond with the Head of Police or somebody else, and find his overcoat, now. . . . Such conduct, for some unknown reason, appeared familiar to the General.

"What are you up to, my dear Sir?" he resumed abruptly. "Don't you know the proper procedure? Where have you come to? Don't you know how matters ought to be conducted? As far as this is concerned, you should have first of all submitted a petition to the Chancellery; it would have gone from there to the head of the proper Division, then would have been transferred to the Secretary, and the Secretary would in due time have brought it to my attention—"

"But, Your Excellency," said Akakii Akakiievich, trying to collect whatever little pinch of presence of mind he had, yet feeling at the same time that he was in a dreadful sweat. "I ventured to trouble you, Your Excellency, because secretaries, now . . . aren't any too much to be relied upon—"

"What? What? What?" said the important person. "Where did you get such a tone from? Where did you get such notions? What sort of rebellious feeling has spread among the young people against the administrators and their superiors?" The important person had, it seems, failed to notice that Akakii Akakiievich would never see fifty again, consequently, even if he could have been called a young man it could be applied only relatively, that is, to someone who was already seventy. "Do you know whom you're saying this to? Do you realize in whose presence you are? Do you realize? Do you realize, I'm asking you!" Here he stamped his foot, bringing his voice to such an overwhelming note that even another than an Akakii Akakiievich would have been frightened. Akakii Akakiievich was simply bereft of his senses, swayed, shook all over, and simply could not stand on his feet. If a couple of doormen had not run up right then and there to support him he would have slumped to the floor; they carried him out in a practically cataleptic state. But the important person, satisfied because the effect had surpassed even anything he had expected, and inebriated by the idea that a word from him could actually deprive a man of his senses, looked out of the corner of his eye to learn how his friend was taking this and noticed, not without satisfaction, that his friend was in a most indeterminate state and was even beginning to experience fear on his own account.

How he went down the stairs, how he came out into the street—that was something Akakii Akakiievich was no longer conscious of. He felt neither his hands nor his feet; never in all his life had he been dragged over such hot coals by a General—and a General outside his bureau, at that! With his mouth gaping, stumbling off the sidewalk, he breasted the blizzard that was whistling and howling through the streets; the wind, as is its wont in Petersburg, blew upon him from all the four quarters, from every cross lane. In a second it had blown a quinsy down his throat, and he crawled home without the strength to utter a word; he became all swollen and took to his bed. That's how effective a proper hauling over the coals can be at times!

On the next day he was running a high fever. Thanks to the magnanimous all-round help of the Petersburg climate, the disease progressed more rapidly than could have been expected, and when the doctor appeared he, after having felt the patient's pulse, could not strike on anything to do save prescribing hot compresses, and that solely so that the sick man might not be left without the beneficial help of medicine; but, on the whole, he announced on the spot that in another day and a half it would be curtains for Akakii Akakiievich, after which he turned to the landlady and said, "As for you, Mother, don't you be losing any time for nothing; order a pine coffin for him right now, because a coffin of oak will be beyond his means."

Whether Akakii Akakiievich heard the doctor utter these words, so fateful for him, and, even if he did hear them, whether they had a staggering effect on him, whether he felt regrets over his life of hard sledding—about that nothing is known, inasmuch as he was all the time running a temperature and was in delirium. Visions, each one stranger than the one before, appeared before him ceaselessly: now he saw Petrovich and was ordering him to make an overcoat with some sort of traps to catch thieves, whom he ceaselessly imagined to be under his bed, at every minute calling his landlady to pull out from under his blanket one of them who had actually crawled under there; then he would ask why his old *negligée* was hanging in front of him, for he had a new overcoat; then once more he had a hallucination that he was standing before the General, getting a proper raking over the coals, and saying, "Forgive me, Your Excellency!"; then, finally, he actually took to swearing foully, uttering such dreadful words that his old landlady could do nothing but cross herself, having never in her life heard anything of the sort from him, all the more so since these words followed immediately after "Your Excellency!"

After that he spoke utter nonsense, so that there was no understanding anything; all one could perceive was that his incoherent words and thoughts all revolved about that overcoat and nothing else.

Finally poor Akakii Akakiievich gave up the ghost. Neither his room nor his things were put under seal; in the first place because he had no heirs, and in the second because there was very little left for anybody to inherit, to wit: a bundle of goose quills, a quire of white governmental paper, three pairs of socks, two or three buttons that had come off his trousers, and the *negligée* which the reader is already familiar with. Who fell heir to all this treasure-trove, God knows; I confess that even the narrator of this tale was not much interested in the matter. They bore Akakii Akakiievich off and buried him. And Petersburg was left without Akakii Akakiievich, as if he had never been therein. There vanished and disappeared a being protected by none, endeared to no one, of no interest to anyone, a being that actually had failed to attract to itself the attention of even a naturalist who wouldn't let a chance slip of sticking an ordinary housefly on a pin and of examining it through a microscope; a being that had submissively endured the jests of the whole chancellery and that had gone to its grave without any extraordinary fuss, but before which, nevertheless, even before the very end of its life, there had flitted a radiant guest in the guise of an overcoat, which had animated for an instant a poor life, and upon which being calamity had come crashing down just as unbearably as it comes crashing down upon the heads of the mighty ones of this earth!

A few days after his death a doorman was sent to his house from the Bureau with an injunction for Akakii Akakiievich to appear immediately; the Chief, now, was asking for him; but the doorman had to return empty-handed, reporting back that "he weren't able to come no more," and to the question, "Why not?" expressed himself in the words, "Why, just so; he up and died; they buried him four days back." Thus did they learn at the Bureau about the death of Akakii Akakiievich, and the very next day a new pettifogger, considerably taller than Akakii Akakiievich, was already sitting in his place and putting down the letters no longer in such a straight hand, but considerably more on the slant and downhill.

But whoever could imagine that this wouldn't be all about Akakii Akakiievich, that he was fated to live for several noisy days after his death, as though in reward for a life that had gone by utterly unnoticed? Yet that is how things fell out, and our poor history is taking on a fantastic ending.

Rumors suddenly spread through Petersburg that near the Kalinkin Bridge, and much farther out still, a dead man had started haunting of nights, in the guise of a petty government clerk, seeking for some overcoat or other that had been purloined from him and, because of that stolen overcoat, snatching from all and sundry shoulders, without differentiating among the various ranks and titles, all sorts of overcoats: whether they had collars of catskin or beaver, whether they were quilted with cotton wool, whether they were lined with raccoon, with fox, with bear—in a word, every sort of fur and skin that man has ever thought of for covering his own hide. One of the clerks in the Bureau had seen the dead man with his own eyes and had immediately recognized in him Akakii Akakiievich. This had inspired him with such horror, however, that he started running for all his legs were worth and for that reason could not make him out very well but had merely seen the other shake his finger at him from afar. From all sides came an uninterrupted flow of complaints that backs and shoulders—it wouldn't matter so much if they were merely those of Titular Councilors, but even those of Privy Councilors were affected—were exposed to the danger of catching thorough colds, because of this oft-repeated snatching-off of overcoats.

An order was put through to the police to capture the dead man, at any cost, dead or alive, and to punish him in the severest manner as an example to others—and they all but succeeded in this. To be precise, a policeman at a sentry box on a certain block of the Kirushkin Lane had already gotten a perfect grip on the dead man by his coat collar, at the very scene of his malefaction, while attempting to snatch off the frieze overcoat of some retired musician, who in his time had tootled a flute. Seizing the dead man by the collar, the policeman had summoned two of his colleagues by shouting and had entrusted the ghost to them to hold him, the while he himself took just a moment to reach down in his bootleg for his snuffbox, to relieve temporarily a nose that had been frostbitten six times in his life; but the snuff, probably, was of such a nature as even a dead man could not stand. Hardly had the policeman, after stopping his right nostril with a finger, succeeded in drawing half a handful of rapee up his left, than the dead man sneezed so heartily that he completely bespattered the eyes of all the three myrmidons. While they were bringing their fists up to rub their eyes, the dead man vanished without leaving as much as a trace, so that they actually did not know whether he had really been in their hands or not.

From then on the policemen developed such a phobia of dead men that they were afraid to lay hands even on living ones and merely shouted from a distance, "Hey, there, get going!" and the dead government clerk began to do his haunting even beyond the Kalinkin Bridge, inspiring not a little fear in all timid folk.

However, we have dropped entirely a certain *important person,* who, in reality, had been all but the cause of the fantastic trend taken by what is, by the bye, a perfectly true story. First of all, a sense of justice compels us to say that the *certain important person,* soon after the departure of the poor Akakii Akakiievich, done to a turn in the raking over the hot coals, had felt something in the nature of compunction. He was no stranger to compassion; many kind impulses found access to his heart, despite the fact that his rank often stood in the way of their revealing themselves. As soon as the visiting friend had left his private office, he actually fell into a brown study over Akakii Akakiievich. And from that time on, almost every day, there appeared before him the pale Akakii Akakiievich, who had not been able to stand up under an administrative hauling over the coals. The thought concerning him disquieted the certain important person to such a degree that, a week later, he even decided to send a clerk to him to find out what the man had wanted, and how he was, and whether it were really possible to help him in some way. And when he was informed that Akakii Akakiievich had died suddenly in a fever he was left actually stunned, hearkening to the reproaches of conscience, and was out of sorts the whole day.

Wishing to distract himself to some extent and to forget the unpleasant impression this news had made upon him, he set out for an evening party to one of his friends, where he found a suitable social gathering, and, what was best of all, all the men there were of almost the same rank, so that he absolutely could not feel constrained in any way. This had an astonishing effect on the state of his spirits. He relaxed, became amiable and pleasant to converse with—in a word, he passed the time very agreeably. At supper he drank off a goblet or two of champagne—a remedy which, as everybody knows, has not at all an ill effect upon one's gaiety. The champagne predisposed him to certain extracurricular considerations; to be precise, he decided not to go home yet but to drop in on a certain lady of his acquaintance, a Caroline Ivanovna—a lady of German extraction, apparently, toward whom his feelings and relations were friendly. It must be pointed out the important person was no longer a young man, that he was a good spouse, a respected *paterfamilias*. He had two sons, one of whom was already serving in a chancellery, and a pretty daughter of sixteen, with a somewhat humped yet very charming little nose, who came to kiss his hand every day, adding, "*Bonjour, papa*," as she did so. His wife, a woman who still had not lost her freshness and was not even in the least hard to look at, would allow him to kiss her hand first, then, turning her own over, kissed the hand that was holding hers.

Yet *the important person,* who, by the bye, was perfectly contented with domestic tendernesses, found it respectable to have a lady friend in another part of the city. This lady friend was not in the least fresher or younger than his wife, but such are the enigmas that exist in this world, and to sit in judgment upon them is none of our affair. And so the important person came down the steps, climbed into his sleigh, and told his driver, "To Caroline Ivanovna's!"—while he himself, after muffling up rather luxuriously in his warm overcoat, remained in that pleasant state than which no better could even be thought of for a Russian—that is, when one isn't even thinking of his own volition, but the thoughts in the meanwhile troop into one's head by themselves, each more pleasant than the other, without giving one even the trouble of pursuing them and seeking them. Filled with agreeable feelings, he lightly recalled all the gay episodes of the evening he had spent, all his *mots* that had made the select circle go off into peals of laughter; many of them he even repeated in a low voice and found that they were still just as amusing as before, and for that reason it is not to be wondered at that even he chuckled at them heartily.

Occasionally, however, he became annoyed with the gusty wind which, suddenly escaping from God knows where and no one knows for what reason, simply cut the face, tossing tatters of snow thereat, making the collar of his overcoat belly out like a sail, or suddenly, with unnatural force, throwing it over his head and in this manner giving him ceaseless trouble in extricating himself from it.

Suddenly the important person felt that someone had seized him rather hard by his collar. Turning around, he noticed a man of no great height, in an old, much worn frock coat, and, not without horror, recognized in him Akakii Akakiievich. The petty clerk's face was wan as snow and looked utterly like the face of a dead man. But the horror of the important person passed all bounds when he saw that the mouth of the man became twisted and, horribly wafting upon him the odor of the grave, uttered the following speech: "Ah, so there you are, now, at last! At last I have collared you, now! Your overcoat is just the one I need! You didn't put yourself out any about mine, and on top of that hauled me over the coals—so now let me have yours!"

The poor important person almost passed away. No matter how firm of character he was in his chancellery and before his inferiors in general, and although after but one look merely at his manly appearance and his figure everyone said, "My, what character he has!"—in this instance, nevertheless, like quite a number of men who have the appearance of doughty knights, he experienced such terror that, not without reason, he even began to fear an attack of some physical disorder. He even hastened to throw his overcoat off his shoulders himself and cried out to the driver in a voice that was not his own. "Go home—fast as you can!"

The driver, on hearing the voice that the important person used only at critical moments and which he often accompanied by something of a far more physical nature, drew his head in between his shoulders just to be on the safe side, swung his whip, and flew off like an arrow. In just a little over six minutes the important person was already at the entrance to his own house. Pale, frightened out of his wits, and minus his overcoat, he had come home instead of to Caroline Ivanovna's, somehow made his way stumblingly to his room, and spent the night in quite considerable distress, so that the next day, during the morning tea, his daughter told him outright, "You're all pale today, papa." But papa kept silent and said not a word to anybody of what had befallen him, and where he had been, and where he had intended to go.

This adventure made a strong impression on him. He even badgered his subordinates at rarer intervals with his, "How dare you? Do you realize in whose presence you are?"—and even if he did utter these phrases he did not do so before he had first heard through to the end just what was what. But still more remarkable is the fact that from that time forth the apparition of the dead clerk ceased its visitations utterly; evidently the General's overcoat fitted him to a *t;* at least, no cases of overcoats being snatched off anybody were heard of any more, anywhere. However, many energetic and solicitous people simply would not calm down and kept on saying from time to time that the dead government clerk was still haunting the remoter parts of the city.

And, sure enough, one policeman at a sentry box in Colomna had with his own eyes seen the apparition coming out of a house; but, being by nature somewhat puny, so that on one occasion an ordinary well-grown shoat, darting out of a private yard, had knocked him off his feet, to the profound amusement of the cab drivers who were standing around, from whom he had exacted a copper each for humiliating him so greatly, to buy snuff with—well, being puny, he had not dared to halt him but simply followed him in the dark until such time as the apparition suddenly looked over its shoulder, and, halting, asked, "What are you after?" and shook a fist at him whose like for size was not to be found among the living. The policeman said, "Nothing," and at once turned back. The apparition, however, was considerably taller by now and was sporting a pair of enormous mustachios; setting its steps apparently in the direction of the Obuhov Bridge, it disappeared utterly in the darkness of night.

Edgar Allan Poe (1809–1849)

The short story was particularly suited to life in the United States where it flourished so well that some critics believe it is essentially an American form of literature. Frontier life remote from the centers of culture and social contact promoted the growth of magazines, and magazines certainly encouraged the writing of short fiction. Edgar Allan Poe became the outstanding American theorist and practitioner of the fledgling genre. He argued that the short story was a legitimate and important literary form, capable of intense emotional and aesthetic effects. Because it relied upon the "single effect" it was, to him, second only to the lyric poem in its ability to "induce an exaltation of the soul." In his own work, he was the most self-conscious of artists.

> I prefer commencing with the consideration of an effect. . . . I say to myself . . . "Of the innumerable effects, or impressions, of which the heart, the intellect, or (more generally) the soul is susceptible, what one shall I, on the present occasion, select?" Having chosen a novel, first, and secondly a vivid effect, I consider whether it can be best wrought by incident or tone—whether by ordinary incidents and peculiar tone or the converse, or by pecu-

liarity both of incident and tone—afterward looking about me (or rather within) for such combinations of event, or tone, as shall best aid me in construction of the effect.

The kinds of effects Poe sought—horror, fear, loathing—are brought about not by showing real people in real situations but by creating a heavily emotional atmosphere. He placed his stories against a dark, mysterious, usually Gothic background. The House of Usher is a "mansion of gloom" beside "the precipitous brink of a black and lurid tarn," and "minute fungi" fall "in a fine tangled webwork from the eaves." Descriptions of the people contribute to the mood. The valet has a "stealthy step" and the physician wears a "mingled expression of low cunning and perplexity." As for Roderick himself, his "cadaverousness of complexion" has given way to "ghostly pallor." What besides horror could be the effect of reading about these people in this place?

Poe's words and the rhythm of his sentences reinforce the other worldly atmosphere and sense of mystery. The stories are told with multisyllable words: "phantasmagoria," "shudderingly," "countenance," "ponderous." It is almost impossible to read Poe rapidly as, say, we can the work of his contemporary Gogol. Poe's rhythms are somber and stately and literary rather than colloquial. Such a vocabulary and such a style leave room for little if any humor or irony.

Poe's work was much admired in Europe, as well as in the United States. Baudelaire translated his fiction and Mallarmé his poems. Debussy attempted to write a symphony based on one of his stories. Elizabeth Barrett Browning said of another story, "The certain thing in the tale in question is the power of the writer, and the faculty he has of making horrible improbabilities seem near and familiar."

Yet the violence and morbidity that so excited and horrified our forebears seem artificial and overheated—even sentimental—to a generation grown up on television atrocities and newspaper sensationalism. But though his stories may not have the effect on adult audiences they once did, Poe must be credited for his major contributions to not only the horror story but also the detective story and science fiction, and indeed to the development of the serious modern short story.

Poe was born in 1809, was orphaned young, adopted, and finally disinherited. He died at the age of forty on the eve of a second marriage. All his life he was plagued by poverty, gambling, alcoholism.

The Fall of the House of Usher

Son cœur est un luth suspendu;
Sitôt qu'on le touche il résonne.
De Béranger.

DURING the whole of a dull, dark, and soundless day in the autumn of the year, when the clouds hung oppressively low in the heavens, I had been passing alone, on horseback, through a singularly dreary tract of country; and at length found myself, as the shades of the evening drew on, within view of the melancholy House of Usher. I know

From *The Complete Works of Edgar Allan Poe,* ed. James A. Harrison, Vol. III, *Tales–Volume II,* AMS Press Inc. New York, 1965 (reproduced from 1902 New York edition).

not how it was—but, with the first glimpse of the building, a sense of insufferable gloom pervaded my spirit. I say insufferable; for the feeling was unrelieved by any of that half-pleasurable, because poetic, sentiment, with which the mind usually receives even the sternest natural images of the desolate or terrible. I looked upon the scene before me— upon the mere house, and the simple landscape features of the domain—upon the bleak walls—upon the vacant eye-like windows—upon a few rank sedges—and upon a few white trunks of decayed trees—with an utter depression of soul which I can compare to no earthly sensation more properly than to the after-dream of the reveller upon opium— the bitter lapse into everyday life—the hideous dropping off of the veil. There was an iciness, a sinking, a sickening of the heart—an unredeemed dreariness of thought which no goading of the imagination could torture into aught of the sublime. What was it—I paused to think—what was it that so unnerved me in the contemplation of the House of Usher? It was a mystery all insoluble; nor could I grapple with the shadowy fancies that crowded upon me as I pondered. I was forced to fall back upon the unsatisfactory conclusion, that while, beyond doubt, there *are* combinations of very simple natural objects which have the power of thus affecting us, still the analysis of this power lies among considerations beyond our depth. It was possible, I reflected, that a mere differ-ent arrangement of the particulars of the scene, of the details of the picture, would be sufficient to modify, or perhaps to annihilate its capacity for sorrowful impression; and, acting upon this idea, I reined my horse to the precipitous brink of a black and lurid tarn that lay in unruffled lustre by the dwelling, and gazed down—but with a shudder even more thrilling than before—upon the remodelled and inverted images of the gray sedge, and the ghastly tree-stems, and the vacant and eye-like windows.

Nevertheless, in this mansion of gloom I now proposed to myself a sojourn of some weeks. Its proprietor, Roderick Usher, had been one of my boon companions in boy-hood; but many years had elapsed since our last meeting. A letter, however, had lately reached me in a distant part of the country—a letter from him—which, in its wildly importunate nature, had admitted of no other than a personal reply. The MS. gave evidence of nervous agitation. The writer spoke of acute bodily illness—of a mental disorder which oppressed him—and of an earnest desire to see me, as his best, and indeed his only personal friend, with a view of attempting, by the cheerfulness of my society, some alleviation of his malady. It was the manner in which all this, and much more, was said—it was the apparent *heart* that went with his request—which allowed me no room for hesitation; and I accordingly obeyed forthwith what I still considered a very singular summons.

Although, as boys, we had been even intimate associates, yet I really knew little of my friend. His reserve had been always excessive and habitual. I was aware, however, that his very ancient family had been noted, time out of mind, for a peculiar sensibility of temperament, displaying itself, through long ages, in many works of exalted art, and manifested, of late, in repeated deeds of munificent yet unobtrusive charity, as well as in a passionate devotion to the intricacies, perhaps even more than to the orthodox and easily recognisable beauties, of musical science. I had learned, too, the very remarkable fact, that the stem of the Usher race, all time-honoured as it was, had put forth, at no period, any enduring branch; in other words, that the entire family lay in the direct line of descent, and had always, with very trifling and very temporary variation, so lain. It was this deficiency, I considered, while running over in thought the perfect keeping of the character of the premises with the accredited character of the people, and while speculating upon the possible influence which the one, in the long lapse of centuries, might have exercised upon the other—it was this deficiency, perhaps, of collateral issue, and the consequent undeviating transmission, from sire to son, of the patrimony with the name, which had, at length, so identified the two as to merge the original title of the estate in the quaint and equivocal appellation of the "House of Usher"—an appellation which seemed to include, in the minds of the peasantry who used it, both the family and the family mansion.

I have said that the sole effect of my somewhat childish experiment—that of looking down within the tarn—had been to deepen the first singular impression. There can be no doubt that the consciousness of the rapid increase of my superstition—for why should I not so term it?—served mainly to accelerate the increase itself. Such, I have long known, is the paradoxical law of all sentiments having terror as a basis. And it might have been for this reason only, that, when I again uplifted my eyes to the house itself, from its image in the pool, there grew in my mind a strange fancy—a fancy so ridiculous, indeed, that I but mention it to show the vivid force of the sensations which oppressed me. I had so worked upon my imagination as really to believe that about the whole mansion and domain there hung an atmosphere peculiar to themselves and their immediate vicinity—an atmosphere which had no affinity with the air of heaven, but which had reeked up from the decayed trees, and the gray wall, and the silent tarn—a pestilent and mystic vapour, dull, sluggish, faintly discernible, and leaden-hued.

Shaking off from my spirit what *must* have been a dream, I scanned more narrowly the real aspect of the building. Its principal feature seemed to be that of an excessive antiquity. The discoloration of ages had been great. Minute fungi overspread the whole exterior, hanging in a fine tangled web-work from the eaves. Yet all this was apart from any extraordinary dilapidation. No portion of the masonry had fallen; and there appeared to be a wild inconsistency between its still perfect adaptation of parts, and the crumbling condition of the individual stones. In this there was much that reminded me of the specious totality of old wood-work which has rotted for long years in some neglected vault, with no disturbance from the breath of the external air. Beyond this indication of extensive decay, however, the fabric gave little token of instability. Perhaps the eye of a scrutinising observer might have discovered a barely perceptible fissure, which, extending from the roof of the building in front, made its way down the wall in a zigzag direction, until it became lost in the sullen waters of the tarn.

Noticing these things, I rode over a short causeway to the house. A servant in waiting took my horse, and I entered the Gothic archway of the hall. A valet, of stealthy step, thence conducted me, in silence, through many dark and intricate passages in my progress to the *studio* of his master. Much that I encountered on the way contributed, I know not how, to heighten the vague sentiments of which I have already spoken. While the objects around me—while the carvings of the ceilings, the sombre tapestries of the walls, the ebon blackness of the floors, and the phantasmagoric armorial trophies which rattled as I strode, were but matters to which, or to such as which, I had been accustomed from my infancy—while I hestitated not to acknowledge how familiar was all this—I still wondered to find how unfamiliar were the fancies which ordinary images were stirring up. On one of the staircases, I met the physician of the family. His countenance, I thought, wore a mingled expression of low cunning and perplexity. He accosted me with trepidation and passed on. The valet now threw open a door and ushered me into the presence of his master.

The room in which I found myself was very large and lofty. The windows were long, narrow, and pointed, and at so vast a distance from the black oaken floor as to be altogether inaccessible from within. Feeble gleams of encrimsoned light made their way through the trellised panes, and served to render sufficiently distinct the more prominent objects around; the eye, however, struggled in vain to reach the remoter angles of the chamber, or the recesses of the vaulted and fretted ceiling. Dark draperies hung upon the walls. The general furniture was profuse, comfortless, antique, and tattered. Many books and musical instruments lay scattered about, but failed to give any vitality to the scene. I felt that I breathed an atmosphere of sorrow. An air of stern, deep, and irredeemable gloom hung over and pervaded all.

Upon my entrance, Usher arose from a sofa on which he had been lying at full length, and greeted me with a vivacious warmth which had much in it, I at first thought, of an overdone cordiality—of the constrained effort of the *ennuyé* man of the world. A glance, however, at his countenance, convinced me of his perfect sincerity. We sat down; and for some moments, while he spoke not, I gazed upon him with a feeling half of pity, half of awe. Surely, man had never before so terribly altered, in so brief a period, as had Roderick Usher! It was with difficulty that I could bring myself to admit the identity of the wan being before me with the companion of my early boyhood. Yet the character of his face had been at all times remarkable. A cadaverousness of complexion; an eye large, liquid, and luminous beyond comparison; lips somewhat thin and very pallid, but of a surpassingly beautiful curve; a nose of a delicate Hebrew model, but with a breadth of nostril unusual in similar formations; a finely moulded chin, speaking, in its want of prominence, of a want of moral energy; hair of a more than web-like softness and tenuity; these features, with an inordinate expansion above the regions of the temple, made up altogether a countenance not easily to be forgotten. And now in the mere exaggeration of the prevailing character of these features, and of the expression they were wont to convey, lay so much of change that I doubted to whom I spoke. The now ghastly pallor of the skin, and the now miraculous lustre of the eye, above all things startled and even awed me. The silken hair, too, had been suffered to grow all unheeded, and as, in its wild gossamer texture, it floated rather than fell about the face, I could not, even with effort, connect its Arabesque expression with any idea of simple humanity.

In the manner of my friend I was at once struck with an incoherence—an inconsistency; and I soon found this to arise from a series of feeble and futile struggles to overcome an habitual trepidancy—an excessive nervous agitation. For something of this nature I had indeed been prepared, no less by his letter, than by reminiscences of certain boyish traits, and by conclusions deduced from his peculiar physical conformation and temperament. His action was alternately vivacious and sullen. His voice varied rapidly from a tremulous indecision (when the animal spirits seemed utterly in abeyance) to that species of energetic concision—that abrupt, weighty, unhurried, and hollow-sounding enunciation—that leaden, self-balanced and perfectly modulated guttural utterance, which may be observed in the lost drunkard, or the irreclaimable eater of opium, during the periods of his most intense excitement.

It was thus that he spoke of the object of my visit, of his earnest desire to see me, and of the solace he expected me to afford him. He entered, at some length, into what he conceived to be the nature of his malady. It was, he said, a constitutional and a family evil, and one for which he despaired to find a remedy—a mere nervous affection, he immediately added, which would undoubtedly soon pass off. It displayed itself in a host of unnatural sensations. Some of these, as he detailed them, interested and bewildered me; although, perhaps, the terms, and the general manner of the narration had their weight. He suffered much from a morbid acuteness of the senses; the most insipid food was alone endurable; he could wear only garments of certain texture; the odours of all flowers were oppressive; his eyes were tortured by even a faint light; and there were but peculiar sounds, and these from stringed instruments, which did not inspire him with horror.

To an anomalous species of terror I found him a bounden slave. "I shall perish," said he, "I *must* perish in this deplorable folly. Thus, thus, and not otherwise, shall I be lost. I dread the events of the future, not in themselves, but in their results. I shudder at the thought of any, even the most trivial, incident, which may operate upon this intolerable agitation of soul. I have, indeed, no abhorrence of danger, except in its absolute effect—in terror. In this unnerved—in this pitiable condition—I feel that the period will sooner or later arrive when I must abandon life and reason together, in some struggle with the grim phantasm, FEAR.''

I learned, moreover, at intervals, and through broken and equivocal hints, another singular feature of his mental condition. He was enchained by certain superstitious impressions in regard to the dwelling which he tenanted, and whence, for many years, he had never ventured forth—in regard to an influence whose supposititious force was conveyed in terms too shadowy here to be re-stated—an influence which some peculiarities in the mere form and substance of his family mansion, had, by dint of long sufferance, he said, obtained over his spirit—an effect which the *physique* of the gray walls and turrets, and of the dim tarn into which they all looked down, had, at length, brought about upon the *morale* of his existence.

He admitted, however, although with hesitation, that much of the peculiar gloom which thus afflicted him could be traced to a more natural and far more palpable origin—to the severe and long-continued illness—indeed to the evidently approaching dissolution—of a tenderly beloved sister—his sole companion for long years—his last and only relative on earth. ''Her decease,'' he said, with a bitterness which I can never forget, ''would leave him (him the hopeless and the frail) the last of the ancient race of the Ushers.'' While he spoke, the lady Madeline (for so was she called) passed slowly through a remote portion of the apartment, and, without having noticed my presence, disappeared. I regarded her with an utter astonishment not unmingled with dread—and yet I found it impossible to account for such feelings. A sensation of stupor oppressed me, as my eyes followed her retreating steps. When a door, at length, closed upon her, my glance sought instinctively and eagerly the countenance of the brother—but he had buried his face in his hands, and I could only perceive that a far more than ordinary wanness had overspread the emaciated fingers through which trickled many passionate tears.

The disease of the lady Madeline had long baffled the skill of her physicians. A settled apathy, a gradual wasting away of the person, and frequent although transient affections of a partially cataleptical character, were the unusual diagnosis. Hitherto she had steadily borne up against the pressure of her malady, and had not betaken herself finally to bed; but, on the closing in of the evening of my arrival at the house, she succumbed (as her brother told me at night with inexpressible agitation) to the prostrating power of the destroyer; and I learned that the glimpse I had obtained of her person would thus probably be the last I should obtain—that the lady, at least while living, would be seen by me no more.

For several days ensuing, her name was unmentioned by either Usher or myself: and during this period I was busied in earnest endeavours to alleviate the melancholy of my friend. We painted and read together; or I listened, as if in a dream, to the wild improvisations of his speaking guitar. And thus, as a closer and still closer intimacy admitted me more unreservedly into the recesses of his spirit, the more bitterly did I perceive the futility of all attempt at cheering a mind from which darkness, as if an inherent positive quality, poured forth upon all objects of the moral and physical universe, in one unceasing radiation of gloom.

I shall ever bear about me a memory of the many solemn hours I thus spent alone with the master of the House of Usher. Yet I should fail in any attempt to convey an idea of the exact character of the studies, or of the occupations, in which he involved me, or led me the way. An excited and highly distempered ideality threw a sulphureous lustre over all. His long improvised dirges will ring forever in my ears. Among other things, I hold painfully in mind a certain singular perversion and amplification of the wild air of the last waltz of Von Weber. From the paintings over which his elaborate fancy brooded, and which grew, touch by touch, into vaguenesses at which I shuddered the more thrillingly, because I shuddered knowing not why;—from these paintings (vivid as their images now are before me) I would in vain endeavour to educe more than a small portion which should lie within the compass of merely written words. By the utter simplicity, by the nakedness of his designs, he arrested and overawed attention. If ever mortal painted an idea, that mortal was Roderick Usher. For me at least—in the circumstances then surrounding me—there arose out of the pure abstractions which the hypochondriac contrived to throw upon his canvas, an intensity of intolerable awe, no shadow of which felt I ever yet in the contemplation of the certainly glowing yet too concrete reveries of Fuseli.

One of the phantasmagoric conceptions of my friend, partaking not so rigidly of the spirit of abstraction, may be shadowed forth, although feebly, in words. A small picture presented the interior of an immensely long and rectangular vault or tunnel, with low walls, smooth, white, and without interruption or device. Certain accessory points of the design served well to convey the idea that this excavation lay at an exceeding depth below the surface of the earth. No outlet was observed in any portion of its vast extent, and no torch, or other artificial source of light was discernible; yet a flood of intense rays rolled throughout, and bathed the whole in a ghastly and inappropriate splendour.

I have just spoken of that morbid condition of the auditory nerve which rendered all music intolerable to the sufferer, with the exception of certain effects of stringed instruments. It was, perhaps, the narrow limits to which he thus confined himself upon the guitar, which gave birth, in great measure, to the fantastic character of his performances. But the fervid *facility* of his *impromptus* could not be so accounted for. They must have been, and were, in the notes, as well as in the words of his wild fantasias (for he not unfrequently accompanied himself with rhymed verbal improvisations), the result of that intense mental collectedness and concentration to which I have previously alluded as observable only in particular moments of the highest artificial excitement. The words of one of these rhapsodies I have easily remembered. I was, perhaps, the more forcibly impressed with it, as he gave it, because, in the under or mystic current of its meaning, I fancied that I perceived, and for the first time, a full consciousness on the part of Usher, of the tottering of his lofty reason upon her throne. The verses, which were entitled "The Haunted Palace," ran very nearly, if not accurately, thus:

I.

In the greenest of our valleys,
   By good angels tenanted,
Once a fair and stately palace—
   Radiant palace—reared its head.
In the monarch Thought's dominion—
   It stood there!
Never seraph spread a pinion
   Over fabric half so fair.

II.

Banners yellow, glorious, golden,
   On its roof did float and flow;

(This—all this—was in the olden
   Time long ago)
And every gentle air that dallied,
   In that sweet day,
Along the ramparts plumed and pallid,
   A winged odour went away.

III.

Wanderers in that happy valley
   Through two luminous windows saw
Spirits moving musically
   To a lute's well-tuned law,
Round about a throne, where sitting
   (Porphyrogene!)
In state his glory well befitting,
   The ruler of the realm was seen.

IV.

And all with pearl and ruby glowing
   Was the fair palace door,
Through which came flowing, flowing, flowing
   And sparkling evermore,
A troop of Echoes whose sweet duty
   Was but to sing,
In voices of surpassing beauty,
   The wit and wisdom of their king.

V.

But evil things, in robes of sorrow,
   Assailed the monarch's high estate;
(Ah, let us mourn, for never morrow
   Shall dawn upon him, desolate!)
And, round about his home, the glory
   That blushed and bloomed
Is but a dim-remembered story
   Of the old time entombed.

VI.

And travellers now within that valley,
   Through the red-litten windows, see
Vast forms that move fantastically
   To a discordant melody;
While, like a rapid ghastly river,
   Through the pale door,
A hideous throng rush out forever,
   And laugh—but smile no more.

    I well remember that suggestions arising from this ballad, led us into a train of thought wherein there became manifest an opinion of Usher's which I mention not so much on account of its novelty, (for other men have thought thus,) as on account of the pertinacity with which he maintained it. This opinion, in its general form, was that of the sentience of all vegetable things. But, in his disordered fancy, the idea had assumed a more daring character, and trespassed, under certain conditions, upon the kingdom of inorganization. I lack words to express the full extent, or the earnest *abandon* of his persuasion. The belief, however, was connected (as I have previously hinted) with the gray stones of the home of his forefathers. The conditions of the sentience had been here, he imagined, fulfilled in the method of collocation of these stones—in the order of their arrangement, as well as in that of the many *fungi* which overspread them, and of the decayed trees which stood around—above all, in the long undisturbed endurance of this arrangement, and in its reduplication in the still waters of the tarn. Its evidence—the evidence of the sentience—was to be seen, he said, (and I here started as he spoke,) in the gradual yet certain condensation of an atmosphere of their own about the waters and the walls. The result was discoverable, he added, in that silent, yet importunate and terrible influence which for centuries had moulded the destinies of his family, and which made *him* what I now saw him—what he was. Such opinions need no comment, and I will make none.

Our books—the books which, for years, had formed no small portion of the mental existence of the invalid—were, as might be supposed, in strict keeping with this character of phantasm. We pored together over such works as the Ververt et Chartreuse of Gresset; the Belphegor of Machiavelli; the Heaven and Hell of Swedenborg; the Subterranean Voyage of Nicholas Klimm by Holberg; the Chiromancy of Robert Flud, of Jean D'Indaginé, and of De la Chambre; the Journey into the Blue Distance of Tieck; and the City of the Sun of Campanella. One favourite volume was a small octavo edition of the *Directorium Inquisitorum*, by the Dominican Eymeric de Gironne; and there were passages in Pomponius Mela, about the old African Satyrs and Ægipans, over which Usher would sit dreaming for hours. His chief delight, however, was found in the perusal of an exceedingly rare and curious book in quarto Gothic—the manual of a forgotten church—the *Vigiliæ Mortuorum secundum Chorum Ecclesiæ Maguntinæ*.

I could not help thinking of the wild ritual of this work, and of its probable influence upon the hypochondriac, when, one evening, having informed me abruptly that the lady Madeline was no more, he stated his intention of preserving her corpse for a fortnight, (previously to its final interment,) in one of the numerous vaults within the main walls of the building. The worldly reason, however, assigned for this singular proceeding, was one which I did not feel at liberty to dispute. The brother had been led to his resolution (so he told me) by consideration of the unusual character of the malady of the deceased, of certain obtrusive and eager inquiries on the part of her medical men, and of the remote and exposed situation of the burial-ground of the family. I will not deny that when I called to mind the sinister countenance of the person whom I met upon the staircase, on the day of my arrival at the house, I had no desire to oppose what I regarded as at best but a harmless, and by no means an unnatural, precaution.

At the request of Usher, I personally aided him in the arrangements for the temporary entombment. The body having been encoffined, we two alone bore it to its rest. The vault in which we placed it (and which had been so long unopened that our torches, half smothered in its oppressive atmosphere, gave us little opportunity for investigation) was small, damp, and entirely without means of admission for light; lying, at great depth, immediately beneath that portion of the building in which was my own sleeping apartment. It had been used, apparently, in remote feudal times, for the worst purposes of a donjon-keep, and, in later days, as a place of deposit for powder, or some other highly combustible substance, as a portion of its floor, and the whole interior of a long archway through which we reached it, were carefully sheathed with copper. The door, of massive iron, had been, also, similarly protected. Its immense weight caused an unusually sharp grating sound, as it moved upon its hinges.

Having deposited our mournful burden upon tressels within this region of horror, we partially turned aside the yet unscrewed lid of the coffin, and looked upon the face of the tenant. A striking similitude between the brother and sister now first arrested my attention; and Usher, divining, perhaps, my thoughts, murmured out some few words from which I learned that the deceased and himself had been twins, and that sympathies of a scarcely intelligible nature had always existed between them. Our glances, however, rested not long upon the dead—for we could not regard her unawed. The disease which had thus entombed the lady in the maturity of youth, had left, as usual in all maladies of a strictly cataleptical character, the mockery of a faint blush upon the bosom and the face, and that suspiciously lingering smile upon the lip which is so terrible in death. We replaced and screwed down the lid, and, having secured the door of iron, made our way, with toil, into the scarcely less gloomy apartments of the upper portion of the house.

And now, some days of bitter grief having elapsed, an observable change came over the features of the mental disorder of my friend. His ordinary manner had vanished. His ordinary occupations were neglected or forgotten. He roamed from chamber to chamber with hurried, unequal, and objectless step. The pallor of his countenance had assumed, if possible, a more ghastly hue—but the luminousness of his eye had utterly gone out. The once occasional huskiness of his tone was heard no more; and a tremulous quaver, as if of extreme terror, habitually characterized his utterance. There were times, indeed, when I thought his unceasingly agitated mind was labouring with some oppressive secret, to divulge which he struggled for the necessary courage. At times, again, I was obliged to resolve all into the mere inexplicable vagaries of madness, for I beheld him gazing upon vacancy for long hours, in an attitude of the profoundest attention, as if listening to some imaginary sound. It was no wonder that his condition terrified—that it infected me. I felt creeping upon me, by slow yet certain degrees, the wild influences of his own fantastic yet impressive superstitions.

It was, especially, upon retiring to bed late in the night of the seventh or eighth day after the placing of the lady Madeline within the donjon, that I experienced the full power of such feelings. Sleep came not near my couch—while the hours waned and waned away. I struggled to reason off the nervousness which had dominion over me. I endeavoured to believe that much, if not all of what I felt, was due to the bewildering influence of the gloomy furniture of the room—of the dark and tattered draperies, which, tortured into motion by the breath of a rising tempest, swayed fitfully to and fro upon the walls, and rustled uneasily about the decorations of the bed. But my efforts were fruitless. An irrepressible tremour gradually pervaded my frame; and, at length, there sat upon my very heart an incubus of utterly causeless alarm. Shaking this off with a gasp and a struggle, I uplifted myself upon the pillows, and, peering earnestly within the intense darkness of the chamber, hearkened—I know not why, except that an instinctive spirit prompted me—to certain low and indefinite sounds which came, through the pauses of the storm, at long intervals, I knew not whence. Overpowered by an intense sentiment of horror, unaccountable yet unendurable, I threw on my clothes with haste (for I felt that I should sleep no more during the night), and endeavoured to arouse myself from the pitiable condition into which I had fallen, by pacing rapidly to and fro through the apartment.

I had taken but few turns in this manner, when a light step on an adjoining staircase arrested my attention. I presently recognised it as that of Usher. In an instant afterward he rapped, with a gentle touch, at my door, and entered, bearing a lamp. His countenance was, as usual, cadaverously wan—but, moreover, there was a species of mad hilarity in his eyes—an evidently restrained *hysteria* in his whole demeanour. His air appalled me—but anything was preferable to the solitude which I had so long endured, and I even welcomed his presence as a relief.

"And you have not seen it?" he said abruptly, after having stared about him for some moments in silence—"you have not then seen it?—but, stay! you shall." Thus speaking, and having carefully shaded his lamp, he hurried to one of the casements, and threw it freely open to the storm.

The impetuous fury of the entering gust nearly lifted us from our feet. It was, indeed, a tempestuous yet sternly beautiful night, and one wildly singular in its terror and its beauty. A whirlwind had apparently collected its force in our vicinity; for there were frequent and violent alterations in the direction of the wind; and the exceeding density of the clouds (which hung so low as to press upon the turrets of the house) did not prevent our perceiving the life-like velocity with which they flew careering from all points against each other, without passing away into the distance. I say that even their exceeding density did not prevent our perceiving this—yet we had no glimpse of the moon or stars—nor was there any flashing forth of the lightning. But the under surfaces of the huge masses of agitated vapour, as well as all terrestrial objects immediately around us, were glowing in the unnatural light of a faintly luminous and distinctly visible gaseous exhalation which hung about and enshrouded the mansion.

"You must not—you shall not behold this!" said I, shudderingly, to Usher, as I led him, with a gentle violence, from the window to a seat. "These appearances, which bewilder you, are merely electrical phenomena not uncommon—or it may be that they have their ghastly origin in the rank miasma of the tarn. Let us close this casement;—the air is chilling and dangerous to your frame. Here is one of your favourite romances. I will read, and you shall listen;—and so we will pass away this terrible night together."

The antique volume which I had taken up was the "Mad Trist" of Sir Launcelot Canning; but I had called it a favourite of Usher's more in sad jest than in earnest; for, in truth, there is little in its uncouth and unimaginative prolixity which could have had interest for the lofty and spiritual ideality of my friend. It was, however, the only book immediately at hand; and I indulged a vague hope that the excitement which now agitated the hypochondriac, might find relief (for the history of mental disorder is full of similar anomalies) even in the extremeness of the folly which I should read. Could I have judged, indeed, by the wild overstrained air of vivacity with which he hearkened, or apparently hearkened, to the words of the tale, I might well have congratulated myself upon the success of my design.

I had arrived at that well-known portion of the story where Ethelred, the hero of the Trist, having sought in vain for peaceable admission into the dwelling of the hermit, proceeds to make good an entrance by force. Here, it will be remembered, the words of the narrative runs thus:

"And Ethelred, who was by nature of a doughty heart, and who was now mighty withal, on account of the powerfulness of the wine which he had drunken, waited no longer to hold parley with the hermit, who, in sooth, was of an obstinate and maliceful turn, but, feeling the rain upon his shoulders, and fearing the rising of the tempest, uplifted his mace outright, and, with blows, made quickly room in the plankings of the door for his gauntleted hand; and now pulling therewith sturdily, he so cracked, and ripped, and tore all asunder, that the noise of the dry and hollow-sounding wood alarumed and reverberated throughout the forest."

At the termination of this sentence I started, and for a moment, paused; for it appeared to me (although I at once concluded that my excited fancy had deceived me)— it appeared to me that, from some very remote portion of the mansion, there came, indistinctly, to my ears, what might have been, in its exact similarity of character, the echo (but a stifled and dull one certainly) of the very cracking and ripping sound which Sir Launcelot had so particularly described. It was, beyond doubt, the coincidence alone which had arrested my attention; for, amid the rattling of the sashes of the casements, and the ordinary commingled noises of the still increasing storm, the sound, in itself, had nothing, surely, which should have interested or disturbed me. I continued the story:

"But the good champion Ethelred, now entering within the door, was sore enraged and amazed to perceive no signal of the maliceful hermit; but, in the stead thereof, a dragon of a scaly and prodigious demeanour, and of a fiery tongue, which sate in guard before a palace of gold, with a floor of silver; and upon the wall there hung a shield of shining brass with this legend enwritten—

Who entereth herein, a conqueror hath bin;
Who slayeth the dragon, the shield he shall win;

And Ethelred uplifted his mace, and struck upon the head of the dragon, which fell before him, and gave up his pesty breath, with a shriek so horrid and harsh, and withal so piercing, that Ethelred had fain to close his ears with his hands against the dreadful noise of it, the like whereof was never before heard."

Here again I paused abruptly, and now with a feeling of wild amazement—for there could be no doubt whatever that, in this instance, I did actually hear (although from what direction it proceeded I found it impossible to say) a low and apparently distant, but harsh, protracted, and most unusual screaming or grating sound—the exact counterpart of what my fancy had already conjured up for the dragon's unnatural shriek as described by the romancer.

Oppressed, as I certainly was, upon the occurrence of the second and most extraordinary coincidence, by a thousand conflicting sensations, in which wonder and extreme terror were predominant, I still retained sufficient presence of mind to avoid exciting, by any observation, the sensitive nervousness of my companion. I was by no means certain that he had noticed the sounds in question; although, assuredly, a strange alteration had, during the last few minutes, taken place in his demeanour. From a position fronting my own, he had gradually brought round his chair, so as to sit with his face to the door of the chamber; and thus I could but partially perceive his features, although I saw that his lips trembled as if he were murmuring inaudibly. His head had dropped upon his breast—yet I knew that he was not asleep, from the wide and rigid opening of the eye as I caught a glance of it in profile. The motion of his body, too, was at variance with this idea—for he rocked from side to side with a gentle yet constant and uniform sway. Having rapidly taken notice of all this, I resumed the narrative of Sir Launcelot, which thus proceeded:

"And now, the champion, having escaped from the terrible fury of the dragon, bethinking himself of the brazen shield, and of the breaking up of the enchantment which was upon it, removed the carcass from out of the way before him, and approached valorously over the silver pavement of the castle to where the shield was upon the wall; which in sooth tarried not for his full coming, but fell down at his feet upon the silver floor, with a mighty great and terrible ringing sound."

No sooner had these syllables passed my lips, than—as if a shield of brass had indeed, at the moment, fallen heavily upon a floor of silver—I became aware of a distinct, hollow, metallic, and clangorous, yet apparently muffled reverberation. Completely unnerved, I leaped to my feet; but the measured rocking movement of Usher was undisturbed. I rushed to the chair in which he sat. His eyes were bent fixedly before him, and throughout his whole countenance there reigned a stony rigidity. But, as I placed my hand upon his shoulder, there came a strong shudder over his whole person; a sickly smile quivered about his lips; and I saw that he spoke in a low, hurried, and gibbering murmur, as if unconscious of my presence. Bending closely over him, I at length drank in the hideous import of his words.

"Not hear it?—yes, I hear it, and *have* heard it. Long—long—long—many minutes, many hours, many days, have I heard it—yet I dared not—oh, pity me, miserable wretch that I am!—I dared not—I *dared* not speak! *We have put her living in the tomb!* Said I not that my senses were acute? I *now* tell you that I heard her first feeble movements in the hollow coffin. I heard them—many, many days ago—yet I dared not—*I dared not speak!* And now—to-night—Ethelred—ha! ha!—the breaking of the hermit's door, and the death-cry of the dragon, and the clangour of the shield!—say, rather, the rending of her coffin, and the grating of the iron hinges of her prison, and her struggles within the coppered archway of the vault! Oh whither shall I fly? Will she not be here anon? Is she not hurrying to upbraid me for my haste? Have I not heard her footstep on the stair? Do I not distinguish that heavy and horrible beating of her heart? MADMAN!" here he sprang furiously to his feet, and shrieked out his syllables, as if in the effort he were giving up his soul—"MADMAN! I TELL YOU THAT SHE NOW STANDS WITHOUT THE DOOR!"

As if in the superhuman energy of his utterance there had been found the potency of a spell—the huge antique panels to which the speaker pointed, threw slowly back, upon the instant, their ponderous and ebony jaws. It was the work of the rushing gust—but then without those doors there DID stand the lofty and enshrouded figure of the lady Madeline of Usher. There was blood upon her white robes, and the evidence of some bitter struggle upon every portion of her emaciated frame. For a moment she remained trembling and reeling to and fro upon the threshold, then, with a low moaning cry, fell heavily inward upon the person of her brother, and in her violent and now final death-agonies, bore him to the floor a corpse, and a victim to the terrors he had anticipated.

From that chamber, and from that mansion, I fled aghast. The storm was still abroad in all its wrath as I found myself crossing the old causeway. Suddenly there shot along the path a wild light, and I turned to see whence a gleam so unusual could have issued; for the vast house and its shadows were alone behind me. The radiance was that of the full, setting, and blood-red moon which now shone vividly through that once barely-discernible fissure of which I have before spoken as extending from the roof of the building, in a zigzag direction, to the base. While I gazed, this fissure rapidly widened—there came a fierce breath of the whirlwind—the entire orb of the satellite burst at once upon my sight—my brain reeled as I saw the mighty walls rushing asunder—there was a long tumultuous shouting sound like the voice of a thousand waters—and the deep and dank tarn at my feet closed sullenly and silently over the fragments of the "HOUSE OF USHER."

Ivan Turgenev (1818–1883)

According to Henry James, *The Hunting Sketches* by Ivan Turgenev was to the freeing of the serfs in Russia what *Uncle Tom's Cabin* was to the emancipation of the slaves in the United States. Yet nothing could appear less propagandistic, less polemical, than Turgenev's book of stories, filled as it is with sensuous and poetic evocation of nature. Turgenev differs from Harriet Beecher Stowe, says James, by "having rather presented the case with an art too insidious for instant recognition, an art that stirred the depths more than the surface."

Turgenev's "insidious" art was perhaps as much a matter of self-preservation as of artistry. He was born in 1818, the son of rich landowners. Because he expressed an admiration for Gogol, who had been exiled after his satire *The Inspector General* had been performed, Turgenev was put under "house arrest." He came to know the serfs of his estate, and his natural sympathies and liberalism focused on their plight. He could not speak out directly for fear of further punishment, and so he wrote the indirect but effective *The Hunting Sketches*. It is said that the Czar himself was influenced by it.

The book, from which the following story comes, is made up of a series of encounters the first-person narrator has on his hunting rounds. The stories have in common the general setting, the narrative voice, and the peasants as subject matter, but they are otherwise discrete. The narrator describes the hunt, the forest, the atmosphere in which he moves. Even in translation, the imagery is lyrical, vibrant, exquisitely physical:

> The water gushes out of a cleft in the bank, which had little by little been turned into a small but deep ravine and, some twenty paces farther, tumbles with merry and chattering noisiness into the river. Scrub oaks grow thickly over the sloping sides of the ravine; short, velvety grass shows green near the wellspring; the rays of the sun hardly ever reach its chill, silvery waters.

The plot of a Turgenev story is almost nil: The hunter meets two men who are fishing; another arrives; they talk; they go their separate ways. That is all. In fact, the real story has nothing to do with the hunter. He is only a witness to the other lives. By the end of "Raspberry Spring," we understand those other lives, the injustices suffered, the patient endurance. We even understand, in the case of Fog, that the patience conceals a full knowledge of the injustice despite the overt acceptance. Henry James says that these sketches "give the impression of life itself, and not of an arrangement." Yet they do more: they indict a whole society and expose the indifference and cruelty of one human being toward another.

Turgenev was the author of many novels, including the famous *Fathers and Sons* (1861) and *Smoke* (1867). He spent most of his adult life in Germany and France and was rejected by many Russians, including Tolstoy and Dostoevsky, for being too "European." Actually he continued to care deeply about Russia and Russian literature and offered hospitality to many exiles. He died in France in 1883.

Raspberry Spring

At the beginning of August the persisting hot spells are often unbearable. At a time like that the most resolute and purposeful man is, from noon to three, in no condition to hunt, and the most faithful dog begins to "polish" the hunter's heels, i.e., it heels him at a slow walk, with its eyes puckered up as if they are aching and its tongue lolling exaggeratedly, while in answer to its master's chidings it wags its tail in humility and its face expresses embarrassment, yet mend its pace the animal will not.

It was on precisely such a day that I happened to be out hunting. I had long been resisting the temptation to lie down somewhere in the shade, if but for a moment; my indefatigable bitch for a long while kept beating about the bushes, even though she herself evidently expected nothing worthwhile from her feverish activity. The stifling sultriness at last compelled me to think of conserving the last of our strength and faculties. Somehow or other I managed to drag myself to the river Ista (which my condescending readers are already familiar with), descended the steep bank, and went on along the yellow and damp sand in the direction of a spring known throughout that district as Raspberry Water. It gushes out of a cleft in the bank, which had little by little been turned into a small but deep ravine and, some twenty paces farther, tumbles with merry and chattering noisiness into the river. Scrub oaks grow thickly over the sloping sides of the ravine; short, velvety grass shows green near the wellspring; the rays of the sun hardly ever reach its chill, silvery waters.

I dragged myself to the spring somehow; lying on the grass was a dipper of birch bark, left by some passing muzhik for the general good. I drank my fill, lay down in the shade, and looked about me. Near the cove formed by the spring falling into the river and thereby covering its surface at that point with perpetual small ripples, two old men were sitting, with their backs to me. One of them, tall and quite stout, in a neat dark caftan and a brimmed cap of beaver felt, was fishing with a pole; the other, ever so spare and ever so small, in a patched little jacket of mouse gray and minus any head covering, was holding a pannikin of worms on his knees and every now and then passed his hand over his small gray head, as though he wished to guard it against the sun. I looked at him more fixedly and recognized him: he was Stepushka, the property of the Shumihins. I ask the reader's permission to introduce this man.

The big settlement of Shumihino, with a stone church reared to honor the names of those most worthy saints, Kozma and Damian, is situated a few miles from my village. Rising up in all its beauty before this church there was at one time a spacious, many-roomed manor house, surrounded by all sorts of outbuildings, offices, workshops, barns, toolsheds, carriage stables, bathhouses, and temporary kitchens, wings for guests and administrative workers, hot-houses, swings for the common folk, and other structures of varying degrees of usefulness. Rich landowners had for a time lived in these spacious quarters, and everything had been going along smoothly when suddenly, one fine morning, all this wealth had burned down to fine ashes. The masters had made their way to another nest; this estate had become deserted. The extensive site of the fire became a truck garden, cluttered here and there with heaps of brick rubble, all that remained of what had been the foundations. Out of the lumber that had escaped the flames a small hut had been slapped together and roofed over with barge strakes which had been bought a decade or so before to build a pavilion in the Gothic manner, and Mitrophan the gardener with his wife Axenia and their seven children had been installed therein. Mitrophan was ordered to supply the masters' table (though the masters were living a hundred miles away) with potherbs and vegetables; Axenia was entrusted with the care of a Tyrolean cow, bought in Moscow for a great sum but, regrettably, altogether incapable of reproducing her kind and which for that reason had not yielded any milk from the day she had been acquired; it was also in Axenia's hands that they had placed tufted, smoke-hued drake, the only "lordly" fowl; the children, because of their tender years, had not been assigned any definite duties—this, however, did not hinder them in the least from becoming thoroughly shiftless.

It was at this gardener's that I had chanced to stay for the night on a couple of occasions; I would, in passing, get cucumbers from him—which, God knows why, were remarkable even in the summertime because of their great size, execrable watery taste, and thick yellow skin. And it was precisely at his house that I had first laid eyes on Stepushka. Outside of Mitrophan and his family, and Gherassim, an old, deaf church-warden who was living on Christ's charity in a cubbyhole in the house of a soldier's wife, lopsided and one-eyed, there wasn't a single domestic person left in Shumihino, inasmuch as Stepushka (with whom I intend to make the reader acquainted) could not be considered either as a person in general or as a domestic in particular.

Every human being has some sort of status in the social structure, has some sort of connections; every domestic is issued, if he gets no wages, at least a flour allotment, so called. Stepushka received no subsistence aids whatsoever, was not related to anybody; nobody was aware of his existence. This being hadn't even a past; people did not speak of him; it was doubtful if he was actually listed in the government's census of serfs. There were vague rumors current that he had been a valet to somebody at some time; but just who he was, whence he had come, whose son he was, how he had come to be of the number of those subject to the Shumihins, in what manner he had acquired the mouse-gray garment he had been wearing time out of mind, where he lived, what he lived on—of these things absolutely no one had the least notion, and besides, truth to tell, these questions did not arouse anybody's interest. Grandpa Trophimych, who knew the genealogy of all the house serfs for four generations back—well, even he said only once that, now, far as he could recall, Stepan was of kin to a Turkish woman whom the late master, Brigadier Alexei Romanych, had deigned to bring captive in a baggage cart on his return from a campaign. Even on gala days, days of good will and being treated to bread and salt, symbolic of hospitality, to pastries stuffed with buckwheat grits, and to green wine, according to the olden Russian custom—even on such days as these Stepushka did not put in an appearance at the food-laden tables and the barrels of spirits, all set out in the open, did not bow low before his masters, did not approach to kiss the master's hand, did not scoff off, at one breath, under the eye of the master and to the master's health, the glass filled by the pudgy hand of an overseer; he got nothing, unless some kind soul, passing by, bestowed a half-eaten piece of pie upon the poor fellow. People did exchange Easter greetings with him; he did not, however, roll up his greasy sleeve and reach in his back pocket for the traditional red-dyed egg, did not proffer it, panting and blinking, to the young masters, or even to the mistress her-self.

In the summer he lived in a cubbyhole back of the henhouse, and in the winter in the entry to the bathhouse; during hard frosts he slept in the hayloft. People were used to the sight of him; every now and then they would even bestow a kick upon him, but no one got into talk with him, while he himself, apparently, had never opened his mouth from the day he was born. After the fire this neglected being had found shelter with (or, as the Orlov folk put it, "leaned up against") Mitrophan, the gardener. The gardener hadn't molested him; he hadn't told him "Live with me," but he hadn't driven him off, either. And Stepushka, if it comes to that, did not actually live at the gardener's: he abode in, he hovered about the truck garden. He walked and moved without any noise whatsoever; he sneezed and coughed into his fist, and even then not without apprehension; he was eternally taken up with cares and fossicking about ever so quietly, unobtru-sively, like an ant—and all for the sake of something to eat, solely for the sake of something to eat. And, sure enough, were he not taken up from morn till night with concern over his sustenance, my Stepushka would have died from hunger. Things are in a bad way when a body doesn't know in the morning what he'll fill his belly with toward nightfall! Stepushka would be squatting close to the fence and gnawing away at a radish, or sucking a carrot, or mincing up a dirt-covered cabbage head, screening it with his body; now he would be lugging a bucket of water somewhere, grunting hard; now making a bit of a fire under a little pot and, taking chunks of something black from the bosom of his shirt, would toss them into the pot; then you would find him in his cubbyhole, tapping away at a scrap of lumber, driving in a nail, putting up a little shelf to place a crust of bread on. And all this he did with nary a chirp out of him, as though he were eyeing you from around a corner: you'd look, and he'd already hidden himself. Or, all of a sudden, he would absent himself for a couple of days or so—of course, nobody noticed his absence; then you might look up, and there he was again, again somewhere close to the fence, shoving tiny chips into the bit of a fire under his little pot of cast iron.

His face is tiny, his little eyes are sort of yellow, his hair straggles down to his very eyebrows, his snip of a nose is ever so sharp, his ears are ever so big, translucent, like a bat's, his beard looks just as if it had been shaved off a fortnight ago, and never gets smaller or bigger. And it was this very Stepushka whom I came upon on the bank of the Ista, in the company of another gaffer.

I walked up, exchanged greetings, and sat down alongside them. In Stepushka's companion I had recognized another acquaintance—he was Michailo Savelich, known under the sobriquet of Fog, a liberated serf of Count Peter Ilyich _____. He was staying with a consumptive burgher of Bolhov, who kept an inn at which I put up quite frequently.

Travelers along the main Orlov highway, young government clerks and other folk who aren't any too busy (merchants, sunk deep in their featherbeds of striped ticking, have other things on their minds) can observe, even to this day, at no great distance from the large settlement of Troitsk, an enormous two-storied house jutting out to the very road, a house utterly neglected, with its roof fallen in and its windows tightly boarded up. At noontide, when the weather is clear and sunny, one can imagine nothing more woeful than this ruin. It was here that Count Peter Ilyich, well known as a hospitable host, as a rich grandee of a time gone by, had once lived. The whole province used to gather at his place, dancing and making merry most gloriously to the deafening music of home-talent musicians, to the crackling of rockets and sputter of Roman candles, and probably more than one little crone, as she now drives by the deserted seignioral mansion, will sigh and recall the times past and past youth. For a long spell did the count feast; for a long spell did he keep promenading, amiably smiling, amid his thronging, fawning guests; unfortunately, however, his estate did not last out his lifetime. Utterly ruined, he set out for Petersburg to find a post for himself, and died in a hotel room after waiting in vain for something definite to turn up.

Fog had served him as a major-domo and had been granted his freedom even during the count's lifetime. He was a man of about seventy, his face pleasant and with regular features. He smiled almost constantly, as only the people of the era of Catherine the Great smile nowadays—good-naturedly and imposingly; when he spoke he would slowly thrust out and compress his lips, pucker up his eyes in a kindly way, and pronounce his words somewhat through his nose. He was likewise deliberate about blowing his nose and taking his snuff, as though he were engaged in a task of some importance.

"Well, now, Michailo Savelich," I began, "have you caught plenty of fish?"

"Why, just take a look in the creel, if you please; I've made sure of two perch and five bullheads. Show them to the gentleman, Stepka."

Stepushka held out the crudely plaited creel to me.

"How are you getting along, Stepan?" I asked.

"Why . . . why . . . why, not . . . not so bad, now, father of mine, in my small way," Stepan answered haltingly, as though he were turning thirty-pound weights with his tongue.

"And Mitrophan—is he in good health?"

"He is, to be . . . to be sure, father of mine." The poor fellow turned away.

"But they're biting rather poorly, somehow," Fog began. "It's mortal hot; the fish, now, are all hiding beneath the underwater roots of the bushes, asleep. Put a worm on the hook, now, Stepa." Stepushka got out a worm, placed it on his palm, smacked it a couple of times, put it on the hook, spat on it, and handed the line to Fog. "Thanks, Stepa. And you, father of mine," he went on, turning to me, "are you after a little hunting?"

"As you see."

"So-o. And what sort of a hound might you have there—English, or some sort of Fourland breed?" The old man loved, when the opportunity offered, to show his mettle, as if to say: "There, now, we too have lived a bit in this world!"

"I don't know the breed, but it's a good dog."

"So-o. And do you like to ride to hounds?"

"I keep two packs."

Fog smiled and shook his head. "That's the way of it, for sure: one man will be wild about dogs, whilst another wouldn't have them for free. To my simple way of thinking, dogs ought to be kept mostly for the grand looks of the thing, so to say. And everything that goes with them should also be fit and proper; the horses, too, ought to be right, and the whippers-in ought to be right, as is fitting, and everything else as well. The late count—may the Kingdom of Heaven be his!—wasn't a hunter born and bred, it must be confessed; yet he did keep hounds, and twice a year was pleased to ride after them. The lads would gather in the yard, in red caftans with gold braid, and blow the horn; His Excellency would deign to come out, and a steed would be led up for His Excellency, whilst the chief huntsman would put His Excellency's dainty feet in the stirrups, doff his cap, and then hand up the reins nested in that cap. His Excellency would snap his long whip—so!—and the whippers-in would begin hallooing and start out from the yard. The chief groom rode off behind the count, meanwhile holding two of the master's favorite little hounds on a silken leash and sort of keeping an eye on every-thing, you know. And he sat high in his Cossack saddle, this chief groom did; such a rosy-cheeked fellow, now, and rolling his huge eyes. Well, there were guests too, naturally, on an occasion like that. It was a diversion, and at the same time all due honor was observed. Ah, he got away, the low-down creature!" he added suddenly, jerking his line.

"Well, now, is it true what they say—about the count's having lived a full life in his day?" I asked.

The old man spat on the worm and cast his line.

"He was a right noble person, to be sure, sir. The foremost people from Peters-burg, you might say, used to come for a stay with him. All rigged out in the blue ribbons of their decorations, they were, as they sat and ate at his table. And, naturally, he was a great hand for treating them. Used to summon me into his presence: 'Fog,' he'd say, 'I must have some live sterlet sturgeons by tomorrow; give orders to get some.'—'Right, Your Excellency!' There were embroidered long coats, wigs, canes, perfumes, *ladeco-logne* of the first sort, snuffboxes, all those big paintings—he used to write away for them all the way to Paris itself, he did. When he'd get set to give a banquet—O Lord, Sovereign of my life!—the fireworks would begin, and the pleasure jaunts. They used to shoot off cannon, even. Of musicians alone there was an active staff of forty. He used to keep a maestro, a German fellow, but that heinie got some high and mighty notions into his head—got to hankering to eat at the same table with the masters, so His Excellency gave orders to send him packing with God's blessings: 'My musicians,' said His Excellency, 'understand their trade even as it is.' You know the way of things: the will of the masters must be obeyed.

"They'd start in to dance and keep dancing till dawn—*lacossaise, matradura*, mostly. Eh, eh, eh—I got you, brother!" The old man pulled a small perch out of the water. "Here you are, Stepa. A master, he was, a right proper master," the old man went on, casting in his line again, "and a right kind soul he had too. He'd give you a beating, now and then, but, first thing you know, he'd forgotten all about it. There was one thing, though: he used to keep mistresses. Oh, those mistresses, the Lord forgive us! It was just them that ruined him. And, mind you, it was from a low class he picked them, for the most part. What more could they want, a body might think: But no—you had to serve them with whatever stuff was most expensive in all of Yurrup. And why not live for one's own pleasure, you might say—that's what masters are for; still, there's no sense in ruining yourself. There was one in particular—Akulina, they called her; she's no longer amongst the living, may the Kingdom of Heaven be hers! A simple wench, she was, the daughter of the constable at Sitov, but what a vile temper she had! Used to slap the count's cheeks for him. She'd bewitched him entirely. Had a nephew of mine cropped for a soldier—he'd overturned some choc'lit on a new dress of hers. Yes. . . . But, after all, them was the good old days!" the old man added with a deep sigh and, casting his eyes down, fell silent.

"But your master was a strict sort, I can see," I began, after a short pause.

"That was all the go then, father of mine," the old man retorted with a shake of his head.

"They no longer do such things nowadays," I remarked without taking my eyes off him.

He gave me a sidelong look: "Things are better nowadays, everybody knows that," he muttered—and cast his line far out.

We were sitting in the shade, but even in the shade it was stifling. The oppressive, sultry air seemed to be holding its breath; one's heated face longingly sought a breeze, yet a breeze was the one thing missing. The sun was simply beating down out of the blue, now darkened sky; straight ahead of us, on the opposite bank, a field of oats showed yellow, with patches of wormwood breaking through here and there—and if but one stalk would stir! On a somewhat lower plane a peasant's horse was standing knee-deep in the river and lazily swishing itself with its wet tail; now and then, but only at long intervals, some large fish would come to the surface under an overhanging bush, let out a few bubbles, and quietly sink to the bottom, leaving light ripples behind. The grasshoppers were whirring away in the grass, now turned to a rusty hue; the quail were calling—halfheartedly, somehow; sparrow hawks were soaring smoothly over the fields and often hovered in one spot, beating their wings fast and fanning out their tails. We sat without moving, crushed by the heat.

There was a sudden noise behind us, in the ravine—someone was making his way down to the spring. I looked over my shoulder and saw a muzhik of fifty, all dusty, in blouse and bast sandals, with a knapsack of plaited birch bark and a rough overcoat slung over his shoulders. He walked up to the spring, drank his fill avidly, and stood up again.

"That you, Vlass?" Fog cried out after a good look at him. "Greetings, brother. Whence has God brought you?"

"Greetings, Michaila Savelich," said the muzhik, walking up to us. "I've come a long way."

"Where have you been keeping yourself so long?" Fog asked him.

"Why, I went to Moscow, to see my master."

"What for?"

"I went to petition him."

"To petition him about what?"

"Why, to lower my quitrent, or to hire me out, or to resettle me, or something like that. My son died, so I can't manage things all by myself now."

"Your son died?"

"He did that. He's no longer amongst the living," the muzhik added after a pause. "He was living in Moscow, driving a cab; to tell you the truth, it was him that paid my quitrent for me."

"Come, are you under a quitrent now?"

"I am that."

"Well, what did your master do?"

"Well, what do you expect of a master? He drove me out! 'How dare you come straight to me!' says he. 'That's what stewards are for—you must make a report to the steward first,' he says. 'And besides, where am I to resettle you? You pay your quitrent arrears first,' he says. Got real riled, he did."

"Well, what did you do then? Start back for home?"

"That's just what I did. I wanted to find out if my dead son had left anything behind him, but nothing came of that. I told the man he was working for: 'I'm Philip's father, now.' But he says to me: 'How am I supposed to know that? And besides, your son didn't leave anything. As a matter of fact he was in debt to me.' And so I started out for home."

The muzhik was telling all this with a mocking smile, as though it were somebody else he was talking about, but tears were welling up in his little half-closed eyes; his lips were twitching.

"Well, are you heading for home now?"

"Why, where else? I'm heading home, naturally. My wife must be perishing from hunger right now, I guess."

"You might . . . now. . . ." Stepushka spoke up unexpectedly, then became confused, fell silent, and began fussing with the worms in the pannikin.

"And are you going to the steward?" Fog went on, not without a surprised look at Stepa.

"What would I be going to him for! I'm in arrears as it is. My son was ailing for a year before he died, so he didn't pay in even his own quitrent. Not that I'm grieving over the arrears too much—they can't get anything out of me. Yes, brother, no matter how you twist and turn, you're wasting your time—you can't hold me to anything!" The muzhik broke into laughter. "No matter how he schemes and connives, this Quintilian Seménych, now, it won't get him nowheres, nohow!" Vlass laughed again.

"Well, now. That's bad, brother Vlass," Fog uttered thoughtfully.

"Why, what way is it bad? No. . . ." Here Vlass's voice broke. "What a hot spell we're having," he went on, mopping his face on his sleeve.

"Who's your master?" I asked.

"Valerian Petrovich, Count _____."

"Son of Peter Ilyich?"

"Peter Ilyich's son," Fog answered. "The late Peter Ilyich, whilst he was still alive, gave his son the village Vlass belongs to."

"How is your master—well?"

"He's well, glory be to God," Vlass retorted. "He's grown all red; his face is all bloated, like."

"There, father of mine," Fog went on, turning to me. "Things wouldn't be so bad if he were around Moscow, but he's been put under quitrent here."

"And how much is that for each household?"

"Ninety-five rubles for each house," Vlass muttered in answer.

"There, you see—yet of land there's ever so little; all there is to it is the master's woods."

"And even that has been sold," the muzhik put in.

"There, you see. . . . Let's have a worm, Stepa. Eh, Stepa? Have you fallen asleep, or what?"

Stepushka came to with a start. The muzhik sat down next to us. We again fell silent. Someone on the other side of the river started a long-drawn-out song—and such a dismal song, at that. My poor Vlass slumped over in his misery.

Half an hour later we all went our different ways.

Herman Melville (1819–1891)

In the spring of 1851, struggling to finish *Moby Dick* even as he was seeing its early chapters through the press, Melville wrote Hawthorne: "The calm, the coolness, the silent grass-growing mood in which a man *ought* always to compose,—that, I fear, can seldom be mine. Dollars damn me. . . . What I feel most moved to write, that is banned,—it will not pay. Yet, altogether, write the *other* way I cannot." The *other* way had produced Melville's earlier novels of sea adventure (*Typee*, 1846; *Omoo*, 1847; *Redburn*, 1849; *White-Jacket*, 1850) and it had brought him popular success. Write again that other way he did not, and when *Moby Dick* appeared later in 1851, the public did not buy and the critics did not praise. The broad sweep of his prose style and the habits of a deeply metaphysical mind were mistaken by some for incoherence and even madness. With the publication of his next novel, *Pierre* (1852), an even more spectacular commercial failure, the reviewers turned into downright attackers.

With "Bartleby," Melville turned his hand to shorter fiction. It has been read by some critics—and the interpretation is persuasive—"as a parable having to do with Melville's fate as a writer":

> To begin with, the story *is* about a kind of writer, a "copyist" in a Wall Street lawyer's office. Furthermore, the copyist is a man who obstinately refuses to go on doing the sort of writing demanded of him. Under the circumstances there can be little doubt about the connection between Bartleby's dilemma and Melville's own. . . . "Bartleby" is not only about a writer who refuses to conform to the demands of society, but it is, more relevantly, about a writer who forsakes conventional modes because of an irresistible preoccupation with the most baffling philosophical questions.

In the above reading, Leo Marx asks us to think seriously about the subtitle, "A Story of Wall Street." The setting is clearly that of a commercial society, but the locale is not just Wall Street, New York: "As Melville describes the street it literally becomes a walled street. The walls are the controlling symbols of the story, and in fact it may be said that this is a parable of walls, the walls which hem in the meditative artist and for that matter every reflective man."

Suppose, on the other hand, that we did not have the letter to Hawthorne, that we knew nothing of Melville's professional literary career, that we had only "Bartleby." Who, we might be inclined to ask, is in fact the protagonist—the nameless narrator or the scrivener? Which one, as we later recall the story, stirs more vividly, more insistently in our memory? Is Bartleby's fate, the fate of a gray, semi-automaton, more moving than the graduated enlightenment and understanding—together with moments of love—that humanize the lawyer? For whom are we more happy— if we are happy for anyone—at the end of the tale? The effort to address questions such as these may help us to determine what we have a right, and perhaps what we have only a qualified right, to ask of both literature and biographical history.

Bartleby, the Scrivener: A Story of Wall Street

I am a rather elderly man. The nature of my avocations, for the last thirty years, has brought me into more than ordinary contact with what would seem an interesting and somewhat singular set of men, of whom, as yet, nothing, that I know of, has ever been written:—I mean the lawcopyists or scriveners. I have known very many of them, professionally and privately, and, if I pleased, could relate divers histories, at which good-natured gentlemen might smile, and sentimental souls might weep. But I waive the biographies of all other scriveners for a few passages in the life of Bartleby, who was a scrivener, the strangest I ever saw, or heard of. While, of other law-copyists, I might write the complete life, of Bartleby nothing of that sort can be done. I believe that no materials exist, for a full and satisfactory biography of this man. It is an irreparable loss to literature. Bartleby was one of those beings of whom nothing is ascertainable, except from the original sources, and, in his case, those are very small. What my own astonished eyes saw of Bartleby, *that* is all I know of him, except, indeed, one vague report, which will appear in the sequel.

Ere introducing the scrivener, as he first appeared to me, it is fit I make some mention of myself, my *employées*, my business, my chambers, and general surroundings; because some such description is indispensable to an adequate understanding of the chief character about to be presented.

Imprimis:[1] I am a man who, from his youth upwards, has been filled with a profound conviction that the easiest way of life is the best. Hence, though I belong to a profession proverbially energetic and nervous, even to turbulence, at times, yet nothing of that sort have I ever suffered to invade my peace. I am one of those unambitious lawyers who never addresses a jury, or in any way draws down public applause; but in the cool tranquillity of a snug retreat, do a snug business among rich men's bonds, and mortgages, and title-deeds. All who know me, consider me an eminently *safe* man. The late John Jacob Astor,[2] a personage little given to poetic enthusiasm, had no hesitation

---

[1] In the first place: a legal term.
[2] Astor (1763–1848) was at one time the richest man in the United States.

in pronouncing my first grand point to be prudence; my next, method. I do not speak it in vanity, but simply record the fact, that I was not unemployed in my profession by the late John Jacob Astor; a name which, I admit, I love to repeat; for it hath a rounded and orbicular sound to it, and rings like unto bullion. I will freely add, that I was not insensible to the late John Jacob Astor's good opinion.

Some time prior to the period at which this little history begins, my avocations had been largely increased. The good old office, now extinct in the State of New York, of a Master in Chancery,[3] had been conferred upon me. It was not a very arduous office, but very pleasantly remunerative. I seldom lose my temper; much more seldom indulge in dangerous indignation at wrongs and outrages; but I must be permitted to be rash here and declare, that I consider the sudden and violent abrogation of the office of Master in Chancery, by the new Constitution, as a—premature act; inasmuch as I had counted upon a life-lease of the profits, whereas I only received those of a few short years. But this is by the way.

My chambers were up stairs at No.—Wall Street. At one end they looked upon the white wall of the interior of a spacious skylight shaft, penetrating the building from top to bottom.

This view might have been considered rather tame than otherwise, deficient in what landscape painters call "life." But, if so, the view from the other end of my chambers offered, at least, a contrast, if nothing more. In that direction my windows commanded an unobstructed view of a lofty brick wall, black by age and everlasting shade; which wall required no spyglass to bring out its lurking beauties, but, for the benefit of all near-sighted spectators, was pushed up to within ten feet of my window panes. Owing to the great height of the surrounding buildings, and my chambers being on the second floor, the interval between this wall and mine not a little resembled a huge square cistern.

At the period just preceding the advent of Bartleby, I had two persons as copyists in my employment, and a promising lad as an officeboy. First, Turkey; second, Nippers; third, Ginger Nut. These may seem names, the like of which are not usually found in the Directory. In truth, they were nicknames, mutually conferred upon each other by my three clerks, and were deemed expressive of their respective persons or characters. Turkey was a short, pursy Englishman of about my own age—that is, somewhere not far from sixty. In the morning, one might say, his face was a fine florid hue, but after twelve o'clock, meridian—his dinner hour—it blazed like a grate full of Christmas coals; and continued blazing—but, as it were, with a gradual wane—till 6 o'clock, P.M. or there-abouts, after which I saw no more of the proprietor of the face, which gaining its meridian with the sun, seemed to set with it, to rise, culminate, and decline the following day, with the like regularity and undiminished glory. There are many singular coincidences I have known in the course of my life, not the least among which was the fact, that exactly when Turkey displayed his fullest beams from his red and radiant countenance, just then, too, at that critical moment, began the daily period when I considered his business capacities as seriously disturbed for the remainder of the twenty-four hours. Not that he was absolutely idle, or adverse to business then; far from it. The difficulty was, he was apt to be altogether too energetic. There was a strange, inflamed, flurried, flighty recklessness of activity about him. He would be incautious in dipping his pen into his inkstand. All his blots upon my documents were dropped there after twelve o'clock, meridian. Indeed, not only would he be reckless and sadly given to making blots in the afternoon, but some days he went further, and was rather noisy. At

[3] The Court of Chancery in New York State was abolished in 1847.

such times, too, his face flamed with augmented blazonry, as if cannel coal had been heaped on anthracite.[4] He made an unpleasant racket with his chair; spilled his sand-box; in mending his pens, impatiently split them all to pieces, and threw them on the floor in a sudden passion; stood up and leaned over his table, boxing his papers about in a most indecorous manner, very sad to behold in an elderly man like him. Nevertheless, as he was in many ways a most valuable person to me, and all the time before twelve o'clock, meridian, was the quickest, steadiest creature, too, accomplishing a great deal of work in a style not easy to be matched—for these reasons, I was willing to overlook his eccentricities, though indeed, occasionally, I remonstrated with him. I did this very gently, however, because, though the civilest, nay, the blandest and most reverential of men in the morning, yet, in the afternoon he was disposed, upon provocation, to be slightly rash with his tongue, in fact, insolent. Now, valuing his morning services as I did, and resolved not to lose them—yet, at the same time, made uncomfortable by his inflamed ways after twelve o'clock—and being a man of peace, unwilling by my admoni-tions to call forth unseemly retorts from him, I took upon me, one Saturday noon (he was always worse on Saturdays), to hint to him, very kindly, that, perhaps now that he was growing old, it might be well to abridge his labors; in short, he need not come to my chambers after twelve o'clock, but, dinner over, had best go home to his lodgings, and rest himself till tea-time. But no; he insisted upon his afternoon devotions. His counte-nance became intolerably fervid, as he oratorically assured me—gesticulating with a long ruler at the other end of the room—that if his services in the morning were useful, how indispensable, then, in the afternoon?

"With submission, sir," said Turkey, on this occasion, "I consider myself your right-hand man. In the morning I but marshal and deploy my columns; but in the afternoon I put myself at their head, and gallantly charge the foe, thus"—and he made a violent thrust with the ruler.

"But the blots, Turkey," intimated I.

"True; but, with submission, sir, behold these hairs? I am getting old. Surely, sir, a blot or two of a warm afternoon is not to be severely urged against gray hairs. Old age—even if it blot the page—is honorable. With submission, sir, we *both* are getting old."

This appeal to my fellow-feeling was hardly to be resisted. At all events, I saw that go he would not. So, I made up my mind to let him stay, resolving, nevertheless, to see to it, that during the afternoon he had to do with my less important papers.

Nippers, the second on my list, was a whiskered, sallow, and, upon the whole, rather piratical-looking young man, of about five and twenty. I always deemed him the victim of two evil powers—ambition and indigestion. The ambition was evinced by a certain impatience of the duties of a mere copyist, an unwarrantable usurpation of strictly professional affairs, such as the original drawing up of legal documents. The indigestion seemed betokened in an occasional nervous testiness and grinning irritabil-ity, causing the teeth to audibly grind together over mistakes committed in copying; unnecessary maledictions, hissed, rather than spoken, in the heat of business; and especially by a continual discontent with the height of the table where he worked. Though of a very ingenious mechanical turn, Nippers could never get this table to suit him. He put chips under it, blocks of various sorts, bits of pasteboard, and at last went so far as to attempt an exquisite adjustment by final pieces of folded blotting-paper. But no invention would answer. If, for the sake of easing his back, he brought the table lid at a sharp angle well up towards his chin, and wrote there like a man using the steep roof of a Dutch house for his desk, then he declared that it stopped the circulation in his

[4] Cannel burns brightly; anthracite shows almost no flame.

arms. If now he lowered the table to his waistbands, and stooped over it in writing, then there was a sore aching in his back. In short, the truth of the matter was, Nippers knew not what he wanted. Or, if he wanted anything, it was to be rid of a scrivener's table altogether. Among the manifestations of his diseased ambition was a fondness he had for receiving visits from certain ambiguous-looking fellows in seedy coats, whom he called his clients. Indeed, I was aware that not only was he, at times, considerable of a ward-politician, but he occasionally did a little business at the Justices' courts, and was not unknown on the steps of the Tombs.[5] I have good reason to believe, however, that one individual who called upon him at my chambers, and who, with a grand air, he insisted was his client, was no other than a dun,[6] and the alleged title-deed, a bill. But with all his failings, and the annoyances he caused me, Nippers, like his compatriot Turkey, was a very useful man to me; wrote a neat, swift hand; and, when he chose, was not deficient in a gentlemanly sort of deportment. Added to this, he always dressed in a gentlemanly sort of way; and so, incidentally, reflected credit upon my chambers. Whereas, with respect to Turkey, I had much ado to keep him from being a reproach to me. His clothes were apt to look oily, and smell of eating-houses. He wore his pantaloons very loose and baggy in summer. His coats were execrable; his hat not to be handled. But while the hat was a thing of indifference to me, inasmuch as his natural civility and deference, as a dependent Englishman, always led him to doff it the moment he entered the room, yet his coat was another matter. Concerning his coats, I reasoned with him; but with no effect. The truth was, I suppose, that a man with so small an income, could not afford to sport such a lustrous face and a lustrous coat at one and the same time. As Nippers once observed, Turkey's money went chiefly for red ink. One winter day, I presented Turkey with a highly-respectable looking coat of my own—a padded gray coat, of a most comfortable warmth, and which buttoned straight up from the knee to the neck. I thought Turkey would appreciate the favor, and abate his rashness and obstreperousness of afternoons. But no; I verily believe that buttoning himself up in so downy and blanket-like a coat had a pernicious effect upon him—upon the same principle that too much oats are bad for horses. In fact, precisely as a rash, restive horse is said to feel his oats, so Turkey felt his coat. It made him insolent. He was a man whom prosperity harmed.

Though, concerning the self-indulgent habits of Turkey, I had my own private surmises, yet, touching Nippers, I was well persuaded that, whatever might be his faults in other respects, he was, at least, a temperate young man. But indeed, nature herself seemed to have been his vintner, and at his birth charged him so thoroughly with an irritable, brandy-like disposition, that all subsequent potations were needless. When I consider how, amid the stillness of my chambers, Nippers would sometimes impatiently rise from his seat, and stooping over his table, spread his arms wide apart, seize the whole desk, and move it, and jerk it, with a grim, grinding motion on the floor, as if the table were a perverse voluntary agent, intent on thwarting and vexing him, I plainly perceive that, for Nippers, brandy and water were altogether superfluous.

It was fortunate for me that, owing to its peculiar cause—indigestion—the irritability and consequent nervousness of Nippers, were mainly observable in the morning, while in the afternoon he was comparatively mild. So that, Turkey's paroxysms only coming on about twelve o'clock, I never had to do with their eccentricities at one time. Their fits relieved each other like guards. When Nippers' was on, Turkey's was off; and *vice versa*. This was a good natural arrangement under the circumstances.

[5] A New York City prison.
[6] Bill collector.

Ginger Nut, the third on my list, was a lad, some twelve years old. His father was a carman,[7] ambitious of seeing his son on the bench instead of a cart, before he died. So he sent him to my office as student at law, errand boy, and cleaner and sweeper, at the rate of one dollar a week. He had a little desk to himself, but he did not use it much. Upon inspection, the drawer exhibited a great array of the shells of various sorts of nuts. Indeed, to this quick-witted youth the whole science of the law was contained in a nutshell. Not the least among the employments of Ginger Nut, as well as one which he discharged with the most alacrity, was his duty as cake and apple purveyor for Turkey and Nippers. Copying law papers being proverbially a dry, husky sort of business, my two scriveners were fain to moisten their mouths very often with Spitzenbergs[8] to be had at the numerous stalls nigh the Custom House and Post Office. Also, they sent Ginger Nut very frequently for that peculiar cake—small, flat, round, and very spicy— after which he had been named by them. Of a cold morning when business was but dull, Turkey would gobble up scores of these cakes, as if they were mere wafers—indeed, they sell them at the rate of six or eight for a penny—the scrape of his pen blending with the crunching of the crisp particles in his mouth. Of all the fiery afternoon blunders and flurried rashnesses of Turkey, was his once moistening a ginger-cake between his lips, and clapping it on to a mortgage, for a seal. I came within an ace of dismissing him then. But he mollified me by making an oriental bow, and saying—

"With submission, sir, it was generous of me to find you in[9] stationery on my own account."

Now my original business—that of a conveyancer and title hunter, and drawer-up of recondite documents of all sorts—was considerably increased by receiving the Master's office. There was now great work for scriveners. Not only must I push the clerks already with me, but I must have additional help.

In answer to my advertisement, a motionless young man one morning stood upon my office threshold, the door being open, for it was summer. I can see that figure now— pallidly neat, pitiably respectable, incurably forlorn! It was Bartleby.

After a few words touching his qualifications, I engaged him, glad to have among my corps of copyists a man of so singularly sedate an aspect, which I thought might operate beneficially upon the flighty temper of Turkey, and the fiery one of Nippers.

I should have stated before that ground glass folding-doors divided my premises into two parts, one of which was occupied by my scriveners, the other by myself. According to my humor, I threw open these doors, or closed them. I resolved to assign Bartleby a corner by the folding-doors, but on my side of them, so as to have this quiet man within easy call, in case any trifling thing was to be done. I placed his desk close up to a small side-window in that part of the room, a window which originally had afforded a lateral view of certain grimy backyards and bricks, but which, owing to subsequent erections, commanded at present no view at all, though it gave some light. Within three feet of the panes was a wall, and the light came down from far above, between two lofty buildings, as from a very small opening in a dome. Still further to a satisfactory arrangement, I procured a high green folding screen, which might entirely isolate Bartleby from my sight, though not remove him from my voice. And thus, in a manner, privacy and society were conjoined.

At first, Bartleby did an extraordinary quantity of writing. As if long famishing for something to copy, he seemed to gorge himself on my documents. There was no pause for digestion. He ran a day and night line, copying by sunlight and by candlelight. I

---

[7] Wagon driver
[8] Apples.
[9] Provide you with.

should have been quite delighted with his application, had he been cheerfully industrious. But he wrote on silently, palely, mechanically.

It is, of course, an indispensable part of a scrivener's business to verify the accuracy of his copy, word by word. Where there are two or more scriveners in an office, they assist each other in this examination, one reading from the copy, the other holding the original. It is a very dull, wearisome, and lethargic affair. I can readily imagine that, to some sanguine temperaments, it would be altogether intolerable. For example, I cannot credit that the mettlesome poet, Byron, would have contentedly sat down with Bartleby to examine a law document of, say, five hundred pages, closely written in a crimpy hand.

Now and then, in the haste of business, it had been my habit to assist in comparing some brief document myself, calling Turkey or Nippers for this purpose. One object I had, in placing Bartleby so handy to me behind the screen, was, to avail myself on his services on such trivial occasions. It was on the third day, I think, of his being with me, and before any necessity had arisen for having his own writing examined, that, being much hurried to complete a small affair I had in hand, I abruptly called to Bartleby. In my haste and natural expectancy of instant compliance, I sat with my head bent over the original on my desk, and my right hand sideways, and somewhat nervously extended with the copy, so that, immediately upon emerging from his retreat, Bartleby might snatch it and proceed to business without the least delay.

In this very attitude did I sit when I called to him, rapidly stating what it was I wanted him to do—namely, to examine a small paper with me. Imagine my surprise, nay, my consternation, when without moving from his privacy, Bartleby, in a singularly mild, firm voice, replied, "I would prefer not to."

I sat awhile in perfect silence, rallying my stunned faculties. Immediately it occurred to me that my ears had deceived me, or Bartleby had entirely misunderstood my meaning. I repeated my request in the clearest tone I could assume: but in quite as clear a one came the previous reply, "I would prefer not to."

"Prefer not to," echoed I, rising in high excitement, and crossing the room with a stride. "What do you mean? Are you moon-struck? I want you to help me compare this sheet here—take it," and I thrust it towards him.

"I would prefer not to," said he.

I looked at him steadfastly. His face was leanly composed; his gray eye dimly calm. Not a wrinkle of agitation rippled him. Had there been the least uneasiness, anger, impatience or impertinence in his manner; in other words, had there been anything ordinarily human about him, doubtless I should have violently dismissed him from the premises. But as it was, I should have as soon thought of turning my pale plaster-of-paris bust of Cicero out-of-doors. I stood gazing at him awhile, as he went on with his own writing, and then reseated myself at my desk. This is very strange, thought I. What had one best do? But my business hurried me. I concluded to forget the matter for the present, reserving it for my future leisure. So, calling Nippers from the other room, the paper was speedily examined.

A few days after this, Bartleby concluded four lengthy documents, being quadruplicates of a week's testimony taken before me in my High Court of Chancery. It became necessary to examine them. It was an important suit, and great accuracy was imperative. Having all things arranged I called Turkey, Nippers and Ginger Nut from the next room, meaning to place the four copies in the hands of my four clerks, while I should read from the original. Accordingly, Turkey, Nippers and Ginger Nut had taken their seats in a row, each with his document in hand, when I called to Bartleby to join this interesting group.

"Bartleby! quick, I am waiting."

I heard a slow scrape of his chair legs on the uncarpeted floor, and soon he appeared standing at the entrance of his hermitage.

"What is wanted?" said he mildly.

"The copies, the copies," said I hurriedly. "We are going to examine them. There"—and I held towards him the fourth quadruplicate.

"I would prefer not to," he said, and gently disappeared behind the screen.

For a few moments I was turned into a pillar of salt, standing at the head of my seated column of clerks. Recovering myself, I advanced towards the screen, and demanded the reason for such extraordinary conduct.

"*Why* do you refuse?"

"I would prefer not to."

With any other man I should have flown outright into a dreadful passion, scorned all further words, and thrust him ignominiously from my presence. But there was something about Bartleby that not only strangely disarmed me, but in a wonderful manner touched and disconcerted me. I began to reason with him.

"These are your own copies we are about to examine. It is labor saving to you, because one examination will answer for your four papers. It is common usage. Every copyist is bound to help examine his copy. Is it not so? Will you not speak? Answer!"

"I prefer not to," he replied in a flute-like tone. It seemed to me that while I had been addressing him, he carefully revolved every statement that I made; fully comprehended the meaning; could not gainsay the irresistible conclusion; but, at the same time, some paramount consideration prevailed with him to reply as he did.

"You are decided, then, not to comply with my request—a request made according to common usage and common sense?"

He briefly gave me to understand, that on that point my judgment was sound. Yes: his decision was irreversible.

It is not seldom the case that, when a man is browbeaten in some unprecedented and violently unreasonable way, he begins to stagger in his own plainest faith. He begins, as it were, vaguely to surmise that, wonderful as it may be, all the justice and all the reason is on the other side. Accordingly, if any disinterested persons are present, he turns to them for some reinforcement for his own faltering mind.

"Turkey," said I, "what do you think of this? Am I not right?"

"With submission, sir," said Turkey, with his blandest tone, "I think that you are."

"Nippers," said I, "what do *you* think of it?"

"I think I should kick him out of the office."

(The reader of nice perceptions will here perceive that, it being morning, Turkey's answer is couched in polite and tranquil terms, but Nippers replies in ill-tempered ones. Or, to repeat a previous sentence, Nippers's ugly mood was on duty, and Turkey's off.)

"Ginger Nut," said I, willing to enlist the smallest suffrage in my behalf, "what do *you* think of it?"

"I think, sir, he's a little *luny*," replied Ginger Nut, with a grin.

"You hear what they say," said I, turning towards the screen, "come forth and do your duty."

But he vouchsafed no reply. I pondered a moment in sore perplexity. But once more business hurried me. I determined again to postpone the consideration of this dilemma to my future leisure. With a little trouble we made out to examine the papers without Bartleby, though at every page or two, Turkey deferentially dropped his opinion that this proceeding was quite out of the common; while Nippers, twitching in his chair with a dyspeptic nervousness, ground out between his set teeth occasional hissing maledictions against the stubborn oaf behind the screen. And for his (Nippers's) part, this was the first and the last time he would do another man's business without pay.

Meanwhile Bartleby sat in his hermitage, oblivious to everything but his own peculiar business there.

Some days passed, the scrivener being employed upon another lengthy work. His late remarkable conduct led me to regard his ways narrowly. I observed that he never went to dinner; indeed that he never went anywhere. As yet I had never of my personal knowledge known him to be outside of my office. He was a perpetual sentry in the corner. At about eleven o'clock though, in the morning, I noticed that Ginger Nut would advance toward the opening in Bartleby's screen, as if silently beckoned thither by a gesture invisible to me where I sat. The boy would then leave the office, jingling a few pence, and reappear with a handful of ginger-nuts which he delivered in the hermitage, receiving two of the cakes for his trouble.

He lives, then, on ginger-nuts, thought I; never eats a dinner, properly speaking; he must be a vegetarian, then, but no; he never eats even vegetables, he eats nothing but ginger-nuts. My mind then ran on in reveries concerning the probable effects upon the human constitution of living entirely on ginger-nuts. Ginger-nuts are so called because they contain ginger as one of their peculiar constituents, and the final flavoring one. Now, what was ginger? A hot, spicy thing. Was Bartleby hot and spicy? Not at all. Ginger, then, had no effect upon Bartleby. Probably he preferred it should have none.

Nothing so aggravates an earnest person as a passive resistance. If the individual so resisted be of a not inhumane temper, and the resisting one perfectly harmless in his passivity, then, in the better moods of the former, he will endeavor charitably to construe to his imagination what proves impossible to be solved by his judgment. Even so, for the most part, I regarded Bartleby and his ways. Poor fellow! thought I, he means no mischief; it is plain he intends no insolence; his aspect sufficiently evinces that his eccentricities are involuntary. He is useful to me. I can get along with him. If I turn him away, the chances are he will fall in with some less indulgent employer, and then he will be rudely treated, and perhaps driven forth miserably to starve. Yes. Here I can cheaply purchase a delicious self-approval. To befriend Bartleby; to humor him in his strange wilfulness, will cost me little or nothing, while I lay up in my soul what will eventually prove a sweet morsel for my conscience. But this mood was not invariable with me. The passiveness of Bartleby sometimes irritated me. I felt strangely goaded on to encounter him in new opposition, to elicit some angry spark from him answerable to my own. But indeed I might as well have essayed to strike fire with my knuckles against a bit of Windsor soap. But one afternoon the evil impulse in me mastered me, and the following little scene ensued:

"Bartleby," said I, "when those papers are all copied, I will compare them with you."

"I would prefer not to."

"How? Surely you do not mean to persist in that mulish vagary?"

No answer.

I threw open the folding-doors near by, and turning upon Turkey and Nippers, exclaimed in an excited manner—

"He says, a second time, he won't examine his papers. What do you think of it, Turkey?"

It was afternoon, be it remembered. Turkey sat glowing like a brass boiler, his bald head steaming, his hands reeling among his blotted papers.

"Think of it?" roared Turkey; "I think I'll just step behind his screen, and black his eyes for him!"

So saying, Turkey rose to his feet and threw his arms into a pugilistic position. He was hurrying away to make good his promise, when I detained him, alarmed at the effect of incautiously rousing Turkey's combativeness after dinner.

"Sit down, Turkey," said I, "and hear what Nippers has to say. What do you think of it, Nippers? Would I not be justified in immediately dismissing Bartleby?"

"Excuse me, that is for you to decide, sir. I think his conduct quite unusual, and indeed unjust, as regards Turkey and myself. But it may only be a passing whim."

"Ah," exclaimed I, "you have strangely changed your mind then—you speak very gently of him now."

"All beer," cried Turkey; "gentleness is effects of beer—Nippers and I dined together today. You see how gentle *I* am, sir. Shall I go and black his eyes?"

"You refer to Bartleby, I suppose. No, not today, Turkey," I replied; "pray, put up your fists."

I closed the doors, and again advanced towards Bartleby. I felt additional incentives tempting me to my fate. I burned to be rebelled against again. I remembered that Bartleby never left the office.

"Bartleby," said I, "Ginger Nut is away; just step round to the Post Office, won't you? (it was but a three minutes' walk,) and see if there is anything for me."

"I would prefer not to."

"You *will* not?"

"I *prefer* not."

I staggered to my desk, and sat there in a deep study. My blind inveteracy returned. Was there any other thing in which I could procure myself to be ignominiously repulsed by this lean, penniless wight?—my hired clerk? What added thing is there, perfectly reasonable, that he will be sure to refuse to do?

"Bartleby!"

No answer.

"Bartleby," in a louder tone.

No answer.

"Bartleby," I roared.

Like a very ghost, agreeably to the laws of magical invocation, at the third summons, he appeared at the entrance of his hermitage.

"Got to the next room, and tell Nippers to come to me."

"I prefer not to," he respectfully and slowly said, and mildly disappeared.

"Very good, Bartleby," said I, in a quiet sort of serenely severe self-possessed tone, intimating the unalterable purpose of some terrible retribution very close at hand. At the moment I half intended something of the kind. But upon the whole, as it was drawing towards my dinner-hour, I thought it best to put on my hat and walk home for the day, suffering much from perplexity and distress of mind.

Shall I acknowledge it? The conclusion of this whole business was, that it soon became a fixed fact of my chambers, that a pale young scrivener, by the name of Bartleby, had a desk there; that he copied for me at the usual rate of four cents a folio (one hundred words); but he was permanently exempt from examining the work done by him, that duty being transferred to Turkey and Nippers, out of compliment doubtless to their superior acuteness; moreover, said Bartleby was never on any account to be dispatched on the most trivial errand of any sort; and that even if entreated to take upon him such a matter, it was generally understood that he would "prefer not to"—in other words, that he would refuse point-blank.

As days passed on, I became considerably reconciled to Bartleby. His steadiness, his freedom from all dissipation, his incessant industry (except when he chose to throw himself into a standing revery behind his screen), his great stillness, his unalterableness of demeanor under all circumstances, made him a valuable acquisition. One prime thing was this—*he was always there*—first in the morning, continually through the day, and the last at night. I had a singular confidence in his honesty. I felt my most precious papers perfectly safe in his hands. Sometimes to be sure I could not, for the very soul of me, avoid falling into sudden spasmodic passions with him. For it was exceeding difficult to bear in mind all the time those strange peculiarities, privileges, and unheard of exemptions, forming the tacit stipulations on Bartleby's part under which he remained in my office. Now and then, in the eagerness of dispatching pressing business, I would inadvertently summon Bartleby, in a short, rapid tone, to put his finger, say, on the incipient tie of a bit of red tape with which I was about compressing some papers. Of course, from behind the screen the usual answer, "I prefer not to," was sure to come; and then, how could a human creature with the common infirmities of our nature, refrain from bitterly exclaiming upon such perverseness—such unreasonableness? However, every added repulse of this sort which I received only tended to lessen the probability of my repeating the inadvertence.

Here it must be said, that, according to the custom of most legal gentlemen occupying chambers in densely-populated law buildings, there were several keys to my door. One was kept by a woman residing in the attic, which person weekly scrubbed and daily swept and dusted my apartments. Another was kept by Turkey for convenience sake. The third I sometimes carried in my own pocket. The fourth I knew not who had.

Now, one Sunday morning I happened to go to Trinity Church, to hear a celebrated preacher, and finding myself rather early on the ground, I thought I would walk round to my chambers for a while. Luckily I had my key with me; but upon applying it to the lock, I found it resisted by something inserted from the inside. Quite surprised, I called out; when to my consternation a key was turned from within; and thrusting his lean visage at me, and holding the door ajar, the apparition of Bartleby appeared, in his shirt sleeves, and otherwise in a strangely tattered dishabille, saying quietly that he was sorry, but he was deeply engaged just then, and—preferred not admitting me at present. In a brief word or two, he moreover added, that perhaps I had better walk round the block two or three times, and by that time he would probably have concluded his affairs.

Now, the utterly unsurmised appearance of Bartleby, tenanting my law-chambers of a Sunday morning, with his cadaverously gentlemanly *nonchalance*, yet withal firm and self-possessed, had such a strange effect upon me, that incontinently I slunk away from my own door, and did as desired. But not without sundry twinges of impotent rebellion against the mild effrontery of this unaccountable scrivener. Indeed, it was his wonderful mildness, chiefly, which not only disarmed me, but unmanned me, as it were. For I consider that one, for the time, is sort of unmanned when he tranquilly permits his hired clerk to dictate to him, and order him away from his own premises. Furthermore, I was full of uneasiness as to what Bartleby could possibly be doing in my office in his shirt sleeves, and in an otherwise dismantled condition of a Sunday morning. Was anything amiss going on? Nay, that was out of the question. It was not to be thought of for a moment that Bartleby was an immoral person. But what could he be doing there?—copying? Nay again, whatever might be his eccentricities, Bartleby was an eminently decorous person. He would be the last man to sit down to his desk in any state approaching to nudity. Besides, it was Sunday; and there was something about Bartleby that forbade the supposition that he would by any secular occupation violate the proprieties of the day.

Nevertheless, my mind was not pacified; and full of a restless curiosity, at last I returned to the door. Without hindrance I inserted my key, opened it, and entered.

Bartleby was not to be seen. I looked round anxiously, peeped behind his screen; but it was very plain that he was gone. Upon more closely examining the place, I surmised that for an indefinite period Bartleby must have ate, dressed, and slept in my office, and that too without plate, mirror, or bed. The cushioned seat of a rickety old sofa in one corner bore the faint impress of a lean, reclining form. Rolled away under his desk, I found a blanket under the empty grate, a blacking box[10] and brush; on a chair, a tin basin, with soap and a ragged towel; in a newspaper a few crumbs of ginger-nuts and a morsel of cheese. Yes, thought I, it is evident enough that Bartleby has been making his home here, keeping bachelor's hall all by himself. Immediately then the thought came sweeping across me, What miserable friendlessness and loneliness are here revealed! His poverty is great; but his solitude, how horrible! Think of it. Of a Sunday, Wall Street is deserted as Petra;[11] and every night of every day it is an emptiness. This building too, which of weekdays hums with industry and life, at nightfall echoes with sheer vacancy, and all through Sunday is forlorn. And here Bartleby makes his home; sole spectator of a solitude which he has seen all populous—a sort of innocent and transformed Marius brooding among the ruins of Carthage![12]

For the first time in my life a feeling of overpowering stinging melancholy seized me. Before, I had never experienced aught but a not-unpleasing sadness. The bond of a common humanity now drew me irresistibly to gloom. A fraternal melancholy! For both I and Bartleby were sons of Adam. I remembered the bright silks and sparkling faces I had seen that day, in gala trim, swan-like sailing down the Mississippi of Broadway; and I contrasted them with the pallid copyist, and thought to myself, Ah, happiness courts the light, so we deem the world is gay; but misery hides aloof, so we deem that misery there is none. These sad fancyings—chimeras, doubtless, of a sick and silly brain—led on to other and more special thoughts, concerning the eccentricities of Bartleby. Presentiments of strange discoveries hovered round me. The scrivener's pale form appeared to me laid out, among uncaring strangers, in its shivering winding sheet.

Suddenly I was attracted by Bartleby's closed desk, the key in open sight left in the lock.

I mean no mischief, seek the gratification of no heartless curiosity, thought I; besides, the desk is mine, and its contents too, so I will make bold to look within. Everything was methodically arranged, the papers smoothly placed. The pigeonholes were deep, and removing the files of documents, I groped into their recesses. Presently I felt something there, and dragged it out. It was an old bandanna handkerchief, heavy and knotted. I opened it, and saw it was a savings' bank.

I now recalled all the quiet mysteries which I had noted in the man. I remembered that he never spoke but to answer; that though at intervals he had considerable time to himself, yet I had never seen him reading—no, not even a newspaper; that for long periods he would stand looking out, at his pale window behind the screen, upon the dead brick wall; I was quite sure he never visited any refectory or eating house; while his pale face clearly indicated that he never drank beer like Turkey, or tea and coffee even, like other men; that he never went anywhere in particular that I could learn; never went out for a walk, unless indeed that was the case at present; that he had declined telling who he was, or whence he came, or whether he had any relatives in the world; that though so thin and pale, he never complained of ill health. And more than all, I remembered a

---

[10] Box of black shoe polish.

[11] Ancient city, long in ruins, in present state of Jordan. At one time it had been a major center of caravan routes and trade.

[12] Roman general and consul Gaius Marius (*ca.* 155–86 B.C.), having lost his power and exiled from Rome by Sulla in 88 B.C., brooded among the ruins of Carthage.

certain unconscious air of pallid—how shall I call it?—of pallid haughtiness, say, or rather an austere reserve about him, which had positively awed me into my tame compliance with his eccentricities, when I had feared to ask him to do the slightest incidental thing for me, even though I might know, from his long-continued motionlessness, that behind his screen he must be standing in one of those dead-wall reveries of his.

Revolving all these things, and coupling them with the recently discovered fact, that he made my office his constant abiding place and home, and not forgetful of his morbid moodiness; revolving all these things, a prudential feeling began to steal over me. My first emotions had been those of pure melancholy and sincerest pity; but just in proportion as the forlornness of Bartleby grew and grew to my imagination, did that same melancholy merge into fear, that pity into repulsion. So true it is, and so terrible, too, that up to a certain point the thought or sight of misery enlists our best affections; but, in certain special cases, beyond that point it does not. They err who would assert that invariably this is owing to the inherent selfishness of the human heart. It rather proceeds from a certain hopelessness of remedying excessive and organic ill. To a sensitive being, pity is not seldom pain. And when at last it is perceived that such pity cannot lead to effectual succor, common sense bids the soul be rid of it. What I saw that morning persuaded me that the scrivener was the victim of innate and incurable disorder. I might give alms to his body; but his body did not pain him; it was his soul that suffered, and his soul I could not reach.

I did not accomplish the purpose of going to Trinity Church that morning. Somehow, the things I had seen disqualified me for the time from churchgoing. I walked homeward, thinking what I would do with Bartleby. Finally, I resolved upon this—I would put certain calm questions to him the next morning, touching his history, etc., and if he declined to answer them openly and unreservedly (and I supposed he would prefer not), then to give him a twenty-dollar bill over and above whatever I might owe him, and tell him his services were no longer required; but that if in any other way I could assist him, I would be happy to do so, especially if he desired to return to his native place, wherever that might be, I would willingly help to defray the expenses. Moreover, if, after reaching home, he found himself at any time in want of aid, a letter from him would be sure of a reply.

The next morning came.

"Bartleby," said I, gently calling to him behind his screen.

No reply.

"Bartleby," said I, in a still gentler tone, "come here; I am not going to ask you to do anything you would prefer not to do—I simply wish to speak to you."

Upon this he noiselessly slid into view.

"Will you tell me, Bartleby, where you were born?"

"I would prefer not to."

"Will you tell me *anything* about yourself?"

"I would prefer not to."

"But what reasonable objection can you have to speak to me? I feel friendly towards you."

He did not look at me while I spoke, but kept his glance fixed upon my bust of Cicero, which, as I then sat, was directly behind me, some six inches above my head.

"What is your answer, Bartleby?" said I, after waiting a considerable time for a reply, during which his countenance remained immovable, only there was the faintest conceivable tremor of the white attenuated mouth.

"At present I prefer to give no answer," he said, and retired into his hermitage.

It was rather weak in me I confess, but his manner, on this occasion, nettled me. Not only did there seem to lurk in it a certain calm disdain, but his perverseness seemed ungrateful, considering the undeniable good usage and indulgence he had received from me.

Again I sat ruminating what I should do. Mortified as I was at his behavior, and resolved as I had been to dismiss him when I entered my office, nevertheless I strangely felt something superstitious knocking at my heart, and forbidding me to carry out my purpose, and denouncing me for a villain if I dared to breathe one bitter word against this forlornest of mankind. At last, familiarly drawing my chair behind his screen, I sat down and said: "Bartleby, never mind then about revealing your history; but let me entreat you, as a friend, to comply as far as may be with the usages of this office. Say now, you will help to examine papers tomorrow or next day: in short, say now, that in a day or two you will begin to be a little reasonable:—say so, Bartleby."

"At present I would prefer not to be a little reasonable," was his mildly cadaverous reply.

Just then the folding-doors opened, and Nippers approached. He seemed suffering from an unusually bad night's rest, induced by severer indigestion than common. He overheard those final words of Bartleby.

"*Prefer not,* eh?" gritted Nippers—"I'd *prefer* him, if I were you, sir," addressing me—"I'd *prefer* him; I'd give him preferences, the stubborn mule! What is it, sir, pray, that he *prefers* not to do now?"

Bartleby moved not a limb.

"Mr. Nippers," said I, "I'd prefer that you would withdraw for the present."

Somehow, of late I had got into the way of involuntarily using this word "prefer" upon all sorts of not exactly suitable occasions. And I trembled to think that my contact with the scrivener had already and seriously affected me in a mental way. And what further and deeper aberration might it not yet produce? This apprehension had not been without efficacy in determining me to summary means.

As Nippers, looking very sour and sulky, was departing, Turkey blandly and deferentially approached.

"With submission, sir," said he, "yesterday I was thinking about Bartleby here, and I think that if he would but prefer to take a quart of good ale every day, it would do much towards mending him and enabling him to assist in examining his papers."

"So you have got the word, too," said I, slightly excited.

"With submission, what word, sir?" asked Turkey, respectfully crowding himself into the contracted space behind the screen, and by so doing, making me jostle the scrivener. "What word, sir?"

"I would prefer to be left alone here," said Bartleby, as if offended at being mobbed in his privacy.

"*That's* the word, Turkey," said I—"*that's* it."

"Oh, *prefer?* oh yes—queer word. I never use it myself. But, sir, as I was saying, if he would but prefer—"

"Turkey," interrupted I, "you will please withdraw."

"Oh certainly, sir, if you prefer that I should."

As he opened the folding-door to retire, Nippers at his desk caught a glimpse of me, and asked whether I would prefer to have a certain paper copied on blue paper or white. He did not in the least roguishly accent the word *prefer.* It was plain that it involuntarily rolled from his tongue. I thought to myself, surely I must get rid of a demented man, who already has in some degree turned the tongues, if not the heads of myself and clerks. But I thought it prudent not to break the dismission at once.

The next day I noticed that Bartleby did nothing but stand at his window in his dead-wall revery. Upon asking him why he did not write, he said that he had decided upon doing no more writing.

"Why, how now? what next?" exclaimed I, "do no more writing?"

"No more."

"And what is the reason?"

"Do you not see the reason for yourself," he indifferently replied.

I looked steadfastly at him, and perceived that his eyes looked dull and glazed. Instantly it occurred to me, that his unexampled diligence in copying by his dim window for the first few weeks of his stay with me might have temporarily impaired his vision.

I was touched. I said something in condolence with him. I hinted that of course he did wisely in abstaining from writing for a while; and urged him to embrace that opportunity of taking wholesome exercise in the open air. This, however, he did not do. A few days after this, my other clerks being absent, and being in a great hurry to dispatch certain letters by the mail, I thought that, having nothing else earthly to do, Bartleby would surely be less inflexible than usual, and carry these letters to the post office. But he blankly declined. So, much to my inconvenience, I went myself.

Still added days went by. Whether Bartleby's eyes improved or not, I could not say. To all appearance, I thought they did. But when I asked him if they did, he vouchsafed no answer. At all events, he would do no copying. At last, in reply to my urgings, he informed me that he had permanently given up copying.

"What!" exclaimed I; "suppose your eyes should get entirely well—better than ever before—would you not copy then?"

"I have given up copying," he answered, and slid aside.

He remained, as ever, a fixture in my chamber. Nay—if that were possible—he became still more of a fixture than before. What was to be done? He would do nothing in the office: why should he stay there? In plain fact, he had now become a millstone to me, not only useless as a necklace, but afflictive to bear. Yet I was sorry for him. I speak less than truth when I say that, on his own account, he occasioned me uneasiness. If he would but have named a single relative or friend, I would instantly have written, and urged their taking the poor fellow away to some convenient retreat. But he seemed alone, absolutely alone in the universe. A bit of wreck in the mid-Atlantic. At length, necessities connected with my business tyrannized over all other considerations. Decently as I could, I told Bartleby that in six days' time he must unconditionally leave the office. I wanted him to take measures, in the interval, for procuring some other abode. I offered to assist him in this endeavor, if he himself would but take the first step towards a removal. "And when you finally quit me, Bartleby," added I, "I shall see that you go not away entirely unprovided. Six days from this hour, remember."

At the expiration of that period, I peeped behind the screen, and lo! Bartleby was there.

I buttoned up my coat, balanced myself; advanced slowly towards him, touched his shoulder, and said, "The time has come; you must quit this place; I am sorry for you; here is money; but you must go."

"I would prefer not," he replied, with his back still towards me.

"You *must*."

He remained silent.

Now I had an unbounded confidence in this man's common honesty. He had frequently restored to me sixpences and shillings carelessly dropped upon the floor, for I am apt to be very reckless in such shirt-button affairs. The proceeding then which followed will not be deemed extraordinary.

"Bartleby," said I, "I owe you twelve dollars on account; here are thirty-two; the odd twenty are yours.—Will you take it?" and I handed the bills towards him.

But he made no notion.

"I will leave them here then," putting them under a weight on the table. Then taking my hat and cane and going to the door I tranquilly turned and added—"After you have removed your things from these offices, Bartleby, you will of course lock the door—since everyone is now gone for the day but you—and if you please, slip your key underneath the mat, so that I may have it in the morning. I shall not see you again; so good-bye to you. If hereafter in your new place of abode I can be of any service to you, do not fail to advise me by letter. Goodbye, Bartleby, and fare you well."

But he answered not a word; like the last column of some ruined temple, he remained standing mute and solitary in the middle of the otherwise deserted room.

As I walked home in a pensive mood, my vanity got the better of my pity. I could not but highly plume myself on my masterly management in getting rid of Bartleby. Masterly I call it, and such it must appear to any dispassionate thinker. The beauty of my procedure seemed to consist in its perfect quietness. There was no vulgar bullying, no bravado of any sort, no choleric hectoring, and striding to and fro across the apartment, jerking out vehement commands for Bartleby to bundle himself off with his beggarly traps.[13] Nothing of the kind. Without loudly bidding Bartleby depart—as an inferior genius might have done—I *assumed* the ground that depart he must; and upon the assumption built all I had to say. The more I thought over my procedure, the more I was charmed with it. Nevertheless, next morning, upon awakening, I had my doubts—I had somehow slept off the fumes of vanity. One of the coolest and wisest hours a man has is just after he awakes in the morning. My procedure seemed as sagacious as ever,— but only in theory. How it would prove in practice—there was the rub. It was truly a beautiful thought to have assumed Bartleby's departure; but, after all, that assumption was simply my own, and none of Bartleby's. The great point was, not whether I had assumed that he would quit me, but whether he would prefer to do so. He was more a man of preferences than assumptions.

After breakfast, I walked downtown, arguing the probabilities *pro* and *con*. One moment I thought it would prove a miserable failure, and Bartleby would be found all alive at my office as usual; the next moment it seemed certain that I should see his chair empty. And so I kept veering about. At the corner of Broadway and Canal Street, I saw quite an excited group of people standing in earnest conversation.

"I'll take odds he doesn't," said a voice as I passed.

"Doesn't go?—done!" said I, "put up your money."

I was instinctively putting my hand in my pocket to produce my own, when I remembered that this was an election day. The words I had overheard bore no reference to Bartleby, but to the success or nonsuccess of some candidate for the mayoralty. In my intent frame of mind, I had, as it were, imagined that all Broadway shared in my excitement, and were debating the same question with me. I passed on, very thankful that the uproar of the street screened my momentary absent-mindedness.

As I had intended, I was earlier than usual at my office door. I stood listening for a moment. All was still. He must be gone. I tried the knob. The door was locked. Yes, my procedure had worked to a charm; he indeed must be vanished. Yet a certain melancholy mixed with this: I was almost sorry for my brilliant success. I was fumbling under the door mat for the key, which Bartleby was to have left there for me, when acciden-

---

[13] Personal belongings, luggage.

tally my knee knocked against a panel, producing a summoning sound, and in response a voice came to me from within—"Not yet; I am occupied."

It was Bartleby.

I was thunderstruck. For an instant I stood like the man who, pipe in mouth, was killed one cloudless afternoon long ago in Virginia, by summer lightning; at his own warm open window he was killed, and remained leaning out there upon the dreamy afternoon, till some one touched him, when he fell.

"Not gone!" I murmured at last. But again obeying the wondrous ascendancy which the inscrutable scrivener had over me, and from which ascendancy, for all my chafing, I could not completely escape, I slowly went downstairs and out into the street, and while walking round the block, considered what I should next do in this unheard-of perplexity. Turn the man out by an actual thrusting I could not; to drive him away by calling him hard names would not do; calling in the police was an unpleasant idea; and yet, permit him to enjoy his cadaverous triumph over me—this, too, I could not think of. What was to be done? or, if nothing could be done, was there anything further that I could *assume* in the matter? Yes, as before I had prospectively assumed that Bartleby would depart, so now I might retrospectively assume that departed he was. In the legitimate carrying out of this assumption, I might enter my office in a great hurry, and pretending not to see Bartleby at all, walk straight against him as if he were air. Such a proceeding would in a singular degree have the appearance of a homethrust. It was hardly possible that Bartleby could withstand such an application of the doctrine of assumptions. But upon second thoughts the success of the plan seemed rather dubious. I resolved to argue the matter over with him again.

"Bartleby," said I, entering the office, with a quietly severe expression, "I am seriously displeased. I am pained, Bartleby. I had thought better of you. I had imagined you of such a gentlemanly organization, that in any delicate dilemma a slight hint would suffice—in short, an assumption. But it appears I am deceived. Why," I added, unaffectedly starting, "you have not even touched that money yet," pointing to it, just where I had left it the evening previous.

He answered nothing.

"Will you, or will you not, quit me?" I now demanded in a sudden passion, advancing close to him.

"I would prefer *not* to quit you," he replied gently emphasizing the *not*.

"What earthly right have you to stay here? Do you pay any rent? Do you pay my taxes? Or is this property yours?"

He answered nothing.

"Are you ready to go on and write now? Are your eyes recovered? Could you copy a small paper for me this morning? or help examine a few lines? or step round to the post office? In a word, will you do anything at all, to give a coloring to your refusal to depart the premises?"

He silently retired into his hermitage.

I was now in such a state of nervous resentment that I thought it but prudent to check myself at present from further demonstrations. Bartleby and I were alone. I remembered the tragedy of the unfortunate Adams and the still more unfortunate Colt [14] in the solitary office of the latter; and how poor Colt, being dreadfully incensed by Adams, and imprudently permitting himself to get wildly excited, was at unawares

---

[14] Celebrated New York murder case in 1841. John C. Colt, brother of the famous gun manufacturer, killed Samuel Adams, a printer, with a heavy blow on the head.

hurried into his fatal act—an act which certainly no man could possibly deplore more than the actor himself. Often it had occurred to me in my ponderings upon the subject, that had that altercation taken place in the public street, or at a private residence, it would not have terminated as it did. It was the circumstance of being alone in a solitary office, up stairs, of a building entirely unhallowed by humanizing domestic associations—an uncarpeted office, doubtless, of a dusty, haggard sort of appearance—this it must have been, which greatly helped to enhance the irritable desperation of the hapless Colt.

But when this old Adam of resentment rose in me and tempted me concerning Bartleby, I grappled him and threw him. How? Why, simply by recalling the divine injunction: "A new commandment give I unto you, that ye love one another." Yes, this it was that saved me. Aside from higher considerations, charity often operates as a vastly wise and prudent principle—a great safeguard to its possessor. Men have committed murder for jealousy's sake, and anger's sake, and hatred's sake, and selfishness's sake, and spiritual pride's sake; but no man that ever I heard of, ever committed a diabolical murder for sweet charity's sake. Mere self-interest, then, if no better motive can be enlisted, should, especially with high-tempered men, prompt all beings to charity and philanthropy. At any rate, upon the occasion in question, I strove to drown my exasperated feelings towards the scrivener by benevolently construing his conduct. Poor fellow, poor fellow! thought I, he don't mean anything; and besides, he has seen hard times, and ought to be indulged.

I endeavored also immediately to occupy myself, and at the same time to comfort my despondency. I tried to fancy that in the course of the morning, at such time as might prove agreeable to him, Bartleby, of his own free accord, would emerge from his hermitage, and take up some decided line of march in the direction of the door. But no. Half-past twelve o'clock came; Turkey began to glow in the face, overturn his inkstand, and become generally obstreperous; Nippers abated down into quietude and courtesy; Ginger Nut munched his noon apple; and Bartleby remained standing at his window in one of his profoundest dead-wall reveries. Will it be credited? Ought I to acknowledge it? That afternoon I left the office without saying one further word to him.

Some days now passed, during which, at leisure intervals I looked a little into "Edwards on the Will," and "Priestly on Necessity."[15] Under the circumstances, those books induced a salutary feeling. Gradually I slid into the persuasion that these troubles of mine touching the scrivener, had been all predestinated from eternity, and Bartleby was billeted upon me for some mysterious purpose of an all-wise Providence, which it was not for a mere mortal like me to fathom. Yes, Bartleby, stay there behind your screen, thought I; I shall persecute you no more; you are harmless and noiseless as any of these old chairs; in short, I never feel so private as when I know you are here. At last I see it, I feel it; I penetrate to the predestinated purpose of my life. I am content. Others may have loftier parts to enact; but my mission in this world, Bartleby, is to furnish you with office-room for such period as you may see fit to remain.

I believe that this wise and blessed frame of mind would have continued with me, had it not been for the unsolicited and uncharitable remarks obtruded upon me by my professional friends who visited the rooms. But thus it often is, that the constant friction of illiberal minds wears out at last the best resolves of the more generous. Though to be sure, when I reflected upon it, it was not strange that people entering my office should

---

[15] New England Theologian Jonathan Edwards (1703–1758) argued in *The Freedom of the Will* (1754) that the human will is not free, but subject. Joseph Priestly (1733–1803) was an English clergyman, scientist, and philosopher who also maintained the bondage of the will.

be struck by the peculiar aspect of the unaccountable Bartleby, and so be tempted to throw out some sinister observations concerning him. Sometimes an attorney having business with me, and calling at my office, and finding no one but the scrivener there, would undertake to obtain some sort of precise information from him touching my whereabouts; but without heeding his idle talk, Bartleby would remain standing immovable in the middle of the room. So after contemplating him in that position for a time, the attorney would depart, no wiser than he came.

Also, when a Reference[16] was going on, and the room full of lawyers and witnesses and business was driving fast, some deeply occupied legal gentleman present, seeing Bartleby wholly unemployed, would request him to run round to his (the legal gentleman's) office and fetch some papers for him. Thereupon, Bartleby would tranquilly decline, and yet remain idle as before. Then the lawyer would give a great stare, and turn to me. And what could I say? At last I was made aware that all through the circle of my professional acquaintance, a whisper of wonder was running round, having reference to the strange creature I kept at my office. This worried me very much. And as the idea came upon me of his possibly turning out a long-lived man, and keep occupying my chambers, and denying my authority; and perplexing my visitors; and scandalizing my professional reputation; and casting a general gloom over the premises; keeping soul and body together to the last upon his savings (for doubtless he spent but half a dime a day), and in the end perhaps outlive me, and claim possession of my office by right of his perpetual occupancy: as all these dark anticipations crowded upon me more and more, and my friends continually intruded their relentless remarks upon the apparition in my room; a great change was wrought in me. I resolved to gather all my faculties together, and forever rid me of this intolerable incubus.

Ere resolving any complicated project, however, adapted to this end, I first simply suggested to Bartleby the propriety of his permanent departure. In a calm and serious tone, I commended the idea to his careful and mature consideration. But having taken three days to meditate upon it, he appraised me that his original determination remained the same; in short, that he still preferred to abide with me.

What shall I do? I now said to myself, buttoning up my coat to the last button. What shall I do? what ought I to do? what does conscience say I *should* do with this man, or rather ghost. Rid myself of him, I must; go, he shall. But how? You will not thrust him, the poor, pale, passive mortal—you will not thrust such a helpless creature out of your door? you will not dishonor yourself by such cruelty? No, I will not, I cannot do that. Rather would I let him live and die here, and then mason up his remains in the wall. What then will you do? For all your coaxing, he will not budge. Bribes he leaves under your own paperweight on your table; in short, it is quite plain that he prefers to cling to you.

Then something severe, something unusual must be done. What! surely you will not have him collared by a constable, and commit his innocent pallor to the common jail? And upon what ground could you procure such a thing to be done?—a vagrant, is he? What! he a vagrant, a wanderer, who refuses to budge? It is because he will *not* be a vagrant then, that you seek to count him *as* a vagrant. That is too absurd. No visible means of support: there I have him. Wrong again: for indubitably he *does* support himself, and that is the only unanswerable proof that any man can show of his possessing the means so to do. No more then. Since he will not quit me, I must quit him. I will change my offices; I will move elsewhere; and give him fair notice, that if I find him on my new premises I will then proceed against him as a common trespasser.

[16] Consultation or committee meeting.

Acting accordingly, next day I thus addressed him: "I find these chambers too far from the City Hall; the air is unwholesome. In a word, I propose to remove my offices next week, and shall no longer require your services. I tell you this now, in order that you may seek another place."

He made no reply, and nothing more was said.

On the appointed day I engaged carts and men, proceeded to my chambers, and having but little furniture, everything was removed in a few hours. Throughout, the scrivener remained standing behind the screen, which I directed to be removed the last thing. It was withdrawn; and being folded up like a huge folio, left him the motionless occupant of a naked room. I stood in the entry watching him a moment, while something from within me upbraided me.

I re-entered, with my hand in my pocket—and—and my heart in my mouth.

"Good-bye, Bartleby; I am going—good-bye, and God some way bless you; and take that," slipping something in his hand. But it dropped upon the floor, and then—strange to say—I tore myself from him whom I had so longed to be rid of.

Established in my new quarters, for a day or two I kept the door locked, and started at every footfall in the passages. When I returned to my rooms after any little absence, I would pause at the threshold for an instant, and attentively listen, ere applying my key. But these fears were needless. Bartleby never came nigh me.

I thought all was going well, when a perturbed-looking stranger visited me, inquiring whether I was the person who had recently occupied rooms at No.— Wall Street.

Full of forebodings, I replied that I was.

"Then sir," said the stranger, who proved a lawyer, "you are responsible for the man you left there. He refuses to do any copying; he refuses to do anything; he says he prefers not to; and he refuses to quit the premises."

"I am very sorry, sir," said I, with assumed tranquillity, but an inward tremor, "but, really, the man you allude to is nothing to me—he is no relation or apprentice of mine, that you should hold me responsible for him."

"In mercy's name, who is he?"

"I certainly cannot inform you. I know nothing about him. Formerly I employed him as a copyist; but he has done nothing for me now for some time past."

"I shall settle him then—good morning, sir."

Several days passed, and I heard nothing more, and though I often felt a charitable prompting to call at the place and see poor Bartleby, yet a certain squeamishness of I know not what withheld me.

All is over with him, by this time, thought I at last, when through another week no further intelligence reached me. But coming to my room the day after, I found several persons waiting at my door in a high state of nervous excitement.

"That's the man—here he comes," cried the foremost one, whom I recognized as the lawyer who had previously called upon me alone.

"You must take him away, sir, at once," cried a portly person among them, advancing upon me, and whom I knew to be the landlord of No. — Wall Street. "These gentlemen, my tenants, cannot stand it any longer; Mr. B_____" pointing to the lawyer, "has turned him out of his room, and he now persists in haunting the building generally, sitting upon the banisters of the stairs by day, and sleeping in the entry by night. Everybody is concerned; clients are leaving the offices; some fears are entertained of a mob; something you must do, and that without delay."

Aghast at this torrent, I fell back before it, and would fain have locked myself in my new quarters. In vain I persisted that Bartleby was nothing to me—no more than to anyone else. In vain—I was the last person known to have anything to do with him, and they held me to the terrible account. Fearful, then, of being exposed in the papers (as one person present obscurely threatened) I considered the matter, and at length said, that if the lawyer would give me a confidential interview with the scrivener, in his (the lawyer's) own room, I would that afternoon strive my best to rid them of the nuisance they complained of.

Going upstairs to my old haunt, there was Bartleby silently sitting upon the banister at the landing.

"What are you doing here, Bartleby?" said I.

"Sitting upon the banister," he mildly replied.

I motioned him into the lawyer's room, who then left us.

"Bartleby," said I, "are you aware that you are the cause of great tribulation to me, by persisting in occupying the entry after being dismissed from the office?"

No answer.

"Now one of two things must take place. Either you must do something, or something must be done to you. Now what sort of business would you like to engage in? Would you like to re-engage in copying for someone?"

"No; I would prefer not to make any change."

"Would you like a clerkship in a drygoods store?"

"There is too much confinement about that. No, I would not like a clerkship; but I am not particular."

"Too much confinement," I cried, "why you keep yourself confined all the time!"

"I would prefer not to take a clerkship," he rejoined, as if to settle that little item at once.

"How would a bartender's business suit you? There is no trying of eyesight in that."

"I would not like it at all; though, as I said before, I am not particular."

His unwonted wordiness inspirited me. I returned to the charge.

"Well, then, would you like to travel through the country collecting bills for the merchants? That would improve your health."

"No, I would prefer to be doing something else."

"How then would going as a companion to Europe, to entertain some young gentleman with your conversation,—how would that suit you?"

"Not at all. It does not strike me that there is anything definite about that. I like to be stationary. But I am not particular."

"Stationary you shall be then," I cried, now losing all patience, and for the first time in all my exasperating connection with him fairly flying into a passion. "If you do not go away from these premises before night, I shall feel bound—indeed I *am* bound—to—to—to quit the premises myself!" I rather absurdly concluded, knowing not with what possible threat to try to frighten his immobility into compliance. Despairing of all further efforts, I was precipitately leaving him, when a final thought occurred to me— one which had not been wholly unindulged before.

"Bartleby," said I, in the kindest tone I could assume under such exciting circumstances, "will you go home with me now—not to my office, but my dwelling—and remain there till we can conclude upon some convenient arrangement for you at our leisure? Come, let us start now, right away."

"No: at present I would prefer not to make any change at all."

I answered nothing; but, effectually dodging everyone by the suddenness and rapidity of my flight, rushed from the building, ran up Wall Street toward Broadway, and jumping into the first omnibus was soon removed from pursuit. As soon as tranquillity returned I distinctly perceived that I had now done all that I possibly could, both in respect to the demands of the landlord and his tenants, and with regard to my own desire and sense of duty, to benefit Bartleby, and shield him from rude persecution. I now strove to be entirely carefree and quiescent; and my conscience justified me in the attempt; though, indeed, it was not so successful as I could have wished. So fearful was I of being again hunted out by the incensed landlord and his exasperated tenants, that, surrendering my business to Nippers, for a few days, I drove about the upper part of the town and through the suburbs, in my rockaway; crossed over to Jersey City and Hoboken, and paid fugitive visits to Manhattanville and Astoria. In fact I almost lived in my rockaway for the time.

When again I entered my office, lo, a note from the landlord lay upon the desk. I opened it with trembling hands. It informed me that the writer had sent to the police, and had Bartleby removed to the Tombs as a vagrant. Moreover, since I knew more about him than anyone else, he wished me to appear at that place, and make a suitable statement of the facts. These tidings had a conflicting effect upon me. At first I was indignant; but at last almost approved. The landlord's energetic, summary disposition had led him to adopt a procedure which I do not think I would have decided upon myself; and yet, as a last resort, under such peculiar circumstances, it seemed the only plan.

As I afterwards learned, the poor scrivener, when told that he must be conducted to the Tombs, offered not the slightest obstacle, but in his pale unmoving way, silently acquiesced.

Some of the compassionate and curious bystanders joined the party; and headed by one of the constables arm in arm with Bartleby, the silent procession filed its way through all the noise, and heat, and joy of the roaring thoroughfares at noon.

The same day I received the note I went to the Tombs, or to speak more properly, the Halls of Justice. Seeking the right officer, I stated the purpose of my call, and was informed that the individual I described was indeed within. I then assured the functionary that Bartleby was a perfectly honest man, and greatly to be compassionated, however unaccountably eccentric. I narrated all I knew, and closed by suggesting the idea of letting him remain in as indulgent confinement as possible till something less harsh might be done—though indeed I hardly knew what. At all events, if nothing else could be decided upon, the alms-house must receive him. I then begged to have an interview.

Being under no disgraceful charge, and quite serene and harmless in all his ways, they had permitted him freely to wander about the prison, and especially in the inclosed glass-platted yards thereof. And so I found him there, standing all alone in the quietest of the yards, his face towards a high wall, while all around, from the narrow slits of the jail windows, I thought I saw peering out upon him the eyes of murderers and thieves.

"Bartleby!"

"I know you," he said, without looking round—"and I want nothing to say to you."

"It was not I that brought you here, Bartleby," said I, keenly pained at his implied suspicion. "And to you, this should not be so vile a place. Nothing reproachful attaches to you by being here. And see, it is not so sad a place as one might think. Look, there is the sky, and here is the grass."

"I know where I am," he replied, but would say nothing more, and so I left him.

As I entered the corridor again, a broad meat-like man, in an apron, accosted me, and jerking his thumb over his shoulder said—"Is that your friend?"

"Yes."

"Does he want to starve? If he does, let him live on the prison fare, that's all."

"Who are you?" asked I, not knowing what to make of such an officially-speaking person in such a place.

"I am the grub-man. Such gentlemen as have friends here, hire me to provide them with something good to eat."

"Is this so?" said I, turning to the turnkey.

He said it was.

"Well, then," said I, slipping some silver into the grub-man's hands (for so they called him). "I want you to give particular attention to my friend there; let him have the best dinner you can get. And you must be as polite to him as possible."

"Introduce me, will you?" said the grub-man, looking at me with an expression which seemed to say he was all impatience for an opportunity to give a specimen of his breeding.

Thinking it would prove of benefit to the scrivener, I acquiesced; and asking the grub-man his name, went up with him to Bartleby.

"Bartleby, this is a friend; you will find him very useful to you."

"Your sarvant, sir, your sarvant," said the grub-man, making a low salutation behind his apron. "Hope you find it pleasant here, sir—nice grounds—cool apartments—hope you'll stay with us some time—try to make it agreeable. What will you have for dinner to-day?"

"I prefer not to dine today," said Bartleby, turning away. "It would disagree with me; I am unused to dinners." So saying he slowly moved to the other side of the inclosure, and took up a position fronting the dead-wall.

"How's this?" said the grub-man, addressing me with a stare of astonishment. "He's odd, ain't he?"

"I think he is a little deranged," said I, sadly.

"Deranged? deranged is it? Well now, upon my word, I thought that friend of yourn was a gentleman forger; they are always pale and genteel-like, them forgers. I can't help pity 'em—can't help it, sir. Did you know Monroe Edwards?" he added touchingly, and paused. Then, laying his hand piteously on my shoulder, sighed, "he died of consumption at Sing Sing. So you weren't acquainted with Monroe?"

"No, I was never socially acquainted with any forgers. But I cannot stop longer. Look to my friend yonder. You will not lose by it. I will see you again."

Some few days after this, I again obtained admission to the Tombs, and went through the corridors in quest of Bartleby; but without finding him.

"I saw him coming from his cell not long ago," said a turnkey, "maybe he's gone to loiter in the yards."

So I went in that direction.

"Are you looking for the silent man?" said another turnkey, passing me. "Yonder he lies—sleeping in the yard there. 'Tis not twenty minutes since I saw him lie down."

The yard was entirely quiet. It was not accessible to the common prisoners. The surrounding walls, of amazing thickness, kept off all sounds behind them. The Egyptian character of the masonry weighed upon me with its gloom. But a soft imprisoned turf grew under foot. The heart of the eternal pyramids, it seemed, wherein, by some strange magic, through the clefts, grass-seed, dropped by birds, had sprung.

Strangely huddled at the base of the wall, his knees drawn up, and lying by his side, his head touching the cold stones, I saw the wasted Bartleby. But nothing stirred. I paused; then went close up to him; stooped over, and saw that his dim eyes were open; otherwise he seemed profoundly sleeping. Something prompted me to touch him. I felt his hand, when a tingling shiver ran up my arm and down my spine to my feet.

The round face of the grub-man peered upon me now. "His dinner is ready. Won't he dine to-day, either? Or does he live without dining?"

"Lives without dining," said I, and closed the eyes.

"Eh!—He's asleep, ain't he?"

"With kings and counsellors,"[17] murmured I.

There would seem little need for proceeding further in this history. Imagination will readily supply the meager recital of poor Bartleby's interment. But, ere parting with the reader, let me say, that if this little narrative has sufficiently interested him, to awaken curiosity as to who Bartleby was, and what manner of life he led prior to the present narrator's making his acquaintance, I can only reply, that in such curiosity I fully share, but am wholly unable to gratify it. Yet here I hardly know whether I should divulge one little item of rumor, which came to my ear a few months after the scrivener's decease. Upon what basis it rested, I could never ascertain; and hence, how true it is I cannot now tell. But inasmuch as this vague report has not been without a certain suggestive interest to me, however sad, it may prove the same with others; and so I will briefly mention it. The report was this: that Bartleby had been a subordinate clerk in the Dead Letter Office at Washington, from which he had been suddenly removed by a change in the administration. When I think over this rumor, I cannot adequately express the emotions which seize me. Dead letters! does it not sound like dead men? Conceive a man by nature and misfortune prone to a pallid hopelessness, can any business seem more fitted to heighten it than that of continually handling these dead letters, and assorting them for the flames? For by the cartload they are annually burned. Sometimes from out the folded paper the pale clerk takes a ring:—the finger it was meant for, perhaps, molders in the grave; a banknote sent in swiftest charity—he whom it would relieve, nor eats nor hungers any more; pardon for those who died despairing; hope for those who died unhoping; good tidings for those who died stifled by unrelieved calamities. On errands of life, these letters speed to death.

Ah, Bartleby! Ah, humanity!

---

[17] See *Job* 3:13–14: ". . . then had I been at rest, With kings and counsellors of the earth, which built desolate places for themselves."

Gustave Flaubert (1821–1880)

Flaubert led a singularly uneventful life, except in a literary sense. As a result of a nervous seizure (then diagnosed as epilepsy) in 1844, he retired as a young man to the little Normandy town of Le Croisset and there lived almost as a hermit, devoting himself to writing. Being a man of means, he did not have to rush into print, and his friends dissuaded him from publishing his first efforts—which were in a romantic and semi-autobiographic vein, like his later-published *Salammbô* (1862) and *La Tentation de Saint-Antoine* (1874). They urged him to turn from romance to realism: to turn from fictionalizing a dim past and his own fantasies to the everyday, bourgeois life of a Normandy town. The result was *Madame Bovary* (1857), a novel that made him famous and infamous at once. Though Flaubert was bourgeois himself, he hated the commercialism, vulgarity, and prudery of his own class; and some members of that class saw in the book's realism only "a heap of manure," and sued him for immorality. But others, more discerning, hailed the book as a masterpiece, and it established Flaubert as a seminal influence on later writers. As the poet Allen Tate has said, Flaubert "created modern fiction." His attention to style, to *le mot juste,* to precisely observed detail, set a standard of perfection in fiction that permitted critics thereafter to think of the novel as an art form (as had not been the case before). Baudelaire, imaginatively reconstructing what went on in Flaubert's mind as he composed the book, wrote:

> We shall employ a style that is terse, vivid, subtle, and exact on a subject that is banal. We shall imprison the most burning and passionate feelings within the most commonplace intrigue. The most solemn utterances will come from the most imbecile mouths.

These same effects are all apparent in the short novel "A Simple Heart," that appeared in *Trois Contes* in 1876. But, style apart, there is warmth and humanity here which the polished, perhaps too polished, *Madame Bovary* lacks. Though Flaubert was a furious anti-democrat and snob and could write (in a time of radical change), "I detest my fellow-beings and do not feel that I am their fellow at all," these feelings seem muted in the story. In the ancient serving-woman Félicité, whose life is almost as eventless as Flaubert's own, he finds a nobility beyond the reach of the corrupted middle classes. Yet even here, Flaubert holds Félicité at a great distance, as a specimen, an object to be pitied—which is to say he also holds himself at a great distance, detached. "The artist," he writes, "ought not to appear in his work any more than God in nature." Flaubert does not moralize, he lets the tale speak for itself; and in the emblem (see pp. 21–22) of the parrot, literally the one bright spot in Félicité's gray and exploited life, we both enter the dignity of her suffering and transcend it—until at the end the bird has become for her (and for us) a religious symbol, almost literally a bird of paradise.

But if there is something self-effacing in Flaubert's furious perfectionism, there is also something nihilistic: "What seems beautiful to me," he writes, "what I should like to write, is a book about nothing, a book dependent on nothing external, which would be held together by the strength of its style, just as the earth, suspended in the void, depends on nothing external for its support. . . ." "A Simple Heart" is not that book, but it is interesting that this master of realism should come so close to voicing the credo of the anti-realists with which this collection ends. Flaubert to the last was a conflicted man, as seen in his effort to make his prose "as rhythmical as verse and as precise as the language of science." The "epilepsy" that visited him as a youth plagued him all his life; he died suddenly in 1880, apparently of a cerebral hemorrhage.

A Simple Heart

1

For half a century the women of Pont-l'Évêque envied Mme Aubain her maidservant Félicité.

In return for a hundred francs a year she did all the cooking and the housework, the sewing, the washing, and the ironing. She could bridle a horse, fatten poultry, and churn butter, and she remained faithful to her mistress, who was by no means an easy person to get on with.

Mme Aubain had married a young fellow who was goodlooking but badly-off, and who died at the beginning of 1809, leaving her with two small children and a pile of debts. She then sold all her property except for the farms of Toucques and Geffosses, which together brought in five thousand francs a year at the most, and left her house at Saint-Melaine for one behind the covered market which was cheaper to run and had belonged to her family.

This house had a slate roof and stood between an alley-way and a lane leading down to the river. Inside there were differences in level which were the cause of many a stumble. A narrow entrance-hall separated the kitchen from the parlour, where Mme Aubain sat all day long in a wicker easy-chair by the window. Eight mahogany chairs were lined up against the white-painted wainscoting, and under the barometer stood an old piano loaded with a pyramid of boxes and cartons. On either side of the chimney-piece, which was carved out of yellow marble in the Louis Quinze style, there was a tapestry-covered arm-chair, and in the middle was a clock designed to look like a temple of Vesta.[1] The whole room smelt a little musty, as the floor was on a lower level than the garden.

On the first floor was 'Madame's' bedroom—very spacious, with a patterned wallpaper of pale flowers and a portrait of 'Monsieur' dressed in what had once been the height of fashion. It opened into a smaller room in which there were two cots, without mattresses. Then came the drawing-room, which was always shut up and full of furniture covered with dust-sheets. Next there was a passage leading to the study, where books and papers filled the shelves of a book-case in three sections built round a big writing-table of dark wood. The two end panels were hidden under pen-and-ink drawings, landscapes in gouache, and etchings by Audran,[2] souvenirs of better days and bygone luxury. On the second floor a dormer window gave light to Félicité's room, which looked out over the fields.

Every day Félicité got up at dawn, so as not to miss Mass, and worked until evening without stopping. Then, once dinner was over, the plates and dishes put away, and the door bolted, she piled ashes on the log fire and went to sleep in front of the hearth, with her rosary in her hands. Nobody could be more stubborn when it came to haggling over prices, and as for cleanliness, the shine on her saucepans was the despair of all the other servants. Being of a thrifty nature, she ate slowly, picking up from the table the crumbs from her loaf of bread—a twelve pound loaf which was baked specially for her and lasted twenty days.

All the year round she wore a kerchief of printed calico fastened behind with a pin, a bonnet which covered her hair, grey stockings, a red skirt, and over her jacket a bibbed apron such as hospital nurses wear.

Her face was thin and her voice was sharp. At twenty-five she was often taken for forty; once she reached fifty, she stopped looking any age in particular. Always silent and upright and deliberate in her movements, she looked like a wooden doll driven by clock-work.

2

Like everyone else, she had had her love-story.

Her father, a mason, had been killed when he fell off some scaffolding. Then her mother died, and when her sisters went their separate ways, a farmer took her in, sending her, small as she was, to look after the cows out in the fields. She went about in

---

[1] The Roman goddess of the hearth and the hearth fire. In her temple a fire was tended by the vestal virgins.

[2] Probably by Gérard or Jean Audran (1640–1703) (1667–1756), members of an illustrious family of French engravers.

rags, shivering with cold, used to lie flat on the ground to drink water out of the ponds, would be beaten for no reason at all, and was finally turned out of the house for stealing thirty sous, a theft of which she was innocent. She found work at another farm, looking after the poultry, and as she was liked by her employers the other servants were jealous of her.

One August evening—she was eighteen at the time—they took her off to the fête at Colleville. From the start she was dazed and bewildered by the noise of the fiddles, the lamps in the trees, the medley of gaily coloured dresses, the gold crosses and lace, and the throng of people jigging up and down. She was standing shyly on one side when a smart young fellow, who had been leaning on the shaft of a cart, smoking his pipe, came up and asked her to dance. He treated her to cider, coffee, girdle-cake, and a silk neckerchief, and imagining that she knew what he was after, offered to see her home. At the edge of a field of oats, he pushed her roughly to the ground. Thoroughly frightened, she started screaming for help. He took to his heels.

Another night, on the road to Beaumont, she tried to get past a big, slow-moving waggon loaded with hay, and as she was squeezing by she recognized Théodore.

He greeted her quite calmly, saying that she must forgive him for the way he had behaved to her, as 'it was the drink that did it'.

She did not know what to say in reply and felt like running off.

Straight away he began talking about the crops and the notabilities of the commune, saying that his father had left Colleville for the farm at Les Écots, so that they were now neighbours.

'Ah!' she said.

He added that his family wanted to see him settle but that he was in no hurry and was waiting to find a wife to suit his fancy. She lowered her head. Then he asked her if she was thinking of getting married. She answered with a smile that it was mean of him to make fun of her.

'But I'm not making fun of you!' he said. 'I swear I'm not!'

He put his left arm round her waist, and she walked on supported by his embrace. Soon they slowed down. There was a gentle breeze blowing, the stars were shining, the huge load of hay was swaying about in front of them, and the four horses were raising clouds of dust as they shambled along. Then, without being told, they turned off to the right. He kissed her once more and she disappeared into the darkness.

The following week Théodore got her to grant him several rendezvous.

They would meet at the bottom of a farm-yard, behind a wall, under a solitary tree. She was not ignorant of life as young ladies are, for the animals had taught her a great deal; but her reason and an instinctive sense of honour prevented her from giving way. The resistance she put up inflamed Théodore's passion to such an extent that in order to satisfy it (or perhaps out of sheer naïvety) he proposed to her. At first she refused to believe him, but he swore that he was serious.

Soon afterwards he had a disturbing piece of news to tell her: the year before, his parents had paid a man to do his military service for him, but now he might be called up again any day, and the idea of going into the army frightened him. In Félicité's eyes this cowardice of his appeared to be proof of his affection, and she loved him all the more for it. Every night she would steal out to meet him, and every night Théodore would plague her with his worries and entreaties.

In the end he said that he was going to the Prefecture himself to make inquiries, and that he would come and tell her how matters stood the following Sunday, between eleven and midnight.

At the appointed hour she hurried to meet her sweetheart, but found one of his friends waiting for her instead.

He told her that she would not see Théodore again. To make sure of avoiding conscription, he had married a very rich old woman, Mme Lehoussais of Toucques.

Her reaction was an outburst of frenzied grief. She threw herself on the ground, screaming and calling on God, and lay moaning all alone in the open until sunrise. Then she went back to the farm and announced her intention of leaving. At the end of the month, when she had received her wages, she wrapped her small belongings up in a kerchief and made her way to Pont-l'Évêque.

In front of the inn there, she sought information from a woman in a widow's bonnet, who, as it happened, was looking for a cook. The girl did not know much about cooking, but she seemed so willing and expected so little that finally Mme Aubain ended up by saying: 'Very well, I will take you on.'

A quarter of an hour later Félicité was installed in her house.

At first she lived there in a kind of fearful awe caused by 'the style of the house' and the memory of 'Monsieur' brooding over everything. Paul and Virginie, the boy aged seven and the girl barely four, seemed to her to be made of some precious substance. She used to carry them about pick-a-back, and when Mme Aubain told her not to keep on kissing them she was cut to the quick. All the same, she was happy now, for her pleasant surroundings had dispelled her grief.

On Thursdays, a few regular visitors came in to play Boston, and Félicité got the cards and the footwarmers ready beforehand. They always arrived punctually at eight, and left before the clock struck eleven.

Every Monday morning the second-hand dealer who lived down the alley put all his junk out on the pavement. Then the hum of voices began to fill the town, mingled with the neighing of horses, the bleating of lambs, the grunting of pigs, and the rattle of carts in the streets.

About midday, when the market was in full swing, a tall old peasant with a hooked nose and his cap on the back of his head would appear at the door. This was Robelin, the farmer from Geffosses. A little later, and Liébard, the farmer from Toucques, would arrive—a short, fat, red-faced fellow in a grey jacket and leather gaiters fitted with spurs.

Both men had hens or cheeses they wanted to sell to 'Madame'. But Félicité was up to all their tricks and invariably outwitted them, so that they went away full of respect for her.

From time to time Mme Aubain had a visit from an uncle of hers, the Marquis de Grémanville, who had been ruined by loose living and was now living at Falaise on his last remaining scrap of property. He always turned up at lunch-time, accompanied by a hideous poodle who dirtied all the furniture with its paws. However hard he tried to behave like a gentleman, even going so far as to raise his hat every time he mentioned 'my late father', the force of habit was usually too much for him, for he would start pouring himself one glass after another and telling bawdy stories. Félicité used to push him gently out of the house, saying politely: 'You've had quite enough, Monsieur de Grémanville. See you another time!' and shutting the door on him.

She used to open it with pleasure to M. Bourais, who was a retired solicitor. His white tie and his bald head, his frilled shirt-front and his ample brown frock-coat, the way he had of rounding his arm to take a pinch of snuff, and indeed everything about him made an overwhelming impression on her such as we feel when we meet some outstanding personality.

As he looked after 'Madame's' property, he used to shut himself up with her for hours in 'Monsieur's' study. He lived in dread of compromising his reputation, had a tremendous respect for the Bench, and laid claim to some knowledge of Latin.

To give the children a little painless instruction, he made them a present of a geography book with illustrations. These represented scenes in different parts of the world, such as cannibals wearing feather head-dresses, a monkey carrying off a young lady, Bedouins in the desert, a whale being harpooned, and so on.

Paul explained these pictures to Félicité, and that indeed was all the education she ever had. As for the children, they were taught by Guyot, a poor devil employed at the Town Hall, who was famous for his beautiful handwriting, and who had a habit of sharpening his penknife on his boots.

When the weather was fine the whole household used to set off early for a day on the Geffosses farm.

The farm-yard there was on a slope, with the house in the middle; and the sea, in the distance, looked like a streak of grey. Félicité would take some slices of cold meat out of her basket, and they would have their lunch in a room adjoining the dairy. It was all that remained of a country house which had fallen into ruin, and the wallpaper hung in shreds, fluttering in the draught. Mme Aubain used to sit with bowed head, absorbed in her memories, so that the children were afraid to talk. 'Why don't you run along and play?' she would say, and away they went.

Paul climbed up into the barn, caught birds, played ducks and drakes on the pond, or banged with a stick on the great casks, which sounded just like drums.

Virginie fed the rabbits, or scampered off to pick cornflowers, showing her little embroidered knickers as she ran.

One autumn evening they came home through the fields. The moon, which was in its first quarter, lit up part of the sky, and there was some mist floating like a scarf over the winding Toucques. The cattle, lying out in the middle of the pasture, looked peacefully at the four people walking by. In the third field a few got up and made a half circle in front of them.

'Don't be frightened!' said Félicité, and crooning softly, she stroked the back of the nearest animal. It turned about and the others did the same. But while they were crossing the next field they suddenly heard a dreadful bellowing. It came from a bull which had been hidden by the mist, and which now came towards the two women.

Mme Aubain started to run.

'No! No!' said Félicité. 'Not so fast!'

All the same they quickened their pace, hearing behind them a sound of heavy breathing which came nearer and nearer. The bull's hooves thudded like hammers on the turf, and they realized that it had broken into a gallop. Turning round, Félicité tore up some clods of earth and flung them at its eyes. It lowered its muzzle and thrust its horns forward, trembling with rage and bellowing horribly.

By now Mme Aubain had got to the end of the field with her two children and was frantically looking for a way over the high bank. Félicité was still backing away from the bull, hurling clods of turf which blinded it, and shouting: 'Hurry! Hurry!'

Mme Aubain got down into the ditch, pushed first Virginie and then Paul up the other side, fell once or twice trying to climb the bank, and finally managed it with a valiant effort.

The bull had driven Félicité back against a gate, and its slaver was spurting into her face. In another second it would have gored her, but she just had time to slip between two of the bars, and the great beast halted in amazement.

This adventure was talked about at Pont-l'Évêque for a good many years, but Félicité never prided herself in the least on what she had done, as it never occurred to her that she had done anything heroic.

Virginie claimed all her attention, for the fright had affected the little girl's nerves, and M. Poupart, the doctor, recommended sea-bathing at Trouville.

In those days the resort had few visitors. Mme Aubain made inquiries, consulted Bourais, and got everything ready as though for a long journey.

Her luggage went off in Liébard's cart the day before she left. The next morning he brought along two horses, one of which had a woman's saddle with a velvet back, while the other carried a cloak rolled up to make a kind of seat on its crupper. Mme Aubain sat on this, with Liébard in front. Félicité looked after Virginie on the other horse, and Paul mounted M. Lechaptois's donkey, which he had lent them on condition they took great care of it.

The road was so bad that it took two hours to travel the five miles to Toucques. The horses sank into the mud up to their pasterns and had to jerk their hind-quarters to get out; often they stumbled in the ruts, or else they had to jump. In some places, Liébard's mare came to a sudden stop, and while he waited patiently for her to move off again, he talked about the people whose properties bordered the road, adding moral reflexions to each story. For instance, in the middle of Toucques, as they were passing underneath some windows set in a mass of nasturtiums, he shrugged his shoulders and said:

'There's a Madame Lehoussais lives here. Now instead of taking a young man, she . . .'

Félicité did not hear the rest, for the horses had broken into a trot and the donkey was galloping along. All three turned down a bridle-path, a gate swung open, a couple of boys appeared, and everyone dismounted in front of a manure-heap right outside the farm-house door.

Old Mother Liébard welcomed her mistress with every appearance of pleasure. She served up a sirloin of beef for lunch, with tripe and black pudding, a fricassee of chicken, sparkling cider, a fruit tart and brandy-plums, garnishing the whole meal with compliments to Madame, who seemed to be enjoying better health, to Mademoiselle, who had turned into a 'proper little beauty', and to Monsieur Paul, who had 'filled out a lot'. Nor did she forget their deceased grandparents, whom the Liébards had known personally, having been in the family's service for several generations.

Like its occupants, the farm had an air of antiquity. The ceiling-beams were worm-eaten, the walls black with smoke, and the window-panes grey with dust. There was an oak dresser laden with all sorts of odds and ends—jugs, plates, pewter bowls, wolf-traps, sheep-shears, and an enormous syringe which amused the children. In the three yards outside there was not a single tree without either mushrooms at its base or mistletoe in its branches. Several had been blown down and had taken root again in the middle; all of them were bent under the weight of their apples. The thatched roofs, which looked like brown velvet and varied in thickness, weathered the fiercest winds, but the cart-shed was tumbling down. Mme Aubain said that she would have it seen to, and ordered the animals to be reharnessed.

It took them another half-hour to reach Trouville. The little caravan dismounted to make their way along the Écores, a cliff jutting right out over the boats moored below; and three minutes later they got to the end of the quay and entered the courtyard of the Golden Lamb, the inn kept by Mère David.

After the first few days Virginie felt stronger, as a result of the change of air and the sea-bathing. Not having a costume, she went into the water in her chemise and her maid dressed her afterwards in a customs officer's hut which was used by the bathers.

In the afternoons they took the donkey and went off beyond the Roches-Noires, in the direction of Hennequeville. To begin with, the path went uphill between gentle slopes like the lawns in a park, and then came out on a plateau where pastureland and ploughed fields alternated. On either side there were holly-bushes standing out from the tangle of brambles, and here and there a big dead tree spread its zigzag branches against the blue sky.

They almost always rested in the same field, with Deauville on their left, Le Havre on their right, and the open sea in front. The water glittered in the sunshine, smooth as a mirror, and so still that the murmur it made was scarcely audible; unseen sparrows could be heard twittering, and the sky covered the whole scene with its huge canopy. Mme Aubain sat doing her needlework, Virginie plaited rushes beside her, Félicité gathered lavender, and Paul, feeling profoundly bored, longed to get up and go.

Sometimes they crossed the Touques in a boat and hunted for shells. When the tide went out, sea-urchins, ormers,[3] and jelly-fish were left behind; and the children scampered around, snatching at the foam-flakes carried on the wind. The sleepy waves, breaking on the sand, spread themselves out along the shore. The beach stretched as far as the eye could see, bounded on the land side by the dunes which separated it from the Marais, a broad meadow in the shape of an arena. When they came back that way, Trouville, on the distant hillside, grew bigger at every step, and with its medley of oddly assorted houses seemed to blossom out in gay disorder.

On exceptionally hot days they stayed in their room. The sun shone in dazzling bars of light between the slats of the blind. There was not a sound to be heard in the village, and not a soul to be seen down in the street. Everything seemed more peaceful in the prevailing silence. In the distance caulkers were hammering away at the boats, and the smell of tar was wafted along by a sluggish breeze.

The principal amusement consisted in watching the fishingboats come in. As soon as they had passed the buoys, they started tacking. With their canvas partly lowered and their foresails blown out like balloons they glided through the splashing waves as far as the middle of the harbour, where they suddenly dropped anchor. Then each boat came alongside the quay, and the crew threw ashore their catch of quivering fish. A line of carts stood waiting, and women in cotton bonnets rushed forward to take the baskets and kiss their men.

One day one of these women spoke to Félicité, who came back to the inn soon after in a state of great excitement. She explained that she had found one of her sisters—and Nastasie Barette, now Leroux, made her appearance, with a baby at her breast, another child holding her right hand, and on her left a little sailor-boy, his arms akimbo and his cap over one ear.

Mme Aubain sent her off after a quarter of an hour. From then on they were forever hanging round the kitchen or loitering about when the family went for a walk, though the husband kept out of sight.

Félicité became quite attached to them. She bought them a blanket, several shirts, and a stove; and it was clear that they were bent on getting all they could out of her.

This weakness of hers annoyed Mme Aubain, who in any event disliked the familiar way in which the nephew spoke to Paul. And so, as Virginie had started coughing and the good weather was over, she decided to go back to Pont-l'Évêque.

M. Bourais advised her on the choice of a school; Caen was considered the best, so it was there that Paul was sent. He said good-bye bravely, feeling really rather pleased to be going to a place where he would have friends of his own.

Mme Aubain resigned herself to the loss of her son, knowing that it was unavoid-

---

[3] From French *orielle de mer,* ear of the sea; an abalone shell.

able. Virginie soon got used to it. Félicité missed the din he used to make, but she was given something new to do which served as a distraction: from Christmas onwards she had to take the little girl to catechism every day.

3

After genuflecting at the door, she walked up the centre aisle under the nave, opened the door of Mme Aubain's pew, sat down, and started looking about her.

The choir stalls were all occupied, with the boys on the right and the girls on the left, while the curé stood by the lectern. In one of the stained-glass windows in the apse the Holy Ghost looked down on the Virgin; another window showed her kneeling before the Infant Jesus; and behind the tabernacle there was a wood-carving of St. Michael slaying the dragon.

The priest began with a brief outline of sacred history. Listening to him, Félicité saw in imagination the Garden of Eden, the Flood, the Tower of Babel, cities burning, peoples dying, and idols being overthrown; and this dazzling vision left her with a great respect for the Almighty and profound fear of His wrath.

Then she wept as she listened to the story of the Passion. Why had they crucified Him, when He loved children, fed the multitudes, healed the blind, and had chosen out of humility to be born among the poor, on the litter of a stable? The sowing of the seed, the reaping of the harvest, the pressing of the grapes—all those familiar things of which the Gospels speak had their place in her life. God had sanctified them in passing, so that she loved the lambs more tenderly for love of the Lamb of God, and the doves for the sake of the Holy Ghost.

She found it difficult, however, to imagine what the Holy Ghost looked like, for it was not just a bird but a fire as well, and sometimes a breath. She wondered whether that was its light she had seen flitting about the edge of the marshes at night, whether that was its breath she had felt driving the clouds across the sky, whether that was its voice she had heard in the sweet music of the bells. And she sat in silent adoration, delighting in the coolness of the walls and the quiet of the church.

Of dogma she neither understood nor even tried to understand anything. The curé discoursed, the children repeated their lesson, and she finally dropped off to sleep, waking up suddenly at the sound of their sabots clattering across the flagstones as they left the church.

It was in this manner, simply by hearing it expounded, that she learnt her catechism, for her religious education had been neglected in her youth. From then on she copied all Virginie's observances, fasting when she did and going to confession with her. On the feast of Corpus Christi the two of them made an altar of repose together.

The preparations for Virginie's first communion caused her great anxiety. She worried over her shoes, her rosary, her missal, and her gloves. And how she trembled as she helped Mme Aubain to dress the child!

All through the Mass her heart was in her mouth. One side of the choir was hidden from her by M. Bourais, but directly opposite her she could see the flock of maidens, looking like a field of snow with their white crowns perched on top of their veils; and she recognized her little darling from a distance by her dainty neck and her rapt attitude. The bell tinkled. Every head bowed low, and there was a silence. Then, to the thunderous accompaniment of the organ, choir and congregation joined in singing the *Agnus Dei*. Next the boys' procession began, and after that the girls got up from their seats. Slowly, their hands joined in prayer, they went towards the brightly lit altar, knelt on the first step, received the Host one by one, and went back to their places in the same order.

When it was Virginie's turn, Félicité leant forward to see her, and in one of those imaginative flights born of real affection, it seemed to her that she herself was in the child's place. Virginie's face became her own. Virginie's dress clothed her, Virginie's heart was beating in her breast; and as she closed her eyes and opened her mouth, she almost fainted away.

Early next morning she went to the sacristy and asked M. le Curé to give her communion. She received the sacrament with all due reverence, but did not feel the same rapture as she had the day before.

Mme Aubain wanted her daughter to possess every accomplishment, and since Guyot could not teach her English or music, she decided to send her as a boarder to the Ursuline Convent at Honfleur.

Virginie raised no objection, but Félicité went about sighing at Madame's lack of feeling. Then she thought that perhaps her mistress was right: such matters, after all, lay outside her province.

Finally the day arrived when an old waggonette stopped at their door, and a nun got down from it who had come to fetch Mademoiselle. Félicité hoisted the luggage up on top, gave the driver some parting instructions, and put six pots of jam, a dozen pears, and a bunch of violets in the boot.

At the last moment Virginie burst into a fit of sobbing. She threw her arms round her mother, who kissed her on the forehead, saying: 'Come now, be brave, be brave.' The step was pulled up and the carriage drove away.

Then Mme Aubain broke down, and that evening all her friends, M. and Mme Lormeau, Mme Lechaptois, the Rochefeuille sisters, M. de Houppeville, and Bourais, came in to console her.

To begin with she missed her daughter badly. But she had a letter from her three times a week, wrote back on the other days, walked round her garden, did a little reading, and thus contrived to fill the empty hours.

As for Félicité, she went into Virginie's room every morning from sheer force of habit and looked round it. It upset her not having to brush the child's hair any more, tie her bootlaces, or tuck her up in bed; and she missed seeing her sweet face all the time and holding her hand when they went out together. For want of something to do, she tried making lace, but her fingers were too clumsy and broke the threads. She could not settle to anything, lost her sleep, and, to use her own words, was 'eaten up inside.'

To 'occupy her mind', she asked if her nephew Victor might come and see her, and permission was granted.

He used to arrive after Mass on Sunday, his cheeks flushed, his chest bare, and smelling of the countryside through which he had come. She laid a place for him straight away, opposite hers, and they had lunch together. Eating as little as possible herself, in order to save the expense, she stuffed him so full of food that he fell asleep after the meal. When the first bell for vespers rang, she woke him up, brushed his trousers, tied his tie, and set off for church, leaning on his arm with all a mother's pride.

His parents always told him to get something out of her—a packet of brown sugar perhaps, some soap, or a little brandy, sometimes even money. He brought her his clothes to be mended, and she did the work gladly, thankful for anything that would force him to come again.

In August his father took him on a coasting trip. The children's holidays were just beginning, and it cheered her up to have them home again. But Paul was turning capricious and Virginie was getting too old to be addressed familiarly—a state of affairs which put a barrier of constraint between them.

Victor went to Morlaix, Dunkirk, and Brighton in turn, and brought her a present after each trip. The first time it was a box covered with shells, the second a coffee cup, the third a big gingerbread man. He was growing quite handsome, with his trim figure, his little moustache, his frank open eyes, and the little leather cap that he wore on the back of his head like a pilot. He kept her amused by telling her stories full of nautical jargon.

One Monday—it was the fourteenth of July 1819, a date she never forgot—Victor told her that he had signed on for an ocean voyage, and that on the Wednesday night he would be taking the Honfleur packet to join his schooner, which was due to sail shortly from Le Havre. He might be away, he said, for two years.

The prospect of such a long absence made Félicité extremely unhappy, and she felt she must bid him godspeed once more. So on the Wednesday evening, when Madame's dinner was over, she put on her clogs and swiftly covered the ten miles between Pont-l'Évêque and Honfleur.

When she arrived at the Calvary she turned right instead of left, got lost in the shipyards, and had to retrace her steps. Some people she spoke to advised her to hurry. She went right round the harbour, which was full of boats, constantly tripping over moorings. Then the ground fell away, rays of light criss-crossed in front of her, and for a moment, she thought she was going mad, for she could see horses up in the sky.

On the quayside more horses were neighing, frightened by the sea. A derrick was hoisting them into the air and dropping them into one of the boats, which was already crowded with passengers elbowing their way between barrels of cider, baskets of cheese, and sacks of grain. Hens were cackling and the captain swearing, while a cabin-boy stood leaning on the cats-head, completely indifferent to it all. Félicité, who had not recognized him, shouted: 'Victor!' and he raised his head. She rushed forward, but at that very moment the gangway was pulled ashore.

The packet moved out of the harbour with women singing as they hauled it along, its ribs creaking and heavy waves lashing its bows. The sail swung round, hiding everyone on board from view, and against the silvery, moonlit sea the boat appeared as a dark shape that grew ever fainter, until at last it vanished in the distance.

As Félicité was passing the Calvary, she felt a longing to commend to God's mercy all that she held most dear; and she stood there praying for a long time, her face bathed in tears, her eyes fixed upon the clouds. The town was asleep, except for the customs officers walking up and down. Water was pouring ceaselessly through the holes in the sluice-gate, making as much noise as a torrent. The clocks struck two.

The convent parlour would not be open before daybreak, and Madame would be annoyed if she were late; so, although she would have liked to give a kiss to the other child, she set off for home. The maids at the inn were just waking up as she got to Pont-l'Évêque.

So the poor lad was going to be tossed by the waves for months on end! His previous voyages had caused her no alarm. People came back from England and Brittany; but America, the Colonies, the Islands, were all so far away, somewhere at the other end of the world.

From then on Félicité thought of nothing but her nephew. On sunny days she hoped he was not too thirsty, and when there was a storm she was afraid he would be struck by lightning. Listening to the wind howling in the chimney or blowing slates off the roof, she saw him being buffeted by the very same storm, perched on the top of a broken mast, with his whole body bent backwards under a sheet of foam; or again—and these were reminiscences of the illustrated geography-book—he was being eaten by savages, captured by monkeys in the forest, or dying on a desert shore. But she never spoke of her worries.

Mme Aubain had worries of her own about her daughter. The good nuns said that she was an affectionate child, but very delicate. The slightest emotion upset her, and she had to give up playing the piano.

Her mother insisted on regular letters from the convent. One morning when the postman had not called, she lost patience and walked up and down the room, between her chair and the window. It was really extraordinary! Four days without any news!

Thinking her own example would comfort her, Félicité said:

'I've been six months, Madame, without news.'

'News of whom?'

The servant answered gently:

'Why—of my nephew.'

'Oh, your nephew!' And Mme Aubain started pacing up and down again, with a shrug of her shoulders that seemed to say: 'I wasn't thinking of him—and indeed, why should I? Who cares about a young, good-for-nothing cabin-boy? Whereas my daughter—why, just think!'

Although she had been brought up the hard way, Félicité was indignant with Madame, but she soon forgot. It struck her as perfectly natural to lose one's head where the little girl was concerned. For her, the two children were of equal importance; they were linked together in her heart by a single bond, and their destinies should be the same.

The chemist told her that Victor's ship had arrived at Havana: he had seen this piece of information in a newspaper.

Because of its association with cigars, she imagined Havana as a place where nobody did anything but smoke, and pictured Victor walking about among crowds of Negroes in a cloud of tobacco-smoke. Was it possible, she wondered, 'in case of need' to come back by land? And how far was it from Pont-l'Évêque? To find out she asked M. Bourais.

He reached for his atlas, and launched forth into an explanation of latitudes and longitudes, smiling like the pedant he was at Félicité's bewilderment. Finally he pointed with his pencil at a minute black dot inside a ragged oval patch, saying:

'There it is.'

She bent over the map, but the network of coloured lines meant nothing to her and only tired her eyes. So when Bourais asked her to tell him what was puzzling her, she begged him to show her the house where Victor was living. He threw up his hands, sneezed, and roared with laughter, delighted to come across such simplicity. And Félicité—whose intelligence was so limited that she probably expected to see an actual portrait of her nephew—could not make out why he was laughing.

It was a fortnight later that Liébard came into the kitchen at market-time, as he usually did, and handed her a letter from her brother-in-law. As neither of them could read, she turned to her mistress for help.

Mme Aubain, who was counting the stitches in her knitting, put it down and unsealed the letter. She gave a start, and, looking hard at Félicité, said quietly:

'They have some bad news for you . . . Your nephew . . .'

He was dead. That was all the letter had to say.

Félicité dropped on to a chair, leaning her head against the wall and closing her eyelids, which suddenly turned pink. Then, with her head bowed, her hands dangling, and her eyes set, she kept repeating:

'Poor little lad! Poor little lad!'

Liébard looked at her and sighed. Mme Aubain was trembling slightly. She suggested that she should go and see her sister at Trouville, but Félicité shook her head to indicate that there was no need for that.

There was a silence. Old Liébard thought it advisable to go.

Then Félicité said:

'It doesn't matter a bit, not to them it doesn't.'

Her head fell forward again, and from time to time she unconsciously picked up the knitting needles lying on the work table.

Some women went past carrying a tray full of dripping linen.

Catching sight of them through the window, she remembered her own washing; she had passed the lye through it the day before and today it needed rinsing. So she left the room.

Her board and tub were on the bank of the Toucques. She threw a pile of chemises down by the water's edge, rolled up her sleeves, and picked up her battledore. The lusty blows she gave with it could be heard in all the neighbouring gardens.

The fields were empty, the river rippling in the wind; at the bottom long weeds were waving to and fro, like the hair of corpses floating in the water. She held back her grief, and was very brave until the evening; but in her room she gave way to it completely, lying on her mattress with her face buried in the pillow and her fists pressed against her temples.

Long afterwards she learnt the circumstances of Victor's death from the captain of his ship. He had gone down with yellow fever, and they had bled him too much at the hospital. Four doctors had held him at once. He had died straight away, and the chief doctor had said:

'Good! There goes another!'

His parents had always treated him cruelly. She preferred not to see them again, and they made no advances, either because they had forgotten about her or out of the callousness of the poor.

Meanwhile Virginie was growing weaker. Difficulty in breathing, fits of coughing, protracted bouts of fever, and mottled patches on the cheekbones all indicated some deepseated complaint. M. Poupart had advised a stay in Provence. Mme Aubain decided to follow this suggestion, and, if it had not been for the weather at Pont-l'Évêque, she would have brought her daughter home at once.

She arranged with a jobmaster to drive her out to the convent every Tuesday. There was a terrace in the garden, overlooking the Seine, and there Virginie, leaning on her mother's arm, walked up and down over the fallen vineleaves. Sometimes, while she was looking at the sails in the distance, or at the long stretch of horizon from the Château de Tancarville to the lighthouses of Le Havre, the sun would break through the clouds and make her blink. Afterwards they would rest in the arbor. Her mother had secured a little cask of excellent Malaga, and, laughing at the idea of getting tipsy, Virginie used to drink a thimbleful, but no more.

Her strength revived. Autumn slipped by, and Félicité assured Mme Aubain that there was nothing to fear. But one evening, coming back from some errand in the neighbourhood, she found M. Poupart's gig standing at the door. He was in the hall, and Mme Aubain was tying on her bonnet.

'Give me my foot-warmer, purse, gloves. Quickly now!'

Virginie had pneumonia and was perhaps past recovery.

'Not yet!' said the doctor; and the two of them got into the carriage with snowflakes swirling around them. Night was falling and it was very cold.

Félicité rushed into the church to light a candle, and then ran after the gig. She caught up with it an hour later, jumped lightly behind, and hung on to the fringe. But then a thought struck her: the courtyard had not been locked up, the burglars might get in. So she jumped down again.

At dawn the next day she went to the doctor's. He had come home and gone out again on his rounds. Then she waited at the inn, thinking that somebody who was a stranger to the district might call there with a letter. Finally, when it was twilight, she got into the coach for Lisieux.

The convent was at the bottom of a steep lane. When she was half-way down the hill, she heard a strange sound which she recognized as a death-bell tolling.

'It's for somebody else,' she thought, as she banged the door-knocker hard.

After a few minutes she heard the sound of shuffling feet, the door opened a little way, and a nun appeared.

The good sister said with an air of compunction that 'she had just passed away'. At that moment the bell of Saint-Léonard was tolled more vigorously than ever.

Félicité went up to the second floor. From the doorway of the room she could see Virginie lying on her back, her hands clapsed together, her mouth open, her head tilted back under a black crucifix that leant over her, her face whiter than the curtains that hung motionless on either side. Mme Aubain was clinging to the foot of the bed and sobbing desperately. The Mother Superior stood on the right. Three candlesticks on the chest of drawers added touches of red to the scene, and fog was whitening the windows. Some nuns led Mme Aubain away.

For two nights Félicité never left the dead girl. She said the same prayers over and over again, sprinkled holy water on the sheets, then sat down again to watch. At the end of her first vigil she noticed that the child's face had gone yellow, the lips were turning blue, the nose looked sharper, and the eyes were sunken. She kissed them several times, and would not have been particularly surprised if Virginie had opened them again: to minds like hers the supernatural is a simple matter. She laid her out, wrapped her in a shroud, put her in her coffin, placed a wreath on her, and spread out her hair. It was fair and amazingly long for her age. Félicité cut off a big lock, half of which she slipped into her bosom, resolving never to part with it.

The body was brought back to Pont-l'Évêque at the request of Mme Aubain, who followed the hearse in a closed carriage.

After the Requiem Mass, it took another three-quarters of an hour to reach the cemetery. Paul walked in front, sobbing. Then came M. Bourais, and after him the principal inhabitants of the town, the women all wearing long black veils, and Félicité. She was thinking about her nephew; and since she had been unable to pay him these last honours, she felt an added grief, just as if they were burying him with Virginie.

Mme Aubain's despair passed all bounds. First of all she rebelled against God, considering it unfair of Him to have taken her daughter from her—for she had never done any harm, and her conscience was quite clear. But was it? She ought to have taken Virginie to the south; other doctors would have saved her life. She blamed herself, wished she could have joined her daughter, and cried out in anguish in her dreams. One dream in particular obsessed her. Her husband, dressed like a sailor, came back from a long voyage, and told her amid tears that he had been ordered to take Virginie away— whereupon they put their heads together to discover somewhere to hide her.

One day she came in from the garden utterly distraught. A few minutes earlier— and she pointed to the spot—father and daughter had appeared to her, doing nothing, but simply looking at her.

For several months she stayed in her room in a kind of stupor. Félicité scolded her gently, telling her that she must take care of herself for her son's sake, and also in remembrance of 'her'.

'Her?' repeated Mme Aubain, as if she were waking from a sleep. 'Oh, yes, of course! You don't forget her, do you!' This was an allusion to the cemetery, where she herself was strictly forbidden to go.

Félicité went there every day. She would set out on the stroke of four, going past the houses, up the hill, and through the gate, until she came to Virginie's grave. There was a little column of pink marble with a tablet at its base, and a tiny garden enclosed by chains. The beds were hidden under a carpet of flowers. She watered their leaves and changed the sand, going down on her knees to fork the ground thoroughly. The result was that when Mme Aubain was able to come here, she experienced a feeling of relief, a kind of consolation.

Then the years slipped by, each one like the last, with nothing to vary the rhythm of the great festivals: Easter, the Assumption, All Saints' Day. Domestic events marked dates that later served as points of reference. Thus in 1825 a couple of glaziers white-washed the hall; in 1827 a piece of the roof fell into the courtyard and nearly killed a man; and in the summer of 1828 it was Madame's turn to provide the bread for consecration. About this time Bourais went away in a mysterious fashion; and one by one the old acquaintances disappeared: Guyot, Liébard, Mme Lechaptois, Robelin, and Uncle Gré-manville, who had been paralysed for a long time.

One night the driver of the mail-coach brought Pont-l'Évêque news of the July Revolution. A few days later a new sub-prefect was appointed. This was the Baron de Larsonnière, who had been a consul in America, and who brought with him, besides his wife, his sister-in-law and three young ladies who were almost grown-up. They were to be seen on their lawn, dressed in loose-fitting smocks; and they had a Negro servant and a parrot. They paid a call on Mme Aubain, who made a point of returning it. As soon as Félicité saw them coming, she would run and tell her mistress. But only one thing could really awaken her interest, and that was her son's letters.

He seemed to be incapable of following any career and spent all his time in taverns. She paid his debts, but he contracted new ones, and the sighs Mme Aubain heaved as she knitted by the window reached Félicité at her spinning wheel in the kitchen.

The two women used to walk up and down together beside the espalier, forever talking of Virginie and debating whether such and such a thing would have appealed to her, or what she would have said on such and such an occasion.

All her little belongings were in a cupboard in the children's bedroom. Mme Aubain went through them as seldom as possible. One summer day she resigned herself to doing so, and the moths were sent fluttering out of the cupboard.

Virginie's frocks hung in a row underneath a shelf containing three dolls, a few hoops, a set of toy furniture, and the wash-basin she had used. Besides the frocks, they took out her petticoats, her stockings and her handkerchiefs, and spread them out on the two beds before folding them up again. The sunlight streamed in on these pathetic objects, bringing out the stains and showing up the creases made by the child's move-ments. The air was warm, the sky was blue, a blackbird was singing, and everything seemed to be utterly at peace.

They found a little chestnut-coloured hat, made of plush with a long nap; but the moths had ruined it. Félicité asked if she might have it. The two women looked at each other and their eyes filled with tears. Then the mistress opened her arms, the maid threw herself into them, and they clasped each other in a warm embrace, satisfying their grief in a kiss which made them equal.

It was the first time that such a thing had happened, for Mme Aubain was not of a demonstrative nature. Félicité was as grateful as if she had received a great favour, and henceforth loved her mistress with dog-like devotion and religious veneration.

Her heart grew softer as time went by.

When she heard the drums of a regiment coming down the street she stood at the door with a jug of cider and offered the soldiers a drink. She looked after the people who went down with cholera. She watched over the Polish refugees, and one of them actually expressed a desire to marry her. But they fell out, for when she came back from the Angelus one morning, she found that he had got into her kitchen and was calmly eating an oil-and-vinegar salad.

After the Poles it was Père Colmiche, an old man who was said to have committed fearful atrocities in '93. He lived by the river in a ruined pig-sty. The boys of the town used to peer at him through the cracks in the walls, and threw pebbles at him which landed on the litter where he lay, constantly shaken by fits of coughing. His hair was extremely long, his eyelids inflamed, and on one arm there was a swelling bigger than his head. Félicité brought him some linen, tried to clean out his filthy hovel, and even wondered if she could install him in the wash-house without annoying Madame. When the tumour had burst, she changed his dressings every day, brought him some cake now and then, and put him out in the sun on a truss of hay. The poor old fellow would thank her in a faint whisper, slavering and trembling all the while, fearful of losing her and stretching his hands out as soon as he saw her moving away.

He died, and she had a Mass said for the repose of his soul.

That same day a great piece of good fortune came her way. Just as she was serving dinner, Mme de Larsonnière's Negro appeared carrying the parrot in its cage, complete with perch, chain, and padlock. The Baroness had written a note informing Mme Aubain that her husband had been promoted to a Prefecture and they were leaving that evening; she begged her to accept the parrot as a keepsake and a token of her regard.

This bird had engrossed Félicité's thoughts for a long time, for it came from America, and that word reminded her of Victor. So she had asked the Negro all about it, and once she had even gone so far as to say:

'How pleased Madame would be if it were hers!'

The Negro had repeated this remark to his mistress, who, unable to take the parrot with her, was glad to get rid of it in this way.

4

His name was Loulou. His body was green, the tips of his wings were pink, his poll blue, and his breast golden.

Unfortunately he had a tiresome mania for biting his perch, and also used to pull his feathers out, scatter his droppings everywhere, and upset his bath water. He annoyed Mme Aubain, and so she gave him to Félicité for good.

Félicité started training him, and soon he could say: 'Nice boy! Your servant, sir! Hail, Mary!' He was put near the door, and several people who spoke to him said how strange it was that he did not answer to the name of Jacquot, as all parrots were called Jacquot. They likened him to a turkey or a block of wood, and every sneer cut Félicité to the quick. How odd, she thought, that Loulou should be so stubborn, refusing to talk whenever anyone looked at him!

For all that, he liked having people around him, because on Sundays, while the Rochefeuille sisters, M. Houppeville and some new friends—the apothecary Onfroy,

M. Varin, and Captain Mathieu—were having their game of cards, he would beat on the window-panes with his wings and make such a din that it was impossible to hear oneself speak.

Bourais's face obviously struck him as terribly funny, for as soon as he saw it he was seized with uncontrollable laughter. His shrieks rang round the courtyard, the echo repeated them, and the neighbours came to their windows and started laughing too. To avoid being seen by the bird, M. Bourais used to creep along by the wall, hiding his face behind his hat, until he got to the river, and then come into the house from the garden. The looks he gave the parrot were far from tender.

Loulou had once been cuffed by the butcher's boy for poking his head into his basket; and since then he was always trying to give him a nip through his shirt. Fabu threatened to wring his neck, although he was not a cruel fellow, in spite of his tattooed arms and bushy whiskers. On the contrary, he rather liked the parrot, so much so indeed that in a spirit of jovial camaraderie he tried to teach him a few swear-words. Félicité, alarmed at this development, put the bird in the kitchen. His little chain was removed and he was allowed to wander all over the house.

Coming downstairs, he used to rest the curved part of his beak on each step and then raise first his right foot, then his left; and Félicité was afraid that this sort of gymnastic performance would make him giddy. He fell ill and could neither talk nor eat for there was a swelling under his tongue such as hens sometimes have. She cured him by pulling this pellicule[4] out with her finger-nails. One day M. Paul was silly enough to blow the smoke of his cigar at him; another time Mme Lormeau started teasing him with the end of her parasol, and he caught hold of the ferrule[5] with his beak. Finally he got lost.

Félicité had put him down on the grass in the fresh air, and left him there for a minute. When she came back, the parrot had gone. First of all she looked for him in the bushes, by the river and on the rooftops, paying no attention to her mistress's shouts of: 'Be careful, now! You must be mad!' Next she went over all the gardens in Pont-l'Évêque, stopping passersby and asking them: 'You don't happen to have seen my parrot by any chance?' Those who did not know him already were given a description of the bird. Suddenly she thought she could make out something green flying about behind the mills at the foot of the hill. But up on the hill there was nothing to be seen. A pedlar told her that he had come upon the parrot a short time before in Mère Simon's shop at Saint-Melaine. She ran all the way there, but no one knew what she was talking about. Finally she came back home, worn out, her shoes falling to pieces, and death in her heart. She was sitting beside Madame on the garden-seat and telling her what she had been doing, when she felt something light drop on her shoulder. It was Loulou! What he had been up to, no one could discover: perhaps he had just gone for a little walk round the town.

Félicité was slow to recover from this fright, and indeed never really got over it.

As the result of a chill she had an attack of quinsy, and soon after that her ears were affected. Three years later she was deaf, and she spoke at the top of her voice, even in church. Although her sins could have been proclaimed over the length and breadth of the diocese without dishonour to her or offence to others, M. le Curé thought it advisable to hear her confession in the sacristy.

---

[4] Thin skin or membrane.
[5] Iron ring around the end of a staff.

Imaginary buzzings in the head added to her troubles. Often her mistress would say: 'Heavens, how stupid you are!' and she would reply: 'Yes, Madame,' at the same time looking all around her for something.

The little circle of her ideas grew narrower and narrower, and the pealing of bells and the lowing of cattle went out of her life. Every living thing moved about in a ghostly silence. Only one sound reached her ears now, and that was the voice of the parrot.

As if to amuse her, he would reproduce the click-clack of the turn-spit, the shrill call of a man selling fish, and the noise of the saw at the joiner's across the way; and when the bell rang he would imitate Mme Aubain's 'Félicité! The door, the door!'

They held conversations with each other, he repeating *ad nauseam* the three phrases in his repertory, she replying with words which were just as disconnected but which came from the heart. In her isolation, Loulou was almost a son or a lover to her. He used to climb up her fingers, peck at her lips, and hang on to her shawl; and as she bent over him, wagging her head from side to side as nurses do, the great wings of her bonnet and the wings of the bird quivered in unison.

When clouds banked up in the sky and there was a rumbling of thunder, he would utter piercing cries, no doubt remembering the sudden downpours in his native forests. The sound of the rain falling roused him to frenzy. He would flap excitedly around, shoot up to the ceiling, knocking everything over, and fly out of the window to splash about in the garden. But he would soon come back to perch on one of the firedogs, hopping about to dry his feathers and showing tail and beak in turn.

One morning in the terrible winter of 1837, when she had put him in front of the fire because of the cold she found him dead in the middle of his cage, hanging head down with his claws caught in the bars. He had probably died of a stroke, but she thought he had been poisoned with parsley, and despite the absence of any proof, her suspicions fell on Fabu.

She wept so much that her mistress said to her: 'Why don't you have him stuffed?'

Félicité asked the chemist's advice, remembering that he had always been kind to the parrot. He wrote to Le Havre, and a man called Fellacher agreed to do the job. As parcels sometimes went astray on the mail-coach, she decided to take the parrot as far as Honfleur herself.

On either side of the road stretched an endless succession of apple-trees, all stripped of their leaves, and there was ice in the ditches. Dogs were barking around the farms; and Félicité, with her hands tucked under her mantlet, her little black sabots and her basket, walked briskly along the middle of the road.

She crossed the forest, passed Le Haut-Chêne, and got as far as Saint-Gatien.

Behind her, in a cloud of dust, and gathering speed as the horses galloped downhill, a mail-coach swept along like a whirlwind. When he saw this woman making no attempt to get out of the way, the driver poked his head out above the hood, and he and the postilion shouted at her. His four horses could not be held in and galloped faster, the two leaders touching her as they went by. With a jerk of the reins the driver threw them to one side, and then, in a fury, he raised his long whip and gave her such a lash, from head to waist, that she fell flat on her back.

The first thing she did on regaining consciousness was to open her basket. Fortunately nothing had happened to Loulou. She felt her right cheek burning, and when she touched it her hand turned red; it was bleeding.

She sat down on a heap of stones and dabbed her face with her handkerchief. Then she ate a crust of bread which she had taken the precaution of putting in her basket, and tried to forget her wound by looking at the bird.

As she reached the top of the hill at Ecquemauville, she saw the lights of Honfleur twinkling in the darkness like a host of stars, and the shadowy expanse of the sea beyond. Then a sudden feeling of faintness made her stop; and the misery of her childhood, the disappointment of her first love, the departure of her nephew, and the death of Virginie all came back to her at once like the waves of a rising-tide, and, welling up in her throat, choked her.

When she got to the boat she insisted on speaking to the captain, and without telling him what was in her parcel, asked him to take good care of it.

Fellacher kept the parrot a long time. Every week he promised it for the next; after six months he announced that a box had been sent off, and nothing more was heard of it. It looked as though Loulou would never come back, and Félicité told herself: 'They've stolen him for sure!'

At last he arrived—looking quite magnificent, perched on a branch screwed into a mahogany base, one foot in the air, his head cocked to one side, and biting a nut which the taxidermist, out of love of the grandiose, had gilded.

Félicité shut him up in her room.

This place, to which few people were ever admitted, contained such a quantity of religious bric-à-brac and miscellaneous oddments that it looked like a cross between a chapel and a bazaar.

A big wardrobe prevented the door from opening properly. Opposite the window that overlooked the garden was a little round one looking on to the courtyard. There was a table beside the bed, with a water-jug, a couple of combs, and a block of blue soap in a chipped plate. On the walls there were rosaries, medals, several pictures of the Virgin, and a holy-water stoup made out of a coconut. On the chest of drawers, which was draped with a cloth just like an altar, was the shell box Victor had given her, and also a watering-can and a ball, some copy-books, the illustrated geography book, and a pair of ankle-boots. And on the nail supporting the looking-glass, fastened by its ribbons, hung the little plush hat.

Félicité carried this form of veneration to such lengths that she even kept one of Monsieur's frock-coats. All the old rubbish Mme Aubain had no more use for, she carried off to her room. That was how there came to be artificial flowers along the edge of the chest of drawers, and a portrait of the Comte d'Artois in the window-recess.

With the aid of a wall-bracket, Loulou was installed on a chimney-breast that jutted out into the room. Every morning when she awoke, she saw him in the light of the dawn, and then she remembered the old days, and the smallest details of insignificant actions, not in sorrow but in absolute tranquillity.

Having no intercourse with anyone, she lived in the torpid state of a sleep-walker. The Corpus Christi processions roused her from this condition, for she would go round the neighbours collecting candlesticks and mats to decorate the altar of repose which they used to set up in the street.

In church she was forever gazing at the Holy Ghost, and one day she noticed that it had something of the parrot about it. This resemblance struck her as even more obvious in a colourprint depicting the baptism of Our Lord. With its red wings and its emerald-green body, it was the very image of Loulou.

She bought the print and hung it in the place of the Comte d'Artois, so that she could include them both in a single glance. They were linked together in her mind, the parrot being sanctified by this connexion with the Holy Ghost, which itself acquired new life and meaning in her eyes. God the Father could not have chosen a dove as a means of expressing Himself, since doves cannot talk, but rather one of Loulou's ancestors. And although Félicité used to say her prayers with her eyes on the picture, from time to time she would turn slightly towards the bird.

She wanted to join the Children of Mary, but Mme Aubain dissuaded her from doing so.

An important event now loomed up—Paul's wedding.

After starting as a lawyer's clerk, he had been in business, in the Customs, and in Inland Revenue, and had even begun trying to get into the Department of Woods and Forests, when, at the age of thirty-six, by some heaven-sent inspiration, he suddenly discovered his real vocation—in the Wills and Probate Department. There he proved so capable that one of the auditors had offered him his daughter in marriage and promised to use his influence on his behalf.

Paul, grown serious-minded, brought her to see his mother. She criticized the way things were done at Pont-l'Évêque, put on airs, and hurt Félicité's feelings. Mme Aubain was relieved to see her go.

The following week came news of M. Bourais's death in an inn in Lower Brittany. Rumours that he had committed suicide were confirmed, and doubts arose as to his honesty. Mme Aubain went over her accounts and was soon conversant with the full catalogue of his misdeeds—embezzlement of interest, secret sales of timber, forged receipts, etc. Besides all this, he was the father of an illegitimate child, and had had 'relations with a person at Dozulé'.

These infamies upset Mme Aubain greatly. In March 1853 she was afflicted with a pain in the chest; her tongue seemed to be covered with a film; leeches failed to make her breathing any easier; and on the ninth evening of her illness she died. She had just reached the age of seventy-two.

She was thought to be younger because of her brown hair, worn in bandeaux round her pale, pock-marked face. There were few friends to mourn her, for she had a haughty manner which put people off. Yet Félicité wept for her as servants rarely weep for their masters. That Madame should die before her upset her ideas, seemed to be contrary to the order of things, monstrous and unthinkable.

Ten days later—the time it took to travel hot-foot from Besançon—the heirs arrived. The daughter-in-law ransacked every drawer, picked out some pieces of furniture and sold the rest; and then back they went to the Wills and Probate Department.

Madame's arm-chair, her pedestal table, her foot-warmer, and the eight chairs had all gone. Yellow squares in the centre of the wall-panels showed where the pictures had hung. They had carried off the two cots with their mattresses, and no trace remained in the cupboard of all Virginie's things. Félicité climbed the stairs to her room, numbed with sadness.

The next day there was a notice on the door, and the apothecary shouted in her ear that the house was up for sale.

She swayed on her feet, and was obliged to sit down.

What distressed her most of all was the idea of leaving her room, which was so suitable for poor Loulou. Fixing an anguished look on him as she appealed to the Holy Ghost, she contracted the idolatrous habit of kneeling in front of the parrot to say her prayers. Sometimes the sun, as it came through the little window, caught his glass eye, so that it shot out a great luminous ray which sent her into ecstasies.

She had a pension of three hundred and eighty francs a year which her mistress had left her. The garden kept her in vegetables. As for clothes, she had enough to last her till the end of her days, and she saved on lighting by going to bed as soon as darkness fell.

She went out as little as possible, to avoid the second-hand dealer's shop where some of the old furniture was on display. Ever since her fit of giddiness, she had been dragging one leg; and as her strength was failing, Mère Simon, whose grocery business had come to grief, came in every morning to chop wood and pump water for her.

Her eyes grew weaker. The shutters were not opened any more. Years went by, and nobody rented the house and nobody bought it.

For fear of being evicted, Félicité never asked for any repairs to be done. The laths in the roof rotted, and all through one winter her bolster was wet. After Easter she began spitting blood.

When this happened Mère Simon called in a doctor. Félicité wanted to know what was the matter with her, but she was so deaf that only one word reached her: 'Pneumonia.' It was a word she knew, and she answered gently: 'Ah! like Madame', thinking it natural that she should follow in her mistress's footsteps.

The time to set up the altars of repose was drawing near.

The first altar was always at the foot of the hill, the second in front of the post office, the third about half-way up the street. There was some argument as to the siting of this one, and finally the women of the parish picked on Mme Aubain's courtyard.

The fever and the tightness of the chest grew worse. Félicité fretted over not doing anything for the altar. If only she could have something put on it! Then she thought of the parrot. The neighbours protested that it would not be seemly, but the curé gave his permission, and this made her so happy that she begged him to accept Loulou, the only thing of value she possessed, when she died.

From Tuesday to Saturday, the eve of Corpus Christi, she coughed more and more frequently. In the evening her face looked pinched and drawn, her lips stuck to her gums, and she started vomiting. At dawn the next day, feeling very low, she sent for a priest.

Three good women stood by her while she was given extreme unction. Then she said that she had to speak to Fabu.

He arrived in his Sunday best, very ill at ease in this funereal atmosphere.

'Forgive me,' she said, making an effort to stretch out her arm. 'I thought it was you who had killed him.'

What could she mean by such nonsense? To think that she had suspected a man like him of murder! He got very indignant and was obviously going to make a scene.

'Can't you see', they said, 'that she isn't in her right mind any more?'

From time to time Félicité would start talking to shadows. The women went away. Mère Simon had her lunch.

A little later she picked Loulou up and held him out to Félicité, saying:

'Come now, say good-bye to him.'

Although the parrot was not a corpse, the worms were eating him up. One of his wings was broken, and the stuffing was coming out of his stomach. But she was blind by now, and she kissed him on the forehead and pressed him against her cheek. Mère Simon took him away from her to put him on the altar.

5

The scents of summer came up from the meadows; there was a buzzing of flies; the sun was glittering in the river and warming the slates of the roof. Mère Simon had come back into the room and was gently nodding off to sleep.

The noise of church bells woke her up; the congregation was coming out from vespers. Félicité's delirium abated. Thinking of the procession, she could see it as clearly as if she had been following it.

All the school-children, the choristers, and the firemen were walking along the pavements, while advancing up the middle of the street came the church officer armed with his halberd, the beadle carrying a great cross, the schoolmaster keeping an eye on the boys, and the nun fussing over her little girls—three of the prettiest, looking like curly-headed angels, were throwing rose-petals into the air. Then came the deacon, with both arms outstretched, conducting the band, and a couple of censer-bearers who turned round at every step to face the Holy Sacrament, which the curé, wearing his splendid chasuble, was carrying under a canopy of poppy-red velvet held aloft by four churchwardens. A crowd of people surged along behind, between the white cloths covering the walls of the houses, and eventually they got to the bottom of the hill.

A cold sweat moistened Félicité's temples. Mère Simon sponged it up with a cloth, telling herself that one day she would have to go the same way.

The hum of the crowd increased in volume, was very loud for a moment, then faded away.

A fusillade shook the window-panes. It was the postilions[6] saluting the monstrance.[7] Félicité rolled her eyes and said as loud as she could: 'Is he all right?'—worrying about the parrot.

She entered into her death-agony. Her breath, coming ever faster, with a rattling sound, made her sides heave. Bubbles of froth appeared at the corners of her mouth, and her whole body trembled.

Soon the booming of the ophicleides,[8] the clear voices of the children, and the deep voices of the men could be heard near at hand. Now and then everything was quiet, and the tramping of feet, deadened by a carpet of flowers, sounded like a flock moving across pasture-land.

The clergy appeared in the courtyard. Mère Simon climbed on to a chair to reach the little round window, from which she had a full view of the altar below.

It was hung with green garlands and adorned with a flounce in English needlepoint lace. In the middle was a little frame containing some relics, there were two orange-trees at the corners, and all the way along stood silver candlesticks and china vases holding sunflowers, lilies, peonies, foxgloves, and bunches of hydrangea. This pyramid of bright colours stretched from the first floor right down to the carpet which was spread out over the pavement. Some rare objects caught the eye: a silver-gilt sugar-basin wreathed in violets, some pendants of Alençon gems gleaming on a bed of moss, and two Chinese screens with landscape decorations. Loulou, hidden under roses, showed nothing but his blue poll, which looked like a plaque of lapis lazuli.

The churchwardens, the choristers, and the children lined up along the three sides of the courtyard. The priest went slowly up the steps and placed his great shining gold sun on the lace altar-cloth. Everyone knelt down. There was a deep silence. And the censers, swinging at full tilt, slid up and down their chains.

A blue cloud of incense was wafted up into Félicité's room. She opened her nostrils wide and breathed it in with a mystical, sensuous fervour. Then she closed her eyes. Her lips smiled. Her heart-beats grew slower and slower, each a little fainter and

---

[6] Those who ride the left-hand horse of a two- or four-horse carriage.
[7] The showing of the consecrated Host.
[8] An early brass wind instrument.

gentler, like a fountain running dry, an echo fading away. And as she breathed her last, she thought she could see, in the opening heavens, a gigantic parrot hovering above her head.

Ambrose Bierce (1842–1914?)

Ambrose Bierce was a legend in his own day, a legend largely of his own making. Carey McWilliams, one of his most reliable biographers, writes:

> It is seriously to be doubted if there exists another figure in American litera- ture about whom as much irregular and unreliable critical comment has been written. He has been characterized as great, bitter, idealistic, cynical, mo- rose, frustrated, cheerful, bad, sadistic, obscure, perverted, famous, brutal, kind, a fiend, a God, a misanthrope, a poet, a realist who wrote romances, a fine satirist, and something of a charlatan.

He was many things to many people—and to himself; he lived as well as wrote fiction. He served for four years in the Civil War (1861–1865) and two years in the occupation that followed; he saw action at Shiloh, Stone River, Chickamauga, and other bloody engagements; he was captured and seriously wounded. The war was the most formative and unforgettable experience of his life. As Stuart C. Woodruff says, "Bierce talked about the war, thought about it, wrote about it, all his life, and paid repeated visits to the Civil War battlefields where he had fought." His most important fiction volumes are *Tales of Soldiers and Civilians* (1891), in which "An Occurrence at Owl Creek Bridge" appeared, and *Can Such Things Be?* (1893). But Bierce reacted to the war with a curious ambivalence: on the one hand he felt the heroism and idealism, on the other the terror and disgust, and he never sorted out the conflict within himself. Death stirred a feeling of "resentment" in him; yet it was inseparable from a sense of the exhilaration he felt in battle. Thus does this conflict come out in the story "A Tough Tussle":

> The exhilaration of battle was agreeable to him, but the sight of the dead, with their clay faces, blank eyes and stiff bodies, which when not unnaturally shrunken were unnaturally swollen, had always intolerably affected him. He felt toward them a kind of reasonless antipathy . . . Doubtless this feeling was due to his unusually acute sensibilities—his keen sense of the beautiful, which these hideous things outraged.

For forty years Bierce was famous as a satirical journalist, writing a column for William Randolph Hearst's San Francisco *Examiner* and becoming, as one critic says, "the best hated and the best loved man in California." His satire was vitriolic, personal, slashing, and crude. Yet it was powerful enough to defeat the railroad tycoon Colis P. Huntington in his attempt to milk the U.S. Treasury of millions of dollars; and it was brave enough to take on the war hysteria that led to the Spanish-American War of 1898. This is a sample of his polemics: "We can conquer these people without half trying, for we belong to the race of gluttons and drunkards to whom dominion is given over the abstemious." Not very subtle stuff.

"An Occurrence at Owl Creek Bridge" is Bierce's best story, as his short stories are his best work. His stories had their widest popularity in the 1920s, at a time following World War I when readers were more ready than in the 1890s to accept a bitter, realistic, and wholly unromantic vision of what war is. Bierce's approach is usually too direct and literal for sustained irony, but "An Occurrence at Owl Creek Bridge" is an exception. Here Bierce imagines his way—in entirely realistic terms—into the fantasies of Farquhar at the moment of his hanging; then at the end he yanks us back, as if at a rope's end, from this dream of happiness to death itself. The irony—the illusion snatched away—is all done by technique. But if it is a technical "trick," it is also Bierce's paradoxical and bitter view of the human reality.

In 1913 Bierce disappeared into Mexico—no one quite knows why—and was never heard from again.

An Occurrence at Owl Creek Bridge

1

A man stood upon a railroad bridge in northern Alabama, looking down into the swift water twenty feet below. The man's hands were behind his back, the wrists bound with a cord. A rope closely encircled his neck. It was attached to a stout cross-timber above his head and the slack fell to the level of his knees. Some loose boards laid upon the sleepers supporting the metals of the railway supplied a footing for him and his executioners—two private soldiers of the Federal army, directed by a sergeant who in civil life may have been a deputy sheriff. At a short remove upon the same temporary platform was an officer in the uniform of his rank, armed. He was a captain. A sentinel at each end of the bridge stood with his rifle in the position known as "support," that is to say, vertical in front of the left shoulder, the hammer resting on the forearm thrown straight across the chest—a formal and unnatural position, enforcing an erect carriage of the body. It did not appear to be the duty of these two men to know what was occurring at the centre of the bridge; they merely blockaded the two ends of the foot planking that traversed it.

Beyond one of the sentinels nobody was in sight; the railroad ran straight away into a forest for a hundred yards, then, curving, was lost to view. Doubtless there was an outpost farther along. The other bank of the stream was open ground—a gentle acclivity topped with a stockade of vertical tree trunks, loopholed for rifles, with a single embrasure through which protruded the muzzle of a brass cannon commanding the bridge. Midway of the slope between bridge and fort were the spectators—a single company of infantry in line, at "parade rest," the butts of the rifles on the ground, the barrels inclining slightly backward against the right shoulder, the hands crossed upon the stock. A lieutenant stood at the right of the line, the point of his sword upon the ground, his left hand resting upon his right. Excepting the group of four at the centre of the bridge, not a man moved. The company faced the bridge, staring stonily, motionless. The sentinels, facing the banks of the stream, might have been statues to adorn the bridge. The captain stood with folded arms, silent, observing the work of his subordinates, but making no sign. Death is a dignitary who when he comes announced is to be received with formal manifestations of respect, even by those most familiar with him. In the code of military etiquette silence and fixity are forms of deference.

The man who was engaged in being hanged was apparently about thirty-five years of age. He was a civilian, if one might judge from his habit, which was that of a planter. His features were good—a straight nose, firm mouth, broad forehead, from which his long, dark hair was combed straight back, falling behind his ears to the collar of his well-fitting frock-coat. He wore a mustache and pointed beard, but no whiskers; his eyes were large and dark gray, and had a kindly expression which one would hardly have expected in one whose neck was in the hemp. Evidently this was no vulgar assassin. The liberal military code makes provision for hanging many kinds of persons, and gentlemen are not excluded.

The preparations being complete, the two private soldiers stepped aside and each drew away the plank upon which he had been standing. The sergeant turned to the captain, saluted and placed himself immediately behind that officer, who in turn moved apart one pace. These movements left the condemned man and the sergeant standing on the two ends of the same plank, which spanned three of the cross-ties of the bridge. The end upon which the civilian stood almost, but not quite, reached a fourth. This plank had been held in place by the weight of the captain; it was now held by that of the sergeant. At a signal from the former the latter would step aside, the plank would tilt and the condemned man go down between two ties. The arrangement commended itself to his judgment as simple and effective. His face had not been covered nor his eyes bandaged. He looked a moment at his "unsteadfast footing," then let his gaze wander to the swirling water of the stream racing madly beneath his feet. A piece of dancing driftwood caught his attention and his eyes followed it down the current. How slowly it appeared to move! What a sluggish stream!

He closed his eyes in order to fix his last thoughts upon his wife and children. The water, touched to gold by the early sun, the brooding mists under the banks at some distance down the stream, the fort, the soldiers, the piece of drift—all had distracted him. And now he became conscious of a new disturbance. Striking through the thought of his dear ones was a sound which he could neither ignore nor understand, a sharp, distinct, metallic percussion like the stroke of a blacksmith's hammer upon the anvil; it had the same ringing quality. He wondered what it was, and whether immeasurably distant or near by—it seemed both. Its recurrence was regular, but as slow as the tolling of a death knell. He awaited each stroke with impatience and—he knew not why—apprehension. The intervals of silence grew progressively longer; the delays became maddening. With their greater infrequency the sounds increased in strength and sharpness. They hurt his ear like the thrust of a knife; he feared he would shriek. What he heard was the ticking of his watch.

He unclosed his eyes and saw again the water below him. "If I could free my hands," he thought, "I might throw off the noose and spring into the stream. By diving I could evade the bullets and, swimming vigorously, reach the bank, take to the woods and get away home. My home, thank God, is as yet outside their lines; my wife and little ones are still beyond the invader's farthest advance."

As these thoughts, which have here to be set down in words, were flashed into the doomed man's brain rather than evolved from it the captain nodded to the sergeant. The sergeant stepped aside.

2

Peyton Farquhar was a well-to-do planter, of an old and highly respected Alabama family. Being a slave owner and like other slave owners a politician he was naturally an original secessionist and ardently devoted to the Southern cause. Circumstances of an imperious nature, which it is unnecessary to relate here, had prevented him from taking service with the gallant army that had fought the disastrous campaigns ending with the fall of Corinth, and he chafed under the inglorious restraint, longing for the release of his energies, the larger life of the soldier, the opportunity for distinction. That opportunity, he felt, would come, as it comes to all in war time. Meanwhile he did what he could. No service was too humble for him to perform in aid of the South, no adventure too perilous for him to undertake if consistent with the character of a civilian who was at heart a soldier, and who in good faith and without too much qualification assented to at least a part of the frankly villainous dictum that all is fair in love and war.

One evening while Farquhar and his wife were sitting on a rustic bench near the entrance to his grounds, a gray-clad soldier rode up to the gate and asked for a drink of water. Mrs. Farquhar was only too happy to serve him with her own white hands. While she was fetching the water her husband approached the dusty horseman and inquired eagerly for news from the front.

"The Yanks are repairing the railroads," said the man, "and are getting ready for another advance. They have reached the Owl Creek bridge, put it in order and built a stockade on the north bank. The commandant has issued an order, which is posted everywhere, declaring that any civilian caught interfering with the railroad, its bridges, tunnels or trains will be summarily hanged. I saw the order."

"How far is it to the Owl Creek bridge?" Farquhar asked.

"About thirty miles."

"Is there no force on this side the creek?"

"Only a picket post half a mile out, on the railroad, and a single sentinel at this end of the bridge."

"Suppose a man—a civilian and student of hanging—should elude the picket post and perhaps get the better of the sentinel," said Farquhar, smiling, "what could he accomplish?"

The soldier reflected. "I was there a month ago," he replied. "I observed that the flood of last winter had lodged a great quantity of driftwood against the wooden pier at this end of the bridge. It is now dry and would burn like tow."

The lady had now brought the water, which the soldier drank. He thanked her ceremoniously, bowed to her husband and rode away. An hour later, after nightfall, he repassed the plantation, going northward in the direction from which he had come. He was a federal scout.

3

As Peyton Farquhar fell straight downward through the bridge he lost consciousness and was as one already dead. From this state he was awakened—ages later, it seemed to him—by the pain of a sharp pressure upon his throat, followed by a sense of suffocation. Keen, poignant agonies seemed to shoot from his neck downward through every fibre of his body and limbs. These pains appeared to flash along well-defined lines of ramification and to beat with an inconceivably rapid periodicity. They seemed like streams of pulsating fire heating him to an intolerable temperature. As to his head, he was conscious of nothing but a feeling of fulness—of congestion. These sensations were unaccompanied by thought. The intellectual part of his nature was already effaced; he had power only to feel, and feeling was torment. He was conscious of motion. Encompassed in a luminous cloud, of which he was now merely the fiery heart, without material substance, he swung through unthinkable arcs of oscillation, like a vast pendulum. Then all at once, with terrible suddenness, the light about him shot upward with the noise of a loud plash; a frightful roaring was in his ears, and all was cold and dark. The power of thought was restored; he knew that the rope had broken and he had fallen into the stream. There was no additional strangulation; the noose about his neck was already suffocating him and kept the water from his lungs. To die of hanging at the bottom of a river!—the idea seemed to him ludicrous. He opened his eyes in the darkness and saw above him a gleam of light, but how distant, how inaccessible! He was still sinking, for the light became fainter and fainter until it was a mere glimmer. Then it began to grow and brighten, and he knew that he was rising toward the surface—knew it with reluctance, for he was now very comfortable. "To be hanged and drowned," he thought, "that is not so bad; but I do not wish to be shot. No; I will not be shot; that is not fair."

He was not conscious of an effort, but a sharp pain in his wrist apprised him that he was trying to free his hands. He gave the struggle his attention, as an idler might observe the feat of a juggler, without interest in the outcome. What splendid effort!—what magnificent, what superhuman strength! Ah, that was a fine endeavor! Bravo! The cord fell away; his arms parted and floated upward, the hands dimly seen on each side in the growing light. He watched them with a new interest as first one and then the other pounced upon the noose at his neck. They tore it away and thrust it fiercely aside, its undulations resembling those of a water-snake. "Put it back, put it back!" He thought he shouted these words to his hands, for the undoing of the noose had been succeeded by the direst pang that he had yet experienced. His neck ached horribly; his brain was on fire; his heart, which had been fluttering faintly, gave a great leap, trying to force itself out at his mouth. His whole body was racked and wrenched with an insupportable anguish! But his disobedient hands gave no heed to the command. They beat the water vigorously with quick, downward strokes, forcing him to the surface. He felt his head emerge; his eyes were blinded by the sunlight; his chest expanded convulsively, and with a supreme and crowning agony his lungs engulfed a great draught of air, which instantly he expelled in a shriek!

He was now in full possession of his physical senses. They were, indeed, preternaturally keen and alert. Something in the awful disturbance of his organic system had so exalted and refined them that they made record of things never before perceived. He felt the ripples upon his face and heard their separate sounds as they struck. He looked at the forest on the bank of the stream, saw the individual trees, the leaves and the veining of each leaf—saw the very insects upon them: the locusts, the brilliant-bodied flies, the gray spiders stretching their webs from twig to twig. He noted the prismatic colors in all the dewdrops upon a million blades of grass. The humming of the gnats that danced above the eddies of the stream, the beating of the dragon-flies' wings, the strokes of the water-spiders' legs, like oars which had lifted their boat—all these made audible music. A fish slid along beneath his eyes and he heard the rush of its body parting the water.

He had come to the surface facing down the stream; in a moment the visible world seemed to wheel slowly round, himself the pivotal point, and he saw the bridge, the fort, the soldiers upon the bridge, the captain, the sergeant, the two privates, his executioners. They were in silhouette against the blue sky. They shouted and gesticulated, pointing at him. The captain had drawn his pistol, but did not fire; the others were unarmed. Their movements were grotesque and horrible, their forms gigantic.

Suddenly he heard a sharp report and something struck the water smartly within a few inches of his head, spattering his face with spray. He heard a second report, and saw one of the sentinels with his rifle at his shoulder, a light cloud of blue smoke rising from the muzzle. The man in the water saw the eye of the man on the bridge gazing into his own through the sights of the rifle. He observed that it was a gray eye and remembered having read that gray eyes were keenest, and that all famous markmen had them. Nevertheless, this one had missed.

A counter-swirl had caught Farquhar and turned him half around; he was again looking into the forest on the bank opposite the fort. The sound of a clear, high voice in a monotonous singsong now rang out behind him and came across the water with a distinctness that pierced and subdued all other sounds, even the beating of the ripples in his ears. Although no soldier, he had frequented camps enough to know the dread significance of that deliberate, drawling, aspirated chant; the lieutenant on shore was taking a part in the morning's work. How coldly and pitilessly—with what an even, calm intonation, presaging, and enforcing tranquillity in the men—with what accurately measured intervals fell those cruel words:

"Attention, company! . . . Shoulder arms! . . . Ready! . . . Aim! . . . Fire!"

Farquhar dived—dived as deeply as he could. The water roared in his ears like the voice of Niagara, yet he heard the dulled thunder of the volley and, rising again toward the surface, met shining bits of metal, singularly flattened, oscillating slowly downward. Some of them touched him on the face and hands, then fell away, continuing their descent. One lodged between his collar and neck; it was uncomfortably warm and he snatched it out.

As he rose to the surface, gasping for breath, he saw that he had been a long time under water; he was perceptibly farther down stream—nearer to safety. The soldiers had almost finished reloading; the metal ramrods flashed all at once in the sunshine as they were drawn from the barrels, turned in the air, and thrust into their sockets. The two sentinels fired again, independently and ineffectually.

The hunted man saw all this over his shoulder; he was now swimming vigorously with the current. His brain was as energetic as his arms and legs; he thought with the rapidity of lightning.

"The officer," he reasoned, "will not make that martinet's error a second time. It is as easy to dodge a volley as a single shot. He has probably already given the command to fire at will. God help me, I cannot dodge them all!"

An appalling plash within two yards of him was followed by a loud, rushing sound, *diminuendo,* which seemed to travel back through the air to the fort and died in an explosion which stirred the very river to its deeps! A rising sheet of water curved over him, fell down upon him, blinded him, strangled him! The cannon had taken a hand in the game. As he shook his head free from the commotion of the smitten water he heard the deflected shot humming through the air ahead, and in an instant it was cracking and smashing the branches in the forest beyond.

"They will not do that again," he thought; "the next time they will use a charge of grape. I must keep my eye upon the gun; the smoke will apprise me—the report arrives too late; it lags behind the missile. That is a good gun."

Suddenly he felt himself whirled round and round—spinning like a top. The water, the banks, the forests, the now distant bridge, fort and men—all were commingled and blurred. Objects were represented by their colors only; circular horizontal streaks of color—that was all he saw. He had been caught in a vortex and was being whirled on with a velocity of advance and gyration that made him giddy and sick. In a few moments he was flung upon the gravel at the foot of the left bank of the stream—the southern bank—and behind a projecting point which concealed him from his enemies. The sudden arrest of his motion, the abrasion of one of his hands on the gravel, restored him, and he wept with delight. He dug his fingers into the sand, threw it over himself in handfuls and audibly blessed it. It looked like diamonds, rubies, emeralds; he could think of nothing beautiful which it did not resemble. The trees upon the bank were giant garden plants; he noted a definite order in their arrangement, inhaled the fragrance of their blooms. A strange, roseate light shone through the spaces among their trunks and the wind made in their branches the music of æolian harps. He had no wish to perfect his escape—was content to remain in that enchanting spot until retaken.

A whiz and rattle of grapeshot among the branches high above his head roused him from his dream. The baffled cannoneer had fired him a random farewell. He sprang to his feet, rushed up the sloping bank, and plunged into the forest.

All that day he traveled, laying his course by the rounding sun. The forest seemed interminable; nowhere did he discover a break in it, not even a woodman's road. He had not known that he lived in so wild a region. There was something uncanny in the revelation.

By nightfall he was fatigued, footsore, famishing. The thought of his wife and children urged him on. At last he found a road which led him in what he knew to be the right direction. It was as wide and straight as a city street, yet it seemed untraveled. No fields bordered it, no dwelling anywhere. Not so much as the barking of a dog suggested human habitation. The black bodies of the trees formed a straight wall on both sides, terminating on the horizon in a point, like a diagram in a lesson in perspective. Overhead, as he looked up through this rift in the wood, shone great golden stars looking unfamiliar and grouped in strange constellations. He was sure they were arranged in some order which had a secret and malign significance. The wood on either side was full of singular noises, among which—once, twice, and again—he distinctly heard whispers in an unknown tongue.

His neck was in pain and lifting his hand to it he found it horribly swollen. He knew that it had a circle of black where the rope had bruised it. His eyes felt congested; he could no longer close them. His tongue was swollen with thirst; he relieved its fever by thrusting it forward from between his teeth into the cold air. How softly the turf had carpeted the untraveled avenue—he could no longer feel the roadway beneath his feet!

Doubtless, despite his suffering, he had fallen asleep while walking, for now he sees another scene—perhaps he has merely recovered from a delirium. He stands at the gate of his own home. All is as he left it, and all bright and beautiful in the morning sunshine. He must have traveled the entire night. As he pushes open the gate and passes up the wide white walk, he sees a flutter of female garments; his wife, looking fresh and cool and sweet, steps down from the veranda to meet him. At the bottom of the steps she stands waiting, with a smile of ineffable joy, an attitude of matchless grace and dignity. Ah, how beautiful she is! He springs forward with extended arms. As he is about to clasp her he feels a stunning blow upon the back of the neck; a blinding white light blazes all about him with a sound like the shock of a cannon—then all is darkness and silence!

Peyton Farquhar was dead; his body, with a broken neck, swung gently from side to side beneath the timbers of the Owl Creek bridge.

Henry James (1843–1916)

Henry James was the great theoretician of fictional methods, and generations of young writers have gone to school to his essays, prefaces, letters, notebooks, criticism, as well as to his astonishing number of novels and tales. In "The Art of Fiction" he says that the source of fiction is not mere raw experience but "the power to guess the unseen from the seen, to trace the implication of things, to judge the whole piece by the pattern, the condition of feeling life in general so completely that you are well on your way to knowing any particular corner of it." He insisted, as had few of his predecessors, that fiction writing was a great art, that the aesthetic as well as the ethical element was of the highest importance.

"The Beast in the Jungle" illustrates at once James's importance in the development of fiction and the difficulty some readers may experience with him. He believed that the story ought to tell itself, that the writer should not comment or interfere with the characters or interpret their actions. Everything, he thought, must be rendered, dramatized. And yet his fiction is a monument to the inward, the subtle, the unseen. The practical world of politics and poverty, births, jobs, disease—which had so occupied earlier writers—with him must be inferred from his presentation of a subjective consciousness. Inwardness itself is the stage, the battlefield, where nuances of thought and feeling, gradations of decency and selfishness, play the leading parts. Joseph Conrad said,

> . . . the struggles Mr. James chronicles with such subtle and direct insight are, though only personal contests, desperate in their silence, none the less heroic . . . for the absence of shouted watchwords, clash of arms, and sound of trumpets.

To Conrad, he was "the historian of fine consciences."

James introduced the notion of a "central intelligence" (see introduction, pp. 14–15) through which all information is funneled to the reader. By means of the flow of this consciousness, the reader is privy to the important elements in the story. In *The Craft of Fiction,* Percy Lubbock describes the effect of James's method. "The world of silent thought," he says, "is thrown open, and instead of telling the reader what happened there, the novelist uses the look and behavior of thought as the vehicle by which the story is rendered. . . . The impulses and reactions of . . . mood are the players upon the new scene."

James's style matches the "fine consciences": carefully wrought, precisely qualified, sometimes opaque, sometimes radiant, always subtle and complex. Because he saw the human scene from all around, felt the effect of even the smallest perception, he was not comfortable in the short-story form with its demand for compression. He much preferred what he called "the beautiful and blest nouvelle," which is the form of "The Beast in the Jungle." The nouvelle moves at a stately pace over a period of time, and it gives full measure to the nuances James's prose is capable of. To some readers, James's style may seem precious, excessive, nearly impenetrable with its dashes and commas, its subordinate and coordinate clauses, its myriad qualifications. It is certainly easily parodied, as his contemporary Max Beerbohm demonstrated beautifully long ago. Yet other readers find that his language itself is exciting, arouses deep feeling and serves admirably his complex, deeply moral intentions.

The theme of "The Beast in the Jungle" is typically Jamesian: a man discovers, too late, that his egoism has caused him to miss the one passion of life he might have had. It is told in a fashion that provides rich, typically Jamesian, ironies. All that we know comes through the "central intelligence," John Marcher, and we accept him at his own value. But because of the language in which Marcher's perceptions are presented, we see him as foolish, selfish, unimaginative. And yet his humanity is so clearly and palpably rendered that our deepest sympathies are engaged: there but for the grace of God go I.

Although born in New York, James lived most of his life abroad and became a British subject in 1915. He died in 1916 at the age of seventy-three.

The Beast in the Jungle

What determined the speech that startled him in the course of their encounter scarcely matters, being probably but some words spoken by himself quite without intention— spoken as they lingered and slowly moved together after their renewal of acquaintance. He had been conveyed by friends an hour or two before to the house at which she was staying; the party of visitors at the other house, of whom he was one, and thanks to whom it was his theory, as always, that he was lost in the crowd, had been invited over to luncheon. There had been after luncheon much dispersal, all in the interest of the original move, a view of Weatherend itself and the fine things, intrinsic features, pictures, heirlooms, treasures of all the arts, that made the place almost famous; and the great rooms were so numerous that guests could wander at their will, hang back from the principal group and in cases where they took such matters with the least seriousness give themselves up to mysterious appreciations and measurements. There were persons to be observed, singly or in couples, bending toward objects in out-of-the-way corners with their hands on their knees and their heads nodding quite as with the emphasis of an excited sense of smell. When they were two they either mingled their sounds of ecstasy or melted into silences of even deeper import, so that there were aspects of the occasion that gave it for Marcher much the air of the "look round," previous to a sale highly advertised, that excites or quenches, as may be, the dream of acquisition. The dream of acquisition at Weatherend would have had to be wild indeed, and John Marcher found himself, among such suggestions, disconcerted almost equally by the presence of those who knew too much and by that of those who knew nothing. The great rooms caused so much poetry and history to press upon him that he needed some straying apart to feel in a proper relation with them, though this impulse was not, as happened, like the gloating of some of his companions, to be compared to the movements of a dog sniffing a cupboard. It had an issue promptly enough in a direction that was not to have been calculated.

It led, briefly, in the course of the October afternoon, to his closer meeting with May Bartram, whose face, a reminder, yet not quite a remembrance, as they sat much separated at a very long table, had begun merely by troubling him rather pleasantly. It affected him as the sequel of something of which he had lost the beginning. He knew it, and for the time quite welcomed it, as a continuation, but didn't know what it continued, which was an interest or an amusement the greater as he was also somehow aware—yet without a direct sign from her—that the young woman herself hadn't lost the thread. She hadn't lost it, but she wouldn't give it back to him, he saw, without some putting forth of his hand for it; and he not only saw that, but saw several things more, things odd enough in the light of the fact that at the moment some accident of grouping brought them face to face he was still merely fumbling with the idea that any contact between them in the past would have had no importance. If it had had no importance he scarcely knew why his actual impression of her should so seem to have so much; the answer to which, however, was that in such a life as they all appeared to be leading for the moment one could but take things as they came. He was satisfied, without in the least being able to say why, that this young lady might roughly have ranked in the house as a poor relation; satisfied also that she was not there on a brief visit, but was more or less a part of the establishment—almost a working, a remunerated part. Didn't she enjoy at periods a protection that she paid for by helping, among other services, to show the place and explain it, deal with the tiresome people, answer questions about the dates of the building, the styles of the furniture, the authorship of the pictures, the favourite haunts of the ghost? It wasn't that she looked as if you could have given her shillings—it was impossible to look less so. Yet when she finally drifted toward him, distinctly handsome, though ever so much older—older than when he had seen her before—it might have been as an effect of her guessing that he had, within the couple of hours, devoted more imagination to her than to all the others put together, and had thereby penetrated to a kind of truth that the others were too stupid for. She *was* there on harder terms than any one; she was there as a consequence of things suffered, one way and another, in the interval of years; and she remembered him very much as she was remembered—only a good deal better.

By the time they at last thus came to speech they were alone in one of the rooms—remarkable for a fine portrait over the chimney-place—out of which their friends had passed, and the charm of it was that even before they had spoken they had practically arranged with each other to stay behind to talk. The charm, happily, was in other things too—partly in there being scarce a spot at Weatherend without something to stay behind for. It was in the way the autumn day looked into the high windows as it waned; the way the red light, breaking at the close from under a low sombre sky, reached out in a long shaft and played over old wainscots, old tapestry, old gold, old colour. It was most of all perhaps in the way she came to him as if, since she had been turned on to deal with the simpler sort, he might, should he choose to keep the whole thing down, just take her mild attention for a part of her general business. As soon as he heard her voice, however, the gap was filled up and the missing link supplied; the slight irony he divined in her attitude lost its advantage. He almost jumped at it to get there before her. "I met you years and years ago in Rome. I remember all about it." She confessed to disappointment—she had been so sure he didn't; and to prove how well he did he began to pour forth the particular recollections that popped up as he called for them. Her face and her voice, all at his service now, worked the miracle—the impression operating like the torch of a lamplighter who touches into flame, one by one, a long row of gas-jets. Marcher flattered himself the illumination was brilliant, yet he was really still more pleased on her showing him, with amusement, that in his haste to make everything right he had got most things rather wrong. It hadn't been at Rome—it had been at Naples; and it hadn't been eight years before—it had been more nearly ten. She hadn't been, either, with her uncle and aunt, but with her mother and her brother; in addition to which it was not with the Pembles *he* had been, but with the Boyers, coming down in their company from Rome—a point on which she insisted, a little to his confusion, and as to which she had her evidence in hand. The Boyers she had known, but didn't know the Pembles, though she had heard of them, and it was the people he was with who had made them acquainted. The incident of the thunderstorm that had raged round them with such violence as to drive them for refuge into an excavation—this incident had not occurred at the Palace of the Cæsars, but at Pompeii, on an occasion when they had been present there at an important find.

He accepted her amendments, he enjoyed her corrections, though the moral of them was, she pointed out, that he *really* didn't remember the least thing about her; and he only felt it as a drawback that when all was made strictly historic there didn't appear much of anything left. They lingered together still, she neglecting her office—for from the moment he was so clever she had no proper right to him—and both neglecting the house, just waiting as to see if a memory or two more wouldn't again breathe on them. It hadn't taken them many minutes, after all, to put down on the table, like the cards of a pack, those that constituted their respective hands; only what came out was that the pack was unfortunately not perfect—that the past, invoked, invited, encouraged, could give them, naturally, no more than it had. It had made them anciently meet—her at twenty, him at twenty-five; but nothing was so strange, they seemed to say to each other, as that, while so occupied, it hadn't done a little more for them. They looked at each other as with the feeling of an occasion missed; the present would have been so much better if the other, in the far distance, in the foreign land, hadn't been so stupidly meagre. There weren't apparently, all counted, more than a dozen little old things that had succeeded in coming to pass between them; trivialities of youth, simplicities of freshness, stupidities of ignorance, small possible germs, but too deeply buried—too deeply (didn't it seem?) to sprout after so many years. Marcher could only feel he ought to have rendered her some service—saved her from a capsized boat in the Bay or at least recovered her dressing-bag, filched from her cab in the streets of Naples by a lazzarone with a stiletto. Or it would have been nice if he could have been taken with fever all alone at his hotel, and she could have come to look after him, to write to his people, to drive him out in convalescence. *Then* they would be in possession of the something or other that their actual show seemed to lack. It yet somehow presented itself, this show, as too good to be spoiled; so that they were reduced for a few minutes more to wondering a little helplessly why—since they seemed to know a certain number of the same people—their reunion had been so long averted. They didn't use that name for it, but their delay from minute to minute to join the others was a kind of confession that they didn't quite want it to be a failure. Their attempted supposition of reasons for their not having met but showed how little they knew of each other. There came in fact a moment when Marcher felt a positive pang. It was vain to pretend she was an old friend, for all the communities were wanting, in spite of which it was as an old friend that he saw she would have suited him. He had new ones enough—was surrounded with them for instance on the stage of the other house; as a new one he probably wouldn't have so much as noticed her. He would have liked to invent something, get her to make-believe with him that some passage of a romantic or critical kind *had* originally occurred. He was really almost reaching out in imagination—as against time—for something that would do, and saying to himself that if it didn't come this sketch of a fresh start would show for quite awkwardly bungled. They would separate, and now for no second or no third chance. They would have tried and not succeeded. Then it was, just at the turn, as he afterwards made it out to himself, that, everything else failing, she herself decided to take up the case and, as it were, save the situation. He felt as soon as she spoke that she had been consciously keeping back what she said and hoping to get on without it; a scruple in her that immensely touched him when, by the end of three or four minutes more, he was able to measure it. What she brought out, at any rate, quite cleared the air and supplied the link—the link it was so odd he should frivolously have managed to lose.

"You know you told me something I've never forgotten and that again and again has made me think of you since; it was that tremendously hot day when we went to Sorrento, across the bay, for the breeze. What I allude to was that you said to me, on the way back, as we sat under the awning of the boat enjoying the cool. Have you forgotten?"

He had forgotten and was even more surprised than ashamed. But the great thing was that he saw in this no vulgar reminder of any "sweet" speech. The vanity of women had long memories, but she was making no claim on him of a compliment or a mistake. With another woman, a totally different one, he might have feared the recall possibly even some imbecile "offer." So, in having to say that he had indeed forgotten, he was conscious rather of a loss than of a gain; he already saw an interest in the matter of her mention. "I try to think—but I give it up. Yet I remember the Sorrento day."

"I'm not very sure you do," May Bartram after a moment said; "and I'm not very sure I ought to want you to. It's dreadful to bring a person back at any time to what he was ten years before. If you've lived away from it," she smiled, "so much the better."

"Ah if *you* haven't why should I?" he asked.

"Lived away, you mean, from what I myself was?"

"From what *I* was. I was of course an ass," Marcher went on; "but I would rather know from you just the sort of ass I was than—from the moment you have something in your mind—not know anything."

Still, however, she hesitated. "But if you've completely ceased to be that sort—?"

"Why I can then all the more bear to know. Besides, perhaps I haven't."

"Perhaps. Yet if you haven't," she added, "I should suppose you'd remember. Not indeed that *I* in the least connect with my impression the invidious name you use. If I had only thought you foolish," she explained, "the thing I speak of wouldn't so have remained with me. It was about yourself." She waited as if it might come to him; but as, only meeting her eyes in wonder, he gave no sign, she burnt her ships. "Has it ever happened?"

Then it was that, while he continued to stare, a light broke for him and the blood slowly came to his face, which began to burn with recognition. "Do you mean I told you—?" But he faltered, lest what came to him shouldn't be right, lest he should only give himself away.

"It was something about yourself that it was natural one shouldn't forget—that is if one remembered you at all. That's why I ask you," she smiled, "if the thing you then spoke of has ever come to pass?"

Oh then he saw, but he was lost in wonder and found himself embarrassed. This, he also saw, made her sorry for him, as if her allusion had been a mistake. It took him but a moment, however, to feel it hadn't been, much as it had been a surprise. After the first little shock of it her knowledge on the contrary began, even if rather strangely, to taste sweet to him. She was the only other person in the world then who would have it, and she had had it all these years, while the fact of his having so breathed his secret had unaccountably faded from him. No wonder they couldn't have met as if nothing had happened. "I judge," he finally said, "that I know what you mean. Only I had strangely enough lost any sense of having taken you so far into my confidence."

"Is it because you've taken so many others as well?"

"I've taken nobody. Not a creature since then."

"So that I'm the only person who knows?"

"The only person in the world."

"Well," she quickly replied, "I myself have never spoken. I've never, never repeated of you what you told me." She looked at him so that he perfectly believed her. Their eyes met over it in such a way that he was without a doubt. "And I never will."

She spoke with an earnestness that, as if almost excessive, put him at ease about her possible derision. Somehow the whole question was a new luxury to him—that is from the moment she was in possession. If she didn't take the sarcastic view she clearly took the sympathetic, and that was what he had had, in all the long time, from no one whomsoever. What he felt was that he couldn't at present have begun to tell her, and yet could profit perhaps exquisitely by the accident of having done so of old. "Please don't then. We're just right as it is."

"Oh I am," she laughed, "if you are!" To which she added: "Then you do still feel in the same way?"

It was impossible he shouldn't take to himself that she was really interested, though it all kept coming as perfect surprise. He had thought of himself so long as abominably alone, and lo he wasn't alone a bit. He hadn't been, it appeared, for an hour—since those moments on the Sorrento boat. It was *she* who had been, he seemed to see as he looked at her—she who had been made so by the graceless fact of his lapse of fidelity. To tell her what he had told her—what had it been but to ask something of her? something that she had given, in her charity, without his having, by a remembrance, by a return of the spirit, failing another encounter, so much as thanked her. What he had asked of her had been simply at first not to laugh at him. She had beautifully not done so for ten years, and she was not doing so now. So he had endless gratitude to make up. Only for that he must see just how he had figured to her. "What, exactly, was the account I gave—?"

"Of the way you did feel? Well, it was very simple. You said you had had from your earliest time, as the deepest thing within you, the sense of being kept for something rare and strange, possibly prodigious and terrible, that was sooner or later to happen to you, that you had in your bones the foreboding and the conviction of, and that would perhaps overwhelm you."

"Do you call that very simple?" John Marcher asked.

She thought a moment. "It was perhaps because I seemed, as you spoke, to understand it."

"You do understand it?" he eagerly asked.

Again she kept her kind eyes on him. "You still have the belief?"

"Oh!" he exclaimed helplessly. There was too much to say.

"Whatever it's to be," she clearly made out, "it hasn't yet come."

He shook his head in complete surrender now. "It hasn't yet come. Only, you know, it isn't anything I'm to *do,* to achieve in the world, to be distinguished or admired for. I'm not such an ass as *that.* It would be much better, no doubt, if I were."

"It's to be something you're merely to suffer?"

"Well, say to wait for—to have to meet, to face, to see suddenly break out in my life; possibly destroying all further consciousness, possibly annihilating me; possibly, on the other hand, only altering everything, striking at the root of all my world and leaving me to the consequences, however they shape themselves."

She took this in, but the light in her eyes continued for him not to be that of mockery. "Isn't what you describe perhaps but the expectation—or at any rate the sense of danger, familiar to so many people—of falling in love?"

John Marcher wondered. "Did you ask me that before?"

"No—I wasn't so free-and-easy then. But it's what strikes me now."

"Of course," he said after a moment, "it strikes you. Of course it strikes *me*. Of course what's in store for me may be no more than that. The only thing is," he went on, "that I think if it had been that I should by this time know."

"Do you mean because you've *been* in love?" And then as he but looked at her in silence: "You've been in love, and it hasn't meant such a cataclysm, hasn't proved the great affair?"

"Here I am, you see. It hasn't been overwhelming."

"Then it hasn't been love," said May Bartram.

"Well, I at least thought it was. I took it for that—I've taken it till now. It was agreeable, it was delightful, it was miserable," he explained. "But it wasn't strange. It wasn't what *my* affair's to be."

"You want something all to yourself—something that nobody else knows or *has* known?"

"It isn't a question of what I 'want'—God knows I don't want anything. It's only a question of the apprehension that haunts me—that I live with day by day."

He said this so lucidly and consistently that he could see it further impose itself. If she hadn't been interested before she'd have been interested now. "Is it a sense of coming violence?"

Evidently now too again he liked to talk of it. "I don't think of it as—when it does come—necessarily violent. I only think of it as natural and as of course above all unmistakable. I think of it simply as *the* thing. *The* thing will of itself appear natural."

"Then how will it appear strange?"

Marcher bethought himself. "It won't—to *me*."

"To whom then?"

"Well," he replied, smiling at last, "say to you."

"Oh then I'm to be present?"

"Why you *are* present—since you know."

"I see." She turned it over. "But I mean at the catastrophe."

At this, for a minute, their lightness gave way to their gravity; it was as if the long look they exchanged held them together. "It will only depend on yourself—if you'll watch with me."

"Are you afraid?" she asked.

"Don't leave me *now*," he went on.

"Are you afraid?" she repeated.

"Do you think me simply out of my mind?" he pursued instead of answering. "Do I merely strike you as a harmless lunatic?"

"No," said May Bartram. "I understand you. I believe you."

"You mean you feel how my obsession—poor old thing!—may correspond to some possible reality?"

"To some possible reality."

"Then you *will* watch with me?"

She hesitated, then for the third time put her question. "Are you afraid?"

"Did I tell you I was—at Naples?"

"No, you said nothing about it."

"Then I don't know. And I should *like* to know," said John Marcher. "You'll tell me yourself whether you think so. If you'll watch with me you'll see."

"Very good then." They had been moving by this time across the room, and at the door, before passing out, they paused as for the full wind-up of their understanding. "I'll watch with you," said May Bartram.

2

The fact that she "knew"—knew and yet neither chaffed him nor betrayed him—had in a short time begun to constitute between them a goodly bond, which became more marked when, within the year that followed their afternoon at Weatherend, the opportunities for meeting multiplied. The event that thus promoted these occasions was the death of the ancient lady her great-aunt, under whose wing, since losing her mother, she had to such an extent found shelter, and who, though but the widowed mother of the new successor to the property, had succeeded—thanks to a high tone and a high temper—in not forfeiting the supreme position at the great house. The deposition of this personage arrived but with her death, which, followed by many changes, made in particular a difference for the young woman in whom Marcher's expert attention had recognised from the first a dependent with a pride that might ache though it didn't bristle. Nothing for a long time had made him easier than the thought that the aching must have been much soothed by Miss Bartram's now finding herself able to set up a small home in London. She had acquired property, to an amount that made that luxury just possible, under her aunt's extremely complicated will, and when the whole matter began to be straightened out, which indeed took time, she let him know that the happy issue was at last in view. He had seen her again before that day, both because she had more than once accompanied the ancient lady to town and because he had paid another visit to the friends who so conveniently made of Weatherend one of the charms of their own hospitality. These friends had taken him back there; he had achieved there again with Miss Bartram some quiet detachment; and he had in London succeeded in persuading her to more than one brief absence from her aunt. They went together, on these latter occasions, to the National Gallery and the South Kensington Museum, where, among vivid reminders, they talked of Italy at large—not now attempting to recover, as at first, the taste of their youth and their ignorance. That recovery, the first day at Weatherend, had served its purpose well, had given them quite enough; so that they were, to Marcher's sense, no longer hovering about the headwaters of their stream, but had felt their boat pushed sharply off and down the current.

They were literally afloat together; for our gentleman this was marked, quite as marked as that the fortunate cause of it was just the buried treasure of her knowledge. He had with his own hands dug up this little hoard, brought to light—that is to within reach of the dim day constituted by their discretions and privacies—the object of value the hiding-place of which he had, after putting it into the ground himself, so strangely, so long forgotten. The rare luck of his having again just stumbled on the spot made him indifferent to any other question; he would doubtless have devoted more time to the odd accident of his lapse of memory if he hadn't been moved to devote so much to the sweetness, the comfort, as he felt, for the future, that this accident itself had helped to keep fresh. It had never entered into his plan that any one should "know," and mainly for the reason that it wasn't in him to tell any one. That would have been impossible, for nothing but the amusement of a cold world would have waited on it. Since, however, a mysterious fate had opened his mouth betimes, in spite of him, he would count that a compensation and profit by it to the utmost. That the right person *should* know tempered the asperity of his secret more even than his shyness had permitted him to imagine; and May Bartram was clearly right, because—well, because there she was. Her knowledge simply settled it; he would have been sure enough by this time had she been wrong. There was that in his situation, no doubt, that disposed him too much to see her as a mere confidant, taking all her light for him from the fact—the fact only—of her interest in his predicament; from her mercy, sympathy, seriousness, her consent not to regard him as the funniest of the funny. Aware, in fine, that her price for him was just in her giving him this constant sense of his being admirably spared, he was careful to remember that she had also a life of her own, with things that might happen to *her,* things that in friendship one should likewise take account of. Something fairly remarkable came to pass with him, for that matter, in this connexion—something represented by a certain passage of his consciousness, in the suddenest way, from one extreme to the other.

He had thought himself, so long as nobody knew, the most disinterested person in the world, carrying his concentrated burden, his perpetual suspense, ever so quietly, holding his tongue about it, giving others no glimpse of it nor of its effect upon his life, asking of them no allowance and only making on his side all those that were asked. He hadn't disturbed people with the queerness of their having to know a haunted man, though he had had moments of rather special temptation on hearing them say they were forsooth "unsettled." If they were as unsettled as he was—he who had never been settled for an hour in his life—they would know what it meant. Yet it wasn't, all the same, for him to make them, and he listened to them civilly enough. This was why he had such good—though possibly such rather colourless—manners; this was why, above all, he could regard himself, in a greedy world, as decently—as in fact perhaps even a little sublimely—unselfish. Our point is accordingly that he valued this character quite sufficiently to measure his present danger of letting it lapse, against which he promised himself to be much on his guard. He was quite ready, none the less, to be selfish just a little, since surely no more charming occasion for it had come to him. "Just a little," in a word, was just as much as Miss Bartram, taking one day with another, would let him. He never would be in the least coercive, and would keep well before him the lines on which consideration for her—the very highest—ought to proceed. He would thoroughly establish the heads under which her affairs, her requirements, her peculiarities—he went so far as to give them the latitude of that name—would come into their intercourse. All this naturally was a sign of how much he took the intercourse itself for granted. There was nothing more to be done about *that.* It simply existed; had sprung into being with her first penetrating question to him in the autumn light there at Weatherend. The real form it should have taken on the basis that stood out large was the form of their marrying. But the devil in this was that the very basis itself put marrying out of the question. His conviction, his apprehension, his obsession, in short, wasn't a privilege he could invite a woman to share; and that consequence of it was precisely what was the matter with him. Something or other lay in wait for him, amid the twists and the turns of the months and the years, like a crouching beast in the jungle. It signified little whether the crouching beast were destined to slay him or to be slain. The definite point was the inevitable spring of the creature; and the definite lesson from that was that a man of feeling didn't cause himself to be accompanied by a lady on a tiger-hunt. Such was the image under which he had ended by figuring his life.

They had at first, none the less, in the scattered hours spent together, made no allusion to that view of it; which was a sign he was handsomely alert to give that he didn't expect, that he in fact didn't care, always to be talking about it. Such a feature in one's outlook was really like a hump on one's back. The differences it made every minute of the day existed quite independently of discussion. One discussed of course *like* a hunchback, for there was always, if nothing else, the hunchback face. That remained, and she was watching him; but people watched best, as a general thing, in silence, so that such would be predominantly the manner of their vigil. Yet he didn't want, at the same time, to be tense and solemn; tense and solemn was what he imagined he too much showed for with other people. The thing to be, with the one person who knew, was easy and natural—to make the reference rather than be seeming to avoid it, to avoid it rather than be seeming to make it, and to keep it, in any case, familiar, facetious even, rather than pedantic and portentous. Some such consideration as the latter was doubtless in his mind for instance when he wrote pleasantly to Miss Bartram that perhaps the great thing he had so long felt as in the lap of the gods was no more than this circumstance, which touched him so nearly, of her acquiring a house in London. It was the first allusion they had yet again made, needing any other hitherto so little; but when she replied, after having given him the news, that she was by no means satisfied with such a trifle as the climax to so special a suspense, she almost set him wondering if she hadn't even a larger conception of singularity for him than he had for himself. He was at all events destined to become aware little by little, as time went by, that she was all the while looking at his life, judging it, measuring it, in the light of the thing she knew, which grew to be at last, with the consecration of the years, never mentioned between them save as "the real truth" about him. That had always been his own form of reference to it, but she adopted the form so quietly that, looking back at the end of a period, he knew there was no moment at which it was traceable that she had, as he might say, got inside his idea, or exchanged the attitude of beautifully indulging for that of still more beautifully believing him.

It was always open to him to accuse her of seeing him but as the most harmless of maniacs, and this, in the long run—since it covered so much ground—was his easiest description of their friendship. He had a screw loose for her, but she liked him in spite of it and was practically, against the rest of the world, his kind wise keeper, unremunerated but fairly amused and, in the absence of other near ties, not disreputably occupied. The rest of the world of course thought him queer, but she, she only, knew how, and above all why, queer; which was precisely what enabled her to dispose the concealing veil in the right folds. She took his gaiety from him—since it had to pass with them for gaiety—as she took everything else; but she certainly so far justified by her unerring touch his finer sense of the degree to which he had ended by convincing her. *She* at least never spoke of the secret of his life except as "the real truth about you," and she had in fact a wonderful way of making it seem, as such, the secret of her own life too. That was in fine how he so constantly felt her as allowing for him; he couldn't on the whole call it anything else. He allowed for himself, but she, exactly, allowed still more; partly because, better placed for a sight of the matter, she traced his unhappy perversion through reaches of its course into which he could scarce follow it. He knew how he felt, but, besides knowing that, she knew how he *looked* as well; he knew each of the things of importance he was insidiously kept from doing, but she could add up the amount they made, understand how much, with a lighter weight on his spirit, he might have done, and thereby establish how, clever as he was, he fell short. Above all she was in the secret of the difference between the forms he went through—those of his little office under Government, those of caring for his modest patrimony, for his library, for his garden in the country, for the people in London whose invitations he accepted and repaid—and the detachment that reigned beneath them and that made of all behaviour, all that could in the least be called behaviour, a long act of dissimulation. What it had come to was that he wore a mask painted with the social simper, out of the eye-holes of which there looked eyes of an expression not in the least matching the other features. This the stupid world, even after years, had never more than half-discovered. It was only May Bartram who had, and she achieved, by an art indescribable, the feat of at once—or perhaps it was only alternately—meeting the eyes from in front and mingling her own vision, as from over his shoulder, with their peep through the apertures.

So while they grew older together she did watch with him, and so she let this association give shape and colour to her own existence. Beneath *her* forms as well detachment had learned to sit, and behaviour had become for her, in the social sense, a false account of herself. There was but one account of her that would have been true all the while and that she could give straight to nobody, least of all to John Marcher. Her whole attitude was a virtual statement, but the perception of that only seemed called to take its place for him as one of the many things necessarily crowded out of his consciousness. If she had moreover, like himself, to make sacrifices to their real truth, it was to be granted that her compensation might have affected her as more prompt and more natural. They had long periods, in this London time, during which, when they were together, a stranger might have listened to them without in the least pricking up his ears; on the other hand the real truth was equally liable at any moment to rise to the surface, and the auditor would then have wondered indeed what they were talking about. They had from an early hour made up their mind that society was, luckily, unintelligent, and the margin allowed them by this had fairly become one of their commonplaces. Yet there were still moments when the situation turned almost fresh— usually under the effect of some expression drawn from herself. Her expressions doubtless repeated themselves, but her intervals were generous. "What saves us, you know, is that we answer so completely to so usual an appearance: that of the man and woman whose friendship has become such a daily habit—or almost—as to be at last indispensable." That for instance was a remark she had frequently enough had occasion to make, though she had given it at different times different developments. What we are especially concerned with is the turn it happened to take from her one afternoon when he had come to see her in honour of her birthday. This anniversary had fallen on a Sunday, at a season of thick fog and general outward gloom; but he had brought her his customary offering, having known her now long enough to have established a hundred small traditions. It was one of his proofs to himself, the present he made her on her birthday, that he hadn't sunk into real selfishness. It was mostly nothing more than a small trinket, but it was always fine of its kind, and he was regularly careful to pay for it more than he thought he could afford. "Our habit saves you at least, don't you see? because it makes you, after all, for the vulgar, indistinguishable from other men. What's the most inveterate mark of men in general? Why the capacity to spend endless time with dull women—to spend it I won't say without being bored, but without minding that they are, without being driven off at a tangent by it; which comes to the same thing. I'm your dull woman, a part of the daily bread for which you pray at church. That covers your tracks more than anything."

"And what covers yours?" asked Marcher, whom his dull woman could mostly to this extent amuse. "I see of course what you mean by your saving me, in this way and that, so far as other people are concerned—I've seen it all along. Only what is it that saves *you*? I often think, you know, of that."

She looked as if she sometimes thought of that too, but rather in a different way. "Where other people, you mean, are concerned?"

"Well, you're really so in with me, you know—as a sort of result of my being so in with yourself. I mean of my having such an immense regard for you, being so tremendously mindful of all you've done for me. I sometimes ask myself if it's quite fair. Fair I mean to have so involved and—since one may say it—interested you. I almost feel as if you hadn't really had time to do anything else."

"Anything else but be interested?" she asked. "Ah what else does one ever want to be? If I've been 'watching' with you, as we long ago agreed I was to do, watching's always in itself an absorption."

"Oh certainly," John Marcher said, 'if you hadn't had your curiosity—! Only doesn't it sometimes come to you as time goes on that your curiosity isn't being particularly repaid?''

May Bartram had a pause. "Do you ask that, by any chance, because you feel at all that yours isn't? I mean because you have to wait so long.''

Oh he understood what she meant! "For the thing to happen that never does happen? For the beast to jump out? No, I'm just where I was about it. It isn't a matter as to which I can *choose,* I can decide for a change. It isn't one as to which there *can* be a change. It's in the lap of the gods. One's in the hands of one's law—there one is. As to the form the law will take, the way it will operate, that's its own affair.''

"Yes,'' Miss Bartram replied; "of course one's fate's coming, of course it *has* come in its own form and its own way, all the while. Only, you know, the form and the way in your case were to have been—well, something so exceptional and, as one may say, so particularly *your* own.''

Something in this made him look at her with suspicion. "You say 'were to *have* been,' as if in your heart you had begun to doubt.''

"Oh!'' she vaguely protested.

"As if you believed,'' he went on, "that nothing will now take place.''

She shook her head slowly but rather inscrutably. "You're far from my thought.''

He continued to look at her. "What then is the matter with you?''

"Well,'' she said after another wait, "the matter with me is simply that I'm more sure than ever my curiosity, as you call it, will be but too well repaid.''

They were frankly grave now; he had got up from his seat, had turned once more about the little drawing-room to which, year after year, he brought his inevitable topic; in which he had, as he might have said, tasted their intimate community with every sauce, where every object was as familiar to him as the things of his own house and the very carpets were worn with his fitful walk very much as the desks in old counting-houses are worn by the elbows of generations of clerks. The generations of his nervous moods had been at work there, and the place was the written history of his whole middle life. Under the impression of what his friend had just said he knew himself, for some reason, more aware of these things; which made him, after a moment, stop again before her. "Is it possibly that you've grown afraid?''

"Afraid?'' He thought, as she repeated the word, that his question had made her, a little, change colour; so that, lest he should have touched on a truth, he explained very kindly: "You remember that that was what you asked *me* long ago—that first day at Weatherend.''

"Oh yes, and you told me you didn't know—that I was to see for myself. We've said little about it since, even in so long a time.''

"Precisely,'' Marcher interposed—"quite as if it were too delicate a matter for us to make free with. Quite as if we might find, on pressure, that I *am* afraid. For then,'' he said, "we shouldn't, should we? quite know what to do.''

She had for the time no answer to this question. "There have been days when I thought you were. Only, of course,'' she added, "there have been days when we have thought almost anything.''

"Everything. Oh!'' Marcher softly groaned as with a gasp, half-spent, at the face, more uncovered just then than it had been for a long while, of the imagination always with them. It had always had its incalculable moments of glaring out, quite as with the very eyes of the very Beast, and, used as he was to them, they could still draw from him the tribute of a sigh that rose from the depths of his being. All they had thought, first and last, rolled over him; the past seemed to have been reduced to mere barren speculation. This in fact was what the place had just struck him as so full of—the simplification of everything but the state of suspense. That remained only by seeming to hang in the void surrounding it. Even his original fear, if fear it had been, had lost itself in the desert. "I judge, however," he continued, "that you see I'm not afraid now."

"What I see, as I make it out, is that you've achieved something almost unprecedented in the way of getting used to danger. Living with it so long and so closely you've lost your sense of it; you know it's there, but you're indifferent, and you cease even, as of old, to have to whistle in the dark. Considering what the danger is," May Bartram wound up, "I'm bound to say I don't think your attitude could well be surpassed."

John Marcher faintly smiled. "It's heroic?"

"Certainly—call it that."

It was what he would have liked indeed to call it. "I *am* then a man of courage?"

"That's what you were to show me."

He still, however, wondered. "But doesn't the man of courage know what he's afraid of—or *not* afraid of? I don't know *that,* you see. I don't focus it. I can't name it. I only know I'm exposed."

"Yes, but exposed—how shall I say?—so directly. So intimately. That's surely enough."

"Enough to make you feel then—as what we may call the end and the upshot of our watch—that I'm not afraid?"

"You're not afraid. But it isn't," she said, "the end of our watch. That is it isn't the end of yours. You've everything still to see."

"Then why haven't *you?*" he asked. He had had, all along, to-day, the sense of her keeping something back, and still had it. As this was his first impression of that it quite made a date. The case was the more marked as she didn't at first answer; which in turn made him go on. "You know something I don't." Then his voice, for that of a man of courage, trembled a little. "You know what's to happen." Her silence, with the face she showed, was almost a confession—it made him sure. "You know, and you're afraid to tell me. It's so bad that you're afraid I'll find out."

All this might be true, for she did look as if, unexpectedly to her, he had crossed some mystic line that she had secretly drawn round her. Yet she might, after all, not have worried; and the real climax was that he himself, at all events, needn't. "You'll never find out."

3

It was all to have made, none the less, as I have said, a date; which came out in the fact that again and again, even after long intervals, other things that passed between them wore in relation to this hour but the character of recalls and results. Its immediate effect had been indeed rather to lighten insistence—almost to provoke a reaction; as if their topic had dropped by its own weight and as if moreover, for that matter, Marcher had been visited by one of his occasional warnings against egotism. He had kept up, he felt, and very decently on the whole, his consciousness of the importance of not being selfish, and it was true that he had never sinned in that direction without promptly enough trying to press the scales the other way. He often repaired his fault, the season permitting, by inviting his friend to accompany him to the opera; and it not infrequently thus happened that, to show he didn't wish her to have but one sort of food for her mind, he was the cause of her appearing there with him a dozen nights in the month. It even happened that, seeing her home at such times, he occasionally went in with her to finish, as he called it, the evening, and, the better to make his point, sat down to the frugal but always careful little supper that awaited his pleasure. His point was made, he thought, by his not eternally insisting with her on himself; made for instance, at such hours, when it befell that, her piano at hand and each of them familiar with it, they went over passages of the opera together. It chanced to be on one of these occasions, however, that he reminded her of her not having answered a certain question he had put to her during the talk that had taken place between them on her last birthday. "What is it that saves *you?*"—saved her, he meant, from that appearance of variation from the usual human type. If he had practically escaped remark, as she pretended, by doing, in the most important particular, what most men do—find the answer to life in patching up an alliance of a sort with a woman no better than himself—how had she escaped it, and how could the alliance, such as it was, since they must suppose it had been more or less noticed, have failed to make her rather positively talked about?

"I never said," May Bartram replied, "that it hadn't made me a good deal talked about."

"Ah well then you're not 'saved.' "

"It hasn't been a question for me. If you've had your woman I've had," she said, "my man."

"And you mean that makes you all right?"

Oh it was always as if there were so much to say! "I don't know why it shouldn't make me—humanly, which is what we're speaking of—as right as it makes you."

"I see," Marcher returned. " 'Humanly,' no doubt, as showing that you're living for something. Not, that is, just for me and my secret."

May Bartram smiled. "I don't pretend it exactly showed that I'm not living for you. It's my intimacy with you that's in question."

He laughed as he saw what she meant. "Yes, but since, as you say, I'm only, so far as people make out, ordinary, you're—aren't you?—no more than ordinary either. You help me to pass for a man like another. So if I *am,* as I understand you, you're not compromised. Is that it?"

She had another of her waits, but she spoke clearly enough. "That's it. It's all that concerns me—to help you to pass for a man like another."

He was careful to acknowledge the remark handsomely. "How kind, how beautiful, you are to me! How shall I ever repay you?"

She had her last grave pause, as if there might be a choice of ways. But she chose. "By going on as you are."

It was into this going on as he was that they relapsed, and really for so long a time that the day inevitably came for a further sounding of their depths. These depths, constantly bridged over by a structure firm enough in spite of its lightness and of its occasional oscillation in the somewhat vertiginous air, invited on occasion, in the interest of their nerves, a dropping of the plummet and a measurement of the abyss. A difference had been made moreover, once for all, by the fact that she had all the while not appeared to feel the need of rebutting his charge of an idea within her that she didn't dare to express—a charge uttered just before one of the fullest of their later discussions ended. It had come up for him then that she "knew" something and that what she knew was bad—too bad to tell him. When he had spoken of it as visibly so bad that she was afraid he might find it out, her reply had left the matter too equivocal to be let alone and yet, for Marcher's special sensibility, almost too formidable again to touch. He circled about it at a distance that alternately narrowed and widened and that still wasn't much affected by the consciousness in him that there was nothing she could "know," after all, any better than he did. She had no source of knowledge he hadn't equally—except of course that she might have finer nerves. That was what women had where they were interested; they made out things, where people were concerned, that the people often couldn't have made out for themselves. Their nerves, their sensibility, their imagination, were conductors and revealers, and the beauty of May Bartram was in particular that she had given herself so to his case. He felt in these days what, oddly enough, he had never felt before, the growth of a dread of losing her by some catastrophe—some catastrophe that yet wouldn't at all be *the* catastrophe: partly because she had almost of a sudden begun to strike him as more useful to him than ever yet, and partly by reason of an appearance of uncertainty in her health, coincident and equally new. It was characteristic of the inner detachment he had hitherto so successfully cultivated and to which our whole account of him is a reference, it was characteristic that his complications, such as they were, had never yet seemed so as at this crisis to thicken about him, even to the point of making him ask himself if he were, by any chance, of a truth, within sight or sound, within touch or reach, within the immediate jurisdiction, of the thing that waited.

When the day came, as come it had to, that his friend confessed to him her fear of a deep disorder in her blood, he felt somehow the shadow of a change and the chill of a shock. He immediately began to imagine aggravations and disasters, and above all to think of her peril as the direct menace for himself of personal privation. This indeed gave him one of those partial recoveries of equanimity that were agreeable to him—it showed him that what was still first in his mind was the loss she herself might suffer. "What if she should have to die before knowing, before seeing—?" It would have been brutal, in the early stages of her trouble, to put that question to her; but it had immediately sounded for him to his own concern, and the possibility was what most made him sorry for her. If she did "know," moreover, in the sense of her having had some—what should he think?—mystical irresistible light, this would make the matter not better, but worse, inasmuch as her original adoption of his own curiosity had quite become the basis of her life. She had been living to see what would *be* to be seen, and it would quite lacerate her to have to give up before the accomplishment of the vision. These reflexions, as I say, quickened his generosity; yet, make them as he might, he saw himself, with the lapse of the period, more and more disconcerted. It lapsed for him with a strange steady sweep, and the oddest oddity was that it gave him, independently of the threat of much inconvenience, almost the only positive surprise his career, if career it could be called, had yet offered him. She kept the house as she had never done; he had to go to her to see her—she could meet him nowhere now, though there was scarce a corner of their loved old London in which she hadn't in the past, at one time or another, done so; and he found her always seated by her fire in the deep old-fashioned chair she was less and less able to leave. He had been struck one day, after an absence exceeding his usual measure, with her suddenly looking much older to him than he had ever thought of her being; then he recognized that the suddenness was all on his side—he had just simply and suddenly noticed. She looked older because inevitably, after so many years, she *was* old, or almost; which was of course true in still greater measure of her companion. If she was old, or almost, John Marcher assuredly was, and yet it was her showing of the lesson, not his own, that brought the truth home to him. His surprises began here; when once they had begun they multiplied; they came rather with a rush: it was as if, in the oddest way in the world, they had all been kept back, sown in a thick cluster, for the late afternoon of life, the time at which for people in general the unexpected has died out.

One of them was that he should have caught himself—for he *had* so done—*really* wondering if the great accident would take form now as nothing more than his being condemned to see this charming woman, this admirable friend, pass away from him. He had never so unreservedly qualified her as while confronted in thought with such a possibility; in spite of which there was small doubt for him that as an answer to his long riddle the mere effacement of even so fine a feature of his situation would be an abject anticlimax. It would represent, as connected with his past attitude, a drop of dignity under the shadow of which his existence could only become the most grotesque of failures. He had been far from holding it a failure—long as he had waited for the appearance that was to make it a success. He had waited for quite another thing, not for such a thing as that. The breath of his good faith came short, however, as he recognised how long he had waited, or how long at least his companion had. That she, at all events, might be recorded as having waited in vain—this affected him sharply, and all the more because of his at first having done little more than amuse himself with the idea. It grew more grave as the gravity of her condition grew, and the state of mind it produced in him, which he himself ended by watching as if it had been some definite disfigurement of his outer person, may pass for another of his surprises. This conjoined itself still with another, the really stupefying consciousness of a question that he would have allowed to shape itself had he dared. What did everything mean—what, that is, did *she* mean, she and her vain waiting and her probable death and the soundless admonition of it all— unless that, at this time of day, it was simply, it was overwhelmingly too late? He had never at any stage of his queer consciousness admitted the whisper of such a correction; he had never till within these last few months been so false to his conviction as not to hold that what was to come to him had time, whether *he* struck himself as having it or not. That at last, at last, he certainly hadn't it, to speak of, or had it but in the scantiest measure—such, soon enough, as things went with him, became the inference with which his old obsession had to reckon: and this it was not helped to do by the more and more confirmed appearance that the great vagueness casting the long shadow in which he had lived had, to attest itself, almost no margin left. Since it was in Time that he was to have met his fate, so it was in Time that his fate was to have acted; and as he waked up to the sense of no longer being young, which was exactly the sense of being stale, just as that, in turn, was the sense of being weak, he waked up to another matter beside. It all hung together; they were subject, he and the great vagueness, to an equal and indivisible law. When the possibilities themselves had accordingly turned stale, when the secret of the gods had grown faint, had perhaps even quite evaporated, that, and that only, was failure. It wouldn't have been failure to be bankrupt, dishonoured, pilloried, hanged; it was failure not to be anything. And so, in the dark valley into which his path had taken its unlooked-for twist, he wondered not a little as he groped. He didn't care what awful crash might overtake him, with what ignominy or what monstrosity he might yet be associated—since he wasn't after all too utterly old to suffer—if it would only be decently proportionate to the posture he had kept, all his life, in the threatened presence of it. He had but one desire left—that he shouldn't have been "sold."

4

Then it was that, one afternoon, while the spring of the year was young and new she met all in her own way his frankest betrayal of these alarms. He had gone in late to see her, but evening hadn't settled and she was presented to him in that long fresh light of waning April days which affects us often with a sadness sharper than the greyest hours of autumn. The week had been warm, the spring was supposed to have begun early, and May Bartram sat, for the first time in the year, without a fire; a fact that, to Marcher's sense, gave the scene of which she formed part a smooth and ultimate look, an air of knowing, in its immaculate order and cold meaningless cheer, that it would never see a fire again. Her own aspect—he could scarce have said why—intensified this note.

Almost as white as wax, with the marks and signs in her face as numerous and as fine as if they had been etched by a needle, with soft white draperies relieved by a faded green scarf on the delicate tone of which the years had further refined, she was the picture of a serene and exquisite but impenetrable sphinx, whose head, or indeed all whose person, might have been powdered with silver. She was a sphinx, yet with her white petals and green fronds she might have been a lily too—only an artificial lily, wonderfully imitated and constantly kept, without dust or stain, though not exempt from a slight droop and a complexity of faint creases, under some clear glass bell. The perfection of household care, of high polish and finish, always reigned in her rooms, but they now looked most as if everything had been wound up, tucked in, put away, so that she might sit with folded hands and with nothing more to do. She was "out of it," to Marcher's vision; her work was over; she communicated with him as across some gulf or from some island of rest that she had already reached, and it made him feel strangely abandoned. Was it—or rather wasn't it—that if for so long she had been watching with him the answer to their question must have swum into her ken and taken on its name, so that her occupation was verily gone? He had as much as charged her with this in saying to her, many months before, that she even then knew something she was keeping from him. It was a point he had never since ventured to press, vaguely fearing as he did that it might become a difference, perhaps a disagreement, between them. He had in this later time turned nervous, which was what he in all the other years had never been; and the oddity was that his nervousness should have waited till he had begun to doubt, should have held off so long as he was sure. There was something, it seemed to him, that the wrong word would bring down on his head, something that would so at least ease off his tension. But he wanted not to speak the wrong word; that would make everything ugly. He wanted the knowledge he lacked to drop on him, if drop it could, by its own august weight. If she was to forsake him it was surely for her to take leave. This was why he didn't directly ask her again what she knew; but it was also why, approaching the matter from another side, he said to her in the course of his visit: "What do you regard as the very worst that at this time of day *can* happen to me?"

He had asked her that in the past often enough; they had, with the odd irregular rhythm of their intensities and avoidances, exchanged ideas about it and then had seen the ideas washed away by cool intervals, washed like figures traced in sea-sand. It had ever been the mark of their talk that the oldest allusions in it required but a little dismissal and reaction to come out again, sounding for the hour as new. She could thus at present meet his enquiry quite freshly and patiently. "Oh yes, I've repeatedly thought, only it always seemed to me of old that I couldn't quite make up my mind. I thought of dreadful things, between which it was difficult to choose; and so must you have done."

"Rather! I feel now as if I had scarce done anything else. I appear to myself to have spent my life in thinking of nothing *but* dreadful things. A great many of them I've at different times named to you, but there were others I couldn't name."

"They were too, too dreadful?"

"Too, too dreadful—some of them."

She looked at him a minute, and there came to him as he met it an inconsequent sense that her eyes, when one got their full clearness, were still as beautiful as they had been in youth, only beautiful with a strange cold light—a light that somehow was a part of the effect, if it wasn't rather a part of the cause, of the pale hard sweetness of the season and the hour. "And yet," she said at last, "there are horrors we've mentioned."

It deepened the strangeness to see her, as such a figure in such a picture, talk of "horrors," but she was to do in a few minutes something stranger yet—though even of this he was to take the full measure but afterwards—and the note of it already trembled. It was, for the matter of that, one of the signs that her eyes were having again the high flicker of their prime. He had to admit, however, what she said. "Oh yes, there were times when we did go far." He caught himself in the act of speaking as if it all were over. Well, he wished it were; and the consummation depended for him clearly more and more on his friend.

But she had now a soft smile. "Oh far—!"

It was oddly ironic. "Do you mean you're prepared to go further?"

She was frail and ancient and charming as she continued to look at him, yet it was rather as if she had lost the thread. "Do you consider that we went far?"

"Why I thought it the point you were just making—that we *had* looked most things in the face."

"Including each other?" She still smiled. "But you're quite right. We've had together great imaginations, often great fears; but some of them have been unspoken."

"Then the worst—we haven't faced that. I *could* face it, I believe, if I knew what you think it. I feel," he explained, "as if I had lost my power to conceive such things." And he wondered if he looked as blank as he sounded. "It's spent."

"Then why do you assume," she asked, "that mine isn't?"

"Because you've given me signs to the contrary. It isn't a question for you of conceiving, imagining, comparing. It isn't a question now of choosing." At last he came out with it. "You know something I don't. You've shown me that before."

These last words had affected her, he made out in a moment, exceedingly, and she spoke with firmness. "I've shown you, my dear, nothing."

He shook his head. "You can't hide it."

"Oh, oh!" May Bartram sounded over what she couldn't hide. It was almost a smothered groan.

"You admitted it months ago, when I spoke of it to you as of something you were afraid I should find out. Your answer was that I couldn't, that I wouldn't, and I don't pretend I have. But you had something therefore in mind, and I now see how it must have been, how it still is, the possibility that, of all possibilities, has settled itself for you as the worst. This," he went on, "is why I appeal to you. I'm only afraid of ignorance to-day—I'm not afraid of knowledge." And then as for a while she said nothing: "What makes me sure is that I see in your face and feel here, in this air and amid these appearances, that you're out of it. You've done. You've had your experience. You leave me to my fate."

Well, she listened, motionless and white in her chair, as on a decision to be made, so that her manner was fairly an avowal, though still, with a small fine inner stiffness, an imperfect surrender. "It *would* be the worst," she finally let herself say. "I mean the thing I've never said."

It hushed him a moment. "More monstrous than all the monstrosities we've named?"

"More monstrous. Isn't that what you sufficiently express," she asked, "in calling it the worst?"

Marcher thought. "Assuredly—if you mean, as I do, something that includes all the loss and all the shame that are thinkable."

"It would if it *should* happen," said May Bartram. "What we're speaking of, remember, is only my idea."

"It's your belief," Marcher returned. "That's enough for me. I feel your beliefs are right. Therefore if, having this one, you give me no more light on it, you abandon me."

"No, no!" she repeated. "I'm with you—don't you see?—still." And as to make it more vivid to him she rose from her chair—a movement she seldom risked in these days—and showed herself, all draped and all soft, in her fairness and slimness. "I haven't forsaken you."

It was really, in its effort against weakness, a generous assurance, and had the success of the impulse not, happily, been great, it would have touched him to pain more than to pleasure. But the cold charm in her eyes had spread, as she hovered before him, to all the rest of her person, so that it was for the minute almost a recovery of youth. He couldn't pity her for that; he could only take her as she showed—as capable even yet of helping him. It was as if, at the same time, her light might at any instant go out; wherefore he must make the most of it. There passed before him with intensity the three or four things he wanted most to know; but the question that came of itself to his lips really covered the others. "Then tell me if I shall consciously suffer."

She promptly shook her head. "Never!"

It confirmed the authority he imputed to her, and it produced on him an extraordinary effect. "Well, what's better than that? Do you call that the worst?"

"You think nothing is better?" she asked.

She seemed to mean something so special that he again sharply wondered, though still with the dawn of a prospect of relief. "Why not, if one doesn't *know*?" After which, as their eyes, over his question, met in a silence, the dawn deepened and something to his purpose came prodigiously out of her very face. His own, as he took it in, suddenly flushed to the forehead, and he gasped with the force of a perception to which, on the instant, everything fitted. The sound of his gasp filled the air; then he became articulate. "I see—if I don't suffer!"

In her own look, however, was doubt. "You see what?"

"Why what you mean—what you've always meant."

She again shook her head. "What I mean isn't what I've always meant. It's different."

"It's something new?"

She hung back from it a little. "Something new. It's not what you think. I see what you think."

His divination drew breath then; only her correction might be wrong. "It isn't that I *am* a blockhead?" he asked between faintness and grimness. "It isn't that it's all a mistake?"

"A mistake?" she pityingly echoed. *That* possibility, for her, he saw, would be monstrous; and if she guaranteed him the immunity from pain it would accordingly not be what she had in mind. "Oh no," she declared; "it's nothing of that sort. You've been right."

Yet he couldn't help asking himself if she weren't, thus pressed, speaking but to save him. It seemed to him he should be most in a hole if his history should prove all a platitude. "Are you telling me the truth, so that I shan't have been a bigger idiot than I can bear to know? I *haven't* lived with a vain imagination, in the most besotted illusion? I haven't waited but to see the door shut in my face?"

She shook her head again. "However the case stands *that* isn't the truth. Whatever the reality, it *is* a reality. The door isn't shut. The door's open," said May Bartram.

"Then something's to come?"

She waited once again, always with her cold sweet eyes on him. "It's never too late." She had, with her gliding step, diminished the distance between them, and she stood nearer to him, close to him, a minute, as if still charged with the unspoken. Her movement might have been for some finer emphasis on what she was at once hesitating and deciding to say. He had been standing by the chimney-piece, fireless and sparely adorned, a small perfect old French clock and two morsels of rosy Dresden constituting all its furniture; and her hand grasped the shelf while she kept him waiting, grasped it a little as for support and encouragement. She only kept him waiting, however; that is he only waited. It had become suddenly, from her movement and attitude, beautiful and vivid to him that she had something more to give him; her wasted face delicately shone with it—it glittered almost as with the white lustre of silver in her expression. She was right, incontestably, for what he saw in her face was the truth, and strangely, without consequence, while their talk of it as dreadful was still in the air, she appeared to present it as inordinately soft. This, prompting bewilderment, made him but gape the more gratefully for her revelation, so that they continued for some minutes silent, her face shining at him, her contact imponderably pressing, and his stare all kind but all expectant. The end, none the less, was that what he had expected failed to come to him. Something else took place instead, which seemed to consist at first in the mere closing of her eyes. She gave way at the same instant to a slow fine shudder, and though he remained staring—though he stared in fact but the harder—turned off and regained her chair. It was the end of what she had been intending, but it left him thinking only of that.

"Well, you don't say—?"

She had touched in her passage a bell near the chimney and had sunk back strangely pale. "I'm afraid I'm too ill."

"Too ill to tell me?" It sprang up sharp to him, and almost to his lips, the fear she might die without giving him light. He checked himself in time from so expressing his question, but she answered as if she had heard the words.

"Don't you know—now?"

"Now'—?" She had spoken as if some difference had been made within the moment. But her maid, quickly obedient to her bell, was already with them. "I know nothing." And he was afterwards to say to himself that he must have spoken with odious impatience, such an impatience as to show that, supremely disconcerted, he washed his hands of the whole question.

"Oh!" said May Bartram.

"Are you in pain?" he asked as the woman went to her.

"No," said May Bartram.

Her maid, who had put an arm round her as if to take her to her room, fixed on him eyes that appealingly contradicted her; in spite of which, however, he showed once more his mystification. "What then has happened?"

She was once more, with her companion's help, on her feet, and, feeling withdrawal imposed on him, he had blankly found his hat and gloves and had reached the door. Yet he waited for her answer. "What *was* to," she said.

5

He came back the next day, but she was then unable to see him, and as it was literally the first time this had occurred in the long stretch of their acquaintance he turned away, defeated and sore, almost angry—or feeling at least that such a break in their custom was really the beginning of the end—and wandered alone with his thoughts, especially with the one he was least able to keep down. She was dying and he would lose her; she was dying and his life would end. He stopped in the Park, into which he had passed, and stared before him at his recurrent doubt. Away from her the doubt pressed again; in her presence he had believed her, but as he felt his forlornness he threw himself into the explanation that, nearest at hand, had most of a miserable warmth for him and least of a cold torment. She had deceived him to save him—to put him off with something in which he should be able to rest. What could the thing that was to happen to him be, after all, but just this thing that had begun to happen? Her dying, her death, his consequent solitude—*that* was what he had figured as the Beast in the Jungle, that was what had been in the lap of the gods. He had had her word for it as he left her—what else on earth could she have meant? It wasn't a thing of a monstrous order; not a fate rare and distinguished; not a stroke of fortune that overwhelmed and immortalised; it had only the stamp of the common doom. But poor Marcher at this hour judged the common doom sufficient. It would serve his turn, and even as the consummation of infinite waiting he would bend his pride to accept it. He sat down on a bench in the twilight. He hadn't been a fool. Something had *been,* as she had said, to come. Before he rose indeed it had quite struck him that the final fact really matched with the long avenue through which he had had to reach it. As sharing his suspense and as giving herself all, giving her life, to bring it to an end, she had come with him every step of the way. He had lived by her aid, and to leave her behind would be cruelly, damnably to miss her. What could be more overwhelming than that?

Well, he was to know within the week, for though she kept him a while at bay, left him restless and wretched during a series of days on each of which he asked about her only again to have to turn away, she ended his trial by receiving him where she had always received him. Yet she had been brought out at some hazard into the presence of so many things that were, consciously, vainly, half their past, and there was scant service left in the gentleness of her mere desire, all too visible, to check his obsession and wind up his long trouble. That was clearly what she wanted, the one thing more for her own peace while she could still put out her hand. He was so affected by her state that, once seated by her chair, he was moved to let everything go; it was she herself therefore who brought him back, took up again, before she dismissed him, her last word of the other time. She showed how she wished to leave their business in order. "I'm not sure you understood. You've nothing to wait for more. It *has* come."

Oh how he looked at her! "Really?"

"Really."

"The thing that, as you said, *was* to?"

"The thing that we began in our youth to watch for."

Face to face with her once more he believed her; it was a claim to which he had so abjectly little to oppose. "You mean that it has come as a positive definite occurrence, with a name and a date?"

"Positive. Definite. I don't know about the 'name,' but oh with a date!"

He found himself again too helplessly at sea. "But come in the night—come and passed me by?"

May Bartram had her strange faint smile. "Oh no, it hasn't passed you by!"

"But if I haven't been aware of it and it hasn't touched me—?"

"Ah your not being aware of it"—and she seemed to hesitate an instant to deal with this—"your not being aware of it is the strangeness *in* the strangeness. Its the wonder *of* the wonder." She spoke as with the softness almost of a sick child, yet now at last, at the end of all, with the perfect straightness of a sibyl. She visibly knew that she knew, the effect on him was of something co-ordinate, in its high character, with the law that had ruled him. It was the true voice of the law; so on her lips would the law itself have sounded. "It *has* touched you," she went on. "It has done its office. It has made you all its own."

"So utterly without my knowing it?"

"So utterly without your knowing it." His hand, as he leaned to her, was on the arm of her chair, and, dimly smiling always now, she placed her own on it. "It's enough if *I* know it."

"Oh!" he confusedly breathed, as she herself of late so often had done.

"What I long ago said is true. You'll never know now, and I think you ought to be content. You've *had* it," said May Bartram.

"But had what?"

"Why what was to have marked you out. The proof of your law. It has acted. I'm too glad," she then bravely added, "to have been able to see what it's *not*."

He continued to attach his eyes to her, and with the sense that it was all beyond him, and that *she* was too, he would still have sharply challenged her hadn't he so felt it an abuse of her weakness to do more than take devoutly what she gave him, take it hushed as to a revelation. If he did speak, it was out of the foreknowledge of his loneliness to come. "If you're glad of what it's 'not' it might then have been worse?"

She turned her eyes away, she looked straight before her; with which after a moment: "Well, you know our fears."

He wondered. "It's something then we never feared?"

On this slowly she turned to him. "Did we ever dream, with all our dreams, that we should sit and talk of it thus?"

He tried for a little to make out that they had; but it was as if their dreams, numberless enough, were in solution in some thick cold mist through which thought lost itself. "It might have been that we couldn't talk?"

"Well"—she did her best for him—"not from this side. This, you see," she said, "is the *other* side."

"I think," poor Marcher returned, "that all sides are the same to me." Then, however, as she gently shook her head in correction: "We mightn't, as it were, have got across—?"

"To where we are—no. We're *here*"—she made her weak emphasis.

"And much good does it do us!" was her friend's frank comment.

"It does us the good it can. It does us the good that *it* isn't here. It's past, It's behind," said May Bartram. "Before—" but her voice dropped.

He had got up, not to tire her, but it was hard to combat his yearning. She after all told him nothing but that his light had failed—which he knew well enough without her. "Before—?" he blankly echoed.

"Before, you see, it was always to *come*. That kept it present."

"Oh I don't care what comes now! Besides," Marcher added, "it seems to me I liked it better present, as you say, than I can like it absent with *your* absence."

"Oh mine!"—and her pale hands made light of it.

"With the absence of everything." He had a dreadful sense of standing there before her for—so far as anything but this proved, this bottomless drop was concerned—the last time of their life. It rested on him with a weight he felt he could scarce bear, and this weight it apparently was that still pressed out what remained in him of speakable protest. "I believe you; but I can't begin to pretend I understand. *Nothing,* for me, is past; nothing *will* pass till I pass myself, which I pray my stars may be as soon as possible. Say, however," he added, "that I've eaten my cake, as you contend, to the last crumb—how can the thing I've never felt at all be the thing I was marked out to feel?"

She met him perhaps less directly, but she met him unperturbed. "You take your 'feelings' for granted. You were to suffer your fate. That was not necessarily to know it."

"How in the world—when what is such knowledge but suffering?"

She looked up at him a while in silence. "No—you don't understand."

"I suffer," said John Marcher.

"Don't, don't!"

"How can I help at least *that*?"

"Don't!" May Bartram repeated.

She spoke it in a tone so special, in spite of her weakness, that he stared an instant—stared as if some light, hitherto hidden, had shimmered across his vision. Darkness again closed over it, but the gleam had already become for him an idea. "Because I haven't the right—?"

"Don't *know*—when you needn't," she mercifully urged. "You needn't—for we shouldn't."

"Shouldn't?" If he could but know what she meant!

"No—it's too much."

"Too much?" he still asked but, with a mystification that was the next moment of a sudden to give way. Her words, if they meant something, affected him in this light—the light also of her wasted face—as meaning *all,* and the sense of what knowledge had been for herself came over him with a rush which broke through into a question. "Is it of that then you're dying?"

She but watched him, gravely at first, as to see, with this, where he was, and she might have seen something or feared something that moved her sympathy. "I would live for you still—if I could." Her eyes closed for a little, as if, withdrawn into herself, she were for a last time trying. "But I can't!" she said as she raised them again to take leave of him.

She couldn't indeed, as but too promptly and sharply appeared, and he had no vision of her after this that was anything but darkness and doom. They had parted for ever in that strange talk; access to her chamber of pain, rigidly guarded, was almost wholly forbidden him; he was feeling now moreover, in the face of doctors, nurses, the two or three relatives attracted doubtless by the presumption of what she had to "leave," how few were the rights, as they were called in such cases, that he had to put forward, and how odd it might even seem that their intimacy shouldn't have given him more of them. The stupidest fourth cousin had more, even though she had been nothing in such a person's life. She had been a feature of features in *his,* for what else was it to have been so indispensable? Strange beyond saying were the ways of existence, baffling for him the anomaly of his lack, as he felt it to be, of producible claim. A woman might have been, as it were, everything to him, and it might yet present him in no connexion that any one seemed held to recognise. If this was the case in these closing weeks it was the case more sharply on the occasion of the last offices rendered, in the great grey London cemetery, to what had been mortal, to what had been precious, in his friend. The concourse at her grave was not numerous, but he saw himself treated as scarce more nearly concerned with it than if there had been a thousand others. He was in short from this moment face to face with the fact that he was to profit extraordinarily little by the interest May Bartram had taken in him. He couldn't quite have said what he expected, but he hadn't surely expected this approach to a double privation. Not only had her interest failed him, but he seemed to feel himself unattended—and for a reason he couldn't seize—by the distinction, the dignity, the propriety, if nothing else, of the man markedly bereaved. It was as if in the view of society he had not *been* markedly bereaved, as if there still failed some sign of proof of it, and as if none the less his character could never be affirmed nor the deficiency ever made up. There were moments as the weeks went by when he would have liked, by some almost aggressive act, to take his stand on the intimacy of his loss, in order that it *might* be questioned and his retort, to the relief of his spirit, so recorded; but the moments of an irritation more helpless followed fast on these, the moments during which, turning things over with a good conscience but with a bare horizon, he found himself wondering if he oughtn't to have begun, so to speak, further back.

He found himself wondering indeed at many things, and this last speculation had others to keep it company. What could he have done, after all, in her lifetime, without giving them both, as it were, away? He couldn't have made known she was watching him, for that would have published the superstition of the Beast. This was what closed his mouth now—now that the Jungle had been threshed to vacancy and that the Beast had stolen away. It sounded too foolish and too flat; the difference for him in this particular, the extinction in his life of the element of suspense, was such as in fact to surprise him. He could scarce have said what the effect resembled; the abrupt cessation, the positive prohibition, of music perhaps, more than anything else, in some place all adjusted and all accustomed to sonority and to attention. If he could at any rate have conceived lifting the veil from his image at some moment of the past (what had he done, after all, if not lift it to *her?)* so to do this to-day, to talk to people at large of the Jungle cleared and confide to them that he now felt it as safe, would have been not only to see them listen as to a goodwife's tale, but really to hear himself tell one. What it presently came to in truth was that poor Marcher waded through his beaten grass, where no life stirred, where no breath sounded, where no evil eye seemed to gleam from a possible lair, very much as if vaguely looking for the Beast, and still more as if acutely missing it. He walked about in an existence that had grown strangely more spacious, and, stopping fitfully in places where the undergrowth of life struck him as closer, asked himself yearningly, wondered secretly and sorely, if it would have lurked here or there. It would have at all events *sprung;* what was at least complete was his belief in the truth itself of the assurance given him. The change from his old sense to his new was absolute and final: what was to happen *had* so absolutely and finally happened that he was as little able to know a fear for his future as to know a hope; so absent in short was any question of anything still to come. He was to live entirely with the other question, that of his unidentified past, that of his having to see his fortune impenetrably muffled and masked.

The torment of this vision became then his occupation; he couldn't perhaps have consented to live but for the possibility of guessing. She had told him, his friend, not to guess; she had forbidden him, so far as he might, to know, and she had even in a sort denied the power in him to learn: which were so many things, precisely, to deprive him of rest. It wasn't that he wanted, he argued for fairness, that anything past and done should repeat itself; it was only that he shouldn't, as an anticlimax, have been taken sleeping so sound as not to be able to win back by an effort of thought the lost stuff of consciousness. He declared to himself at moments that he would either win it back or have done with consciousness for ever; he made this idea his one motive in fine, made it so much his passion that none other, to compare with it, seemed ever to have touched him. The lost stuff of consciousness became thus for him as a strayed or stolen child to an unappeasable father; he hunted it up and down very much as if he were knocking at doors and enquiring of the police. This was the spirit in which, inevitably, he set himself to travel; he started on a journey that was to be as long as he could make it; it danced before him that, as the other side of the globe couldn't possibly have less to say to him, it might, by a possibility of suggestion, have more. Before he quitted London, however, he made a pilgrimage to May Bartram's grave, took his way to it through the endless avenues of the grim suburban metropolis, sought it out in the wilderness of tombs, and though he had come but for the renewal of the act of farewell, found himself, when he had at last stood by it, beguiled into long intensities. He stood for an hour, powerless to turn away and yet powerless to penetrate the darkness of death; fixing with his eyes her inscribed name and date, beating his forehead against the fact of the secret they kept, drawing his breath, while he waited, as if some sense would in pity of him rise from the stones. He kneeled on the stones, however, in vain; they kept what they concealed; and if the face of the tomb did become a face for him it was because her two names became a pair of eyes that didn't know him. He gave them a last long look, but no palest light broke.

6

He stayed away, after this, for a year; he visited the depths of Asia, spending himself on scenes of romantic interest, of superlative sanctity; but what was present to him everywhere was that for a man who had known what *he* had known the world was vulgar and vain. The state of mind in which he had lived for so many years shone out to him, in reflexion, as a light that coloured and refined, a light beside which the glow of the East was garish, cheap and thin. The terrible truth was that he had lost—with everything else—a distinction as well; the things he saw couldn't help being common when he had become common to look at them. He was simply now one of them himself—he was in the dust, without a peg for the sense of difference; and there were hours when, before the temples of gods and the sepulchres of kings, his spirit turned for nobleness of association to the barely discriminated slab in the London suburb. That had become for him, and more intensely with time and distance, his one witness of a past glory. It was all that was left to him for proof or pride, yet the past glories of Pharaohs were nothing to him as he thought of it. Small wonder then that he came back to it on the morrow of his return. He was drawn there this time as irresistibly as the other, yet with a confidence, almost, that was doubtless the effect of the many months that had elapsed. He had lived, in spite of himself, into his change of feeling, and in wandering over the earth had wandered, as might be said, from the circumference to the centre of his desert. He had settled to his safety and accepted perforce his extinction; figuring to himself, with some colour, in the likeness of certain little old men he remembered to have seen, of whom, all meagre and wizened as they might look, it was related that they had in their time fought twenty duels or been loved by ten princesses. They indeed had been wondrous for others while he was but wondrous for himself; which, however, was exactly the cause of his haste to renew the wonder by getting back, as he might put it, into his own presence. That had quickened his steps and checked his delay. If his visit was prompt it was because he had been separated so long from the part of himself that alone he now valued.

It's accordingly not false to say that he reached his goal with a certain elation and stood there again with a certain assurance. The creature beneath the sod *knew* of his rare experience, so that, strangely now, the place had lost for him its mere blankness of expression. It met him in mildness—not, as before, in mockery; it wore for him the air of conscious greeting that we find, after absence, in things that have closely belonged to us and which seem to confess of themselves to the connexion. The plot of ground, the graven tablet, the tended flowers affected him so as belonging to him that he resembled for the hour a contented landlord reviewing a piece of property. Whatever had happened—well, had happened. He had not come back this time with the vanity of that question, his former worrying "What, *what*?" now practically so spent. Yet he would none the less never again so cut himself off from the spot; he would come back to it every month, for if he did nothing else by its aid he at least held up his head. It thus grew for him, in the oddest way, a positive resource; he carried out his idea of periodical returns, which took their place at last among the most inveterate of his habits. What it all amounted to, oddly enough, was that in his finally so simplified world this garden of death gave him the few square feet of earth on which he could still most live. It was as if, being nothing anywhere else for any one, nothing even for himself, he were just every-thing here, and if not for a crowd of witnesses or indeed for any witness but John Marcher, then by clear right of the register that he could scan like an open page. The open page was the tomb of his friend, and *there* were the facts of the past, there the truth of his life, there the backward reaches in which he could lose himself. He did this from time to time with such effect that he seemed to wander through the old years with his hand in the arm of a companion who was, in the most extraordinary manner, his other, his younger self; and to wander, which was more extraordinary yet, round and round a third presence—not wandering she, but stationary, still, whose eyes, turning with his resolution, never ceased to follow him, and whose seat was his point, so to speak, of orientation. Thus in short he settled to live—feeding all on the sense that he once *had* lived, and dependent on it not alone for a support but for an identity.

It sufficed him in its way for months and the year elapsed; it would doubtless even have carried him further but for an accident, superficially slight, which moved him, quite in another direction, with a force beyond any of his impressions of Egypt or of India. It was a thing of the merest chance—the turn, as he afterwards felt, of a hair, though he was indeed to live to believe that if light hadn't come to him in this particular fashion it would still have come in another. He was to live to believe this, I say, though he was not to live, I may not less definitely mention, to do much else. We allow him at any rate the benefit of the conviction, struggling up for him at the end, that, whatever might have happened or not happened, he would have come round of himself to the light. The incident of an autumn day had put the match to the train laid from of old by his misery. With the light before him he knew that even of late his ache had only been smothered. It was strangely drugged, but it throbbed; at the touch it began to bleed. And the touch, in the event, was the face of a fellow mortal. This face, one grey afternoon when the leaves were thick in the alleys, looked into Marcher's own, at the cemetery, with an expression like the cut of a blade. He felt it, that is, so deep down that he winced at the steady thrust. The person who so mutely assaulted him was a figure he had noticed, on reaching his own goal, absorbed by a grave a short distance away, a grave apparently fresh, so that the emotion of the visitor would probably match it for frank-ness. This fact alone forbade further attention, though during the time he stayed he remained vaguely conscious of his neighbour, a middle-aged man apparently, in mourn-ing, whose bowed back, among the clustered monuments and mortuary yews, was constantly presented. Marcher's theory that these were elements in contact with which he himself revived, had suffered, on this occasion, it may be granted, a marked, an excessive check. The autumn day was dire for him as none had recently been, and he rested with a heaviness he had not yet known on the low stone table that bore May Bartram's name. He rested without power to move, as if some spring in him, some spell vouchsafed, had suddenly been broken for ever. If he could have done that moment as he wanted he would simply have stretched himself on the slab that was ready to take him, treating it as a place prepared to receive his last sleep. What in all the wide world had he now to keep awake for? He stared before him with the question, and it was then that, as one of the cemetery walks passed near him, he caught the shock of the face.

His neighbour at the other grave had withdrawn, as he himself, with force enough in him, would have done by now, and was advancing along the path on his way to one of the gates. This brought him close, and his pace was slow, so that—and all the more as there was a kind of hunger on his look—the two men were for a minute directly confronted. Marcher knew him at once for one of the deeply stricken—a perception so sharp that nothing else in the picture comparatively lived, neither his dress, his age, nor his presumable character and class; nothing lived but the deep ravage of the features he showed. He *showed* them—that was the point; he was moved, as he passed, by some impulse that was either a signal for sympathy or, more possibly, a challenge to an opposed sorrow. He might already have been aware of our friend, might at some previous hour have noticed in him the smooth habit of the scene, with which the state of his own senses so scantly consorted, and might thereby have been stirred as by an overt discord. What Marcher was at all events conscious of was in the first place that the image of scarred passion presented to him was conscious too—of something that profaned the air; and in the second that, roused, startled, shocked, he was yet the next moment looking after it, as it went, with envy. The most extraordinary thing that had happened to him—though he had given that name to other matters as well—took place, after his immediate vague stare, as a consequence of this impression. The stranger passed, but the raw glare of his grief remained, making our friend wonder in pity what wrong, what wound it expressed, what injury not to be healed. What had the man *had,* to make him by the loss of it so bleed and yet live?

Something—and this reached him with a pang—that *he,* John Marcher, hadn't; the proof of which was precisely John Marcher's arid end. No passion had ever touched him, for this was what passion meant; he had survived and maundered and pined, but where had been *his* deep ravage? The extraordinary thing we speak of was the sudden rush of the result of this question. The sight that had just met his eyes named to him, as in letters of quick flame, something he had utterly, insanely missed, and what he had missed made these things a train of fire, made them mark themselves in an anguish of inward throbs. He had seen *outside* of his life, not learned it within, the way a woman was mourned when she had been loved for herself: such was the force of his conviction of the meaning of the stranger's face, which still flared for him as a smoky torch. It hadn't come to him, the knowledge, on the wings of experience; it had brushed him, jostled him, upset him, with the disrespect of chance, the insolence of accident. Now that the illumination had begun, however, it blazed to the zenith, and what he presently stood there gazing at was the sounded void of his life. He gazed, he drew breath, in pain; he turned in his dismay, and, turning, he had before him in sharper incision than ever the open page of his story. The name on the table smote him as the passage of his neighbour had done, and what it said to him, full in the face, was that *she* was what he had missed. This was the awful thought, the answer to all the past, the vision at the dread clearness of which he grew as cold as the stone beneath him. Everything fell together, confessed, explained, overwhelmed; leaving him most of all stupefied at the blindness he had cherished. The fate he had been marked for he had met with a vengeance—he had emptied the cup to the lees; he had been the man of his time, *the* man, to whom nothing on earth was to have happened. That was the rare stroke—that was his visitation. So he saw it, as we say, in pale horror, while the pieces fitted and fitted. So *she* had seen it while he didn't, and so she served at this hour to drive the truth home. It was the truth, vivid and monstrous, that all the while he had waited the wait was itself his portion. This the companion of his vigil had at a given moment made out, and she had then offered him the chance to baffle his doom. One's doom, however, was never baffled, and on the day she told him his own had come down she had seen him but stupidly stare at the escape she offered him.

The escape would have been to love her; then, *then* he would have lived. *She* had lived—who could say now with what passion?—since she had loved him for himself;

whereas he had never thought of her (ah how it hugely glared at him!) but in the chill of his egotism and the light of her use. Her spoken words came back to him—the chain stretched and stretched. The Beast had lurked indeed, and the Beast, at its hour, had sprung; it had sprung in that twilight of the cold April when, pale, ill, wasted, but all beautiful, and perhaps even then recoverable, she had risen from her chair to stand before him and let him imaginably guess. It had sprung as he didn't guess; it had sprung as she hopelessly turned from him, and the mark, by the time he left her, had fallen where it *was* to fall. He had justified his fear and achieved his fate; he had failed, with the last exactitude, of all he was to fail of; and a moan now rose to his lips as he remembered she had prayed he mightn't know. This horror of waking—*this* was knowledge, knowledge under the breath of which the very tears in his eyes seemed to freeze. Through them, none the less, he tried to fix it and hold it; he kept it there before him so that he might feel the pain. That at least, belated and bitter, had something of the taste of life. But the bitterness suddenly sickened him, and it was as if, horribly, he saw, in the truth, in the cruelty of his image, what had been appointed and done. He saw the Jungle of his life and saw the lurking Beast; then, while he looked, perceived it, as by a stir of the air, rise, huge and hideous, for the leap that was to settle him. His eyes darkened—it was close; and, instinctively turning, in his hallucination, to avoid it, he flung himself, face down, on the tomb.

Guy de Maupassant (1850–1893)

Guy de Maupassant was born in Normandy in 1850, the son of a well-to-do stockbroker. Gustave Flaubert was a family friend and called the young Maupassant "my disciple." "For seven years," says Maupassant of this relationship, "I wrote verses, short stories, longer stories, even a wretched play. Nothing survived. The master read everything. Then, the following Sunday at lunch, developed his criticisms." Flaubert taught him to write so that the reader will know "by means of a single word, wherein one cab-horse does not resemble the fifty others ahead of it. . . ." Exact description, *le mot juste*, became the outstanding quality of Maupassant's work.

Through Flaubert, the young writer met such great literary men of Europe as James and Turgenev—but most important was Emile Zola. In 1880, the Zola circle of naturalists published a volume of stories on the Franco-Prussian War, which had been a humiliating disaster for France; Maupassant's contribution "Boule de Suif"—a devastating picture of bourgeois hypocrisy—was almost unanimously hailed as the book's prize.

Maupassant's stories move swiftly and dramatically toward their point of illumination (see Introduction pp. 8–10). His narrative line is compact and elegant, avoiding the digressions and lengthy explanations of earlier writers. In "The Avenger," the narrative covers a friendship, a marriage, a death, and a remarriage in less than a page, and then shifts to drama for the rest of the story. Maupassant can suggest a character in a quick summary ("She was pretty, well-mannered, and smart. She married Souris for his money") or a gesture ("She said nothing, only letting out a malicious little giggle and burying her face in her husband's neck"). He conveys a social class in a picture (the family in "A Country Outing" driving from Paris in a milkman's two-wheeled cart) and a whole life in a brief scene (the grandmother chasing the stray cat, "showering it in vain with affectionate pet names"). Under his influence, compression became the hallmark of the short story.

In a critical essay, Henry James says, "As a commentator, Maupassant is slightly common, while as an artist he is wonderfully rare. . . . His [instrument of art] is that of the senses, and it is through them alone, or almost alone, that life appeals to him; it is almost alone by their help that he . . . produces brilliant works." His was no mean talent: he is unsurpassed in his ability to render sense impressions. The opening passages of "A Country Outing" provide a vivid scene as the cart, with the reader, moves toward the country: "Here and there, tall factory chimneys sprang out of the barren soil, the only vegetation in those putrid fields across which the light spring breezes spread the aroma of kerosene and soot mixed with another smell, even less alluring." And sounds: the nightingale "was singing full-throatedly. It emitted trills and warbles, then let out great vibrating sounds that filled the air and seemed to fade somewhere beyond the horizon." And feelings: the girl "abandoned herself to the gentle sensation of gliding over the water. . . . A vague need for sensuous pleasure, a fermentation of the blood, ran through her flesh. . . ."

Maupassant has been compared, usually to his detriment, to his slightly younger contemporary Anton Chekhov. They are perhaps equally responsible for technical advances that moved the short story toward greater intensity through compression. Both had a wide range of characters and subjects. Their difference is in their relation to their characters. Chekhov views his characters—even the seducer Gurov in "The Lady With The Pet Dog"—with a sympathetic irony. But, except for the young girl in whom he expresses a wholly sexual interest, Maupassant views his characters from an ironic distance. The mother with her fat thighs, the father with his dull egotism, the boy, the grandmother—all are dealt with at arm's length and rather coldly. Maupassant had immense technical skill, but he shared some of Flaubert's contempt for his fellow human beings.

Although he died at the age of forty-three of paresis, he had written enough to fill thirty volumes, including over three-hundred stories.

A Country Outing

For five months they had been talking of having lunch outside Paris on the saint's day of Madame Dufour, whose first name was Pétronille. And since they had been waiting impatiently for this outing for a long time, they got up very early that morning.

Monsieur Dufour had borrowed the milkman's cart, which he drove himself. The two-wheeled cart was quite presentable; its top was supported by four iron rods with curtains attached to them—curtains that were rolled up now, the better to admire the landscape. Only the curtain in the rear had been left loose, and it was flapping like a flag.

The wife, sitting next to her husband, had blossomed forth in an extraordinary, cherry-colored silk dress. Behind them, on two chairs, sat the old grandmother and a young girl, and one could also see the yellow thatch of a young fellow who, since there was nothing for him to sit on, had sprawled out in the bottom of the cart so that only his head showed.

When they had driven down the Champs Elysées and passed the fortifications at the Porte Maillot, the party began to admire the countryside.

When they reached the Neuilly Bridge, Monsieur Dufour announced: "Here we are, in the country at last," and at this signal, his wife became very emotional about nature.

When they reached the traffic circle of Courbevoie, they were filled with admiration at the vast expanse of the horizon. To the right, at a distance, lay Argenteuil with its church tower standing out; above it appeared the Sannois hills and the Orgemont mill. To the left, the aqueduct of Marly was outlined against the pale morning sky and, farther away, one could also see the high ground of Saint Germain; directly ahead of them, at the end of a chain of hills, the upturned earth indicated the site of the new fort of Cormeilles. And very, very far away, at an impressive distance, they caught a glimpse of the dark green line of the forest.

The sun began to scorch their faces and the dust kept getting into their eyes as, on either side of the road, a barren, dirty, stinking countryside unfolded. One would have thought it had been ravaged by a leprosy that had attacked even the houses, for the skeletons of gutted and abandoned dwellings and of huts that hadn't been finished because the builders couldn't be paid showed nothing to the world but four roofless walls.

Here and there, tall factory chimneys sprang out of the barren soil, the only vegetation in those putrid fields across which the light spring breezes spread the aroma of kerosene and soot mixed with another smell, even less alluring.

Finally they crossed the Seine for a second time, giving rein to their delight as they rolled over the bridge. The river was bursting with light—a haze rose from it, drawn up by the sun. A sweet feeling of peace came over them and they felt refreshed as they breathed a cleaner air that was no longer filled with the black smoke of the factories and stenches from the refuse dumps.

A man who passed by told them the name of the place: Bezons.

The carriage stopped and Monsieur Dufour started to read an inviting sign posted over an eating-place: "Restaurant Poulin, Fish Stews and Fish Fries, Dining Rooms for Private Parties, Garden and Swings."

"Well, what do you say, Madame Dufour—does this suit you? Will you finally make up your mind?"

Madame Dufour read the sign in her turn, after which she examined the house at length.

It was a white country inn, standing by the side of the road. Through the open door one could see the shining zinc of the counter at which two workers dressed in their Sunday best were standing.

Finally Madame Dufour decided:

"Yes, it looks all right," she said; "besides, there's the view."

The cart rolled onto the spacious grounds planted with large trees that extended behind the inn and that were only separated from the Seine by the towpath.

They got out. The husband jumped down first and opened his arms to receive his wife. The footboard, supported by two iron brackets, was very low, so that to reach it, Madame Dufour had to uncover a leg whose erstwhile slenderness was vanishing under the invasion of flesh coming down from her thighs.

Monsieur Dufour, already aroused by the countryside, quickly pinched her calf and then, catching her under the arms, deposited her heavily on the ground as if she were a huge package.

She patted her silk dress with the palms of her hands to shake the dust off it, and began to examine the place she had come to.

She was a woman of thirty-six or so, well fleshed, blooming, and pleasant to look at. She breathed painfully, held in the stranglehold of her corset, and the pressure of that contraption squeezed the quivering mass of her over-abundant bosom right up to her double chin.

Then came the young girl who, placing her hand on her father's shoulder, jumped down lightly without any further help. The yellow-haired boy had climbed down by himself, using the spokes of the wheel, and now helped Monsieur Dufour to unload the grandmother.

After that they unharnessed the horse and tied it to a tree, letting the cart fall on its nose with the two shafts on the ground. The men removed their coats, washed their hands in a bucket of water, and then joined the ladies who were already installed on the swings.

Mademoiselle Dufour was trying to swing herself by standing up on the board, but couldn't manage to give herself a sufficiently vigorous send-off. She was a handsome girl between eighteen and twenty, one of those women who, met in the street, fill a man with a sudden, whipping desire and leave the vague disturbance and agitation of the senses with him until he goes to sleep. Tall, slender at the waist, broad at the hip, she had a very dark complexion and very black hair. Her dress clearly revealed the full curves of her flesh, further accentuated by the movement of her hips as she tried to set the swing going. Her arms were stretched upward as she held on to the ropes above her head so that her breast bulged smoothly at each push she gave. Her hat, carried away by a gust of wind, had fallen behind her. Finally the swing set into motion, revealing her legs, which were quite slender, up to the knee with each swing; and throwing into the faces of the two men who were laughingly watching her the gossamer of her skirts, headier than wine vapors.

Sitting on the other swing, Madame Dufour kept moaning constantly and monotonously:

"Come over here and push me, Cyprien; come, Cyprien, give me a push."

Finally he went over to her. Rolling up the sleeves of his shirt as though he were going to start on a heavy job, he made a tremendous effort and set his wife into motion.

Grasping the ropes tightly, she held her legs out straight to avoid the ground and was delighted by the feeling of dizziness the rhythmic motion of the swing gave her. Her shaken body quivered like a jelly in a dish. But as the motion of the swing increased, she became dizzy and frightened. At each descent she let out a piercing scream that attracted the urchins of the neighborhood, so that she vaguely saw in front of her a row of mischievous faces peering over the garden hedge and distorted in a variety of ways by their laughter.

A maidservant came out from the inn and they ordered lunch.

"A fish fry from the Seine, a sautéed rabbit, a salad, and dessert," Madame Dufour spelled out with an important air.

"Bring two liters of ordinary wine and a bottle of Bordeaux," her husband said.

And their daughter added:

"We'll have our meal on the grass."

The grandmother had been seized by a feeling of tenderness at the sight of the inn's cat and had been chasing it for ten minutes, showering it in vain with affectionate pet names. The animal, although probably secretly flattered by these attentions, remained constantly close at hand without ever allowing her to get hold of it; it walked quietly around the trees, rubbing itself against them with its tail in the air and emitting little purrs of satisfaction.

"Look at that!" the blond young man cried suddenly. He had been ferreting around the grounds. "What swell boats!"

They went to have a look. Two splendid skiffs, fine and worked like costly pieces of furniture, hung in a little wooden boathouse. The boats rested side by side like two tall young maidens, stretched out in all their slender length, evoking a desire to glide over the water on gentle evenings or on bright summer mornings, to slip along past the flower-covered banks where the trees dip their branches in the water, where the eternally shivering reeds tremble and from which the lively kingfishers take off like blue streaks of lightning.

The entire family admired them reverently.

"They sure are beautiful," Monsieur Dufour repeated, examining them like a connoisseur. He had done his share of rowing when he was young, he told the others. Indeed, when he was pulling on those things—and he pretended to be pulling on oars—he didn't care a hoot for the rest of the world. He had, in his time, outraced many of those Englishmen at Joinville. . . . Then he made a few puns about the word *dames*, as oarsmen call oarlocks, saying that rowing men never went out without their *dames*, and for good reason. He got all excited as he spoke and insisted on betting that, with a boat like one of these, he could easily go fifteen miles in an hour, and without even hurrying.

"It's ready," the servant announced, appearing in the doorway.

They hurried off to eat, but they found that the spot Madame Dufour had mentally picked out as the best for their lunch was already occupied. Two young men were having their lunch there. They were obviously the owners of the boats, for they were dressed as oarsmen.

They were reclining—almost stretched out—in their chairs. Their faces were blackened by the sun and their chests were covered by the thin, white cotton jerseys from which their bare arms, as powerful as blacksmiths', emerged. They were two solid fellows, very powerfully muscled, but displaying in all their movements that graceful looseness of limb which is acquired through exercise and which is so different from the deformation produced in the worker by the repetition of the same painful effort again and again.

They exchanged a quick smile when they saw the mother and a look when they saw the daughter.

"Let's give them our place," one of the young men said; "that way we'll make their acquaintance."

The other immediately got up and, holding his half-black, half-red cap in his hand, gallantly offered the ladies the only spot in the garden unreached by the sun. His offer was accepted after a chorus of protestations and then, so that they would feel more as if they were in the country, the family installed themselves on the grass, scorning table and chairs.

The young men carried their plates a few steps away and resumed their lunch. Their bare arms, which they showed off constantly, disturbed the girl somewhat and she even turned her head away and pretended not to notice them, while Madame Dufour, bolder and impelled by a feminine curiosity that was perhaps really desire, kept looking at them constantly, probably comparing them to the concealed ugliness of her husband.

She was sitting on the grass with her legs bent and crossed tailor-fashion, and she kept wriggling constantly on the pretext that ants had got under her clothes somewhere. Monsieur Dufour, soured by the presence of the two strangers and by their amiability, was looking for a comfortable position, which he couldn't find. As to the young man with yellow hair, he was silently tucking away food like an ogre.

"What wonderful weather, monsieur," big Madame Dufour said to one of the oarsmen, trying to be amiable because they had so gallantly yielded their place.

"Oh yes, ma'am," the man replied. "Do you often come out of town?"

"Well, only once or twice a year, to breathe some fresh air. And what about you, monsieur?"

"I come out here every evening and spend the night."

"Oh, that must be ever so nice!"

"It certainly is, ma'am."

And he expanded poetically on his daily life in a way that awakened in the hearts of these shopkeepers, deprived of grass and hungry for a walk across the fields, that silly love of nature which haunts such people throughout the year as they stand behind the counters of their shops.

Moved, the girl raised her eyes and glanced at the oarsman. Then Monsieur Dufour spoke for the first time.

"That's the real life," he said, and turning to his wife: "Could you eat a bit more of this rabbit, dearie?"

"No thank you, my dear," she said and again turned toward the two young men. She indicated their bare arms and asked: "Aren't you ever cold like that?"

They laughed and proceeded to shock the family with tales of their prodigious feats of endurance, of going swimming while they were in a sweat, of long rows through night and fog. And as they spoke, they kept thumping their chests to emphasize each word with the sound it made.

"Ah, you sure look sturdy!" Monsieur Dufour said.

He no longer held forth about the times he had inflicted those wallopings on the English oarsmen.

The girl examined them out of the corner of her eye. The yellow-haired young clerk, whose wine had gone down the wrong way, started to choke and cough, splattering the cherry-colored dress of his lady employer, who angrily demanded some water with which to wash off the stains.

In the meantime, it was growing terribly hot. The sparkling river seemed to radiate waves of heat and the wine fumes mounted to their heads.

Monsieur Dufour, shaken by violent hiccoughs, had unbottoned his waistcoat and the top button of his trousers. His wife, feeling suffocated, was gradually unhooking her dress. Their clerk was gaily shaking his shock of yellow hair and kept filling his glass. The grandmother, feeling a little tipsy, sat stiffly, looking very dignified.

As to the young girl, she remained impassive, except that a faint sparkle appeared in her eyes and the dark skin of her cheeks turned rather pink.

The coffee finished them off completely. They decided to sing, each singing his own couplet while the others applauded frantically. Then, with some difficulty, they got up. While the two women, rather dizzy, stood there getting their breath, the two men, who were quite drunk, tried to perform some acrobatic exercises.

Heavy, flabby, their faces congested, they hung limply on the rings, quite unable to pull themselves up, while their shirts constantly threatened to escape from their trousers and wave in the wind like flags.

The oarsmen, who had put their boats into the water, now came up and politely offered to take the ladies for a row on the river.

"May I, dear? Please!" Madame Dufour cried.

Her husband stared at her drunkenly, without understanding.

Then one of the oarsmen, holding two fishing rods in his hand, walked over to him. The hope of catching a gudgeon flashed through his head. That shopkeeper's dream lit up his mournful stare. He gave his sanction to everything and installed himself in the shade under the bridge, his feet hanging over the water. The yellow-haired clerk sat down beside him and immediately fell asleep.

One of the oarsmen sacrificed himself and took the mother.

"To the little wood on the Île-aux-Anglais!" he called out, rowing away.

The other skiff proceeded at a slower pace. The man at the oars was staring so hard at his companion that he couldn't concentrate on anything else. A certain emotion had taken hold of him and was sapping his strength.

The girl, sitting on the coxswain's seat, abandoned herself to the gentle sensation of gliding over the water. She felt the ability to think deserting her; her limbs felt supremely relaxed; she was as free of herself as if permeated by total intoxication. She had turned very red and her breath came short. Dizziness caused by the wine and amplified by the heat waves shimmering around her made all the trees along the bank seem to bow to her in salutation. A vague need for sensuous pleasure, a fermentation of the blood, ran through her flesh which was excited by the ardors of the day; she was also stirred by this tête-à-tête on the water in the midst of a countryside emptied by the blazing sky, with this young man who thought her beautiful—whose eye caressed her skin and whose desire was as penetrating as the sun.

Their inability to speak further increased their emotion and they kept looking at the water around them. Then making an effort, he asked her name.

"Henriette," she said.

"Ah, really? Mine's Henri."

The sound of their own voices had a calming effect upon them and they became interested in the river bank. The other skiff had stopped there and seemed to be waiting for them. The other oarsman called out to them:

"We'll join you in the woods. We're going to Robinson's now because Madame is thirsty."

He leaned heavily on his oars and moved off so quickly that in no time he was out of sight.

In the meantime a continuous roar that they had vaguely discerned before was rapidly growing nearer to them. The river itself seemed to tremble as if the deadened sound was emerging from its depths.

"What's that noise?" she inquired.

It was the water falling from the dam that cut the river in two at the tip of the island. He was becoming entangled in this explanation when, through the roar of the cascade, they were struck by a bird's song that seemed to come from very far off.

"Imagine that!" he said. "The nightingales are singing during the day now. The hens must be hatching."

A nightingale! She had never heard nightingales sing. The thought of hearing one now aroused tender, poetic notions in her heart.

A nightingale! That invisible witness of love-trysts invoked by Juliet on her balcony; that heavenly music bestowed upon humans to accompany their kisses; that eternal inspiration of all the languorous romances that open up an azure ideal to the poor little hearts of young girls trembling with emotion!

So she was going to hear a nightingale.

"Don't let's make any noise," her companion said. "We could go ashore by the wood and sit down quite close to it."

The skiff seemed to be gliding on ice. The tree-lined bank was so low that their eyes seemed to plunge into the depth of the wood. They stopped. The skiff was tied up. Henriette leaned on Henri's arm and they made their way among the branches.

"Bend down," he said.

She did so and they made their way through an inextricable tangle of creepers, leaves, and reeds, into a shelter that had to be known to be found and that the young man laughingly called his "private study."

Immediately above their heads the bird was singing full-throatedly. It emitted trills and warbles, then let out great vibrating sounds that filled the air and seemed to fade somewhere beyond the horizon, rolling off along the river and flying away over the meadows, through the blazing silence that weighed on the countryside.

They didn't speak for fear of frightening the bird and making it fly away. They sat next to each other and slowly Henri's arm slipped around Henriette's waist, exerting a gentle pressure. Without anger, she took that bold hand and pushed it farther away from her. And she did so whenever he brought his hand closer. She felt no embarrassment whatever at his caress, as if it were quite natural. And she pushed it off most naturally too.

Lost in a sort of ecstasy, she listened to the bird. She was filled with infinite desires, with sudden tender impulses, with revelations of superhuman poetry, and with such a softening of the nerves and heart that she began to cry without knowing why.

The young man pressed her against him, but now she didn't push him away, didn't even think of doing so.

Suddenly the nightingale fell silent. A distant voice called:

"Henriette!"

"Don't answer," her companion whispered, "or you'll scare away the bird."

She hadn't even thought of answering.

For some time they remained sitting there like that. Madame Dufour must also have been sitting somewhere, for from time to time, they would hear the shrill little cries of the big lady whom the other oarsman must have been fondling.

The girl, still crying, was filled with delightful sensations, her skin hot and prickled all over by an unfamiliar tingling. Henri's head was on her shoulder.

Suddenly he kissed her on the lips. She drew back, furious, and to avoid him, threw herself down on her back. But he threw himself on top of her, covering her with his entire body. He had to pursue that fleeting mouth for a long time before he caught it and welded it to his. Then maddened by a formidable desire, she responded to his kiss, pressing him against her breast. All her resistance collapsed as if crushed by a weight too heavy for it.

Everything around them was quiet. The bird resumed his song. It burst out at first in three strident notes that seemed an appeal for love, then after a moment's silence, it again sang in a weakened tone, in very slow trills.

A soft breeze slipped by, causing the leaves to murmur, and from beneath the tangle of branches came two ardent sighs which blended with the song of the nightingale and the gentle breath of the wood.

Drunkenness seemed to overcome the bird, and its voice, gradually gaining in momentum like a fire flaring up or like a mounting passion, seemed to accompany the crackling of kisses under the tree. Then, the delirium in its throat was let loose in complete abandon. It went through long, drawn-out swoons, great melodious spasms.

Now and then it would stop to rest, threading out only two or three light sounds that ended suddenly on a strident note. Or else it would go off at a mad pace, with gushing scales, with shudders and jerks—a sort of fierce, furious hymn of love followed by cries of triumph.

But then the bird fell silent, hearing below it a moan so deep that one might have taken it for a soul taking leave of this world. The sound lasted for a while and then culminated in a sob.

They were both quite pale as they left their green bed. The sky seemed to them to have become overcast; to their eyes, the glowing sun had been extinguished; they were aware of their loneliness and of the silence around them. They walked quickly, side by side, without touching each other, without talking, for they seemed to have become irreconcilable enemies—as if disgust had sprung up between their bodies and hatred between their spirits.

Occasionally Henriette would call: "Mamma!"

There was a stir beneath a bush. Henri thought he saw a white underskirt quickly pulled over a thick calf. Then the huge lady emerged, a bit embarrassed and even redder than before, her eyes aglow and her stormy bosom perhaps a bit too close to her companion. As for him, he must have witnessed some rather funny things, for his face was furrowed by an irrepressible hilarity that kept bursting out despite all his efforts.

Madame Dufour took his arm affectionately and they returned to the boats. Henri, who was walking in front next to the girl, thought at one point that he heard a hard kiss that was intended to be noiseless.

Finally they returned to Bezons.

Monsieur Dufour, now sober, was impatient. The blond clerk was having a bite to eat before leaving the inn. The cart, already harnessed, was waiting for them in the courtyard. The grandmother was already in her seat, very worried that they might be overtaken by darkness before reaching Paris, for the countryside was none too safe.

Hands were shaken and the Dufour family left.

"So long!" the oarsmen shouted, and received a sigh and a tear in reply.

Two months later, passing along the Rue des Martyrs. Henri saw a sign over a door which read: "Dufour—Hardware Merchant." He went in.

The big lady was displaying her rotundity across the counter. They recognized each other right away. After a thousand polite remarks, he inquired:

"And how's Mademoiselle Henriette?"

"She's fine, thank you. In fact, she got married."

"Ah . . ." he said, seized by emotion. "And whom did she marry?"

"The young man who was with us then, you know. . . . He'll be the one to take over the business."

"Yes, yes, I remember very well. . . ."

He started to leave, feeling very sad without knowing why. Madame Dufour called him back.

"And how is your friend?" she asked shyly.

"He's fine."

"Please give him our best and tell him to drop in on us whenever he comes by." She turned very red and added: "Tell him I'd like him to do that very much."

"I certainly will tell him. Good-bye."

"No. . . . See you very soon!"

A year later, on a very sultry summer Sunday, every detail of the adventure he had always remembered came back to Henri; the recollection was so vivid and he felt such nostalgia that he returned all alone to his "private study" in the little wood.

As he crept in, he received a shock. She was there. She was sitting on the grass looking very sad, while next to her, still in his shirt sleeves, the yellow-haired young man was stretched out asleep. He had given himself entirely to his sleep, like an animal.

She turned very pale when she saw Henri and he thought she was about to faint. But then they started to talk quite naturally, as if nothing had ever happened between them.

As he was telling her that he often came to this place on Sundays to rest and to relive many past memories, she looked lengthily into his eyes.

"Me," she said, "I think of it every night."

"Well, dear," her husband mumbled, yawning, "I guess it's time we were on our way back."

The Avenger

When Antoine Leuillet married the widowed Mathilde Souris, he had been in love with her for almost ten years.

Souris had been his friend, an old schoolmate. Leuillet had been rather fond of him, although he had thought him a bit dumb.

"Poor old Souris," he used to say. "He'll certainly never set the world on fire."

When Souris married Mademoiselle Mathilde Duvall, Leuillet was surprised and slightly vexed because he was a little sweet on her himself. She was the daughter of a local haberdasher who had put aside a tiny bit of capital and retired. She was pretty, well-mannered, and smart. She married Souris for his money.

After that Leuillet looked at her with different eyes and started pursuing his friend's wife with his attentions. He was a handsome man, not stupid, and also rather well off. He felt confident of success. He failed. So then he really fell in love and his love was made discreet, shy, and awkward because of his close friendship with her husband. For her part, Madame Souris, thinking that he had given up his ideas of seduction, relaxed and treated him with sincere fondness. And that went on for nine years.

Then one morning, Leuillet received a desperate note from the poor woman: Souris had died suddenly of coronary thrombosis.

It was a frightful shock to him because he and Souris were exactly the same age. But the first shock was almost immediately followed by a deep joy and feeling of infinite relief that filled him body and soul. Madame Souris was free now.

Nevertheless, he managed to put on an appropriate air of grief to let the necessary time elapse, and in general, to observe all the conventional proprieties. Fifteen months later, he married the widow.

People considered his behavior natural, even noble: he had acted as a loyal friend and an honest man.

Now, at last, his happiness was complete.

They understood each other immediately and lived in a very close, warm intimacy. They had no secrets and shared their most private thoughts. Leuillet now loved his wife with a relaxed and trusting love and treating her like a loyal and tender companion, an equal and a confidante. However, there still lingered in his heart a strange and unaccountable resentment against the late Souris who had been the first to possess his wife— who had picked the flower of her youth and her girlish heart and had thus somewhat marred the poetic quality of it all. The memory of the dead husband spoiled the bliss of the living one, and gradually this jealously came to torment Leuillet night and day.

He kept returning to the subject of Souris, questioning her on thousands of intimate and secret details, insisting on being told all the dead man's habits and then pursuing him into his grave with sarcasms and sneers, emphasizing his inadequacies.

At any moment he was likely to call his wife from the other end of the house:

"Hey, Mathilde!"

"Yes, dear, what is it?"

"Here, I'd like to tell you something. . . ."

And she'd come to him, always smiling, knowing very well that he was going to talk to her about Souris and quite willing to gratify her new husband's harmless mania.

"Say, do you remember the day when Souris tried to convince me that small guys are always loved more than big guys?"

And he'd launch into a series of remarks that were disparaging to the dead man, who had been small, and discreetly flattering to himself, Leuillet, who was big.

And Madame Leuillet would make him feel that he was right, absolutely right; and she would laugh wholeheartedly, quietly making fun of her former husband for the greater comfort of her present one, who always concluded thus:

"Well, never mind, he was a bit dumb, poor Souris!"

They were happy, extremely happy, and Leuillet continued to prove his unabated love to his wife by all the usual means.

Then one night, as they were prevented from sleeping by a renewal of youthful ardor, Leuillet, who was holding his wife tightly in his arms and kissing her with great zest on the mouth, suddenly asked her:

"Tell me something, darling."

"What?"

"Now, Souris. . . . This is rather an awkward question for me to ask. . . . Well, anyway, was he very amorous, Souris?"

She gave him a big, noisy kiss and murmured in his ear:

"Not as much as you are, my sweet."

His male pride was flattered and he said:

"So he wasn't too good in these things, was he?"

She said nothing, only letting out a malicious little giggle and burying her face in her husband's neck. He insisted:

"He was a bit simple, I bet. Not too effective, if you see what I mean. Didn't have a very fine touch?"

She made a slight movement of the head that signified, "No, no touch whatever."

"So I suppose he annoyed you at night, didn't he?"

This time, in an access of frankness, she said emphatically:

"Ah, he certainly did!"

He kissed her on hearing that and whispered:

"Ah, the awkward brute! You weren't happy with him, were you?"

"No," she said, "it certainly wasn't very gay. . . ."

Leuillet was delighted, setting up in his mind a very flattering comparison between the former state of affairs and the present one.

For some time he remained silent, then suddenly, shaking with merriment, he said:

"Tell me something."

"What?"

"Will you be absolutely frank with me?"

"Of course, darling."

"Well, tell me then, were you ever tempted to deceive . . . to cheat on that poor imbecile Souris?"

Madame Leuillet let out a coy "Oh!" and buried her face even deeper in her husband's chest. But he realized she was laughing. He insisted:

"No, really tell me. He had—well, the face of a husband whose wife cheats on him, the poor idiot! It would've been funny, really funny! Ah, poor Souris! Come, darling, you can tell me about it now! You can tell me, you know!"

He stressed the "me," certain that if she'd had any idea of being unfaithful to

Souris, she'd have chosen him, Leuillet, for her accomplice. And he was fretting with gleeful impatience to hear her confess, fully confident that if she hadn't been the virtuous woman she was, she would've been his then too.

But she didn't say anything—just laughed as though she had remembered something that struck her as infinitely funny.

Leuillet laughed too then, at the thought that he could have cuckolded poor Souris all that time! Ah, wouldn't that have been funny! What a trick to have played on the fool! Ah, it would've been enough to make you really roll on the ground with laughter! And he stammered through his laughter:

"Ah, poor Souris sure would have looked the part! Ah, that's for sure."

Madame Leuillet was now twisting about under the sheets, laughing till she almost cried, almost screaming as Leuillet kept repeating:

"Come on, admit it, confess it, be frank with me! You must realize that it wouldn't be the least bit unpleasant for me now."

Finally, choking, she brought out: "Yes . . . yes. . . ."

Her husband insisted:

"Yes what? Come on, tell me everything."

Now she was only laughing a little. She brought her mouth close to his ear, and as he waited for the titillating admission, she said:

"Yes, I was unfaithful to him."

An icy shiver shook him to his bones. He stammered:

"You . . . you what? You actually . . . did it?"

She, still thinking that he was finding the thing infinitely titillating, went on:

"Yes . . . I did . . . I actually did."

He had to sit up, his breath cut short. He was almost as shocked as if someone had come and informed him that Mathilde had been unfaithful to him, Leuillet. He was at a loss for words and it was only after a while that he said simply:

"Ah!"

She had stopped laughing, realizing her mistake when it was too late.

Finally Leuillet inquired:

"Who with?"

She remained silent, trying to think of some way out, but he said again:

"Who with?"

At last she murmured:

"With a young man."

He turned on her abruptly and said in a rasping voice:

"I suspected it wasn't with a kitchenmaid. I want to know who the young man was."

She didn't answer. Then, he tore away the sheet she had pulled over her head, repeating:

"I must know which young man, do you understand!"

She said painfully:

"I was only joking. . . ."

But he was trembling with rage.

"So you were joking, were you? You were just pulling my leg? Well, I want you to know you can't get around me like that! I want his name!"

She said nothing and lay motionless on her back. He seized her arm and squeezed it violently.

"Don't you hear me? I demand that you answer when I speak to you!"

She answered nervously:

"I think you've gone mad. Leave me alone!"

He was trembling in his fury; he shook her with all his might, repeating again and again:

"D'you hear! . . . d'you hear! . . ."

She made a sharp movement to free herself and her fingertips grazed his nose. Then he, thinking she had intentionally struck him, flung himself upon her, held her down, and slapped her as hard as he could, shouting:

"Here, take that, take that, you whore! Here, that's for you, take that, you slut, take that, you whore, you whore!"

When he was out of breath and tired, he got up and went over to the cupboard to get himself a glass of orangeade because he was afraid he was going to faint.

And she, she was crying in the bed, sobbing loudly, and feeling this was the end of her happiness and through her own fault.

Then, between her sobs, she mumbled:

"Listen, Antoine, come here. I lied to you. I'll explain. Listen. . . ."

Prepared to salvage whatever was left and armed with ready arguments and cunning, she raised her disheveled head in its nightcap that had slipped to one side.

He turned toward her, ashamed of himself for having struck her but aware that there was now an inexhaustible hatred in his husband's heart for this woman who had deceived her previous husband—Souris.

Anton Chekhov (1860–1904)

For many critics, Anton Chekhov is *the* master of the short-story form. Beginning with comic potboilers to help support his family while he was a medical student, he wrote over six hundred stories, many among the finest ever done. Only when he discovered, in 1886, that his work was highly regarded in St. Petersburg did he begin to take himself seriously as a writer. Even so, he called medicine his wife, literature his mistress.

To the editor who first encouraged him, Chekhov—the son of a slave who failed as a shopkeeper—wrote an appealing self-portrait:

> Write a story, do, about a young man, the son of a serf, a former grocery boy, a choir singer, a high school pupil and university student, brought up to respect rank, to kiss the hands of priests, to truckle to the ideas of others—a young man who expressed thanks for every piece of bread, who was whipped many times, who went without galoshes to do his tutoring, who used his fists, tortured animals, was fond of dining with rich relatives, was a hypocrite in his dealings with God and men, needlessly, solely out of a realization of his own insignificance—write how this young man squeezes the slave out of himself, drop by drop, and how, on awaking one fine morning, he feels that the blood coursing through his veins is no longer that of a slave but that of a real human being.

Chekhov was immensely influential in the development of the short story, affecting both its form and subject matter. Rather than writing of immense crises, he writes of small sins and common misfortunes: self-deceit, lack of consideration, wounded vanity, disappointed hopes, failed human connections. Even when his subject matter is potentially overwhelming—like the death of the son in "Heartache"—he resists the grand emotions, keeps the tragedy within a human range. His characters come from all walks of life: landowners, peasants, shopkeepers, doctors, teachers, foolish men and foolish women, and neglected children. He views each of them not as a cog in a social wheel but as an individual.

His technique is disarmingly simple. Relatively plotless, his stories have no resounding upbeat ending. He introduces a character or two, gives a little background, shifts to the people themselves, and allows them to move around, talk, interact. Little happens: a cabbie talks to his horse, a *ménage a trois* is tacitly agreed to, married lovers recognize their plight. As H. E. Bates says, there is "no grandiose staying of the scene."

The reader is apt to feel a little uncomfortable at the end of a Chekhov story. Justice has hardly triumphed just because the cuckolded husband accepts the lover or because an adulterer realizes he truly loves. The good is not amply served by the horse that merely stands still for the desperate cabbie. In fact, Chekhov's stories almost always seem to die away at the end.

Yet something has happened. A situation is clarified or a character is revealed. A tension is relaxed, a rough edge worn smooth, a hidden self has surfaced. And it is right, the truth has been served. We have been with the people, have understood them in their complexity and venality, have better understood ourselves. Virginia Woolf said that "as we read these little stories about nothing at all, the horizon widens; the soul gains an astonishing sense of freedom."

Although never successful in writing a novel, Chekhov became one of the greatest playwrights of the modern age. His most frequently produced plays are *The Sea Gull* (1896), *Uncle Vanya* (1897), *The Cherry Orchard* (1904), and *The Three Sisters* (1900), which has been called the finest play since Shakespeare. Like his stories, his plays emphasize the everyday moments that define his characters.

Ninochka: A Love Story

The door opened quietly and my good friend Pavel Sergeyevich Vikhlyenev entered. Although a young man, he was sickly, old-looking, and, in general—with his round shoulders, long nose, and gaunt features—unattractive. But, on the other hand, his face was so bland, soft, and undefined that every time you looked at it you experienced a strange desire to get hold of it with your five fingers and to feel, as it were, the doughy soft-heartedness and warmth of my friend. Like all bookish people, he was quiet, diffident, and shy; besides which, at this time he was paler than usual, and for some reason violently agitated.

"What's the matter with you?" I asked, glancing at his white face and faintly trembling lips. "Are you sick, or has there been another misunderstanding with your wife? You don't look yourself."

After hesitating for a moment Vikhlyenev coughed slightly, then with a gesture of despair said "Yes . . . with Ninochka again. I've been so miserable I couldn't sleep all night, and, as you see, I'm barely alive. Damn it all! Other people don't let things get them down; they take injury, loss, or pain lightly. But it requires a mere trifle to depress and upset me.''

"But what happened?''

"A trifle—a little domestic drama. But I'll tell you the whole story, if you like. Yesterday my Ninochka did not go out. She took it into her head to spend an evening with me and stayed at home. I was, of course, overjoyed. She usually goes out to a meeting somewhere at night, and since that's the only time I'm at home, you can imagine how I was . . . well . . . I was overjoyed. But then, you have never been married, so you don't know how cozy and warm it feels when you come home from work to find the woman you live for . . . . Ah!''

Vikhlyenev made an inventory of the charms of married life. Then he wiped the perspiration from his forehead, and continued. "Ninochka thought she'd like to spend an evening with me. Well, you know how I am—dull, heavy, and far from clever. It's not much fun to be with me; I'm forever at my drafting board or my soil filters; I never play, or dance, or joke. And you must admit that Ninochka is pleasure-loving. Youth has its rights, don't you think so? Well, I began by showing her various little things, photographs and one thing and another, told her some stories, and then I suddenly remembered that I had some old letters in my desk, among them some that were very funny. In my student days I had friends who wrote devilishly clever letters: you read them and you split your guts laughing! I pulled these letters out of the desk and commenced reading them to Ninochka. I read her one, then another, then a third, and suddenly—the whole thing broke down! In one letter she came across the phrase: 'Katya sends her regards.' To a jealous wife such a phrase is like a sharp knife, and my Ninochka—an Othello in petticoats! The questions rained down on my unfortunate head: Who is this Katya? And how? And why? I explained to her that she was in some way a kind of first love, something out of my young student life, my salad days, to which it was impossible to attach any significance whatsoever. Every youth, I told her, has his Katya; it would be impossible not to—but my Ninochka wouldn't listen. She imagined—God knows what!—and started to cry. After the tears, hysterics. 'You're vile, filthy,' she screamed. 'You hid your past from me! You probably have some kind of a Katya even now, and you're hiding it from me!' I tried and I tried to reassure her, but to no avail. Masculine logic never convinced a woman. In the end I begged her forgiveness—on my knees. I crawled, and where did it get me? She went to bed in hysterics— she in the bedroom and I on the sofa in my study. This morning she was pouting, wouldn't look at me, and spoke to me as though I were a stranger. She threatens to move to her mother's, and she probably will—I know her!''

"Hm-m. Not a very pleasant story.''

"Women are incomprehensible to me! Granting that Ninochka is young, pure, fastidious, and can't help being shocked by something so earthy—is that so hard to forgive? I may be guilty, but I begged her forgiveness—I crawled on my knees! I even, if you must know, wept!''

"Yes, women are a great riddle.''

"My dear friend, you have a strong influence over Ninochka. She respects you; she sees in you an authority. Please, go and see her. Exert your influence, and make her understand how wrong she is. I am suffering, my friend. If this goes on one more day I won't be able to endure it. Go—be a friend!''

"But do you think that would be . . . proper?''

"Why not? You and she have been friends almost since childhood. She trusts you. As a friend, please go!''

Vikhlyenev's tearful pleading touched me. I dressed and went to see his wife. I found Ninochka engaged in her favorite occupation: she was sitting on the sofa, one leg crossed over the other, blinking her beautiful eyes and doing nothing. When I came in she jumped up and ran to me; then she glanced round, quietly closed the door, and, with the lightness of a feather, clung to my neck. (You must not think, dear reader, that this is a misprint. For a year now, I had been sharing with Vikhlyenev his conjugal obligations.)

"What deviltry have you thought up now?" I asked Ninochka, seating her beside me.

"What do you mean?"

"Again you have managed to torment your better half. He came to see me today and told me all about it."

"Oh—that! So he found someone to complain to!"

"What actually happened?"

"Oh, not much. I was bored last night . . . and got angry because I had no place to go, so, out of spite, I started nagging him about his Katya. I cried simply from boredom—and how can I explain that to him?"

"But you know, my darling, that's cruel and inhuman. He's so nervous, and yet you plague him with your scenes."

"Oh, that's nothing. He loves it when I act jealous. And there's no better blind than fictitious jealousy. But let's drop it. I don't like it when you start talking about my milksop; I'm fed up with him! Let's have tea."

"Well, in any case, stop tormenting him. You know, he's pathetic: he describes his happiness and his faith in your love so frankly and sincerely that it makes one uncomfortable. Do control yourself somehow; show him some affection; lie! One word from you and he's in seventh heaven."

Ninochka frowned and pouted, but a little later when Vikhlyenev came in and timidly looked into my face, she gaily and affectionately smiled at him.

"You're just in time for tea!" she said to him. "How clever of you, my pet, never to be late. Lemon or cream for you?"

Vikhlyenev, not expecting such a welcome, was moved; he kissed his wife's hand warmly, and embraced me. This embrace was so absurd and so untimely that both Ninochka and I blushed.

"Blessed are the peacemakers!" clucked the happy husband. "You've made her listen to reason; and why? Because you're a man of the world; you mingle in society, and you know all the fine points of a woman's heart! Ha! Ha! Ha! I'm a clumsy ox; when one word is needed, I say ten; when I should kiss her hand or something, I start to find fault! Ha! Ha!"

After tea Vikhlyenev led me into his study, buttonholed me, and mumbled, "I don't know how to thank you, my dear friend. Believe me, I suffered; I was tortured; and now I am so happy—I'm simply overwhelmed! And this isn't the first time that you've pulled me out of a terrible situation. My dear friend—now, don't refuse me—I have here a little something. . . . It's just a little model locomotive that I made myself; I got a medal for it at the exposition. Take it as a token of my gratitude . . . my friendship. Do me this favor!"

Naturally, I refused in every possible way, but Vikhlyenev was insistent and, like it or not, I had to accept his precious gift.

Days, weeks, months passed. Sooner or later the ugly truth was bound to be revealed to him in all its enormity. When, by accident, he did find out, he turned frightfully pale, sat down on the sofa, and stared dully at the ceiling without saying a word. A heartache has to express itself in some kind of movement, and he began to turn from side to side on the sofa in an agonizing way. Even these movements were circumscribed by his milksop nature.

A week later, somewhat recovered from the shock of this news, he came to see me. We were both embarrassed and avoided looking at each other. I began to spout some sort of nonsense about free love, marital selfishness, submission to fate.

"It wasn't about that—" he interrupted meekly, "all that I understand perfectly. In matters of the heart, no one is guilty. What concerns me is the other side of the business . . . the purely practical. You see, I don't know life at all, and where the actual arrangements . . . the social conventions are concerned, I'm a real greenhorn. So, help me, my friend! Tell me, what is Ninochka supposed to do now? Should she go on living with me, or do you think it would be better if she moved in with you?"

Having deliberated briefly, we left it at this: Ninochka would continue to live at Vikhlyenev's; I would go to see her whenever I liked, and he would take the corner room, which formerly had been the storeroom, for himself. This room was rather dark and damp, and the entrance to it was through the kitchen, but, on the other hand, he could perfectly well shut himself up in it and not be a nuisance to anyone.

Heartache

"To whom shall I tell my sorrow?"[1]

Evening twilight. Large flakes of wet snow are circling lazily about the street lamps which have just been lighted, settling in a thin soft layer on roofs, horses' backs, peoples' shoulders, caps. Iona Potapov, the cabby, is all white like a ghost. As hunched as a living body can be, he sits on the box without stirring. If a whole snowdrift were to fall on him, even then, perhaps, he would not find it necessary to shake it off. His nag, too, is white and motionless. Her immobility, the angularity of her shape, and the sticklike straightness of her legs make her look like a penny gingerbread horse. She is probably lost in thought. Anyone who has been torn away from the plow, from the familiar gray scenes, and cast into this whirlpool full of monstrous lights, of ceaseless uproar and hurrying people, cannot help thinking.

Iona and his nag have not budged for a long time. They had driven out of the yard before dinnertime and haven't had a single fare yet. But now evening dusk is descending upon the city. The pale light of the street lamps changes to a vivid color and the bustle of the street grows louder.

"Sleigh to the Vyborg District!" Iona hears. "Sleigh!"

Iona starts, and through his snow-plastered eyelashes sees an officer in a military overcoat with a hood.

"To the Vyborg District!" repeats the officer. "Are you asleep, eh? To the Vyborg District!"

As a sign of assent Iona gives a tug at the reins, which sends layers of snow flying from the horse's back and from his own shoulders. The officer gets into the sleigh. The

[1] From an old Russian folksong.

driver clucks to the horse, cranes his neck like a swan, rises in his seat and, more from habit than necessity, flourishes his whip. The nag, too, stretches her neck, crooks her sticklike legs and irresolutely sets off.

"Where are you barging in, damn you?" Iona is promptly assailed by shouts from the massive dark wavering to and fro before him. "Where the devil are you going? Keep to the right!"

"Don't you know how to drive? Keep to the right," says the officer with vexation.

A coachman driving a private carriage swears at him; a pedestrian who was crossing the street and brushed against the nag's nose with his shoulder, looks at him angrily and shakes the snow off his sleeve. Iona fidgets on the box as if sitting on needles and pins, thrusts out his elbows and rolls his eyes like a madman, as though he did not know where he was or why he was there.

"What rascals they all are," the officer jokes. "They are doing their best to knock into you or be trampled by the horse. It's a conspiracy."

Iona looks at his fare and moves his lips. He wants to say something, but the only sound that comes out is a wheeze.

"What is it?" asks the officer.

Iona twists his mouth into a smile, strains his throat and croaks hoarsely: "My son, sir . . . er, my son died this week."

"H'm, what did he die of?"

Iona turns his whole body around to his fare and says, "Who can tell? It must have been a fever. He lay in the hospital only three days and then he died. . . . It is God's will."

"Get over, you devil!" comes out of the dark. "Have you gone blind, you old dog? Keep your eyes peeled!"

"Go on, go on," says the officer. "We shan't get there until tomorrow at this rate. Give her the whip!"

The driver cranes his neck again, rises in his seat, and with heavy grace swings his whip. Then he looks around at the officer several times, but the latter keeps his eyes closed and is apparently indisposed to listen. Letting his fare off in the Vyborg District, Iona stops by a teahouse and again sits motionless and hunched on the box. Again the wet snow paints him and his nag white. One hour passes, another . . .

Three young men, two tall and lanky, one short and hunchbacked, come along swearing at each other and loudly pound the pavement with their galoshes.

"Cabby, to the Police Bridge!" the hunchback shouts in a cracked voice. "The three of us . . . twenty kopecks!"

Iona tugs at the reins and clucks to his horse. Twenty kopecks is not fair, but his mind is not on that. Whether it is a ruble or five kopecks, it is all one to him now, so long as he has a fare. . . . The three young men, jostling each other and using foul language, go up to the sleigh and all three try to sit down at once. They start arguing about which two are to sit and who shall be the one to stand. After a long ill-tempered and abusive altercation, they decide that the hunchback must stand up because he is the shortest.

"Well, get going," says the hunchback in his cracked voice, taking up his station and breathing down Iona's neck. "On your way! What a cap you've got, brother! You won't find a worse one in all Petersburg—"

"Hee, hee . . . hee, hee . . ." Iona giggles, "as you say—"

"Well, then, 'as you say,' drive on. Are you going to crawl like this all the way, eh? D'you want to get it in the neck?"

"My head is splitting," says one of the tall ones. "At the Dukmasov's yesterday, Vaska and I killed four bottles of cognac between us."

"I don't get it, why lie?" says the other tall one angrily. "He is lying like a trouper."

"Strike me dead, it's the truth!"

"It is about as true as that a louse sneezes."

"Hee, hee," giggles Iona. "The gentlemen are feeling good!"

"Faugh, the devil take you!" cries the hunchback indignantly. "Will you get a move on, you old pest, or won't you? Is that the way to drive? Give her a crack of the whip! Giddap, devil! Giddap! Let her feel it!"

Iona feels the hunchback's wriggling body and quivering voice behind his back. He hears abuse addressed to him, sees people, and the feeling of loneliness begins little by little to lift from his heart. The hunchback swears till he chokes on an elaborate three-decker oath and is overcome by cough. The tall youths begin discussing a certain Nadezhda Petrovna. Iona looks round at them. When at last there is a lull in the conversation for which he has been waiting, he turns around and says: "This week . . . er . . . my son died."

"We shall all die," says the hunchback, with a sigh wiping his lips after his coughing fit. "Come, drive on, drive on. Gentlemen, I simply cannot stand this pace! When will he get us there?"

"Well, you give him a little encouragement. Biff him in the neck!"

"Do you hear, you old pest? I'll give it to you in the neck. If one stands on ceremony with fellows like you, one may as well walk. Do you hear, you old serpent? Or don't you give a damn what we say?"

And Iona hears rather than feels the thud of a blow on his neck.

"Hee, hee," he laughs. "The gentlemen are feeling good. God give you health!"

"Cabby, are you married?" asks one of the tall ones.

"Me? Hee, hee! The gentlemen are feeling good. The only wife for me now is the damp earth . . . Hee, haw, haw! The grave, that is! . . . Here my son is dead and me alive . . . It is a queer thing, death comes in at the wrong door . . . It don't come for me, it comes for my son. . . ."

And Iona turns round to tell them how his son died, but at that point the hunchback gives a sigh of relief and announces that, thank God, they have arrived at last. Having received his twenty kopecks, for a long while Iona stares after the revelers, who disappear into a dark entrance. Again he is alone and once more silence envelops him. The grief which has been allayed for a brief space comes back again and wrenches his heart more cruelly than ever. There is a look of anxiety and torment in Iona's eyes as they wander restlessly over the crowds moving to and fro on both sides of the street. Isn't there someone among those thousands who will listen to him? But the crowds hurry past, heedless of him and his grief. His grief is immense, boundless. If his heart were to burst and his grief to pour out, it seems that it would flood the whole world, and yet no one sees it. It has found a place for itself in such an insignificant shell that no one can see it in broad daylight.

Iona notices a doorkeeper with a bag and makes up his mind to speak to him.

"What time will it be, friend?" he asks.

"Past nine. What have you stopped here for? On your way!"

Iona drives a few steps away, hunches up and surrenders himself to his grief. He feels it is useless to turn to people. But before five minutes are over, he draws himself up, shakes his head as though stabbed by a sharp pain and tugs at the reins . . . He can bear it no longer.

"Back to the yard!" he thinks. "To the yard!"

And his nag, as though she knew his thoughts, starts out at a trot. An hour and a half later, Iona is sitting beside a large dirty stove. On the stove, on the floor, on benches are men snoring. The air is stuffy and foul. Iona looks at the sleeping figures, scratches himself and regrets that he has come home so early.

"I haven't earned enough to pay for the oats," he reflects. "That's what's wrong with me. A man that knows his job . . . who has enough to eat and has enough for his horse don't need to fret."

In one of the corners a young driver gets up, hawks sleepily and reaches for the water bucket.

"Thirsty?" Iona asks him.

"Guess so."

"H'm, may it do you good, but my son is dead, brother . . . did you hear? This week in the hospital. . . . What a business!"

Iona looks to see the effect of his words, but he notices none. The young man has drawn his cover over his head and is already asleep. The old man sighs and scratches himself. Just as the young man was thirsty for water so he thirsts for talk. It will soon be a week since his son died and he hasn't talked to anybody about him properly. He ought to be able to talk about it, taking his time, sensibly. He ought to tell how his son was taken ill, how he suffered, what he said before he died, how he died. . . . He ought to describe the funeral, and how he went to the hospital to fetch his son's clothes. His daughter Anisya is still in the country. . . . And he would like to talk about her too. Yes, he has plenty to talk about now. And his listener should gasp and moan and keen. . . . It would be even better to talk to women. Though they are foolish, two words will make them blubber.

"I must go out and have a look at the horse," Iona thinks. "There will be time enough for sleep. You will have enough sleep, no fear. . . ."

He gets dressed and goes into the stable where his horse is standing. He thinks about oats, hay, the weather. When he is alone, he dares not think of his son. It is possible to talk about him with someone, but to think of him when one is alone, to evoke his image is unbearably painful.

"You chewing?" Iona asks his mare seeing her shining eyes. "There, chew away, chew away. . . . If we haven't earned enough for oats, we'll eat hay. . . . Yes. . . . I've grown too old to drive. My son had ought to be driving, not me. . . . He was a real cabby. . . . He had ought to have lived. . . ."

Iona is silent for a space and then goes on: "That's how it is, old girl. . . . Kuzma Ionych is gone. . . . Departed this life. . . . He went and died to no purpose. . . . Now let's say you had a little colt, and you were that little colt's own mother. And suddenly, let's say, that same little colt departed this life. . . . You'd be sorry, wouldn't you?"

The nag chews, listens and breathes on her master's hands. Iona is carried away and tells her everything.

The Lady with the Pet Dog

1

They were saying a new face had been seen on the esplanade: a lady with a pet dog. Dmitry Dmitrich Gurov, who had already spent two weeks in Yalta and regarded himself as an old hand, was beginning to show an interest in new faces. He was sitting in Vernet's coffeehouse when he saw a young lady, blonde and fairly tall, wearing a beret and walking along the esplanade. A white Pomeranian was trotting behind her.

Later he encountered her several times a day in the public gardens or in the square. She walked alone, always wearing the same beret, and always accompanied by the Pomeranian. No one knew who she was, and people called her simply "the lady with the pet dog."

"If she is here alone without a husband or any friends," thought Gurov, "then it wouldn't be a bad idea to make her acquaintance."

He was under forty, but he already had a twelve-year-old daughter and two boys at school. He had married young, when still a second-year student at college, and by now his wife looked nearly twice as old as he did. She was a tall, erect woman with dark eyebrows, dignified and imposing, who called herself a thinking person. She read a good deal, used simplified spelling in her letters, and called her husband Dimitry instead of Dmitry. Though he secretly regarded her as a woman of limited intelligence, narrow-minded and rather dowdy, he stood in awe of her and disliked being at home. Long ago he had begun being unfaithful to her, and he was now constantly unfaithful, and perhaps that was why he nearly always spoke ill of women, and whenever they were discussed in his presence he would call them "the lower race."

It seemed to him that he had been so schooled by bitter experience that he was entitled to call them anything he liked, but he was unable to live for even two days without "the lower race." In the company of men he was bored, cold, ill at ease, and uncommunicative, but felt at home among women, and knew what to say to them and how to behave; and even when he was silent in their presence he felt at ease. In his appearance, in his character, in his whole nature, there was something charming and elusive, which made him attractive to women and cast a spell over them. He knew this, and was himself attracted to them by some mysterious power.

Repeated and bitter experience had taught him that every fresh intimacy, which at first seems to give the spice of variety to life and a sense of delightful and easy conquest, inevitably ends by introducing excessively complicated problems, and creating intolerable situations—this is particularly true of the well-intentioned Moscow people, who are irresolute and slow to embark on adventures. But with every new encounter with an interesting woman he forgot all about his former experiences, and the desire to live surged in him, and everything suddenly seemed simple and amusing.

One evening when he was dining in the public gardens, the lady in the beret came strolling up and sat down at the next table. Her expression, her clothes, her way of walking, the way she did her hair, suggested that she belonged to the upper classes, that she was married, that she was paying her first visit to Yalta, and that she was alone and bored. . . . Stories told about immorality in Yalta are largely untrue, and for his part Gurov despised them, knowing they were mostly invented by people who were only too ready to sin, if they had the chance. . . . But when the lady sat down at the next table a few yards away from him, he remembered all those stories of easy conquests and trips to the mountains, and he was suddenly possessed with the tempting thought of a quick and temporary liaison, a romance with an unknown woman of whose very name he was ignorant.

He beckoned invitingly at the Pomeranian, and when the little dog came up to him, he shook his finger at it. The Pomeranian began to bark. Then Gurov wagged his finger again.

The lady glanced up at him and immediately lowered her eyes.

"He doesn't bite!" she said, and blushed.

"May I give him a bone?" Gurov said, and when she nodded, he asked politely: "Have you been long in Yalta?"

"Five days."

"And I am dragging through my second week."

There was silence for a while.

"Time passes so quickly, and it is so dull here," she said without looking at him.

"It's quite the fashion to say it is boring here," he replied. "People who live out their lives in places like Belevo or Zhizdro are not bored, but when they come here they say: 'How dull! All this dust!' One would think they live in Granada!"

She laughed. Then they both went on eating in silence, like complete strangers, but after dinner they walked off together and began to converse lightly and playfully like people who are completely at their ease and contented with themselves, and it is all the same to them where they go or what they talk about. They walked and talked about the strange light of the sea, the soft warm lilac color of the water, and the golden pathway made by the moonlight. They talked of how sultry it was after a hot day. Gurov told her he came from Moscow, that he had been trained as a philologist, though he now worked in a bank, that at one time he had trained to be an opera singer, but had given it up, and he told her about the two houses he owned in Moscow. From her he learned that she grew up in St. Petersburg and had been married in the town of S_____, where she had been living for the past two years, that she would stay another month in Yalta, and perhaps her husband, who also needed a rest, would come to join her. She was not sure whether her husband was a member of a government board or on the zemstvo council, and this amused her. Gurov learned that her name was Anna Sergeyevna.

Afterwards in his room at the hotel he thought about her, and how they would surely meet on the following day. It was inevitable. Getting into bed, he recalled that only a little while ago she was a schoolgirl, doing lessons like his own daughter, and he remembered how awkward and timid she was in her laughter and in her manner of talking with a stranger—it was probably the first time in her life that she had found herself alone, in a situation where men followed her, gazed at her, and talked with her, always with a secret purpose she could not fail to guess. He thought of her slender and delicate throat and her lovely gray eyes.

"There's something pathetic about her," he thought, as he fell asleep.

2

A week had passed since they met. It was a holiday. Indoors it was oppressively hot, but the dust rose in clouds out of doors, and the people's hats whirled away. All day long Gurov was plagued with thirst, and kept going to the soft-drink stand to offer Anna Sergeyevna a soft drink or an ice cream. There was no refuge from the heat.

In the evening when the wind dropped they walked to the pier to watch the steamer come in. There were a great many people strolling along the pier: they had come to welcome friends, and they carried bunches of flowers. Two peculiarities of a festive Yalta crowd stood out distinctly: the elderly ladies were dressed like young women, and there were innumerable generals.

Because there was a heavy sea, the steamer was late, and already the sun was going down. The steamer had to maneuver for a long time before it could take its place beside the jetty. Anna Sergeyevna scanned the steamer and the passengers through her lorgnette, as though searching for someone she knew, and when she turned to Gurov her eyes were shining. She talked a good deal, with sudden abrupt questions, and quickly forgot what she had been saying; and then she lost her lorgnette in the crush.

The smartly dressed people went away, and it was now too dark to recognize faces. The wind had dropped, but Gurov and Anna Sergeyevna still stood there as though waiting for someone to come off the steamer. Anna Sergeyevna had fallen silent, and every now and then she would smell her flowers. She did not look at Gurov.

"The weather is better this evening," he said. "Where shall we go now? We might go for a drive."

He gazed at her intently and suddenly embraced her and kissed her on the lips, overwhelmed by the perfume and moisture of the flowers. And then, frightened, he looked around—had anyone observed them?

"Let us go to your . . ." he said softly.

They walked away quickly.

Her room was oppressively hot, and there was the scent of the perfume she had bought at a Japanese shop. Gurov gazed at her, and all the while he was thinking: "How strange are our meetings!" Out of the past there came to him the memory of other careless, good-natured women, happy in their love-making, grateful for the joy he gave them, however short, and then he remembered other women, like his wife, whose caresses were insincere and who talked endlessly in an affected and hysterical manner, with an expression which said this was not love or passion but something far more meaningful; and then he thought of the few very beautiful cold women on whose faces there would suddenly appear the glow of a fierce flame, a stubborn desire to take, to wring from life more than it can give: women who were no longer in their first youth, capricious, imprudent, unreflecting, and domineering, and when Gurov grew cold to them, their beauty aroused his hatred, and the lace trimming of their lingerie reminded him of fish scales.

But here there was all the shyness and awkwardness of inexperienced youth: a feeling of embarrassment, as though someone had suddenly knocked on the door. Anna Sergeyevna, "the lady with the pet dog," accepted what had happened in her own special way, gravely and seriously, as though she had accomplished her own downfall, an attitude which he found odd and disconcerting. Her features faded and drooped away, and on both sides of her face the long hair hung mournfully down, while she sat musing disconsolately like an adulteress in an antique painting.

"It's not right," she said. "You're the first person not to respect me."

There was a watermelon on the table. Gurov cut off a slice and began eating it slowly. For at least half an hour they were silent.

There was something touching about Anna Sergeyevna, revealing the purity of a simple and naïve woman who knew very little about life. The single candle burning on the table barely illuminated her face, but it was clear that she was deeply unhappy.

"Why should I not respect you?" Gurov said. "You don't know what you are saying."

"God forgive me!" she said, and her eyes filled with tears. "It's terrible!"

"You don't have to justify yourself."

"How can I justify myself? No, I am a wicked, fallen woman! I despise myself, and have no desire to justify myself! It isn't my husband I have deceived, but myself! And not only now, I have been deceiving myself for a long time. My husband may be a good, honest man, but he is also a flunky! I don't know what work he does, but I know he is a flunky! When I married him I was twenty. I was devoured with curiosity. I longed for something better! Surely, I told myself, there is another kind of life! I wanted to live! To live, only to live! I was burning with curiosity. You won't understand, but I swear by God I was no longer in control of myself! Something strange was going on in me. I could not hold back. I told my husband I was ill, and I came here. . . . And now I have been walking about as though in a daze, like someone who has gone out of his senses. . . . And now I am nothing else but a low, common woman, and anyone may despise me!"

Gurov listened to her, bored to death. He was irritated with her naïve tone, and with her remorse, so unexpected and so out of place. But for the tears in her eyes, he would have thought she was joking or playing a part.

"I don't understand," he said gently. "What do you want?"

She laid her face against his chest and pressed close to him.

"Believe me, believe me, I beg you," she said. "I love all that is honest and pure in life, and sin is hateful to me. I don't know what I am doing. There are simple people who say: 'The Evil One led her astray,' and now I can say of myself that the Evil One has led me astray."

"Don't say such things," he murmured.

Then he gazed into her frightened, staring eyes, kissed her, spoke softly and affectionately, and gradually he was able to quieten her, and she was happy again; and then they both began to laugh.

Afterwards when they went out, there was not a soul on the esplanade. The town with its cypresses looked like a city of the dead, but the sea still roared and hurled itself against the shore. A single boat was rocking on the waves, and the lantern on it shone with a sleepy light.

They found a cab and drove to Oreanda.

"I discovered your name in the foyer just now," he said. "It was written up on the board—von Diederichs. Is your husband German?"

"No, I believe his grandfather was German, but he himself is an Orthodox Russian."

At Oreanda they sat on a bench not far from the church and gazed below at the sea and were lost in silence. Yalta was scarcely visible through the morning mist. Motionless white clouds covered the mountaintops. No leaves rustled, but the cicadas sang, and the monotonous muffled thunder of the sea, coming up from below, spoke of the peace, the eternal sleep awaiting us. This muffled thunder rose from the sea when neither Yalta nor Oreanda existed, and so it roars and will roar, dully, indifferently, after we have passed away. In this constancy of the sea, in her perfect indifference to our living and dying, there lies perhaps the promise of our eternal salvation, the unbroken stream of life on earth, and its unceasing movement toward perfection. Sitting beside the young woman, who looked so beautiful in the dawn, Gurov was soothed and enchanted by the fairylike scene—the sea and the mountains, the clouds and the broad sky. He pondered how everything in the universe, if properly understood, would be entirely beautiful, but for our own thoughts and actions when we lose sight of the higher purposes of life and our human dignity.

Someone came up to them—probably a coast guard—looked at them and then walked away. His coming seemed full of mystery and beauty. Then in the glow of the early dawn they saw the steamer coming from Feodossia, its lights already doused.

"There is dew on the grass," said Anna Sergeyevna after a silence.

"Yes, it's time to go home."

They went back to the town.

Thereafter they met every day at noon on the esplanade, lunched and dined together, went out on excursions, and admired the sea. She complained of sleeping badly and of the violent beating of her heart, and she kept asking the same questions over and over again, alternately surrendering to jealousy and the fear that he did not really respect her. And often in the square or in the public gardens, when there was no one near, he would suddenly draw her to him and kiss her passionately. Their perfect idleness, those kisses in the full light of day, exchanged circumspectly and furtively for fear that anyone should see them, the heat, the smell of the sea, the continual glittering procession of idle, fashionable, well-fed people—all this seemed to give him a new lease of life. He kept telling Anna Sergeyevna how beautiful and seductive she was; he was impatient and passionate for her; and he never left her side, while she brooded continually, always trying to make him confess that he had no respect for her, did not love her at all, and saw in her nothing but a loose woman. Almost every evening at a late hour they would leave the town and drive out to Oreanda or to the waterfall, and these excursions were invariably a success, while the sensations they enjoyed were invariably beautiful and sublime.

All this time they were waiting for her husband to come, but he sent a letter saying he was having trouble with his eyes and imploring her to come home as soon as possible. Anna Sergeyevna made haste to obey.

"It's a good thing I am going away," she told Gurov. "It is fate."

She took a carriage to the railroad station, and he went with her. The drive took nearly a whole day. When she had taken her seat in the express train, and when the second bell had rung, she said: "Let me have one more look at you! Just one more! Like that!"

She did not cry, but looked sad and ill, and her face trembled.

"I shall always think of you and remember you," she said. "God be with you! Think kindly of me! We shall never meet again—that's all for the good, for we should never have met. God bless you!"

The train moved off rapidly, and soon its lights vanished, and in a few moments the sound of the engine grew silent, as though everything were conspiring to put an end to this sweet oblivion, this madness. Alone on the platform, gazing into the dark distance, Gurov listened to the crying of the cicadas and the humming of the telegraph wires with the feeling that he had only just this moment woken up. And he told himself that this was just one more of the many adventures in his life, and it was now over, and there remained only a memory. . . . He was confused, sad, and filled with a faint sensation of remorse. After all, this young woman whom he would never meet again, had not been happy with him. He had been affectionate and sincere, but in his manner, his tone, his caresses, there had always been a suggestion of irony, the insulting arrogance of a successful male who was almost twice her age. And always she had called him kind, exceptional, noble: obviously he had seemed to her different from what he really was, and unintentionally he had deceived her. . . .

Here at the railroad station there was the scent of autumn in the air; and the evening was cold.

"It's time for me to go north, too," Gurov thought as he left the platform. "High time!"

3

At home in Moscow winter was already at hand. The stoves were heated, and it was still dark when the children got up to go to school, and the nurse would light the lamp for a short while. Already there was frost. When the first snow falls, and people go out for the first time on sleighs, it is good to see the white ground, the white roofs: one breathes easily and lightly, and one remembers the days of one's youth. The old lime trees and birches have a kindly look about them: they lie closer to one's heart than cypresses and palms; and below their branches one has no desire to dream of mountains and the sea.

Gurov, a native of Moscow, arrived there on a fine, frosty day, and when he put on his fur coat and warm gloves and went for a stroll along the Petrovka, and when on Saturday evening he heard the church bells ringing, then his recent travels and all the places he had visited lost their charm for him. Little by little he became immersed in Moscow life, eagerly read three newspapers a day, and declared that on principle he never read Moscow newspapers. Once more he was caught up in a whirl of restaurants, clubs, banquets, and celebrations, and it was flattering to have famous lawyers and actors visiting his house, and flattering to play cards with a professor at the doctors' club. He could eat a whole portion of *selyanka*, a cabbage stew, straight off the frying pan. . . .

So a month would pass, and the image of Anna Sergeyevna, he thought, would vanish into the mists of memory, and only rarely would she visit his dreams with her touching smile, like the other women who appeared in his dreams. But more than a month went by, soon it was the dead of winter, and the memory of Anna Sergeyevna remained as vivid as if he had parted from her only the day before. And these memories kept glowing with an even stronger flame. Whether it was in the silence of the evening when he was in his study and heard the voices of his children preparing their lessons, or listening to a song or the music in a restaurant or a storm howling in the chimney, suddenly all his memories would spring to life again: what happened on the pier, the misty mountains in the early morning, the steamer coming in from Feodossia, their kisses. He would pace up and down the room for a long while, remembering it all and smiling to himself, and later these memories would fill his dreams, and in his imagination the past would mingle with the future. When he closed his eyes, he saw her as though she were standing before him in the flesh, younger, lovelier, tenderer than she had really been; and he imagined himself a finer person than he had been in Yalta. In the evenings she peered at him from the bookshelves, the fireplace, a corner of the room; he heard her breathing and the soft rustle of her skirts. In the street he followed the women with his eyes, looking for someone who resembled her.

He began to feel an overwhelming desire to share his memories with someone. But in his home it was impossible for him to talk of his love, and away from home—there was no one. The tenants who lived in his house and his colleagues at the bank were equally useless. And what could he tell them? Had he really been in love? Was there anything beautiful, poetic, edifying, or even interesting, in his relations with Anna Sergeyevna? He found himself talking about women and love in vague generalities, and nobody guessed what he meant, and only his wife twitched her dark eyebrows and said: "Really, Dimitry, the role of a coxcomb does not suit you at all!"

One evening he was coming out of the doctors' club with one of his card partners, a government official, and he could not prevent himself from saying: "If you only knew what a fascinating woman I met in Yalta!"

The official sat down in the sleigh, and was driving away when he suddenly turned round and shouted: "Dmitry Dmitrich!"

"What?"

"You were quite right just now! The sturgeon wasn't fresh!"

These words, in themselves so commonplace, for some reason aroused Gurov's indignation: they seemed somehow dirty and degrading. What savage manners, what awful faces! What wasted nights, what dull days devoid of interest! Frenzied card playing, gluttony, drunkenness, endless conversations about the same thing. Futile pursuits and conversations about the same topics taking up the greater part of the day and the greater part of a man's strength, so that he was left to live out a curtailed, bobtailed life with his wings clipped—an idiotic mess—impossible to run away or escape—one might as well be in a madhouse or a convict settlement.

Gurov, boiling with indignation, did not sleep a wink that night, and all the next day he suffered from a headache. On the following nights, too, he slept badly, sitting up in bed, thinking, or pacing the floor of his room. He was fed up with his children, fed up with the bank, and had not the slightest desire to go anywhere or talk about anything.

During the December holidays he decided to go on a journey and told his wife he had to go to St. Petersburg on some business connected with a certain young friend of his. Instead he went to the town of S_____. Why? He hardly knew himself. He wanted to see Anna Sergeyevna and talk with her and if possible arrange a rendezvous.

He arrived at S_____ during the morning and took the best room in the hotel, where the floor was covered with gray army cloth and on the table there was an inkstand, gray with dust, topped by a headless rider holding a hat in his raised hand. The porter gave him the necessary information: von Diederichs lived on Old Goncharnaya Street in a house of his own not far from the hotel; lived on a grand scale, luxuriously, and kept his own horses; the whole town knew him. The porter pronounced the name "Driderits."

He was in no hurry. He walked along Old Goncharnaya Street and found the house. In front of the house stretched a long gray fence studded with nails.

"You'd run away from a fence like that," Gurov thought, glancing now at the windows of the house, now at the fence.

He thought: "Today is a holiday, and her husband is probably at home. In any case it would be tactless to go up to the house and upset her. And if I sent her a note it might fall into her husband's hands and bring about a catastrophe! The best thing is to trust to chance." So he kept walking up and down the street by the fence, waiting for the chance. He saw a beggar entering the gates, only to be attacked by dogs, and about an hour later he heard someone playing on a piano, but the sounds were very faint and indistinct. Probably Anna Sergeyevna was playing. Suddenly the front door opened, and an old woman came out, followed by the familiar white Pomeranian. Gurov thought of calling out to the dog, but his heart suddenly began to beat violently and he was so excited he could not remember the dog's name.

As he walked on, he came to hate the gray fence more and more, and it occurred to him with a sense of irritation that Anna Sergeyevna had forgotten him and was perhaps amusing herself with another man, and that was very natural in a young woman who had nothing to look at from morning to night but that damned fence. He went back to his hotel room and for a long while sat on the sofa, not knowing what to do. Then he ordered dinner and took a long nap.

"How absurd and tiresome it is!" he thought when he woke and looked at the dark windows, for evening had fallen. "Well, I've had some sleep, and what is there to do tonight?"

He sat up in the bed, which was covered with a cheap gray blanket of the kind seen in hospitals, and he taunted himself with anger and vexation.

"You and your lady with the pet dog. . . . There's a fine adventure for you! You're in a nice fix now!"

However, at the railroad station that morning his eye had been caught by a playbill advertising in enormous letters the first performance of *The Geisha*. He remembered this, and drove to the theater.

"It's very likely that she goes to first nights," he told himself.

The theater was full. There, as so often in provincial theaters, a thick haze hung above the chandeliers, and the crowds in the gallery were fidgeting noisily. In the first row of the orchestra the local dandies were standing with their hands behind their backs, waiting for the curtain to rise, while in the governor's box the governor's daughter, wearing a boa, sat in front, the governor himself sitting modestly behind the drapes, with only his hands visible. The curtain was swaying; the orchestra spent a long time tuning up. While the audience was coming in and taking their seats, Gurov was looking impatiently around him.

And then Anna Sergeyevna came in. She sat in the third row, and when Gurov looked at her his heart seemed to stop, and he understood clearly that the whole world contained no one nearer, dearer, and more important than Anna. This slight woman, lost amid a provincial rabble, in no way remarkable, with her silly lorgnette in her hands, filled his whole life: she was his sorrow and his joy, the only happiness he desired for himself; and to the sounds of the wretched orchestra, with its feeble provincial violins, he thought how beautiful she was. He thought and dreamed.

There came with Anna Sergeyevna a young man with small side whiskers, very tall and stooped, who inclined his head at every step and seemed to be continually bowing. Probably this was the husband she once described as a flunky one day in Yalta when she was in a bitter mood. And indeed in his lanky figure, his side whiskers, his small bald patch, there was something of a flunky's servility. He smiled sweetly, and in his button-hole there was an academic badge like the number worn by a waiter.

During the first intermission the husband went away to smoke, and she remained in her seat. Gurov, who was also sitting in the orchestra, went up to her and said in a trembling voice, with a forced smile: "How are you?"

She looked up at him and turned pale, then glanced at him again in horror, unable to believe her eyes, tightly gripping the fan and the lorgnette, evidently fighting to overcome a feeling of faintness. Both were silent. She sat, he stood, and he was frightened by her distress, and did not dare sit beside her. The violins and flutes sang out as they were tuned. Suddenly he was afraid, as it occurred to him that all the people in the boxes were staring down at them. She stood up and walked quickly to the exit; he followed her, and both of them walked aimlessly up and down the corridors, while crowds of lawyers, teachers, and civil servants, all wearing the appropriate uniforms and badges, flashed past; and the ladies, and the fur coats hanging from pegs, also flashed past; and the draft blew through the place, bringing with it the odor of cigar stubs. Gurov, whose heart was beating wildly, thought: "Oh Lord, why are these people here and this orchestra?"

At that moment he recalled how, when he saw Anna Sergeyevna off at the station in the evening, he had told himself it was all over and they would never meet again. But how far away the end seemed to be now!

Anna paused on a narrow dark stairway which bore the inscription: "This way to the upper balcony."

"How you frightened me!" she said, breathing heavily, pale and stunned. "How you frightened me! I am half dead! Why did you come? Why?"

"Do try to understand, Anna—please understand . . ." he said in a hurried whisper. "I implore you, please understand . . ."

She looked at him with dread, with entreaty, with love, intently, to retain his features all the more firmly in her memory.

"I've been so unhappy," she went on, not listening to him. "All this time I've thought only of you, I've lived on thoughts of you. I tried to forget, to forget—why, why have you come?"

A pair of schoolboys were standing on the landing above them, smoking and peering down, but Gurov did not care, and drawing Anna to him, he began kissing her face, her cheeks, her hands.

"What are you doing? What are you doing?" she said in terror, pushing him away from her. "We have both lost our senses! Go away now—tonight! . . . I implore you by everything you hold sacred. . . . Someone is coming!"

Someone was climbing up the stairs.

"You must go away . . ." Anna Sergeyevna went on in a whisper. "Do you hear, Dmitry Dmitrich? I'll come and visit you in Moscow. I have never been happy. I am miserable now, and I shall never be happy again, never! Don't make me suffer any more! I swear I'll come to Moscow! We must separate now. My dear precious darling, we have to separate!"

She pressed his hand and went quickly down the stairs, all the while gazing back at him, and it was clear from the expression in her eyes that she was miserable. For a while Gurov stood there, listening to her footsteps, and then all sounds faded away, and he went to look for his coat and left the theater.

4

And Anna Sergeyevna began coming to see him in Moscow. Every two or three months she would leave the town of S_____, telling her husband she was going to consult a specialist in women's disorders, and her husband neither believed her nor disbelieved her. In Moscow she always stayed at the Slavyansky Bazaar Hotel, and the moment she arrived she would send a red-capped hotel messenger to Gurov. He would visit her, and no one in Moscow ever knew about their meetings.

One winter morning he was going to visit her as usual. (The messenger from the hotel had come the evening before, but he was out.) His daughter accompanied him. He was taking her to school, and the school lay on the way to the hotel. Great wet flakes of snow were falling.

"Three degrees above freezing, and it's still snowing," he told his daughter. "That's only the surface temperature of the earth—the other layers of the atmosphere have other temperatures."

"Yes, Papa. But why are there no thunderstorms in winter?"

He explained that, too. He talked, and all the while he was thinking about his meeting with the beloved, and not a living soul knew of it, and probably no one would ever know. He was living a double life: an open and public life visible to all who had any need to know, full of conventional truth and conventional lies, exactly like the lives of his friends and acquaintances, and another which followed a secret course. And by one of those strange and perhaps accidental circumstances everything that was to him meaningful, urgent, and important, everything about which he felt sincerely and did not deceive himself, everything that went to shape the very core of his existence, was concealed from others, while everything that was false and the shell where he hid in order to hide the truth about himself—his work at the bank, discussions at the club, conversations about women as "an inferior race," and attending anniversary celebrations with his wife—all this was on the surface. Judging others by himself, he refused to believe the evidence of his eyes, and therefore he imagined that all men led their real and meaningful lives under a veil of mystery and under cover of darkness. Every man's intimate existence revolved around mysterious secrets, and it was perhaps partly for this reason that all civilized men were so nervously anxious to protect their privacy.

Leaving his daughter at the school, Gurov went on to the Slavyansky Bazaar Hotel. He removed his fur coat in the lobby, and then went upstairs and knocked softly on the door. Anna Sergeyevna had been exhausted by the journey and the suspense of waiting for his arrival—she had in fact expected him the previous evening. She was wearing her favorite gray dress. She was pale, and she looked at him without smiling, and he had scarcely entered the room when she threw herself in his arms. Their kisses were lingering and prolonged, as though two years had passed since they had seen each other.

"How were things down there?" he said. "Anything new?"

"Please wait. . . . I'll tell you in a moment. . . . I can't speak yet!"

She could not speak because she was crying. She turned away from him, pressing a handkerchief to her eyes.

"Let her have her cry," he thought. "I'll sit down and wait." And he sat down in an armchair.

Then he rang and ordered tea, and while he drank the tea she remained standing with her face turned to the window. . . . She was crying from the depth of her emotions, in the bitter knowledge that their life together was so weighed down with sadness, because they could only meet in secret and were always hiding from people like thieves. And that meant surely that their lives were shattered!

"Oh, do stop crying!" he said.

It was evident to him that their love affair would not soon be over, and there was no end in sight. Anna Sergeyevna was growing more and more passionately fond of him, and it was beyond belief that he would ever tell her it must one day end; and if he had told her, she would not have believed him.

He went up to her and put his hands on her shoulders, intending to console her with some meaningless words and to fondle her; and then he saw himself in the mirror.

His hair was turning gray. It struck him as strange that he should have aged so much in these last years, and lost his good looks. Her shoulders were warm and trembling at his touch. He felt pity for her, who was so warm and beautiful, though probably it would not be long before she would begin to fade and wither, as he had done. Why did she love him so much? Women had always believed him to be other than what he was, and they loved in him not himself but the creature who came to life in their imagination, the man they had been seeking eagerly all their lives, and when they had discovered their mistake, they went on loving him. And not one of them was ever happy with him. Time passed, he met other women, became intimate with them, parted from them, never having loved them. It was anything you please, but it was not love.

And now at last, when his hair was turning gray, he had fallen in love—real love— for the first time in his life.

Anna Sergeyevna and he loved one another as people who are very close and dear love one another: they were like deeply devoted friends, like husband and wife. It seemed to them that Fate had intended them for one another, and it was beyond understanding that one had a wife, the other a husband. It was as though they were two birds of passage, one male, one female, who had been trapped and were now compelled to live in different cages. They had forgiven one another for all they were ashamed of in the past, they forgave everything in the present, and felt that this love of theirs changed them both.

Formerly in moments of depression he had consoled himself with the first argument that came into his head, but now all such arguments were foreign to him. He felt a deep compassion for her, and desired to be tender and sincere. . . .

"Don't cry, my darling," he said. "You've cried enough. Now let us talk, and we'll think of something. . . ."

Then they talked it over for a long time, trying to discover some way of avoiding secrecy and deception, and living in different towns, and being separated for long periods. How could they free themselves from their intolerable chains?

"How? How?" he asked, holding his head in his hands. "How?"

And it seemed as though in a little while the solution would be found and a lovely new life would begin for them; and to both of them it was clear that the end was still very far away, and the hardest and most difficult part was only beginning.

Edith Wharton (1862–1937)

How does a writer create sympathy? How is the reader distanced or brought closer? Focusing on the way Edith Wharton controls our attitude toward Mrs. Slade and Mrs. Ansley in "Roman Fever" can tell us a lot about writing. Seen from the outside at the beginning, Mrs. Slade is clearly the more dynamic and attractive of the two women, and throughout the story we spend more time in her mind than in the pale Mrs. Ansley's. Yet Wharton does not let us become too committed to her. Something inhibits our sympathy, perhaps that "determined nose supported by vigorous black eyebrows," perhaps the way she uses money to buy off the head waiter, perhaps the contempt she feels for her friend. Although, perhaps for reasons of plot suspense, we are never fully privy to Mrs. Ansley's thoughts, gradually our sympathy shifts toward her: she is more sensitive, kinder, and more mysterious. The story gathers momentum largely through the intensification of Mrs. Slade's hostility. As the disclosure approaches, we fear that it will, as it does, cost Mrs. Ansley. By then, we are not surprised by Mrs. Slade's cruelty—such hostility combined with such pride will surely find its occasion—and because we have subtly taken Mrs. Ansley's side we are pleased by Mrs. Slade's comeuppance. Wharton has subtly reversed our sympathies, and indeed our sense of which woman is the more interesting—very likely without our noticing.

Though written relatively late in a long career, this story serves as a wonderful introduction to a major American writer. It sounds many of the notes sounded in her novels. Born in 1862 to the confining, watchful, narrow New York aristocracy, Wharton wrote extensively about the restrictions and repressions of a rich though insecure society. This society placed a higher premium on good form and conventional behavior than on love and happiness. Those individuals who go their own way—Lily Bart in *The House of Mirth*, Ellen Olenska in *The Age of Innocence*—are destroyed or cast out. Wharton seems to have known everything there was to know about the money, manners, and morals of this society, and about the hollowness at its heart. She also knew, as she shows in the character of Mrs. Ansley, that a belief in the supremacy of sentiment and the surrender to passion can give meaning to an otherwise dull life.

Wharton has often been called a disciple of Henry James. Indeed, they had much in common (in addition to being New Yorkers and good friends). Both wrote of the leisured classes and international travelers as well as of artists and writers. Both believed in the seriousness of fiction as a high calling. Both were consummate artists. But their style and their technique are different. For Wharton the major drama is not, as it is for James, in the feelings and thoughts of the characters, but on the public stage where the potential outlaw confronts society's power and wrath, and suffers the consequences. And—as we see when we compare "Roman Fever" to "The Beast in the Jungle"—Wharton is more direct and dramatic in the way she presents her stories.

Wharton completed more than twenty novels, three volumes of poetry, two plays, ten volumes of stories, as well as books on travel and interior design. Her best known novels, in addition to the ones mentioned above, are *The Custom of the Country* and *Ethan Frome*. She died in 1937.

Roman Fever

1

From the table at which they had been lunching two American ladies of ripe but well-cared-for middle age moved across the lofty terrace of the Roman restaurant and, leaning on its parapet, looked first at each other, and then down on the outspread glories of the Palatine and the Forum, with the same expression of vague but benevolent approval.

As they leaned there a girlish voice echoed up gaily from the stairs leading to the court below. "Well, come along, then," it cried, not to them but to an invisible companion, "and let's leave the young things to their knitting"; and a voice as fresh laughed back: "Oh, look here, Babs, not actually *knitting*—" "Well, I mean figuratively," rejoined the first. "After all, we haven't left our poor parents much else to do . . ." and at that point the turn of the stairs engulfed the dialogue.

The two ladies looked at each other again, this time with a tinge of smiling embarrassment, and the smaller and paler one shook her head and coloured slightly.

"Barbara!" she murmured, sending an unheard rebuke after the mocking voice in the stairway.

The other lady, who was fuller, and higher in colour, with a small determined nose supported by vigorous black eyebrows, gave a good-humoured laugh. "That's what our daughters think of us!"

Her companion replied by a deprecating gesture. "Not of us individually. We must remember that. It's just the collective modern idea of Mothers. And you see—" Half guiltily she drew from her handsomely mounted black hand-bag a twist of crimson silk run through by two fine knitting needles. "One never knows," she murmured. "The new system has certainly given us a good deal of time to kill; and sometimes I get tired just looking—even at this." Her gesture was now addressed to the stupendous scene at their feet.

The dark lady laughed again, and they both relapsed upon the view, contemplating it in silence, with a sort of diffused serenity which might have been borrowed from the spring effulgence of the Roman skies. The luncheon-hour was long past, and the two had their end of the vast terrace to themselves. At its opposite extremity a few groups, detained by a lingering look at the outspread city, were gathering up guide-books and fumbling for tips. The last of them scattered, and the two ladies were alone on the air-washed height.

"Well, I don't see why we shouldn't just stay here," said Mrs. Slade, the lady of the high colour and energetic brows. Two derelict basket-chairs stood near, and she pushed them into the angle of the parapet, and settled herself in one, her gaze upon the Palatine. "After all, it's still the most beautiful view in the world."

"It always will be, to me," assented her friend Mrs. Ansley, with so slight a stress on the "me" that Mrs. Slade, though she noticed it, wondered if it were not merely accidental, like the random underlinings of old-fashioned letter-writers.

"Grace Ansley was always old-fashioned," she thought; and added aloud, with a retrospective smile: "It's a view we've both been familiar with for a good many years. When we first met here we were younger than our girls are now. You remember?"

"Oh, yes, I remember," murmured Mrs. Ansley, with the same undefinable stress.—"There's that head-waiter wondering," she interpolated. She was evidently far less sure than her companion of herself and of her rights in the world.

"I'll cure him of wondering," said Mrs. Slade, stretching her hand toward a bag as discreetly opulent-looking as Mrs. Ansley's. Signing to the head-waiter, she explained that she and her friend were old lovers of Rome, and would like to spend the end of the afternoon looking down on the view—that is, if it did not disturb the service? The head-waiter, bowing over her gratuity, assured her that the ladies were most welcome, and would be still more so if they would condescend to remain for dinner. A full moon night, they would remember . . .

Mrs. Slade's black brows drew together, as though references to the moon were out-of-place and even unwelcome. But she smiled away her frown as the head-waiter retreated. "Well, why not? We might do worse. There's no knowing, I suppose, when the girls will be back. Do you even know back from *where*? I don't!"

Mrs. Ansley again coloured slightly. "I think those young Italian aviators we met at the Embassy invited them to fly to Tarquinia for tea. I suppose they'll want to wait and fly back by moonlight."

"Moonlight—moonlight! What a part it still plays. Do you suppose they're as sentimental as we were?"

"I've come to the conclusion that I don't in the least know what they are," said Mrs. Ansley. "And perhaps we didn't know much more about each other."

"No; perhaps we didn't."

Her friend gave her a shy glance. "I never should have supposed you were sentimental, Alida."

"Well, perhaps I wasn't." Mrs. Slade drew her lids together in retrospect; and for a few moments the two ladies, who had been intimate since childhood, reflected how little they knew each other. Each one, of course, had a label ready to attach to the other's name; Mrs. Delphin Slade, for instance, would have told herself, or any one who asked her, that Mrs. Horace Ansley, twenty-five years ago, had been exquisitely lovely—no, you wouldn't believe it, would you? . . . though, of course, still charming, distinguished . . . Well, as a girl she had been exquisite; far more beautiful than her daughter Barbara, though certainly Babs, according to the new standards at any rate, was more effective—had more *edge*, as they say. Funny where she got it, with those two nullities as parents. Yes; Horace Ansley was—well, just the duplicate of his wife. Museum specimens of old New York. Good-looking, irreproachable, exemplary. Mrs. Slade and Mrs. Ansley had lived opposite each other—actually as well as figuratively—for years. When the drawing-room curtains in No. 20 East 73rd Street were renewed, No. 23, across the way, was always aware of it. And of all the movings, buyings, travels, anniversaries, illnesses—the tame chronicle of an estimable pair. Little of it escaped Mrs. Slade. But she had grown bored with it by the time her husband made his big *coup* in Wall Street, and when they bought in upper Park Avenue had already begun to think: "I'd rather live opposite a speak-easy for a change; at least one might see it raided." The idea of seeing Grace raided was so amusing that (before the move) she launched it at a woman's lunch. It made a hit, and went the rounds—she sometimes wondered if it had crossed the street, and reached Mrs. Ansley. She hoped not, but didn't much mind. Those were the days when respectability was at a discount, and it did the irreproachable no harm to laugh at them a little.

A few years later, and not many months apart, both ladies lost their husbands. There was an appropriate exchange of wreaths and condolences, and a brief renewal of intimacy in the half-shadow of their mourning; and now, after another interval, they had run across each other in Rome, at the same hotel, each of them the modest appendage of a salient daughter. The similarity of their lot had again drawn them together, lending itself to mild jokes, and the mutual confession that, if in old days it must have been tiring to "keep up" with daughters, it was now, at times, a little dull not to.

No doubt, Mrs. Slade reflected, she felt her unemployment more than poor Grace ever would. It was a big drop from being the wife of Delphin Slade to being his widow. She had always regarded herself (with a certain conjugal pride) as his equal in social gifts, as contributing her full share to the making of the exceptional couple they were: but the difference after his death was irremediable. As the wife of the famous corporation lawyer, always with an international case or two on hand, every day brought its exciting and unexpected obligation: the impromptu entertaining of eminent colleagues from abroad, the hurried dashes on legal business to London, Paris or Rome, where the entertaining was so handsomely reciprocated; the amusement of hearing in her wake: "What, that handsome woman with the good clothes and the eyes is Mrs. Slade—*the* Slade's wife? Really? Generally the wives of celebrities are such frumps."

Yes; being *the* Slade's widow was a dullish business after that. In living up to such a husband all her faculties had been engaged; now she had only her daughter to live up to, for the son who seemed to have inherited his father's gifts had died suddenly in boyhood. She had fought through that agony because her husband was there, to be helped and to help; now, after the father's death, the thought of the boy had become unbearable. There was nothing left but to mother her daughter; and dear Jenny was such a perfect daughter that she needed no excessive mothering. "Now with Babs Ansley I don't know that I *should* be so quiet," Mrs. Slade sometimes half-enviously reflected; but Jenny, who was younger than her brilliant friend, was that rare accident, an extremely pretty girl who somehow made youth and prettiness seem as safe as their absence. It was all perplexing—and to Mrs. Slade a little boring. She wished that Jenny would fall in love—with the wrong man, even; that she might have to be watched, out-manoeuvred, rescued. And instead, it was Jenny who watched her mother, kept her out of draughts, made sure that she had taken her tonic . . .

Mrs. Ansley was much less articulate than her friend, and her mental portrait of Mrs. Slade was slighter, and drawn with fainter touches. "Alida Slade's awfully brilliant; but not as brilliant as she thinks," would have summed it up; though she would have added, for the enlightenment of strangers, that Mrs. Slade had been an extremely dashing girl; much more so than her daughter, who was pretty, of course, and clever in a way, but had none of her mother's—well, "vividness", some one had once called it. Mrs. Ansley would take up current words like this, and cite them in quotation marks, as unheard-of audacities. No; Jenny was not like her mother. Sometimes Mrs. Ansley thought Alida Slade was disappointed; on the whole she had had a sad life. Full of failures and mistakes; Mrs. Ansley had always been rather sorry for her . . .

So these two ladies visualized each other, each through the wrong end of her little telescope.

2

For a long time they continued to sit side by side without speaking. It seemed as though, to both, there was a relief in laying down their somewhat futile activities in the presence of the vast Memento Mori which faced them. Mrs. Slade sat quite still, her eyes fixed on the golden slope of the Palace of the Cæsars, and after a while Mrs. Ansley ceased to fidget with her bag, and she too sank into meditation. Like many intimate friends, the two ladies had never before had occasion to be silent together, and Mrs. Ansley was slightly embarrassed by what seemed, after so many years, a new stage in their intimacy, and one with which she did not yet know how to deal.

Suddenly the air was full of that deep clangour of bells which periodically covers Rome with a roof of silver. Mrs. Slade glanced at her wrist-watch. "Five o'clock already," she said, as though surprised.

Mrs. Ansley suggested interrogatively: "There's bridge at the Embassy at five." For a long time Mrs. Slade did not answer. She appeared to be lost in contemplation, and Mrs. Ansley thought the remark had escaped her. But after a while she said, as if speaking out of a dream: "Bridge, did you say? Not unless you want to . . . But I don't think I will, you know."

"Oh, no," Mrs. Ansley hastened to assure her. "I don't care to at all. It's so lovely here; and so full of old memories, as you say." She settled herself in her chair, and almost furtively drew forth her knitting. Mrs. Slade took sideway note of this activity, but her own beautifully cared-for hands remained motionless on her knee.

"I was just thinking," she said slowly, "what different things Rome stands for to each generation of travellers. To our grandmothers, Roman fever; to our mothers, sentimental dangers—how we used to be guarded!—to our daughters, no more dangers than the middle of Main Street. They don't know it—but how much they're missing!"

The long golden light was beginning to pale, and Mrs. Ansley lifted her knitting a little closer to her eyes. "Yes; how we were guarded!"

"I always used to think," Mrs. Slade continued, "that our mothers had a much more difficult job than our grandmothers. When Roman fever stalked the streets it must have been comparatively easy to gather in the girls at the danger hour; but when you and I were young, with such beauty calling us, and the spice of disobedience thrown in, and no worse risk than catching cold during the cool hour after sunset, the mothers used to be put to it to keep us in—didn't they?"

She turned again toward Mrs. Ansley, but the latter had reached a delicate point in her knitting. "One, two, three—slip two; yes, they must have been," she assented, without looking up.

Mrs. Slade's eyes rested on her with a deepened attention. "She can knit—in the face of *this*! How like her . . ."

Mrs. Slade leaned back, brooding, her eyes ranging from the ruins which faced her to the long green hollow of the Forum, the fading glow of the church fronts beyond it, and the outlying immensity of the Colosseum. Suddenly she thought: "It's all very well to say that our girls have done away with sentiment and moonlight. But if Babs Ansley isn't out to catch that young aviator—the one who's a Marchese—then I don't know anything. And Jenny has no chance beside her. I know that too. I wonder if that's why Grace Ansley likes the two girls to go everywhere together? My poor Jenny as a foil—!" Mrs. Slade gave a hardly audible laugh, and at the sound Mrs. Ansley dropped her knitting.

"Yes—?"

"I—oh, nothing, I was only thinking how your Babs carries everything before her. That Campolieri boy is one of the best matches in Rome. Don't look so innocent, my dear—you know he is. And I was wondering, ever so respectfully, you understand . . . wondering how two such exemplary characters as you and Horace had managed to produce anything quite so dynamic." Mrs. Slade laughed again, with a touch of asperity.

Mrs. Ansley's hands lay inert across her needles. She looked straight out at the great accumulated wreckage of passion and splendour at her feet. But her small profile was almost expressionless. At length she said: "I think you overrate Babs, my dear."

Mrs. Slade's tone grew easier. "No; I don't. I appreciate her. And perhaps envy you. Oh, my girl's perfect; if I were a chronic invalid I'd—well, I think I'd rather be in Jenny's hands. There must be times . . . but there! I always wanted a brilliant daughter . . . and never quite understood why I got an angel instead."

Mrs. Ansley echoed her laugh in a faint murmur. "Babs is an angel too."

"Of course—of course! But she's got rainbow wings. Well, they're wandering by the sea with their young men; and here we sit . . . and it all brings back the past a little too acutely."

Mrs. Ansley had resumed her knitting. One might almost have imagined (if one had known her less well, Mrs. Slade reflected) that, for her also, too many memories rose from the lengthening shadows of those august ruins. But no; she was simply absorbed in her work. What was there for her to worry about? She knew that Babs would almost certainly come back engaged to the extremely eligible Campolieri. "And she'll sell the New York house, and settle down near them in Rome, and never be in their way . . . she's much too tactful. But she'll have an excellent cook, and just the right people in for bridge and cocktails . . . and a perfectly peaceful old age among her grandchildren."

Mrs. Slade broke off this prophetic flight with a recoil of self-disgust. There was no one of whom she had less right to think unkindly than of Grace Ansley. Would she never cure herself of envying her? Perhaps she had begun too long ago.

She stood up and leaned against the parapet, filling her troubled eyes with the tranquillizing magic of the hour. But instead of tranquillizing her the sight seemed to increase her exasperation. Her gaze turned toward the Colosseum. Already its golden flank was drowned in purple shadow, and above it the sky curved crystal clear, without light or colour. It was the moment when afternoon and evening hang balanced in mid-heaven.

Mrs. Slade turned back and laid her hand on her friend's arm. The gesture was so abrupt that Mrs. Ansley looked up, startled.

"The sun's set. You're not afraid, my dear?"

"Afraid—?"

"Of Roman fever or pneumonia? I remember how ill you were that winter. As a girl you had a very delicate throat, hadn't you?"

"Oh, we're all right up here. Down below, in the Forum, it does get deathly cold, all of a sudden . . . but not here."

"Ah, of course you know because you had to be so careful." Mrs. Slade turned back to the parapet. She thought: "I must make one more effort not to hate her." Aloud she said: "Whenever I look at the Forum from up here, I remember that story about a great-aunt of yours, wasn't she? A dreadfully wicked great-aunt?"

"Oh, yes; Great-aunt Harriet. The one who was supposed to have sent her young sister out to the Forum after sunset to gather a night-blooming flower for her album. All our great-aunts and grand-mothers used to have albums of dried flowers."

Mrs. Slade nodded. "But she really sent her because they were in love with the same man—"

"Well, that was the family tradition. They said Aunt Harriet confessed it years afterward. At any rate, the poor little sister caught the fever and died. Mother used to frighten us with the story when we were children."

"And you frightened *me* with it, that winter when you and I were here as girls. The winter I was engaged to Delphin."

Mrs. Ansley gave a faint laugh. "Oh, did I? Really frightened you? I don't believe you're easily frightened."

"Not often; but I was then. I was easily frightened because I was too happy. I wonder if you know what that means?"

"I—yes . . ." Mrs. Ansley faltered.

"Well, I suppose that was why the story of your wicked aunt made such an impression on me. And I thought: 'There's no more Roman fever, but the Forum is deathly cold after sunset—especially after a hot day. And the Colosseum's even colder and damper'."

"The Colosseum—?"

"Yes. It wasn't easy to get in, after the gates were locked for the night. Far from easy. Still, in those days it could be managed; it *was* managed, often. Lovers met there who couldn't meet elsewhere. You knew that?"

"I—I daresay. I don't remember."

"You don't remember? You don't remember going to visit some ruins or other one evening, just after dark, and catching a bad chill? You were supposed to have gone to see the moon rise. People always said that expedition was what caused your illness."

There was a moment's silence; then Mrs. Ansley rejoined: "Did they? It was all so long ago."

"Yes. And you got well again—so it didn't matter. But I suppose it struck your friends—the reason given for your illness, I mean—because everybody knew you were so prudent on account of your throat, and your mother took such care of you . . . You *had* been out late sight-seeing, hadn't you, that night?"

"Perhaps I had. The most prudent girls aren't always prudent. What made you think of it now?"

Mrs. Slade seemed to have no answer ready. But after a moment she broke out: "Because I simply can't bear it any longer—!"

Mrs. Ansley lifted her head quickly. Her eyes were wide and very pale. "Can't bear what?"

"Why—your not knowing that I've always known why you went."

"Why I went—?"

"Yes. You think I'm bluffing, don't you? Well, you went to meet the man I was engaged to—and I can repeat every word of the letter that took you there."

While Mrs. Slade spoke Mrs. Ansley had risen unsteadily to her feet. Her bag, her knitting and gloves, slid in a panic-stricken heap to the ground. She looked at Mrs. Slade as though she were looking at a ghost.

"No, no—don't," she faltered out.

"Why not? Listen, if you don't believe me. 'My one darling, things can't go on like this. I must see you alone. Come to the Colosseum immediately after dark tomorrow. There will be somebody to let you in. No one whom you need fear will suspect'—but perhaps you've forgotten what the letter said?"

Mrs. Ansley met the challenge with an unexpected composure. Steadying herself against the chair she looked at her friend, and replied: "No; I know it by heart too."

"And the signature? 'Only *your* D.S.' Was that it? I'm right, am I? That was the letter that took you out that evening after dark?"

Mrs. Ansley was still looking at her. It seemed to Mrs. Slade that a slow struggle was going on behind the voluntarily controlled mask of her small quiet face. "I shouldn't have thought she had herself so well in hand," Mrs. Slade reflected, almost resentfully. But at this moment Mrs. Ansley spoke. "I don't know how you knew. I burnt that letter at once."

"Yes; you would, naturally—you're so prudent!" The sneer was open now. "And if you burnt the letter you're wondering how on earth I know what was in it. That's it, isn't it?"

Mrs. Slade waited, but Mrs. Ansley did not speak.

"Well, my dear, I know what was in that letter because I wrote it!"

"You wrote it?"

"Yes."

The two women stood for a minute staring at each other in the last golden light. Then Mrs. Ansley dropped back into her chair. "Oh," she murmured, and covered her face with her hands.

Mrs. Slade waited nervously for another word or movement. None came, and at length she broke out: "I horrify you."

Mrs. Ansley's hands dropped to her knee. The face they uncovered was streaked with tears. "I wasn't thinking of you. I was thinking—it was the only letter I ever had from him!"

"And I wrote it. Yes; I wrote it! But I was the girl he was engaged to. Did you happen to remember that?"

Mrs. Ansley's head drooped again. "I'm not trying to excuse myself . . . I remembered . . ."

"And still you went?"

"Still I went."

Mrs. Slade stood looking down on the small bowed figure at her side. The flame of her wrath had already sunk, and she wondered why she had ever thought there would be any satisfaction in inflicting so purposeless a wound on her friend. But she had to justify herself.

"You do understand? I'd found out—and I hated you, hated you. I knew you were in love with Delphin—and I was afraid; afraid of you, of your quiet ways, your sweetness . . . your . . . well, I wanted you out of the way, that's all. Just for a few weeks; just till I was sure of him. So in a blind fury I wrote that letter . . . I don't know why I'm telling you now."

"I suppose," said Mrs. Ansley slowly, "it's because you've always gone on hating me."

"Perhaps. Or because I wanted to get the whole thing off my mind." She paused. "I'm glad you destroyed the letter. Of course I never thought you'd die."

Mrs. Ansley relapsed into silence, and Mrs. Slade, leaning above her, was conscious of a strange sense of isolation, of being cut off from the warm current of human communion. "You think me a monster!"

"I don't know . . . It was the only letter I had, and you say he didn't write it?"

"Ah, how you care for him still!"

"I cared for that memory," said Mrs. Ansley.

Mrs. Slade continued to look down on her. She seemed physically reduced by the blow—as if, when she got up, the wind might scatter her like a puff of dust. Mrs. Slade's jealousy suddenly leapt up again at the sight. All these years the woman had been living on that letter. How she must have loved him, to treasure the mere memory of its ashes! The letter of the man her friend was engaged to. Wasn't it she who was the monster?

"You tried your best to get him away from me, didn't you? But you failed; and I kept him. That's all."

"Yes. That's all."

"I wish now I hadn't told you. I'd no idea you'd feel about it as you do; I thought you'd be amused. It all happened so long ago, as you say; and you must do me the justice to remember that I had no reason to think you'd ever taken it seriously. How could I, when you were married to Horace Ansley two months afterward? As soon as you could get out of bed your mother rushed you off to Florence and married you. People were rather surprised—they wondered at its being done so quickly; but I thought I knew. I had an idea you did it out of *pique*—to be able to say you'd got ahead of Delphin and me. Girls have such silly reasons for doing the most serious things. And your marrying so soon convinced me that you'd never really cared."

"Yes. I suppose it would," Mrs. Ansley assented.

The clear heaven overhead was emptied of all its gold. Dusk spread over it, abruptly darkening the Seven Hills. Here and there lights began to twinkle through the foliage at their feet. Steps were coming and going on the deserted terrace—waiters looking out of the doorway at the head of the stairs, then reappearing with trays and napkins and flasks of wine. Tables were moved, chairs straightened. A feeble string of electric lights flickered out. Some vases of faded flowers were carried away, and brought back replenished. A stout lady in a dust-coat suddenly appeared, asking in broken Italian if any one had seen the elastic band which held together her tattered Baedeker. She poked with her stick under the table at which she had lunched, the waiters assisting.

The corner where Mrs. Slade and Mrs. Ansley sat was still shadowy and deserted. For a long time neither of them spoke. At length Mrs. Slade began again: "I suppose I did it as a sort of joke—"

"A joke?"

"Well, girls are ferocious sometimes, you know. Girls in love especially. And I remember laughing to myself all that evening at the idea that you were waiting around there in the dark, dodging out of sight, listening for every sound, trying to get in—. Of course I was upset when I heard you were so ill afterward."

Mrs. Ansley had not moved for a long time. But now she turned slowly toward her companion. "But I didn't wait. He'd arranged everything. He was there. We were let in at once," she said.

Mrs. Slade sprang up from her leaning position. "Delphin there? They let you in?— Ah, now you're lying!" She burst out with violence.

Mrs. Ansley's voice grew clearer, and full of surprise. "But of course he was there. Naturally he came—"

"Came? How did he know he'd find you there? You must be raving!"

Mrs. Ansley hesitated, as though reflecting. "But I answered the letter. I told him I'd be there. So he came."

Mrs. Slade flung her hands up to her face. "Oh, God—you answered! I never thought of your answering . . ."

"It's odd you never thought of it, if you wrote the letter."

"Yes, I was blind with rage."

Mrs. Ansley rose, and drew her fur scarf about her. "It is cold here. We'd better go . . . I'm sorry for you," she said, as she clasped the fur about her throat.

The unexpected words sent a pang through Mrs. Slade. "Yes; we'd better go." She gathered up her bag and cloak. "I don't know why you should be sorry for me," she muttered.

Mrs. Ansley stood looking away from her toward the dusky secret mass of the Colosseum. "Well—because I didn't have to wait that night."

Mrs. Slade gave an unquiet laugh. "Yes; I was beaten there. But I oughtn't to begrudge it to you, I suppose. At the end of all these years. After all, I had everything; I had him for twenty-five years. And you had nothing but that one letter that he didn't write."

Mrs. Ansley was again silent. At length she turned toward the door of the terrace. She took a step, and turned back, facing her companion.

"I had Barbara," she said, and began to move ahead of Mrs. Slade toward the stairway.

Stephen Crane (1871–1900)

Stephen Crane could be thought of as a funnel through which the forces of nine-teenth-century literature entered the American twentieth century. He was at once a naturalist, a realist, an impressionist, and a symbolist. And though he died before the age of twenty-nine in 1900, he is a towering figure in American fiction. His influence went to both technique and subject matter. He was, said his contempo-rary H. G. Wells, "the first expression of the opening mind of a new period."

Maggie: A Girl of the Streets (1892) was the first American novel to use the techniques of naturalism derived from Flaubert and Zola. Its fearless portrayal of American society and its sympathy for the underside of our culture were shocking at the time, and despite the support of established writers like William Dean How-ells and Hamlin Garland, Crane had a hard time giving away copies of the book. *The Red Badge of Courage* (1895), written in the realist tradition of his befrienders, made more of a splash, especially in England. Although Crane claimed to believe that personal experience was the basis for literature, this work was pure invention: Crane was born six years after the end of the Civil War which it depicted so movingly.

"The Open Boat" was indeed based on personal experience. As a correspon-dent in search of adventure, Crane had been shipwrecked off Cuba, and in his story he attempted faithfully to render the experience. Yet despite its historical basis and its colloquial, even breezy, language, this story must be read symboli-cally. The sea and the little craft and the men working together are symbols of Crane's beliefs about the harsh indifferent universe, and man's indomitable will, and the spiritual brotherhood of survivors. These symbols are as important in this story as the white whale in *Moby Dick.*

Crane had a sharp eye for the exact detail that could convey a whole scene and its meaning. He describes the little boat on the sea: "As the boat bounced from the top of each wave the wind tore through the hair of the hatless men, and as the craft plopped her stern down again the spray splashed past them." He describes the cook: "His sleeves were rolled over his fat forearms, and the two flaps of his unbuttoned vest dangled as he bent to bail out the boat." Though pictorial and precise, his prose can without awkwardness present the weight of meaning, psychological and philosophical, that underlies the concrete details: "The injured captain, lying in the bow, was at this time buried in that profound dejection and indifference which comes, temporarily at least, to even the bravest and most enduring. . . ." These passages illustrate two of the advantages of the omniscient point of view (see introduction, p. 12): a distance sufficient to allow perspective on more than one character, and a chance for authorial comment without destroying the mood of the story.

Many critics have called attention to the story's magnificent opening lines which rivet the reader's attention so tightly to the perilous situation. The closing line, too, deserves attention. It seems to release the story from its specific and confining moorings and allow it to ascend into universal significance. What this last line expresses, of course, is the hope and ambition of Crane, and of all writers and artists:

> When it came night, the white waves paced to and fro in the moonlight, and the wind brought the sound of the great sea's voice to the men on the shore, and they felt that they could then be interpreters.

The Open Boat

A TALE INTENDED TO BE AFTER THE FACT. BEING THE EXPERIENCE OF FOUR MEN FROM THE SUNK STEAMER *COMMODORE*.

None of them knew the color of the sky. Their eyes glanced level, and were fastened upon the waves that swept toward them. These waves were of the hue of slate, save for the tops, which were of foaming white, and all of the men knew the colors of the sea. The horizon narrowed and widened, and dipped and rose, and at all times its edge was jagged with waves that seemed thrust up in points like rocks. Many a man ought to have a bathtub larger than the boat which here rode upon the sea. These waves were most wrongfully and barbarously abrupt and tall, and each froth-top was a problem in small-boat navigation.

The cook squatted in the bottom and looked with both eyes at the six inches of gunwale which separated him from the ocean. His sleeves were rolled over his fat forearms, and the two flaps of his unbuttoned vest dangled as he bent to bail out the boat. Often he said: "Gawd! That was a narrow clip." As he remarked it he invariably gazed eastward over the broken sea.

The oiler, steering with one of the two oars in the boat, sometimes raised himself suddenly to keep clear of water that swirled in over the stern. It was a thin little oar and it seemed often ready to snap.

The correspondent, pulling at the other oar, watched the waves and wondered why he was there.

The injured captain, lying in the bow, was at this time buried in that profound dejection and indifference which comes, temporarily at least, to even the bravest and most enduring when, willy nilly, the firm fails, the army loses, the ship goes down. The mind of the master of a vessel is rooted deep in the timbers of her, though he command for a day or a decade, and this captain had on him the stern impression of a scene in the greys of dawn of seven turned faces, and later a stump of a top-mast with a white ball on it that slashed to and fro at the waves, went low and lower, and down. Thereafter there was something strange in his voice. Although steady, it was deep with mourning, and of a quality beyond oration or tears.

"Keep 'er a little more south, Billie," said he.

" 'A little more south,' sir," said the oiler in the stern.

A seat in this boat was not unlike the seat upon a bucking broncho, and by the same token, a broncho is not much smaller. The craft pranced and reared, and plunged like an animal. As each wave came, and she rose for it, she seemed like a horse making at a fence outrageously high. The manner of her scramble over these walls of water is a mystic thing, and, moreover, at the top of them were ordinarily these problems in white water, the foam racing down from the summit of each wave, requiring a new leap, and a leap from the air. Then, after scornfully bumping a crest, she would slide, and race, and splash down a long incline, and arrive bobbing and nodding in front of the next menace.

A singular disadvantage of the sea lies in the fact that after successfully surmounting one wave you discover that there is another behind it just as important and just as nervously anxious to do something effective in the way of swamping boats. In a ten-foot dinghy one can get an idea of the resources of the sea in the line of waves that is not probable to the average experience which is never at sea in a dinghy. As each slatey wall of water approached, it shut all else from the view of the men in the boat, and it was not difficult to imagine that this particular wave was the final outburst of the ocean, the last effort of the grim water. There was a terrible grace in the move of the waves, and they came in silence, save for the snarling of the crests.

In the wan light, the faces of the men must have been grey. Their eyes must have glinted in strange ways as they gazed steadily astern. Viewed from a balcony, the whole thing would doubtless have been weirdly picturesque. But the men in the boat had no time to see it, and if they had had leisure there were other things to occupy their minds. The sun swung steadily up the sky, and they knew it was broad day because the color of the sea changed from slate to emerald-green, streaked with amber lights, and the foam was like tumbling snow. The process of the breaking day was unknown to them. They were aware only of this effect upon the color of the waves that rolled toward them.

In disjointed sentences the cook and the correspondent argued as to the difference between a life-saving station and a house of refuge. The cook had said: "There's a house of refuge just north of the Mosquito Inlet Light, and as soon as they see us, they'll come off in their boat and pick us up."

"As soon as who see us?" said the correspondent.

"The crew," said the cook.

"Houses of refuge don't have crews," said the correspondent. "As I understand them, they are only places where clothes and grub are stored for the benefit of ship-wrecked people. They don't carry crews."

"Oh, yes, they do," said the cook.

"No, they don't," said the correspondent.

"Well, we're not there yet, anyhow," said the oiler, in the stern.

"Well," said the cook, "perhaps it's not a house of refuge that I'm thinking of as being near Mosquito Inlet Light. Perhaps it's a life-saving station."

"We're not there yet," said the oiler, in the stern.

2

As the boat bounced from the top of each wave, the wind tore through the hair of the hatless men, and as the craft plopped her stern down again the spray splashed past them. The crest of each of these waves was a hill, from the top of which the men surveyed, for a moment, a broad tumultuous expanse, shining and wind-riven. It was probably splendid. It was probably glorious, this play of the free sea, wild with lights of emerald and white and amber.

"Bully good thing it's an on-shore wind," said the cook. "If not, where would we be? Wouldn't have a show."

"That's right," said the correspondent.

The busy oiler nodded his assent.

Then the captain, in the bow, chuckled in a way that expressed humor, contempt, tragedy, all in one. "Do you think we've got much of a show now, boys?" said he.

Whereupon the three were silent, save for a trifle of hemming and hawing. To express any particular optimism at this time they felt to be childish and stupid, but they all doubtless possessed this sense of the situation in their mind. A young man thinks doggedly at such times. On the other hand, the ethics of their condition was decidely against any open suggestion of hopelessness. So they were silent.

"Oh, well," said the captain, soothing his children, "we'll get ashore all right."

But there was that in his tone which made them think, so the oiler quoth: "Yes! If this wind holds!"

The cook was bailing: "Yes! If we don't catch hell in the surf."

Canton-flannel gulls flew near and far. Sometimes they sat down on the sea, near patches of brown seaweed that rolled on the waves with a movement like carpets on a line in a gale. The birds sat comfortably in groups, and they were envied by some in the dinghy, for the wrath of the sea was no more to them than it was to a covey of prairie chickens a thousand miles inland. Often they came very close and stared at the men with black bead-like eyes. At these times they were uncanny and sinister in their unblinking scrutiny, and the men hooted angrily at them, telling them to be gone. One came, and evidently decided to alight on the top of the captain's head. The bird flew parallel to the boat and did not circle, but made short sidelong jumps in the air in chicken-fashion. His black eyes were wistfully fixed upon the captain's head. "Ugly brute," said the oiler to the bird. "You look as if you were made with a jack-knife." The cook and the correspondent swore darkly at the creature. The captain naturally wished to knock it away with the end of the heavy painter; but he did not dare do it, because anything resembling an emphatic gesture would have capsized this freighted boat, and so with his open hand, the captain gently and carefully waved the gull away. After it had been discouraged from the pursuit the captain breathed easier on account of his hair, and others breathed easier because the bird struck their minds at this time as being somehow gruesome and ominous.

In the meantime the oiler and the correspondent rowed. And also they rowed. They sat together in the same seat, and each rowed an oar. Then the oiler took both oars; then the correspondent took both oars; then the oiler; then the correspondent. They rowed and they rowed. The very ticklish part of the business was when the time came for the reclining one in the stern to take his turn at the oars. By the very last star of truth, it is easier to steal eggs from under a hen that it was to change seats in the dinghy. First the man in the stern slid his hand along the thwart and moved with care, as if he were of Sèvres. Then the man in the rowing seat slid his hand along the other thwart. It was all done with the most extraordinary care. As the two sidled past each other, the whole party kept watchful eyes on the coming wave, and the captain cried: "Look out now! Steady there!"

The brown mats of seaweed that appeared from time to time were like islands, bits of earth. They were traveling, apparently, neither one way nor the other. They were, to all intents, stationary. They informed the men in the boat that it was making progress slowly toward the land.

The captain, rearing cautiously in the bow, after the dinghy soared on a great swell, said that he had seen the lighthouse at Mosquito Inlet. Presently the cook remarked that he had seen it. The correspondent was at the oars then and for some reason he too wished to look at the lighthouse, but his back was toward the far shore and the waves were important, and for some time he could not seize an opportunity to turn his head. But at last there came a wave more gentle than the others, and when at the crest of it he swiftly scoured the western horizon.

"See it?" said the captain.

"No," said the correspondent slowly, "I didn't see anything."

"Look again," said the captain. He pointed. "It's exactly in that direction."

At the top of another wave, the correspondent did as he was bid, and this time his eyes chanced on a small still thing on the edge of the swaying horizon. It was precisely like the point of a pin. It took an anxious eye to find a lighthouse so tiny.

"Think we'll make it, captain?"

"If this wind holds and the boat don't swamp, we can't do much else," said the captain.

The little boat, lifted by each towering sea, and splashed viciously by the crests, made progress that in the absence of seaweed was not apparent to those in her. She seemed just a wee thing wallowing, miraculously top up, at the mercy of five oceans. Occasionally, a great spread of water, like white flames, swarmed into her.

"Bail her, cook," said the captain serenely.

"All right, captain," said the cheerful cook.

3

It would be difficult to describe the subtle brotherhood of men that was here established on the seas. No one said that it was so. No one mentioned it. But it dwelt in the boat, and each man felt it warm him. They were a captain, an oiler, a cook, and a correspondent, and they were friends, friends in a more curiously iron-bound degree than may be common. The hurt captain, lying against the water-jar in the bow, spoke always in a low voice and calmly, but he could never command a more ready and swiftly obedient crew than the motley three of the dinghy. It was more than a mere recognition of what was best for the common safety. There was surely in it a quality that was personal and heartfelt. And after this devotion to the commander of the boat there was this comrade-ship that the correspondent, for instance, who had been taught to be cynical of men, knew even at the time was the best experience of his life. But no one said that it was so. No one mentioned it.

"I wish we had a sail," remarked the captain, "We might try my overcoat on the end of an oar and give you two boys a chance to rest." So the cook and the correspondent held the mast and spread wide the overcoat. The oiler steered, and the little boat made good way with her new rig. Sometimes the oiler had to scull sharply to keep a sea from breaking into the boat, but otherwise sailing was a success.

Meanwhile the lighthouse had been growing slowly larger. It had now almost assumed color, and appeared like a little grey shadow on the sky. The man at the oars could not be prevented from turning his head rather often to try for a glimpse of this little grey shadow.

At last, from the top of each wave the men in the tossing boat could see land. Even as the lighthouse was an upright shadow on the sky, this land seemed but a long black shadow on the sea. It certainly was thinner than paper. "We must be about opposite New Smyrna," said the cook, who had coasted this shore often in schooners. "Captain, by the way, I believe they abandoned that life-saving station there about a year ago."

"Did they?" said the captain.

The wind slowly died away. The cook and the correspondent were not now obliged to slave in order to hold high the oar. But the waves continued their old impetuous swooping at the dinghy, and the little craft, no longer under way, struggled woundily over them. The oiler or the correspondent took the oars again.

Shipwrecks are à propos of nothing. If men could only train for them and have them occur when the men had reached pink condition, there would be less drowning at sea. Of the four in the dinghy none had slept any time worth mentioning for two days and two nights previous to embarking in the dinghy, and in the excitement of clambering about the deck of a foundering ship they had also forgotten to eat heartily.

For these reasons, and for others, neither the oiler nor the correspondent was fond of rowing at this time. The correspondent wondered ingenuously how in the name of all that was sane could there be people who thought it amusing to row a boat. It was not an amusement; it was a diabolical punishment, and even a genius of mental aberrations could never conclude that it was anything but a horror to the muscles and a crime against the back. He mentioned to the boat in general how the amusement of rowing struck him, and the weary-faced oiler smiled in full sympathy. Previously to the foundering, by the way, the oiler had worked double-watch in the engine-room of the ship.

"Take her easy, now, boys," said the captain. "Don't spend yourselves. If we have to run a surf you'll need all your strength, because we'll sure have to swim for it. Take your time."

Slowly the land arose from the sea. From a black line it became a line of black and a line of white, trees and sand. Finally, the captain said that he could make out a house on the shore. "That's the house of refuge, sure," said the cook. "They'll see us before long, and come out after us."

The distant lighthouse reared high. "The keeper ought to be able to make us out now, if he's looking through a glass," said the captain. "He'll notify the life-saving people."

"None of those other boats could have got ashore to give word of the wreck," said the oiler, in a low voice. "Else the lifeboat would be out hunting us."

Slowly and beautifully the land loomed out of the sea. The wind came again. It had veered from the north-east to the south-east. Finally, a new sound struck the ears of the men in the boat. It was the low thunder of the surf on the shore. "We'll never be able to make the lighthouse now," said the captain. "Swing her head a little more north, Billie," said he.

"A little more north,' sir," said the oiler.

Whereupon the little boat turned her nose once more down the wind, and all but the oarsman watched the shore grow. Under the influence of this expansion doubt and direful apprehension was leaving the minds of the men. The management of the boat was still most absorbing, but it could not prevent a quiet cheerfulness. In an hour, perhaps, they would be ashore.

Their backbones had become thoroughly used to balancing in the boat, and they now rode this wild colt of a dinghy like circus men. The correspondent thought that he had been drenched to the skin, but happening to feel in the top pocket of his coat, he found therein eight cigars. Four of them were soaked with sea-water; four were perfectly scathless. After a search, somebody produced three dry matches, and thereupon the four waifs rode impudently in their little boat and, with an assurance of an impending rescue shining in their eyes, puffed at the big cigars and judged well and ill of all men. Everybody took a drink of water.

4

"Cook," remarked the captain, "there don't seem to be any signs of life about your house of refuge."

"No," replied the cook. "Funny they don't see us!"

A broad stretch of lowly coast lay before the eyes of the men. It was of dunes topped with dark vegetation. The roar of the surf was plain, and sometimes they could see the white lip of a wave as it spun up the beach. A tiny house was blocked out black upon the sky. Southward, the slim lighthouse lifted its little grey length.

Tide, wind, and waves were swinging the dinghy northward. "Funny they don't see us," said the men.

The surf's roar was here dulled, but its tone was, nevertheless, thunderous and mighty. As the boat swam over the great rollers, the men sat listening to this roar. "We'll swamp sure," said everybody.

It is fair to say here that there was not a life-saving station within twenty miles in either direction, but the men did not know this fact, and in consequence they made dark and opprobrious remarks concerning the eyesight of the nation's life-savers. Four scowling men sat in the dinghy and surpassed records in the invention of epithets.

"Funny they don't see us."

The lightheartedness of a former time had completely faded. To their sharpened minds it was easy to conjure pictures of all kinds of incompetency and blindness and, indeed, cowardice. There was the shore of the populous land, and it was bitter and bitter to them that from it came no sign.

"Well," said the captain, ultimately, "I suppose we'll have to make a try for ourselves. If we stay out here too long, we'll none of us have strength left to swim after the boat swamps."

And so the oiler, who was at oars, turned the boat straight for the shore. There was a sudden tightening of muscle. There was some thinking.

"If we don't all get ashore—" said the captain. "If we don't all get ashore, I suppose you fellows know where to send news of my finish?"

They then briefly exchanged some addresses and admonitions. As for the reflections of men, there was a great deal of rage in them. Perchance they might be formulated thus: "If I am going to be drowned—if I am going to be drowned—if I am going to be drowned, why in the name of the seven mad gods who rule the sea, was I allowed to come thus far and contemplate sand and trees? Was I brought here merely to have my nose dragged away as I was about to nibble the sacred cheese of life? It is preposterous. If this old ninny-woman, Fate, cannot do better than this, she should be deprived of the management of men's fortunes. She is an old hen who knows not her intention. If she has decided to drown me, why did she not do it in the beginning and save me all this trouble? The whole affair is absurd. . . . But no, she cannot mean to drown me. She dare not drown me. She cannot drown me. Not after all this work.'' Afterward the man might have had an impulse to shake his fist at the clouds: ''Just you drown me, now, and then hear what I call you!''

The billows that came at this time were more formidable. They seemed always just about to break and roll over the little boat in a turmoil of foam. There was a preparatory and long growl in the speech of them. No mind unused to the sea would have concluded that the dinghy could ascend these sheer heights in time. The shore was still afar. The oiler was a wily surfman. ''Boys,'' he said swiftly, ''she won't live three minutes more, and we're too far out to swim. Shall I take her to sea again, captain?''

''Yes! Go ahead!'' said the captain.

This oiler, by a series of quick miracles, and fast and steady oarsmanship, turned the boat in the middle of the surf and took her safely to sea again.

There was a considerable silence as the boat bumped over the furrowed sea to deeper water. Then somebody in gloom spoke. ''Well, anyhow, they must have seen us from the shore by now.''

The gulls went in slanting flight up the wind toward the grey desolate east. A squall, marked by dingy clouds, and clouds, brick-red, like smoke from a burning building, appeared from the south-east.

''What do you think of those life-saving people? Ain't they peaches?''

''Funny they haven't seen us.''

''Maybe they think we're out here for sport! Maybe they think we're fishin'. Maybe they think we're damned fools.''

It was a long afternoon. A changed tide tried to force them southward, but the wind and wave said northward. Far ahead, where coast-line, sea, and sky formed their mightly angle, there were little dots which seemed to indicate a city on the shore.

''St. Augustine?''

The captain shook his head. ''Too near Mosquito Inlet.''

And the oiler rowed, and then the correspondent rowed. Then the oiler rowed. It was a weary business. The human back can become the seat of more aches and pains than are registered in books for the composite anatomy of a regiment. It is a limited area, but it can become the theatre of innumerable muscular conflicts, tangles, wrenches, knots, and other comforts.

''Did you ever like to row, Billie?'' asked the correspondent.

''No,'' said the oiler. ''Hang it!''

When one exchanged the rowing-seat for a place in the bottom of the boat, he suffered a bodily depression that caused him to be careless of everything save an obligation to wiggle one finger. There was cold sea-water swashing to and fro in the boat, and he lay in it. His head, pillowed on a thwart, was within an inch of the swirl of a wave crest, and sometimes a particularly obstreperous sea came in-board and drenched him once more. But these matters did not annoy him. It is almost certain that if the boat had capsized he would have tumbled comfortably out upon the ocean as if he felt sure that it was a great soft mattress.

''Look! There's a man on the shore!''

''Where?''

''There! See 'im? See 'im?''

''Yes, sure! He's walking along.''

''Now he's stopped. Look! He's facing us!''

''He's waving at us!''

"So he is! By thunder!"

"Ah, now we're all right! Now we're all right! There'll be a boat out here for us in half-an-hour."

"He's going on. He's running. He's going up to that house there."

The remote beach seemed lower than the sea, and it required a searching glance to discern the little black figure. The captain saw a floating stick and they rowed to it. A bath-towel was by some weird chance in the boat, and, tying this on the stick, the captain waved it. The oarsman did not dare turn his head, so he was obliged to ask questions.

"What's he doing now?"

"He's standing still again. He's looking, I think. . . . There he goes again. Toward the house. . . . Now he's stopped again."

"Is he waving at us?"

"No, not now! He was, though."

"Look! There comes another man!"

"He's running."

"Look at him go, would you."

"Why, he's on a bicycle. Now he's met the other man. They're both waving at us. Look!"

"There comes something up the beach."

"What the devil is that thing?"

"Why it looks like a boat."

"Why, certainly it's a boat."

"No, it's on wheels."

"Yes, so it is. Well, that must be the life-boat. They drag them along shore on a wagon."

"That's the life-boat, sure."

"No, by God, it's—it's an omnibus."

"I tell you it's a life-boat."

"It is not! It's an omnibus. I can see it plain. See? One of these big hotel omnibuses."

"By thunder, you're right. It's an omnibus, sure as fate. What do you suppose they are doing with an omnibus? Maybe they are going around collecting the life-crew, hey?"

"That's it, likely. Look! There's a fellow waving a little black flag. He's standing on the steps of the omnibus. There come those other two fellows. Now they're all talking together. Look at the fellow with the flag. Maybe he ain't waving it."

"That ain't a flag, is it? That's his coat. Why, certainly, that's his coat."

"So it is. It's his coat. He's taken it off and is waving it around his head. But would you look at him swing it."

"Oh, say, there isn't any life-saving station there. That's just a winter resort hotel omnibus that has brought over some of the boarders to see us drown."

"What's that idiot with the coat mean? What's he signaling, anyhow?"

"It looks as if he were trying to tell us to go north. There must be a life-saving station up there."

"No! He thinks we're fishing. Just giving us a merry hand. See? Ah, there, Willie!"

"Well, I wish I could make something out of those signals. What do you suppose he means?"

"He don't mean anything. He's just playing."

"Well, if he'd just signal us to try the surf again, or to go to sea and wait, or go north, or go south, or go to hell—there would be some reason in it. But look at him. He just stands there and keeps his coat revolving like a wheel. The ass!"

"There come more people."

"Now there's quite a mob. Look! Isn't that a boat?"

"Where? Oh, I see where you mean. No, that's no boat."

"That fellow is still waving his coat."

"He must think we like to see him do that. Why don't he quit it? It don't mean anything."

"I don't know. I think he is trying to make us go north. It must be that there's a life-saving station there somewhere."

"Say, he ain't tired yet. Look at 'im wave."

"Wonder how long he can keep that up. He's been revolving his coat ever since he caught sight of us. He's an idiot. Why aren't they getting men to bring a boat out? A fishing boat—one of those big yawls—could come out here all right. Why don't he do something?"

"Oh, it's all right, now."

"They'll have a boat out here for us in less than no time, now that they've seen us."

A faint yellow tone came into the sky over the low land. The shadows on the sea slowly deepened. The wind bore coldness with it, and the men began to shiver.

"Holy smoke!" said one, allowing his voice to express his impious mood, "if we keep on monkeying out here! If we've got to flounder out here all night!"

"Oh, we'll never have to stay here all night! Don't you worry. They've seen us now, and it won't be long before they'll come chasing out after us."

The shore grew dusky. The man waving a coat blended gradually into this gloom, and it swallowed in the same manner the omnibus and the group of people. The spray, when it dashed uproariously over the side, made the voyagers shrink and swear like men who were being branded.

"I'd like to catch the chump who waved the coat. I feel like socking him one, just for luck."

"Why? What did he do?"

"Oh, nothing, but then he seemed so damned cheerful."

In the meantime the oiler rowed, and then the correspondent rowed, and then the oiler rowed. Grey-faced and bowed forward, they mechanically, turn by turn, plied the leaden oars. The form of the lighthouse had vanished from the southern horizon, but finally a pale star appeared, just lifting from the sea. The streaked saffron in the west passed before the all-merging darkness, and the sea to the east was black. The land had vanished, and was expressed only by the low and drear thunder of the surf.

"If I am going to be drowned—if I am going to be drowned—if I am going to be drowned, why, in the name of the seven mad gods who rule the sea, was I allowed to come thus far and contemplate sand and trees? Was I brought here merely to have my nose dragged away as I was about to nibble the sacred cheese of life?"

The patient captain, drooped over the water-jar, was sometimes obliged to speak to the oarsman.

"Keep her head up! Keep her head up!"

"Keep her head up, sir." The voices were weary and low.

This was surely a quiet evening. All save the oarsman lay heavily and listlessly in the boat's bottom. As for him, his eyes were just capable of noting the tall black waves that swept forward in a most sinister silence, save for an occasional subdued growl of a crest.

The cook's head was on a thwart, and he looked without interest at the water under his nose. He was deep in other scenes. Finally he spoke. "Billie," he murmured, dreamfully, "what kind of pie do you like best?"

5

"Pie," said the oiler and the correspondent, agitatedly. "Don't talk about those things, blast you!"

"Well," said the cook, "I was just thinking about ham sandwiches and—"

A night on the sea in an open boat is a long night. As darkness settled finally, the shine of the light, lifting from the sea in the south, changed to full gold. On the northern horizon a new light appeared, a small bluish gleam on the edge of the waters. These two lights were the furniture of the world. Otherwise there was nothing but waves.

Two men huddled in the stern, and distances were so magnificent in the dinghy that the rower was enabled to keep his feet partly warmed by thrusting them under his companions. Their legs indeed extended far under the rowing-seat until they touched the feet of the captain forward. Sometimes, despite the efforts of the tired oarsman, a wave came piling into the boat, an icy wave of the night, and the chilling water soaked them anew. They would twist their bodies for a moment and groan, and sleep the dead sleep once more, while the water in the boat gurgled about them as the craft rocked.

The plan of the oiler and the correspondent was for one to row until he lost the ability, and then arouse the other from his sea-water couch in the bottom of the boat.

The oiler plied the oars until his head drooped forward, and the overpowering sleep blinded him. And he rowed yet afterward. Then he touched a man in the bottom of the boat, and called his name. "Will you spell me for a little while?" he said, meekly.

"Sure, Billie," said the correspondent, awakening and dragging himself to a sitting position. They exchanged places carefully, and the oiler, cuddling down in the sea-water at the cook's side, seemed to go to sleep instantly.

The particular violence of the sea had ceased. The waves came without snarling. The obligation of the man at the oars was to keep the boat headed so that the tilt of the rollers would not capsize her, and to preserve her from filling when the crests rushed past. The black waves were silent and hard to be seen in the darkness. Often one was almost upon the boat before the oarsman was aware.

In a low voice the correspondent addressed the captain. He was not sure that the captain was awake, although this iron man seemed to be always awake. "Captain, shall I keep her making for that light north, sir?"

The same steady voice answered him. "Yes. Keep it about two points off the port bow."

The cook had tied a life-belt around himself in order to get even the warmth which this clumsy cork contrivance could donate, and he seemed almost stove-like when a rower, whose teeth invariably chattered wildly as soon as he ceased his labor, dropped down to sleep.

The correspondent, as he rowed, looked down at the two men sleeping underfoot. The cook's arm was around the oiler's shoulders, and, with their fragmentary clothing and haggard faces, they were the babes of the sea, a grotesque rendering of the old babes in the wood.

Later he must have grown stupid at his work, for suddenly there was a growling of water, and a crest came with a roar and a swash into the boat, and it was a wonder that it did not set the cook afloat in his life-belt. The cook continued to sleep, but the oiler sat up, blinking his eyes and shaking with the new cold.

"Oh, I'm awful sorry, Billie," said the correspondent contritely.

"That's all right, old boy," said the oiler, and lay down again and was asleep.

Presently it seemed that even the captain dozed, and the correspondent thought that he was the one man afloat on all the oceans. The wind had a voice as it came over the waves, and it was sadder than the end.

There was a long, loud swishing astern of the boat, and a gleaming trail of phosphorescence, like blue flame, was furrowed on the black waters. It might have been made by a monstrous knife.

Then there came a stillness, while the correspondent breathed with open mouth and looked at the sea.

Suddenly there was another swish and another long flash of bluish light, and this time it was alongside the boat, and might almost have been reached with an oar. The correspondent saw an enormous fin speed like a shadow through the water, hurling the crystalline spray and leaving the long glowing trail.

The correspondent looked over his shoulder at the captain. His face was hidden, and he seemed to be asleep. He looked at the babes of the sea. They certainly were asleep. So, being bereft of sympathy, he leaned a little way to one side and swore softly in to the sea.

But the thing did not then leave the vicinity of the boat. Ahead or astern, on one side or the other, at intervals long or short, fled the long sparkling streak, and there was to be heard the whirroo of the dark fin. The speed and power of the thing was greatly to be admired. It cut the water like a gigantic and keen projectile.

The presence of this biding thing did not affect the man with the same horror that it would if he had been a picnicker. He simply looked at the sea dully and swore in an undertone.

Nevertheless, it is true that he did not wish to be alone, He wished one of his companions to awaken by chance and keep him company with it. But the captain hung motionless over the water-jar, and the oiler and the cook in the bottom of the boat were plunged in slumber.

6

"If I am going to be drowned—if I am going to be drowned—if I am going to be drowned, why, in the name of the seven mad gods who rule the sea, was I allowed to come thus far and contemplate sand and trees?"

During this dismal night, it may be remarked that a man would conclude that it was really the intention of the seven mad gods to drown him, despite the abominable injustice of it. For it was certainly an abominable injustice to drown a man who had worked so hard, so hard. The man felt it would be a crime most unnatural. Other people had drowned at sea since galleys swarmed with painted sails, but still—

When it occurs to a man that nature does not regard him as important, and that she feels she would not maim the universe by disposing of him, he at first wishes to throw bricks at the temple, and he hates deeply the fact that there are no brick and no temples. Any visible expression of nature would surely be pelleted with his jeers.

Then, if there be no tangible thing to hoot he feels, perhaps, the desire to confront a personification and indulge in pleas, bowed to one knee, and with hands supplicant, saying: "Yes, but I love myself."

A high cold star on a winter's night is the word he feels that she says to him. Thereafter he knows the pathos of his situation.

The men in the dinghy had not discussed these matters, but each had, no doubt, reflected upon them in silence and according to his mind. There was seldom any expression upon their faces save the general one of complete weariness. Speech was devoted to the business of the boat.

To chime the notes of his emotion, a verse mysteriously entered the correspondent's head. He had even forgotten that he had forgotten this verse, but it suddenly was in his mind.

"A soldier of the Legion lay dying in Algiers.
There was a lack of woman's nursing, there was dearth of woman's tears;
But a comrade stood beside him, and he took that comrade's hand,
And he said: 'I shall never see my own, my native land.' "

In his childhood, the correspondent had been made acquainted with the fact that a soldier of the Legion lay dying in Algiers, but he had never regarded the fact as important. Myriads of his school-fellows had informed him of the soldier's plight, but the dinning had naturally ended by making him perfectly indifferent. He had never considered it his affair that a soldier of the Legion lay dying in Algiers, nor had it appeared to him as a matter for sorrow. It was less to him than the breaking of a pencil's point.

Now, however, it quaintly came to him as a human, living thing. It was no longer merely a picture of a few throes in the breast of a poet, meanwhile drinking tea and warming his feet at the grate; it was an actuality—stern, mournful, and fine.

The correspondent plainly saw the soldier. He lay on the sand with his feet out straight and still. While his pale left hand was upon his chest in an attempt to thwart the going of life, the blood came between his fingers. In the far Algerian distance, a city of low square forms was set against a sky that was faint with the last sunset hues. The correspondent, plying the oars and dreaming of the slow and slower movements of the lips of the soldier, was moved by a profound and perfectly impersonal comprehension. He was sorry for the soldier of the Legion who lay dying in Algiers.

The thing which had followed the boat and waited had evidently grown bored at the delay. There was no longer to be heard the slash of the cut-water, and there was no longer the flame of the long trail. The light in the north still glimmered, but it was apparently no nearer to the boat. Sometimes the boom of the surf rang in the correspondent's ears, and he turned the craft seaward then and rowed harder. Southward, some one had evidently built a watch-fire on the beach. It was too low and too far to be seen, but it made a shimmering, roseate reflection upon the bluff back of it, and this could be discerned from the boat. The wind came stronger, and sometimes a wave suddenly raged out like a mountain cat, and there was to be seen the sheen and sparkle of a broken crest.

The captain, in the bow, moved on his water-jar and sat erect. "Pretty long night," he observed to the correspondent. He looked at the shore, "Those life-saving people take their time."

"Did you see that shark playing around?"

"Yes, I saw him. He was a big fellow, all right."

"Wish I had known you were awake."

Later the correspondent spoke into the bottom of the boat.

"Billie!" There was a slow and gradual disentanglement. "Billie, will you spell me?" "Sure," said the oiler.

As soon as the correspondent touched the cold comfortable sea-water in the bottom of the boat, and had huddled close to the cook's lifebelt he was deep in sleep, despite the fact that his teeth played all the popular airs. This sleep was so good to him that it was but a moment before he heard a voice call his name in a tone that demonstrated the last stages of exhaustion. "Will you spell me?"

"Sure, Billie."

The light in the north had mysteriously vanished, but the correspondent took his course from the wide-awake captain.

Later in the night they took the boat further out to sea, and the captain directed the cook to take one oar at the stern and keep the boat facing the seas. He was to call out if he should hear the thunder of the surf. This plan enabled the oiler and the correspondent to get respite together. "We'll give those boys a chance to get into shape again," said the captain. They curled down and, after a few preliminary chatterings and trembles, slept once more the dead sleep. Neither knew they had bequeathed to the cook the company of another shark, or perhaps the same shark.

As the boat caroused on the waves, spray occasionally bumped over the side and gave them a fresh soaking, but this had no power to break their repose. The ominous slash of the wind and the water affected them as it would have affected mummies.

"Boys," said the cook, with the notes of every reluctance in his voice, "she's drifted in pretty close. I guess one of you had better take her to sea again." The correspondent, aroused, heard the crash of the toppled crests.

As he was rowing, the captain gave him some whisky-and-water, and this steadied the chills out of him. "If I ever get ashore and anybody shows me even a photograph of an oar—"

At last there was a short conversation.

"Billie. . . . Billie, will you spell me?"

"Sure," said the oiler.

7

When the correspondent again opened his eyes, the sea and the sky were each of the grey hue of the dawning. Later, carmine and gold was painted upon the waters. The morning appeared finally, in its splendor, with a sky of pure blue, and the sunlight flamed on the tips of the waves.

On the distant dunes were set many little black cottages, and a tall white windmill reared above them. No man, nor dog, nor bicycle appeared on the beach. The cottages might have formed a deserted village.

The voyagers scanned the shore. A conference was held in the boat. "Well," said the captain, "if no help is coming we might better try a run through the surf right away. If we stay out here much longer we will be too weak to do anything for ourselves at all." The others silently acquiesced in this reasoning. The boat was headed for the beach. The correspondent wondered if none ever ascended the tall wind-tower, and if then they never looked seaward. This tower was a giant, standing with its back to the plight of the ants. It represented in a degree, to the correspondent, the serenity of nature amid the struggles of the individual—nature in the wind, and nature in the vision of men. She did not seem cruel to him then, nor beneficient, nor treacherous, nor wise. But she was indifferent, flatly indifferent. It is, perhaps, plausible that a man in this situation, impressed with the unconcern of the universe, should see the innumerable flaws of his life, and have them taste wickedly in his mind and wish for another chance. A distinction between right and wrong seems absurdly clear to him, then, in this new ignorance of the grave-edge, and he understands that if he were given another opportunity he would mend his conduct and his words, and be better and brighter during an introduction or at a tea.

"Now, boys," said the captain, "she is going to swamp, sure. All we can do is to work her in as far as possible, and then when she swamps, pile out and scramble for the beach. Keep cool now, and don't jump until she swamps sure."

The oiler took the oars. Over his shoulders he scanned the surf. "Captain," he said, "I think I'd better bring her about, and keep her head-on to the seas and back her in."

"All right, Billie," said the captain. "Back her in." The oiler swung the boat then and, seated in the stern, the cook and the correspondent were obliged to look over their shoulders to contemplate the lonely and indifferent shore.

The monstrous in-shore rollers heaved the boat high until the men were again enabled to see the white sheets of water scudding up the slanted beach. "We won't get in very close," said the captain. Each time a man could wrest his attention from the rollers, he turned his glance toward the shore, and in the expression of the eyes during this contemplation there was a singular quality. The correspondent, observing the others, knew that they were not afraid, but the full meaning of their glances was shrouded.

As for himself, he was too tired to grapple fundamentally with the fact. He tried to coerce his mind into thinking of it, but the mind was dominated at this time by the muscles, and the muscles said they did not care. It merely occurred to him that if he should drown it would be a shame.

There were no hurried words, no pallor, no plain agitation. The men simply looked at the shore. "Now, remember to get well clear of the boat when you jump," said the captain.

Seaward the crest of a roller suddenly fell with a thunderous crash, and the long white comber came roaring down upon the boat.

"Steady now," said the captain. The men were silent. They turned their eyes from the shore to the comber and waited. The boat slid up the incline, leaped at the furious top, bounced over it, and swung down the long back of the wave. Some water had been shipped and the cook bailed it out.

But the next crest crashed also. The tumbling, boiling flood of white water caught the boat and whirled it almost perpendicular. Water swarmed in from all sides. The correspondent had his hands on the gunwale at this time, and when the water entered at that place he swiftly withdrew his fingers, as if he objected to wetting them.

The little boat, drunken with this weight of water, reeled and snuggled deeper into the sea.

"Bail her out, cook! Bail her out," said the captain.

"All right, captain," said the cook.

"Now, boys, the next one will do for us, sure," said the oiler. "Mind to jump clear of the boat."

The third wave moved forward, huge, furious, implacable. It fairly swallowed the dinghy, and almost simultaneously the men tumbled into the sea. A piece of lifebelt had lain in the bottom of the boat, and as the correspondent went overboard he held this to his chest with his left hand.

The January water was icy, and he reflected immediately that it was colder than he had expected to find it on the coast of Florida. This appeared to his dazed mind as a fact important enough to be noted at the time. The coldness of the water was sad; it was tragic. This fact was somehow so mixed and confused with his opinion of his own situation that it seemed almost a proper reason for tears. The water was cold.

When he came to the surface he was conscious of little but the noisy water. Afterward he saw his companions in the sea. The oiler was ahead in the race. He was swimming strongly and rapidly. Off to the correspondent's left, the cook's great white and corked back bulged out of the water, and in the rear the captain was hanging with his one good hand to the keel of the overturned dinghy.

There is a certain immovable quality to a shore, and the correspondent wondered at it amid the confusion of the sea.

It seemed also very attractive, but the correspondent knew that it was a long journey, and he paddled leisurely. The piece of life-preserver lay under him, and sometimes he whirled down the incline of a wave as if he were on a hand-sled.

But finally he arrived at a place in the sea where travel was beset with difficulty. He did not pause swimming to inquire what manner of current had caught him, but there his progress ceased. The shore was set before him like a bit of scenery on a stage, and he looked at it and understood with his eyes each detail of it.

As the cook passed, much further to the left, the captain was calling to him, "Turn over on your back, cook! Turn over on your back and use the oar."

"All right, sir." The cook turned on his back, and, paddling with an oar, went ahead as if he were a canoe.

Presently the boat also passed to the left of the correspondent with the captain clinging with one hand to the keel. He would have appeared like a man raising himself to look over a board fence, if it were not for the extraordinary gymnastics of the boat. The correspondent marvelled that the captain could still hold to it.

They passed on, nearer to shore—the oiler, the cook, the captain—and following them went the water-jar, bouncing gaily over the seas.

The correspondent remained in the grip of this strange new enemy—a current. The shore, with its white slope of sand and its green bluff, topped with little silent cottages, was spread like a picture before him. It was very near to him then, but he was impressed as one who in a gallery looks at a scene from Brittany or Holland.

He thought: "I am going to drown? Can it be possible? Can it be possible? Can it be possible?" Perhaps an individual must consider his own death to be the final phenomenon of nature.

But later a wave perhaps whirled him out of this small, deadly current, for he found suddenly that he could again make progress toward the shore. Later still, he was aware that the captain, clinging with one hand to the keel of the dinghy, had his face turned away from the shore and toward him, and was calling his name. "Come to the boat! Come to the boat!"

In his struggle to reach the captain and the boat, he reflected that when one gets properly wearied, drowning must really be a comfortable arrangement, a cessation of hostilities accompanied by a large degree of relief, and he was glad of it, for the main thing in his mind for some moments had been horror of the temporary agony. He did not wish to be hurt.

Presently he saw a man running along the shore. He was undressing with most remarkable speed. Coat, trousers, shirt, everything flew magically off him.

"Come to the boat," called the captain.

"All right, captain." As the correspondent paddled, he saw the captain let himself down to bottom and leave the boat. Then the correspondent performed his one little marvel of the voyage. A large wave caught him and flung him with ease and supreme speed completely over the boat and far beyond it. It struck him even then as an event in gymnastics, and a true miracle of the sea. An over-turned boat in the surf is not a plaything to a swimming man.

The correspondent arrived in water that reached only to his waist, but his condition did not enable him to stand for more than a moment. Each wave knocked him into a heap, and the under-tow pulled at him.

Then he saw the man who had been running and undressing, and undressing and running, come bounding into the water. He dragged ashore the cook, and then waded towards the captain, but the captain waved him away, and sent him to the correspondent. He was naked, naked as a tree in winter, but a halo was about his head, and he shone like a saint. He gave a strong pull, and a long drag, and a bully heave at the correspondent's hand. The correspondent, schooled in the minor formulæ, said: "Thanks, old man." But suddenly the man cried: "What's that?" He pointed a swift finger. The correspondent said: "Go."

In the shallows, face downward, lay the oiler. His forehead touched sand that was periodically, between each wave, clear of the sea.

The correspondent did not know all that transpired afterward. When he achieved safe ground he fell, striking the sand with each particular part of his body. It was as if he had dropped from a roof, but the thud was grateful to him.

It seems that instantly the beach was populated with men with blankets, clothes, and flasks, and women with coffeepots and all the remedies sacred to their minds. The welcome of the land to the men from the sea was warm and generous, but a still and dripping shape was carried slowly up the beach, and the land's welcome for it could only be the different and sinister hospitality of the grave.

When it came night, the white waves paced to and fro in the moonlight, and the wind brought the sound of the great sea's voice to the men on shore, and they felt that they could then be interpreters.

Part Three

The Golden Age

Thomas Mann (1875–1955)

Thomas Mann has been compared with Marcel Proust and James Joyce in literary achievement and influence. He is one of the towering intellects of the modern age. His interests range from the Bible to twelve-tone music, from medicine to mythology, from artistic consciousness to fascism, from history to science to psychoanalysis. His writing displays a prodigious scholarship.

For Mann, mental aberration and genius lie close together; often, he seemed to believe, the artistic urge is based on an affinity with death. In *The Magic Mountain* (1926), for which Mann received the Nobel Prize for Literature in 1929, these themes are explored with subtlety and drama. Hans Castorp, a young bourgeois, visits his cousin at a tuberculosis sanitarium and—seduced by the heightened sentience and sensuality of the diseased—stays seven years. He becomes the battleground of opposing intellectual and artistic forces of various people at the sanitarium. Finally, when World War I breaks out, he leaves the mountain; but he is no longer the stolid bourgeois: through his experience he has achieved a new sensibility and a complex fulfillment.

In *Joseph and His Brothers*, a tetralogy which occupied Mann from 1926 to 1943, the themes are further developed through use of biblical stories. Mann sees Joseph as both the genius with the power to interpret dreams and a practical man who saves his family.

Although in his early work Mann seemed to accept the authoritarian aspect of German culture, he was intensely anti-Nazi and became a self-exile in 1933. In

1948, *Doctor Faustus* appeared. It is a modern version of the Faust legend: Adrian Leverkühn, a composer, bargains away to the Devil his capacity for human love in exchange for genius. Although primarily an embodiment of Mann's views of the connection between the creativity and the destructiveness of genius, Leverkühn symbolizes the demonic forces in German life.

The English translations of his short stories by H. T. Lowe-Porter were collected as *Stories of Three Decades* (1935), which contains three great novellas (see p. 604) as well: *Tonio Kröger, Death in Venice,* and *Mario and the Magician.* Mann's was not essentially a short-story skill. He insisted upon the full complexity of scenes and situations that interested him. The details that saturate the early pages of *Mario and the Magician*—the social climate of Torre di Venere, the intense August heat, the insulting hotelkeepers, the hostility of the Italians towards foreigners—are vital components of this richly textured plot. This is the Italy of Mussolini, and we can feel the onset of fascism like a spreading cancer, poisoning human relationships. Particularly disturbing is the prudery, which made an official case out of an eight-year-old girl's nudity on a public beach: "all the emotionalism of the sense-loving south . . . in the service of morality and discipline." But fascism's chief representative here is Cipolla the magician, the dapper, cocksure sadist, whose whole performance is aimed at the humiliation—chiefly sexual humiliation—of the simple subjects he hypnotizes. The debasement of innocence is everywhere in this story, and the children—who play an important part—"did not know where the comedy left off and the tragedy began." But the adults were not laughing when this story ends.

One must not be satisfied with the surface of the drama in a work by Thomas Mann. The reader will find beneath the surface the play of a complex idea, perhaps an esoteric theory, a myth clothed in modern dress, a philosophic argument.

Mann was born in Lübeck, Germany, in the year 1875 and died in Zürich in 1955.

Mario and the Magician

The atmosphere of Torre di Venere remains unpleasant in the memory. From the first moment the air of the place made us uneasy, we felt irritable, on edge; then at the end came the shocking business of Cipolla, that dreadful being who seemed to incorporate, in so fateful and so humanly impressive a way, all the peculiar evilness of the situation as a whole. Looking back, we had the feeling that the horrible end of the affair had been preordained and lay in the nature of things; that the children had to be present at it was an added impropriety, due to the false colours in which the weird creature presented himself. Luckily for them, they did not know where the comedy left off and the tragedy began; and we let them remain in their happy belief that the whole thing had been a play up till the end.

Torre di Venere lies some fifteen kilometres from Portoclemente, one of the most popular summer resorts on the Tyrrhenian Sea. Portoclemente is urban and elegant and full to overflowing for months on end. Its gay and busy main street of shops and hotels runs down to a wide sandy beach covered with tents and pennanted sand-castles and sunburnt humanity, where at all times a lively social bustle reigns, and much noise. But this same spacious and inviting fine-sanded beach, this same border of pine grove and near, presiding mountains, continues all the way along the coast. No wonder then that some competition of a quiet kind should have sprung up further on. Torre di Venere—the tower that gave the town its name is gone long since, one looks for it in vain—is an offshoot of the larger resort, and for some years remained an idyll for the few, a refuge for more unworldly spirits. But the usual history of such places repeated itself: peace has had to retire further along the coast, to Marina Petriera and dear knows where else. We all know how the world at once seeks peace and puts her to flight—rushing upon her in the fond idea that they two will wed, and where she is, there it can be at home. It will even set up its Vanity Fair in a spot and be capable of thinking that peace is still by its side. Thus Torre—though its atmosphere so far is more modest and contemplative than that of Portoclemente—has been quite taken up, by both Italians and foreigners. It is no longer the thing to go to Portoclemente—though still so much the thing that it is as noisy and crowded as ever. One goes next door, so to speak: to Torre. So much more refined, even, and cheaper to boot. And the attractiveness of these qualities persists, though the qualities themselves long ago ceased to be evident. Torre has got a Grand Hotel. Numerous pensions have sprung up, some modest, some pretentious. The people who own or rent the villas and pinetas overlooking the sea no longer have it all their own way on the beach. In July and August it looks just like the beach at Portoclemente: it swarms with a screaming, squabbling, merrymaking crowd, and the sun, blazing down like mad, peels the skin off their necks. Garish little flat-bottomed boats rock on the glittering blue, manned by children, whose mothers hover afar and fill the air with anxious cries of Nino! and Sandro! and Bice! and Maria! Pedlars step across the legs of recumbent sun-bathers, selling flowers and corals, oysters, lemonade, and *cornetti al burro,* and crying their wares in the breathy, full-throated southern voice.

Such was the scene that greeted our arrival in Torre: pleasant enough, but after all, we thought, we had come too soon. It was the middle of August, the Italian season was still at its height, scarcely the moment for strangers to learn to love the special charms of the place. What an afternoon crowd in the cafés on the front! For instance, in the Esquisito, where we sometimes sat and were served by Mario, that very Mario of whom I shall have presently to tell. It is well-nigh impossible to find a table; and the various orchestras contend together in the midst of one's conversation with bewildering effect. Of course, it is in the afternoon that people come over from Portoclemente. The excursion is a favourite one for the restless denizens of that pleasure resort, and a Fiat motor-bus plies to and fro, coating inch-thick with dust the oleander and laurel hedges along the highroad—a notable if repulsive sight.

Yes, decidedly one should go to Torre in September, when the great public has left. Or else in May, before the water is warm enough to tempt the Southerner to bathe. Even in the before and after seasons Torre is not empty, but life is less national and more subdued. English, French, and German prevail under the tent-awnings and in the pension dining-rooms; whereas in August—in the Grand Hotel, at least, where, in default of private addresses, we had engaged rooms—the stranger finds the field so occupied by Florentine and Roman society that he feels quite isolated and even temporarily *dé-classé.*

We had, rather to our annoyance, this experience on the evening we arrived, when we went in to dinner and were shown to our table by the waiter in charge. As a table, it had nothing against it, save that we had already fixed our eyes upon those on the veranda beyond, built out over the water, where little red-shaded lamps glowed—and there were still some tables empty, though it was as full as the dining-room within. The children went into raptures at the festive sight, and without more ado we announced our intention to take our meals by preference in the veranda. Our words, it appeared, were prompted by ignorance; for we were informed, with somewhat embarrassed politeness, that the cosy nook outside was reserved for the clients of the hotel: *ai nostri clienti.* Their clients? But we were their clients. We were not tourists or trippers, but boarders for a stay of some three or four weeks. However, we forbore to press for an explanation of the difference between the likes of us and that clientèle to whom it was vouchsafed to eat out there in the glow of the red lamps, and took our dinner by the prosaic common light of the dining-room chandelier—a thoroughly ordinary and monotonous hotel bill of fare, be it said. In Pensione Eleonora, a few steps landward, the table, as we were to discover, was much better.

And thither it was that we moved, three or four days later, before we had had time to settle in properly at the Grand Hotel. Not on account of the veranda and the lamps. The children, straightway on the best of terms with waiters and pages, absorbed in the joys of life on the beach, promptly forgot those colourful seductions. But now there arose, between ourselves and the veranda clientèle—or perhaps more correctly with the compliant management—one of those little unpleasantnesses which can quite spoil the pleasure of a holiday. Among the guests were some high Roman aristocracy, a Principe X and his family. These grand folk occupied rooms close to our own, and the Principessa, a great and a passionately maternal lady, was thrown into a panic by the vestiges of a whooping-cough which our little ones had lately got over, but which now and then still faintly troubled the unshatterable slumbers of our youngest-born. The nature of this illness is not clear, leaving some play for the imagination. So we took no offence at our elegant neighbour for clinging to the widely held view that whooping-cough is acoustically contagious and quite simply fearing lest her children yield to the bad example set by ours. In the fullness of her feminine self-confidence she protested to the management, which then, in the person of the proverbial frock-coated manager, hastened to represent to us, with many expressions of regret, that under the circumstances they were obliged to transfer us to the annexe. We did our best to assure him that the disease was in its very last stages, that it was actually over, and presented no danger of infection to anybody. All that we gained was permission to bring the case before the hotel physician—not one chosen by us—by whose verdict we must then abide. We agreed, convinced that thus we should at once pacify the Princess and escape the trouble of moving. The doctor appeared, and behaved like a faithful and honest servant of science. He examined the child and gave his opinion: the disease was quite over, no danger of contagion was present. We drew a long breath and considered the incident closed—until the manager announced that despite the doctor's verdict it would still be necessary for us to give up our rooms and retire to the *dépendance.* Byzantinism like this outraged us. It is not likely that the Principessa was responsible for the wilful breach of faith. Very likely the fawning management had not even dared to tell her what the physician said. Anyhow, we made it clear to his understanding that we preferred to leave the hotel altogether and at once—and packed our trunks. We could do so with a light heart, having already set up casual friendly relations with Casa Eleonora. We had noticed its pleasant exterior and formed the acquaintance of its proprietor, Signora Angiolieri, and her husband: she slender and black-haired, Tuscan in type, probably at the beginning of the thirties, with the dead ivory complexion of the southern woman, he quiet and bald and carefully dressed. They owned a larger establishment in Florence and presided only in summer and early autumn over the branch in Torre di Venere. But earlier, before her marriage, our new landlady had been companion, fellow-traveller, wardrobe mistress, yes, friend, of Eleonora Duse and manifestly regarded that period as the crown of her career. Even at our first visit she spoke of it with animation. Numerous photographs of the great actress, with affectionate inscriptions, were displayed about the drawing-room, and other souvenirs of their life together adorned the little tables and étagères. This cult of a so interesting past was calculated, of course, to heighten the advantages of the signora's present business. Nevertheless our pleasure and interest were quite genuine as we were conducted through the house by its owner and listened to her sonorous and staccato Tuscan voice relating anecdotes of that immortal mistress, depicting her suffering saintliness, her genius, her profound delicacy of feeling.

Thither, then, we moved our effects, to the dismay of the staff of the Grand Hotel, who, like all Italians, were very good to children. Our new quarters were retired and pleasant, we were within easy reach of the sea through the avenue of young plane trees that ran down to the esplanade. In the clean, cool dining-room Signora Angiolieri daily served the soup with her own hands, the service was attentive and good, the table capital. We even discovered some Viennese acquaintances, and enjoyed chatting with them after luncheon, in front of the house. They, in their turn, were the means of our finding others—in short, all seemed for the best, and we were heartily glad of the change we had made. Nothing was now wanting to a holiday of the most gratifying kind.

And yet no proper gratification ensued. Perhaps the stupid occasion of our change of quarters pursued us to the new ones we had found. Personally, I admit that I do not easily forget these collisions with ordinary humanity, the naïve misuse of power, the injustice, the sycophantic corruption. I dwelt upon the incident too much, it irritated me in retrospect—quite futilely, of course, since such phenomena are only all too natural and all too much the rule. And we had not broken off relations with the Grand Hotel. The children were as friendly as ever there, the porter mended their toys, and we sometimes took tea in the garden. We even saw the Principessa. She would come out, with her firm and delicate tread, her lips emphatically corallined, to look after her children, playing under the supervision of their English governess. She did not dream that we were anywhere near, for so soon as she appeared in the offing we sternly forbade our little one even to clear his throat.

The heat—if I may bring it in evidence—was extreme. It was African. The power of the sun, directly one left the border of the indigo-blue wave, was so frightful, so relentless, that the mere thought of the few steps between the beach and luncheon was a burden, clad though one might be only in pyjamas. Do you care for that sort of thing? Weeks on end? Yes, of course, it is proper to the south, it is classic weather, the sun of Homer, the climate wherein human culture came to flower—and all the rest of it. But after a while it is too much for me, I reach a point where I begin to find it dull. The burning void of the sky, day after day, weighs one down; the high coloration, the enormous naïveté of the unrefracted light—they do, I dare say, induce light-heartedness, a carefree mood born of immunity from downpours and other meteorological caprices. But slowly, slowly, there makes itself felt a lack: the deeper, more complex needs of the northern soul remain unsatisfied. You are left barren—even, it may be, in time, a little contemptuous. True, without that stupid business of the whooping-cough I might not have been feeling these things. I was annoyed, very likely I wanted to feel them and so half-unconsciously seized upon an idea lying ready to hand to induce, or if not to induce, at least to justify and strengthen, my attitude. Up to this point, then, if you like, let us grant some ill will on our part. But the sea; and the mornings spent extended upon the fine sand in face of its eternal splendours—no, the sea could not conceivably induce such feelings. Yet it was none the less true that, despite all previous experience, we were not at home on the beach, we were not happy.

It was too soon, too soon. The beach, as I have said, was still in the hands of the middle-class native. It is a pleasing breed to look at, and among the young we saw much shapeliness and charm. Still, we were necessarily surrounded by a great deal of very average humanity—a middle-class mob, which, you will admit, is not more charming under this sun than under one's own native sky. The voices these women have! It was sometimes hard to believe that we were in the land which is the western cradle of the art of song. *"Fuggièro!"* I can still hear that cry, as for twenty mornings long I heard it close behind me, breathy, full-throated, hideously stressed, with a harsh open *e*, uttered in accents of mechanical despair. *"Fuggièro! Rispondi almeno!"* Answer when I call you! The *sp* in *rispondi* was pronounced like *shp,* as Germans pronounce it; and this, on top of what I felt already, vexed my sensitive soul. The cry was addressed to a repulsive youngster whose sunburn had made disgusting raw sores on his shoulders. He outdid anything I have ever seen for ill-breeding, refractoriness, and temper and was a great coward to boot, putting the whole beach in an uproar, one day, because of his outrageous sensitiveness to the slightest pain. A sand-crab had pinched his toe in the water, and the minute injury made him set up a cry of heroic proportions—the shout of an antique hero in his agony—that pierced one to the marrow and called up visions of some frightful tragedy. Evidently he considered himself not only wounded, but poisoned as well; he crawled out on the sand and lay in apparently intolerable anguish, groaning *"Ohi!"* and *"Ohimè!"* and threshing about with arms and legs to ward off his mother's tragic appeals and the questions of the bystanders. An audience gathered round. A doctor was fetched—the same who had pronounced objective judgment on our whooping-cough—and here again acquitted himself like a man of science. Good-naturedly he reassured the boy, telling him that he was not hurt at all, he should simply go into the water again to relieve the smart. Instead of which, Fuggièro was borne off the beach, followed by a concourse of people. But he did not fail to appear next morning, nor did he leave off spoiling our children's sand-castles. Of course, always by accident. In short, a perfect terror.

And this twelve-year-old lad was prominent among the influences that, imperceptibly at first, combined to spoil our holiday and render it unwholesome. Somehow or other, there was a stiffness, a lack of innocent enjoyment. These people stood on their dignity—just why, and in what spirit, it was not easy at first to tell. They displayed much self-respectingness; towards each other and towards the foreigner their bearing was that of a person newly conscious of a sense of honour. And wherefore? Gradually we realized the political implications and understood that we were in the presence of a national ideal. The beach, in fact, was alive with patriotic children—a phenomenon as unnatural as it was depressing. Children are a human species and a society apart, a nation of their own, so to speak. On the basis of their common form of life, they find each other out with the greatest ease, no matter how different their small vocabularies. Ours soon played with natives and foreigners alike. Yet they were plainly both puzzled and disappointed at times. There were wounded sensibilities, displays of assertiveness—or rather hardly assertiveness, for it was too self-conscious and too didactic to deserve the name. There were quarrels over flags, disputes about authority and precedence. Grownups joined in, not so much to pacify as to render judgment and enunciate principles. Phrases were dropped about the greatness and dignity of Italy, solemn phrases that spoilt the fun. We saw our two little ones retreat, puzzled and hurt, and were put to it to explain the situation. These people, we told them, were just passing through a certain stage, something rather like an illness, perhaps; not very pleasant, but probably unavoidable.

We had only our own carelessness to thank that we came to blows in the end with this "stage"—which, after all, we had seen and sized up long before now. Yes, it came to another "cross-purposes," so evidently the earlier ones had not been sheer accident. In a word, we became an offence to the public morals. Our small daughter—eight years old, but in physical development a good year younger and thin as a chicken—had had a good long bathe and gone playing in the warm sun in her wet costume. We told her that she might take off her bathing-suit, which was stiff with sand, rinse it in the sea, and put it on again, after which she must take care to keep it cleaner. Off goes the costume and she runs down naked to the sea, rinses her little jersey, and comes back. Ought we to have foreseen the outburst of anger and resentment which her conduct, and thus our conduct, called forth? Without delivering a homily on the subject, I may say that in the last decade our attitude towards the nude body and our feelings regarding it have undergone, all over the world, a fundamental change. There are things we "never think about" any more, and among them is the freedom we had permitted to this by no means provocative little childish body. But in these parts it was taken as a challenge. The patriotic children hooted. Fuggièro whistled on his fingers. The sudden buzz of conversation among the grown people in our neighbourhood boded no good. A gentleman in city togs, with a not very apropos bowler hat on the back of his head, was assuring his outraged womenfolk that he proposed to take punitive measures; he stepped up to us, and a philippic descended on our unworthy heads, in which all the emotionalism of the sense-loving south spoke in the service of morality and discipline. The offence against decency of which we had been guilty was, he said, the more to be condemned because it was also a gross ingratitude and an insulting breach of his country's hospitality. We had criminally injured not only the letter and spirit of the public bathing regulations, but also the honour of Italy; he, the gentleman in the city togs, knew how to defend that honour and proposed to see to it that our offence against the national dignity should not go unpunished.

We did our best, bowing respectfully, to give ear to this eloquence. To contradict the man, overheated as he was, would probably be to fall from one error into another. On the tips of our tongues we had various answers: as, that the word "hospitality," in its strictest sense, was not quite the right one, taking all the circumstances into consideration. We were not literally the guests of Italy, but of Signora Angiolieri, who had assumed the rôle of dispenser of hospitality some years ago on laying down that of familiar friend to Eleonora Duse. We longed to say that surely this beautiful country had not sunk so low as to be reduced to a state of hypersensitive prudishness. But we confined ourselves to assuring the gentleman that any lack of respect, any provocation on our parts, had been the furthest from our thoughts. And as a mitigating circumstance we pointed out the tender age and physical slightness of the little culprit. In vain. Our protests were waved away, he did not believe in them; our defence would not hold water. We must be made an example of. The authorities were notified, by telephone, I believe, and their representative appeared on the beach. He said the case was *"molto grave."* We had to go with him to the Municipio up in the Piazza, where a higher official confirmed the previous verdict of *"molto grave,"* launched into a stream of the usual didactic phrases—the selfsame tune and words as the man in the bowler hat—and levied a fine and ransom of fifty lire. We felt that the adventure must willy-nilly be worth to us this much of a contribution to the economy of the Italian government; paid, and left. Ought we not at this point to have left Torre as well?

If we only had! We should thus have escaped that fatal Cipolla. But circumstances combined to prevent us from making up our minds to a change. A certain poet says that it is indolence that makes us endure uncomfortable situations. The *aperçu* may serve as an explanation for our inaction. Anyhow, one dislikes voiding the field immediately upon such an event. Especially if sympathy from other quarters encourages one to defy it. And in the Villa Eleonora they pronounced as with one voice upon the injustice of our punishment. Some Italian after-dinner acquaintances found that the episode put their country in a very bad light, and proposed taking the man in the bowler hat to task, as one fellow-citizen to another. But the next day he and his party had vanished from the beach. Not on our account, of course. Though it might be that the consciousness of his impending departure had added energy to his rebuke; in any case his going was a relief. And, furthermore, we stayed because our stay had by now become remarkable in our own eyes, which is worth something in itself, quite apart from the comfort or discomfort involved. Shall we strike sail, avoid a certain experience so soon as it seems not expressly calculated to increase our enjoyment or our self-esteem? Shall we go away whenever life looks like turning in the slightest uncanny, or not quite normal, or even rather painful and mortifying? No, surely not. Rather stay and look matters in the face, brave them out; perhaps precisely in so doing lies a lesson for us to learn. We stayed on and reaped as the awful reward of our constancy the unholy and staggering experience with Cipolla.

I have not mentioned that the after season had begun, almost on the very day we were disciplined by the city authorities. The worshipful gentleman in the bowler hat, our denouncer, was not the only person to leave the resort. There was a regular exodus, on every hand you saw luggage-carts on their way to the station. The beach denationalized itself. Life in Torre, in the cafés and the pinetas, became more homelike and more European. Very likely we might even have eaten at a table in the glass veranda, but we refrained, being content at Signora Angiolieri's—as content, that is, as our evil star would let us be. But at the same time with this turn for the better came a change in the weather: almost to an hour it showed itself in harmony with the holiday calendar of the general public. The sky was overcast; not that it grew any cooler, but the unclouded heat of the entire eighteen days since our arrival, and probably long before that, gave place to a stifling sirocco air, while from time to time a little ineffectual rain sprinkled the velvety surface of the beach. Add to which, that two-thirds of our intended stay at Torre had passed. The colourless, lazy sea, with sluggish jellyfish floating in its shallows, was at least a change. And it would have been silly to feel retrospective longings after a sun that had caused us so many sighs when it burned down in all its arrogant power.

At this juncture, then, it was that Cipolla announced himself. Cavaliere Cipolla he was called on the posters that appeared one day stuck up everywhere, even in the dining-room of Pensione Eleonora. A travelling virtuoso, an entertainer, *"forzatore, illusionista, prestidigatore,"* as he called himself, who proposed to wait upon the highly respectable population of Torre di Venere with a display of extraordinary phenomena of a mysterious and staggering kind. A conjuror! The bare announcement was enough to turn our children's heads. They had never seen anything of the sort, and now our present holiday was to afford them this new excitement. From that moment on they besieged us with prayers to take tickets for the performance. We had doubts, from the first, on the score of the lateness of the hour, nine o'clock; but gave way, in the idea that we might see a little of what Cipolla had to offer, probably no great matter, and then go home. Besides, of course, the children could sleep late next day. We bought four tickets of Signora Angiolieri herself, she having taken a number of the stalls on commission to sell them to her guests. She could not vouch for the man's performance, and we had no great expectations. But we were conscious of a need for diversion, and the children's violent curiosity proved catching.

The Cavaliere's performance was to take place in a hall where during the season there had been a cinema with a weekly programme. We had never been there. You reached it by following the main street under the wall of the *"palazzo,"* a ruin with a "For sale" sign, that suggested a castle and had obviously been built in lordlier days. In the same street were the chemist, the hairdresser, and all the better shops; it led, so to speak, from the feudal past the bourgeois into the proletarian, for it ended off between two rows of poor fishing-huts, where old women sat mending nets before the doors. And here, among the proletariat, was the hall, not much more, actually, than a wooded shed, though a large one, with a turreted entrance, plastered on either side with layers of gay placards. Some while after dinner, then, on the appointed evening, we wended our way thither in the dark, the children dressed in their best and blissful with the sense of so much irregularity. It was sultry, as it had been for days; there was heat lightning now and then, and a little rain; we proceeded under umbrellas. It took us a quarter of an hour.

Our tickets were collected at the entrance, our places we had to find ourselves. They were in the third row left, and as we sat down we saw that, late though the hour was for the performance, it was to be interpreted with even more laxity. Only very slowly did an audience—who seemed to be relied upon to come late—begin to fill the stalls. These comprised the whole auditorium; there were no boxes. This tardiness gave us some concern. The children's cheeks were already flushed as much with fatigue as with excitement. But even when we entered, the standing-room at the back and in the side aisles was already well occupied. There stood the manhood of Torre di Venere, all and sundry, fisherfolk, rough-and-ready youths with bare forearms crossed over their striped jerseys. We were well pleased with the presence of this native assemblage, which always adds colour and animation to occasions like the present; and the children were frankly delighted. For they had friends among these people—acquaintances picked up on afternoon strolls to the further ends of the beach. We would be turning homeward, at the hour when the sun dropped into the sea, spent with the huge effort it had made and gilding with reddish gold the oncoming surf; and we would come upon bare-legged fisherfolk standing in rows, bracing and hauling with long-drawn cries as they drew in the nets and harvested in dripping baskets their catch, often so scanty, of *frutta di mare*. The children looked on, helped to pull, brought out their little stock of Italian words, made friends. So now they exchanged nods with the "standing-room" clientèle; there was Guiscardo, there Antonio, they knew them by name and waved and called across in half-whispers, getting answering nods and smiles that displayed rows of healthy white teeth. Look, there is even Mario, Mario from the Esquisito, who brings us the chocolate. He wants to see the conjuror, too, and he must have come early, for he is almost in front; but he does not see us, he is not paying attention; that is a way he has, even though he is a waiter. So we wave instead to the man who lets out the little boats on the beach; he is there too, standing at the back.

It had got to a quarter past nine, it got to almost half past. It was natural that we should be nervous. When would the children get to bed? It had been a mistake to bring them, for now it would be very hard to suggest breaking off their enjoyment before it had got well under way. The stalls had filled in time; all Torre, apparently, was there: the guests of the Grand Hotel, the guests of Villa Eleonora, familiar faces from the beach. We heard English and German and the sort of French that Rumanians speak with Italians. Madame Angiolieri herself sat two rows behind us, with her quiet, bald-headed spouse, who kept stroking his moustache with the two middle fingers of his right hand. Everybody had come late, but nobody too late. Cipolla made us wait for him.

He made us wait. That is probably the way to put it. He heightened the suspense by his delay in appearing. And we could see the point of this, too—only not when it was carried to extremes. Towards half past nine the audience began to clap—an amiable way of expressing justifiable impatience, evincing as it does an eagerness to applaud. For the little ones, this was a joy in itself—all children love to clap. From the popular sphere came loud cries of *"Pronti!" "Cominciamo!"* And lo, it seemed now as easy to begin as before it had been hard. A gong sounded, greeted by the standing rows with a many-voiced "Ah-h!" and the curtains parted. They revealed a platform furnished more like a schoolroom than like the theatre of a conjuring performance—largely because of the blackboard in the left foreground. There was a common yellow hat-stand, a few ordinary straw-bottomed chairs, and further back a little round table holding a water carafe and glass, also a tray with a liqueur glass and a flask of pale yellow liquid. We had still a few seconds of time to let these things sink in. Then, with no darkening of the house, Cavaliere Cipolla made his entry.

He came forward with a rapid step that expressed his eagerness to appear before his public and gave rise to the illusion that he had already come a long way to put himself at their service—whereas, of course, he had only been standing in the wings. His costume supported the fiction. A man of an age hard to determine, but by no means young; with a sharp, ravaged face, piercing eyes, compressed lips, small black waxed moustache, and a so-called imperial in the curve between mouth and chin. He was dressed for the street with a sort of complicated evening elegance, in a wide black pelerine with velvet collar and satin lining; which, in the hampered state of his arms, he held together in front with his white-gloved hands. He had a white scarf round his neck; a top hat with a curving brim sat far back on his head. Perhaps more than anywhere else the eighteenth century is still alive in Italy, and with it the charlatan and mountebank type so characteristic of the period. Only there, at any rate, does one still encounter really well-preserved specimens. Cipolla had in his whole appearance much of the historic type; his very clothes helped to conjure up the traditional figure with its blatantly, fantastically foppish air. His pretentious costume sat upon him, or rather hung upon him, most curiously, being in one place drawn too tight, in another a mass of awkward folds. There was something not quite in order about his figure, both front and back—that was plain later on. But I must emphasize the fact that there was not a trace of personal jocularity or clownishness in his pose, manner, or behaviour. On the contrary, there was complete seriousness, an absence of any humorous appeal; occasionally even a cross-grained pride, along with that curious, self-satisfied air so characteristic of the deformed. None of all this, however, prevented his appearance from being greeted with laughter from more than one quarter of the hall.

All the eagerness had left his manner. The swift entry had been merely an expression of energy, not of zeal. Standing at the footlights he negligently drew off his gloves, to display long yellow hands, one of them adorned with a seal ring with a lapis-lazuli in a high setting. As he stood there, his small hard eyes, with flabby pouches beneath them, roved appraisingly about the hall, not quickly, rather in a considered examination, pausing here and there upon a face with his lips clipped together, not speaking a word. Then with a display of skill as surprising as it was casual, he rolled his gloves into a ball and tossed them across a considerable distance into the glass on the table. Next from an inner pocket he drew forth a packet of cigarettes; you could see by the wrapper that they were the cheapest sort the government sells. With his fingertips he pulled out a cigarette and lighted it, without looking, from a quick-firing benzine lighter. He drew the smoke deep into his lungs and let it out again, tapping his foot, with both lips drawn in an arrogant grimace and the grey smoke streaming out between broken and saw-edged teeth.

With a keenness equal to his own his audience eyed him. The youths at the rear scowled as they peered at this cocksure creature to search out his secret weaknesses. He betrayed none. In fetching out and putting back the cigarettes his clothes got in his way. He had to turn back his pelerine, and in so doing revealed a riding-whip with a silver claw-handle that hung by a leather thong from his left forearm and looked decidedly out of place. You could see that he had on not evening clothes but a frock-coat, and under this, as he lifted it to get at his pocket, could be seen a striped sash worn about the body. Somebody behind me whispered that this sash went with his title of Cavaliere. I give the information for what it may be worth—personally, I never heard that the title carried such insignia with it. Perhaps the sash was sheer pose, like the way he stood there, without a word, casually and arrogantly puffing smoke into his audience's face.

People laughed, as I said. The merriment had become almost general when somebody in the "standing seats," in a loud, dry voice, remarked: *"Buona sera."*

Cipolla cocked his head. "Who was that?" asked he, as though he had been dared. "Who was that just spoke? Well? First so bold and now so modest? *Paura,* eh?" He spoke with a rather high, asthmatic voice, which yet had a metallic quality. He waited.

"That was me," a youth at the rear broke into the stillness, seeing himself thus challenged. He was not far from us, a handsome fellow in a woollen shirt, with his coat hanging over one shoulder. He wore his curly, wiry hair in a high, dishevelled mop, the style affected by the youth of the awakened Fatherland; it gave him an African appearance that rather spoiled his looks. *"Bè!* That was me. It was your business to say it first, but I was trying to be friendly."

More laughter. The chap had a tongue in his head. *"Ha sciolto la scilinguágnolo,"* I heard near me. After all, the retort was deserved.

"Ah, bravo!" answered Cipolla. "I like you, *giovanotto.* Trust me, I've had my eye on you for some time. People like you are just in my line. I can use them. And you are the pick of the lot, that's plain to see. You do what you like. Or is it possible you have ever not done what you liked—or even, maybe, what you didn't like? What somebody else liked, in short? Hark ye, my friend, that might be a pleasant change for you, to divide up the willing and the doing and stop tackling both jobs at once. Division of labour, *sistema americano, sa'!* For instance, suppose you were to show your tongue to this select and honourable audience here—your whole tongue, right down to the roots?"

"No, I won't," said the youth, hostilely. "Sticking out your tongue shows a bad bringing-up."

"Nothing of the sort," retorted Cipolla. "You would only be *doing* it. With all due respect to your bringing-up, I suggest that before I count ten, you will perform a right turn and stick out your tongue at the company here further than you knew yourself that you could stick it out."

He gazed at the youth, and his piercing eyes seemed to sink deeper into their sockets. *"Uno!"* said he. He had let his riding-whip slide down his arm and made it whistle once through the air. The boy faced about and put out his tongue, so long, so extendedly, that you could see it was the very uttermost in tongue which he had to offer. Then turned back, stony-faced, to his former position.

"That was me," mocked Cipolla, with a jerk of his head towards the youth. *"Bè!* That was me." Leaving the audience to enjoy its sensations, he turned towards the little round table, lifted the bottle, poured out a small glass of what was obviously cognac, and tipped it up with a practised hand.

The children laughed with all their hearts. They had understood practically nothing of what had been said, but it pleased them hugely that something so funny should happen, straightaway, between that queer man up there and somebody out of the audience. They had no preconception of what an "evening" would be like and were quite ready to find this a priceless beginning. As for us, we exchanged a glance and I remember that involuntarily I made with my lips the sound that Cipolla's whip had made when it cut the air. For the rest, it was plain that people did not know what to make of a preposterous beginning like this to a sleight-of-hand performance. They could not see why the *giovanotto,* who after all in a way had been their spokesman, should suddenly have turned on them to vent his incivility. They felt that he had behaved like a silly ass and withdrew their countenances from him in favour of the artist, who now came back from his refreshment table and addressed them as follows:

"Ladies and gentlemen," said he, in his wheezing, metallic voice, "you saw just now that I was rather sensitive on the score of the rebuke this hopeful young linguist saw fit to give me"—"*questo linguista di belle speranze*" was what he said, and we all laughed at the pun. "I am a man who sets some store by himself, you may take it from me. And I see no point in being wished a good-evening unless it is done courteously and in all seriousness. For anything else there is no occasion. When a man wishes me a good-evening he wishes himself one, for the audience will have one only if I do. So this lady-killer of Torre di Venere" (another thrust) "did well to testify that I have one tonight and that I can dispense with any wishes of his in the matter. I can boast of having good evenings almost without exception. One not so good does come my way now and again, but very seldom. My calling is hard and my health not of the best. I have a little physical defect which prevented me from doing my bit in the war for the greater glory of the Fatherland. It is perforce with my mental and spiritual parts that I conquer life— which after all only means conquering oneself. And I flatter myself that my achievements have aroused interest and respect among the educated public. The leading news-papers have lauded me, the *Corriere della Sera* did me the courtesy of calling me a phenomenon, and in Rome the brother of the *Duce* honoured me by his presence at one of my evenings. I should not have thought that in a relatively less important place" (laughter here, at the expense of poor little Torre) "I should have to give up the small personal habits which brilliant and elevated audiences had been ready to overlook. Nor did I think I had to stand being heckled by a person who seems to have been rather spoilt by the favours of the fair sex." All this of course at the expense of the youth whom Cipolla never tired of presenting in the guise of *donnaiuolo* and rustic Don Juan. His persistent thin-skinnedness and animosity were in striking contrast to the self-confi-dence and the worldly success he boasted of. One might have assumed that the *giovanotto* was merely the chosen butt of Cipolla's customary professional sallies, had not the very pointed witticisms betrayed a genuine antagonism. No one looking at the physical parts of the two men need have been at a loss for the explanation, even if the deformed man had not constantly played on the other's supposed success with the fair sex. "Well," Cipolla went on, "before beginning our entertainment this evening, per-haps you will permit me to make myself comfortable."

And he went towards the hat-stand to take off his things.

"*Parla benissimo,*" asserted somebody in our neighbourhood. So far, the man had done nothing; but what he had said was accepted as an achievement, by means of that he had made an impression. Among southern peoples speech is a constituent part of the pleasure of living, it enjoys far livelier social esteem than in the north. That national cement, the mother tongue, is paid symbolic honours down here, and there is something blithely symbolical in the pleasure people take in their respect for its forms and phonetics. They enjoy speaking, they enjoy listening; and they listen with discrimination. For the way a man speaks serves as a measure of his personal rank; carelessness and clumsiness are greeted with scorn, elegance and mastery are rewarded with social éclat. Wherefore the small man too, where it is a question of geting his effect, chooses his phrase nicely and turns it with care. On this count, then, at least, Cipolla had won his audience; though he by no means belonged to the class of men which the Italian, in a singular mixture of moral and aesthetic judgments, labels "*simpatico.*"

After removing his hat, scarf, and mantle he came to the front of the stage, settling his coat, pulling down his cuffs with their large cuff-buttons, adjusting his absurd sash. He had very ugly hair; the top of his head, that is, was almost bald, while a narrow, black-varnished frizz of curls ran from front to back as though stuck on; the side hair, likewise blackened, was brushed forward to the corners of the eyes—it was, in short, the hairdressing of an old-fashioned circus-director, fantastic, but entirely suited to his outmoded personal type and worn with so much assurance as to take the edge off the public's sense of humour. The little physical defect of which he had warned us was now all too visible, though the nature of it was even now not very clear: the chest was too high, as is usual in such cases; but the corresponding malformation of the back did not sit between the shoulders, it took the form of a sort of hips or buttocks hump, which did not indeed hinder his movements but gave him a grotesque and dipping stride at every step he took. However, by mentioning his deformity beforehand he had broken the shock of it, and a delicate propriety of feeling appeared to reign throughout the hall.

"At your service," said Cipolla. "With your kind permission, we will begin the evening with some arithmetical tests."

Arithmetic? That did not sound much like sleight-of-hand. We began to have our suspicions that the man was sailing under a false flag, only we did not yet know which was the right one. I felt sorry on the children's account; but for the moment they were content simply to be there.

The numerical test which Cipolla now introduced was as simple as it was baffling. He began by fastening a piece of paper to the upper right-hand corner of the blackboard; then lifting it up, he wrote something underneath. He talked all the while, relieving the dryness of his offering by a constant flow of words, and showed himself a practised speaker, never at a loss for conversational turns of phrase. It was in keeping with the nature of his performance, and at the same time vastly entertained the children, that he went on to eliminate the gap between stage and audience, which had already been bridged over by the curious skirmish with the fisher lad: he had representatives from the audience mount the stage, and himself descended the wooden steps to seek personal contact with his public. And again, with individuals, he fell into his former taunting tone. I do not know how far that was a deliberate feature of his system; he preserved a serious, even a peevish air, but his audience, at least the more popular section, seemed convinced that that was all part of the game. So then, after he had written something and covered the writing by the paper, he desired that two persons should come up on the platform and help to perform the calculations. They would not be difficult, even for people not clever at figures. As usual, nobody volunteered, and Cipolla took care not to molest the more select portion of his audience. He kept to the populace. Turning to two sturdy young louts standing behind us, he beckoned them to the front, encouraging and scolding by turns. They should not stand there gaping, he said, unwilling to oblige the company. Actually, he got them in motion; with clumsy tread they came down the middle aisle, climbed the steps, and stood in front of the blackboard, grinning sheepishly at their comrades' shouts and applause. Cipolla joked with them for a few minutes, praised their heroic firmness of limb and the size of their hands, so well calculated to do this service for the public. Then he handed one of them the chalk and told him to write down the numbers as they were called out. But now the creature declared that he could not write! *"Non so scrivere,"* said he in his gruff voice, and his companion added that neither did he.

God knows whether they told the truth or whether they wanted to make game of Cipolla. Anyhow, the latter was far from sharing the general merriment which their confession aroused. He was insulted and disgusted. He sat there on a straw-bottomed chair in the centre of the stage with his legs crossed, smoking a fresh cigarette out of his cheap packet; obviously it tasted the better for the cognac he had indulged in while the yokels were stumping up the steps. Again he inhaled the smoke and let it stream out between curling lips. Swinging his leg, with his gaze sternly averted from the two shamelessly chuckling creatures and from the audience as well, he stared into space as one who withdraws himself and his dignity from the contemplation of an utterly despicable phenomenon.

"Scandalous," said he, in a sort of icy snarl. "Go back to your places! In Italy everybody can write—in all her greatness there is no room for ignorance and un-enlightenment. To accuse her of them, in the hearing of this international company, is a cheap joke, in which you yourselves cut a very poor figure and humiliate the government and the whole country as well. If it is true that Torre di Venere is indeed the last refuge of such ignorance, then I must blush to have visited the place—being, as I already was, aware of its inferiority to Rome in more than one respect—"

Here Cipolla was interrupted by the youth with the Nubian coiffure and his jacket across his shoulder. His fighting spirit, as we now saw, had only abdicated temporarily, and he now flung himself into the breach in defence of his native heath. "That will do," said he loudly. "That's enough jokes about Torre. We all come from the place and we won't stand strangers making fun of it. These two chaps are our friends. Maybe they are no scholars, but even so they may be straighter than some folks in the room who are so free with their boasts about Rome, though they did not build it either."

That was capital. The young man had certainly cut his eyeteeth. And this sort of spectacle was good fun, even though it still further delayed the regular performance. It is always fascinating to listen to an altercation. Some people it simply amuses, they take a sort of kill-joy pleasure in not being principals. Others feel upset and uneasy, and my sympathies are with these latter, although on the present occasion I was under the impression that all this was part of the show—the analphabetic yokels no less than the *giovanotto* with the jacket. The children listened well pleased. They understood not at all, but the sound of the voices made them hold their breath. So this was a "magic evening"—at least it was the kind they have in Italy. They expressly found it "lovely."

Cipolla had stood up and with two of his scooping strides was at the footlights.

"Well, well, see who's here!" said he with grim cordiality. "An old acquaintance! A young man with his heart at the end of his tongue" (he used the word *linguaccia,* which means a coated tongue, and gave rise to much hilarity). "That will do, my friends," he turned to the yokels. "I do not need you now, I have business with this deserving young man here, *con questo torregiano di Venere,* this tower of Venus, who no doubt expects the gratitude of the fair as a reward for his prowess—"

"Ah, non scherziamo! We're talking earnest," cried out the youth. His eyes flashed, and he actually made as though to pull off his jacket and proceed to direct methods of settlement.

Cipolla did not take him too seriously. We had exchanged apprehensive glances; but he was dealing with a fellow-countryman and had his native soil beneath his feet. He kept quite cool and showed complete mastery of the situation. He looked at his audience, smiled, and made a sideways motion of the head towards the young cockerel as though calling the public to witness how the man's bumptiousness only served to betray the simplicity of his mind. And then, for the second time, something strange happened, which set Cipolla's calm superiority in an uncanny light, and in some mysterious and irritating way turned all the explosiveness latent in the air into matter for laughter.

Cipolla drew still nearer to the fellow, looking him in the eye with a peculiar gaze. He even came half-way down the steps that led into the auditorium on our left, so that he stood directly in front of the trouble-maker, on slightly higher ground. The riding-whip hung from his arm.

"My son, you do not feel much like joking," he said. "It is only too natural, for anyone can see that you are not feeling too well. Even your tongue, which leaves something to be desired on the score of cleanliness, indicates acute disorder of the gastric system. An evening entertainment is no place for people in your state; you yourself, I can tell, were of several minds whether you would not do better to put on a flannel bandage and go to bed. It was not good judgment to drink so much of that very sour white wine this afternoon. Now you have such a colic you would like to double up with the pain. Go ahead, don't be embarrassed. There is a distinct relief that comes from bending over, in cases of intestinal cramp."

He spoke thus, word for word, with quiet impressiveness and a kind of stern sympathy, and his eyes, plunged the while deep in the young man's, seemed to grow very tired and at the same time burning above their enlarged tear-ducts—they were the strangest eyes, you could tell that not manly pride alone was preventing the young adversary from withdrawing his gaze. And presently, indeed, all trace of its former arrogance was gone from the bronzed young face. He looked open-mouthed at the Cavaliere and the open mouth was drawn in a rueful smile.

"Double over," repeated Cipolla. "What else can you do? With a colic like that you *must* bend. Surely you will not struggle against the performance of a perfectly natural action just because somebody suggests it to you?"

Slowly the youth lifted his forearms, folded and squeezed them across his body; it turned a little sideways, then bent, lower and lower, the feet shifted, the knees turned inward, until he had become a picture of writhing pain, until he all but grovelled upon the ground. Cipolla let him stand for some seconds thus, then made a short cut through the air with his whip and went with his scooping stride back to the little table, where he poured himself out a cognac.

"*Il boit beaucoup,*" asserted a lady behind us. Was that the only thing that struck her? We could not tell how far the audience grasped the situation. The fellow was standing upright again, with a sheepish grin—he looked as though he scarcely knew how it had all happened. The scene had been followed with tense interest and applauded at the end; there were shouts of "*Bravo, Cipolla!*" and "*Bravo, giovanotto!*" Apparently the issue of the duel was not looked upon as a personal defeat for the young man. Rather the audience encouraged him as one does an actor who succeeds in an unsympathetic rôle. Certainly his way of screwing himself up with cramp had been highly picturesque, its appeal was directly calculated to impress the gallery—in short, a fine dramatic performance. But I am not sure how far the audience were moved by that natural tactfulness in which the south excels, or how far it penetrated into the nature of what was going on.

The Cavaliere, refreshed, had lighted another cigarette. The numerical tests might now proceed. A young man was easily found in the back row who was willing to write down on the blackboard the numbers as they were dictated to him. Him too we knew; the whole entertainment had taken on an intimate character through our acquaintance with so many of the actors. This was the man who worked at the greengrocer's in the main street; he had served us several times, with neatness and dispatch. He wielded the chalk with clerkly confidence, while Cipolla descended to our level and walked with his deformed gait through the audience, collecting numbers as they were given, in two, three, and four places, and calling them out to the grocer's assistant, who wrote them down in a column. In all this, everything on both sides was calculated to amuse, with its jokes and its oratorical asides. The artist could not fail to hit on foreigners, who were not ready with their figures, and with them he was elaborately patient and chivalrous, to the great amusement of the natives, whom he reduced to confusion in their turn, by making them translate numbers that were given in English or French. Some people gave dates concerned with great events in Italian history. Cipolla took them up at once and made patriotic comments. Somebody shouted "Number one!" The Cavaliere, incensed at this as at every attempt to make game of him, retorted over his shoulder that he could not take less than two-place figures. Whereupon another joker cried out "Number two!" and was greeted with the applause and laughter which every reference to natural functions is sure to win among southerners.

When fifteen numbers stood in a long straggling row on the board, Cipolla called for a general adding-match. Ready reckoners might add in their heads, but pencil and paper were not forbidden. Cipolla, while the work went on, sat on his chair near the blackboard, smoked and grimaced, with the complacent, pompous air cripples so often have. The five-place addition was soon done. Somebody announced the answer, somebody else confirmed it, a third had arrived at a slightly different result, but the fourth agreed with the first and second. Cipolla got up, tapped some ash from his coat, and lifted the paper at the upper right-hand corner of the board to display the writing. The correct answer, a sum close on a million, stood there; he had written it down beforehand.

Astonishment, and loud applause. The children were overwhelmed. How had he done that, they wanted to know. We told them it was a trick, not easily explainable offhand. In short, the man was a conjuror. This was what a sleight-of-hand evening was like, so now they knew. First the fisherman had cramp, and then the right answer was written down beforehand—it was all simply glorious, and we saw with dismay that despite the hot eyes and the hand of the clock at almost half past ten, it would be very hard to get them away. There would be tears. And yet it was plain that this magician did not "magick"—at least not in the accepted sense, of manual dexterity—and that the entertainment was not at all suitable for children. Again, I do not know, either, what the audience really thought. Obviously there was grave doubt whether its answers had been given of "free choice"; here and there an individual might have answered of his own motion, but on the whole Cipolla certainly selected his people and thus kept the whole procedure in his own hands and directed it towards the given result. Even so, one had to admire the quickness of his calculations, however much one felt disinclined to admire anything else about the performance. Then his patriotism, his irritable sense of dignity— the Cavaliere's own countrymen might feel in their element with all that and continue in a laughing mood; but the combination certainly gave us outsiders food for thought.

Cipolla himself saw to it—though without giving them a name—that the nature of his powers should be clear beyond a doubt to even the least-instructed person. He alluded to them, of course, in his talk—and he talked without stopping—but only in vague, boastful, self-advertising phrases. He went on awhile with experiments on the same lines as the first, merely making them more complicated by introducing operations in multiplying, subtracting, and dividing; then he simplified them to the last degree in order to bring out the method. He simply had numbers "guessed" which were previously written under the paper; and the guess was nearly always right. One guesser admitted that he had had in mind to give a certain number, when Cipolla's whip went whistling through the air, and a quite different one slipped out, which proved to be the "right" one. Cipolla's shoulders shook. He pretended admiration for the powers of the people he questioned. But in all his compliments there was something fleering and derogatory; the victims could scarcely have relished them much, although they smiled, and although they might easily have set down some part of the applause to their own credit. Moreover, I had not the impression that the artist was popular with his public. A certain ill will and reluctance were in the air, but courtesy kept such feelings in check, as did Cipolla's competency and his stern self-confidence. Even the riding-whip, I think, did much to keep rebellion from becoming overt.

From tricks with numbers he passed to tricks with cards. There were two packs, which he drew out of his pockets, and so much I still remember, that the basis of the tricks he played with them was as follows: from the first pack he drew three cards and thrust them without looking at them inside his coat. Another person then drew three out of the second pack, and these turned out to be the same as the first three—not invariably all the three, for it did happen that only two were the same. But in the majority of cases Cipolla triumphed, showing his three cards with a little bow in acknowledgment of the applause with which his audience conceded his possession of strange powers—strange whether for good or evil. A young man in the front row to our right, an Italian, with proud, finely chiselled features, rose up and said that he intended to assert his own will in his choice and consciously to resist any influence, of whatever sort. Under these circumstances, what did Cipolla think would be the result? "You will," answered the Cavaliere, "make my task somewhat more difficult thereby. As for the result, your resistance will not alter it in the least. Freedom exists, and also the will exists; but freedom of the will does not exist, for a will that aims at its own freedom aims at the unknown. You are free to draw or not to draw. But if you draw, you will draw the right cards—the more certainly, the more wilfully obstinate your behaviour."

One must admit that he could not have chosen his words better, to trouble the waters and confuse the mind. The refractory youth hesitated before drawing. Then he pulled out a card and at once demanded to see if it was among the chosen three. "But why?" queried Cipolla. "Why do things by halves?" Then, as the other defiantly insisted, *"E servito,"* said the juggler, with a gesture of exaggerated servility; and held out the three cards fanwise, without looking at them himself. The left-hand card was the one drawn.

Amid general applause, the apostle of freedom sat down. How far Cipolla employed small tricks and manual dexterity to help out his natural talents, the deuce only knew. But even without them the result would have been the same: the curiosity of the entire audience was unbounded and universal, everybody both enjoyed the amazing character of the entertainment and unanimously conceded the professional skill of the performer. *"Lavora bene,"* we heard, here and there in our neighbourhood; it signified the triumph of objective judgment over antipathy and repressed resentment.

After his last, incomplete, yet so much the more telling success, Cipolla had at once fortified himself with another cognac. Truly he did "drink a lot," and the fact made a bad impression. But obviously he needed the liquor and the cigarettes for the replenishment of his energy, upon which, as he himself said, heavy demands were made in all directions. Certainly in the intervals he looked very ill, exhausted and hollow-eyed. Then the little glassful would redress the balance, and the flow of lively, self-confident chatter run on, while the smoke he inhaled gushed out grey from his lungs. I clearly recall that he passed from the card-tricks to parlour games—the kind based on certain powers which in human nature are higher or else lower than human reason: on intuition and "magnetic" transmission; in short, upon a low type of manifestation. What I do not remember is the precise order things came in. And I will not bore you with a description of these experiments; everybody knows them, everybody has at one time or another taken part in this finding of hidden articles, this blind carrying out of a series of acts, directed by a force that proceeds from organism to organism by unexplored paths. Everybody has had his little glimpse into the equivocal, impure, inexplicable nature of the occult, has been conscious of both curiosity and contempt, has shaken his head over the human tendency of those who deal in it to help themselves out with humbuggery, though, after all, the humbuggery is no disproof whatever of the genuineness of the other elements in the dubious amalgam. I can only say here that each single circumstance gains in weight and the whole greatly in impressiveness when it is a man like Cipolla who is the chief actor and guiding spirit in the sinister business. He sat smoking at the rear of the stage, his back to the audience while they conferred. The object passed from hand to hand which it was his task to find, with which he was to perform some action agreed upon beforehand. Then he would start to move zigzag through the hall, with his head thrown back and one hand outstretched, the other clasped in that of a guide who was in the secret but enjoined to keep himself perfectly passive, with his thoughts directed upon the agreed goal. Cipolla moved with the bearing typical in these experiments: now groping upon a false start, now with a quick forward thrust, now pausing as though to listen and by sudden inspiration correcting his course. The rôles seemed reversed, the stream of influence was moving in the contrary direction, as the artist himself pointed out, in his ceaseless flow of discourse. The suffering, receptive, performing part was now his, the will he had before imposed on others was shut out, he acted in obedience to a voiceless common will which was in the air. But he made it perfectly clear that it all came to the same thing. The capacity for self-surrender, he said, for becoming a tool, for the most unconditional and utter self-abnegation, was but the reverse side of that other power to will and to command. Commanding and obeying formed together one single principle, one indissoluble unity; he who knew how to obey knew also how to command, and conversely; the one idea was comprehended in the other, as people and leader were comprehended in one another. But that which was *done*, the highly exacting and exhausting performance, was in every case his, the leader's and mover's, in whom the will became obedience, the obedience will, whose person was the cradle and womb of both, and who thus suffered enormous hardship. Repeatedly he emphasized the fact that his lot was a hard one—presumably to account for his need of stimulant and his frequent recourse to the little glass.

Thus he groped his way forward, like a blind seer, led and sustained by the mysterious common will. He drew a pin set with a stone out of its hiding-place in an Englishwoman's shoe, carried it, halting and pressing on by turns, to another lady—Signora Angiolieri—and handed it to her on bended knee, with the words it had been agreed he was to utter. "I present you with this in token of my respect," was the sentence. Their sense was obvious, but the words themselves not easy to hit upon, for the reason that they had been agreed on in French; the language complication seemed to us a little malicious, implying as it did a conflict between the audience's natural interest in the success of the miracle, and their desire to witness the humiliation of this presumptuous man. It was a strange sight: Cipolla on his knees before the signora, wrestling, amid efforts at speech, after knowledge of the preordained words. "I must say something," he said, "and I feel clearly what it is I must say. But I also feel that if it passed my lips it would be wrong. Be careful not to help me unintentionally!" he cried out, though very likely that was precisely what he was hoping for. *"Pensez très fort,"* he cried all at once, in bad French, and then burst out with the required words—in Italian, indeed, but with the final substantive pronounced in the sister tongue, in which he was probably far from fluent: he said *vénération* instead of *venerazione,* with an impossible nasal. And this partial success, after the complete success before it, the finding of the pin, the presentation of it on his knees to the right person—was almost more impressive than if he had got the sentence exactly right, and evoked bursts of admiring applause.

Cipolla got up from his knees and wiped the perspiration from his brow. You understand that this experiment with the pin was a single case, which I describe because it sticks in my memory. But he changed his method several times and improvised a number of variations suggested by his contact with his audience; a good deal of time thus went by. He seemed to get particular inspiration from the person of our landlady; she drew him on to the most extraordinary displays of clairvoyance. "It does not escape me, madame," he said to her, "that there is something unusual about you, some special and honourable distinction. He who has eyes to see descries about your lovely brow an aureola—if I mistake not, it once was stronger than now—a slowly paling radiance . . . hush, not a word! Don't help me. Beside you sits your husband—yes?" He turned towards the silent Signor Angiolieri. "You are the husband of this lady, and your happiness is complete. But in the midst of this happiness memories rise . . . the past, signora, so it seems to me, plays an important part in your present. You knew a king . . . has not a king crossed your path in bygone days?"

"No," breathed the dispenser of our midday soup, her golden-brown eyes gleaming in the noble pallor of her face.

"No? No, not a king; I meant that generally, I did not mean literally a king. Not a king, not a prince, and a prince after all, a king of a loftier realm; it was a great artist, at whose side you once—you would contradict me, and yet I am not wholly wrong. Well, then! It was a woman, a great, a world-renowned woman artist, whose friendship you enjoyed in your tender years, whose sacred memory overshadows and transfigures your whole existence. Her name? Need I utter it, whose fame has long been bound up with the Fatherland's, immortal as its own? Eleonora Duse," he finished, softly and with much solemnity.

The little woman bowed her head, overcome. The applause was like a patriotic demonstration. Nearly everyone there knew about Signora Angiolieri's wonderful past; they were all able to confirm the Cavaliere's intuition—not least the present guests of Casa Eleonora. But we wondered how much of the truth he had learned as the result of professional inquiries made on his arrival. Yet I see no reason at all to cast doubt, on rational grounds, upon powers which, before our very eyes, became fatal to their possessor.

At this point there was an intermission. Our lord and master withdrew. Now I confess that almost ever since the beginning of my tale I have looked forward with dread to this moment in it. The thoughts of men are mostly not hard to read; in this case they are very easy. You are sure to ask why we did not choose this moment to go away—and I must continue to owe you an answer. I do not know why. I cannot defend myself. By this time it was certainly eleven, probably later. The children were asleep. The last series of tests had been too long, nature had had her way. They were sleeping in our laps, the little one on mine, the boy on his mother's. That was, in a way, a consolation; but at the same time it was also ground for compassion and a clear leading to take them home to bed. And I give you my word that we wanted to obey this touching admonition, we seriously wanted to. We roused the poor things and told them it was now high time to go. But they were no sooner conscious than they began to resist and implore—you know how horrified children are at the thought of leaving before the end of a thing. No cajoling has any effect, you have to use force. It was so lovely, they wailed. How did we know what was coming next? Surely we could not leave until after the intermission; they liked a little nap now and again—only not go home, only not go to bed, while the beautiful evening was still going on!

We yielded, but only for the moment, of course—so far as we knew—only for a little while, just a few minutes longer. I cannot excuse our staying, scarcely can I even understand it. Did we think, having once said A, we had to say B—having once brought the children hither we had to let them stay? No, it is not good enough. Were we ourselves so highly entertained? Yes, and no. Our feelings for Cavaliere Cipolla were of a very mixed kind, but so were the feelings of the whole audience, if I mistake not, and nobody left. Were we under the sway of a fascination which emanated from this man who took so strange a way to earn his bread; a fascination which he gave out independently of the programme and even between the tricks and which paralysed our resolve? Again, sheer curiosity may account for something. One was curious to know how such an evening turned out; Cipolla in his remarks having all along hinted that he had tricks in his bag stranger than any he had yet produced.

But all that is not it—or at least it is not all of it. More correct it would be to answer the first question with another. Why had we not left Torre di Venere itself before now? To me the two questions are one and the same, and in order to get out of the impasse I might simply say that I had answered it already. For, as things had been in Torre in general: queer, uncomfortable, troublesome, tense, oppressive, so precisely they were here in this hall tonight. Yes, more than precisely. For it seemed to be the fountainhead of all the uncanniness and all the strained feelings which had oppressed the atmosphere of our holiday. This man whose return to the stage we were awaiting was the personification of all that; and, as we had not gone away in general, so to speak, it would have been inconsistent to do it in the particular case. You may call this an explanation, you may call it inertia, as you see fit. Any argument more to the purpose I simply do not know how to adduce.

Well, there was an interval of ten minutes, which grew into nearly twenty. The children remained awake. They were enchanted by our compliance, and filled the break to their own satisfaction by renewing relations with the popular sphere, with Antonio, Guiscardo, and the canoe man. They put their hands to their mouths and called messages across, appealing to us for the Italian words. "Hope you have a good catch tomorrow, a whole netful!" They called to Mario, Esquisito Mario: *"Mario, una cioccolata e biscotti!"* And this time he heeded and answered with a smile: *"Subito, signorini!"* Later we had reason to recall this kindly, if rather absent and pensive smile.

Thus the interval passed, the gong sounded. The audience, which had scattered in conversation, took their places again, the children sat up straight in their chairs with their hands in their laps. The curtain had not been dropped. Cipolla came forward again, with his dipping stride, and began to introduce the second half of the programme with a lecture.

Let me state once for all that this self-confident cripple was the most powerful hypnotist I have ever seen in my life. It was pretty plain now that he threw dust in the public eye and advertised himself as a prestidigitator on account of police regulations which would have prevented him from making his living by the exercise of his powers. Perhaps this eye-wash is the usual thing in Italy; it may be permitted or even connived at by the authorities. Certainly the man had from the beginning made little concealment of the actual nature of his operations; and this second half of the programme was quite frankly and exclusively devoted to one sort of experiment. While he still practised some rhetorical circumlocutions, the tests themselves were one long series of attacks upon the will-power, the loss or compulsion of volition. Comic, exciting, amazing by turns, by midnight they were still in full swing; we ran the gamut of all the phenomena this natural-unnatural field has to show, from the unimpressive at one end of the scale to the monstrous at the other. The audience laughed and applauded as they followed the grotesque details; shook their heads, clapped their knees, fell very frankly under the spell of this stern, self-assured personality. At the same time I saw signs that they were not quite complacent, not quite unconscious of the peculiar ignominy which lay, for the individual and for the general, in Cipolla's triumphs.

Two main features were constant in all the experiements: the liquor glass and the claw-handled riding-whip. The first was always invoked to add fuel to his demoniac fires; without it, apparently, they might have burned out. On this score we might even have felt pity for the man; but the whistle of his scourge, the insulting symbol of his domination, before which we all cowered, drowned out every sensation save a dazed and outbraved submission to his power. Did he then lay claim to our sympathy to boot? I was struck by a remark he made—it suggested no less. At the climax of his experiments, by stroking and breathing upon a certain young man who had offered himself as a subject and already proved himself a particularly susceptible one, he had not only put him into the condition known as deep trance and extended his insensible body by neck and feet across the backs of two chairs, but had actually sat down on the rigid form as on a bench, without making it yield. The sight of this unholy figure in a frock-coat squatted on the stiff body was horrible and incredible; the audience, convinced that the victim of this scientific diversion must be suffering, expressed its sympathy: *"Ah, poveretto!"* Poor soul, poor soul! *"Poor soul!"* Cipolla mocked them, with some bitterness. "Ladies and gentlemen, you are barking up the wrong tree. *Sono io il poveretto.* I am the person who is suffering, I am the one to be pitied." We pocketed the information. Very good. Maybe the experiment was at his expense, maybe it was he who had suffered the cramp when the *giovanotto* over there had made the faces. But appearances were all against it; and one does not feel like saying *poveretto* to a man who is suffering to bring about the humiliation of others.

I have got ahead of my story and lost sight of the sequence of events. To this day my mind is full of the Cavaliere's feats of endurance; only I do not recall them in their order—which does not matter. So much I do know: that the longer and more circumstantial tests, which got the most applause, impressed me less than some of the small ones which passed quickly over. I remember the young man whose body Cipolla converted into a board, only because of the accompanying remarks which I have quoted. An elderly lady in a cane-seated chair was lulled by Cipolla in the delusion that she was on a voyage to India and gave a voluble account of her adventures by land and sea. But I found this phenomenon less impressive than one which followed immediately after the intermission. A tall, well-built, soldierly man was unable to lift his arm, after the hunchback had told him that he could not and given a cut through the air with his whip. I can still see the face of that stately, mustachioed colonel smiling and clenching his teeth as he struggled to regain his lost freedom of action. A staggering performance! He seemed to be exerting his will, and in vain; the trouble, however, was probably simply that he could not will. There was involved here that recoil of the will upon itself which paralyses choice—as our tyrant had previously explained to the Roman gentleman.

Still less can I forget the touching scene, at once comic and horrible, with Signora Angiolieri. The Cavaliere, probably in his first bold survey of the room, had spied out her ethereal lack of resistance to his power. For actually he bewitched her, literally drew her out of her seat, out of her row, and away with him whither he willed. And in order to enhance his effect, he bade Signor Angiolieri call upon his wife by her name, to throw, as it were, all the weight of his existence and his rights in her into the scale, to rouse by the voice of her husband everything in his spouse's soul which could shield her virtue against the evil assaults of magic. And how vain it all was! Cipolla was standing at some distance from the couple, when he made a single cut with his whip through the air. It caused our landlady to shudder violently and turn her face towards him. "Sofronia!" cried Signor Angiolieri—we had not known that Signora Angiolieri's name was Sofronia. And he did well to call, everybody saw that there was no time to lose. His wife kept her face turned in the direction of the diabolical Cavaliere, who with his ten long yellow fingers was making passes at his victim, moving backwards as he did so, step by step. Then Signora Angiolieri, her pale face gleaming, rose up from her seat, turned right round, and began to glide after him. Fatal and forbidding sight! Her face as though moonstruck, stiff-armed, her lovely hands lifted a little at the wrists, the feet as it were together, she seemed to float slowly out of her row and after the tempter. "Call her, sir, keep on calling," prompted the redoubtable man. And Signor Angiolieri, in a weak voice, called: "Sofronia!" Ah, again and again he called; as his wife went further off he even curved one hand round his lips and beckoned with the other as he called. But the poor voice of love and duty echoed unheard, in vain, behind the lost one's back; the signora swayed along, moonstruck, deaf, enslaved; she glided into the middle aisle and down it towards the fingering hunchback, towards the door. We were convinced, we were driven to the conviction, that she would have followed her master, had he so willed it, to the ends of the earth.

"Accidente!" cried out Signor Angiolieri, in genuine affright, springing up as the exit was reached. But at the same moment the Cavaliere put aside, as it were, the triumphal crown and broke off. "Enough, signora, I thank you," he said, and offered his arm to lead her back to her husband. "Signor," he greeted the latter, "here is your wife. Unharmed, with my compliments, I give her into your hands. Cherish with all the strength of your manhood a treasure which is so wholly yours, and let your zeal be quickened by knowing that there are powers stronger than reason or virtue, and not always so magnanimously ready to relinquish their prey!"

Poor Signor Angiolieri, so quiet, so bald! He did not look as though he would know how to defend his happiness, even against powers much less demoniac than these which were now adding mockery to frightfulness. Solemnly and pompously the Cavaliere retired to the stage, amid applause to which his eloquence gave double strength. It was this particular episode, I feel sure, that set the seal upon his ascendancy. For now he made them dance, yes, literally; and the dancing lent a dissolute, abandoned, topsy-turvy air to the scene, a drunken abdication of the critical spirit which had so long resisted the spell of this man. Yes, he had had to fight to get the upper hand—for instance against the animosity of the young Roman gentleman, whose rebellious spirit threatened to serve others as a rallying-point. But it was precisely upon the importance of example that the Cavaliere was so strong. He had the wit to make his attack at the weakest point and to choose at his first victim that feeble, ecstatic youth whom he had previously made into a board. The master had but to look at him, when this young man would fling himself back as though struck by lightening, place his hands rigidly at his sides, and fall into a state of military somnambulism, in which it was plain to any eye that he was open to the most absurd suggestion that might be made to him. He seemed quite content in his abject state, quite pleased to be relieved of the burden of voluntary choice. Again and again he offered himself as a subject and gloried in the model facility he had in losing consciousness. So now he mounted the platform, and a single cut of the whip was enough to make him dance to the Cavaliere's orders, in a kind of complacent ecstasy, eyes closed, head nodding, lank limbs flying in all directions.

It looked unmistakably like enjoyment, and other recruits were not long in coming forward: two other young men, one humbly and one well dressed, were soon jigging alongside the first. But now the gentleman from Rome bobbed up again, asking defiantly if the Cavaliere would engage to make him dance too, even against his will.

"Even against your will," answered Cipolla, in unforgettable accents. That frightful *"anche se non vuole"* still rings in my ears. The struggle began. After Cipolla had taken another little glass and lighted a fresh cigarette he stationed the Roman at a point in the middle aisle and himself took up a position some distance behind him, making his whip whistle through the air as he gave the order: *"Balla!"* His opponent did not stir. *"Balla!"* repeated the Cavaliere incisively, and snapped his whip. You saw the young man move his neck round in his collar; at the same time one hand lifted slightly at the wrist, one ankle turned outward. But that was all, for the time at least; merely a tendency to twitch, now sternly repressed, now seeming about to get the upper hand. It escaped nobody that here a heroic obstinacy, a fixed resolve to resist, must needs be conquered; we were beholding a gallant effort to strike out and save the honour of the human race. He twitched but danced not; and the struggle was so prolonged that the Cavaliere had to divide his attention between it and the stage, turning now and then to make his riding-whip whistle in the direction of the dancers, as it were to keep them in leash. At the same time he advised the audience that no fatigue was involved in such activities, however long they went on, since it was not the automatons up there who danced, but himself. Then once more his eye would bore itself into the back of the Roman's neck and lay siege to the strength of purpose which defied him.

One saw it waver, that strength of purpose, beneath the repeated summons and whip-crackings. Saw with an objective interest which yet was not quite free from traces of sympathetic emotion—from pity, even from a cruel kind of pleasure. If I understand what was going on, it was the negative character of the young man's fighting position which was his undoing. It is likely that *not* willing is not a practicable state of mind; *not* to want to do something may be in the long run a mental content impossible to subsist on. Between not willing a certain thing and not willing at all—in other words, yielding to another person's will—there may lie too small a space for the idea of freedom to squeeze into. Again, there were the Cavaliere's persuasive words, woven in among the whip-crackings and commands, as he mingled effects that were his own secret with others of a bewilderingly psychological kind. *"Balla!"* said he. "Who wants to torture himself like that? Is forcing yourself your idea of freedom? *Una ballatina!* Why, your arms and legs are aching for it. What a relief to give way to them—there, you are dancing already! That is no struggle any more, it is a pleasure!" And so it was. The jerking and twitching of the refractory youth's limbs had at last got the upper hand; he lifted his arms, then his knees, his joints quite suddenly relaxed, he flung his legs and danced, and amid bursts of applause the Cavaliere led him to join the row of puppets on the stage. Up there we could see his face as he "enjoyed" himself; it was clothed in a broad grin and the eyes were half-shut. In a way, it was consoling to see that he was having a better time than he had had in the hour of his pride.

His "fall" was, I may say, an epoch. The ice was completely broken, Cipolla's triumph had reached its height. The Circe's wand, that whistling leather whip with the claw handle, held absolute sway. At one time—it must have been well after midnight— not only were there eight or ten persons dancing on the little stage, but in the hall below a varied animation reigned, and a long-toothed Anglo-Saxoness in a pince-nez left her seat of her own motion to perform a tarantella in the centre aisle. Cipolla was lounging in a cane-seated chair at the left of the stage, gulping down the smoke of a cigarette and breathing it impudently out through his bad teeth. He tapped his foot and shrugged his shoulders, looking down upon the abandoned scene in the hall; now and then he snapped his whip backwards at a laggard upon the stage. The children were awake at the moment. With shame I speak of them. For it was not good to be here, least of all for them; that we had not taken them away can only be explained by saying that we had caught the general devil-may-careness of the hour. By that time it was all one. Anyhow, thank goodness, they lacked understanding for the disreputable side of the entertainment, and in their innocence were perpetually charmed by the unheard-of indulgence which permitted them to be present at such a thing as a magician's "evening." Whole quarter-hours at a time they drowsed on our laps, waking refreshed and rosy-cheeked, with sleep-drunken eyes, to laugh to bursting at the leaps and jumps the magician made those people up there make. They had not thought it would be so jolly; they joined with their clumsy little hands in every round of applause. And jumped for joy upon their chairs, as was their wont, when Cipolla beckoned to their friend Mario from the Esquisito, beckoned to him just like a picture in a book, holding his hand in front of his nose and bending and straightening the forefinger by turns.

Mario obeyed. I can see him now going up the stairs to Cipolla, who continued to beckon him, in that droll, picture-book sort of way. He hesitated for a moment at first; that, too, I recall quite clearly. During the whole evening he had lounged against a wooden pillar at the side entrance, with his arms folded, or else with his hands thrust into his jacket pockets. He was on our left, near the youth with the militant hair, and had followed the performance attentively, so far as we had seen, if with no particular animation and God knows how much comprehension. He could not much relish being summoned thus, at the end of the evening. But it was only too easy to see why he obeyed. After all, obedience was his calling in life; and then, how should a simple lad like him find it within his human capacity to refuse compliance to a man so throned and crowned as Cipolla at that hour? Willy-nilly he left his column and with a word of thanks to those making way for him he mounted the steps with a doubtful smile on his full lips.

Picture a thickset youth of twenty years, with clipt hair, a low forehead, and heavy-lidded eyes of an indefinite grey, shot with green and yellow. These things I knew from having spoken with him, as we often had. There was a saddle of freckles on the flat nose, the whole upper half of the face retreated behind the lower, and that again was dominated by thick lips that parted to show the salivated teeth. These thick lips and the veiled look of the eyes lent the whole face a primitive melancholy—it was that which had drawn us to him from the first. In it was not the faintest trace of brutality—indeed, his hands would have given the lie to such an idea, being unusually slender and delicate even for a southerner. They were hands by which one liked being served.

We knew him humanly without knowing him personally, if I may make that distinction. We saw him nearly every day, and felt a certain kindness for his dreamy ways, which might at times be actual inattentiveness, suddenly transformed into a redeeming zeal to serve. His mien was serious, only the children could bring a smile to his face. It was not sulky, but uningratiating, without intentional effort to please—or, rather, it seemed to give up being pleasant in the conviction that it could not succeed. We should have remembered Mario in any case, as one of those homely recollections of travel which often stick in the mind better than more important ones. But of his circumstances we knew no more than that his father was a petty clerk in the Municipio and his mother took in washing.

His white waiter's-coat became him better than the faded striped suit he wore, with a gay coloured scarf instead of a collar, the ends tucked into his jacket. He neared Cipolla, who however did not leave off that motion of his finger before his nose, so that Mario had to come still closer, right up to the chair-seat and the master's legs. Whereupon the latter spread out his elbows and seized the lad, turning him so that we had a view of his face. Then gazed him briskly up and down, with a careless, commanding eye.

"Well, *ragazzo mio,* how comes it we make acquaintance so late in the day? But believe me, I made yours long ago. Yes, yes, I've had you in my eye this long while and known what good stuff you were made of. How could I go and forget you again? Well, I've had a good deal to think about. . . . Now tell me, what is your name? The first name, that's all I want."

"My name is Mario," the young man answered, in a low voice.

"Ah, Mario. Very good. Yes, yes, there is such a name, quite a common name, a classic name too, one of those which preserve the heroic traditions of the Fatherland. *Bravo! Salve!*" And he flung up his arm slantingly above his crooked shoulder, palm outward, in the Roman salute. He may have been slightly tipsy by now, and no wonder; but he spoke as before, clearly, fluently, and with emphasis. Though about this time there had crept into his voice a gross, autocratic note, and a kind of arrogance was in his sprawl.

"Well, now, Mario *mio,*" he went on, "it's a good thing you came this evening, and that's a pretty scarf you've got on; it is becoming to your style of beauty. It must stand you in good stead with the girls, the pretty pretty girls of Torre—"

From the row of youths, close by the place where Mario had been standing, sounded a laugh. It came from the youth with the militant hair. He stood there, his jacket over his shoulder, and laughed outright, rudely and scornfully.

Mario gave a start. I think it was a shrug, but he may have started and then hastened to cover the movement by shrugging his shoulders, as much as to say that the neckerchief and the fair sex were matters of equal indifference to him.

The Cavaliere gave a downward glance.

"We needn't trouble about him," he said. "He is jealous, because your scarf is so popular with the girls, maybe partly because you and I are so friendly up here. Perhaps he'd like me to put him in mind of his colic—I could do it free of charge. Tell me, Mario. You've come here this evening for a bit of fun—and in the daytime you work in an ironmonger's shop?"

"In a café," corrected the youth.

"Oh, in a café. That's where Cipolla nearly came a cropper! What you are is a cupbearer, a Ganymede—I like that, it is another classical allusion—*Salvietta!*" Again the Cavaliere saluted, to the huge gratification of his audience.

Mario smiled too. "But before that," he interpolated, in the interest of accuracy, "I worked for a while in a shop in Portoclemente." He seemed visited by a natural desire to assist the prophecy by dredging out its essential features.

"There, didn't I say so? In an ironmonger's shop?"

"They kept combs and brushes," Mario got round it.

"Didn't I say that you were not always a Ganymede? Not always at the sign of the serviette? Even when Cipolla makes a mistake, it is a kind that makes you believe in him. Now tell me: Do you believe in me?"

An indefinite gesture.

"A half-way answer," commented the Cavaliere. "Probably it is not easy to win your confidence. Even for me, I can see, it is not so easy. I see in your features a reserve, a sadness, *un tratto di malinconia* . . . tell me" (he seized Mario's hand persuasively) "have you troubles?"

"Nossignore," answered Mario, promptly and decidedly.

"You *have* troubles," insisted the Cavaliere, bearing down the denial by the weight of his authority. "Can't I see? Trying to pull the wool over Cipolla's eyes, are you? Of course, about the girls—it is a girl, isn't it? You have love troubles?"

Mario gave a vigorous head-shake. And again the *giovanotto's* brutal laugh rang out. The Cavaliere gave heed. His eyes were roving about somewhere in the air; but he cocked an ear to the sound, then swung his whip backwards, as he had once or twice before in his conversation with Mario, that none of his puppets might flag in their zeal. The gesture had nearly cost him his new prey: Mario gave a sudden start in the direction of the steps. But Cipolla had him in his clutch.

"Not so fast," said he. "That would be fine, wouldn't it? So you want to skip, do you, Ganymede, right in the middle of the fun, or, rather, when it is just beginning? Stay with me, I'll show you something nice. I'll convince you. You have no reason to worry, I promise you. This girl—you know her and others know her too—what's her name? Wait! I read the name in your eyes, it is on the tip of my tongue and yours too—"

"Silvestra!" shouted the *giovanotto* from below.

The Cavaliere's face did not change.

"Aren't there the forward people?" he asked, not looking down, more as in undisturbed converse with Mario. "Aren't there the young fighting-cocks that crow in season and out? Takes the word out of your mouth, the conceited fool, and seems to think he has some special right to it. Let him be. But Silvestra, your Silvestra—ah, what a girl that is! What a prize! Brings your heart into your mouth to see her walk or laugh or breathe, she is so lovely. And her round arms when she washes, and tosses her head back to get the hair out of her eyes! An angel from paradise!"

Mario stared at him, his head thrust forward. He seemed to have forgotten the audience, forgotten where he was. The red rings round his eyes had got larger, they looked as though they were painted on. His thick lips parted.

"And she makes you suffer, this angel," went on Cipolla, "or, rather, you make yourself suffer for her—there is a difference, my lad, a most important difference, let me tell you. There are misunderstandings in love, maybe nowhere else in the world are there so many. I know what you are thinking: what does this Cipolla, with his little physical defect, know about love? Wrong, all wrong, he knows a lot. He has a wide and powerful understanding of its workings, and it pays to listen to his advice. But let's leave Cipolla out, cut him out altogether and think only of Silvestra, your peerless Silvestra! What! Is she to give any young gamecock the preference, so that he can laugh while you cry? To prefer him to a chap like you, so full of feeling and so sympathetic? Not very likely, is it? It is impossible—we know better, Cipolla and she. If I were to put myself in her place and choose between the two of you, a tarry lout like that—a codfish, a sea-urchin—and a Mario, a knight of the serviette, who moves among gentlefolk and hands round refreshments with an air—my word, but my heart would speak in no uncertain tones—it knows to whom I gave it long ago. It is time that he should see and understand, my chosen one! It is time that you see me and recognize me, Mario, my beloved! Tell me, who am I?"

It was grisly, the way the betrayer made himself irresistible, wreathed and coquetted with his crooked shoulder, languished with the puffy eyes, and showed his splintered teeth in a sickly smile. And alas, at his beguiling words, what was come of our Mario? It is hard for me to tell, hard as it was for me to see; for here was nothing less than an utter abandonment of the inmost soul, a public exposure of timid and deluded passion and rapture. He put his hands across his mouth, his shoulders rose and fell with his pantings. He could not, it was plain, trust his eyes and ears for joy, and the one thing he forgot was precisely that he could not trust them. "Silvestra!" he breathed, from the very depths of his vanquished heart.

"Kiss me!" said the hunchback. "Trust me, I love thee. Kiss me here." And with the tip of his index finger, hand, arm, and little finger outspread, he pointed to his cheek, near the mouth. And Mario bent and kissed him.

It had grown very still in the room. That was a monstrous moment, grotesque and thrilling, the moment of Mario's bliss. In that evil span of time, crowded with a sense of the illusiveness of all joy, one sound became audible, and that not quite at once, but on the instant of the melancholy and ribald meeting between Mario's lips and the repulsive flesh which thrust itself forward for his caress. It was the sound of a laugh, from the *giovanotto* on our left. It broke into the dramatic suspense of the moment, coarse, mocking, and yet—or I must have been grossly mistaken—with an undertone of compassion for the poor bewildered, victimized creature. It had a faint ring of that *"Poveretto"* which Cipolla had declared was wasted on the wrong person, when he claimed the pity for his own.

The laugh still rang in the air when the recipient of the caress gave his whip a little swish, low down, close to his chair-leg, and Mario started up and flung himself back. He stood in that posture staring, his hands one over the other on those desecrated lips. Then he beat his temples with his clenched fists, over and over; turned and staggered down the steps, while the audience applauded, and Cipolla sat there with his hands in his lap, his shoulders shaking. Once below, and even while in full retreat, Mario hurled himself round with legs flung wide apart; one arm flew up, and two flat shattering detonations crashed through applause and laughter.

There was instant silence. Even the dancers came to a full stop and stared about, struck dumb. Cipolla bounded from his seat. He stood with his arms spread out, slanting as though to ward everybody off, as though next moment he would cry out: "Stop! Keep back! Silence! What was that?" Then, in that instant, he sank back in his seat, his head rolling on his chest; in the next he had fallen sideways to the floor, where he lay motionless, a huddled heap of clothing, with limbs awry.

The commotion was indescribable. Ladies hid their faces, shuddering, on the breasts of their escorts. There were shouts for a doctor, for the police. People flung themselves on Mario in a mob, to disarm him, to take away the weapon that hung from his fingers—that small, dull-metal, scarcely pistol-shaped tool with hardly any barrel—in how strange and unexpected a direction had fate levelled it!

And now—now finally, at last—we took the children and led them towards the exit, past the pair of *carabinieri* just entering. Was that the end, they wanted to know, that they might go in peace? Yes, we assured them, that was the end. An end of horror, a fatal end. And yet a liberation—for I could not, and I cannot, but find it so!

Sherwood Anderson (1876–1941)

When Henry James, commenting on Turgenev's *The Hunting Sketches,* said that they "give the impression of life itself, and not of an arrangement," he could as easily have been speaking of Sherwood Anderson. Maxwell Geismar, Anderson's editor, wrote on the "apparent formlessness" of his stories, of "the sudden, shifting associations of thought and feeling which come, apparently at the writer's whim, and actually by the most meticulous use of detail." Each of those comments may serve as a guide to the special quality of Anderson's art. What we get is an arrangement, seemingly unarranged, of carefully selected, realistic detail (see Introduction, p. 23). Though he employs only a limited number of sensory brushstrokes in what may seem "artless," often fragmentary, clusters, Anderson nevertheless conveys indelibly the impression made upon his backward-looking narrator by the experiences he observes. Those impressions, those observations, become ours.

All of Anderson's best writing deals with the soil, sidewalks, and people of small-town Midwestern America. He was himself born in Camden, Ohio, and, much like the narrators of some of his stories, spent his youth drifting with his family from town to town. Following an irregular, interrupted education, he went to Chicago as a laborer. Then came brief service in the Spanish-American War, after which he returned to the Midwest, first as an advertising writer, then as a paint manufacturer in Elyria, Ohio. Though he prospered financially, he (by his own account) felt choked spiritually, and in 1913 he returned to Chicago, walking out on both his business and the first of what were to be four wives. The so-called Chicago "little renaissance" brought him in touch with a number of newly emerging voices in American letters, notably Dreiser, Lindsay, Masters, and Sandburg (nearly all of whom, like Anderson, experienced their first literary achievement and acclaim in middle age). With their encouragement—however expert—he managed to publish three utterly unsuccessful novels. But in the year 1919, when Anderson was forty-three, there appeared *Winesburg, Ohio,* a group of interrelated stories that explore with compassion and psychological acuity the loneliness and frustration of small-town lives. The book won him international recognition and is usually regarded as his masterpiece, though many readers argue that certain stories in *The Triumph of the Egg* (1921) excel anything in the earlier collection. In his later years he edited newspapers in Virginia and wrote articles about American industrial conditions. He died in Panama in 1941.

"Fictions are for finding things out," writes Frank Kermode (see p. 2). Anderson's stories are full of this search. The narrator of one of his stories, puzzled by experience, tentatively concludes: "One in time gets to know many unexplainable things." The narrator of "I Want to Know Why" asks the question of the title. Translated, the question means: Why must ideals be tarnished? Why must innocence be lost? Why must knowledge lead to disillusionment? For that is the course experience seems to take in Anderson's stories, and their poignancy draws from that American setting where an ideal of innocence could still be entertained. To the boy-narrator, everything and everybody connected with thoroughbred horses is clean and good, and his love is infectious: "Nothing smells better than coffee and manure and horses and niggers and bacon frying and pipes being smoked out of doors on a morning like that." But the white man proves unworthy of the horses. Why did he besmirch himself? The boy wants to know why, and it is up to the reader to tell him—if he or she can.

I Want to Know Why

We got up at four in the morning, that first day in the east. On the evening before we had climbed off a freight train at the edge of town, and with the true instinct of Kentucky boys had found our way across town and to the racetrack and the stables at once. Then we knew we were all right. Hanley Turner right away found a nigger we knew. It was Bildad Johnson who in the winter works at Ed Becker's livery barn in our home town, Beckersville. Bildad is a good cook as almost all our niggers are and of course he, like everyone in our part of Kentucky who is anyone at all, likes the horses. In the spring Bildad begins to scratch around. A nigger from our country can flatter and wheedle anyone into letting him do most anything he wants. Bildad wheedles the stable men and the trainers from the horse farms in our country around Lexington. The trainers come into town in the evening to stand around and talk and maybe get into a poker game. Bildad gets in with them. He is always doing little favors and telling about things to eat, chicken browned in a pan, and how is the best way to cook sweet potatoes and corn bread. It makes your mouth water to hear him.

When the racing season comes on and the horses go to the races and there is all the talk on the streets in the evenings about the new colts, and everyone says when they are going over to Lexington or to the spring meeting at Churchill Downs or to Latonia, and the horsemen that have been down to New Orleans or maybe at the winter meeting at Havana in Cuba come home to spend a week before they start out again, at such a time when everything talked about in Beckersville is just horses and nothing else and the outfits start out and horse racing is in every breath of air you breathe, Bildad shows up with a job as cook for some outfit. Often when I think about it, his always going all season to the races and working in the livery barn in the winter where horses are and where men like to come and talk about horses, I wish I was a nigger. It's a foolish thing to say, but that's the way I am about being around horses, just crazy. I can't help it.

Well, I must tell you about what we did and let you in on what I'm talking about. Four of us boys from Beckersville, all whites and sons of men who live in Beckersville regular, made up our minds we were going to the races, not just to Lexington or Louisville, I don't mean, but to the big eastern track we were always hearing our Beckersville men talk about, to Saratoga. We were all pretty young then. I was just turned fifteen and I was the oldest of the four. It was my scheme. I admit that and I talked the others into trying it. There was Hanley Turner and Henry Rieback and Tom Tumberton and myself. I had thirty-seven dollars I had earned during the winter working nights and Saturdays in Enoch Myer's grocery. Henry Rieback had eleven dollars and the others, Hanley and Tom, had only a dollar or two each. We fixed it all up and laid low until the Kentucky spring meetings were over and some of our men, the sportiest ones, the ones we envied the most, had cut out—then we cut out too.

I won't tell you the trouble we had beating our way on freights and all. We went through Cleveland and Buffalo and other cities and saw Niagara Falls. We bought things there, souvenirs and spoons and cards and shells with pictures of the falls on them for our sisters and mothers, but thought we had better not send any of the things home. We didn't want to put the folks on our trail and maybe be nabbed.

We got into Saratoga as I said at night and went to the track. Bildad fed us up. He showed us a place to sleep in hay over a shed and promised to keep still. Niggers are all right about things like that. They won't squeal on you. Often a white man you might meet, when you had run away from home like that, might appear to be all right and give

you a quarter or a half dollar or something, and then go right and give you away. White
men will do that, but not a nigger. You can trust them. They are squarer with kids. I
don't know why.

At the Saratoga meeting that year there were a lot of men from home. Dave
Williams and Arthur Mulford and Jerry Myers and others. Then there was a lot from
Louisville and Lexington Henry Rieback knew but I didn't. They were professional
gamblers and Henry Rieback's father is one too. He is what is called a sheet writer and
goes away most of the year to tracks. In the winter when he is home in Beckersville he
don't stay there much but goes away to cities and deals faro. He is a nice man and
generous, is always sending Henry presents, a bicycle and a gold watch and a boy scout
suit of clothes and things like that.

My own father is a lawyer. He's all right, but don't make much money and can't
buy me things and anyway I'm getting so old now I don't expect it. He never said
nothing to me against Henry, but Hanley Turner and Tom Tumberton's fathers did.
They said to their boys that money so come by is no good and they didn't want their
boys brought up to hear gamblers' talk and be thinking about such things and maybe
embrace them.

That's all right and I guess the men know what they are talking about, but I don't
see what it's got to do with Henry or with horses either. That's what I'm writing this
story about. I'm puzzled. I'm getting to be a man and want to think straight and be
O.K., and there's something I saw at the race meeting at the eastern track I can't figure
out.

I can't help it, I'm crazy about thoroughbred horses. I've always been that way.
When I was ten years old and saw I was growing to be big and couldn't be a rider I was
so sorry I nearly died. Harry Hellinfinger in Beckersville, whose father is Postmaster, is
grown up and too lazy to work, but likes to stand around in the street and get up jokes on
boys like sending them to a hardware store for a gimlet to bore square holes and other
jokes like that. He played one on me. He told me that if I would eat a half a cigar I would
be stunted and not grow any more and maybe could be a rider. I did it. When father
wasn't looking I took a cigar out of his pocket and gagged it down some way. It made me
awful sick and the doctor had to be sent for, and then it did no good. I kept right on
growing. It was a joke. When I told what I had done and why most fathers would have
whipped me but mine didn't.

Well, I didn't get stunted and didn't die. It serves Harry Hellinfinger right. Then I
made up my mind I would like to be a stable boy, but had to give that up too. Mostly
niggers do that work and I knew father wouldn't let me go into it. No use to ask him.

If you've never been crazy about thoroughbreds it's because you've never been
around where they are much and don't know any better. They're beautiful. There isn't
anything so lovely and clean and full of spunk and honest and everything as some
race horses. On the big horse farms that are all around our town Beckersville there are
tracks and the horses run in the early morning. More than a thousand times I've got out
of bed before daylight and walked two or three miles to the tracks. Mother wouldn't of
let me go but father always says, "Let him alone." So I got some bread out of the bread
box and some butter and jam, gobbled it and lit out.

At the tracks you sit on the fence with men, whites and niggers, and they chew
tobacco and talk, and then the colts are brought out. It's early and the grass is covered
with shiny dew and in another field a man is plowing and they are frying things in a shed
where the track niggers sleep, and you know how a nigger can giggle and laugh and say
things that make you laugh. A white man can't do it and some niggers can't but a track
nigger can every time.

And so the colts are brought out and some are just galloped by stable boys, but almost every morning on a big track owned by a rich man who lives maybe in New York, there are always, nearly every morning, a few colts and some of the old race horses and geldings and mares that are cut loose.

It brings a lump up into my throat when a horse runs. I don't mean all horses but some. I can pick them nearly every time. It's in my blood like in the blood of race-track niggers and trainers. Even when they just go slop-jogging along with a little nigger on their backs I can tell a winner. If my throat hurts and it's hard for me to swallow, that's him. He'll run like Sam Hill when you let him out. If he don't win every time it'll be a wonder and because they've got him in a pocket behind another or he was pulled or got off bad at the post or something. If I wanted to be a gambler like Henry Rieback's father I could get rich. I know I could and Henry says so too. All I would have to do is to wait 'til that hurt comes when I see a horse and then bet every cent. That's what I would do if I wanted to be a gambler, but I don't.

When you're at the tracks in the morning—not the race tracks but the training tracks around Beckersville—you don't see a horse, the kind I've been talking about, very often, but it's nice anyway. Any thoroughbred, that is sired right and out of a good mare and trained by a man that knows how, can run. If he couldn't what would he be there for and not pulling a plow?

Well, out of the stables they come and the boys are on their backs and it's lovely to be there. You hunch down on top of the fence and itch inside you. Over in the sheds the niggers giggle and sing. Bacon is being fried and coffee made. Everything smells lovely. Nothing smells better than coffee and manure and horses and niggers and bacon frying and pipes being smoked out of doors on a morning like that. It just gets you, that's what it does.

But about Saratoga. We was there six days and not a soul from home seen us and everything came off just as we wanted it to, fine weather and horses and races and all. We beat our way home and Bildad gave us a basket with fried chicken and bread and other eatables in, and I had eighteen dollars when we got back to Beckersville. Mother jawed and cried but Pop didn't say much. I told everything we done except one thing. I did and saw that alone. That's what I'm writing about. It got me upset. I think about it at night. Here it is.

At Saratoga we laid up nights in the hay in the shed Bildad had showed us and ate with the niggers early and at night when the race people had all gone away. The men from home stayed mostly in the grandstand and betting field, and didn't come out around the places where the horses are kept except to the paddocks just before a race when the horses are saddled. At Saratoga they don't have paddocks under an open shed as at Lexington and Churchill Downs and other tracks down in our country, but saddle the horses right out in an open place under trees on a lawn as smooth and nice as Banker Bohon's front yard here in Beckersville. It's lovely. The horses are sweaty and nervous and shine and the men come out and smoke cigars and look at them and the trainers are there and the owners, and your heart thumps so you can hardly breathe.

Then the bugle blows for post and the boys that ride come running out with their silk clothes on and you run to get a place by the fence with the niggers.

I always am wanting to be a trainer or owner, and at the risk of being seen and caught and sent home I went to the paddocks before every race. The other boys didn't but I did.

We got to Saratoga on a Friday and on Wednesday the next week the big Mullford Handicap was to be run. Middlestride was in it and Sunstreak. The weather was fine and the track fast. I couldn't sleep the night before.

What had happened was that both these horses are the kind it makes my throat hurt to see. Middlestride is long and looks awkward and is a gelding. He belongs to Joe Thompson, a little owner from home who only has a half dozen horses. The Mullford Handicap is for a mile and Middlestride can't untrack fast. He goes away slow and is always way back at the half, then he begins to run and if the race is a mile and a quarter he'll just eat up everything and get there.

Sunstreak is different. He is a stallion and nervous and belongs on the biggest farm we've got in our country, the Van Riddle place that belongs to Mr. Van Riddle of New York. Sunstreak is like a girl you think about sometimes but never see. He is hard all over and lovely too. When you look at his head you want to kiss him. He is trained by Jerry Tillford who knows me and has been good to me lots of times, lets me walk into a horse's stall to look at him close and other things. There isn't anything as sweet as that horse. He stands at the post quiet and not letting on, but he is just burning up inside. Then when the barrier goes up he is off like his name, Sunstreak. It makes you ache to see him. It hurts you. He just lays down and runs like a bird dog. There can't anything I ever see run like him except Middlestride when he gets untracked and stretches himself.

Gee! I ached to see that race and those two horses run, ached and dreaded it too. I didn't want to see either of our horses beaten. We had never sent a pair like that to the races before. Old men in Beckersville said so and the niggers said so. It was a fact.

Before the race I went over to the paddocks to see. I looked a last look at Middlestride, who isn't such a much standing in a paddock that way, then I went to see Sunstreak.

It was his day. I knew when I see him. I forgot all about being seen myself and walked right up. All the men from Beckersville were there and no one noticed me except Jerry Tillford. He saw me and something happened. I'll tell you about that.

I was standing looking at that horse and aching. In some way, I can't tell how, I knew just how Sunstreak felt inside. He was quiet and letting the niggers rub his legs and Mr. Van Riddle himself put the saddle on, but he was just a raging torrent inside. He was like the water in the river at Niagara Falls just before it goes plunk down. That horse wasn't thinking about running. He don't have to think about that. He was just thinking about holding himself back 'til the time for the running came. I knew that. I could just in a way see right inside him. He was going to do some awful running and I knew it. He wasn't bragging or letting on much or prancing or making a fuss, but just waiting. I knew it and Jerry Tillford his trainer knew. I looked up and then that man and I looked into each other's eyes. Something happened to me. I guess I loved the man as much as I did the horse because he knew what I knew. Seemed to me there wasn't anything in the world but that man and the horse and me. I cried and Jerry Tillford had a shine in his eyes. Then I came away to the fence to wait for the race. The horse was better than me, more steadier, and now I know better than Jerry. He was the quietest and he had to do the running.

Sunstreak ran first of course and he busted the world's record for a mile. I've seen that if I never see anything more. Everything came out just as I expected. Middlestride got left at the post and was way back and closed up to be second, just as I knew he would. He'll get a world's record too some day. They can't skin the Beckersville country on horses.

I watched the race calm because I knew what would happen. I was sure. Hanley Turner and Henry Rieback and Tom Tumberton were all more excited than me.

A funny thing had happened to me. I was thinking about Jerry Tillford the trainer and how happy he was all through the race. I liked him that afternoon even more than I ever liked my own father. I almost forgot the horses thinking that way about him. It was because of what I had seen in his eyes as he stood in the paddocks beside Sunstreak before the race started. I knew he had been watching and working with Sunstreak since the horse was a baby colt, had taught him to run and be patient and when to let himself out and not to quit, never. I knew that for him it was like a mother seeing her child do something brave or wonderful. It was the first time I ever felt for a man like that.

After the race that night I cut out from Tom and Hanley and Henry. I wanted to be by myself and I wanted to be near Jerry Tillford if I could work it. Here is what happened.

The track in Saratoga is near the edge of town. It is all polished up and trees around, the evergreen kind, and grass and everything painted and nice. If you go past the track you get to a hard road made of asphalt for automobiles, and if you go along this for a few miles there is a road turns off to a little rummy-looking farmhouse set in a yard.

That night after the race I went along that road because I had seen Jerry and some other men go that way in an automobile. I didn't expect to find them. I walked for a ways and then sat down by a fence to think. It was the direction they went in. I wanted to be as near Jerry as I could. I felt close to him. Pretty soon I went up the side road—I don't know why—and came to the rummy farmhouse. I was just lonesome to see Jerry, like wanting to see your father at night when you are a young kid. Just then an automobile came along and turned in. Jerry was in it and Henry Rieback's father, and Arthur Bedford from home, and Dave Williams and two other men I didn't know. They got out of the car and went into the house, all but Henry Rieback's father who quarreled with them and said he wouldn't go. It was only about nine o'clock, but they were all drunk and the rummy looking farmhouse was a place for bad women to stay in. That's what it was. I crept up along a fence and looked through a window and saw.

It's what give me the fantods. I can't make it out. The women in the house were all ugly mean-looking women, not nice to look at or be near. They were homely too, except one who was tall and looked a little like the gelding Middlestride, but not clean like him, but with a hard ugly mouth. She had red hair. I saw everything plain. I got up by an old rosebush by an open window and looked. The women had on loose dresses and sat around in chairs. The men came in and some sat on the women's laps. The place smelled rotten and there was rotten talk, the kind a kid hears around a livery stable in a town like Beckersville in the winter but don't ever expect to hear talked when there are women around. It was rotten. A nigger wouldn't go into such a place.

I looked at Jerry Tillford. I've told you how I had been feeling about him on account of his knowing what was going on inside of Sunstreak in the minute before he went to the post for the race in which he made a world's record.

Jerry bragged in that bad woman house as I know Sunstreak wouldn't never have bragged. He said that he made that horse, that it was him that won the race and made the record. He lied and bragged like a fool. I never heard such silly talk.

And then, what do you suppose he did! He looked at the woman in there, the one that was lean and hard-mouthed and looked a little like the gelding Middlestride, but not clean like him, and his eyes began to shine just as they did when he looked at me and at Sunstreak in the paddocks at the track in the afternoon. I stood there by the window—gee!—but I wished I hadn't gone away from the tracks, but had stayed with the boys and the niggers and the horses. The tall rotten looking woman was between us just as Sunstreak was in the paddocks in the afternoon.

Then, all of a sudden, I began to hate that man. I wanted to scream and rush in the room and kill him. I never had such a feeling before. I was so mad clean through that I cried and my fists were doubled up so my finger nails cut my hands.

And Jerry's eyes kept shining and he waved back and forth, and then he went and kissed that woman and I crept away and went back to the tracks and to bed and didn't sleep hardly any, and then next day I got the other kids to start home with me and never told them anything I seen.

I been thinking about it ever since. I can't make it out. Spring has come again and I'm nearly sixteen and go to the tracks mornings same as always, and I see Sunstreak and Middlestride and a new colt named Strident I'll bet will lay them all out, but no one thinks so but me and two or three niggers.

But things are different. At the tracks the air don't taste as good or smell as good. It's because a man like Jerry Tillford, who knows what he does, could see a horse like Sunstreak run, and kiss a woman like that the same day. I can't make it out. Darn him, what did he want to do like that for? I keep thinking about it and it spoils looking at horses and smelling things and hearing niggers laugh and everything. Sometimes I'm so mad about it I want to fight someone. It gives me the fantods. What did he do it for? I want to know why.

E. M. Forster (1879–1970)

E. M. Forster, a fringe member of the so-called "Bloomsbury Group," is best known for his novels, *Where Angels Fear to Tread* (1905), *The Longest Journey* (1907), *A Room With a View* (1908), *Howards End* (1910), and *A Passage to India* (1924), but he has also had a tremendous influence—particularly on a post-World War II generation—with his short stories and his two volumes of essays, *Abinger Harvest* (1936) and *Two Cheers for Democracy* (1951). He is honored not only as a fiction writer but as a liberal humanist, as a believer in "personal relations" in an age of bigness, monopoly, and totalitarianism, where the individual counts for less and less. One of his radical statements in his essay "What I Believe" is: "If I had to choose between betraying my country and betraying my friend, I hope I should have the guts to betray my country." He believes in democracy because it allows free speech, but he does not idealize it—hence, he gives it only two cheers, not three. Chief honors go to the individual and to art, which respect the individual. Actually, Forster believes in aristocracy rather than the common man, but it is an aristocracy of character rather than of class, an aristocracy of "the sensitive, the considerate, and the plucky."

Since his death in 1970, two important posthumous volumes have appeared: *Maurice* (written in 1913 but suppressed because of its homosexual theme) and *The Life To Come* (1972), containing mainly hitherto unpublished stories. Forster's earlier stories, appearing in *The Celestial Omnibus* (1911) and *The Eternal Moment* (1928), were all fantasies, full of—in his words—"all beings who inhabit the lower air, the shallow water, and the smaller hills, all Fauns and Dryads and slips of the memory, all verbal coincidences, Pans and puns. . . ." But light as these stories are, they are also exercises in criticism, delivering comeuppance to those stuffy guardians of Late Victorian conventions that Forster suffered under as a boy. The unpublished stories do the same, but they go further, dealing in large part with that forbidden subject—homosexuality—which throughout most of Forster's life had to be carefully hidden. Inferior, by and large, to the published stories, they all have the Forster touch, the casual, witty manner that, upon close examination, is a carrier of great wisdom and serious moral purpose.

Forster called "Dr Woolacott," written in 1927, "the best thing I've done and . . . unlike anyone else's work." To the reader who knows *Howards End* or *A Passage to India* or even some of his earlier stories, that is bound to seem an extravagant comment; what is behind it is the fact that this story deals with homosexuality. To deal with this forbidden subject presented great difficulties for Forster, and his homosexual stories appeared only posthumously, two years after his death. Of the lot, this story, with the possible exception of "The Other Boat," is by far the most mature and interesting.

In most of Forster's stories there is an ego-character who, more or less, represents Forster himself; he is invariably an upper-middle-class lad, repressed by parents and guardians, who seeks freedom—class freedom as well as sexual freedom. But to "overleap" class—as Maurice tries to do—was not easy, and it is interesting that Forster's privileged ego-character achieves sexual love, as opposed to "spiritual" relationships, only with members of the lower classes. Like the other stories, this is a story of repression and escape from repression; but here Clesant does not escape the consequences of his love, he dies for it. Although Clesant's lover is a fantasy—there was no one in the gun-room just as there was no one in his bed—at least he dies embracing his fantasy rather than living the death-in-life of Dr Woolacott's sterile regimen. Forster, who again and again used the New Testament as a point of reference, would doubtless agree that the story could be read as a kind of secular illustration of John 12:25: "He that loveth his life shall lose it; and he that hateth his life in this world shall keep it unto life eternal."

Dr Woolacott

For this, from stiller seats we came
Cymbeline v. iv

1

People, several of them, crossing the park. . . .

Clesant said to himself, "There is no reason I should not live for years now that I have given up the violin," and leant back with the knowledge that he had faced a fact. From where he lay, he could see a little of the garden and a little of the park, a little of the fields and the river, and hear a little of the tennis; a little of everything was what was good for him, and what Dr Woolacott had prescribed. Every few weeks he must expect a relapse, and he would never be able to travel or marry or manage the estates, still there, he didn't want to much, he didn't much want to do anything. An electric bell connected him with the house, the strong beautiful slightly alarming house where his father had died, still there, not so very alarming, not so bad lying out in the tepid sun and watching the colourless shapeless country people. . . .

No, there was no reason he should not live for years.

"In 1990, why even 2000 is possible, I am young," he thought. Then he frowned, for Dr Woolacott was bound to be dead by 2000, and the treatment might not be continued intelligently. The anxiety made his head ache, the trees and grass turned black or crimson, and he nearly rang his bell. Soothed by the advancing figures, he desisted. Looking for mushrooms apparently, they soothed him because of their inadequacy. No mushrooms grew in the park. He felt friendly and called out in his gentle voice, "Come here."

"Oh aye," came the answer.

"I'm the squire, I want you a moment, it's all right."

Set in motion, the answerer climbed over the park fence. Clesant had not intended him to do this, and fearful of being bored said: "You'll find no mushrooms here, but they'll give you a drink or anything else you fancy up at the house."

"Sir, the squire, did you say?"

"Yes; I pass for the squire."

"The one who's sick?"

"Yes, that one."

"I'm sorry."

"Thank you, thanks," said the boy, pleased by the unexpected scrap of sympathy. "Sir . . ."

"All right, what is it?" he smiled encouragingly.

"Sick of what illness?"

Clesant hesitated. As a rule he resented that question, but this morning it pleased him, it was as if he too had been detected by friendly eyes zigzagging in search of a treasure which did not exist. He replied: "Of being myself perhaps! Well, what they call functional. Nothing organic. I can't possibly die, but my heart makes my nerves go wrong, my nerves my digestion, then my head aches, so I can't sleep, which affects my heart, and round we go again. However, I'm better this morning."

"When shall you be well?"

He gave the contemptuous laugh of the chronic invalid. "Well? That's a very different question. It depends. It depends on a good many things. On how carefully I live. I must avoid all excitement, I must never get tired, I mustn't be—" He was going to say "mustn't be intimate with people," but it was no use employing expressions which would be meaningless to a farm-worker, and such the man appeared to be, so he changed it to "I must do as Dr Woolacott tells me."

"Oh, Woolacott . . ."

"Of course you know him, everyone round here does, marvellous doctor."

"Yes, I know Woolacott."

Clesant looked up, intrigued by something positive in the tone of the voice.

"Woolacott, Woolacott, so I must be getting on." Not quite as he had come, he vaulted over the park palings, paused, repeated "Woolacott" and walked rapidly after his companions, who had almost disappeared.

A servant now answered the bell. It had failed to ring the first time, which would have been annoying had the visitor proved tedious. The little incident was over now, and nothing else disturbed the peace of the morning. The park, the garden, the sounds from the tennis, all reassumed their due proportions, but it seemed to Clesant that they were pleasanter and more significant than they had been, that the colours of the grass and the shapes of the trees had beauty, that the sun wandered with a purpose through the sky, that the little clouds, wafted by westerly airs, were moving against the course of doom and fate, and were inviting him to follow them.

2

Continuance of convalescence . . . tea in the gun-room. The gun-room, a grand place in the old squire's time, much energy had flowed through it, intellectual and bodily. Now the bookcases were locked, the trophies between them desolate, the tall shadow cupboard designed for fishing-rods and concealed in the wainscoting contained only medicine-bottles and air cushions. Still, it was Clesant's nearest approach to normality, for the rest of his household had tea in the gun-room too. There was innocuous talk as they flitted out and in, pursuing their affairs like birds, and troubling him only with the external glint of their plumage. He knew nothing about them, although they were his guardians and familiars; even their sex left no impression on his mind. Throned on the pedestal of a sofa, he heard them speak of their wishes and plans, and give one another to understand that they had passionate impulses, while he barricaded himself in the circle of his thoughts.

He was thinking about music.

Was it quite out of the question that he should take up the violin again? He felt better, the morning in the garden had started him upon a good road, a refreshing sleep had followed. Now a languorous yearning filled him, which might not the violin satisfy? The effect might be the contrary, the yearning might turn to pain, yet even pain seemed unlikely in this kindly house, this house which had not always been kindly, yet surely this afternoon it was accepting him.

A stranger entered his consciousness—a young man in good if somewhat provincial clothes, with a pleasant and resolute expression upon his face. People always were coming into the house on some business or other, and then going out of it. He stopped in the middle of the room, evidently a little shy. No one spoke to him for the reason that no one remained: they had all gone away while Clesant followed his meditations. Obliged to exert himself for a moment, Clesant said: "I'm sorry—I expect you're wanting one of the others."

He smiled and twiddled his cap.

"I'm afraid I mustn't entertain you myself. I'm something of an invalid, and this is my first day up. I suffer from one of those wretched functional troubles—fortunately nothing organic."

Smiling more broadly, he remarked: "Oh aye."

Clesant clutched at his heart, jumped up, sat down, burst out laughing. It was that farm-worker who had been crossing the park.

"Thought I'd surprise you, thought I'd give you a turn," he cried gaily. "I've come for that drink you promised."

Clesant couldn't speak for laughing, the whole room seemed to join in, it was a tremendous joke.

"I was around in my working-kit when you invited me this morning, so I thought after I'd washed myself up a bit and had a shave my proper course was to call and explain," he continued more seriously. There was something fresh and rough in his voice which caught at the boy's heart.

"But who on earth are you, who are you working for?"

"For you."

"Oh nonsense, don't be silly."

" 'Tisn't nonsense, I'm not silly, I'm one of your farm-hands. Rather an unusual one, if you like. Still, I've been working here for the last three months, ask your bailiff if I haven't. But I say—I've kept thinking about you—how are you?"

"Better—because I saw you this morning!"

"That's fine. Now you've seen me this afternoon you'll be well."

But this last remark was flippant, and the visitor through making it lost more than the ground he had gained. It reminded Clesant that he had been guilty of laughter and of rapid movement, and he replied in reproving tones: "To be well and to be better are very different. I'm afraid one can't get well from one's self. Excuse me if we don't talk any more. It's so bad for my heart." He closed his eyes. He opened them again immediately. He had had, during that instant of twilight, a curious and pleasurable sensation. However, there was the young man still over at the further side of the room. He was smiling. He was attractive—fresh as a daisy, strong as a horse. His shyness had gone.

"Thanks for that tea, a treat," he said, lighting a cigarette. "Now for who I am. I'm a farmer—or rather, going to be a farmer. I'm only an agricultural labourer now— exactly what you took me for this morning. I wasn't dressing up or posing with that broad talk. It's come natural to say 'Oh aye', especially when startled."

"Did I startle you?"

"Yes, you weren't in my mind."

"I thought you were looking for mushrooms."

"So I was. We all do when we're shifting across, and when there's a market we sell them. I've been living with that sort all the summer, your regular hands, temporaries like myself, tramps, sharing their work, thinking their thoughts when they have any." He paused. "I like them."

"Do they like you?"

"Oh well. . . ." He laughed, drew a ring off his finger, laid it on the palm of his hand, looked at it for a moment, put it on again. All his gestures were definite and a trifle unusual. "I've no pride anyway, nor any reason to have. I only have my health, and I didn't always have that. I've known what it is to be an invalid, though no one guesses it now." He looked across gently at Clesant. He seemed to say: "Come to me, and you shall be as happy as I am and as strong." He gave a short account of his life. He dealt in facts, very much so when they arrived—and the tale he unfolded was high-spirited and a trifle romantic here and there, but in no way remarkable. Aged twenty-two, he was the son of an engineer at Wolverhampton, his two brothers were also engineers, but he himself had always taken after his mother's family, and preferred country life. All his holidays on a farm. The war. After which he took up agriculture seriously, and went through a course at Cirencester. The course terminated last spring, he had done well, his people were about to invest money in him, but he himself felt "too scientific" after it all. He was determined to "get down into the manure" and feel people instead of thinking about them. "Later on it's too late." So off he went and roughed it, with a few decent clothes in a suitcase, and now and then, just for the fun of the thing, he took them out and dressed up. He described the estate, how decent the bailiff was, how sorry people seemed to be about the squire's illness, how he himself got a certain amount of time off, practically any evening. Extinguishing his cigarette, he put back what was left of it into his case for future use, laid a hand upon either knee, smiled.

There was a silence. Clesant could not think of anything to say, and began to tremble.

"Oh, my name—"

"Oh yes, of course, what's your name?"

"Let me write it down, my address too. Both my Wolverhampton address I'll give you, also where I'm lodging here, so if ever—got a pencil?"

"Yes."

"Don't get up."

He came over and sat on the sofa; his weight sent a tremor, the warmth and sweetness of his body began casting nets.

"And now we've no paper."

"Never mind," said Clesant, his heart beating violently.

"Talking's better, isn't it?"

"Yes."

"Or even not talking." His hand came nearer, his eyes danced round the room, which began to fill with a golden haze. He beckoned, and Clesant moved into his arms. Clesant had often been proud of his disease but never, never of his body, it had never occurred to him that he could provoke desire. The sudden revelation shattered him, he fell from his pedestal, but not alone, there was someone to cling to, broad shoulders, a sunburnt throat, lips that parted as they touched him to murmur—"And to hell with Woolacott."

Woolacott! He had completely forgotten the doctor's existence. Woolacott! The word crashed between them and exploded with a sober light, and he saw in the light of the years that had passed and would come how ridiculously he was behaving. To hell with Woolacott, indeed! What an idea! His charming new friend must be mad. He started, recoiled, and exclaimed: "What ever made you say that?"

The other did not reply. He looked rather foolish, and he too recoiled, and leant back in the opposite corner of the sofa, wiping his forehead. At last he said: "He's not a good doctor."

"Why, he's our family doctor, he's everyone's doctor round here!"

"I didn't mean to be rude—it slipped out. I just had to say it, it must have sounded curious."

"Oh, all right then," said the boy, willing enough to be mollified. But the radiance had passed and no effort of theirs could recall it.

The young man took out his unfinished cigarette, and raised it towards his lips. He was evidently a good deal worried. "Perhaps I'd better explain what I meant," he said.

"As you like, it doesn't matter."

"Got a match?"

"I'm afraid I haven't."

He went for one to the further side of the room, and sat down there again. Then he began: "I'm perfectly straight—I'm not trying to work in some friend of my own as your doctor. I only can't bear to think of this particular one coming to your house—this grand house—you so rich and important at the first sight and yet so awfully undefended and deceived." His voice faltered. "No, we won't talk it over. You're right. We've found each other, nothing else matters, it's a chance in a million we've found each other. I'd do anything for you, I'd die if I could for you, and there's this one thing you must do straight away for me: sack Woolacott."

"Tell me what you've got against him instead of talking sentimentally."

He hardened at once. "Sentimental, was I? All right, what I've got against Woolacott is that he never makes anyone well, which seems a defect in a doctor. I may be wrong."

"Yes, you're wrong," said Clesant; the mere repetition of the doctor's name was steadying him. "I've been under him for years."

"So I should think."

"Of course, I'm different, I'm not well, it's not natural for me to be well, I'm not a fair test, but other people—"

"Which other people?"

The names of Dr Woolacott's successful cases escaped him for the moment. They filled the centre of his mind, yet the moment he looked at them they disappeared.

"Quite so," said the other. "Woolacott," he kept on saying. "Woolacott! I've my eye on him. What's life after twenty-five? Impotent, blind, paralytic. What's life before it unless you're fit? Woolacott! Even the poor can't escape. The crying, the limping, the nagging, the medicine-bottles, the running sores—in the cottages too; kind Dr Woolacott won't let them stop. . . . You think I'm mad, but it's not your own thought you're thinking: Woolacott stuck it ready diseased into your mind."

Clesant sighed. He looked at the arms, now folded hard against each other, and longed to feel them around him. He had only to say, "Very well, I'll change doctors," and immediately. . . . But he never hesitated. Life until 1990 or 2000 retained the prior claim. "He keeps people alive," he persisted.

"Alive for what?"

"And there's always the marvellously unselfish work he did during the war."

"Did he not. I saw him doing it."

"Oh—it was in France you knew him?"

"Was it not. He was at his marvellously unselfish work night and day, and not a single man he touched ever got well. Woolacott dosed, Woolacott inoculated, Woolacott operated, Woolacot spoke a kind word even, and there they were and here they are."

"Were you in hospital yourself?"

"Oh aye, a shell. This hand—ring and all mashed and twisted, the head—hair's thick enough on it now, but brain stuck out then, so did my guts, I was a butcher's shop. A perfect case for Woolacott. Up he came with his 'Let me patch you up, do let me just patch you up,' oh, patience itself and all that, but I took his measure, I was only a boy then, but I refused."

"Can one refuse in a military hospital?"

"You can refuse anywhere."

"I hadn't realized you'd been wounded. Are you all right now?"

"Yes, thanks," and he resumed his grievances. The pleasant purple-gray suit, the big well-made shoes and soft white collar, all suggested a sensible country lad on his holiday, perhaps on courtship—farm-hand or farmer, countrified anyway. Yet with them went this wretched war-obsession, this desire to be revenged on a man who had never wronged him and must have forgotten his existence. "He is stronger than I am," he said angrily. "He can fight alone, I can't. My great disadvantage—never could fight alone. I counted on you to help, but you prefer to let me down, you pretended at first you'd join up with me—you're no good."

"Look here, you'll have to be going. So much talk is fatal for me, I simply mustn't get overtired. I've already far exceeded my allowance, and anyhow I can't enter into this sort of thing. Can you find your own way out, or shall I ring this bell?" For inserted into the fabric of the sofa was an electric bell.

"I'll go. I know where I'm not wanted. Don't you worry, you'll never see me again." And he slapped his cap onto his head and swung to the door. The normal life of the house entered the gun-room as he opened it—servants, inmates, talking in the passages, in the hall outside. It disconcerted him, he came back with a complete change of manner, and before ever he spoke Clesant had the sense of an incredible catastrophe moving up towards them both.

"Is there another way out?" he inquired anxiously.

"No, of course not. Go out the way you came in."

"I didn't tell you, but the fact is I'm in trouble."

"How dare you, I mustn't be upset, this is the kind of thing that makes me ill," he wailed.

"I can't meet those people—they've heard of something I did out in France."

"What was it?"

"I can't tell you."

In the sinister silence, Clesant's heart resumed its violent beating, and though the door was now closed voices could be heard through it. They were coming. The stranger rushed at the window and tried to climb out. He plunged about, soiling his freshness, and whimpering, "Hide me."

"There's nowhere."

"There must be . . ."

"Only that cupboard," said Clesant in a voice not his own.

"I can't find it," he gasped, thumping stupidly on the panelling.

"Do it for me. Open it. They're coming."

Clesant dragged himself up and across the floor, he opened the cupboard, and the man bundled in and hid, and that was how it ended.

Yes, that's how it ends, that's what comes of being kind to handsome strangers and wanting to touch them. Aware of all his weaknesses, Dr Woolacott had warned him against this one. He crawled back to the sofa, where a pain stabbed him through the heart and another struck between the eye. He was going to be ill.

The voices came nearer, and with the cunning of a sufferer he decided what he must do. He must betray his late friend and pretend to have trapped him on purpose in the cupboard, cry "Open it. . . ."

The voices entered. They spoke of the sounds of a violin. A violin had apparently been heard playing in the great house for the last half-hour, and no one could find out where it was. Playing all sorts of music, gay, grave and passionate. But never completing a theme. Always breaking off. A beautiful instrument. Yet so unsatisfying . . . leaving the hearers much sadder than if it had never performed. What was the use (someone asked) of music like that? Better silence absolute than this aimless disturbance of our peace. The discussion broke off, his distress had been observed, and like a familiar refrain rose up "Telephone, nurse, doctor . . ." Yes, it was coming again—the illness, merely functional, the heart had affected the nerves, the muscles, the brain. He groaned, shrieked, but love died last; as he writhed in convulsions he cried: "Don't go to the cupboard, no one's there."

So they went to it. And no one was there. It was as it had always been since his father's death—shallow, tidy, a few medicine-bottles on the upper shelf, a few cushions stored on the lower.

3

Collapse. . . . He fell back into the apparatus of decay without further disaster, and in a few hours any other machinery for life became unreal. It always was like this, increasingly like this, when he was ill. Discomfort and pain brought their compensation, because they were so superbly organized. His bedroom, the anteroom where the night-nurse sat, the bathroom and tiny kitchen, throbbed like a nerve in the corner of the great house, and elsewhere normal life proceeded, people pursued their avocations in channels which did not disturb him.

Delirium. . . . The nurse kept coming in, she performed medical incantations and took notes against the doctor's arrival. She did not make him better, he grew worse, but disease knows its harmonies as well as health, and through its soft advances now rang the promise, "You shall live to grow old."

"I did something wrong, tell me, what was it?" It made him happy to abase himself before his disease, nor was this colloquy their first.

"Intimacy," the disease replied.

"I remember. . . . Do not punish me this once, let me live and I will be careful. Oh, save me from him."

"No—from yourself. Not from him. He does not exist. He is an illusion, whom you created in the garden because you wanted to feel you were attractive."

"I know I am not attractive, I will never excite myself again, but he does exist, I think."

"No."

"He may be death, but he does exist."

"No. He never came into the gun-room. You only wished that he would. He never sat down on the sofa by your side and made love. You handed a pencil, but he never took it, you fell into his arms, but they were not there, it has all been a daydream of the kind forbidden. And when the others came in and opened the cupboard: your muscular and intelligent farm-hand, your saviour from Wolverhampton in his Sunday suit—was he there?"

"No, he was not," the boy sobbed.

"No, he was not," came an echo, "but perhaps I am here."

The disease began to crouch and gurgle. There was the sound of a struggle, a spewing sound, a fall. Clesant, not greatly frightened, sat up and peered into the chaos. The nightmare passed, he felt better. Something survived from it, an echo that said "Here, here." And, he not dissenting, bare feet seemed to walk to the little table by his side, and hollow, filled with the dark, a shell of nakedness bent towards him and sighed "Here."

Clesant declined to reply.

"Here is the end, unless you. . . ." Then silence. Then, as if emitted by a machine, the syllables "Oh aye."

Clesant, after thought, put out his hand and touched the bell.

"I put her to sleep as I passed her, this is my hour, I can do that much. . . ." He seemed to gather strength from any recognition of his presence, and to say, "Tell my story for me, explain how I got here, pour life into me and I shall live as before when our bodies touched." He sighed. "Come home with me now, perhaps it is a farm. I have just enough power. Come away with me for an evening to my earthly lodging, easily managed by a . . . the . . . such a visit would be love. Ah, that was the word—love—why they pursued me and still know I am in the house; love was the word they cannot endure, I have remembered it at last."

Then Clesant spoke, sighing in his turn. "I don't even know what is real, so how can I know what is love? Unless it is excitement, and of that I am afraid. Do not love me, whatever you are; at all events this is my life and no one shall disturb it; a little sleep followed by a little pain."

And his speech evoked strength. More powerfully the other answered now, giving instances and arguments, throwing into sentences the glow they had borne during daylight. Clesant was drawn into a struggle, but whether to reach or elude the hovering presence he did not know. There was always a barrier either way, always his own nature. He began calling for people to come, and the adversary, waxing lovely and powerful, struck them dead before they could waken and help. His household perished, the whole earth was thinning, one instant more, and he would be alone with his ghost—and then through the walls of the house he saw the lights of a car rushing across the park.

It was Dr Woolacott at last.

Instantly the spell broke, the dead revived, and went downstairs to receive life's universal lord; and he—he was left with a human being who had somehow trespassed and been caught, and blundered over the furniture in the dark, bruising his defenceless body, and whispering, "Hide me."

And Clesant took pity on him again, and lifted the clothes of the bed, and they hid.

Voices approached, a great company, Dr Woolacott leading his army. They touched, their limbs intertwined, they gripped and grew mad with delight, yet through it all sounded the tramp of that army.

"They are coming."

"They will part us."

"Clesant, shall I take you away from all this?"

"Have you still the power?"

"Yes, until Woolacott sees me."

"Oh, what is your name?"

"I have none."

"Where is your home?"

"Woolacott calls it the grave."

"Shall I be with you in it?"

"I can promise you that. We shall be together for ever and ever, we shall never be ill, and never grow old."

"Take me."

They entwined more closely, their lips touched never to part, and then something gashed him where life had concentrated, and Dr Woolacott, arriving too late, found him dead on the floor.

The doctor examined the room carefully. It presented its usual appearance, yet it reminded him of another place. Dimly, from France, came the vision of a hospital ward, dimly the sound of his own voice saying to a mutilated recruit, "Do let me patch you up, oh but you must just let me patch you up. . . ."

James Joyce (1882–1941)

After half a century of controversy, during which he was thought by turns to be obscene and obscure, James Joyce has achieved his place as one of the giants of the modern age. His output was small: two volumes of verse, a play, fifteen short stories, three novels, a few critical pieces. Yet he is unsurpassed in achievement, perhaps unmatched in influence upon the development of present-day fiction.

James Augustine Aloysius Joyce was born in Ireland in 1882 to a genteel family on the downward slope of respectability. The two great influences on him were the Catholic faith of his mother and the nationalism of his father. In 1912 he departed Ireland never to return, but he never wrote of anything else. And though he renounced his faith, he replied when asked if he had found a substitute, "I have lost my faith, I have not lost my mind."

His growth as an artist charted the course of twentieth-century fiction. *Dubliners* (1914), a collection of stories, was written in the tradition of naturalism. "My intention," he wrote his publisher,

> was to write a chapter of the moral history of my country and I chose Dublin for the scene because that city seemed to me the centre of paralysis. . . . I have written it for the most part in a style of scrupulous meanness and with the conviction that he is a very bold man who dares to alter in the present- ment, still more to deform, whatever he has seen and heard.

A Portrait of the Artist as a Young Man (1916) chronicles the early life of Stephen Dedalus. It is lyrical and impressionistic in its imagery. Notable is the growing complexity and sophistication of the language as Stephen matures in the book.

Ulysses (1922) covers a day, June 16, 1904, in the lives of Stephen Dedalus, Leopold Bloom, and Molly Bloom. The book is realistic, yet richly symbolic and lyrical. Katherine Mansfield said, "I can't get over the feeling of wet linoleum and unemptied pails and far worse horrors in the house of his mind." T. S. Eliot was more prophetic: "I hold this book to be the most important expression which the present age has found; it is a book to which we are all indebted, and from which none of us can escape."

Finnegans Wake (1939) is raucous and erudite, a coarse comedy and an ency- clopedia of religion, a descent into the unconscious and a history of civilization. For the casual reader, it may seem gibberish; for some critics, it is the highest achievement of the human imagination in our century.

Joyce was not accepted by a wide public during his lifetime. He supported his family by giving language lessons and doing office tasks. He died, nearly blind, in 1941.

Joyce's technique combines seemingly disparate elements: poetic mysticism and naturalism (see Glossary p. 603); pictorial exactness and deep concern for sound and cadence; a pervasive sympathy and a "scrupulous meanness," to use Joyce's term. By scrupulous meanness, Joyce apparently meant that his language would faithfully mirror his subject matter. He wrote that "he is a very bold man who dares alter in the presentment, still more to deform, whatever he has seen and heard."

In "A Painful Case," scrupulous meanness takes several forms. Joyce uses the passive voice ("A bookcase had been made. . . ." "The bed was clothed. . . ." "The books . . . were arranged. . . .") to underscore the absence of the human touch in Mr Duffy's life. The room is all hard surfaces, angularity, absence of color. Indeed, in referring to the protagonist always as "Mr," Joyce further establishes Duffy's emotional rigidity. But unlike most of the characters in *Dubliners,* Mr. Duffy comes to understand and regret that he is an "outcast from life's feast." The reader shares this moving epiphany (see p. 9).

A Painful Case

Mr James Duffy lived in Chapelizod because he wished to live as far as possible from the city of which he was a citizen and because he found all the other suburbs of Dublin mean, modern and pretentious. He lived in an old sombre house and from his windows he could look into the disused distillery or upwards along the shallow river on which Dublin is built. The lofty walls of his uncarpeted room were free from pictures. He had himself bought every article of furniture in the room: a black iron bedstead, an iron washstand, four cane chairs, a clothes-rack, a coal scuttle, a fender and irons and a square table on which lay a double desk. A bookcase had been made in an alcove by means of shelves of white wood. The bed was clothed with white bed-clothes and a black and scarlet rug covered the floor. A little hand-mirror hung above the washstand and during the day a white-shaded lamp stood as the sole ornament of the mantelpiece. The books on the white wooden shelves were arranged from below upwards according to bulk. A complete Wordsworth stood at one end of the lowest shelf and a copy of the *Maynooth Catechism,* sewn into the cloth cover of a notebook, stood at one end of the top shelf. Writing materials were always on the desk. In the desk lay a manuscript translation of Hauptmann's *Michael Kramer,* the stage directions of which were written in purple ink, and a little sheaf of papers held together by a brass pin. In these sheets a sentence was inscribed from time to time and, in an ironical moment, the headline of an advertisement for *Bile Beans* had been pasted on to the first sheet. On lifting the lid of the desk a faint fragrance escaped—the fragrance of new cedarwood pencils or of a bottle of gum or of an over-ripe apple which might have been left there and forgotten.

Mr Duffy abhorred anything which betokened physical or mental disorder. A mediæval doctor would have called him saturnine. His face, which carried the entire tale of his years, was of the brown tint of Dublin streets. On his long and rather large head grew dry black hair and a tawny moustache did not quite cover an unamiable mouth. His cheekbones also gave his face a harsh character; but there was no harshness in the eyes which, looking at the world from under their tawny eyebrows, gave the impression of a man ever alert to greet a redeeming instinct in others but often disappointed. He lived at a little distance from his body, regarding his own acts with doubtful side-glances. He had an odd autobiographical habit which led him to compose in his mind from time to time a short sentence about himself containing a subject in the third person and a predicate in the past tense. He never gave alms to beggars and walked firmly, carrying a stout hazel.

He had been for many years cashier of a private bank in Baggot Street. Every morning he came in from Chapelizod by tram. At midday he went to Dan Burke's and took his lunch—a bottle of lager beer and a small trayful of arrowroot biscuits. At four o'clock he was set free. He dined in an eating-house in George's Street where he felt himself safe from the society of Dublin's gilded youth and where there was a certain plain honesty in the bill of fare. His evenings were spent either before his landlady's piano or roaming about the outskirts of the city. His liking for Mozart's music brought him sometimes to an opera or a concert: these were the only dissipations of his life.

He had neither companions nor friends, church nor creed. He lived his spiritual life without any communion with others, visiting his relatives at Christmas and escorting them to the cemetery when they died. He performed these two social duties for old dignity' sake but conceded nothing further to the conventions which regulate the civic life. He allowed himself to think that in certain circumstances he would rob his bank but, as these circumstances never arose, his life rolled out evenly—an adventure-less tale.

One evening he found himself sitting beside two ladies in the Rotunda. The house, thinly peopled and silent, gave distressing prophecy of failure. The lady who sat next him looked round at the deserted house once or twice and then said:

—What a pity there is such a poor house to-night! It's so hard on people to have to sing to empty benches.

He took the remark as an invitation to talk. He was surprised that she seemed so little awkward. While they talked he tried to fix her permanently in his memory. When he learned that the young girl beside her was her daughter he judged her to be a year or so younger than himself. Her face, which must have been handsome, had remained intelligent. It was an oval face with strongly marked features. The eyes were very dark blue and steady. Their gaze began with a defiant note but was confused by what seemed a deliberate swoon of the pupil into the iris, revealing for an instant a temperament of great sensibility. The pupil reasserted itself quickly, this half-disclosed nature fell again under the reign of prudence, and her astrakhan jacket, moulding a bosom of a certain fulness, struck the note of defiance more definitely.

He met her again a few weeks afterwards at a concert in Earlsfort Terrace and seized the moments when her daughter's attention was diverted to become intimate. She alluded once or twice to her husband but her tone was not such as to make the allusion a warning. Her name was Mrs Sinico. Her husband's great-great-grandfather had come from Leghorn. Her husband was captain of a mercantile boat plying between Dublin and Holland; and they had one child.

Meeting her a third time by accident he found courage to make an appointment. She came. This was the first of many meetings; they met always in the evening and chose the most quiet quarters for their walks together. Mr Duffy, however, had a distaste for underhand ways and, finding that they were compelled to meet stealthily, he forced her to ask him to her house. Captain Sinico encouraged his visits, thinking that his daughter's hand was in question. He had dismissed his wife so sincerely from his gallery of pleasures that he did not suspect that anyone else would take an interest in her. As the husband was often away and the daughter out giving music lessons Mr Duffy had many opportunities of enjoying the lady's society. Neither he nor she had had any such adventure before and neither was conscious of any incongruity. Little by little he entangled his thoughts with hers. He lent her books, provided her with ideas, shared his intellectual life with her. She listened to all.

Sometimes in return for his theories she gave out some fact of her own life. With almost maternal solicitude she urged him to let his nature open to the full; she became his confessor. He told her that for some time he had assisted at the meetings of an Irish Socialist Party where he had felt himself a unique figure amidst a score of sober work-men in a garret lit by an inefficient oil-lamp. When the party had divided into three sections, each under its own leader and in its own garret, he had discontinued his attendances. The workmen's discussions, he said, were too timorous; the interest they took in the question of wages was inordinate. He felt that they were hard-featured realists and that they resented an exactitude which was the product of a leisure not within their reach. No social revolution, he told her, would be likely to strike Dublin for some centuries.

She asked him why did he not write out his thoughts. For what, he asked her, with careful scorn. To compete with phrasemongers, incapable of thinking consecutively for sixty seconds? To submit himself to the criticisms of an obtuse middle class which entrusted its morality to policemen and its fine arts to impresarios?

He went often to her little cottage outside Dublin; often they spent their evenings alone. Little by little, as their thoughts entangled, they spoke of subjects less remote. Her companionship was like a warm soil about an exotic. Many times she allowed the dark to fall upon them, refraining from lighting the lamp. The dark discreet room, their isolation, the music that still vibrated in their ears united them. This union exalted him, wore away the rough edges of his character, emotionalised his mental life. Sometimes he caught himself listening to the sound of his own voice. He thought that in her eyes he would ascend to an angelical stature; and, as he attached the fervent nature of his companion more and more closely to him, he heard the strange impersonal voice which he recognised as his own, insisting on the soul's incurable loneliness. We cannot give ourselves, it said: we are our own. The end of these discourses was that one night during which she had shown every sign of unusual excitement, Mrs Sinico caught up his hand passionately and pressed it to her cheek.

Mr Duffy was very much surprised. Her interpretation of his words disillusioned him. He did not visit her for a week; then he wrote to her asking her to meet him. As he did not wish their last interview to be troubled by the influence of their ruined confessional they met in a little cakeshop near the Parkgate. It was cold autumn weather but in spite of the cold they wandered up and down the roads of the Park for nearly three hours. They agreed to break off their intercourse: every bond, he said, is a bond to sorrow. When they came out of the Park they walked in silence towards the tram; but here she began to tremble so violently that, fearing another collapse on her part, he bade her good-bye quickly and left her. A few days later he received a parcel containing his books and music.

Four years passed. Mr Duffy returned to his even way of life. His room still bore witness of the orderliness of his mind. Some new pieces of music encumbered the music-stand in the lower room and on his shelves stood two volumes by Nietzsche: *Thus Spake Zarathustra* and *The Gay Science*. He wrote seldom in the sheaf of papers which lay in his desk. One of his sentences, written two months after his last interview with Mrs Sinico, read: Love between man and man is impossible because there must not be sexual intercourse and friendship between man and woman is impossible because there must be sexual intercourse. He kept away from concerts lest he should meet her. His father died; the junior partner of the bank retired. And still every morning he went into the city by tram and every evening walked home from the city after having dined moderately in George's Street and read the evening paper for dessert.

One evening as he was about to put a morsel of corned beef and cabbage into his mouth his hand stopped. His eyes fixed themselves on a paragraph in the evening paper which he had propped against the water-carafe. He replaced the morsel of food on his plate and read the paragraph attentively. Then he drank a glass of water, pushed his plate to one side, doubled the paper down before him between his elbows and read the paragraph over and over again. The cabbage began to deposit a cold white grease on his plate. The girl came over to him to ask was his dinner not properly cooked. He said it was very good and ate a few mouthfuls of it with difficulty. Then he paid his bill and went out.

He walked along quickly through the November twilight, his stout hazel stick striking the ground regularly, the fringe of the buff *Mail* peeping out of a side-pocket of his tight reefer over-coat. On the lonely road which leads from the Parkgate to Chapelizod he slackened his pace. His stick struck the ground less emphatically and his breath, issuing irregularly, almost with a sighing sound, condensed in the wintry air. When he reached his house he went up at once to his bedroom and, taking the paper from his pocket, read the paragraph again by the failing light of the window. He read it not aloud, but moving his lips as a priest does when he reads the prayers *Secreto*. This was the paragraph:

DEATH OF A LADY AT SYDNEY PARADE
A Painful Case

To-day at the City of Dublin Hospital the Deputy Coroner (in the absence of Mr Leverett) held an inquest on the body of Mrs Emily Sinico, aged forty-three years, who was killed at Sydney Parade station yesterday evening. The evidence showed that the deceased lady, while attempting to cross the line, was knocked down by the engine of the ten o'clock slow train from Kingstown, thereby sustaining injuries of the head and right side which led to her death.

James Lennon, driver of the engine, stated that he had been in the employment of the railway company for fifteen years. On hearing the guard's whistle he set the train in motion and a second or two afterwards brought it to rest in response to loud cries. The train was going slowly.

P. Dunne, railway porter, stated that as the train was about to start he observed a woman attempting to cross the lines. He ran towards her and shouted but, before he could reach her, she was caught by the buffer of the engine and fell to the ground.

A juror—You saw the lady fall?

Witness—Yes.

Police Sergeant Croly deposed that when he arrived he found the deceased lying on the platform apparently dead. He had the body taken to the waiting-room pending the arrival of the ambulance.

Constable 57E corroborated.

Dr Halpin, assistant house surgeon of the City of Dublin Hospital, stated that the deceased had two lower ribs fractured and had sustained severe contusions of the right shoulder. The right side of the head had been injured in the fall. The injuries were not sufficient to have caused death in a normal person. Death, in his opinion, had been probably due to shock and sudden failure of the heart's action.

Mr H. B. Patterson Finlay, on behalf of the railway company, expressed his deep regret at the accident. The company had always taken every precaution to prevent people crossing the lines except by the bridges, both by placing notices in every station and by the use of patent spring gates at level crossings. The deceased had been in the habit of crossing the lines late at night from platform to platform and, in view of certain other circumstances of the case, he did not think the railway officials were to blame.

Captain Sinico, of Leoville, Sydney Parade, husband of the deceased, also gave evidence. He stated that the deceased was his wife. He was not in Dublin at the time of the accident as he had arrived only that morning from Rotterdam. They had been married for twenty-two years and had lived happily until about two years ago when his wife began to be rather intemperate in her habits.

Miss Mary Sinico said that of late her mother had been in the habit of going out at night to buy spirits. She, witness, had often tried to reason with her mother and had induced her to join a league. She was not at home until an hour after the accident.

The jury returned a verdict in accordance with the medical evidence and exonerated Lennon from all blame.

The Deputy Coroner said it was a most painful case, and expressed great sympathy with Captain Sinico and his daughter. He urged on the railway company to take strong measures to prevent the possibility of similar accidents in the future. No blame attached to anyone.

Mr Duffy raised his eyes from the paper and gazed out of his window on the cheerless evening landscape. The river lay quiet beside the empty distillery and from time to time a light appeared in some house on the Lucan road. What an end! The whole narrative of her death revolted him and it revolted him to think that he had ever spoken to her of what he held sacred. The threadbare phrases, the inane expressions of sympathy, the cautious words of a reporter won over to conceal the details of a commonplace vulgar death attacked his stomach. Not merely had she degraded herself; she had degraded him. He saw the squalid tract of her vice, miserable and malodorous. His soul's companion! He thought of the hobbling wretches whom he had seen carrying cans and bottles to be filled by the barman. Just God, what an end! Evidently she had been unfit to live, without any strength of purpose, an easy prey to habits, one of the wrecks on which civilisation has been reared. But that she could have sunk so low! Was it possible he had deceived himself so utterly about her? He remembered her outburst of that night and interpreted it in a harsher sense than he had ever done. He had no difficulty now in approving of the course he had taken.

As the light failed and his memory began to wander he thought her hand touched his. The shock which had first attacked his stomach was now attacking his nerves. He put on his overcoat and hat quickly and went out. The cold air met him on the threshold; it crept into the sleeves of his coat. When he came to the public-house at Chapelizod Bridge he went in and ordered a hot punch.

The proprietor served him obsequiously but did not venture to talk. There were five or six working-men in the shop discussing the value of a gentleman's estate in County Kildare. They drank at intervals from their huge pint tumblers and smoked, spitting often on the floor and sometimes dragging the sawdust over their spits with their heavy boots. Mr Duffy sat on his stool and gazed at them, without seeing or hearing them. After a while they went out and he called for another punch. He sat a long time over it. The shop was very quiet. The proprietor sprawled on the counter reading the *Herald* and yawning. Now and again a tram was heard swishing along the lonely road outside.

As he sat there, living over his life with her and evoking alternately the two images in which he now conceived her, he realised that she was dead, that she had ceased to exist, that she had become a memory. He began to feel ill at ease. He asked himself what else could he have done. He could not have carried on a comedy of deception with her; he could not have lived with her openly. He had done what seemed to him best. How was he to blame? Now that she was gone he understood how lonely her life must have been, sitting night after night alone in that room. His life would be lonely too until he, too, died, ceased to exist, became a memory—if anyone remembered him.

It was after nine o'clock when he left the shop. The night was cold and gloomy. He entered the Park by the first gate and walked along under the gaunt trees. He walked through the bleak alleys where they had walked four years before. She seemed to be near him in the darkness. At moments he seemed to feel her voice touch his ear, her hand touch his. He stood still to listen. Why had he withheld life from her? Why had he sentenced her to death? He felt his moral nature falling to pieces.

When he gained the crest of the Magazine Hill he halted and looked along the river towards Dublin, the lights of which burned redly and hospitably in the cold night. He looked down the slope and, at the base, in the shadow of the wall of the Park, he saw some human figures lying. Those venal and furtive loves filled him with despair. He gnawed the rectitude of his life; he felt that he had been outcast from life's feast. One human being had seemed to love him and he had denied her life and happiness: he had sentenced her to ignominy, a death of shame. He knew that the prostrate creatures down by the wall were watching him and wished him gone. No one wanted him; he was outcast from life's feast. He turned his eyes to the grey gleaming river, winding along towards Dublin. Beyond the river he saw a goods train winding out of Kingsbridge station, like a worm with a fiery head winding through the darkness, obstinately and laboriously. It passed slowly out of sight; but still he heard in his ears the laborious drone of the engine reiterating the syllables of her name.

He turned back the way he had come, the rhythm of the engine pounding in his ears. He began to doubt the reality of what memory told him. He halted under a tree and allowed the rhythm to die away. He could not feel her near him in the darkness nor her voice touch his ear. He waited for some minutes listening. He could hear nothing: the night was perfectly silent. He listened again: perfectly silent. He felt that he was alone.

Virginia Woolf (1882–1941)

Virginia Woolf, like E. M. Forster a member of the so-called "Bloomsbury Group," began her serious career as a writer with the appearance in 1915 of her first novel, *The Voyage Out,* which had taken her seven years to write. It is a more or less conventional novel, but in the works that followed—notably *Jacob's Room* (1922), *Mrs. Dalloway* (1925), *To the Lighthouse* (1927), *The Waves* (1931), and *Between the Acts* (1941)—Virginia Woolf developed more and more radical techniques for rendering her sense of "life" and "reality." In the essay "Mr. Bennett and Mrs. Brown" she expressed her profound dissatisfaction with the "reality" of the fictional world of naturalistic writers like John Galsworthy, H. G. Wells, and Arnold Bennett. "Life is not," she says elsewhere, "a series of gig-lamps symmetrically arranged; life is a luminous halo, a semi-transparent envelope surrounding us from the beginning of consciousness to the end." To penetrate this envelope, to render "life itself," one must capture "the stream of thought, of consciousness" which is its subjective vehicle. In pursuit of this end, Woolf eliminated more and more externals, seeking a fictional structure that would be "miraculously habitable without the help of walls, staircases, or partitions"—an effort that caused her good friend and critic E. M. Forster to wonder whether she hadn't gone too far: "She does not tell a story or weave a plot, and—can she create character?" A character in her first novel says, "I want to write a novel about Silence, about the things people don't say," and by the time of her penultimate novel, *The Waves,* she has very nearly succeeded. The ambition expressed in her *Writer's Dairy* of eliminating "all waste, deadness, superfluity" and "to give the moment whole; whatever it includes" is close to realization. Gone are story and plot, dialogue, and characterization (as it is usually conceived); instead we have the flow of the six characters' thoughts and feelings, presented as a kind of reverie. One cannot in this space describe the excitement and beauty of Virginia Woolf's writing: but writing was her very life, and in a very real sense her stay against madness and death.

"The Mark on the Wall" is as unconventional a "story" as *The Waves* is a "novel," but it beautifully illustrates her technique. The narrator (clearly Woolf herself) remembers a mark on the wall. What was it? At the end we learn what it was—and that, so to speak, is the "plot." But the plot is not the point, just as the satisfying of such curiosity is not the point of life. The point is that the mark becomes the focus of a whole series of free associations, ranging from Shakespeare to women's rights, but all returning to those fundamental questions of Woolf's art—the nature of "reality" and of "life itself." "If I should get up . . . and ascertain that the mark on the wall is really . . . the head of a . . . nail . . . what should I gain? Knowledge? . . . And what is knowledge?" She plays with the epistemological question. And life? "Why, if one wants to compare life to anything, one must liken it to being blown through the Tube at fifty miles an hour—landing at the other end without a single hairpin in one's hair. Shot out at the feet of God entirely naked!" But such marks, like the grain of sand around which the oyster builds a pearl, were the nuclei of Woolf's art, and her perilous tie to order and sanity. In 1941 she committed suicide by drowning in the River Ouse. As the story tells us, "One by one the fibres snap beneath the immense cold pressure of the earth. . . ."

The Mark on the Wall

Perhaps it was the middle of January in the present year that I first looked up and saw the mark on the wall. In order to fix a date it is necessary to remember what one saw. So now I think of the fire; the steady film of yellow light upon the page of my book; the three chrysanthemums in the round glass bowl on the mantelpiece. Yes, it must have been the winter time, and we had just finished our tea, for I remember that I was smoking a cigarette when I looked up and saw the mark on the wall for the first time. I looked up through the smoke of my cigarette and my eye lodged for a moment upon the burning coals, and that old fancy of the crimson flag flapping from the castle tower came into my mind, and I thought of the cavalcade of red knights riding up the side of the black rock. Rather to my relief the sight of the mark interrupted the fancy, for it is an old fancy, an automatic fancy, made as a child perhaps. The mark was a small round mark, black upon the white wall, about six or seven inches above the mantelpiece.

How readily our thoughts swarm upon a new object, lifting it a little way, as ants carry a blade of straw so feverishly, and then leave it. . . . If that mark was made by a nail, it can't have been for a picture, it must have been for a miniature—the miniature of a lady with white powdered curls, powder-dusted cheeks, and lips like red carnations. A fraud of course, for the people who had this house before us would have chosen pictures in that way—an old picture for an old room. That is the sort of people they were—very interesting people, and I think of them so often, in such queer places, because one will never see them again, never know what happened next. They wanted to leave this house because they wanted to change their style of furniture, so he said, and he was in process of saying that in his opinion art should have ideas behind it when we were torn asunder, as one is torn from the old lady about to pour out tea and the young man about to hit the tennis ball in the back garden of the suburban villa as one rushes past in the train.

But for that mark, I'm not sure about it; I don't believe it was made by a nail after all; it's too big, too round, for that. I might get up, but if I got up and looked at it, ten to one I shouldn't be able to say for certain; because once a thing's done, no one ever knows how it happened. Oh! dear me, the mystery of life; the inaccuracy of thought! The ignorance of humanity! To show how very little control of our possessions we have—what an accidental affair this living is after all our civilization—let me just count over a few of the things lost in one lifetime, beginning, for that seems always the most mysterious of losses—what cat would gnaw, what rat would nibble—three pale blue canisters of book-binding tools? Then there were the bird cages, the iron hoops, the steel skates, the Queen Anne coal-scuttle, the bagatelle board, the hand organ—all gone, and jewels, too. Opals and emeralds, they lie about the roots of turnips. What a scraping paring affair it is to be sure! The wonder is that I've any clothes on my back, that I sit surrounded by solid furniture at this moment. Why, if one wants to compare life to anything, one must liken it to being blown through the Tube at fifty miles an hour—landing at the other end without a single hairpin in one's hair! Shot out at the feet of God entirely naked! Tumbling head over heels in the asphodel meadows like brown paper parcels pitched down a shoot in the post office! With one's hair flying back like the tail of a race-horse. Yes, that seems to express the rapidity of life, the perpetual waste and repair; all so casual, all so haphazard. . . .

But after life. The slow pulling down of thick green stalks so that the cup of the flower, as it turns over, deluges one with purple and red light. Why, after all, should one not be born there as one is born here, helpless, speechless, unable to focus one's eyesight, groping at the roots of the grass, at the toes of the Giants? As for saying which are trees, and which are men and women, or whether there are such things, that one won't be in a condition to do for fifty years or so. There will be nothing but spaces of light and dark, intersected by thick stalks, and rather higher up perhaps, rose-shaped blots of an indistinct colour—dim pinks and blues—which will, as time goes on, become more definite, become—I don't know what. . . .

And yet that mark on the wall is not a hole at all. It may even be caused by some round black substance, such as a small rose leaf, left over from the summer, and I, not being a very vigilant housekeeper—look at the dust on the mantelpiece, for example, the dust which, so they say, buried Troy three times over, only fragments of pots utterly refusing annihilation, as one can believe.

The tree outside the window taps very gently on the pane. . . . I want to think quietly, calmly, spaciously, never to be interrupted, never to have to rise from my chair, to slip easily from one thing to another, without any sense of hostility, or obstacle. I want to sink deeper and deeper, away from the surface, with its hard separate facts. To steady myself, let me catch hold of the first idea that passes . . . Shakespeare. . . . Well, he will do as well as another. A man who sat himself solidly in an arm-chair, and looked into the fire, so—A shower of ideas fell perpetually from some very high Heaven down through his mind. He leant his forehead on his hand, and people, looking in through the open door—for this scene is supposed to take place on a summer's evening—But how dull this is, this historical fiction! It doesn't interest me at all. I wish I could hit upon a pleasant track of thought, a track indirectly reflecting credit upon myself, for those are the pleasantest thoughts, and very frequent even in the minds of modest mouse-coloured people, who believe genuinely that they dislike to hear their own praises. They are not thoughts directly praising oneself; that is the beauty of them; they are thoughts like this:

"And then I came into the room. They were discussing botany. I said how I'd seen a flower growing on a dust heap on the site of an old house in Kingsway. The seed, I said, must have been sown in the reign of Charles the First. What flowers grew in the reign of Charles the First?'' I asked—(But I don't remember the answer.) Tall flowers with purple tassels to them perhaps. And so it goes on. All the time I'm dressing up the figure of myself in my own mind, lovingly, stealthily, not openly adoring it, for if I did that, I should catch myself out, and stretch my hand at once for a book in self-protection. Indeed, it is curious how instinctively one protects the image of oneself from idolatry or any other handling that could make it ridiculous, or too unlike the original to be believed in any longer. Or is it not so very curious after all? It is a matter of great importance. Suppose the looking-glass smashes, the image disappears, and the romantic figure with the green of forest depths all about it is there no longer, but only that shell of a person which is seen by other people—what an airless, shallow, bald, prominent world it becomes! A world not to be lived in. As we face each other in omnibuses and underground railways we are looking into the mirror; that accounts for the vagueness, the gleam of glassiness, in our eyes. And the novelists in future will realize more and more the importance of these reflections, for of course there is not one reflection but an almost infinite number; those are the depths they will explore, those the phantoms they will pursue, leaving the description of reality more and more out of their stories, taking a knowledge of it for granted, as the Greeks did and Shakespeare perhaps—but these generalizations are very worthless. The military sound of the world is enough. It recalls leading articles, cabinet ministers—a whole class of things indeed which, as a child, one thought the thing itself, the standard thing, the real thing, from which one could not depart save at the risk of nameless damnation. Generalizations bring back somehow Sunday in London, Sunday afternoon walks, Sunday luncheons, and also ways of speaking of the dead, clothes, and habits—like the habit of sitting all together in one room until a certain hour, although nobody liked it. There was a rule for everything. The rule for tablecloths at that particular period was that they should be made of tapestry with little yellow compartments marked upon them, such as you may see in photographs of the carpets in the corridors of the royal palaces. Tablecloths of a different kind were not real tablecloths. How shocking, and yet how wonderful it was to discover that these real things, Sunday luncheons, Sunday walks, country houses, and tablecloths were not entirely real, were indeed half phantoms, and the damnation which visited the disbeliever in them was only a sense of illegitimate freedom. What now takes the place of those things I wonder, those real standard things? Men perhaps, should you be a woman; the masculine point of view which governs our lives, which sets the standard, which establishes Whitaker's Table of Precedency,[1] which has become, I suppose, since the war, half a phantom to many men and women, which soon, one may hope, will be laughed into the dustbin where the phantoms go, the mahogany sideboards and the Landseer prints, Gods and Devils, Hell and so forth, leaving us all with an intoxicating sense of illegitimate freedom—if freedom exists. . . .

In certain lights that mark on the wall seems actually to project from the wall. Nor is it entirely circular. I cannot be sure, but it seems to cast a perceptible shadow, suggesting that if I ran my finger down that strip of the wall it would, at a certain point, mount and descend a small tumulus, a smooth tumulus like those barrows on the South Downs which are, they say, either tombs or camps. Of the two I should prefer them to be tombs, desiring melancholy like most English people, and finding it natural at the end of a walk to think of the bones stretched beneath the turf. . . . There must be some book about it. Some antiquary must have dug up those bones and given them a name. . . .

---

[1] A table listing the rank order of the British aristocracy and notables in *Whitaker's Almanak,* (est. 1868), an annual publication like the *World Almanac* in The United States.

What sort of a man is an antiquary, I wonder? Retired Colonels for the most part, I daresay, leading parties of aged labourers to the top here, examining clods of earth and stone, and getting into correspondence with the neighbouring clergy, which, being opened at breakfast time, gives them a feeling of importance, and the comparison of arrow-heads necessitates cross-country journeys to the county towns, an agreeable necessity both to them and to their elderly wives, who wish to make plum jam or to clean out the study, and have every reason for keeping that great question of the camp or the tomb in perpetual suspension, while the Colonel himself feels agreeably philosophic in accumulating evidence on both sides of the question. It is true that he does finally incline to believe in the camp; and, being opposed, indites a pamphlet which he is about to read at the quarterly meeting of the local society when a stroke lays him low, and his last conscious thoughts are not of wife or child, but of the camp and that arrow-head there, which is now in the case at the local museum, together with the foot of a Chinese murderess, a handful of Elizabethan nails, a great many Tudor clay pipes, a piece of Roman pottery, and the wineglass that Nelson drank out of—proving I really don't know what.

No, no, nothing is proved, nothing is known. And if I were to get up at this very moment and ascertain that the mark on the wall is really—what shall we say?—the head of a gigantic old nail, driven in two hundred years ago, which has now, owing to the patient attrition of many generations of housemaids, revealed its head above the coat of paint, and is taking its first view of modern life in the sight of a white-walled fire-lit room, what should I gain?—Knowledge? Matter for further speculation? I can think sitting still as well as standing up. And what is knowledge? What are our learned men save the descendants of witches and hermits who crouched in caves and in woods brewing herbs, interrogating shrew-mice and writing down the language of the stars? And the less we honour them as our superstitions dwindle and our respect for beauty and health of mind increases. . . . Yes, one could imagine a very pleasant world. A quiet, spacious world, with the flowers so red and blue in the open fields. A world without professors or specialists or house-keepers with the profiles of policemen, a world which one could slice with one's thought as a fish slices the water with his fin, grazing the stems of the water-lilies, hanging suspended over nests of white sea eggs. . . . How peaceful it is down here, rooted in the centre of the world and gazing up through the grey waters, and their sudden gleams of light, and their reflections—if it were not for Whitaker's Almanack—if it were not for the Table of Precedency!

I must jump up and see for myself what that mark on the wall really is—a nail, a rose-leaf, a crack in the wood?

Here is nature once more at her old game of self-preservation. This train of thought, she perceives, is threatening mere waste of energy, even some collision with reality, for who will ever be able to lift a finger against Whitaker's Table of Precedency? The Archbishop of Canterbury is followed by the Lord High Chancellor; the Lord High Chancellor is followed by the Archbishop of York. Everybody follows somebody, such is the philosophy of Whitaker; and the great thing is to know who follows whom. Whitaker knows, and let that, so Nature counsels, comfort you, instead of enraging you; and if you can't be comforted, if you must shatter this hour of peace, think of the mark on the wall.

I understand Nature's game—her prompting to take action as a way of ending any thought that theatens to excite or to pain. Hence, I suppose, comes our slight contempt for men of action—men, we assume, who don't think. Still, there's no harm in putting a full stop to one's disagreeable thoughts by looking at a mark on the wall.

Indeed, now that I have fixed my eyes upon it, I feel that I have grasped a plank in the sea; I feel a satisfying sense of reality which at once turns the two Archbishops and the Lord High Chancellor to the shadows of shades. Here is something definite, something real. Thus, waking from a midnight dream of horror, one hastily turns on the light and lies quiescent, worshipping the chest of drawers, worshipping solidity, worshipping reality, worshipping the impersonal world which is a proof of some existence other than ours. That is what one wants to be sure of. . . . Wood is a pleasant thing to think about. It comes from a tree; and trees grow, and we don't know how they grow. For years and years they grow, without paying any attention to us, in meadows, in forests, and by the side of rivers—all things one likes to think about. The cows swish their tails beneath them on hot afternoons; they paint rivers so green that when a moorhen dives one expects to see its feathers all green when it comes up again. I like to think of the fish balanced against the stream like flags blown out; and of water-beetles slowly raising domes of mud upon the bed of the river. I like to think of the tree itself: first of the close dry sensation of being wood; then the grinding of the storm; then the slow, delicious ooze of sap; I like to think of it, too, on winter's nights standing in the empty field with all leaves close-furled, nothing tender exposed to the iron bullets of the moon, a naked mast upon an earth that goes tumbling, tumbling, all night long. The song of birds must sound very loud and strange in June; and how cold the feet of insects must feel upon it, as they make laborious progresses up the creases of the bark, or sun themselves upon the thin green awning of the leaves, and look straight in front of them with diamond-cut red eyes. . . . One by one the fibres snap beneath the immense cold pressure of the earth, then the last storm comes and, falling, the highest branches drive deep into the ground again. Even so, life isn't done with; there are a million patient, watchful lives still for a tree, all over the world, in bedrooms, in ships, on the pavement, lining rooms, where men and women sit after tea, smoking cigarettes. It is full of peaceful thoughts, happy thoughts, this tree. I should like to take each one separately—but something is getting in the way. . . . Where was I? What has it all been about? A tree? A river? The Downs? Whitaker's Almanack? The fields of asphodel? I can't remember a thing. Everything's moving, falling, slipping, vanishing. . . . There is a vast upheaval of matter. Someone is standing over me and saying:

"I'm going out to buy a newspaper."

"Yes?"

"Though it's no good buying newspapers. . . . Nothing ever happens. Curse this war; God damn this war! . . . All the same, I don't see why we should have a snail on our wall."

Ah, the mark on the wall! It was a snail.

Franz Kafka (1883–1924)

At least one reader has suggested that the best description of Kafka's fictional world—more exactly, of our response to its symbolic labyrinths—is to be found in a portion of a sentence from "A Country Doctor": "The air was almost unbreathable; . . . I wanted to push open a window." In his stories and novels we often feel as though we were experiencing a waking nightmare, the more terrifying because at the end of the tale we have not waked up. Yet, as Philip Rahv reminds us, it is important to perceive that Kafka is considerably more than a neurotic artist; "he is also an artist of neurosis." His greatness is by now fully established, but the character and meaning of his work are still much in dispute. Claimed as one of their own by Freudians, existentialists, expressionists, antitotalitarians, and by Jews and Christians, Kafka continues to baffle even as he magnetizes his readers.

He was born into an upper-middle-class Jewish family in Prague in 1883. From youth onward the central force in his life was his father, an authoritarian figure who generated in his son ambivalent feelings of admiration and fear. So profound was his father's effect on him that, while he spoke easily and well in the company of others, in the presence of the disquieting parent he stuttered. The need for his father's approval was obsessive, and it stayed with Kafka to the end of his life. Many critics find the father- or authority-figure, in its multiple symbolic manifestations, indispensable to any accounting of what happens in Kafka's fiction. For example, in "A Hunger Artist," the impresario rules the external life of the hunger artist with an absolute authority, against which the artist maintains his freedom only by clinging to his self-sacrificial role. Consider the scene at the end of the artist's forty-day fast: "The impresario . . . lifted his arms in the air above the artist, as if inviting Heaven to look down upon its creature here in the straw, this suffering martyr."

The events of Kafka's adult life are quickly told. He received a doctorate in jurisprudence in 1906 and entered the civil service two years later, already a writer in private. Although his duties were not in themselves taxing, he experienced only annoyance in his position, and his fear of bureaucracy became terror in his fiction. In 1917 he discovered that he had tuberculosis and resigned. Treatment was unsuccessful; he died in 1924, known only to a small literary circle.

During his life Kafka published very little. He owes his fame to his friend and literary executor, Max Brod, who, against Kafka's expressed wish, refused to burn his unpublished manuscripts, much the greater part of his work. Following their initial publication in the decade after Kafka's death, the stories and novels began to appear in English translation in 1930. All of the novels—*The Trial, The Castle,* and *Amerika*—focus on the impotence, felt sinfulness, and frustration of man brought before a tribunal that seems to exist outside of time, a perpetual court of perpetual conviction. No innocent verdicts are rendered. There is not hope, because for man hope may not even be conceptualized.

Like all of Kafka's stories, "A Hunger Artist" has been given a wide variety of allegorical interpretations. Perhaps the most convincing is that the artist is a kind of modern holy man who, as the world grows more materialistic and secularized, gradually loses his credibility and his following. But the story is full of ambiguities. At the very moment of death, for example, the artist claims he didn't eat "because I couldn't find the food I liked." Is this a last desperate attempt of this deeply alienated man to make common sense of a world that scorned him? The next-to-last paragraph of the story is saturated with such ambiguities; but perhaps none is greater than the fact that, in his miserable death—starved to death in a cage among circus animals—he found his fulfillment; for it had always been his boast that he could fast infinitely longer than the forty days the impresario permitted him.

A Hunger Artist

During these last decades the interest in professional fasting has markedly diminished. It used to pay very well to stage such great performances under one's own management, but today that is quite impossible. We live in a different world now. At one time the whole town took a lively interest in the hunger artist; from day to day of his fast the excitement mounted; everybody wanted to see him at least once a day; there were people who bought season tickets for the last few days and sat from morning till night in front of his small barred cage; even in the nighttime there were visiting hours, when the whole effect was heightened by torch flares; on fine days the cage was set out in the open air, and then it was the children's special treat to see the hunger artist; for their elders he was often just a joke that happened to be in fashion, but the children stood openmouthed, holding each other's hands for greater security, marveling at him as he sat there pallid in black tights, with his ribs sticking out so prominently, not even on a seat but down among straw on the ground, sometimes giving a courteous nod, answering questions with a constrained smile, or perhaps stretching an arm through the bars so that one might feel how thin it was, and then again withdrawing deep into himself, paying no attention to anyone or anything, not even to the all-important striking of the clock that was the only piece of furniture in his cage, but merely staring into vacancy with half-shut eyes, now and then taking a sip from a tiny glass of water to moisten his lips.

Besides casual onlookers there were also relays of permanent watchers selected by the public, usually butchers, strangely enough, and it was their task to watch the hunger artist day and night, three of them at a time, in case he should have some secret recourse to nourishment. This was nothing but a formality, instituted to reassure the masses, for the initiates knew well enough that during his fast the artist would never in any circumstances, not even under forcible compulsion, swallow the smallest morsel of food; the honor of his profession forbade it. Not every watcher, of course, was capable of understanding this, there were often groups of night watchers who were very lax in carrying out their duties and deliberately huddled together in a retired corner to play cards with great absorption, obviously intending to give the hunger artist the chance of a little refreshment, which they supposed he could draw from some private hoard. Nothing annoyed the artist more than such watchers; they made him miserable; they made his fast seem unendurable; sometimes he mastered his feebleness sufficiently to sing during their watch for as long as he could keep going, to show them how unjust their suspicions were. But that was of little use; they only wondered at his cleverness in being able to fill his mouth even while singing. Much more to his taste were the watchers who sat close up to the bars, who were not content with the dim night lighting of the hall but focused him in the full glare of the electric pocket torch given them by the impresario. The harsh light did not trouble him at all, in any case he could never sleep properly, and he could always drowse a little, whatever the light, at any hour, even when the hall was thronged with noisy onlookers. He was quite happy at the prospect of spending a sleepless night with such watchers; he was ready to exchange jokes with them, to tell them stories out of his nomadic life, anything at all to keep them awake and demonstrate to them again that he had no eatables in his cage and that he was fasting as not one of them could fast. But his happiest moment was when the morning came and an enormous breakfast was brought them, at his expense, on which they flung themselves with the keen appetite of healthy men after a weary night of wakefulness. Of course there were people who argued that this breakfast was an unfair attempt to bribe the watchers, but that was going rather too far, and when they were invited to take on a night's vigil without a breakfast, merely for the sake of the cause, they made themselves scarce, although they stuck stubbornly to their suspicions.

Such suspicions, anyhow, were a necessary accompaniment to the profession of fasting. No one could possibly watch the hunger artist continuously, day and night, and so no one could produce first-hand evidence that the fast had really been rigorous and continuous; only the artist himself could know that, he was therefore bound to be the sole completely satisfied spectator of his own fast. Yet for other reasons he was never satisfied; it was not perhaps mere fasting that had brought him to such skeleton thinness that many people had regretfully to keep away from his exhibitions, because the sight of him was too much for them, perhaps it was dissatisfaction with himself that had worn him down. For he alone knew, what no other initiate knew, how easy it was to fast. It was the easiest thing in the world. He made no secret of this, yet people did not believe him, at the best they set him down as modest, most of them, however, thought he was out for publicity or else was some kind of cheat who found it easy to fast because he had discovered a way of making it easy, and then had the impudence to admit the fact, more or less. He had to put up with all that, and in the course of time had got used to it, but his inner dissatisfaction always rankled, and never yet, after any term of fasting—this must be granted to his credit—had he left the cage of his own free will. The longest period of fasting was fixed by his impresario at forty days, beyond that term he was not allowed to go, not even in great cities, and there was good reason for it, too. Experience had proved that for about forty days the interest of the public could be stimulated by a steadily increasing pressure of advertisement, but after that the town began to lose interest, sympathetic support began notably to fall off; there were of course local variations as between one town and another or one country and another, but as a general rule forty days marked the limit. So on the fortieth day the flower-bedecked cage was opened, enthusiastic spectators filled the hall, a military band played, two doctors entered the cage to measure the results of the fast, which were announced through a megaphone, and finally two young ladies appeared, blissful at having been selected for the honor, to help the hunger artist down the few steps leading to a small table on which was spread a carefully chosen invalid repast. And at this very moment the artist always turned stubborn. True, he would entrust his bony arms to the out-stretched helping hands of the ladies bending over him, but stand up he would not. Why stop fasting at this particular moment, after forty days of it? He had held out for a long time, an illimitably long time; why stop now, when he was in his best fasting form, or rather, not yet quite in his best fasting form? Why should he be cheated of the fame he would get for fasting longer, for being not only the record hunger artist of all time, which presumbly he was already, but for beating his own record by a performance beyond human imagination, since he felt that there were no limits to his capacity for fasting? His public pretended to admire him so much, why should it have so little patience with him; if he could endure fasting longer, why shouldn't the public endure it? Besides, he was tired, he was comfortable sitting in the straw, and now he was supposed to lift himself to his full height and go down to a meal the very thought of which gave him a nausea that only the presence of the ladies kept him from betraying, and even that with an effort. And he looked up into the eyes of the ladies who were apparently so friendly and in reality so cruel, and shook his head, which felt too heavy on its strengthless neck. But then there happened yet again what always happened. The impresario came forward, without a word—for the band made speech impossible—lifted his arms in the air above the artist, as if inviting Heaven to look down upon its creature here in the straw, this suffering martyr, which indeed he was, although in quite another sense; grasped him around the emaciated waist, with exaggerated caution, so that the frail condition he was in might be appreciated; and committed him to the care of the blenching ladies, not without secretly giving him a shaking so that his legs and body tottered and swayed. The artist now submitted completely; his head lolled on his breast as if it had landed there by chance; his body was hollowed out; his legs in a spasm of self-preservation clung close to each other at the knees, yet scraped on the ground as if it were not really solid ground, as if they were only trying to find solid ground; and the whole weight of his body, a featherweight after all, relapsed onto one of the ladies, who, looking around for help and panting a little—this post of honor was not at all what she had expected it to be—first stretched her neck as far as she could to keep her face at least free from contact with the artist, then finding this impossible, and her more fortunate companion not coming to her aid but merely holding extended in her own trembling hand the little bunch of knucklebones that was the artist's, to the great delight of the spectators burst into tears and had to be replaced by an attendant who had long been stationed in readiness. Then came the food, a little of which the impresario managed to get between the artist's lips, while he sat in a kind of half-fainting trance, to the accompaniment of cheerful patter designed to distract the public's attention from the artist's condition; after that, a toast was drunk to the public, supposedly prompted by a whisper from the artist in the impresario's ear; the band confirmed it with a mighty flourish, the spectators melted away, and no one had any cause to be dissatisfied with the proceedings, no one except the hunger artist himself, he only, as always.

So he lived for many years, with small regular intervals of recuperation, in visible glory, honored by the world, yet in spite of that troubled in spirit, and all the more troubled because no one would take his trouble seriously. What comfort could he possibly need? What more could he possibly wish for? And if some good-natured person, feeling sorry for him, tried to console him by pointing out that his melancholy was probably caused by fasting, it could happen, especially when he had been fasting for some time, that he reacted with an outburst of fury and to the general alarm began to shake the bars of his cage like a wild animal. Yet the impresario had a way of punishing these outbreaks which he rather enjoyed putting into operation. He would apologize publicly for the artist's behavior, which was only to be excused, he admitted, because of the irritability caused by fasting; a condition hardly to be understood by well-fed people; then by natural transition he went on to mention the artist's equally incomprehensible boast that he could fast for much longer than he was doing; he praised the high ambition, the good will, the great self-denial undoubtedly implicit in such a statement; and then quite simply countered it by bringing out photographs, which were also on sale to the public, showing the artist on the fortieth day of a fast lying in bed almost dead from exhaustion. This perversion of the truth, familiar to the artist though it was, always unnerved him afresh and proved too much for him. What was a consequence of the premature ending of his fast was here presented as the cause of it! To fight against this lack of understanding, against a whole world of nonunderstanding, was impossible. Time and again in good faith he stood by the bars listening to the impresario, but as soon as the photographs appeared he always let go and sank with a groan back onto his straw, and the reassured public could once more come close and gaze at him.

A few years later when the witnesses of such scenes called them to mind, they often failed to understand themselves at all. For meanwhile the aforementioned change in public interest had set in; it seemed to happen almost overnight; there may have been profound causes for it, but who was going to bother about that; at any rate the pampered hunger artist suddenly found himself deserted one fine day by the amusement-seekers, who went streaming past him to other more-favored attractions. For the last time the impresario hurried him over half Europe to discover whether the old interest might still survive here and there; all in vain; everywhere, as if by secret agreement, a positive revulsion from professional fasting was in evidence. Of course it could not really have sprung up so suddenly as all that, and many premonitory symptoms which had not been sufficiently remarked or suppressed during the rush and glitter of success now came retrospectively to mind, but it was now too late to take any countermeasures. Fasting would surely come into fashion again at some future date, yet that was no comfort for those living in the present. What, then, was the hunger artist to do? He had been applauded by thousands in his time and could hardly come down to showing himself in a street booth at village fairs, and as for adopting another profession, he was not only too old for that but too fanatically devoted to fasting. So he took leave of the impresario, his partner in an unparalleled career, and hired himself to a large circus; in order to spare his own feelings he avoided reading the conditions of his contract.

A large circus with its enormous traffic in replacing and recruiting men, animals, and apparatus can always find a use for people at any time, even for a hunger artist, provided of course that he does not ask too much, and in this particular case anyhow it was not only the artist who was taken on but his famous and long-known name as well, indeed considering the peculiar nature of his performance, which was not impaired by advancing age, it could not be objected that here was an artist past his prime, no longer at the height of his professional skill, seeking a refuge in some quiet corner of a circus; on the contrary, the hunger artist averred that he could fast as well as ever, which was entirely credible, he even alleged that if he were allowed to fast as he liked, and this was at once promised him without more ado, he could astound the world by establishing a record never yet achieved, a statement that certainly provoked a smile among the other professionals, since it left out of account the change in public opinion, which the hunger artist in his zeal conveniently forgot.

He had not, however, actually lost his sense of the real situation and took it as a matter of course that he and his cage should be stationed, not in the middle of the ring as a main attraction, but outside, near the animal cages, on a site that was after all easily accessible. Large and gaily painted placards made a frame for the cage and announced what was to be seen inside it. When the public came thronging out in the intervals to see the animals, they could hardly avoid passing the hunger artist's cage and stopping there for a moment, perhaps they might even have stayed longer had not those pressing behind them in the narrow gangway, who did not understand why they should be held up on their way toward the excitements of the menagerie, made it impossible for anyone to stand gazing quietly for any length of time. And that was the reason why the hunger artist, who had of course been looking forward to these visiting hours as the main achievement of his life, began instead to shrink from them. At first he could hardly wait for the intervals; it was exhilarating to watch the crowds come streaming his way, until only too soon—not even the most obstinate self-deception, clung to almost consciously, could hold out against the fact—the conviction was borne in upon him that these people, most of them, to judge from their actions, again and again, without exception, were all on their way to the menagerie. And the first sight of them from the distance remained the best. For when they reached his cage he was at once deafened by the storm of shouting and abuse that arose from the two contending factions, which renewed themselves continuously, of those who wanted to stop and stare at him—he soon began to dislike them more than the others—not out of real interest but only out of obstinate self-assertiveness, and those who wanted to go straight on to the animals. When the first great rush was past, the stragglers came along, and these, whom nothing could have prevented from stopping to look at him as long as they had breath, raced past with long strides, hardly even glancing at him, in their haste to get to the menagerie in time. And all too rarely did it happen that he had a stroke of luck, when some father of a family fetched up before him with his children, pointed a finger at the hunger artist, and explained at length what the phenomenon meant, telling stories of earlier years when he himself had watched similar but much more thrilling performances, and the children, still rather uncomprehending, since neither inside nor outside school had they been sufficiently prepared for this lesson—what did they care about fasting?—yet showed by the brightness of their intent eyes that new and better times might be coming. Perhaps, said the hunger artist to himself many a time, things would be a little better if his cage were set not quite so near the menagerie. That made it too easy for people to make their choice, to say nothing of what he suffered from the stench of the menagerie, the animals' restlessness by night, the carrying past of raw lumps of flesh for the beasts of prey, the roaring at feeding times, which depressed him continually. But he did not dare to lodge a complaint with the management; after all, he had the animals to thank for the troops of people who passed his cage, among whom there might always be one here and there to take an interest in him, and who could tell where they might seclude him if he called attention to his existence and thereby to the fact that, strictly speaking, he was only an impediment on the way to the menagerie.

A small impediment, to be sure, one that grew steadily less. People grew familiar with the strange idea that they could be expected, in times like these, to take an interest in a hunger artist, and with this familiarity the verdict went out against him. He might fast as much as he could, and he did so; but nothing could save him now, people passed him by. Just try to explain to anyone the art of fasting! Anyone who has no feeling for it cannot be made to understand it. The fine placards grew dirty and illegible, they were torn down; the little notice board telling the number of fast days achieved, which at first was changed carefully every day, had long stayed at the same figure, for after the first few weeks even this small task seemed pointless to the staff; and so the artist simply fasted on and on, as he had once dreamed of doing, and it was no trouble to him, just as he had always foretold, but no one counted the days, no one, not even the artist himself, knew what records he was already breaking, and his heart grew heavy. And when once in a while some leisurely passer-by stopped, made merry over the old figure on the board, and spoke of swindling, that was in its way the stupidest lie ever invented by indifference and inborn malice, since it was not the hunger artist who was cheating, he was working honestly, but the world was cheating him of his reward.

Many more days went by, however, and that too came to an end. An overseer's eye fell on the cage one day and he asked the attendants why this perfectly good cage should be left standing there unused with dirty straw inside it; nobody knew, until one man, helped out by the notice board, remembered about the hunger artist. They poked into the straw with sticks and found him in it. "Are you still fasting?" asked the overseer, "when on earth do you mean to stop?" "Forgive me, everybody," whispered the hunger artist; only the overseer, who had his ear to the bars, understood him. "Of course," said the overseer, and tapped his forehead with a finger to let the attendants know what state the man was in, "we forgive you." "I always wanted you to admire my fasting," said the hunger artist. "We do admire it," said the overseer, affably. "But you shouldn't admire it," said the hunger artist. "Well then we don't admire it," said the overseer, "but why shouldn't we admire it?" "Because I have to fast, I can't help it," said the hunger artist. "What a fellow you are," said the overseer, "and why can't you help it?" "Because," said the hunger artist, lifting his head a little and speaking, with his lips pursed, as if for a kiss, right into the overseer's ear, so that no syllable might be lost, "because I couldn't find the food I liked. If I had found it, believe me, I should have made no fuss and stuffed myself like you or anyone else." These were his last words, but in his dimming eyes remained the firm though no longer proud persuasion that he was still continuing to fast.

"Well, clear this out now!" said the overseer, and they buried the hunger artist, straw and all. Into the cage they put a young panther. Even the most insensitive felt it refreshing to see this wild creature leaping around the cage that had so long been dreary. The panther was all right. The food he liked was brought him without hesitation by the attendants; he seemed not even to miss his freedom; his noble body, furnished almost to the bursting point with all that it needed, seemed to carry freedom around with it too; somewhere in his jaws it seemed to lurk; and the joy of life streamed with such ardent passion from his throat that for the onlookers it was not easy to stand the shock of it. But they braced themselves, crowded around the cage, and did not want ever to move away.

D. H. Lawrence (1885–1930)

D. H. Lawrence was born in England's coal-mining country, the son of a miner. His father was a black-bearded, irreligious, heavy drinking man who spoke the rough Nottinghamshire dialect; his mother was a "refined" chapel-goer who had been a schoolteacher and spoke the King's English. Between these two there developed deep tensions, and *Sons and Lovers* (1913), Lawrence's first important novel, is the unforgettable story of how a mother sought to *possess* her son, and how this possessiveness corrupted his sexual relations with other women. At her death Lawrence said to Jessie Chambers, with whom he had sought a "spiritual" relationship: "I've *loved* her, like a lover. That's why I could never love you." This œdipal conflict appears in many guises in Lawrence's later novels, in *The Rainbow* (1915), *Women in Love* (1920), and *Lady Chatterley's Lover* (1928), to name but a few. Again and again, we see characters struggling to relate to others and at the same time struggling to break free; and part of the struggle is often the individual's difficulty in sorting out the male and female, the earthy and the refined, the intellectual and the passional, the homo- and the heterosexual sides of his being. The ideal was, as Lawrence expressed it in *Women in Love*, a "star-equilibrium," in which two beings are held each to each by forces of attraction, but never fusing, never losing their individuality. The ideal was more easily stated than demonstrated, however, and his short stories (which many think constitute his best work) render these struggles in a protean variety of ways.

Lawrence saw the modern world as anathema to love; he saw its ugliness, its mechanization, its economics of greed as invading human personality and impairing that *flow* of life, that wholeness, which can only occur when the "dark self" of the unconscious and the "knowing self" of the conscious are in relation with each other. "My great religion," he wrote in 1913, "is a belief in the blood, the flesh, as being wiser than the intellect." That faith in the "blood" led Lawrence into some strange corners (including a kind of flirtation with fascism), but what he wanted essentially was wholeness, an end to the alienation and disintegration brought on by the "hopeless squalor of industrialism, the huge cemetery of human hopes."

The two short stories "Tickets, Please" and "The Horse Dealer's Daughter" are quintessential Lawrence. The one, cast in a time of war, glimpses another kind of war: the war between the sexes brought on, so Lawrence implies, by the brutal alienations of industrialism. Machines dominate this setting, especially the tram-cars, driven by cripples and conducted by women, which connect the ugliness of the Midland industrial towns. But the ugliest machine is the machine-lover, John Thomas, who treats the women under his authority as sex objects, as things to be manipulated and used. Against him Annie stirs up a terrible Dionysiac revenge; but she is not just avenging a jilt, she is reasserting the values of a world where community was more than "a competition of mere acquisition," and where the warm flow between the sexes was still a possibility.

Again, in "The Horse Dealer's Daughter" we see an exploited woman, abandoned by her coarse and brutal brothers to a kind of emotional exile. In her presence, they talk about her in the third person, as if she didn't exist. She turns as dumb and silent as the great horses on the now bankrupt farm. But she is called out of her dark despair by the doctor Fergusson, who prevents her suicide by drowning and wraps her shivering body in a blanket and warms her before the hearth. "You undressed me?" she asked. Then her next question: "Do you love me, then?" "He had no intention of loving her. . . . It was horrible," but "with an inward groan he gave way, and let his heart yield towards her." Out of the dark unconscious comes a force, anonymous and impersonal, that defies the will. It is in response to this force that "star-equilibrium" is achieved.

Lawrence led a tempestuous and nomadic life, traveling with his wife Frieda through Europe and to the American Southwest and Mexico. He died of tuberculosis in southern France in 1930.

The Horse Dealer's Daughter

"Well, Mabel, and what are you going to do with yourself?" asked Joe, with foolish flippancy. He felt quite safe himself. Without listening for an answer, he turned aside, worked a grain of tobacco to the tip of his tongue, and spat it out. He did not care about anything, since he felt safe himself.

The three brothers and the sister sat round the desolate breakfast-table, attempting some sort of desultory consultation. The morning's post had given the final tap to the family fortunes, and all was over. The dreary dining-room itself, with its heavy mahogany furniture, looked as if it were waiting to be done away with.

But the consultation amounted to nothing. There was a strange air of ineffectuality about the three men, as they sprawled at table, smoking and reflecting vaguely on their own condition. The girl was alone, a rather short, sullen-looking young woman of twenty-seven. She did not share the same life as her brothers. She would have been good-looking, save for the impressive fixity of her face, 'bull-dog', as her brothers called it.

There was a confused tramping of horses' feet outside. The three men all sprawled round in their chairs to watch. Beyond the dark holly bushes that separated the strip of lawn from the high-road, they could see a cavalcade of shire horses swinging out of their own yard, being taken for exercise. This was the last time. These were the last horses that would go through their hands. The young men watched with critical, callous look. They were all frightened at the collapse of their lives, and the sense of disaster in which they were involved left them no inner freedom.

Yet they were three fine, well-set fellows enough. Joe, the eldest, was a man of thirty-three, broad and handsome in a hot, flushed way. His face was red, he twisted his black moustache over a thick finger, his eyes were shallow and restless. He had a sensual way of uncovering his teeth when he laughed, and his bearing was stupid. Now he watched the horses with a glazed look of helplessness in his eyes, a certain stupor of downfall.

The great draught-horses swung past. They were tied head to tail, four of them, and they heaved along to where a lane branched off from the high-road, planting their great hoofs floutingly in the fine black mud, swinging their great rounded haunches sumptuously, and trotting a few sudden steps as they were led into the lane, round the corner. Every movement showed a massive, slumbrous strength, and a stupidity which held them in subjection. The groom at the head looked back, jerking the leading rope. And the cavalcade moved out of sight up the lane, the tail of the last horse, bobbed up tight and stiff, held out taut from the swinging great haunches as they rocked behind the hedges in a motion-like sleep.

Joe watched with glazed hopeless eyes. The horses were almost like his own body to him. He felt he was done for now. Luckily he was engaged to a woman as old as himself, and therefore her father, who was steward of a neighbouring estate, would provide him with a job. He would marry and go into harness. His life was over, he would be a subject animal now.

He turned uneasily aside, the retreating steps of the horses echoing in his ears. Then, with foolish restlessness, he reached for the scraps of bacon-rind from the plates, and making a faint whistling sound, flung them to the terrier that lay against the fender. He watched the dog swallow them, and waited till the creature looked into his eyes. Then a faint grin came on his face, and in a high, foolish voice he said:

"You won't get much more bacon, shall you, you little b——?"

The dog faintly and dismally wagged his tail, then lowered its haunches, circled round, and lay down again.

There was another helpless silence at the table. Joe sprawled uneasily in his seat, not willing to go till the family conclave was dissolved. Fred Henry, the second brother, was erect, clean-limbed, alert. He had watched the passing of the horses with more *sang-froid*. If he was an animal, like Joe, he was an animal which controls, not one which is controlled. He was master of any horse, and he carried himself with a well-tempered air of mastery. But he was not master of the situations of life. He pushed his coarse brown moustache upwards, off his lip, and glanced irritably at his sister, who sat impassive and inscrutable.

"You'll go and stop with Lucy for a bit, shan't you?" he asked. The girl did not answer.

"I don't see what else you can do," persisted Fred Henry.

"Go as a skivvy," Joe interpolated laconically.

The girl did not move a muscle.

"If I was her, I should go in for training for a nurse," said Malcolm, the youngest of them all. He was the baby of the family, a young man of twenty-two, with a fresh, jaunty *museau*.

But Mabel did not take any notice of him. They had talked at her and round her for so many years, that she hardly heard them at all.

The marble clock on the mantelpiece softly chimed the half-hour, the dog rose uneasily from the hearth-rug and looked at the party at the breakfast-table. But still they sat on in ineffectual conclave.

"Oh, all right," said Joe suddenly, apropos of nothing. "I'll get a move on."

He pushed back his chair, straddled his knees with a downward jerk, to get them free, in horsey fashion, and went to the fire. Still he did not go out of the room; he was curious to know what the others would do or say. He began to charge his pipe, looking down at the dog and saying in a high, affected voice:

"Going wi' me? Going wi' me are ter? Tha'rt goin' further than tha counts on just now, dost hear?"

The dog faintly wagged its tail, the man stuck out his jaw and covered his pipe with his hands, and puffed intently, losing himself in the tobacco, looking down all the while at the dog with an absent brown eye. The dog looked up at him in mournful distrust. Joe stood with his knees stuck out, in real horsey fashion.

"Have you had a letter from Lucy?" Fred Henry asked of his sister.

"Last week," came the neutral reply.

"And what does she say?"

There was no answer.

"Does she *ask* you to go and stop there?" persisted Fred Henry.

"She says I can if I like."

"Well, then, you'd better. Tell her you'll come on Monday."

This was received in silence.

"That's what you'll do then, is it?" said Fred Henry, in some exasperation.

But she made no answer. There was a silence of futility and irritation in the room. Malcolm grinned fatuously.

"You'll have to make up your mind between now and next Wednesday," said Joe loudly, "or else find yourself lodgings on the kerbstone."

The face of the young woman darkened, but she sat on immutable.

"Here's Jack Ferguson!" exclaimed Malcolm, who was looking aimlessly out of the window.

"Where?" exclaimed Joe loudly.

"Just gone past."

"Coming in?"

Malcom craned his neck to see the gate.

"Yes, he said.

There was a silence. Mabel sat on like one condemned, at the head of the table. Then a whistle was heard from the kitchen. The dog got up and barked sharply. Joe opened the door and shouted:

"Come on."

After a moment a young man entered. He was muffled up in overcoat and a purple woollen scarf, and his tweed cap, which he did not remove, was pulled down on his head. He was of medium height, his face was rather long and pale, his eyes looked tired.

"Hello, Jack! Well, Jack!" exclaimed Malcolm and Joe. Fred Henry merely said: "Jack."

"What's doing?" asked the newcomer, evidently addressing Fred Henry.

"Same. We've got to be out by Wednesday. Got a cold?"

"I have—got it bad, too."

"Why don't you stop in?"

"*Me* stop in? When I can't stand on my legs, perhaps I shall have a chance." The young man spoke huskily. He had a slight Scotch accent.

"It's a knock-out, isn't it," said Joe, boisterously, "if a doctor goes round croaking with a cold. Looks bad for the patients, doesn't it?"

The young doctor looked at him slowly.

"Anything the matter with *you*, then?" he asked sarcastically.

"Not as I know of. Damn your eyes, I hope not. Why?"

"I thought you were very concerned about the patients, wondered if you might be one yourself."

"Damn it, no, I've never been patient to no flaming doctor, and hope I never shall be," returned Joe.

At this point Mabel rose from the table, and they all seemed to become aware of her existence. She began putting the dishes together. The young doctor looked at her, but did not address her. He had not greeted her. She went out of the room with the tray, her face impassive and unchanged.

"When are you off then, all of you?" asked the doctor.

"I'm catching the eleven-forty," replied Malcolm. "Are you goin' down wi' th' trap, Joe?"

"Yes, I've told you I'm going down wi' th' trap, haven't I?"

"We'd better be getting her in then. So long, Jack, if I don't see you before I go," said Malcolm, shaking hands.

He went out, followed by Joe, who seemed to have his tail between his legs.

"Well, this is the devil's own," exclaimed the doctor, when he was left alone with Fred Henry. "Going before Wednesday, are you?"

"That's the orders," replied the other.

"Where, to Northampton?"

"That's it."

"The devil!" exclaimed Ferguson, with quiet chagrin.

And there was silence between the two.

"All settled up, are you?" asked Ferguson.

"About."

There was another pause.

"Well, I shall miss yer, Freddy, boy," said the young doctor.

"And I shall miss thee, Jack," returned the other.

"Miss you like hell," mused the doctor.

Fred Henry turned aside. There was nothing to say. Mabel came in again, to finish clearing the table.

"What are *you* going to do, then, Miss Pervin?" asked Ferguson. "Going to your sister's, are you?"

Mabel looked at him with her steady, dangerous eyes, that always made him uncomfortable, unsettling his superficial ease.

"No," she said.

"Well, what in the name of fortune *are* you going to do? Say what you mean to do," cried Fred Henry, with futile intensity.

But she only averted her head, and continued her work. She folded the white tablecloth, and put on the chenille cloth.

"The sulkiest bitch that ever trod!" muttered her brother.

But she finished her task with perfectly impassive face, the young doctor watching her interestedly all the while. Then she went out.

Fred Henry stared after her, clenching his lips, his blue eyes fixing in sharp antagonism, as he made a grimace of sour exasperation.

"You could bray her into bits, and that's all you'd get out of her," he said, in a small, narrowed tone.

The doctor smiled faintly.

"What's she *going* to do, then?" he asked.

"Strike me if *I* know!" returned the other.

There was a pause. Then the doctor stirred.

"I'll be seeing you to-night, shall I?" he said to his friend.

"Ay—where's it to be? Are we going over to Jessdale?"

"I don't know. I've got such a cold on me. I'll come round to the 'Moon and Stars', anyway."

"Let Lizzie and May miss their night for once, eh?"

"That's it—if I feel as I do now."

"All's one——"

The two young men went through the passage and down to the back door together. The house was large, but it was servantless now, and desolate. At the back was a small bricked house-yard and beyond that a big square, gravelled fine and red, and having stables on two sides. Sloping, dank, winter-dark fields stretched away on the open sides.

But the stables were empty. Joseph Pervin, the father of the family, had been a man of no education, who had become a fairly large horse dealer. The stables had been full of horses, there was a great turmoil and come-and-go of horses and of dealers and grooms. Then the kitchen was full of servants. But of late things had declined. The old man had married a second time, to retrieve his fortunes. Now he was dead and everything was gone to the dogs, there was nothing but debt and threatening.

For months, Mabel had been servantless in the big house, keeping the home together in penury for her ineffectual brothers. She had kept house for ten years. But previously it was with unstinted means. Then, however brutal and coarse everything was, the sense of money had kept her proud, confident. The men might be foul-mouthed, the women in the kitchen might have bad reputations, her brothers might have illegitimate children. But so long as there was money, the girl felt herself established, and brutally proud, reserved.

No company came to the house, save dealers and coarse men. Mabel had no associates of her own sex, after her sister went away. But she did not mind. She went regularly to church, she attended to her father. And she lived in the memory of her mother, who had died when she was fourteen, and whom she had loved. She had loved her father, too, in a different way, depending upon him, and feeling secure in him, until at the age of fifty-four he married again. And then she had set hard against him. Now he had died and left them all hopelessly in debt.

She had suffered badly during the period of poverty. Nothing, however, could shake the curious, sullen, animal pride that dominated each member of the family. Now, for Mabel, the end had come. Still she would not cast about her. She would follow her own way just the same. She would always hold the keys of her own situation. Mindless and persistent, she endured from day to day. Why should she think? Why should she answer anybody? It was enough that this was the end, and there was no way out. She need not pass any more darkly along the main street of the small town, avoiding every eye. She need not demean herself any more, going into the shops and buying the cheapest food. This was at an end. She thought of nobody, not even of herself. Mindless and persistent, she seemed in a sort of ecstasy to be coming nearer to her fulfilment, her own glorification, approaching her dead mother, who was glorified.

In the afternoon she took a little bag, with shears and sponge and a small scrubbing-brush, and went out. It was a grey, wintry day, with saddened, dark green fields and an atmosphere blackened by the smoke of foundries not far off. She went quickly, darkly along the causeway, heeding nobody, through the town to the churchyard.

There she always felt secure, as if no one could see her, although as a matter of fact she was exposed to the stare of everyone who passed along under the churchyard wall. Nevertheless, once under the shadow of the great looming church, among the graves, she felt immune from the world, reserved within the thick churchyard wall as in another country.

Carefully she clipped the grass from the grave, and arranged the pinky white, small chrysanthemums in the tin cross. When this was done, she took an empty jar from a neighbouring grave, brought water, and carefully, most scrupulously sponged the marble headstone and the coping-stone.

It gave her sincere satisfaction to do this. She felt in immediate contact with the world of her mother. She took minute pains, went through the park in a state bordering on pure happiness, as if in performing this task she came into a subtle, intimate connection with her mother. For the life she followed here in the world was far less real than the world of death she inherited from her mother.

The doctor's house was just by the church. Ferguson, being a mere hired assistant, was slave to the country-side. As he hurried now to attend to the out-patients in the surgery, glancing across the graveyard with his quick eye, he saw the girl at her task at the grave. She seemed so intent and remote, it was like looking into another world. Some mystical element was touched in him. He slowed down as he walked, watching her as if spellbound.

She lifted her eyes, feeling him looking. Their eyes met. And each looked again at once, each feeling, in some way, found out by the other. He lifted his cap and passed on down the road. There remained distinct in his consciousness, like a vision, the memory of her face, lifted from the tombstone in the churchyard, and looking at him with slow, large, portentous eyes. It *was* portentous, her face. It seemed to mesmerise him. There was a heavy power in her eyes which laid hold of his whole being, as if he had drunk some powerful drug. He had been feeling weak and done before. Now the life came back into him, he felt delivered from his own fretted, daily self.

He finished his duties at the surgery as quickly as might be, hastily filling up the bottles of the waiting people with cheap drugs. Then, in perpetual haste, he set off again to visit several cases in another part of his round, before tea-time. At all times he preferred to walk if he could, but particularly when he was not well. He fancied the motion restored him.

The afternoon was falling. It was grey, deadened, and wintry, with a slow, moist, heavy coldness sinking in and deadening all the faculties. But why should he think or notice? He hastily climbed the hill and turned across the dark green fields, following the black cinder-track. In the distance, across a shallow dip in the country, the small town was clustered like smouldering ash, a tower, a spire, a heap of low, raw, extinct houses. And on the nearest fringe of the town, sloping into the dip, was Oldmeadow, the Pervins' house. He could see the stables and the outbuildings distinctly, as they lay towards him on the slope. Well, he would not go there many more times! Another resource would be lost to him, another place gone: the only company he cared for in the alien, ugly little town he was losing. Nothing but work, drudgery, constant hastening from dwelling to dwelling among the colliers and the iron-workers. It wore him out, but at the same time he had a craving for it. It was a stimulant to him to be in the homes of the working people, moving, as it were, through the innermost body of their life. His nerves were excited and gratified. He could come so near, into the very lives of the rough, inarticulate, powerfully emotional men and women. He grumbled, he said he hated the hellish hole. But as a matter of fact it excited him, the contact with the rough, strongly-feeling people was a stimulant applied direct to his nerves.

Below Oldmeadow, in the green, shallow, soddened hollow of fields, lay a square, deep pond. Roving across the landscape, the doctor's quick eye detected a figure in black passing through the gate of the field, down towards the pond. He looked again. It would be Mabel Pervin. His mind suddenly became alive and attentive.

Why was she going down there? He pulled up on the path on the slope above, and stood staring. He could just make sure of the small black figure moving in the hollow of the failing day. He seemed to see her in the midst of such obscurity, that he was like a clairvoyant, seeing rather with the mind's eye than with ordinary sight. Yet he could see her positively enough, whilst he kept his eye attentive. He felt, if he looked away from her, in the thick, ugly falling dusk, he would lose her altogether.

He followed her minutely as she moved, direct and intent, like something transmitted rather than stirring in voluntary activity, straight down the field towards the pond. There she stood on the bank for a moment. She never raised her head. Then she waded slowly into the water.

He stood motionless as the small black figure walked slowly and deliberately towards the centre of the pond, very slowly, gradually moving deeper into the motionless water, and still moving forward as the water got up to her breast. Then he could see her no more in the dusk of the dead afternoon.

"There!" he exclaimed. "Would you believe it?"

And he hastened straight down, running over the wet, soddened fields, pushing through the hedges, down into the depression of callous wintry obscurity. It took him several minutes to come to the pond. He stood on the bank, breathing heavily. He could see nothing. His eyes seemed to penetrate the dead water. Yes, perhaps that was the dark shadow of her black clothing beneath the surface of the water.

He slowly ventured into the pond. The bottom was deep, soft clay, he sank in, and the water clasped dead cold round his legs. As he stirred he could smell the cold, rotten clay that fouled up into the water. It was objectionable in his lungs. Still, repelled and yet not heeding, he moved deeper into the pond. The cold water rose over his thighs, over his loins, upon his abdomen. The lower part of his body was all sunk in the hideous cold element. And the bottom was so deeply soft and uncertain, he was afraid of pitching with his mouth underneath. He could not swim, and was afraid.

He crouched a little, spreading his hands under the water and moving them round, trying to feel for her. The dead cold pond swayed upon his chest. He moved again, a little deeper, and again, with his hands underneath, he felt all around under the water. And he touched her clothing. But it evaded his fingers. He made a desperate effort to grasp it.

And so doing he lost his balance and went under, horribly, suffocating in the foul earthy water, struggling madly for a few moments. At last, after what seemed an eternity, he got his footing, rose again into the air and looked around. He gasped, and knew he was in the world. Then he looked at the water. She had risen near him. He grasped her clothing, and drawing her nearer, turned to take his way to land again.

He went very slowly, carefully, absorbed in the slow progress. He rose higher, climbing out of the pond. The water was now only about his legs; he was thankful, full of relief to be out of the clutches of the pond. He lifted her and staggered on to the bank, out of the horror of wet, grey clay.

He laid her down on the bank. She was quite unconscious and running with water. He made the water come from her mouth, he worked to restore her. He did not have to work very long before he could feel the breathing begin again in her; she was breathing naturally. He worked a little longer. He could feel her live beneath his hands; she was coming back. He wiped her face, wrapped her in his overcoat, looked round into the dim, dark grey world, then lifted her and staggered down the bank and across the fields.

It seemed an unthinkably long way, and his burden so heavy he felt he would never get to the house. But at last he was in the stable-yard, and then in the house-yard. He opened the door and went into the house. In the kitchen he laid her down on the hearth-rug and called. The house was empty. But the fire was burning in the grate.

Then again he kneeled to attend to her. She was breathing regularly, her eyes were wide open and as if conscious, but there seemed something missing in her look. She was conscious in herself, but unconscious of her surroundings.

He ran upstairs, took blankets from a bed, and put them before the fire to warm. Then he removed her saturated, earthy-smelling clothing, rubbed her dry with a towel, and wrapped her naked in the blankets. Then he went into the dining-room to look for spirits. There was a little whisky. He drank a gulp himself, and put some into her mouth.

The effect was instantaneous. She looked full into his face, as if she had been seeing him for some time, and yet had only just become conscious of him.

"Dr. Ferguson?" she said.

"What?" he answered.

He was divesting himself of his coat, intending to find some dry clothing upstairs. He could not bear the smell of the dead, clayey water, and he was mortally afraid for his own health.

"What did I do?" she asked.

"Walked into the pond," he replied. He had begun to shudder like one sick, and could hardly attend to her. Her eyes remained full on him, he seemed to be going dark in his mind, looking back at her helplessly. The shuddering became quieter in him, as life came back to him, dark and unknowing, but strong again.

"Was I out of my mind?" she asked, while her eyes were fixed on him all the time.

"Maybe, for the moment," he replied. He felt quiet, because his strength had come back. The strange fretful strain had left him.

"Am I out of my mind now?" she asked.

"Are you?" he reflected a moment. "No," he answered truthfully, "I don't see that you are." He turned his face aside. He was afraid now, because he felt dazed, and felt dimly that her power was stronger than his, in this issue. And she continued to look at him fixedly all the time. "Can you tell me where I shall find some dry things to put on?" he asked.

"Did you dive into the pond for me?" she asked.

"No," he answered. "I walked in. But I went in overhead as well."

There was silence for a moment. He hesitated. He very much wanted to go up-stairs to get into dry clothing. But there was another desire in him. And she seemed to hold him. His will seemed to have gone to sleep, and left him, standing there slack before her. But he felt warm inside. He did not shudder at all, though his clothes were sodden on him.

"Why did you?" she asked.

"Because I didn't want you to do such a foolish thing," he said.

"It wasn't foolish," she said, still gazing at him as she lay on the floor, with a sofa cushion under her head. "It was the right thing to do. *I* knew best, then."

"I'll go and shift these wet things," he said. But still he had not the power to move out of her presence, until she sent him. It was as if she had the life of his body in her hands, and he could not extricate himself. Or perhaps he did not want to.

Suddenly she sat up. Then she became aware of her own immediate condition. She felt the blankets about her, she knew her own limbs. For a moment it seemed as if her reason were going. She looked round, with wild eye, as if seeking something. He stood still with fear. She saw her clothing lying scattered.

"Who undressed me?" she asked, her eyes resting full and inevitable on his face.

"I did," he replied, "to bring you round."

For some moments she sat and gazed at him awfully, her lips parted.

"Do you love me, then?" she asked.

He only stood and stared at her, fascinated. His soul seemed to melt.

She shuffled forward on her knees, and put her arms round him, round his legs, as he stood there, pressing her breasts against his knees and thighs, clutching him with strange, convulsive certainty, pressing his thighs against her, drawing him to her face, her throat, as she looked up at him with flaring, humble eyes of transfiguration, triumphant in first possession.

"You love me," she murmured, in strange transport, yearning and triumphant and confident. "You love me. I know you love me, I know."

And she was passionately kissing his knees, through the wet clothing, passionately and indiscriminately kissing his knees, his legs, as if unaware of everything.

He looked down at the tangled wet hair, the wild, bare, animal shoulders. He was amazed, bewildered, and afraid. He had never thought of loving her. He had never wanted to love her. When he rescued her and restored her, he was a doctor, and she was a patient. He had had no single personal thought of her. Nay, this introduction of the personal element was very distasteful to him, a violation of his professional honour. It was horrible to have her there embracing his knees. It was horrible. He revolted from it, violently. And yet—and yet—he had not the power to break away.

She looked at him again, with the same supplication of powerful love, and that same transcendent, frightening light of triumph. In view of the delicate flame which seemed to come from her face like a light, he was powerless. And yet he had never intended to love her. He had never intended. And something stubborn in him could not give way.

"You love me," she repeated in a murmur of deep, rhapsodic assurance. "You love me."

Her hands were drawing him, drawing him down to her. He was afraid, even a little horrified. For he had, really, no intention of loving her. Yet her hands were drawing him towards her. He put out his hand quickly to steady himself, and grasped her bare shoulder. A flame seemed to burn the hand that grasped her soft shoulder. He had no intention of loving her: his whole will was against his yielding. It was horrible. And yet wonderful was the touch of her shoulders, beautiful the shining of her face. Was she perhaps mad? He had a horror of yielding to her. Yet something in him ached also.

He had been staring away at the door, away from her. But his hand remained on her shoulder. She had gone suddenly very still. He looked down at her. Her eyes were now wide with fear, with doubt, the light was dying from her face, a shadow of terrible greyness was returning. He could not bear the touch of her eyes' question upon him, and the look of death behind the question.

With an inward groan he gave way, and let his heart yield towards her. A sudden gentle smile came on his face. And her eyes, which never left his face, slowly, slowly filled with tears. He watched the strange water rise in her eyes, like some slow fountain coming. And his heart seemed to burn and melt away in his breast.

He could not bear to look at her any more. He dropped on his knees and caught her head with his arms and pressed her face against his throat. She was very still. His heart, which seemed to have broken, was burning with a kind of agony in his breast. And he felt her slow, hot tears wetting his throat. But he could not move.

He felt the hot tears wet his neck and the hollows of his neck, and he remained motionless, suspended through one of man's eternities. Only now it had become indispensable to him to have her face pressed close to him; he could never let her go again. He could never let her head go away from the close clutch of his arm. He wanted to remain like that for ever, with his heart hurting him in a pain that was also life to him. Without knowing, he was looking down on her damp, soft brown hair.

Then, as it were suddenly, he smelt the horrid stagnant smell of that water. And at the same moment she drew away from him and looked at him. Her eyes were wistful and unfathomable. He was afraid of them, and he fell to kissing her, not knowing what he was doing. He wanted her eyes not to have that terrible, wistful, unfathomable look.

When she turned her face to him again, a faint delicate flush was glowing, and there was again dawning that terrible shining of joy in her eyes, which really terrified him, and yet which he now wanted to see, because he feared the look of doubt still more.

"You love me?" she said, rather faltering.

"Yes." The word cost him a painful effort. Not because it wasn't true. But because it was too newly true, the *saying* seemed to tear open again his newly-torn heart. And he hardly wanted it to be true, even now.

She lifted her face to him, and he bent forward and kissed her on the mouth, gently, with the one kiss that is an eternal pledge. And as he kissed her his heart strained again in his breast. He never intended to love her. But now it was over. He had crossed over the gulf to her, and all that he had left behind had shrivelled and become void.

After the kiss, her eyes again slowly filled with tears. She sat still, away from him, with her face dropped aside, and her hands folded in her lap. The tears fell very slowly. There was complete silence. He too sat there motionless and silent on the hearth-rug. The strange pain of his heart that was broken seemed to consume him. That he should love her? That this was love! That he should be ripped open in this way! Him, a doctor! How they would all jeer if they knew! It was agony to him to think they might know.

In the curious naked pain of the thought he looked again to her. She was sitting there dropped into a muse. He saw a tear fall, and his heart flared hot. He saw for the first time that one of her shoulders was quite uncovered, one arm bare, he could see one of her small breasts; dimly, because it had become almost dark in the room.

"Why are you crying?" he asked, in an altered voice.

She looked up at him, and behind her tears the consciousness of her situation for the first time brought a dark look of shame to her eyes.

"I'm not crying, really," she said, watching him, half frightened.

He reached his hand, and softly closed it on her bare arm.

"I love you! I love you!" he said in a soft, low vibrating voice, unlike himself.

She shrank, and dropped her head. The soft, penetrating grip of his hand on her arm distressed her. She looked up at him.

"I want to go," she said. "I want to go and get you some dry things."

"Why?" he said. "I'm all right."

"But I want to go," she said. "And I want you to change your things."

He released her arm, and she wrapped herself in the blanket, looking at him rather frightened. And still she did not rise.

"Kiss me," she said wistfully.

He kissed her, but briefly, half in anger.

Then, after a second, she rose nervously, all mixed up in the blanket. He watched her in her confusion as she tried to extricate herself and wrap herself up so that she could walk. He watched her relentlessly, as she knew. And as she went, the blanket trailing, and as he saw a glimpse of her feet and her white leg, he tried to remember her as she was when he had wrapped her in the blanket. But then he didn't want to remember, because she had been nothing to him then, and his nature revolted from remembering her as she was when she was nothing to him.

A tumbling, muffled noise from within the dark house startled him. Then he heard her voice: "There are clothes." He rose and went to the foot of the stairs, and gathered up the garments she had thrown down. Then he came back to the fire, to rub himself down and dress. He grinned at his own appearance when he had finished.

The fire was sinking, so he put on coal. The house was now quite dark, save for the light of a street-lamp that shone in faintly from beyond the holly trees. He lit the gas with matches he found on the mantelpiece. Then he emptied the pockets of his own clothes, and threw all his wet things in a heap into the scullery. After which he gathered up her sodden clothes, gently, and put them in a separate heap on the copper-top in the scullery.

It was six o'clock on the clock. His own watch had stopped. He ought to go back to the surgery. He waited, and still she did not come down. So he went to the foot of the stairs and called:

"I shall have to go."

Almost immediately he heard her coming down. She had on her best dress of black voile, and her hair was tidy, but still damp. She looked at him—and in spite of herself, smiled.

"I don't like you in those clothes," she said.

"Do I look a sight?" he answered.

They were shy of one another.

"I'll make you some tea," she said.

"No, I must go."

"Must you?" And she looked at him again with the wide, strained, doubtful eyes. And again, from the pain of his breast, he knew how he loved her. He went and bent to kiss her, gently, passionately, with his heart's painful kiss.

"And my hair smells so horrible," she murmured in distraction. "And I'm so awful, I'm so awful! Oh no, I'm too awful." And she broke into bitter, heart-broken sobbing. "You can't want to love me, I'm horrible."

"Don't be silly, don't be silly," he said, trying to comfort her, kissing her, holding her in his arms. "I want you, I want to marry you, we're going to be married, quickly, quickly—to-morrow if I can."

But she only sobbed terribly, and cried:

"I feel awful. I feel awful. I feel I'm horrible to you."

"No, I want you, I want you," was all he answered, blindly, with that terrible intonation which frightened her almost more than her horror lest he should *not* want her.

Tickets, Please

There is in the Midlands a single-line tramway system which boldly leaves the county town and plunges off into the black, industrial country-side, up hill and down dale, through the long ugly villages of workmen's houses, over canals and railways, past churches perched high and nobly over the smoke and shadows, through stark, grimy cold little market-places, tilting away in a rush past cinemas and shops down to the hollow where the collieries are, then up again, past a little rural church, under the ash trees, on in a rush to the terminus, the last little ugly place of industry, the cold little town that shivers on the edge of the wild, gloomy country beyond. There the green and creamy coloured tram-cars seem to pause and purr with curious satisfaction. But in a few minutes—the clock on the turret of the Co-operative Wholesale Society's shops gives the time—away it starts once more on the adventure. Again there are the reckless swoops downhill, bouncing the loops: again the chilly wait in the hill-top market-place: again the breathless slithering round the precipitous drop under the church: again the patient halts at the loops, waiting for the outcoming car: so on and on, for two long hours, till at last the city looms beyond·the fat gas-works, the narrow factories draw near, we are in the sordid streets of the great town, once more we sidle to a standstill at our terminus, abashed by the great crimson and cream-coloured city cars, but still perky, jaunty, somewhat dare-devil, green as a jaunty sprig of parsley out of a black colliery garden.

To ride on these cars is always an adventure. Since we are in war-time, the drivers are men unfit for active service: cripples and hunchbacks. So they have the spirit of the devil in them. The ride becomes a steeplechase. Hurray! we have leapt in a clear jump over the canal bridge—now for the four-lane corner. With a shriek and a trail of sparks we are clear again. To be sure, a tram often leaps the rails—but what matter! It sits in a ditch till other trams come to haul it out. It is quite common for a car, parked with one solid mass of living people, to come to a dead halt in the midst of unbroken blackness, the heart of nowhere on a dark night, and for the driver and the girl conductor to call: "All get off—car's on fire!" Instead, however, of rushing out in a panic, the passengers stolidly reply: "Get on—get on! We're not coming out. We're stopping where we are. Push on, George." So till flames actually appear.

The reason for this reluctance to dismount is that the nights are howlingly cold, black, and windswept, and a car is a haven of refuge. From village to village the miners travel, for a change of cinema, of girl, of pub. The trams are desperately packed. Who is going to risk himself in the black gulf outside, to wait perhaps an hour for another tram, then to see the forlorn notice 'Depot Only', because there is something wrong! Or to greet a unit of three bright cars all so tight with people that they sail past with a howl of derision. Trams that pass in the night.

This, the most dangerous tram-service in England, as the authorities themselves declare, with pride, is entirely conducted by girls, and driven by rash young men, a little crippled, or by delicate young men, who creep forward in terror. The girls are fearless young hussies. In their ugly blue uniform, skirts up to their knees, shapeless old peaked caps on their heads, they have all the *sang-froid* of an old non-commissioned officer. With a tram packed with howling colliers, roaring hymns downstairs and a sort of antiphony of obscenities upstairs, the lasses are perfectly at their ease. They pounce on the youths who try to evade their ticket-machine. They push off the men at the end of their distance. They are not going to be done in the eye—not they. They fear nobody—and everybody fears them.

"Hello, Annie!"

"Hello, Ted!"

"Oh, mind my corn, Miss Stone. It's my belief you've got a heart of stone, for you've trod on it again."

"You should keep it in your pocket," replies Miss Stone, and she goes sturdily upstairs in her high boots.

"Tickets, please."

She is peremptory, suspicious, and ready to hit first. She can hold her own against ten thousand. The step of that tram-car is her Thermopylæ.

Therefore, there is a certain wild romance aboard these cars—and in the sturdy bosom of Annie herself. The time for soft romance is in the morning, between ten o'clock and one, when things are rather slack: that is, except market-day and Saturday. Thus Annie has time to look about her. Then she often hops off her car and into a shop where she has spied something, while the driver chats in the main road. There is very good feeling between the girls and the drivers. Are they not companions in peril, shipments aboard this careering vessel of a tram-car, for ever rocking on the waves of a stormy land.

Then, also, during the easy hours, the inspectors are most in evidence. For some reason, everybody employed in this tram-service is young: there are no grey heads. It would not do. Therefore the inspectors are of the right age, and one, the chief, is also good-looking. See him stand on a wet, gloomy morning, in his long oilskin, his peaked cap well down over his eyes, waiting to board a car. His face ruddy, his small brown moustache is weathered, he has a faint impudent smile. Fairly tall and agile, even in his waterproof, he springs aboard a car and greets Annie.

"Hello, Annie! Keeping the wet out?"

"Trying to."

There are only two people in the car. Inspecting is soon over. Then for a long and impudent chat on the foot-board, a good, easy, twelve-mile chat.

The inspector's name is John Thomas Raynor—always called John Thomas, except sometimes, in malice, Coddy. His face sets in fury when he is addressed, from a distance, with this abbreviation. There is considerable scandal about John Thomas in half a dozen villages. He flirts with the girl conductors in the morning, and walks out with them in the dark night, when they leave their tram-car at the depôt. Of course, the girls quit the service frequently. Then he flirts and walks out with the newcomer: always providing she is sufficiently attractive, and that she will consent to walk. It is remarkable, however, that most of the girls are quite comely, they are all young, and this roving life aboard the car gives them a sailor's dash and recklessness. What matter how they behave when the ship is in port? To-morrow they will be aboard again.

Annie, however, was something of a Tartar, and her sharp tongue had kept John Thomas at arm's length for many months. Perhaps, therefore, she liked him all the more: for he always came up smiling, with impudence. She watched him vanquish one girl, then another. She could tell by the movement of his mouth and eyes, when he flirted with her in the morning, that he had been walking out with this lass, or the other, the night before. A fine cock-of-the-walk he was. She could sum him up pretty well.

In this subtle antagonism they knew each other like old friends, they were as shrewd with one another almost as man and wife. But Annie had always kept him sufficiently at arm's length. Besides, she had a boy of her own.

The Statutes fair, however, came in November, at Bestwood. It happened that Annie had the Monday night off. It was a drizzling ugly night, yet she dressed herself up and went to the fair-ground. She was alone, but she expected soon to find a pal of some sort.

The roundabouts were veering round and grinding out their music, the side-shows were making as much commotion as possible. In the coconut shies there were no coconuts, but artificial war-time substitutes, which the lads declared were fastened into the irons. There was a sad decline in brilliance and luxury. None the less, the ground was muddy as ever, there was the same crush, the press of faces lighted up by the flares and the electric lights, the same smell of naphtha and a few potatoes, and of electricity.

Who should be the first to greet Miss Annie on the show-ground but John Thomas. He had a black overcoat buttoned up to his chin, and a tweed cap pulled down over his brows, his face between was ruddy and smiling and handy as ever. She knew so well the way his mouth moved.

She was very glad to have a 'boy'. To be at the Statutes without a fellow was no fun. Instantly, like the gallant he was, he took her on the Dragons, grim-toothed, roundabout switchbacks. It was not nearly so exciting as a tram-car actually. But, then, to be seated in a shaking, green dragon, uplifted above the sea of bubble faces, careering in a rickety fashion in the lower heavens, whilst John Thomas leaned over her, his cigarette in his mouth, was after all the right style. She was a plump, quick, alive little creature. So she was quite excited and happy.

John Thomas made her stay on for the next round. And therefore she could hardly for shame repulse him when he put his arm around her and drew her a little nearer to him, in a very warm and cuddly manner. Besides, he was fairly discreet, he kept his movement as hidden as possible. She looked down, and saw that his red, clean hand was out of sight of the crowd. And they knew each other so well. So they warmed up to the fair.

After the dragons they went on the horses. John Thomas paid each time, so she could but be complaisant. He, of course, sat astride on the outer horse—named 'Black Bess'—and she sat sideways, towards him, on the inner horse—named 'Wildfire'. But of course John Thomas was not going to sit discreetly on 'Black Bess', holding the brass bar. Round they spun and heaved, in the light. And round he swung on his wooden steed, flinging one leg across her mount, and perilously tipping up and down, across the space, half lying back, laughing at her. He was perfectly happy; she was afraid her hat was on one side, but she was excited.

He threw quoits on a table, and won for her two large, pale blue hat-pins. And then, hearing the noise of the cinemas, announcing another performance, they climbed the boards and went in.

Of course, during these performances pitch darkness falls from time to time, when the machine goes wrong. Then there is a wild whooping, and a loud smacking of simulated kisses. In these moments John Thomas drew Annie towards him. After all, he had a wonderfully warm, cosy way of holding a girl with his arm, he seemed to make such a nice fit. And, after all, it was pleasant to be so held: so very comforting and cosy and nice. He leaned over her and she felt his breath on her hair; she knew he wanted to kiss her on the lips. And, after all, he was so warm and she fitted in to him so softly. After all, she wanted him to touch her lips.

But the light sprang up; she also started electrically, and put her hat straight. He left his arm lying nonchalantly behind her. Well, it was fun, it was exciting to be at the Statutes with John Thomas.

When the cinema was over they went for a walk across the dark, damp fields. He had all the arts of love-making. He was especially good at holding a girl, when he sat with her on a stile in the black, drizzling darkness. He seemed to be holding her in space, against his own warmth and gratification. And his kisses were soft and slow and searching.

So Annie walked out with John Thomas, though she kept her own boy dangling in the distance. Some of the tram-girls chose to be huffy. But there, you must take things as you find them, in this life.

There was no mistake about it, Annie liked John Thomas a good deal. She felt so rich and warm in herself whenever he was near. And John Thomas really liked Annie, more than usual. The soft, melting way in which she could flow into a fellow, as if she melted into his very bones, was something rare and good. He fully appreciated this.

But with a developing acquaintance there began a developing intimacy. Annie wanted to consider him a person, a man: she wanted to take an intelligent interest in him, and to have an intelligent response. She did not want a mere nocturnal presence, which was what he was so far. And she prided herself that he could not leave her.

Here she made a mistake. John Thomas intended to remain a nocturnal presence; he had no idea of becoming an all-round individual to her. When she started to take an intelligent interest in him and his life and his character, he sheered off. He hated intelligent interest. And he knew that the only way to stop it was to avoid it. The possessive female was aroused in Annie. So he left her.

It is no use saying she was not surprised. She was at first startled, thrown out of her count. For she had been so *very* sure of holding him. For a while she was staggered, and everything became uncertain to her. Then she wept with fury, indignation, desolation, and misery. Then she had a spasm of despair. And then, when he came, still impudently, on to her car, still familiar, but letting her see by the movement of his head that he had gone away to somebody else for the time being, and was enjoying pastures new, then she determined to have her own back.

She had a very shrewd idea what girls John Thomas had taken out. She went to Nora Purdy. Nora was a tall, rather pale, but well-built girl, with beautiful yellow hair. She was rather secretive.

"Hey!" said Annie, accosting her; then softly: "Who's John Thomas on with now?"

"I don't know," said Nora.

"Why, tha does," said Annie, ironically lapsing into dialect. "Tha knows as well as I do."

"Well, I do, then," said Nora. "It isn't me, so don't bother."

"It's Cissy Meakin, isn't it?"

"It is, for all I know."

"Hasn't he got a face on him!" said Annie. "I don't half like his cheek. I could knock him off the foot-board when he comes round at me."

"He'll get dropped on one of these days," said Nora.

"Ay, he will, when somebody makes up their mind to drop it on him. I should like to see him taken down a peg or two, shouldn't you?"

"I shouldn't mind," said Nora.

"You've got quite as much cause to as I have," said Annie. "But we'll drop on him one of these days, my girl. What? Don't you want to?"

"I don't mind," said Nora.

But as a matter of fact, Nora was much more vindictive than Annie.

One by one Annie went the round of the old flames. It so happened that Cissy Meakin left the tramway service in quite a short time. Her mother made her leave. Then John Thomas was on the *qui vive*. He cast his eyes over his old flock. And his eyes lighted on Annie. He thought she would be safe now. Besides, he liked her.

She arranged to walk home with him on Sunday night. It so happened that her car would be in the depôt at half-past nine: the last car would come in at 10:15. So John Thomas was to wait for her there.

At the depôt the girls had a little waiting-room of their own. It was quite rough, but cosy, with a fire and an oven and a mirror, and table and wooden chairs. The half-dozen girls who knew John Thomas only too well had arranged to take service this Sunday afternoon. So, as the cars began to come in, early, the girls dropped into the waiting-room. And instead of hurrying off home, they sat around the fire and had a cup of tea. Outside was the darkness and lawlessness of war-time.

John Thomas came on the car after Annie, at about a quarter to ten. He poked his head easily into the girls' waiting-room.

"Prayer-meeting?" he asked.

"Ay," said Laura Sharp. "Ladies only."

"That's me!" said John Thomas. It was one of his favourite exclamations.

"Shut the door, boy," said Muriel Baggaley.

"Oh, which side of me?" said John Thomas.

"Which tha likes," said Polly Birkin.

He had come in and closed the door behind him. The girls moved in their circle, to make a place for him near the fire. He took off his great-coat and pushed back his hat.

"Who handles the teapot?" he said.

Nora Purdy silently poured him out a cup of tea.

"Want a bit o' my bread and drippin'?" said Muriel Baggaley to him.

"Ay, give us a bit."

And he began to eat his piece of bread.

"There's no place like home, girls," he said.

They all looked at him as he uttered this piece of impudence. He seemed to be sunning himself in the presence of so many damsels.

"Especially if you're not afraid to go home in the dark," said Laura Sharp.

"Me! By myself I am."

They sat till they heard the last tram come in. In a few minutes Emma Houselay entered.

"Come on, my old duck!" cried Polly Birkin.

"It *is* perishing," said Emma, holding her fingers to the fire.

"But—I'm afraid to, go home in, the dark," sang Laura Sharp, the tune having got into her mind.

"Who're you going with to-night, John Thomas?" asked Muriel Baggaley coolly.

"To-night?" said John Thomas. "Oh, I'm going home by myself to-night—all on my lonely-o."

"That's me!" said Nora Purdy, using his own ejaculation.

The girls laughed shrilly.

"Me as well, Nora," said John Thomas.

"Don't know what you mean," said Laura.

"Yes, I'm toddling," said he, rising and reaching for his overcoat.

"Nay, said Polly. "We're all here waiting for you."

"We've got to be up in good time in the morning," he said, in the benevolent official manner.

They all laughed.

"Nay," said Muriel. "Don't leave us all lonely, John Thomas. Take one!"

"I'll take the lot, if you like," he responded gallantly.

"That you won't, either," said Muriel. "Two's company, seven's too much of a good thing."

"Nay—take one," said Laura. "Fair and square, all above board and say which."

"Ay," cried Annie, speaking for the first time. "Pick, John Thomas; let's hear thee."

"Nay," he said. "I'm going home quiet to-night. Feeling good, for once."

"Whereabouts?" said Annie. "Take a good 'un, then. But tha's got to take one of us!"

"Nay, how can I take one," he said, laughing uneasily. "I don't want to make enemies."

"You'd only make *one*," said Annie.

"The chosen *one*," added Laura.

"Oh, my! Who said girls!" exclaimed John Thomas, again turning, as if to escape. "Well—good-night."

"Nay, you've got to make your pick," said Muriel. "Turn your face to the wall, and say which one touches you. Go on—we shall only just touch your back—one of us. Go on—turn your face to the wall, and don't look, and say which one touches you."

He was uneasy, mistrusting them. Yet he had not the courage to break away. They pushed him to a wall and stood him there with his face to it. Behind his back they all grimaced, tittering. He looked so comical. He looked around uneasily.

"Go on!" he cried.

"You're looking—you're looking!" they shouted.

He turned his head away. And suddenly, with a movement like a swift cat, Annie went forward and fetched him a box on the side of the head that sent his cap flying and himself staggering. He started round.

But at Annie's signal they all flew at him, slapping him, pinching him, pulling his hair, though more in fun than in spite or anger. He, however, saw red. His blue eyes flamed with strange fear as well as fury, and he butted through the girls to the door. It was locked. He wrenched at it. Roused, alert, the girls stood round and looked at him. He faced them, at bay. At that moment they were rather horrifying to him, as they stood in their short uniforms. He was distinctly afraid.

"Come on, John Thomas! Come on! Choose!" said Annie.

"What are you after? Open the door," he said.

"We shan't—not till you've chosen!" said Muriel.

"Chosen what?" he said.

"Chosen the one you're going to marry," she replied.

He hesitated a moment.

"Open the blasted door," he said, "and get back to your senses." He spoke with official authority.

"You've got to choose!" cried the girls.

"Come on!" cried Annie, looking him in the eye. "Come on! Come on!"

He went forward, rather vaguely. She had taken off her belt, and swinging it, she fetched him a sharp blow over the head with the buckle end. He sprang and seized her. But immediately the other girls rushed upon him, pulling and tearing and beating him. Their blood was now thoroughly up. He was their sport now. They were going to have their own back, out of him. Strange, wild creatures, they hung on him and rushed at him to bear him down. His tunic was torn right up the back, Nora had hold at the back of his collar, and was actually strangling him. Luckily the button burst. He struggled in a wild frenzy of fury and terror, almost mad terror. His tunic was simply torn off his back, his shirt-sleeves were torn away, his arms were naked. The girls rushed at him, clenched their hands on him and pulled at him: or they rushed at him and pushed him, butted him with all their might: or they struck him wild blows. He ducked and cringed and struck sideways. They became more intense.

At last he was down. They rushed on him, kneeling on him. He had neither breath nor strength to move. His face was bleeding with a long scratch, his brow was bruised.

Annie knelt on him, the other girls knelt and hung on to him. Their faces were flushed, their hair wild, their eyes were all glittering strangely. He lay at last quite still, with face averted, as an animal lies when it is defeated and at the mercy of the captor. Sometimes his eye glanced back at the wild faces of the girls. His breast rose heavily, his wrists were torn.

"Now, then, my fellow!" gasped Annie at length. "Now then—now——"

At the sound of her terrifying, cold triumph, he suddenly started to struggle as an animal might, but the girls threw themselves upon him with unnatural strength and power, forcing him down.

"Yes—now, then!" gasped Annie at length.

And there was a dead silence, in which the thud of heartbeating was to be heard. It was a suspense of pure silence in every soul.

"Now you know where you are," said Annie.

The sight of his white, bare arm maddened the girls. He lay in a kind of trance of fear and antagonism. They felt themselves filled with supernatural strength.

Suddenly Polly started to laugh—to giggle wildly—helplessly—and Emma and Muriel joined in. But Annie and Nora and Laura remained the same, tense, watchful, with gleaming eyes. He winced away from these eyes.

"Yes," said Annie, in a curious low tone, secret and deadly. "Yes! You've got it now. You know what you've done, don't you? You know what you've done."

He made no sound nor sign, but lay with bright, averted eyes, and averted, bleeding face.

"You ougnt to be *killed*, that's what you ought," said Annie, tensely. "You ought to be *killed*." And there was a terrifying lust in her voice.

Polly was ceasing to laugh, and giving long-drawn Oh-h-hs and sighs as she came to herself.

"He's got to choose," she said vaguely.

"Oh, yes, he has," said Laura, with vindictive decision.

"Do you hear—do you hear?" said Annie. And with a sharp movement, that made him wince, she turned his face to her.

"Do you hear?" she repeated, shaking him.

But he was quite dumb. She fetched him a sharp slap on the face. He started, and his eyes widened. Then his face darkened with defiance, after all.

"Do you hear?" she repeated.

He only looked at her with hostile eyes.

"Speak!" she said, putting her face devilishly near his.

"What?" he said, almost overcome.

"You've got to *choose*!" she cried, as if it were some terrible menace, and as if it hurt her that she could not exact more.

"What?" he said, in fear.

"Choose your girl, Coddy. You've got to choose her now. And you'll get your neck broken if you play any more of your tricks, my boy. You're settled now."

There was a pause. Again he averted his face. He was cunning in his overthrow. He did not give in to them really—no, not if they tore him to bits.

"All right, then," he said, "I choose Annie." His voice was strange and full of malice. Annie let go of him as if he had been a hot coal.

"He's chosen Annie!" said the girls in chorus.

"Me!" cried Annie. She was still kneeling, but away from him. He was still lying prostrate, with averted face. The girls grouped uneasily around.

"Me!" repeated Annie, with a terrible bitter accent.

Then she got up, drawing away from him with strange disgust and bitterness.

"I wouldn't touch him," she said.

But her face quivered with a kind of agony, she seemed as if she would fall. The other girls turned aside. He remained lying on the floor, with his torn clothes and bleeding, averted face.

"Oh, if he's chosen——" said Polly.

"I don't want him—he can choose again," said Annie, with the same rather bitter hopelessness.

"Get up," said Polly, lifting his shoulder. "Get up."

He rose slowly, a strange, ragged, dazed creature. The girls eyed him from a distance, curiously, furtively, dangerously.

"Who wants him?" cried Laura, roughly.

"Nobody," they answered, with contempt. Yet each one of them waited for him to look at her, hoped he would look at her. All except Annie, and something was broken in her.

He, however, kept his face closed and averted from them all. There was a silence of the end. He picked up the torn pieces of his tunic, without knowing what to do with them. The girls stood about uneasily, flushed, panting, tidying their hair and their dress unconsciously, and watching him. He looked at none of them. He espied his cap in a corner, and went and picked it up. He put it on his head, and one of the girls burst into a shrill, hysteric laugh at the sight he presented. He, however, took no heed, but went straight to where his overcoat hung on a peg. The girls moved away from contact with him as if he had been an electric wire. He put on his coat and buttoned it down. Then he rolled his tunic-rags into a bundle, and stood before the locked door, dumbly.

"Open the door, somebody," said Laura.

"Annie's got the key," said one.

Annie silently offered the key to the girls. Nora unlocked the door.

"Tit for tat, old man," she said. "Show yourself a man, and don't bear a grudge."

But without a word or sign he had opened the door and gone, his face closed, his head dropped.

"That'll learn him," said Laura.

"Coddy!" said Nora.

"Shut up, for God's sake!" cried Annie fiercely, as if in torture.

"Well, I'm about ready to go, Polly. Look sharp!" said Muriel.

The girls were all anxious to be off. They were tidying themselves hurriedly, with mute, stupefied faces.

Katherine Mansfield (1888–1923)

Like several other important short-story writers (Chekhov, Maupassant, Poe), Katherine Mansfield died quite young. After an ultra-Bohemian life, she succumbed to tuberculosis in 1923. Her reputation as a writer rests upon forty-two short stories, a volume of critical pieces, a group of revealing letters, and a remarkable journal.

Born Kathleen Beauchamp, daughter of a well-to-do New Zealand banker, Mansfield went to England as a schoolgirl of fifteen, and except for a visit the next year, she never went home again. Yet some of her best stories take place in the New Zealand of her childhood. As an adult, she was always an alien, an outsider. She traveled in Europe, lived in England, Germany, Italy, died in France, stayed on the fringes of groups like Bloomsbury or the mystics among whom she spent her last days at Fontainebleau. Her friends were Bohemians and artists. Gudrun in Lawrence's *Women in Love* and Beatrice Gilray in Aldous Huxley's *Point Counterpoint* seem to be modeled after her. She and Virginia Woolf were uneasy friends. The great relationship of her adult life was with John Middleton Murry, whom she married in 1918. After her death, Murry edited her letters and journals and did much to promote the cult of Katherine Mansfield as the doomed artist who lived to the hilt all the time.

Mansfield read Chekhov in German translation before his work appeared in English, and he was the great influence on her development as a writer. At least five of her stories are closely modeled after stories by him. Like Chekhov, Mansfield uses small moments to reveal large significance in the lives of people, and, like him, she develops the irony inherent in so many human situations.

But she must be credited with her own substantial contributions to the development of the short story, its language, and its structure. Under her influence the language of the genre became more lyrical and expressive. She does not merely denote or describe the feelings and thoughts of her characters, she recreates them. Her language closely tracks their sensitivity, perception, intensity; in short, the slang, the cadence, the phrasing reproduce the personality of the character. This technique at its best draws the reader very close to the emotional center of the story, so that the writer, the reader, and the protagonist all seem to be occupying the same space and experiencing the same emotions.

Because, true romantic that she was, she cared so much about intensity of feeling, Mansfield attempted to remove all that did not directly contribute to the emotional impact. She concentrated the presentation of plot into a brief time span covering only the most dramatic moments (see Introduction pp. 7–8). Time past, present, and future all seem to be occurring now in the mind of the protagonist. The whole weight of a life—or of a marriage—is compressed in a moment.

Her main characters are extremely vulnerable to experience and their own emotions. And by concentrating so intensely on their sensitivity, Mansfield sometimes oversimplifies her people and their experience. Occasionally, as in her "Life of Ma Parker," her stories slide into sentimentality. But "The Garden Party" is saved from this fate. Because the narrator is young, because the reader can sympathize with the family members who don't want their party ruined, and because Laura goes through contrasting experiences and emotional shifts, Mansfield fully earns her ending: " 'Isn't life,' she stammered, 'isn't life——' But what life was she couldn't explain."

The Garden-Party

And after all the weather was ideal. They could not have had a more perfect day for a garden-party if they had ordered it. Windless, warm, the sky without a cloud. Only the blue was veiled with a haze of light gold, as it is sometimes in early summer. The gardener had been up since dawn, mowing the lawns and sweeping them, until the grass and the dark flat rosettes where the daisy plants had been seemed to shine. As for the roses, you could not help feeling they understood that roses are the only flowers that impress people at garden-parties; the only flowers that everybody is certain of knowing. Hundreds, yes, literally hundreds, had come out in a single night; the green bushes bowed down as though they had been visited by archangels.

Breakfast was not yet over before the men came to put up the marquee.

"Where do you want the marquee put, mother?"

"My dear child, it's no use asking me. I'm determined to leave everything to you children this year. Forget I am your mother. Treat me as an honoured guest."

But Meg could not possibly go and supervise the men. She had washed her hair before breakfast, and she sat drinking her coffee in a green turban, with a dark wet curl stamped on each cheek. Jose, the butterfly, always came down in a silk petticoat and a kimono jacket.

"You'll have to go, Laura; you're the artistic one."

Away Laura flew, still holding her piece of bread-and-butter. It's so delicious to have an excuse for eating out of doors, and besides, she loved having to arrange things; she always felt she could do it so much better than anybody else.

Four men in their shirt-sleeves stood grouped together on the garden path. They carried staves covered with rolls of canvas, and they had big tool-bags slung on their backs. They looked impressive. Laura wished now that she had not got the bread-and-butter, but there was nowhere to put it, and she couldn't possibly throw it away. She blushed and tried to look severe and even a little bit short-sighted as she came up to them.

"Good morning," she said, copying her mother's voice. But that sounded so fearfully affected that she was ashamed, and stammered like a little girl, "Oh—er—have you come—is it about the marquee?"

"That's right, miss," said the tallest of the men, a lanky, freckled fellow, and he shifted his tool-bag, knocked back his straw hat and smiled down at her. "That's about it."

His smile was so easy, so friendly that Laura recovered. What nice eyes he had, small, but such a dark blue! And now she looked at the others, they were smiling too. "Cheer up, we won't bite," their smile seemed to say. How very nice workmen were! And what a beautiful morning! She mustn't mention the morning; she must be business-like. The marquee.

"Well, what about the lily-lawn? Would that do?"

And she pointed to the lily-lawn with the hand that didn't hold the bread-and-butter. They turned, they stared in the direction. A little fat chap thrust out his under-lip, and the tall fellow frowned.

"I don't fancy it," he said. "Not conspicuous enough. You see, with a thing like a marquee," and he turned to Laura in his easy way, "you want to put it somewhere where it'll give you a bang slap in the eye, if you follow me."

Laura's upbringing made her wonder for a moment whether it was quite respectful of a workman to talk to her of bangs slap in the eye. But she did quite follow him.

"A corner of the tennis-court," she suggested. "But the band's going to be in one corner."

"H'm, going to have a band, are you?" said another of the workmen. He was pale. He had a haggard look as his dark eyes scanned the tennis-court. What was he thinking?

"Only a very small band," said Laura gently. Perhaps he wouldn't mind so much if the band was quite small. But the tall fellow interrupted.

"Look here, miss, that's the place. Against those trees. Over there. That'll do fine."

Against the karakas. Then the karaka trees would be hidden. And they were so lovely, with their broad, gleaming leaves, and their clusters of yellow fruit. They were like trees you imagined growing on a desert island, proud, solitary, lifting their leaves and fruits to the sun in a kind of silent splendour. Must they be hidden by a marquee?

They must. Already the men had shouldered their staves and were making for the place. Only the tall fellow was left. He bent down, pinched a sprig of lavender, put his thumb and forefinger to his nose and snuffed up the smell. When Laura saw that gesture she forgot all about the karakas in her wonder at him caring for things like that—caring for the smell of lavender. How many men that she knew would have done such a thing? Oh, how extraordinarily nice workmen were, she thought. Why couldn't she have workmen for friends rather than the silly boys she danced with and who came to Sunday night supper? She would get on much better with men like these.

It's all the fault, she decided, as the tall fellow drew something on the back of an envelope, something that was to be looped up or left to hang, of these absurd class distinctions. Well, for her part, she didn't feel them. Not a bit, not an atom. . . . And now there came the chock-chock of wooden hammers. Some one whistled, some one sang out, "Are you right there, matey?" "Matey!" The friendliness of it, the—the— Just to prove how happy she was, just to show the tall fellow how at home she felt, and how she despised stupid conventions, Laura took a big bite of her bread-and-butter as she stared at the little drawing. She felt just like a work-girl.

"Laura, Laura, where are you? Telephone, Laura!" a voice cried from the house.

"Coming!" Away she skimmed, over the lawn, up the path, up the steps, across the verandah, and into the porch. In the hall her father and Laurie were brushing their hats ready to go to the office.

"I say, Laura," said Laurie very fast, "you might just give a squiz at my coat before this afternoon. See if it wants pressing."

"I will," said she. Suddenly she couldn't stop herself. She ran at Laurie and gave him a small, quick squeeze. "Oh, I do love parties, don't you?" gasped Laura.

"Ra-ther," said Laurie's warm, boyish voice, and he squeezed his sister too, and gave her a gentle push. "Dash off to the telephone, old girl."

The telephone. "Yes, yes; oh yes. Kitty? Good morning, dear. Come to lunch? Do, dear. Delighted of course. It will only be a very scratch meal—just the sandwich crusts and broken meringue-shells and what's left over. Yes, isn't it a perfect morning? Your white? Oh, I certainly should. One moment—hold the line. Mother's calling." And Laura sat back. "What, mother? Can't hear."

Mrs. Sheridan's voice floated down the stairs. "Tell her to wear that sweet hat she had on last Sunday."

"Mother says you're to wear that *sweet* hat you had on last Sunday. Good. One o'clock. Bye-bye."

Laura put back the receiver, flung her arms over her head, took a deep breath, stretched and let them fall. "Huh," she sighed, and the moment after the sigh she sat up quickly. She was still, listening. All the doors in the house seemed to be open. The house was alive with soft, quick steps and running voices. The green baize door that led to the kitchen regions swung open and shut with a muffled thud. And now there came a long, chuckling absurd sound. It was the heavy piano being moved on its stiff castors. But the air! If you stopped to notice, was the air always like this? Little faint winds were playing chase, in at the tops of the windows, out at the doors. And there were two tiny spots of sun, one on the inkpot, one on a silver photograph frame, playing too. Darling little spots. Especially the one on the inkpot lid. It was quite warm. A warm little silver star. She could have kissed it.

The front door bell pealed, and there sounded the rustle of Sadie's print skirt on the stairs. A man's voice murmured; Sadie answered, careless, "I'm sure I don't know. Wait. I'll ask Mrs. Sheridan."

"What is it, Sadie?" Laura came into the hall.

"It's the florist, Miss Laura."

It was, indeed. There, just inside the door, stood a wide, shallow tray full of pots of pink lilies. No other kind. Nothing but lilies—canna lilies, big pink flowers, wide open, radiant, almost frighteningly alive on bright crimson stems.

"O-oh, Sadie!" said Laura, and the sound was like a little moan. She crouched down as if to warm herself at that blaze of lilies; she felt they were in her fingers, on her lips, growing in her breast.

"It's some mistake," she said faintly. "Nobody ever ordered so many. Sadie, go and find mother."

But at that moment Mrs. Sheridan joined them.

"It's quite right," she said calmly. "Yes, I ordered them. Aren't they lovely?" She pressed Laura's arm. "I was passing the shop yesterday, and I saw them in the window. And I suddenly thought for once in my life I shall have enough canna lilies. The garden-party will be a good excuse."

"But I thought you said you didn't mean to interfere," said Laura. Sadie had gone. The florist's man was still outside at his van. She put her arm round her mother's neck and gently, very gently, she bit her mother's ear.

"My darling child, you wouldn't like a logical mother, would you? Don't do that. Here's the man."

He carried more lilies still, another whole tray.

"Bank them up, just inside the door, on both sides of the porch, please," said Mrs. Sheridan. "Don't you agree, Laura?"

"Oh, I *do* mother."

In the drawing-room Meg, Jose and good little Hans had at last succeeded in moving the piano.

"Now, if we put this chesterfield against the wall and move everything out of the room except the chairs, don't you think?"

"Quite."

"Hans, move these tables into the smoking-room, and bring a sweeper to take these marks off the carpet and—one moment, Hans—" Jose loved giving orders to the servants, and they loved obeying her. She always made them feel they were taking part in some drama. "Tell mother and Miss Laura to come here at once."

"Very good, Miss Jose."

She turned to Meg. "I want to hear what the piano sounds like, just in case I'm asked to sing this afternoon. Let's try over 'This life is Weary.'"

Pom! Ta-ta-ta *Tee*-ta! The piano burst out so passionately that Jose's face changed. She clasped her hands. She looked mournfully and enigmatically at her mother and Laura as they came in.

> This Life is *Wee*-ary,
> A Tear—a Sigh.
> A Love that *Chan*-ges,
>   This Life is *Wee*-ary,
> A Tear—a Sigh.
> A Love that *Chan*-ges,
> And then . . . Good-bye!

But at the word "Good-bye," and although the piano sounded more desperate than ever, her face broke into a brilliant, dreadfully unsympathetic smile.

"Aren't I in good voice, mummy?" she beamed.

> This Life is *Wee*-ary,
> Hope comes to Die.
> A Dream—a *Wa*-kening.

But now Sadie interrupted them. "What is it, Sadie?"

"If you please, m'm, cook says have you got the flags for the sandwiches?"

"The flags for the sandwiches, Sadie? echoed Mrs. Sheridan dreamily. And the children knew by her face that she hadn't got them. "Let me see." And she said to Sadie firmly, "Tell cook I'll let her have them in ten minutes."

Sadie went.

"Now, Laura," said her mother quickly. "Come with me into the smoking-room. I've got the names somewhere on the back of an envelope. You'll have to write them out for me. Meg, go upstairs this minute and take that wet thing off your head. Jose, run and finish dressing this instant. Do you hear me, children, or shall I have to tell your father when he comes home to-night? And—and, Jose, pacify cook if you do go into the kitchen, will you? I'm terrified of her this morning."

The envelope was found at last behind the dining-room clock, though how it had got there Mrs. Sheridan could not imagine.

"One of you children must have stolen it out of my bag, because I remember vividly—cream cheese and lemon-curd. Have you done that?"

"Yes."

"Egg and—" Mrs. Sheridan held the envelope away from her. "It looks like mice. It can't be mice, can it?"

"Olive, pet," said Laura, looking over her shoulder.

"Yes, of course, olive. What a horrible combination it sounds. Egg and olive."

They were finished at last, and Laura took them off to the kitchen. She found Jose there pacifying the cook, who did not look at all terrifying.

"I have never seen such exquisite sandwiches," said Jose's rapturous voice. "How many kinds did you say there were, cook? Fifteen?"

"Fifteen, Miss Jose."

"Well, cook, I congratulate you."

Cook swept up crusts with the long sandwich knife, and smiled broadly.

"Godber's has come," announced Sadie, issuing out of the pantry. She had seen the man pass the window.

That meant the cream puffs had come. Godber's were famous for their cream puffs. Nobody ever thought of making them at home.

"Bring them in and put them on the table, my girl," ordered cook.

Sadie brought them in and went back to the door. Of course Laura and Jose were far too grown-up to really care about such things. All the same, they couldn't help agreeing that the puffs looked very attractive. Very. Cook began arranging them, shaking off the extra icing sugar.

"Don't they carry one back to all one's parties?" said Laura.

"I suppose they do," said practical Jose, who never like to be carried back. "They look beautifully light and feathery, I must say."

"Have one each, my dears," said cook in her comfortable voice. "Yer ma won't know."

Oh, impossible. Fancy cream puffs so soon after breakfast. The very idea made one shudder. All the same, two minutes later Jose and Laura were licking their fingers with that absorbed inward look that only comes from whipped cream.

"Let's go into the garden, out by the back way," suggested Laura. "I want to see how the men are getting on with the marquee. They're such awfully nice men."

But the back door was blocked by cook, Sadie, Godber's man and Hans.

Something had happened.

"Tuk-tuk-tuk," clucked cook like an agitated hen. Sadie had her hand clapped to her cheek as though she had toothache. Hans's face was screwed up in the effort to understand. Only Godber's man seemed to be enjoying himself; it was his story.

"What's the matter? What's happened?"

"There's been a horrible accident," said cook. "A man killed."

"A man killed! Where? How? When?"

But Godber's man wasn't going to have his story snatched from under his very nose.

"Know those little cottages just below here, miss?" Know them? Of course, she knew them. "Well, there's a young chap living there, name of Scott, a carter. His horse shied at a traction-engine, corner of Hawke Street this morning, and he was thrown out on the back of his head. Killed."

"Dead!" Laura stared at Godber's man.

"Dead when they picked him up," said Godber's man with relish. "They were taking the body home as I come up here." And he said to the cook, "He's left a wife and five little ones."

"Jose, come here." Laura caught hold of her sister's sleeve and dragged her through the kitchen to the other side of the green baize door. There she paused and leaned against it. "Jose!" she said, horrified, "however are we going to stop everything?"

"Stop everything, Laura!" cried Jose in astonishment. "What do you mean?"

"Stop the garden-party, of course." Why did Jose pretend?

But Jose was still more amazed. "Stop the garden-party? My dear Laura, don't be so absurd. Of course we can't do anything of the kind. Nobody expects us to. Don't be so extravagant."

"But we can't possibly have a garden-party with a man dead just outside the front gate."

That really was extravagant, for the little cottages were in a lane to themselves at the very bottom of a steep rise that led up to the house. A broad road ran between. True, they were far too near. They were the greatest possible eyesore, and they had no right to be in that neighbourhood at all. They were little mean dwellings painted a chocolate brown. In the garden patches there was nothing but cabbage stalks, sick hens and tomato cans. The very smoke coming out of their chimneys was poverty-stricken. Little rags and shreds of smoke, so unlike the great silvery plumes that uncurled from the Sheridans' chimneys. Washerwomen lived in the lane and sweeps and a cobbler, and a man whose house-front was studded all over with minute bird-cages. Children swarmed. When the Sheridans were little they were forbidden to set foot there because of the revolting language and of what they might catch. But since they were grown up, Laura and Laurie on their prowls sometimes walked through. It was disgusting and sordid. They came out with a shudder. But still one must go everywhere; one must see everything. So through they went.

"And just think of what the band would sound like to that poor woman," said Laura.

"Oh, Laura!" Jose began to be seriously annoyed. "If you're going to stop a band playing every time some one has an accident, you'll lead a very strenuous life. I'm every bit as sorry about it as you. I feel just as sympathetic." Her eyes hardened. She looked at her sister just as she used to when they were little and fighting together. "You won't bring a drunken workman back to life by being sentimental," she said softly.

"Drunk! Who said he was drunk?" Laura turned furiously on Jose. She said, just as they had used to say on those occasions, "I'm going straight up to tell mother."

"Do, dear," cooed Jose.

"Mother, can I come into your room?" Laura turned the big glass door-knob.

"Of course, child. Why, what's the matter? What's given you such a colour?" And Mrs. Sheridan turned round from her dressing table. She was trying on a new hat.

"Mother, a man's been killed," began Laura.

"*Not* in the garden?" interrupted her mother.

"No, no!"

"Oh, what a fright you gave me!" Mrs. Sheridan sighed with relief, and took off the big hat and held it on her knees.

"But listen, mother," said Laura. Breathless, half-choking, she told the dreadful story. "Of course, we can't have our party, can we?" she pleaded. "The band and everybody arriving. They'd hear us, mother; they're nearly neighbours!"

To Laura's astonishment her mother behaved just like Jose, it was harder to bear because she seemed amused. She refused to take Laura seriously.

"But, my dear child, use your common sense. It's only by accident we've heard of it. If some one had died there normally—and I can't understand how they keep alive in those poky little holes—we should still be having our party, shouldn't we?"

Laura had to say "yes" to that, but she felt it was all wrong. She sat down on her mother's sofa and pinched the cushion frill.

"Mother, isn't it really terribly heartless of us?" she asked.

"Darling!" Mrs. Sheridan got up and came over to her, carrying the hat. Before Laura could stop her she had popped it on. "My child!" said her mother, "the hat is yours. It's made for you. It's much too young for me. I have never seen you look such a picture. Look at yourself!" And she held up her hand-mirror.

"But, mother," Laura began again. She couldn't look at herself; she turned aside.

This time Mrs. Sheridan lost patience just as Jose had done.

"You are being very absurd, Laura," she said coldly. "People like that don't expect sacrifices from us. And it's not very sympathetic to spoil everybody's enjoyment as you're doing now."

"I don't understand," said Laura, and she walked quickly out of the room into her own bedroom. There, quite by chance, the first thing she saw was this charming girl in the mirror, in her black hat trimmed with gold daisies, and a long black velvet ribbon. Never had she imagined she could look like that. Is mother right? she thought. And now she hoped her mother was right. Am I being extravagant? Perhaps it was extravagant. Just for a moment she had another glimpse of that poor woman and those little children, and the body being carried into the house. But it all seemed blurred, unreal, like a picture in the newspaper. I'll remember it again after the party's over, she decided. And somehow that seemed quite the best plan. . . .

Lunch was over by half past one. By half past two they were all ready for the fray. The green-coated band had arrived and was established in a corner of the tennis-court.

"My dear!" trilled Kitty Maitland, "aren't they too like frogs for words? You ought to have arranged them round the pond with the conductor in the middle on a leaf."

Laurie arrived and hailed them on his way to dress. At the sight of him Laura remembered the accident again. She wanted to tell him. If Laurie agreed with the others, then it was bound to be all right. And she followed him into the hall.

"Laurie!"

"Hallo!" He was half-way upstairs, but when he turned round and saw Laura he suddenly puffed out his cheeks and goggled his eyes at her. "My word, Laura; you do look stunning," said Laurie. "What an absolutely topping hat!"

Laura said faintly "Is it?" and smiled up at Laurie, and didn't tell him after all.

Soon after that people began coming in streams. The band struck up; the hired waiters ran from the house to the marquee. Wherever you looked there were couples strolling, bending to the flowers, greeting, moving on over the lawn. They were like bright birds that had alighted in the Sheridans' garden for this one afternoon, on their way to—where? Ah, what happiness it is to be with people who all are happy, to press hands, press cheeks, smile into eyes.

"Darling Laura, how well you look!"

"What a becoming hat, child!"

"Laura, you look quite Spanish. I've never seen you look so striking."

And Laura, glowing, answered softly, "Have you had tea? Won't you have an ice? The passion-fruit ices really are rather special." She ran to her father and begged him. "Daddy darling, can't the band have something to drink?"

And the perfect afternoon slowly ripened, slowly faded, slowly its petals closed.

"Never a more delightful garden-party . . . " "The greatest success . . . " "Quite the most . . . "

Laura helped her mother with the good-byes. They stood side by side in the porch till it was all over.

"All over, all over, thank heaven," said Mrs. Sheridan. "Round up the others, Laura. Let's go and have some fresh coffee. I'm exhausted. Yes, it's been very success-ful. But oh, these parties, these parties! Why will you children insist on giving parties!" And they all of them sat down in the deserted marquee.

"Have a sandwich, daddy dear. I wrote the flag."

"Thanks." Mr. Sheridan took a bite and the sandwich was gone. He took another. "I suppose you didn't hear of a beastly accident that happened to-day?" he said.

"My dear," said Mrs. Sheridan, holding up her hand, "we did. It nearly ruined the party. Laura insisted we should put it off."

"Oh, mother!" Laura didn't want to be teased about it.

"It was a horrible affair all the same," said Mr. Sheridan. "The chap was married too. Lived just below in the lane, and leaves a wife and half a dozen kiddies, so they say."

An awkward little silence fell. Mrs. Sheridan fidgeted with her cup. Really, it was very tactless of father . . .

Suddenly she looked up. There on the table were all those sandwiches, cakes, puffs, all uneaten, all going to be wasted. She had one of her brilliant ideas.

"I know," she said. "Let's make up a basket. Let's send that poor creature some of this perfectly good food. At any rate, it will be the greatest treat for the children.

Don't you agree? And she's sure to have neighbours calling in and so on. What a point to have it all ready prepared. Laura!'' She jumped up. ''Get me the big basket out of the stairs cupboard.''

''But, mother, do you really think it's a good idea?'' said Laura.

Again, how curious, she seemed to be different from them all. To take scraps from their party. Would the poor woman really like that?

''Of course! What's the matter with you to-day? An hour or two ago you were insisting on us being sympathetic, and now—''

Oh, well! Laura ran for the basket. It was filled, it was heaped by her mother.

''Take it yourself, darling,'' said she. ''Run down just as you are. No, wait, take the arum lilies too. People of that class are so impressed by arum lilies.''

''The stems will ruin her lace frock,'' said practical Jose.

So they would. Just in time. ''Only the basket, then. And, Laura!''—her mother followed her out of the marquee—''don't on any account—''

''What, mother?''

No, better not put such ideas into the child's head! ''Nothing! Run along.''

It was just growing dusky as Laura shut their garden gates. A big dog ran by like a shadow. The road gleamed white, and down below in the hollow the little cottages were in deep shade. How quiet it seemed after the afternoon. Here she was going down the hill to somewhere where a man lay dead, and she couldn't realize it. Why couldn't she? She stopped a minute. And it seemed to her that kisses, voices, tinkling spoons, laughter, the smell of crushed grass were somehow inside her. She had no room for anything else. How strange! She looked up at the pale sky, and all she thought was, ''Yes, it was the most successful party.''

Now the broad road was crossed. The lane began, smoky and dark. Women in shawls and men's tweed caps hurried by. Men hung over the palings; the children played in the doorways. A low hum came from the mean little cottages. In some of them there was a flicker of light, and a shadow, crab-like, moved across the window. Laura bent her head and hurried on. She wished now she had put on a coat. How her frock shone! And the big hat with the velvet streamer—if only it was another hat! Were the people looking at her? They must be. It was a mistake to have come; she knew all along it was a mistake. Should she go back even now?

No, too late. This was the house. It must be. A dark knot of people stood outside. Beside the gate an old, old woman with a crutch sat in a chair, watching. She had her feet on a newspaper. The voices stopped as Laura drew near. The group parted. It was as though she was expected, as though they had known she was coming here.

Laura was terribly nervous. Tossing the velvet ribbon over her shoulder, she said to a woman standing by, ''Is this Mrs. Scott's house?'' and the woman, smiling queerly, said, ''It is, my lass.''

Oh, to be away from this! She actually said, ''Help me, God,'' as she walked up the tiny path and knocked. To be away from those staring eyes, or to be covered up in anything, one of those women's shawls even. I'll just leave the basket and go, she decided. I shan't even wait for it to be emptied.

Then the door opened. A little woman in black showed in the gloom.

Laura said, ''Are you Mrs. Scott?'' But to her horror the woman answered, ''Walk in please, miss,'' and she was shut in the passage.

''No,'' said Laura, ''I don't want to come in. I only want to leave this basket. Mother sent—''

The little woman in the gloomy passage seemed not to have heard her. ''Step this way, please, miss,'' she said in an oily voice, and Laura followed her.

She found herself in a wretched little low kitchen lighted by a smoky lamp. There was a woman sitting before the fire.

"Em," said the little creature who had let her in. "Em! It's a young lady." She turned to Laura. She said meaningly, "I'm 'er sister, miss. You'll excuse 'er, won't you?"

"Oh, but of course!" said Laura. "Please, please don't disturb her. I—I only want to leave—"

But at that moment the woman at the fire turned round. Her face, puffed up, red, with swollen eyes and swollen lips, looked terrible. She seemed as though she couldn't understand why Laura was there. What did it mean? Why was this stranger standing in the kitchen with a basket? What was it all about? And the poor face puckered up again.

"All right, my dear," said the other. "I'll thenk the young lady."

And again she began, "You'll excuse her, miss, I'm sure," and her face, swollen too, tried an oily smile.

Laura only wanted to get out, to get away. She was back in the passage. The door opened. She walked straight through into the bedroom, where the dead man was lying.

"You'd like a look at 'im, wouldn't you?" said Em's sister, and she brushed past Laura over to the bed. "Don't be afraid, my lass,—" and now her voice sounded fond and sly, and fondly she drew down the sheet—" 'e looks a picture. There's nothing to show. Come along, my dear."

Laura came.

There lay a young man, fast asleep—sleeping so soundly, so deeply, that he was far, far away from them both. Oh, so remote, so peaceful. He was dreaming. Never wake him up again. His head was sunk in the pillow, his eyes were closed; they were blind under the closed eyelids. He was given up to his dream. What did garden-parties and baskets and lace frocks matter to him? He was far from all those things. He was wonderful, beautiful. While they were laughing and while the band was playing, this marvel had come to the lane. Happy . . . happy. . . . All is well, said that sleeping face. This is just as it should be. I am content.

But all the same you had to cry, and she couldn't go out of the room without saying something to him. Laura gave a loud childish sob.

"Forgive my hat," she said.

And this time she didn't wait for Em's sister. She found her way out of the door, down the path, past all those dark people. At the corner of the lane she met Laurie.

He stepped out of the shadow. "Is that you, Laura?"

"Yes."

"Mother was getting anxious. Was it all right?"

"Yes, quite. Oh, Laurie!" She took his arm, she pressed up against him.

"I say, you're not crying, are you?" asked her brother.

Laura shook her head. She was.

Laurie put his arm round her shoulder. "Don't cry," he said in his warm, loving voice. "Was it awful?"

"No," sobbed Laura. "It was simply marvellous. But, Laurie—" She stopped, she looked at her brother. "Isn't life," she stammered, "isn't life—" But what life was she couldn't explain. No matter. He quite understood.

"*Isn't* it, darling?" said Laurie.

Conrad Aiken (1889–1973)

Until his death in August 1973, Conrad Aiken had enjoyed a long and distinguished career as poet, critic, and writer of fiction. He began his undergraduate studies at Harvard in 1908 with a freshman class which included T. S. Eliot (whom Aiken nicknamed *tsetse*), Van Wyck Brooks, John Reed, and Robert Benchley. During his senior year he was placed on probation for poor class attendance; indignant, he took off for Europe. Six months later he returned and completed his degree in June 1912. Between 1916 and 1922 he wrote poetry and fiction, as well as serving actively as a reviewer-critic for the *Dial, The New Republic,* and various London journals. Except for one brief stint in 1927–1928 as tutor in English at Harvard, Aiken seems to have functioned throughout his long and productive career wholly as a professional writer and editor. While his work brought him many honors— Pulitzer Prize (1930), Library of Congress Chair of Poetry (1950), National Book Award (1954), Bollingen Prize (1956)—he was always thought to be somewhat outside the main currents of American literary fashion.

Behind any and all of the externals of Aiken's life and career lay a shattering experience of boyhood. At age eleven and a half, in the year 1900, he heard two pistol shots and discovered that his father had killed his mother and himself. Here is how Aiken writes of that terrible event years later in his autobiographical *Ushant* (1952):

> He was retaining all this, and re-enacting it, even to the final scene of all: when, after the desultory early-morning quarrel, came the half-stifled scream, and then the sound of his father's voice counting three, and the two loud pistol-shots; and he had tiptoed into the dark room, where the two bodies lay motionless, and apart, and finding them dead, *found himself possessed of them forever.*

We may only guess what the long-term effects of that profound wound were to be. Much of Aiken's criticism is Freudian, and Freudian psychoanalysis did become important to him. Enlargement of consciousness, human relationships, individual isolation—all these are central themes and tensions in his poems, novels, and stories. But any full study of his work will reveal that he went beyond Freudianism. As Henry A. Murray, psychoanalyst and close friend, put it: "Aiken allowed the Freudian dragon to swallow him, and then, after a sufficient sojourn in its maw, cut his way out to a new freedom."

"Silent Snow, Secret Snow" belongs to a gathering of Aiken's short stories published in 1934 under the title *Among the Lost People.* Other stories in the collection set forth configurations of separation and isolation (the lonely child, the lonely old man), but none more dramatically than this one. Among all those lost people of the volume, no one gets lost so sheerly, so completely, so *purely* as does Paul. Some readers take the snow as representing death or a metaphoric means to death. And yet Paul's final condition suggests a living death. The action commences in the preliminary stages of schizophrenia and moves through stages of intensification to the final and permanent withdrawal from an irrecoverable objective reality—Paul's end being not death, but a state of ultimate, autistic catatonia. The ending of Aiken's story brings to mind the end of Ibsen's play *Ghosts,* where Oswald, suffering the final ravages of syphilis, sits motionless, staring at an eclipsing sun, going blind and mad all at once.

Whatever their final interpretation, readers have uniformly regarded this as Aiken's most powerful tale. We are led into the center of the story gradually, but with a kind of relentless suspense that will not let us go. Part of Aiken's technique is to arouse within us the expectation that the snow stands for, or contains, some deeper meaning or reality that will eventually be revealed, perhaps in some kind of confrontation scene, in which we will share recognition with Paul (or his parents) of what they come to recognize. But it doesn't happen; we never get beyond the snow itself, "whose meanings remain secret." One of the most judicious commentaries on the story is that of Frederick J. Hoffman:

> The narrative consistently stays within the boy's mind, moving with it toward his destruction, never suggesting or stating reasons or trying to probe "psychologically" into the boy's injured spirit. It is a psychic scene of remarkable purity; the adult world stays always dimly at the fringe of the boy's awareness and of his sense of his relationship. What has caused the aberration is never revealed, but his desire to withdraw from human communication is faithfully followed to its ultimate, total rejection of the family and submission to the vision.

Silent Snow, Secret Snow

Just why it should have happened, or why it should have happened just when it did, he could not, of course, possibly have said; nor perhaps could it even have occurred to him to ask. The thing was above all a secret, something to be preciously concealed from Mother and Father; and to that very fact it owed an enormous part of its deliciousness. It was like a peculiarly beautiful trinket to be carried unmentioned in one's trouser-pocket—a rare stamp, an old coin, a few tiny gold links found trodden out of shape on the path in the park, a pebble of carnelian,[1] a sea shell distinguishable from all others by an unusual spot or stripe—and, as if it were any one of these, he carried around with him everywhere a warm and persistent and increasingly beautiful sense of possession. Nor was it only a sense of possession—it was also a sense of protection. It was as if, in some delightful way, his secret gave him a fortress, a wall behind which he could retreat into heavenly seclusion. This was almost the first thing he had noticed about it—apart from the oddness of the thing itself—and it was this that now again, for the fiftieth time, occurred to him, as he sat in the little schoolroom. It was the half hour for geography. Miss Buell was revolving with one finger, slowly, a huge terrestrial globe which had been placed on her desk. The green and yellow continents passed and repassed, questions were asked and answered, and now the little girl in front of him, Deirdre, who had a funny little constellation of freckles on the back of her neck, exactly like the Big Dipper, was standing up and telling Miss Buell that the equator was the line that ran around the middle:

---

[1] A reddish quartz, used in jewelry.

Miss Buell's face, which was old and grayish and kindly, with gray stiff curls beside the cheeks, and eyes that swam very brightly, like little minnows, behind thick glasses, wrinkled itself into a complication of amusements.

"Ah! I see. The earth is wearing a belt, or a sash. Or someone drew a line round it!"

"Oh, no—not that—I mean—"

In the general laughter, he did not share, or only a very little. He was thinking about the Arctic and Antarctic regions, which of course, on the globe, were white. Miss Buell was now telling them about the tropics, the jungles, the steamy heat of equatorial swamps, where the birds and butterflies, and even the snakes, were like living jewels. As he listened to these things, he was already, with a pleasant sense of half-effort, putting his secret between himself and the words. Was it really an effort at all? For effort implied something voluntary, and perhaps even something one did not especially want; whereas this was distinctly pleasant, and came almost of its own accord. All he needed to do was to think of that morning, the first one, and then of all the others—

But it was all so absurdly simple! It had amounted to so little. It was nothing, just an idea—and just why it should have become so wonderful, so permanent, was a mystery—a very pleasant one, to be sure, but also, in an amusing way, foolish. However, without ceasing to listen to Miss Buell, who had now moved up to the north temperate zone, he deliberately invited his memory of the first morning. It was only a moment or two after he had waked up—or perhaps the moment itself. But was there, to be exact, an exact moment? Was one awake all at once? Or was it gradual? Anyway, it was after he had stretched a lazy hand up towards the headrail, and yawned, and then relaxed again among his warm covers, all the more grateful on a December morning, that the thing had happened. Suddenly, for no reason, he had thought of the postman, he remembered the postman. Perhaps there was nothing so odd in that. After all, he heard the postman almost every morning in his life—his heavy boots could be heard clumping round the corner at the top of the little cobbled hill-street, and then, progressively nearer, progressively louder, the double knock at each door, the crossings and re-crossings of the street, till finally the clumsy steps came stumbling across to the very door, and the tremendous knock came which shook the house itself.

(Miss Buell was saying "Vast wheat-growing areas in North America and Siberia.")

Deirdre had for the moment placed her left hand across the back of her neck.)

But on this particular morning, the first morning, as he lay there with his eyes closed, he had for some reason *waited* for the postman. He wanted to hear him come round the corner. And that was precisely the joke—he never did. He never came. He never had come—*round the corner*—again. For when at last the steps *were* heard, they had already, he was quite sure, come a little down the hill, to the first house; and even so, the steps were curiously different—they were softer, they had a new secrecy about them, they were muffled and indistinct; and while the rhythm of them was the same, it now said a new thing—it said peace, it said remoteness, it said cold, it said sleep. And he had understood the situation at once—nothing could have seemed simpler—there had been snow in the night, such as all winter he had been longing for; and it was this which had rendered the postman's first footsteps inaudible, and the later ones faint. Of course! How lovely! And even now it must be snowing—it was going to be a snowy day—the long white ragged lines were drifting and sifting across the street, across the faces of the old houses, whispering and hushing, making little triangles of white in the corners between cobblestones, seething a little when the wind blew them over the ground to a drifted corner; and so it would be all day, getting deeper and deeper and silenter and silenter.

(Miss Buell was saying "Land of perpetual snow.")

All this time, of course (while he lay in bed), he had kept his eyes closed, listening to the nearer progress of the postman, the muffled footsteps thumping and slipping on the snow-sheathed cobbles; and all the other sounds—the double knocks, a frosty far-off voice or two, a bell ringing thinly and softly as if under a sheet of ice—had the same slightly abstracted quality, as if removed by one degree from actuality—as if everything in the world had been insulated by snow. But when at last, pleased, he opened his eyes, and turned them towards the window, to see for himself this long-desired and now so clearly imagined miracle—what he saw instead was brilliant sunlight on a roof; and when, astonished, he jumped out of bed and stared down into the street, expecting to see the cobbles obliterated by the snow, he was nothing but the bare bright cobbles themselves.

Queer, the effect this extraordinary surprise had had upon him—all the following morning he had kept with him a sense as of snow falling about him, a secret screen of new snow between himself and the world. If he had not dreamed such a thing—and how could he have dreamed it while awake?—how else could one explain it? In any case, the delusion had been so vivid as to affect his entire behavior. He could not now remember whether it was on the first or the second morning—or was it even the third?—that his mother had drawn attention to some oddness in his manner.

"But my darling"—she had said at the breakfast table—"what has come over you? You don't seem to be listening. . . . "

And how often that very thing had happened since!

(Miss Buell was now asking if anyone knew the difference between the North Pole and the Magnetic Pole. Deirdre was holding up her flickering brown hand, and he could see the four white dimples that marked the knuckles.)

Perhaps it hadn't been either the second or third morning—or even the fourth or fifth. How could he be sure? How could he be sure just when the delicious *progress* had become clear? Just when it had really *begun*? The intervals weren't very precise. . . . All he now knew was, that at some point or other—perhaps the second day, perhaps the sixth—he had noticed that the presence of the snow was a little more insistent, the sound of it clearer; and, conversely, the sound of the postman's footsteps more indistinct. Not only could he not hear the steps come round the corner, he could not even hear them at the first house. It was below the first house that he heard them; and then, a few days later, it was below the second house that he heard them; and a few days later again, below the third. Gradually, gradually, the snow was becoming heavier, the sound of its seething louder, the cobblestones more and more muffled. When he found, each morning, on going to the window, after the ritual of listening, that the roofs and cobbles were as bare as ever, it made no difference. This was, after all, only what he had expected. It was even what pleased him, what rewarded him: the thing was his own, belonged to no one else. No one else knew about it, not even his mother and father. There, outside, were the bare cobbles; and here, inside, was the snow. Snow growing heavier each day, muffling the world, hiding the ugly, and deadening increasingly—above all—the steps of the postman.

"But my darling"—she had said at the luncheon table—"what has come over you? You don't seem to listen when people speak to you. That's the third time I've asked you to pass your plate. . . . "

How was one to explain this to Mother? or to Father? There was, of course, nothing to be done about it, nothing. All one could do was to laugh embarrassedly, pretend to be a little ashamed, apologize, and take a sudden and somewhat disingenuous interest in what was being done or said. The cat had stayed out all night. He had a curious swelling on his left cheek—perhaps somebody had kicked him, or a stone had struck him. Mrs. Kempton was or was not coming to tea. The house was going to be house cleaned, or "turned out," on Wednesday instead of Friday. A new lamp was provided for his evening work—perhaps it was eyestrain which accounted for this new and so peculiar vagueness of his—Mother was looking at him with amusement as she said this, but with something else as well. A new lamp? A new lamp. Yes Mother, No Mother, Yes Mother. School is going very well. The geometry is very easy. The history is very dull. The geography is very interesting—particularly when it takes one to the North Pole. Why the North Pole? Oh, well, it would be fun to be an explorer. Another Peary or Scott or Shackleton. And then abruptly he found his interest in the talk at an end, stared at the pudding on his plate, listened, waited, and began once more—ah, how heavenly, too, the first beginnings—to hear or feel—for could he actually hear it?—the silent snow, the secret snow.

(Miss Buell was telling them about the search for the Northwest Passage, about Hendrik Hudson, the Half Moon.)

This had been, indeed, the only distressing feature of the new experience: the fact that it so increasingly had brought him into a kind of mute misunderstanding, or even conflict, with his father and mother. It was as if he were trying to lead a double life. On the one hand he had to be Paul Hasleman, and keep up the appearance of being that person—dress, wash, and answer intelligently when spoken to—; on the other, he had to explore this new world which had been opened to him. Nor could there be the slightest doubt—not the slightest—that the new world was the profounder and more wonderful of the two. It was irresistible. It was miraculous. Its beauty was simply beyond any-thing—beyond speech as beyond thought—utterly incommunicable. But how then, be-tween the two worlds, of which he was thus constantly aware, was he to keep a balance? One must get up, one must go to breakfast, one must talk with Mother, go to school, do one's lessons—and, in all this, try not to appear too much of a fool. But if all the while one was also trying to extract the full deliciousness of another and quite separate existence, one which could not easily (if at all) be spoken of—how was one to manage? How was one to explain? Would it be safe to explain? Would it be absurd? Would it merely mean that he would get into some obscure kind of trouble?

These thoughts came and went, came and went, as softly and secretly as the snow; they were not precisely a disturbance, perhaps they were even a pleasure; he liked to have them; their presence was something almost palpable, something he could stroke with his hand, without closing his eyes, and without ceasing to see Miss Buell and the schoolroom and the globe and the freckles on Deirdre's neck; nevertheless he did in a sense cease to see, or to see the obvious external world, and substituted for this vision the vision of snow, the sound of snow, and the slow, almost soundless, approach of the postman. Yesterday, it had been only at the sixth house that the postman had become audible; the snow was much deeper now, it was falling more swiftly and heavily, the sound of its seething was more distinct, more soothing, more persistent. And this morning, it had been—as nearly as he could figure—just above the seventh house— perhaps only a step or two above: at most, he had heard two or three footsteps before the knock had sounded. . . . And with each such narrowing of the sphere, each nearer approach of the limit at which the postman was first audible, it was odd how sharply was increased the amount of illusion which had to be carried into the ordinary business of daily life. Each day it was harder to get out of bed, to go to the window, to look out at the—as always—perfectly empty and snowless street. Each day it was more difficult to go through the perfunctory motions of greeting Mother and Father at breakfast, to reply to their questions, to put his books together and go to school. And at school, how extraordinarily hard to conduct with success simultaneously the public life and the life that was secret. There were times when he longed—positively ached—to tell everyone about it—to burst out with it—only to be checked almost at once by a far-off feeling as of some faint absurdity which was inherent in it—but *was* it absurd?—and more importantly by a sense of mysterious power in his very secrecy. Yes: it must be kept secret. That, more and more, became clear. At whatever cost to himself, whatever pain to others—

(Miss Buell looked straight at him, smiling, and said, "Perhaps we'll ask Paul. I'm sure Paul will come out of his day-dream long enough to be able to tell us. Won't you, Paul?" He rose slowly from his chair, resting one hand on the brightly varnished desk, and deliberately stared through the snow towards the blackboard. It was an effort, but it was amusing to make it. "Yes," he said slowly, "it was what we now call the Hudson River. This he thought to be the Northwest Passage. He was disappointed." He sat down again, and as he did so Deirdre half turned in her chair and gave him a shy smile, of approval and admiration.)

At whatever pain to others.

This part of it was very puzzling, very puzzling. Mother was very nice, and so was Father. Yes, that was all true enough. He wanted to be nice to them, to tell them everything—and yet, was it really wrong of him to want to have a secret place of his own?

At bedtime, the night before, Mother had said, "If this goes on, my lad, we'll have to see a doctor, we will! We can't have our boy—" But what was it she had said? "Live in another world"? "Live so far away"? The word "far" had been in it, he was sure, and then Mother had taken up a magazine again and laughed a little, but with an expression which wasn't mirthful. He had felt sorry for her. . . .

The bell rang for dismissal. The sound came to him through long curved parallels of falling snow. He saw Deirdre rise, and had himself risen almost as soon—but not quite as soon—as she.

2

On the walk homeward, which was timeless, it pleased him to see through the accompaniment, or counterpoint, of snow, the items of mere externality on his way. There were many kinds of bricks in the sidewalks, and laid in many kinds of pattern. The garden walls too were various, some of wooden palings, some of plaster, some of stone. Twigs of bushes leaned over the walls; the little hard green winter-buds of lilac, on gray stems, sheathed and fat; other branches very thin and fine and black and desiccated. Dirty sparrows huddled in the bushes, as dull in color as dead fruit left in leafless trees. A single starling creaked on a weather vane. In the gutter, beside a drain, was a scrap of torn and dirty newspaper, caught in a little delta of filth: the word ECZEMA appeared in large capitals, and below it was a letter from Mrs. Amelia D. Cravath, 2100 Pine Street, Fort Worth, Texas, to the effect that after being a sufferer for years she had been cured by Caley's Ointment. In the little delta, beside the fan-shaped and deeply runneled continent of brown mud, were lost twigs, descended from their parent trees, dead matches, a rusty horse-chestnut burr, a small concentration of sparkling gravel on the lip of the sewer, a fragment of eggshell, a streak of yellow sawdust which had been wet and was now dry and congealed, a brown pebble, and a broken feather. Further on was a cement sidewalk, ruled into geometrical parallelograms, with a brass inlay at one end commemorating the contractors who had laid it, and, halfway across, an irregular and random series of dog-tracks, immortalized in synthetic stone. He knew these well, and always stepped on them; to cover the little hollows with his own foot had always been a queer pleasure; today he did it once more, but perfunctorily and detachedly, all the while thinking of something else. That was a dog, a long time ago, who had made a mistake and walked on the cement while it was still wet. He had probably wagged his tail, but that hadn't been recorded. Now, Paul Hasleman, aged twelve, on his way home from school, crossed the same river, which in the meantime had frozen into rock. Homeward through the snow, the snow falling in bright sunshine. Homeward?

Then came the gateway with the two posts surmounted by egg-shaped stones which had been cunningly balanced on their ends, as if by Columbus, and mortared in the very act of balance: a source of perpetual wonder. On the brick wall just beyond, the letter H had been stenciled, presumably for some purpose. H? H.

The green hydrant, with a little green-painted chain attached to the brass screwcap.

The elm tree, with the great gray wound in the bark, kidney-shaped, into which he always put his hand—to feel the cold but living wood. The injury, he had been sure, was due to the gnawings of a tethered horse. But now it deserved only a passing palm, a merely tolerant eye. There were more important things. Miracles. Beyond the thoughts of trees, mere elms. Beyond the thoughts of sidewalks, mere stone, mere brick, mere cement. Beyond the thoughts even of his own shoes, which trod these sidewalks obediently, bearing a burden—far above—of elaborate mystery. He watched them. They were not very well polished; he had neglected them, for a very good reason: they were one of the many parts of the increasing difficulty of the daily return to daily life, the morning struggle. To get up, having at last opened one's eyes, to go to the window, and discover no snow, to wash, to dress, to descend the curving stairs to breakfast—

At whatever pain to others, nevertheless, one must persevere in severance, since the incommunicability of the experience demanded it. It was desirable of course to be kind to Mother and Father, especially as they seemed to be worried, but it was also desirable to be resolute. If they should decide—as appeared likely—to consult the doctor, Doctor Howells, and have Paul inspected, his heart listened to through a kind of dictaphone, his lungs, his stomach—well, that was all right. He would go through with it. He would give them answer for question, too—perhaps such answers as they hadn't expected? No. That would never do. For the secret world must, at all costs, be preserved.

The bird-house in the apple-tree was empty—it was the wrong time of year for wrens. The little round black door had lost its pleasure. The wrens were enjoying other houses, other nests, remoter trees. But this too was a notion which he only vaguely and grazingly entertained—as if, for the moment, he merely touched an edge of it; there was something further on, which was already assuming a sharper importance; something which already teased at the corners of his eyes, teasing also at the corner of his mind. It was funny to think that he so wanted this, so awaited it—and yet found himself enjoying this momentary dalliance with the bird-house, as if for a quite deliberate postponement and enhancement of the approaching pleasure. He was aware of his delay, of his smiling and detached and now almost uncomprehending gaze at the little bird-house; he knew what he was going to look at next: it was his own little cobbled hill-street, his own house, the little river at the bottom of the hill, the grocer's shop with the cardboard man in the window—and now, thinking of all this, he turned his head, still smiling, and looking quickly right and left through the snow-laden sunlight.

And the mist of snow, as he had foreseen, was still on it—a ghost of snow falling in the bright sunlight, softly and steadily floating and turning and pausing, soundlessly meeting the snow that covered, as with a transparent mirage, the bare bright cobbles. He loved it—he stood still and loved it. Its beauty was paralyzing—beyond all words, all experience, all dream. No fairy-story he had ever read could be compared with it—none had ever given him this extraordinary combination of ethereal loveliness with a something else, unnameable, which was just faintly and deliciously terrifying. What was this thing? As he thought of it, he looked upward toward his own bedroom window, which was open—and it was as if he looked straight into the room and saw himself lying half awake in his bed. There he was—at this very instant he was still perhaps actually there—more truly there than standing here at the edge of the cobbled hill-street, with one hand lifted to shade his eyes against the snow-sun. Had he indeed ever left his room, in all this time? since that very first morning? Was the whole progress still being enacted there, was it still the same morning, and himself not yet wholly awake? And even now, had the postman not yet come round the corner? . . .

This idea amused him, and automatically, as he thought of it, he turned his head and looked toward the top of the hill. There was, of course, nothing there—nothing and no one. The street was empty and quiet. And all the more because of its emptiness it occurred to him to count the houses—a thing which, oddly enough, he hadn't before thought of doing. Of course, he had known there weren't many—many, that is, on his own side of the street, which were the ones that figured in the postman's progress—but nevertheless it came to him as something of a shock to find that there were precisely *six*, above his own house—his own house was the seventh.

Six!

Astonished, he looked at his own house—looked at the door, on which was the number thirteen—and then realized that the whole thing was exactly and logically and absurdly what he ought to have known. Just the same, the realization gave him abruptly, and even a little frighteningly, a sense of hurry. He was being hurried—he was being rushed. For—he knit his brows—he couldn't be mistaken—it was just above the *seventh* house, his *own* house, that the postman had first been audible this very morning. But in that case—in that case—did it mean that tomorrow he would hear nothing? The knock he had heard must have been the knock of their own door. Did it mean—and this was an idea which gave him a really extraordinary feeling of surprise—that he would never hear the postman again?—that tomorrow morning the postman would already have passed the house, in a snow by then so deep as to render his footsteps completely inaudible? That he would have made his approach down the snow-filled street so soundlessly, so secretly, that he, Paul Hasleman, there lying in bed, would not have waked in time, or, waking, would have heard nothing?

But how could that be? Unless even the knocker should be muffled in the snow—frozen tight, perhaps? . . . But in that case—

A vague feeling of disappointment came over him; a vague sadness, as if he felt himself deprived of something which he had long looked forward to, something much prized. After all this, all this beautiful progress, the slow delicious advance of the postman through the silent and secret snow, the knock creeping closer each day, and the footsteps nearer, the audible compass of the world thus daily narrowed, narrowed, narrowed, as the snow soothingly and beautifully encroached and deepened, after all this, was he to be defrauded of the one thing he had so wanted—to be about to count, as it were, the last two or three solemn footsteps, as they finally approached his own door? Was it all going to happen, at the end, so suddenly? or indeed, had it already happened? with no slow and subtle gradations of menace, in which he could luxuriate?

He gazed upward again, toward his own window which flashed in the sun: and this time almost with a feeling that it would be better if he *were* still in bed, in that room; for in that case this must still be the first morning, and there would be six more mornings to come—or, for that matter, seven or eight or nine—how could he be sure?—or even more.

3

After supper, the inquisition began. He stood before the doctor, under the lamp, and submitted silently to the usual thumpings and tappings.

"Now will you please say 'Ah!'?"

"Ah!"

"Now again please, if you don't mind."

"Ah."

"Say it slowly and hold it if you can—"

"Ah-h-h-h-h-h—"

"Good."

How silly all this was. As if it had anything to do with his throat! Or his heart or lungs!

Relaxing his mouth, of which the corners, after all this absurd stretching, felt uncomfortable, he avoided the doctor's eyes, and stared towards the fireplace, past his mother's feet (in gray slippers) which projected from the green chair, and his father's feet (in brown slippers) which stood neatly side by side on the hearth rug.

"Hm. There is certainly nothing wrong there . . . "

He felt the doctor's eyes fixed upon him, and, as if merely to be polite, returned the look, but with a feeling of justifiable evasiveness.

"Now, young man, tell me,—do you feel all right?"

"Yes, sir, quite all right."

"No headaches? No dizziness?"

"No, I don't think so."

"Let me see. Let's get a book, if you don't mind—yes, thank you, that will do splendidly—and now, Paul, if you'll just read it, holding it as you would normally hold it—"

He took the book and read:

"And another praise have I to tell for this the city our mother, the gift of a great god, a glory of the land most high; the might of horses, the might of young horses, the might of the sea. . . . For thou, son of Cronus, our lord Poseidon, hast throned herein this pride, since in these roads first thou didst show forth the curb that cures the rage of steeds. And the shapely oar, apt to men's hands, hath a wonderous speed on the brine, following the hundred-footed Nereids. . . . O land that art praised above all lands, now is it for thee to make those bright praises seen in deeds."

He stopped, tentatively, and lowered the heavy book.

"No—as I thought—there is certainly no superficial sign of eyestrain."

Silence thronged the room, and he was aware of the focused scrutiny of the three people who confronted him. . . .

"We could have his eyes examined—but I believe it is something else."

"What could it be?" This was his father's voice.

"It's only this curious absent-minded—" This was his mother's voice.

In the presence of the doctor, they both seemed irritatingly apologetic.

"I believe it is something else. Now, Paul—I would like very much to ask you a question or two. You will answer them, won't you—you know I'm an old, old friend of yours, eh? That's right! . . . "

His back was thumped twice by the doctor's fat fist—then the doctor was grinning at him with false amiability, while with one finger-nail he was scratching the top button of his waistcoat. Beyond the doctor's shoulder was the fire, the fingers of flame making light prestidigitation against the sooty fireback, the soft sound of their random flutter the only sound.

"I would like to know—is there anything that worries you?"

The doctor was again smiling, his eyelids low against the little black pupils, in each of which was a tiny white bead of light. Why answer him? Why answer him at all? "At whatever pain to others"—but it was all a nuisance, this necessity for resistance, this necessity for attention: it was as if one had been stood up on a brilliantly lighted stage, under a great round blaze of spotlight; as if one were merely a trained seal, or a performing dog, or a fish, dipped out of an aquarium and held up by the tail. It would serve them right if he were merely to bark or growl. And meanwhile, to miss these last few precious hours, these hours of which every minute was more beautiful than the last, more menacing—? He still looked, as if from a great distance, at the beads of light in the doctor's eyes, at the fixed false smile, and then, beyond, once more at his mother's slippers, his father's slippers, the soft flutter of the fire. Even here, even amongst these hostile presences, and in this arranged light, he could see the snow, he could hear it—it was in the corners of the room, where the shadow was deepest, under the sofa, behind the half-opened door which led to the dining room. It was gentler here, softer, its seethe the quietest of whispers, as if, in deference to a drawing room, it had quite deliberately put on its "manners"; it kept itself out of sight, obliterated itself, but distinctly with an air of saying, "Ah, but just wait! Wait till we are alone together! Then I will begin to tell you something new! Something white! something cold! something sleepy! something of cease, and peace, and the long bright curve of space! Tell them to go away. Banish them. Refuse to speak. Leave them, go upstairs to your room, turn out the light and get into bed—I will go with you, I will be waiting for you, I will tell you a better story than Little Kay of the Skates, or The Snow Ghost—I will surround your bed, I will close the windows, pile a deep drift against the door, so that none will ever again be able to enter. Speak to them! . . . " It seemed as if the little hissing voice came from a slow white spiral of falling flakes in the corner by the front window—but he could not be sure. He felt himself smiling, then, and said to the doctor, but without looking at him, looking beyond him still—

"Oh, no, I think not—"

"But are you sure, my boy?"

His father's voice came softly and coldly then—the familiar voice of silken warning. . . .

"You needn't answer at once, Paul—remember we're trying to help you—think it over and be quite sure, won't you?"

He felt himself smiling again, at the notion of being quite sure. What a joke! As if he weren't so sure that reassurance was no longer necessary, and all this cross-examination a ridiculous farce, a grotesque parody! What could they know about it? These gross intelligences, these humdrum minds so bound to the usual, the ordinary? Impossible to tell them about it! Why, even now, even now, with the proof so abundant, so formidable, so imminent, so appallingly present here in this very room, could they believe it?—could even his mother believe it? No—it was only too plain that if anything were said about it, the merest hint given, they would be incredulous—they would laugh—they would say "Absurd!"—think things about him which weren't true. . . .

"Why no, I'm not worried—why should I be?"

He looked then straight at the doctor's low-lidded eyes, looked from one of them to the other, from one bead of light to the other, and gave a little laugh.

The doctor seemed to be disconcerted by this. He drew back in his chair, resting a fat white hand on either knee. The smile faded slowly from his face.

"Well, Paul!" he said, and paused gravely, "I'm afraid you don't take this quite seriously enough. I think you perhaps don't quite realize—don't quite realize—" He took a deep quick breath, and turned, as if helpless, at a loss for words, to the others. But Mother and Father were both silent—no help was forthcoming.

"You must surely know, be aware, that you have not been quite yourself, of late? Don't you know that? . . . ."

It was amusing to watch the doctor's renewed attempt at a smile, a queer disorganized look, as of confidential embarrassment.

"I feel all right, sir," he said, and again gave the little laugh.

"And we're trying to help you." The doctor's tone sharpened.

"Yes, sir, I know. But why? I'm all right. I'm just *thinking*, that's all."

His mother made a quick movement forward, resting a hand on the back of the doctor's chair.

"Thinking?" she said. "But my dear, about what?"

This was a direct challenge—and would have to be directly met. But before he met it, he looked again into the corner by the door, as if for reassurance. He smiled again at what he saw, at what he heard. The little spiral was still there, still softly whirling, like the ghost of a white kitten chasing the ghost of a white tail, and making as it did so the faintest of whispers. It was all right! If only he could remain firm, everything was going to be all right.

"Oh, about anything, about nothing.—*you* know the way you do!"

"You mean—day-dreaming?"

"Oh, no—thinking!"

"But thinking about *what*?"

"Anything."

He laughed a third time—but this time, happening to glance upward towards his mother's face, he was appalled at the effect his laughter seemed to have upon her. Her mouth had opened in an expression of horror. . . . This was too bad! Unfortunate! He had known it would cause pain, of course—but he hadn't expected it to be quite so bad as this. Perhaps—perhaps if he just gave them a tiny gleaming hint—?

"About the snow," he said.

"What on earth!" This was his father's voice. The brown slippers came a step nearer on the hearth-rug.

"But my dear, what do you mean!" This was his mother's voice.

The doctor merely stared.

"Just *snow*, that's all. I like to think about it."

"Tell us about it, my boy."

"But that's all it is. There's nothing to tell. *You* know what snow is."

This he said almost angrily, for he felt that they were trying to corner him. He turned sideways so as no longer to face the doctor, and the better to see the inch of blackness between the window-sill and the lowered curtains,—the cold inch of beckoning and delicious night. At once he felt better, more assured.

"Mother—can I go to bed, now, please? I've got a headache."

"But I thought you said—"

"It's just come. It's all these questions—! Can I, Mother?"

"You can go as soon as the doctor has finished."

"Don't you think this thing ought to be gone into thoroughly, and *now*?" This was Father's voice. The brown slippers again came a step nearer, the voice was the well-known "punishment" voice, resonant and cruel.

"Oh, what's the use, Norman—"

Quite suddenly, everyone was silent. And without precisely facing them, nevertheless he was aware that all three of them were watching him with an extraordinary intensity—staring hard at him—as if he had done something monstrous, or was himself some kind of monster. He could hear the soft irregular flutter of the flames; the cluck-click-cluck-click of the clock; far and faint, two sudden spurts of laughter from the kitchen, as quickly cut off as begun; a murmur of water in the pipes; and then, the silence seemed to deepen, to spread out, to become worldlong and worldwide, to become timeless and shapeless, and to center inevitably and rightly, with a slow and sleepy but enormous concentration of all power, on the beginning of a new sound. What this new sound was going to be, he knew perfectly well. It might begin with a hiss, but it would end with a roar—there was no time to lose—he must escape. It mustn't happen here—

Without another word, he turned and ran up the stairs.

4

Not a moment too soon. The darkness was coming in long white waves. A prolonged sibilance filled the night—a great seamless seethe of wild influence went abruptly across it—a cold low humming shook the windows. He shut the door and flung off his clothes in the dark. The bare black floor was like a little raft tossed in waves in snow, almost overwhelmed, washed under whitely, up again, smothered in curled billows of feather. The snow was laughing: it spoke from all sides at once: it pressed closer to him as he ran and jumped exulting into his bed.

"Listen to us!" it said. "Listen! We have come to tell you the story we told you about. You remember? Lie down. Shut your eyes, now—you will no longer see much—in this white darkness who could see, or want to see? We will take the place of every-thing. . . . Listen—"

A beautiful varying dance of snow began at the front of the room, came forward and then retreated, flattened out toward the floor, then rose fountain-like to the ceiling, swayed, recruited itself from a new stream of flakes which poured laughing in through the humming window, advanced again, lifted long white arms. It said peace, it said remoteness, it said cold—it said—

But then a gash of horrible light fell brutally across the room from the opening door—the snow drew back hissing—something alien had come into the room—some-thing hostile. This thing rushed at him, clutched at him, shook him—and he was not merely horrified, he was filled with such a loathing as he had never known. What was this? this cruel disturbance? this act of anger and hate? It was as if he had to reach up a hand toward another world for any understanding of it—an effort of which he was only barely capable. But of that other world he still remembered just enough to know the exorcising words. They tore themselves from his other life suddenly—

"Mother! Mother! Go away! I hate you!"

And with that effort, everything was solved, everything became all right: the seamless hiss advanced once more, the long white wavering lines rose and fell like enormous whispering sea-waves, the whisper becoming louder, the laughter more nu-merous.

"Listen!" it said. "We'll tell you the last, the most beautiful and secret story—shut your eyes—it is a very small story—a story that gets smaller and smaller—it comes inward instead of opening like a flower—it is a flower becoming a seed—a little cold seed—do you hear? We are leaning closer to you—"

The hiss was now becoming a roar—the whole world was a vast moving screen of snow—but even now it said peace, it said remoteness, it said cold, it said sleep.

Katherine Anne Porter (1890–1980)

Katherine Anne Porter was born in Texas in 1890 to a prominent Catholic family. Her first marriage was at sixteen, her first divorce at nineteen. Two more of each followed. She traveled extensively, lived in many foreign and American cities, settled at last in a suburb of Washington, D.C. She writes, "I am the grandchild of a lost War, and I have blood-knowledge of what life can be in a defeated country on the bare bones of privation." Many of her stories are set in the South of her childhood, and almost all of them deal with loss and reconciliation.

Although critics and other writers have rated her work among the best, she did not achieve general popularity until her only novel, *Ship of Fools*, was published in 1962. It was a best seller of mammoth proportions and was made into a film.

"My whole attempt," she says, in discussing her work,

> has been to discover and understand human motives, human feelings, to make a distillation of what human relations and experiences my mind has been able to absorb. I have never known an uninteresting human being, and I have never known two alike.

A writer, she says, begins with

> *first a theme*, and then a point of view, a certain knowledge of human nature and strong feelings about it, and style—that is to say, his own special way of telling a thing that makes it precisely his own and no one else's.

Porter's style is not so instantly recognizable as, say, Faulkner's or Hemingway's. But her range is tremendous. Sometimes naïve, sometimes sophisticated, or ironic, sardonic, anguished, or remote, objective, her style seems to follow theme and subject matter. But always her language is beautifully exact, pictorial, rhythmically balanced. She is not afraid of adjectives and rich imagery. The first sentence of the second paragraph of "The Grave" illustrates her skill. The reader's imagination moves from the abstract ("family cemetery") to a slightly more concrete image ("pleasant, small, neglected garden") to a carefully chosen and precisely qualified description of objects in the garden. At the end of the sentence, the reader is submerged in the "uncropped sweet-smelling wild grass." Each noun and adjective brings the reader deeper into the story.

This sentence also contains the themes of the story, the intermingling of sweetness and death and corruption. It places the reader, metaphorically and literally, in the middle of the world where the story takes place. The themes are developed as much through language as through plot. After a graceful, stately opening, the language adjusts to the coarser sensibilities of the children ("scratching," "scooped," "leaped"). When Miranda puts on the ring, the subordinate theme of women and men is introduced, and the language reflects the difference between the children. Paul talks of "get[ting] your bird" and "bulls'-eyes" while Miranda has "vague stirrings of desire for luxury," a sensual image which reinforces her emerging awareness of herself. When the experience with the rabbits emphasizes the dominant theme of death and corruption, the language reflects the changed sensibility of Miranda.

The epiphany is borne to Miranda, and the reader, not alone by memory of the rabbits aroused by the little sugar figures but by the vision of her brother "standing in the blazing sunshine, again twelve years old, a pleased sober smile in his eyes, turning the silver dove over and over in his hands." More by means of the sounds and the imagery than by what could be paraphrased as meaning, the reader understands that Miranda has become reconciled with the "mingled sweetness and corruption" of her life.

The Grave

The grandfather, dead for more than thirty years, had been twice disturbed in his long repose by the constancy and possessiveness of his widow. She removed his bones first to Louisiana and then to Texas as if she had set out to find her own burial place, knowing well she would never return to the places she had left. In Texas she set up a small cemetery in a corner of her first farm, and as the family connection grew, and oddments of relations came over from Kentucky to settle, it contained at last about twenty graves. After the grandmother's death, part of her land was to be sold for the benefit of certain of her children, and the cemetery happened to lie in the part set aside for sale. It was necessary to take up the bodies and bury them again in the family plot in the big new public cemetery, where the grandmother had been buried. At last her husband was to lie beside her for eternity, as she had planned.

The family cemetery had been a pleasant small neglected garden of tangled rose bushes and ragged cedar trees and cypress, the simple flat stones rising out of un-cropped sweet-smelling wild grass. The graves were lying open and empty one burning day when Miranda and her brother Paul, who often went together to hunt rabbits and doves, propped their twenty-two Winchester rifles carefully against the rail fence, climbed over and explored among the graves. She was nine years old and he was twelve.

They peered into the pits all shaped alike with such purposeful accuracy, and looking at each other with pleased adventurous eyes, they said in solemn tones: "These were graves!" trying by words to shape a special, suitable emotion in their minds, but they felt nothing except an agreeable thrill of wonder: they were seeing a new sight, doing something they had not done before. In them both there was also a small disappointment at the entire commonplaceness of the actual spectacle. Even if it had once contained a coffin for years upon years, when the coffin was gone a grave was just a hole in the ground. Miranda leaped into the pit that had held her grandfather's bones. Scratching around aimlessly and pleasurably as any young animal, she scooped up a lump of earth and weighted in her palm. It had a pleasantly sweet, corrupt smell, being mixed with cedar needles and small leaves, and as the crumbs fell apart, she saw a silver dove no larger than a hazel nut, with spread wings and a neat fan-shaped tail. The breast had a deep round hollow in it. Turning it up to the fierce sunlight, she saw that the inside of the hollow was cut in little whorls. She scrambled out, over the pile of loose earth that had fallen back into one end of the grave, calling to Paul that she had found something, he must guess what. . . . His head appeared smiling over the rim of another grave. He waved a closed hand at her. "I've got something too!" They ran to compare treasures, making a game of it, so many guesses each, all wrong, and a final showdown with opened palms. Paul had found a thin wide gold ring carved with intricate flowers and leaves. Miranda was smitten at sight of the ring and wished to have it. Paul seemed more impressed by the dove. They made a trade, with some little bickering. After he had got the dove in his hand, Paul said, "Don't you know what this is? This is a screw head for a *coffin!* . . . I'll bet nobody else in the world has one like this!"

Miranda glanced at it without covetousness. She had the gold ring on her thumb; it fitted perfectly. "Maybe we ought to go now," she said, "maybe one of the niggers 'll see us and tell somebody." They knew the land had been sold, the cemetery was no longer theirs, and they felt like trespassers. They climbed back over the fence, slung their rifles loosely under their arms—they had been shooting at targets with various kinds of firearms since they were seven years old—and set out to look for the rabbits and doves or whatever small game might happen along. On these expeditions Miranda always followed at Paul's heels along the path, obeying instructions about handling her gun when going through fences; learning how to stand it up properly so it would not slip and fire unexpectedly; how to wait her time for a shot and not just bang away in the air without looking, spoiling shots for Paul, who really could hit things if given a chance. Now and then, in her excitement at seeing birds whizz up suddenly before her face, or a rabbit leap across her very toes, she lost her head, and almost without sighting she flung her rifle up and pulled the trigger. She hardly ever hit any sort of mark. She had no proper sense of hunting at all. Her brother would be often completely disgusted with her. "You don't care whether you get your bird or not," he said. "That's no way to hunt." Miranda could not understand his indignation. She had seen him smash his hat and yell with fury when he had missed his aim. "What I like about shooting," said Miranda, with exasperating inconsequence, "is pulling the trigger and hearing the noise."

"Then, by golly," said Paul, "whyn't you go back to the range and shoot at bulls'-eyes?"

"I'd just as soon," said Miranda, "only like this, we walk around more."

"Well, you just stay behind and stop spoiling my shots," said Paul, who, when he made a kill, wanted to be certain he had made it. Miranda, who alone brought down a bird once in twenty rounds, always claimed as her own any game they got when they fired at the same moment. It was tiresome and unfair and her brother was sick of it.

"Now, the first dove we see, or the first rabbit, is mine," he told her. "And the next will be yours. Remember that and don't get smarty."

"What about snakes?" asked Miranda idly. "Can I have the first snake?"

Waving her thumb gently and watching her gold ring glitter, Miranda lost interest in shooting. She was wearing her summer roughing outfit: dark blue overalls, a light blue shirt, a hired-man's straw hat, and thick brown sandals. Her brother had the same outfit except his was a sober hickory-nut color. Ordinarily Miranda preferred her overalls to any other dress, though it was making rather a scandal in the countryside, for the year was 1903, and in the back country the law of female decorum had teeth in it. Her father had been criticized for letting his girls dress like boys and go careering around astride barebacked horses. Big sister Maria, the really independent and fearless one, in spite of her rather affected ways, rode at a dead run with only a rope knotted around her horse's nose. It was said the motherless family was running down, with the Grandmother no longer there to hold it together. It was known that she had discriminated against her son Harry in her will, and that he was in straits about money. Some of his old neighbors reflected with vicious satisfaction that now he would probably not be so stiffnecked, nor have any more high-stepping horses either. Miranda knew this, though she could not say how. She had met along the road old women of the kind who smoked corn-cob pipes, who had treated her grandmother with most sincere respect. They slanted their gummy old eyes side-ways at the granddaughter and said, "Ain't you ashamed of yoself, Missy? It's aginst the Scriptures to dress like that. Whut yo Pappy thinkin about?" Miranda, with her powerful social sense, which was like a fine set of antennae radiating from every pore of her skin, would feel ashamed because she knew well it was rude and ill-bred to shock anybody, even bad-tempered old crones, though she had faith in her father's judgment and was perfectly comfortable in the clothes. Her father had said, "They're just what you need, and they'll save your dresses for school . . . " This sounded quite simple and natural to her. She had been brought up in rigorous economy. Wastefulness was vulgar. It was also a sin. These were truths; she had heard them repeated many times and never once disputed.

Now the ring, shining with the serene purity of fine gold on her rather grubby thumb, turned her feelings against her overalls and sockless feet, toes sticking through the thick brown leather straps. She wanted to go back to the farmhouse, take a good cold bath, dust herself with plenty of Maria's violet talcum powder—provided Maria was not present to object, of course—put on the thinnest, most becoming dress she owned, with a big sash, and sit in a wicker chair under the trees . . . These things were not all she wanted, of course; she had vague stirrings of desire for luxury and a grand way of living which could not take precise form in her imagination but were founded on family legend of past wealth and leisure. These immediate comforts were what she could have, and she wanted them at once. She lagged rather far behind Paul, and once she thought of just turning back without a word and going home. She stopped, thinking that Paul would never do that to her, and so she would have to tell him. When a rabbit leaped, she let Paul have it without dispute. He killed it with one shot.

When she came up with him, he was already kneeling, examining the wound, the rabbit trailing from his hands. "Right through the head," he said complacently, as if he had aimed for it. He took out his sharp, competent bowie knife and started to skin the body. He did it very cleanly and quickly. Uncle Jimbilly knew how to prepare the skins so that Miranda always had fur coats for her dolls, for though she never cared much for her dolls she liked seeing them in fur coats. The children knelt facing each other over the dead animal. Miranda watched admiringly while her brother stripped the skin away as if he were taking off a glove. The flayed flesh emerged dark scarlet, sleek, firm; Miranda with thumb and finger felt the long fine muscles with the silvery flat strips binding them to the joints. Brother lifted the oddly bloated belly. "Look," he said, in a low amazed voice. "It was going to have young ones."

Very carefully he slit the thin flesh from the center ribs to the flanks, and a scarlet bag appeared. He slit again and pulled the bag open, and there lay a bundle of tiny rabbits, each wrapped in a thin scarlet veil. The brother pulled these off and there they were, dark gray, their sleek wet down lying in minute even ripples, like a baby's head just washed, their unbelievably small delicate ears folded close, their little blind faces almost featureless.

Miranda said, "Oh, I want to *see*," under her breath. She looked and looked—excited but not frightened, for she was accustomed to the sight of animals killed in hunting—filled with pity and astonishment and a kind of shocked delight in the wonderful little creatures for their own sakes, they were so pretty. She touched one of them ever so carefully. "Ah, there's blood running over them," she said and began to tremble without knowing why. Yet she wanted most deeply to see and to know. Having seen, she felt at once as if she had known all along. The very memory of her former ignorance faded, she had always known just this. No one had ever told her anything outright, she had been rather unobservant of the animal life around her because she was so accustomed to animals. They seemed simply disorderly and unaccountably rude in their habits, but altogether natural and not very interesting. Her brother had spoken as if he had known about everything all along. He may have seen all this before. He had never said a word to her, but she knew now a part at least of what he knew. She understood a little of the secret, formless intuitions in her own mind and body, which had been clearing up, taking form, so gradually and so steadily she had not realized that she was learning what she had to know. Paul said cautiously, as if he were talking about something forbidden: "They were just about ready to be born." His voice dropped on the last word. "I know," said Miranda, "like kittens. I know, like babies." She was quietly and terribly agitated, standing again with her rifle under her arm, looking down at the bloody heap. "I don't want the skin," she said, "I won't have it." Paul buried the young rabbits again in their mother's body, wrapped the skin around her, carried her to a clump of sage bushes, and hid her away. He came out again at once and said to Miranda, with an eager friendliness, a confidential tone quite unusual in him, as if he were taking her into an important secret on equal terms: "Listen now. Now you listen to me, and don't ever forget. Don't you ever tell a living soul that you saw this. Don't tell a soul. Don't tell Dad because I'll get into trouble. He'll say I'm leading you into things you ought not to do. He's always saying that. So now don't you go and forget and blab out sometime the way you're always doing . . . Now, that's a secret. Don't you tell."

Miranda never told, she did not even wish to tell anybody. She thought about the whole worrisome affair with confused unhappiness for a few days. Then it sank quietly into her mind and was heaped over by accumulated thousands of impressions, for nearly twenty years. One day she was picking her path among the puddles and crushed refuse of a market street in a strange city of a strange country, when without warning, plain and clear in its true colors as if she looked through a frame upon a scene that had not stirred nor changed since the moment it happened, the episode of that far-off day leaped from its burial place before her mind's eye. She was so reasonlessly horrified she halted suddenly staring, the scene before her eyes dimmed by the vision back of them. An Indian vendor had held up before her a tray of dyed sugar sweets, in the shapes of all kinds of small creatures: birds, baby chicks, baby rabbits, lambs, baby pigs. They were in gay colors and smelled of vanilla, maybe. . . . It was a very hot day and the smell in the market, with its piles of raw flesh and wilting flowers, was like the mingled sweetness and corruption she had smelled that other day in the empty cemetery at home: the day she had remembered always until now vaguely as the time she and her brother had found treasure in the opened graves. Instantly upon this thought the dreadful vision faded, and she saw clearly her brother, whose childhood face she had forgotten, standing again in the blazing sunshine, again twelve years old, a pleased sober smile in his eyes, turning the silver dove over and over in his hands.

Isaac Babel (1894–1941)

Contradiction and anomaly marked the life of Isaac Babel. A Jew, he glorified his people's age-old enemy, the Cossacks. A scholar, he romanticized violence. An intellectual, he exalted the military. To celebrate the Red Army, he wrote stories of it that were heavy with irony. His accounts of violence are written with elegance; his scenes of disorder are painted with precision. One of the few authentic voices of the Russian Revolution, by the 1930s he had become, in his words, "the past master of silence." To serve the Party, he withdrew from literature. A Communist loyalist, he died in a Russian concentration camp. His output was small: some fifty stories. His achievement was enormous: he is perhaps the greatest Russian short-story writer since Anton Chekhov.

Babel was born in Odessa in 1894, the son of a Jewish warehousekeeper. In 1916 he met Gorki: "I owe everything to this meeting, and to this day I speak the name of Alexei Maximovich with love and reverence." Gorki told him to get experience before trying to write. The next seven years Babel spent as a Red Army soldier, a production supervisor, and a journalist.

His literary career began in earnest in 1924 with the publication of half a dozen stories. By 1925, he was a celebrity, the rage of Moscow. Although his wife, mother, and sister emigrated, Babel apparently believed that his talent could not flourish outside Russia. But with the advent of Stalin and the increased demand for conformity, Babel's output declined precipitately. When Gorki died in 1936, Babel lost his great friend and protector, and over the next few years his existence grew more precarious. He was arrested in 1939 and was seen no more. The official date of his death was given as March 17, 1941. The final irony was the revocation, in 1954, by the Supreme Court of the USSR of the sentence imposed on Babel.

At the heart of Babel's fiction is the conflict between violence and compassion. The violence is often romanticized, as in "My First Goose," and the compassion is often ironic, as in "The Sin of Jesus." His stories are usually quite short and pungent. Even in translation the language is subtle and rich in imagery. He keeps exposition to a minimum: drama is all. There is almost always a host of lively energetic characters cavorting through his scenes in amusing, telling, sometimes frightening or touching ways. (See Introduction, pp. 10, 20.)

In "My First Goose" a Jewish intellectual cruelly destroys a goose in order to win acceptance from the Cossacks. The first-person narrator never expresses judgment of the violent Cossack way of life; yet the changing tone of metaphors in the story prepares the reader to recognize, in the epiphany (see pp. 9–10), the divided heart of the narrator.

There are some elements of humor in that grim, violent story. In "The Sin of Jesus," humor is the vital force and is established in the first paragraph. The reader knows from the first he will be entertained (see Introduction, p. 15). But in the second paragraph a new note is presented: Arina is helpless, foolish, mistreated. When Seryoga "took off his belt and beat her like a hero," the terrible tension is established and the reader uneasily shifts from hilarity to horror. And when Arina asks Jesus Christ for help, the full complexity of Babel's intention is revealed. From then on the story veers from farce to realism to naturalism and almost to myth, but its tone is always compassionate toward poor foolish Arina, who is, even in her relations with Jesus Christ, more sinned against than sinning. In such a brief space, and in so amused a tone, Babel has managed to do full justice to Arina's humanity, and in the end it is not Arina we scorn, but rather the cruelty of the world and of fate.

My First Goose

Savitsky, Commander of the VI Division, rose when he saw me, and I wondered at the beauty of his giant's body. He rose, the purple of his riding breeches and the crimson of his little tilted cap and the decorations stuck on his chest cleaving the hut as a standard cleaves the sky. A smell of scent and the sickly sweet freshness of soap emanated from him. His long legs were like girls sheathed to the neck in shining riding boots.

He smiled at me, struck his riding whip on the table, and drew toward him an order that the Chief of Staff had just finished dictating. It was an order for Ivan Chesnokov to advance on Chugunov-Dobryvodka with the regiment entrusted to him, to make contact with the enemy and destroy the same.

"For which destruction," the Commander began to write, smearing the whole sheet, "I make this same Chesnokov entirely responsible, up to and including the supreme penalty, and will if necessary strike him down on the spot; which you, Chesnokov, who have been working with me at the front for some months now, cannot doubt."

The Commander signed the order with a flourish, tossed it to his orderlies and turned upon me gray eyes that danced with merriment.

I handed him a paper with my appointment to the Staff of the Division.

"Put it down in the Order of the Day," said the Commander. "Put him down for every satisfaction save the front one. Can you read and write?"

"Yes, I can read and write," I replied, envying the flower and iron of that youthfulness. "I graduated in law from St. Petersburg University."

"Oh, are you one of those grinds?" he laughed. "Specs on your nose, too! What a nasty little object! They've sent you along without making any enquiries; and this is a hot place for specs. Think you'll get on with us?"

The quartermaster carried my trunk on his shoulder. Before us stretched the village street. The dying sun, round and yellow as a pumpkin, was giving up its roseate ghost to the skies.

We went up to a hut painted over with garlands. The quartermaster stopped, and said suddenly, with a guilty smile:

"Nuisance with specs. Can't do anything to stop it, either. Not a life for the brainy type here. But you go and mess up a lady, and a good lady too, and you'll have the boys patting you on the back."

He hesitated, my little trunk on his shoulder; then he came quite close to me, only to dart away again despairingly and run to the nearest yard. Cossacks were sitting there, shaving one another.

"Here, you soldiers," said the quartermaster, setting my little trunk down on the ground. "Comrade Savitsky's orders are that you're to take this chap in your billets, so no nonsense about it, because the chap's been through a lot in the learning line."

The quartermaster, purple in the face, left us without looking back. I raised my hand to my cap and saluted the Cossacks. A lad with long straight flaxen hair and the handsome face of the Ryazan Cossacks[1] went over to my little trunk and tossed it out at the gate. Then he turned his back on me and with remarkable skill emitted a series of shameful noises.

"To your guns—number double-zero!" an older Cossack shouted at him, and burst out laughing. "Running fire!"

[1] Noted cavalrymen from southern Russia.

His guileless art exhausted, the lad made off. Then, crawling over the ground, I began to gather together the manuscripts and tattered garments that had fallen out of the trunk. I gathered them up and carried them to the other end of the yard. Near the hut, on a brick stove, stood a cauldron in which pork was cooking. The steam that rose from it was like the far-off smoke of home in the village, and it mingled hunger with desperate loneliness in my head. Then I covered my little broken trunk with hay, turning it into a pillow, and lay down on the ground to read in *Pravda* Lenin's speech at the Second Congress of the Comintern. The sun fell upon me from behind the toothed hillocks, the Cossacks trod on my feet, the lad made fun of me untiringly, the beloved lines came toward me along a thorny path and could not reach me. Then I put aside the paper and went out to the landlady, who was spinning on the porch.

"Landlady," I said, "I've got to eat."

The old woman raised to me the diffused whites of her purblind eyes and lowered them again.

"Comrade," she said, after a pause, "what with all this going on, I want to go and hang myself."

"Christ!" I muttered, and pushed the old woman in the chest with my fist. "You don't suppose I'm going to go into explanations with you, do you?"

And turning around I saw somebody's sword lying within reach. A severe-looking goose was waddling about the yard, inoffensively preening its feathers. I overtook it and pressed it to the ground. Its head cracked beneath my boot, cracked and emptied itself. The white neck lay stretched out in the dung, the wings twitched.

"Christ!" I said, digging into the goose with my sword. "Go and cook it for me, landlady."

Her blind eyes and glasses glistening, the old woman picked up the slaughtered bird, wrapped it in her apron, and started to bear it off toward the kitchen.

"Comrade," she said to me, after a while, "I want to go and hang myself." And she closed the door behind her.

The Cossacks in the yard were already sitting around their cauldron. They sat motionless, stiff as heathen priests at a sacrifice, and had not looked at the goose.

"The lad's all right," one of them said, winking and scooping up the cabbage soup with his spoon.

The Cossacks commenced their supper with all the elegance and restraint of peasants who respect one another. And I wiped the sword with sand, went out at the gate, and came in again, depressed. Already the moon hung above the yard like a cheap earring.

"Hey, you," suddenly said Surovkov, an older Cossack. "Sit down and feed with us till your goose is done."

He produced a spare spoon from his boot and handed it to me. We supped up the cabbage soup they had made, and ate the pork.

"What's in the newspaper?" asked the flaxen-haired lad, making room for me.

"Lenin writes in the paper," I said, pulling out *Pravda*. "Lenin writes that there's a shortage of everything."

And loudly, like a triumphant man hard of hearing, I read Lenin's speech out to the Cossacks.

Evening wrapped about me the quickening moisture of its twilight sheets; evening laid a mother's hand upon my burning forehead. I read on and rejoiced, spying out exultingly the secret curve of Lenin's straight line.

"Truth tickles everyone's nostrils," said Surovkov, when I had come to the end. "The question is, how's it to be pulled from the heap. But he goes and strikes at it straight off like a hen pecking at a grain!"

This remark about Lenin was made by Surovkov, platoon commander of the Staff Squadron; after which we lay down to sleep in the hayloft. We slept, all six of us, beneath a wooden roof that let in the stars, warming one another, our legs intermingled. I dreamed: and in my dreams saw women. But my heart, stained with bloodshed, grated and brimmed over.

The Sin of Jesus

Arina was a servant at the hotel. She lived next to the main staircase, while Seryoga, the janitor's helper, lived over the back stairs. Between them there was shame. On Palm Sunday Arina gave Seryoga a present—twins. Water flows, stars shine, a man lusts, and soon Arina was big again, her sixth month was rolling by—they're slippery, a woman's months. And now Seryoga must go into the army. There's a mess for you!

So Arina goes and says: "No sense, Seryoga. There's no sense in my waiting for you. For four years we'll be parted, and in four years, whichever way you look at it, I'll be sure to bring two or three more into this world. It's like walking around with your skirt turned up, working at the hotel. Whoever stops here, he's your master, let him be a Jew, let him be anybody at all. By the time you come home, my insides will be no good any more. I'll be a used-up woman, no match for you."

"That's so," Seryoga nodded.

"There's many that want me. Trofimych the contractor—but he's no gentleman. And Isai Abramych, the warden of Nikolo-Svyatsky Church, a feeble old man, but anyway I'm sick to the stomach of your murderous strength. I tell you this now, I say it like I would at confession, I've got the wind plain knocked out of me. I'll spill my load in three months, then I'll take the baby to the orphanage and marry the old man."

When Seryoga heard this, he took off his belt and beat her like a hero, right on the belly.

"Look out there," Arina say to him, "go soft on the belly. It's your stuffing, no one else's."

There was no end to the beating, no end to the man's tears and the woman's blood, but that is neither here nor there.

Then the woman came to Jesus Christ.

"So on and so forth," she says, "Lord Jesus, I am the woman from the Hotel Madrid and Louvre, the one on Tverskaya Street. Working at the hotel, it's just like going around with your skirt up. Just let a man stop there, and he's your lord and master, let him be a Jew, let him be anyone at all. There is another slave of yours walking the earth, the janitor's helper, Seryoga. Last year on Palm Sunday I bore him twins."

And so she described it all to the Lord.

"And what if Seryoga were not to go into the army after all?" the Saviour suggested.

"Try and get away with it—not with the policeman around. He'll drag him off as sure as daylight."

"Oh yes, the policeman," the Lord bowed His head, "I never thought of him. Then perhaps you ought to live in purity for a while?"

"For four years?" the woman cried. "To hear you talk, all people should deny their animal nature. That's just your old ways all over again. And where will the increase come from? No, you'd better give me some sensible advice."

The Lord's cheeks turned scarlet, the woman's words had touched a tender spot. But He said nothing. You cannot kiss your own ear—even God knows that.

"I'll tell you what, God's servant, glorious sinner, maiden Arina," the Lord proclaimed in all His glory, "I have a little angel here in heaven, hanging around uselessly. His name is Alfred. Lately he's gotten out of hand altogether, keeps crying and nagging all the time: 'What have you done to me, Lord? Why do you turn me into an angel in my twentieth year, and me a hale young fellow?' So I'll give you Alfred the angel as a husband for four years. He'll be your prayer, he'll be your protection, and he'll be your solace. And as for offspring, you've nothing to worry about—you can't bear a duckling from him, let alone a baby, for there's a lot of fun in him, but no seriousness."

"That's just what I need," the maid Arina wept gratefully. "Their seriousness takes me to the doorstep of the grave three times every two years."

"You'll have a sweet respite, God's child Arina. May your prayer be light as a song. Amen."

And so it was decided. Alfred was brought in—a frail young fellow, delicate, two wings fluttering behind his pale-blue shoulders, rippling with rosy light like two doves playing in heaven. Arina threw her hefty arms about him, weeping out of tenderness, out of her woman's soft heart.

"Alfred, my soul, my consolation, my bridegroom . . . "

In parting, the Lord gave her strict instructions to take off the angel's wings every night before he went to bed. His wings were attached to hinges, like a door, and every night she was to take them off and wrap them in a clean sheet, because they were brittle, his wings, and could snap as he tossed in bed—for what were they made of but the sighs of babes, no more than that.

For the last time the Lord blessed the union, while the choir of bishops, called in for the occasion, rendered thunderous praises. No food was served, not a crumb—that wasn't the style in heaven—and then Arina and Alfred, their arms about each other, ran down a silken ladder, straight back to earth. They came to Petrovka, the street where nothing but the best is sold. The woman would do right by her Alfred for he, if one might say so, not only lacked socks, but was altogether as natural as when his mother bore him. And she bought him patent-leather half-boots, checked jersey trousers, a fine hunting jacket, and an electric-blue vest.

"The rest," she says, "we'll find at home."

That day Arina begged off from work. Seryoga came and raised a fuss, but she did not even come out to him, only said from behind her locked door:

"Sergey Nifantyich, I am at present a-washing my feet and beg you to retire without further noise."

He went away without a word—the angel's power was already beginning to manifest itself!

In the evening Arina set out a supper fit for a merchant—the woman had devilish vanity! A half-pint of vodka, wine on the side, a Danube herring with potatoes, a samovar of tea. When Alfred had partaken of all these earthly blessings, he keeled over in a dead sleep. Quick as a wink, Arina lifted off his wings from the hinges, packed them away, and carried him to bed in her arms.

There it lies, the snowy wonder on the eiderdown pillows of her tattered, sinful bed, sending forth a heavenly radiance: moon-silver shafts of light pass and repass, alternate with red ones, float across the floor, sway over his shining feet. Arina weeps and rejoices, sings and prays. Arina, thou hast been granted a happiness unheard of on this battered earth. Blessed art thou among women!

They had drunk the vodka to the last drop, and now it took effect. As soon as they fell asleep, she went and rolled over on top of Alfred with her hot, six-months-big belly. Not enough for her to sleep with an angel, not enough that nobody beside her spat at the wall, snored and snorted—that wasn't enough for the clumsy, ravening slut. No, she had to warm her belly too, her burning belly big with Seryoga's lust. And so she smothered him in her fuddled sleep, smothered him like a week-old babe in the midst of her rejoicing, crushed him under her bloated weight, and he gave up the ghost, and his wings, wrapped in her sheet, wept pale tears.

Dawn came—and all the trees bowed low to the ground. In distant northern forests each fir tree turned into a priest, each fir tree bent its knees in silent worship.

Once more the woman stands before the Lord's throne. She is broad in the shoulders, mighty, the young corpse drooping in her huge red arms.

"Behold, Lord . . ."

But here the gentle heart of Jesus could endure no more, and He cursed the woman in His anger:

"As it is on earth, so shall it be with you, Arina, from this day on."

"How is it then, Lord?" the woman replied in a scarcely audible voice. "Was it I who made my body heavy, was it I that brewed vodka on earth, was it I that created a woman's soul, stupid and lonely?"

"I don't wish to be bothered with you," exclaimed the Lord Jesus. "You've smothered my angel, you filthy scum."

And Arina was thrown back to earth on a putrid wind, straight down to Tverskaya Street, to the Hotel Madrid and Louvre, where she was doomed to spend her days. And once there, the sky was the limit. Seryoga was carousing, drinking away his last days, seeing as he was a recruit. The contractor Trofimych, just come from Kolomna, took one look at Arina, hefty and red-cheeked: "Oh, you cute little belly," he said, and so on and so forth.

Isai Abramych, the old codger, heard about this cute little belly, and he was right there too, wheezing toothlessly:

"I cannot wed you lawfully," he said, "after all that happened. However, I can lie with you the same as anyone."

The old man ought to be lying in cold mother earth instead of thinking of such things, but no, he too must take his turn at spitting into her soul. It was as though they had all slipped the chain—kitchen-boys, merchants, foreigners. A fellow in trade—he likes to have his fun.

And that is the end of my tale.

Before she was laid up, for three months had rolled by in the meantime, Arina went out into the back yard, behind the janitor's rooms, raised her monstrous belly to the silken sky, and said stupidly:

"See, Lord, what a belly! They hammer at it like peas falling in a colander. And what sense there's in it I just can't see. But I've had enough."

With His tears Jesus laved Arina when He heard these words. The Saviour fell on His knees before her.

"Forgive me, little Arina. Forgive your sinful God for all He has done to you . . ."

But Arina shook her head and would not listen.

"There's no forgiveness for you, Jesus Christ," she said. "No forgiveness, and never will be."

F. Scott Fitzgerald (1896–1940)

F. Scott Fitzgerald once claimed that he had coined the term "The Jazz Age" to denote that decade of easy money, booze, music, and sex between the end of the First World War and the Crash of 1929. Coiner or not, he was ideally suited to be its chronicler, its most famous representative, and its victim. His first novel, *This Side of Paradise* (1920), launched him and his wife Zelda—an international beauty, a would-be dancer, a frustrated writer—into a decade's long party of recklessness, extravagance, drunken pranks, public squabbles, and used, abused, and squandered talent. By the end of the period, Fitzgerald was, as he said, "a cracked plate, the kind that one wonders whether it was worth preserving. . . . It can never be warmed on the stove, nor shuffled with the other plates in the dishpan; it will not be brought out for company, but it will do to hold crackers late at night or to go into the ice box under left-overs." His life ended in Hollywood, where he was a poorly paid, almost forgotten, hardly respected screen writer. His contemporary and friend Glenway Wescott wrote, "He was our darling, our genius, our fool."

But even during the long party, and intermittently for the next ten years, Fitzgerald showed that he was one of the most talented and accomplished writers in a richly talented generation. He wrote five novels, the most important being *The Great Gatsby* (1925), *Tender Is the Night* (1934), and the unfinished *The Last Tycoon* (1941), over a hundred short stories, and one play. His letters to his daughter are among the most tender, touching, and yet rigorous ever written by a father. He was a supreme stylist. His prose is stripped of both emotional excess and unnecessary detail. His goal was clarity and his means was economy and the result indicated, in John Cheever's phrase, "an angelic austerity of spirit."

Yet he was able to convey as much about his time and place as any of his contemporaries. As Cheever noted, "In Fitzgerald there is a thrilling sense of knowing exactly where one is—the city, the resort, the hotel, the decade, and the time of day." He is a trustworthy social historian, whether writing about a mechanic's life in a greasy garage on Long Island or about the idle rich in the fanciest hotels on the French Riviera.

His subject was usually some variation on his own experience and he himself can be identified with his protagonists. They spend their days chasing after their dreams of the good life, glamor, luxury, excitement, beautiful women, infinite possibility. They and their friends and lovers are "a whole race going hedonistic, deciding on pleasure." They have no politics and apparently no social conscience. This part of Fitzgerald's vision is innocent, childlike, amoral. But the other part is tragic, dark, profoundly moral. The piper is paid in full: Gatsby mistakenly murdered, Dick Diver morally and emotionally destroyed. Life, Fitzgerald wrote his daughter, "is essentially a cheat and its conditions are those of defeat." But he adds that "the redeeming things are not 'happiness and pleasure' but the deeper satisfaction that comes of struggle."

The story that follows beautifully encapsulates both parts of the vision, and explains their connection, more succinctly than do the novels. Charlie Wales has lived the reckless, extravagant, careless life to the hilt, and he has lost everything that he loves and values—his wife, his child, his self-respect. "I heard you lost a lot in the crash," the head barman says to Charlie. With heartbreaking irony, Charlie answers, "I did, but I lost everything I wanted in the boom."

Babylon Revisited

"And where's Mr. Campbell?" Charlie asked.

"Gone to Switzerland. Mr. Campbell's a pretty sick man, Mr. Wales."

"I'm sorry to hear that. And George Hardt?" Charlie inquired.

"Back in America, gone to work."

"And where is the Snow Bird?"

"He was in here last week. Anyway, his friend, Mr. Schaeffer, is in Paris."

Two familiar names from the long list of a year and a half ago. Charlie scribbled an address in his notebook and tore out the page.

"If you see Mr. Schaeffer, give him this," he said. "It's my brother-in-law's address. I haven't settled on a hotel yet."

He was not really disappointed to find Paris was so empty. But the stillness in the Ritz bar was strange and portentous. It was not an American bar any more—he felt polite in it, and not as if he owned it. It had gone back into France. He felt the stillness from the moment he got out of the taxi and saw the doorman, usually in a frenzy of activity at this hour, gossiping with a *chasseur* by the servants' entrance.

Passing through the corridor, he heard only a single, bored voice in the once-clamorous women's room. When he turned into the bar he travelled the twenty feet of green carpet with his eyes fixed straight ahead by old habit; and then, with his foot firmly on the rail, he turned and surveyed the room, encountering only a single pair of eyes that fluttered up from a newspaper in the corner. Charlie asked for the head barman, Paul, who in the latter days of the bull market had come to work in his own custom-built car—disembarking, however, with due nicety at the nearest corner. But Paul was at his country house today and Alix giving him information.

"No, no more," Charlie said, "I'm going slow these days."

Alix congratulated him: "You were going pretty strong a couple of years ago."

"I'll stick to it all right," Charlie assured him. "I've stuck to it for over a year and a half now."

"How do you find conditions in America?"

"I haven't been to America for months. I'm in business in Prague, representing a couple of concerns there. They don't know about me down there."

Alix smiled.

"Remember the night of George Hardt's bachelor dinner here?" said Charlie. "By the way, what's become of Claude Fessenden?"

Alix lowered his voice confidentially: "He's in Paris, but he doesn't come here any more. Paul doesn't allow it. He ran up a bill of thirty thousand francs, charging all his drinks and his lunches, and usually his dinner, for more than a year. And when Paul finally told him he had to pay, he gave him a bad check."

Alix shook his head sadly.

"I don't understand it, such a dandy fellow. Now he's all bloated up—" He made a plump apple of his hands.

Charlie watched a group of strident queens installing themselves in a corner.

"Nothing affects them," he thought. "Stocks rise and fall, people loaf or work, but they go on forever.'' The place oppressed him. He called for the dice and shook with Alix for the drink.

"Here for long, Mr. Wales?"

"I'm here for four or five days to see my little girl."

"Oh-h! You have a little girl?"

Outside, the fire-red, gas-blue, ghost-green signs shone smokily through the tranquil rain. It was late afternoon and the streets were in movement; the *bistros* gleamed. At the corner of the Boulevard des Capucines he took a taxi. The Place de la Concorde moved by in pink majesty; they crossed the logical Seine, and Charlie felt the sudden provincial quality of the Left Bank.

Charlie directed his taxi to the Avenue de l'Opera, which was out of his way. But he wanted to see the blue hour spread over the magnificent façade, and imagine that the cab horns, playing endlessly the first few bars of *Le Plus que Lent,* were the trumpets of the Second Empire. They were closing the iron grill in front of Brentano's Bookstore, and people were already at dinner behind the trim little bourgeois hedge of Duval's. He had never eaten at a really cheap restaurant in Paris. Five-course dinner, four francs fifty, eighteen cents, wine included. For some odd reason he wished that he had.

As they rolled on to the Left Bank and he felt its sudden provincialism, he thought, "I spoiled this city for myself. I didn't realize it, but the days came along one after another, and then two years were gone, and everything was gone, and I was gone."

He was thirty-five, and good to look at. The Irish mobility of his face was sobered by a deep wrinkle between his eyes. As he rang his brother-in-law's bell in the Rue Palatine, the wrinkle deepened till it pulled down his brows; he felt a cramping sensation in his belly. From behind the maid who opened the door darted a lovely little girl of nine who shrieked "Daddy!" and flew up, struggling like a fish, into his arms. She pulled his head around by one ear and set her cheek against his.

"My old pie," he said.

"Oh, daddy, daddy, daddy, daddy, dads, dads, dads!"

She drew him into the salon, where the family waited, a boy and a girl his daughter's age, his sister-in-law and her husband. He greeted Marion with his voice pitched carefully to avoid either feigned enthusiasm or dislike, but her response was more frankly tepid, though she minimized her expression of unalterable distrust by directing her regard toward his child. The two men clasped hands in a friendly way and Lincoln Peters rested his for a moment on Charlie's shoulder.

The room was warm and comfortably American. The three children moved intimately about, playing through the yellow oblongs that led to other rooms; the cheer of six o'clock spoke in the eager smacks of the fire and the sounds of French activity in the kitchen. But Charlie did not relax; his heart sat up rigidly in his body and he drew confidence from his daughter, who from time to time came close to him, holding in her arms the doll he had brought.

"Really extremely well," he declared in answer to Lincoln's question. "There's a lot of business there that isn't moving at all, but we're doing even better than ever. In fact, damn well. I'm bringing my sister over from America next month to keep house for me. My income last year was bigger than it was when I had money. You see, the Czechs—"

His boasting was for a specific purpose; but after a moment, seeing a faint restiveness in Lincoln's eye, he changed the subject:

"Those are fine children of yours, well brought up, good manners."

"We think Honoria's a great little girl too."

Marion Peters came back from the kitchen. She was a tall woman with worried eyes, who had once possessed a fresh American loveliness. Charlie had never been sensitive to it and was always surprised when people spoke of how pretty she had been. From the first there had been an instinctive antipathy between them.

"Well, how do you find Honoria?" she asked.

"Wonderful. I was astonished how much she's grown in ten months. All the children are looking well."

"We haven't had a doctor for a year. How do you like being back in Paris?"

"It seems very funny to see so few Americans around."

"I'm delighted," Marion said vehemently. "Now at least you can go into a store without their assuming you're a millionaire. We've suffered like everybody, but on the whole it's a good deal pleasanter."

"But it was nice while it lasted," Charlie said. "We were a sort of royalty, almost infallible, with a sort of magic around us. In the bar this afternoon"—he stumbled, seeing his mistake—"there wasn't a man I knew."

She looked at him keenly. "I should think you'd have had enough of bars."

"I only stayed a minute. I take one drink every afternoon, and no more."

"Don't you want a cocktail before dinner?" Lincoln asked.

"I take only one drink every afternoon, and I've had that."

"I hope you keep to it," said Marion.

Her dislike was evident in the coldness with which she spoke, but Charlie only smiled; he had larger plans. Her very aggressiveness gave him an advantage, and he knew enough to wait. He wanted them to initiate the discussion of what they knew had brought him to Paris.

At dinner he couldn't decide whether Honoria was most like him or her mother. Fortunate if she didn't combine the traits of both that had brought them to disaster. A great wave of protectiveness went over him. He thought he knew what to do for her. He believed in character; he wanted to jump back a whole generation and trust in character again as the eternally valuable element. Everything else wore out.

He left soon after dinner, but not to go home. He was curious to see Paris by night with clearer and more judicious eyes than those of other days. He bought a *strapontin* for the Casino and watched Josephine Baker go through her chocolate arabesques.

After an hour he left and strolled toward Montmartre, up the Rue Pigalle into the Place Blanche. The rain had stopped and there were a few people in evening clothes disembarking from taxis in front of cabarets, and *cocottes* prowling singly or in pairs, and many Negroes. He passed a lighted door from which issued music, and stopped with the sense of familiarity; it was Bricktop's, where he had parted with so many hours and so much money. A few doors farther on he found another ancient rendezvous and incautiously put his head inside. Immediately an eager orchestra burst into sound, a pair of professional dancers leaped to their feet and a maître d'hôtel swooped toward him, crying, "Crowd just arriving, sir!" But he withdrew quickly.

"You have to be damn drunk," he thought.

Zelli's was closed, the bleak and sinister cheap hotels surrounding it were dark; up in the Rue Blanche there was more light and a local, colloquial French crowd. The Poet's Cave had disappeared, but the two great mouths of the Café of Heaven and the Café of Hell still yawned—even devoured, as he watched, the meager contents of a tourist bus—a German, a Japanese, and an American couple who glanced at him with frightened eyes.

So much for the effort and ingenuity of Montmartre. All the catering to vice and waste was on an utterly childish scale, and he suddenly realized the meaning of the word "dissipate"—to dissipate into thin air; to make nothing out of something. In the little hours of the night every move from place to place was an enormous human jump, an increase of paying for the privilege of slower and slower motion.

He remembered thousand-franc notes given to an orchestra for playing a single number, hundred-franc notes tossed to a doorman for calling a cab.

But it hadn't been given for nothing.

It had been given, even the most wildly squandered sum, as an offering to destiny that he might not remember the things most worth remembering, the things that now he would always remember—his child taken from his control, his wife escaped to a grave in Vermont.

In the glare of a *brasserie* a woman spoke to him. He bought her some eggs and coffee, and then, eluding her encouraging stare, gave her a twenty-franc note and took a taxi to his hotel.

2

He woke upon a fine fall day—football weather. The depression of yesterday was gone and he liked the people on the streets. At noon he sat opposite Honoria at Le Grand Vatel, the only restaurant he could think of not reminiscent of champagne dinners and long luncheons that began at two and ended in a blurred and vague twilight.

"Now, how about vegetables? Oughtn't you to have some vegetables?"

"Well, yes."

"Here's *épinards* and *chou-fleur* and carrots and *haricots*."

"I'd like *chou-fleur*."

"Wouldn't you like to have two vegetables?"

"I usually only have one at lunch."

The waiter was pretending to be inordinately fond of children. *"Qu'elle est mignonne la petite! Elle parle exactement comme une Française."*

"How about dessert? Shall we wait and see?"

The waiter disappeared. Honoria looked at her father expectantly.

"What are we going to do?"

"First, we're going to that toy store in the Rue Saint-Honoré and buy you anything you like. And then we're going to the vaudeville at the Empire."

She hesitated. "I like it about the vaudeville, but not the toy store."

"Why not?"

"Well, you brought me this doll." She had it with her. "And I've got lots of things. And we're not rich any more, are we?"

"We never were. But today you are to have anything you want."

"All right," she agreed resignedly.

When there had been her mother and a French nurse he had been inclined to be strict; now he extended himself, reached out for a new tolerance; he must be both parents to her and not shut any of her out of communication.

"I want to get to know you," he said gravely. "First let me introduce myself. My name is Charles J. Wales, of Prague."

"Oh, daddy!" her voice cracked with laughter.

"And who are you, please?" he persisted, and she accepted a rôle immediately: "Honoria Wales, Rue Palatine, Paris."

"Married or single?"

"No, not married. Single."

He indicated the doll. "But I see you have a child, madame."

Unwilling to disinherit it, she took it to her heart and thought quickly: "Yes, I've been married, but I'm not married now. My husband is dead."

He went on quickly, "And the child's name?"

"Simone. That's after my best friend at school."

"I'm very pleased that you're doing so well at school."

"I'm third this month," she boasted. "Elsie"—that was her cousin—"is only about eighteenth, and Richard is about at the bottom."

"You like Richard and Elsie, don't you?"

"Oh, yes. I like Richard quite well and I like her all right."

Cautiously and casually he asked: "And Aunt Marion and Uncle Lincoln—which do you like best?"

"Oh, Uncle Lincoln, I guess."

He was increasingly aware of her presence. As they came in, a murmur of ". . . adorable" followed them, and now the people at the next table bent all their silences upon her, staring as if she were something no more conscious than a flower.

"Why don't I live with you?" she asked suddenly. "Because mamma's dead?"

"You must stay here and learn more French. It would have been hard for daddy to take care of you so well."

"I don't really need much taking care of any more. I do everything for myself."

Going out of the restaurant, a man and a woman unexpectedly hailed him!

"Well, the old Wales!"

"Hello there, Lorraine. . . . Dunc."

Sudden ghosts out of the past: Duncan Schaeffer, a friend from college. Lorraine Quarrles, a lovely, pale blonde of thirty; one of a crowd who had helped them make months into days in the lavish times of three years ago.

"My husband couldn't come this year," she said, in answer to his question. "We're poor as hell. So he gave me two hundred a month and told me I could do my worst on that. . . . This your little girl?"

"What about coming back and sitting down?" Duncan asked.

"Can't do it." He was glad for an excuse. As always, he felt Lorraine's passionate, provocative attraction, but his own rhythm was different now.

"Well, how about dinner?" she asked.

"I'm not free. Give me your address and let me call you."

"Charlie, I believe you're sober," she said judicially. "I honestly believe he's sober, Dunc. Pinch him and see if he's sober."

Charlie indicated Honoria with his head. They both laughed.

"What's your address?" said Duncan skeptically.

He hesitated, unwilling to give the name of his hotel.

"I'm not settled yet. Id better call you. We're going to see the vaudeville at the Empire."

"There! That's what I want to do," Lorraine said. "I want to see some clowns and acrobats and jugglers. That's just what we'll do, Dunc."

"We've got to do an errand first," said Charlie. "Perhaps we'll see you there."

"All right, you snob. . . . Good-bye, beautiful little girl."

"Good-by."

Honoria bobbed politely.

Somehow, an unwelcome encounter. They liked him because he was functioning, because he was serious; they wanted to see him, because he was stronger than they were now, because they wanted to draw a certain sustenance from his strength.

At the Empire, Honoria proudly refused to sit upon her father's folded coat. She was already an individual with a code of her own, and Charlie was more and more absorbed by the desire of putting a little of himself into her before she crystallized utterly. It was hopeless to try to know her in so short a time.

Between the acts they came upon Duncan and Lorraine in the lobby where the band was playing.

"Have a drink?"

"All right, but not up at the bar. We'll take a table."

"The perfect father."

Listening abstractedly to Lorraine, Charlie watched Honoria's eyes leave their table, and he followed them wistfully about the room, wondering what they saw. He met her glance and she smiled.

"I liked that lemonade," she said.

What had she said? What had he expected? Going home in a taxi afterward, he pulled her over until her head rested against his chest.

"Darling, do you ever think about your mother?"

"Yes, sometimes," she answered vaguely.

"I don't want you to forget her. Have you got a picture of her?"

"Yes, I think so. Anyhow, Aunt Marion has. Why don't you want me to forget her?"

"She loved you very much."

"I loved her too."

They were silent for a moment.

"Daddy, I want to come and live with you," she said suddenly.

His heart leaped; he had wanted it to come like this.

"Aren't you perfectly happy?"

"Yes, but I love you better than anybody. And you love me better than anybody, don't you, now that mummy's dead?"

"Of course I do. But you won't always like me best, honey. You'll grow up and meet somebody your own age and go marry him and forget you ever had a daddy."

"Yes, that's true," she agreed tranquilly.

He didn't go in. He was coming back at nine o'clock and he wanted to keep himself fresh and new for the thing he must say then.

"When you're safe inside, just show yourself in that window."

"All right. Good-by, dads, dads, dads, dads."

He waited in the dark street until she appeared, all warm and glowing, in the window above and kissed her fingers out into the night.

3

They were waiting, Marion sat behind the coffee service in a dignified black dinner dress that just faintly suggested mourning. Lincoln was walking up and down with the animation of one who had already been talking. They were as anxious as he was to get into the question. He opened it almost immediately:

"I suppose you know what I want to see you about—why I really came to Paris."

Marion played with the black stars on her necklace and frowned.

"I'm awfully anxious to have a home," he continued. "And I'm awfully anxious to have Honoria in it. I appreciate your taking in Honoria for her mother's sake, but things have changed now"—he hesitated and then continued more forcibly—"changed radically with me, and I want to ask you to reconsider the matter. It would be silly for me to deny that about three years ago I was acting badly—"

Marion looked up at him with hard eyes.

"—but all that's over. As I told you, I haven't had more than a drink a day for over a year, and I take that drink deliberately, so that the idea of alcohol won't get too big in my imagination. You see the idea?"

"No," said Marion succinctly.

"It's a sort of stunt I set myself. It keeps the matter in proportion."

"I get you," said Lincoln. "You don't want to admit it's got any attraction for you."

"Something like that. Sometimes I forget and don't take it. But I try to take it. Anyhow, I couldn't afford to drink in my position. The people I represent are more than satisfied with what I've done, and I'm bringing my sister over from Burlington to keep house for me, and I want awfully to have Honoria too. You know that even when her mother and I weren't getting along well we never let anything that happened touch Honoria. I know she's fond of me and I know I'm able to take care of her and—well, there you are. How do you feel about it?"

He knew that now he would have to take a beating. It would last an hour or two hours, and it would be difficult, but if he modulated his inevitable resentment to the chastened attitude of the reformed sinner, he might win his point in the end.

Keep your temper, he told himself. You don't want to be justified. You want Honoria.

Lincoln spoke first: "We've been talking it over ever since we got your letter last month. We're happy to have Honoria here. She's a dear little thing, and we're glad to be able to help her, but of course that isn't the question—"

Marion interrupted suddenly. "How long are you going to stay sober, Charlie?" she asked.

"Permanently, I hope."

"How can anybody count on that?"

"You know I never did drink heavily until I gave up business and came over here with nothing to do. Then Helen and I began to run around with—"

"Please leave Helen out of it. I can't bear to hear you talk about her like that."

He stared at her grimly; he had never been certain how fond of each other the sisters were in life.

"My drinking only lasted about a year and a half—from the time we came over until I—collapsed."

"It was time enough."

"It was time enough," he agreed.

"My duty is entirely to Helen," she said. "I try to think what she would have wanted me to do. Frankly, from the night you did that terrible thing you haven't really existed for me. I can't help that. She was my sister."

"Yes."

"When she was dying she asked me to look out for Honoria. If you hadn't been in a sanitarium then, it might have helped matters."

He had no answer.

"I'll never in my life be able to forget the morning when Helen knocked at my door, soaked to the skin and shivering and said you'd locked her out."

Charlie gripped the sides of the chair. This was more difficult than he expected; he wanted to launch out into a long expostulation and explanation, but he only said: "The night I locked her out—" and she interrupted, "I don't feel up to going over that again."

After a moment's silence Lincoln said: "We're getting off the subject. You want Marion to set aside her legal guardianship and give you Honoria. I think the main point for her is whether she has confidence in you or not."

"I don't blame Marion," Charlie said slowly, "but I think she can have entire confidence in me. I had a good record up to three years ago. Of course, it's within human possibilities I might go wrong any time. But if we wait much longer I'll lose Honoria's childhood and my chance for a home." He shook his head, "I'll simply lose her, don't you see?"

"Yes, I see," said Lincoln.

"Why didn't you think of all this before?" Marion asked.

"I suppose I did, from time to time, but Helen and I were getting along badly. When I consented to the guardianship, I was flat on my back in a sanitarium and the market had cleaned me out. I knew I'd acted badly, and I thought if it would bring any peace to Helen, I'd agree to anything. But now it's different. I'm functioning, I'm behaving damn well, so far as—"

"Please don't swear at me," Marion said.

He looked at her, startled. With each remark the force of her dislike became more and more apparent. She had built up all her fear of life into one wall and faced it toward him. This trivial reproof was possibly the result of some trouble with the cook several hours before. Charlie became increasingly alarmed at leaving Honoria in this atmosphere of hostility against himself; sooner or later it would come out, in a word here, a shake of the head there, and some of that distrust would be irrevocably implanted in Honoria. But he pulled his temper down out of his face and shut it up inside him; he had won a point, for Lincoln realized the absurdity of Marion's remark and asked her lightly since when she had objected to the word "damn."

"Another thing," Charlie said: "I'm able to give her certain advantages now. I'm going to take a French governess to Prague with me. I've got a lease on a new apartment—"

He stopped, realizing that he was blundering. They couldn't be expected to accept with equanimity the fact that his income was again twice as large as their own.

"I suppose you can give her more luxuries than we can," said Marion. "When you were throwing away money we were living along watching every ten francs. . . . I suppose you'll start doing it again."

"Oh, no," he said. "I've learned. I worked hard for ten years, you know—until I got lucky in the market, like so many people. Terribly lucky. It won't happen again."

There was a long silence. All of them felt their nerves straining, and for the first time in a year Charlie wanted a drink. He was sure now that Lincoln Peters wanted him to have his child.

Marion shuddered suddenly; part of her saw that Charlie's feet were planted on the earth now, and her own maternal feeling recognized the naturalness of his desire; but she had lived for a long time with a prejudice—a prejudice founded on a curious disbelief in her sister's happiness, and which, in the shock of one terrible night, had turned to hatred for him. It had all happened at a point in her life where the discouragement of ill health and adverse circumstances made it necessary for her to believe in tangible villainy and a tangible villain.

"I can't help what I think!" she cried out suddenly. "How much you were responsible for Helen's death, I don't know. It's something you'll have to square with your own conscience."

An electric current of agony surged through him; for a moment he was almost on his feet, an unuttered sound echoing in his throat. He hung on to himself for a moment, another moment.

"Hold on there," said Lincoln uncomfortably. "I never thought you were responsible for that."

"Helen died of heart trouble," Charlie said dully.

"Yes, heart trouble." Marion spoke as if the phrase had another meaning for her.

Then, in the flatness that followed her outburst, she saw him plainly and she knew he had somehow arrived at control over the situation. Glancing at her husband, she found no help from him, and as abruptly as if it were a matter of no importance, she threw up the sponge.

"Do what you like!" she cried, springing up from her chair. "She's your child. I'm not the person to stand in your way. I think if it were my child I'd rather see her—" She managed to check herself. "You two decide it. I can't stand this. I'm sick. I'm going to bed."

She hurried from the room; after a moment Lincoln said:

"This has been a hard day for her. You know how strongly she feels—" His voice was almost apologetic: "When a woman gets an idea in her head."

"Of course."

"It's going to be all right. I think she sees now that you—can provide for the child, and so we can't very well stand in your way or Honoria's way."

"Thank you, Lincoln."

"I'd better go along and see how she is."

"I'm going."

He was still trembling when he reached the street, but a walk down the Rue Bonaparte to the *quais* set him up, and as he crossed the Seine, fresh and new by the *quai* lamps, he felt exultant. But back in his room he couldn't sleep. The image of Helen haunted him. Helen whom he had loved so until they had senselessly begun to abuse each other's love, tear it into shreds. On that terrible February night that Marion remembered so vividly, a slow quarrel had gone on for hours. There was a scene at the Florida, and then he attempted to take her home, and then she kissed young Webb at a table; after that there was what she had hysterically said. When he arrived home alone he turned the key in the lock in wild anger. How could he know she would arrive an hour later alone, that there would be a snowstorm in which she wandered about in slippers, too confused to find a taxi? Then the aftermath, her escaping pneumonia by a miracle, and all the attendant horror. They were "reconciled," but that was the beginning of the end, and Marion, who had seen with her own eyes and who imagined it to be one of many scenes from her sister's martyrdom, never forgot.

Going over it again brought Helen nearer, and in the white, soft light that steals upon half sleep near morning he found himself talking to her again. She said that he was perfectly right about Honoria and that she wanted Honoria to be with him. She said she was glad he was being good and doing better. She said a lot of other things—very friendly things—but she was in a swing in a white dress, and swinging faster and faster all the time, so that at the end he could not hear clearly all that she said.

4

He woke up feeling happy. The door of the world was open again. He made plans, vistas, futures for Honoria and himself, but suddenly he grew sad, remembering all the plans he and Helen had made. She had not planned to die. The present was the thing— work to do and someone to love. But not to love too much, for he knew the injury that a father can do to a daughter or a mother to a son by attaching them too closely: afterward, out in the world, the child would seek in the marriage partner the same blind tenderness and, failing probably to find it, turn against love and life.

It was another bright, crisp day. He called Lincoln Peters at the bank where he worked and asked if he could count on taking Honoria when he left for Prague. Lincoln agreed that there was no reason for delay. One thing—the legal guardianship. Marion wanted to retain that a while longer. She was upset by the whole matter, and it would oil things if she felt that the situation was still in her control for another year. Charlie agreed, wanting only the tangible, visible child.

Then the question of a governess. Charlie sat in a gloomy agency and talked to a cross Béarnaise and to a buxom Breton peasant, neither of whom he could have endured. There were others whom he would see tomorrow.

He lunched with Lincoln Peters at Griffons, trying to keep down his exultation.

"There's nothing quite like your own child," Lincoln said. "But you understand how Marion feels too."

"She's forgotten how hard I worked for seven years there," Charlie said. "She just remembers one night."

"There's another thing." Lincoln hesitated. "While you and Helen were tearing around Europe throwing money away, we were just getting along. I didn't touch any of the prosperity because I never got ahead enough to carry anything but my insurance. I think Marion felt there was some kind of injustice in it—you not even working toward the end, and getting richer and richer."

"It went just as quick as it came," said Charlie.

"Yes, a lot of it stayed in the hands of *chasseurs* and saxophone players and maîtres d'hôtel—well, the big party's over now. I just said that to explain Marion's feeling about those crazy years. If you drop in about six o'clock tonight before Marion's too tired, we'll settle the details on the spot."

Back at his hotel, Charlie found a *pneumatique* that had been redirected from the Ritz bar where Charlie had left his address for the purpose of finding a certain man.

"DEAR CHARLIE: You were so strange when we saw you the other day that I wondered if I did something to offend you. If so, I'm not conscious of it. In fact, I have thought about you too much for the last year, and it's always been in the back of my mind that I might see you if I came over here. We *did* have such good times that crazy spring, like the night you and I stole the butcher's tricycle, and the time we tried to call on the president and you had the old derby rim and the wire cane. Everybody seems so old lately, but I don't feel old a bit. Couldn't we get together some time today for old time's sake? I've got a vile hang-over for the moment, but will be feeling better this afternoon and will look for you about five in the sweat-shop at the Ritz.

"Always devotedly,

"LORRAINE."

His first feeling was one of awe that he had actually, in his mature years, stolen a tricycle and pedalled Lorraine all over the Étoile between the small hours and dawn. In retrospect it was a nightmare. Locking out Helen didn't fit in with any other act of his life, but the tricycle incident did—it was one of many. How many weeks or months of dissipation to arrive at that condition of utter irresponsibility?

He tried to picture how Lorraine had appeared to him then—very attractive; Helen was unhappy about it, though she said nothing. Yesterday, in the restaurant, Lorraine had seemed trite, blurred, worn away. He emphatically did not want to see her, and he was glad Alix had not given away his hotel address. It was a relief to think, instead, of Honoria, to think of Sundays spent with her and saying good morning to her and of knowing she was there in his house at night, drawing her breath in the darkness.

At five he took a taxi and bought presents for all the Peters—a piquant cloth doll, a box of Roman soldiers, flowers for Marion, big linen handkerchiefs for Lincoln.

He saw, when he arrived in the apartment, that Marion had accepted the inevitable. She greeted him now as though he were a recalcitrant member of the family, rather than a menacing outsider. Honoria had been told she was going; Charlie was glad to see that her tact made her conceal her excessive happiness. Only on his lap did she whisper her delight and the question "When?" before she slipped away with the other children.

He and Marion were alone for a minute in the room, and on an impulse he spoke out boldly:

"Family quarrels are bitter things. They don't go according to any rules. They're not like aches or wounds; they're more like splits in the skin that won't heal because there's not enough material. I wish you and I could be on better terms."

"Some things are hard to forget," she answered. "It's a question of confidence." There was no answer to this and presently she asked, "When do you propose to take her?"

"As soon as I can get a governess. I hoped the day after tomorrow."

"That's impossible. I've got to get her things in shape. Not before Saturday."

He yielded. Coming back into the room, Lincoln offered him a drink.

"I'll take my daily whisky," he said.

It was warm here, it was a home, people together by a fire. The children felt very safe and important; the mother and father were serious, watchful. They had things to do for the children more important than his visit here. A spoonful of medicine was, after all, more important than the strained relations between Marion and himself. They were not dull people, but they were very much in the grip of life and circumstances. He wondered if he couldn't do something to get Lincoln out of his rut at the bank.

A long peal at the door-bell; the *bonne à toute faire* passed through and went down the corridor. The door opened upon another long ring, and then voices, and the three in the salon looked up expectantly; Richard moved to bring the corridor within his range of vision, and Marion rose. Then the maid came back along the corridor, closely followed by the voices, which developed under the light into Duncan Schaeffer and Lorraine Quarrles.

They were gay, they were hilarious, they were roaring with laughter. For a moment Charlie was astounded; unable to understand how they ferreted out the Peters' address.

"Ah-h-h!" Duncan wagged his finger roguishly at Charlie. "Ah-h-h!"

They both slid down another cascade of laughter. Anxious and at a loss, Charlie shook hands with them quickly and presented them to Lincoln and Marion. Marion nodded, scarcely speaking. She had drawn back a step toward the fire; her little girl stood beside her, and Marion put an arm about her shoulder.

With growing annoyance at the intrusion, Charlie waited for them to explain themselves. After some concentration Duncan said:

"We came to invite you out to dinner. Lorraine and I insist that all this shishi, cagy business 'bout your address got to stop."

Charlie came closer to them, as if to force them backward down the corridor.

"Sorry, but I can't. Tell me where you'll be and I'll phone you in half an hour."

This made no impression. Lorraine sat down suddenly on the side of a chair, and focusing her eyes on Richard, cried, "Oh, what a nice little boy! Come here, little boy." Richard glanced at his mother, but did not move. With a perceptible shrug of her shoulders, Lorraine turned back to Charlie:

"Come and dine. Sure your cousins won' mine. See you so sel'om. Or solemn."

"I can't," said Charlie sharply. "You two have dinner and I'll phone you."

Her voice became suddenly unpleasant. "All right, we'll go. But I remember once when you hammered on my door at four A.M. I was enough of a good sport to give you a drink. Come on, Dunc."

Still in slow motion, with blurred, angry faces, with uncertain feet, they retired along the corridor.

"Good night," Charlie said.

"Good night!" responded Lorraine emphatically.

When he went back into the salon Marion had not moved, only now her son was standing in the circle of her other arm. Lincoln was still swinging Honoria back and forth like a pendulum from side to side.

"What an outrage!" Charlie broke out. "What an absolute outrage!"

Neither of them answered. Charlie dropped into an armchair, picked up his drink, set it down again and said:

"People I haven't seen for two years having the colossal nerve—"

He broke off. Marion had made the sound "Oh!" in one swift, furious breath, turned her body from him with a jerk and left the room.

Lincoln set down Honoria carefully.

"You children go in and start your soup," he said, and when they obeyed, he said to Charlie:

"Marion's not well and she can't stand shocks. That kind of people make her really physically sick."

"I didn't tell them to come here. They wormed your name out of somebody. They deliberately—"

"Well, it's too bad. It doesn't help matters. Excuse me a minute."

Left alone, Charlie sat tense in his chair. In the next room he could hear the children eating, talking in monosyllables, already oblivious to the scene between their elders. He heard a murmur of conversation from a farther room and then the ticking bell of a telephone receiver picked up, and in a panic he moved to the other side of the room and out of earshot.

In a minute Lincoln came back. "Look here, Charlie. I think we'd better call off dinner for tonight. Marion's in bad shape."

"Is she angry with me?"

"Sort of," he said, almost roughly. "She's not strong and—"

"You mean she's changed her mind about Honoria?"

"She's pretty bitter right now. I don't know. You phone me at the bank to-morrow."

"I wish you'd explain to her I never dreamed these people would come here. I'm just as sore as you are."

"I couldn't explain anything to her now."

Charlie got up. He took his coat and hat and started down the corridor. Then he opened the door of the dining room and said in a strange voice, "Good night, children."

Honoria rose and ran around the table to hug him.

"Good night, sweetheart," he said vaguely, and then trying to make his voice more tender, trying to conciliate something, "Good night, dear children."

5

Charlie went directly to the Ritz bar with the furious idea of finding Lorraine and Duncan, but they were not there, and he realized that in any case there was nothing he could do. He had not touched his drink at the Peters', and now he ordered a whisky-and-soda. Paul came over to say hello.

"It's a great change," he said sadly. "We do about half the business we did. So many fellows I hear about back in the States lost everything, maybe not in the first crash, but then in the second. Your friend George Hardt lost every cent, I hear. Are you back in the States?"

"No. I'm in business in Prague."

"I heard that you lost a lot in the crash."

"I did," and he added grimly, "but I lost everything I wanted in the boom."

"Selling short."

"Something like that."

Again the memory of those days swept over him like a nightmare—the people they had met traveling; then people who couldn't add a row of figures or speak a coherent sentence. The little man Helen had consented to dance with at the ship's party, who had insulted her ten feet from the table; the women and girls carried screaming with drink or drugs out of public places—

—The men who locked their wives out in the snow, because the snow of twenty-nine wasn't real snow. If you didn't want it to be snow, you just paid some money.

He went to the phone and called the Peters' apartment; Lincoln answered.

"I called up because this thing is on my mind. Has Marion said anything definite?"

"Marion's sick," Lincoln answered shortly. "I know this thing isn't altogether your fault, but I can't have her go to pieces about it. I'm afraid we'll have to let it slide for six months; I can't take the chance of working her up to this state again."

"I see."

"I'm sorry, Charlie."

He went back to his table. His whisky glass was empty, but he shook his head when Alix looked at it questioningly. There wasn't much he could do now except send Honoria some things; he would send her a lot of things tomorrow. He thought rather angrily that this was just money—he had given so many people money. . . .

"No, no more," he said to another waiter. "What do I owe you?"

He would come back some day; they couldn't make him pay forever. But he wanted his child, and nothing was much good now, beside that fact. He wasn't young any more, with a lot of nice thoughts and dreams to have by himself. He was absolutely sure Helen wouldn't have wanted him to be so alone.

William Faulkner (1897–1962)

William Faulkner was born in Mississippi in 1897. He was never an expatriate as were many of his writing contemporaries, notably Hemingway and Fitzgerald. He spent almost all his life in Oxford, the site of the University of Mississippi. He says, "I discovered that my own little postage stamp of native soil was worth writing about and that I would never live long enough to exhaust it." The fruit of this discovery is a self-contained world of fiction:

"Jefferson, Yoknapatawpha Co., Mississippi
Area, 2400 Square Miles—Population, Whites, 6298; Negroes, 9313
William Faulkner, Sole Owner & Proprietor."

A map of this mythical place appears at the end of *Absalom, Absalom!* (1936). From book to book, story to story, Faulkner fills in the background, rivers, and cross-roads, businesses, and homesteads. He provides a rich legend of Indian begin-nings and early times of white settlement, slavery, and the Civil War, and the struggle for the soul of the modern South. This world is one of the great constructs of the human imagination.

His primary intention as a writer, however, was not to create a fictionalized social history, as did, say, Balzac in his *La Comédie Humaine.* "I have been writing all the time," Faulkner says, "about honor, truth, pity, consideration, the capacity to endure well grief and misfortune and injustice and then endure again." This theme was restated in his eloquent address upon receiving the Nobel Prize for Literature in 1949. Few writers can match him in the largeness of his themes and his passionate commitment to them. Isaac Rosenfeld says that Faulkner "would certainly be a homiletic writer were it not for the fact that he is pointing up no trite morality."

There is no trite morality in "That Evening Sun." Faulkner is writing about irresponsibility, passion, violence, and betrayals of trust. The story is many-layered and the opposing forces are complex and various: blacks and whites, the power-less individual and the community, women and men, and—as is common in Faulkner's work—the old South and the new. Although in the first two paragraphs Quentin portrays the new South (about 1918) as bloated, shadeless, and imper-sonal, the picture he presents of the old South (1902) is of an ignorant Nancy left to her fate by a selfish, neurasthenic Mrs. Compson and a—finally—irresponsible Mr. Compson. The myth of mutual solicitude between masters and servants is shown to be false. By the end of the story, we can have no doubt that she is doomed.

Because Nancy is not a true tragic heroine (she is disloyal, taunting, and terrified), the story might have fallen into bathos—that is, a ludicrous straining after immense feeling. Faulkner avoids this by distancing the reader in two ways. Most of the dialogue hardly touches the central concern. The real story moves along underneath the comings and goings of the children and their constant bick-ering. And the humorous exchanges—the unconsciously funny talk of the children and the witty, if threatening, confrontations of Nancy and Jesus—provide relief from the underlying horror. A story at once funny and horrible is quite an achieve-ment.

Faulkner was the author of many volumes of poems, stories, and novels. The novels considered most significant are *The Sound and the Fury* (1929), *Light in August* (1932), and *Absalom, Absalom!* (1936). He died in 1962 in Oxford, Missis-sippi, estranged, because of his moderate views on civil rights, from the people of the postage stamp he had made immortal.

That Evening Sun

Monday is no different from any other weekday in Jefferson now. The streets are paved now, and the telephone and electric companies are cutting down more and more of the shade trees—the water oaks, the maples and locusts and elms—to make room for iron poles bearing clusters of bloated and ghostly and bloodless grapes, and we have a city laundry which makes the rounds on Monday morning, gathering the bundles of clothes into bright-colored, specially-made motor cars: the soiled wearing of a whole week now flees apparitionlike behind alert and irritable electric horns, with a long diminishing noise of rubber and asphalt like tearing silk, and even the Negro women who still take in white people's washing after the old custom, fetch and deliver it in automobiles.

But fifteen years ago, on Monday morning the quiet, dusty, shady streets would be full of Negro women with, balanced on their steady, turbaned heads, bundles of clothes tied up in sheets, almost as large as cotton bales, carried so without touch of hand between the kitchen door of the white house and the blackened washpot beside a cabin door in Negro Hollow.

Nancy would set her bundle on the top of her head, then upon the bundle in turn she would set the black straw sailor hat which she wore winter and summer. She was tall, with a high, sad face sunken a little where her teeth were missing. Sometimes we would go a part of the way down the lane and across the pasture with her, to watch the balanced bundle and the hat that never bobbed nor wavered, even when she walked down into the ditch and up the other side and stooped through the fence. She would go down on her hands and knees and crawl through the gap, her head rigid, uptilted, the bundle steady as a rock or a balloon, and rise to her feet again and go on.

Sometimes the husbands of the washing women would fetch and deliver the clothes, but Jesus never did that for Nancy, even before father told him to stay away from our house, even when Dilsey was sick and Nancy would come to cook for us.

And then about half the time we'd have to go down the lane to Nancy's cabin and tell her to come on and cook breakfast. We would stop at the ditch, because father told us to not have anything to do with Jesus—he was a short black man, with a razor scar down his face—and we would throw rocks at Nancy's house until she came to the door, leaning her head around it without any clothes on.

"What yawl mean, chunking my house?" Nancy said. "What you little devils mean?"

"Father says for you to come on and get breakfast," Caddy said. "Father says it's over a half an hour now, and you've got to come this minute."

"I aint studying no breakfast," Nancy said. "I going to get my sleep out."

"I bet you're drunk," Jason said. "Father says you're drunk. Are you drunk, Nancy?"

"Who says I is?" Nancy said. "I got to get my sleep out. I aint studying no breakfast."

So after a while we quit chunking the cabin and went back home. When she finally came, it was too late for me to go to school. So we thought it was whisky until that day they arrested her again and they were taking her to jail and they passed Mr Stovall. He was the cashier in the bank and a deacon in the Baptist church, and Nancy began to say:

"When you going to pay me, white man? When you going to pay me, white man? It's been three times now since you paid me a cent—" Mr Stovall knocked her down, but she kept on saying, "When you going to pay me, white man? It's been three times now since—" until Mr Stovall kicked her in the mouth with his heel and the marshal caught Mr Stovall back, and Nancy lying in the street, laughing. She turned her head and spat out some blood and teeth and said, "It's been three times now since he paid me a cent."

That was how she lost her teeth, and all that day they told about Nancy and Mr Stovall, and all that night the ones that passed the jail could hear Nancy singing and yelling. They could see her hands holding to the window bars, and a lot of them stopped along the fence, listening to her and to the jailer trying to make her stop. She didn't shut up until almost daylight, when the jailer began to hear a bumping and scraping upstairs and he went up there and found Nancy hanging from the window bar. He said that it was cocaine and not whisky, because no nigger would try to commit suicide unless he was full of cocaine, because a nigger full of cocaine wasn't a nigger any longer.

The jailer cut her down and revived her; then he beat her, whipped her. She had hung herself with her dress. She had fixed it all right, but when they arrested her she didn't have on anything except a dress and so she didn't have anything to tie her hands with and she couldn't make her hands let go of the window ledge. So the jailer heard the noise and ran up there and found Nancy hanging from the window, stark naked, her belly already swelling out a little, like a little balloon.

When Dilsey was sick in her cabin and Nancy was cooking for us, we could see her apron swelling out; that was before father told Jesus to stay away from the house. Jesus was in the kitchen, sitting behind the stove, with his razor scar on his black face like a piece of dirty string. He said it was a watermelon that Nancy had under her dress.

"It never come off of your vine, though," Nancy said.

"Off of what vine?" Caddy said.

"I can cut down the vine it did come off of," Jesus said.

"What makes you want to talk like that before these chillen?" Nancy said. "Whyn't you go on to work? You done et. You want Mr Jason to catch you hanging around his kitchen, talking that way before these chillen?"

"Talking what way?" Caddy said. "What vine?"

"I cant hang around white man's kitchen," Jesus said. "But white man can hang around mine. White man can come in my house, but I cant stop him. When white man want to come in my house, I aint got no house. I cant stop him, but he cant kick me outen it. He cant do that."

Dilsey was still sick in her cabin. Father told Jesus to stay off our place. Dilsey was still sick. It was a long time. We were in the library after supper.

"Isn't Nancy through in the kitchen yet?" mother said. "It seems to me that she has had plenty of time to have finished the dishes."

"Let Quentin go and see," father said. "Go and see if Nancy is through, Quentin. Tell her she can go on home."

I went to the kitchen. Nancy was through. The dishes were put away and the fire was out. Nancy was sitting in a chair, close to the cold stove. She looked at me.

"Mother wants to know if you are through," I said.

"Yes," Nancy said. She looked at me. "I done finished." She looked at me.

"What is it?" I said. "What is it?"

"I aint nothing but a nigger," Nancy said. "It aint none of my fault."

She looked at me, sitting in the chair before the cold stove, the sailor hat on her head. I went back to the library. It was the cold stove and all, when you think of a kitchen being warm and busy and cheerful. And with a cold stove and the dishes all put away, and nobody wanting to eat at that hour.

"Is she through?" mother said.

"Yessum," I said.

"What is she doing?" mother said.

"She's not doing anything. She's through."

"I'll go and see," father said.

"Maybe she's waiting for Jesus to come and take her home," Caddy said.

"Jesus is gone," I said. Nancy told us how one morning she woke up and Jesus was gone.

"He quit me," Nancy said. "Done gone to Memphis, I reckon. Dodging them city *po*-lice for a while, I reckon."

"And a good riddance," father said. "I hope he stays there."

"Nancy's scaired of the dark," Jason said.

"So are you," Caddy said.

"I'm not," Jason said.

"Scairy cat," Caddy said.

"I'm not," Jason said.

"You, Candace!" mother said. Father came back.

"I am going to walk down the lane with Nancy," he said. "She says that Jesus is back."

"Has she seen him?" mother said.

"No. Some Negro sent her word that he was back in town. I wont be long."

"You'll leave me alone, to take Nancy home?" mother said. "Is her safety more precious to you than mine?"

"I wont be long," father said.

"You'll leave these children unprotected, with that Negro about?"

"I'm going too," Caddy said. "Let me go, father."

"What would he do with them, if he were unfortunate enough to have them?" father said.

"I want to go, too," Jason said.

"Jason!" mother said. She was speaking to father. You could tell that by the way she said the name. Like she believed that all day father had been trying to think of doing the thing she wouldn't like the most, and that she knew all the time that after a while he would think of it. I stayed quiet, because father and I both knew that mother would want him to make me stay with her if she just thought of it in time. So father didn't look at me. I was the oldest. I was nine and Caddy was seven and Jason was five.

"Nonsense," father said. "We wont be long."

Nancy had her hat on. We came to the lane. "Jesus always been good to me," Nancy said. "Whenever he had two dollars, one of them was mine." We walked in the lane. "If I can just get through the lane," Nancy said, "I be all right then."

The lane was always dark. "This is where Jason got scared on Hallowe'en," Caddy said.

"I didn't," Jason said.

"Cant Aunt Rachel do anything with him?" father said. Aunt Rachel was old. she lived in a cabin beyond Nancy's, by herself. She had white hair and she smoked a pipe in the door, all day long; she didn't work any more. They said she was Jesus' mother. Sometimes she said she was and sometimes she said she wasn't any kin to Jesus.

"Yes, you did," Caddy said. "You were scairder then Frony. You were scairder than T. P. even. Scairder than niggers."

"Cant nobody do nothing with him," Nancy said. "He say I done woke up the devil in him and aint but one thing going to lay it down again."

"Well, he's gone now," father said. "There's nothing for you to be afraid of now. And if you'd just let white men alone."

"Let what white men alone?" Caddy said. "How let them alone?"

"He aint gone nowhere," Nancy said. "I can feel him. I can feel him now, in this lane. He hearing us talk, every word, hid somewhere, waiting. I aint seen him, and I aint going to see him again but once more, with that razor in his mouth. That razor on that string down his back, inside his shirt. And then I aint going to be even surprised."

"I wasn't scaired," Jason said.

"If you'd behave yourself, you'd have kept out of this," father said. "But it's all right now. He's probably in St. Louis now. Probably got another wife by now and forgot all about you."

"If he has, I better not find out about it," Nancy said. "I'd stand there right over them, and every time he wropped her, I'd cut that arm off. I'd cut his head off and I'd slit her belly and I'd shove—"

"Hush," father said.

"Slit whose belly, Nancy?" Caddy said.

"I wasn't scaired," Jason said. "I'd walk right down this lane by myself."

"Yah," Caddy said. "You wouldn't dare to put your foot down in it if we were not here too."

2

Dilsey was still sick, so we took Nancy home every night until mother said, "How much longer is this going on? I to be left alone in this big house while you take home a frightened Negro?"

We fixed a pallet in the kitchen for Nancy. One night we waked up, hearing the sound. It was not singing and it was not crying, coming up the dark stairs. There was a light in mother's room and we heard father going down the hall, down the back stairs, and Caddy and I went into the hall. The floor was cold. Our toes curled away from it while we listened to the sound. It was like singing and it wasn't like singing, like the sounds that Negroes make.

Then it stopped and we heard father going down the back stairs, and we went to the head of the stairs. Then the sound began again, in the stairway, not loud, and we could see Nancy's eyes halfway up the stairs, against the wall. They looked like cat's eyes do, like a big cat against the wall, watching us. When we came down the steps to where she was, she quit making the sound again, and we stood there until father came back up from the kitchen, with his pistol in his hand. He went back down with Nancy and they came back with Nancy's pallet.

We spread the pallet in our room. After the light in mother's room went off, we could see Nancy's eyes again. "Nancy," Caddy whispered, "are you asleep, Nancy?"

Nancy whispered something. It was oh or no, I dont know which. Like nobody had made it, like it came from nowhere and went nowhere, until it was like Nancy was not there at all; that I had looked so hard at her eyes on the stairs that they had got printed on my eyeballs, like the sun does when you have closed your eyes and there is no sun. "Jesus," Nancy whispered. "Jesus."

"Was it Jesus?" Caddy said. "Did he try to come into the kitchen?"

"Jesus," Nancy said. Like this: Jeeeeeeeeeeeeeeeesus, until the sound went out, like a match or a candle does.

"It's the other Jesus she means," I said.

"Can you see us, Nancy?" Caddy whispered. "Can you see our eyes too?"

"I aint nothing but a nigger," Nancy said. "God knows. God knows."

"What did you see down there in the kitchen?" Caddy whispered. "What tried to get in?"

"God knows," Nancy said. We could see her eyes. "God knows."

Dilsey got well. She cooked dinner. "You'd better stay in bed a day or two longer," father said.

"What for?" Dilsey said. "If I had been a day later, this place would be to rack and ruin. Get on out of here now, and let me get my kitchen straight again."

Dilsey cooked supper too. And that night, just before dark, Nancy came into the kitchen.

"How do you know he's back?" Dilsey said. "You aint seen him."

"Jesus is a nigger," Jason said.

"I can feel him," Nancy said. "I can feel him laying yonder in the ditch."

"Tonight?" Dilsey said. "Is he there tonight?"

"Dilsey's a nigger too," Jason said.

"You try to eat something," Dilsey said.

"I dont want nothing," Nancy said.

"I aint a nigger," Jason said.

"Drink some coffee," Dilsey said. She poured a cup of coffee for Nancy. "Do you know he's out there tonight? How come you know it's tonight?"

"I know," Nancy said. "He's there, waiting. I know. I done lived with him too long. I know what he is fixing to do fore he know it himself."

"Drink some coffee," Dilsey said. Nancy held the cup to her mouth and blew into the cup. Her mouth pursed out like a spreading adder's, like a rubber mouth, like she had blown all the color out of her lips with blowing the coffee.

"I aint a nigger," Jason said. "Are you a nigger, Nancy?"

"I hellborn, child," Nancy said. "I wont be nothing soon. I going back where I come from soon."

3

She began to drink the coffee. While she was drinking, holding the cup in both hands, she began to make the sound again. She made the sound into the cup and the coffee sploshed out onto her hands and her dress. Her eyes looked at us and she sat there, her elbows on her knees, holding the cup in both hands, looking at us across the wet cup, making the sound. "Look at Nancy," Jason said. "Nancy cant cook for us now. Dilsey's got well now."

"You hush up," Dilsey said. Nancy held the cup in both hands, looking at us, making the sound, like there were two of them: one looking at us and the other making the sound. "Whyn't you let Mr Jason telefoam the marshal?" Dilsey said. Nancy stopped then, holding the cup in her long brown hands. She tried to drink some coffee again, but it sploshed out of the cup, onto her hands and her dress, and she put the cup down. Jason watched her.

"I cant swallow it," Nancy said. "I swallows but it wont go down me."

"You go down to the cabin," Dilsey said. "Frony will fix you a pallet and I'll be there soon."

"Wont no nigger stop him," Nancy said.

"I aint a nigger," Jason said. "Am I, Dilsey?"

"I reckon not," Dilsey said. She looked at Nancy. "I dont reckon so. What you going to do, then?"

Nancy looked at us. Her eyes went fast, like she was afraid there wasn't time to look, without hardly moving at all. She looked at us, at all three of us at one time. "You member that night I stayed in yawls' room?" she said. She told about how we waked up early the next morning, and played. We had to play quiet, on her pallet, until father woke up and it was time to get breakfast. "Go and ask your maw to let me stay here tonight," Nancy said. "I wont need no pallet. We can play some more."

Caddy asked mother. Jason went too. "I cant have Negroes sleeping in the bedrooms," mother said. Jason cried. He cried until mother said he couldn't have any dessert for three days if he didn't stop. Then Jason said he would stop if Dilsey would make a chocolate cake. Father was there.

"Why dont you do something about it?" mother said. "What do we have officers for?"

"Why is Nancy afraid of Jesus?" Caddy said. "Are you afraid of father, mother?"

"What could the officers do?" father said. "If Nancy hasn't seen him, how could the officers find him?"

"Then why is she afraid?" mother said.

"She says he is there. She says she knows he is there tonight."

"Yet we pay taxes," mother said. "I must wait here alone in this big house while you take a Negro woman home."

"You know that I am not lying outside with a razor," father said.

"I'll stop if Dilsey will make a chocolate cake," Jason said. Mother told us to go out and father said he didn't know if Jason would get a chocolate cake or not, but he knew what Jason was going to get in about a minute. We went back to the kitchen and told Nancy.

"Father said for you to go home and lock the door, and you'll be all right," Caddy said. "All right from what, Nancy? Is Jesus mad at you?" Nancy was holding the coffee cup in her hands again, her elbows on her knees and her hands holding the cup between her knees. She was looking into the cup. "What have you done that made Jesus mad?" Caddy said. Nancy let the cup go. It didn't break on the floor, but the coffee spilled out, and Nancy sat there with her hands still making the shape of the cup. She began to make the sound again, not loud. Not singing and not unsinging. We watched her.

"Here," Dilsey said. "You quit that, now. You get aholt of yourself. You wait here. I going to get Versh to walk home with you." Dilsey went out.

We looked at Nancy. Her shoulders kept shaking, but she quit making the sound. We watched her, "What's Jesus going to do to you?" Caddy said. "He went away."

Nancy looked at us. "We had fun that night I stayed in yawls' room, didn't we?"

"I didn't," Jason said. "I didn't have any fun."

"You were asleep in mother's room," Caddy said. "You were not there."

"Let's go down to my house and have some more fun," Nancy said.

"Mother wont let us," I said. "It's too late now."

"Dont bother her," Nancy said. "We can tell her in the morning. She wont mind."

"She wouldn't let us," I said.

"Dont ask her now," Nancy said. "Dont bother her now."

"She didn't say we couldn't go," Caddy said.

"We didn't ask," I said.

"If you go, I'll tell," Jason said.

"We'll have fun," Nancy said. "They wont mind, just to my house. I been working for yawl a long time. They won't mind."

"I'm not afraid to go," Caddy said. "Jason is the one that's afraid. He'll tell."

"I'm not," Jason said.

"Yes, you are," Caddy said. "You'll tell."

"I won't tell," Jason said. "I'm not afraid."

"Jason aint afraid to go with me," Nancy said. "Is you, Jason?"

"Jason is going to tell," Caddy said. The lane was dark. We passed the pasture gate. "I bet if something was to jump out from behind that gate, Jason would holler."

"I wouldn't," Jason said. We walked down the lane. Nancy was talking loud.

"What are you talking so loud for, Nancy?" Caddy said.

"Who; me?" Nancy said. "Listen at Quentin and Caddy and Jason saying I'm talking loud."

"You talk like there was five of us here," Caddy said. "You talk like father was here too."

"Who; me talking loud, Mr Jason?" Nancy said.

"Nancy called Jason 'Mister,' " Caddy said.

"Listen how Caddy and Quentin and Jason talk," Nancy said.

"We're not talking loud," Caddy said. "You're the one that's talking like father—"

"Hush," Nancy said; "hush, Mr Jason."

"Nancy called Jason 'Mister' aguh—"

"Hush," Nancy said. She was talking loud when we crossed the ditch and stooped through the fence where she used to stoop through with the clothes on her head. Then we came to her house. We were going fast then. She opened the door. The smell of the house was like the lamp and the smell of Nancy was like the wick, like they were waiting for one another to begin to smell. She lit the lamp and closed the door and put the bar up. Then she quit talking loud, looking at us.

"What're we going to do?" Caddy said.

"What do yawl want to do?" Nancy said.

"You said we would have some fun," Caddy said.

There was something about Nancy's house; something you could smell besides Nancy and the house. Jason smelled it, even. "I dont want to stay here," he said. "I want to go home."

"Go home, then," Caddy said.

"I dont want to go by myself," Jason said.

"We're going to have some fun," Nancy said.

"How?" Caddy said.

Nancy stood by the door. She was looking at us, only it was like she had emptied her eyes, like she had quit using them. "What do you want to do?" she said.

"Tell us a story," Caddy said. "Can you tell a story?"

"Yes," Nancy said.

"Tell it," Caddy said. We looked at Nancy. "You dont know any stories."

"Yes," Nancy said. "Yes, I do."

She came and sat in a chair before the hearth. There was a little fire there. Nancy built it up, when it was already hot inside. She built a good blaze. She told a story. She talked like her eyes looked, like her eyes watching us and her voice talking to us did not belong to her. Like she was living somewhere else, waiting somewhere else. She was outside the cabin. Her voice was inside and the shape of her, the Nancy that could stoop under a barbed wire fence with a bundle of clothes balanced on her head as though without weight, like a balloon, was there. But that was all. "And so this here queen come walking up to the ditch, where that bad man was hiding. She was walking up to the ditch, and she say, 'If I can just get past this here ditch,' was what she say . . ."

"What ditch?" Caddy said. "A ditch like that one out there? Why did a queen want to go into a ditch?"

"To get to her house," Nancy said. She looked at us. "She had to cross the ditch to get into her house quick and bar the door."

"Why did she want to go home and bar the door?" Caddy said.

4

Nancy looked at us. She quit talking. She looked at us. Jason's legs stuck straight out of his pants where he sat on Nancy's lap. "I dont think that's a good story," he said. "I want to go home."

"Maybe we had better," Caddy said. She got up from the floor. "I bet they are looking for us right now." She went toward the door.

"No," Nancy said. "Dont open it." She got up quick and passed Caddy. She didn't touch the door, the wooden bar.

"Why not?" Caddy said.

"Come back to the lamp," Nancy said. "We'll have fun. You dont have to go."

"We ought to go," Caddy said. "Unless we have a lot of fun." She and Nancy came back to the fire, the lamp.

"I want to go home," Jason said. "I'm going to tell."

"I know another story," Nancy said. She stood close to the lamp. She looked at Caddy, like when your eyes look up at a stick balanced on your nose. She had to look down to see Caddy, but her eyes looked like that, like when you are balancing a stick.

"I wont listen to it," Jason said. "I'll bang on the floor."

"It's a good one," Nancy said. "It's better than the other one."

"What's it about?" Caddy said. Nancy was standing by the lamp. Her hand was on the lamp, against the light, long and brown.

"Your hand is on that hot globe," Caddy said. "Don't it feel hot to your hand?"

Nancy looked at her hand on the lamp chimney. She took her hand away, slow. She stood there, looking at Caddy, wringing her long hand as though it were tied to her wrist with a string.

"Let's do something else," Caddy said.

"I want to go home," Jason said.

"I got some popcorn," Nancy said. She looked at Caddy and then at Jason and then at me and then at Caddy again. "I got some popcorn."

"I don't like popcorn," Jason said. "I'd rather have candy."

Nancy looked at Jason. "You can hold the popper." She was still wringing her hand; it was long and limp and brown.

"All right," Jason said. "I'll stay a while if I can do that. Caddy cant hold it. I'll want to go home again if Caddy holds the popper."

Nancy built up the fire. "Look at Nancy putting her hands in the fire," Caddy said. "What's the matter with you, Nancy?"

"I got popcorn," Nancy said. "I got some." She took the popper from under the bed. It was broken. Jason began to cry.

"Now we cant have any popcorn," he said.

"We ought to go home, anyway," Caddy said. "Come on, Quentin."

"Wait," Nancy said; "wait. I can fix it. Dont you want to help me fix it?"

"I dont think I want any," Caddy said. "It's too late now."

"You help me, Jason," Nancy said. "Dont you want to help me?"

"No," Jason said. "I want to go home."

"Hush," Nancy said; "hush. Watch. Watch me. I can fix it so Jason can hold it and pop the corn." She got a piece of wire and fixed the popper.

"It wont hold good," Caddy said.

"Yes, it will," Nancy said. "Yawl watch. Yawl help me shell some corn."

The popcorn was under the bed too. We shelled it into the popper and Nancy helped Jason hold the popper over the fire.

"It's not popping," Jason said. "I want to go home."

"You wait," Nancy said. "It'll begin to pop. We'll have fun then." She was sitting close to the fire. The lamp was turned up so high it was beginning to smoke.

"Why dont you turn it down some?" I said.

"It's all right," Nancy said. "I'll clean it. Yawl wait. The popcorn will start in a minute."

"I dont believe it's going to start," Caddy said. "We ought to start home, anyway. They'll be worried."

"No," Nancy said. "It's going to pop. Dilsey will tell um yawl with me. I been working for yawl long time. They won't mind if yawl at my house. You wait, now. It'll start popping any minute now."

Then Jason got some smoke in his eyes and he began to cry. He dropped the popper into the fire. Nancy got a wet rag and wiped Jason's face, but he didn't stop crying.

"Hush," she said. "Hush." But he didn't hush. Caddy took the popper out of the fire.

"It's burned up," she said. "You'll have to get some more popcorn, Nancy."

"Did you put all of it in?" Nancy said.

"Yes," Caddy said. Nancy looked at Caddy. Then she took the popper and opened it and poured the cinders into her apron and began to sort the grains, her hands long and brown, and we watching her.

"Haven't you got any more?" Caddy said.

"Yes," Nancy said; "yes. Look. This here aint burnt. All we need to do is—"

"I want to go home, " Jason said. "I'm going to tell."

"Hush," Caddy said. We all listened. Nancy's head was already turned toward the barred door, her eyes filled with red lamplight. "Somebody is coming," Caddy said.

Then Nancy began to make that sound again, not loud, sitting there above the fire, her long hands dangling between her knees; all of a sudden water began to come out on her face in big drops, running down her face, carrying in each one a little turning ball of firelight like a spark until it dropped off her chin. "She's not crying," I said.

"I aint crying," Nancy said. Her eyes were closed. "I aint crying. Who is it?"

"I dont know," Caddy said. She went to the door and looked out. "We've got to go now," she said. "Here comes father."

"I'm going to tell," Jason said. "Yawl made me come."

The water still ran down Nancy's face. She turned in her chair. "Listen. Tell him. Tell him we going to have fun. Tell him I take good care of yawl until in the morning. Tell him to let me come home with yawl and sleep on the floor. Tell him I wont need no pallet. We'll have fun. You member last time how we had so much fun?"

"I didn't have fun," Jason said. "You hurt me. You put smoke in my eyes. I'm going to tell."

5

Father came in. He looked at us. Nancy did not get up.

"Tell him," she said.

"Caddy made us come down here," Jason said. "I didn't want to."

Father came to the fire. Nancy looked up at him. "Cant you go to Aunt Rachel's and stay?" he said. Nancy looked up at father, her hands between her knees. "He's not here," father said. "I would have seen him. There's not a soul in sight."

"He in the ditch," Nancy said. "He waiting in the ditch yonder."

"Nonsense," father said. He looked at Nancy. "Do you know he's there?"

"I got the sign," Nancy said.

"What sign?"

"I got it. It was on the table when I come in. It was a hogbone, with blood meat still on it, laying by the lamp. He out there. When yawl walk out that door, I gone."

"Gone where, Nancy?" Caddy said.

"I'm not a tattletale," Jason said.

"Nonsense," father said.

"He out there," Nancy said. "He looking through that window this minute, waiting for yawl to go. Then I gone."

"Nonsense," father said. "Lock up your house and we'll take you on to Aunt Rachel's."

" 'Twont do no good," Nancy said. She didn't look at father now, but he looked down at her, at her long, limp, moving hands. "Putting it off wont do no good."

"Then what do you want to do?" father said.

"I dont know," Nancy said. "I cant do nothing. Just put it off. And that don't do no good. I reckon it belong to me. I reckon what I going to get aint no more than mine."

"Get what?" Caddy said. "What's yours?"

"Nothing," father said. "You all must get to bed."

"Caddy made me come," Jason said.

"Go on to Aunt Rachel's," father said.

"It wont do no good," Nancy said. She sat before the fire, her elbows on her knees, her long hands between her knees. "When even your own kitchen wouldn't do no good. When even if I was sleeping on the floor in the room with your chillen, and the next morning there I am, and blood—"

"Hush," father said. "Lock the door and put out the lamp and go to bed."

"I scared of the dark," Nancy said. "I scared for it to happen in the dark."

"You mean you're going to sit right here with the lamp lighted?" father said. Then Nancy began to make the sound again, sitting before the fire, her long hands between her knees. "Ah, damnation," father said. "Come along, chillen. It's past bedtime."

"When yawl go home, I gone," Nancy said. She talked quieter now, and her face looked quiet, like her hands. "Anyway, I got my coffin money saved up with Mr. Lovelady." Mr. Lovelady was a short, dirty man who collected the Negro insurance, coming around to the cabins or the kitchens every Saturday morning, to collect fifteen cents. He and his wife lived at the hotel. One morning his wife committed suicide. They had a child, a little girl. He and the child went away. After a week or two he came back alone. We would see him going along the lanes and the back streets on Saturday mornings.

"Nonsense," father said. "You'll be the first thing I'll see in the kitchen tomorrow morning."

"You'll see what you'll see, I reckon," Nancy said. "But it will take the Lord to say what that will be."

6

We left her sitting before the fire.

"Come and put the bar up," father said. But she didn't move. She didn't look at us again, sitting quietly there between the lamp and the fire. From some distance down the lane we could look back and see her through the open door.

"What, father?" Caddy said. "What's going to happen?"

"Nothing," father said. Jason was on father's back, so Jason was the tallest of all of us. We went down into the ditch. I looked at it, quiet. I couldn't see much where the moonlight and the shadows tangled.

"If Jesus is hid here, he can see us, cant he?" Caddy said.

"He's not there," father said. "He went away a long time ago."

"You made me come," Jason said, high; against the sky it looked like father had two heads, a little one and a big one. "I didn't want to."

We went up out of the ditch. We could still see Nancy's house and the open door, but we couldn't see Nancy now, sitting before the fire with the door open, because she was tired. "I just done got tired," she said. "I just a nigger. It aint no fault of mine."

But we could hear her, because she began just after we came up out of the ditch, the sound that was not singing and not unsinging. "Who will do our washing now father?" I said.

"I'm not a nigger," Jason said, high and close above father's head.

"You're worse," Caddy said, "you are a tattletale. If something was to jump out, you'd be scairder than a nigger."

"I wouldn't," Jason said.

"You'd cry," Caddy said.

"Caddy," father said.

"I wouldn't!" Jason said.

"Scairy cat," Caddy said.

"Candace!" father said.

Ernest Hemingway (1899–1961)

The stories of Ernest Hemingway are at once an expression of disillusionment bordering on nihilism and a celebration of the ethic of courage or, as he put it, "grace under pressure." His style is closely parallel to his theme: terse, spare, somber, stripped of the verbiage and stylistic "elegance" he disliked in much turn-of-the-century writing. His prose is marked by an understatement that may seem to suggest lack of adequate feeling, yet its very terseness arouses a great emotional response from many readers. Both in his technical development and in his tone and themes, he has exercised an immense influence on American fiction.

Although he was himself a man of action and celebrated protagonists who had experienced physically dangerous situations—war, the hunt, violent sports— his stories are not particularly action-packed or heavily plotted. As in the story which follows, dialogue is often the whole of the action, and he has been justly admired for its power and realism. A Hemingway story can beautifully demonstrate that what people in fiction say to each other is what they do to each other. (See Introduction, p. 13.) "Hills Like White Elephants" takes place almost entirely within quotation marks. Practically all we know of the characters we learn through what they say. The man through speech slowly manipulates the girl toward the operation. "I wouldn't have you do it if you didn't want to," he says. "But I know it's perfectly simple." His frequent repetition of the word "perfectly" defines his insincerity. And, after the girl acquiesces, he begins to manipulate himself out of responsibility until the girl says she'll scream; because she says that, we learn that she is not completely swayed by him.

In the spaces outside quotation marks, Hemingway builds not so much with verbs as with nouns, and he almost totally eschews adjectives and qualifiers.

Though his descriptive passages are short and infrequent, they count heavily in two ways. First, the setting can create the atmosphere, the mood, of the story, and can serve as a kind of Greek chorus. In the following story, the controlling symbols come from the scene and the scenery: the hills, the river, the little crossroads station leading anywhere, nowhere, the barren fields that connote the barrenness of the lives. Description also provides a sense of movement, as Hemingway directs the eye of the reader's imagination from object to object, "panning" as a movie does. The opening paragraph illustrates this technique. The reader has the feeling that the story is moving.

Hemingway was born in Oak Park, Illinois, in 1899. He became an ambulance driver in the First World War and was wounded while serving on the Italian Front. This experience formed the basis for many of his stories and for his most popular novel, *A Farewell To Arms* (1929). After the war, dissatisifed with life in America, he went to Paris as correspondent for the Toronto *Star.* He lived most of his life in Europe and Cuba.

Hemingway's work was greatly influenced by Stephen Crane and Joseph Conrad in theme—the test, the ordeal—and by Sherwood Anderson and Gertrude Stein in the use of simple, colloquial language. According to Frank O'Connor, he learned from Joyce the power of repeating key words in order to build a reader's mood.

Besides his short stores, which have been acclaimed as among the very best in the world, his novels *The Sun Also Rises* (1926) and *The Old Man and the Sea* (1952) brought him the highest critical praise. When he won the Nobel Prize for Literature in 1954, he was cited for his "powerful, style-making mastery of the art of modern narration." He died of a self-inflicted gunshot wound in 1961.

Hills Like White Elephants

The hills across the valley of the Ebro were long and white. On this side there was no shade and no trees and the station was between two lines of rails in the sun. Close against the side of the station there was the warm shadow of the building and a curtain, made of strings of bamboo beads, hung across the open door into the bar, to keep out flies. The American and the girl with him sat at a table in the shade, outside the building. It was very hot and the express from Barcelona would come in forty minutes. It stopped at this junction for two minutes and went on to Madrid.

"What should we drink?" the girl asked. She had taken off her hat and put it on the table.

"It's pretty hot," the man said.

"Let's drink beer."

"Dos cervezas," the man said into the curtain.

"Big ones?" a woman asked from the doorway.

"Yes. Two big ones."

The woman brought two glasses of beer and two felt pads. She put the felt pads and the beer glasses on the table and looked at the man and the girl. The girl was looking off at the line of hills. They were white in the sun and the country was brown and dry.

"They look like white elephants," she said.

"I've never seen one," the man drank his beer.

"No, you wouldn't have."

"I might have," the man said. "Just because you say I wouldn't have doesn't prove anything."

The girl looked at the bead curtain. "They've painted something on it," she said. "What does it say?"

"Anis del Toro. It's a drink."

"Could we try it?"

The man called "Listen" through the curtain. The woman came out from the bar.

"Four reales."

"We want two Anis del Toro."

"With water?"

"Do you want it with water?"

"I don't know," the girl said, "Is it good with water?"

"It's all right."

"You want them with water?" asked the woman.

"Yes, with water."

"It tastes like licorice," the girl said and put the glass down.

"That's the way with everything."

"Yes," said the girl. "Everything tastes of licorice. Especially all the things you've waited so long for, like absinthe."

"Oh, cut it out."

"You started it," the girl said. "I was being amused. I was having a fine time."

"Well, let's try to have a fine time."

"All right. I was trying. I said the mountains looked like white elephants. Wasn't that bright?"

"That was bright."

"I wanted to try this new drink. That's all we do, isn't it—look at things and try new drinks?"

"I guess so."

The girl looked across at the hills.

"They're lovely hills," she said. "They don't really look like white elephants. I just meant the coloring of their skin through the trees."

"Should we have another drink?"

"All right."

The warm wind blew the bead curtain against the table.

"The beer's nice and cool," the man said.

"It's lovely," the girl said.

"It's really an awfully simple operation, Jig," the man said. "It's not really an operation at all."

The girl looked at the ground the table legs rested on.

"I know you wouldn't mind it, Jig. It's really not anything. It's just to let the air in."

The girl did not say anything.

"I'll go with you and I'll stay with you all the time. They just let the air in and then it's all perfectly natural."

"Then what will we do afterward?"

"We'll be fine afterward. Just like we were before."

"What makes you think so?"

"That's the only thing that bothers us. It's the only thing that's made us unhappy."

The girl looked at the bead curtain, put her hand out and took hold of two of the strings of beads.

"And you think then we'll be all right and be happy."

"I know we will. You don't have to be afraid. I've known lots of people that have done it."

"So have I," said the girl. "And afterward they were all so happy."

"Well," the man said, "if you don't want to you don't have to. I wouldn't have you do it if you didn't want to. But I know it's perfectly simple."

"And you really want to?"

"I think it's the best thing to do. But I don't want you to do it if you don't really want to."

"And if I do it you'll be happy and things will be like they were and you'll love me?"

"I love you now. You know I love you."

"I know. But if I do it, then it will be nice again if I say things are like white elephants, and you'll like it?"

"I'll love it. I love it now but I just can't think about it. You know how I get when I worry."

"If I do it you won't ever worry?"

"I won't worry about that because it's perfectly simple."

"Then I'll do it. Because I don't care about me."

"What do you mean?"

"I don't care about me."

"Well, I care about you."

"Oh, yes. But I don't care about me. And I'll do it and then everything will be fine."

"I don't want you to do it if you feel that way."

The girl stood up and walked to the end of the station. Across, on the other side, were fields of grain and trees along the banks of the Ebro. Far away, beyond the river, were mountains. The shadow of a cloud moved across the field of grain and she saw the river through the trees.

"And we could have all this," she said. "And we could have everything and every day we make it more impossible."

"What did you say?"

"I said we could have everything."

"We can have everything."

"No, we can't."

"We can have the whole world."

"No, we can't."

"We can go everywhere."

"No, we can't. It isn't ours any more."

"It's ours."

"No, it isn't. And once they take it away, you never get it back."

"But they haven't taken it away."

"We'll wait and see."

"Come on back in the shade," he said. "You mustn't feel that way."

"I don't feel any way," the girl said. "I just know things."

"I don't want you to do anything that you don't want to do——"

"Nor that isn't good for me," she said. "I know. Could we have another beer?"

"All right. But you've got to realize——"

"I realize," the girl said. "Can't we maybe stop talking?"

They sat down at the table and the girl looked across at the hills on the dry side of the valley and the man looked at her and at the table.

"You've got to realize," he said, "that I don't want you to do it if you don't want to. I'm perfectly willing to go through with it if it means anything to you."

"Doesn't it mean anything to you? We could get along."

"Of course it does. But I don't want anybody but you. I don't want any one else. And I know it's perfectly simple."

"Yes, you know it's perfectly simple."

"It's all right for you to say that, but I do know it."

"Would you do something for me now?"

"I'd do anything for you."

"Would you please please please please please please please stop talking?"

He did not say anything but looked at the bags against the wall of the station. There were labels on them from all the hotels where they had spent nights.

"But I don't want you to," he said. "I don't care anything about it."

"I'll scream," said the girl.

The woman came out through the curtains with two glasses of beer and put them down on the damp felt pads. "The train comes in five minutes," she said.

"What did she say?" asked the girl.

"That the train is coming in five minutes."

The girl smiled brightly at the woman, to thank her.

"I'd better take the bags over to the other side of the station," the man said. She smiled at him.

"All right. Then come back and we'll finish the beer."

He picked up the two heavy bags and carried them around the station to the other tracks. He looked up the tracks but could not see the train. Coming back, he walked through the barroom, where people waiting for the train were drinking. He drank an Anis at the bar and looked at the people. They were all waiting reasonably for the train. He went out through the bead curtain. She was sitting at the table and smiled at him.

"Do you feel better?" he asked.

"I feel fine," she said. "There's nothing wrong with me. I feel fine."

Richard Wright (1908–1960)

Richard Wright was perhaps the most significant and influential black writer of the 1930s and 1940s. By opening up black ghetto experience to serious fictional treatment, he helped arouse a somnolent American conscience. Of Wright's great early novel, Irving Howe wrote, "The day *Native Son* appeared, American culture was changed forever. No matter how much qualifying the book might need, it made impossible a repetition of the old lies. In all its crudeness, melodrama and claustrophobia of vision, Richard Wright's novel brought out into the open, as no one ever had before, the hatred, fear and violence that have crippled and may yet destroy our culture."

Born in Mississippi in 1908, Wright was the grandson of a slave, the son of a sharecropper who deserted his family. Despite the fact that his mother had been a teacher, his schooling was intermittent at best, caught on the run between family disasters. Yet he was a voracious reader, and when he went to Chicago in 1928 he could hold his own with the intellectual radicals who became his friends. He joined the Communist Party, and his writing—largely polemical at this point—began to appear regularly in Communist publications. But he began to chafe under the party discipline and to question the purity of its motives, and in 1944 he resigned his membership.

Wright's most important work, *Native Son* (1940), was an instant success. It is the story of Bigger Thomas, product of the Chicago ghetto, a murderer, surely one of the first anti-heroes in American fiction. Many readers were deeply affected by the unusual glimpse it provided of the underside of black society. Wright's black predecessors had often so idealized black culture and relationships that an ignorant reader might wonder if segregation was really evil. Wright changed that, exposed honestly the effects of repression and poverty. The technique of naturalism which he used in his work was common to proletarian writers and social realists in the 1930s, but he achieved particularly deep and lasting effects. He did not view his subjects from a distance or through a microscope. Bigger—and Dave in "The Man Who Was Almost a Man"—are not examples or symbols or representatives of a remote social order. Their experience was his experience, for he had lived in the same circumstances. Thus he combined the authenticity of honest observation with the deeper authenticity of personal experience. His work, didactic though it may be, is passionately felt.

Wright's novels and stories are valuable not only as a portrayal of the black society he knew so well, but as the forerunner of a new motif in American fiction. No wonder that when he moved permanently to France in 1947 he found kinship with French existentialists: Bigger and Dave are in a real sense existential anti-heroes. They seek to realize themselves by escaping to freedom from a harsh, oppressive environment. For Bigger, the escape ends inexorably in his execution, for he has become the outlaw, guilty of a useless murder. After reading "The Man Who Was Almost a Man," we can have little more hope for Dave, whose passion for the gun, representing his chance to escape from being just a "boy"—that is, young, black, inferior—has already started him toward violence.

Wright died in Paris in 1960. Black writers he had befriended and inspired—Ellison, Himes, Baldwin—have built on his accomplishment, and black experience is now an integral part of the mainstream of American fiction.

The Man Who Was Almost a Man

Dave struck out across the fields, looking homeward through paling light. Whut's the usa talkin wid em niggers in the field? Anyhow, his mother was putting supper on the table. Them niggers can't understan nothing. One of these days he was going to get a gun and practice shooting, then they can't talk to him as though he were a little boy. He slowed, looking at the ground. Shucks, Ah ain scareda them even ef they are biggern me! Aw, Ah know whut Ahma do. . . . Ahm going by ol Joe's sto n git that Sears Roebuck catlog n look at them guns. Mabbe Ma will lemme buy one when she gits mah pay from ol man Hawkins. Ahma beg her t gimme some money. Ahm ol ernough to hava gun. Ahm seventeen. Almos a man. He strode, feeling his long, loose-jointed limbs. Shucks, a man oughta hava little gun aftah he done worked hard all day. . . .

He came in sight of Joe's store. A yellow lantern glowed on the front porch. He mounted steps and went through the screen door, hearing it bang behind him. There was a strong smell of coal oil and mackerel fish. He felt very confident until he saw fat Joe walk in through the rear door, then his courage began to ooze.

"Howdy, Dave! Whutcha want?"

"How yuh, Mistah Joe? Aw, Ah don wanna buy nothing. Ah jus wanted t see ef yuhd lemme look at tha ol catlog erwhile."

"Sure! You wanna see it here?"

"Nawsuh. Ah wans t take it home wid me. Ahll bring it back termorrow when Ah come in from the fiels."

"You plannin on buyin something?"

"Yessuh."

"Your ma letting you have your own money now?"

"Shucks. Mistah Joe, Ahm gittin t be a man like anybody else!"

Joe laughed and wiped his greasy white face with a red bandanna.

"Whut you plannin on buyin?"

Dave looked at the floor, scratched his head, scratched his thigh, and smiled. Then he looked up shyly.

"Ahll tell yuh, Mistah Joe, ef yuh promise yuh won't tell."

"I promise."

"Waal, Ahma buy a gun."

"A gun? Whut you want with a gun?"

"Ah wanna keep it."

"You ain't nothing but a boy. You don't need a gun."

"Aw, lemme have the catlog, Mistah Joe. Ahll bring it back."

Joe walked through the rear door. Dave was elated. He looked around at barrels of sugar and flour. He heard Joe coming back. He craned his neck to see if he were bringing the book. Yeah, he's got it! Gawddog, he's got it!

"Here, but be sure you bring it back. It's the only one I got."

"Sho, Mistah Joe."

"Say, if you wanna buy a gun, why don't you buy one from me? I gotta gun to sell."

"Will it shoot?"

"Sure it'll shoot."

"Whut kind is it?"

"Oh, it's kinda old. . . . A lefthand Wheeler. A pistol. A big one."

"Is it got bullets in it?"

"It's loaded."

"Kin Ah see it?"

"Where's your money?"

"Whut yuh wan fer it?"

"I'll let you have it for two dollars."

"Just two dollahs? Shucks, Ah could buy tha when Ah git mah pay."

"I'll have it here when you want it."

"Awright, suh. Ah be in fer it."

He went through the door, hearing it slam again behind him. Ahma git some money from Ma n buy me a gun! Only two dollahs! He tucked the thick catalogue under his arm and hurried.

"Where yuh been, boy?" His mother held a steaming dish of black-eyed peas.

"Aw, Ma, Ah jus stopped down the road t talk wid th boys."

"Yuh know bettah than t keep suppah waitin."

He sat down, resting the catalogue on the edge of the table.

"Yuh git up from there and git to the well n wash yosef! Ah ain feedin no hogs in mah house!"

She grabbed his shoulder and pushed him. He stumbled out of the room, then came back to get the catalogue.

"Whut this?"

"Aw, Ma, it's jusa catlog."

"Who yuh git it from?"

"From Joe, down at the sto."

"Waal, thas good. We kin use it around the house."

"Naw, Ma." He grabbed for it. "Gimme mah catlog, Ma."

She held onto it and glared at him.

"Quit hollerin at me! Whut's wrong wid yuh? Yuh crazy?"

"But Ma, please. It ain mine! It's Joe's! He tol me t bring it back t im termorrow."

She gave up the book. He stumbled down the back steps, hugging the thick book under his arm. When he had splashed water on his face and hands, he groped back to the kitchen and fumbled in a corner for the towel. He bumped into a chair; it clattered to the floor. The catalogue sprawled at his feet. When he had dried his eyes, he snatched up the book and held it again under his arm. His mother stood watching him.

"Now, ef yuh gonna acka fool over that ol book, Ahll take it n burn it up."

"Naw, Ma, please."

"Waal, set down n be still!"

He sat down and drew the oil lamp close. He thumbed page after page, unaware of the food his mother set on the table. His father came in. Then his small brother.

"Whutcha got there, Dave?" his father asked.

"Jusa catalog," he answered, not looking up.

"Yawh, here they is!" His eyes glowed at blue and black revolvers. He glanced up, feeling sudden guilt. His father was watching him. He eased the book under the table and rested it on his knees. After the blessing was asked, he ate. He scooped up peas and swallowed fat meat without chewing. Buttermilk helped to wash it down. He did not want to mention money before his father. He would do much better by cornering his mother when she was alone. He looked at his father uneasily out of the edge of his eye.

"Boy, how come yuh don quit foolin wid tha book n eat yo suppah."

"Yessuh."

"How yuh n ol man Hawkins gittin erlong?"

"Suh?"

"Can't yuh hear. Why don yuh listen? Ah ast yuh how wuz yuh n ol man Hawkins gittin erlong?"

"Oh, swell, Pa. Ah plows mo lan than anybody over there."

"Waal, yuh oughta keep yo min on whut yuh doin."

"Yessuh."

He poured his plate full of molasses and sopped at it slowly with a chunk of cornbread. When all but his mother had left the kitchen he still sat and looked again at the guns in the catalogue. Lawd, ef Ah only had the pretty one! He could almost feel the slickness of the weapon with his fingers. If he had a gun like that he would polish it and keep it shining so it would never rust. N Ahd keep it loaded, by Gawd!

"Ma?"

"Hunh?"

"Ol man Hawkins give yuh mah money yit?"

"Yeah, but ain no usa yuh thinkin bout thowin nona it erway. Ahm keepin tha money sos yuh kin have cloes t go to school this winter."

He rose and went to her side with the open catalogue in his palms. She was washing dishes, her head bent low over a pan. Shyly he raised the open book. When he spoke his voice was husky, faint.

"Ma, Gawd know Ah wans one of these."

"One of whut?" she asked, not raising her eyes.

"One of these," he said again, not daring even to point. She glanced up at the page, then at him with wide eyes.

"Nigger, is yuh gone plum crazy?"

"Aw, Ma—"

"Git outta here! Don't yuh talk t me bout no gun! Yuh a fool!"

"Ma, Ah kin buy one fer two dollahs."

"Not ef Ah knows it yuh ain!"

"But yuh promised me one—"

"Ah don care whut Ah promised! Yuh ain nothing but a boy yit!"

"Ma, ef yuh lemme buy one Ahll never ast yuh fer nothing no mo."

"Ah tol yuh t git outta here! Yuh ain gonna toucha penny of tha money fer no gun! Thas how come Ah has Mistah Hawkins pay yo wages t me, cause Ah knows yuh ain got no sense."

"But Ma, we needa gun. Pa ain got no gun. We needa gun in the house. Yuh kin never tell whut might happen."

"Now don yuh try to maka fool outta me, boy! Ef we did hava gun yuh wouldn't have it!"

He laid the catalogue down and slipped his arm around her waist. "Aw, Ma, Ah done worked hard alla summer n ain ast yuh fer nothing, is Ah, now?"

"Thas whut yuh spose t do!"

"But Ma. Ah wants a gun. Yuh kin lemme have two dollahs outa mah money. Please Ma. I kin give it to Pa. . . . Please, Ma! Ah loves yuh, Ma."

When she spoke her voice came soft and low.

"What yuh wan wida gun, Dave? Yuh don need no gun. Yuhll git in trouble. N ef yo Pa jus thought Ah letyuh have money t buy a gun he'd hava fit."

"Ahll hide it, Ma. It ain but two dollahs."

"Lawd, chil, whuts wrong wid yuh?"

"Ain nothing wrong, Ma. Ahm almos a man now. Ah wants a gun."

"Who gonna sell yuh a gun?"

"Ol Joe at the sto."

"N it don cos but two dollahs?"

"Thas all, Ma. Just two dollahs. Please, Ma."

She was stacking the plates away; her hands moved slowly, reflectively. Dave kept an anxious silence. Finally she turned to him.

"Ahll let yuh git the gun ef yuh promise me one thing."

"Whuts tha, Ma?"

"Yuh bring it straight back t me, yuh hear? It'll be fer Pa."

"Yessum! Lemme go now, Ma."

She stooped, turned slightly to one side, raised the hem of her dress, rolled down the top of her stocking, and came up with a slender wad of bills.

"Here," she said. "Lawd knows yuh don need no gun. But yer Pa does. Yuh bring it right back t me, yuh hear. Ahma put it up. Now ef yuh don, Ahma have yuh Pa lick yuh so hard yuh won ferget it."

"Yessum."

He took the money, ran down the steps, and across the yard.

"Dave! Yuuuuuuh Daaaaaave!"

He heard, but he was not going to stop now. "Naw, Lawd!"

The first movement he made the following morning was to reach under his pillow for the gun. In the gray light of dawn he held it loosely, feeling a sense of power. Could killa man wida gun like this. Kill anybody, black or white. And if he were holding this gun in his hand nobody could run over him; they would have to respect him. It was a big gun, with a long barrel and a heavy handle. He raised and lowered it in his hand, marveling at its weight.

He had not come straight home with it as his mother had asked; instead he had stayed out in the fields, holding the weapon in his hand, aiming it now and then at some imaginary foe. But he had not fired it; he had been afraid that his father might hear. Also he was not sure he knew how to fire it.

To avoid surrendering the pistol he had not come into the house until he knew that all were asleep. When his mother had tiptoed to his bedside late that night and demanded the gun, he had first played 'possum; then he had told her that the gun was hidden outdoors, that he would bring it to her in the morning. Now he lay turning it slowly in his hands. He broke it, took out the cartridges, felt them, and then put them back.

He slid out of bed, got a long strip of old flannel from a trunk, wrapped the gun in it, and tied it to his naked thigh while it was still loaded. He did not go in to breakfast. Even though it was not yet daylight, he started for Jim Hawkins's plantation. Just as the sun was rising he reached the barns where the mules and plows were kept.

"Hey! That you, Dave?"

He turned. Jim Hawkins stood eyeing him suspiciously.

"What're yuh doing here so early?"

"Ah didn't know Ah wuz gittin up so early, Mistah Hawkins. Ah wuz fixing t hitch up ol Jenny n take her t the fiels."

"Good. Since you're here so early, how about plowing that stretch down by the woods?"

"Suits me, Mistah Hawkins."

"O.K. Go to it!"

He hitched Jenny to a plow and started across the fields. Hot dog! This was just what he wanted. If he could get down by the woods, he could shoot his gun and nobody would hear. He walked behind the plow, hearing the traces creaking, feeling the gun tied tight to his thigh.

When he reached the woods, he plowed two whole rows before he decided to take out the gun. Finally he stopped, looked in all directions, then untied the gun and held it in his hand. He turned to the mule and smiled.

"Know whut this is, Jenny? Naw, yuh wouldn't know! Yuhs jus a ol mule! Anyhow, this is a gun, n it kin shoot, by Gawd!"

He held the gun at arm's length. Whut t hell, Ahma shoot this thing! He looked at Jenny again.

"Lissen here, Jenny! When Ah pull this ol trigger Ah don wan yuh t run n acka fool now."

Jenny stood with head down, her short ears pricked straight. Dave walked off about twenty feet, held the gun far out from him, at arms' length, and turned his head. Hell, he told himself, Ah ain afraid. The gun felt loose in his fingers; he waved it wildly for a moment. Then he shut his eyes and tightened his forefinger. Bloom! The report half-deafened him and he thought his right hand was torn from his arm. He heard Jenny whinnying and galloping over the field, and he found himself on his knees squeezing his fingers hard between his legs. His hand was numb; he jammed it into his mouth, trying to warm it, trying to stop the pain. The gun lay at his feet. He did not quite know what had happened. He stood up and stared at the gun as though it were a living thing. He gritted his teeth and kicked the gun. Yuh almos broke mah arm! He turned to look for Jenny; she was far over the fields, tossing her head and kicking wildly.

"Hol on there, ol mule!"

When he caught up with her she stood trembling, walling her big white eyes at him. The plow was far away; the traces had broken. Then Dave stopped short, looking, not believing. Jenny was bleeding. Her left side was red and wet with blood. He went closer. Lawd, have mercy! Wondah did Ah shoot this mule? He grabbed for Jenny's mane. She flinched, snorted, whirled, tossing her head.

"Hol on now! Hol on."

Then he saw the hole in Jenny's side, right between the ribs. It was round, wet, red. A crimson stream streaked down the front leg, flowing fast. Good Gawd! Ah wuzn't shootin at tha mule. He felt panic. He knew he had to stop that blood, or Jenny would bleed to death. He had never seen so much blood in all his life. He chased the mule for half a mile, trying to catch her. Finally she stopped, breathing hard, stumpy tail half arched. He caught her mane and led her back to where the plow and gun lay. Then he stopped and grabbed handfuls of damp black earth and tried to plug the bullet hole. Jenny shuddered, whinnied, and broke from him.

"Hol on! Hol on now!"

He tried to plug it again, but blood came anyhow. His fingers were hot and sticky. He rubbed dirt into his palms, trying to dry them. Then again he attempted to plug the bullet hole, but Jenny shied away, kicking her heels high. He stood helpless. He had to do something. He ran at Jenny; she dodged him. He watched a red stream of blood flow down Jenny's leg and form a bright pool at her feet.

"Jenny . . . Jenny . . ." he called weakly.

His lips trembled! She's bleeding t death! He looked in the direction of home, wanting to go back, wanting to get help. But he saw the pistol lying in the damp black clay. He had a queer feeling that if he only did something, this would not be; Jenny would not be there bleeding to death.

When he went to her this time, she did not move. She stood with sleepy, dreamy eyes; and when he touched her she gave a low-pitched whinny and knelt to the ground, her front knees slopping in blood.

"Jenny . . . Jenny . . ." he whispered.

For a long time she held her neck erect; then her head sank, slowly. Her ribs swelled with a mighty heave and she went over.

Dave's stomach felt empty, very empty. He picked up the gun and held it gingerly between his thumb and forefinger. He buried it at the foot of a tree. He took a stick and tried to cover the pool of blood with dirt—but what was the use? There was Jenny lying with her mouth open and her eyes walled and glassy. He could not tell Jim Hawkins he had shot his mule. But he had to tell him something. Yeah, Ahll tell em Jenny started gittin wil n fell on the joint of the plow. . . . But that would hardly happen to a mule. He walked across the field slowly, head down.

It was sunset. Two of Jim Hawkins's men were over near the edge of the woods digging a hole in which to bury Jenny. Dave was surrounded by a knot of people; all of them were looking down at the dead mule.

"I don't see how in the world it happened," said Jim Hawkins for the tenth time.

The crowd parted and Dave's mother, father, and small brother pushed into the center.

"Where Dave?" his mother called.

"There he is," said Jim Hawkins.

His mother grabbed him.

"Whut happened, Dave? Whut yuh done?"

"Nothing."

"C'mon, boy, talk," his father said.

Dave took a deep breath and told the story he knew nobody believed.

"Waal," he drawled. "Ah brung ol Jenny down here sos Ah could do mah plowin. Ah plowed bout two rows, just like yuh see." He stopped and pointed at the long rows of upturned earth. "Then something musta been wrong wid ol Jenny. She wouldn't ack right a-tall. She started snortin n kickin her heels. Ah tried to hol her, but she pulled erway, rearin n goin on. Then when the point of the plow was stickin up in the air, she swung erroun n twisted herself back on it. . . . She stuck herself n started t bleed. N fo Ah could do anything, she wuz dead."

"Did you ever hear of anything like that in all your life?" asked Jim Hawkins.

There were white and black standing in the crowd. They murmured. Dave's mother came close to him and looked hard into his face.

"Tell the truth, Dave," she said.

"Looks like a bullet hole ter me," said one man.

"Dave, whut yuh do wid the gun?" his mother asked.

The crowd surged in, looking at him. He jammed his hands into his pockets, shook his head slowly from left to right, and backed away. His eyes were wide and painful.

"Did he hava gun?" asked Jim Hawkins.

"By Gawd, Ah tol yuh tha wuz a gunwound," said a man, slapping his thigh.

His father caught his shoulders and shook him till his teeth rattled.

"Tell whut happened, yuh rascal! Tell whut . . ."

Dave looked at Jenny's stiff legs and began to cry.

"Whut yuh do wid tha gun?" his mother asked.

"Come on and tell the truth," said Hawkins. "Ain't nobody going to hurt you. . . ."

His mother crowded close to him.

"Did yuh shoot tha mule, Dave?"

Dave cried, seeing blurred white and black faces.

"Ahh ddinnt gggo tt sshoooot hher. . . . Ah ssswear off Gawd Ahh ddint. . . . Ah wuz a-tryin t sssee ef the ol gggun would sshoot—"

"Where yuh git the gun from?" his father asked.

"Ah got it from Joe, at the sto."

"Where yuh git the money?"

"Ma give it t me."

"He kept worryin me, Bob. . . . Ah had t. . . . Ah tol im t bring the gun right back t me. . . It was fer yuh, the gun."

"But how yuh happen to shoot that mule?" asked Jim Hawkins.

"Ah wuznt shootin at the mule, Mistah Hawkins. The gun jumped when Ah pulled the trigger . . . N for Ah knowed anything Jenny wuz there a-bleedin."

Somebody in the crowd laughed. Jim Hawkins walked close to Dave and looked into his face.

"Well, looks like you have bought you a mule, Dave."

"Ah swear for Gawd, Ah didn't go t kill the mule, Mistah Hawkins!"

"But you killed her!"

All the crowd was laughing now. They stood on tiptoe and poked heads over one another's shoulders.

"Well, boy, looks like yuh done bought a dead mule! Hahaha!"

"Ain tha ershame."

"Hohohohoho."

Dave stood, head down, twisting his feet in the dirt.

"Well, you needn't worry about it, Bob," said Jim Hawkins to Dave's father. "Just let the boy keep on working and pay me two dollars a month."

"Whut yuh wan fer yo mule, Mistah Hawkins?"

Jim Hawkins screwed up his eyes.

"Fifty dollars."

"Whut yuh do wid tha gun?" Dave's father demanded.

Dave said nothing.

"Yuh wan me t take a tree lim n beat yuh till yuh talk!"

"Nawsuh!"

"What yuh do wid it?"

"Ah thowed it erway."

"Where?"

"Ah . . . Ah thowed it in the creek."

"Waal, c mon home. N firs thing in the mawnin git to tha creek n fin tha gun."

"Yessuh."

"Whut yuh pay fer it?"

"Two dollahs."

"Take tha gun n git yo money back n carry it t Mistah Hawkins, yuh hear? N don fergit Ahma lam you black bottom good fer this! Now march yosef on home, suh!"

Dave turned and walked slowly. He heard people laughing. Dave glared, his eyes welling with tears. Hot anger bubbled in him. Then he swallowed and stumbled on.

That night Dave did not sleep. He was glad that he had gotten out of killing the mule so easily, but he was hurt. Something hot seemed to turn over inside him each time he remembered how they had laughed. He tossed on his bed, feeling his hard pillow. N Pa says he's gonna beat me. . . . He remembered other beatings, and his back quivered. Naw, naw, Ah sho don wan im t beat me tha way no mo. . . . Dam em all! Nobody ever gave him anything. All he did was work. They treat me lika mule. . . . N then they beat me. . . . He gritted his teeth. N Ma had t tell on me.

Well, if he had to, he would take old man Hawkins that two dollars. But that meant selling the gun. And he wanted to keep that gun. Fifty dollahs fer a dead mule.

He turned over, thinking how he had fired the gun. He had an itch to fire it again. Ef other men kin shoota gun, by Gawd, Ah kin! He was still listening. Mebbe they all sleepin now. . . . The house was still. He heard the soft breathing of his brother. Yes, now! He would go down an get that gun and see if he could fire it! He eased out of bed and slipped into overalls.

The moon was bright. He ran almost all the way to the edge of the woods. He stumbled over the ground, looking for the spot where he had buried the gun. Yeah, here it is. Like a hungry dog scratching for a bone he pawed it up. He puffed his black cheeks and blew dirt from the trigger and barrel. He broke it and found four cartridges unshot. He looked around; the fields were filled with silence and moonlight. He clutched the gun stiff and hard in his fingers. But as soon as he wanted to pull the trigger, he shut his eyes and turned his head. Naw, Ah can't shoot wid mah eyes closed n mah head turned. With effort he held his eyes open; then he squeezed. Bloooom! He was stiff, not breathing. The gun was still in his hands. Dammit, he'd done it! He fired again. Blooom! He smiled. Bloooom! Bloooom! Click, click. There! It was empty. If anybody could shoot a gun, he could. He put the gun into his hip pocket and started across the fields.

When he reached the top of a ridge he stood straight and proud in the moonlight, looking at Jim Hawkins's big white house, feeling the gun sagging in his pocket. Lawd, ef Ah had jus one mo bullet Ahd taka shot at tha house. Ahd like t scare ol man Hawkins jussa little. . . . Jussa enough t let im know Dave Sanders is a man.

To his left the road curved, running to the tracks of the Illinois Central. He jerked his head, listening. From far off came a faint hoooof-hoooof; hoooof-hoooof; hoooof-hoooof. . . . That's number eight. He took a swift look at Jim Hawkins's white house; he thought of Pa, of Ma, of his little brother, and the boys. He thought of the dead mule and heard hooof-hooof; hooof-hooof; hooof-hooof. . . . He stood rigid. Two dollahs a mont. Les see now . . . Tha mans itll take bout two years. Shucks! Ahll be dam! He started down the road, toward the tracks. Yeah, here she comes! He stood beside the track and held himself stiffly. Here she comes, erroun the ben. . . . C mon, yuh slow poke! C mon! He had his hand on his gun; something quivered in his stomach. Then the train thundered past, the gray and brown boxcars rumbling and clinking. He gripped the gun tightly; then he jerked his hand out of his pocket. Ah betcha Bill wouldn't do it! Ah betcha. . . . The cars slid past, steel grinding upon steel. Ahm riding yuh ternight so hep me Gawd! He was hot all over. He hesitated just a moment; then he grabbed, pulled atop of a car, and lay flat. He felt his pocket; the gun was still there. Ahead the long rails were glinting in moonlight, stretching away, away to somewhere, somewhere where he could be a man. . . .

Part Four

The Contemporary Scene: The Ongoing Tradition

Eudora Welty (1909–   )

Eudora Welty, who makes her home in Jackson, Mississippi, is one of the leading writers in the so-called "Southern Renascence" (which includes William Faulkner, Robert Penn Warren, John Crowe Ransom, Flannery O'Connor, and others), and belongs firmly in that tradition beginning with Chekhov and extending through Henry James and Katherine Anne Porter. Her interest is not primarily in plot or action, but in the effect of action on character—on the motions of experience that occur in the inner life. Unlike James or Woolf, she does not use stream of consciousness in tapping the inner life, but instead depends on an exquisite manipulation of detail, mood, and accent. As Ruth Vande Kieft says, in comparing Welty with those in the Chekhovian tradition: "They invest with maximum significance each detail, each small piece of dialogue, narration or description; and they endow each metaphor with an emotional resonance comparable to that of poetic metaphor." The lyric intensity of her stories gives them the kind of unity that Poe called for (see Introduction, pp. 5–6), and to hear Eudora Welty read aloud (several of her stories are on records) is a unique delight.

    Though she was born in Jackson, she is in some ways less "Southern" than the other Renascence writers, less preoccupied with the tragic courses of Southern history—slavery, the Civil War, industrialism, the land, the race problem; her subject is the plight of the individual and, as Vande Kieft says, "the general hostility of life to man's fulfillment." She makes "what one might call an attempt to escape from the South," writes Isaac Rosenfeld, but this is an escape from great public issues, not from the land or its people. Early in her career as "Junior Publicity Agent" for the WPA, a job that required her to travel about the state of Mississippi interviewing people, taking pictures, and writing newspaper copy, she developed that keen eye for detail so evident in her art. That was but one of many part-time jobs she held in those Depression years (1930 to 1936)—in advertising, radio scriptwriting, public relations—following her graduation from the University of Wisconsin and a year's study of advertising at Columbia. Welty has remembered these early experiences in her recent *One Time, One Place: Mississippi in the Depression* (1971).

Her first story appeared in *Manuscript* in 1936 and her first volume of stories, *A Curtain of Green* (with a generous introduction by Katherine Anne Porter), in 1941. Stories and novels since have included *Delta Wedding* (1946), *The Golden Apples* (1949), *The Ponder Heart* (1954), *The Bridge of Innisfallen and Other Stories* (1955), and—more recently—*The Optimist's Daughter* (1972).

"A Worn Path" is perhaps Eudora Welty's classic story. Without raising her voice or any social banner—and without abandoning her rich sense of humor (which here in no way demeans her serious subject)—she presents in the lonely walk of Old Phoenix along the Natchez Trace to get free medicine for her sick grandson something of the quintessence of all suffering and all oppression. "Out of my way, all you foxes, owls, beetles, jack rabbits, coons, and wild animals! . . . Keep out from under these feet, little bobwhites. . . . Keep the big wild hogs out of my path. . . . I got a long way." She is almost at one with the animals; defenseless, she endures—yet there is no suggestion of sentimentality here, just as there is none of bitterness. Of all the stories heard by black children in a Jackson Freedom School in 1964, this was their favorite. Here, in this exploited ex-slave, rendered by Welty with such tenderness and love, was their own dear mother; here with no political issues raised, was the call for justice they best understood.

A Worn Path

It was December—a bright frozen day in the early morning. Far out in the country there was an old Negro woman with her head tied in a red rag, coming along a path through the pinewoods. Her name was Phoenix Jackson. She was very old and small and she walked slowly in the dark pine shadows, moving a little from side to side in her steps, with the balanced heaviness and lightness of a pendulum in a grandfather clock. She carried a thin, small cane made from an umbrella, and with this she kept tapping the frozen earth in front of her. This made a grave and persistent noise in the still air, that seemed meditative like the chirping of a solitary little bird.

She wore a dark striped dress reaching down to her shoe tops, and an equally long apron of bleached sugar sacks, with a full pocket: all neat and tidy, but every time she took a step she might have fallen over her shoe-laces, which dragged from her unlaced shoes. She looked straight ahead. Her eyes were blue with age. Her skin had a pattern all its own of numberless branching wrinkles and as though a whole little tree stood in the middle of her forehead, but a golden color ran underneath, and the two knobs of her cheeks were illuminated by a yellow burning under the dark. Under the red rag her hair came down on her neck in the frailest of ringlets, still black, and with an odor like copper.

Now and then there was a quivering in the thicket. Old Phoenix said, "Out of my way, all you foxes, owls, beetles, jack rabbits, coons, and wild animals! . . . Keep out from under these feet, little bob-whites. . . . Keep the big wild hogs out of my path. Don't let none of those come running my direction. I got a long way." Under her small black-freckled hand her cane, limber as a buggy whip, would switch at the brush as if to rouse up any hiding things.

On she went. The woods were deep and still. The sun made the pine needles almost too bright to look at, up where the wind rocked. The cones dropped as light as feathers. Down in the hollow was the mourning dove—it was not too late for him.

The path ran up a hill. "Seem like there is chains about my feet, time I get this far," she said, in the voice of argument old people keep to use with themselves. "Something always take a hold of me on this hill—pleads I should stay."

After she got to the top she turned and gave a full, severe look behind her where she had come. "Up through pines," she said at length. "Now down through oaks."

Her eyes opened their widest, and she started down gently. But before she got to the bottom of the hill a bush caught her dress.

Her fingers were busy and intent, but her skirts were full and long, so that before she could pull them free in one place they were caught in another. It was not possible to allow the dress to tear. "I in the thorny bush," she said. "Thorns, you doing your appointed work. Never want to let folks pass—no sir. Old eyes thought you was a pretty little *green* bush."

Finally, trembling all over, she stood free, and after a moment dared to stoop for her cane.

"Sun so high!" she cried, leaning back and looking, while the thick tears went over her eyes. "The time getting all gone here."

At the foot of this hill was a place where a log was laid across the creek.

"Now comes the trial," said Phoenix.

Putting her right foot out, she mounted the log and shut her eyes. Lifting her skirt, levelling her cane fiercely before her, like a festival figure in some parade, she began to march across. Then she opened her eyes and she was safe on the other side.

"I wasn't as old as I thought," she said.

But she sat down to rest. She spread her skirts on the bank around her and folded her hands over her knees. Up above her was a tree in a pearly cloud of mistletoe. She did not dare to close her eyes, and when a little boy brought her a little plate with a slice of marble-cake on it she spoke to him. "That would be acceptable," she said. But when she went to take it there was just her own hand in the air.

So she left that tree, and had to go through a barbed-wire fence. There she had to creep and crawl, spreading her knees and stretching her fingers like a baby trying to climb the steps. But she talked loudly to herself: she could not let her dress be torn now, so late in the day, and she could not pay for having her arm or her leg sawed off if she got caught fast where she was.

At last she was safe through the fence and risen up out in the clearing. Big dead trees, like black men with one arm, were standing in the purple stalks of the withered cotton field. There sat a buzzard.

"Who you watching?"

In the furrow she made her way along.

"Glad this not the season for bulls," she said, looking sideways, "and the good Lord made his snakes to curl up and sleep in the winter. A pleasure I don't see no two-headed snake coming around that tree, where it come once. It took a while to get by him, back in the summer."

She passed through the old cotton and went into a field of dead corn. It whispered and shook and was taller than her head. "Through the maze now," she said, for there was no path.

Then there was something tall, black, and skinny there, moving before her.

At first she took it for a man. It could have been a man dancing in the field. But she stood still and listened, and it did not make a sound. It was as silent as a ghost.

"Ghost," she said sharply, "who be you the ghost of? For I have heard of nary death close by."

But there was no answer—only the ragged dancing in the wind.

She shut her eyes, reached out her hand, and touched a sleeve. She found a coat and inside that an emptiness, cold as ice.

"You scarecrow," she said. Her face lighted. "I ought to be shut up for good," she said with laughter. "My senses is gone. I too old. I the oldest people I ever know. Dance, old scarecrow," she said, "while I dancing with you."

She kicked her foot over the furrow, and with mouth drawn down, shook her head once or twice in a little strutting way. Some husks blew down and whirled in streamers about her skirts.

Then she went on, parting her way from side to side with the cane, through the whispering field. At last she came to the end, to a wagon track where the silver grass blew between the red ruts. The quail were walking around like pullets, seeming all dainty and unseen.

"Walk pretty," she said. "This the easy place. This the easy going."

She followed the track, swaying through the quiet bare fields, through the little strings of trees silver in their dead leaves, past cabins silver from weather, with the doors and windows boarded shut, all like old women under a spell sitting there. "I walking in their sleep," she said, nodding her head vigorously.

In a ravine she went where a spring was silently flowing through a hollow log. Old Phoenix bent and drank. "Sweet-gum makes the water sweet," she said, and drank more. "Nobody know who made this well, for it was here when I was born."

The track crossed a swampy part where the moss hung as white as lace from every limb. "Sleep on, alligators, and blow your bubbles." Then the track went into the road.

Deep, deep the road went down between the high green-colored banks. Overhead the live-oaks met, and it was as dark as a cave.

A black dog with a lolling tongue came up out of the weeds by the ditch. She was meditating, and not ready, and when he came at her she only hit him a little with her cane. Over she went in the ditch, like a little puff of milk-weed.

Down there, her senses drifted away. A dream visited her, and she reached her hand up, but nothing reached down and gave her a pull. So she lay there and presently went to talking. "Old woman," she said to herself, "that black dog come up out of the weeds to stall you off, and now there he sitting on his fine tail, smiling at you."

A white man finally came along and found her—a hunter, a young man, with his dog on a chain.

"Well, Granny!" he laughed. "What are you doing there?"

"Lying on my back like a June-bug waiting to be turned over, mister," she said, reaching up her hand.

He lifted her up, gave her a swing in the air, and set her down, "Anything broken, Granny?"

"No sir, them old dead weeds is springy enough," said Phoenix, when she had got her breath. "I thank you for your trouble."

"Where do you live, Granny?" he asked, while the two dogs were growling at each other.

"Away back yonder, sir, behind the ridge. You can't even see it from here."

"On your way home?"

"No, sir, I going to town."

"Why, that's too far! That's as far as I walk when I come out myself, and I get something for my trouble." He patted the stuffed bag he carried, and there hung down a little closed claw. It was one of the bob-whites, with its beak hooked bitterly to show it was dead. "Now you go on home, Granny!"

"I bound to go to town, mister," said Phoenix. "The time come around."

He gave another laugh, filling the whole landscape. "I know you old colored people! Wouldn't miss going to town to see Santa Claus!"

But something held Old Phoenix very still. The deep lines in her face went into a fierce and different radiation. Without warning, she had seen with her own eyes a flashing nickel fall out of the man's pocket onto the ground.

"How old are you, Granny?" he was saying.

"There is no telling, mister," she said, "no telling."

Then she gave a little cry and clapped her hands and said, "Git on away from here, dog! Look! Look at that dog!" She laughed as if in admiration. "He ain't scared of nobody. He a big black dog." She whispered, "Sic him!"

"Watch me get rid of that cur," said the man. "Sic him, Pete! Sic him!"

Phoenix heard the dogs fighting, and heard the man running and throwing sticks. She even heard a gunshot. But she was slowly bending forward by that time, further and further forward, the lids stretched down over her eyes, as if she were doing this in her sleep. Her chin was lowered almost to her knees. The yellow palm of her hand came out from the fold of her apron. Her fingers slid down and along the ground under the piece of money with the grace and care they would have in lifting an egg from under a sitting hen. Then she slowly straightened up, she stood erect, and the nickel was in her apron pocket. A bird flew by. Her lips moved. "God watching me the whole time. I come to stealing."

The man came back, and his own dog panted about them. "Well, I scared him off that time," he said, and then he laughed and lifted his gun and pointed it at Phoenix.

She stood straight and faced him.

"Doesn't the gun scare you?" he said, still pointing it.

"No, sir, I seen plenty go off closer by, in my day, and for less than what I done," she said, holding utterly still.

He smiled, and shouldered the gun. "Well, Granny," he said, "you must be a hundred years old, and scared of nothing. I'd give you a dime if I had any money with me. But you take my advice and stay home, and nothing will happen to you."

"I bound to go on my way, mister," said Phoenix. She inclined her head in the red rag. Then they went in different directions, but she could hear the gun shooting again and again over the hill.

She walked on. The shadows hung from the oak trees to the road like curtains. Then she smelled wood-smoke, and smelled the river, and she saw a steeple and the cabins on their steep steps. Dozens of little black children whirled around her. There ahead was Natchez shining. Bells were ringing. She walked on.

In the paved city it was Christmas time. There were red and green electric lights strung and crisscrossed everywhere, and all turned on in the daytime. Old Phoenix would have been lost if she had not distrusted her eyesight and depended on her feet to know where to take her.

She paused quietly on the sidewalk where people were passing by. A lady came along in the crowd, carrying an armful of red-, green-, and silver-wrapped presents; she gave off perfume like the red roses in hot summer, and Phoenix stopped her.

"Please, missy, will you lace up my shoe?" She held up her foot.

"What do you want, Grandma?"

"See my shoe," said Phoenix. "Do all right for out in the country, but wouldn't look right to go in a big building."

"Stand still then, Grandma," said the lady. She put her packages down on the sidewalk beside her and laced and tied both shoes tightly.

"Can't lace 'em with a cane," said Phoenix. "Thank you, missy. I doesn't mind asking a nice lady to tie up my shoe, when I gets out on the street."

Moving slowly and from side to side, she went into the big building and into a tower of steps, where she walked up and around and around until her feet knew to stop.

She entered a door, and there she saw nailed up on the wall the document that had been stamped with the gold seal and framed in the gold frame, which matched the dream that was hung up in her head.

"Here I be," she said. There was a fixed and ceremonial stiffness over her body.

"A charity case, I suppose," said an attendant who sat at the desk before her.

But Phoenix only looked above her head. There was sweat on her face, the wrinkles in her skin shone like a bright net.

"Speak up, Grandma," the woman said. "What's your name? We must have your history, you know. Have you been here before? What seems to be the trouble with you?"

Old Phoenix only gave a twitch to her face as if a fly were bothering her.

"Are you deaf?" cried the attendant.

But then the nurse came in.

"Oh, that's just old Aunt Phoenix," she said. "She doesn't come for herself—she has a little grandson. She makes these trips just as regular as clockwork. She lives away back off the Old Natchez Trace." She bent down. "Well, Aunt Phoenix, why don't you just take a seat? We won't keep you standing after your long trip." She pointed.

The old woman sat down, bolt upright in the chair.

"Now, how is the boy?" asked the nurse.

Old Phoenix did not speak.

"I said, how is the boy?"

But Phoenix only waited and stared straight ahead, her face very solemn and withdrawn into rigidity.

"Is his throat any better?" asked the nurse. "Aunt Phoenix, don't you hear me? Is your grandson's throat any better since the last time you came for the medicine?"

With her hands on her knees, the old woman waited, silent, erect and motionless, just as if she were in armour.

"You mustn't take up our time this way, Aunt Phoenix," the nurse said. "Tell us quickly about your grandson, and get it over. He isn't dead, is he?"

At last there came a flicker and then a flame of comprehension across her face, and she spoke.

"My grandson. It was my memory had left me. There I sat and forgot why I made my long trip."

"Forgot?" The nurse frowned. "After you came so far?"

Then Phoenix was like an old woman begging a dignified forgiveness for waking up frightened in the night. "I never did go to school, I was too old at the Surrender," she said in a soft voice. "I'm an old woman without an education. It was my memory fail me. My little grandson, he is just the same, and I forgot it in the coming."

"Throat never heals, does it?" said the nurse, speaking in a loud, sure voice to Old Phoenix. By now she had a card with something written on it, a little list. "Yes. Swallowed lye. When was it—January—two-three years ago—"

Phoenix spoke unasked now. "No, missy, he not dead, he just the same. Every little while his throat begin to close up again, and he not able to swallow. He not get his breath. He not able to help himself. So the time come around, and I go on another trip for the soothingmedicine."

"All right. The doctor said as long as you came to get it, you could have it," said the nurse. "But it's an obstinate case."

"My little grandson, he sit up there in the house all wrapped up, waiting by himself," Phoenix went on. "We is the only two left in the world. He suffer and it don't seem to put him back at all. He got a sweet look. He going to last. He wear a little patch quilt and peep out holding his mouth open like a little bird. I remembers so plain now. I not going to forget him again, no, the whole enduring time. I could tell him from all the others in creation."

"All right." The nurse was trying to hush her now. She brought her a bottle of medicine. "Charity," she said, making a check mark in a book.

Old Phoenix held the bottle close to her eyes and then carefully put it into her pocket.

"I thank you," she said.

"It's Christmas time, Grandma," said the attendant. "Could I give you a few pennies out of my purse?"

"Five pennies is a nickel," said Phoenix stiffly.

"Here's a nickel," said the attendant.

Phoenix rose carefully and held out her hand. She received the nickel and then fished the other nickel out of her pocket and laid it beside the new one. She stared at her palm closely, with her head on one side.

Then she gave a tap with her cane on the floor.

"This is what come to me to do," she said. "I going to the store and buy my child a little windmill they sells, made out of paper. He going to find it hard to believe there such a thing in the world. I'll march myself back where he waiting, holding it straight up in this hand."

She lifted her free hand, gave a little nod, turned round, and walked out of the doctor's office. Then her slow step began on the stairs, going down.

John Cheever (1912–1982)

John Cheever has long been recognized as one of the most finished short-story craftsmen of our time. And yet when his retrospective collection, *The Short Stories of John Cheever,* appeared in 1978, nearly every reviewer said the same thing: all of the stories seemed even better than anyone remembered, the whole adding up to a richly varied and significant body of creative work. In recognition of the book's excellence, Cheever received the Critics' Circle Award and the Pulitzer Prize.

The segment of American life that Cheever writes about is, typically, upper middle class. Most of his settings will be found on Manhattan's Upper East Side, in summer houses in New Hampshire, Martha's Vineyard, Nantucket, or in the wealthy suburban communities of Westchester County, New York, or Fairfield County, Connecticut. He writes, as one critic remarks, about "a world of doormen and elevator men, of private schools, of riding lessons, skiing lessons, sailing classes, dancing classes, of cocktail parties, dinner parties, and church on Sunday." Yet most readers will find Cheever country a world of familiar human beings—husbands, wives, mothers, fathers, children, neighbors friendly and hostile, babysitters—striving to keep up appearances, clinging to gentility, and longing for affection. A "typical" Cheever story has been described as a satire on suburbia viewed against the background of a fading Protestant ethic. But Cheever treats his characters not so much satirically as with a kind of "troubled affection." His stories are drenched in nostalgia; his major characters, at their most typical, *yearn*. For example, from a story called "O Youth and Beauty!":

> He feels as if the figures in the next yard are the specters from some party in that past where all his tastes and desires lie, and from which he has been cruelly removed. He feels like a ghost of the summer evening. He is sick with longing.

Though not heavily plotted, Cheever's stories have a remarkable unity, based largely on language and mood. They usually chronicle the experiences of a man, husband, father, at or approaching forty, and subject to any and all the crises and temptations of early middle age. Such a figure is Francis Weed in the story that follows. Weed experiences a sequence of shocks and reactions that at once illuminate and threaten his life. He survives the turbulence and finally is said to be happy. But the careful reader will wonder about the ironies of the last line: "Then it is dark; it is a night where kings in golden suits ride elephants over the mountains."

Perhaps nothing strikes us more forcefully than the poetic quality of Cheever's writing. He writes stories, but his impulse is lyric, and he fixes moment, place, and event in terms of their precise sensory qualities of sight, taste, hearing, smell, and touch:

> Kneeling on the floor to unlock a trunk, he broke a spider web with his lips. The frail web covered his mouth as if a hand had been put over it. He wiped it impatiently, but also with the feeling of having been gagged.

> The noise of the train is muffled in the heavy foliage, and the long car windows look like a string of lighted aquarium tanks before they flicker out of sight.

Of his stories, Cheever once remarked that many of them were generated from "the interrupted event." Full of moral insights and moral urgencies, they frequently focus on what one critic calls "domestic poignancies." And many are marvelously funny. We observe his characters experiencing the limitations and disappointments of this life, but the presiding tone is not pessimism or bitterness. As he says, he wants his fiction to draw together disparate incidents so that they relate to one another and confirm the feeling that life itself is a creative process, that one thing is put purposefully upon another, that what is lost in one encounter is replenished in the next, and that we possess some power to make sense of what takes place.

The Country Husband

To begin at the beginning, the airplane from Minneapolis in which Francis Weed was traveling East ran into heavy weather. The sky had been a hazy blue, with the clouds below the plane lying so close together that nothing could be seen of the earth. Then mist began to form outside the windows, and they flew into a white cloud of such density that it reflected the exhaust fires. The color of the cloud darkened to gray, and the plane began to rock. Francis had been in heavy weather before, but he had never been shaken up so much. The man in the seat beside him pulled a flask out of his pocket and took a drink. Francis smiled at his neighbor, but the man looked away; he wasn't sharing his pain killer with anyone. The plane began to drop and flounder wildly. A child was crying. The air in the cabin was overheated and stale, and Francis' left foot went to sleep. He read a little from a paper book that he had bought at the airport, but the violence of the storm divided his attention. It was black outside the ports. The exhaust fires blazed and shed sparks in the dark, and, inside, the shaded lights, the stuffiness, and the window curtains gave the cabin an atmosphere of intense and misplaced domesticity. Then the lights flickered and went out. "You know what I've always wanted to do?" the man beside Francis said suddenly. "I've always wanted to buy a farm in New Hampshire and raise beef cattle." The stewardess announced that they were going to make an emergency landing. All but the children saw in their minds the spreading wings of the Angel of Death. The pilot could be heard singing faintly, "I've got sixpence, jolly, jolly sixpence. I've got sixpence to last me all my life . . ." There was no other sound.

The loud groaning of the hydraulic valves swallowed up the pilot's song, and there was a shrieking high in the air, like automobile brakes, and the plane hit flat on its belly in a cornfield and shook them so violently that an old man up forward howled, "Me kidneys! Me kidneys!" The stewardess flung open the door, and someone opened an emergency door at the back, letting in the sweet noise of their continuing mortality—the idle splash and smell of a heavy rain. Anxious for their lives, they filed out of the doors and scattered over the cornfield in all directions, praying that the thread would hold. It did. Nothing happened. When it was clear that the plane would not burn or explode, the crew and the stewardess gathered the passengers together and led them to the shelter of a barn. They were not far from Philadelphia, and in a little while a string of taxis took them into the city. "It's just like the Marne," someone said, but there was surprisingly little relaxation of that suspiciousness with which many Americans regard their fellow travelers.

In Philadelphia, Francis Weed got a train to New York. At the end of that journey, he crossed the city and caught just as it was about to pull out the commuting train that he took five nights a week to his home in Shady Hill.

He sat with Trace Bearden. "You know, I was in that plane that just crashed outside Philadelphia," he said. "We came down in a field . . ." He had traveled faster than the newspapers or the rain, and the weather in New York was sunny and mild. It was a day in late September, as fragrant and shapely as an apple. Trace listened to the story, but how could he get excited? Francis had no powers that would let him re-create a brush with death—particularly in the atmosphere of a commuting train, journeying through a sunny countryside where already, in the slum gardens, there were signs of harvest. Trace picked up his newspaper, and Francis was left alone with his thoughts. He said good night to Trace on the platform at Shady Hill and drove in his secondhand Volkswagen up to the Blenhollow neighborhood, where he lived.

The Weeds' Dutch Colonial house was larger than it appeared to be from the driveway. The living room was spacious and divided like Gaul into three parts. Around an ell to the left as one entered from the vestibule was the long table, laid for six, with candles and a bowl of fruit in the center. The sounds and smells that came from the open kitchen door were appetizing, for Julia Weed was a good cook. The largest part of the living room centered on a fireplace. On the right were some bookshelves and a piano. The room was polished and tranquil, and from the windows that opened to the west there was some late-summer sunlight, brilliant and as clear as water. Nothing here was neglected; nothing had not been burnished. It was not the kind of household where, after prying open a stuck cigarette box, you would find an old shirt button and a tarnished nickel. The hearth was swept, the roses on the piano were reflected in the polish of the broad top, and there was an album of Schubert waltzes on the rack. Louisa Weed, a pretty girl of nine, was looking out the western windows. Her younger brother Henry was standing beside her. Her still younger brother, Toby, was studying the figures of some tonsured monks drinking beer on the polished brass of the woodbox. Francis, taking off his hat and putting down his paper, was not consciously pleased with the scene; he was not that reflective. It was his element, his creation, and he returned to it with that sense of lightness and strength with which any creature returns to his home. "Hi, everybody," he said. "The plane from Minneapolis . . ."

Nine times out of ten, Francis would be greeted with affection, but tonight the children are absorbed in their own antagonisms. Francis had not finished his sentence about the plane crash before Henry plants a kick in Louisa's behind. Louisa swings around, saying, "*Damn* you!" Francis makes the mistake of scolding Louisa for bad language before he punishes Henry. Now Louisa turns on her father and accuses him of favoritism. Henry is always right; she is persecuted and lonely; her lot is hopeless. Francis turns to his son, but the boy has justification for the kick—she hit him first; she hit him on the ear, which is dangerous. Louisa agrees with this passionately. She hit him on the ear, and she *meant* to hit him on the ear, because he messed up her china collection. Henry says that this is a lie. Little Toby turns away from the woodbox to throw in some evidence for Louisa. Henry claps his hand over little Toby's mouth. Francis separates the two boys but accidentally pushes Toby into the woodbox. Toby begins to cry. Louisa is already crying. Just then, Julia Weed comes into that part of the room where the table is laid. She is a pretty, intelligent woman, and the white in her hair is premature. She does not seem to notice the fracas. "Hello, darling," she says serenely to Francis. "Wash your hands, everyone. Dinner is ready." She strikes a match and lights the six candles in this vale of tears.

This simple announcement, like the war cries of the Scottish chieftains, only refreshes the ferocity of the combatants. Louisa gives Henry a blow on the shoulder. Henry, although he seldom cries, has pitched nine innings and is tired. He bursts into tears. Little Toby discovers a splinter in his hand and begins to howl. Francis says loudly that he has been in a plane crash and that he is tired. Julia appears again from the kitchen and, still ignoring the chaos, asks Francis to go upstairs and tell Helen that everything is ready. Francis is happy to go; it is like getting back to headquarters company. He is planning to tell his oldest daughter about the airplane crash, but Helen is lying on her bed reading a *True Romance* magazine, and the first thing Francis does is to take the magazine from her hand and remind Helen that he has forbidden her to buy it. She did not buy it, Helen replies. It was given to her by her best friend, Bessie Black. Everybody reads *True Romance*. Bessie Black's father reads *True Romance*. There isn't a girl in Helen's class who doesn't read *True Romance*. Francis expresses his detestation of the magazine and then tells her that dinner is ready—although from the sounds downstairs it doesn't seem so. Helen follows him down the stairs. Julia has seated herself in the candlelight and spread a napkin over her lap. Neither Louisa nor Henry has come to the table. Little Toby is still howling, lying face down on the floor. Francis speaks to him gently: "Daddy was in a plane crash this afternoon, Toby. Don't you want to hear about it?" Toby goes on crying. "If you don't come to the table now, Toby," Francis says, "I'll have to send you to bed without any supper." The little boy rises, gives him a cutting look, flies up the stairs to his bedroom, and slams the door. "Oh dear," Julia says, and starts to go after him. Francis says that she will spoil him. Julia says that Toby is ten pounds underweight and has to be encouraged to eat. Winter is coming, and he will spend the cold months in bed unless he has his dinner. Julia goes upstairs. Francis sits down at the table with Helen. Helen is suffering from the dismal feeling of having read too intently on a fine day, and she gives her father and the room a jaded look. She doesn't understand about the plane crash, because there wasn't a drop of rain in Shady Hill.

Julia returns with Toby, and they all sit down and are served. "Do I have to look at that big, fat slob?" Henry says, of Louisa. Everybody but Toby enters into this skirmish, and it rages up and down the table for five minutes. Toward the end, Henry puts his napkin over his head and, trying to eat that way, spills spinach all over his shirt. Francis asks Julia if the children couldn't have their dinner earlier. Julia's guns are loaded for this. She can't cook two dinners and lay two tables. She paints with lightning strokes that panorama of drudgery in which her youth, her beauty, and her wit have been lost. Francis says that he must be understood; he was nearly killed in an airplane crash, and he doesn't like to come home every night to a battlefield. Now Julia is deeply concerned. Her voice trembles. He doesn't come home every night to a battlefield. The accusation is stupid and mean. Everything was tranquil until he arrived. She stops speaking, puts down her knife and fork, and looks into her plate as if it is a gulf. She begins to cry. "Poor Mummy!" Toby says, and when Julia gets up from the table, drying her tears with a napkin, Toby goes to her side. "Poor Mummy," he says. "Poor Mummy!" And they climb the stairs together. The other children drift away from the battlefield, and Francis goes into the back garden for a cigarette and some air.

It was a pleasant garden, with walks and flower beds and places to sit. The sunset had nearly burned out, but there was still plenty of light. Put into a thoughtful mood by the crash and the battle, Francis listened to the evening sounds of Shady Hill. "Varmints! Rascals!" old Mr. Nixon shouted to the squirrels in his bird-feeding station. "Avaunt and quit my sight!" A door slammed. Someone was cutting grass. Then Donald Goslin, who lived at the corner, began to play the "Moonlight Sonata." He did this nearly every night. He threw the tempo out the window and played it *rubato* from beginning to end, like an outpouring of tearful petulance, lonesomeness, and self-pity—of everything it was Beethoven's greatness not to know. The music rang up and down the street beneath the trees like an appeal for love, for tenderness, aimed at some lovely housemaid—some fresh-faced, homesick girl from Galway, looking at old snapshots in her third-floor room. "Here, Jupiter, here, Jupiter," Francis called to the Mercers' retriever. Jupiter crashed through the tomato vines with the remains of a felt hat in his mouth.

Jupiter was an anomaly. His retrieving instincts and his high spirits were out of place in Shady Hill. He was as black as coal, with a long, alert, intelligent, rakehell face. His eyes gleamed with mischief, and he held his head high. It was the fierce, heavily collared dog's head that appears in heraldry, in tapestry, and that used to appear on umbrella handles and walking sticks. Jupiter went where he pleased, ransacking waste-baskets, clotheslines, garbage pails, and shoe bags. He broke up garden parties and tennis matches, and got mixed up in the processional at Christ Church on Sunday, barking at the men in red dresses. He crashed through old Mr. Nixon's rose garden two or three times a day, cutting a wide swath through the Condesa de Sastagos, and as soon as Donald Goslin lighted his barbecue fire on Thursday nights, Jupiter would get the scent. Nothing the Goslins did could drive him away. Sticks and stones and rude commands only moved him to the edge of the terrace, where he remained, with his gallant and heraldic muzzle, waiting for Donald Goslin to turn his back and reach for the salt. Then he would spring onto the terrace, lift the steak lightly off the fire, and run away with the Goslins' dinner. Jupiter's days were numbered. The Wrightsons' German gardener or the Farquarsons' cook would soon poison him. Even old Mr. Nixon might put some arsenic in the garbage that Jupiter loved. "Here, Jupiter, Jupiter!" Francis called, but the dog pranced off, shaking the hat in his white teeth. Looking at the windows of his house, Francis saw that Julia had come down and was blowing out the candles.

Julia and Francis Weed went out a great deal. Julia was well liked and gregarious, and her love of parties sprang from a most natural dread of chaos and loneliness. She went through her morning mail with real anxiety, looking for invitations, and she usually found some, but she was insatiable, and if she had gone out seven nights a week, it would not have cured her of a reflective look—the look of someone who hears distant music—for she would always suppose that there was a more brilliant party somewhere else. Francis limited her to two week-night parties, putting a flexible interpretation on Friday, and rode through the weekend like a dory in a gale. The day after the airplane crash, the Weeds were to have dinner with the Farquarsons.

Francis got home late from town, and Julia got the sitter while he dressed, and then hurried him out of the house. The party was small and pleasant, and Francis settled down to enjoy himself. A new maid passed the drinks. Her hair was dark, and her face was round and pale and seemed familiar to Francis. He had not developed his memory as a sentimental faculty. Wood smoke, lilac, and other such perfumes did not stir him, and his memory was something like his appendix—a vestigial repository. It was not his limitation at all to be unable to escape the past; it was perhaps his limitation that he had escaped it so successfully. He might have seen the maid at other parties, he might have seen her taking a walk on Sunday afternoons, but in either case he would not be searching his memory now. Her face was, in a wonderful way, a moon face—Norman or Irish—but it was not beautiful enough to account for his feeling that he had seen her before, in circumstances that he ought to be able to remember. He asked Nellie Farquarson who she was. Nellie said that the maid had come through an agency, and that her home was Trenon, in Normandy—a small place with a church and a restaurant that Nellie had once visited. While Nellie talked on about her travels abroad, Francis realized where he had seen the woman before. It had been at the end of the war. He had left a replacement depot with some other men and taken a three-day pass in Trenon. On their second day, they had walked out to a crossroads to see the public chastisement of a young woman who had lived with the German commandant during the Occupation.

It was a cool morning in the fall. The sky was overcast, and poured down onto the dirt crossroads a very discouraging light. They were on high land and could see how like one another the shapes of the clouds and the hills were as they stretched off toward the sea. The prisoner arrived sitting on a three-legged stool in a farm cart. She stood by the cart while the Mayor read the accusation and the sentence. Her head was bent and her face was set in that empty half smile behind which the whipped soul is suspended. When the Mayor was finished, she undid her hair and let it fall across her back. A little man with a gray mustache cut off her hair with shears and dropped it on the ground. Then, with a bowl of soapy water and a straight razor, he shaved her skull clean. A woman approached and began to undo the fastenings of her clothes, but the prisoner pushed her aside and undressed herself. When she pulled the chemise over her head and threw it on the ground, she was naked. The women jeered; the men were still. There was no change in the falseness or the plaintiveness of the prisoner's smile. The cold wind made her white skin rough and hardened the nipples of her breasts. The jeering ended gradually, put down by the recognition of their common humanity. One woman spat on her, but some inviolable grandeur in her nakedness lasted through the ordeal. When the crowd was quiet, she turned—she had begun to cry—and, with nothing on but a pair of worn black shoes and stockings, walked down the dirt road alone away from the village. The round white face had aged a little, but there was no question but that the maid who passed his cocktails and later served Francis his dinner was the woman who had been punished at the crossroads.

The war seemed now so distant and that world where the cost of partisanship had been death or torture so long ago. Francis had lost track of the men who had been with him in Vesey. He could not count on Julia's discretion. He could not tell anyone. And if he had told the story now, at the dinner table, it would have been a social as well as a human error. The people in the Farquarsons' living room seemed united in their tacit claim that there had been no past, no war—that there was no danger or trouble in the world. In the recorded history of human arrangements, this extraordinary meeting would have fallen into place, but the atmosphere of Shady Hill made the memory unseemly and impolite. The prisoner withdrew after passing the coffee, but the encounter left Francis feeling languid; it had opened his memory and his senses, and left them dilated. Julia went into the house. Francis stayed in the car to take the sitter home.

Expecting to see Mrs. Henlein, the old lady who usually stayed with the children, he was surprised when a young girl opened the door and came out onto the lighted stoop. She stayed in the light to count her textbooks. She was frowning and beautiful. Now, the world is full of beautiful young girls, but Francis saw here the difference between beauty and perfection. All those endearing flaws, moles, birthmarks, and healed wounds were missing, and he experienced in his consciousness that moment when music breaks glass, and felt a pang of recognition as strange, deep, and wonderful as anything in his life. It hung from her frown, from an impalpable darkness in her face—a look that impressed him as a direct appeal for love. When she had counted her books, she came down the steps and opened the car door. In the light, he saw that her cheeks were wet. She got in and shut the door.

"You're new," Francis said.

"Yes. Mrs. Henlein is sick. I'm Anne Murchison."

"Did the children give you any trouble?"

"Oh, no, no." She turned and smiled at him unhappily in the dim dashboard light. Her light hair caught on the collar of her jacket, and she shook her head to set it loose.

"You've been crying."

"Yes."

"I hope it was nothing that happened in our house."

"No, no, it was nothing that happened in your house." Her voice was bleak. "It's no secret. Everybody in the village knows. Daddy's an alcoholic, and he just called me from some saloon and gave me a piece of his mind. He thinks I'm immoral. He called just before Mrs. Weed came back."

"I'm sorry."

"Oh, *Lord!*" She gasped and began to cry. She turned toward Francis, and he took her in his arms and let her cry on his shoulder. She shook in his embrace, and this movement accentuated his sense of the fineness of her flesh and bone. The layers of their clothing felt thin, and when her shuddering began to diminish, it was so much like a paroxysm of love that Francis lost his head and pulled her roughly against him. She drew away. "I live on Belleview Avenue," she said. "You go down Lansing Street to the railroad bridge."

"All right." He stared the car.

"You turn left at that traffic light. . . . Now you turn right here and go straight on toward the tracks."

The road Francis took brought him out of his own neighborhood, across the tracks, and toward the river, to a street where the near-poor lived, in houses whose peaked gables and trimmings of wooden lace conveyed the purest feelings of pride and romance, although the houses themselves could not have offered much privacy or comfort, they were all so small. The street was dark, and, stirred by the grace and beauty of the troubled girl, he seemed, in turning into it, to have come into the deepest part of some submerged memory. In the distance, he saw a porch light burning. It was the only one, and she said that the house with the light was where she lived. When he stopped the car, he could see beyond the porch light into a dimly lighted hallway with an old-fashioned clothes tree. "Well, here we are," he said, conscious that a young man would have said something different.

She did not move her hands from the books, where they were folded, and she turned and faced him. There were tears of lust in his eyes. Determinedly—not sadly—he opened the door on his side and walked around to open hers. He took her free hand, letting his fingers in between hers, climbed at her side the two concrete steps, and went up a narrow walk through a front garden where dahlias, marigolds, and roses—things that had withstood the light frosts—still bloomed, and made a bittersweet smell in the night air. At the steps, she freed her hand and then turned and kissed him swiftly. Then she crossed the porch and shut the door. The porch light went out, then the light in the hall. A second later, a light went on upstairs at the side of the house, shining into a tree that was still covered with leaves. It took her only a few minutes to undress and get into bed, and then the house was dark.

Julia was asleep when Francis got home. He opened a second window and got into bed to shut his eyes on that night, but as soon as they were shut—as soon as he had dropped off to sleep—the girl entered his mind, moving with perfect freedom through its shut doors and filling chamber after chamber with her light, her perfume, and the music of her voice. He was crossing the Atlantic with her on the old *Mauretania* and, later, living with her in Paris. When he woke from his dream, he got up and smoked a cigarette at the open window. Getting back into bed, he cast around in his mind for something he desired to do that would injure no one, and he thought of skiing. Up through the dimness in his mind rose the image of a mountain deep in snow. It was late in the day. Wherever his eyes looked, he saw broad and heartening things. Over his shoulder, there was a snow-filled valley, rising into wooded hills where the trees dimmed the whiteness like a sparse coat of hair. The cold deadened all sound but the loud, iron clanking of the lift machinery. The light on the trails was blue, and it was harder than it had been a minute or two earlier to pick the turns, harder to judge—now that the snow was all deep blue— the crust, the ice, the bare spots, and the deep piles of dry powder. Down the mountain he swung, matching his speed against the contours of a slope that had been formed in the first ice age, seeking with ardor some simplicity of feeling and circumstances. Night fell then, and he drank a Martini with some old friend in a dirty country bar.

In the morning, Francis' snow-covered mountain was gone, and he was left with his vivid memories of Paris and the *Mauretania*. He had been bitten gravely. He washed his body, shaved his jaws, drank his coffee, and missed the seven-thirty-one. The train pulled out just as he brought his car to the station, and the longing he felt for the coaches as they drew subbornly away from him reminded him of the humors of love. He waited for the eight-two, on what was now an empty platform. It was a clear morning; the morning seemed thrown like a gleaming bridge of light over his mixed affairs. His spirits were feverish and high. The image of the girl seemed to put him into a relationship to the world that was mysterious and enthralling. Cars were beginning to fill up the parking lot, and he noticed that those that had driven down from the high land above Shady Hill were white with hoarfrost. This first clear sign of autumn thrilled him. An express train—a night train from Buffalo or Albany—came down the tracks between the plat- forms, and he saw that the roofs of the foremost cars were covered with a skin of ice. Struck by the miraculous physicalness of everything, he smiled at the passengers in the dining car, who could be seen eating eggs and wiping their mouths with napkins as they traveled. The sleeping-car compartments, with their soiled bed linen, trailed through the fresh morning like a string of rooming-house windows. Then he saw an extraordinary thing; at one of the bedroom windows sat an unclothed woman of exceptional beauty, combing her golden hair. She passed like an apparition through Shady Hill, combing and combing her hair, and Francis followed her with his eyes until she was out of sight. Then old Mrs. Wrightson joined him on the platform and began to talk.

"Well, I guess you must be surprised to see me here the third morning in a row," she said, "but because of my window curtains I'm becoming a regular commuter. The curtains I bought on Monday I returned on Tuesday, and the curtains I bought Tuesday I'm returning today. On Monday, I got exactly what I wanted—it's a wool tapestry with roses and birds—but when I got them home, I found they were the wrong length. Well, I exchanged them yesterday, and when I got them home, I found they were still the wrong length. Now I'm praying to high heaven that the decorator will have them in the right length, because you know my house, you *know* my living-room windows, and you can imagine what a problem they present. I don't know what to do with them."

"I know what to do with them," Francis said.

"What?"

"Paint them black on the inside, and shut up."

There was a gasp from Mrs. Wrightson, and Francis looked down at her to be sure that she knew he meant to be rude. She turned and walked away from him, so damaged in spirit that she limped. A wonderful feeling enveloped him, as if light were being shaken about him, and he thought again of Venus combing and combing her hair as she drifted through the Bronx. The realization of how many years had passed since he had enjoyed being deliberately impolite sobered him. Among his friends and neighbors, there were brilliant and gifted people—he saw that—but many of them, also, were bores and fools, and he had made the mistake of listening to them all with equal attention. He had confused a lack of discrimination with Christian love, and the confusion seemed general and destructive. He was grateful to the girl for this bracing sensation of indepen- dence. Birds were singing—cardinals and the last of the robins. The sky shone like enamel. Even the smell of ink from his morning paper honed his appetite for life, and the world that was spread out around him was plainly a paradise.

If Francis had believed in some hierarchy of love—in spirits armed with hunting bows, in the capriciousness of Venus and Eros—or even in magical potions, philters, and stews, in scapulae and quarters of the moon, it might have explained his susceptibility and his feverish high spirits. The autumnal loves of middle ages are well publicized, and he guessed that he was face to face with one of these, but there was not a trace of autumn in what he felt. He wanted to sport in the green woods, scratch where he itched, and drink from the same cup.

His secretary, Miss Rainey, was late that morning—she went to a psychiatrist three mornings a week—and when she came in, Francis wondered what advice a psychiatrist would have for him. But the girl promised to bring back into his life something like the sound of music. The realization that this music might lead him straight to a trial for statutory rape at the county courthouse collapsed his happiness. The photograph of his four children laughing into the camera on the beach at Gay Head reproached him. On the letterhead of his firm there was a drawing of the Laocoön, and the figure of the priest and his sons in the coils of the snake appeared to him to have the deepest meaning.

He had lunch with Pinky Trabert. At a conversational level, the mores of his friends were robust and elastic, but he knew that the moral card house would come down on them all—on Julia and the children as well—if he got caught taking advantage of a baby-sitter. Looking back over the recent history of Shady Hill for some precedent, he found there was none. There was no turpitude; there had not been a divorce since he lived there; there had not even been a breath of scandal. Things seemed arranged with more propriety even than in the Kingdom of Heaven. After leaving Pinky, Francis went to a jeweler's and bought the girl a bracelet. How happy this clandestine purchase made him, how stuffy and comical the jeweler's clerks seemed, how sweet the women who passed at his back smelled! On Fifth Avenue, passing Atlas with his shoulders bent under the weight of the world, Francis thought of the strenuousness of containing his physicalness within the patterns he had chosen.

He did not know when he would see the girl next. He had the bracelet in his inside pocket when he got home. Opening the door of his house, he found her in the hall. Her back was to him, and she turned when she heard the door close. Her smile was open and living. Her perfection stunned him like a fine day—a day after a thunderstorm. He seized her and covered her lips with his, and she struggled but she did not have to struggle for long, because just then little Gertrude Flannery appeared from somewhere and said, "Oh, Mr. Weed . . ."

Gertrude was a stray. She had been born with a taste for exploration, and she did not have it in her to center her life with her affectionate parents. People who did not know the Flannerys concluded from Gertrude's behavior that she was the child of a bitterly divided family, where drunken quarrels were the rule. This was not true. The fact that little Gertrude's clothing was ragged and thin was her own triumph over her mother's struggle to dress her warmly and neatly. Garrulous, skinny, and unwashed, she drifted from house to house around the Blenhollow neighborhood, forming and breaking alliances based on an attachment to babies, animals, children her own age, adolescents, and sometimes adults. Opening your front door in the morning, you would find Gertrude sitting on your stoop. Going into the bathroom to shave, you would find Gertrude using the toilet. Looking into your son's crib, you would find it empty, and, looking further, you would find that Gertrude had pushed him in his baby carriage into the next village. She was helpful, pervasive, honest, hungry, and loyal. She never went home of her own choice. When the time to go arrived, she was indifferent to all signs.

"Go home, Gertrude," people could be heard saying in one house or another, night after night. "Go home, Gertrude. It's time for you to go home now, Gertrude." "You had better go home and get your supper, Gertrude." "I told you to go home twenty minutes ago, Gertrude." "Your mother will be worrying about you, Gertrude." "Go home, Gertrude, go home."

There are times when the lines around the human eye seem like shelves of eroded stone and when the staring eye itself strikes us with such a wilderness of animal feeling that we are at a loss. The look Francis gave the little girl was ugly and queer, and it frightened her. He reached into his pockets—his hands were shaking—and took out a quarter. "Go home, Gertrude, go home, and don't tell anyone, Gertrude. Don't—" He choked and ran into the living room as Julia called down to him from upstairs to hurry and dress.

The thought that he would drive Anne Murchison home later that night ran like a golden thread through the events of the party that Francis and Julia went to, and he laughed uproariously at dull jokes, dried a tear when Mabel Mercer told him about the death of her kitten, and stretched, yawned, sighed, and grunted like any other man with a rendezvous at the back of his mind. The bracelet was in his pocket. As he sat talking, the smell of grass was in his nose, and he was wondering where he would park the car. Nobody lived in the old Parker mansion, and the driveway was used as a lovers' lane. Townsend Street was a dead end, and he could park there, beyond the last house. The old lane that used to connect Elm Street to the riverbanks was overgrown, but he had walked there with his children, and he could drive his car deep enough into the brush-woods to be concealed.

The Weeds were the last to leave the party, and their host and hostess spoke of their own married happiness while they all four stood in the hallway saying good night. "She's my girl," their host said, squeezing his wife. "She's my blue sky. After sixteen years, I still bite her shoulders. She makes me feel like Hannibal crossing the Alps."

The Weeds drove home in silence. Francis brought the car up the driveway and sat still, with the motor running. "You can put the car in the garage," Julia said as she got out. "I told the Murchison girl she could leave at eleven. Someone drove her home." She shut the door, and Francis sat in the dark. He would be spared nothing then, it seemed, that a fool was not spared: ravening lewdness, jealousy, this hurt to his feelings that put tears in his eyes, even scorn—for he could see clearly the image he now presented, his arms spread over the steering wheel and his head buried in them for love.

Francis had been a dedicated Boy Scout when he was young, and, remembering the precepts of his youth, he left his office early the next afternoon and played some round-robin squash, but, with his body toned up by exercise and a shower, he realized that he might better have stayed at his desk. It was a frosty night when he got home. The air smelled sharply of change. When he stepped into the house, he sensed an unusual stir. The children were in their best clothes, and when Julia came down, she was wearing a lavender dress and her diamond sunburst. She explained the stir: Mr. Hubber was coming at seven to take their photograph for the Christmas card. She had put out Francis' blue suit and a tie with some color in it, because the picture was going to be in color this year. Julia was lighthearted at the thought of being photographed for Christmas. It was the kind of ceremony she enjoyed.

Francis went upstairs to change his clothes. He was tired from the day's work and tired with longing, and sitting on the edge of the bed had the effect of deepening his weariness. He thought of Anne Murchison, and the physical need to express himself, instead of being restrained by the pink lamps of Julia's dressing table, engulfed him. He went to Julia's desk, took a piece of writing paper, and began to write on it. "Dear Anne, I love you, I love you, I love you . . ." No one would see the letter, and he used no restraint. He used phrases like "heavenly bliss," and "love nest." He salivated, sighed, and trembled. When Julia called him to come down, the abyss between his fantasy and the practical world opened so wide that he felt it affected the muscles of his heart.

Julia and the children were on the stoop, and the photographer and his assistant had set up a double battery of floodlights to show the family and the architectural beauty of the entrance to their house. People who had come home on a late train slowed their cars to see the Weeds being photographed for their Christmas card. A few waved and called to the family. It took half an hour of smiling and wetting their lips before Mr. Hubber was satisfied. The heat of the lights made an unfresh smell in the frosty air, and when they were turned off, they lingered on the retina of Francis' eyes.

Later that night, while Francis and Julia were drinking their coffee in the living room, the doorbell rang. Julia answered the door and let in Clayton Thomas. He had come to pay for some theatre tickets that she had given his mother some time ago, and that Helen Thomas had scrupulously insisted on paying for, though Julia had asked her not to. Julia invited him in to have a cup of coffee. "I won't have any coffee," Clayton said, "but I will come in for a minute." He followed her into the living room, said good evening to Francis, and sat awkwardly in a chair.

Clayton's father had been killed in the war, and the young man's fatherlessness surrounded him like an element. This may have been conspicuous in Shady Hill because the Thomases were the only family that lacked a piece; all the other marriages were intact and productive. Clayton was in his second or third year of college, and he and his mother lived alone in a large house, which she hoped to sell. Clayton had once made some trouble. Years ago, he had stolen some money and run away; he had got to California before they caught up with him. He was tall and homely, wore horn-rimmed glasses, and spoke in a deep voice.

"When do you go back to college, Clayton?" Francis asked.

"I'm not going back," Clayton said. "Mother doesn't have the money, and there's no sense in all this pretense. I'm going to get a job, and if we sell the house, we'll take an apartment in New York."

"Won't you miss Shady Hill?" Julia asked.

"No," Clayton said. "I don't like it."

"Why not?" Francis asked.

"Well, there's a lot here I don't approve of," Clayton said gravely. "Things like the club dances. Last Saturday night, I looked in toward the end and saw Mr. Granner trying to put Mrs. Minot into the trophy case. They were both drunk. I disapprove of so much drinking."

"It was Saturday night," Francis said.

"And all the dovecotes are phony," Clayton said. "And the way people clutter up their lives. I've thought about it a lot, and what seems to me to be really wrong with Shady Hill is that it doesn't have any future. So much energy is spent in perpetuating the place—in keeping out undesirables, and so forth—that the only idea of the future anyone has is just more and more commuting trains and more parties. I don't think that's healthy. I think people ought to be able to dream big dreams about the future. I think people ought to be able to dream great dreams."

"It's too bad you couldn't continue with college," Julia said.

"I wanted to go to divinity school," Clayton said.

"What's your church?" Francis asked.

"Unitarian, Theosophist, Transcendentalist, Humanist," Clayton said.

"Wasn't Emerson a transcendentalist?" Julia asked.

"I mean the English transcendentalists," Clayton said. "All the American transcendentalists were goops."

"What kind of job do you expect to get?" Francis asked.

"Well, I'd like to work for a publisher," Clayton said, "but everyone tells me there's nothing doing. But it's the kind of thing I'm interested in. I'm writing a long verse play about good and evil. Uncle Charlie might get me into a bank, and that would be good for me. I need the discipline. I have a long way to go in forming my character. I have some terrible habits. I talk too much. I think I ought to take vows of silence. I ought to try not to speak for a week, and discipline myself. I've thought of making a retreat at one of the Episcopalian monasteries, but I don't like Trinitarianism."

"Do you have any girl friends?" Francis asked.

"I'm engaged to be married," Clayton said. "Of course, I'm not old enough or rich enough to have my engagement observed or respected or anything, but I bought a simulated emerald for Anne Murchison with the money I made cutting lawns this summer. We're going to be married as soon as she finishes school."

Francis recoiled at the mention of the girl's name. Then a dingy light seemed to emanate from his spirit, showing everything—Julia, the boy, the chairs—in their true colorlessness. It was like a bitter turn of the weather.

"We're going to have a large family," Clayton said. "Her father's a terrible rummy, and I've had my hard times, and we want to have lots of children. Oh, she's wonderful, Mr. and Mrs. Weed, and we have so much in common. We like all the same things. We sent out the same Christmas card last year without planning it, and we both have an allergy to tomatoes, and our eyebrows grow together in the middle. Well, goodnight."

Julia went to the door with him. When she returned, Francis said that Clayton was lazy, irresponsible, affected, and smelly. Julia said that Francis seemed to be getting intolerant; the Thomas boy was young and should be given a chance. Julia had noticed other cases where Francis had been short-tempered. "Mrs. Wrightson has asked everyone in Shady Hill to her anniversary party but us," she said.

"I'm sorry, Julia."

"Do you know why they didn't ask us?"

"Why?"

"Because you insulted Mrs. Wrightson."

"Then you know about it?"

"June Masterson told me. She was standing behind you."

Julia walked in front of the sofa with a small step that expressed, Francis knew, a feeling of anger.

"I did insult Mrs. Wrightson, Julia, and I meant to. I've never liked her parties, and I'm glad she's dropped us."

"What about Helen?"

"How does Helen come into this?"

"Mrs. Wrightson's the one who decides who goes to the assemblies."

"You mean she can keep Helen from going to the dances?"

"Yes."

"I hadn't thought of that."

"Oh. I knew you hadn't thought of it," Julia cried, thrusting hilt-deep into this chink of his armor. "And it makes me furious to see this kind of stupid thoughtlessness wreck everyone's happiness."

"I don't think I've wrecked anyone's happiness."

"Mrs. Wrightson runs Shady Hill and has run it for the last forty years. I don't know what makes you think that in a community like this you can indulge every impulse you have to be insulting, vulgar, and offensive."

"I have very good manners," Francis said, trying to give the evening a turn toward the light.

"Damn you, Francis Weed!" Julia cried, and the spit of her words struck him in the face. "I've worked hard for the social position we enjoy in this place, and I won't stand by and see you wreck it. You must have understood when you settled here that you couldn't expect to live like a bear in a cave."

"I've got to express my likes and dislikes."

"You can conceal your dislikes. You don't have to meet everything head on, like a child. Unless you're anxious to be a social leper. It's no accident that we get asked out a great deal! It's no accident that Helen has so many friends. How would you like to spend your Saturday nights at the movies? How would you like to spend your Sundays raking up dead leaves? How would you like it if your daughter spent the assembly nights sitting at her window, listening to the music from the club? How would you like it—" He did something then that was, after all, not so unaccountable, since her words seemed to raise up between them a wall so deadening that he gagged. He struck her full in the face. She staggered and then, a moment later, seemed composed. She went up the stairs to their room. She didn't slam the door. When Francis followed, a few minutes later, he found her packing a suitcase.

"Julia, I'm very sorry."

"It doesn't matter," she said. She was crying.

"Where do you think you're going?"

"I don't know. I just looked at a timetable. There's an eleven-sixteen into New York. I'll take that."

"You can't go, Julia."

"I can't stay. I know that."

"I'm sorry about Mrs. Wrightson, Julia, and I'm—"

"It doesn't matter about Mrs. Wrightson. That isn't the trouble."

"What is the trouble?"

"You don't love me."

"I do love you, Julia."

"No, you don't."

"Julia, I do love you, and I would like to be as we were—sweet and bawdy and dark—but now there are so many people."

"You hate me."

"I don't hate you, Julia."

"You have no idea of how much you hate me. I think it's subconscious. You don't realize the cruel things you've done."

"What cruel things, Julia?"

"The cruel acts your subconscious drives you to in order to express your hatred of me."

"What, Julia?"

"I've never complained."

"Tell me."

"You don't know what you're doing."

"Tell me."

"Your clothes."

"What do you mean?"

"I mean the way you leave your dirty clothes around in order to express your subconscious hatred of me."

"I don't understand."

"I mean your dirty socks and your dirty pajamas and your dirty underwear and your dirty shirts!" She rose from kneeling by the suitcase and faced him, her eyes blazing and her voice ringing with emotion. "I'm talking about the fact that you've never learned to hang up anything. You just leave your clothes all over the floor where they drop, in order to humiliate me. You do it on purpose!" She fell on the bed, sobbing.

"Julia, darling!" he said, but when she felt his hand on her shoulder she got up.

"Leave me alone," she said. "I have to go." She brushed past him to the closet and came back with a dress. "I'm not taking any of the things you've given me," she said. "I'm leaving my pearls and the fur jacket."

"Oh, Julia!" Her figure, so helpless in its self-deceptions, bent over the suitcase made him nearly sick with pity. She did not understand how desolate her life would be without him. She didn't understand the hours that working women have to keep. She didn't understand that most of her friendships existed within the framework of their marriage, and that without this she would find herself alone. She didn't understand about travel, about hotels, about money. "Julia, I can't let you go! What you don't understand, Julia, is that you've come to be dependent on me."

She tossed her head back and covered her face with her hands. "Did you say that *I* was dependent on *you*?" she asked. "Is that what you said? And who is it that tells you what time to get up in the morning and when to go to bed at night? Who is it that prepares your meals and picks up your dirty clothes and invites your friends to dinner? If it weren't for me, your neckties would be greasy and your clothing would be full of moth holes. You were alone when I met you, Francis Weed, and you'll be alone when I leave. When Mother asked you for a list to send out invitations to our wedding, how many names did you have to give her? Fourteen!"

"Cleveland wasn't my home, Julia."

"And how many of your friends came to the church? Two!"

"Cleveland wasn't my home, Julia."

"Since I'm not taking the fur jacket," she said quietly, "you'd better put it back into storage. There's an insurance policy on the pearls that comes due in January. The name of the laundry and the maid's telephone number—all those things are in my desk. I hope you won't drink too much, Francis. I hope that nothing bad will happen to you. If you do get into serious trouble, you can call me."

"Oh, my darling, I can't let you go!" Francis said. "I can't let you go, Julia!" He took her in his arms.

"I guess I'd better stay and take care of you for a little while longer," she said.

Riding to work in the morning, Francis saw the girl walk down the aisle of the coach. He was surprised; he hadn't realized that the school she went to was in the city, but she was carrying books, she seemed to be going to school. His surprise delayed his reaction, but then he got up clumsily and stepped into the aisle. Several people had come between them, but he could see her ahead of him, waiting for someone to open the car door, and then, as the train swerved, putting out her hand to support herself as she crossed the platform into the next car. He followed her through that car and halfway through another before calling her name—"Anne! Anne!"—but she didn't turn. He followed her into still another car, and she sat down in an aisle seat. Coming up to her, all his feelings warm and bent in her direction, he put his hand on the back of her seat—even this touch warmed him—and leaning down to speak to her, he saw that it was not

Anne. It was an older woman wearing glasses. He went on deliberately into another car, his face red with embarrassment and the much deeper feeling of having his good sense challenged; for if he couldn't tell one person from another, what evidence was there that his life with Julia and the children had as much reality as his dreams of iniquity in Paris or the litter, the grass smell, and the cave-shaped trees in Lovers' Lane.

Late that afternoon, Julia called to remind Francis that they were going out for dinner. A few minutes later, Trace Bearden called. "Look, fellar," Trace said. "I'm calling for Mrs. Thomas. You know? Clayton, that boy of hers, doesn't seem able to get a job, and I wondered if you could help. If you'd call Charlie Bell—I know he's indebted to you—and say a good word for the kid, I think Charlie would—"

"Trace, I hate to say this," Francis said, "but I don't feel that I can do anything for that boy. The kid's worthless. I know it's a harsh thing to say, but it's a fact. Any kindness done for him would backfire in everybody's face. He's just a worthless kid, Trace, and there's nothing to be done about it. Even if we got him a job, he wouldn't be able to keep it for a week. I know that to be a fact. It's an awful thing, Trace, and I know it is, but instead of recommending that kid, I'd feel obligated to warn people against him—people who knew his father and would naturally want to step in and do something. I'd feel obliged to warn them. He's a thief . . . "

The moment this conversation was finished, Miss Rainey came in and stood by his desk. "I'm not going to be able to work for you any more, Mr. Weed," she said. "I can stay until the seventeenth if you need me, but I've been offered a whirlwind of a job, and I'd like to leave as soon as possible."

She went out, leaving him to face alone the wickedness of what he had done to the Thomas boy. His children in their photograph laughed and laughed, glazed with all the bright colors of summer, and he remembered that they had met a bagpiper on the beach that day and he had paid the piper a dollar to play them a battle song of the Black Watch. The girl would be at the house when he got home. He would spend another evening among his kind neighbors, picking and choosing dead-end streets, cart tracks, and the driveways of abandoned houses. There was nothing to mitigate his feeling—nothing that laughter or a game of softball with the children would change—and, thinking back over the plane crash, the Farquarsons' new maid, and Anne Murchison's difficulties with her drunken father, he wondered how he could have avoided arriving at just where he was. He was in trouble. He had been lost once in his life, coming back from a trout stream in the north woods, and he had now the same bleak realization that no amount of cheerfulness or hopefulness or valor or perseverance could help him find, in the gathering dark, the path that he'd lost. He smelled the forest. The feeling of bleakness was intolerable, and he saw clearly that he had reached the point where he would have to make a choice.

He could go to a psychiatrist, like Miss Rainey; he could go to church and confess his lusts; he could go to a Danish massage parlor in the West Seventies that had been recommended by a salesman; he could rape the girl or trust that he would somehow be prevented from doing this; or he could get drunk. It was his life, his boat, and, like every other man, he was made to be the father of thousands, and what harm could there be in a tryst that would make them both feel more kindly toward the world? This was the wrong train of thought, and he came back to the first, the psychiatrist. He had the telephone number of Miss Rainey's doctor, and he called and asked for an immediate appointment. He was insistent with the doctor's secretary—it was his manner in business—and when she said that the doctor's schedule was full for the next few weeks, Francis demanded an appointment that day and was told to come at five.

The psychiatrist's office was in a building that was used mostly by doctors and dentists, and the hallways were filled with the candy smell of mouthwash and memories of pain. Francis' character had been formed upon a series of private resolves—resolves about cleanliness, about going off the high diving board or repeating any other feat that challenged his courage, about punctuality, honesty, and virtue. To abdicate the perfect loneliness in which he had made his most vital decisions shattered his concept of character and left him now in a condition that felt like shock. He was stupefied. The scene for his *miserere mei Deus* was, like the waiting room of so many doctor's offices, a crude token gesture toward the sweets of domestic bliss: a place arranged with antiques, coffee tables, potted plants, and etchings of snow-covered bridges and geese in flight, although there were no children, no marriage bed, no stove, even, in this travesty of a house, where no one had ever spent the night and where the curtained windows looked straight onto a dark air shaft. Francis gave his name and address to a secretary and then saw, at the side of the room, a policeman moving toward him. "Hold it, hold it," the policeman said. "Don't move. Keep your hands where they are."

"I think it's all right, Officer," the secretary began. "I think it will be—"

"Let's make sure," the policeman said, and he began to slap Francis' clothes, looking for what—pistols, knives, an icepick? Finding nothing, he went off and the secretary began a nervous apology: "When you called on the telephone, Mr. Weed, you seemed very excited, and one of the doctor's patients has been threatening his life, and we have to be careful. If you want to go in now?" Francis pushed open a door connected to an electrical chime, and in the doctor's lair sat down heavily, blew his nose into a handkerchief, searched in his pockets for cigarettes, for matches, for something, and said hoarsely, with tears in his eyes, "I'm in love, Dr. Herzog."

It is a week or ten days later in Shady Hill. The seven-fourteen has come and gone, and here and there dinner is finished and the dishes are in the dish-washing machine. The village hangs, morally and economically, from a thread; but it hangs by its thread in the evening light. Donald Goslin has begun to worry the "Moonlight Sonata" again. *Marcato ma sempre pianissimo!* He seems to be wringing out a wet bath towel, but the housemaid does not heed him. She is writing a letter to Arthur Godfrey. In the cellar of his house, Francis Weed is building a coffee table. Dr. Herzog recommends woodwork as a therapy, and Francis finds some true consolation in the simple arithmetic involved and in the holy smell of new wood. Francis is happy. Upstairs, little Toby is crying, because he is tired. He puts off his cowboy hat, gloves, and fringed jacket, unbuckles the belt studded with gold and rubies, the silver bullets and holsters, slips off his suspenders, his checked shirt, and Levi's, and sits on the edge of his bed to pull off his high boots. Leaving this equipment in a heap, he goes to the closet and takes his space suit off a nail. It is a struggle for him to get into the long tights, but he succeeds. He loops the magic cape over his shoulders and, climbing onto the footboard of his bed, he spreads his arms and flies the short distance to the floor, landing with a thump that is audible to everyone in the house but himself.

"Go home, Gertrude, go home," Mrs. Masterson says. "I told you to go home an hour ago, Gertrude. It's way past your suppertime, and your mother will be worried. Go home!" A door on the Babcocks' terrace flies open, and out comes Mrs. Babcock without any clothes on, pursued by a naked husband. (Their children are away at boarding school, and their terrace is screened by a hedge.) Over the terrace they go and in at the kitchen door, as passionate and handsome a nymph and satyr as you will find on any wall in Venice. Cutting the last of the roses in her garden, Julia hears old Mr. Nixon shouting at the squirrels in his bird-feeding station. "Rapscallions! Varmints! Avaunt and quit my sight!" A miserable cat wanders into the garden, sunk in spiritual and physical discomfort. Tied to its head is a small straw hat—a doll's hat—and it is securely buttoned into a doll's dress, from the skirts of which protrudes its long, hairy tail. As it walks, it shakes its feet, as if it had fallen into water.

"Here, pussy, pussy, pussy!" Julia calls.

"Here, pussy, here, poor pussy!" But the cat gives her a skeptical look and stumbles away in its skirts. The last to come is Jupiter. He prances through the tomato vines, holding in his generous mouth the remains of an evening slipper. Then it is dark; it is a night where kings in golden suits ride elephants over the mountains.

Bernard Malamud (1914–   )

Bernard Malamud's first novel *The Natural* (1952) was a mythic treatment of a baseball player; it signaled the advent of a writer who combines fantasy and realism to create works of imagination that are fresh, humorous, and profound. His imagery, cadences, metaphors, his themes, plots, and characters express a unique modern tragicomic vision. He is easily one of the most distinctive voices in American fiction, and he seems equally at home in the short story and the novel. In 1957 his novel *The Assistant* appeared and instantly won a high place among American novels of our era, and in 1959 his volume of short stories *The Magic Barrel*, whose title story follows this note, received the National Book Award. He has since published several volumes of stories and several novels.

Although his work transcends its subject matter and has universal implications for our age, it deals almost always with the Jewish experience, an experience which provided him an approach to reality and a tone for presenting it. The mixture of the tragic and comic is common in the literature of the people whose will to survive was fueled in part by comic irony.

Malamud's characters, like Leo Finkle in "The Magic Barrel," are often caught in a "ghetto" of the spirit, unable to experience human love or understanding. Suffering and defeat are their lot, but out of suffering comes a hint of redemption and out of defeat perhaps an approximate victory of the spirit. But Malamud's endings hardly provide the kind of uplift the reader may hope for: for at the heart of his vision lies ironic ambiguity.

Thus, after Finkle has persuaded the reader that he will "convert [the prostitute] to goodness, himself to God," and "Violins and lit candles revolved in the sky," then Malamud points out that "Around the corner, Salzman leaning against the wall, chanted prayers for the dead." Prayers for the dead! Just as the reader relaxes into satisfaction, the writer undercuts him.

Hopes dashed can be hard on a reader. What makes this ending endurable is the comic quality which has prepared us to expect almost anything. All of Malamud has this comic quality (even *The Fixer*, which takes place largely in a prison). Theodore Solotaroff says that Malamud's is an "implacably comic world of absurd reversals and last straws and of uncertain stairs that lead seemingly nowhere."

Often, as in "The Magic Barrel," the beginning of a Malamud story is flat, matter-of-fact, comically prosaic, accepting the bizarre (the rabbinical student who seeks a wife in order to get a better congregation) as if it were perfectly usual. That same flat tone tells the reader that the matchmaker "appeared one night out of the dark fourth-floor hallway" and was of "slight but dignified build" and "smelled frankly of fish." These hints prepare the reader to accept the later fantasy.

Soon the incongruities deepen: between piety and rascality, the satiric and the portentous, the ironic and the spiritual. The most significant disparity is between naturalism (lonely widows, elderly spinsters, lame girls, all craving love, all losers) and the marvelous (the sudden appearances of the matchmaker, the picture of his daughter falling from the packet). And over the whole story hovers the quality of Yiddish speech: inversions, questions, analogies, exaggerations, the persistent rhythms, the cadence.

But comedy is certainly not the whole story. Important notions find expression. Leo comes to understand that his life has been empty. He suffers, and out of his suffering, a little miracle occurs, and he is redeemed. Or is he?

The Magic Barrel

Not long ago there lived in uptown New York, in a small almost meager room, though crowded with books, Leo Finkle, a rabbinical student in the Yeshivah University. Finkle, after six years of study, was to be ordained in June and had been advised by an acquaintance that he might find it easier to win himself a congregation if he were married. Since he had no present prospects of marriage, after two tormented days of turning it over in his mind, he called in Pinye Salzman, a marriage broker whose two-line advertisement he had read in the *Forward*.

The matchmaker appeared one night out of the dark fourth-floor hallway of the graystone rooming house where Finkle lived, grasping a black, strapped portfolio that had been worn thin with use. Salzman, who had been long in the business, was of slight but dignified build, wearing an old hat, and an overcoat too short and tight for him. He smelled frankly of fish, which he loved to eat, and although he was missing a few teeth, his presence was not displeasing, because of an amiable manner curiously contrasted with mournful eyes. His voice, his lips, his wisp of beard, his bony fingers were animated, but give him a moment of repose and his mild blue eyes revealed a depth of sadness, a characteristic that put Leo a little at ease although the situation, for him, was inherently tense.

He at once informed Salzman why he had asked him to come, explaining that his home was in Cleveland, and that but for his parents, who had married comparatively late in life, he was alone in the world. He had for six years devoted himself almost entirely to his studies, as a result of which, understandably, he had found himself without time for a social life and the company of young women. Therefore he thought it the better part of trial and error—of embarrassing fumbling—to call in an experienced person to advise him on these matters. He remarked in passing that the function of the marriage broker was ancient and honorable, highly approved in the Jewish community, because it made practical the necessary without hindering joy. Moreover, his own parents had been brought together by a matchmaker. They had made, if not a financially profitable marriage—since neither had possessed any worldly goods to speak of—at least a successful one in the sense of their everlasting devotion to each other. Salzman listened in embarrassed surprise, sensing a sort of apology. Later, however, he experienced a glow of pride in his work, an emotion that had left him years ago, and he heartily approved of Finkle.

The two went to their business. Leo had led Salzman to the only clear place in the room, a table near a window that overlooked the lamp-lit city. He seated himself at the matchmaker's side but facing him, attempting by an act of will to suppress the unpleasant tickle in his throat. Salzman eagerly unstrapped his portfolio and removed a loose rubber band from a thin packet of much-handled cards. As he flipped through them, a gesture and sound that physically hurt Leo, the student pretended not to see and gazed steadfastly out the window. Although it was still February, winter was on its last legs, signs of which he had for the first time in years begun to notice. He now observed the round white moon, moving high in the sky through a cloud menagerie, and watched with half-open mouth as it penetrated a huge hen, and dropped out of her like an egg laying itself. Salzman, though pretending through eyeglasses he had just slipped on, to be engaged in scanning the writing on the cards, stole occasional glances at the young man's distinguished face, noting with pleasure the long, severe scholar's nose, brown eyes heavy with learning, sensitive yet ascetic lips, and a certain, almost hollow quality of the dark cheeks. He gazed around at shelves upon shelves of books and let out a soft, contented sigh.

When Leo's eyes fell upon the cards, he counted six spread out in Salzman's hand.

"So few?" he asked in disappointment.

"You wouldn't believe me how much cards I got in my office," Salzman replied. "The drawers are already filled to the top, so I keep them now in a barrel, but is every girl good for a new rabbi?"

Leo blushed at this, regretting all he had revealed of himself in a curriculum vitae he had sent to Salzman. He had thought it best to acquaint him with his strict standards and specifications, but in having done so, felt he had told the marriage broker more than was absolutely necessary.

He hesitantly inquired, "Do you keep photographs of your clients on file?"

"First comes family, amount of dowry, also what kind promises," Salzman replied, unbuttoning his tight coat and settling himself in the chair. "After comes pictures, rabbi."

"Call me Mr. Finkle. I'm not yet a rabbi."

Salzman said he would, but instead called him doctor, which he changed to rabbi when Leo was not listening too attentively.

Salzman adjusted his horn-rimmed spectacles, gently cleared his throat and read in an eager voice the contents of the top card:

"Sophie P. Twenty four years. Widow one year. No children. Educated high school and two years college. Father promises eight thousand dollars. Has wonderful wholesale business. Also real estate. On the mother's side comes teachers, also one actor. Well known on Second Avenue."

Leo gazed up in surprise. "Did you say a widow?"

"A widow don't mean spoiled, rabbi. She lived with her husband maybe four months. He was a sick boy she made a mistake to marry him."

"Marrying a widow has never entered my mind."

"This is because you have no experience. A widow, especially if she is young and healthy like this girl, is a wonderful person to marry. She will be thankful to you the rest of her life. Believe me, if I was looking now for a bride, I would marry a widow."

Leo reflected, then shook his head.

Salzman hunched his shoulders in an almost imperceptible gesture of disappointment. He placed the card down on the wooden table and began to read another:

"Lily H. High school teacher. Regular. Not a substitute. Has savings and new Dodge car. Lived in Paris one year. Father is successful dentist thirty-five years. Interested in professional man. Well Americanized family. Wonderful opportunity."

"I knew her personally," said Salzman. "I wish you could see this girl. She is a doll. Also very intelligent. All day you could talk to her about books and theyater and what not. She also knows current events."

"I don't believe you mentioned her age?"

"Her age?" Salzman said, raising his brows. "Her age is thirty-two years."

Leo said after a while, "I'm afraid that seems a little too old."

Salzman let out a laugh. "So how old are you, rabbi?"

"Twenty-seven."

"So what is the difference, tell me, between twenty-seven and thirty-two? My own wife is seven years older than me. So what did I suffer?—Nothing. If Rothschild's a daughter wants to marry you, would you say on account her age, no?"

"Yes," Leo said dryly.

Salzman shook off the no in the yes. "Five years don't mean a thing. I give you my word that when you will live with her for one week you will forget her age. What does it mean five years—that she lived more and knows more than somebody who is younger? On this girl, God bless her, years are not wasted. Each one that it comes makes better the bargain."

"What subject does she teach in high school?"

"Languages. If you heard the way she speaks French, you will think it is music. I am in the business twenty-five years, and I recommend her with my whole heart. Believe me, I know what I'm talking, rabbi."

"What's on the next card?" Leo said abruptly.

Salzman reluctantly turned up the third card:

"Ruth K. Nineteen years. Honor student. Father offers thirteen thousand cash to the right bridegroom. He is a medical doctor. Stomach specialist with marvelous practice. Brother in law owns own garment business. Particular people."

Salzman looked as if he had read his trump card.

"Did you say nineteen?" Leo asked with interest.

"On the dot."

"Is she attractive?" He blushed. "Pretty?"

Salzman kissed her finger tips. "A little doll. On this I give you my word. Let me call the father tonight and you will see what means pretty."

But Leo was troubled. "You're sure she's that young?"

"This I am positive. The father will show you the birth certificate."

"Are you positive there isn't something wrong with her?" Leo insisted.

"Who says there is wrong?"

"I don't understand why an American girl her age should go to a marriage broker."

A smile spread over Salzman's face.

"So for the same reason you went, she comes."

Leo flushed. "I am pressed for time."

Salzman, realizing he had been tactless, quickly explained. "The father came, not her. He wants she should have the best, so he looks around himself. When we will locate the right boy he will introduce him and encourage. This makes a better marriage than if a young girl without experience takes for herself. I don't have to tell you this."

"But don't you think this young girl believes in love?" Leo spoke uneasily.

Salzman was about to guffaw but caught himself and said soberly, "Love comes with the right person, not before."

Leo parted dry lips but did not speak. Noticing that Salzman had snatched a glance at the next card, he cleverly asked, "How is her health?"

"Perfect," Salzman said, breathing with difficulty. "Of course, she is a little lame on her right foot from an auto accident that it happened to her when she was twelve years, but nobody notices on account she is so brilliant and also beautiful."

Leo got up heavily and went to the window. He felt curiously bitter and upbraided himself for having called in the marriage broker. Finally, he shook his head.

"Why not?" Salzman persisted, the pitch of his voice rising.

"Because I detest stomach specialists."

"So what do you care what is his business? After you marry her do you need him? Who says he must come every Friday night in your house?"

Ashamed of the way the talk was going, Leo dismissed Salzman, who went home with heavy, melancholy eyes.

Though he had felt only relief at the marriage broker's departure, Leo was in low spirits the next day. He explained it as arising from Salzman's failure to produce a suitable bride for him. He did not care for this type of clientele. But when Leo found himself hesitating whether to seek out another matchmaker, one more polished than Pinye, he wondered if it could be—his protestations to the contrary, and although he honored his father and mother—that he did not, in essence, care for the matchmaking institution? This thought he quickly put out of mind yet found himself still upset. All day he ran around in the woods—missed an important appointment, forgot to give out his laundry, walked out of a Broadway cafeteria without paying and had to run back with the ticket in his hand; had even not recognized his landlady in the street when she passed with a friend and courteously called out, "A good evening to you, Doctor Finkle." By nightfall, however, he had regained sufficient calm to sink his nose into a book and there found peace from his thoughts.

Almost at once there came a knock on the door. Before Leo could say enter, Salzman, commercial cupid, was standing in the room. His face was gray and meager, his expression hungry, and he looked as if he would expire on his feet. Yet the marriage broker managed, by some trick of the muscles, to display a broad smile.

"So good evening. I am invited?"

Leo nodded, disturbed to see him again, yet unwilling to ask the man to leave.

Beaming still, Salzman laid his portfolio on the table, "Rabbi, I got for you tonight good news."

"I've asked you not to call me rabbi. I'm still a student."

"Your worries are finished. I have for you a first-class bride."

"Leave me in peace concerning this subject." Leo pretended lack of interest.

"The world will dance at your wedding."

"Please, Mr. Salzman, no more."

"But first must come back my strength," Salzman said weakly. He fumbled with the portfolio straps and took out of the leather case an oily paper bag, from which he extracted a hard, seeded roll and a small, smoked white fish. With a quick motion of his hand he stripped the fish out of its skin and began ravenously to chew. "All day in a rush," he muttered.

Leo watched him eat.

"A sliced tomato you have maybe?" Salzman hesitantly inquired.

"No."

The marriage broker shut his eyes and ate. When he had finished he carefully cleaned up the crumbs and rolled up the remains of the fish, in the paper bag. His spectacled eyes roamed the room until he discovered, amid some piles of books, a one-burner gas stove. Lifting his hat he humbly asked, "A glass tea you got, rabbi?"

Conscience-stricken, Leo rose and brewed the tea. He served it with a chunk of lemon and two cubes of lump sugar, delighting Salzman.

After he had drunk his tea, Salzman's strength and good spirits were restored.

"So tell me, rabbi," he said amiably, "you consider some more the three clients I mentioned yesterday?"

"There was no need to consider."

"Why not?"

"None of them suits me."

"What then suits you?"

Leo let it pass because he could give only a confused answer.

Without waiting for a reply, Salzman asked, "You remember this girl I talked to you—the high school teacher?"

"Age thirty-two?"

But, surprisingly, Salzman's face lit in a smile. "Age twenty-nine."

Leo shot him a look. "Reduced from thirty-two?"

"A mistake," Salzman avowed, "I talked today with the dentist. He took me to his safety deposit box and showed me the birth certificate. She was twenty-nine years last August. They made her a party in the mountains where she went for her vacation. When her father spoke to me the first time I forgot to write the age and I told you thirty-two, but now I remember this was a different client, a widow."

"The same one you told me about? I thought she was twenty-four?"

"A different. Am I responsible that the world is filled with widows?"

"No, but I'm not interested in them, nor for that matter, in school teachers."

Salzman pulled his clasped hands to his breast. Looking at the ceiling he devoutly exclaimed, "Yiddishe kinder, what can I say to somebody that he is not interested in high school teachers? So what then you are interested?"

Leo flushed but controlled himself.

"In what else will you be interested," Salzman went on, "if you are not interested in this fine girl that speaks four languages and has personally in the bank ten thousand dollars? Also her father guarantees further twelve thousand. Also she has a new car, wonderful clothes, talks on all subjects, and she will give you a first-class home and children. How near do we come in our life to paradise?"

"If she's so wonderful, why hasn't she married ten years ago?"

"Why?" said Salzman with a heavy laugh. "—Why? Because she is *partikiler*. This is why. She wants the *best*."

Leo was silent, amused at how he had entangled himself. But Salzman had aroused his interest in Lily H., and he began seriously to consider calling on her. When the marriage broker observed how intently Leo's mind was at work on the facts he had supplied, he felt certain they would soon come to an agreement.

Late Saturday afternoon, conscious of Salzman, Leo Finkle walked with Lily Hirschorn along Riverside Drive. He walked briskly and erectly, wearing with distinction the black fedora he had that morning taken with trepidation out of the dusty hat box on his closet shelf, and the heavy black Saturday coat he had thoroughly whisked clean. Leo also owned a walking stick, a present from a distant relative, but quickly put temptation aside and did not use it. Lily, petite and not unpretty, had on something signifying the approach of spring. She was au courant, animatedly, with all sorts of subjects, and he weighed her words and found her surprisingly sound—score another for Salzman, whom he uneasily sensed to be somewhere around, hiding perhaps high in a tree along the street, flashing the lady signals with a pocket mirror; or perhaps a cloven-hoofed Pan, piping nuptial ditties as he danced his invisible way before them, strewing wild buds on the walk and purple grapes in their path, symbolizing fruit of a union, though there was of course still none.

Lily startled Leo by remarking, "I was thinking of Mr. Salzman, a curious figure, wouldn't you say?"

Not certain what to answer, he nodded.

She bravely went on, blushing, "I for one am grateful for his introducing us. Aren't you?"

He courteously replied, "I am."

"I mean," she said with a little laugh—and it was all in good taste, or at least gave the effect of being not in bad—"do you mind that we came together so?"

He was not displeased with her honesty, recognizing that she meant to set the relationship aright, and understanding that it took a certain amount of experience in life, and courage, to want to do it quite that way. One had to have some sort of past to make that kind of beginning.

He said that he did not mind. Salzman's function was traditional and honorable— valuable for what it might achieve, which, he pointed out, was frequently nothing.

Lily agreed with a sigh. They walked on for a while and she said after a long silence, again with a nervous laugh, "Would you mind if I asked you something a little bit personal? Frankly, I find the subject fascinating." Although Leo shrugged, she went on half embarrassedly, "How was it that you came to your calling? I mean was it a sudden passionate inspiration?"

Leo, after a time, slowly replied, "I was always interested in the Law."

"You saw revealed in it the presence of the Highest?"

He nodded and changed the subject. "I understand that you spent a little time in Paris, Miss Hirschorn?"

"Oh, did Mr. Salzman tell you, Rabbi Finkle?" Leo winced but she went on, "It was ages ago and almost forgotten. I remember I had to return for my sister's wedding."

And Lily would not be put off. "When," she asked in a trembly voice, "did you become enamored of God?"

He stared at her. Then it came to him that she was talking not about Leo Finkle, but of a total stranger, some mystical figure, perhaps even passionate prophet that Salzman had dreamed up for her—no relation to the living or dead. Leo trembled with rage and weakness. The trickster had obviously sold her a bill of goods, just as he had him, who'd expected to become acquainted with a young lady of twenty-nine, only to behold, the moment he laid eyes upon her strained and anxious face, a woman past thirty-five and aging rapidly. Only his self control had kept him this long in her presence.

"I am not," he said gravely, "a talented religious person," and in seeking words to go on, found himself possessed by shame and fear. "I think," he said in a strained manner, "that I came to God not because I loved Him, but because I did not."

This confession he spoke harshly because its unexpectedness shook him.

Lily wilted. Leo saw a profusion of loaves of bread go flying like ducks high over his head, not unlike the winged loaves by which he had counted himself to sleep last night. Mercifully, then, it snowed, which he would not put past Salzman's machinations.

He was infuriated with the marriage broker and swore he would throw him out of the room the minute he reappeared. But Salzman did not come that night, and when Leo's anger had subsided, an unaccountable despair grew in its place. At first he thought this was caused by his disappointment in Lily, but before long it became evident that he had involved himself with Salzman without a true knowledge of his own intent. He gradually realized—with an emptiness that seized him with six hands—that he had called in the broker to find him a bride because he was incapable of doing it himself. This terrifying insight he had derived as a result of his meeting and conversation with Lily Hirschorn. Her probing questions had somehow irritated him into revealing—to himself more than her—the true nature of his relationship to God, and from that it had come upon him, with shocking force, that apart from his parents, he had never loved anyone. Or perhaps it went the other way, that he did not love God so well as he might, because he had not loved man. It seemed to Leo that his whole life stood starkly revealed and he saw himself for the first time as he truly was—unloved and loveless. This bitter but somehow not fully unexpected revelation brought him to a point of panic, controlled only by extraordinary effort. He covered his face with his hands and cried.

The week that followed was the worst of his life. He did not eat and lost weight. His beard darkened and grew ragged. He stopped attending seminars and almost never opened a book. He seriously considered leaving the Yeshivah, although he was deeply troubled at the thought of the loss of all his years of study—saw them like pages torn from a book, strewn over the city—and at the devastating effect of this decision upon his parents. But he had lived without knowledge of himself, and never in the Five Books and all the Commentaries—mea culpa—had the truth been revealed to him. He did not know where to turn, and in all this desolating loneliness there was no *to whom*, although he often thought of Lily but not once could bring himself to go downstairs and make the call. He became touchy and irritable, especially with his landlady, who asked him all manner of personal questions; on the other hand, sensing his own disagreeableness, he waylaid her on the stairs and apologized abjectly, until mortified, she ran from him. Out of this, however, he drew the consolation that he was a Jew and that a Jew suffered. But gradually, as the long and terrible week drew to a close, he regained his composure and some idea of purpose in life: to go on as planned. Although he was imperfect, the ideal was not. As for his quest for a bride, the thought of continuing afflicted him with anxiety and heartburn, yet perhaps with this new knowledge of himself he would be more successful than in the past. Perhaps love would now come to him and a bride to that love. And for this sanctified seeking who needed a Salzman?

The marriage broker, a skeleton with haunted eyes, returned that very night. He looked, withal, the picture of frustrated expectancy—as if he had steadfastly waited the week at Miss Lily Hirschorn's side for a telephone call that never came.

Casually coughing, Salzman came immediately to the point: "So how did you like her?"

Leo's anger rose and he could not refrain from chiding the matchmaker: "Why did you lie to me, Salzman?"

Salzman's pale face went dead white, the world had snowed on him.

"Did you not state that she was twenty-nine?" Leo insisted.

"I give you my word—"

"She was thirty-five, if a day. *At least* thirty-five."

"Of this don't be too sure. Her father told me—"

"Never mind. The worst of it was that you lied to her."

"How did I lie to her, tell me?"

"You told her things about me that weren't true. You made me out to be more, consequently less than I am. She had in mind a totally different person, a sort of semimystical Wonder Rabbi."

"All I said, you was a religious man."

"I can imagine."

Salzman sighed. "This is my weakness that I have," he confessed. "My wife says to me I shouldn't be a salesman, but when I have two fine people that they would be wonderful to be married, I am so happy that I talk too much." He smiled wanly. "This is why Salzman is a poor man."

Leo's anger left him. "Well, Salzman, I'm afraid that's all."

The marriage broker fastened hungry eyes on him.

"You don't want any more a bride?"

"I do," said Leo, "but I have decided to seek her in a different way. I am no longer interested in an arranged marriage. To be frank, I now admit the necessity of premarital love. That is, I want to be in love with the one I marry."

"Love?" said Salzman, astounded. After a moment he remarked, "For us, our love is our life, not for the ladies. In the ghetto they—"

"I know, I know," said Leo. "I've thought of it often. Love, I have said to myself, should be a by-product of living and worship rather than its own end. Yet for myself I find it necessary to establish the level of my need and fulfill it."

Salzman shrugged but answered, "Listen, rabbi, if you want love, this I can find for you also. I have such beautiful clients that you will love them the minute your eyes will see them."

Leo smiled unhappily. "I'm afraid you don't understand."

But Salzman hastily unstrapped his portfolio and withdrew a manila packet from it.

"Pictures," he said, quickly laying the envelope on the table.

Leo called after him to take the pictures away, but as if on the wings of the wind, Salzman had disappeared.

March came. Leo had returned to his regular routine. Although he felt not quite himself yet—lacked energy—he was making plans for a more active social life. Of course it would cost something, but he was an expert in cutting corners; and when there were no corners left he would make circles rounder. All the while Salzman's pictures had lain on the table, gathering dust. Occasionally as Leo sat studying, or enjoying a cup of tea, his eyes fell on the manila envelope, but he never opened it.

The days went by and no social life to speak of developed with a member of the opposite sex—it was difficult, given the circumstances of his situation. One morning Leo toiled up the stairs to his room and stared out the window at the city. Although the day was bright his view of it was dark. For some time he watched the people in the street below hurrying along and then turned with a heavy heart to his little room. On the table was the packet. With a sudden relentless gesture he tore it open. For a half-hour he stood by the table in a state of excitement, examining the photographs of the ladies Salzman had included. Finally, with a deep sigh he put them down. There were six, of varying degrees of attractiveness, but look at them long enough and they all became Lily Hirschorn: all past their prime, all starved behind bright smiles, not a true personality in the lot. Life, despite their frantic yoohooings, had passed them by; they were pictures in a brief case that stank of fish. After a while, however, as Leo attempted to return the photographs into the envelope, he found in it another, a snapshot of the type taken by a machine for a quarter. He gazed at it a moment and let out a cry.

Her face deeply moved him. Why, he could at first not say. It gave him the impression of youth—spring flowers, yet age—a sense of having been used to the bone, wasted; this came from the eyes which were hauntingly familiar, yet absolutely strange. He had a vivid impression that he had met her before, but try as he might he could not place her although he could almost recall her name, as if he had read it in her own handwriting. No, this couldn't be; he would have remembered her. It was not, he affirmed, that she had an extraordinary beauty—no, though her face was attractive enough; it was that *something* about her moved him. Feature for feature, even some of the ladies of the photographs could do better; but she leaped forth to his heart—had *lived,* or wanted to—more than just wanted, perhaps regretted how she had lived—had somehow deeply suffered: it could be seen in the depths of those reluctant eyes, and from the way the light enclosed and shone from her, and within her, opening realms of possibility: this was her own. Her he desired. His head ached and eyes narrowed with the intensity of his gazing, then as if an obscure fog had blown up in the mind, he experienced fear of her and was aware that he had received an impression, somehow, of evil. He shuddered, saying softly, it is thus with us all. Leo brewed some tea in a small pot and sat sipping it without sugar, to calm himself. But before he had finished drinking, again with excitement he examined the face and found it good: good for Leo Finkle. Only such a one could understand him and help him seek whatever he was seeking. She might, perhaps, love him. How she had happened to be among the discards in Salzman's barrel he could never guess, but he must urgently go find her.

Leo rushed downstairs, grabbed up the Bronx telephone book, and searched for Salzman's home address. He was not listed, nor was his office. Neither was he in the Manhattan book. But Leo remembered having written down the address on a slip of paper after he had read Salzman's advertisement in the "personals" column of the *Forward.* He ran up to his room and tore through his papers, without luck. It was exasperating. Just when he needed the matchmaker he was nowhere to be found. Fortunately Leo remembered to look in his wallet. There on a card he found his name written and a Bronx address. No phone number was listed, the reason—Leo now recalled—he had originally communicated with Salzman by letter. He got on his coat, put a hat on over his skull cap and hurried to the subway station. All the way to the far end of the Bronx he sat on the edge of his seat. He was more than once tempted to take out the picture and see if the girl's face was as he remembered it, but he refrained, allowing the snapshot to remain in his inside coat pocket, content to have her so close. When the train pulled into the station he was waiting at the door and bolted out. He quickly located the street Salzman had advertised.

The building he sought was less than a block from the subway, but it was not an office building, nor even a loft, nor a store in which one could rent office space. It was a very old tenement house. Leo found Salzman's name in pencil on a soiled tag under the bell and climbed three dark flights to his apartment. When he knocked, the door was opened by a thin, asthmatic, gray-haired woman, in felt slippers.

"Yes?" she said, expecting nothing. She listened without listening. He could have sworn he had seen her, too, before but knew it was an illusion.

"Salzman—does he live here? Pinye Salzman," he said, "the matchmaker?"

She stared at him a long minute. "Of course."

He felt embarrassed. "Is he in?"

"No." Her mouth, though left open, offered nothing more.

"The matter is urgent. Can you tell me where his office is?"

"In the air." She pointed upward.

"You mean he has no office?" Leo asked.

"In his socks."

He peered into the apartment. It was sunless and dingy, one large room divided by a half-open curtain, beyond which he could see a sagging metal bed. The near side of a room was crowded with rickety chairs, old bureaus, a three-legged table, racks of cooking utensils, and all the apparatus of a kitchen. But there was no sign of Salzman or his magic barrel, probably also a figment of the imagination. An odor of frying fish made Leo weak to the knees.

"Where is he?" he insisted. "Ive got to see your husband."

At length she answered, "So who knows where he is? Every time he thinks a new thought he runs to a different place. Go home, he will find you."

"Tell him Leo Finkle."

She gave no sign she had heard.

He walked downstairs, depressed.

But Salzman, breathless, stood waiting at his door.

Leo was astounded and overjoyed. "How did you get here before me?"

"I rushed."

"Come inside."

They enetered. Leo fixed tea, and a sardine sandwich for Salzman. As they were drinking he reached behind him for the packet of pictures and handed them to the marriage broker.

Salzman put down his glass and said expectantly, "You found somebody you like?"

"Not among these."

The marriage broker turned away.

"Here is the one I want." Leo held forth the snapshot.

Salzman slipped on his glasses and took the picture into his trembling hand. He turned ghastly and let out a groan.

"What's the matter?" cried Leo.

"Excuse me. Was an accident this picture. She isn't for you."

Salzman frantically shoved the manila packet into his portfolio. He thrust the snapshot into his pocket and fled down the stairs.

Leo, after momentary paralysis, gave chase and cornered the marriage broker in the vestibule. The landlady made hysterical outcries but neither of them listened.

"Give me back the picture, Salzman."

"No." The pain in his eyes was terrible.

"Tell me who she is then."

"This I can't tell you. Excuse me."

He made to depart, but Leo, forgetting himself, seized the matchmaker by his tight coat and shook him frenziedly.

"Please," sighed Salzman. "*Please*."

Leo ashamedly let him go. "Tell me who she is," he begged. "It's very important for me to know."

"She is not for you. She is a wild one—wild, without shame. This is not a bride for a rabbi."

"What do you mean wild?"

"Like an animal. Like a dog. For her to be poor was a sin. This is why to me she is dead now."

"In God's name, what do you mean?"

"Her I can't introduce to you," Salzman cried.

"Why are you so excited?"

"Why, he asks," Salzman said, bursting into tears. "This is my baby, my Stella, she should burn in hell."

Leo hurried up to bed and hid under the covers. Under the covers he thought his life through. Although he soon fell asleep he could not sleep her out of his mind. He woke, beating his breast. Though he prayed to be rid of her, his prayers went unanswered. Through days of torment he endlessly struggled not to love her; fearing success, he escaped it. He then concluded to convert her to goodness, himself to God. The idea alternately nauseated and exalted him.

He perhaps did not know that he had come to a final decision until he encountered Salzman in a Broadway cafeteria. He was sitting alone at a rear table, sucking the bony remains of a fish. The marriage broker appeared haggard, and transparent to the point of vanishing.

Salzman looked up at first without recognizing him. Leo had grown a pointed beard and his eyes were weighted with wisdom.

"Salzman," he said, "love has at last come to my heart."

"Who can love from a picture?" mocked the marriage broker.

"It is not impossible."

"If you can love her, then you can love anybody. Let me show you some new clients that they just sent me their photographs. One is a little doll."

"Just her I want," Leo murmured.

"Don't be a fool, doctor. Don't bother with her."

"Put me in touch with her, Salzman," Leo said humbly. "Perhaps I can be of service."

Salzman had stopped eating and Leo understood with emotion that it was now arranged.

Leaving the cafeteria, he was, however, afflicted by a tormenting suspicion that Salzman had planned it all to happen this way.

Leo was informed by letter that she would meet him on a certain corner, and she was there one spring night, waiting under a street lamp. He appeared, carrying a small bouquet of violets and rosebuds. Stella stood by the lamp post, smoking. She wore white with red shoes, which fitted his expectations, although in a troubled moment he had imagined the dress red, and only the shoes white. She waited uneasily and shyly. From afar he saw that her eyes—clearly her father's —were filled with desperate innocence. He pictured, in her, his own redemption. Violins and lit candles revolved in the sky. Leo ran forward with flowers outthrust.

Around the corner, Salzman, leaning against a wall, chanted prayers for the dead.

Carson McCullers (1917–1967)

Carson McCullers was born in Columbus, Georgia, and, as with so many Southern writers, the South is a powerful presence in nearly all of her fiction. Her original ambition was to become a concert pianist, and at the age of seventeen she came to New York to attend the Juilliard School of Music. Unfortunately, she lost her tuition money in the subway on her second day in the city. Her musical career thus quickly ended, she found work to support herself while taking writing courses at Columbia University. Between 4 A.M. and 8 A.M. she worked at her writing and then set off to a full-time clerical job. One of her reviewers reported that she lost one job when her boss caught her reading Proust. In 1936 she suffered a severe attack of rheumatic fever, the first in an almost unbelievable series of illnesses and accidents. In 1940 her first novel, *The Heart is a Lonely Hunter*, was published. It caused an immediate sensation, and to many critics it seemed incredible that it had been written by someone only twenty-two years old. Her next novel, *Reflections in a Golden Eye* (1941), was a critical disaster, but in 1946 she published *The Member of the Wedding*, and in 1951 the dramatic version of that third novel opened on Broadway to overwhelming critical and popular success. In that same year she had the pleasure, at age thirty-four, of seeing a single volume of her collected works appear, the three novels, six stories, and a moving new novella that served as a title piece, *The Ballad of the Sad Café*. From this point on, however, her health and her personal life began to fall apart, and the work she published during the last sixteen years of her life fell far short of the promise and achievement she had already realized. She died of a stroke in 1967.

Many readers have felt the influence of Sherwood Anderson on Carson McCullers's work. Her characters, who are often physically, mentally, or sexually deformed, are "grotesques" in the Anderson tradition. Her constant theme is the search of those alienated misfits for love and understanding. As Louise Gossett says,

> The motif of Carson Smith McCullers' fiction is love, its modes, demands, successes, defeats, grace, and shame. Whatever force, instinct, or need holds the human community together, this is love. The falling apart of the community is signaled by the breakdown of communications between persons, by physical and spiritual isolation, by hatred and fear, by sexual perversion, or by economic and racial injustice, and violence accompanies all negations. Within each negation, however, there is a drive toward a positive alliance. No matter how distorted the relationship may be, Mrs. McCullers has compassion for every attempt of the human being to become a *we* instead of an *I*. . . . Thus the author is charitable toward the violence and grotesqueness which develop when the impulse to love goes astray, and she treats deviations more with mercy than with horror.

We have discussed "A Tree * A Rock * A Cloud" with some fullness in our main introduction. The ending of the story—the old man leaving the boy, going "cautious" into the "gray damp light of the early morning"—receives a most sensitive reaction from Mark Schorer: "They move off, each into his own separateness. The very periods in her title suggest the character of the human situation as she saw it."

A Tree * A Rock * A Cloud

It was raining that morning, and still very dark. When the boy reached the streetcar café he had almost finished his route and he went in for a cup of coffee. The place was an all-night café owned by a bitter and stingy man called Leo. After the raw, empty street, the café seemed friendly and bright: along the counter there were a couple of soldiers, three spinners from the cotton mill, and in a corner a man who sat hunched over with his nose and half his face down in a beer mug. The boy wore a helmet such as aviators wear. When he went into the café he unbuckled the chin strap and raised the right flap up over his pink little ear; often as he drank his coffee someone would speak to him in a friendly way. But this morning Leo did not look into his face and none of the men were talking. He paid and was leaving the café when a voice called out to him:

"Son! Hey Son!"

He turned back and the man in the corner was crooking his finger and nodding to him. He had brought his face out of the beer mug and he seemed suddenly very happy. The man was long and pale, with a big nose and faded orange hair.

"Hey Son!"

The boy went toward him. He was an undersized boy of about twelve, with one shoulder drawn higher than the other because of the weight of the paper sack. His face was shallow, freckled, and his eyes were round child eyes.

"Yeah Mister?"

The man laid one hand on the paper boy's shoulders, then grasped the boy's chin and turned his face slowly from one side to the other. The boy shrank back uneasily.

"Say! What's the big idea?"

The boy's voice was shrill; inside the café it was suddenly very quiet.

The man said slowly: "I love you."

All along the counter the men laughed. The boy, who had scowled and sidled away, did not know what to do. He looked over the counter at Leo, and Leo watched him with a weary, brittle jeer. The boy tried to laugh also. But the man was serious and sad.

"I did not mean to tease you, Son," he said. "Sit down and have a beer with me. There is something I have to explain."

Cautiously, out of the corner of his eye, the paper boy questioned the men along the counter to see what he should do. But they had gone back to their beer or their breakfast and did not notice him. Leo put a cup of coffee on the counter and a little jug of cream.

"He is a minor," Leo said.

The paper boy slid himself up onto the stool. His ear beneath the upturned flap of the helmet was very small and red. The man was nodding at him soberly. "It is important," he said. Then he reached in his hip pocket and brought out something which he held up in the palm of his hand for the boy to see.

"Look very carefully," he said.

The boy stared, but there was nothing to look at very carefully. The man held in his big, grimy palm a photograph. It was the face of a woman, but blurred, so that only the hat and the dress she was wearing stood out clearly.

"See?" the man asked.

The boy nodded and the man placed another picture in his palm. The woman was standing on a beach in a bathing suit. The suit made her stomach very big, and that was the main thing you noticed.

"Got a good look?" He leaned over close and finally asked: "You ever seen her before?"

The boy sat motionless, staring slantwise at the man. "Not so I know of."

"Very well." The man blew on the photographs and put them back into his pocket. "That was my wife."

"Dead?" the boy asked.

Slowly the man shook his head. He pursed his lips as though about to whistle and answered in a long-drawn way; "Nuuu—" he said. "I will explain."

The beer on the counter before the man was in a large brown mug. He did not pick it up to drink. Instead he bent down and, putting his face over the rim, he rested there for a moment. Then with both hands he tilted the mug and sipped.

"Some night you'll go to sleep with your nose in a mug and drown," said Leo. "Prominent transient drowns in beer. That would be a cute death."

The paper boy tried to signal to Leo. While the man was not looking he screwed up his face and worked his mouth to question soundless: "Drunk?" But Leo only raised his eyebrows and turned away to put some pink strips of bacon on the grill. The man pushed the mug away from him, straightened himself, and folded his loose crooked hands on the counter. His face was sad as he looked at the paper boy. He did not blink, but from time to time the lids closed down with delicate gravity over his pale green eyes. It was nearing dawn and the boy shifted the weight of the paper sack.

"I am talking about love," the man said. "With me it is a science."

The boy half slid down from the stool. But the man raised his forefinger, and there was something about him that held the boy and would not let him go away.

"Twelve years ago I married the woman in the photograph. She was my wife for one year, nine months, three days, and two nights. I loved her. Yes . . . ." He tightened his blurred, rambling voice and said again: "I loved her. I thought also that she loved me. I was a railroad engineer. She had all home comforts and luxuries. It never crept into my brain that she was not satisfied. But do you know what happened?"

"Mgneeow!" said Leo.

The man did not take his eyes from the boy's face. "She left me. I came in one night and the house was empty and she was gone. She left me."

"With a fellow?" the boy asked.

Gently the man placed his palm down on the counter. "Why naturally, Son. A woman does not run off like that alone."

The café was quiet, the soft rain black and endless in the street outside. Leo pressed down the frying bacon with the prongs of his long fork. "So you have been chasing the floozie for eleven years. You frazzled old rascal!"

For the first time the man glanced at Leo. "Please don't be vulgar. Besides, I was not speaking to you." He turned back to the boy and said in a trusting and secretive undertone: "Let's not pay any attention to him. O.K.?"

The paper boy nodded doubtfully.

"It was like this," the man continued. "I am a person who feels many things. All my life one thing after another has impressed me. Moonlight. The leg of a pretty girl. One thing after another. But the point is that when I had enjoyed anything there was a peculiar sensation as though it was laying around loose in me. Nothing seemed to finish itself up or fit in with the other things. Women? I had my portion of them. The same. Afterwards laying around loose in me. I was a man who had never loved."

Very slowly he closed his eyelids, and the gesture was like a curtain drawn at the end of a scene in a play. When he spoke again his voice was excited and the words came fast—the lobes of his large, loose ears seemed to tremble.

"Then I met this woman. I was fifty-one years old and she always said she was thirty. I met her at a filling station and we were married within three days. And do you know what it was like? I just can't tell you. All I had ever felt was gathered together around this woman. Nothing lay around loose in me any more but was finished up by her."

The man stopped suddenly and stroked his long nose. His voice sank down to a steady and reproachful undertone: "I'm not explaining this right. What happened was this. There were these beautiful feelings and loose little pleasures inside me. And this woman was something like an assembly line for my soul. I run these little pieces of myself through her and I come out complete. Now do you follow me?''

"What was her name?" the boy asked.

"Oh," he said. "I called her Dodo. But that is immaterial."

"Did you try to make her come back?"

The man did not seem to hear. "Under the circumstances you can imagine how I felt when she left me."

Leo took the bacon from the grill and folded two strips of it between a bun. He had a gray face, with slitted eyes, and a pinched nose saddled by faint blue shadows. One of the mill workers signaled for more coffee and Leo poured it. He did not give refills on coffee free. The spinner ate breakfast there very morning, but the better Leo knew his customers the stingier he treated them. He nibbled his own bun as though he grudged it to himself.

"And you never got hold of her again?"

The boy did not know what to think of the man, and his child's face was uncertain with mingled curiosity and doubt. He was new on the paper route; it was still strange to him to be out in the town in the black, queer early morning.

"Yes," the man said. "I took a number of steps to get her back. I went around trying to locate her. I went to Tulsa where she had folks. And to Mobile. I went to every town she had ever mentioned to me, and I hunted down every man she had formerly been connected with. Tulsa, Atlanta, Chicago, Cheehaw, Memphis. . . . For the better part of two years I chased around the country trying to lay hold of her."

"But the pair of them had vanished from the face of the earth!" said Leo.

"Don't listen to him," the man said confidentially. "And also just forget those two years. They are not important. What matters is that around the third year a curious thing begun to happen to me."

"What?" the boy asked.

The man leaned down and tilted his mug to take a sip of beer. But as he hovered over the mug his nostrils fluttered slightly; he sniffed the staleness of the beer and did not drink. "Love is a curious thing to begin with. At first I thought only of getting her back. It was a kind of mania. But then as time went on I tried to remember her. But do you know what happened?"

"No," the boy said.

"When I laid myself down on a bed and tried to think about her my mind became a blank. I couldn't see her. I would take out her pictures and look. No good. Nothing doing. A blank. Can you imagine it?"

"Say Mac!" Leo called down the counter. "Can you imagine this bozo's mind a blank!"

Slowly, as though fanning away flies, the man waved his hand. His green eyes were concentrated and fixed on the shallow little face of the paper boy.

"But a sudden piece of glass on a sidewalk. Or a nickel tune in a music box. A shadow on a wall at night. And I would remember. It might happen in a street and I would cry or bang my head against a lamppost. You follow me?"

"A piece of glass . . . " the boy said.

"Anything. I would walk around and I had no power of how and when to remember her. You think you can put up a kind of shield. But remembering don't come to a man face forward—it corners around sideways. I was at the mercy of everything I saw and heard. Suddenly instead of me combing the countryside to find her she begun to chase me around in my very soul. *She* chasing *me*, mind you! And in my soul."

The boy asked finally: "What part of the country were you in then?"

"Ooh," the man groaned. "I was a sick mortal. It was like smallpox. I confess, Son, that I boozed. I fornicated. I committed any sin that suddenly appealed to me. I am loath to confess it but I will do so. When I recall that period it is all curdled in my mind, it was so terrible."

The man leaned his head down and tapped his forehead on the counter. For a few seconds he stayed bowed over in this position, the back of his stringy neck covered with orange furze, his hands with their long warped fingers held palm to palm in an attitude of prayer. Then the man straightened himself; he was smiling and suddenly his face was bright and tremulous and old.

"It was in the fifth year that it happened," he said. "And with it I started my science."

Leo's mouth jerked with a pale, quick grin. "Well none of we boys are getting any younger," he said. Then with sudden anger he balled up a dishcloth he was holding and threw it down hard on the floor. "You draggle-tailed old Romeo!"

"What happened?" the boy asked.

The old man's voice was high and clear: "Peace," he answered.

"Huh?"

"It is hard to explain scientifically, Son," he said. "I guess the logical explanation is that she and I had fleed around from each other for so long that finally we just got tangled up together and lay down and quit. Peace. A queer and beautiful blankness. It was spring in Portland and the rain came every afternoon. All evening I just stayed there on my bed in the dark. And that is how the science come to me."

The windows in the streetcar were pale blue with light. The two soldiers paid for their beers and opened the door—one of the soldiers combed his hair and wiped off his muddy puttees before they went outside. The three mill workers bent silently over their breakfasts. Leo's clock was ticking on the wall.

"It is this. And listen carefully. I meditated on love and reasoned it out. I realized what is wrong with us. Men fall in love for the first time. And what do they fall in love with?"

The boy's soft mouth was partly open and he did not answer.

"A woman," the old man said. "Without science, with nothing to go by, they undertake the most dangerous and sacred experience in God's earth. They fall in love with a woman. Is that correct, Son?"

"Yeah," the boy said faintly.

"They start at the wrong end of love. They begin at the climax. Can you wonder it is so miserable? Do you know how men should love?"

The old man reached over and grasped the boy by the collar of his leather jacket. He gave him a gentle little shake and his green eyes gazed down unblinking and grave.

"Son, do you know how love should be begun?"

The boy sat small and listening and still. Slowly he shook his head. The old man leaned closer and whispered:

"A tree. A rock. A cloud."

It was still raining outside in the street: a mild, gray, endless rain. The mill whistle blew for the six o'clock shift and the three spinners paid and went away. There was no one in the café but Leo, the old man, and the little paper boy.

"The weather was like this in Portland." he said. "At the time my science was begun. I meditated and I started very cautious. I would pick up something from the street and take it home with me. I bought a goldfish and I concentrated on the goldfish and I loved it. I graduated from one thing to another. Day by day I was getting this technique. On the road from Portland to San Diego—"

"Aw shut up!" screamed Leo suddenly. "Shut up! Shut up!"

The old man still held the collar of the boy's jacket; he was trembling and his face was earnest and bright and wild. "For six years now I have gone around by myself and built up my science. And now I am a master. Son. I can love anything. No longer do I have to think about it even. I see a street full of people and a beautiful light comes in me. I watch a bird in the sky. Or I meet a traveler on the road. Everything, Son. And anybody. All stranger and all loved! Do you realize what a science like mine can mean?"

The boy held himself stiffly, his hands curled tight around the counter edge. Finally he asked: "Did you ever really find that lady?"

"What? What say, Son?"

"I mean," the boy asked timidly. "Have you fallen in love with a woman again?"

The old man loosened his grasp on the boy's collar. He turned away and for the first time his green eyes had a vague and scattered look. He lifted the mug from the counter, drank down the yellow beer. His head was shaking slowly from side to side. Then finally he answered: "No, Son. You see that is the last step in my science. I go cautious. And I am not quite ready yet."

"Well!" said Leo. "Well well well!"

The old man stood in the open doorway. "Remember," he said. Framed there in the gray damp light of the early morning he looked shrunken and seedy and frail. But his smile was bright. "Remember I love you." he said with a last nod. And the door closed quietly behind him.

The boy did not speak for a long time. He pulled down the bangs on his forehead and slid his grimy little forefinger around the rim of his empty cup. When without looking at Leo he finally asked:

"Was he drunk?"

"No," said Leo shortly.

The boy raised his clear voice higher. "Then was he a dope fiend?"

"No."

The boy looked up at Leo, and his flat little face was desperate, his voice urgent and shrill. "Was he crazy? Do you think he was a lunatic?" The paper boy's voice dropped suddenly with doubt. "Leo? Or not?"

But Leo would not answer him. Leo had run a night café for fourteen years, and he held himself to be a critic of craziness. There were the town characters and also the transients who roamed in from the night. He knew the manias of all of them. But he did not want to satisfy the questions of the waiting child. He tightened his pale face and was silent.

So the boy pulled down the right flap of his helmet and as he turned to leave he made the only comment that seemed safe to him, the only remark that could not be laughed down and despised:

"He sure has done a lot of traveling."

Aleksandr Isayevich Solzhenitsyn (1918–   )

The poet, writes Czeslaw Milosz, "should be God-fearing, love his country and his native tongue, rely upon his conscience, avoid alliances with evil, and be attached to tradition." Though Milosz, a 1980 Nobel Prize-winning poet, was paraphrasing

the beliefs of the Russian poet Joseph Brodsky, he could as well have been paraphrasing those of Aleksandr Solzhenitsyn. For in spite of the fact that Solzhenitsyn—himself a winner of the 1970 Nobel Prize in literature—spent eight years in
various Soviet prisons and work camps for criticizing Stalin (1945–1953), three
more years exiled to the desert region of Kazakhstan (1953–1956), and was finally
exiled permanently from Russia in 1974, he remains a loyal and patriotic Russian.
"Russia," he wrote, "is to the Soviet Union as a man is to the disease afflicting him.
We do not confuse a man with his illness: we do not refer to him by the name of
that illness or curse him for it." Solzhenitsyn, though a philosophical skeptic in his
youth and educated in mathematics, physics, and philology, is a deeply religious
man. At the height of his first fame, he surprised the Russian intellectual world by
publishing, of all things, a "prayer." "It was not a literary device," write his biographers David Burg and George Feifer, "but a wholly personal address to God" that
combined "his bewildered and grateful surprise over his fame, his confirmed
sense of mission and the relief of abandoning the secrecy of his work. . . ." His
religious impulses are inseparable from Russia: his love of his native language, his
passion for history and the great nineteenth-century Russian classics, and his
unshakable belief that literature performs a moral function. "In our age," he has
said, "when technology is gaining control of life, when material well-being is
considered the most important goal, when the influence of religion has been weakened everywhere in the world, a special responsibility lies upon the writer. He must
fill more than one vacated function."

Solzhenitsyn came to fame in 1962—during the "thaw" of the Krushchev era
following the death of Stalin—with the publication of *One Day in the Life of Ivan
Denisovich*, an account of a "good day" in the life of an inmate of one of Stalin's
work camps. At last the truth could be told. But the thaw was short-lived; in 1969
Solzhenitsyn was expelled from the Soviet Union of Writers; in 1970 was prevented
from going to Sweden to receive the Nobel Prize; and in 1972 was permanently
exiled from his homeland. He managed to publish a few stories before his exile—
"An Incident at Krechetovka Station," "Matryona's Place," and "Zakhar the
Pouch"—but other stories (including "The Right Hand") and his novels *Cancer
Ward* (1968), *The First Circle* (1968), and *August 1914* (1972) were never published
in Russia, except in underground *Samizdat* editions. Later works, such as *The
Gulag Archipelago* (1974, 1975, 1976) and *The Oak and the Calf* (1975), of course
met the same fate.

"The Right Hand," written in 1964, deals with the period of Solzhenitsyn's first
exile when he was stricken with cancer and allowed to make his way to a Tashkent
hospital for treatment. He was physically and mentally exhausted and near death;
but this moment marked the beginning of his return to life—as a man and as a
writer. In writing this story, he is beginning to fulfill the writer's sacred duty to
remember the suffering of the Stalin years—and to tell others. In this simple story,
with its simple irony (the decorated citizen who has escaped from Stalin's camps is
worse off than the exile who barely survived them), Solzhenitsyn lets us feel something of the pain, humiliation, despair—and immense compassion—that comes to
those who have been *in extremis* and surmounted it. Donald Fanger quotes Tolstoy
as saying, "The hero of my tale, the one I love with all the power of my soul . . .
is Truth," and comments: "Aside from Solzhenitsyn, it is hard to think of a
major writer today who could use these terms without irony or extensive qualification."

Solzhenitsyn is now living and writing in the United States.

The Right Hand

When I arrived in Tashkent that winter I was practically a corpse. I came there expecting to die.

But I was given another lease of life.

A month passed, then another and a third. Outside, the vivid Tashkent spring unfolded and advanced into summer; it was already very warm and lush greenery was everywhere when I started to venture out of doors on my shaky legs.

I still did not dare to admit to myself that I was getting better; in my wildest dreams I still measured my extra span of life not in years but in months. I would tread slowly along the gravel and asphalt paths in the park which was laid out between the blocks of the clinic. I would often have to sit down for a rest and sometimes, when overcome with nausea, I had to lie down with my head as low as possible.

I was like the sick people all around me, and yet I was different; I had fewer rights than they had and was forced to be more silent. People came to visit them, relatives wept for them, and their one concern, their one aim in life was to get well again. But if I recovered, it would be almost pointless: I was thirty-five years of age and yet in that spring I had no one I could call my own in the whole world. I did not even own a passport, and if I were to recover, I should have to leave this green, abundant land and go back to my desert where I had been exiled "in perpetuity." There I was under open surveillance, reported on every fortnight, and for a long time the local police headquarters had not even allowed me, a dying man, to go away for treatment.

I could not talk about all this to the free patients around me; had I done so, they would not have understood. On the other hand, I had ten years of long and careful reflection behind me and already knew the truth of the saying that the true savour of life is not to be gained by big things but from little ones—things like my ability to shuffle along hesitantly on my weakened legs; my cautious breathing, to avoid stabbing pains in the chest; and a single potato, undamaged by the frost, that I fished out of my soup.

So for me this spring was the most painful and the loveliest of my life.

I was surrounded by things I had either forgotten or had never seen, so everything interested me—even the ice-cream cart, the roadsweeper with his hose, the women selling bunches of long radishes, and especially the foal who had strayed through a gap in the wall onto the grass.

With every passing day I dared to wander farther away from the clinic, through the park, which must have been laid out at the end of the last century, when these good, sturdy buildings, with their ornamental brickwork at the corners, were also put up. From the magnificent sunrise, throughout the long southern day, and deep into the electric-yellow evening, the park was alive with movement. The healthy people would scurry around while the sick would make their unhurried promenade.

At the point where several avenues merged into the one leading to the main gates, there stood a large white alabaster Stalin, grinning sarcastically behind his stone whiskers. Other, smaller statutes were spaced out evenly along the path leading to the gates.

Then there was a stationer's kiosk. It sold plastic pencils and tempting notebooks. But I decided it was better to do without them, not merely because I had to keep a strict watch on my spending but also because previous notebooks of mine had fallen into the wrong hands.

"The Right Hand" from *Stories and Prose Poems* by Alexander Solzhenitsyn, translated by Michael Glenny. Translation Copyright © 1970, 1971 by Michael Glenny.

A fruit stall and a teahouse were situated right by the gates. We patients in our striped pyjamas were not allowed into the teahouse, but you could watch what was going on through the openwork fence. I had never in my life seen a real teahouse, with those individual pots of green or black tea for each person. The teahouse had a European section with small tables, and an Uzbek section with a large dais. The people at the tables ate and drank quickly, left a small payment in an empty bowl, and departed. But on the dais people sat or sprawled around for hours on end, some of them even for days. On sackcloth mats beneath a rush awning which had been put up at the beginning of the hot weather, they consumed pot after pot of tea while playing dice, as if the whole long day was completely free of cares.

The fruit stall did sell to the patients, but the few kopecks I had earned in exile shied away from the prices. I stared hard at the piles of dried apricots, raisins, and fresh cherries, then walked away.

Farther on there was a high wall; the patients were not allowed beyond the gates. Two or three times a day the strains of a band playing funeral marches would waft over this wall into the hospital grounds.

The city had a million inhabitants, but the cemetery was right next door to us. We could hear the slow funeral processions for about ten minutes, until they had passed the grounds. The sound of the drum produced an odd result: its rhythm had no effect on the crowd of mourners, whose jerky movements were always slightly faster than the beat; the healthy bystanders would hardly stop to look around before hurrying off again to wherever they had to go (and they all knew exactly where they had to go); but the patients would stop when they heard these marches, poke their heads out of the windows of the wards, and listen for a long time.

The clearer it grew that I was recovering from the disease, and the more certain I became that I would remain alive, the more wistfully I looked around: I was already sorry to be leaving all this.

In the medical students' sports ground, white figures were hitting white tennis balls to each other. All my life I had wanted to play tennis, but I had never had the chance. Beneath its steep bank, the muddy yellow water of the river Salar was gurgling furiously. Wide-branching oak trees grew in the park, shady maples and delicate Japanese acacias. The octagonal fountain was throwing up fresh, slender streams of silver as high as they could reach. And what grass on the lawns!—succulent and mercifully disregarded, unlike the grass in the prison camps, which the authorities ordered to be weeded out like an enemy, while in my place of exile grass could not grow at all. Just to lie in it face downwards, peacefully breathing in its herbal fragrance and its sun-warmed exhalation, was a taste of paradise.

I was not the only one lying there in the grass. Dotted about were students from the Medical Institute, slogging away at their bulky textbooks. Some of them, however, were absorbed in reading short stories which were not part of the examination syllabus, while others, the athletic ones, emerged from the changing rooms swinging their sports holdalls. In the evening girls, indistinct and therefore three times more attractive, would walk round the fountain in creased or well-ironed frocks, crunching the gravel of the paths under their feet.

My heart was bursting with pity for someone: it might have been for myself and my contemporaries, frozen to death near Demiansk, burnt alive in Auschwitz, harried to exhaustion in Djezkazgan, or dying in the wastes of Siberia, because these girls would never belong to us. Or it might have been for these girls, because of the things I could never tell them and which they would never find out.

The whole day long, women—women, women!—would flow along the gravel and asphalt paths, young doctors, nurses, laboratory assistants, clerks, housekeepers, dispensers, and relatives visiting patients. They would pass me by in their austere white coats and their bright southern dresses, often semi-transparent, the richer ones in bright blues and pinks slowly twirling fashionable bamboo-handled Chinese parasols over their heads. Each one, as she flashed past, momentarily made up a complete plot for a novel: her past, the (nonexistent) chance of my getting to know her.

I was a pitiful wreck. My emaciated face bore the stamp of what I had been through—the wrinkles caused by the enforced gloom of camp life, the ashen colour of death on my leathery skin, the more recent poisoning caused by a venomous disease and toxic medicines which had added a greenish tinge to my cheeks. My back was hunched from the defensive habit of submission and self-effacement. My clown-like striped jacket barely reached as far as my stomach, my striped trousers ended above my ankles, and the edges of my footcloths, brown from long wear, were hanging out of the canvas uppers of my blunt-toed prison-camp boots.

Not one of these women would have dared to walk beside me. But I could not see myself, and the world impinged upon my consciousness through eyes that were as sensitive as theirs.

One day, towards evening, I was standing by the main gates, looking around me at the usual stream of people rushing past; parasols bobbed along, silk dresses and tussore trousers with bright sashes, embroidered shirts and skullcaps flickered by. There was a buzz of voices. People were selling fruit; behind the fence, others were drinking tea and throwing dice. At the same time, leaning against the fence, a small, ungainly man who looked like a beggar was addressing the crowd from time to time in a voice gasping for breath: "Comrades . . . Comrades . . . "

The busy, gaily-coloured crowd was not listening to him. I went up to him. "What's the matter, brother?"

The man had an enormous belly, larger than a pregnant woman's, which hung down like a sack. It had burst through his dirty khaki tunic and trousers. His shoes, their soles worn away, were clumsy and dusty. His thick, unbuttoned overcoat with its soiled collar and frayed cuffs, unsuitable for this weather, weighed down his shoulders. On his head he wore an ancient, torn peaked cap, fit for a garden scarecrow. His eyes, swollen with dropsy, were glazed.

With great effort he raised one clenched hand, and I pulled a sweaty, crumpled piece of paper out of it. It was an application from citizen Bobrov, written in an angular hand with a pen that had scratched the paper, requesting admission to hospital; slanting across the application were two stamps, one in blue ink and one in red. The one in blue ink was from the Town Health Committee giving reasoned grounds for its refusal to admit him. The one in red ink, however, ordered the clinic of the Medical Institute to accept the man as an in-patient. The blue ink bore yesterday's date; the red ink—today's.

"Look," I explained to him loudly, as if he were deaf. "You've got to go to Reception, in Ward One. So just go straight on past these . . . statues . . . "

But then I noticed that his strength had abandoned him at the very moment that he reached the goal of his journey; not only was he incapable of asking any more questions or dragging his feet over the smooth asphalt path; he was even too weak to carry his shabby bag, which weighed no more than three or four pounds. So I made up my mind and said: "All right, old fellow, I'll take you. Let's go. Give me your bag."

He understood. He handed me his bag with relief, leaned on my proffered arm, and moved forward by dragging his shoes along the asphalt path, hardly lifting his feet off the ground. I guided him by his elbow, holding on to his coat, which was reddish-brown from the dust. His swollen stomach seemed to pull the old man forward and downwards. He frequently heaved a deep sigh.

Thus we advanced, two dishevelled figures, along the same avenue where, in my thoughts, I had linked arms with the most beautiful girls in Tashkent. For a long time we slowly dragged ourselves past the alabaster statues.

At last we turned off. Beside our path stood a bench with a back rest. My companion asked to sit down for a while. I too could feel an attack of nausea coming on, as I had been standing too long. We sat down. From here we could see the fountain.

While we were still walking along, the old man had said a few things to me, and now that he had recovered his breath, he resumed his story. He had to get to the Urals, and the residence permit in his passport was for the Urals, which was the whole trouble. He had been taken ill somewhere near Takhia-Tashem (where, I remember, they had started building a canal). At Urgench they had kept him in hospital for a month, drained the water from his stomach and legs, made him worse, and then discharged him. He had interrupted his journey at Chardzhou and then at Ursatevskaya, but wherever he went for treatment he was turned away; instead, they had sent him on to the Urals, because that was his official place of residence. He had felt too weak to go there by train, and anyway he did not have enough money for the ticket. So two days ago he had managed to get to Tashkent in the hope of being admitted to hospital.

I did not ask what he was doing down south or what had brought him here. His illness was, according to his medical certificates, "advanced," but a glance at the man was enough to tell you that it was terminal. I had seen a lot of patients and I could tell that he no longer had the will to live. He had lost control of his lips, his speech was indistinct, and his eyes had a dull lifelessness about them.

Even his cap was a burden to him. With great difficulty he pulled it off his head, down onto his knees. He struggled to raise his arm again and wiped the sweat off his forehead with his dirty sleeve. The top of his head was bald, though it was ringed by some sparse, untidy hair, still pale red under its coating of dust. It was not old age that had reduced him to this state but disease.

Folds of superfluous skin hung from his neck, which had grown pitifully thin, like a chicken's, and his triangular Adam's apple protruded visibly. I wondered how he held his head up, and we had scarcely sat down when it lolled forward onto his chest, supported by his chin.

There he collapsed, with his cap on his knees and his eyes closed. He seemed to have forgotten that we had only sat down for a moment to recover our breath and that he had to go on to Reception.

Before our eyes, the almost noiseless jet of the fountain was casting its silver thread upwards. Beyond it, two girls passed, side by side. I watched them walk away. One was wearing an orange skirt, the other a maroon one. I found both of them extremely attractive.

My neighbour signed audibly, rolled his head across his chest, and, raising his yellowish-grey lashes, squinted up at me. "Do you happen to have a cigarette, comrade?"

"You can forget that idea, old fellow," I barked at him. "You and I haven't got a hope unless we give up smoking. Take a look at yourself in a mirror. A cigarette! Really!" (I had only just succeeded in breaking myself of the habit a month before.)

Panting for breath, he again raised his eyes and looked at me from underneath his yellow lashes, rather like a dog. "All the same, comrade, give us three roubles."

I thought about whether to give them to him or not. After all, I was still a prisoner, while he was a free man. For all the years I had worked in prison camps I had been paid nothing. And when they did start to pay me they took all of it back in deductions: for the

escort, for lighting the perimeter, for police dogs, for the officers, for the prison
stew.

I took my oilskin purse out of the small breast pocket of my clown's jacket and
inspected the notes in it. I sighed, then handed the old man a three-rouble note.

"Thanks," he said hoarsely. Struggling to hold his arm out, he took the note and
put it in his pocket; at once his arm flopped down and slapped against his knee. His chin
sagged forward until his head was again resting on his chest.

We fell silent. A woman passed by, then two more girl students. I found all three of
them very attractive. It had been years since I had heard girls' voices or the tapping of
their stiletto heels.

"You're lucky they gave you an admission form, otherwise you might have had to
hang around here for a week or so. It often happens. Lots of people have to put up with
it."

He pulled his chin away from his chest and turned towards me. In his eyes a spark
of sense glinted, his voice quivered, and he spoke more distinctly: "They're putting me
in here, son, because I'm a deserving case. I'm a veteran of the Revolution. Sergey
Mironovich Kirov personally shook me by the hand during the fighting at Tsaritsyn. I
should be getting a special pension."

A slight movement of his cheeks and lips—the shadow of a proud smile—registered on his unshaven face.

I examined his rags, then looked him over once more. "Why don't you get it,
then?"

"That's life," he sighed. "Now they don't even acknowledge my existence. Some
of the records were burnt, others were lost. And I can't get any witnesses. Sergey
Mironovich was murdered . . . It's all my fault. I didn't keep my documents . . . I've
just one thing here . . . "

He lifted his right hand and fumbled in his pocket with his round, swollen finger
joints, but here his burst of activity expired, and he again dropped his arm and his head
and sat stock-still.

The sun was already sinking behind the hospital buildings and we would have to
hurry to Reception (it was still a hundred paces away). In my experience, getting
admitted to a hospital is always beset with difficulties.

I took the old man by the shoulder. "Wake up, old fellow. Look, see that door
over there? See it? I'm going over there to start persuading them. Come on your own if
you can, but if not, wait for me. I'll take your bag."

He nodded as if he understood.

Reception was part of a large, shabby hall, divided off by rough partitions; at one
time there had been a communal bathroom, a dressing room, and a hairdresser's here.
In the daytime it was always crowded with patients whiling away the long hours until
they would be admitted, but now, to my surprise, there was not a soul there. I knocked
at the plywood hatch, which was closed. A very young nurse with a snub nose opened
it; her lips were painted not red but a thick violet.

"What do you want?" She was sitting at a table reading a spy comic, as far as I
could see.

She had very lively eyes.

I gave her the application with the two stamps on it and explained: "He can hardly
walk. I've just brought him in."

"How dare you bring anyone in!" she cried sharply, without even looking at the
piece of paper. "Don't you know the routine? We only admit patients at nine a.m.!"

She was the one who did not know the "routine." I stuck my head through the hatch and as much of my arm as I could manage, so that she could not slam it shut on me. Twisting my lower lip and pulling a face like a gorilla, I hissed in a menacing voice: "Listen, woman. And get this into your head—I'm not going to be bossed about by you!"

She took fright, moved her chair farther back into her little room, and said: "There's no admission, citizen. Only at nine a.m."

"Look . . . read this bit of paper!" I growled at her in my nastiest voice.

She read it.

"Well, so what? The normal routine applies. And there may not be any places tomorrow. There weren't any this morning."

She announced that there had been no places that morning with a sort of satisfaction, as if the remark would puncture me.

"But the man's just passing through, don't you see? He's got nowhere to go."

As I backed out of the hatch and stopped talking in my harsh prison-camp rasp, her face took on its former expression of cheerful callousness. "They're all passing through. Where can we put them? They have to wait. He'll have to find a room somewhere."

"But just come and have a look. You'll see the condition he's in."

"Whatever next? Do you expect me to go round collecting patients? I'm not an orderly, you know!"

And she proudly twitched her snub nose. Her reply was as snappy and as automatic as clockwork.

"Then what the hell are you doing sitting here?"

I banged on the plywood wall with my fist, and a thin layer of whitewash scattered like pollen. "Lock the place up!"

"No one asked for your opinion, you lout!" She exploded with anger, jumped up, ran round, and appeared out of the narrow corridor. "Who do you think you are, anyway? Don't you teach me how to do my job! The ambulance'll bring him in."

Except for her crude violet lips and her matching nail varnish, she would not have been at all bad-looking. Her nose was her attractive feature, and she made great play with her eyebrows. Because it was so stuffy, she had undone the top buttons on her white coat and I could see her nice little pink scarf and Komsomol badge.

"What? If he hadn't come here by himself but had been picked up in the street by an ambulance, you would have admitted him? Is that your rule?"

She stared haughtily at my absurd figure and I stared back at her. I had completely forgotten that my footcloths were poking out of my boots. She snorted, looked at me coldly, and continued: "Yes, *patient*. That *is* the rule."

And she went back behind the partition.

I heard a rustling sound behind me. I looked around. My companion was already standing there. He had heard and understood everything. Clutching onto the wall and hauling himself towards the large bench put there for visitors, he was scarcely able to wave his right hand, which was clutching a tattered piece of paper.

"Here you are," he appealed to me in a faint voice. " . . . Here you are, show her this . . . let her . . . here . . . "

I managed to support him and lowered him onto the bench. With helpless fingers he tried to pull his only certificate out of his wallet but just could not manage it.

I took the top piece of paper from him, which was stuck down along its folds because it was falling apart, and opened it. On it were typed, in violet ink, lines with the letters dancing up and down over the creases:

Workers of the World Unite!

This certificate is presented to Comrade Bobrov N.K. for active service in 1921 in the distinguished "World Revolution" Special Detachment of _____ Province for personally eliminating large numbers of counterrevolutionary terrorists.

Signed: Commissar _____

A pale violet seal was attached to it.

Scratching my chest, I asked him quietly: "What's this 'Special Detachment'? What did it do?"

"Aha," he replied, scarcely able to keep his eyes open. "Show it to her."

I noticed his hand, his right hand—so small, with its brown, swollen veins and its round, puffed joints, practically incapable of pulling a certificate out of his wallet. And I remembered the way horsemen used to strike down men on foot with a single, sweeping backhand stroke.

Strange . . . That right hand had once swung a sabre in a full arc and chopped off heads, necks, and shoulders. And now it could not even hold a scrap of paper . . .

I went up to the plywood hatch and again tried to persuade her to listen. The registrar did not raise her head but continued reading her comic. On the open page I saw a handsome man in uniform leaping onto a windowsill with a pistol.

I quietly placed the torn certificate on top of her book and turned away. I kept rubbing my chest to avoid being sick as I walked towards the door. I had to lie down as quickly as possible.

"What have you put this paper here for? Take it away!" the girl shot at me through the hatch as I walked away.

The veteran shrank into the bench. His head and even his shoulders seemed to sink into his torso. His helpless fingers dangled, outspread. His unbuttoned coat hung down, his bulbous, unbelievably swollen belly sagging into the fold of his thighs.

Richard Wilbur (1921–   )

"A Game of Catch" is Richard Wilbur's only published short story. He is primarily a poet—one of America's most distinguished—but in this effort at story writing he has shown, for a poet, remarkable talents. We say *for a poet* neither to denigrate poets nor to minimize Wilbur's fine achievement, but only to emphasize that what makes a great poet is not necessarily what makes a great story writer. A poet can probe internal states and play innumerable changes on a single emotion, but the short-story writer has no time or space for meditative or introspective voyaging. He or she must make a quick entry into a limited world and emerge as quickly, having in the meantime evoked a point or hint of action. One critic has said, "Mr. Wilbur's voice is quiet and tense, and is at its best describing in elegies and eulogies . . . and in exploring inward and private emotions." That would not suggest the talents of a short-story writer, but Wilbur has other qualities as well: a highly developed dramatic sense, a sure-footed sense of words, and a compassionate sense of humor. The style of "A Game of Catch"—economical, witty, gently ironic—is the same style we find in such delicately funny poems as "Museum Piece" or "Playboy." A certain elegance and polish characterize these poems—indeed all of Wilbur's work—and they must be read as wholes; their quality is not easily caught by excerpting a few lines. Wilbur's poems, writes Donald Hall, "move carefully and elegantly, step by calculated step, to a sure conclusion." They are in a sense plotted, even as this story is, and one is always aware, in reading Wilbur, of his sense of design.

These qualities have led some critics to call Wilbur "passionless," but such criticism, writes Paul F. Cummins, "would limit passion solely to the physical, sexual, violent aspects of experience. Wilbur's poetry does in fact reveal a deep passion: for minute particulars of the external world; for odd and unique sounds and colors and shapes; . . . for the human mind, the imagination . . . ; and for the necessity of maintaining balance and perspective in a paradoxical, mysterious, and fallen world." And, one could add, for the world of childhood, into which Wilbur enters with wit, tenderness, and a sharp memory for how it was—as his children's book *Opposites* (1973) attests.

Wilbur was born in New York City, was educated at Amherst College and Harvard, and served with the 36th Infantry Division in Europe. "It was not until World War II took me to Cassio, Anzio, and the Siegfried Line that I began to versify in earnest," he writes. His first volume of poems, *The Beautiful Changes,* appeared in 1947, followed by *Ceremony* (1950), *Things of this World* (1956), *Advice to a Prophet* (1961), *Walking to Sleep* (1969), and *The Mind Reader* (1976). He has also published *A Bestiary* (1955); written most of the lyrics for a comic operetta on Voltaire called *Candide*; and translated four plays by Moliere into verse: *The Misanthrope* (1955), *Tartuffe* (1963), *The School for Wives* (1971), and *The Learned Ladies* (1978). A volume of prose pieces called *Responses* appeared in 1976.

Here in this story Scho is wracked by passions that, in the hands of another writer, could emerge in scenes of violent revenge. But Wilbur controls the situation almost ritualistically, letting Scho have his revenge and retrieve his dignity via words rather than fists: "I want you to do whatever you're going to do for the whole rest of your life!" Scho is a poet in the making—a poet very like Wilbur—who persuades us again and again that word magic has power enough to effect "beautiful changes."

A Game of Catch

Monk and Glennie were playing catch on the side lawn of the firehouse when Scho caught sight of them. They were good at it, for seventh-graders, as anyone could see right away. Monk, wearing a catcher's mitt, would lean easily sidewise and back, with one leg lifted and his throwing hand almost down to the grass, and then lob the white ball straight up into the sunlight. Glennie would shield his eyes with his left hand and, just as the ball fell past him, snag it with a little dart of his glove. Then he would burn the ball straight toward Monk, and it would spank into the round mitt and sit, like a still-life apple on a plate, until Monk flipped it over into his right hand and, with a negligent flick of his hanging arm, gave Glennie a fast grounder.

They were going on and on like that, in a kind of slow, mannered, luxurious dance in the sun, their faces perfectly blank and entranced, when Glennie noticed Scho dawdling along the other side of the street and called hello to him. Scho crossed over and stood at the front edge of the lawn, near an apple tree, watching.

"Got your glove?" asked Glennie after a time. Scho obviously hadn't.

"You could give me some easy grounders," said Scho. "But don't burn 'em."

"All right," Glennie said. He moved off a little, so the three of them formed a triangle, and they passed the ball around for about five minutes, Monk tossing easy grounders to Scho, Scho throwing to Glennie, and Glennie burning them in to Monk. After a while, Monk began to throw them back to Glennie once or twice before he let Scho have his grounder, and finally Monk gave Scho a fast, bumpy grounder that hopped over his shoulder and went into the brake on the other side of the street.

"Not so hard," called Scho as he ran across to get it.

"You should've had it," Monk shouted.

It took Scho a little while to find the ball among the ferns and dead leaves, and when he saw it, he grabbed it up and threw it toward Glennie. It struck the trunk of the apple tree, bounced back at an angle, and rolled steadily and stupidly onto the cement apron in front of the firehouse, where one of the trucks was parked. Scho ran hard and stopped it just before it rolled under the truck, and this time he carried it back to his former position on the lawn and threw it carefully to Glennie.

"I got an idea," said Glennie. "Why don't Monk and I catch for five minutes more, and then you can borrow one of our gloves?"

"That's all right with me," said Monk. He socked his fist into his mitt, and Glennie burned one in.

"All right," Scho said, and went over and sat under the tree. There in the shade he watched them resume their skillful play. They threw lazily fast or lazily slow—high, low, or wide—and always handsomely, their expressions serene, changeless, and forgetful. When Monk missed a low backhand catch, he walked indolently after the ball and, hardly even looking, flung it sidearm for an imaginary put-out. After a good while of this, Scho said, "Isn't it five minutes yet?"

"One minute to go," said Monk with a fraction of a grin.

Scho stood up and watched the ball slap back and forth for several minutes more, and then he turned and pulled himself up into the crotch of the tree.

"Where you going?" Monk asked.

"Just up the tree," Scho said.

"I guess he doesn't want to catch," said Monk.

Scho went up and up through the fat light-gray branches until they grew slender and bright and gave under him. He found a place where several supple branches were knit to make a dangerous chair, and sat there with his head coming out of the leaves into the sunlight. He could see the two other boys down below, the ball going back and forth between them as if they were bowling on the grass, and Glennie's crew-cut head looking like a sea urchin.

"I found a wonderful seat up here," Scho said loudly. "If I don't fall out." Monk and Glennie didn't look up or comment, and so he began jouncing gently in his chair of branches and singing "Yo-ho, heave ho" in an exaggerated way.

"Do you know what, Monk?" he announced in a few moments. "I can make you two guys do anything I want. Catch that ball, Monk! Now you catch it, Glennie!"

"I was going to catch it anyway," Monk suddenly said. "You're not making anybody do anything when they're already going to do it anyway."

"I made you say what you just said," Scho replied joyfully.

"No, you didn't," said Monk, still throwing and catching but now less serenely absorbed in the game.

"That's what I wanted you to say," Scho said.

The ball bounded off the rim of Monk's mitt and plowed into a gladiolus bed beside the firehouse, and Monk ran to get it while Scho jounced in his treetop and sang, "I wanted you to miss that. Anything you do is what I wanted you to do."

"Let's quit for a minute," Glennie suggested.

"We might as well, until the peanut gallery shuts up," Monk said.

They went over and sat cross-legged in the shade of the tree. Scho looked down between his legs and saw them on the dim, spotty ground, saying nothing to one another. Glennie soon began abstractedly spinning his glove between his palms; Monk pulled his nose and stared out across the lawn.

"I want you to mess around with your nose, Monk," said Scho, giggling. Monk withdrew his hand from his face.

"Do that with your glove, Glennie," Scho persisted. "Monk, I want you to pull up hunks of grass and chew on it."

Glennie looked up and saw a self-delighted, intense face staring down at him through the leaves. "Stop being a dope and come down and we'll catch for a few minutes," he said.

Scho hesitated, and then said, in a tentatively mocking voice, "That's what I wanted you to say."

"All right, then, nuts to you," said Glennie.

"Why don't you keep quiet and stop bothering people?" Monk asked.

"I made you say that," Scho replied, softly.

"Shut up," Monk said.

"I made you say that, and I want you to be standing there looking sore. And I want you to climb up the tree. I'm making you do it!"

Monk was scrambling up through the branches, awkward in his haste, and getting snagged on twigs. His face was furious and foolish, and he kept telling Scho to shut up, shut up, shut up, while the other's exuberant and panicky voice poured down upon his head.

"*Now* you shut up or you'll be sorry," Monk said, breathing hard as he reached up and threatened to shake the cradle of slight branches in which Scho was sitting.

"I want—" Scho screamed as he fell. Two lower branches broke his rustling, crackling fall, but he landed on his back with a deep thud and lay still, with a strangled look on his face and his eyes clenched. Glennie knelt down and asked breathlessly, "Are you O.K., Scho? Are you O.K.?," while Monk swung down through the leaves crying that honestly he hadn't even touched him, the crazy guy just let go. Scho doubled up and turned over on his right side, and now both the other boys knelt beside him, pawing at his shoulder and begging to know how he was.

Then Scho rolled away from them and sat partly up, still struggling to get his wind but forcing a species of smile onto his face.

"I'm sorry, Scho," Monk said. "I didn't mean to make you fall."

Scho's voice came out weak and gravelly, in gasps. "I meant—you to do it. You— had to. You can't do—anything—unless I want—you to."

Glennie and Monk looked helplessly at him as he sat there, breathing a bit more easily and smiling fixedly, with tears in his eyes. Then they picked up their gloves and the ball, walked over to the street, and went slowly away down the sidewalk, Monk punching his fist into the mitt, Glennie juggling the ball between glove and hand.

From under the apple tree, Scho, still bent over a little for lack of breath, croaked after them in triumph and misery, "I want you to do whatever you're going to do for the whole rest of your life!"

Grace Paley (1922–   )

Grace Paley is a writer's writer. That is, young writers, would-be writers, even established writers hope by studying her stories to create simple yet powerful works like hers. Though many have tried to imitate her, no one has come close to producing the poignancy of her vision, the brilliance of her personality, or the originality of her craft.

On its surface, Paley's work does seem simple. She tells her stories as though she were gossiping with a friend. There is no grasping after elegance, no pretense of "literary language." What occurs seems natural, homely, not far from experiences most of us have known first- or second-hand. An ex-husband comes to visit children he has long ignored. A mother resents her son's wife. A father is dying. A friend dies. So—what accounts for the enormous effect these stories have on us? It is, in Sean O'Faolain's words, the "punch and poetry" that are distinctively Paley's own.

The punch—if indeed the two qualities can be separated—is provided by the dominant female character in the best of the stories. This character— frequently named Faith—is, like Paley herself, a political radical, a pacifist, an anarchist of sorts, but not especially feminist. She functions in the bedroom and kitchen, not the boardroom or the office. Her resentments are caused not by the historical oppression of women but by the disloyalty, vanity, and irresponsibility of lovers and husbands. But she lives by a combination of hope and acceptance of reality. Paley says of one character that her "capacity for survival has not been overwhelmed by her susceptibility to abuse." Her creed is comply, resent, accept, go on, laugh.

The poetry is the wonderfully original voice of Grace Paley. Paley's accents are ironic and sometimes bizarre. One narrator says that a man's remark, "like a plumber's snake, could work its way through the ear down the throat, half-way to my heart. He would then disappear, leaving me choking with equipment." A mother says of her son's girlfriend that " . . . every wild boy on the block has been leaning his thumbs on her titties like she was a Carvel dairy counter. . . . " A woman enters the room where a man who has been bitten by a child sits: "The stationary sun, the breathless air in which the planets swing were empowered now to make him well, to act, in their remarkable art, like aspirin." Few writers take such risks with imagery; few can match her triumphs.

The four women in "Friends" are true Grace Paley women. The fact of friendship between women—shared concern and support, lasting affection, loyalty even to each other's self-deceptions—is, Paley-Faith says, a bond "at least as useful as the vow we'd all sworn with husbands to whom we're no longer married." Faith is older, but still hopeful, still realistic. Things are not that bad, not that good.

Grace Paley was born in 1922 in New York City. Her first book of stories, *The Little Disturbances of Man*, appeared in 1959. Her second, *Enormous Changes at the Last Minute*, appeared in 1974.

Friends

To put us at our ease, to quiet our hearts as she lay dying, our dear friend Selena said, Life, after all, has not been an unrelieved horror—you know, I *did* have many wonderful years with her.

She pointed to a child who leaned out of a portrait on the wall—long brown hair, white pinafore, head and shoulders forward.

Eagerness, said Susan. Ann closed her eyes.

On the same wall three little girls were photographed in a schoolyard. They were in furious discussion; they were holding hands. Right in the middle of the coffee table, framed, in autumn colors, a handsome young woman of eighteen sat on an enormous horse—aloof, disinterested, a rider. One night this young woman, Selena's child, was found in a rooming house in a distant city, dead. The police called. They said, Do you have a daughter named Abby?

And with *him*, too, our friend Selena said. We had good times, Max and I. You know that.

There were no photographs of *him*. He was married to another woman and had a new, stalwart girl of about six, to whom no harm would ever come, her mother believed.

Our dear Selena had gotten out of bed. Heavily but with a comic dance, she soft-shoed to the bathroom, singing "Those were the days, my friend . . ."

Later that evening, Ann, Susan, and I were enduring our five-hour train ride to home. After one hour of silence and one hour of coffee and the sandwiches Selena had given us (she actually stood, leaned her big soft excavated body against the kitchen table to make those sandwiches), Ann said, Well, we'll never see *her* again.

Who says? Anyway, listen, said Susan. Think of it. Abby isn't the only kid who died. What about that great guy, remember Bill Dalrymple—he was a non-coöperator or a deserter? And Bob Simon. They were killed in automobile accidents. Matthew, Jeannie, Mike. Remember Al Lurie—he was murdered on Sixth Street—and that little kid Brenda, who O.D.'d on your roof, Ann? The tendency, I suppose, is to forget. You people don't remember them.

What do you mean, "you people"? Ann asked. You're talking to *us*.

I began to apologize for not knowing them all. Most of them were older than my kids, I said.

Of course, the child Abby was exactly in my time of knowing and in all my places of paying attention—the park, the school, our street. But oh! It's true! Selena's Abby was not the only one of that beloved generation of our children murdered by cars, lost to war, to drugs, to madness.

Selena's main problem, Ann said—you know, she didn't tell the truth.

What?

A few hot human truthful words are powerful enough, Ann thinks, to steam all God's chemical mistakes and society's slimy lies out of her life. We all believe in that power, my friends and I, but sometimes . . . the heat.

Anyway, I always thought Selena had told us a lot. For instance, we knew she was an orphan. There were six, seven other children. She was the youngest. She was forty-two years old before someone informed her that her mother had *not* died in childbirthing her. It was some terrible sickness. And she had lived close to her mother's body—at her breast, in fact—until she was eight months old. Whew! said Selena. What a relief! I'd always felt I was the one who'd killed her.

Your family stinks, we told her. They really held you up for grief.

Oh, people, she said. Forget it. They did a lot of nice things for me, too. Me and Abby. Forget it. Who has the time?

That's what I mean, said Ann. Selena should have gone after them with an axe.

More information: Selena's two sisters brought her to a Home. They were ashamed that at sixteen and nineteen they could not take care of her. They kept hugging her. They were sure she'd cry. They took her to her room—not a room, a dormitory with about eight beds. This is your bed, Lena. This is your table for your things. This little drawer is for your toothbrush. All for me? she asked. No one else can use it? Only me. That's all? Artie can't come? Franky can't come? Right?

Believe me, Selena said, those were happy days at Home.

Facts, said Ann, just facts. Not necessarily the *truth*.

I don't think it's right to complain about the character of the dying or start hustling all their motives into the spotlight like that. Isn't it amazing enough, the bravery of that private inclusive intentional community?

It wouldn't help not to be brave, said Selena. You'll see.

She wanted to get back to bed. Susan moved to help her.

Thanks, our Selena said, leaning on another person for the first time in her entire life. The trouble is, when I stand, it hurts me here all down my back. Nothing they can do about it. All the chemotherapy. No more chemistry left in me to therapeut. Ha! Did you know before I came to New York and met you I used to work in that hospital? I was supervisor in gynecology. Nursing. They were my friends, the doctors. They weren't so snotty then. David Clark, big surgeon. He couldn't look at me last week. He kept saying, Lena . . . Lena . . . Like that. We were in North Africa the same year—'44, I think. I told him, Davy, I've been around a long enough time. I haven't missed too much. He knows it. But I didn't want to make him look at me. Ugh, my damn feet are a pain in the neck.

Recent research, said Susan, tells us that it's the neck that's a pain in the feet.

Always something new, said Selena, our dear friend.

On the way back to the bed, she stopped at her desk. There were about twenty snapshots scattered across it—the baby, the child, the young woman. Here, she said to me, take this one. It's a shot of Abby and your Richard in front of the school—third grade? What a day! The show those kids put on! What a bunch of kids! What's Richard doing now?

Oh, who knows? Horsing around someplace. Spain. These days, it's Spain. Who knows where he is? They're all the same.

Why did I say that? I knew exactly where he was. He writes. In fact, he found a broken phone and was able to call every day for a week—mostly to give orders to his brother but also to say, Are you O.K., Ma? How's your new boyfriend, did he smile yet?

The kids, they're all the same, I said.

It was only politeness, I think, not to pour my boy's light, noisy face into that dark afternoon. Richard used to say in his early mean teens, You'd sell us down the river to keep Selena happy and innocent. It's true. Whenever Selena would say, I don't know, Abby has some peculiar friends, I'd answer for stupid comfort, You should see Richard's.

Still, he's in Spain, Selena said. At least you know that. It's probably interesting. He'll learn a lot. Richard is a wonderful boy, Faith. He acts like a wise guy but he's not. You know the night Abby died, when the police called me and told me? That was my first night's sleep in two years. I *knew* where she was.

Selena said this very matter-of-factly—just offering a few informative sentences.

But Ann, listening, said, Oh!—she called out to us all, Oh!—and began to sob. Her straightforwardness had become an arrow and gone right into her own heart.

Then a deep tear-drying breath: I want a picture, too, she said.

Yes. Yes, wait, I have one here someplace. Abby and Judy and that Spanish kid Victor. Where is it? Ah. Here!

Three nine-year-old children sat high on that long-armed sycamore in the park, dangling their legs on someone's patient head—smooth dark hair, parted in the middle. Was that head Kitty's?

Our dear friend laughed. Another great day, she said. Wasn't it? I remember you two sizing up the men. I *had* one at the time—I thought. Some joke. Here, take it. I have two copies. But you ought to get it enlarged. When this you see, remember me. Ha-ha. Well, girls—excuse me, I mean ladies—it's time for me to rest.

She took Susan's arm and continued that awful walk to her bed.

We didn't move. We had a long journey ahead of us and had expected a little more comforting before we set off.

No, she said. You'll only miss the express. I'm not in much pain. I've got lots of painkiller. See?

The tabletop was full of little bottles.

I just want to lie down and think of Abby.

It was true, the local could cost us an extra two hours at least. I looked at Ann. It had been hard for her to come at all. Still, we couldn't move. We stood there before Selena in a row. Three old friends. Selena pressed her lips together, ordered her eyes into cold distance.

I know that face. Once, years ago, when the children were children, it had been placed modestly in front of J. Hoffner, the principal of the elementary school.

He'd said, No! Without training you cannot tutor these kids. There are real problems. You have to know *how to teach*.

Our P.-T.A. had decided to offer some one-to-one tutorial help for the Spanish kids, who were stuck in crowded classrooms with exhausted teachers among little middle-class achievers. He had said, in a written communication to show seriousness and then in personal confrontation to *prove* seriousness, that he could not allow it. And the board of ed itself had said no. (All this no-ness was to lead to some terrible events in the schools and neighborhoods of our poor yes-requiring city.) But most of the women in our P.-T.A. were independent—by necessity and disposition. We were, in fact, the soft-speaking tough souls of anarchy.

I had Fridays off that year. At about 11 A.M. I'd bypass the principal's office and run up to the fourth floor. I'd take Robert Figueroa to the end of the hall, and we'd work away at story-telling for about twenty minutes. Then we would write the beautiful letters of the alphabet invented by smart foreigners long ago to fool time and distance.

That day, Selena and her stubborn face remained in the office for at least two hours. Finally, Mr. Hoffner, besieged, said that because she was a nurse, she would be allowed to help out by taking the littlest children to the modern difficult toilet. Some of them, he said, had just come from the barbarous hills beyond Maricao. Selena said O.K., she'd do that. In the toilet she taught the little girls which way to wipe, as she had taught her own little girl a couple of years earlier. At three o'clock she brought them home for cookies and milk. The children of that year ate cookies in her kitchen until the end of the sixth grade.

Now, what did we learn in that year of my Friday afternoons off? The following:

Though the world cannot be changed by talking to one child at a time, it may at least be known.

Anyway, Selena placed into our eyes for long remembrance that useful stubborn face. She said, No. Listen to me, you people. Please. I don't have lots of time. What I want . . . I want to lie down and think about Abby. Nothing special. Just think about her, you know.

In the train Susan fell asleep immediately. She woke up from time to time, because the speed of the new wheels and the resistance of the old track gave us some terrible jolts. Once, she opened her eyes wide and said, You know, Ann's right. You don't get sick like that for nothing. I mean, she didn't even mention him.

Why should she? She hasn't even see him, I said. Susan, you still have him-itis, the dread disease of females.

Yeah? And you don't? Anyway, he *was* around quite a bit. He was there every day, nearly, when the kid died.

Abby. I didn't like to hear "the kid." I wanted to say "Abby" the way I've said "Selena"—so those names can take thickness and strength and fall back into the world with their weight.

Abby, you know, was a wonderful child. She was in Richard's classes every class till high school. Good-hearted little girl from the beginning, noticeably kind—for a kid, I mean. Smart.

That's true, said Ann, very kind. She'd give away Selena's last shirt. Oh, yes, they were all wonderful little girls and wonderful little boys.

Chrissy *is* wonderful, Susan said.

She *is*, I said.

Middle kids aren't supposed to be, but she is. She put herself through college—I didn't have a cent—and now she has this fellowship. And, you know, she never did take any crap from boys. She's something.

Ann went swaying up the aisle to the bathroom. First she said, Oh, all of them— just wohunderful.

I loved Selena, Susan said, but she never talked to me enough. Maybe she talked to you women more, about things. Men.

Then Susan fell asleep.

Ann sat down opposite me. She looked straight into my eyes with a narrow squint. It often connotes accusation.

Be careful—you're wrecking your laugh lines, I said.

Screw you, she said. You're kidding around. Do you realize I don't know where Mickey is? You know, you've been lucky. You always have been. Since you were a little kid. Papa and Mama's darling.

As usual in conversations, I said a couple of things out loud and kept a few structured remarks for interior mulling and righteousness. I thought: She's never even met my folks. I thought: What a rotten thing to say. Luck—isn't it something like an insult?

I said, Annie, I'm only forty-eight. There's lots of time for me to be totally wrecked—if I live, I mean.

Then I tried to knock wood, but we were sitting in plush and leaning on plastic. Wood! I shouted. Please, some wood! Anybody here have a matchstick?

Oh, shut up, she said. Anyway, death doesn't count.

I tried to think of a couple of sorrows as irreversible as death. But truthfully nothing in my life can compare to hers: a son, a boy of fifteen, who disappears before your very eyes into a darkness or a light behind his own, from which neither hugging nor hitting can bring him. If you shout, Come back, come back, he won't come. Mickey, Mickey, Mickey, we once screamed, as though he were twenty miles away instead of right in front of us in a kitchen chair; but he refused to return. And when he did, twelve hours later, he left immediately for California.

Well, some bad things have happened in my life, I said.

What? You were born a woman? Is that it?

She was, of course, mocking me this time, referring to an old discussion about feminism and Judaism. Actually, on the prism of isms, both of those do have to be looked at together once in a while.

Well, I said, my mother died a couple of years ago and I still feel it. I think *Ma* sometimes and I lose my breath. I miss her. You understand that. Your mother's seventy-six. You have to admit it's nice still having her.

She's very sick, Ann said, Half the time she's out of it.

I decided not to describe my mother's death. I could have done so and made Ann even more miserable. But I thought I'd save that for her next attack on me. These constrictions of her spirit were coming closer and closer together. Probably a great enmity was about to be born.

Susan's eyes opened. The death or dying of someone near or dear often makes people irritable, she stated. (She's been taking a course in relationships *and* interrelationships.) The real name of my seminar is Skills: Personal Friendship and Community. It's a very good course despite your snide remarks.

While we talked, a number of cities passed us, going in the opposite direction. I had tried to look at New London through the dusk of the windows. Now I was missing New Haven. The conductor explained, smiling: Lady, if the windows were clean, half of you'd be dead. The tracks are lined with sharpshooters.

Do you believe that? I hate people to talk that way.

He may be exaggerating, Susan said, but don't wash the window.

A man leaned across the aisle. Ladies, he said, I do believe it. According to what I hear of this part of the country, it don't seem unplausible.

Susan turned to see if he was worth engaging in political dialogue.

You've forgotten Selena already, Ann said. All of us have. Then you'll make this nice memorial service for her and everyone will stand up and say a few words and then we'll forget her again—for good. What'll you say at the memorial, Faith?

It's not right to talk like that. She's not dead yet, Annie.

Yes, she is, said Ann.

We discovered the next day that give or take an hour or two, Ann had been correct. It was a combination—David Clark, surgeon, said—of being sick unto real death and having a tabletop full of little bottles.

Now, why are you taking all those hormones? Susan had asked Selena a couple of years earlier. They were visiting New Orleans. It was Mardi Gras.

Oh, they're mostly vitamins, Selena said. Besides, I want to be young and beautiful. She made a joking pirouette.

Susan said, That's absolutely ridiculous.

But Susan's seven or eight years younger than Selena. What did she know? Because: People *do* want to be young and beautiful. When they meet in the street, male or female, if they're getting older they look at each other's faces a little ashamed. It's clear they want to say, Excuse me, I didn't mean to draw attention to mortality and gravity all at once. I didn't want to remind you, my dear friend, of our coming eviction, first from liveliness, then from life. To which, most of the time, the friend's eyes will courteously reply, My dear, it's nothing at all. I hardly noticed.

Luckily, I learned recently how to get out of that deep well of melancholy. Anyone can do it. You grab at roots of the littlest future, sometimes just stubs of conversation. Though some believe you miss a great deal of depth by not sinking down down down.

Susan, I asked, you still seeing Ed Flores?

Went back to his wife.

Lucky she didn't kill you, said Ann. I'd never fool around with a Spanish guy. They all have tough ladies back in the barrio.

No, said Susan, she's unusual. I met her at a meeting. We had an amazing talk. Luisa is a very fine woman. She's one of the office-worker organizers I told you about. She only needs him two more years, she says. Because the kids—they're girls—need to be watched a little in their neighborhood. The neighborhood is definitely not good. He's a good father but not such a great husband.

I'd call that a word to the wise.

Well, you know me—I don't want a husband. I like a male person around. I hate to do without. Anyway, listen to this. She, Luisa, whispers in my ear the other day, she whispers, Suzie, in two years you still want him, I promise you, you got him. Really, I may still want him then. He's only about forty-five now. Still got a lot of spunk. I'll have my degree in two years. Chrissy will be out of the house.

Two years! In two years we'll all be dead, said Ann.

I know she didn't mean all of us. She meant Mickey. That boy of hers would surely be killed in one of the drugstores or whorehouses of Chicago, New Orleans, San Francisco. I'm in a big beautiful city, he said when he called last month. Makes New York look like a garbage tank.

Mickey! Where?

Ha-ha, he said and hung up.

Soon he'd be picked up for vagrancy, dealing, small thievery, or simply screaming dirty words at night under a citizen's window. Then Ann would fly to the town or not fly to the town to disentangle him, depending on a confluence of financial reality and psychiatric advice.

How *is* Mickey? Selena had said. In fact, that was her first sentence when we came, solemn and embarrassed, into her sunny front room that was full of the light and shadow of windy courtyard trees. We said, each in her own way, How are you feeling, Selena? She said, O.K., first things first. Let's talk about important things. How's Richard? How's Tonto? How's John? How's Chrissy? How's Judy? How's Mickey?

I don't want to talk about Mickey, said Ann.

Oh, let's talk about him, talk about him, Selena said, taking Ann's hand. Let's all think before it's too late. How did it start? Oh, for God's sake talk about him.

Susan and I were smart enough to keep our mouths shut.

Nobody knows, nobody knows anything. Why? Where? Everybody has an idea, theories, and writes articles. Nobody knows.

Ann said this sternly. She didn't whine. She wouldn't lean too far into Selena's softness, but listening to Selena speak Mickey's name, she could sit in her chair more easily. I watched. It was interesting. Ann breathed deeply in and out the way we've learned in our Thursday-night yoga class. She was able to rest her body a little bit.

We were riding the rails of the trough called Park Avenue-in-the-Bronx. Susan had turned from us to talk to the man across the aisle. She was explaining that the war in Vietnam was not yet over and would not be, as far as she was concerned, until we repaired the dikes we'd bombed and paid for some of the hopeless ecological damage. He didn't see it that way. Fifty thousand American lives, our own boys—we'd paid, he said. He asked us if we agreed with Susan. Every word, we said.

You don't look like hippies. He laughed. Then his face changed. As the resident face-reader, I decided he was thinking: Adventure. He may have hit a mother lode of late counter-culture in three opinionated left-wing ladies. That was the nice part of his face. The other part was the sly out-of-town-husband-in-New-York look.

I'd like to see you again, he said to Susan.

Oh? Well, come to dinner day after tomorrow. Only two of my kids will be home. You ought to have at least one decent meal in New York.

Kids? His face thought it over. Thanks. Sure, he said. I'll come.

Ann muttered, She's impossible. She did it again.

Oh, Susan's O.K., I said. She's just right in there. Isn't that good?

This is a long ride, said Ann.

Then we were in the darkness that precedes Grand Central.

We're irritable, Susan explained to her new pal. We're angry with our friend Selena for dying. The reason is, we want her to be present when we're dying. We all require a mother or mother-surrogate to fix our pillows on that final occasion, and we were counting on her to be that person.

I know just what you mean, he said. You'd like to have someone around. A little fuss, maybe.

Something like that. Right, Faith?

It always takes me a minute to slide under the style of her public-address system. I agreed. Yes.

The train stopped hard, in a grinding agony of opposing technologies.

Right. Wrong. Who cares? Ann said. She didn't have to die. She really wrecked everything.

Oh, Annie, I said.

Shut up, will you? Both of you, said Ann, nearly breaking our knees as she jammed past us and out of the train.

Then Susan, like a New York hostess, began to tell that man all our private troubles—the mistake of the World Trade Center, Westway, the decay of the South Bronx, the rage in Williamsburg. She rose with him on the escalator, gabbing into evening friendship and a happy night.

At home Anthony, my youngest son, said, Hello, you just missed Richard. He's in Paris now. He had to call collect.

Collect? From Paris?

He saw my sad face and made one of the herb teas used by his peer group to calm their overwrought natures. He does want to improve my pretty good health and spirits. His friends have a book that says a person should, if properly nutritioned, live forever. He wants me to give it a try. He also believes that the human race, its brains and good looks, will end in his time.

At about eleven-thirty he went out to live the pleasures of his eighteen-year-old nighttime life.

At 3 A.M. he found me washing the floors and making little apartment repairs.

More tea, Mom? he asked. He sat down to keep me company. O.K., Faith. I know you feel terrible. But how come Selena never realized about Abby?

Anthony, what the hell do I realize about you?

Come on, you had to be blind. I was just a little kid, and *I* saw. Honest to God, Ma.

Listen, Tonto. Basically Abby was O.K. She was. You don't know yet what their times can do to a person.

Here she goes with her goody-goodies—everything is so groovy wonderful far-out terrific. Next thing, you'll say people are darling and the world is *so* nice and round that Union Carbide will never blow it up.

I have never said anything as hopeful as that. And why to all our knowledge of that sad day did Tonto at 3 A.M. have to add the fact of the world?

The next night Max called from North Carolina. How's Selena? I'm flying up, he said. I have one early-morning appointment. Then I'm cancelling everything.

At 7 A.M. Annie called. I had barely brushed my morning teeth. It was hard, she said. The whole damn thing. I don't mean Selena. All of us. In the train. None of you seemed real to me.

Real? Reality, huh? Listen, how about coming over for breakfast—I don't have to get going until after nine? I have this neat sourdough rye?

No, she said. Oh Christ, no. No!

I remember Ann's eyes and the hat she wore the day we first looked at each other. Our babies had just stepped howling out of the sandbox on their new walking legs. We picked them up. Over their sandy heads we smiled. I think a bond was sealed then, at least as useful as the vow we'd all sworn with husbands to whom we're no longer married. Hindsight, usually looked down upon, is probably as valuable as foresight, since it does include a few facts.

Meanwhile, Anthony's world—poor, dense, defenseless thing—rolls round and round. Living and dying are fastened to its surface and stuffed into its softer parts.

He was right to call my attention to its suffering and danger. He was right to harass my responsible nature. But I was right to invent for my friends and our children a report on these private deaths and the condition of our lifelong attachments.

Flannery O'Connor (1925–1964)

Flannery O'Connor was a woman, a Southerner, physically handicapped, and a Catholic and, though all her complex background and experience find their way into her fiction, the theme that runs most strongly is religion. She wrote:

> I see from the standpoint of Christian orthodoxy. This means that for me the meaning of life is centered in our Redemption by Christ and what I see in the world I see in its relation to that.

Hers is no simple or easily grasped vision. She said that she discovered from reading her work that "my subject in fiction is the action of grace in territory held largely by the devil."

Sometimes the violence of the action and the grotesqueness of the characters seem to preclude the manifestation of grace. But she believed that when the audience viewed the repugnant as normal, the writer must shock: "To the hard of hearing you shout and for the almost-blind you draw large and startling pictures." She also found that "violence is strangely capable of returning my characters to reality and preparing them to accept their moment of grace."

But she is not propagandistic, and the reader who does not share her theology or values can still enjoy and benefit from her work. She does not oversimplify human experience in order to fit it neatly into a mold or to prove a point. Though often her characters seem larger than life, perhaps caricatured, they lead their own lives, find their own destinies, make their own hells. Also, O'Connor tells good, exciting yarns in which important things happen to people, usually her fellow Georgians.

In a letter about Ruby Turpin, the main character in "Revelation," O'Connor wrote that "You got to be a very big woman to shout at the Lord across a hogpen. She's a country female Jacob." And a wonderfully comic creation, a devious, self-willed, smug country woman, a favorite O'Connor target. She thinks of herself as particularly blessed by God, but it is exactly when she shouts out her gratitude for being so wonderful ("Oh, thank you, Jesus, Jesus, thank you") that she is brought low. She is attacked by a young intellectual woman, another favorite target of the author's, who says, "Go back to hell where you came from, you old wart hog." Only after this humbling is there any hope for redemption for Ruby Turpin. In her final vision, she sees a "vast horde of souls rumbling toward heaven." First in line are the least in this world, "white trash," "niggers," and lunatics. And last are the respectable, smug, materialistic people like herself, "even their virtues burned away." This vision, O'Connor says, is purgatorial. Mrs. Turpin is now worthy of salvation.

This story, "Parker's Back," and "Judgment Day" were written in the last year of O'Connor's life, after her health had deteriorated radically. The three are the clearest and most moving statements of O'Connor's religious beliefs and feelings.

But despite the seriousness of her themes and the power of her commitment, Flannery O'Connor is a comic writer. She can make a reader laugh out loud, at the outrageous imagery, at the twists of countrified speech, at characters who are exaggerated and grotesque but somehow not horrible, and even at the comic absurdity she sees in the spiritual condition of modern humanity.

Revelation

The doctor's waiting room, which was very small, was almost full when the Turpins entered and Mrs. Turpin, who was very large, made it look even smaller by her presence. She stood looming at the head of the magazine table set in the center of it, a living demonstration that the room was inadequate and ridiculous. Her little bright black eyes took in all the patients as she sized up the seating situation. There was one vacant chair and a place on the sofa occupied by a blond child in a dirty blue romper who should have been told to move over and make room for the lady. He was five or six, but Mrs. Turpin saw at once that no one was going to tell him to move over. He was slumped down in the seat, his arms idle at his sides and his eyes idle in his head; his nose ran unchecked.

Mrs. Turpin put a firm hand on Claud's shoulder and said in a voice that included anyone who wanted to listen, "Claud, you sit in that chair there," and gave him a push down into the vacant one. Claud was florid and bald and sturdy, somewhat shorter than Mrs. Turpin, but he sat down as if he were accustomed to doing what she told him to.

Mrs. Turpin remained standing. The only man in the room besides Claud was a lean stringy old fellow with a rusty hand spread out on each knee, whose eyes were closed as if he were asleep or dead or pretending to be so as not to get up and offer her his seat. Her gaze settled agreeably on a well-dressed gray-haired lady whose eyes met hers and whose expression said: if that child belonged to me, he would have some manners and move over—there's plenty of room there for you and him too.

Claud looked up with a sigh and made as if to rise.

"Sit down," Mrs. Turpin said. "You know you're not supposed to stand on that leg. He has an ulcer on his leg," she explained.

Claud lifted his foot onto the magazine table and rolled his trouser leg up to reveal a purple swelling on a plump marble-white calf.

"My!" the pleasant lady said. "How did you do that?"

"A cow kicked him," Mrs. Turpin said.

"Goodness!" said the lady.

Claud rolled his trouser leg down.

"Maybe the little boy would move over," the lady suggested, but the child did not stir.

"Somebody will be leaving in a minute," Mrs. Turpin said. She could not understand why a doctor—with as much money as they made charging five dollars a day to just stick their head in the hospital door and look at you—couldn't afford a decent-sized waiting room. This one was hardly bigger than a garage. The table was cluttered with limp-looking magazines and at one end of it there was a big green glass ash tray full of cigarette butts and cotton wads with little blood spots on them. If she had had anything to do with the running of the place, that would have been emptied every so often. There were no chairs against the wall at the head of the room. It had a rectangular-shaped panel in it that permitted a view of the office where the nurse came and went and the secretary listened to the radio. A plastic fern in a gold pot sat in the opening and trailed its fronds down almost to the floor. The radio was softly playing gospel music.

Just then the inner door opened and a nurse with the highest stack of yellow hair Mrs. Turpin had ever seen put her face in the crack and called for the next patient. The woman sitting beside Claud grasped the two arms of her chair and hoisted herself up; she pulled her dress free from her legs and lumbered through the door where the nurse had disappeared.

Mrs. Turpin eased into the vacant chair, which held her tight as a corset. "I wish I could reduce," she said, and rolled her eyes and gave a comic sigh.

"Oh, *you* aren't fat," the stylish lady said.

"Ooooo I am too," Mrs. Turpin said. "Claud he eats all he wants to and never weighs over one hundred and seventy-five pounds, but me I just look at something good to eat and I gain some weight," and her stomach and shoulders shook with laughter. "You can eat all you want to, can't you, Claud?" she asked, turning to him.

Claud only grinned.

"Well, as long as you have such a good disposition," the stylish lady said, "I don't think it makes a bit of difference what size you are. You just can't beat a good disposition."

Next to her was a fat girl of eighteen or nineteen, scowling into a thick blue book which Mrs. Turpin saw was entitled *Human Development*. The girl raised her head and directed her scowl at Mrs. Turpin as if she did not like her looks. She appeared annoyed that anyone should speak while she tried to read. The poor girl's face was blue with acne and Mrs. Turpin thought how pitiful it was to have a face like that at that age. She gave the girl a friendly smile but the girl only scowled the harder. Mrs. Turpin herself was fat but she had always had good skin, and, though she was forty-seven years old, there was not a wrinkle in her face except around her eyes from laughing too much.

Next to the ugly girl was the child, still in exactly the same position, and next to him was a thin leathery old woman in a cotton print dress. She and Claud had three sacks of chicken feed in their pump house that was in the same print. She had seen from the first that the child belonged with the old woman. She could tell by the way they sat—kind of vacant and white-trashy, as if they would sit there until Doomsday if nobody called and told them to get up. And at right angles but next to the well-dressed pleasant lady was a lank-faced woman who was certainly the child's mother. She had on a yellow sweat shirt and wine-colored slacks, both gritty-looking, and the rims of her lips were stained with snuff. Her dirty yellow hair was tied behind with a little piece of red paper ribbon. Worse than niggers any day, Mrs. Turpin thought.

The gospel hymn playing was, "When I looked up and He looked down," and Mrs. Turpin, who knew it, supplied the last line mentally, "And wona these days I know I'll we-eara crown."

Without appearing to, Mrs. Turpin always noticed people's feet. The well-dressed lady had on red and gray suede shoes to match her dress. Mrs. Turpin had on her good black patent leather pumps. The ugly girl had on Girl Scout shoes and heavy socks. The old woman had on tennis shoes and the white-trashy mother had on what appeared to be bedroom slippers, black straw with gold braid threaded through them—exactly what you would have expected her to have on.

Sometimes at night when she couldn't go to sleep, Mrs. Turpin would occupy herself with the question of who she would have chosen to be if she couldn't have been herself. If Jesus had said to her before he made her, "There's only two places available for you. You can either be a nigger or white-trash," what would she have said? "Please, Jesus, please," she would have said, "just let me wait until there's another place available," and he would have said, "No, you have to go right now and I have only those two places so make up your mind." She would have wiggled and squirmed and begged and pleaded but it would have been no use and finally she would have said, "All right, make me a nigger then—but that don't mean a trashy one." And he would have made her a neat clean respectable Negro woman, herself but black.

Next to the child's mother was a red-headed youngish woman, reading one of the magazines and working a piece of chewing gum, hell for leather, as Claud would say. Mrs. Turpin could not see the woman's feet. She was not white-trash, just common. Sometimes Mrs. Turpin occupied herself at night naming the classes of people. On the bottom of the heap were most colored people, not the kind she would have been if she had been one, but most of them; then next to them—not above, just away from—were the white-trash; then above them were the home-owners, and above them the home-and-land owners, to which she and Claud belonged. Above she and Claud were people with a lot of money and much bigger houses and much more land. But here the complexity of it would begin to bear in on her, for some of the people with a lot money were common and ought to be below she and Claud and some of the people who had good blood had lost their money and had to rent and then there were colored people who owned their homes and land as well. There was a colored dentist in town who had two red Lincolns and a swimming pool and a farm with registered white-face cattle on it. Usually by the time she had fallen asleep all the classes of people were moiling and roiling around in her head, and she would dream they were all crammed in together in a box car, being ridden off to be put in a gas oven.

"That's a beautiful clock," she said and nodded to her right. It was a big wall clock, the face encased in a brass sunburst.

"Yes, it's very pretty," the stylish lady said agreeably. "And right on the dot too," she added, glancing at her watch.

The ugly girl beside her cast an eye upward at the clock, smirked, then looked directly at Mrs. Turpin and smirked again. Then she returned her eyes to her book. She was obviously the lady's daughter because, although they didn't look anything alike as to disposition, they both had the same shape of face and the same blue eyes. On the lady they sparkled pleasantly but in the girl's seared face they appeared alternately to smolder and to blaze.

What if Jesus had said, "All right, you can be white-trash or a nigger or ugly"!

Mrs. Turpin felt an awful pity for the girl, though she thought it was one thing to be ugly and another to act ugly.

The woman with the snuff-stained lips turned around in her chair and looked up at the clock. Then she turned back and appeared to look a little to the side of Mrs. Turpin. There was a cast in one of her eyes. "You want to know wher you can get you one of themther clocks?" she asked in a loud voice.

"No, I already have a nice clock," Mrs. Turpin said. Once somebody like her got a leg in the conversation, she would be all over it.

"You can get you one with green stamps," the woman said. "That's most likely wher he got hisn. Save you up enough, you can get you most anythang. I got me some joo'ry."

Ought to have got you a wash rag and some soap, Mrs. Turpin thought.

"I get contour sheets with mine," the pleasant lady said.

The daughter slammed her book shut. She looked straight in front of her, directly through Mrs. Turpin and on through the yellow curtain and the plate glass window which made the wall behind her. The girl's eyes seemed lit all of a sudden with a peculiar light, an unnatural light like night road signs give. Mrs. Turpin turned her head to see if there was anything going on outside that she should see, but she could not see anything. Figures passing cast only a pale shadow through the curtain. There was no reason the girl should single her out for her ugly looks.

"Miss Finley," the nurse said, cracking the door. The gum-chewing woman got up and passed in front of her and Claud and went into the office. She had on red high-heeled shoes.

Directly across the table, the ugly girl's eyes were fixed on Mrs. Turpin as if she had some very special reason for disliking her.

"This is wonderful weather, isn't it?" the girl's mother said.

"It's good weather for cotton if you can get the niggers to pick it," Mrs. Turpin said, "but niggers don't want to pick cotton any more. You can't get the white folks to pick it and now you can't get the niggers—because they got to be right up there with the white folks."

"They gonna *try* anyways," the white-trash woman said, leaning forward.

"Do you have one of the cotton-picking machines?" the pleasant lady asked.

"No," Mrs. Turpin said, "they leave half the cotton in the field. We don't have much cotton anyway. If you want to make it farming now, you have to have a little of everything. We got a couple of acres of cotton and a few hogs and chickens and just enough white-face that Claud can look after them himself."

"One thang I don't want," the white-trash woman said, wiping her mouth with the back of her hand. "Hogs. Nasty stinking things, a-gruntin and a-rootin all over the place."

Mrs. Turpin gave her the merest edge of her attention. "Our hogs are not dirty and they don't stink," she said. "They're cleaner than some children I've seen. Their feet never touch the ground. We have a pig-parlor—that's where you raise them on concrete," she explained to the pleasant lady, "and Claud scoots them down with the hose every afternoon and washes off the floor." Cleaner by far than that child right there, she thought. Poor nasty little thing. He had not moved except to put the thumb of his dirty hand into his mouth.

The woman turned her face away from Mrs. Turpin. "I know I wouldn't scoot down no hog with no hose," she said to the wall.

You wouldn't have no hog to scoot down, Mrs. Turpin said to herself.

"A-gruntin and a-rootin and a-groanin," the woman muttered.

"We got a little of everything," Mrs. Turpin said to the pleasant lady. "It's no use in having more than you can handle yourself with help like it is. We found enough niggers to pick our cotton this year but Claud he has to go after them and take them home again in the evening. They can't walk that half a mile. No they can't. I tell you," she said and laughed merrily, "I sure am tired of buttering up niggers, but you got to love em if you want em to work for you. When they come in the morning, I run out and I say, 'Hi yawl this morning?' and when Claud drives them off to the field I just wave to beat the band and they just wave back." And she waved her hand rapidly to illustrate.

"Like you read out of the same book," the lady said, showing she understood perfectly.

"Child, yes," Mrs. Turpin said. "And when they come in from the field, I run out with a bucket of icewater. That's the way it's going to be from now on," she said. "You may as well face it."

"One thang I know," the white-trash woman said. "Two thangs I ain't going to do: love no niggers or scoot down no hog with no hose." And she let out a bark of contempt.

The look that Mrs. Turpin and the pleasant lady exchanged indicated they both understood that you had to *have* certain things before you could *know* certain things. But every time Mrs. Turpin exchanged a look with the lady, she was aware that the ugly girl's peculiar eyes were still on her, and she had trouble bringing her attention back to the conversation.

"When you got something," she said, "you got to look after it." And when you ain't got a thing but breath and britches, she added to herself, you can afford to come to town every morning and just sit on the Court House coping and spit.

A grotesque revolving shadow passed across the curtain behind her and was thrown palely on the opposite wall. Then a bicycle clattered down against the outside of the building. The door opened and a colored boy glided in with a tray from the drugstore. It had two large red and white paper cups on it with tops on them. He was a tall, very black boy in discolored white pants and a green nylon shirt. He was chewing gum slowly, as if to music. He set the tray down in the office opening next to the fern and stuck his head through to look for the secretary. She was not in there. He rested his arms on the ledge and waited, his narrow bottom stuck out, swaying to the left and right. He raised a hand over his head and scratched the base of his skull.

"You see that button there, boy?" Mrs. Turpin said. "You can punch that and she'll come. She's probably in the back somewhere."

"Is thas right?" the boy said agreeably, as if he had never seen the button before. He leaned to the right and put his finger on it. "She sometime out," he said and twisted around to face his audience, his elbows behind him on the counter. The nurse appeared and he twisted back again. She handed him a dollar and he rooted in his pocket and made the change and counted it out to her. She gave him fifteen cents for a tip and he went out with the empty tray. The heavy door swung to slowly and closed at length with the sound of suction. For a moment no one spoke.

"They ought to send all them niggers back to Africa," the white-trash woman said. "That's wher they come from in the first place."

"Oh, I couldn't do without my good colored friends," the pleasant lady said.

"There's a heap of things worse than a nigger," Mrs. Turpin agreed. "It's all kinds of them just like it's all kinds of us."

"Yes, and it takes all kinds to make the world go round," the lady said in her musical voice.

As she said it, the raw-complexioned girl snapped her teeth together. Her lower lip turned downwards and inside out, revealing the pale pink inside of her mouth. After a second it rolled back up. It was the ugliest face Mrs. Turpin had ever seen anyone make and for a moment she was certain that the girl had made it at her. She was looking at her as if she had known and disliked her all her life—all of Mrs. Turpin's life, it seemed too, not just all the girl's life. Why, girl, I don't even know you, Mrs. Turpin said silently.

She forced her attention back to the discussion. "It wouldn't be practical to send them back to Africa," she said. "They wouldn't want to go. They got it too good here."

"Wouldn't be what they wanted—if I had anythang to do with it," the woman said.

"It wouldn't be a way in the world you could get all the niggers back over there," Mrs. Turpin said. "They'd be hiding out and lying down and turning sick on you and wailing and hollering and raring and pitching. It wouldn't be a way in the world to get them over there."

"They got over here," the trashy woman said. "Get back like they got over."

"It wasn't so many of them then," Mrs. Turpin explained.

The woman looked at Mrs. Turpin as if here was an idiot indeed but Mrs. Turpin was not bothered by the look, considering where it came from.

"Nooo," she said, "they're going to stay here where they can go to New York and marry white folks and improve their color. That's what they all want to do, every one of them, improve their color."

"You know what comes of that, don't you?" Claud asked.

"No, Claud, what?" Mrs. Turpin said.

Claud's eyes twinkled. "White-faced niggers," he said with never a smile.

Everybody in the office laughed except the white-trash and the ugly girl. The girl gripped the book in her lap with white fingers. The trashy woman looked around her from face to face as if she thought they were all idiots. The old woman in the feed sack dress continued to gaze expressionless across the floor at the high-top shoes of the man opposite her, the one who had been pretending to be asleep when the Turpins came in. He was laughing heartily, his hands still spread out on his knees. The child had fallen to the side and was lying now almost face down in the old woman's lap.

While they recovered from their laughter, the nasal chorus on the radio kept the room from silence.

> *"You go to blank blank*
> *And I'll go to mine*
> *But we'll all blank along*
> *To-geth-ther,*
> *And all along the blank*
> *We'll hep eachother out*
> *Smile-ling in any kind of*
> *Weath-ther!"*

Mrs. Turpin didn't catch every word but she caught enough to agree with the spirit of the song and it turned her thoughts sober. To help anybody out that needed it was her philosophy of life. She never spared herself when she found somebody in need, whether they were white or black, trash or decent. And of all she had to be thankful for, she was most thankful that this was so. If Jesus had said, "You can be high society and have all the money you want and be thin and svelte-like, but you can't be a good woman with it," she would have had to say, "Well don't make me that then. Make me a good woman and it don't matter what else, how fat or how ugly or how poor!" Her heart rose. He had not made her a nigger or white-trash or ugly! He had made her herself and given her a little of everything. Jesus, thank you! she said. Thank you thank you thank you! Whenever she counted her blessings she felt as buoyant as if she weighed one hundred and twenty-five pounds instead of one hundred and eighty.

"What's wrong with your little boy?" the pleasant lady asked the white-trashy woman.

"He has a ulcer," the woman said proudly. "He ain't give me a minute's peace since he was born. Him and her are just alike," she said, nodding at the old woman, who was running her leathery fingers through the child's pale hair. "Look like I can't get nothing down them two but Co' Cola and candy."

That's all you try to get down em, Mrs. Turpin said to herself. Too lazy to light the fire. There was nothing you could tell her about people like them that she didn't know already. And it was not just that they didn't have anything. Because if you gave them everything, in two weeks it would all be broken or filthy or they would have chopped it up for lightwood. She knew all this from her own experience. Help them you must, but help them you couldn't.

All at once the ugly girl turned her lips inside out again. Her eyes fixed like two drills on Mrs. Turpin. This time there was no mistaking that there was something urgent behind them.

Girl, Mrs. Turpin exclaimed silently, I haven't done a thing to you! The girl might be confusing her with somebody else. There was no need to sit by and let herself be intimidated. "You must be in college," she said boldly, looking directly at the girl. "I see you reading a book there."

The girl continued to stare and pointedly did not answer.

Her mother blushed at this rudeness. "The lady asked you a question, Mary Grace," she said under her breath.

"I have ears," Mary Grace said.

The poor mother blushed again. "Mary Grace goes to Wellesley College," she explained. She twisted one of the buttons on her dress. "In Massachusetts," she added with a grimace. "And in the summer she just keeps right on studying. Just reads all the time, a real book worm. She's done real well at Wellesley; she's taking English and Math and History and Psychology and Social Studies," she rattled on, "and I think it's too much. I think she ought to get out and have fun."

The girl looked as if she would like to hurl them all through the plate glass window.

"Way up north," Mrs. Turpin murmured and thought, well, it hasn't done much for her manners.

"I'd almost rather to have him sick," the white-trash woman said, wrenching the attention back to herself. "He's so mean when he ain't. Look like some children just take natural to meanness. It's some gets bad when they get sick but he was the opposite. Took sick and turned good. He don't give me no trouble now. It's me waitin to see the doctor," she said.

If I was going to send anybody back to Africa, Mrs. Turpin thought, it would be your kind, woman. "Yes, indeed," she said aloud, but looking up at the ceiling, "it's a heap of things worse than a nigger." And dirtier than a hog, she added to herself.

"I think people with bad dispositions are more to be pitied than anyone on earth," the pleasant lady said in a voice that was decidedly thin.

"I thank the Lord he has blessed me with a good one," Mrs. Turpin said. "The day has never dawned that I couldn't find something to laugh at."

"Not since she married me anyways," Claud said with a comical straight face.

Everybody laughed except the girl and the white-trash.

Mrs. Turpin's stomach shook. "He's such a caution," she said, "that I can't help but laugh at him."

The girl made a loud ugly noise through her teeth.

Her mother's mouth grew thin and tight. "I think the worst thing in the world," she said, "is an ungrateful person. To have everything and not appreciate it. I know a girl," she said, "who has parents who would give her anything, a little brother who loves her dearly, who is getting a good education, who wears the best clothes, but who can never say a kind word to anyone, who never smiles, who just criticizes and complains all day long."

"Is she too old to paddle?" Claud asked.

The girl's face was almost purple.

"Yes," the lady said, "I'm afraid there's nothing to do but leave her to her folly. Some day she'll wake up and it'll be too late."

"It never hurt anyone to smile," Mrs. Turpin said. "It just makes you feel better all over."

"Of course," the lady said sadly, "but there are just some people you can't tell anything to. They can't take criticism."

"If it's one thing I am," Mrs. Turpin said with feeling, "it's grateful. When I think who all I could have been besides myself and what all I got, a little of everything, and a good disposition besides, I just feel like shouting, 'Thank you, Jesus, for making everything the way it is!' It could have been different!" For one thing, somebody else could have got Claud. At the thought of this, she was flooded with gratitude and a terrible pang of joy ran through her. "Oh thank you, Jesus, Jesus, thank you!" she cried aloud.

The book struck her directly over her left eye. It struck almost at the same instant that she realized the girl was about to hurl it. Before she could utter a sound, the raw face came crashing across the table toward her, howling. The girl's fingers sank like clamps into the soft flesh of her neck. She heard the mother cry out and Claud shout, "Whoa!" There was an instant when she was certain that she was about to be in an earthquake.

All at once her vision narrowed and she saw everything as if it were happening in a small room far away, or as if she were looking at it through the wrong end of a telescope. Claud's face crumpled and fell out of sight. The nurse ran in, then out, then in again. Then the gangling figure of the doctor rushed out of the inner door. Magazines flew this way and that as the table turned over. The girl fell with a thud and Mrs. Turpin's vision suddenly reversed itself and she saw everything large instead of small. The eyes of the white-trashy woman were staring hugely at the floor. There the girl, held down on one side by the nurse and on the other by her mother, was wrenching and turning in their grasp. The doctor was kneeling astride her, trying to hold her arm down. He managed after a second to sink a long needle into it.

Mrs. Turpin felt entirely hollow except for her heart which swung from side to side as if it were agitated in a great empty drum of flesh.

"Somebody that's not busy call for the ambulance," the doctor said in the off-hand voice young doctors adopt for terrible occasions.

Mrs. Turpin could not have moved a finger. The old man who had been sitting next to her skipped nimbly into the office and made the call, for the secretary still seemed to be gone.

"Claud!" Mrs. Turpin called.

He was not in his chair. She knew she must jump up and find him but she felt like some one trying to catch a train in a dream, when everything moves in slow motion and the faster you try to run the slower you go.

"Here I am," a suffocated voice, very unlike Claud's, said.

He was doubled up in the corner of the floor, pale as paper, holding his leg. She wanted to get up and go to him but she could not move. Instead, her gaze was drawn slowly downward to the churning face on the floor, which she could see over the doctor's shoulder.

The girl's eyes stopped rolling and focused on her. They seemed a much lighter blue than before, as if a door that had been tightly closed behind them was now open to admit light and air.

Mrs. Turpin's head cleared and her power of motion returned. She leaned forward until she was looking directly into the fierce brilliant eyes. There was no doubt in her mind that the girl did know her, knew her in some intense and personal way, beyond time and place and condition. "What you got to say to me?" she asked hoarsely and held her breath, waiting, as for a revelation.

The girl raised her head. Her gaze locked with Mrs. Turpin's. "Go back to hell where you came from, you old wart hog," she whispered. Her voice was low but clear. Her eyes burned for a moment as if she saw with pleasure that her message had struck its target.

Mrs. Turpin sank back in her chair.

After a moment the girl's eyes closed and she turned her head wearily to the side.

The doctor rose and handed the nurse the empty syringe. He leaned over and put both hands for a moment on the mother's shoulders, which were shaking. She was sitting on the floor, her lips pressed together, holding Mary Grace's hand in her lap. The girl's fingers were gripped like a baby's around her thumb. "Go on to the hospital," he said. "I'll call and make the arrangements."

"Now let's see that neck," he said in a jovial voice to Mrs. Turpin. He began to inspect her neck with his first two fingers. Two little moon-shaped lines like pink fish bones were indented over her windpipe. There was the beginning of an angry red swelling above her eye. His fingers passed over this also.

"Lea' me be," she said thickly and shook him off. "See about Claud. She kicked him."

"I'll see about him in a minute," he said and felt her pulse. He was a thin gray-haired man, given to pleasantries. "Go home and have yourself a vacation the rest of the day," he said and patted her on the shoulder.

Quit your pattin me, Mrs. Turpin growled to herself.

"And put an ice pack over that eye," he said. Then he went and squatted down beside Claud and looked at his leg. After a moment he pulled him up and Claud limped after him into the office.

Until the ambulance came, the only sounds in the room were the tremulous moans of the girl's mother, who continued to sit on the floor. The white-trash woman did not take her eyes off the girl. Mrs. Turpin looked straight ahead at nothing. Presently the ambulance drew up, a long dark shadow, behind the curtain. The attendants came in and set the stretcher down beside the girl and lifted her expertly onto it and carried her out. The nurse helped the mother gather up her things. The shadow of the ambulance moved silently away and the nurse came back in the office.

"That ther girl is going to be a lunatic, ain't she?" the white-trash woman asked the nurse, but the nurse kept on to the back and never answered her.

"Yes, she's going to be a lunatic," the white-trash woman said to the rest of them.

"Po' critter," the old woman murmured. The child's face was still in her lap. His eyes looked idly out over her knees. He had not moved during the disturbance except to draw one leg up under him.

"I thank Gawd," the white-trash woman said fervently, "I ain't a lunatic."

Claud came limping out and the Turpins went home.

As their pick-up truck turned into their own dirt road and made the crest of the hill, Mrs. Turpin gripped the window ledge and looked out suspiciously. The land sloped gracefully down through a field dotted with lavender weeds and at the start of the rise their small yellow frame house, with its little flower beds spread out around it like a fancy apron, sat primly in its accustomed place between two giant hickory trees. She would not have been startled to see a burnt wound between two blackened chimneys.

Neither of them felt like eating so they put on their house clothes and lowered the shade in the bedroom and lay down, Claud with his leg on a pillow and herself with a damp washcloth over her eye. The instant she was flat on her back, the image of a razor-backed hog with warts on its face and horns coming out behind its ears snorted into her head. She moaned, a low quiet moan.

"I am not," she said tearfully, "a wart hog. From hell." But the denial had no force. The girl's eyes and her words, even the tone of her voice, low but clear, directed only to her, brooked no repudiation. She had been singled out for the message, though there was trash in the room to whom it might justly have been applied. The full force of this fact struck her only now. There was a woman there who was neglecting her own child but she had been overlooked. The message had been given to Ruby Turpin, a respectable, hard-working, church-going woman. The tears dried. Her eyes began to burn instead with wrath.

She rose on her elbow and the washcloth fell into her hand. Claud was lying on his back, snoring. She wanted to tell him what the girl had said. At the same time, she did not wish to put the image of herself as a wart hog from hell into his mind.

"Hey, Claud," she muttered and pushed his shoulder.

Claud opened one pale baby blue eye.

She looked into it warily. He did not think about anything. He just went his way.

"Wha, whasit?" he said and closed the eye again.

"Nothing," she said. "Does your leg pain you?"

"Hurts like hell," Claud said.

"It'll quit terreckly," she said and lay back down. In a moment Claud was snoring again. For the rest of the afternoon they lay there. Claud slept. She scowled at the ceiling. Occasionally she raised her fist and made a small stabbing motion over her chest as if she was defending her innocence to invisible guests who were like the comforters of Job, reasonable-seeming but wrong.

About five-thirty Claud stirred. "Got to go after those niggers," he sighed, not moving.

She was looking straight up as if there were unintelligible handwriting on the ceiling. The protuberance over her eye had turned a greenish-blue. "Listen here," she said.

"What?"

"Kiss me."

Claud leaned over and kissed her loudly on the mouth. He pinched her side and their hands interlocked. Her expression of ferocious concentration did not change. Claud got up, groaning and growling, and limped off. She continued to study the ceiling.

She did not get up until she heard the pick-up truck coming back with the Negroes. Then she rose and thrust her feet in her brown oxfords, which she did not bother to lace, and stumped out onto the back porch and got her red plastic bucket. She emptied a tray of ice cubes into it and filled it half full of water and went out into the back yard. Every afternoon after Claud brought the hands in, one of the boys helped him put out hay and the rest waited in the back of the truck until he was ready to take them home. The truck was parked in the shade under one of the hickory trees.

"Hi yawl this evening?" Mrs. Turpin asked grimly, appearing with the bucket and the dipper. There were three women and a boy in the truck.

"Us doin nicely," the oldest woman said. "Hi you doin?" and her gaze stuck immediately on the dark lump on Mrs. Turpin's forehead. "You done fell down, ain't you?" she asked in a solicitous voice. The old woman was dark and almost toothless. She had on an old felt hat of Claud's set back on her head. The other two women were younger and lighter and they both had new bright green sunhats. One of them had hers on her head; the other had taken hers off and the boy was grinning beneath it.

Mrs. Turpin set the bucket down on the floor of the truck. "Yawl hep yourselves," she said. She looked around to make sure Claud had gone. "No, I didn't fall down," she said, folding her arms. "It was something worse than that."

"Ain't nothing bad happen to you!" the old woman said. She said it as if they all knew that Mrs. Turpin was protected in some special way by Divine Providence. "You just had you a little fall."

"We were in town at the doctor's office for where the cow kicked Mr. Turpin," Mrs. Turpin said in a flat tone that indicated they could leave off their foolishness. "And there was this girl there. A big fat girl with her face all broke out. I could look at that girl and tell she was peculiar but I couldn't tell how. And me and her mama was just talking and going along and all of a sudden WHAM! She throws this big book she was reading at me and . . . ."

"Naw!" the old woman cried out.

"And then she jumps over the table and commences to choke me."

"Naw!" they all exclaimed, "naw!"

"Hi come she do that?" the old woman asked. "What ail her?"

Mrs. Turpin only glared in front of her.

"Somethin ail her," the old woman said.

"They carried her off in an ambulance," Mrs. Turpin continued, "but before she went she was rolling on the floor and they were trying to hold her down to give her a shot and she said something to me." She paused. "You know what she said to me?"

"What she say?" they asked.

"She said," Mrs. Turpin began, and stopped, her face very dark and heavy. The sun was getting whiter and whiter, blanching the sky overhead so that the leaves of the hickory tree were black in the face of it. She could not bring forth the words. "Something real ugly," she muttered.

"She sho shouldn't said nothin ugly to you," the old woman said. "You so sweet. You the sweetest lady I know."

"She pretty too," the one with the hat on said.

"And stout," the other one said. "I never knowed no sweeter white lady."

"That's the truth befo' Jesus," the old woman said. "Amen! You des as sweet and pretty as you can be."

Mrs. Turpin knew exactly how much Negro flattery was worth and it added to her rage. "She said," she began again and finished this time with a fierce rush of breath, "that I was an old wart hog from hell."

There was an astounded silence.

"Where she at?" the youngest woman cried in a piercing voice.

"Lemme see her. I'll kill her!"

"I'll kill her with you! the other one cried.

"She b'long in the sylum," the old woman said emphatically. "You the sweetest white lady I know."

"She pretty too," the other two said. "Stout as she can be and sweet. Jesus satisfied with her!"

"Deed he is," the old woman declared.

Idiots! Mrs. Turpin growled to herself. You could never say anything intelligent to a nigger. You could talk at them but not with them. "Yawl ain't drunk your water," she said shortly. "Leave the bucket in the truck when you're finished with it. I got more to do than just stand around and pass the time of day," and she moved off and into the house.

She stood for a moment in the middle of the kitchen. The dark protuberance over her eye looked like a miniature tornado cloud which might any moment sweep across the horizon of her brow. Her lower lip protruded dangerously. She squared her massive shoulders. Then she marched into the front of the house and out the side door and started down the road to the pig parlor. She had the look of a woman going single-handed, weaponless, into battle.

The sun was a deep yellow now like a harvest moon and was riding westward very fast over the far tree line as if it meant to reach the hogs before she did. The road was rutted and she kicked several good-sized stones out of her path as she strode along. The pig parlor was on a little knoll at the end of a lane that ran off from the side of the barn. It was a square of concrete as large as a small room, with a board fence about four feet high around it. The concrete floor sloped slightly so that the hog wash could drain off into a trench where it was carried to the field for fertilizer. Claud was standing on the outside, on the edge of the concrete, hanging onto the top board, hosing down the floor inside. The hose was connected to the faucet of a water trough nearby.

Mrs. Turpin climbed up beside him and glowered down at the hogs inside. There were seven long-snouted bristly shoats in it—tan with liver-colored spots—and an old sow a few weeks off from farrowing. She was lying on her side grunting. The shoats were running about shaking themselves like idiot children, their little slit pig eyes searching the floor for anything left. She had read that pigs were the most intelligent animal. She doubted it. They were supposed to be smarter than dogs. There had even been a pig astronaut. He had performed his assignment perfectly but died of a heart attack afterwards because they left him in his electric suit, sitting upright throughout his examination when naturally a hog should be on all fours.

A-gruntin and a-rootin and a-groanin.

"Gimme that hose," she said, yanking it away from Claud. "Go on and carry them niggers home and then get off that leg."

"You look like you might have swallowed a mad dog," Claud observed, but he got down and limped off. He paid no attention to her humors.

Until he was out of earshot, Mrs. Turpin stood on the side of the pen, holding the hose and pointing the stream of water at the hind quarters of any shoat that looked as if it might try to lie down. When he had had time to get over the hill, she turned her head slightly and her wrathful eyes scanned the path. He was nowhere in sight. She turned back again and seemed to gather herself up. Her shoulders rose and she drew in her breath.

"What do you send me a message like that for?" she said in a low fierce voice, barely above a whisper but with the force of a shout in its concentrated fury. "How am I a hog and me both? How am I saved and from hell too?" Her free fist was knotted and with the other she gripped the hose, blindly pointing the stream of water in and out of the eye of the old sow whose outraged squeal she did not hear.

The pig parlor commanded a view of the back pasture where their twenty beef cows were gathered around the hay-bales Claud and the boy had put out. The freshly cut pasture sloped down to the highway. Across it was their cotton field and beyond that a dark green dusty wood which they owned as well. The sun was behind the wood, very red, looking over the paling of trees like a farmer inspecting his own hogs.

"Why me?" she rumbled. "It's no trash around here, black or white, that I haven't given to. And break my back to the bone every day working. And do for the church."

She appeared to be the right size woman to command the arena before her. "How am I a hog?" she demanded. "Exactly how am I like them?" and she jabbed the stream of water at the shoats. "There was plenty of trash there. It didn't have to be me.

"If you like trash better, go get yourself some trash then," she railed. "You could have made me trash. Or a nigger. If trash is what you wanted why didn't you make me trash?" She shook her fist with the hose in it and a watery snake appeared momentarily in the air. "I could quit working and take it easy and be filthy," she growled. "Lounge about the sidewalks all day drinking root beer. Dip snuff and spit in every puddle and have it all over my face. I could be nasty.

"Or you could have made me a nigger. It's too late for me to be a nigger," she said with deep sarcasm, "but I could act like one. Lay down in the middle of the road and stop traffic. Roll on the ground."

In the deepening light everything was taking on a mysterious hue. The pasture was growing a peculiar glassy green and the streak of highway had turned lavender. She braced herself for a final assault and this time her voice rolled out over the pasture. "Go on," she yelled, "call me a hog! Call me a hog again. From hell. Call me a wart hog from hell. Put that bottom rail on top. There'll still be a top and bottom!"

A garbled echo returned to her.

A final surge of fury shook her and she roared, "Who do you think you are?"

The color everything, field and crimson sky, burned for a moment with a transparent intensity. The question carried over the pasture and across the highway and the cotton field and returned to her clearly like an answer from beyond the wood.

She opened her mouth but no sound came out of it.

A tiny truck, Claud's, appeared on the highway, heading rapidly out of sight. Its gears scraped thinly. It looked like a child's toy. At any moment a bigger truck might smash into it and scatter Claud's and the niggers' brains all over the road.

Mrs. Turpin stood there, her gaze fixed on the highway, all her muscles rigid, until in five or six minutes the truck reappeared, returning. She waited until it had had time to turn into their own road. Then like a monumental statue coming to life, she bent her head slowly and gazed, as if through the very heart of mystery, down into the pig parlor at the hogs. They had settled all in one corner around the old sow who was grunting softly. A red glow suffused them. They appeared to pant with a secret life.

Until the sun slipped finally behind the tree line, Mrs. Turpin remained there with her gaze bent to them as if she were absorbing some abysmal life-giving knowledge. At last she lifted her head. There was only a purple streak in the sky, cutting through a field of crimson and leading, like an extension of the highway, into the descending dusk. She raised her hands from the side of the pen in a gesture hieratic and profound. A visionary light settled in her eyes. She saw the streak as a vast swinging bridge extending upward from the earth through a field of living fire. Upon it a vast horde of souls were rumbling toward heaven. There were whole companies of white-trash, clean for the first time in their lives, and bands of black niggers in white robes, and battalions of freaks and lunatics shouting and clapping and leaping like frogs. And bringing up the end of the procession was a tribe of people whom she recognized at once as those who, like herself and Claud, had always had a little of everything and the God-given wit to use it right. She leaned forward to observe them closer. They were marching behind the others with great dignity, accountable as they had always been for good order and common sense and respectable behavior. They alone were on key. Yet she could see by their shocked and altered faces that even their virtues were being burned away. She lowered her hands and gripped the rail of the hog pen, her eyes small but fixed unblinkingly on what lay ahead. In a moment the vision faded but she remained where she was, immobile.

At length she got down and turned off the faucet and made her slow way on the darkening path to the house. In the woods around her the invisible cricket choruses had struck up, but what she heard were the voices of the souls climbing upward into the starry field and shouting hallelujah.

Yukio Mishima (1925–1970)

In November 1970 Yukio Mishima, together with some of his fanatical followers from the ultranationalistic Shield Society (which he had founded in 1968), broke into the headquarters of Japan's Eastern Defense Forces armed with swords and daggers, overpowered some aides, tied up the commanding general, and demanded that the troops be assembled to hear a speech. Mishima, wearing a kamikaze headband, addressed the troops for ten minutes, inciting them to rebel against the constitutional government (imposed by the United States) that had, in his words, "turned Japan spineless." Receiving only ridicule in response, he returned to the general's office and there, before the general's unbelieving eyes, proceeded to kill himself in strict accordance with the traditional samurai ritual of *seppuku,* or hara-kiri. After Mishima had driven a dagger deep into his left abdomen, one of his aides severed his head with a sword. The aide likewise killed himself and was beheaded; the others surrendered.

In 1936 there had been a similar revolt and, though equally unsuccessful, it had foreshadowed the repressive regime of General Tojo that was to stage the attack on Pearl Harbor in 1941. That earlier revolt is the one referred to in "Patriotism," one of Mishima's most powerful stories. Here life and fiction become joined. The act of *seppuku* was for Mishima (born Kimitake Hiraoka) a fulfillment, "the ultimate dream of my life." Born of an ancient samurai family, he longed to die a hero's death in accordance with the ancient samurai code; but his weak body kept him from service in the war, and he had to compensate through body-building (he became expert at *karate* and *kendo*) and, most important, through the discipline of writing. In his short lifetime he turned out twenty novels, thirty-three plays, many essays, and more than eighty stories; he also produced, directed, and acted in movies, and even sang on stage. His first book of stories, *A Forest in Flower,* appeared in 1943, but it was *Confessions of a Mask* (1948), dealing with the meditations of a young man of homosexual leanings in a repressive society, that brought him fame. A later book, *Forbidden Colors* (1968), also dealt with homosexuality, revealing that strain of aestheticism and even decadence which, throughout Mishima's work, seems strangely out of place in one so given to the samurai spirit. But his love of death was itself erotic, a kind of *liebestod,* and his self-discipline inseparable from a desire to create a body beautiful enough to be sacrificed. His last book, *Spring Snow* (1971), was the first of a four-volume posthumous cycle entitled *The Sea of Fertility,* of which the others are *Runaway Horses* (1973), *The Temple of Dawn* (1973), and *The Decay of the Angel* (1974). This last novel, translated by Edward G. Seidensticker, has been called "a death rattle in prose," but "a surpassingly chilling, subtle, and original novel" as well.

Mishima has been called "Japan's Hemingway," while others have compared him to "aesthetic" writers like Walter Pater and Oscar Wilde. He is not easy to define. His writing sometimes approaches the slick and the sentimental, but at its best—as in "Patriotism"—it is elegant, polished, austere. From an outsider's point of view there can be something simply silly or melodramatic about the enactment of archaic rituals that, for most, have lost their meaning; but Mishima by his heroic seriousness has, at least in his art, redeemed the ceremonial. He was a man out of his time. He hated, in Lawrence Olson's words, "the gritty selfishness and hypocrisy of much of postwar Japanese society," and this—together with his disposition toward theatricalism and sexual fantasy—"set him to writing books about young men in search of perfect beauty." In "Patriotism" we see the disciplined ardor of a fanatical romantic.

Patriotism

On the twenty-eighth of February, 1936 (on the third day, that is, of the February 26 Incident), Lieutenant Shinji Takeyama of the Konoe Transport Battalion—profoundly disturbed by the knowledge that his closest colleagues had been with the mutineers from the beginning, and indignant at the imminent prospect of Imperial troops attacking Imperial troops—took his officer's sword and ceremonially disemboweled himself in the eight-mat room of his private residence in the sixth block of Aoba-chō, in Yotsuya Ward. His wife, Reiko, followed him, stabbing herself to death. The lieutenant's farewell note consisted of one sentence: "Long live the Imperial Forces." His wife's, after apologies for her unfilial conduct in thus preceding her parents to the grave, concluded: "The day which, for a soldier's wife, had to come, has come. . . ." The last moments of this heroic and dedicated couple were such as to make the gods themselves weep. The lieutenant's age, it should be noted, was thirty-one, his wife's twenty-three; and it was not half a year since the celebration of their marriage.

2

Those who saw the bride and bridegroom in the commemorative photograph—perhaps no less than those actually present at the lieutenant's wedding—had exclaimed in wonder at the bearing of this handsome couple. The lieutenant, majestic in military uniform, stood protectively beside his bride, his right hand resting upon his sword, his officer's cap held at his left side. His expression was severe, and his dark brows and wide-gazing eyes well conveyed the clear integrity of youth. For the beauty of the bride in her white over-robe no comparisons were adequate. In the eyes, round beneath soft brows, in the slender, finely shaped nose, and in the full lips, there was both sensuousness and refinement. One hand, emerging shyly from a sleeve of the over-robe, held a fan, and the tips of the fingers, clustering delicately, were like the bud of a moonflower.

After the suicide, people would take out this photograph and examine it, and sadly reflect that too often there was a curse on these seemingly flawless unions. Perhaps it was no more than imagination, but looking at the picture after the tragedy it almost seemed as if the two young people before the gold-lacquered screen were gazing, each with equal clarity, at the deaths which lay before them.

Thanks to the good offices of their go-between, Lieutenant General Ozeki, they had been able to set themselves up in a new home at Aoba-chō in Yotsuya. "New home" is perhaps misleading. It was an old three-room rented house backing onto a small garden. As neither the six- nor the four-and-a-half mat room downstairs was favored by the sun, they used the upstairs eight-mat room as both bedroom and guest room. There was no maid, so Reiko was left alone to guard the house in her husband's absence.

The honeymoon trip was dispensed with on the grounds that these were times of national emergency. The two of them had spent the first night of their marriage at this house. Before going to bed, Shinji, sitting erect on the floor with his sword laid before him, had bestowed upon his wife a soldierly lecture. A woman who had become the wife of a soldier should know and resolutely accept that her husband's death might come at any moment. It could be tomorrow. It could be the day after. But, no matter when it came—he asked—was she steadfast in her resolve to accept it? Reiko rose to her feet, pulled open a drawer of the cabinet, and took out what was the most prized of her new possessions, the dagger her mother had given her. Returning to her place, she laid the dagger without a word on the mat before her, just as her husband had laid his sword. A silent understanding was achieved at once, and the lieutenant never again sought to test his wife's resolve.

In the first few months of her marriage Reiko's beauty grew daily more radiant, shining serene like the moon after rain.

As both were possessed of young, vigorous bodies, their relationship was passionate. Nor was this merely a matter of the night. On more than one occasion, returning home straight from maneuvers, and begrudging even the time it took to remove his mud-splashed uniform, the lieutenant had pushed his wife to the floor almost as soon as he had entered the house. Reiko was equally ardent in her response. For a little more or a little less than a month, from the first night of their marriage Reiko knew happiness, and the lieutenant, seeing this, was happy too.

Reiko's body was white and pure, and her swelling breasts conveyed a firm and chaste refusal; but, upon consent, those breasts were lavish with their intimate, welcoming warmth. Even in bed these two were frighteningly and awesomely serious. In the very midst of wild, intoxicating passions, their hearts were sober and serious.

By day the lieutenant would think of his wife in the brief rest periods between training; and all day long, at home, Reiko would recall the image of her husband. Even when apart, however, they had only to look at the wedding photograph for their happiness to be once more confirmed. Reiko felt not the slightest surprise that a man who had been a complete stranger until a few months ago should not have become the sun about which her whole world revolved.

All these things had a moral basis, and were in accordance with the Education Rescript's injunction that "husband and wife should be harmonious." Not once did Reiko contradict her husband, nor did the lieutenant ever find reason to scold his wife.

On the god shelf below the stairway, alongside the tablet from the Great Ise Shrine, were set photographs of their Imperial Majesties, and regularly every morning, before leaving for duty, the lieutenant would stand with his wife at this hallowed place and together they would bow their heads low. The offering water was renewed each morning, and the sacred sprig of *sasaki* was always green and fresh. Their lives were lived beneath the solemn protection of the gods and were filled with an intense happiness which set every fiber in their bodies trembling.

3

Although Lord Privy Seal Saitō's house was in their neighborhood, neither of them heard any noise of gunfire on the morning of February 26. It was a bugle, sounding muster in the dim, snowy dawn, when the ten-minute tragedy had already ended, which first disrupted the lieutenant's slumbers. Leaping at once from his bed, and without speaking a word, the lieutenant donned his uniform, buckled on the sword held ready for him by his wife, and hurried swiftly out into the snow-covered streets of the still darkened morning. He did not return until the evening of the twenty-eighth.

Later, from the radio news, Reiko learned the full extent of this sudden eruption of violence. Her life throughout the subsequent two days was lived alone, in complete tranquillity, and behind locked doors.

In the lieutenant's face, as he hurried silently out into the snowy morning, Reiko had read the determination to die. If her husband did not return, her own decision was made: she too would die. Quietly she attended to the disposition of her personal possessions. She chose her sets of visiting kimonos as keepsakes for friends of her schooldays, and she wrote a name and address on the stiff paper in which each was folded. Constantly admonished by her husband never to think of the morrow, Reiko had not even kept a diary and was now denied the pleasure of assiduously rereading her record of the happiness of the past few months and consigning each page to the fire as she did so. Ranged across the top of the radio were a small china dog, a rabbit, a squirrel, a bear, and a fox. There were also a small vase and a water pitcher. These comprised Reiko's one and only collection. But it would hardly do, she imagined, to give such things as keepsakes. Nor again would it be quite proper to ask specifically for them to be included in the coffin. It seemed to Reiko, as these thoughts passed through her mind, that the expressions on the small animals' faces grew even more lost and forlorn.

Reiko took the squirrel in her hand and looked at it. And then, her thoughts turning to a realm far beyond these childlike affections, she gazed up into the distance at the great sunlike principle which her husband embodied. She was ready, and happy, to be hurtled along to her destruction in that gleaming sun chariot—but now, for these few moments of solitude, she allowed herself to luxuriate in this innocent attachment to trifles. The time when she had genuinely loved these things, however, was long past. Now she merely loved the memory of having once loved them, and their place in her heart had been filled by more intense passions, by a more frenzied happiness. . . . For Reiko had never, even to herself, thought of those soaring joys of the flesh as a mere pleasure. The February cold, and the icy touch of the china squirrel, had numbed Reiko's slender fingers; yet, even so, in her lower limbs, beneath the ordered repetition of the pattern which crossed the skirt of her trim *meisen* kimono, she could feel now, as she thought of the lieutenant's powerful arms reaching out toward her, a hot moistness of the flesh which defied the snows.

She was not in the least afraid of the death hovering in her mind. Waiting alone at home, Reiko firmly believed that everything her husband was feeling or thinking now, his anguish and distress, was leading her—just as surely as the power in his flesh—to a welcome death. She felt as if her body could melt away with ease and be transformed to the merest fraction of her husband's thought.

Listening to the frequent announcements on the radio, she heard the names of several of her husband's colleagues mentioned among those of the insurgents. This was news of death. She followed the developments closely, wondering anxiously, as the situation became daily more irrevocable, why no Imperial ordinance was sent down, and watching what had at first been taken as a movement to restore the nation's honor come gradually to be branded with the infamous name of mutiny. There was no communication from the regiment. At any moment, it seemed, fighting might commence in the city streets where the remains of the snow still lay.

Toward sundown on the twenty-eighth Reiko was startled by a furious pounding on the front door. She hurried downstairs. As she pulled with fumbling fingers at the bolt, the shape dimly outlined beyond the frosted-glass panel made no sound, but she knew it was her husband. Reiko had never known the bolt on the sliding door to be so stiff. Still it resisted. The door just would not open.

In a moment, almost before she knew she had succeeded, the lieutenant was standing before her on the cement floor inside the porch, muffled in a khaki greatcoat, his top boots heavy with slush from the street. Closing the door behind him, he returned the bolt once more to its socket. With what significance, Reiko did not understand.

"Welcome home."

Reiko bowed deeply, but her husband made no response. As he had already unfastened his sword and was about to remove his greatcoat, Reiko moved around behind to assist. The coat, which was cold and damp and had lost the odor of horse dung it normally exuded when exposed to the sun, weighed heavily upon her arm. Draping it across a hanger, and cradling the sword and leather belt in her sleeves, she waited while her husband removed his top boots and then followed behind him into the "living room." This was the six-mat room downstairs.

Seen in the clear light from the lamp, her husband's face, covered with a heavy growth of bristle, was almost unrecognizably wasted and thin. The cheeks were hollow, their luster and resilience gone. In his normal good spirits he would have changed into old clothes as soon as he was home and have pressed her to get supper at once, but now he sat before the table still in his uniform, his head drooping dejectedly. Reiko refrained from asking whether she should prepare the supper.

After an interval the lieutenant spoke.

"I knew nothing. They hadn't asked me to join. Perhaps out of consideration, because I was newly married. Kanō, and Homma too, and Yamaguchi."

Reiko recalled momentarily the faces of high-spirited young officers, friends of her husband, who had come to the house occasionally as guests.

"There may be an Imperial ordinance sent down tomorrow. They'll be posted as rebels, I imagine. I shall be in command of a unit with orders to attack them. . . . I can't do it. It's impossible to do a thing like that."

He spoke again.

"They've taken me off guard duty, and I have permission to return home for one night. Tomorrow morning, without question, I must leave to join the attack. I can't do it, Reiko."

Reiko sat erect with lowered eyes. She understood clearly that her husband had spoken of his death. The lieutenant was resolved. Each word, being rooted in death, emerged sharply and with powerful significance against this dark, unmovable background. Although the lieutenant was speaking of his dilemma, already there was no room in his mind for vacillation.

However, there was a clarity, like the clarity of a stream fed from melting snows, in the silence which rested between them. Sitting in his own home after the long two-day ordeal, and looking across at the face of his beautiful wife, the lieutenant was for the first time experiencing true peace of mind. For he had at once known, though she said nothing, that his wife divined the resolve which lay beneath his words.

"Well, then . . ." The lieutenant's eyes opened wide. Despite his exhaustion they were strong and clear, and now for the first time they looked straight into the eyes of his wife. "Tonight I shall cut my stomach."

Reiko did not flinch.

Her round eyes showed tension, as taut as the clang of a bell.

"I am ready," she said. "I ask permission to accompany you."

The lieutenant felt almost mesmerized by the strength in those eyes. His words flowed swiftly and easily, like the utterances of a man in delirium, and it was beyond his understanding how permission in a matter of such weight could be expressed so casually.

"Good. We'll go together. But I want you as a witness, first, for my own suicide. Agreed?"

When this was said a sudden release of abundant happiness welled up in both their hearts. Reiko was deeply affected by the greatness of her husband's trust in her. It was vital for the lieutenant, whatever else might happen, that there should be no irregularity in his death. For that reason there had to be a witness. The fact that he had chosen his wife for this was the first mark of his trust. The second, and even greater mark, was that though he had pledged that they should die together he did not intend to kill his wife first—he had deferred her death to a time when he would no longer be there to verify it. If the lieutenant had been a suspicious husband, he would doubtless, as in the usual suicide pact, have chosen to kill his wife first.

When Reiko said, "I ask permission to accompany you," the lieutenant felt these words to be the final fruit of the education which he had himself given his wife, starting on the first night of their marriage, and which had schooled her, when the moment came, to say what had to be said without a shadow of hesitation. This flattered the lieutenant's opinion of himself as a self-reliant man. He was not so romantic or conceited as to imagine that the words were spoken spontaneously, out of love for her husband.

With happiness welling almost too abundantly in their hearts, they could not help smiling at each other. Reiko felt as if she had returned to her wedding night.

Before her eyes was neither pain nor death. She seemed to see only a free and limitless expanse opening out into vast distances.

"The water is hot. Will you take your bath now?"

"Ah yes, of course."

"And supper . . .?"

The words were delivered in such level, domestic tones that the lieutenant came near to thinking, for the fraction of a second, that everything had been a hallucination.

"I don't think we'll need supper. But perhaps you could warm some sake?"

"As you wish."

As Reiko rose and took a *tanzen* gown from the cabinet for after the bath, she purposely directed her husband's attention to the opened drawer. The lieutenant rose, crossed to the cabinet, and looked inside. From the ordered array of paper wrappings he read, one by one, the addresses of the keepsakes. There was no grief in the lieutenant's response to this demonstration of heroic resolve. His heart was filled with tenderness. Like a husband who is proudly shown the childish purchases of a young wife, the lieutenant, overwhelmed by affection, lovingly embraced his wife from behind and implanted a kiss upon her neck.

Reiko felt the roughness of the lieutenant's unshaven skin against her neck. This sensation, more than being just a thing of this world, was for Reiko almost the world itself, but now—with the feeling that it was soon to be lost forever—it had freshness beyond all her experience. Each moment had its own vital strength, and the senses in every corner of her body were reawakened. Accepting her husband's caresses from behind, Reiko raised herself on the tips of her toes, letting the vitality seep through her entire body.

"First the bath, and then, after some sake . . . lay out the bedding upstairs, will you?"

The lieutenant whispered the words into his wife's ear. Reiko silently nodded.

Flinging off his uniform, the lieutenant went to the bath. To faint background noises of slopping water Reiko tended the charcoal brazier in the living room and began the preparations for warming the sake.

Taking the *tanzen,* a sash, and some underclothes, she went to the bathroom to ask how the water was. In the midst of a coiling cloud of steam the lieutenant was sitting cross-legged on the floor, shaving, and she could dimly discern the rippling movements of the muscles on his damp, powerful back as they responded to the movement of his arms.

There was nothing to suggest a time of any special significance. Reiko, going busily about her tasks, was preparing side dishes from odds and ends in stock. Her hands did not tremble. If anything, she managed even more efficiently and smoothly than usual. From time to time, it is true, there was a strange throbbing deep within her breast. Like distant lightning, it had a moment of sharp intensity and then vanished without trace. Apart from that, nothing was in any way out of the ordinary.

The lieutenant, shaving in the bathroom, felt his warmed body miraculously healed at last of the desperate tiredness of the days of indecision and filled—in spite of the death which lay ahead—with pleasurable anticipation. The sound of his wife going about her work came to him faintly. A healthy physical craving, submerged for two days, reasserted itself.

The lieutenant was confident there had been no impurity in that joy they had experienced when resolving upon death. They had both sensed at that moment—though not, of course, in any clear and conscious way—that those permissible pleasures which they shared in private were once more beneath the protection of Righteousness and Divine Power, and of a complete and unassailable morality. On looking into each other's eyes and discovering there an honorable death, they had felt themselves safe once more behind steel walls which none could destroy, encased in an impenetrable armor of Beauty and Truth. Thus, so far from seeing any inconsistency or conflict between the urges of his flesh and the sincerity of his patriotism, the lieutenant was even able to regard the two as parts of the same thing.

Thrusting his face close to the dark, cracked, misted wall mirror, the lieutenant shaved himself with great care. This would be his death face. There must be no unsightly blemishes. The clean-shaven face gleamed once more with a youthful luster, seeming to brighten the darkness of the mirror. There was a certain elegance, he even felt, in the association of death with this radiantly healthy face.

Just as it looked now, this would become his death face! Already, in fact, it had half departed from the lieutenant's personal possession and had become the bust above a dead soldier's memorial. As an experiment he closed his eyes tight. Everything was wrapped in blackness, and he was no longer a living, seeing creature.

Returning from the bath, the traces of the shave glowing faintly blue beneath his smooth cheeks, he seated himself beside the now well-kindled charcoal brazier. Busy though Reiko was, he noticed, she had found time lightly to touch up her face. Her cheeks were gay and her lips moist. There was no shadow of sadness to be seen. Truly, the lieutenant felt, as he saw this mark of his young wife's passionate nature, he had chosen the wife he ought to have chosen.

As soon as the lieutenant had drained his sake cup he offered it to Reiko. Reiko had never before tasted sake, but she accepted without hesitation and sipped timidly.

"Come here," the lieutenant said.

Reiko moved to her husband's side and and was embraced as she leaned backward across his lap. Her breast was in violent commotion, as if sadness, joy, and the potent sake were mingling and reacting within her. The lieutenant looked down into his wife's face. It was the last face he would see in this world, the last face he would see of his wife. The lieutenant scrutinized the face minutely, with the eyes of a traveler bidding farewell to splendid vistas which he will never revisit. It was a face he could not tire of looking at—the features regular yet not cold, the lips lightly closed with a soft strength. The lieutenant kissed those lips, unthinkingly. And suddenly, though there was not the slightest distortion of the face into the unsightliness of sobbing, he noticed that tears were welling slowly from beneath the long lashes of the closed eyes and brimming over into a glistening stream.

When, a little later, the lieutenant urged that they should move to the upstairs bedroom, his wife replied that she would follow after taking a bath. Climbing the stairs alone to the bedroom, where the air was already warmed by the gas heater, the lieutenant lay down on the bedding with arms outstretched and legs apart. Even the time at which he lay waiting for his wife to join him was no later and no earlier than usual.

He folded his hands beneath his head and gazed at the dark boards of the ceiling in the dimness beyond the range of the standard lamp. Was it death he was now waiting for? Or a wild ecstasy of the senses? The two seemed to overlap, almost as if the object of this bodily desire was death itself. But, however that might be, it was certain that never before had the lieutenant tasted such total freedom.

There was the sound of a car outside the window. He could hear the screech of its tires skidding in the snow piled at the side of the street. The sound of its horn reechoed from near-by walls. . . . Listening to these noises he had the feeling that this house rose like a solitary island in the ocean of a society going as restlessly about its business as ever. All around, vastly and untidily, stretched the country for which he grieved. He was to give his life for it. But would that great country, with which he was prepared to remonstrate to the extent of destroying himself, take the slightest heed of his death? He did not know; and it did not matter. His was a battlefield without glory, a battlefield where none could display deeds of valor: it was the front line of the spirit.

Reiko's footsteps sounded on the stairway. The steep stairs in this old house creaked badly. There were fond memories in that creaking, and many a time, while waiting in bed, the lieutenant had listened to its welcome sound. At the thought that he would hear it no more he listened with intense concentration, striving for every corner of every moment of this precious time to be filled with the sound of those soft footfalls on the creaking stairway. The moments seemed transformed to jewels, sparkling with inner light.

Reiko wore a Nagoya sash about the waist of her *yukata,* but as the lieutenant reached toward it, its redness sobered by the dimness of the light, Reiko's hand moved to his assistance and the sash fell away, slithering swiftly to the floor. As she stood before him, still in her *yukata,* the lieutenant inserted his hands through the side slits beneath each sleeve, intending to embrace her as she was; but at the touch of his finger tips upon the warm naked flesh, and as the armpits closed gently about his hands, his whole body was suddenly aflame.

In a few moments the two lay naked before the glowing gas heater.

Neither spoke the thought, but their hearts, their bodies, and their pounding breasts blazed with the knowledge that this was the very last time. It was as if the words "The Last Time" were spelled out, in invisible brushstrokes, across every inch of their bodies.

The lieutenant drew his wife close and kissed her vehemently. As their tongues explored each other's mouths, reaching out into the smooth, moist interior, they felt as if the still unknown agonies of death had tempered their senses to the keenness of red-hot steel. The agonies they could not yet feel, the distant pains of death, had refined their awareness of pleasure.

"This is the last time I shall see your body," said the lieutenant. "Let me look at it closely." And, tilting the shade on the lampstand to one side, he directed the rays along the full length of Reiko's outstretched form.

Reiko lay still with her eyes closed. The light from the low lamp clearly revealed the majestic sweep of her white flesh. The lieutenant, not without a touch of egocentricity, rejoiced that he would never see this beauty crumble in death.

At his leisure, the lieutenant allowed the unforgettable spectacle to engrave itself upon his mind. With one hand he fondled the hair, with the other he softly stroked the magnificent face, implanting kisses here and there where his eyes lingered. The quiet coldness of the high, tapering forehead, the closed eyes with their long lashes beneath faintly etched brows, the set of the finely shaped nose, the gleam of teeth glimpsed between full, regular lips, the soft cheeks and the small, wise chin . . . these things conjured up in the lieutenant's mind the vision of a truly radiant death face, and again and again he pressed his lips tight against the white throat—where Reiko's own hand was soon to strike—and the throat reddened faintly beneath his kisses. Returning to the mouth he laid his lips against it with the gentlest of pressures, and moved them rhythmically over Reiko's with the light rolling motion of a small boat. If he closed his eyes, the world became a rocking cradle.

Wherever the lieutenant's eyes moved his lips faithfully followed. The high, swelling breasts, surmounted by nipples like the buds of a wild cherry, hardened as the lieutenant's lips closed about them. The arms flowed smoothly downward from each side of the breast, tapering toward the wrists, yet losing nothing of their roundness or symmetry, and at their tips were those delicate fingers which had held the fan at the wedding ceremony. One by one, as the lieutenant kissed them, the fingers withdrew behind their neighbor as if in shame. . . . The natural hollow curving between the bosom and the stomach carried in its lines a suggestion not only of softness but of resilient strength, and while it gave forewarning of the rich curves spreading outward from here to the hips it had, in itself, an appearance only of restraint and proper discipline. The whiteness and richness of the stomach and hips was like milk brimming in a great bowl, and the sharply shadowed dip of the navel could have been the fresh impress of a raindrop, fallen there that very moment. Where the shadows gathered more thickly, hair clustered, gentle and sensitive, and as the agitation mounted in the now no longer passive body there hung over this region a scent like the smoldering of fragrant blossoms, growing steadily more pervasive.

At length, in a tremulous voice. Reiko spoke.

"Show me. . . . Let me look too, for the last time."

Never before had he heard from his wife's lips so strong and unequivocal a request. It was as if something which her modesty had wished to keep hidden to the end had suddenly burst its bonds of constraint. The lieutenant obediently lay back and surrendered himself to his wife. Lithely she raised her white, trembling body, and—

burning with an innocent desire to return to her husband what he had done for her—placed two white fingers on the lieutenant's eyes, which gazed fixedly up at her, and gently stroked them shut.

Suddenly overwhelmed by tenderness, her cheeks flushed by a dizzying uprush of emotion, Reiko threw her arms about the lieutenant's close-cropped head. The bristly hairs rubbed painfully against her breast, the prominent nose was cold as it dug into her flesh, and his breath was hot. Relaxing her embrace, she gazed down at her husband's masculine face. The severe brows, the closed eyes, the splendid bridge of the nose, the shapely lips drawn firmly together . . . the blue, cleanshaven cheeks reflecting the light and gleaming smoothly. Reiko kissed each of these. She kissed the broad nape of the neck, the strong, erect shoulders, the powerful chest with its twin circles like shields and its russet nipples. In the armpits, deeply shadowed by the ample flesh of the shoulders and chest, a sweet and melancholy odor emanated from the growth of hair, and in the sweetness of this odor was contained, somehow, the essence of young death. The lieutenant's naked skin glowed like a field of barley, and everywhere the muscles showed in sharp relief, converging on the lower abdomen about the small, unassuming navel. Gazing at the youthful, firm stomach, modestly covered by a vigorous growth of hair, Reiko thought of it as it was soon to be, cruelly cut by the sword, and she laid her head upon it, sobbing in pity, and bathed it with kisses.

At the touch of his wife's tears upon his stomach the lieutenant felt ready to endure with courage the cruelest agonies of his suicide.

What ecstasies they experienced after these tender exchanges may well be imagined. The lieutenant raised himself and enfolded his wife in a powerful embrace, her body now limp with exhaustion after her grief and tears. Passionately they held their faces close, rubbing cheek against cheek. Reiko's body was trembling. Their breasts, moist with sweat, were tightly joined, and every inch of the young and beautiful bodies had become so much one with the other that it seemed impossible there should ever again be a separation. Reiko cried out. From the heights they plunged into the abyss, and from the abyss they took wing and soared once more to dizzying heights. The lieutenant panted like the regimental standard-bearer on a route march. . . . As one cycle ended, almost immediately a new wave of passion would be generated, and together—with no trace of fatigue—they would climb again in a single breathless movement to the very summit.

4

When the lieutenant at last turned away, it was not from weariness. For one thing, he was anxious not to undermine the considerable strength he would need in carrying out his suicide. For another, he would have been sorry to mar the sweetness of these last memories by overindulgence.

Since the lieutenant had clearly desisted, Reiko too, with her usual compliance, followed his example. The two lay naked on their backs, with fingers interlaced, staring fixedly at the dark ceiling. The room was warm from the heater, and even when the sweat had ceased to pour from their bodies they felt no cold. Outside, in the hushed night, the sounds of passing traffic had ceased. Even the noises of the trains and streetcars around Yotsuya station did not penetrate this far. After echoing through the region bounded by the moat, they were lost in the heavily wooded park fronting the broad driveway before Akasaka Palace. It was hard to believe in the tension gripping this whole quarter, where the two factions of the bitterly divided Imperial Army now confronted each other, poised for battle.

Savoring the warmth glowing within themselves, they lay still and recalled the ecstasies they had just known. Each moment of the experience was relived. They remembered the taste of kisses which had never wearied, the touch of naked flesh, episode after episode of dizzying bliss. But already, from the dark boards of the ceiling, the face of death was peering down. These joys had been final, and their bodies would never know them again. Not that joy of this intensity—and the same thought had occurred to them both—was ever likely to be reexperienced, even if they should live on to old age.

The feel of their fingers intertwined—this too would soon be lost. Even the wood-grain patterns they now gazed at on the dark ceiling boards would be taken from them. They could feel death edging in, nearer and nearer. There could be no hesitation now. They must have the courage to reach out to death themselves, and to seize it.

"Well, let's make our preparations," said the lieutenant. The note of determination in the words was unmistakable, but at the same time Reiko had never heard her husband's voice so warm and tender.

After they had risen, a variety of tasks awaited them.

The lieutenant, who had never once before helped with the bedding, now cheerfully slid back the door of the closet, lifted the mattress across the room by himself, and stowed it away inside.

Reiko turned off the gas heater and put away the lamp standard. During the lieutenant's absence she had arranged this room carefully, sweeping and dusting it to a fresh cleanness, and now—if one overlooked the rosewood table drawn into one corner—the eight-mat room gave all the appearance of a reception room ready to welcome an important guest.

"We've seen some drinking here, haven't we? With Kanō and Homma and Noguchi . . ."

"Yes, they were great drinkers, all of them."

"We'll be meeting them before long, in the other world. They'll tease us, I imagine, when they find I've brought you with me."

Descending the stairs, the lieutenant turned to look back into this calm clean room, now brightly illuminated by the ceiling lamp. There floated across his mind the faces of the young officers who had drunk there, and laughed, and innocently bragged. He had never dreamed then that he would one day cut open his stomach in this room.

In the two rooms downstairs husband and wife busied themselves smoothly and serenely with their respective preparations. The lieutenant went to the toilet, and then to the bathroom to wash. Meanwhile Reiko folded away her husband's padded robe, placed his uniform tunic, his trousers, and a newly cut bleached loincloth in the bathroom, and set out sheets of paper on the livingroom table for the farewell notes. Then she removed the lid from the writing box and began rubbing ink from the ink tablet. She had already decided upon the wording of her own note.

Reiko's fingers pressed hard upon the cold gilt letters of the ink tablet, and the water in the shallow well at once darkened, as if a black cloud had spread across it. She stopped thinking that this repeated action, this pressure from her fingers, this rise and fall of faint sound, was all and solely for death. It was a routine domestic task, a simple paring away of time until death should finally stand before her. But somehow, in the increasingly smooth motion of the tablet rubbing on the stone, and in the scent from the thickening ink, there was unspeakable darkness.

Neat in his uniform, which he now wore next to his skin, the lieutenant emerged from the bathroom. Without a word he seated himself at the table, bolt upright, took a brush in his hand, and stared undecidedly at the paper before him.

Reiko took a white silk kimono with her and entered the bathroom. When she reappeared in the living room, clad in the white kimono and with her face lightly made up, the farewell note lay completed on the table beneath the lamp. The thick black brushstrokes said simply:

"Long Live the Imperial Forces—Army Lieutenant Takeyama Shinji."

While Reiko sat opposite him writing her own note, the lieutenant gazed in silence, intensely serious, at the controlled movement of his wife's pale fingers as they manipulated the brush.

With their respective notes in their hands—the lieutenant's sword strapped to his side, Reiko's small dagger thrust into the sash of her white Kimono—the two of them stood before the god shelf and silently prayed. Then they put out all the downstairs lights. As he mounted the stairs the lieutenant turned his head and gazed back at the striking, white-clad figure of his wife, climbing behind him, with lowered eyes, from the darkness beneath.

The farewell notes were laid side by side in the alcove of the upstairs room. They wondered whether they ought not to remove the hanging scroll, but since it had been written by their go-between, Lieutenant General Ozeki, and consisted, moreover, of two Chinese characters signifying "Sincerity," they left it where it was. Even if it were to become stained with splashes of blood, they felt that the lieutenant general would understand.

The lieutenant sitting erect with his back to the alcove, laid his sword on the floor before him.

Reiko set facing him, a mat's width away. With the rest of her so severely white the touch of rouge on her lips seemed remarkably seductive.

Across the dividing mat they gazed intently into each other's eyes. The lieutenant's sword lay before his knees. Seeing it, Reiko recalled their first night and was overwhelmed with sadness. The lieutenant spoke, in a hoarse voice:

"As I have no second to help me I shall cut deep. It may look unpleasant, but please do not panic. Death of any sort is a fearful thing to watch. You must not be discouraged by what you see. Is that all right?"

"Yes."

Reiko nodded deeply.

Looking at the slender white figure of his wife the lieutenant experienced a bizarre excitement. What he was about to perform was an act in his public capacity as a soldier, something he had never previously shown his wife. It called for a resolution equal to the courage to enter battle; it was a death of no less degree and quality than death in the front line. It was his conduct on the battlefield that he was now to display.

Momentarily the thought led the lieutenant to a strange fantasy. A lonely death on the battlefield, a death beneath the eyes of his beautiful wife . . . in the sensation that he was now to die in these two dimensions, realizing an impossible union of them both, there was sweetness beyond words. This must be the very pinnacle of good fortune, he thought. To have every moment of his death observed by those beautiful eyes—it was like being borne to death on a gentle, fragrant breeze. There was some special favor here. He did not understand precisely what it was, but it was a domain unknown to others: a dispensation granted to no one else had been permitted to himself. In the radiant, bridelike figure of his white-robed wife the lieutenant seemed to see a vision of all those things he had loved and for which he was to lay down his life—the Imperial Household, the Nation, the Army Flag. All these, no less than the wife who sat before him, were presences observing him closely with clear and never-faltering eyes.

Reiko too was gazing intently at her husband, so soon to die, and she thought that never in this world had she seen anything so beautiful. The lieutenant always looked well in uniform, but now, as he contemplated death with severe brows and firmly closed lips, he revealed what was perhaps masculine beauty at its most superb.

"It's time to go," the lieutenant said at last.

Reiko bent her body low to the mat in a deep bow. She could not raise her face. She did not wish to spoil her make-up with tears, but the tears could not be held back.

When at length she looked up she saw hazily through the tears that her husband had wound a white bandage around the blade of his now unsheathed sword, leaving five or six inches of naked steel showing at the point.

Resting the sword in its cloth wrapping on the mat before him, the lieutenant rose from his knees, resettled himself cross-legged, and unfastened the hooks of his uniform collar. His eyes no longer saw his wife. Slowly, one by one, he undid the flat brass buttons. The dusky brown chest was revealed, and then the stomach. He unclasped his belt and undid the buttons of his trousers. The pure whiteness of the thickly coiled loincloth showed itself. The lieutenant pushed the cloth down with both hands, further to ease his stomach, and then reached for the white-bandaged blade of his sword. With his left hand he massaged his abdomen, glancing downward as he did so.

To reassure himself on the sharpness of his sword's cutting edge the lieutenant folded back the left trouser flap, exposing a little of his thigh, and lightly drew the blade across the skin. Blood welled up in the wound at once, and several streaks of red trickled downward, glistening in the strong light.

It was the first time Reiko had ever seen her husband's blood, and she felt a violent throbbing in her chest. She looked at her husband's face. The lieutenant was looking at the blood with calm appraisal. For a moment—though thinking at the same time that it was hollow comfort—Reiko experienced a sense of relief.

The lieutenant's eyes fixed his wife with an intense, hawk-like stare. Moving the sword around to his front, he raised himself slightly on his hips and let the upper half of his body lean over the sword point. That he was mustering his whole strength was apparent from the angry tension of the uniform at his shoulders. The lieutenant aimed to strike deep into the left of his stomach. His sharp cry pierced the silence of the room.

Despite the effort he had himself put into the blow, the lieutenant had the impression that someone else had struck the side of his stomach agonizingly with a thick rod of iron. For a second or so his head reeled and he had no idea what had happened. The five or six inches of naked point had vanished completely into his flesh, and the white bandage, gripped in his clenched fist, pressed directly against his stomach.

He returned to consciousness. The blade had certainly pierced the wall of the stomach, he thought. His breathing was difficult, his chest thumped violently, and in some far deep region, which he could hardly believe was a part of himself, a fearful and excruciating pain came welling up as if the ground had split open to disgorge a boiling stream of molten rock. The pain came suddenly nearer, with terrifying speed. The lieutenant bit his lower lip and stiffled an instinctive moan.

Was this *seppuku?*—he was thinking. It was a sensation of utter chaos, as if the sky had fallen on his head and the world was reeling drunkenly. His will power and courage, which had seemed so robust before he made the incision, had now dwindled to something like a single hairlike thread of steel, and he was assailed by the uneasy feeling that he must advance along this thread, clinging to it with desperation. His clenched fist had grown moist. Looking down, he saw that both his hand and the cloth were drenched in blood. His loincloth too was dyed a deep red. It struck him as incredible that, amidst this terrible agony, things which could be seen could still be seen, and existing things existed still.

The moment the lieutenant thrust the sword into his left side and she saw the deathly pallor fall across his face, like an abruptly lowered curtain, Reiko had to struggle to prevent herself from rushing to his side. Whatever happened, she must watch. She must be a witness. That was the duty her husband had lain upon her. Opposite her, a mat's space away, she could clearly see her husband biting his lip to stifle the pain. The pain was there, with absolute certainty, before her eyes. And Reiko had no means of rescuing him from it.

The sweat glistened on her husband's forehead. The lieutenant closed his eyes, and then opened them again, as if experimenting. The eyes had lost their luster, and seemed innocent and empty like the eyes of a small animal.

The agony before Reiko's eyes burned as strong as the summer sun, utterly remote from the grief which seemed to be tearing herself apart within. The pain grew steadily in stature, stretching upward. Reiko felt that her husband had already become a man in a separate world, a man whose whole being had resolved into pain, a prisoner in a cage of pain where no hand could reach out to him. But Reiko felt no pain at all. Her grief was not pain. As she thought about this, Reiko began to feel as if someone had raised a cruel wall of glass high between herself and her husband.

Ever since her marriage her husband's existence had been her own existence, and every breath of his had been a breath drawn by herself. But now, while her husband's existence in pain was a vivid reality, Reiko could find in this grief of hers no certain proof at all of her own existence.

With only his right hand on the sword the lieutenant began to cut sideways across his stomach. But as the blade became entangled with the entrails it was pushed constantly outward by their soft resilience; and the lieutenant realized that it would be necessary, as he cut, to use both hands to keep the point pressed deep into his stomach. He pulled the blade across. It did not cut as easily as he had expected. He directed the strength of his whole body into his right hand and pulled again. There was a cut of three or four inches.

The pain spread slowly outward from the inner depths until the whole stomach reverberated. It was like the wild clanging of a bell. Or like a thousand bells which jangled simultaneously at every breath he breathed and every throb of his pulse, rocking his whole being. The lieutenant could no longer stop himself from moaning. But by now the blade had cut its way through to below the navel, and when he noticed this he felt a sense of satisfaction, and a renewal of courage.

The volume of blood had steadily increased, and now it spurted from the wound as if propelled by the beat of the pulse. The mat before the lieutenant was drenched red with splattered blood, and more blood overflowed onto it from pools which gathered in folds of the lieutenant's khaki trousers. A spot, like a bird, came flying across to Reiko and settled on the lap of her white silk kimono.

By the time the lieutenant had at last drawn the sword across to the right side of his stomach, the blade was already cutting shallow and had revealed its naked tip, slippery with blood and grease. But, suddenly stricken by a fit of vomiting, the lieutenant cried out hoarsely. The vomiting made the fierce pain fiercer still, and the stomach, which had thus far remained firm and compact, now abruptly heaved, opening wide its wound, and the entrails burst through, as if the wound too were vomiting. Seemingly ignorant of their master's suffering, the entrails gave an impression of robust health and almost disagreeable vitality as they slipped smoothly out and spilled over into the crotch. The lieutenant's head dropped, his shoulders heaved, his eyes opened to narrow slits, and a thin trickle of saliva dribbled from his mouth. The gold markings on his epaulettes caught the light and glinted.

Blood was scattered everywhere. The lieutenant was soaked in it to his knees, and he sat now in a crumpled and listless posture, one hand on the floor. A raw smell filled the room. The lieutenant his head dropping, retched repeatedly, and the movement showed vividly in his shoulders. The blade of the sword, now pushed back by the entrails and exposed to its tip, was still in the lieutenant's right hand.

It would be difficult to imagine a more heroic sight than that of the lieutenant at this moment, as he mustered his strength and flung back his head. The movement was performed with sudden violence, and the back of his head struck with a sharp crack against the alcove pillar. Reiko had been sitting until now with her face lowered; gazing in fascination at the tide of blood advancing toward her knees, but the sound took her by surprise and she looked up.

The lieutenant's face was not the face of a living man. The eyes were hollow, the skin parched, the once so lustrous cheeks and lips the color of dried mud. The right hand alone was moving. Laboriously gripping the sword, it hovered shakily in the air like the hand of a marionette and strove to direct the point at the base of the lieutenant's throat. Reiko watched her husband make this last, most heart-rending, futile exertion. Glistening with blood and grease, the point was thrust at the throat again and again. And each time it missed its aim. The strength to guide it was no longer there. The straying point struck the collar and the collar badges. Although its hooks had been unfastened, the still military collar had closed together again and was protecting the throat.

Reiko could bear the sight no longer. She tried to go to her husband's help, but she could not stand. She moved through the blood on her knees, and her white skirts grew deep red. Moving to the rear of her husband, she helped no more than by loosening the collar. The quivering blade at last contacted the naked flesh of the throat. At that moment Reiko's impression was that she herself had propelled her husband forward; but that was not the case. It was a movement planned by the lieutenant himself, his last exertion of strength. Abruptly he threw his body at the blade, and the blade pierced his neck, emerging at the nape. There was a tremendous spurt of blood and the lieutenant lay still, cold blue-tinged steel protruding from his neck at the back.

5

Slowly, her socks slippery with blood, Reiko descended the stairway. The upstairs room was not completely still.

Switching on the ground-floor lights, she checked the gas jet and the main gas plug and poured water over the smoldering, half-buried charcoal in the brazier. She stood before the upright mirror in the four-and-a-half-mat room and held up her skirts. The blood stains made it seem as if a bold, vivid pattern was printed across the lower half of her white kimono. When she sat down before the mirror, she was conscious of the dampness and coldness of her husband's blood in the region of her thighs, and she shivered. Then, for a long while, she lingered over her toilet preparations. She applied the rouge generously to her cheeks, and her lips too she painted heavily. This was no longer make-up to please her husband. It was make-up for the world which she would leave behind, and there was a touch of the magnificent and the spectacular in her brushwork. When she rose, the mat before the mirror was wet with blood. Reiko was not concerned about this. Returning from the toilet, Reiko stood finally on the cement floor of the porchway. When her husband had bolted the door here last night it had been in preparation for death. For a while she stood immersed in the consideration of a simple problem. Should she now leave the bolt drawn? If she were to lock the door, it could be that the neighbors might not notice their suicide for several days. Reiko did not relish the thought of their two corpses putrifying before discovery. After all, it seemed, it would be best to leave it open. . . . She released the bolt, and also drew open the frosted-glass door a fraction. . . . At once a chill wind blew in. There was no sign of anyone in the midnight streets and stars glittered ice-cold through the trees in the large house opposite.

Leaving the door as it was, Reiko mounted the stairs. She had walked here and there for some time and her socks were no longer slippery. About halfway up, her nostrils were already assailed by a peculiar smell.

The lieutenant was lying on his face in a sea of blood. The point protruding from his neck seemed to have grown even more prominent than before. Reiko walked heedlessly across the blood. Sitting beside the lieutenant's corpse, she stared intently at the face, which lay on one cheek on the mat. The eyes were opened wide, as if the lieutenant's attention had been attracted by something. She raised the head, folding it in her sleeve, wiped the blood from the lips, and bestowed a last kiss.

Then she rose and took from the closet a new white blanket and a waist cord. To prevent any derangement of her skirts, she wrapped the blanket about her waist and bound it there firmly with the cord.

Reiko sat herself on a spot about a foot distant from the lieutenant's body. Drawing the dagger from her sash, she examined its dully gleaming blade intently, and held it to her tongue. The taste of the polished steel was slightly sweet.

Reiko did not linger. When she thought how the pain which had previously opened such a gulf between herself and her dying husband was now to become a part of her own experience, she saw before her only the joy of herself entering a realm her husband had already made his own. In her husband's agonized face there had been something inexplicable which she was seeing for the first time. Now she would solve that riddle. Reiko sensed that at last she too would be able to taste the true bitterness and sweetness of that great moral principle in which her husband believed. What had until now been tasted only faintly through her husband's example she was about to savor directly with her own tongue.

Reiko rested the point of the blade against the base of her throat. She thrust hard. The wound was only shallow. Her head blazed, and her hands shook uncontrollably. She gave the blade a strong pull sideways. A warm substance flooded into her mouth, and everything before her eyes reddened, in a vision of spouting blood. She gathered her strength and plunged the point of the blade deep into her throat.

Cynthia Ozick (1928–   )

Recipient of a number of prizes, among them an O'Henry Award, a National Book Award, and the Award for Literature of the American Academy of Arts and Letters, Cynthia Ozick is a novelist and storyteller of great range and versatility. She is the author of *Trust,* a novel published in 1966, *The Pagan Rabbi and Other Stories* (1971), and *Bloodshed and Three Novellas* (1976). She has also written poetry, essays, criticism, reviews, and translations. "The Shawl" was first published in *The New Yorker* magazine in 1980.

Nearly all of Ozick's work is centrally concerned with the idea of Jewishness. Not "Judaism" as an abstract idea or as a force in intellectual and cultural history, but as a consciousness at once individual and collective, something we feel as a dominating *presence,* even though in her stories and novellas we are regularly following the particular thoughts, movements, and acts of particular characters.

"The Shawl" belongs to the literature of the Holocaust. It is a recalling, at once impressionistic and precise, of the horrors of a Dachau or an Auschwitz. It is the story of a brutal extinction vividly told. The destroyer's helmet glints in the light, its crested spike a seeming goblet in savage toast to the sacrifice; his booted legs propel him as he hurls the child. And then all the voices *hum* together. Harsh and clear as the story is, there are ambiguities and mysteries. Fifteen-month-old Magda did not resemble her mother: ". . . it was another kind of face altogether, eyes blue as air, smooth feathers of hair nearly as yellow as the Star sewn into Rosa's coat. You could think she was one of *their* babies." Perhaps she is, the illegitimate child of Rosa and a Nazi. Is this why she must be first hidden, then destroyed? Consider the following questions for further understanding. Is Stella also Rosa's daughter? Why does *she* pronounce Magda "Aryan"? What is the significance of the several references to Magda's death? How does the alternating imagery of wetness and dryness, water and aridity, contribute to the story's meaning? How should we interpret the shawl?

The world that the story represents—and in so doing interprets—is a world of hunger and thirst, withering and survival, birth, life, death. It is a symbolic world in which liquid and life are extracted from a shawl, a shawl that is also used to choke grief and hysteria, a world in which the first sounds a baby utters are echoed in an electrified fence. It is a real world of excrement, blood, steel fences, yet bounded by green meadows, violets, and tiger lilies. It is a world in which the flowers of innocence and evil flourish simultaneously. Our sensibilities are symbolically assaulted and our senses overwhelmingly engaged: ". . . the bad wind with pieces of black in it." There is no mistaking the smell.

In the preface to *Bloodshed,* Ozick speaks of "the Creator of the Universe, who admitted Auschwitz into His creation," but she does not elaborate the implication. She also says: "I believe that stories ought to judge and interpret the world." "The Shawl" most assuredly sits in majestic moral judgment.

The Shawl

Stella, cold, cold, the coldness of hell. How they walked on the roads together, Rosa with Magda curled up between sore breasts, Magda wound up in the shawl. Sometimes Stella carried Magda. But she was jealous of Magda. A thin girl of fourteen, too small, with thin breasts of her own, Stella wanted to be wrapped in a shawl, hidden away, asleep, rocked by the march, a baby, a round infant in arms. Magda took Rosa's nipple, and Rosa never stopped walking, a walking cradle. There was not enough milk; sometimes Magda sucked air; then she screamed. Stella was ravenous. Her knees were tumors on sticks, her elbows chicken bones.

Rosa did not feel hunger; she felt light, not like someone walking but like someone in a faint, in trance, arrested in a fit, someone who is already a floating angel, alert and seeing everything, but in the air, not there, not touching the road. As if teetering on the tips of her fingernails. She looked into Magda's face through a gap in the shawl: a squirrel in a nest, safe, no one could reach her inside the little house of the shawl's windings. The face, very round, a pocket mirror of a face: but it was not Rosa's bleak complexion, dark like cholera, it was another kind of face altogether, eyes blue as air, smooth feathers of hair nearly as yellow as the Star sewn into Rosa's coat. You could think she was one of *their* babies.

Rosa, floating, dreamed of giving Magda away in one of the villages. She could leave the line for a minute and push Magda into the hands of any woman on the side of the road. But if she moved out of line they might shoot. And even if she fled the line for half a second and pushed the shawl-bundle at a stranger, would the woman take it? She might be surprised, or afraid; she might drop the shawl, and Magda would fall out and strike her head and die. The little round head. Such a good child, she gave up screaming, and sucked now only for the taste of the drying nipple itself. The neat grip of the tiny gums. One mite of a tooth tip sticking up in the bottom gum, how shining, an elfin tombstone of white marble gleaming there. Without complaining, Magda relinquished Rosa's teats, first the left, then the right; both were cracked, not a sniff of milk. The duct crevice extinct, a dead volcano, blind eye, chill hole, so Magda took the corner of the shawl and milked it instead. She sucked and sucked, flooding the threads with wetness. The shawl's good flavor, milk of linen.

It was a magic shawl, it could nourish an infant for three days and three nights. Magda did not die, she stayed alive, although very quiet. A peculiar smell, of cinnamon and almonds, lifted out of her mouth. She held her eyes open every moment, forgetting how to blink or nap, and Rosa and sometimes Stella studied their blueness. On the road they raised one burden of a leg after another and studied Magda's face. "Aryan," Stella said, in a voice grown as thin as a string; and Rosa thought how Stella gazed at Magda like a young cannibal. And the time that Stella said "Aryan," it sounded to Rosa as if Stella had really said "Let us devour her."

But Magda lived to walk. She lived that long, but she did not walk very well, partly because she was only fifteen months old, and partly because the spindles of her legs could not hold up her fat belly. It was fat with air, full and round. Rosa gave almost all her food to Magda, Stella gave nothing; Stella was ravenous, a growing child herself, but not growing much. Stella did not menstruate. Rosa did not menstruate. Rosa was ravenous, but also not; she learned from Magda how to drink the taste of a finger in one's mouth. They were in a place without pity, all pity was annihilated in Rosa, she looked at Stella's bones without pity. She was sure that Stella was waiting for Magda to die so she could put her teeth into the little thighs.

Rosa knew Magda was going to die very soon; she should have been dead already, but she had been buried away deep inside the magic shawl, mistaken there for the shivering mound of Rosa's breasts; Rosa clung to the shawl as if it covered only herself. No one took it away from her. Magda was mute. She never cried. Rosa hid her in the barracks, under the shawl, but she knew that one day someone would inform; or one day someone, not even Stella, would steal Magda to eat her. When Magda began to walk Rosa knew that Magda was going to die very soon, something would happen. She was afraid to fall asleep; she slept with the weight of her thigh on Magda's body; she was afraid she would smother Magda under her thigh. The weight of Rosa was becoming less and less; Rosa and Stella were slowly turning into air.

Magda was quiet, but her eyes were horribly alive, like blue tigers. She watched. Sometimes she laughed—it seemed a laugh, but how could it be? Magda had never seen anyone laugh. Still, Magda laughed at her shawl when the wind blew its corners, the bad wind with pieces of black in it, that made Stella's and Rosa's eyes tear. Magda's eyes were always clear and tearless. She watched like a tiger. She guarded her shawl. No one could touch it; only Rosa could touch it. Stella was not allowed. The shawl was Magda's own baby, her pet, her little sister. She tangled herself up in it and sucked on one of the corners when she wanted to be very still.

Then Stella took the shawl away and made Magda die.

Afterward Stella said: "I was cold."

And afterward she was always cold, always. The cold went into her heart: Rosa saw that Stella's heart was cold. Magda flopped onward with her little pencil legs scribbling this way and that, in search of the shawl; the pencils faltered at the barracks opening, where the light began. Rosa saw and pursued. But already Magda was in the square outside the barracks, in the jolly light. It was the roll-call arena. Every morning Rosa had to conceal Magda under the shawl against a wall of the barracks and go out and stand in the area with Stella and hundreds of others, sometimes for hours, and Magda, deserted, was quiet under the shawl, sucking on her corner. Every day Magda was silent, and so she did not die. Rosa saw that today Magda was going to die, and at the same time a fearful joy ran in Rosa's two palms, her fingers were on fire, she was astonished, febrile: Magda, in the sunlight, swaying on her pencil legs, was howling. Ever since the drying up of Rosa's nipples, ever since Magda's last scream on the road, Magda had been devoid of any syllable; Magda was a mute. Rosa believed that something had gone wrong with her vocal cords, with her windpipe, with the cave of her larynx; Magda was defective, without a voice; perhaps she was deaf; there might be something amiss with her intelligence; Magda was dumb. Even the laugh that came when the ash-stippled wind made a clown out of Magda's shawl was only the air-blown showing of her teeth. Even when the lice, head lice and body lice, crazed her so that she became as wild as one of the big rats that plundered the barracks at daybreak looking for carrion, she rubbed and scratched and kicked and bit and rolled without a whimper. But now Magda's mouth was spilling a long viscous rope of clamor.

"Maaaa—"

It was the first noise Magda had ever sent out from her throat since the drying up of Rosa's nipples.

"Maaaa . . . aaa!"

Again! Magda was wavering in the perilous sunlight of the arena, scribbling on such pitiful little bent shins. Rosa saw. She saw that Magda was grieving for the loss of her shawl, she saw that Magda was going to die. A tide of commands hammered in Rosa's nipples: Fetch, get, bring! But she did not know which to go after first. Magda or the shawl. If she jumped out into the arena to snatch Magda up, the howling would not stop, because Magda would still not have the shawl; but if she ran back into the barracks to find the shawl, and if she found it, and if she came after Magda holding it and shaking it, then she would get Magda back, Magda would put the shawl in her mouth and turn dumb again.

Rosa entered the dark. It was easy to discover the shawl. Stella was heaped under it, asleep in her thin bones. Rosa tore the shawl free and flew—she could fly, she was only air—into the arena. The sunheat murmured of another life, of butterflies in summer. The light was placid, mellow. On the other side of the steel fence, far away, there were green meadows speckled with dandelions and deep-colored violets; beyond them, even farther, innocent tiger lilies, tall, lifting their orange bonnets. In the barracks they spoke of "flowers," of "rain": excrement, thick turd-braids, and the slow stinking maroon waterfall that slunk down from the upper bunks, the stink mixed with a bitter fatty floating smoke that greased Rosa's skin. She stood for an instant at the margin of the arena. Sometimes the electricity inside the fence would seem to hum; even Stella said it was only an imagining, but Rosa heard real sounds in the wire: grainy sad voices. The farther she was from the fence, the more clearly the voices crowded at her. The lamenting voices strummed so convincingly, so passionately, it was impossible to suspect them of being phantoms. The voices told her to hold up the shawl, high; the voices told her to shake it, to whip with it, to unfurl it like a flag. Rosa lifted, shook, whipped, unfurled. Far off, very far, Magda leaned across her air-fed belly, reaching out with the rods of her arms. She was high up, elevated, riding someone's shoulder. But the shoulder that carried Magda was not coming toward Rosa and the shawl, it was drifting away, the speck of Magda was moving more and more into the smoky distance. Above the shoulder a helmet glinted. The light tapped the helmet and sparkled it into a goblet. Below the helmet a black body like a domino and a pair of black boots hurled themselves in the direction of the electrified fence. The electric voices began to chatter wildly. "Maamaa, maaamaaa," they all hummed together. How far Magda was from Rosa now, across the whole square, past a dozen barracks, all the way on the other side! She was no bigger than a moth.

All at once Magda was swimming through the air. The whole of Magda traveled through loftiness. She looked like a butterfly touching a silver vine. And the moment Magda's feathered round head and her pencil legs and balloonish belly and zigzag arms splashed against the fence, the steel voices went mad in their growling, urging Rosa to run and run to the spot where Magda had fallen from her flight against the electrified fence; but of course Rosa did not obey them. She only stood, because if she ran they would shoot, and if she tried to pick up the sticks of Magda's body they would shoot, and if she let the wolf's screech ascending now through the ladder of her skeleton break out, they would shoot; so she took Magda's shawl and filled her own mouth with it, stuffed it in and stuffed it in, until she was swallowing up the wolf's screech and tasting the cinnamon and almond depth of Magda's saliva; and Rosa drank Magda's shawl until it dried.

John Updike (1932–   )

Perhaps no important writer of his generation can lay claim to a more prodigious and varied output than John Updike. Born in 1932, he has published nine novels, seven collections of short stories, five volumes of verse, a play, two libretti, a children's book, and a volume of prose pieces. Since his twenties he has been considered one of the outstanding writers of America.

For the most part, his fiction is traditional and his concern is the middle range of experience. His characters are not of heroic measure, nor are they evil, cruel, bizarre, or mad, as are many of the characters of his contemporaries. The hero of his most acclaimed works *Rabbit, Run* and *Rabbit Is Rich,* is a former basketball star, now a salesman of kitchen gadgets, who makes one failed effort to shake off the mediocrity and "quiet desperation" of his middle-American life. *The Centaur*

(1963) is about the family of a high school science teacher. Even the protagonist of *Bech: a Book* (1970), albeit a writer of celebrated novels, is only a man who works at his craft and leads a relatively normal life. Basically, he is no more unusual and eccentric than any man next door.

Updike's characters, in both his novels and short stories, are concerned with common experiences: the loss of youth, sexuality, the generation gap, marriage and its discontents, religious faith, the saving grace of love, even in-law conflicts. His fiction is a transformation of material familiar to most of us. Though his subject matter is plain, his style is far from it. It seems to be an expression of his early training as a painter, his continuing experience as a poet, and his concern for the homely facts of real life. His rhythms are pronounced, his perceptions are precisely delineated, his language is exact and yet surprising, his imagery is often luscious.

"Leaves" is not a typical Updike story; it is, as Updike himself says, "in a mode of mine, the abstract-personal, not a favorite with my critics." It is more of a meditation than a story. The narrator is remembering: there has been a divorce and there is a wife-to-be, but what is front-stage in this story is the pain, pain and explosive guilt.

How does he deal with this pain and guilt? He invests it in something nonhuman outside himself, making external the inner landscape. It is a process that writers know well: that of investing an "emblem" with meaning (see pp. 8, 21–22), making symbols out of the neutral artifacts of existence. Here it is "Nature" that so serves, Nature made concrete in the bird and the leaves, especially the leaves, that focus his attention as he stares out the window. Out of his need he defines Nature this morning as "that which exists without guilt." And finally the leaves of paper on which he is writing serve the same purpose: "Why do I produce them but to thrust, by some subjective photosynthesis, my guilt into Nature, where there is no guilt?" The next day the shadows on the leaves look different, and as he opens the door to let in a promise of warmth, "sunlight falls flat at my feet like a penitent." Such purgation is inseparable from the images that convey it. Updike's own comment on this story seems perfect:

> It was written after long silence, swiftly, unerringly as a sleepwalker walks. No memory of any revision mars my backwards impression of it. The way the leaves become the pages, the way the bird becomes his description, the way the bright and multiform world of nature is felt rubbing against the dark world of the trapped ego—all strike me as beautiful, and of the order of artistic "happiness" that is given rather than attained.

Leaves

The grape leaves outside my window are curiously beautiful. "Curiously" because it comes upon me as strange, after the long darkness of self-absorption and fear and shame in which I have been living, that things are beautiful, that independent of our catastrophes they continue to maintain the casual precision, the effortless abundance of inventive "effect," which is the hallmark and specialty of Nature. Nature: this morning it seems to me very clear that Nature may be defined as that which exists without guilt. Our bodies are in Nature; our shoes, their laces, the little plastic tips of the laces—everything around us and about us is in Nature, and yet something holds us away from it, like the upward push of water which keeps us from touching the sandy bottom, ribbed and glimmering with crescental fragments of oyster shell, so clear to our eyes.

A blue jay lights on a twig outside my window. Momentarily sturdy, he stands astraddle, his dingy rump toward me, his head alertly frozen in silhouette, the predatory curve of his beak stamped on a sky almost white above the misting tawny marsh. See him? I do, and, snapping the chain of my thought, I have reached through glass and seized him and stamped him on this page. Now he is gone. And yet, there, a few lines above, he still is, "astraddle," his rump "dingy," his head "alertly frozen." A curious trick, possibly useless, but mine.

The grape leaves where they are not in each other's shadows are golden. Flat leaves, they take the sun flatly, and turn the absolute light, sum of the spectrum and source of all life, into the crayon yellow with which children render it. Here and there, wilt transmutes this lent radiance into a glowing orange, and the green of the still tender leaves—for green persists long into autumn, if we look—strains from the sunlight a fine-veined chartreuse. The shadows these leaves cast upon each other, though vagrant and nervous in the wind that sends friendly scavenging rattles scurrying across the roof, are yet quite various and definite, containing innumerable barbaric suggestions of scimitars, flanged spears, prongs, and menacing helmets. The net effect, however, is innocent of menace. On the contrary, its intricate simultaneous suggestion of shelter and openness, warmth and breeze, invites me outward; my eyes venture into the leaves beyond. I am surrounded by leaves. The oak's are tenacious claws of purplish rust; the elm's, scant feathers of a feminine yellow; the sumac's, a savage, toothed blush. I am upheld in a serene and burning universe of leaves. Yet something plucks me back, returns me to that inner darkness where guilt is the sun.

The events need to be sorted out. I am told I behaved wantonly, and it will take time to integrate this unanimous impression with the unqualified righteousness with which our own acts, however admittedly miscalculated, invest themselves. And once the events are sorted out—the actions given motivations, the actors assigned psychologies, the miscalculations tabulated, the abnormalities named, the whole furious and careless growth pruned by explanation and rooted in history and returned, as it were, to Nature—what then? Is not such a return spurious? Can our spirits really enter Time's haven of mortality and sink composedly among the mulching leaves? No: we stand at the intersection of two kingdoms, and there is no advance and no retreat, only a sharpening of the edge where we stand.

I remember most sharply the black of my wife's dress as she left our house to get her divorce. The dress was a soft black sheath, with a V neckline, and Helen always looked handsome in it; it flattered her pallor. This morning she looked especially handsome, her face utterly white with fatigue. Yet her body, that natural thing, ignored our catastrophe, and her shape and gestures were incongruously usual. She kissed me lightly in leaving, and we both felt the humor of this trip's being insufficiently unlike any other of her trips to Boston—to Symphony, to Bonwit's. The same search for the car keys, the same harassed instructions to the complacent baby-sitter, the same little dip and thrust of her head as she settled behind the wheel of her car. And I, satisfied at last, divorced, studied my children with the eyes of one who had left them, examined my house as one does a set of snapshots from an irrevocable time, drove through the turning landscape as a man in asbestos cuts through a fire, met my wife-to-be—weeping yet smiling, stunned yet brave—and felt, unstoppably, to my horror, the inner darkness burst my skin and engulf us both and drown our love. The natural world, where our love had existed, ceased to exist. My heart shied back; it shies back still. I retreated. As I drove back, the leaves of the trees along the road stated their shapes to me. There is no more story to tell. By telephone I plucked my wife back; I clasped the black of her dress to me, and braced for the pain.

It does not stop coming. The pain does not stop coming. Almost every day, a new installment arrives by mail or face or phone. Every time the telephone rings, I expect it to uncoil some new convolution of consequence. I have come to hide in this cottage, but even here, there is a telephone, and the scraping sounds of wind and branch and unseen animal are charged with its electric silence. At any moment, it may explode, and the curious beauty of the leaves will be eclipsed again.

In nervousness, I rise, and walk across the floor. A spider like a white asterisk hangs in air in front of my face. I look at the ceiling and cannot see where its thread is attached. The ceiling is smooth plasterboard. The spider hesitates. It feels a huge alien presence. Its exquisite white legs spread warily and of its own dead weight it twirls on its invisible thread. I catch myself in the quaint and antique pose of the fabulist seeking to draw a lesson from a spider, and become self-conscious. I dismiss self-consciousness and do earnestly attend to this minute articulated star hung so pointedly before my face; and am unable to read the lesson. The spider and I inhabit contiguous but incompatible cosmoses. Across the gulf we feel only fear. The telephone remains silent. The spider reconsiders its spinning. The wind continues to stir the sunlight. In walking in and out of this cottage, I have tracked the floor with a few dead leaves, pressed flat like scraps of dark paper.

And what are these pages but leaves? Why do I produce them but to thrust, by some subjective photosynthesis, my guilt into Nature, where there is no guilt? Now the marsh, level as a carpet, is streaked with faint green amid the shades of brown—russet, ochre, tan, *marron*—and on the far side, where the land lifts above tide level, evergreens stab upwards sullenly. Beyond them, there is a low blue hill; in this coastal region, the hills are almost too modest to bear names. But I *see* it; for the first time in months I see it. I see it as a child, fingers gripping and neck straining, glimpses the roof of a house over a cruelly high wall. Under my window, the lawn is lank and green and mixed with leaves shed from a small elm, and I remember how, the first night I came to this cottage, thinking I was leaving my life behind me, I went to bed alone and read, in the way one reads stray books in a borrowed house, a few pages of an old edition of *Leaves of Grass*. And my sleep was a loop, so that in awaking I seemed still in the book, and the light-struck sky quivering through the stripped branches of the young elm seemed another page of Whitman, and I was entirely open, and lost, like a woman in passion, and free, and in love, without a shadow in any corner of my being. It was a beautiful awakening, but by the next night I had returned to my house.

The precise barbaric shadows on the grape leaves have shifted. The angle of illumination has altered. I imagine warmth leaning against the door, and open the door to let it in; sunlight falls flat at my feet like a penitent.

Raymond Carver (1938–   )

Raymond Carver is not concerned with the privileged, self-conscious upper-middle class of the big city and its suburbs. His characters live in small cities and towns, teach high school, guard banks, wait on tables. They are not particularly witty or insightful. Carver writes about ordinary people in ordinary situations, the Silent Majority of Middle America. And yet after finishing a Carver story, we feel the deep chill and the menace of modern life.

In the stories something happens to disturb the protagonist—an infidelity is acknowledged years later, a loutish husband is exposed, or in "Neighbors," a profound envy revealed. He suffers shame or guilt; feels rejected or disappointed. He doesn't know what action to follow or even what attitude to take. Carver's people are not self-aware enough to understand their feelings or articulate enough to discuss their lives. Although a rare Carver story ends in actual violence, usually his protagonist will simply go on with the old life. It will, of course, never be the same.

Unlike many of his contemporaries, Carver has not attempted to develop a new, elaborate language for fiction. He writes in a traditional, rather laconic style. His prose is as sparse and flat as the prose of Hemingway (although their characters and themes are very different), almost devoid of metaphor or simile. There are no extra words, no acrobatics. He tells us what we need to know as directly as he can—the fuzzy white spread on the bed, the tell-tale white lint on the wife's back. Again like Hemingway, he does not dwell on psychology or spend time rummaging in the minds of his protagonists. They are what they say and what they do. Yet the reader understands them, their sense of inadequacy, the violence just below the surface.

Herein lies Carver's enormous skill. Speech and gesture are so exactly right that the small detail reveals the large meaning. In "Neighbors," when Bill reaches "in back for the bottle of Chivas Regal," we know that he has watched with envy as Jim hid the bottle. When he looks at the door across the hall and immediately says to Arlene, "Let's go to bed," we understand the excitement he feels at the prospect of changing lives with the Stones. In the hands of this writer, less *is* more.

"Neighbors" is a typical Carver story. Envy and mild discontent lead decent, unexceptional people into a disturbing self-awareness. As they adopt the good life of their neighbors, changes occur in their own relationship. They become at once more secretive and more sexual. Disaster ensues. Yet the ending is ambiguous. Caught in the corridor between the two apartments, are they now excluded from both? Or are they more united?

We don't necessarily know what will now happen—will the Millers call a locksmith?—but that is irrelevant. The important thing has already occurred: they share an awful truth about themselves. It is awful, and yet ordinary, human, perhaps inevitable. There but for the grace of God go I. Like Chekhov, Carver writes stories that are small in scope and large in the truths they reveal.

Carver was born in Clatskanie, Oregon, in 1938. He is the author of several volumes of poetry and two collections of stories. His first, *Will You Please Be Quiet, Please?*, was nominated for the National Book Award in 1977. When *What We Talk About When We Talk About Love* appeared in 1981, Michael Wood wrote that in it Carver "has invented a country of his own, like no other except the very world, as Wordsworth said, which is the world of all of us."

Neighbors

Bill and Arlene Miller were a happy couple. But now and then they felt they alone among their circle had been passed by somehow, leaving Bill to attend to his bookkeeping duties and Arlene occupied with secretarial chores. They talked about it sometimes, mostly in comparison with the lives of their neighbors, Harriet and Jim Stone. It seemed to the Millers that the Stones lived a fuller and brighter life. The Stones were always going out for dinner, or entertaining at home, or traveling about the country somewhere in connection with Jim's work.

The Stones lived across the hall from the Millers. Jim was a salesman for a machine-parts firm and often managed to combine business with pleasure trips, and on this occasion the Stones would be away for ten days, first to Cheyenne, then on to St. Louis to visit relatives. In their absence, the Millers would look after the Stones' apartment, feed Kitty, and water the plants.

Bill and Jim shook hands beside the car. Harriet and Arlene held each other by the elbows and kissed lightly on the lips.

"Have fun," Bill said to Harriet.

"We will," said Harriet. "You kids have fun too."

Arlene nodded.

Jim winked at her. "Bye, Arlene. Take good care of the old man."

"I will," Arlene said.

"Have fun," Bill said.

"You bet," Jim said, clipping Bill lightly on the arm. "And thanks again, you guys."

The Stones waved as they drove away, and the Millers waved too.

"Well, I wish it was us," Bill said.

"God knows, we could use a vacation," Arlene said. She took his arm and put it around her waist as they climbed the stairs to their apartment.

After dinner Arlene said, "Don't forget. Kitty gets liver flavor the first night." She stood in the kitchen doorway folding the handmade tablecloth that Harriet had bought for her last year in Santa Fe.

Bill took a deep breath as he entered the Stones' apartment. The air was already heavy and it was vaguely sweet. The sunburst clock over the television said half past eight. He remembered when Harriet had come home with the clock, how she had crossed the hall to show it to Arlene, cradling the brass case in her arms and talking to it through the tissue paper as if it were an infant.

Kitty rubbed her face against his slippers and then turned onto her side, but jumped up quickly as Bill moved to the kitchen and selected one of the stacked cans from the gleaming drainboard. Leaving the cat to pick at her food, he headed for the bathroom. He looked at himself in the mirror and then closed his eyes and then looked again. He opened the medicine chest. He found a container of pills and read the label—*Harriet Stone. One each day as directed*—and slipped it into his pocket. He went back to the kitchen, drew a pitcher of water, and returned to the living room. He finished watering, set the pitcher on the rug, and opened the liquor cabinet. He reached in back for the bottle of Chivas Regal. He took two drinks from the bottle, wiped his lips on his sleeve, and replaced the bottle in the cabinet.

From *Will You Please Be Quiet, Please?* by Raymond Carver. © 1976 by Raymond Carver. Reprinted by permission of McGraw-Hill Book Company and Raymond Carver.

Kitty was on the couch sleeping. He switched off the lights, slowly closing and checking the door. He had the feeling he had left something.

"What kept you?" Arlene said. She sat with her legs turned under her, watching television.

"Nothing. Playing with Kitty," he said, and went over to her and touched her breasts.

"Let's go to bed, honey," he said.

The next day Bill took only ten minutes of the twenty-minute break allotted for the afternoon and left at fifteen minutes before five. He parked the car in the lot just as Arlene hopped down from the bus. He waited until she entered the building, then ran up the stairs to catch her as she stepped out of the elevator.

"Bill! God, you scared me. You're early," she said.

He shrugged. "Nothing to do at work," he said.

She let him use her key to open the door. He looked at the door across the hall before following her inside.

"Let's go to bed," he said.

"Now?" She laughed. "What's gotten into you?"

"Nothing. Take your dress off." He grabbed for her awkwardly, and she said, "Good God, Bill."

He unfastened his belt.

Later they sent out for Chinese food, and when it arrived they ate hungrily, without speaking, and listened to records.

"Let's not forget to feed Kitty," she said.

"I was just thinking about that," he said. "I'll go right over."

He selected a can of fish flavor for the cat, then filled the pitcher and went to water. When he returned to the kitchen, the cat was scratching in her box. She looked at him steadily before she turned back to the litter. He opened all the cupboards and examined the canned goods, the cereals, the packaged foods, the cocktail and wine glasses, the china, the pots and pans. He opened the refrigerator. He sniffed some celery, took two bites of cheddar cheese, and chewed on an apple as he walked into the bedroom. The bed seemed enormous, with a fluffy white bedspread draped to the floor. He pulled out a nightstand drawer, found a half-empty package of cigarets and stuffed them into his pocket. Then he stepped to the closet and was opening it when the knock sounded at the front door.

He stopped by the bathroom and flushed the toilet on his way.

"What's been keeping you?" Arlene said. "You've been over here more than an hour."

"Have I really?" he said.

"Yes, you have," she said.

"I had to go to the toilet," he said.

"You have your own toilet," she said.

"I couldn't wait," he said.

That night they made love again.

In the morning he had Arlene call in for him. He showered, dressed, and made a light breakfast. He tried to start a book. He went out for a walk and felt better. But after a while, hands still in his pockets, he returned to the apartment. He stopped at the Stones' door on the chance he might hear the cat moving about. Then he let himself in at his own door and went to the kitchen for the key.

Inside it seemed cooler than his apartment, and darker too. He wondered if the plants had something to do with the temperature of the air. He looked out the window, and then he moved slowly through each room considering everything that fell under his gaze, carefully, one object at a time. He saw ashtrays, items of furniture, kitchen utensils, the clock. He saw everything. At last he entered the bedroom, and the cat appeared at his feet. He stroked her once, carried her into the bathroom, and shut the door.

He lay down on the bed and stared at the ceiling. He lay for a while with his eyes closed, and then he moved his hand under his belt. He tried to recall what day it was. He tried to remember when the Stones were due back, and then he wondered if they would ever return. He could not remember their faces or the way they talked and dressed. He sighed and with effort rolled off the bed to lean over the dresser and look at himself in the mirror.

He opened the closet and selected a Hawaiian shirt. He looked until he found Bermudas, neatly pressed and hanging over a pair of brown twill slacks. He shed his own clothes and slipped into the shorts and the shirt. He looked in the mirror again. He went to the living room and poured himself a drink and sipped it on his way back to the bedroom. He put on a blue shirt, a dark suit, a blue and white tie, black wing-tip shoes. The glass was empty and he went for another drink.

In the bedroom again, he sat on a chair, crossed his legs, and smiled, observing himself in the mirror. The telephone rang twice and fell silent. He finished the drink and took off the suit. He rummaged through the top drawers until he found a pair of panties and a brassiere. He stepped into the panties and fastened the brassiere, then looked through the closet for an outfit. He put on a black and white checkered skirt and tried to zip it up. He put on a burgundy blouse that buttoned up the front. He considered her shoes, but understood they would not fit. For a long time he looked out the living-room window from behind the curtain. Then he returned to the bedroom and put everything away.

He was not hungry. She did not eat much, either. They looked at each other shyly and smiled. She got up from the table and checked that the key was on the shelf and then she quickly cleared the dishes.

He stood in the kitchen doorway and smoked a cigaret and watched her pick up the key.

"Make yourself comfortable while I go across the hall," she said. "Read the paper or something." She closed her fingers over the key. He was, she said, looking tired.

He tried to concentrate on the news. He read the paper and turned on the television. Finally he went across the hall. The door was locked.

"It's me. Are you still there, honey?" he called.

After a time the lock released and Arlene stepped outside and shut the door. "Was I gone so long?" she said.

"Well, you were," he said.

"Was I?" she said. "I guess I must have been playing with Kitty."

He studied her, and she looked away, her hand still resting on the doorknob.

"It's funny," she said. "You know—to go in someone's place like that."

He nodded, took her hand from the knob, and guided her toward their own door. He let them into their apartment.

"It *is* funny," he said.

He noticed white lint clinging to the back of her sweater, and the color was high in her cheeks. He began kissing her on the neck and hair and she turned and kissed him.

"Oh, damn," she said. "Damn, damn," she sang, girlishly clapping her hands. "I just remembered. I really and truly forgot to do what I went over there to do. I didn't feed Kitty or do any watering." She looked at him. "Isn't that stupid?"

"I don't think so," he said. "Just a minute. I'll get my cigarets and go back with you."

She waited until he had closed and locked their door, and then she took his arm at the muscle and said, "I guess I should tell you. I found some pictures."

He stopped in the middle of the hall. "What kind of pictures?"

"You can see for yourself," she said, and she watched him.

"No kidding." He grinned. "Where?"

"In a drawer," she said.

"No kidding," he said.

And then she said, "Maybe they won't come back," and was at once astonished at her words.

"It could happen," he said. "Anything could happen."

"Or maybe they'll come back and . . ." but she did not finish.

They held hands for the short walk across the hall, and when he spoke she could barely hear his voice.

"The key," he said. "Give it to me."

"What?" she said. She gazed at the door.

"The key," he said. "You have the key."

"My God," she said, "I left the key inside."

He tried the knob. It was locked. Then she tried the knob. It would not turn. Her lips were parted, and her breathing was hard, expectant. He opened his arms and she moved into them.

"Don't worry," he said into her ear. "For God's sake, don't worry."

They stayed there. They held each other. They leaned into the door as if against a wind, and braced themselves.

Joyce Carol Oates (1938–   )

"I would be unable to write about anything that did not seem to me both unique and universal," says Joyce Carol Oates,

—an event I have lived through myself, or experienced intensely through my imagination, and an event that has some larger appeal, which may go far beyond the temporal limitations of the subject. If art has any general evolutionary function, it must be to enhance the race, to work somehow toward an essential unity and harmony—survival and growth—and perhaps an integration of the human world with the natural world.

This is the credo of a young writer who burst, as it were, full-armed upon the world of fiction. Born in upstate New York in 1938, by the time she was thirty-one she had already received the National Book Award for her fourth novel, *them.* By 1981, she had published twelve novels, twelve volumes of short stories, three volumes of poems, and three volumes of critical pieces. She is perhaps the most prolific serious writer in America.

Oates recognizes two distinct kinds of fiction. "When a work of art pleases us it is often because it recounts for us an experience close to our own, something we can recognize." This kind of fiction reassures us. But there is a kind that unnerves us, "works of art that explain nothing, that dispel order and sanity; works of art that contradict our experience and are therefore deeply offensive; works of art that refuse to make sense, that are perhaps dangerous because they are unforgettable." Oates is capable of writing both kinds, but she is at her best when her subject is the violent, the insane, the threatening.

Oates's characters are usually victims, of someone else's violence or of their own obsessions: a middle-class girl imprisoned for compulsive shoplifting, an ordinary man who kills in vengeance and shatters his life, a college girl who becomes obsessed with the wife of her professor-lover, a nun whose rejection of a young student makes her realize that she lives in hell in the region of ice.

The tone (see Introduction, pp. 15-16) of an Oates story underscores the threatening, obsessive quality. Devoid of irony, the language collapses the distance between the subject and us. We become prey to the same unexplained feelings as do the characters. In the story that follows, the atmosphere is feverish and threatening. From the first description of Connie, our nerves are taut. She is reckless, overstimulated, nubile, and we sense danger. But even though we know that nothing pleasant will come of reading, we find it difficult not to go on. That steady, strong current of words pulls us along despite ourselves and at the end we are as excruciatingly vulnerable to the irrational as Connie is.

And that is exactly what Oates wants. She says, "It is only through disruption and confusion that we grow, jarred out of ourselves by the collision of someone else's private world with our own." And, she might have added, at the same time thrust deeper into ourselves. For though an Oates story may contradict our actual experience, it uncovers our own dark fantasies and nightmares.

Where Are You Going, Where Have You Been?

FOR BOB DYLAN

Her name was Connie. She was fifteen and she had a quick, nervous giggling habit of craning her neck to glance into mirrors or checking other people's faces to make sure her own was all right. Her mother, who noticed everything and knew everything and who hadn't much reason any longer to look at her own face, always scolded Connie about it. "Stop gawking at yourself. Who are you? You think you're so pretty?" she would say. Connie would raise her eyebrows at these familiar old complaints and look right through her mother, into a shadowy vision of herself as she was right at that moment: she knew she was pretty and that was everything. Her mother had been pretty once too, if you could believe those old snapshots in the album, but now her looks were gone and that was why she was always after Connie.

"Why don't you keep your room clean like your sister? How've you got your hair fixed—what the hell stinks? Hair spray? You don't see your sister using that junk."

Her sister June was twenty-four and still lived at home. She was a secretary in the high school Connie attended, and if that wasn't bad enough—with her in the same building—she was so plain and chunky and steady that Connie had to hear her praised all the time by her mother and her mother's sisters. June did this, June did that, she saved money and helped clean the house and cooked and Connie couldn't do a thing, her mind was all filled with trashy daydreams. Their father was away at work most of the time and when he came home he wanted supper and he read the newspaper at supper and after supper he went to bed. He didn't bother talking much to them, but around his bent head Connie's mother kept picking at her until Connie wished her mother was dead and she herself was dead and it was all over. "She makes me want to throw up some- times," she complained to her friends. She had a high, breathless, amused voice that made everything she said sound a little forced, whether it was sincere or not.

There was one good thing: June went places with girl friends of hers, girls who were just as plain and steady as she, and so when Connie wanted to do that her mother had no objections. The father of Connie's best girl friend drove the girls the three miles to town and left them at a shopping plaza so they could walk through the stores or go to a movie, and when he came to pick them up again at eleven he never bothered to ask what they had done.

They must have been familiar sights, walking around the shopping plaza in their shorts and flat ballerina slippers that always scuffed on the sidewalk, with charm brace- lets jingling on their thin wrists; they would lean together to whisper and laugh secretly if someone passed who amused or interested them. Connie had long dark blond hair that drew anyone's eye to it, and she wore part of it pulled up on her head and puffed out and the rest of it she let fall down her back. She wore a pull-over jersey blouse that looked one way when she was at home and another way when she was away from home. Everything about her had two sides to it, one for home and one for anywhere that was not home: her walk, which could be childlike and bobbing, or languid enough to make anyone think she was hearing music in her head; her mouth, which was pale and smirking most of the time, but bright and pink on these evenings out; her laugh, which was cynical and drawling at home—"Ha, ha, very funny,"—but highpitched and ner- vous anywhere else, like the jingling of the charms on her bracelet.

Sometimes they did go shopping or to a movie, but sometimes they went across the highway, ducking fast across the busy road, to a drive-in restaurant where older kids hung out. The restaurant was shaped like a big bottle, though squatter than a real bottle, and on its cap was a revolving figure of a grinning boy holding a hamburger aloft. One night in midsummer they ran across, breathless with daring, and right away someone leaned out a car window and invited them over, but it was just a boy from high school they didn't like. It made them feel good to be able to ignore him. They went up through the maze of parked and cruising cars to the bright-lit, fly-infested restaurant, their faces pleased and expectant as if they were entering a sacred building that loomed up out of the night to give them what haven and blessing they yearned for. They sat at the counter and crossed their legs at the ankles, their thin shoulders rigid with excitement, and listened to the music that made everything so good: the music was always in the background, like music at a church service; it was something to depend upon.

A boy named Eddie came in to talk with them. He sat backwards on his stool, turning himself jerkily around in semicircles and then stopping and turning back again, and after a while he asked Connie if she would like something to eat. She said she would and so she tapped her friend's arm on her way out—her friend pulled her face up into a brave, droll look—and Connie said she would meet her at eleven, across the way. "I just hate to leave her like that," Connie said earnestly, but the boy said that she wouldn't be alone for long. So they went out to his car, and on the way Connie couldn't help but let her eyes wander over the windshields and faces all around her, her face gleaming with a joy that had nothing to do with Eddie or even this place; it might have been the music. She drew her shoulders up and sucked in her breath with the pure pleasure of being alive, and just at that moment she happened to glance at a face just a few feet away from hers. It was a boy with shaggy black hair, in a convertible jalopy painted gold. He stared at her and then his lips widened into a grin. Connie slit her eyes at him and turned away, but she couldn't help glancing back and there he was, still watching her. He wagged a finger and laughed and said, "Gonna get you, baby," and Connie turned away again without Eddie noticing anything.

She spent three hours with him, at the restaurant where they ate hamburgers and drank Cokes in wax cups that were always sweating, and then down an alley a mile or so away, and when he left her off at five to eleven only the movie house was still open at the plaza. Her girl friend was there, talking with a boy. When Connie came up, the two girls smiled at each other and Connie said, "How was the movie?" and the girl said, "*You* should know." They rode off with the girl's father, sleepy and pleased, and Connie couldn't help but look back at the darkened shopping plaza with its big empty parking lot and its signs that were faded and ghostly now, and over at the drive-in restaurant where cars were still circling tirelessly. She couldn't hear the music at this distance.

Next morning June asked her how the movie was and Connie said, "So-so."

She and that girl and occasionally another girl went out several times a week, and the rest of the time Connie spent around the house—it was summer vacation—getting in her mother's way and thinking, dreaming about the boys she met. But all the boys fell back and dissolved into a single face that was not even a face but an idea, a feeling, mixed up with the urgent insistent pounding of the music and the humid night air of July. Connie's mother kept dragging her back to the daylight by finding things for her to do or saying suddenly, "What's this about the Pettinger girl?"

And Connie would say nervously, "Oh, her. That dope." She always drew thick clear lines between herself and such girls, and her mother was simple and kind enough to believe it. Her mother was so simple, Connie thought, that it was maybe cruel to fool her so much. Her mother went scuffling around the house in old bedroom slippers and complained over the telephone to one sister about the other, then the other called up and the two of them complained about the third one. If June's name was mentioned her mother's tone was approving, and if Connie's name was mentioned it was disapproving. This did not really mean she disliked Connie, and actually Connie thought that her mother preferred her to June just because she was prettier, but the two of them kept up a pretense of exasperation, a sense that they were tugging and struggling over something of little value to either of them. Sometimes, over coffee, they were almost friends, but something would come up —some vexation that was like a fly buzzing suddenly around their heads—and their faces went hard with contempt.

One Sunday Connie got up at eleven—none of them bothered with church—and washed her hair so that it could dry all day long in the sun. Her parents and sister were going to a barbecue at an aunt's house and Connie said no, she wasn't interested, rolling her eyes to let her mother know just what she thought of it. "Stay home alone then," her mother said sharply. Connie sat out back in a lawn chair and watched them drive away, her father quiet and bald, hunched around so that he could back the car out, her mother with a look that was still angry and not at all softened through the windshield, and in the back seat poor old June, all dressed up as if she didn't know what a barbecue was, with all the running yelling kids and the flies. Connie sat with her eyes closed in the sun, dreaming and dazed with the warmth about her as if this were a kind of love, the caresses of love, and her mind slipped over onto thoughts of the boy she had been with the night before and how nice he had been, how sweet it always was, not the way someone like June would suppose but sweet, gentle, the way it was in movies and promised in songs; and when she opened her eyes she hardly knew where she was, the back yard ran off into weeds and a fence-like line of trees and behind it the sky was perfectly blue and still. The asbestos "ranch house" that was now three years old startled her—it looked small. She shook her head as if to get awake.

It was too hot. She went inside the house and turned on the radio to drown out the quiet. She sat on the edge of her bed, barefoot, and listened for an hour and a half, to a program called XYZ Sunday Jamboree, record after record of hard, fast, shrieking songs she sang along with, interspersed by exclamations from "Bobby King": "An' look here, you girls at Napoleon's—Son and Charley want you to pay real close attention to this song coming up!"

And Connie paid close attention herself, bathed in a glow of slow-pulsed joy that seemed to rise mysteriously out of the music itself and lay languidly about the airless little room, breathed in and breathed out with each gentle rise and fall of her chest.

After a while she heard a car coming up the drive. She sat up at once, startled, because it couldn't be her father so soon. The gravel kept crunching all the way in from the road—the driveway was long—and Connie ran to the window. It was a car she didn't know. It was an open jalopy, painted a bright gold that caught the sunlight opaquely. Her heart began to pound and her fingers snatched at her hair, checking it, and she whispered, "Christ, Christ," wondering how she looked. The car came to a stop at the side door and the horn sounded four short taps, as if this were a signal Connie knew.

She went into the kitchen and approached the door slowly, then hung out the screen door, her bare toes curling down off the step. There were two boys in the car and now she recognized the driver: he had shaggy, shabby black hair that looked crazy as a wig and he was grinning at her.

"I ain't late, am I?" he said.

"Who the hell do you think you are?" Connie said.

"Toldja I'd be out, didn't I?"

"I don't even know who you are."

She spoke sullenly, careful to show no interest or pleasure, and he spoke in a fast, bright monotone. Connie looked past him to the other boy, taking her time. He had fair brown hair, with a lock that fell onto his forehead. His sideburns gave him a fierce, embarrassed look, but so far he hadn't even bothered to glance at her. Both boys wore sunglasses. The driver's glasses were metallic and mirrored everything in miniature.

"You wanta come for a ride?" he said.

Connie smirked and let her hair fall loose over one shoulder.

"Don'tcha like my car? New paint job," he said. "Hey."

"What?"

"You're cute."

She pretended to fidget, chasing flies away from the door.

"Don'tcha believe me, or what?" he said.

"Look, I don't even know who you are," Connie said in disgust.

"Hey, Ellie's got a radio, see. Mine broke down." He lifted his friend's arm and showed her the little transistor radio the boy was holding, and now Connie began to hear the music. It was the same program that was playing inside the house.

"Bobby King?" she said.

"I listen to him all the time. I think he's great."

"He's kind of great," Connie said reluctantly.

"Listen, that guy's *great*. He knows where the action is."

Connie blushed a little, because the glasses made it impossible for her to see just what this boy was looking at. She couldn't decide if she liked him or if he was a jerk, and so she dawdled in the doorway and wouldn't come down or go back inside. She said, "What's all that stuff painted on your car?"

"Can'tcha read it?" He opened the door very carefully, as if he were afraid it might fall off. He slid out just as carefully, planting his feet firmly on the ground, the tiny metallic world in his glasses slowing down like gelatine hardening, and in the midst of it Connie's bright green blouse. "This here is my name, to begin with," he said. ARNOLD FRIEND was written in tarlike black letters on the side, with a drawing of a round, grinning face that reminded Connie of a pumpkin, except it wore sunglasses. "I wanta introduce myself. I'm Arnold Friend and that's my real name and I'm gonna be your friend, honey, and inside the car's Ellie Oscar, he's kinda shy." Ellie brought his transistor radio up to his shoulder and balanced it there. "Now, these numbers are a secret code, honey," Arnold Friend explained. He read off the numbers 33, 19, 17 and raised his eyebrows at her to see what she thought of that, but she didn't think much of it. The left rear fender had been smashed and around it was written, on the gleaming gold background: DONE BY CRAZY WOMAN DRIVER. Connie had to laugh at that. Arnold Friend was pleased at her laughter and looked up at her. "Around the other side's a lot more—you wanta come and see them?"

"No."

"Why not?"

"Why should I?"

"Don'tcha wanta see what's on the car? Don'tcha wanta go for a ride?"

"I don't know."

"Why not?"

"I got things to do."

"Like what?"

"Things."

He laughed as if she had said something funny. He slapped his thighs. He was standing in a strange way, leaning back against the car as if he were balancing himself. He wasn't tall, only an inch or so taller than she would be if she came down to him. Connie liked the way he was dressed, which was the way all of them dressed: tight faded jeans stuffed into black, scuffed boots, a belt that pulled his waist in and showed how lean he was, and a white pull-over shirt that was a little soiled and showed the hard small muscles of his arms and shoulders. He looked as if he probably did hard work, lifting and carrying things. Even his neck looked muscular. And his face was a familiar face, somehow; the jaw and chin and cheeks slightly darkened because he hadn't shaved for a day or two, and the nose long and hawklike, sniffing as if she were a treat he was going to gobble up and it was all a joke.

"Connie, you ain't telling the truth. This is your day set aside for a ride with me and you know it," he said, still laughing. The way he straightened and recovered from his fit of laughing showed that it had been all fake.

"How do you know what my name is?" she said suspiciously.

"It's Connie."

"Maybe and maybe not."

"I know my Connie," he said, wagging his finger. Now she remembered him even better, back at the restaurant, and her cheeks warmed at the thought of how she had sucked in her breath just at the moment she passed him—how she must have looked to him. And he had remembered her. "Ellie and I come out here especially for you." he said. "Ellie can sit in back. How about it?"

"Where?"

"Where what?"

"Where're we going?"

He looked at her. He took off the sunglasses and she saw how pale the skin around his eyes was, like holes that were not in shadow but instead in light. His eyes were like chips of broken glass that catch the light in an amiable way. He smiled. It was as if the idea of going for a ride somewhere, to someplace, was a new idea to him.

"Just for a ride, Connie sweetheart."

"I never said my name was Connie," she said.

"But I know what it is. I know your name and all about you, lots of things," Arnold Friend said. He had not moved yet but stood still leaning back against the side of his jalopy. "I took a special interest in you, such a pretty girl, and found out all about you—like I know your parents and sister are gone somewheres and I know where and how long they're going to be gone, and I know who you were with last night, and your best girl friend's name is Betty, Right?"

He spoke in a simple lilting voice, exactly as if he were reciting the words to a song. His smile assured her that everything was fine. In the car Ellie turned up the volume on his radio and did not bother to look around at them.

"Ellie can sit in the back seat," Arnold Friend said. He indicated his friend with a casual jerk of his chin, as if Ellie did not count and she should not bother with him.

"How'd you find out all that stuff?" Connie said.

"Listen: Betty Schultz and Tony Fitch and Jimmy Pettinger and Nancy Pettinger," he said in a chant. "Raymond Stanley and Bob Hutter—"

"Do you know all those kids?"

"I know everybody."

"Look, you're kidding. You're not from around here."

"Sure."

"But—how come we never saw you before?"

"Sure you saw me before," he said. He looked down at his boots, as if he were a little offended. "You just don't remember."

"I guess I'd remember you," Connie said.

"Yeah?" He looked up at this, beaming. He was pleased. He began to mark time with the music from Ellie's radio, tapping his fists lightly together. Connie looked away from his smile to the car, which was painted so bright it almost hurt her eyes to look at it. She looked at that name, ARNOLD FRIEND. And up at the front fender was an expression that was familiar—MAN THE FLYING SAUCERS. It was an expression kids had used the year before but didn't use this year. She looked at it for a while as if the words meant something to her that she did not yet know.

"What're you thinking about? Huh?" Arnold Friend demanded. "Not worried about your hair blowing around in the car, are you?"

"No."

"Think I maybe can't drive good?"

"How do I know?"

"You're a hard girl to handle. How come?" he said. "Don't you know I'm your friend? Didn't you see me put my sign in the air when you walked by?"

"What sign?"

"My sign." And he drew an X in the air, leaning out toward her. They were maybe ten feet apart. After his hand fell back to his side the X was still in the air, almost visible. Connie let the screen door close and stood perfectly still inside it, listening to the music from her radio and the boy's blend together. She stared at Arnold Friend. He stood there so stiffly relaxed, pretending to be relaxed, with one hand idly on the door handle as if he were keeping himself up that way and had no intention of ever moving again. She recognized most things about him, the tight jeans that showed his thighs and buttocks and the greasy leather boots and the tight shirt, and even that slippery friendly smile of his, that sleepy dreamy smile that all the boys used to get across ideas they didn't want to put into words. She recognized all this and also the sing-song way he talked, slightly mocking, kidding, but serious and a little melancholy, and she recognized the way he tapped one fist against the other in homage to the perpetual music behind him. But all these things did not come together.

She said suddenly, " 'Hey, how old are you?"

His smile faded. She could see then that he wasn't a kid, he was much older—thirty, maybe more. At this knowledge her heart began to pound faster.

"That's a crazy thing to ask. Can'tcha see I'm your own age?"

"Like hell you are."

"Or maybe a coupla years older. I'm eighteen."

"Eighteen?" she said doubtfully.

He grinned to reassure her and lines appeared at the corners of his mouth. His teeth were big and white. He grinned so broadly his eyes became slits and she saw how thick the lashes were, thick and black as if painted with a black tarlike material. Then, abruptly, he seemed to become embarrassed and looked over his shoulder at Ellie. "*Him*, he's crazy," he said. "Ain't he a riot? He's a nut, a real character." Ellie was still listening to the music. His sunglasses told nothing about what he was thinking. He wore a bright orange shirt unbuttoned halfway to show his chest, which was a pale, bluish chest and not muscular like Arnold Friend's. His shirt collar was turned up all around and the very tips of the collar pointed out past his chin as if they were protecting him. He was pressing the transistor radio up against his ear and sat there in a kind of daze, right in the sun.

"He's kinda strange," Connie said.

"Hey, she says you're kinda strange! Kinda strange!" Arnold Friend cried. He pounded on the car to get Ellie's attention. Ellie turned for the first time and Connie saw with shock that he wasn't a kid either—he had a fair, hairless face, cheeks reddened slightly as if the veins grew too close to the surface of his skin, the face of a forty-year-old baby. Connie felt a wave of dizziness rise in her at this sight and she stared at him as if waiting for something to change the shock of the moment, make it all right again. Ellie's lips kept shaping words, mumbling along with the words blasting in his ear.

"Maybe you two better go away," Connie said faintly.

"What? How come?" Arnold Friend cried. "We come out here to take you for a ride. It's Sunday." He had the voice of the man on the radio now. It was the same voice, Connie thought. "Don'tcha know it's Sunday all day? And honey, no matter who you were with last night, today you're with Arnold Friend and don't you forget it! Maybe you better step out here," he said, and this last was in a different voice. It was a little flatter, as if the heat was finally getting to him.

"No. I got things to do."

"Hey."

"You two better leave."

"We ain't leaving until you come with us."

"Like hell I am—"

"Connie, don't fool around with me. I mean—I mean, don't fool *around*," he said, shaking his head. He laughed incredulously. He placed his sunglasses on top of his head, carefully, as if he were indeed wearing a wig, and brought the stems down behind his ears. Connie stared at him, another wave of dizziness and fear rising in her so that for a moment he wasn't even in focus but was just a blur standing there against his gold car, and she had the idea that he had driven up the driveway all right but had come from nowhere before that and belonged nowhere and that everything about him and even about the music that was so familiar to her was only half real.

"If my father comes and sees you—"

"He ain't coming. He's at a barbecue."

"How do you know that?"

"Aunt Tillie's. Right now they're—uh—they're drinking. Sitting around," he said vaguely, squinting as if he were staring all the way to town and over to Aunt Tillie's back yard. Then the vision seemed to get clear and he nodded energetically. "Yeah. Sitting around. There's your sister in a blue dress, huh? And high heels, the poor sad bitch—nothing like you, sweetheart! And your mother's helping some fat woman with the corn, they're cleaning the corn—husking the corn—"

"What fat woman?" Connie cried.

"How do I know what fat woman, I don't know every goddamn fat woman in the world!" Arnold Friend laughed.

"Oh, that's Mrs. Hornsby. . . . Who invited her?" Connie said. She felt a little lightheaded. Her breath was coming quickly.

"She's too fat. I don't like them fat. I like them the way you are, honey," he said, smiling sleepily at her. They stared at each other for a while through the screen door. He said softly, "Now, what you're going to do is this: you're going to come out that door. You're going to sit up front with me and Ellie's going to sit in the back, the hell with Ellie, right? This isn't Ellie's date. You're my date. I'm your lover, honey."

"What? You're crazy—"

"Yes. I'm your lover. You don't know what that is but you will," he said. "I know that too. I know all about you. But look: it's real nice and you couldn't ask for nobody better than me, or more polite. I always keep my word. I'll tell you how it is, I'm always nice at first, the first time. I'll hold you so tight you won't think you have to try to get away or pretend anything because you'll know you can't. And I'll come inside you where it's all secret and you'll give in to me and you'll love me—"

"Shut up! You're crazy!" Connie said. She backed away from the door. She put her hands up against her ears as if she'd heard something terrible, something not meant for her. "People don't talk like that, you're crazy," she muttered. Her heart was almost too big now for her chest and its pumping made sweat break out all over her. She looked out to see Arnold Friend pause and then take a step toward the porch, lurching. He almost fell. But, like a clever drunken man, he managed to catch his balance. He wobbled in his high boots and grabbed hold of one of the porch posts.

"Honey?" he said. "You still listening?"

"Get the hell out of here!"

"Be nice, honey. Listen."

"I'm going to call the police—"

He wobbled again and out of the side of his mouth came a fast spat curse, an aside not meant for her to hear. But even this "Christ!" sounded forced. Then he began to smile again. She watched this smile come, awkward as if he were smiling from inside a mask. His whole face was a mask, she thought wildly, tanned down to his throat but then running out as if he had plastered makeup on his face but had forgotten about his throat.

"Honey—? Listen, here's how it is. I always tell the truth and I promise you this: I ain't coming in that house after you."

"You better not! I'm going to call the police if you—if you don't—"

"Honey," he said, talking right through her voice, "honey. I'm not coming in there but you are coming out here. You know why?"

She was panting. The kitchen looked like a place she had never seen before, some room she had run inside but that wasn't good enough, wasn't going to help her. The kitchen window had never had a curtain, after three years, and there were dishes in the sink for her to do—probably—and if you ran your hand across the table you'd probably feel something stick there.

"You listening, honey? Hey?"

"—going to call the police—"

"Soon as you touch the phone I don't need to keep my promise and can come inside. You won't want that."

She rushed forward and tried to lock the door. Her fingers were shaking. "But why lock it," Arnold Friend said gently, talking right into her face. "It's just a screen door. It's just nothing." One of his boots was at a strange angle, as if his foot wasn't in it. It pointed out to the left, bent at the ankle. "I mean, anybody can break through a screen door and glass and wood and iron or anything else if he needs to, anybody at all, and especially Arnold Friend. If the place got lit up with a fire, honey, you'd come runnin' out into my arms, right into my arms an' safe at home—like you knew I was your lover and'd stopped fooling around. I don't mind a nice shy girl but I don't like no fooling around." Part of those words were spoken with a slight rhythmic lilt, and Connie somehow recognized them—the echo of a song from last year, about a girl rushing into her boy friend's arms and coming home again—

Connie stood barefoot on the linoleum floor, staring at him. "What do you want?" she whispered.

"I want you," he said.

"What?"

"Seen you that night and thought, that's the one, yes sir. I never needed to look anymore."

"But my father's coming back. He's coming to get me. I had to wash my hair first—" She spoke in a dry, rapid voice, hardly raising it for him to hear.

"No, your daddy is not coming and yes, you had to wash your hair and you washed it for me. It's nice and shining and all for me. I thank you sweetheart," he said with a mock bow, but again he almost lost his balance. He had to bend and adjust his boots. Evidently his feet did not go all the way down; the boots must have been stuffed with something so that he would seem taller. Connie stared out at him and behind him at Ellie in the car, who seemed to be looking off toward Connie's right, into nothing. This Ellie said, pulling the words out of the air one after another as if he were just discovering them, "You want me to pull out the phone?"

"Shut your mouth and keep it shut," Arnold Friend said, his face red from bending over or maybe from embarrassment because Connie had seen his boots. "This ain't none of your business."

"What—what are you doing? What do you want?" Connie said. "If I call the police they'll get you, they'll arrest you—"

"Promise was not to come in unless you touch that phone, and I'll keep that promise," he said. He resumed his erect position and tried to force his shoulders back. He sounded like a hero in a movie, declaring something important. But he spoke too loudly and it was as if he were speaking to someone behind Connie. "I ain't made plans for coming in that house where I don't belong but just for you to come out to me, the way you should. Don't you know who I am?"

"You're crazy," she whispered. She backed away from the door but did not want to go into another part of the house, as if this would give him permission to come through the door. "What do you . . . you're crazy, you. . . ."

"Huh? What're you saying, honey?"

Her eyes darted everywhere in the kitchen. She could not remember what it was, this room.

"This is how it is, honey: you come out and we'll drive away, have a nice ride. But if you don't come out we're gonna wait till your people come home and then they're all going to get it."

"You want that telephone pulled out?" Ellie said. He held the radio away from his ear and grimaced, as if without the radio the air was too much for him.

"I toldja shut up, Ellie," Arnold Friend said, "you're deaf, get a hearing aid, right? Fix yourself up. This little girl's no trouble and's gonna be nice to me, so Ellie keep to yourself, this ain't your date—right? Don't hem in on me, don't hog, don't crush, don't bird dog, don't trail me," he said in a rapid, meaningless voice, as if he were running through all the expressions he'd learned but was no longer sure which of them was in style, then rushing on to new ones, making them up with his eyes closed. "Don't crawl under my fence, don't squeeze in my chipmunk hole, don't sniff my glue, suck my popsicle, keep your own greasy fingers on yourself!" He shaded his eyes and peered in at Connie, who was backed against the kitchen table. "Don't mind him, honey, he's just a creep. He's a dope. Right? I'm the boy for you and like I said, you come out here nice like a lady and give me your hand, and nobody else gets hurt, I mean, your nice old bald-headed daddy and your mummy and your sister in her high heels. Because listen: why bring them in this?"

"Leave me alone," Connie whispered.

"Hey, you know that old woman down the road, the one with the chickens and stuff—you know her?"

"She's dead!"

"Dead? What? You know her?" Arnold Friend said.

"She's dead—."

"Don't you like her?"

"She's dead—she's—she isn't here any more—"

"But don't you like her, I mean, you got something against her? Some grudge or something?" Then his voice dipped as if he were conscious of a rudeness. He touched the sunglasses perched up on top of his head as if to make sure they were still there. "Now, you be a good girl."

"What are you going to do?"

"Just two things, or maybe three," Arnold Friend said. "But I promise it won't last long and you'll like me the way you get to like people you're close to. You will. It's all over for you here, so come on out. You don't want your people in any trouble, do you?"

She turned and bumped against a chair or something, hurting her leg, but she ran into the back room and picked up the telephone. Something roared in her ear, a tiny roaring, and she was so sick with fear that she could do nothing but listen to it—the telephone was clammy and very heavy and her fingers groped down to the dial but were too weak to touch it. She began to scream into the phone, into the roaring. She cried out, she cried for her mother, she felt her breath start jerking back and forth in her lungs as if it were something Arnold Friend was stabbing her with again and again with no tenderness. A noisy sorrowful wailing rose all about her and she was locked inside it the way she was locked inside this house.

After a while she could hear again. She was sitting on the floor with her wet back against the wall.

Arnold Friend was saying from the door, "That's a good girl. Put the phone back."

She kicked the phone away from her.

"No, honey. Pick it up. Put it back right."

She picked it up and put it back. The dial tone stopped.

"That's a good girl. Now, you come outside."

She was hollow with what had been fear but what was now just an emptiness. All that screaming had blasted it out of her. She sat, one leg cramped under her, and deep inside her brain was something like a pinpoint of light that kept going and would not let her relax. She thought, I'm not going to see my mother again. She thought, I'm not going to sleep in my bed again. Her bright green blouse was all wet.

Arnold Friend said, in a gentle-loud voice that was like a stage voice, "The place where you came from ain't there any more, and where you had in mind to go is cancelled out. This place you are now—inside your daddy's house—is nothing but a cardboard box I can knock down any time. You know that and always did know it. You hear me?"

She thought, I have got to think. I have got to know what to do.

"We'll go out to a nice field, out in the country here where it smells so nice and it's sunny," Arnold Friend said. "I'll have my arms tight around you so you won't need to try to get away and I'll show you what love is like, what it does. The hell with this house! It looks solid all right," he said. He ran his fingernail down the screen and the noise did not make Connie shiver, as it would have the day before. "Now, put your hand on your heart, honey. Feel that? That feels solid too but we know better. Be nice to me, be sweet like you can because what else is there for a girl like you but to be sweet and pretty and give in?—and get away before her people get back?"

She felt her pounding heart. Her hand seemed to enclose it. She thought for the first time in her life that it was nothing that was hers, that belonged to her, but just a pounding, living thing inside this body that wasn't really hers either.

"You don't want them to get hurt," Arnold Friend went on. "Now, get up, honey. Get up all by yourself."

She stood.

"Now, turn this way. That's right. Come over here to me.—Ellie, put that away, didn't I tell you? You dope. You miserable creepy dope," Arnold Friend said. His words were not angry but only part of an incantation. The incantation was kindly. "Now, come out through the kitchen to me, honey, and let's see a smile, try it, you're a brave, sweet little girl and now they're eating corn and hot dogs cooked to bursting over an outdoor fire, and they don't know one thing about you and never did and honey, you're better than them because not a one of them would have done this for you."

Connie felt the linoleum under her feet; it was cool. She brushed her hair back out of her eyes. Arnold Friend let go of the post tentatively and opened his arms for her, his elbows pointing in toward each other and his wrists limp, to show that this was an embarrassed embrace and a little mocking, he didn't want to make her self-conscious.

She put out her hand against the screen. She watched herself push the door slowly open as if she were back safe somewhere in the other doorway, watching this body and this head of long hair moving out into the sunlight where Arnold Friend waited.

"My sweet little blue-eyed girl," he said in a half-sung sigh that had nothing to do with her brown eyes but was taken up just the same by the vast sunlit reaches of the land behind him and on all sides of him—so much land that Connie had never seen before and did not recognize except to know that she was going to it.

Toni Cade Bambara (1939–   )

Toni Cade Bambara is a black writer and a woman writer, and these two aspects cannot be separated. As one critic says, she writes of "black women at the edge of a new awareness . . . who create their own choices about the kind of women they will be." She published her early work under the name Toni Cade, but added the "Bambara"—a maternal family name—in tribute to the Bambara people of the Sudan. Her reputation as a writer was established by two volumes of short stories: *Gorilla, My Love* (1972) and *The Sea Birds Are Still Alive* (1977). In these stories critics recognized a powerful, if flawed, talent of great promise; with the appearance of her novel, *The Salt Eaters* (1980), many felt that that promise was fulfilled. Almost all her work deals with the black experience, and Bambara's style is alive with the rhythms and idiom of her subject matter. The verbal energy of her writing is astonishing. "The stories start and stop like rapid-fire conversations conducted in a rhythmic, black-inflected, sweet-and-sour language," writes one critic; her plots are not linear but built around situations, "like improvisations on a melody." Her characters, writes another critic, "live on their nerve endings." In this single long sentence from "A Sort of Preface" that begins *Gorilla, My Love*, we get a good example of her tough, vital, fast-paced idiom:

> It does no good to write autobiographical fiction cause the minute the book hits the stand here comes your mama screamin how could you and sighin death where is thy sting and she snatches you up out your bed to grill you about what was going down back there in Brooklyn when she was working three jobs and trying to improve the quality of your life and come to find on page 42 that you were messin around with that nasty boy up the block and breaks into sobs and quite naturally your family strolls in all sleepy-eyed to catch the floor show at 5:00 A.M. but as far as your mama is concerned, it is nineteen-forty-and-something and you ain't too grown to have your ass whipped.

She is "so full of life that she almost bursts from the page," writes Robie Macauley. "Shrewd, tough, cat-smart and, at the same time, both sentimental and humane, she's an original."

Bambara has had a richly varied career. Born in New York and educated at Queens College, she has studied Commedia dell'Arte in Florence, mime in Paris, linguistics at New York University, and film production at the Harlem Film Institute. She has been social worker, recreation director, freelance writer, mother, film-maker, teacher of Afro-American and women's studies, and, recently, writer-in-residence at Spelman College, Atlanta. She has won many honors and held professorial posts at Rutgers, Duke, and other institutions.

"Raymond's Run" (from *Gorilla, My Love*) is quintessential Bambara: sassy, witty, high-spirited, breathless, and full of never-say-die spirit. Like all of Bambara's fictional spokeswomen, this one runs to win. But there is more than competitiveness in this narrator, and at the end she makes a concession that is (in Bambara's fictional world) the same thing as love: "We stand there with this big smile of respect between us. It's about as real a smile as girls can do for each other, considering we don't practice real smiling every day, you know. . . ."

Raymond's Run

I don't have much work to do around the house like some girls. My mother does that. And I don't have to earn my pocket money by hustling; George runs errands for the big boys and sells Christmas cards. And anything else that's got to get done, my father does. All I have to do in life is mind my brother Raymond, which is enough.

Sometimes I slip and say my little brother Raymond. But as any fool can see he's much bigger and he's older too. But a lot of people call him my little brother cause he needs looking after cause he's not quite right. And a lot of smart mouths got lots to say about that too, especially when George was minding him. But now, if anybody has anything to say to Raymond, anything to say about his big head, they have to come by me. And I don't play the dozens or believe in standing around with somebody in my face doing a lot of talking. I much rather just knock you down and take my chances even if I am a little girl with skinny arms and a squeaky voice, which is how I got the name Squeaky. And if things get too rough, I run. And as anybody can tell you, I'm the fastest thing on two feet.

There is no track meet that I don't win the first place medal. I used to win the twenty-yard dash when I was a little kid in kindergarten. Nowadays, it's the fifty-yard dash. And tomorrow I'm subject to run the quarter-meter relay all by myself and come in first, second, and third. The big kids call me Mercury cause I'm the swiftest thing in the neighborhood. Everybody knows that—except two people who know better, my father and me. He can beat me to Amsterdam Avenue with me having a two fire-hydrant headstart and him running with his hands in his pockets and whistling. But that's private information. Cause can you imagine some thirty-five-year-old man stuffing himself into PAL shorts to race little kids? So as far as everyone's concerned, I'm the fastest and that goes for Gretchen, too, who has put out the tale that she is going to win the first-place medal this year. Ridiculous. In the second place, she's got short legs. In the third place, she's got freckles. In the first place, no one can beat me and that's all there is to it.

I'm standing on the corner admiring the weather and about to take a stroll down Broadway so I can practice my breathing exercises, and I've got Raymond walking on the inside close to the buildings, cause he's subject to fits of fantasy and starts thinking he's a circus performer and that the curb is a tightrope strung high in the air. And sometimes after a rain he likes to step down off his tightrope right into the gutter and slosh around getting his shoes and cuffs wet. Then I get hit when I get home. Or sometimes if you don't watch him he'll dash across traffic to the island in the middle of

Broadway and give the pigeons a fit. Then I have to go behind him apologizing to all the old people sitting around trying to get some sun and getting all upset with the pigeons fluttering around them, scattering their newspapers and upsetting the waxpaper lunches in their laps. So I keep Raymond on the inside of me, and he plays like he's driving a stage coach which is O.K. by me so long as he doesn't run me over or interrupt my breathing exercises, which I have to do on account of I'm serious about my running, and I don't care who knows it.

Now some people like to act like things come easy to them, won't let on that they practice. Not me. I'll high-prance down 34th Street like a rodeo pony to keep my knees strong even if it does get my mother uptight so that she walks ahead like she's not with me, don't know me, is all by herself on a shopping trip, and I am somebody else's crazy child. Now you take Cynthia Procter for instance. She's just the opposite. If there's a test tomorrow, she'll say something like, "Oh, I guess I'll play handball this afternoon and watch television tonight," just to let you know she ain't thinking about the test. Or like last week when she won the spelling bee for the millionth time, "A good thing you got 'receive,' Squeaky, cause I would have got it wrong. I completely forgot about the spelling bee." And she'll clutch the lace on her blouse like it was a narrow escape. Oh, brother. But of course when I pass her house on my early morning trots around the block, she is practicing the scales on the piano over and over and over and over. Then in music class she always lets herself get bumped around so she falls accidently on purpose onto the piano stool and is so surprised to find herself sitting there that she decides just for fun to try out the ole keys. And what do you know—Chopin's waltzes just spring out of her fingertips and she's the most surprised thing in the world. A regular prodigy. I could kill people like that. I stay up all night studying the words for the spelling bee. And you can see me any time of day practicing running. I never walk if I can trot, and shame on Raymond if he can't keep up. But of course he does, cause if he hangs back someone's liable to walk up to him and get smart, or take his allowance from him, or ask him where he got that great big pumpkin head. People are so stupid sometimes.

So I'm strolling down Broadway breathing out and breathing in on counts of seven, which is my lucky number, and here comes Gretchen and her sidekicks: Mary Louise, who used to be a friend of mine when she first moved to Harlem from Baltimore and got beat up by everybody till I took up for her on account of her mother and my mother used to sing in the same choir when they were young girls, but people ain't grateful, so now she hangs out with the new girl Gretchen and talks about me like a dog; and Rosie, who is as fast as I am skinny and has a big mouth where Raymond is concerned and is too stupid to know that there is not a big deal of difference between herself and Raymond and that she can't afford to throw stones. So they are steady coming up Broadway and I see right away that it's going to be one of those Dodge City scenes cause the street ain't that big and they're close to the buildings just as we are. First I think I'll step into the candy store and look over the new comics and let them pass. But that's chicken and I've got a reputation to consider. So then I think I'll just walk straight on through them or even over them if necessary. But as they get to me, they slow down. I'm ready to fight, cause like I said I don't feature a whole lot of chit-chat, I much prefer to just knock you down right from the jump and save everybody a lotta precious time.

"You signing up for the May Day races?" smiles Mary Louise, only it's not a smile at all. A dumb question like that doesn't deserve an answer. Besides, there's just me and Gretchen standing there really, so no use wasting my breath talking to shadows.

"I don't think you're going to win this time," says Rosie, trying to signify with her hands on her hips all salty, completely forgetting that I have whupped her behind many times for less salt than that.

"I always win cause I'm the best," I say straight at Gretchen who is, as far as I'm concerned, the only one talking in this ventriloquist-dummy routine. Gretchen smiles, but it's not a smile, and I'm thinking that girls never really smile at each other because they don't know how and don't want to know how and there's probably no one to teach us how, cause grown-up girls don't know either. Then they all look at Raymond who has just brought his mule team to a standstill. And they're about to see what trouble they can get into through him.

"What grade you in now, Raymond?"

"You got anything to say to my brother, you say it to me, Mary Louise Williams of Raggedy Town, Baltimore."

"What are you, his mother?" sasses Rosie.

"That's right, Fatso. And the next word out of anybody and I'll be *their* mother too." So they just stand there and Gretchen shifts from one leg to the other and so do they. Then Gretchen puts her hands on her hips and is about to say something with her freckle-face self but doesn't. Then she walks around me looking me up and down but keeps walking up Broadway, and her sidekicks follow her. So me and Raymond smile at each other and he says, "Gidyap" to his team and I continue with my breathing exercises, strolling down Broadway toward the ice man on 145th with not a care in the world cause I am Miss Quicksilver herself.

I take my time getting to the park on May Day because the track meet is the last thing on the program. The biggest thing on the program is the May Pole dancing, which I can do without, thank you, even if my mother thinks it's a shame I don't take part and act like a girl for a change. You'd think my mother'd be grateful not to have to make me a white organdy dress with a big satin sash and buy me new white baby-doll shoes that can't be taken out of the box till the big day. You'd think she'd be glad her daughter ain't out there prancing around a May Pole getting the new clothes all dirty and sweaty and trying to act like a fairy or a flower or whatever you're supposed to be when you should be trying to be yourself, whatever that is, which is, as far as I am concerned, a poor Black girl who really can't afford to buy shoes and a new dress you only wear once a lifetime cause it won't fit next year.

I was once a strawberry in a Hansel and Gretel pageant when I was in nursery school and didn't have no better sense than to dance on tiptoe with my arms in a circle over my head doing umbrella steps and being a perfect fool just so my mother and father could come dressed up and clap. You'd think they'd know better than to encourage that kind of nonsense. I am not a strawberry. I do not dance on my toes. I run. That is what I am all about. So I always come late to the May Day program, just in time to get my number pinned on and lay in the grass till they announce the fifty-yard dash.

I put Raymond in the little swings, which is a tight squeeze this year and will be impossible next year. Then I look around for Mr. Pearson, who pins the numbers on. I'm really looking for Gretchen if you want to know the truth, but she's not around. The park is jam-packed. Parents in hats and corsages and breast-pocket handkerchiefs peeking up. Kids in white dresses and light-blue suits. The parkees unfolding chairs and chasing the rowdy kids from Lenox as if they had no right to be there. The big guys with their caps on backwards, leaning against the fence swirling the basketballs on the tips of their fingers, waiting for all these crazy people to clear out the park so they can play. Most of the kids in my class are carrying bass drums and glockenspiels and flutes. You'd think they'd put in a few bongos or something for real like that.

Then here comes Mr. Pearson with his clipboard and his cards and pencils and whistles and safety pins and fifty million other things he's always dropping all over the place with his clumsy self. He sticks out in a crowd because he's on stilts. We used to call him Jack and the Beanstalk to get him mad. But I'm the only one that can outrun him and get away, and I'm too grown for that silliness now.

"Well, Squeaky," he says, checking my name off the list and handing me number seven and two pins. And I'm thinking he's got no right to call me Squeaky, if I can't call him Beanstalk.

"Hazel Elizabeth Deborah Parker," I correct him and tell him to write it down on his board.

"Well, Hazel Elizabeth Deborah Parker, going to give someone else a break this year?" I squint at him real hard to see if he is seriously thinking I should lose the race on purpose just to give someone else a break. "Only six girls running this time," he continues, shaking his head sadly like it's my fault all of New York didn't turn out in sneakers. "That new girl should give you a run for your money." He looks around the park for Gretchen like a periscope in a submarine movie. "Wouldn't it be a nice gesture if you were . . . to ahhh . . . ."

I give him such a look he couldn't finish putting that idea into words. Grownups got a lot of nerve sometimes. I pin number seven to myself and stomp away, I'm so burnt. And I go straight for the track and stretch out on the grass while the band winds up with "Oh, the Monkey Wrapped His Tail Around the Flag Pole," which my teacher calls by some other name. The man on the loudspeaker is calling everyone over to the track and I'm on my back looking at the sky, trying to pretend I'm in the country, but I can't, because even grass in the city feels hard as sidewalk, and there's just no pretending you are anywhere but in a "concrete jungle" as my grandfather says.

The twenty-yard dash takes all of two minutes cause most of the little kids don't know no better than to run off the track or run the wrong way or run smack into the fence and fall down and cry. One little kid, though, has got the good sense to run straight for the white ribbon up ahead so he wins. Then the second-graders line up for the thirty-yard dash and I don't even bother to turn my head to watch cause Raphael Perez always wins. He wins before he even begins by psyching the runners, telling them they're going to trip on their shoelaces and fall on their faces or lose their shorts or something, which he doesn't really have to do since he is very fast, almost as fast as I am. After that is the forty-yard dash which I use to run when I was in first grade. Raymond is hollering from the swings cause he knows I'm about to do my thing cause the man on the loudspeaker has just announced the fifty-yard dash, although he might just as well be giving a recipe for angel food cake cause you can hardly make out what he's sayin for the static. I get up and slip off my sweat pants and then I see Gretchen standing at the starting line, kicking her legs out like a pro. Then as I get into place I see that ole Raymond is on line on the other side of the fence, bending down with his fingers on the ground just like he knew what he was doing. I was going to yell at him but then I didn't. It burns up your energy to holler.

Every time, just before I take off in a race, I always feel like I'm in a dream, the kind of dream you have when you're sick with fever and feel all hot and weightless. I dream I'm flying over a sandy beach in the early morning sun, kissing the leaves of the trees as I fly by. And there's always the smell of apples, just like in the country when I was little and used to think I was a choo-choo train, running through the fields of corn and chugging up the hill to the orchard. And all the time I'm dreaming this, I get lighter and lighter until I'm flying over the beach again, getting blown through the sky like a feather that weighs nothing at all. But once I spread my fingers in the dirt and crouch over the Get on Your Mark, the dream goes and I am solid again and am telling myself, Squeaky you must win, you must win, you are the fastest thing in the world, you can even beat your father up Amsterdam if you really try. And then I feel my weight coming back just behind my knees then down to my feet then into the earth and the pistol shot explodes in my blood and I am off and weightless again, flying past the other runners, my arms pumping up and down and the whole world is quiet except for the crunch as I zoom over the gravel in the track. I glance to my left and there is no one. To the right, a blurred Gretchen, who's got her chin jutting out as if it would win the race all by itself. And on the other side of the fence is Raymond with his arms down to his side and the palms tucked up behind him, running in his very own style, and it's the first time I ever saw that and I almost stop to watch my brother Raymond on his first run. But the white ribbon is bouncing toward me and I tear past it, racing into the distance till my feet with a mind of their own start digging up footfuls of dirt and brake me short. Then all the kids standing on the side pile on me, banging me on the back and slapping my head with their May Day programs, for I have won again and everybody on 151st Street can walk tall for another year.

"In first place . . ." the man on the loudspeaker is clear as a bell now. But then he pauses and the loudspeaker starts to whine. Then static. And I lean down to catch my breath and here comes Gretchen walking back, for she's overshot the finish line too, huffing and puffing with her hands on her hips taking it slow, breathing in steady time like a real pro and I sort of like her a little for the first time. "In first place . . ." and then three or four voices get all mixed up on the loudspeaker and I dig my sneaker into the grass and stare at Gretchen who's staring back, we both wondering just who did win. I can hear old Beanstalk arguing with the man on the loudspeaker and then a few others running their mouths about what the stopwatches say. Then I hear Raymond yanking at the fence to call me and I wave to shush him, but he keeps rattling the fence like a gorilla in a cage like in them gorilla movies, but then like a dancer or something he starts climbing up nice and easy but very fast. And it occurs to me, watching how smoothly he climbs hand over hand and remembering how he looked running with his arms down to his side and with the wind pulling his mouth back and his teeth showing and all, it occurred to me that Raymond would make a very fine runner. Doesn't he always keep up with me on my trots? And he surely knows how to breathe in counts of seven cause he's always doing it at the dinner table, which drives my brother George up the wall. And I'm smiling to beat the band cause if I've lost this race, or if me and Gretchen tied, or even if I've won, I can always retire as a runner and begin a whole new career as a coach with Raymond as my champion. After all, with a little more study I can beat Cynthia and her phony self at the spelling bee. And if I bugged my mother, I could get piano lessons and become a star. And I have a big rep as the baddest thing around. And I've got a roomful of ribbons and medals and awards. But what has Raymond got to call his own?

So I stand there with my new plans, laughing out loud by this time as Raymond jumps down from the fence and runs over with his teeth showing and his arms down to the side, which no one before him has quite mastered as a running style. And by the time he comes over I'm jumping up and down so glad to see him—my brother Raymond, a great runner in the family tradition. But of course everyone thinks I'm jumping up and down because the men on the loudspeaker have finally gotten themselves together and compared notes and are announcing "In first place—Miss Hazel Elizabeth Deborah Parker." (Dig that.) "In second place—Miss Gretchen P. Lewis." And I look over at

Gretchen wondering what the "P" stands for. And I smile. Cause she's good, no doubt about it. Maybe she'd like to help me coach Raymond; she obviously is serious about running, as any fool can see. And she nods to congratulate me and then she smiles. And I smile. We stand there with this big smile of respect between us. It's about as real a smile as girls can do for each other, considering we don't practice real smiling every day, you know, cause maybe we too busy being flowers or fairies or strawberries instead of something honest and worthy of respect . . . you know . . . like being people.

Part Five

The Contemporary Scene: Break with Tradition

Jorge Luis Borges (1899–   )

Jorge Luis Borges is considered by many to be the greatest living master of Spanish prose. Born in Buenos Aires in 1899, he was educated in Switzerland; in 1919 he went to Spain, where he met a number of writers interested in European avant-garde literary movements. When he returned to Argentina in 1921, he helped found *Ultraísmo,* a movement of Argentinian and Spanish poets trying to develop Spanish into an instrument of the new poetry. One of their magazines, *Prisma, revista mural*, was devised to be stuck on walls in order to bring poetry to the people. Here is an excerpt from one of the manifestos appearing in that magazine:

> We have synthesized poetry into its primordial element: the metaphor, to which we grant the greatest independence, beyond the little games of those who compare things like each other *to* each other, equating a circus with the moon. Each line of our poems has its individual life and represents an original vision. Ultraísmo thus propounds the formation of an emotional, changeable, varied mythology.

By the early thirties Borges had turned from poetry to the short story, but some of the same principles were evident in his new efforts. Granting "the greatest independence" to his metaphors, he turned out a dazzling series of stories in a modernist and experimental mode. His first important collection of stories was

Ficciones (1945) (translated into English in 1962). These "fictions" were a unique blending of the essay and the short story, and a demonstration of his fundamental artistic contention: that truth eludes matter-of-fact. Works that followed were *El Aleph* in 1949; *El hacedor* (containing "Borges and I") in 1960, and translated as *Dreamtigers* in 1964; and *Antologia personal* in 1961, a volume containing Borges's favorite short stories, sketches, essays, and poems. In 1962 a number of Borges's stories and other writings were collected in a volume called *Labyrinths*—including the three selections reproduced here. This is but a fraction of Borges's work; he is probably the most widely known and translated author in Latin America today.

"The fantastic structure of Borges's stories," writes Victor Lange, "conjured as though by magic or sleight of hand, are the product of acts of calculated deception. What is in one breath stated as corroborated fact is at the same time obscured and blurred by doubts, denials, and open questions." The dream, the labyrinth, the mirror, and the double are characteristic devices by which the "coolly cerebral" Borges achieves and manipulates this deception, confusing the line between subject and object, history and fantasy, appearance and reality. His fictions are flights of imagination; they are also models of scholarly erudition. As Victor Lange says, his marshaling of recondite learning with such "ceremonious care" is itself an irony, "and points to his fundamental conviction of the fictitious character of reality." In "The Waiting" we hover between sleep and waking, fantasy and reality, as the fugitive—who had often dreamed of the two men and Villari coming to kill him—is confronted by the actual assassins and, in his last moments, turns in his bed to face the wall "so that the murderers would be a dream." "He was in this act of magic when the blast obliterated him."

In "Everything and Nothing," that brilliant parable (see pp. 38–39), we engage in a search for identity in a dream within a dream: the Shakespeare who has imagined so many selves desires to be "one and myself," but God denies him, saying, "Neither am I anyone; I have dreamt the world as you dreamt your work, my Shakespeare. . . . " And in "Borges and I"—more a sketch than a story—the author confronts himself as "other" in a similar, but more personal and exacting, search for identity. "I live, let myself go on living, so that Borges may contrive his literature"—and in this exchange between person and persona we are never given the easy comfort of knowing which is which.

Borges has been called a "calculating hallucinator," but his fictional sleights of hand exist not only to baffle, tease, and amuse, but to probe the unknown for "the one word that contains the universe." Some "engaged" critics feel that these practices make Borges an irrelevant aesthete, but most honor him as the artistic genius who did more than anyone to turn Spanish into a vehicle for the new literature.

The Waiting

The cab left him at number four thousand four on that street in the northwest part of Buenos Aires. It was not yet nine in the morning; the man noted with approval the spotted plane trees, the square plot of earth at the foot of each, the respectable houses with their little balconies, the pharmacy alongside, the dull lozenges of the paint and hardware store. A long windowless hospital wall backed the sidewalk on the other side of the street; the sun reverberated, farther down, from some greenhouses. The man thought that these things (now arbitrary and accidental and in no special order, like the things one sees in dreams) would in time, if God willed, become invariable, necessary and familiar. In the pharmacy window porcelain letters spelled out the name "Breslauer"; the Jews were displacing the Italians, who had displaced the Creoles. It was better that way; the man prefered not to mingle with people of his kind.

The cabman helped him take down his trunk; a woman with a distracted or tired air finally opened the door. From his seat, the cabman returned one of the coins to him, a Uruguayan twenty-centavo piece which had been in his pocket since that night in the hotel at Melo. The man gave him forty centavos and immediately felt: "I must act so that everyone will forgive me. I have made two errors: I have used a foreign coin and I have shown that the mistake matters to me."

Led by the woman, he crossed the entrance hall and the first patio. The room they had reserved for him opened, happily, onto the second patio. The bed was of iron, deformed by the craftsman into fantastic curves representing branches and tendrils; there was also a tall pine wardrobe, a bedside table, a shelf with books at floor level, two odd chairs and a washstand with its basin, jar, soap dish and bottle of turbid glass. A map of the province of Buenos Aires and a crucifix adorned the walls; the wallpaper was crimson, with a pattern of huge spread-tailed peacocks. The only door opened onto the patio. It was necessary to change the placement of the chairs in order to get the trunk in. The roomer approved of everything; when the woman asked him his name, he said Villari, not as a secret challenge, not to mitigate the humiliation which actually he did not feel, but because that name troubled him, because it was impossible for him to think of any other. Certainly he was not seduced by the literary error of thinking that assumption of the enemy's name might be an astute maneuver.

Mr. Villari, at first, did not leave the house; after a few weeks, he took to going out for a while at sundown. One night he went into the movie theater three blocks away. He never went beyond the last row of seats; he always got up a little before the end of the feature. He would see tragic stories of the underworld; these stories, no doubt, contained errors; these stories, no doubt, contained images which were also those of his former life; Villari took no notice of them because the idea of a coincidence between art and reality was alien to him. He would submissively try to like the things; he wanted to anticipate the intention with which they were shown. Unlike people who read novels, he never saw himself as a character in a work of art.

No letters nor even a circular ever arrived for him, but with vague hope he would always read one of the sections of the newspaper. In the afternoons, he would put one of the chairs by the door and gravely make and drink his maté, his eyes fixed on the vine covering the wall of the several-storied building next door. Years of solitude had taught him that, in one's memory, all days tend to be the same, but that there is not a day, not even in jail or in the hospital, which does not bring surprises, which is not a translucent network of minimal surprises. In other confinements, he had given in to the temptation of counting the days and the hours, but this confinement was different, for it had no end—unless one morning the newspaper brought news of Alejandro Villari's death. It was also possible that Villari *had already died* and in that case this life was a dream. This possibility disturbed him, because he could never quite understand whether it seemed a relief or a misfortune; he told himself it was absurd and discounted it. In distant days, less distant because of the passage of time than because of two or three irrevocable acts, he had desired many things with an unscrupulous passion; this powerful will, which had moved the hatred of men and the love of some women, no longer wanted any particular thing: it only wanted to endure, not to come to an end. The taste of the maté, the taste of black tobacco, the growing line of shadows gradually covering the patio—these were sufficient incentives.

In the house there was a wolf-dog, now old. Villari made friends with him. He spoke to him in Spanish, in Italian, in the few words he still retained of the rustic dialect of his childhood. Villari tried to live in the simple present, with no memories or anticipation; the former mattered less to him than the latter. In an obscure way, he thought he could see that the past is the stuff time is made of; for that reason, time immediately turns into the past. His weariness, one day, was like a feeling of contentment; in moments like this, he was not much more complex than the dog.

One night he was left astonished and trembling by an intimate discharge of pain in the back of his mouth. This horrible miracle recurred in a few minutes and again towards dawn. Villari, the next day, sent for a cab which left him at a dentist's office in the Once section. There he had the tooth pulled. In this ordeal he was neither more cowardly nor more tranquil than other people.

Another night, returning from the movies, he felt that he was being pushed. With anger, with indignation, with secret relief, he faced the insolent person. He spat out a coarse insult; the other man, astonished, stammered an excuse. He was tall, young, with dark hair, accompanied by a German-looking woman; that night, Villari repeated to himself that he did not know them. Nevertheless, four or five days went by before he went out into the street.

Amongst the books on the shelf there was a copy of the *Divine Comedy*, with the old commentary by Andreoli. Prompted less by curiosity than by a feeling of duty, Villari undertook the reading of this capital work; before dinner, he would read a canto and then, in rigorous order, the notes. He did not judge the punishments of hell to be unbelievable or excessive and did not think Dante would have condemned him to the last circle, where Ugolino's teeth endlessly gnaw Ruggieri's neck.

The peacocks on the crimson wallpaper seemed destined to be food for tenacious nightmares, but Mr. Villari never dreamed of a monstrous arbor inextricably woven of living birds. At dawn he would dream a dream whose substance was the same, with varying circumstances. Two men and Villari would enter the room with revolvers or they would attack him as he left the movie house or all three of them at once would be the stranger who had pushed him or they would sadly wait for him in the patio and seem not to recognize him. At the end of the dream, he would take his revolver from the drawer of the bedside table (and it was true he kept a revolver in that drawer) and open fire on the men. The noise of the weapon would wake him, but it was always a dream and in another dream the attack would be repeated and in another dream he would have to kill them again.

One murky morning in the month of July, the presence of strange people (not the noise of the door when they opened it) woke him. Tall in the shadows of the room, curiously simplified by those shadows (in the fearful dreams they had always been clearer), vigilant, motionless and patient, their eyes lowered as if weighted down by the heaviness of their weapons, Alejandro Villari and a stranger had overtaken him at last. With a gesture, he asked them to wait and turned his face to the wall, as if to resume his sleep. Did he do it to arouse the pity of those who killed him, or because it is less difficult to endure a frightful happening than to imagine it and endlessly await it, or—and this is perhaps most likely—so that the murderers would be a dream, as they had already been so many times, in the same place, at the same hour?

He was in this act of magic when the blast obliterated him.

Borges and I

The other one, the one called Borges, is the one things happen to. I walk through the streets of Buenos Aires and stop for a moment, perhaps mechanically now, to look at the arch of an entrance hall and the grillwork on the gate; I know of Borges from the mail and see his name on a list of professors or in a biographical dictionary. I like hourglasses, maps, eighteenth-century typography, the taste of coffee and the prose of Stevenson;[1] he shares these preferences, but in a vain way that turns them into the attributes of an actor. It would be an exaggeration to say that ours is a hostile relationship; I live, let myself go on living, so that Borges may contrive his literature, and this literature justifies me. It is no effort for me to confess that he has achieved some valid pages, but those pages cannot save me, perhaps because what is good belongs to no one, not even to him, but rather to the language and to tradition. Besides, I am destined to perish, definitively, and only some instant of myself can survive in him. Little by little, I am giving over everything to him, though I am quite aware of his perverse custom of falsifying and magnifying things. Spinoza knew that all things long to persist in their being; the stone eternally wants to be a stone and the tiger a tiger. I shall remain in Borges, not in myself (if it is true that I am someone), but I recognize myself less in his books than in many others or in the laborious strumming of a guitar. Years ago I tried to free myself from him and went from the mythologies of the suburbs to the games with time and infinity, but those games belong to Borges now and I shall have to imagine other things. Thus my life is a flight and I lose everything and everything belongs to oblivion, or to him.

I do not know which of us has written this page.

[1] Robert Louis Stevenson. Borges in 1955 was appointed Professor of English and American Literature at the University of Buenos Aires.

Everything and Nothing

There was no one in him; behind his face (which even through the bad paintings of those times resembles no other) and his words, which were copious, fantastic and stormy, there was only a bit of coldness, a dream dreamt by no one. At first he thought that all people were like him, but the astonishment of a friend to whom he had begun to speak of this emptiness showed him his error and made him feel always that an individual should not differ in outward appearance. Once he thought that in books he would find a cure for his ill and thus he learned the small Latin and less Greek a contemporary would speak of; later he considered that what he sought might well be found in an elemental rite of humanity, and let himself be initiated by Anne Hathaway one long June afternoon. At the age of twenty-odd years he went to London. Instinctively he had already become proficient in the habit of simulating that he was someone, so that others would not discover his condition as no one; in London he found the profession to which he was predestined, that of the actor, who on a stage plays at being another before a gathering of people who play at taking him for that other person. His histrionic tasks brought him a singular satisfaction, perhaps the first he had ever known; but once the last verse had been acclaimed and the last dead man withdrawn from the stage, the hated flavor of unreality returned to him. He ceased to be Ferrex or Tamerlane[1] and became no one again. Thus hounded, he took to imagining other heroes and other tragic fables. And so, while his flesh fulfilled its destiny as flesh in the taverns and brothels of London, the soul that inhabited him was Caesar, who disregards the augur's admonition, and Juliet, who abhors the lark, and Macbeth, who converses on the plain with the witches who are also Fates. No one has ever been so many men as this man, who like the Egyptian Proteus could exhaust all the guises of reality. At times he would leave a confession hidden away in some corner of his work, certain that it would not be deciphered; Richard affirms that in his person he plays the part of many and Iago claims with curious words "I am not what I am." The fundamental identity of existing, dreaming and acting inspired famous passages of his.

For twenty years he persisted in that controlled hallucination, but one morning he was suddenly gripped by the tedium and the terror of being so many kings who die by the sword and so many suffering lovers who converge, diverge and melodiously expire. That very day he arranged to sell his theater. Within a week he had returned to his native village, where he recovered the trees and rivers of his childhood and did not relate them to the others his muse had celebrated, illustrious with mythological allusions and Latin terms. He had to be someone; he was a retired impresario who had made his fortune and concerned himself with loans, lawsuits and petty usury. It was in this character that he dictated the arid will and testament known to us, from which he deliberately excluded all traces of pathos or literature. His friends from London would visit his retreat and for them he would take up again his role as poet.

History adds that before or after dying he found himself in the presence of God and told Him: "I who have been so many men in vain want to be one and myself." The voice of the Lord answered from a whirlwind: "Neither am I anyone; I have dreamt the world as you dreamt your work, my Shakespeare, and among the forms in my dream are you, who like myself are many and no one."

---

[1] See *Ferrex and Porrex* (c. 1570), one of the earliest English tragedies, and *Tamerlane* (1590), a play by Christopher Marlowe.

Samuel Beckett (1906–   )

Samuel Beckett was born near Dublin of a prosperous middle-class family and educated at Trinity College, Dublin, where he received a B.A. in French and Italian in 1927, and an M.A. in 1931. After lecturing at the École Normale Supérieure in Paris for two years (1928–1930), he accepted a three-year post as Lecturer in French at Trinity. But after two years he abruptly resigned. He hated this return to Dublin: the city bored him after Paris, he was often ill, and he disliked teaching, saying that he "could not bear the absurdity of teaching to others what he did not know himself." Between 1932 and 1936 he traveled extensively in England and Europe and then settled permanently in Paris, where in the 1930s he helped James Joyce (then nearly blind) in the preparation of *Finnegans Wake*. But he has mainly devoted himself to his own writing—commonly writing first in French and then translating his own work into English.

From the first—and long before he met Joyce—Beckett was fascinated with wordplay, and such early writings as *Whoroscope* (1930), *A Dream of Fair to Middling Women* (written in 1932), and *More Pricks than Kicks* (1934) are full of puns, parodies, and extravagant comic invention. Here, for example, from *Dream* is a fragment of a one-sentence paragraph in which he parodies some lusty Elizabethan language: "Come come and cull me bonny bony doublebed cony swiftly my springal and my thin twingletwangler comfort my days of roses days of beauty week of redness with mad shame . . ." and so on for fifteen more lines. But along with these experiments in language—and the hilarious comedy—went a vision of the human condition that is as despairing as anything in modern literature. "The reality of the individual . . . is an incoherent reality," Beckett says, "and must be expressed incoherently."

After World War II Beckett published three related novels, *Molloy, Malone Dies,* and *The Unnamable*, which appeared in an omnibus English edition in 1959; but his leap to fame came with the production of his play *Waiting for Godot* in Paris in 1953. *Endgame* (1958), *Krapp's Last Tape* (1958) and other plays followed which have made Beckett—along with Ionesco, Genet, and Pinter—a leading figure in what Martin Esslin has called "the theatre of the absurd." But whether Beckett is writing plays, poems, or novels, he expresses the same vision of reality: a profound and almost absolute pessimism. As George Wellwarth puts it: "Throughout Beckett's work we can find evidence of his conviction that everything is hopeless, meaningless, purposeless, and, above all, agonizing to endure. Beckett's people are levelled off and merged into each other by being all more or less physically disabled—as if this were really the common condition on earth . . . . Beckett is a prophet of negation and sterility."

"The End," originally published in 1946, and translated by Beckett and Richard Seaver for *Stories and Texts for Nothing* (1967), is a representative example of this negative and despairing vision. Here is man, dragging himself to a miserable, lonely, and sordid death—a suitable theme, perhaps, for an author who had lived in a Paris occupied by the Nazis, and who had fought in the Resistance. Yet despair is not the true end of this story. It is redeemed by humor, by the power of Beckett's words—"a language in which the emptiness of conventional speech is charged with new emotion"—to hint at a new Word. As Harold Pinter says, "He leaves no stone unturned and no maggot lonely. He brings forth a body of beauty. His work is beautiful." Here, in extremis, we feel a kind of redemption through what Robert Polhemus has called "comic faith." That is not the whole story, none of Beckett's stories is the whole story, and at the end he mentions "the story I might have told"—"A story in the likeness of my life . . . without the courage to end or the strength to go on."

The End

They clothed me and gave me money. I knew what the money was for, it was to get me started. When it was gone I would have to get more, if I wanted to go on. The same for the shoes, when they were worn out I would have to get them mended, or get myself another pair, or go on barefoot, if I wanted to go on. The same for the coat and trousers, needless to say, with this difference, that I could go on in my shirt-sleeves, if I wanted. The clothes—shoes, socks, trousers, shirt, coat, hat—were not new, but the deceased must have been about my size. That is to say, he must have been a little shorter, a little thinner, for the clothes did not fit me so well in the beginning as they did at the end, the shirt especially, and it was many a long day before I could button it at the neck, or profit by the collar that went with it, or pin the tails together between my legs in the way my mother had taught me. He must have put on his Sunday best to go to the consultation, perhaps for the first time, unable to bear it any longer. Be that as it may the hat was a bowler, in good shape. I said, Keep your hat and give me back mine. I added, Give me back my greatcoat. They replied that they had burnt them, together with my other clothes. I understood then that the end was near, at least fairly near. Later on I tried to exchange this hat for a cap, or a slouch which could be pulled down over my face, but without much success. And yet I could not go about bare-headed, with my skull in the state it was. At first this hat was too small, then it got used to me. They gave me a tie, after long discussion. It seemed a pretty tie to me, but I didn't like it. When it came at last I was too tired to send it back. But in the end it came in useful. It was blue, with kinds of little stars. I didn't feel well, but they told me I was well enough. They didn't say in so many words that I was as well as I would ever be, but that was the implication. I lay inert on the bed and it took three women to put on my trousers. They didn't seem to take much interest in my private parts which to tell the truth were nothing to write home about, I didn't take much interest in them myself. But they might have passed some remark. When they had finished I got up and finished dressing unaided. They told me to sit on the bed and wait. All the bedding had disappeared. It made me angry that they had not let me wait in the familiar bed, instead of leaving me standing in the cold, in these clothes that smelt of sulphur. I said, You might have left me in the bed till the last moment. Men all in white came in with mallets in their hands. They dismantled the bed and took away the pieces. One of the women followed them out and came back with a chair which she set before me. I had done well to pretend I was angry. But to make it quite clear to them how angry I was that they had not left me in my bed I gave the chair a kick that sent it flying. A man came in and made a sign to me to follow him. In the hall he gave me a paper to sign. What's this, I said, a safe-conduct? It's a receipt, he said, for the clothes and money you have received. What money? I said. It was then I received the money. To think I had almost departed without a penny in my pocket. The sum was not large, compared to other sums, but to me it seemed large. I saw the familiar objects, companions of so many bearable hours. The stool, for example, dearest of all. The long afternoons together, waiting for it to be time for bed. At times I felt its wooden life invade me, till I myself became a piece of old wood. There was even a hole for my cyst. Then the window pane with the patch of frosting gone, where I used to press my eye in the hour of need, and rarely in vain. I am greatly obliged to you, I said, is there a law which prevents you from throwing me out naked and penniless? That would damage our reputation in the long run, he replied. Could they not possibly keep me a little longer, I said, I could make myself useful. Useful, he said, joking apart you would be willing to make yourself useful? A moment later he went on, If they believed you were really willing to make yourself useful they would keep you, I am sure. The number of times I had said I was going to make myself useful, I wasn't going to start that again. How weak I felt! Perhaps, I said, they would consent to take back the money and keep me a little longer. This is a charitable institution, he said, and the money is a gift you receive when you leave. When it is gone you will have to get more, if you want to go on. Never come back here whatever you do, you would not be let in. Don't go to any of our branches either, they would turn you away. Exelmans! I cried. Come come, he said, and anyway no one understands a tenth of what you say. I'm so old, I said. You are not so old as all that, he said. May I stay here just a little longer, I said, till the rain is over? You may wait in the cloister, he said, the rain will go on all day. You may wait in the cloister till six o'clock, you will hear the bell. If anyone challenges you, you need only say you have permission to shelter in the cloister. Whose name will I give? I said. Weir, he said.

I had not been long in the cloister when the rain stopped and the sun came out. It was low and I reckoned it must be getting on for six, considering the season. I stayed there looking through the archway at the sun as it went down behind the cloister. A man appeared and asked me what I was doing. What do you want? were the words he used. Very friendly. I replied that I had Mr. Weir's permission to stay in the cloister till six o'clock. He went away, but came back immediately. He must have spoken to Mr. Weir in the interim, for he said, You must not loiter in the cloister now the rain is over.

Now I was making my way through the garden. There was that strange light which follows a day of persistent rain, when the sun comes out and the sky clears too late to be of any use. The earth makes a sound as of sighs and the last drops fall from the emptied cloudless sky. A small boy, stretching out his hands and looking up at the blue sky, asked his mother how such a thing was possible. Fuck off, she said. I suddenly remembered I had not thought of asking Mr. Weir for a piece of bread. He would surely have given it to me. I had as a matter of fact thought of it during our conversation in the hall, I had said to myself, Let us first finish our conversation, then I'll ask. I knew well they would not keep me. I would gladly have turned back, but I was afraid one of the guards would stop me and tell me I would never see Mr. Weir again. That might have added to my sorrow. And anyway I never turned back on such occasions.

In the street I was lost. I had not set foot in this part of the city for a long time and it seemed greatly changed. Whole buildings had disappeared, the palings had changed position and on all sides I saw, in great letters, the names of tradesmen I had never seen before and would have been at a loss to pronounce. There were streets where I remembered none, some I did remember had vanished and others had completely changed their names. The general impression was the same as before. It is true I did not know the city very well. Perhaps it was quite a different one. I did not know where I was supposed to be going. I had the great good fortune, more than once, not to be run over. My appearance still made people laugh, with that hearty jovial laugh so good for the health. By keeping the red part of the sky as much as possible on my right hand I came at last to the river. Here all seemed at first sight more or less as I had left it. But if I had looked more closely I would doubtless have discovered many changes. And indeed I subsequently did so. But the general appearance of the river, flowing between its quays and under its bridges, had not changed. Yes, the river still gave the impression it was flowing in the wrong direction. That's all a pack of lies I feel. My bench was still there. It was shaped to fit the curves of the seated body. It stood beside a watering trough, gift of a Mrs. Maxwell to the city horses, according to the inscription. During the short time I rested there several horses took advantage of this monument. The iron shoes approached and the jingle of the harness. Then silence. That was the horse looking at me. Then the noise of pebbles and mud that horses make when drinking. Then the silence again. That was the horse looking at me again. Then the pebbles again. Then the silence again. Till the horse had finished drinking or the driver deemed it had drunk its fill. The horses were uneasy. Once, when the noise stopped, I turned and saw the horse looking at me. The driver too was looking at me. Mrs. Maxwell would have been pleased if she could have seen her trough rendering such services to the city horses. When it was night, after a tedious twilight, I took off my hat which was paining me. I longed to be under cover again, in an empty place, close and warm, with artificial light, an oil lamp for choice, with a pink shade for preference. From time to time someone would come to make sure I was all right and needed nothing. It was long since I had longed for anything and the effect on me was horrible.

In the days that followed I visited several lodgings, without much success. They usually slammed the door in my face, even when I showed my money and offered to pay a week in advance, or even two. It was in vain I put on my best manners, smiled and spoke distinctly, they slammed the door in my face before I could even finish my little speech. It was at this time I perfected a method of doffing my hat at once courteous and discreet, neither servile or insolent. I slipped it smartly forward, held it a second poised in such a way that the person addressed could see my skull, then slipped it back. To do that naturally, without creating an unfavourable impression, is no easy matter. When I deemed that to tip my hat would suffice, I naturally did no more than tip it. But to tip one's hat is no easy matter either. I subsequently solved this problem, always fundamental in time of adversity, by wearing a kepi and saluting in military fashion, no, that must be wrong, I don't know, I had my hat at the end. I never made the mistake of wearing medals. Some landladies were in such need of money that they let me in immediately and showed me the room. But I couldn't come to an agreement with any of them. Finally I found a basement. With this woman I came to an agreement at once. My oddities, that's the expression she used, did not alarm her. She nevertheless insisted on making the bed and cleaning the room once a week, instead of once a month as I requested. She told me that while she was cleaning, which would not take long, I could wait in the area. She added, with a great deal of feeling, that she would never put me out in bad weather. This woman was Greek, I think, or Turkish. She never spoke about herself. I somehow got the idea she was a widow or at least that her husband had left her. She had a strange accent. But so had I with my way of assimilating the vowels and omitting the consonants.

Now I didn't know where I was. I had a vague vision, not a real vision, I didn't see anything, of a big house five or six stories high, one of a block perhaps. It was dusk when I got there and I did not pay the same heed to my surroundings as I might have done if I had suspected they were to close about me. And by then I must have lost all hope. It is true that when I left this house it was a glorious day, but I never look back when leaving. I must have read somewhere, when I was small and still read, that it is better not to look back when leaving. And yet I sometimes did. But even without looking back it seems to me I should have seen something when leaving. But there it is. All I remember is my feet emerging from my shadow, one after the other. My shoes had stiffened and the sun brought out the cracks in the leather.

I was comfortable enough in this house, I must say. Apart from a few rats I was alone in the basement. The woman did her best to respect our agreement. About noon she brought me a big tray of food and took away the tray of the previous day. At the same time she brought me a clean chamber-pot. The chamber-pot had a large handle which she slipped over her arm so that both her hands were free to carry the tray. The rest of the day I saw no more of her except sometimes when she peeped in to make sure nothing had happened to me. Fortunately I did not need affection. From my bed I saw the feet coming and going on the sidewalk. Certain evenings, when the weather was fine and I felt equal to it, I fetched my chair into the area and sat looking up into the skirts of the women passing by. Once I sent for a crocus bulb and planted it in the dark area, in an old pot. It must have been coming up to spring, it was probably not the right time for it. I left the pot outside, attached to a string I passed through the window. In the evening, when the weather was fine, a little light crept up the wall. Then I sat down beside the window and pulled on the string to keep the pot in the light and warmth. That can't have been easy, I don't see how I managed it. It was probably not the right thing for it. I manured it as best I could and pissed on it when the weather was dry. It may not have been the right thing for it. It sprouted, but never any flowers, just a wilting stem and a few chlorotic leaves. I would have liked to have a yellow crocus, or a hyacinth, but there, it was not to be. She wanted to take it away, but I told her to leave it. She wanted to buy me another, but I told her I didn't want another. What lacerated me most was the din of the newspaper boys. They went pounding by every day at the same hours, their heels thudding on the sidewalk, crying the names of their papers and even the headlines. The house noises disturbed me less. A little girl, unless it was a little boy, sang every evening at the same hour, somewhere above me. For a long time I could not catch the words. But hearing them day after day I finally managed to catch a few. Strange words for a little girl, or a little boy. Was it a song in my head or did it merely come from without? It was a sort of lullaby, I believe. It often sent me to sleep, even me. Sometimes it was a little girl who came. She had long red hair hanging down in two braids. I didn't know who she was. She lingered awhile in the room, then went away without a word. One day I had a visit from a policeman. He said I had to be watched, without explaining why. Suspicious, that was it, he told me I was suspicious. I let him talk. He didn't dare arrest me. Or perhaps he had a kind heart. A priest too, one day I had a visit from a priest. I informed him I belonged to a branch of the reformed church. He asked me what kind of clergyman I would like to see. Yes, there's that about the reformed church, you're lost, it's unavoidable. Perhaps he had a kind heart. He told me to let him know if I ever needed a helping hand. A helping hand! He gave me his name and explained where I could reach him. I should have made a note of it.

One day the woman made me an offer. She said she was in urgent need of cash and that if I could pay her six months in advance she would reduce my rent by one fourth during that period, something of that kind. This had the advantage of saving six weeks' (?) rent and the disadvantage of almost exhausting my small capital. But could you call that a disadvantage? Wouldn't I stay on in any case till my last penny was gone, and even longer, till she put me out? I gave her the money and she gave me a receipt.

One morning, not long after this transaction, I was awakened by a man shaking my shoulder. It could not have been much past eleven. He requested me to get up and leave his house immediately. He was most correct, I must say. His surprise, he said, was no less than mine. It was his house. His property. The Turkish woman had left the day before. But I saw her last night, I said. You must be mistaken, he said, for she brought the keys to my office no later than yesterday afternoon. But I just paid her six months' rent in advance, I said. Get a refund, he said. But I don't even know her name, I said, let alone her address. You don't know her name? he said. He must have thought I was lying. I'm sick, I said, I can't leave like this, without any notice. You're not so sick as all that, he said. He offered to send for a taxi, even an ambulance if I preferred. He said he needed the room immediately for his pig which even as he spoke was catching cold in a cart before the door and no one to look after him but a stray urchin whom he had never set eyes on before and who was probably busy tormenting him. I asked if he couldn't let me have another place, any old corner where I could lie down long enough to recover from the shock and decide what to do. He said he could not. Don't think I'm being unkind, he added. I could live here with the pig, I said, I'd look after him. The long months of peace, wiped out in an instant! Come now, come now, he said, get a grip on yourself, be a man, get up, that's enough. After all it was no concern of his. He had really been most patient. He must have visited the basement while I was sleeping.

I felt weak. Perhaps I was. I stumbled in the blinding light. A bus took me into the country. I sat down in a field in the sun. But it seems to me that was much later. I stuck leaves under my hat, all the way round, to make a shade. The night was cold. I wandered for hours in the fields. At last I found a heap of dung. The next day I started back to the city. They made me get off three buses. I sat down by the roadside and dried my clothes in the sun. I enjoyed doing that. I said to myself, There's nothing more to be done now, not a thing, till they are dry. When they were dry I brushed them with a brush, I think a kind of curry-comb, that I found in a stable. Stables have always been my salvation. Then I went to the house and begged a glass of milk and a slice of bread and butter. They gave me everything except the butter. May I rest in the stable? I said. No, they said. I still stank, but with a stink that pleased me. I much preferred it to my own which moreover it prevented me from smelling, except a waft now and then. In the days that followed I took the necessary steps to recover my money. I don't know exactly what happened, whether I couldn't find the address, or whether there was no such address, or whether the Greek woman was unknown there. I ransacked my pockets for the receipt, to try and decipher the name. It wasn't there. Perhaps she had taken it back while I was sleeping. I don't know how long I wandered thus, resting now in one place, now in another, in the city and in the country. The city had suffered many changes. Nor was the country as I remembered it. The general effect was the same. One day I caught sight of my son. He was striding along with a briefcase under his arm. He took off his hat and bowed and I saw he was as bald as a coot. I was almost certain it was he. I turned round to gaze after him. He went bustling along on his duck feet, bowing and scraping and flourishing his hat left and right. The insufferable son of a bitch.

One day I met a man I had known in former times. He lived in a cave by the sea. He had an ass that grazed winter and summer, over the cliffs, or along the little tracks leading down to the sea. When the weather was very bad this ass came down to the cave of his own accord and sheltered there till the storm was past. So they had spent many a night huddled together, while the wind howled and the sea pounded on the shore. With the help of this ass he could deliver sand, seawrack and shells to the townsfolk, for their gardens. He couldn't carry much at a time, for the ass was old and small and the town was far. But in this way he earned a little money, enough to keep him in tobacco and matches and to buy a piece of bread from time to time. It was during one of these excursions that he met me, in the suburbs. He was delighted to see me, poor man. He begged me to go home with him and spend the night. Stay as long as you like, he said. What's wrong with your ass? I said. Don't mind him, he said, he doesn't know you. I reminded him that I wasn't in the habit of staying more than two or three minutes with anyone and that the sea did not agree with me. He seemed deeply grieved to hear it. So you won't come, he said. But to my amazement I got up on the ass and off we went, in the shade of the red chestnuts springing from the sidewalk. I held the ass by the mane, one hand in front of the other. The little boys jeered and threw stones, but their aim was poor, for they only hit me once, on the hat. A policeman stopped us and accused us of disturbing the peace. My friend replied that we were as nature had made us, the boys too were as nature had made them. It was inevitable, under these conditions, that the peace should be disturbed from time to time. Let us continue on our way, he said, and order will soon be restored throughout your beat. We followed the quiet, dustwhite inland roads with their hedges of hawthorn and fuchsia and their footpaths fringed with wild grass and daisies. Night fell. The ass carried me right to the mouth of the cave, for in the dark I could not have found my way down the path winding steeply to the sea. Then he climbed back to his pasture.

I don't know how long I stayed there. The cave was nicely arranged, I must say. I treated my crablice with salt water and seaweed, but a lot of nits must have survived. I put compresses of seaweed on my skull, which gave me great relief, but not for long. I lay in the cave and sometimes looked out at the horizon. I saw above me a vast trembling expanse without islands or promontories. At night a light shone into the cave at regular intervals. It was here I found the phial in my pocket. It was not broken, for the glass was not real glass. I thought Mr. Weir had confiscated all my belongings. My host was out most of the time. He fed me on fish. It is easy for a man, a proper man, to live in a cave, far from everybody. He invited me to stay as long as I liked. If I preferred to be alone he would gladly prepare another cave for me further on. He would bring me food every day and drop in from time to time to make sure I was all right and needed nothing. He was kind. Unfortunately I did not need kindness. You wouldn't know of a lake dwelling? I said. I couldn't bear the sea, its splashing and heaving, its tides and general convulsiveness. The wind at least sometimes stops. My hands and feet felt as though they were full of ants. This kept me awake for hours on end. If I stayed here something awful would happen to me, I said, and a lot of good that would do me. You'd get drowned, he said. Yes, I said, or jump off the cliff. And to think I couldn't live anywhere else, he said, in my cabin in the mountains I was wretched. Your cabin in the mountains? I said. He repeated the story of his cabin in the mountains, I had forgotten it, it was as though I were hearing it for the first time. I asked him if he still had it. He replied he had not seen it since the day he fled from it, but that he believed it was still there, a little decayed no doubt. But when he urged me to take the key I refused, saying I had other plans. You will always find me here, he said, if you ever need me. Ah people. He gave me his knife.

What he called his cabin in the mountains was a sort of wooden shed. The door had been removed, for firewood, or for some other purpose. The glass had disappeared from the window. The roof had fallen in at several places. The interior was divided, by the remains of a partition, into two unequal parts. If there had been any furniture it was gone. The vilest acts had been committed on the ground and against the walls. The floor was strewn with excrements, both human and animal, with condoms and vomit. In a cowpad a heart had been traced, pierced by an arrow. And yet there was nothing to attract tourists. I noticed the remains of abandoned nosegays. They had been greedily gathered, carried for miles, then thrown away, because they were cumbersome or already withered. This was the dwelling to which I had been offered the key.

The scene was the familiar one of grandeur and desolation.

Nevertheless it was a roof over my head. I rested on a bed of ferns, gathered at great labour with my own hands. One day I couldn't get up. The cow saved me. Goaded by the icy mist she came in search of shelter. It was probably not the first time. She can't have seen me. I tried to suck her, without much success. Her udder was covered with dung. I took off my hat and, summoning all my energy, began to milk her into it. The milk fell to the ground and was lost, but I said to myself, No matter, it's free. She dragged me across the floor, stopping from time to time only to kick me. I didn't know our cows too could be so inhuman. She must have recently been milked. Clutching the dug with one hand I kept my hat under it with the other. But in the end she prevailed. For she dragged me across the threshold and out into the giant streaming ferns, where I was forced to let go.

As I drank the milk I reproached myself with what I had done. I could no longer count on this cow and she would warn the others. More master of myself I might have made a friend of her. She would have come every day, perhaps accompanied by other cows. I might have learnt to make butter, even cheese. But I said to myself, No, all is for the best.

Once on the road it was all downhill. Soon there were carts, but they all refused to take me up. In other clothes, with another face, they might have taken me up. I must have changed since my expulsion from the basement. The face notably seemed to have attained its climacteric. The humble, ingenuous smile would no longer come, nor the expression of candid misery, showing the stars and the distaff. I summoned them, but they would not come. A mask of dirty old hairy leather, with two holes and a slit, it was too far gone for the old trick of please your honour and God reward you and pity upon me. It was disastrous. What would I crawl with in future? I lay down on the side of the road and began to writhe each time I heard a cart approaching. That was so they would not think I was sleeping or resting. I tried to groan, Help! Help! But the tone that came out was that of polite conversation. My hour was not yet come and I could no longer groan. The last time I had cause to groan I had groaned as well as ever, and no heart within miles of me to melt. What was to become of me? I said to myself, I'll learn again. I lay down across the road at a narrow place, so that the carts could not pass without passing over my body, with one wheel at least, or two if there were four. But the day came when, looking round me, I was in the suburbs, and from there to the old haunts it was not far, beyond the stupid hope of rest or less pain.

So I covered the lower part of my face with a black rag and went and begged at a sunny corner. For it seemed to me my eyes were not completely spent, thanks perhaps to the dark glasses my tutor had given me. He had given me the *Ethics* of Geulincz. They were a man's glasses, I was a child. They found him dead, crumpled up in the water closet, his clothes in awful disorder, struck down by an infarctus. Ah what peace. The *Ethics* had his name (Ward) on the fly-leaf, the glasses had belonged to him. The bridge, at the time I am speaking of, was of brass wire, of the kind used to hang pictures and big mirrors, and two long black ribbons served as wings. I wound them round my ears and then down under my chin where I tied them together. The lenses had suffered, from rubbing in my pocket against each other and against the other objects there. I thought Mr. Weir had confiscated all my belongings. But I had no further need of these glasses and used them merely to soften the glare of the sun. I should never have mentioned them. The rag gave me a lot of trouble. I got it in the end from the lining of my greatcoat, no, I had no greatcoat now, of my coat then. The result was a grey rag rather than a black, perhaps even chequered, but I had to make do with it. Till afternoon I held my face raised towards the southern sky, then towards the western till night. The bowl gave me a lot of trouble. I couldn't use my hat because of my skull. As for holding out my hand, that was quite out of the question. So I got a tin and hung it from a button of my greatcoat, what's the matter with me, of my coat, at pubis level. It did not hang plumb, it leaned respectfully towards the passer-by, he had only to drop his mite. But that obliged him to come up close to me, he was in danger of touching me. In the end I got a bigger tin, a kind of big tin box, and I placed it on the sidewalk at my feet. But people who give alms don't much care to toss them, there's something contemptuous about this gesture which is repugnant to sensitive natures. To say nothing of their having to aim. They are prepared to give, but not for their gift to go rolling under the passing feet or under the passing wheels, to be picked up perhaps by some undeserving person. So they don't give. There are those, to be sure, who stoop, but generally speaking people who give alms don't much care to stoop. What they like above all is to sight the wretch from afar, get ready their penny, drop it in their stride and hear the God bless you dying away in the distance. Personally I never said that, nor anything like it, I wasn't much of a believer, but I did make a noise with my mouth. In the end I got a kind of board or tray and tied it to my neck and waist. It jutted out just at the right height, pocket height, and its edge was far enough from my person for the coin to be bestowed without danger. Some days I strewed it with flowers, petals, buds and that herb which men call fleabane, I believe, in a word whatever I could find. I didn't go out of my way to look for them, but all the pretty things of this description that came my way were for the board. They must have thought I loved nature. Most of the time I looked up at the sky, but without focusing it, for why focus it? Most of the time it was a mixture of white, blue and grey, and then at evening all the evening colours. I felt it weighing softly on my face, I rubbed my face against it, one cheek after the other, turning my head from side to side. Now and then to rest my neck I dropped my head on my chest. Then I could see the board in the distance, a haze of many colours. I leaned against the wall, but without nonchalance, I shifted my weight from one foot to the other and my hands clutched the lapels of my coat. To beg with your hands in your pockets makes a bad impression, it irritates the workers, especially in winter. You should never wear gloves either. There were guttersnipes who swept away all I had earned, under cover of giving me a coin. It was to buy sweets. I unbuttoned my trousers discreetly to scratch myself. I scratched myself in an upward direction, with four nails. I pulled on the hairs, to get relief. It passed the time, time flew when I scratched myself. Real scratching is superior to masturbation, in my opinion. One can masturbate up to the age of seventy, and even beyond, but in the end it becomes a mere habit. Whereas to scratch myself properly I would have needed a dozen hands. I itched all over, on the privates, in the bush up to the navel, under the arms, in the arse, and then patches of eczema and psoriasis that I could set raging merely by thinking of them. It was in the arse I had the most pleasure, I stuck in my forefinger up to the knuckle. Later, if I had to shit, the pain was atrocious. But I hardly shat any more. Now and then a flying machine flew by, sluggishly it seemed to me. Often at the end of the day I discovered the legs of my trousers all wet. That must have been the dogs. I personally pissed very little. If by chance the need came on me a little squirt in my fly was enough to relieve it. Once at my post I did not leave it till nightfall. I had no appetite, God tempered the wind to me. After work I bought a bottle of milk and drank it in the evening in the shed. Better still, I got a little boy to buy it for me, always the same, they wouldn't serve me, I don't know why. I gave him a penny for his pains. One day I witnessed a strange scene. Normally I didn't see a great deal. I didn't hear a great deal either. I didn't pay attention. Strictly speaking I wasn't there. Strictly speaking I believe I've never been anywhere. But that day I must have come back. For some time past a sound had been scarifying me. I did not investigate the cause, for I said to myself, It's going to stop. But as it did not stop I had no choice but to find out the cause. It was a man perched on the roof of a car and haranguing the passers-by. That at least was my interpretation. He was bellowing so loud that snatches of his discourse reached my ears. Union . . . brothers . . . Marx . . . capital . . . bread and butter . . . love. It was all Greek to me. The car was drawn up against the kerb, just in front of me, I saw the orator from behind. All of a sudden he turned and pointed at me, as at an exhibit. Look at this down and out, he vociferated, this leftover. If he doesn't go down on all fours, it's for fear of being impounded. Old, lousy, rotten, ripe for the muckheap. And there are a thousand like him, worse than him, ten thousand, twenty thousand—. A voice, Thirty thousand. Every day you pass them by, resumed the orator, and when you have backed a winner you fling them a farthing. Do you ever think? The voice, God forbid. A penny, resumed the orator, tuppence—. The voice, thruppence. It never enters your head, resumed the orator, that your charity is a crime, an incentive to slavery, stultification and organized murder. Take a good look at this living corpse. You may say it's his own fault. Ask him if it's his own fault. The voice, Ask him yourself. Then he bent forward and took me to task. I had perfected my board. It now consisted of two boards hinged together, which enabled me, when my work was done, to fold it and carry it under my arm. I liked doing little odd jobs. So I took off the rag, pocketed the few coins I had earned, untied the board, folded it and put it under my arm. Do you hear me, you crucified bastard! cried the orator. Then I went away, although it was still light. But generally speaking it was a quiet corner, busy but not overcrowded, thriving and well-frequented. He must have been a religious fanatic, I could find no other explanation. Perhaps he was an escaped lunatic. He had a nice face, a little on the red side.

I did not work every day. I had practically no expenses. I even managed to put a little aside, for my very last days. The days I did not work I spent lying in the shed. The shed was on a private estate, or what had once been a private estate, on the riverside. This estate, the main entrance to which opened on a narrow, dark and silent street, was enclosed with a wall, except of course on the river front, which marked its northern boundary for a distance of about thirty yards. From the last quays beyond the water the eyes rose to a confusion of low houses, wasteland, hoardings, chimneys, steeples and towers. A kind of parade ground was also to be seen, where soldiers played football all the year round. Only the ground-floor windows—no, I can't. The estate seemed abandoned. The gates were locked and the paths overgrown with grass. Only the ground-floor windows had shutters. The others were sometimes lit at night, faintly, now one, now another. At least that was my impression. Perhaps it was reflected light. In this shed, the day I adopted it, I found a boat, upside down. I righted it, chocked it up with stones and pieces of wood, took out the thwarts and made my bed inside. The rats had difficulty in getting at me, because of the bulge of the hull. And yet they longed to. Just think of it, living flesh, for in spite of everything I was still living flesh. I had lived too long among rats, in my chance dwellings, to share the dread they inspire in the vulgar. I even had a soft spot in my heart for them. They came with such confidence towards me, it seemed without the least repugnance. They made their toilet with catlike gestures. Toads at evening, motionless for hours, lap flies from the air. They like to squat where cover ends and open air begins, they favour thresholds. But I had to contend now with water rats, exceptionally lean and ferocious. So I made a kind of lid with stray boards. It's incredible the number of boards I've come across in my lifetime, I never needed a board but there it was, I had only to stoop and pick it up. I liked doing little odd jobs, no, not particularly, I didn't mind. It completely covered the boat, I'm referring again to the lid. I pushed it a little towards the stern, climbed into the boat by the bow, crawled to the stern, raised my feet and pushed the lid back towards the bow till it covered me completely. But what did my feet push against? They pushed against a cross-bar I nailed to the lid for that purpose, I liked these little odd jobs. But it was better to climb into the boat by the stern and pull back the lid with my hands till it completely covered me, then push it forward in the same way when I wanted to get out. As holds for my hands I planted two spikes just where I needed them. These little odds and ends of carpentry, if I may so describe it, carried out with whatever tools and material I chanced to find, gave me a certain pleasure. I knew it would soon be the end, so I played the part, you know, the part of—how shall I say, I don't know. I was comfortable enough in this boat, I must say. The lid fitted so well I had to pierce a hole. It's no good closing your eyes, you must leave them open in the dark, that is my opinion. I am not speaking of sleep, I am speaking of what I believe is called waking. In any case, I slept very little at this period, I wasn't sleepy, or I was too sleepy, I don't know, or I was afraid, I don't know. Flat then on my back I saw nothing except, dimly, just above my head, through the tiny chinks, the grey light of the shed. To see nothing at all, no, that's too much. I heard faintly the cries of the gulls ravening about the mouth of the sewer near by. In a spew of yellow foam, if my memory serves me right, the filth gushed into the river and the slush of birds above screaming with hunger and fury. I heard the lapping of water against the slip and against the bank and the other sound, so different, of open wave, I heard it too.

I too, when I moved, felt less boat than wave, or so it seemed to me, and my stillness was the stillness of eddies. That may seem impossible. The rain too, I often heard it, for it often rained. Sometimes a drop, falling through the roof of the shed, exploded on me. All that composed a rather liquid world. And then of course there was the voice of the wind or rather those, so various, of its playthings. But what does it amount to? Howling, soughing, moaning, sighing. What I would have liked was hammer strokes, bang bang bang, clanging in the desert. I let farts to be sure, but hardly ever a real crack, they oozed out with a sucking noise, melted in the mighty never. I don't know how long I stayed there. I was very snug in my box, I must say. It seemed to me I had grown more independent of recent years. That no one came any more, that no one could come any more to ask me if I was all right and needed nothing, distressed me then but little. I was all right, yes, quite so, and the fear of getting worse was less with me. As for my needs, they had dwindled as it were to my dimensions and become, if I may say so, of so exquisite a quality as to exclude all thought of succour. To know I had a being, however faint and false, outside of me, had once had the power to stir my heart. You become unsociable, it's inevitable. It's enough to make you wonder sometimes if you are on the right planet. Even the words desert you, it's as bad as that. Perhaps it's the moment when the vessels stop communicating, you know, the vessels. There you are still between the two murmurs, it must be the same old song as ever, but Christ you wouldn't think so. There were times when I wanted to push away the lid and get out of the boat and couldn't, I was so indolent and weak, so content deep down where I was. I felt them hard upon me, the icy, tumultuous streets, the terrifying faces, the noises that slash, pierce, claw, bruise. So I waited till the desire to shit, or even to piss, lent me wings. I did not want to dirty my nest! And yet it sometimes happened, and even more and more often. Arched and rigid I edged down my trousers and turned a little on my side, just enough to free the hole. To contrive a little kingdom, in the midst of the universal muck, then shit on it, ah that was me all over. The excrements were me too, I know, I know, but all the same. Enough, enough, the next thing I was having visions, I who never did, except sometimes in my sleep, who never had, real visions, I'd remember, except perhaps as a child, my myth will have it so. I knew they were visions because it was night and I was alone in my boat. What else could they have been? So I was in my boat and gliding on the waters. I didn't have to row, the ebb was carrying me out. Anyway I saw no oars, they must have taken them away. I had a board, the remains of a thwart perhaps, which I used when I came too close to the bank, or when a pier came bearing down on me or a barge at its moorings. There were stars in the sky, quite a few. I didn't know what the weather was doing, I was neither cold nor warm and all seemed calm. The banks receded more and more, it was inevitable, soon I saw them no more. The lights grew fainter and fewer as the river widened. There on the land men were sleeping, bodies were gathering strength for the toil and joys of the morrow. The boat was not gliding now, it was tossing, buffeted by the choppy waters of the bay. All seemed calm and yet foam was washing aboard. Now the sea air was all about me, I had no other shelter than the land, and what does it amount to, the shelter of the land, at such a time. I saw the beacons, four in all, including a lightship. I knew them well, even as a child I had known them well. It was evening, I was with my father on a height, he held my hand. I would have liked him to draw me close with a gesture of protective love, but his mind was on other things. He also taught me the names of the mountains. But to have done with these visions I also saw the lights of the buoys, the sea seemed full of them, red and green and to my surprise even yellow. And on the slopes of the mountain, now rearing its unbroken bulk behind the town, the fires turned from gold to red, from red to gold. I knew what it was, it was the gorse burning. How often I had set a match to it myself, as a child. And hours later, back in my home, before I climbed into bed, I watched from my high window the fires I had lit. That night then, all aglow with distant fires, on sea, on land and in the sky, I drifted with the currents and the tides. I noticed that my hat was tied, with a string I suppose, to my buttonhole. I got up from my seat in the stern and a great clanking was heard. That was the chain. One end was fastened to the bow and the other round my waist. I must have pierced a hole beforehand in the floor-boards, for there I was down on my knees prying out the plug with my knife. The hole was small and the water rose slowly. It would take a good half hour, everything included, barring accidents. Back now in the stern-sheets, my legs stretched out, my back well propped against the sack stuffed with grass I used as a cushion, I swallowed my calmative. The sea, the sky, the mountains and the islands closed in and crushed me in a mighty systole, then scattered to the uttermost confines of space. The memory came faint and cold of the story I might have told, a story in the likeness of my life, I mean without the courage to end or the strength to go on.

Tommaso Landolfi (1908–   )

Gogol was a Russian writer, the author of the second modern short story in this collection. Landolfi is an Italian writer who has been profoundly influenced by his reading of nineteenth-century Russian literature—Tolstoy and, especially, Dostoevsky. Gogol may have been a case of adolescent arrest: he never married and apparently never felt an erotic interest in women, though there is no evidence of homosexuality. He died, mad, in 1852. It is also reported authoritatively that his descent into madness was accompanied by an accelerating sensation of coldness, plus an intensifying vision of steadily accumulating snow (enough to arouse and rivet the recollection of anyone who has read Conrad Aiken's "Silent Snow, Secret Snow," p. 348).

We may begin by wondering how much Landolfi might have known of Gogol's life and career. Something, surely; how else to account for the title of the story and for references to such Russian critics of Gogol as Belinsky and Vershiny? But the story's point is no more the historical Gogol than the point of Woolfs' "The Mark on the Wall" (p. 306) is what that mark actually was. At the same time we may remember Gogol's extraordinary importance to contemporary Russian authors (pp. 80–81), a reputation and influence the scholarly monologist of this story assumes we are perfectly familiar with: "so lofty a genius," "these privileged natures," "the Master." The setting, then, formally considered, is perfectly clear: we are in the presence of an official biographer, probably young, diffident, hesitant, but one who has run into something disturbing in the course of his research on "the Master," and who, given his own uncertainties about "the present stage of development of Gogol studies," seems to have to talk himself into disclosing what he has discovered.

Given everything that follows in the story, that whole pose becomes hilarious, if hilariously unnerving. It is, however, a fine example of Landolfi's characteristic technique as described by the Italian critic Giacomo Debenedetti:

Imagine that you have come as a guest to a castle and the host, accompanying you to the room set aside for you, opens the shutters, shows you the beautiful view and acquaints you with the room's comforts and conveniences. But when night falls you begin to hear all around you an insidious concert of squeaks and groans. The next morning, after a sleepless night, you learn that this is the room haunted by ghosts. And the host's politeness and exaggerated concern now appear to you in another light.

When we come to the climactic last evening of the story, our modest biographer alludes to "the famous 'pyre of vanities'—the burning of his manuscripts"—as though we had all heard of how Gogol, near the end of his life and in precipitously deteriorating health, had in fact burned the manuscript of the sequel he was trying to write to his novel *Dead Souls.* And when Caracas hits the coals, the only commentary we are offered is that Gogol, "like all Russians, had a passion for throwing important things in the fire."

A more strictly symbolic reading of the story (see Introduction, p. 21)—without reference to the historical Gogol—might suggest that as the doll-like "wife" begins to take on a life and character of her own, the husband cannot stand it, in fact wants her and her offspring dead. She has, after all, never *really* existed in her own right. And the minute she begins to emerge into vascular and circulatory existence (symbolized by her one spoken utterance?), steps have to be taken. Is not a death wish implicit in all such ego-centered, alienated "love"? And—more unnerving still—may not Caracas symbolize what can happen when we turn life into art?

Landolfi has been Italy's preeminent avant-garde short-story writer for a good many years now, and he is also well known as a critic and translator of Russian literature. Two volumes of his stories have recently become available in English: *Cancerqueen and Other Stories* (1971) and *Gogol's Wife and Other Stories* (1961).

Gogol's Wife

At this point, confronted with the whole complicated affair of Nikolai Vassilevitch's wife, I am overcome by hesitation. Have I any right to disclose something which is unknown to the whole world, which my unforgettable friend himself kept hidden from the world (and he had his reasons), and which I am sure will give rise to all sorts of malicious and stupid misunderstandings? Something, moreover, which will very probably offend the sensibilities of all sorts of base, hypocritical people, and possibly of some honest people too, if there are any left? And finally, have I any right to disclose something before which my own spirit recoils, and even tends toward a more or less open disapproval?

But the fact remains that, as a biographer, I have certain firm obligations. Believing as I do that every bit of information about so lofty a genius will turn out to be of value to us and to future generations, I cannot conceal something which in any case has no hope of being judged fairly and wisely until the end of time. Moreover, what right have we to condemn? Is it given to us to know, not only what intimate needs, but even what higher and wider ends may have been served by those very deeds of a lofty genius which perchance may appear to us vile? No indeed, for we understand so little of these privileged natures. "It is true," a great man once said, "that I also have to pee, but for quite different reasons."

But without more ado I will come to what I know beyond doubt, and can prove beyond question, about this controversial matter, which will now—I dare to hope—no longer be so. I will not trouble to recapitulate what is already known of it, since I do not think this should be necessary at the present stage of development of Gogol studies.

Let me say it at once: Nikolai Vassilevitch's wife was not a woman. Nor was she any sort of human being, nor any sort of living creature at all, whether animal or vegetable (although something of the sort has sometimes been hinted). She was quite simply a balloon. Yes, a balloon; and this will explain the perplexity, or even indignation, of certain biographers who were also the personal friends of the Master, and who complained that, although they often went to his house, they never saw her and "never even heard her voice." From this they deduced all sorts of dark and disgraceful complications—yes, and criminal ones too. No, gentlemen, everything is always simpler than it appears. You did not hear her voice simply because she could not speak, or to be more exact, she could only speak in certain conditions, as we shall see. And it was always, except once, in a tête-à-tête with Nikolai Vassilevitch. So let us not waste time with any cheap or empty refutations but come at once to as exact and complete a description as possible of the being or object in question.

Gogol's so-called wife was an ordinary dummy made of thick rubber, naked at all seasons, buff in tint, or as is more commonly said, flesh-colored. But since women's skins are not all of the same color, I should specify that hers was a light-colored, polished skin, like that of certain brunettes. It, or she, was, it is hardly necessary to add, of feminine sex. Perhaps I should say at once that she was capable of very wide alterations of her attributes without, of course, being able to alter her sex itself. She could sometimes appear to be thin, with hardly any breasts and with narrow hips more like a young lad than a woman, and at other times to be excessively well-endowed or— let us not mince matters—fat. And she often changed the color of her hair, both on her head and elsewhere on her body, though not necessarily at the same time. She could also seem to change in all sorts of other tiny particulars, such as the position of moles, the vitality of the mucous membranes and so forth. She could even to a certain extent change the very color of her skin. One is faced with the necessity of asking oneself who she really was, or whether it would be proper to speak of a single "person"—and in fact we shall see that it would be imprudent to press this point.

The cause of these changes, as my readers will already have understood, was nothing else but the will of Nikolai Vassilevitch himself. He would inflate her to a greater or lesser degree, would change her wig and her other tufts of hair, would grease her with ointments and touch her up in various ways so as to obtain more or less the type of woman which suited him at that moment. Following the natural inclinations of his fancy, he even amused himself sometimes by producing grotesque or monstrous forms; as will be readily understood, she became deformed when inflated beyond a certain point or if she remained below a certain pressure.

But Gogol soon tired of these experiments, which he held to be "after all, not very respectful" to his wife, whom he loved in his own way—however inscrutable it may remain to us. He loved her, but which of these incarnations, we may ask ourselves, did he love? Alas, I have already indicated that the end of the present account will furnish some sort of an answer. And how can I have stated above that it was Nikolai Vassilevitch's will which ruled that woman? In a certain sense, yes, it is true; but it is equally certain that she soon became no longer his slave but his tyrant. And here yawns the abyss, or if you prefer it, the Jaws of Tartarus. But let us not anticipate.

I have said that Gogol obtained with his manipulations *more or less* the type of woman which he needed from time to time. I should add that when, in rare cases, the form he obtained perfectly incarnated his desire, Nikolai Vassilevitch fell in love with it "exclusively," as he said in his own words, and that this was enough to render "her" stable for a certain time—until he fell out of love with "her." I counted no more than three or four of these violent passions—or, as I suppose they would be called today, infatuations—in the life (dare I say in the conjugal life?) of the great writer. It will be convenient to add here that a few years after what one may call his marriage, Gogol had even given a name to his wife. It was Caracas, which is, unless I am mistaken, the capital of Venezuela. I have never been able to discover the reason for this choice: great minds are so capricious!

Speaking only of her normal appearance, Caracas was what is called a fine woman—well built and proportioned in every part. She had every smallest attribute of her sex properly disposed in the proper location. Particularly worthy of attention were her genital organs (if the adjective is permissible in such a context). They were formed by means of ingenious folds in the rubber. Nothing was forgotten, and their operation was rendered easy by various devices, as well as by the internal pressure of the air.

Caracas also had a skeleton, even though a rudimentary one. Perhaps it was made of whalebone. Special care had been devoted to the construction of the thoracic cage, of the pelvic basin and of the cranium. The first two systems were more or less visible in accordance with the thickness of the fatty layer, if I may so describe it, which covered them. It is a great pity that Gogol never let me know the name of the creator of such a fine piece of work. There was an obstinacy in his refusal which was never quite clear to me.

Nikolai Vassilevitch blew his wife up through the anal sphincter with a pump of his own invention, rather like those which you hold down with your two feet and which are used today in all sorts of mechanical workshops. Situated in the anus was a little one-way valve, or whatever the correct technical description would be, like the mitral valve of the heart, which, once the body was inflated, allowed more air to come in but none to go out. To deflate, one unscrewed a stopper in the mouth, at the back of the throat.

And that, I think, exhausts the description of the most noteworthy peculiarities of this being. Unless perhaps I should mention the splendid rows of white teeth which adorned her mouth and the dark eyes which, in spite of their immobility, perfectly simulated life. Did I say simulate? Good heavens, simulate is not the word! Nothing seems to be the word, when one is speaking of Caracas! Even these eyes could undergo a change of color, by means of a special process to which, since it was long and tiresome, Gogol seldom had recourse. Finally, I should speak of her voice, which it was only once given to me to hear. But I cannot do that without going more fully into the relationship between husband and wife, and in this I shall no longer be able to answer to the truth of everything with absolute certitude. On my conscience I could not—so confused, both in itself and in my memory, is that which I now have to tell.

Here, then, as they occur to me, are some of my memories.

The first and, as I said, the last time I ever heard Caracus speak to Nikolai Vassilevitch was one evening when we were absolutely alone. We were in the room where the woman, if I may be allowed the expression, lived. Entrance to this room was strictly forbidden to everybody. It was furnished more or less in the Oriental manner, had no windows and was situated in the most inaccessible part of the house. I did know that she could talk, but Gogol had never explained to me the circumstances under which this happened. There were only the two of us, or three, in there. Nikolai Vassilevitch and I were drinking vodka and discussing Butkov's[1] novel. I remember that we left this topic, and he was maintaining the necessity for radical reforms in the laws of inheritance. We had almost forgotten her. It was then that, with a husky and submissive voice, like Venus on the nuptial couch, she said point-blank: "I want to go poo poo."

I jumped, thinking I had misheard, and looked across at her. She was sitting on a pile of cushions against the wall; that evening she was a soft, blonde beauty, rather well-covered. Her expression seemed commingled of shrewdness and slyness, childishness and irresponsibility. As for Gogol, he blushed violently and, leaping on her, stuck two fingers down her throat. She immediately began to shrink and to turn pale; she took on once again that lost and astonished air which was especially hers, and was in the end reduced to no more than a flabby skin on a perfunctory bony armature. Since, for practical reasons which will readily be divined, she had an extraordinarily flexible backbone, she folded up almost in two, and for the rest of the evening she looked up at us from where she had slithered to the floor, in utter abjection.

All Gogol said was: "She only does it for a joke, or to annoy me, because as a matter of fact she does not have such needs." In the presence of other people, that is to say of me, he generally made a point of treating her with a certain disdain.

We went on drinking and talking, but Nikolai Vassilevitch seemed very much disturbed and absent in spirit. Once he suddenly interrupted what he was saying, seized my hand in his and burst into tears. "What can I do now?" he exclaimed. "You understand, Foma Paskalovitch, that I loved her?"

It is necessary to point out that it was impossible, except by a miracle, ever to repeat any of Caracas' forms. She was a fresh creation every time, and it would have been wasted effort to seek to find again the exact proportions, the exact pressure, and so forth, of a former Caracas. Therefore the plumpish blonde of that evening was lost to Gogol from that time forth forever; this was in fact the tragic end of one of those few loves of Nikolai Vassilevitch, which I described above. He gave me no explanation; he sadly rejected my proffered comfort, and that evening we parted early. But his heart had been laid bare to me in that outburst. He was no longer so reticent with me, and soon had hardly any secrets left. And this, I may say in parenthesis, caused me very great pride.

It seems that things had gone well for the "couple" at the beginning of their life together. Nikolai Vassilevitch had been content with Caracas and slept regularly with her in the same bed. He continued to observe this custom till the end, saying with a timid smile that no companion could be quieter or less importunate than she. But I soon began to doubt this, especially judging by the state he was sometimes in when he woke up. Then, after several years, their relationship began strangely to deteriorate.

All this, let it be said once and for all, is no more than a schematic attempt at an explanation. About that time the woman actually began to show signs of independence or, as one might say, of autonomy. Nikolai Vassilevitch had the extraordinary impression that she was acquiring a personality of her own, indecipherable perhaps, but still distinct from his, and one which slipped through his fingers. It is certain that some sort of continuity was established between each of her appearances—between all those bru-

---

[1] This is probably *Peter Burgskie Vershiny,* 2 vols., 1844–45. The novels of Yakov Petrovich Butkov (1815–1856) showed Gogol's influence.

nettes, those blondes, those redheads and auburn-headed girls, between those plump, those slim, those dusky or snowy or golden beauties, there was a certain something in common. At the beginning of this chapter I cast some doubt on the propriety of considering Caracas as a unitary personality; nevertheless I myself could not quite, whenever I saw her, free myself of the impression that, however unheard of it may seem, this was fundamentally the same woman. And it may be that this was why Gogol felt he had to give her a name.

An attempt to establish in what precisely subsisted the common attributes of the different forms would be quite another thing. Perhaps it was no more and no less than the creative afflatus of Nikolai Vassilevitch himself. But no, it would have been too singular and strange if he had been so much divided off from himself, so much averse to himself. Because whoever she was, Caracas was a disturbing presence and even—it is better to be quite clear—a hostile one. Yet neither Gogol nor I ever succeeded in formulating a remotely tenable hypothesis as to her true nature; when I say formulate, I mean in terms which would be at once rational and accessible to all. But I cannot pass over an extraordinary event which took place at this time.

Caracas fell ill of a shameful disease—or rather Gogol did—though he was not then having, nor had he ever had, any contact with other women. I will not even try to describe how this happened, or where the filthy complaint came from; all I know is that it happened. And that my great, unhappy friend would say to me: "So, Foma Paskalovitch, you see what lay at the heart of Caracas; it was the spirit of syphilis."

Sometimes he would even blame himself in a quite absurd manner; he was always prone to self-accusation. This incident was a real catastrophe as far as the already obscure relationship between husband and wife, and the hostile feelings of Nikolai Vassilevitch himself, were concerned. He was compelled to undergo long-drawn-out and painful treatment—the treatment of those days—and the situation was aggravated by the fact that the disease in the woman did not seem to be easily curable. Gogol deluded himself for some time that, by blowing his wife up and down and furnishing her with the most widely divergent aspects, he could obtain a woman immune from the contagion, but he was forced to desist when no results were forthcoming.

I shall be brief, seeking not to tire my readers, and also because what I remember seems to become more and more confused. I shall therefore hasten to the tragic conclusion. As to this last, however, let there be no mistake. I must once again make it clear that I am very sure of my ground. I was an eyewitness. Would that I had not been!

The years went by. Nikolai Vassilevitch's distaste for his wife became stronger, though his love for her did not show any signs of diminishing. Toward the end, aversion and attachment struggled so fiercely with each other in his heart that he became quite stricken, almost broken up. His restless eyes, which habitually assumed so many different expressions and sometimes spoke so sweetly to the heart of his interlocutor, now almost always shone with a fevered light, as if he were under the effect of a drug. The strangest impulses arose in him, accompanied by the most senseless fears. He spoke to me of Caracas more and more often, accusing her of unthinkable and amazing things. In these regions I could not follow him, since I had but a sketchy acquaintance with his wife, and hardly any intimacy—and above all since my sensibility was so limited compared with his. I shall accordingly restrict myself to reporting some of his accusations, without reference to my personal impressions.

"Believe it or not, Foma Paskalovitch," he would, for example, often say to me: "Believe it or not, *she's aging!*" Then, unspeakably moved, he would, as was his way, take my hands in his. He also accused Caracas of giving herself up to solitary pleasures, which he had expressly forbidden. He even went so far as to charge her with betraying him, but the things he said became so extremely obscure that I must excuse myself from any further account of them.

One thing that appears certain is that toward the end Caracas, whether aged or not, had turned into a bitter creature, querulous, hypocritical and subject to religious excess. I do not exclude the possibility that she may have had an influence on Gogol's moral position during the last period of his life, a position which is sufficiently well known. The tragic climax came one night quite unexpectedly when Nikolai Vassilevitch and I were celebrating his silver wedding—one of the last evenings we were to spend together. I neither can nor should attempt to set down what it was that led to his decision, at a time when to all appearances he was resigned to tolerating his consort. I know not what new events had taken place that day. I shall confine myself to the facts; my readers must make what they can of them.

That evening Nikolai Vassilevitch was unusually agitated. His distaste for Caracas seemed to have reached an unprecedented intensity. The famous "pyre of vanities"— the burning of his manuscripts—had already taken place; I should not like to say whether or not at the instigation of his wife. His state of mind had been further inflamed by other causes. As to his physical condition, this was ever more pitiful, and strengthened my impression that he took drugs. All the same, he began to talk in a more or less normal way about Belinsky,[2] who was giving him some trouble with his attacks on the *Selected Correspondence*. Then suddenly, tears rising to his eyes, he interrupted himself and cried out: "No. No. It's too much, too much. I can't go on any longer," as well as other obscure and disconnected phrases which he would not clarify. He seemed to be talking to himself. He wrung his hands, shook his head, got up and sat down again after having taken four or five anxious steps round the room. When Caracas appeared, or rather when we went in to her later in the evening in her Oriental chamber, he controlled himself no longer and began to behave like an old man, if I may so express myself, in his second childhood, quite giving way to his absurd impulses. For instance, he kept nudging me and winking and senselessly repeating: "There she is, Foma Paskalovitch; there she is!" Meanwhile she seemed to look up at us with a disdainful attention. But behind these "mannerisms" one could feel in him a real repugnance, a repugnance which had, I suppose, now reached the limits of the endurable. Indeed . . .

After a certain time Nikolai Vassilevitch seemed to pluck up courage. He burst into tears, but somehow they were more manly tears. He wrung his hands again, seized mine in his, and walked up and down, muttering: "That's enough! We can't have any more of this. This is an unheard of thing. How can such a thing be happening to me? How can a man be expected to put up with *this?*"

He then leapt furiously upon the pump, the existence of which he seemed just to have remembered, and, with it in his hand, dashed like a whirlwind to Caracas. He inserted the tube in her anus and began to inflate her. . . . Weeping the while, he shouted like one possessed: "Oh, how I love her, how I love her, my poor, poor darling! . . . But she's going to burst! Unhappy Caracas, most pitiable of God's creatures! But die she must!"

Caracas was swelling up. Nikolai Vassilevitch sweated, wept and pumped. I wished to stop him but, I know not why, I had not the courage. She began to become deformed and shortly assumed the most monstrous aspect; and yet she had not given

---

[2] Vissarion Grigoryevitch Belinsky (1811–1848), the founder of literary criticism in Russia, who wrote a famous *Letter to Gogol* in 1847 in which he attacked the czarist autocracy and Gogol's "conversion" to reaction.

any signs of alarm—she was used to these jokes. But when she began to feel unbearably full, or perhaps when Nikolai Vassilevitch's intentions became plain to her, she took on an expression of bestial amazement, even a little beseeching, but still without losing that disdainful look. She was afraid, she was even committing herself to his mercy, but still she could not believe in the immediate approach of her fate; she could not believe in the frightful audacity of her husband. He could not see her face because he was behind her. But I looked at her with fascination, and did not move a finger.

At last the internal pressure came through the fragile bones at the base of her skull, and printed on her face an indescribable rictus. Her belly, her thighs, her lips, her breasts and what I could see of her buttocks had swollen to incredible proportions. All of a sudden she belched, and gave a long hissing groan; both these phenomena one could explain by the increase in pressure, which had suddenly forced a way out through the valve in her throat. Then her eyes bulged frantically, threatening to jump out of their sockets. Her ribs flared wide apart and were no longer attached to the sternum, and she resembled a python digesting a donkey. A donkey, did I say? An ox! An elephant! At this point I believed her already dead, but Nikolai Vassilevitch, sweating, weeping and repeating: "My dearest! My beloved! My best!" continued to pump.

She went off unexpectedly and, as it were, all of a piece. It was not one part of her skin which gave way and the rest which followed, but her whole surface at the same instant. She scattered in the air. The pieces fell more or less slowly, according to their size, which was in no case above a very restricted one. I distinctly remember a piece of her cheek, with some lip attached, hanging on the corner of the mantlepiece. Nikolai Vassilevitch stared at me like a madman. Then he pulled himself together and, once more with furious determination, he began carefully to collect those poor rags which once had been the shining skin of Caracas, and all of her.

"Good-by, Caracas," I thought I heard him murmur, "Good-by! You were too pitiable!" And then suddenly and quite audibly: "The fire! The fire! She too must end up in the fire." He crossed himself—with his left hand, of course. Then, when he had picked up all those shriveled rags, even climbing on the furniture so as not to miss any, he threw them straight on the fire in the hearth, where they began to burn slowly and with an excessively unpleasant smell. Nikolai Vassilevitch, like all Russians, had a passion for throwing important things in the fire.

Red in the face, with an inexpressible look of despair, and yet of sinister triumph too, he gazed on the pyre of those miserable remains. He had seized my arm and was squeezing it convulsively. But those traces of what had once been a being were hardly well alight when he seemed yet again to pull himself together, as if he were suddenly remembering something or taking a painful decision. In one bound he was out of the room.

A few seconds later I heard him speaking to me through the door in a broken, plaintive voice: "Foma Paskalovitch, I want you to promise not to look. *Golubchik,* promise not to look at me when I come in."

I don't know what I answered, or whether I tried to reassure him in any way. But he insisted, and I had to promise him, as if he were a child, to hide my face against the wall and only turn round when he said I might. The door opened violently and Nikolai Vassilevitch burst into the room and ran to the fireplace.

And here I must confess my weakness, though I consider it justified by the extraordinary circumstances. I looked round before Nikolai Vassilevitch told me I could; it was stronger than me. I was just in time to see him carrying something in his arms, something which he threw on the fire with all the rest, so that it suddenly flared up. At that, since the desire to *see* had entirely mastered every other thought in me, I dashed to the fireplace. But Nikolai Vassilevitch placed himself betwen me and it and pushed me back with a strength of which I had not believed him capable. Meanwhile the object was burning and giving off clouds of smoke. And before he showed any sign of calming down there was nothing left but a heap of silent ashes.

The true reason why I wished to see was because I had already glimpsed. But it was only a glimpse, and perhaps I should not allow myself to introduce even the slightest element of uncertainty into this true story. And yet, an eyewitness account is not complete without a mention of that which the witness knows with less than complete certainty. To cut a long story short, that something was a baby. Not a flesh and blood baby, of course, but more something in the line of a rubber doll or a model. Something, which, to judge by its appearance, could have been called *Caracas' son*.

Was I mad too? That I do not know, but I do know that this was what I saw, not clearly, but with my own eyes. And I wonder why it was that when I was writing this just now I didn't mention that when Nikolai Vassilevitch came back into the room he was muttering between his clenched teeth: "Him too! Him too!"

And that is the sum of my knowledge of Nikolai Vassilevitch's wife. In the next chapter I shall tell what happened to him afterwards, and that will be the last chapter of his life. But to give an interpretation of his feelings for his wife, or indeed for anything, is quite another and more difficult matter, though I have attempted it elsewhere in this volume, and refer the reader to that modest effort. I hope I have thrown sufficient light on a most controversial question and that I have unveiled the mystery, if not of Gogol, then at least of his wife. In the course of this I have implicitly given the lie to the insensate accusation that he ill-treated or even beat his wife, as well as other like absurdities. And what else can be the goal of a humble biographer such as the present writer but to serve the memory of that lofty genius who is the object of his study?

Fredric Brown (1906–1972)

Fredric Brown, born October 29, 1906 in Cincinnati, Ohio, once made that city the setting of one of his science fiction stories, "Armageddon."

> It happened—of all places—in Cincinnati. Not that there is anything wrong with Cincinnati, save that it is not the center of the Universe, nor even of the State of Ohio. It's a nice old town, and, in its way, second to none. But even the Chamber of Commerce would admit it lacks cosmic significance.

This—often comic—joining of the familiar and the farfetched is Fredric Brown's special *métier*. He began his career in the Midwest as a newspaperman and magazine writer, but with the success of his first mystery novel, *The Fabulous Clip Joint,* in 1947—which won the Edgar Allan Poe Award of Mystery Writers for that year— he turned entirely to the writing of mystery, fantasy, and science fiction, in both novel and short-story form. Before his death he had written some thirty books, including the short-story volumes *Angels and Spaceships* (1954), *Nightmares and Geezenstacks* (1961), and the posthumous collection *Paradox Lost* (1973). In the 1950s he wrote a number of TV plays and movie scripts, and his novel *The Screaming Mimi* (1949) was made into a film of that name; but this kind of writing did not appeal to him, and he went back to writing fiction. A simple list of some of his titles gives an idea of his wit and imaginative vigor—and subject-matter: *What Mad Universe* (1949), *Compliments of a Fiend* (1950), *Death Has Many Doors* (1951), *Space on My Hands* (1951), *The Lights in the Sky Are Stars* (1953), *Martians, Go Home* (1955), and *Honeymoon in Hell* (1958). His novel *Here Comes a Candle*, a favorite of Fredric Brown's wife, was called by one reviewer a "perfect psychological thriller."

In "Solipsist" Brown takes us lightheartedly into the center of one of the most intractable problems in philosophy—the question, raised most powerfully by David Hume, as to whether what we see *out there* is really *out there.* Skepticism was never carried further: we *know*, said Hume, only mental pictures, the sensory evidence recorded in the subjective individual mind, and we have no actual "proof" of the concrete existence of objects. Hume left us with a *solipsism of the present moment* as the fundamental condition of our knowledge—a condition that the philosopher Immanuel Kant spent his lifetime trying to save us from. But solipsism need not be met as a formal philosophic problem. Self-centeredness and the search for the self are both "modern" critical worries. So Brown is *playing* with an important topic even if he is not *dealing* with it. He enjoys making plots that end us up where we came in, that suggest a world of entrapment, of circularity, of no exit. Brown does it for fun—here in this "minimal" story (see p. 4) doing little more than dramatizing a pun on the word "solipsist" and the Genesis creation myth (see pp. 24–29)—but behind that play of word and idea is a serious theme. Brown may not be seeking "truth" exactly, but he rides his imagination and wit to some strange, far-out intellectual frontiers.

Solipsist

Walter B. Jehovah, for whose name I make no apology since it really *was* his name, had been a solipsist all his life. A solipsist, in case you don't happen to know the word, is one who believes that he himself is the only thing that really exists, that other people and the universe in general exist only in his imagination, and that if he quit imagining them they would cease to exist.

One day Walter B. Jehovah became a practicing solipsist. Within a week his wife had run away with another man, he'd lost his job as a shipping clerk and he had broken his leg chasing a black cat to keep it from crossing his path.

He decided, in his bed at the hospital, to end it all.

Looking out the window, staring up at the stars, he wished them out of existence, and they weren't there any more. Then he wished all other people out of existence and the hospital became strangely quiet even for a hospital. Next, the world, and he found himself suspended in a void. He got rid of his body quite as easily and then took the final step of willing *himself* out of existence.

Nothing happened.

Strange, he thought, can there be a limit to solipsism?

"Yes," a voice said.

"Who are you?" Walter B. Jehovah asked.

Reprinted by permission of the author and the author's agents, Scott Meredith Literary Agency, Inc., 845 Third Avenue, New York, New York 10022.

"I am the one who created the universe which you have just willed out of existence. And now that you have taken my place—" There was a deep sigh. "—I can finally cease my own existence, find oblivion, and let you take over."

"But—how can *I* cease to exist? That's what I'm trying to do, you know."

"Yes, I know," said the voice. "You must do it the same way *I* did. Create a universe. Wait until someone in it really believes what you believed and wills it out of existence. Then you can retire and let him take over. Good-by now."

And the voice was gone.

Walter B. Jehovah was alone in the void and there was only one thing he could do. He created the heaven and the earth.

It took him seven days.

Delmore Schwartz (1913–1966)

Delmore Schwartz, short-story writer, critic, teacher, poet, and famed talker, was born in Brooklyn in 1913. A brilliant student, Schwartz took a degree in philosophy at New York University in 1935, and continued at Harvard in literature. He taught on and off at universities most of his life (Harvard, New York University, Kenyon, Princeton, Chicago, State University of New York at Buffalo, and elsewhere): he was an editor of the *Partisan Review* (1943 to 1955) and poetry editor of *The New Republic* (1955 to 1957). *Summer Knowledge* (1959), a volume of his selected poems, won the Bollingen Prize and the Shelley Memorial Award for 1960.

Schwartz's first book, *In Dreams Begin Responsibilities* (1938), was published when the author was twenty-five and still at Harvard. It included the story that follows as well as poems, a lyric drama, and a play. His recognition as a poet and storywriter was immediate, and Robert Lowell, John Berryman, and Randall Jarrell, to name but a few, admired his work and became lifelong friends. Five volumes of poetry, translations from the French, a book of essays, and other collections of short stories—including *The World Is a Wedding* (1948) and *Successful Love, and Other Stories* (1961)—appeared over the next twenty years. But the precocious, perpetually "young" man lived as close to despair as the characters in his created work. "Even paranoids have real enemies," he once said. He spent years in and out of mental hospitals, and when he died in July, 1966 he was alone in a New York hotel room. His friends had not seen him for a year and were to find a large body of unpublished writings among his papers.

"In Dreams Begin Responsibilities" (the title is a line from John Butler Yeats) reveals the complexity of his thought and the kind of unresolved contradictions that beset him throughout his life. Dreams, we might believe, are a part of life for which we are not responsible, but dreams to Schwartz, a Freudian, were anything but free knowledge. They were fruit stolen from the tree of knowledge by night. The scene of the theft starts hesitantly, with images flickering jumpily across a movie screen: "I think it is the year 1909," the narrator tells us, as the silent movie begins. "The light is bad." By the end we realize that the movie is going on within a dream and that its content (the day the narrator's future father proposed to his future mother in a Coney Island restaurant) had condemned him to live with its knowledge forever. He awakens to the day of his twenty-first birthday; the dream was a ritual coming-of-age. The "omniscient" narrator has subsumed his parents, and suffers not only for himself but for their unhappy marriage as well. At first a passive spectator, he cannot hold back from becoming an actor in their courtship: at the end of the "film" he rises from his seat to yell at his still unmarried parents, "Don't do it! It's not too late to change your minds, both of you. Nothing good will come of it, only remorse, hatred, scandal, and two children whose characters are monstrous." His parents vanish before the light of day, replaced by the *audience*—which plays a decisive role in the story. At first it is sympathetic (an old lady even comforts the narrator), but finally the audience turns on him, his grief having interrupted the story once too often; an usher throws him out, saying, "You can't act like this even if other people aren't about!" The monologist, the compulsive talker, offends others even in his dreams: the narrator's self-pity has interfered with the audience's pleasure, and the audience *must* be entertained.

Irving Howe has called Schwartz a "comedian of alienation." He must turn his own nightmare into a half-comic movie in order to please the audience, an audience he hates but needs, since he must have listeners for his confession. A later generation of American writers often insults that audience, since they feel more hopeless about their alienation.

In Dreams Begin Responsibilities

1

I think it is the year 1909. I feel as if I were in a moving-picture theatre, the long arm of light crossing the darkness and spinning, my eyes fixed upon the screen. It is a silent picture, as if an old Biograph one, in which the actors are dressed in ridiculously old-fashioned clothes, and one flash succeeds another with sudden jumps, and the actors, too, seem to jump about, walking too fast. The shots are full of rays and dots, as if it had been raining when the picture was photographed. The light is bad.

It is Sunday afternoon, June 12th, 1909, and my father is walking down the quiet streets of Brooklyn on his way to visit my mother. His clothes are newly pressed, and his tie is too tight in his high collar. He jingles the coins in his pocket, thinking of the witty things he will say. I feel as if I had by now relaxed entirely in the soft darkness of the theatre; the organist peals out the obvious approximate emotions on which the audience rocks unknowingly. I am anonymous. I have forgotten myself: it is always so when one goes to a movie, it is, as they say, a drug.

My father walks from street to street of trees, lawns and houses, once in a while coming to an avenue on which a streetcar skates and gnaws, progressing slowly. The motorman, who has a handle-bar mustache, helps a young lady wearing a hat like a feathered bowl onto the car. He leisurely makes change and rings his bell as the passengers mount the car. It is obviously Sunday, for everyone is wearing Sunday clothes and the streetcar's noises emphasize the quiet of the holiday (for Brooklyn is said to be the city of churches). The shops are closed and their shades drawn but for an occasional stationery store or drugstore with great green balls in the window.

My father has chosen to take this long walk because he likes to walk and think. He thinks about himself in the future and so arrives at the place he is to visit in a mild state of exaltation. He pays no attention to the houses he is passing, in which the Sunday dinner is being eaten, nor to the many trees which line each street, now coming to their full green and the time when they will enclose the whole street in leafy shadow. An occasional carriage passes, the horses' hooves falling like stones in the quiet afternoon, and once in a while an automobile, looking like an enormous upholstered sofa, puffs and passes.

My father thinks of my mother, of how lady-like she is, and of the pride which will be his when he introduces her to his family. They are not yet engaged and he is not yet sure that he loves my mother, so that, once in a while, he becomes panicky about the bond already established. But then he reassures himself by thinking of the big men he admires who are married: William Randolph Hearst and William Howard Taft, who has just become the President of the United States.

My father arrives at my mother's house. He has come too early and so is suddenly embarrassed. My aunt, my mother's younger sister, answers the loud bell with her napkin in her hand, for the family is still at dinner. As my father enters, my grandfather rises from the table and shakes hands with him. My mother has run upstairs to tidy herself. My grandmother asks my father if he has had dinner and tells him that my mother will be down soon. My grandfather opens the conversation by remarking about the mild June weather. My father sits uncomfortably near the table, holding his hat in his hand. My grandmother tells my aunt to take my father's hat. My uncle, twelve years old, runs into the house, his hair tousled. He shouts a greeting to my father, who has often given him nickels, and then runs upstairs, as my grandmother shouts after him. It is evident that the respect in which my father is held in this house is tempered by a good deal of mirth. He is impressive, but also very awkward.

2

Finally, my mother comes downstairs and my father, being at the moment engaged in conversation with my grandfather, is made uneasy by her entrance, for he does not know whether to greet my mother or to continue the conversation. He gets up from his chair clumsily and says "Hello" gruffly. My grandfather watches this, examining their congruence, such as it is, with a critical eye, and meanwhile rubbing his bearded cheek roughly, as he always does when he reasons. He is worried; he is afraid that my father will not make a good husband for his oldest daughter. At this point something happens to the film, just as my father says something funny to my mother: I am awakened to myself and my unhappiness just as my interest has become most intense. The audience begins to clap impatiently. Then the trouble is attended to, but the film has been returned to a portion just shown, and once more I see my grandfather rubbing his bearded cheek, pondering my father's character. It is difficult to get back into the picture once more and forget myself, but as my mother giggles at my father's words, the darkness drowns me.

My father and mother depart from the house, my father shaking hands with my grandfather once more, out of some unknown uneasiness. I stir uneasily also, slouched in the hard chair of the theatre. Where is the older uncle, my mother's older brother? He is studying in his bedroom upstairs, studying for his final examinations at the College of the City of New York, having been dead of lobar pneumonia for the last twenty-one years. My mother and father walk down the same quiet streets once more. My mother is holding my father's arm and telling him of the novel she has been reading and my father utters judgments of the characters as the plot is made clear to him. This is a habit which he very much enjoys, for he feels the utmost superiority and confidence when he is approving or condemning the behavior of other people. At times he feels moved to utter a brief "Ugh," whenever the story becomes what he would call sugary. My mother feels satisfied by the interest she has awakened; and she is showing my father how intelligent she is and how interesting.

They reach the avenue, and the streetcar leisurely arrives. They are going to Coney Island this afternoon, although my mother really considers such pleasures inferior. She had made up her mind to indulge only in a walk on the boardwalk and a pleasant dinner, avoiding the riotous amusements as being beneath the dignity of so dignified a couple.

My father tells my mother how much money he has made in the week just past, exaggerating an amount which need not have been exaggerated. But my father has always felt that actualities somehow fall short, no matter how fine they are. Suddenly I begin to weep. The determined old lady who sits next to me in the theatre is annoyed and looks at me with an angry face, and being intimidated, I stop. I drag out my handkerchief and dry my face, licking the drop which has fallen near my lips. Meanwhile I have missed something, for here are my father and mother alighting from the streetcar at the last stop, Coney island.

3

They walk toward the boardwalk and my mother commands my father to inhale the pungent air from the sea. They both breathe in deeply, both of them laughing as they do so. They have in common a great interest in health, although my father is strong and husky, and my mother is frail. They are both full of theories about what is good to eat and not good to eat, and sometimes have heated discussions about it, the whole matter ending in my father's announcement, made with a scornful bluster, that you have to die sooner or later anyway. On the boardwalk's flagpole, the American flag is pulsing in an intermittent wind from the sea.

My father and mother go to the rail of the boardwalk and look down on the beach where a good many bathers are casually walking about. A few are in the surf. A peanut-whistle pierces the air with its pleasant and active whine, and my father goes to buy peanuts. My mother remains at the rail and stares at the ocean. The ocean seems merry to her; it pointedly sparkles and again and again the pony waves are released. She notices the children digging in the wet sand, and the bathing costumes of the girls who are her own age. My father returns with the peanuts. Overhead the sun's lightning strikes and strikes, but neither of them are at all aware of it. The boardwalk is full of people dressed in their Sunday clothes and casually strolling. The tide does not reach as far as the boardwalk, and the strollers would feel no danger if it did. My father and mother lean on the rail of the boardwalk and absently stare at the ocean. The ocean is becoming rough; the waves come in slowly, tugging strength from far back. The moment before they somersault, the moment when they arch their backs so beautifully, showing white veins in the green and black, that moment is intolerable. They finally crack, dashing fiercely upon the sand, actually driving, full force downward, against it, bouncing upward and forward, and at last petering out into a small stream of bubbles which slides up the beach and then is recalled. The sun overhead does not disturb my father and my mother. They gaze idly at the ocean, scarcely interested in its harshness. But I stare at the terrible sun which breaks up sight, and the fatal merciless passionate ocean. I forget my parents. I stare fascinated, and finally, shocked by their indifference, I burst out weeping once more. The old lady next to me pats my shoulder and says "There, there, young man, all of this is only a movie, only a movie"—but I look up once more at the terrifying sun and the terrifying ocean, and being unable to control my tears I get up and go to the men's room, stumbling over the feet of the other people seated in my row.

4

When I return, feeling as if I had just awakened in the morning sick for lack of sleep, several hours have apparently passed and my parents are riding on the merry-go-round. My father is on a black horse, my mother on a white one, and they seem to be making an eternal circuit for the single purpose of snatching the nickel rings which are attached to an arm of one of the posts. A hand organ is playing; it is inseparable from the ceaseless circling of the merry-go-round.

For a moment is seems that they will never get off the carousel, for it will never stop, and I feel as if I were looking down from the fiftieth story of a building. But at length they do get off; even the hand-organ has ceased for a moment. There is a sudden and sweet stillness, as if the achievement of so much motion.* My mother has acquired only two rings, my father, however, ten of them, although it was my mother who really wanted them.

They walk on along the boardwalk as the afternoon descends by imperceptible degrees into the incredible violet of dusk. Everything fades into a relaxed glow, even the ceaseless murmuring from the beach. They look for a place to have dinner. My father suggests the best restaurant on the boardwalk and my mother demurs, according to her principles of economy and housewifeliness.

However they do go to the best place, asking for a table near the window so that they can look out upon the boardwalk and the mobile ocean. My father feels omnipotent as he places a quarter in the waiter's hand in asking for a table. The place is crowded and here too there is music, this time from a kind of string-trio. My father orders with a fine confidence.

As their dinner goes on, my father tells of his plans for the future and my mother shows with expressive face how interested she is, and how impressed. My father becomes exultant, lifted up by the waltz that is being played, and his own future begins to intoxicate him. My father tells my mother that he is going to expand his business, for there is a great deal of money to be made. He wants to settle down. After all, he is twenty-nine, he has lived by himself since his thirteenth year, he is making more and more money, and he is envious of his friends when he visits them in the security of their homes, surrounded, it seems, by the calm domestic pleasures, and by delightful children, and then as the waltz reaches the moment when the dancers all swing madly, then, then with awful daring, then he asks my mother to marry him, although awkwardly enough and puzzled as to how he had arrived at the question, and she, to make the whole business worse, begins to cry, and my father looks nervously about, not knowing at all what to do now, and my mother says: "It's all I've wanted from the first moment I saw you," sobbing, and he finds all of this very difficult, scarcely to his taste, scarcely as he thought it would be, on his long walks over Brooklyn Bridge in the revery of a fine cigar and it was then, at that point, that I stood up in the theatre and shouted: "Don't do it! It's not too late to change your minds, both of you. Nothing good will come of it, only remorse, hatred, scandal, and two children whose characters are monstrous." The whole audience turned to look at me, annoyed, the usher came hurrying down the aisle flashing his searchlight, and the old lady next to me tugged me down into my seat, saying: "Be quiet. You'll be put out, and you paid thirty-five cents to come in." And so I shut my eyes because I could not bear to see what was happening. I sat there quietly.

* This sentence was omitted from the revised version.

5

But after awhile I begin to take brief glimpses and at length I watch again with thirsty interest, like a child who tries to maintain his sulk when he is offered the bribe of candy. My parents are now having their picture taken in a photographer's booth along the boardwalk. The place is shadowed in the mauve light which is apparently necessary. The camera is set to the side on its tripod and looks like a Martian man. The photographer is instructing my parents in how to pose. My father has his arm over my mother's shoulder, and both of them smile emphatically. The photographer brings my mother a bouquet of flowers to hold in her hand, but she holds it at the wrong angle. Then the photographer covers himself with the black cloth which drapes the camera, and all that one sees of him is one protruding arm and the hand with which he holds tightly to the rubber ball which he squeezes when the picture is taken. But he is not satisfied with their appearance. He feels that somehow there is something wrong in their pose. Again and again he comes out from his hiding place with new directions. Each suggestion merely makes matters worse. My father is becoming impatient. They try a seated pose. The photographer explains that he has his pride, he wants to make beautiful pictures, he is not merely interested in all of this for the money. My father says: "Hurry up, will you? We haven't got all night." But the photographer only scurries about apologetically, issuing new directions. The photographer charms me, and I approve of him with all my heart, for I know exactly how he feels, and as he criticizes each revised pose according to some obscure idea of rightness, I become quite hopeful. But then my father says angrily: "Come on, you've had enough time, we're not going to wait any longer." And the photographer, sighing unhappily, goes back into the black covering, and holds out his hand, saying: "One, two, three, Now!", and the picture is taken, with my father's smile turned to a grimace and my mother's bright and false. It takes a few minutes for the picture to be developed and as my parents sit in the curious light they become depressed.

6

They have passed a fortune-teller's booth and my mother wishes to go in, but my father does not. They begin to argue about it. My mother becomes stubborn, my father once more impatient. What my father would like to do now is walk off and leave my mother there, but he knows that that would never do. My mother refuses to budge. She is near tears, but she feels an uncontrollable desire to hear what the palm-reader will say. My father consents angrily and they both go into the booth which is, in a way, like the photographer's, since it is draped in black cloth and its light is colored and shadowed. The place is too warm, and my father keeps saying that this is all nonsense, pointing to the crystal ball on the table. The fortune-teller, a short, fat woman garbed in robes supposedly exotic, comes into the room and greets them, speaking with an accent. But suddenly my father feels that the whole thing is intolerable; he tugs at my mother's arm but my mother refuses to budge. And then, in terrible anger, my father lets go of my mother's arm and strides out, leaving my mother stunned. She makes a movement as if to go after him, but the fortune-teller holds her and begs her not to do so, and I in my seat in the darkness am shocked and horrified. I feel as if I were walking a tight-rope one hundred feet over a circus audience and suddenly the rope is showing signs of breaking, and I get up from my seat and begin to shout once more the first words I can think of to communicate my terrible fear, and once more the usher comes hurrying down the aisle flashing his searchlight, and the old lady pleads with me, and the shocked audience has turned to stare at me, and I keep shouting: "What are they doing? Don't they know what they are doing? Why doesn't my mother go after my father and beg him not to be angry? If she does not do that, what will she do? Doesn't my father know what he is doing?" But the usher has seized my arm, and is dragging me away, and as he does so, he says: "What are *you* doing? Don't you know you can't do things like this, you can't do whatever you want to do, even if other people aren't about? You will be sorry if you do not do what you should do. You can't carry on like this, it is not right, you will find that out soon enough, everything you do matters too much," and as he said that, dragging me through the lobby of the theatre, into the cold light, I woke up into the bleak winter morning of my twenty-first birthday, the window-sill shining with its lip of snow, and the morning already begun.

Julio Cortázar (1914–   )

Literature in Latin America is experiencing a new burst of energy which has lifted it from obscurity into international importance. As Jean Franco says, "At the moment when many European countries are going through a dead period in the novel, the genre has attained totally new dimensions in Spanish America."

A major element of this quickening is "magic realism." This term was first used in the late forties to describe a new kind of writing in Spanish America that went beyond regionalism, social realism, and imitation of European literary modes. Magic realism combines reality and fantasy, sometimes by way of folktales and supernaturalism or myth, and sometimes by way of purely intellectual constructs that express the disorientation of modern culture. Although the language can be beautifully lyrical, the imagery is often grotesque or surreal. Time and space are distorted, the vision is frequently apocalyptic. Among the magic realists are Jorge Luis Borges, Gabriel García Márquez, Alejo Carpentier, Carlos Fuentes, and Julio Cortázar. Cortázar has taken one strand of magic realism and in novels and short stories like "Axolōtl" has carried it to an unusual extreme, where it transects some aspects of antirealist fiction in the United States.

Cortázar was born in 1914 in Brussels of Argentine parentage. He grew up in Buenos Aires. At the age of twenty he took a post as provincial teacher and there began his long and deliberate apprenticeship as a writer. He was especially influenced by Poe, whose work he spent two years translating; William Faulkner, whose influence has been great throughout Latin America; and Borges, who befriended Cortázar and helped to promote his career. In 1941, Cortázar published a book of sonnets but nothing after that until 1949, when *Los Reyes*, a dramatic prose poem based on the legend of the minotaur, came out. In 1951 he moved permanently to Paris. Three volumes of short stories appeared in the fifties, one of which was the basis of the movie *Blow Up*. His first novel, *Los Premios,* came out in 1960. His most acclaimed work, *Rayuela* (1963), which was translated as *Hopscotch,* is in the antinovel tradition. Of it Jean Franco says that "the entire form of the book is a questioning of literature and . . . art in its relation to reality" and that "it represents the disintegration of all that constitutes culture and morality, and the demonstration of the conventional nature of thought, action, and literary activity.'' He has since published more stories and several novels in the same vein.

In an interview Cortázar said of his stories, ''They're charms, they're a way out, but above all, they're exorcisms. Many of these stories . . . are purgative, a sort of self-analysis.'' Although in view of his later work, his stories ''may seem like games,'' Cortázar said,

> When I wrote them I didn't think of them that way at all. They were glimpses, dimensions, or hints of possibilities that terrified or fascinated me and that I had to exhaust by working them off in the story.

''Sometimes,'' he says, ''It takes six months of tension to produce a long story that comes out in a single night. . . . The best are packed full of a sort of explosive charge.''

Whether ''Axolōtl'' is a glimpse or a possibility, fascinating or terrifying, may depend on the reader. As the narrator himself, through an act of perception, becomes the axolōtl, so may the reader. The act of apprehending (to grasp mentally) is one and the same as the act of being apprehended (taken into custody). For some readers, this may seem a bewitching game; for others, it may create a moment of existential terror. This story carries the literary trend toward subjectivity to its furthest reaches.

Axolōtl

There was a time when I thought a great deal about the axolōtls. I went to see them in the aquarium at the Jardin des Plantes[1] and stayed for hours watching them, observing their immobility, their faint movements. Now I am an axolōtl.

I got to them by chance one spring morning when Paris was spreading its peacock tail after a wintry Lent. I was heading down the boulevard Port-Royal, then I took Saint-Marcel and L'Hôpital and saw green among all that grey and remembered the lions. I was friend of the lions and panthers, but had never gone into the dark, humid building that was the aquarium. I left my bike against the gratings and went to look at the tulips. The lions were sad and ugly and my panther was asleep. I decided on the aquarium, looked obliquely at banal fish until, unexpectedly, I hit it off with the axolōtls. I stayed watching them for an hour and left, unable to think of anything else.

In the library at Sainte-Geneviève, I consulted a dictionary and learned that axolōtls are the larval stage (provided with gills) of a species of salamander of the genus Ambystoma. That they were Mexican I knew already by looking at them and their little pink Aztec faces and the placard at the top of the tank. I read that specimens of them had been found in Africa capable of living on dry land during the periods of drought, and continuing their life under water when the rainy season came. I found their Spanish name, *ajolote,* and the mention that they were edible, and that their oil was used (no longer used, it said) like cod-liver oil.

[1] In Paris.

I didn't care to look up any of the specialized works, but the next day I went back to the Jardin des Plantes. I began to go every morning, morning and afternoon some days. The aquarium guard smiled perplexedly taking my ticket. I would lean up against the iron bar in front of the tanks and set to watching them. There's nothing strange in this, because after the first minute I knew that we were linked, that something infinitely lost and distant kept pulling us together. It had been enough to detain me that first morning in front of the sheet of glass where some bubbles rose through the water. The axolōtls huddled on the wretched narrow (only I can know how narrow and wretched) floor of moss and stone in the tank. There were nine specimens, and the majority pressed their heads against the glass, looking with their eyes of gold at whoever came near them. Disconcerted, almost ashamed, I felt it a lewdness to be peering at these silent and immobile figures heaped at the bottom of the tank. Mentally I isolated one, situated on the right and somewhat apart from the others, to study it better. I saw a rosy little body, translucent (I thought of those Chinese figurines of milky glass), looking like a small lizard about six inches long, ending in a fish's tail of extraordinary delicacy, the most sensitive part of our body. Along the back ran a transparent fin which joined with the tail, but what obsessed me was the feet, of the slenderest nicety, ending in tiny fingers with minutely human nails. And then I discovered its eyes, its face. Inexpressive features, with no other trait save the eyes, two orifices, like brooches, wholly of transparent gold, lacking any life but looking, letting themselves be penetrated by my look, which seemed to travel past the golden level and lose itself in a diaphanous interior mystery. A very slender black halo ringed the eye and etched it onto the pink flesh, onto the rosy stone of the head, vaguely triangular, but with curved and irregular sides which gave it a total likeness to a statuette corroded by time. The mouth was masked by the triangular plane of the face, its considerable size would be guessed only in profile; in front a delicate crevice barely slit the lifeless stone. On both sides of the head where the ears should have been, there grew three tiny sprigs red as coral, a vegetal outgrowth, the gills, I suppose. And they were the only thing quick about it; every ten or fifteen seconds the sprig pricked up stiffly and again subsided. Once in a while a foot would barely move, I saw the diminutive toes poise mildly on the moss. It's that we don't enjoy moving a lot, and the tank is so cramped—we barely move in any direction and we're hitting one of the others with our tail or our head—difficulties arise, fights, tiredness. The time feels like it's less if we stay quietly.

It was their quietness that made me lean toward them fascinated the first time I saw the axolōtls. Obscurely I seemed to understand their secret will, to abolish space and time with an indifferent immobility. I knew better later; the gill contraction, the tentative reckoning of the delicate feet on the stones, the abrupt swimming (some of them swim with a simple undulation of the body) proved to me that they were capable of escaping that mineral lethargy in which they spent whole hours. Above all else, their eyes obsessed me. In the standing tanks on either side of them, different fishes showed me the simple stupidity of their handsome eyes so similar to our own. The eyes of the axolōtls spoke to me of the presence of a different life, of another way of seeing. Glueing my face to the glass (the guard would cough fussily once in a while), I tried to see better those diminutive golden points, that entrance to the infinitely slow and remote world of these rosy creatures. It was useless to tap with one finger on the glass directly in front of their faces; they never gave the least reaction. The golden eyes continued burning with their soft, terrible light; they continued looking at me from an unfathomable depth which made me dizzy.

And nevertheless they were close. I knew it before this, before being an axolōtl. I learned it the day I came near them for the first time. The anthropomorphic features of a monkey reveal the reverse of what most people believe, the distance that is traveled from them to us. The absolute lack of similarity between axolōtls and human beings proved to me that my recognition was valid, that I was not propping myself up with easy analogies. Only the little hands . . . But an eft, the common newt, has such hands also, and we are not at all alike. I think it was the axolōtls' heads, that triangular pink shape with the tiny eyes of gold. That looked and knew. That laid the claim. They were not *animals*.

It would seem easy, almost obvious, to fall into mythology. I began seeing in the axolōtls a metamorphosis which did not succeed in revoking a mysterious humanity. I imagined them aware, slaves of their bodies, condemned infinitely to the silence of the abyss, to a hopeless meditation. Their blind gaze, the diminutive gold disc without expression and nonetheless terribly shining, went through me like a message: "Save us, save us." I caught myself mumbling words of advice, conveying childish hopes. They continued to look at me, immobile; from time to time the rosy branches of the gills stiffened. In that instant I felt a muted pain; perhaps they were seeing me, attracting my strength to penetrate into the impenetrable thing of their lives. They were not human beings, but I had found in no animal such a profound relation with myself. The axolōtls were like witnesses of something, and at times like horrible judges. I felt ignoble in front of them; there was such a terrifying purity in those transparent eyes. They were larvas, but larva means disguise and also phantom. Behind those Aztec faces, without expression but of an implacable cruelty, what semblance was awaiting its hour?

I was afraid of them. I think that had it not been for feeling the proximity of other visitors and the guard, I would not have been bold enough to remain alone with them. "You eat them alive with your eyes, hey," the guard said, laughing; he likely thought I was a little cracked. What he didn't notice was that it was they devouring me slowly with their eyes, in a cannabalism of gold. At any distance from the aquarium, I had only to think of them, it was as though I were being affected from a distance. It got to the point that I was going every day, and at night I thought of them immobile in the darkness, slowly putting a hand out which immediately encountered another. Perhaps their eyes could see in the dead of night, and for them the day continued indefinitely. The eyes of axolōtls have no lids.

I know now that there was nothing strange, that that had to occur. Leaning over in front of the tank each morning, the recognition was greater. They were suffering, every fiber of my body reached toward that stifled pain, that stiff torment at the bottom of the tank. They were lying in wait for something, a remote dominion destroyed, an age of liberty when the world had been that of the axolōtls. Not possible that such a terrible expression which was attaining the overthrow of that forced blankness on their stone faces should carry any message other than one of pain, proof of that eternal sentence, of that liquid hell they were undergoing. Hopelessly, I wanted to prove to myself that my own sensibility was projecting a nonexistent consciousness upon the axolōtls. They and I knew. So there was nothing strange in what happened. My face was pressed against the glass of the aquarium, my eyes were attempting once more to penetrate the mystery of those eyes of gold without iris, without pupil. I saw from very close up the face of an axolōtl immobile next to the glass. No transition and no surprise, I saw my face against the glass, I saw it on the outside of the tank, I saw it on the other side of the glass. Then my face drew back and I understood.

Only one thing was strange: to go on thinking as usual, to know. To realize that was, for the first moment, like the horror of a man buried alive awaking to his fate. Outside, my face came close to the glass again, I saw my mouth, the lips compressed with the effort of understanding the axolōtls. I was an axolōtl and now I knew instantly that no understanding was possible. He was outside the aquarium, his thinking was a thinking outside the tank. Recognizing him, being him himself, I was an axolōtl and in my world. The horror began—I learned in the same moment—of believing myself prisoner in the body of an axolōtl, metamorphosed into him with my human mind intact, buried alive in an axolōtl, condemned to move lucidly among unconscious creatures. But that stopped when a foot just grazed my face, when I moved just a little to one side and saw an axolōtl next to me who was looking at me, and understood that he knew also, no communication possible, but very clearly. Or I was also in him, or all of us were thinking humanlike, incapable of expression, limited to the golden splendor of our eyes looking at the face of the man pressed against the aquarium.

He returned many times, but he comes less often now. Weeks pass without his showing up. I saw him yesterday, he looked at me for a long time and left briskly. It seemed to me that he was not so much interested in us any more, that he was coming out of habit. Since the only thing I do is think, I could think about him a lot. It occurs to me that at the beginning we continued to communicate, that he felt more than ever one with the mystery which was claiming him. But the bridges were broken between him and me, because what was his obsession is now an axolōtl, alien to his human life. I think that at the beginning I was capable of returning to him in a certain way—ah, only in a certain way—and of keeping awake his desire to know us better. I am an axolōtl for good now, and if I think like a man it's only because every axolōtl thinks like a man inside his rosy stone resemblance. I believe that all this succeeded in communicating something to him in those first days, when I was still he. And in this final solitude to which he no longer comes, I console myself by thinking that perhaps he is going to write a story about us, that, believing he's making up a story, he's going to write all this about axolōtls.

Heinrich Böll (1917–   )

Heinrich Böll was born in Cologne of Catholic parents. His youth was overshadowed by the emergence of Hitler's regime, and he was forced to serve in the Nazi infantry from 1939 to 1945. It was the experience of World War II and of postwar Germany that provided him with his subjects when he began to write, and his was the strongest literary voice to arise from Germany of the 1950s. According to W. B. Fleishmann, the books and plays of that period record "the brutalities of racial persecution, the lethal vacuity of *Wehrmacht* life, and the grim aspects of daily existence under the Nazis, which allows the full horror of recent German existence to emerge. . . ." In his attacks on the corruptions and spiritual sterility of postwar bourgeois society he was no more sparing.

Böll's experiments with language, his use of symbolism, his mordant satire—though often tempered by a playful and wistful strain—all constitute a continuous and major contribution to experimental literature of the continent over the past quarter century. Among his more important works that have been translated into English are *Acquainted with the Night* (1954), *Traveller, If You Come to Spa* (1956), *The Train Was on Time* (1956), *Billiards at Half-Past Nine* (1962), *The Clown* (1965), *18 Stories* (1966), and *End of a Mission* (1968). His works brought him the Nobel Prize for Literature in 1972, the citation acknowledging his part in aiding the "renewal of German literature." In recent years he has been somewhat eclipsed in vogue by newer German writers like Günter Grass and Peter Handke, but he still ranks preeminent among those experimental writers who have tried with high seriousness to make the short story an expressive vehicle for the mixed horror and absurdity of our time.

"Like a Bad Dream" is a kind of *Macbeth* story in that a strong and decisive wife steels her timid and vacillating husband to an evil action. But in this instance the action is not murder; it is the petty corruption of a "kickback" in a business deal. The tone of the story is everyday, matter-of-fact, mundane, as if to suggest that there is nothing unusual about this little crime. That is, of course, Böll's point: corruption in our day, especially in the business world, is part of the routine. The story brings to mind Hannah Arendt's memorable phrase, "the banality of evil." Though Arendt was referring to the way the Nazi death-camp operators treated their ghastly work as a "job" like any other, to be done with virtuous efficiency, we can here see the same moral indifference. The corruption is "like a bad dream" to the narrator, but he is implicated in an evil he does nothing to fight. Everything is sacrificed to convention—to pleasing the boss. Bertha squeezed the mayonnaise onto the appetizers "very nicely," put dinner on the table "very nicely too," and made it all "so attractive and yet so natural." That word "natural" is heavy with irony. And the narrator continually emphasizes his wife's hands even as hands figure unforgettably in *Macbeth*. After the murder, Macbeth cries:

> Will all great Neptune's ocean wash this blood
> Clean from my hand? No; this my hand will rather
> The multitudinous seas incarnadine,
> Making the green one red.

But here hands serve as less intense symbols: "I looked at Bertha's small, brown hands on the steering wheel, so confident and quiet. Hands, I thought, that sign checks and squeeze mayonnaise tubes. . . ." Tragedy has become banality.

Like a Bad Dream

That evening we had invited the Zumpens over for dinner, nice people; it was through my father-in-law that we had got to know them: ever since we have been married he has helped me to meet people who can be useful to me in business, and Zumpen can be useful: he is chairman of a committee which places contracts for large housing projects, and I have married into the excavating business.

I was tense that evening, but Bertha, my wife, reassured me. "The fact," she said, "that he's coming at all is promising. Just try and get the conversation round to the contract. You know it's tomorrow they're going to be awarded."

I stood looking through the net curtains of the glass front door, waiting for Zumpen. I smoked, ground the cigarette butts under my foot, and shoved them under the mat. Next I took up a position at the bathroom window and stood there wondering why Zumpen had accepted the invitation; he couldn't be that interested in having dinner with us, and the fact that the big contract I was involved in was going to be awarded tomorrow must have made the whole thing as embarrassing to him as it was to me.

I thought about the contract too: it was a big one, I would make 20,000 marks on the deal, and I wanted the money.

Bertha had decided what I was to wear: a dark jacket, trousers a shade lighter and a conservative tie. That's the kind of thing she learned at home, and at boarding school from the nuns. Also what to offer guests: when to pass the cognac, and when the vermouth, how to arrange dessert. It is comforting to have a wife who knows all about such things.

But Bertha was tense too: as she put her hands on my shoulders, they touched my neck, and I felt her thumbs damp and cold against it.

"It's going to be all right," she said, "You'll get the contract."

"Christ," I said, "it means 20,000 marks to me, and you know how we need the money."

"One should never," she said gently, "mention Christ's name in connection with money!"

A dark car drew up in front of our house, a make I didn't recognize, but it looked Italian. "Take it easy," Bertha whispered, "wait till they've rung, let them stand there for a couple of seconds, then walk slowly to the door and open it."

I watched Mr. and Mrs. Zumpen come up the steps: he is slender and tall, with graying temples, the kind of man who fifty years ago would have been known as a "ladies' man"; Mrs. Zumpen is one of those thin dark women who always make me think of lemons. I could tell from Zumpen's face that it was a frightful bore for him to have dinner with us.

Then the doorbell rang, and I waited one second, two seconds, walked slowly to the door and opened it.

"Well," I said, "how nice of you to come!"

Cognac glasses in hand, we went from room to room in our apartment, which the Zumpens wanted to see. Bertha stayed in the kitchen to squeeze some mayonnaise out of a tube onto the appetizers; she does this very nicely: hearts, loops, little houses. The Zumpens complimented us on our apartment; they exchanged smiles when they saw the big desk in my study, at that moment it seemed a bit too big even to me.

Zumpen admired a small rococo cabinet, a wedding present from my grandmother, and a baroque Madonna in our bedroom.

By the time we got back to the dining room, Bertha had dinner on the table; she had done this very nicely too, it was all so attractive yet so natural, and dinner was pleasant and relaxed. We talked about movies and books, about the recent elections, and Zumpen praised the assortment of cheeses, and Mrs. Zumpen praised the coffee and the pastries. Then we showed the Zumpens our honeymoon pictures: photographs of the Breton coast, Spanish donkeys, and street scenes from Casablanca.

After that we had some more cognac, and when I stood up to get the box with the photos of the time when we were engaged, Bertha gave me a sign, and I didn't get the box. For two minutes there was absolute silence, because we had nothing more to talk about, and we all thought about the contract; I thought of the 20,000 marks, and it struck me that I could deduct the bottle of cognac from my income tax. Zumpen looked at his watch and said: "Too bad, it's ten o'clock; we have to go. It's been such a pleasant evening!" And Mrs. Zumpen said: "It was really delightful, and I hope you'll come to us one evening."

"We would love to," Bertha said, and we stood around for another half-minute, all thinking again about the contract, and I felt Zumpen was waiting for me to take him aside and bring up the subject. But I didn't. Zumpen kissed Bertha's hand, and I went ahead, opened the doors, and held the car door open for Mrs. Zumpen down below.

"Why," said Bertha gently, "didn't you mention the contract to him? You know it's going to be awarded tomorrow."

"Well," I said, "I didn't know how to bring the conversation round to it."

"Now look," she said in a quiet voice, "you could have used any excuse to ask him into your study, that's where you should have talked to him. You must have noticed how interested he is in art. You ought to have said: I have an eighteenth-century crucifix in there you might like to have a look at, and then . . ."

I said nothing, and she sighed and tied on her apron. I followed her into the kitchen; we put the rest of the appetizers back in the refrigerator, and I crawled about on the floor looking for the top of the mayonnaise tube. I put away the remains of the cognac, counted the cigars: Zumpen had smoked only one. I emptied the ashtrays, ate another pastry, and looked to see if there was any coffee left in the pot. When I went back to the kitchen, Bertha was standing there with the car key in her hand.

"What's up?" I asked.

"We have to go over there, of course," she said.

"Over where?"

"To the Zumpens," she said, "where do you think?"

"It's nearly half past ten."

"I don't care if it's midnight," Bertha said, "all I know is, there's 20,000 marks involved. Don't imagine they're squeamish."

She went into the bathroom to get ready, and I stood behind her watching her wipe her mouth and draw in new outlines, and for the first time I noticed how wide and primitive that mouth is. When she tightened the knot of my tie I could have kissed her, the way I always used to when she fixed my tie, but I didn't.

Downtown the cafés and restaurants were brightly lit. People were sitting outside on the terraces, and the light from the street lamps was caught in the silver ice-cream dishes and ice buckets. Bertha gave me an encouraging look; but she stayed in the car when we stopped in front of the Zumpens' house, and I pressed the bell at once and was surprised how quickly the door was opened. Mrs. Zumpen did not seem surprised to see me; she had on some black lounging pajamas with loose full trousers embroidered with yellow flowers, and this made me think more than ever of lemons.

"I beg your pardon," I said, "I would like to speak to your husband."

"He's gone out again," she said, "he'll be back in half an hour."

In the hall I saw a lot of Madonnas, gothic and baroque, even rococo Madonnas, if there is such a thing.

"I see," I said, "well then, if you don't mind, I'll come back in half an hour."

Bertha had bought an evening paper; she was reading it and smoking, and when I sat down beside her she said: "I think you could have talked about it to her too."

"But how do you know he wasn't there?"

"Because I know he is at the Gaffel Club playing chess, as he does every Wednesday evening at this time."

"You might have told me that earlier."

"Please try and understand," said Bertha, folding the newspaper. "I am trying to help you, I want you to find out for yourself how to deal with such things. All we had to do was call up Father and he would have settled the whole thing for you with one phone call, but I want you to get the contract on your own."

"All right," I said, "then what'll we do: wait here half an hour, or go up right away and have a talk with her?"

"We'd better go up right away," said Bertha.

We got out of the car and went up in the elevator together. "Life," said Bertha, "consists of making compromises and concessions."

Mrs. Zumpen was no more surprised now than she had been earlier, when I had come alone. She greeted us, and we followed her into her husband's study. Mrs. Zumpen brought some cognac, poured it out, and before I could say anything about the contract she pushed a yellow folder toward me: "Housing Project Fir Tree Haven," I read, and looked up in alarm at Mrs. Zumpen, at Bertha, but they both smiled, and Mrs. Zumpen said: "Open the folder," and I opened it; inside was another one, pink, and on this I read: "Housing Project Fir Tree Haven—Excavation Work." I opened this too, saw my estimate lying there on top of the pile; along the upper edge someone had written in red: "Lowest bid."

I could feel myself flushing with pleasure, my heart thumping, and I thought of the 20,000 marks.

"Christ," I said softly, and closed the file, and this time Bertha forgot to rebuke me.

"*Prost,*" said Mrs. Zumpen with a smile, "let's drink to it then."

We drank, and I stood up and said: "It may seem rude of me, but perhaps you'll understand that I would like to go home now."

"I understand perfectly," said Mrs. Zumpen, "there's just one small item to be taken care of." She took the file, leafed through it, and said: "Your price per square meter is thirty pfennigs below that of the next-lowest bidder. I suggest you raise your price by fifteen pfennigs: that way you'll still be the lowest and you'll have made an extra four thousand five hundred marks. Come on, do it now!" Bertha took her pen out of her purse and offered it to me, but I was in too much of a turmoil to write; I gave the file to Bertha and watched her alter the price with a steady hand, re-write the total, and hand the file back to Mrs. Zumpen.

"And now," said Mrs. Zumpen, "just one more little thing. Get out your check book and write a check for three thousand marks; it must be a cash check and endorsed by you."

She had said this to me, but it was Bertha who pulled our check book out of her purse and made out the check.

"It won't be covered," I said in a low voice.

"When the contract is awarded, there will be an advance, and then it will be covered," said Mrs. Zumpen.

Perhaps I failed to grasp what was happening at the time. As we went down in the elevator, Bertha said she was happy, but I said nothing.

Bertha chose a different way home, we drove through quiet residential districts, I saw lights in open windows, people sitting on balconies drinking wine; it was a clear, warm night.

"I suppose the check was for Zumpen?" was all I said, softly, and Bertha replied, just as softly: "Of course."

I looked at Bertha's small, brown hands on the steering wheel, so confident and quiet. Hands, I thought, that sign checks and squeeze mayonnaise tubes, and I looked higher—at her mouth, and still felt no desire to kiss it.

That evening I did not help Bertha put the car away in the garage, nor did I help her with the dishes. I poured myself a large cognac, went up to my study, and sat down at my desk, which was much too big for me. I was wondering about something. I got up, went into the bedroom and looked at the baroque Madonna, but even there I couldn't put my finger on the thing I was wondering about.

The ringing of the phone interrupted my thoughts; I lifted the receiver and was not surprised to hear Zumpen's voice.

"Your wife," he said, "made a slight mistake. She raised the price by twenty-five pfennigs instead of fifteen."

I thought for a moment and then said: "That wasn't a mistake, she did it with my consent."

He was silent for a second or two, then said with a laugh: "So you had already discussed the various possibilities?"

"Yes," I said.

"All right, then make out another check for a thousand."

"Five hundred," I said, and I thought: It's like a bad dream—that's what it's like.

"Eight hundred," he said, and I said with a laugh: "Six hundred," and I knew, although I had no experience to go on, that he would now say seven hundred and fifty, and when he did I said "Yes" and hung up.

It was not yet midnight when I went downstairs and over to the car to give Zumpen the check; he was alone and laughed as I reached in to hand him the folded check. When I walked slowly back into the house, there was no sign of Bertha; she didn't appear when I went back into my study; she didn't appear when I went downstairs again for a glass of milk from the refrigerator, and I knew what she was thinking; she was thinking: he has to get over it, and I have to leave him alone; this is something he has to understand.

But I never did understand. It is beyond understanding.

Alain Robbe-Grillet (1922–   )

The fictional techniques and concerns of Alain Robbe-Grillet are an extension of his existential philosophy. According to Bruce Morrissette, the existential author "must, to express the content of consciousness, attach himself to objects, reject-ing the verbiage of psychological analysis, ideological commentary, and omni-scient rumination." This is what Robbe-Grillet does. His purpose is to render not concepts, or abstract thoughts, but percepts, or the sensory building blocks of experience. For some critics, he is the most original, innovative and influential exponent of "antirealist" fiction.

His approach to point of view and narrative voice is at the heart of his fiction. He attempts to eliminate the narrative voice that analyzes, summarizes, and evalu-ates and that controls the reader's moral and psychological relation to the story. (See Introduction, pp. 2–3.) By confining the reader to the character's sense im-pressions rendered as objectively as possible, he seeks to collapse the distance between the reader and the material of the story. The reader perceives not the character but what the character perceives. Personality (often sadomasochistic in Robbe-Grille) must be inferred from the sense impressions. No motives, ideas, generalities, or values are allowed into the work. Even the action must be inferred from the recorded sensations of the actor. The reader is locked into the reality of the character. In discussing Robbe-Grillet's novel *Jealousy* (1959), Wayne Booth writes that

The effect of such a novel is of an extended dramatic monologue, an intense expression of one quality of mind and soul, deliberately not judged, deliberately left unplaced, isolated from the rest of human experience. It is, thus, less closely related to the traditional forms of fiction than to lyric poetry.

Robbe-Grillet was born in Brest, France, in 1922. His first occupation was as an agronomist, and from this perhaps he learned the skills of minute observation we see in his work. He abandoned agronomy for literature, and his first novel, *The Erasers,* appeared in 1953. In 1961, his film script "Last Year at Marienbad" was produced by Resnais and became an instant source of controversy. It was as startling and inaccessible to many viewers as his novels and stories have been to many readers. But it, like the fiction, forged new possibilities of aesthetic excitement and meaning. Some themes reappear throughout his work: psychosadism, uncertainty, accident.

The story we have included in this volume is a rendering of three children walking along the beach, a common setting for Robbe-Grillet who grew up on the Breton seacoast. The reader is placed at the center of a sensuous awareness that is focused on the children. Everything is rendered sharply and objectively: the tracks the children leave in the sand, the recurrent waves, the birds circling, the bell. Robbe-Grillet has eliminated all except the external objects. Yet there remains a sinister element, an unspoken threat as the awareness relentlessly tracks the children.

The Shore

Three children are walking along a beach. They walk side by side, holding each other by the hand. They are about the same height, and probably the same age: about twelve. The one in the center, nevertheless, is slightly shorter than the other two.

Except for these three children, the long shore is empty. The band of sand is fairly wide, unbroken, free of scattered rocks and water holes, sloping gently from the steep cliff, which seems unending, to the sea.

The weather is fine. The sun illuminates the yellow sand with a violent, vertical light. There is not a single cloud in the sky. Nor is there any wind. The water is blue, calm, without a trace of a swell coming in from the distance, although the beach faces the open sea and the horizon.

But at regular intervals, a quick wave, always the same, originating a few yards from the shore, suddenly rises and immediately breaks, always along the same line. The water does not seem to move forward, and then rush back; it is rather as if the whole movement occurred in a stationary position. The swelling of the water produces first a shallow trough, along the side next to the shore, and the wave draws back slightly, with a rustling noise of gravel rolling; then it bursts and spreads milkily over the slope of the beach's edge, but only to recover the space which it had lost. At most, a stronger surge rises, here and there, to moisten, for a moment, a few extra inches of sand.

And all is again motionless, the sea, flat and blue, stationary at precisely the same height on the yellow sand of the beach, on which the three children walk side by side.

They are blond, and almost the same color as the sand: their skin a little darker, their hair a little lighter. All three are dressed in the same way, short trousers and sleeveless shirts, both of a faded thick blue cloth. They are walking side by side, holding each other by the hand, in a straight line, parallel to the sea and parallel to the cliff, almost equidistant between the two, yet a little closer to the water. The sun, now at the zenith, throws no shadow at their feet.

In front of them the sand is absolutely unmarked, yellow and smooth from the rock cliff to the water. The children walk forward in a straight line, at a constant pace, without the slightest movement to either side, calmly and holding each other by the hand. Behind them the sand, barely damp, is marked by three lines of footprints left by their bare feet, three regular series of similar and equally spaced prints, clearly hollowed out, and without a seam.

The children look straight ahead. They never glance at the high cliff, on their left, or at the sea, with its little waves breaking periodically, in the other direction. Nor, even more certainly, do they turn around to look behind them at the space which they have covered. They continue on their way with a rapid and uniform step.

In front of them, a flock of sea birds walk briskly along the shore, just at the edge of the waves. They move parallel with the children, in the same direction, about a hundred yards farther on. But, as the birds do not move as fast as they, the children gain upon them. And while the sea constantly wipes out the starry tracks of the birds, the children's footsteps remain clearly inscribed in the barely damp sand, in which the three lines of footsteps grow longer and longer.

The depth of these footprints is unchanging: a little less than an inch. They are not deformed either by a crumbling of the edges or by an excessively deep impression of the heel, or of the toe. They appear as if punched out by machine in an upper, and more malleable, crust of the beach.

Thus their triple line extends, always farther, and seems at the same time to grow narrower, to slow down, to blend into a single line, which separates the beach into two bands, throughout its length, and which comes to an end in a tiny mechanical movement, far off, occurring as if in a stationary position: the alternate lifting and setting down of six bare feet.

But as the bare feet move farther along, they gain upon the birds. Not only do they cover the ground rapidly, but the relative distance which separates the two groups diminishes even faster, compared with the space already covered. Soon there is only the gap of a few steps between them. . . .

But, when the children finally seem about to catch up with the birds, there is a flapping of wings as the birds take flight, first one, then two, then ten. . . . And the whole flock, white and gray, describes a curve above the sea as it returns to light upon the sand and begins to walk quickly again, always in the same direction, just at the edge of the waves, about a hundred yards farther on.

At this distance, the movements of the water are almost imperceptible, except for a sudden change in color, every ten seconds, at the moment when the dazzling foam shines in the sunlight.

Heedless of the footprints that they continue to press so precisely into the bare sand, indifferent to the little waves on their right, to the birds—now flying, now walking—that advance before them, the three blond children walk along side by side, with a rapid and uniform step, holding each other by the hand.

Their three sunburned faces, darker than their hair, look alike. They have the same expression: serious, thoughtful, perhaps concerned. Their features are also identical, although, obviously, two of the children are boys and the third a girl. The girl's hair is just a little longer, a little bit more curly, and her limbs appear a shade more slender. But her clothes are exactly the same: short trousers and sleeveless shirt, both of a faded thick blue cloth.

The girl is at the far right, next to the sea. At her left walks the boy who is slightly less tall. The other boy, nearest the cliff, is as tall as the girl.

Before them extends the smooth, unbroken sand, as far as the eye can see. On their left rises the wall of brown rock, almost vertical, and seemingly unending. On their right, motionless and blue out to the horizon, is the flat surface of the water, bordered by a sudden hem, which immediately bursts and spreads out in white foam.

Then, ten seconds later, the wave which wells up hollows out again the same shallow trough, on the side next to the beach, with a rustling noise of gravel rolling.

The tiny wave unfurls; the milky foam again climbs up the slope of sand, recovering the few inches of lost space. During the silence that follows, the tolling of a bell, from very far away, reverberates dimly in the quiet air.

"There's the bell," says the smallest of the children, the boy who is walking in the middle.

But the noise of the gravel sucked in by the sea muffles the weak echoes of the bell. Only at the end of the wave cycle can a few sounds, distorted by the distance, be heard again.

"It's the first bell," says the tall boy.

The tiny wave unfurls, on their right.

When silence returns, they hear nothing further. The three blond children still walk at the same regular pace, holding each other by the hand. In front of them the flock of birds, only a few steps away, is suddenly overcome by a contagious excitement. The birds flap their wings and fly upward.

They describe the same curve above the sea, and return to light upon the sand and begin to walk quickly again, always in the same direction, just at the edge of the waves, about a hundred yards farther on.

"Maybe it isn't the first," says the small boy, "maybe we didn't hear the other one, before. . . ."

"We would have heard it the same as this one," the tall boy answers.

The children have not in any way changed their pace; and the same footprints, behind them, continue to appear, as they walk forward, under the six bare feet.

"We weren't as near before," says the girl.

After a moment, the taller of the two boys, the one next to the cliff, says:

"We still aren't near."

And all three walk on in silence.

They remain silent thus until the bell, still just as faint, sounds again in the quiet air. The taller of the boys says then, "There's the bell." The others make no answer.

The birds, as the children are about to overtake them, flap their wings and fly upward, first one, then two, then ten. . . .

Then the whole flock is again back upon the sand, moving along the shore, about a hundred yards ahead of the children.

The sea continually wipes out the starry tracks left by their feet. The children, on the other hand, who are walking closer to the cliff, side by side, holding each other by the hand, leave behind them deep prints, in a triple line which stretches out parallel to the seashore, down the long beach.

On the right, near the edge of the motionless, flat water, and always at the same spot, the same small wave wells up and breaks.

Gabriel García Márquez (1928–   )

The publication of *One Hundred Years of Solitude* not only heralded a major talent, Gabriel García Márquez, but also called the world's attention to the growing power, indeed primacy, of Latin American literature. There had been earlier acknowledged Hispanic masters; stories by two, Borges and Cortázar, appear in this book. But after *One Hundred Years of Solitude,* a large reading public recognized that something special was happening in Latin America. For at a time when many literatures seemed either repetitious or overly cerebral and contrived, this one was vital and rich and humane.

According to Jean Franco, this novel is as popular among Spanish speakers as is *Don Quixote,* which in its inventiveness and richness it resembles. In accounting for the book's popularity, John S. Brushwood says,

> Three general characteristics form the basis for its wide appeal. First, the author insists on the artist's right to invent his own reality. . . . Second, the book has . . . unusual people, fantasy, and plot suspense. Third, it is a very funny novel—a fact which does not make it a frivolous book, but a profound, humane one.

The novel chronicles the Buendia family, founders of the mythical town of Macondo in a country very like García Márquez's Colombia. The Buendias are proud and defiant figures, imaginative and obsessive. Each pursues his or her own obsession—knowledge, pleasure, memory, fame—but they share a pervading self-absorption and ultimate solitude. Although the vision is finally bleak, this is not at all a solemn book. Wondrous things happen to all the Buendias: one is always surrounded by butterflies; one has the tail of a pig; one survives a firing squad and spends the rest of his days making, melting, remaking goldfish; another expects surgery to be performed telepathically. Though clearly a satire of a people and a culture, the book is a modern myth of man's search for, in Franco's words, "individual authenticity within an unjust society."

The story that follows (in Spanish, *"La Prodigiosa tarde de Baltazar"*) shares many of the novel's concerns. It, too, is a tall tale and wonderfully inventive, and, despite its unhappy, even bitter, conclusion, it is very funny. But unlike the Buendias, Balthazar does not withdraw into narcissism. He is an artist, a maker of beautiful things which he shares with the world. However noble and generous he is in his art, he is proud and even foolish in his person. Mistreated by a commercial society, in order to save face he compounds misfortune to the point of disaster. Yet such a defeat is surely some kind of victory of the human spirit.

García Márquez was born in 1928 and after attending the University of Bogota worked as a newspaper reporter and film critic and began writing fiction. *One Hundred Years of Solitude* appeared in English in 1970; *The Autumn of the Patriarchs* followed in 1976. Two volumes of short stories have also been translated. Fearing that his life was in danger because of his antigovernment opinions, he sought refuge in Mexico in 1980.

Balthazar's Marvelous Afternoon

The cage was finished. Balthazar hung it under the eave, from force of habit, and when he finished lunch everyone was already saying that it was the most beautiful cage in the world. So many people came to see it that a crowd formed in front of the house, and Balthazar had to take it down and close the shop.

"You have to shave," Ursula, his wife, told him. "You look like a Capuchin."

"It's bad to shave after lunch," said Balthazar.

He had two weeks' growth, short, hard, and bristly hair like the mane of a mule, and the general expression of a frightened boy. But it was a false expression. In February he was thirty; he had been living with Ursula for four years, without marrying her and without having children, and life had given him many reasons to be on guard but none to be frightened. He did not even know that for some people the cage he had just made was the most beautiful one in the world. For him, accustomed to making cages since childhood, it had been hardly any more difficult than the others.

"Then rest for a while," said the woman. "With that beard you can't show yourself anywhere."

While he was resting, he had to get out of his hammock several times to show the cage to the neighbors. Ursula had paid little attention to it until then. She was annoyed because her husband had neglected the work of his carpenter's shop to devote himself entirely to the cage, and for two weeks had slept poorly, turning over and muttering incoherencies, and he hadn't thought of shaving. But her annoyance dissolved in the face of the finished cage. When Balthazar woke up from his nap, she had ironed his pants and a shirt; she had put them on a chair near the hammock and had carried the cage to the dining table. She regarded it in silence.

"How much will you charge?" she asked.

"I don't know," Balthazar answered. "I'm going to ask for thirty pesos to see if they'll give me twenty."

"Ask for fifty," said Ursula. "You've lost a lot of sleep in these two weeks. Furthermore, it's rather large. I think it's the biggest cage I've ever seen in my life."

Balthazar began to shave.

"Do you think they'll give me fifty pesos?"

"That's nothing for Mr. Chepe Montiel, and the cage is worth it," said Ursula. "You should ask for sixty."

The house lay in the stifling shadow. It was the first week of April and the heat seemed less bearable because of the chirping of the cicadas. When he finished dressing, Balthazar opened the door to the patio to cool off the house, and a group of children entered the dining room.

The news had spread. Dr. Octavio Giraldo, an old physician, happy with life but tired of his profession, thought about Balthazar's cage while he was eating lunch with his invalid wife. On the inside terrace, where they put the table on hot days, there were many flowerpots and two cages with canaries. His wife liked birds, and she liked them so much that she hated cats because they could eat them up. Thinking about her, Dr. Giraldo went to see a patient that afternoon, and when he returned he went by Balthazar's house to inspect the cage.

There were a lot of people in the dining room. The cage was on display on the table: with its enormous dome of wire, three stories inside, with passageways and compartments especially for eating and sleeping and swings in the space set aside for the birds' recreation, it seemed like a small-scale model of a gigantic ice factory. The doctor inspected it carefully, without touching it, thinking that in effect the cage was better than its reputation, and much more beautiful than any he had ever dreamed of for his wife.

"This is a flight of the imagination," he said. He sought out Balthazar among the group of people and, fixing his maternal eyes on him, added, "You would have been an extraordinary architect."

Balthazar blushed.

"Thank you," he said.

"It's true," said the doctor. He was smoothly and delicately fat, like a woman who had been beautiful in her youth, and he had delicate hands. His voice seemed like that of a priest speaking Latin. "You wouldn't even need to put birds in it," he said, making the cage turn in front of the audience's eyes as if he were auctioning it off. "It would be enough to hang it in the trees so it could sing by itself." He put it back on the table, thought a moment, looking at the cage, and said:

"Fine, then I'll take it."

"It's sold," said Ursula.

"It belongs to the son of Mr. Chepe Montiel," said Balthazar. "He ordered it specially."

The doctor adopted a respectful attitude.

"Did he give you the design?"

"No," said Balthazar. "He said he wanted a large cage, like this one, for a pair of troupials."

The doctor looked at the cage.

"But this isn't for troupials."

"Of course it is, Doctor," said Balthazar, approaching the table. The children surrounded him. "The measurements are carefully calculated," he said, pointing to the different compartments with his forefinger. Then he struck the dome with his knuckles, and the cage filled with resonant chords.

"It's the strongest wire you can find, and each joint is soldered outside and in," he said.

"It's even big enough for a parrot," interrupted one of the children.

"That it is," said Balthazar.

The doctor turned his head.

"Fine, but he didn't give you the design," he said. "He gave you no exact specifications, aside from making it a cage big enough for troupials. Isn't that right?"

"That's right," said Balthazar.

"Then there's no problem," said the doctor. "One thing is a cage big enough for troupials, and another is this cage. There's no proof that this one is the one you were asked to make."

"It's this very one," said Balthazar, confused. "That's why I made it."

The doctor made an impatient gesture.

"You could make another one," said Ursula, looking at her husband. And then, to the doctor: "You're not in any hurry."

"I promised it to my wife for this afternoon," said the doctor.

"I'm very sorry, Doctor," said Balthazar, "but I can't sell you something that's sold already."

The doctor shrugged his shoulders. Drying the sweat from his neck with a handkerchief, he contemplated the cage silently with the fixed unfocused gaze of one who looks at a ship which is sailing away.

"How much did they pay you for it?"

Balthazar sought out Ursula's eyes without replying.

"Sixty pesos," she said.

The doctor kept looking at the cage. "It's very pretty." He sighed. "Extremely pretty." Then, moving toward the door, he began to fan himself energetically, smiling, and the trace of that episode disappeared forever from his memory.

"Montiel is very rich," he said.

In truth, José Montiel was not as rich as he seemed, but he would have been capable of doing anything to become so. A few blocks from there, in a house crammed with equipment, where no one had ever smelled a smell that couldn't be sold, he remained indifferent to the news of the cage. His wife, tortured by an obsession with death, closed the doors and windows after lunch and lay for two hours with her eyes opened to the shadow of the room, while José Montiel took his siesta. The clamor of many voices surprised her there. Then she opened the door to the living room and found a crowd in front of the house, and Balthazar with the cage in the middle of the crowd, dressed in white, freshly shaved, with that expression of decorous candor with which the poor approach the houses of the wealthy.

"What a marvelous thing!" José Montiel's wife exclaimed, with a radiant expression, leading Balthazar inside. "I've never seen anything like it in my life," she said, and added, annoyed by the crowd which piled up at the door:

"But bring it inside before they turn the living room into a grandstand."

Balthazar was no stranger to José Montiel's house. On different occasions, because of his skill and forthright way of dealing, he had been called in to do minor carpentry jobs. But he never felt at ease among the rich. He used to think about them, about their ugly and argumentative wives, about their tremendous surgical operations, and he always experienced a feeling of pity. When he entered their houses, he couldn't move without dragging his feet.

"Is Pepe home?" he asked.

He had put the cage on the dining-room table.

"He's at school," said José Montiel's wife. "But he shouldn't be long," and she added, "Montiel is taking a bath."

In reality, José Montiel had not had time to bathe. He was giving himself an urgent alcohol rub, in order to come out and see what was going on. He was such a cautious man that he slept without an electric fan so he could watch over the noises of the house while he slept.

"Adelaide!" he shouted. "What's going on?"

"Come and see what a marvelous thing!" his wife shouted.

José Montiel, obese and hairy, his towel draped around his neck, appeared at the bedroom window.

"What is that?"

"Pepe's cage," said Balthazar.

His wife looked at him perplexedly.

"Whose?"

"Pepe's," replied Balthazar. And then, turning toward José Montiel, "Pepe ordered it."

Nothing happened at that instant, but Balthazar felt as if someone had just opened the bathroom door on him. José Montiel came out of the bedroom in his underwear.

"Pepe!" he shouted.

"He's not back," whispered his wife, motionless.

Pepe appeared in the doorway. He was about twelve, and had the same curved eyelashes and was as quietly pathetic as his mother.

"Come here," José Montiel said to him. "Did you order this?"

The child lowered his head. Grabbing him by the hair, José Montiel forced Pepe to look him in the eye.

"Answer me."

The child bit his lip without replying.

"Montiel," whispered his wife.

José Montiel let the child go and turned toward Balthazar in a fury. "I'm very sorry, Balthazar," he said. "But you should have consulted me before going on. Only to you would it occur to contract with a minor." As he spoke, his face recovered its serenity. He lifted the cage without looking at it and gave it to Balthazar.

"Take it away at once, and try to sell it to whomever you can," he said. "Above all, I beg you not to argue with me." He patted him on the back and explained, "The doctor has forbidden me to get angry."

The child had remained motionless, without blinking, until Balthazar looked at him uncertainly with the cage in his hand. Then he emitted a guttural sound, like a dog's growl, and threw himself on the floor screaming.

José Montiel looked at him, unmoved, while the other tried to pacify him. "Don't even pick him up," he said. "Let him break his head on the floor, and then put salt and lemon on it so he can rage to his heart's content." The child was shrieking tearlessly while his mother held him by the wrists.

"Leave him alone," José Montiel insisted.

Balthazar observed the child as he would have observed the death throes of a rabid animal. It was almost four o'clock. At that hour, at his house, Ursula was singing a very old song and cutting slices of onion.

"Pepe," said Balthazar.

He approached the child, smiling, and held the cage out to him. The child jumped up, embraced the cage which was almost as big as he was, and stood looking at Balthazar through the wirework without knowing what to say. He hadn't shed one tear.

"Balthazar," said José Montiel softly. "I told you already to take it away."

"Give it back," the woman ordered the child.

"Keep it," said Balthazar. And then, to José Montiel: "After all, that's what I made it for."

José Montiel followed him into the living room.

"Don't be foolish, Balthazar," he was saying, blocking his path. "Take your piece of furniture home and don't be silly. I have no intention of paying you a cent."

"It doesn't matter," said Balthazar. "I made it expressly as a gift for Pepe. I didn't expect to charge anything for it."

As Balthazar made his way through the spectators who were blocking the door, José Montiel was shouting in the middle of the living room. He was very pale and his eyes were beginning to get red.

"Idiot!" he was shouting. "Take your trinket out of here. The last thing we need is for some nobody to give orders in my house. Son of a bitch!"

In the pool hall, Balthazar was received with an ovation. Until that moment, he thought that he had made a better cage than ever before, that he'd had to give it to the son of José Montiel so he wouldn't keep crying, and that none of these things was particularly important. But then he realized that all of this had a certain importance for many people, and he felt a little excited.

"So they gave you fifty pesos for the cage."

"Sixty," said Balthazar.

"Score one for you," someone said. "You're the only one who has managed to get such a pile of money out of Mr. Chepe Montiel. We have to celebrate."

They bought him a beer, and Balthazar responded with a round for everybody. Since it was the first time he had ever been out drinking, by dusk he was completely drunk, and he was talking about a fabulous project of a thousand cages, at sixty pesos each, and then a million cages, till he had sixty million pesos. "We have to make a lot of things to sell to the rich before they die," he was saying, blind drunk. "All of them are sick, and they're going to die. They're so screwed up they can't even get angry any more." For two hours he was paying for the jukebox, which played without interruption. Everybody toasted Balthazar's health, good luck, and fortune, and the death of the rich, but at mealtime they left him alone in the pool hall.

Ursula had waited for him until eight, with a dish of fried meat covered with slices of onion. Someone told her that her husband was in the pool hall, delirious with happiness, buying beers for everyone, but she didn't believe it, because Balthazar had never got drunk. When she went to bed, almost at midnight, Balthazar was in a lighted room where there were little tables, each with four chairs, and an outdoor dance floor, where the plovers were walking around. His face was smeared with rouge, and since he couldn't take one more step, he thought he wanted to lie down with two women in the same bed. He had spent so much that he had had to leave his watch in pawn, with the promise to pay the next day. A moment later, spread-eagled in the street, he realized that his shoes were being taken off, but he didn't want to abandon the happiest dream of his life. The women who passed on their way to five-o'clock Mass didn't dare look at him, thinking he was dead.

John Barth (1930–   )

John Barth has been called a cheerful nihilist, a fabulator, a black humorist, a comic athlete, a player of literary games. He is so protean in his talents that all these terms and more fit him. He is widely acknowledged as one of the wittiest and most inventive of the "innovative fictionists," his term for the experimental style. Before he took his place in the avant-garde, he was esteemed as a writer of realistic fiction. His first two novels—*The Floating Opera* (1956) and *The End of the Road* (1958)—are straightforward narratives about recognizable characters. Yet even in them we can detect the innovator: the stories are told in a witty, self-conscious, disconcerting style and the themes, e.g., absurdity and nihilism, are modernist themes.

In his next two novels, the antirealist takes full charge. Barth believes that the forms of realistic fiction are "used up," the possibilities "exhausted." Appropriate to our age is new fiction, a fiction about fiction, parody, spoof, burlesque. Thus, his *The Sot-Weed Factor* (1960) and *Giles Goat Boy* (1966) are "novels which imitate the form of the Novel, by an author who imitates the role of Author." They are, however, far from ponderous or obscure experiments. Barth intends his work to be "accessible, entertaining, perhaps moving; for I have no use for merely cerebral inventions, merely formalistic tours de force." Filled with puns and paradoxes, with sexual excess and athleticism, with what Robert Scholes calls "an excremental gaiety," Barth's work is wildly funny, outrageous, and bawdy.

But there is more to it than verbal games and hilarity. He is a black humorist, that is, one who laughs and confronts rather than cringes and runs away from the horrible or the merely numbing and demeaning. Black humorists, says Scholes, have a "subtle faith in the humanizing value of laughter." By making us laugh at the deadly serious, Barth helps us to deal with the knowledge of impending nuclear holocaust as well as the corrosive triviality of our everyday concerns.

"Petition" is an excellent example of black humor. Imagine what a story of Siamese twins might have been like if written by a realistic writer, say Sherwood Anderson or Joyce Carol Oates. The subject is horrible because we know it can happen. We could hardly bear to read it. But we don't feel threatened by the Barth story. Its tone is pretentiously literary and mock-serious and the events are outrageous, even ridiculous. This discontinuity distances us and we never forget that we are reading fiction. We can read the story without feeling swamped. Yet the story is not frivolous or merely funny. As our imaginations are quickened, so our sympathies are expanded.

"Petition" appears in the collection of short pieces *Lost in the Funhouse* (1968). Since then Barth has published *Chimera* (1972), which won the National Book Award, and *Letters : A Novel* (1979). Barth was born in Cambridge, Maryland in 1930. He teaches at Johns Hopkins University, of which he is a graduate.

Petition

April 21, 1931

His Most Gracious Majesty Prajadhipok, Descendant
  of Buddha, King of North and South, Supreme Arbiter of
  the Ebb and Flow of the Tide, Brother of the Moon, Half-
  Brother of the Sun, Possessor of the Four-and-Twenty Golden
  Umbrellas
Ophir Hall
White Plains, New York

Sir:
    Welcome to America. An ordinary citizen extends his wish that your visit with us be pleasant, your surgery successful.

    Though not myself a native of your kingdom, I am and have been most alive to its existence and concerns—unlike the average American, alas, to whose imagination the name of that ancient realm summons only white elephants and blue-eyed cats. I am aware, for example, that it was Queen Rambai's father's joke that he'd been inside the Statue of Liberty but never in the United States, having toured the Paris foundry while that symbol was a-casting; in like manner I may say that I have dwelt in a figurative Bangkok all my life. My brother, with whose presumption and other faults I hope further to acquaint you in the course of this petition, has even claimed (in his cups) descent from the mad King Phaya Takh Sin, whose well-deserved assassination—like the surgical excision of a cataract, if I may be so bold—gave to a benighted land the luminous dynasty of Chakkri, whereof Your Majesty is the latest and brightest son. Here as elsewhere my brother lies or is mistaken: we are Occidental, for better or worse, and while our condition is freakish, our origin is almost certainly commonplace. Yet though my brother's claim is false and (should he press it upon you, as he might) in contemptible taste, it may serve the purpose of introducing to you his character, my wretched situation, and my petition to your magnanimity.

The reign of the Chakkris began in violence and threatens to end in blindness; my own history commences with a kind of blindness and threatens to terminate in murder. Happily, our American surgeons are equal to the former threat; my prayer is that Your Majesty—reciprocally, as it were—may find it in his heart to address himself to the latter. The press reports your pledge to liberate three thousand inmates of your country's prisons by April next, to celebrate both the restoration of your eyesight and the sesquicentennial of your dynasty: a regal gesture. But there are prisoners and prisoners; *my* hope is for another kind of release, from what may not unfairly be termed life-imprisonment for no crime whatever, only the misfortune of being born my brother's brother. That the prerogative of kings yet retains, even in the New World, some trace of its old divinity, is amply proved by President Hoover's solicitude for your comfort and all my countrymen's eagerness to serve you. The magazines proclaim the triflingest details of your daily round; society talks of nothing else but your comings and goings; a word from you sends government officers scurrying, reroutes express-trains, stops presses, marshals the finest medical talents in the nation. Give commands, then, that I be liberated at long last from a misery absolute as your monarchy!

Will you counsel resignation to my estate, even affirmation of it? Will you cite the example of Chang and Eng, whom your ancestor thought to put to death and ended by blessing? But Chang and Eng were different from my brother and me, because so much the same; Chang and Eng were as the left hand to the right; Chang and Eng were bound heart to heart: their common navel, which to prick was to injure both, was an emblem of their fraternity, as was the manner of their sitting, each with an arm about the other's shoulders. Haven't I wept with envy of sturdy Chang, loyal Eng? Haven't I invoked them, vainly, as exemplars not only of moral grace but of practical efficiency? Their introduction of the "double chop" for cutting logs, a method still employed by pairs of Carolina woodsmen; their singular skill at driving four-horse teams down the lumber trails of their adopted state; their good-humored baiting of railway conductors, to whom they would present a single ticket, acknowledging that one might be put off the train, but insisting on the other's right to transportation; their resourceful employment of the same reasoning on the occasion of one's arrest, when the other loyally threatened to sue if he too were jailed; their happy marriage to a pair of sisters, who bore them twenty-two healthy children in their separate households; their alternation of authority and residence every three days, rain or shine, each man master under his own roof—a schedule followed faithfully until Chang's death at sixty-three; Eng's touching last request, as he himself expired of sympathy and terror three hours later, that his brother's dead body be moved even closer—didn't I recite these marvels like a litany to *my* brother in the years when I still could hope we might get along?

Yet it may surprise you to learn that even Chang and Eng, those paragons of cooperation, had their differences. Chang was a tippler, Eng a teetotaller; Eng liked all-night checker games, Chang was no gambler; in at least one election they cast their votes for opposing candidates; the arrest aforementioned, though it came to nothing, was for the crime of assault—committed by one against the other. Especially following marriage their differences increased, and if upon returning to the exhibition stage (after the Civil War) they made a show of unanimity, it was to raise money in the hope that some surgeon could part them at last. All this, mind, between veritable Heavenly Twins, sons of the mystical East, whose religions and philosophies—no criticism intended—have ever minimized distinctions, denying even the difference between Sameness and Difference. How altogether contrary is the case of my brother and me! (*He*, as might be expected, denies that the cases are different, contradicts this denial by denying at the same time that we are two in the first place—and would no doubt deny the contradiction as well, with equal obstinacy, should Your Majesty point it out to him.) Only consider: whereas Chang and Eng were bound breast to breast by a good long band that allowed them to walk, sit, and sleep side by side, my brother and I are fastened front to rear—my belly to the small of his back—by a leash of flesh heartbreakingly short. In consequence he never lays eyes on the wretch he forever drags about—no wonder he denies me, agrees with the doctors that such a union is impossible, and claims my utterance and inspiration for his own!—while I see nothing else the day long (unless over his shoulder) but his stupid neck-nape, which I know better than my name. He obscures my view, sits in my lap (never mind how his weight impedes my circulation), smothers me in his wraps. What I suffer in the bathroom is too disgusting for Your Majesty's ears. By night it's scramble or be crushed when he tosses in our bed, pitching and snoring so in his dreams that my own are nightmares; by day I must match his stride like the hinder half of a vaudeville horse until, exhausted, I clamber on him pick-a-back. Small comfort that I may outlast him, despite his greater strength, by riding him thus; when he goes I go, Eng after Chang, and in the meanwhile I must go *where* he goes as well, and suffer his insults along the way. No matter to him that in one breath he denies my existence, in the next affirms it with his oaths and curses: I am Anchises to his Aeneas, he will have it; Old Man of the Sea to his Sinbad; I am his cross, his albatross; I, lifelong victim of his beastliness, he calls the monkey on his back!

No misery, of course, but has its little compensations, however hollow or theoretical. What couldn't we accomplish if he'd cooperate, with me as his back-up man! Only let me count cadence and him go more regularly, there'd be no stumbling; I could prod, tickle, goose him into action if he'd not ignore me; I'd be the eyes in the back of his head, his unobserved prompter and mentor. Cloaked in the legal immunity of Chang-Eng's gambit we could do what we pleased, be wealthy in no time. Even within the law we'd have the world for our oyster, our capacity twice any rival's. Strangers to loneliness, we could make rich our leisure hours: bicycle in tandem, sing close harmony, play astonishing piano, read Plato aloud, assemble mahjongg tiles in half the time. I'd be no prude were we as close in temperament as in body; we could make any open-minded woman happy beyond her most amorous reveries—or, lacking women, delight each other in ways that Chang and Eng could never. . . .

Vain dreams; we are nothing alike. I am slight, my brother is gross. He's incoherent but vocal; I'm articulate and mute. He's ignorant but full of guile; I think I may call myself reasonably educated, and if ingenuous, no more so I hope than the run of scholars. My brother is gregarious: he deals with the public; earns and spends our income; tends (but slovenly) the house and grounds; makes, entertains, and loses friends; indulges in hobbies; pursues ambitions and women. For my part, I am by nature withdrawn, even solitary: an observer of life, a meditator, a taker of notes, a dreamer if you will—yet not a brooder; it's he who moods and broods, today hilarious, tomorrow despondent; I myself am stoical, detached as it were—of necessity, or I'd have long since perished of despair. More to the point, what intelligence my brother has is inclined to synthesis, mine to analysis; he denies that we are two, yet refuses to compromise and cooperate; I affirm our difference—all the difference in the world!—but have endeavored in vain to work out with him a reasonable cohabitation. Untutored and clumsy, he will nevertheless make flatulent noises upon the trombone, write ungainly verses, dance awkwardly with women, hold grunting conversations, jerrybuild a roof over our heads; I, whose imagination encompasses Aristotle, Shakespeare, Bach—I'd never so presume; yet let me point out to him, however diplomatically, however constructively, the shortcomings of his efforts beside genuine creation: he flies into a rage, shreds his doggerel, dents his horn, quarrels with his "sweetheart" (who perhaps was laughing at him all along), abandons carpentry, beats his chest in heroical self-pity, or sulks in a corner for days together. I don't even mention his filthy personal habits: what consolation that he swipes his bum and occasionally soaps his stinking body? Only the sinner needs absolution, and one sin breeds another: because I ride on his back and am content to nourish myself with infrequent sips of tea, I neither perspire nor defecate, but merely emit a discreet vapor, of neutral scent, and tiny puffs of what could pass for talc. Other sustenance I draw less from our common bond, as he might claim, than from books, from introspection, most of all from revery and fancy, without which I'd soon enough starve. But he, he eats anything, lusts after anything, goes to any length to make me wretched. His very excrements he will sniff and savor; he belches up gases, farts in my lap; not content that I must ride atop him, as on a rutting stallion, while he humps his whores, he will torment me in the shower-bath by bending over to draw me against him and pinching at me with his hairy cheeks. Yet let me flinch away, or in a frenzy of disgust attempt to rupture our bond though it kill us (as I sometimes strained to do in years gone by): he turns my revulsion into horrid sport, runs out and snaps back like a paddle-ball or plays crack-the-whip at every turn in our road. Why go on? We have nothing in common but the womb that bore, the flesh that shackles, the grave that must soon receive us. If my situation has any advantage it's only that I can see him without his seeing me; can therefore study and examine our bond, how ever to dissolve it, and take certain surreptitious measures to that end, such as writing this petition. Futile perhaps; desperate certainly. The alternative is madness.

All very well, you may say: lamentable as our situation is, it's nothing new; we were born this way and have somehow muddled through thirty-five years; not even a king has his own way in everything; in the matter of congenital endowment it's potluck for all of us, we must grin and bear it, the weakest to the wall, et cetera. God knows I am no whiner; I've broken heart and spirit to make the best of a bad hand of cards; at the slimmest hint of sympathy from my brother, the least suggestion of real fraternity, I melt with gratitude, must clamber aboard lest I swoon of joy; my tears run in his hair and down the courses of his face, one would think it was he who wept. And were it simply a matter of accumulated misery, or the mere happenstance of your visit, I'd not burden you (and my own sensibility) with this complaint. What prompts my plea is the coincidence of your arrival and a critical turn in our history and situation.

I pass over the details of our past, a tiresome chronicle. Some say our mother died a-bearing us, others that she perished of dismay soon after; just as possibly, she merely put us out. The man we called Father exhibited us throughout our childhood, but the age was more hardened to monstrosity than Chang's and Eng's; we never prospered; indeed we were scarcely noticed. In earliest babyhood I didn't realize I was two; it was the intractability of that creature always before me—going left when I would go right, bawling for food when I would sleep, laughing when I wept—that opened my eyes to the possibility he was other than myself; the teasing of playmates, who mocked our contretemps, verified that suspicion, and I began my painful schooling in detachment. Early on I proposed to my brother a judicious alliance (with myself, naturally, as director of our activities and final arbiter of our differences, he being utterly a creature of impulse); he would none of my proposal. Through childhood our antipathies merely smoldered, as we both submitted perforce, however grudgingly, to Father (who at least never denied our twoness, which, to be sure, was his livelihood); it was upon our fleeing his government, in adolescence, that they flamed. My attempt to direct our partnership ended in my brother's denying first my efficacy, then my authority, finally my reality. He pretended to believe, offstage as well as on, that the audience's interest was in him as a solo performer and not in the pair of us as a freak; hidden from the general view, unable to speak except in whispers, I could take only feeblest revenge: I would wave now and then between the lines of his stupid performances, grimace behind his back and over his shoulder, make signs to mock or contradict his asseverations. Let him deny me, he couldn't ignore me; I tripped him up, confused, confounded him, and though in the end he usually prevailed, I pulled against him every step of his way, spoiled his pleasure, halved his force, and on more than one occasion stalled him entirely.

The consequent fiascos, the rages and rampages of his desperation, are too dreadful to recount; them too I pass over, with a shudder. For some time now our connection has been an exasperated truce punctuated with bitter bursts of hostility, as between old mismatched spouses or weary combatants; the open confrontations are less frequent because more vicious, the interim resentments more deep because more resigned. Each new set-to, legatee of all its predecessors, is more destructive than the last; at the merest popgun-pop, artillery bristles. However radically, therefore, our opposition restricts our freedom, we each had come to feel, I believe, that the next real violence between us would be the last, fatal to one and thus to both, and so were more or less resigned to languishing, disgruntled, in our impasse, for want of alternatives. Then between us came Thalia, love, the present crisis.

It will scarcely surprise you that we arrived late at sexuality. Ordinary girls fled from our advances, or cruelly mocked us; had our bookings not fetched us to the capitals of Europe, whose liberal ladies sought us out for novelty's sake, we'd kept our chastity perforce till affluent maturity, for common prostitutes raised their fees, at sight of us, beyond our adolescent means. Even so, it was my brother did all the clipping, I being out of reach except to surrogate gratifications; only when a producer of unusual motion pictures in Berlin, with the resourcefulness characteristic of his nation, discovered Thalia and brought her to us, did I know directly the experience of coition. I did not enjoy it.

More accurately, I was rent by emotions as at odds as I and my brother. Thalia—a pretty young contortionist of good family obliged by the misery of the times to prostitute her art in exotic nightclubs and films—I admired tremendously, not alone for her merry temper and the talent wherewith she achieved our connection, but for her silent forbearance, not unlike my own, in the face as it were of my brother's abuse. But how expect me to share the universal itch to copulate, whose soul lusts only for disjunction? Even our modest coupling (chaste beside *his* performances), rousing as it was to tickly sense, went so counter to my principles I'd hardly have enjoyed it even had my brother not indignified her the while. Not content to be double already, he must attach himself to everyone, everything; hug, devour, absorb! Heads or tails, it's all one to Brother; he clamped his shaggy thighs about the poor girl's ears as greedily as he engorges a potroast or smothers me into the mattress, threatening with a laugh to squash and ingest me.

After a series of such meetings (the film director, whether as artist or as Teuton, was a perfectionist) we discovered ourselves in love: I with Thalia, my brother likewise in his fashion, and laughing Thalia . . . with me, with me, I'm sure of it! At least in the beginning. She joined our act, inspired or composed fresh material for us; we played with profit the naughty stages of a dozen nations, my brother still pretending he had no brother despite our billing: *The Eternal Triangle*. Arranged in parallel, isosceles, or alphaic fashion, we slept in the same hotel beds, and while it was he who salivated and grunted upon her night after night, as he does yet, still it pleased me to imagine that Thalia permitted him her supple favors out of love for me, and humored his pretense that I did not exist in order to be with me. By gay example she taught me to make fun of our predicament, chuckle through the teeth of anguish, turn woe into wit. In the heights of his barbarous passion our eyes meet, and I have seen her wink; as he roars in his transports, her chin rests on his shoulder; she grins, and I chastely kiss her brow. More than once I have been moved to put my love into written words, to no avail; what profit to be articulate, when he seizes every message like a jealous censor and either obscures its tender sentiments past deciphering or translates them into his own coarse idiom? I reach to comfort her; he thrusts my hand into her crotch; she takes it for his and pretends delight. Agile creature that she is, she would enfold us both in her honey limbs, so to touch the one she loves; as if aware, he thwarts her into some yoga position, Bandha Padmāsana, Dhanurāsana. Little wonder our love remains tentative with him between us, who for aught I know may garble even this petition; little wonder we doubt and mistake each other. Indeed, I can only forgive her, however broken-heartedly, if the worst of my suspicions should prove true: that, hardened by despair, Thalia is becoming her disguise: the vulgar creature who ignores my signals, denies my presence, growls with feral joy beneath her ravisher! My laughter sticks in my throat; either Thalia has lost her sense of humor or I've lost mine. Mirth passes; our wretchedness endures and brutalizes. Truth to tell, she has become a stranger; with the best will in the world I can't always persuade my heart that her refusal to acknowledge me is but a stratagem of love, her teasing and fondling of the man I abhor mere feminine duplicity, to inspire my ardor and cover our tracks. What tracks, Thalia? Of late, particularly, she behaves on occasion as if *I* stood in the way of her contentment, and in darkest moments I can even wonder whether her demand that my brother "pull himself together" is owing to her secret desire for me or a secret wish to see me gone.

This ultimatum she pronounced on our thirty-fifth birthday, three weeks past. We were vacationing between a profitable Mardi-Gras engagement in New Orleans and a scheduled post-Lenten tour of Western speakeasies; indeed, despite Prohibition and Depression, perhaps because of them, we'd had an uncommonly prosperous season; the demand for our sort of spectacle had never been so great; people crowded into basement caves to drink illicit liquors and applaud our repertoire of unnatural combinations and obscene gymnastics. One routine in particular was lining our pockets, a lubricious soft-shoe burlesque of popular songs beginning with *Me and My Shadow* and culminating in *When We're Alone*; it was Thalia's invention, and doubtless inspired both my brother's birthday proposal and her response. She had bought a cake to celebrate the occasion (for both of us, I was sure, though seventy candles would clearly have been too many); my brother, who ordinarily blew out all the candles and clawed into the frosting with both hands before I could draw a breath, had been distracted all day, and managed only thirty-four; eagerly I puffed out the last, over his shoulder, my first such opportunity in three decades and a half, whereat he threw off his mood with a laugh and revealed his wish: to join himself to Thalia in marriage. In his blurting fashion he enounced a whole mad program: he would put the first half of his life altogether behind him, quit show business, use our savings to learn an honest trade, perhaps husbandry, perhaps welding, and raise a family!

"Two can live cheap as one," he grumbled at the end—somewhat defensively, for Thalia showed neither surprise, pleasure, nor dismay, but heard him out with a neutral expression as if the idea were nothing new. I searched her face for assurance that she was revolted; I waved my arms and shook my head, turned out my pockets to find the *NO*-sign I always carried with me, so often was it needed, and flung it in her direction when she wouldn't look at it. Long time she studied him, twirling a sprig of ivy between her fingers; cross with suspense, he admitted he'd been no model companion, but a moody, difficult, irresolute fellow plagued with tensions and contradictions. I mouthed antic sneers over his shoulders. But with her assistance he would become a new man, he declared, and promised ominously to "get rid," "one way or another," of "the monkey on his back," which had kept him to date from single-minded application to anything. It was his first employment of the epithet; I shuddered at his resolve. She was his hope of redemption, he went on, becoming fatuous and sentimental now in his anxiety; without her he was no better than a beast (as if he weren't beastly *with* her!), no more than half a man; let her but consent, therefore and however, to become as the saying was his better half, he'd count himself saved!

Why did she not laugh in his face, throw up to him his bestialities, declare once for all that she endured him solely on my account? She rose from table, leaning upon the cane she always danced with; I held out my arms to her and felt on each elbow the tears my brother forced to dramatize his misery. Oh, he is a cunning animal! I even attempted tears myself, but flabbergastment dried my eyes. At the door Thalia turned to gaze as if it were through him—the last time, I confess, that I was able to believe she might be looking at me. Then bending with a grunt to retrieve my crumpled message, which she tossed unread into the nearest ashtray, she replied that she was indeed weary of acrobatics: let him make good his aforementioned promise, one way or another; then she'd see.

No sooner had she spoken than the false tears ceased; my brother chased her squealing into the kitchen, nor troubled even to ask her leave, but swinish as ever fetched down her tights with the cane-crook and rogered her fair athwart the dish drain, all the while snorting through her whoop and giggle: "You'll see what you'll see!"

Highness, I live in terror of what she'll see! Nothing is beyond my brother. He has put himself on a diet, avowedly to trim his grossness for her sake; but I perceive myself weaker in consequence, and am half-convinced he means to starve me on the vine, as it were, and absorb me through the bond that joins us. He has purchased medical insurance, playing the family man, and remarks as if idly on its coverage of massive skin grafts; for all I know he may be planning to install me out of sight inside him by surgical means. I don't eat; I daren't sleep. Thalia, my hope and consolation—why has she forsaken me?

If indeed she has. For a curious fancy has taken me of late, not impossibly the figment of a mind deranged for want of love (and rest, and sustenance): that Thalia is less simple than she appears. I suspect, in fact, or begin to . . . that there are two Thalias! Don't mistake me: not two as Chang and Eng were two, or as my brother and I are two; not one Thalia joined to another—but a Thalia *within* a Thalia, like the dolls-within-dolls Your Majesty's countrymen and neighbors fashion so cleverly: a Thalia incarcerate in the iron maiden my brother embraces!

I first observed her not long after that fell birthday. No moraler for all his protestations, my brother has devised for our next performance a new stunt based on an old lubricity, and to "get the hang of it" (so he claims) sleeps now arsyturvy with his "fiancée," like shoes in a box or the ancient symbol for Yang and Yin. Sometimes she rests her head on his knees, and thus it happened, late one night, that when I looked down upon the Thalia who'd betrayed me, I found her looking back, sleepless as I, upside down in the first spring moonlight. Yet lo, it was not the same Thalia! Her face—I should say, her sister's face—was inverted, but I realized suddenly that her eyes were not; it was a different woman, a stranger, who regarded me with upright, silent stare through the other's face. I perspired with dismay—my first experience of sweat. Luckily my brother slept, a-pitch with dreams. There was no mistaking it, another woman looked out at me from behind that mask: a prisoner like myself, whose gaze remained level and detached however her heartless warden grinned and grimaced. I saw her the next night and the next, earnest, mute; by day she disappears in the other Thalia; I live only for the night, to rehearse before her steadfast eyes the pity and terror of our situation. She it is (once separate like myself, it may be, then absorbed by her smirking sister) I now adore—if with small hope and much apprehension. Does she see me winking and waving, or is my face as strange to her as her sister's to me? Why does she gaze at me so evenly, as if in unremitting appraisal? Can she too be uncertain of my reality, my love? Too much to bear!

In any case, there's little time. "Thalia" grows restive; now that she has the upper hand with my brother she makes no bones about her reluctance to go back on the road, her yen for a little farm, her dissatisfaction with his progress in "making a man of himself" and the like. Last night, I swear it, I felt him straining to suck me in through our conjunction, and clung to the sheets in terror. Momently I expect him to play some unsuspected trump; have at me for good and all. When he does, I will bite through the tie that binds us and so kill us both. It is a homicide God will forgive, and my beloved will at least be free of what she suffers, through her sister, at my brother's hands.

Yet given the daily advances of science and the inspiring circumstance of Your Majesty's visit, I dare this final hope: that at your bidding the world's most accomplished surgeons may successfully divide my brother from myself, in a manner such that one of us at least may survive, free of the other. After all, we were both joined once to our unknown mother, and safely detached to begin our misery. Or if a bond to *something* is necessary in our case, let it be something more congenial and sympathetic: graft my brother's Thalia in my place, and fasten me . . . to my own navel, to anything but him, if the Thalia I love can't be freed to join me! Perhaps she has another sister. . . . Death itself I would embrace like a lover, if I might share the grave with no other company. To be one: paradise! To be two: bliss! But to be both and neither is unspeakable. Your Highness may imagine with what eagerness His reply to this petition is awaited by

Yours truly,

Donald Barthelme (1933–   )

"Fragments are the only forms I trust," Barthelme has said, and it is a social as well as aesthetic statement. For his fiction tells us, in funny as well as frightening detail, of the mechanical nature of modern life, of the endlessness of the "damned accumulations" of a mass-production society in which the gross national product becomes ever more gross. *Dreck* is one of his favorite terms, by which he means—as Tony Tanner in *City of Words* reminds us—the flow of things, trash, junk, stuff, and sludge that fills and is filling our environment. In his novel *Snow White* a voice says: "The percapita production of trash in this country is up from 2.75 pounds per day in 1920 to 4.5 pounds per day in 1965 . . . that rate will probably go up, because it's *been* going up, and I hazard that we may very well soon reach a point where it's 100 percent. Now at such a point you will agree, the question turns from a question of disposing of this 'trash' to a question of appreciating its qualities, because, after all, it's 100 percent, right?'' Part of that *dreck* is words, the words and syntax of the mass media, corrupting the language for the purposes of commercialism, militarism, and official lying. Barthelme's world, says Tony Tanner, is "a language circus." But though one hears the dance of death in that circus, one is laughing all the time—and no writer of our time has fiddled at our doom with more wry delight.

Besides the novels *Snow White* (1967) and *The Dead Father* (1975), Barthelme has published six volumes of short stories: *Unspeakable Practices, Unnatural Acts* (1967), *City Life* (1970), *Sadness* (1972), *Come Back, Dr. Caligari* (1974), *Amateurs* (1976), and *Great Days* (1979)—as well as a volume of nonfiction called *Guilty Pleasures* (1974) and a children's book. Of Barthelme's personal life we know very little. He was born in Philadelphia and raised and educated in Houston, Texas, where his father, an architect, imparted to him something of his love for the forms of modernism. Barthelme has worked as a newspaperman, magazine editor, curator of an art gallery, and a university public relations director; he has served in the army in Korea and Japan. His earliest fiction attracted the attention of the editors of *The New Yorker*, and he has been a frequent contributor to that magazine ever since. He makes his home in New York's Greenwich Village.

"At the End of the Mechanical Age" is the last story in the collection *Amateurs*, whose dust jacket quotes Richard Todd as saying, "He speaks dozens of the specialized dialects that make up our language, and he mocks their pretension and the pretentious surety of those who use them." Here human relations are "shiny-brite," if temporary, and the marriage of Mrs. Davis and the narrator is a union "of a technical nature, such as nut with bolt, wood with wood screw, aircraft with Plane-Mate." They are replaceable parts, as is appropriate in the mechanical age, and are part of its "end." God is a character in this story: he reads electric meters, dressed in "His blue jump suit with the flashlight stuck in the back pocket," checking to see how much grace has been used up in a given month. Comedy has been defined as "the mechanical encrusted on the living"; here the aptness of that formula is brilliantly shown. Pressed too far, the mechanical encrusted on the living is the stuff of nightmare. But here, as Mrs. Davis and the narrator "huddle and cling" to make life bearable, we laugh instead of shudder.

At the End of the Mechanical Age

I went to the grocery store to buy some soap. I stood for a long time before the soaps in their attractive boxes, RUB and FAB and TUB and suchlike, I couldn't decide so I closed my eyes and reached out blindly and when I opened my eyes I found her hand in mine.

Her name was Mrs. Davis, she said, and TUB was best for important cleaning experiences, in her opinion. So we went to lunch at a Mexican restaurant which as it happened she owned, she took me into the kitchen and showed me her stacks of handsome beige tortillas and the steam tables which were shiny-brite. I told her I wasn't very good with women and she said it didn't matter, few men were, and that nothing mattered, now that Jake was gone, but I would do as an interim project and sit down and have a Carta Blanca. So I sat down and had a cool Carta Blanca, God was standing in the basement reading the meters to see how much grace had been used up in the month of June. Grace is electricity, science has found, it is not *like* electricity, it *is* electricity and God was down in the basement reading the meters in His blue jump suit with the flashlight stuck in the back pocket.

"The mechanical age is drawing to a close," I said to her.

"Or has already done so," she replied.

"It was a good age," I said. "I was comfortable in it, relatively. Probably I will not enjoy the age to come quite so much. I don't like its look."

"One must be fair. We don't know yet what kind of an age the next one will be. Although I feel in my bones that it will be an age inimical to personal well-being and comfort, and that is what I like, personal well-being and comfort."

"Do you suppose there is something to be done?" I asked her.

"Huddle and cling," said Mrs. Davis. "We can huddle and cling. It will pall, of course, everything palls, in time . . . ."

Then we went back to my house to huddle and cling, most women are two different colors when they remove their clothes especially in summer but Mrs. Davis was all one color, an ocher. She seemed to like huddling and clinging, she stayed for many days. From time to time she checked the restaurant keeping everything shiny-brite and distributing sums of money to the staff, returning with tortillas in sacks, cases of Carta Blanca, buckets of guacamole, but I paid her for it because I didn't want to feel obligated.

There was a song I sang her, a song of great expectations.

"Ralph is coming," I sang, *"Ralph is striding in his suit of lights over moons and mountains, over parking lots and fountains, toward your silky side. Ralph is coming, he has a coat of many colors and all major credit cards and he is striding to meet you and culminate your foggy dreams in an explosion of blood and soil, at the end of the mechanical age. Ralph is coming preceded by fifty running men with spears and fifty dancing ladies who are throwing leaf spinach out of little baskets, in his path. Ralph is perfect,"* I sang, *"but he is also full of interesting tragic flaws, and he can drink fifty running men under the table without breaking his stride and he can have congress with fifty dancing ladies without breaking his stride, even his socks are ironed, so natty is Ralph, but he is also right down in the mud with the rest of us, he markets the mud at high prices for specialized industrial uses and he is striding, striding, striding, toward your waiting heart. Of course you may not like him, some people are awfully picky . . . Ralph is coming,"* I sang to her, *"he is striding over dappled plains and crazy rivers and he will change your life for the better, probably, you will be fainting with glee at the simple touch of his grave gentle immense hand although I am aware that some people can't stand prosperity, Ralph is coming, I hear his hoofsteps on the drumhead of history, he is striding as he has been all his life toward you, you, you."*

"Yes," Mrs. Davis said, when I finished singing, "that is what I deserve, all right. But probably I will not get it. And in the meantime, there is you."

God then rained for forty days and forty nights, when the water tore away the front of the house we got into the boat, Mrs. Davis liked the way I maneuvered the boat off the trailer and out of the garage, she was provoked into a memoir of Jake.

"Jake was a straight-ahead kind of man," she said, "he was simpleminded and that helped him to be the kind of man that he was." She was staring into her Scotch-and-floodwater rather moodily I thought, debris bouncing on the waves all around us but she paid no attention. "That is the type of man I like," she said, "a strong and simpleminded man. The case-study method was not Jake's method, he went right through the middle of the line and never failed to gain yardage, no matter what the game was. He had a lust for life, and life had a lust for him. I was inconsolable when Jake passed away." Mrs. Davis was drinking the Scotch for her nerves, she had no nerves of course, she was nerveless and possibly heartless also but that is another question, gutless she was not, she had a gut and a very pretty one ocher in color but that was another matter. God was standing up to His neck in the raging waters with a smile of incredible beauty on His visage, He seemed to be enjoying His creation, the disaster, the waters all around us were raging louder now, raging like a mighty tractor-trailer tailgating you on the highway.

Then Mrs. Davis sang to me, a song of great expectations.

"Maude is waiting for you," Mrs. Davis sang to me, "Maude is waiting for you in all her seriousness and splendor, under her gilded onion dome, in that city which I cannot name at this time, Maude waits. Maude is what you lack, the profoundest of your lacks. Your every yearn since the first yearn has been a yearn for Maude, only you did not know it until I, your dear friend, pointed it out. She is going to heal your scrappy and generally unsatisfactory life with the balm of her Maudeness, luckiest of dogs, she waits only for you. Let me give you just one instance of Maude's inhuman sagacity. Maude named the tools. It was Maude who thought of calling the rattail file a rattail file. It was Maude who christened the needle-nose pliers. Maude named the rasp. Think of it. What else could a rasp be but a rasp? Maude in her wisdom went right to the point, and called it rasp. It was Maude who named the maul. Similarly the sledge, the wedge, the ballpeen hammer, the adz, the shim, the hone, the strop. The handsaw, the hacksaw, the bucksaw, and the fretsaw were named by Maude, peering into each saw and intuiting at once its specialness. The scratch awl, the scuffle hoe, the prick punch and the countersink—I could go on and on. The tools came to Maude, tool by tool in a long respectful line, she gave them their names. The vise. The gimlet. The cold chisel. The reamer, the router, the gouge. The plumb bob. How could she have thought up the rough justice of these wonderful cognomens? Looking languidly at a pair of tin snips, and then deciding to call them tin snips—what a burst of glory! And I haven't even cited the bush hook, the grass snath, or the plumber's snake, or the C-clamp, or the nippers, or the scythe. What a tall achievement, naming the tools! And this is just one of Maude's contributions to our worldly estate, there are others. What delights will come crowding," Mrs. Davis sang to me, "delight upon delight, when the epithalamium is ground out by the hundred organ grinders who are Maude's constant attendants, on that good-quality day of her own choosing, which you have desperately desired all your lean life, only you weren't aware of it until I, your dear friend, pointed it out. And Maude is young but not too young," Mrs. Davis sang to me, "she is not too old either, she is just right and she is waiting for you with her tawny limbs and horse sense, when you receive Maude's nod your future and your past will begin."

There was a pause, or pall.

"Is that true," I asked, "that song?"

"It is a metaphor," said Mrs. Davis, "it has metaphorical truth."

"And the end of the mechanical age," I said, "is that a metaphor?"

"The end of the mechanical age," said Mrs. Davis, "is in my judgment an actuality straining to become a metaphor. One must wish it luck, I suppose. One must cheer it on. Intellectual rigor demands that we give these damned metaphors every chance, even if they are inimical to personal well-being and comfort. We have a duty to understand everything, whether we like it or not—a duty I would scant if I could." At that moment the water jumped into the boat and sank us.

At the wedding Mrs. Davis spoke to me kindly.

"Tom," she said, "you are not Ralph, but you are all that is around at the moment. I have taken in the whole horizon with a single sweep of my practiced eye, no giant figure looms there and that is why I have decided to marry you, temporarily, with Jake gone and an age ending. It will be a marriage of convenience all right, and when Ralph comes, or Maude nods, then our arrangement will automatically self-destruct, like the tinted bubble that it is. You were very kind and considerate, when we were drying out, in the tree, and I appreciated that. That counted for something. Of course kindness and consideration are not what the great songs, the Ralph-song and the Maude-song, promise. They are merely flaky substitutes for the terminal experience. I realize that and want you to realize it. I want to be straight with you. That is one of the most admirable things about me, that I am always straight with people, from the sweet beginning to the bitter end. Now I will return to the big house where my handmaidens will proceed with the robing of the bride."

It was cool in the meadow by the river, the meadow Mrs. Davis had selected for the travesty, I walked over to the tree under which my friend Blackie was standing, he was the best man, in a sense.

"This disgusts me," Blackie said, "this hollow pretense and empty sham and I had to come all the way from Chicago."

God came to the wedding and stood behind a tree with just part of His effulgence showing, I wondered whether He was planning to bless this makeshift construct with His grace, or not. It's hard to imagine what He was thinking of in the beginning when He planned everything that was ever going to happen, planned everything exquisitely right down to the tiniest detail such as what I was thinking at this very moment, my thought about His thought, planned the end of the mechanical age and detailed the new age to follow, and then the bride emerged from the house with her train, all ocher in color and very lovely.

"And do you, Anne," the minister said, "promise to make whatever mutually satisfactory accommodations necessary to reduce tensions and arrive at whatever previously agreed-upon goals both parties have harmoniously set in the appropriate planning sessions?"

"I do," said Mrs. Davis.

"And do you, Thomas, promise to explore all differences thoroughly with patience and inner honesty ignoring no fruitful avenues of discussion and seeking at all times to achieve rapprochement while eschewing advantage in conflict situations?"

"Yes," I said.

"Well, now we are married," said Mrs. Davis, "I think I will retain my present name if you don't mind, I have always been Mrs. Davis and your name is a shade graceless, no offense, dear."

"O.K.," I said.

Then we received the congratulations and good wishes of the guests, who were mostly employees of the Mexican restaurant, Raul was there and Consuelo, Pedro, and Pepe came crowding around with outstretched hands and Blackie came crowding around with outstretched hands, God was standing behind the caterer's tables looking at the enchiladas and chalupas and chile con queso and chicken mole as if He had never seen such things before but that was hard to believe.

I started to speak to Him as all of the world's great religions with a few exceptions urge, from the heart, I started to say "Lord, Little Father of the Poor, and all that, I was just wondering now that an age, the mechanical age, is ending and a new age beginning or so they say, I was just wondering if You could give me a hint, sort of, not a Sign, I'm not asking for a Sign, but just the barest hint as to whether what we have been told about Your nature and our nature is, forgive me and I know how You feel about doubt or rather what we have been told You feel about it, but if You could just let drop the slightest indication as to whether what we have been told is authentic or just a bunch of apocryphal heterodoxy—"

But He had gone away with an insanely beautiful smile on His lighted countenance, gone away to read the meters and get a line on the efficacy of grace in that area, I surmised, I couldn't blame Him, my question had not been so very elegantly put, had I been able to express it mathematically He would have been more interested, maybe, but I have never been able to express anything mathematically.

After the marriage Mrs. Davis explained marriage to me.

Marriage, she said, an institution deeply enmeshed with the mechanical age.

Pairings smiled upon by law were but reifications of the laws of mechanics, inspired by unions of a technical nature, such as nut with bolt, wood with wood screw, aircraft with Plane-Mate.

Permanence or impermanence of the bond a function of (1) materials and (2) technique.

Growth of literacy a factor, she said.

Growth of illiteracy also.

The center will not hold if it has been spot-welded by an operator whose deepest concern is not with the weld but with his lottery ticket.

God interested only in grace—keeping things humming.

Blackouts, brownouts, temporary dimmings of household illumination all portents not of Divine displeasure but of Divine indifference to executive-development programs at middle-management levels.

He likes to get out into the field Himself, she said. With His flashlight. He is doing the best He can.

We two, she and I, no exception to general ebb/flow of world juice and its concomitant psychological effects, she said.

Bitter with the sweet, she said.

After the explanation came the divorce.

"Will you be wanting to contest the divorce?" I asked Mrs. Davis.

"I think not," she said calmly, "although I suppose one of us should, for the fun of the thing. An uncontested divorce always seems to me contrary to the spirit of divorce."

"That is true," I said, "I have had the same feeling myself, not infrequently."

After the divorce the child was born. We named him A. F. of L. Davis and sent him to that part of Russia where people live to be one hundred and ten years old. He is living there still, probably, growing in wisdom and beauty. Then we shook hands, Mrs. Davis and I, and she set out Ralphward, and I, Maudeward, the glow of hope not yet extinguished, the fear of pall not yet triumphant, standby generators ensuring the flow of grace to all of God's creatures at the end of the mechanical age.

Alternative Tables of Contents: Theme and Subject

For readers who want alternative entries into these stories, we have listed below some themes and subjects represented in this volume. A theme must be distinguished from a subject. A story may have *war* as its subject, but *self-discovery* as its theme. The subject is the raw material of the story, its subject *matter,* but the theme is its meaning, its *point.*

Themes are obviously, from a critical point of view, more important than subjects, but the two are often closely allied (and sometimes indistinguishable). We have, therefore, included both, themes under Part I and subjects under Part II.

No such lists as these can be more than crude indicators, since the categories overlap, and since we cannot possibly be exhaustive. It would be the rare story whose theme, by another reader, could not be called by another name: one reader might call the theme of Joyce's "A Painful Case" "self-discovery," while another might call it "alienation." Likewise, a story might have "war" as its subject, but it surely has "human nature" or "courage" or "suffering" as subjects as well. Therefore, we have listed stories under more than one heading. We believe that a careful look at these lists will help readers to compare and distinguish the stories and thus to increase their understanding and response.

PART I: THEMES

In naming the following themes, we have followed the image of a widening circle, beginning in childhood and expanding outward to the experiences of adulthood and of responsibility.

PART ONE: THEME

I. Childhood and Youth

Edith Wharton	*Roman Fever*
Thomas Mann	*Mario and the Magician*
Sherwood Anderson	*I Want to Know Why*
E. M. Forster	*Dr Woolacott*
Katherine Mansfield	*The Garden-Party*
Conrad Aiken	*Silent Snow, Secret Snow*
William Faulkner	*That Evening Sun*
Richard Wilbur	*A Game of Catch*
Toni Cade Bambara	*Raymond's Run*
Delmore Schwartz	*In Dreams Begin Responsibilities*

II. Rites of Passage

Thomas Mann	*Mario and the Magician*
Sherwood Anderson	*I Want to Know Why*
Katherine Mansfield	*The Garden-Party*
Katherine Anne Porter	*The Grave*
F. Scott Fitzgerald	*Babylon Revisited*
Richard Wright	*The Man Who Was Almost a Man*
Richard Wilbur	*A Game of Catch*
Joyce Carol Oates	*Where Are You Going, Where Have You Been?*
Toni Cade Bambara	*Raymond's Run*
Delmore Schwartz	*In Dreams Begin Responsibilities*
F. Scott Fitzgerald	*Babylon Revisited*

III. Identity and Self-Discovery

Nikolai Gogol	*The Overcoat*
Henry James	*The Beast in the Jungle*
Anton Chekhov	*The Lady with the Pet Dog*
Thomas Mann	*Mario and the Magician*
James Joyce	*A Painful Case*
Virginia Woolf	*The Mark on the Wall*
D. H. Lawrence	*The Horse Dealer's Daughter*
John Cheever	*The Country Husband*
Flannery O'Connor	*Revelation*
Gabriel García Márquez	*Balthazar's Marvelous Afternoon*
John Barth	*Petition*

IV. Fantasy and Absurdity

Nikolai Gogol	*The Overcoat*
Edgar Allan Poe	*The Fall of the House of Usher*
Ambrose Bierce	*The Occurrence at Owl Creek Bridge*
E. M. Forster	*Dr Woolacott*
Franz Kafka	*A Hunger Artist*
Jorge Luis Borges	*Borges and I*
	Everything and Nothing
Tommaso Ladolfi	*Gogol's Wife*
Fredric Brown	*Solipsist*

Bernard Malamud   *The Magic Barrel*
Heinrich Böll   *Like a Bad Dream*
Julio Cortàzar   *Axolōtl*
John Barth   *Petition*
Donald Barthelme   *At the End of the Mechanical Age*

V. Adventure and Mystery

Nathaniel Hawthorne   *The Minister's Black Veil*
Edgar Allan Poe   *The Fall of the House of Usher*
Ambrose Bierce   *The Occurrence at Owl Creek Bridge*
Stephen Crane   *The Open Boat*
Jorge Luis Borges   *The Waiting*
Julio Cortàzar   *Axolōtl*
Alain Robbe-Grillet   *The Shore*
Sir Thomas Malory   *The Great Tournament*

VI. Loneliness and Alienation

Nathaniel Hawthorne   *The Minister's Black Veil*
Nikolai Gogol   *The Overcoat*
Edgar Allan Poe   *The Fall of the House of Usher*
Ivan Turgenev   *Raspberry Spring*
Herman Melville   *Bartleby, the Scrivener*
Gustave Flaubert   *A Simple Heart*
Thomas Mann   *Mario and the Magician*
E. M. Forster   *Dr Woolacott*
James Joyce   *A Painful Case*
Isaac Babel   *My First Goose*
F. Scott Fitzgerald   *Babylon Revisited*
Ernest Hemingway   *Hills Like White Elephants*
Eudora Welty   *A Worn Path*
John Cheever   *The Country Husband*
Aleksandr Solzhenitsyn   *The Right Hand*
John Updike   *Leaves*

VII. Love and Sex

Henry James   *The Beast in the Jungle*
Guy de Maupassant   *The Avenger*
                             A Country Outing
Anton Chekhov   *Ninochka: A Love Story*
                             The Lady with the Pet Dog
Edith Wharton   *Roman Fever*
Thomas Mann   *Mario and the Magician*
Sherwood Anderson   *I Want to Know Why*
E. M. Forster   *Dr Woolacott*
James Joyce   *A Painful Case*
D. H. Lawrence   *Tickets, Please*
                             The Horse Dealer's Daughter
Isaac Babel   *The Sin of Jesus*
William Faulkner   *That Evening Sun*
Ernest Hemingway   *Hills Like White Elephants*
John Cheever   *The Country Husband*

Bernard Malamud	*The Magic Barrel*
Carson McCullers	*A Tree * A Rock * A Cloud*
Grace Paley	*Friends*
John Updike	*Leaves*
Raymond Carver	*Neighbors*
Joyce Carol Oates	*Where Are You Going, Where Have You Been?*

VIII. Justice and Injustice

Nikolai Gogol	*The Overcoat*
Ivan Turgenev	*Raspberry Spring*
Ambrose Bierce	*The Occurrence at Owl Creek Bridge*
Thomas Mann	*Mario and the Magician*
E. M. Forster	*Dr Woolacott*
D. H. Lawrence	*Tickets, Please*
William Faulkner	*That Evening Sun*
Aleksandr Solzhenitsyn	*The Right Hand*
Cynthia Ozick	*The Shawl*
Jorge Luis Borges	*The Waiting*
Heinrich Böll	*Like a Bad Dream*
Gabriel García Márquez	*Balthazar's Marvelous Afternoon*

IX. Cruelty and Suffering

Nathaniel Hawthorne	*The Minister's Black Veil*
Edgar Allan Poe	*The Fall of the House of Usher*
Ivan Turgenev	*Raspberry Spring*
Ambrose Bierce	*The Occurrence at Owl Creek Bridge*
Guy de Maupassant	*The Avenger*
Anton Chekhov	*Heartache*
	The Lady with the Pet Dog
Edith Wharton	*Roman Fever*
Thomas Mann	*Mario and the Magician*
James Joyce	*A Painful Case*
Franz Kafka	*A Hunger Artist*
D. H. Lawrence	*Tickets, Please*
William Faulkner	*That Evening Sun*
Aleksandr Solzhenitsyn	*The Right Hand*
Flannery O'Connor	*Revelation*
Cynthia Ozick	*The Shawl*
Samuel Beckett	*The End*

X. Decline and Loss

Nikolai Gogol	*The Overcoat*
Herman Melville	*Bartleby, the Scrivener*
Gustave Flaubert	*A Simple Heart*
Ambrose Bierce	*The Occurrence at Owl Creek Bridge*
Edith Wharton	*Roman Fever*
James Joyce	*A Painful Case*
F. Scott Fitzgerald	*Babylon Revisited*
Jorge Luis Borges	*The Waiting*
Yukio Mishima	*Patriotism*
Samuel Beckett	*The End*
Donald Barthelme	*At the End of the Mechanical Age*

PART II: SUBJECTS

I. Dreams and Daydreams

Nikolai Gogol	*The Overcoat*
Edgar Allan Poe	*The Fall of the House of Usher*
Gustave Flaubert	*A Simple Heart*
Henry James	*The Beast in the Jungle*
Virginia Woolf	*The Mark on the Wall*
Conrad Aiken	*Silent Snow, Secret Snow*
Richard Wilbur	*A Game of Catch*
Raymond Carver	*Neighbors*
Jorge Luis Borges	*Borges and I*
	Everything and Nothing
Tommaso Landolfi	*Gogol's Wife*
Delmore Schwartz	*In Dreams Begin Responsibilities*
Julio Cortázar	*Axolōtl*

II. Journeys Inward and Outward

John Bunyan	*The Pilgrim's Progress*
Nathaniel Hawthorne	*The Minister's Black Veil*
Edgar Allan Poe	*The Fall of the House of Usher*
Ivan Turgenev	*Raspberry Spring*
Ambrose Bierce	*The Occurrence at Owl Creek Bridge*
Thomas Mann	*Mario and the Magician*
Sherwood Anderson	*I Want to Know Why*
Virginia Woolf	*The Mark on the Wall*
Conrad Aiken	*Silent Snow, Secret Snow*
Katherine Anne Porter	*The Grave*
Eudora Welty	*A Worn Path*
John Updike	*Leaves*
Jorge Luis Borges	*Everything and Nothing*
Samuel Beckett	*The End*
Fredric Brown	*Solipsism*

III. Sex, Marriage, Family, Children

Guy de Maupassant	*A Country Outing*
	The Avenger
Anton Chekhov	*Ninochka: A Love Story*
	The Lady with the Pet Dog
Edith Wharton	*Roman Fever*
E. M. Forster	*Dr Woolacott*
James Joyce	*A Painful Case*
D. H. Lawrence	*Tickets, Please*
	The Horse Dealer's Daughter
Katherine Mansfield	*The Garden-Party*
Ernest Hemingway	*Hills Like White Elephants*
Carson McCullers	*A Tree * A Rock * A Cloud*
Bernard Malamud	*The Magic Barrel*
Yukio Mishima	*Patriotism*
John Updike	*Leaves*

Joyce Carol Oates	*Where Are You Going, Where Have You Been?*
Tommaso Landolfi	*Gogol's Wife*
John Barth	*Petition*

IV. Animals and People

Aesop	*Fables*
Kiowa Indians	*Kiowa Legends*
Seneca Indians	*The Origin of Stories*
Gustave Flaubert	*A Simple Heart*
Sherwood Anderson	*I Want to Know Why*
D. H. Lawrence	*The Horse Dealer's Daughter*
Isaac Babel	*My First Goose*
Flannery O'Connor	*Revelation*
Julio Cortázar	*Axolōtl*

V. Country and City

Guy de Maupassant	*A Country Outing*
Sherwood Anderson	*I Want to Know Why*
Eudora Welty	*A Worn Path*
John Cheever	*The Country Husband*
Flannery O'Connor	*Revelation*

VI. Clerks and Bureaucrats

Nikolai Gogol	*The Overcoat*
Herman Melville	*Bartleby, the Scrivener*
Anton Chekhov	*The Lady with the Pet Dog*
Aleksandr Solzhenitsyn	*The Right Hand*
Heinrich Böll	*Like a Bad Dream*
Donald Barthelme	*At the End of the Mechanical Age*

VII. Money, Property, and Poverty

Matthew 25	*The Parable of the Talents*
Ivan Turgenev	*Raspberry Spring*
Herman Melville	*Bartleby, the Scrivener*
Edith Wharton	*Roman Fever*
William Faulkner	*That Evening Sun*
F. Scott Fitzgerald	*Babylon Revisited*
Eudora Welty	*A Worn Path*
John Cheever	*The Country Husband*
Flannery O'Connor	*Revelation*
Heinrich Böll	*Like a Bad Dream*
Gabriel García Márquez	*Balthazar's Marvelous Afternoon*

VIII. Crime and Punishment

Genesis 1–3	*The Story of Adam and Eve*
Edgar Allan Poe	*The Fall of the House of Usher*
Ambrose Bierce	*The Occurrence at Owl Creek Bridge*
Guy de Maupassant	*The Avenger*
Richard Wright	*The Man Who Was Almost a Man*
Yukio Mishima	*Patriotism*

| Joyce Carol Oates | *Where Are You Going, Where Have You Been?* |
| Jorge Luis Borges | *The Waiting* |

IX. Prejudice

Ivan Turgenev	*Raspberry Spring*
James Joyce	*A Painful Case*
Isaac Babel	*My First Goose*
Katherine Mansfield	*The Garden-Party*
F. Scott Fitzgerald	*Babylon Revisited*
William Faulkner	*That Evening Sun*
Eudora Welty	*A Worn Path*
John Barth	*Petition*

X. Simpletons and Underdogs

Matthew 25	*The Parable of the Ten Virgins*
Geoffrey Chaucer	*The Miller's Tale*
Ivan Turgenev	*Raspberry Spring*
Gustave Flaubert	*A Simple Heart*
Anton Chekhov	*Heartache*
Franz Kafka	*A Hunger Artist*
Isaac Babel	*The Sin of Jesus*
Richard Wright	*The Man Who Was Almost a Man*
Eudora Welty	*A Worn Path*
Carson McCullers	*A Tree * A Rock * A Cloud*
Gabriel García Márquez	*Balthazar's Marvelous Afternoon*

XI. The Timid and the Brave

Nikolai Gogol	*The Overcoat*
Henry James	*The Beast in the Jungle*
Gustave Flaubert	*A Simple Heart*
Thomas Mann	*Mario and the Magician*
Franz Kafka	*A Hunger Artist*
Isaac Babel	*My First Goose*
Richard Wilbur	*A Game of Catch*
Grace Paley	*Friends*
Yukio Mishima	*Patriotism*
John Updike	*Leaves*
Raymond Carver	*Neighbors*
Toni Cade Bambara	*Raymond's Run*

XII. War and Peace

Ambrose Bierce	*The Occurrence at Owl Creek Bridge*
Thomas Mann	*Mario and the Magician*
Aleksandr Solzhenitsyn	*The Right Hand*
Yukio Mishima	*Patriotism*
Cynthia Ozick	*The Shawl*

XIII. Entropy and Death

| Nathaniel Hawthorne | *The Minister's Black Veil* |
| Edgar Allan Poe | *The Fall of the House of Usher* |

Henry James	*The Beast in the Jungle*
Stephen Crane	*The Open Boat*
E. M. Forster	*Dr Woolacott*
James Joyce	*A Painful Case*
Ernest Hemingway	*Hills Like White Elephants*
Cynthia Ozick	*The Shawl*
Samuel Beckett	*The End*
Donald Barthelme	*At the End of the Mechanical Age*

Brief Glossary of Terms

The following are some brief and necessarily simple definitions of the genres represented in this volume.

ALLEGORY   (See discussion p. 39.)

ANTIREALISM   Antirealists reject traditional techniques of fiction—plots, character, point of view, "showing" versus "telling"—which they believe are inadequate for modern experience. They are drawn to the farther reaches of imagination—fairy tales, fantasy, grotesquerie, utter subjectivity, absurdity, outrageous satire, wild-inventive humor. (See discussions, pp. 3–5.)

AVANT-GARDE   (See Modernism.)

COMEDY   It is impossible to define comedy in a short space, but it may be of value to suggest some of its parameters. In his essay "Laughter," Henri Bergson says that we laugh whenever we encounter "the mechanical encrusted on the living." When a human being acts like a robot instead of the living creature he is supposed to be, then we laugh—unconsciously trying to laugh him out of his mechanicalness and back into his humanity. But *comedy* is a bigger word than *laugher;* it exists on a spectrum stretching from lighthearted farce and horseplay (at which we laugh) to such deadly serious forms as "black humor" or "gallows humor" which are, quite literally, no laughing matter—though we sometimes laugh anyway. Irony (see pp. 15–16) can be comic or not, depending on the context. Comedy, in short, is a profound and complex subject, as is shown by the fact that it can apply to stories as various as Cheever's "The Country Husband" and Beckett's "The End" or Malamud's "The Magic Barrel" and Barth's "Petition."

EXPRESSIONISM   Expressionism began in the late nineteenth century as a reaction against realism, which was thought to be inadequate for expressing the anguish of modern experience. Expressionists project onto external objects and events internal states of mind. This inner experience is apt to be troubled, anxious, or otherwise abnormal. Chief exponents have been the playwrights August Strindberg (1849–1912) and Bertolt Brecht (1899–1956) and the painters Edvard Münch (1863–1944) and Émile Nolde (1867–1956). Though not frequently used in relation to fiction, the term can be useful in understanding certain antirealists and absurdists in whose work chronology is disrupted, time dislocated, place distorted in order to express the inner condition.

FABLE   (See discussion, pp. 38–41.)

FABLIAU   (See discussion, p. 44.)

FANTASY   Fantasy is as old as fairy tales, as old as dreams, and as new as Antirealism, or Modernism. In fiction, it is the tapping of the world of imagination or dream as opposed to the world of actuality. The elements of play, sport, whimsy, and lighthearted absurdity are often strong in fantasy, but Freud said: "A happy person never fantasies, only an unsatisfied one . . . every single fantasy is the fulfillment of a wish, a correction of unsatisfied reality." (See discussion, pp. 3–4.)

FOLKTALE   (See discussion, pp. 1–2, 24–26.)

GOTHIC TALE (GOTHICISM)   The word *Gothic* (from *Goths,* a German tribe) came to refer to a style of medieval architecture, to stone-vaulted churches and castles with pointed arches and grotesque decorations. Popular in the late eighteenth and early nineteenth centuries were novels set against backgrounds of Gothic architecture, tales fraught with horror, supernaturalism, perversity. The term has come to signify any fiction that is violent and melodramatic, with abnormal characters and a chilling atmosphere, as in the works of Poe and the "Southern Gothic" writers. (See discussion, pp. 101–102.)

IMPRESSIONISM   In literature, as in art and music, impressionism is the effort to portray the effects of experience on consciousness rather than to render reality objectively. Impressionist painters—Monet, Renoir, Pissarro, among others—eschewed formal "Academy" approaches and explored ways of representing the effects of light and air in broken color. To them the "feel" of the scene was more important than attention to detail. Likewise in music, impressionists—like Debussy and Ravel—broke with traditional methods of composition in their desire to evoke a "mood" in the listener.

IRONY   (See discussion, pp. 15–16.)

LEGEND   (See discussion, pp. 24–26.)

MODERNISM   Modernism (including postmodernism) as an artistic movement is a response to the discontinuities, illogicalities, and fragmentation of culture and society in the present day. It refers to the tendency to experiment in radical new techniques, themes, moods, and structures. Atonalism in music, surrealism in painting, *vers libre* in poetry, functionalism in architecture are a few of its manifestations. Modernist writers of fiction eschew the traditional techniques (characterization, plot, consistent point of view, etc.) in favor of a broad range of experimental inventions and developments and generally convey an ironic rather than a reverent view of human life.

MYTH   (See discussions, pp. 1–2, 24–26.)

NATURALISM   Naturalism is a literary movement based on the belief that man is the product of heredity and environment, and that his behavior is completely—or mainly—controlled by social, economic, and biologic forces. Naturalist writers, therefore, tend to render reality in cross section, as a "slice of life," much as a scientist might dissect a specimen for study. As James T. Farrell put it, "Just as science helps man to understand nature, literature helps man to understand himself." Characteristically, naturalist writers tend to be concerned with people in the lower economic strata of society who are victimized by a destructive social environment. Their mode of narration tends to be detached, remote, yet sometimes brutally frank about sexual behavior, bodily functions, and the bestial aspects of human beings. The movement took root in nineteenth century France in the work of Flaubert, Daudet, Maupassant, and especially Émile Zola. In the United States a vigorous school of naturalist writers grew up, led by Stephen Crane, Theodore Dreiser, Frank Norris, and James T. Farrell. Thomas Hardy, among other British writers, also shows the influence of the movement.

NOVELLA   The novella is a novelette, a prose fiction of middle length, and could as well be called a short novel. The term derives from the Italian *novella* ("a little new thing") of which the tales of Boccaccio's *Decameron* are classic examples. (See discussion, p. 43.) Examples of the novella in this volume are Melville's *Bartleby, the Scrivener,* James's *The Beast in the Jungle,* Flaubert's *A Simple Heart,* and Mann's *Mario and the Magician.*

ORIENTAL TALE   (See mention, p. 44.)

PARABLE   (See discussion, pp. 38–39.)

REALISM   Realism in fiction took its rise from writers like Flaubert in France and George Eliot in England. It is an attempt to render "actual" life in recognizable verisimilitude, to present scenes so that the reader has the sense of witnessing everyday experiences. Realism is opposed to Romance, since the characters in realistic fiction are life-size and the events subject to credible cause-effect sequence. No one has put the case for realism better than George Eliot in her novel *Adam Bede:* "I turn, without shrinking, from cloud-borne angels, from prophets, sibyls, and heroic warriors, to an old woman bending over her flower-pot, or eating her solitary dinner, while the noonday light, softened perhaps by a screen of leaves, falls on her mob-cap, and just touches the rim of her spinning wheel, and her stone jug, and all those cheap common things which are the precious necessaries of life to her. . . ."

ROMANCE   Romance is best defined in contrast to Realism. Northrop Frye says, "The romancer does not attempt to create 'real people' so much as stylized figures which expand into psychological archetypes. . . . The romance, which deals with heroes, is intermediate between the novel, which deals with men, and the myth, which deals with gods." The traditional subject matter of romance is courtly love and chivalric deeds often made mysterious with magic and marvels. But in reference to the short story Romance is a generic term embracing a wide range of nonrealistic writing, from allegories and fables to fantasies and Gothic tales.

SATIRE   Satire in fiction is an exposure of the follies and foibles, the vices and shortcomings, of men or societies, or almost anything. It is a conservative genre since the satirist does not wish to destroy but to reinvoke normalcy, to rebuild. Satire can be gentle or harsh, laughter-provoking or denunciatory. Irony is often employed in satire; invective is just as likely.

SCIENCE FICTION   This genre goes far back in literature and includes such works as the Faust legend and Mary Wollstonecraft Shelley's *Frankenstein.* It is an attempt to explore and present in fictional terms the wonders of science, past and future. Although it has tended to portray utopias, science fiction recently has rendered dystopias as well—visions of science become master rather than servant of man.

Although no story in this volume is strictly or exclusively science fiction, many stories contain elements of it, and many of the writers here represented have worked in or near it, most notably Poe and Brown, but also Hawthorne, Forster, Cortázar, Barthelme.

SURREALISM   The intention of surrealists is to release the energy and knowledge of the unconscious mind. Dreams, nightmares, free associations, hallucinations (occasionally drug-induced) are its subject matter. The movement became important in the twenties, and though more influential in painting (de Chirico, Dali, Magritte), it had an important impact on prose, sometimes directly (as with its founder André Breton) and sometimes indirectly (as with Henry Miller and William Burroughs). It is a near relation to Dadaism, an art movement that exploited the absurd, the meaningless, and the irreverent in order to tell a vicious modern society that it too was irrational and without values. In surrealism (though it is less radical) some of the same impulses survive, and stories like Böll's "Like a Bad Dream" embody some of these qualities. (See discussion, pp. 3–4.)

SYMBOLISM   (See discussion pp. 21–22.)

List of Useful Books

Aldridge, John W., ed. *Critiques and Essays on Modern Fiction,* 1920–1951. New York: Ronald Press Co., 1952.

Anderson, Imbert, Enrique. *Teoría y técnica del cuento.* Buenos Aires: Ediciones Marymar, 1979.

Auerbach, Erich. *Mimesis.* Princeton: Princeton University Press, 1953.

Bates, H. E. *The Modern Short Story, A Critical Survey.* Boston: The Writer, Inc., 1941.

Booth, Wayne C. *The Rhetoric of Fiction.* Chicago: University of Chicago Press, 1961.

Bosch, Juan. *Teoría del cuento: tres ensayos.* Mérida, Venezuela: Universidad de los Andes, 1967.

Brooks, Cleanth, Jr., and Robert Penn Warren, eds. *Understanding Fiction.* New York: Appleton-Century-Crofts, Inc., 1943.

Canby, Henry Siedel, and Alfred Dashiel. *A Study of the Short Story.* Revised. New York: Henry Holt, 1935.

Chekhov, Anton. *Letters of Anton Chekhov,* Avram Yarmolinsky, ed. New York: The Viking Press, 1973.

Cowley, Malcolm, ed. *Writers at Work: The Paris Review Interviews.* New York: The Viking Press, 1958.

Current-García, Eugene, ed. *What Is the Short Story?* Glenview, Illinois: Scott Foresman and Co., 1974.

Current-García, Eugene, and Walton R. Patrick, eds. *Realism and Romanticism in Fiction.* Chicago: Scott, Foresman and Co., 1962.

Dietrich, R. F. and Roger H. Sundall. *The Art of Fiction: A Handbook and Anthology*. New York: Holt, Rinehart and Winston, 1967.

Ferguson, Suzanne. *Formal Developments in the English Short Story, 1880–1910*. Ph.D. Thesis. Stanford University, 1966.

Fletcher, Angus. *Allegory. The Theory of a Symbolic Mode*. Ithaca: Cornell University Press, 1964.

Forster, E. M. *Aspects of the Novel*. New York: Harcourt, Brace, & World, Inc., 1927.

Franco, Jean. *Spanish American Literature Since Independence*. New York: Barnes and Noble Publications, 1973.

Gass, William. *Fiction and the Figures of Life*. New York: Alfred A. Knopf, Inc., 1970.

Gordon, Caroline, and Allen Tate. *The House of Fiction*. New York: Charles Scribner's Sons, 1960.

Hersey, John, ed. *The Writer's Craft*. New York: Alfred A. Knopf, Inc., 1974.

Hills, Rust. *Writing in General and the Short Story in Particular: An Informal Textbook*. Boston: Houghton Mifflin, 1977.

James, Henry. *The Art of Fiction and Other Essays*. Morris Roberts, ed. New York: Oxford University Press, 1948.

Kazin, Alfred. *Bright Book of Life: American Novelists and Storytellers from Hemingway to Mailer*. Boston: Little, Brown & Co., 1973.

Kenner, Hugh, ed. *Studies in Change: A Book of the Short Story*. Englewood Cliffs, N.J.: Prentice-Hall, 1965.

Kermode, Frank. *The Sense of an Ending: Studies in the Theory of Fiction*. London and New York: Oxford University Press, 1966.

Klinkowitz, Jerome, and John Somer, eds. *Innovative Fiction Stories for the Seventies*. New York: Dell Publishing Co., Inc., 1972.

Levin, Harry. *The Gates of Horn: A Study of Five French Realists*. London and New York: Oxford University Press, 1963.

Lubbock, Percy. *The Craft of Fiction*. New York: The Viking Press, 1957.

Matthews, Brander. *The Philosophy of the Short Story*. New York: Folcroft, 1912.

May, Charles E., ed. *Short Story Theories*. Athens, Ohio: Ohio University Press, 1976.

Mirrielees, Edith R. *Story Writing*. Boston: The Writer, Inc., 1947.

O'Connor, Flannery. *Mystery and Manners*. Sally and Robert Fitzgerald, eds. New York: Farrar, Straus & Giroux, 1969.

O'Connor, Frank [Michael O'Donovan, pseud.]. *The Lonely Voice*. New York: The World Publishing Co., 1962.

O'Connor, William Van, ed. *Form of Modern Fiction*. Bloomington: Indiana University Press, 1948.

O'Faolain, Sean. *The Short Story*. Old Greenwich, Conn.: The Devin-Adair Co., 1964.

Peden, William. *The American Short Story: Front Line in the National Defense of Literature*. Boston: Houghton Mifflin, 1964.

Reid, Ian. *The Short Story*. London: Methuen; New York: Barnes and Noble Publications, 1977.

Ross, Danforth. *The American Short Story*. Minneapolis: The University of Minnesota Press, 1961.

Sarraute, Nathalie. *The Age of Suspicion: Essays on the Novel*. New York: George Braziller, Inc., 1963.

Stegner, Wallace. *Teaching the Short Story*. Berkeley: University of California Press, 1965.

Steiner, George. *Language and Silence: Essays on Language, Literature and the Inhuman*. New York: Atheneum, 1967.

Stevick, Philip, ed. *Anti-Story: An Anthology of Experimental Fiction*. New York and London: The Free Press and Collier-Macmillan Ltd., 1971.

Strzetelski, Jerzy. *Some Problems of Short Fiction: The Dramatic Short Story*. Crakow: Naktadeu Uniwersytetu Jagiellouskiego, 1976.

Sukenick, Ronald. *The Death of the Novel and Other Stories*. New York: The Dial Press, 1969.

Tanner, Tony. *City of Words: American Fiction 1950–1970*. New York: Harper & Row, 1971.

Trilling, Lionel. *The Liberal Imagination: Essays on Literature and Society*. New York: The Viking Press, Inc., 1950.

Walker, Warren S. *Twentieth-Century Short Story Explication,* 3d ed. Hamden, Connecticut: Shoe String Press, 1977.

Wellek, René, and Austin Warren. *Theory of Literature*. New York: Harcourt Brace & Co., 1942. See Chapter XVI, "The Nature and Modes of Narrative Fiction."

Woolf, Virginia. *A Writer's Diary*. New York: Harcourt, Brace & World, Inc., 1953.

Woolf, Virginia. "Mr. Bennett and Mrs. Brown" in *The Captain's Death Bed and Other Essays*. London: Hogarth Press, 1950.

Wright, Austin McGiffert. *The American Short Story in the Twenties*. Chicago: University of Chicago Press, 1965.

Additional
Acknowledgments

Toni Cade Bambara, from *Gorilla, My Love*. New York: Random House, 1972, p. ix.

Donald Barthelme, from *Snow White*. Copyright © 1967. With permission of Atheneum Publishers.

John S. Brushwood, from *The Spanish American Novel*.

E. Caracciolo-Trejo, from *The Penguin Book of Latin American Verse*. Copyright © 1971. With permission of Penguin Books, Ltd.

Giacomo Debendetti, from "A Note on Landolfi," in *Cancerqueen and Other Stories*, translated by Raymond Rosenthal. With permission of The Dial Press.

William Faulkner in *Writers at Work, The 'Paris Review' Interviews, First Series*, edited by Malcolm Cowley. With permission of Martin Secker & Warburg Ltd.

Suzanne Carol Ferguson, from *Formal Development in the English Short Story*, 1966. With permission of the author.

David Galloway, from Edgar Allan Poe's *Selected Writings*. Copyright © 1967. With permission of Penguin Books Ltd.

William H. Gass, from *Fiction and the Figures of Life*. New York: Knopf, 1970, pp. 105–106.

Louise Y. Gossett, from *Violence in Recent Southern Fiction*. Copyright © 1973. With permission of Duke University Press.

Robert Halsband, from "Sketch Potpourri," in *The Saturday Review*, May 7, 1949. With permission of the publisher.

Rust Hills (ed.), from *Writer's Choice*. New York: David McKay Co., 197■ p. 391.

Index

Index

"A Tree * A Rock * A Cloud" (Carson McCullers), 7, 17, 22, 444–449

Abinger Harvest (E. M. Forster), 289

Absalom, Absalom! (William Faulkner), 384

Absurdity, the absurd, 3, 80, 364, 433, 567, 580, 595

Acquainted with the Night (Heinrich Böll), 566

Adventure and mystery (thematic topic), 596

Advice to a Prophet (Richard Wilbur), 458

Aesop's *Fables*, 21, 22, 39–40

Age of Innocence, The (Edith Wharton), 230

Aiken, Conrad, 22, 347–348, 546

Allegory, 3, 38–39, 602

Allegory: The Theory of a Symbolic Mode (Angus Fletcher), 39

Amateurs (Donald Barthelme), 589

Amerika (Franz Kafka), 311

Among the Lost People (Conrad Aiken), 347

Anderson, Sherwood, 23, 283, 396, 444, 581

Angels and Spaceships (Fredric Brown), 554

Animals and people (thematic topic), 599

Anti-realism, anti-fiction, 3–4, 10, 17, 144–145, 562–563, 571–572, 580, 595, 602
(*See also* Modern fiction)

Anti-story (Philip Stevick), 4, 10, 17

Anton Chekhov: Selected Stories, 213

Arendt, Hannah, 567

Art of Fiction, The (Henry James), 173

Aspects of the Novel (E. M. Forster), 16

Assistant, The (Bernard Malamud), 432

"At the End of the Mechanical Age" (Donald Barthelme), 3, 4, 589–593

August 1914 (Aleksandr I. Solzhenitsyn), 450

Autumn of the Patriarchs, The (Gabriel García Márquez), 575

"Avenger, The" (Guy de Maupassant), 20, 209–212

"Axolōtl" (Julio Cortázar), 4, 21, 563–566

Babel, Isaac, 2, 10, 20, 21, 364

"Babylon Revisited" (F. Scott Fitzgerald), 371–383

Baldick, Robert, 145

Baldwin, James, 400

Ballad of the Sad Café, The (Carson McCullers), 444

"Balthazar's Marvelous Afternoon" (Gabriel García Márquez), 20

Balzac, Honoré, 384

Bambara, Toni Cade, 522–523

Barrett, Elizabeth, 102

Barrie, Sir James, 44

Barth, John, 3, 4, 16, 19, 580–581

Barthelme, Donald, 3, 4, 38, 588

"Bartleby, the Scrivener: A Story of Wall Street" (Herman Melville), 4, 7, 19, 20, 122–144

Bates, H. E., 5, 213

Baudelaire, Charles, 102, 145

Baum, L. Frank, 44

"Beast in the Jungle, The" (Henry James), 14, 174–200, 231

Beautiful Changes, The (Richard Wilbur), 458

Bech: A Book (John Updike), 503

Beckett, Samuel, 2, 4, 25, 534–535

Beerbohm, Max, 173

Belinsky, Vissarion Grigoryevitch, 552

Bellow, Saul, 25

Bennett, Arnold, 305

Beowulf, 2

Bergson, Henri, 3

Bernstein, J. S., 576

Berryman, John, 566

Bestiary, A (Richard Wilbur), 458

Between the Acts (Virginia Woolf), 305

Bierce, Ambrose, 166

Billiards at Half-Past Nine (Heinrich Böll), 566

Black writing, 399–400, 522–523

Blackburn, Paul, 563

Blithedale Romance, The (Nathaniel Hawthorne), 71

Bloodshed and Three Novellas (Cynthia Ozick), 498

Bloomsbury Group, The, 289, 306, 337

Blow-Up (Julio Cortázar), 562

"Blue Beard, The," 44, 67–70

Boccaccio, Giovanni, 43–45

Böll, Heinrich, 2, 25, 39, 566–567

Booth, Wayne, 571

Borges, Jorge Luis, 4, 17, 39, 529–530, 562, 575

"Borges and I" (Jorge Luis Borges), 17, 39, 533

"Boule de Suif" (Guy de Maupassant), 200

Bowen, Elizabeth, 5, 7, 18, 20

Brevity (*see* Compression)

Bride of Innesfallen and Other Stories, The (Eudora Welty), 410

Brod, Max, 311

Brodsky, Joseph, 450

Brown, Fredric, 4, 21, 38, 554–555

Browning, Elizabeth Barrett, 102

Brushwood, John S., 575

Bunyan, John, 21, 39, 42–43, 71

Burg, David, 450

Campbell, Joseph, 21
Can Such Things Be? (Ambrose
    Bierce), 166
Cancer Ward (Aleksandr I. Solzhen-
    itsyn), 450
Cancerqueen and Other Stories
    (Tommaso Landolfi), 547
Canterbury Tales, The (Geoffrey
    Chaucer), 43, 44, 52
Carpentier, Alejo, 562
Carver, Raymond, 506
Castle, The (Franz Kafka), 311
Celestial Omnibus, The (E. M. For-
    ster), 289
Centaur, The (John Updike), 502
"Central Intelligence," 14, 173–174
Ceremony (Richard Wilbur), 458
Character, characterization, 5, 8–10,
    16, 19–21, 200–201, 230,
    239–240, 305, 359–360, 409–410,
    416, 432–433, 469–470,
    502–503, 506, 571–572
Chaucer, Geoffrey, 43, 44, 52
Cheever, John, 4, 370, 415–417
Chekhov, Anton, 5–8, 14–18, 22, 23,
    201, 212–213, 337, 364, 409–506
Cherry Orchard, The (Anton Chek-
    hov), 213
Childhood and youth (thematic
    topic), 595
Chimera (John Barth), 581
"Cinderella," 44
*City of Words: American Fiction
    1950–1970* (Tony Tanner),
    588–589
Clerks and bureaucrats (thematic
    topic), 599
Clown, The (Heinrich Böll), 566
Coghill, Nevill, 52
Collected Impressions (Elizabeth
    Bowen), 5, 20
Collected Stories, The (Isaac Babel),
    367
*Collected Stories of William Faulk-
    ner, The*, 384

Come Back, Dr. Caligari (Donald
    Barthelme), 589
Comédie Humaine, La, (Honoré
    Balzac), 384
Comedy, the comic, tragicomic, hu-
    mor, 44, 364, 416, 432–433,
    457–458, 470, 535, 554, 557,
    580–581, 588–589, 602
Complication, 17
Compliments of a Fiend (Fredric
    Brown), 555
Compression, 5–8, 457
Confessions of a Mask (Yukio Mish-
    ima), 483
Conrad, Joseph, 6, 173, 396
Contemporary Scene, The: The
    Break with Tradition, 529–593
Contemporary Scene, The: The On-
    going Tradition, 409–528
Cortázar, Julio, 4, 21, 562–563, 575
Cory, Herbert Ellsworth, 7
Country and city (thematic topic),
    599
"Country Husband, The" (John
    Cheever), 417–432
"Country Outing, A" (Guy de Mau-
    passant), 2, 8, 13, 19, 201–209
Craft of Fiction, The (Percy Lub-
    bock), 174
Crane, Stephen, 12, 19, 239–240, 396
Creation myth, 24–29
Crime and punishment (thematic
    topic), 599
Crisis, 17
Cruelty and suffering (thematic
    topic), 597
Cummins, Paul F., 458
Curtain of Green, A (Eudora Welty),
    410
Custom of the Country, The (Edith
    Wharton), 231

Dead Father, The (Donald Bar-
    thelme), 589

Dead Souls (Nikolai Gogol), 81, 547
Death Has Many Doors (Fredric Brown), 555
Death in Midsummer and Other Stories (Yukio Mishima), 484
Death in Venice (Thomas Mann), 257
Debenedetti, Giacomo, 546
Debussy, Claude, 102
Decameron, The (Giovanni Boccaccio), 43, 45–52
Decay of the Angel (Yukio Mishima), 484
Decline and loss (thematic topic), 597
Delta Wedding (Eudora Welty), 410
Denouement, 17
Description, 18–19, 200, 372–373, 395–396, 409–410, 571–572
Dialogue, 18–19, 305, 395–396
Dialogues (St. Gregory), 41–42
Dickens, Charles, 20
Direct observer (point of view), 13, 571–572
Distance, 145, 201, 240, 571–572
Doctor Faustus (Thomas Mann), 257
"Dr. Woolacott" (E. M. Forster), 290–298
"Dog in the Manger, The" (Aesop), 40
Dostoevsky, Feodor, 80, 114, 546
Dream of Fair to Middling Women, A (Samuel Beckett), 535
Dreams and daydreams (thematic topic), 598
Dreamtigers (Jorge Luis Borges), 530
Dreiser, Theodore, 283
Dubliners (James Joyce), 299
Dunnigan, Ann, 213

Early stories, 24–70
18 Stories (Heinrich Böll), 566
Eliot, T. S., 3, 19, 299, 347

Ellison, Ralph, 400
Emblem, 8, 22, 145, 359
"End, The" (Samuel Beckett), 2, 4, 25, 535–546
End of a Mission (Heinrich Böll), 566
End of the Game and Other Stories (Julio Cortázar), 563
End of the Road (John Barth), 580
Endgame (Samuel Beckett), 535
Enormous Changes at the Last Minute (Grace Paley), 461
Entropy and death (thematic topic), 600
Epiphany, 9, 10, 299, 360, 364, 366
Erasers, The (Alain Robbe-Grillet), 572
Escape (*see* Fantasy)
Esslin, Martin, 535
Eternal Moment, The (E. M. Forster), 289
Ethan Frome (Edith Wharton), 231
"Everything and Nothing" (Jorge Luis Borges), 4, 39, 533–534
Exemplum, 38–39, 41–42
Existential, existentialism, 311, 399–400, 563, 571
Expressionism, 311, 603

Fable, 38–39, 580, 603
Fabliau, 44, 52, 603
Fabulous Clip Joint, The (Fredric Brown), 554
Fairytale, 44
"Fall of the House of Usher, The" (Edgar Allan Poe), 15, 21, 102–113
Falling action, 17
Fanger, Donald, 450
Fantasy, 3, 4, 81, 166, 405, 432, 530, 546–547, 554–557, 562–563, 575, 589, 595
Farewell to Arms, A (Ernest Hemingway), 396

Fathers and Sons (Ivan Turgenev), 114

Faulkner, William, 5, 11, 23, 359, 383–384, 409, 562

Feifer, George, 450

Finnegans Wake (James Joyce), 299, 534

First Circle, The (Aleksandr I. Solzhenitsyn), 450

First-person (point of view), 13–14

Fitzgerald, F. Scott, 370

Fixer, The (Bernard Malamud), 432

Flaubert, Gustave, 11, 20, 144–145, 200, 201, 239

Fleishmann, W. B., 566

Fletcher, Angus, 39

Floating Opera, The (John Barth), 580

Folklore, folktales, 1, 24, 25, 29–34, 562, 603

Forbidden Colors (Yukio Mishima), 483

Forest in Flower (Yukio Mishima), 483

Forster, E. M., 16, 20, 289–290, 305

"Fox and the Crow, The" (Aesop), 39

Franco, Jean, 562, 575

Frankenstein (Mary Wollstonecraft Shelley), 604

Freud, Sigmund (also Freudian), 3, 22, 311, 347, 556

"Friends" (Grace Paley), 461–469

Fuentes, Carlos, 562

Galsworthy, John, 305

"Game of Catch, A" (Richard Wilbur), 457–461

García Márquez, Gabriel, 20, 562, 575

"Garden Party, The" (Katherine Mansfield), 25, 338–346

Garland, Hamlin, 239

Geismar, Maxwell, 283

Genesis, 24–29

Genet, Jean, 535

Ghosts (Henrik Ibsen), 347

Gide, André, 6n.

Giles Goat Boy (John Barth), 580

Gilgamesh, 2

Gogol, Nikolai, 2, 6, 11, 18, 20, 80–81, 114, 547

"Gogol's Wife" (Tommaso Landolfi), 3, 4, 11, 16, 19, 547–554

Gogol's Wife and Other Stories (Tommaso Landolfi), 547

Golden Age, The, 256–408

Golden Apples, The (Eudora Welty), 410

Gorilla, My Love (Toni Cade Bambara), 523

Gorki, Maxim, 8, 364

Gossett, Louise, 444

Gothic, gothic tale, 44, 71, 603

Grahame, Kenneth, 44

Grass, Günter, 567

"Grave, The" (Katherine Anne Porter), 14–15, 360–363

Great Days (Donald Barthelme), 589

Great Gatsby, The (F. Scott Fitzgerald), 370

"Great Tournament, The" (Sir Thomas Malory), 25, 34–38

Grimm, Jacob, 44

Grimm, Wilhelm, 44

Grotesque, grotesques, 444, 562, 603

Guerney, Bernard Guilbert, 81, 114

Guilty Pleasures (Donald Barthelme), 589

Gulag Archipelago (Aleksandr I. Solzhenitsyn), 450

Hall, Donald, 458

Handke, Peter, 567

"Hansel and Gretel," 44

Haunted House and Other Stories, The (Virginia Woolf), 306

Hawkes, John, 6n.
Hawthorne, Nathaniel, 38, 71–72, 121–122, 546
Heart is a Lonely Hunter, The (Carson McCullers), 443
"Heartache" (Anton Chekhov), 216–219
Hemingway, Ernest, 6–8, 13, 15, 359, 395–396, 484
Here Comes a Candle (Fredric Brown), 555
Hesse, Herman, 6n.
"Hills Like White Elephants" (Ernest Hemingway), 6, 8, 13, 396–399
Himes, Chester, 400
Hoffman, Frederick J., 348
Honeymoon in Hell (Fredric Brown), 555
Hopscotch (Julio Cortázar), 562
"Horse Dealer's Daughter, The" (D. H. Lawrence), 16, 318–328
House of Mirth (Edith Wharton), 230
House of the Seven Gables, The (Nathaniel Hawthorne), 71
Howards End (E. M. Forster), 289, 290
Howe, Irving, 399, 557
Humor (*see* Comedy, the comic, tragicomic, humor)
"Hunger Artist, The" (Franz Kafka), 312–317
Hunting Sketches, The (Ivan Turgenev), 113, 114, 283
Huxley, Aldous, 337

"I Want to Know Why" (Sherwood Anderson), 23, 284–289
Ibsen, Henrik, 347
Identity and self-discovery (thematic topic), 595
Imagery, 409, 432, 461, 499, 562
(*See also* Emblem)
Imbert, Enrique Anderson, 4

Impressionism, 22, 239, 603
"In Dreams Begin Responsibilities" (Delmore Schwartz), 3, 4, 14, 15, 557–562
"Incident at Krechetovka Station" (Aleksandr I. Solzhenitsyn), 450
Inspector General, The (Nikolai Gogol), 81, 114
Intensity (*see* Compression)
Ionesco, Eugene, 535
Irby, James E., viii
Irony, ironic, 12, 16, 102, 167, 174, 201, 337, 364, 432, 450, 461, 603

Jacob's Room (Virginia Woolf), 305
James, Henry, 6, 10, 14, 16, 20, 113, 173–174, 200, 201, 230, 231, 283, 379, 409
Jarrell, Randall, 556
Jealousy (Alain Robbe-Grillet), 571
Joseph and His Brothers (Thomas Mann), 256
Journeys, inward and outward (thematic topic), 598
Joyce, James, 9, 11, 298–299, 396, 534, 535
"Judgement Day" (Flannery O'Connor), 470
Jung, Carl, 21
Justice and injustice (thematic topic), 597

Kafka, Franz, 7, 39, 310, 311
Kermode, Frank, 2, 21, 283
Kiowa (tribe), 25, 29–31
Krapp's Last Tape (Samuel Beckett), 535

Labyrinths (Jorge Luis Borges), 530
Lady Chatterley's Lover (D. H. Lawrence), 317
"Lady with the Pet Dog, The" (Anton Chekhov), 6, 16, 20, 201, 220–230

Landolfi, Tommaso, 4, 16, 19, 546

Lange, Victor, 530

Last Tycoon, The (F. Scott Fitzgerald), 370

Last Year at Marienbad (Alain Robbe-Grillet), 572

Lawrence, D. H., 16, 23, 317–318, 337

Leaning Tower and Other Stories, The (Katherine Anne Porter), 360

"Leaves" (John Updike), 3, 8, 14, 21, 503–505

Legend, 1, 24–26, 603

Letters: A Novel (John Barth), 581

"Life of Ma Parker, The" (Katherine Mansfield), 337

Life to Come, The (E. M. Forster), 289

Light in August (William Faulkner), 384

Lights in the Sky Are Stars, The (Fredric Brown), 555

"Like a Bad Dream" (Heinrich Böll), 2, 23, 25, 567–571

Lindsay, Vachel, 283

Little Disturbances of Man, The (Grace Paley), 461

Loneliness and alienation (thematic topic), 596

Lonely Voice, The (Frank O'Connor), 81

Longest Journey, The (E. M. Forster), 289

Lost in the Funhouse (John Barth), 581

Love and sex (thematic topic), 596

Lowe-Porter, H. T., 257

Lowell, Robert, 556

Lubbock, Percy, 173

Luthi, Max, 44

Lyric, lyrical, 5, 114, 337, 416, 457, 461, 562

MacAndrew, Andrew R., 201

Macauley, Robie, 522

McCullers, Carson, 7, 17, 22, 443–444

McWilliams, Carey, 166

Madame Bovary (Gustave Flaubert), 144, 145

Maggie: A Girl of the Streets (Stephen Crane), 239

"Magic Barrel, The" (Bernard Malamud), 15, 17, 20, 432–443

Magic Barrel, The (Bernard Malamud), 432

Magic Mountain, The (Thomas Mann), 256

Magic realism, 562

Malamud, Bernard, 4, 16, 17, 20, 22, 432–433

Mallarmé, Stéphane, 2, 102

Malone Dies (Samuel Beckett), 535

Malory, Sir Thomas, 26

"Man Who Was Almost a Man, The" (Richard Wright), 2, 400–408

Mann, Thomas, 6, 15, 25, 256–257

Mansfield, Katherine, 25, 299, 337

Marble Faun, The (Nathaniel Hawthorne), 71

"Mario and the Magician" (Thomas Mann), 25, 257–282

"Mark on the Wall, The" (Virginia Woolf), 306–310

Martians Go Home (Fredric Brown), 555

Marx, Leo, 21

Masters, Edgar Lee, 283

"Matryona's Place" (Aleksandr I. Solzhenitsyn), 450

Matthew, St., 40–41

Maugham, Somerset, 17

Maupassant, Guy de, 2, 8, 13, 18, 19, 200–201, 337

Maurice (E. M. Forster), 289

Melville, Herman, 4, 7, 71, 121–122

Member of the Wedding, The (Carson McCullers), 444

Miller's Tale, The (Geoffrey Chaucer), 44, 52–67

Milosz, Czeslaw, 449
Mind Reader, The (Richard Wilbur), 458
"Minister's Black Veil, The" (Nathaniel Hawthorne), 72–80
Mishima, Yukio, 2, 12, 483–484
Moby Dick (Herman Melville), 71, 121, 239
Modern fiction, 2–5, 10, 144, 298–299, 529–530, 566–567, 588–589
(*See also* Anti-realism, anti-fiction)
Modernism, 603
Molloy (Samuel Beckett), 535
Momaday, N. Scott, 25
Money, property and poverty (thematic topic), 599
Mood (*see* Tone)
More Pricks Than Kicks (Samuel Beckett), 535
Morison, Walter, 365, 367
Morrissette, Bruce, 571
Morte d'Arthur, 25
"Mr. Bennett and Mrs. Brown" (Virginia Woolf), 305
Mrs. Dalloway (Virginia Woolf), 305
Muir, Edwin, vii
Muir, Willa, vii
Murray, Henry A., 347
Murry, John Middleton, 337
"Museum Piece" (Richard Wilbur), 458
"My First Goose" (Isaac Babel), 10, 20, 22, 365–367
Myth, 1, 2, 24–26, 364, 432, 554, 562, 603

Nabokov, Vladimir, 80
Narration, narrative, narrator, 11–16, 283, 364, 396, 409, 556–557, 571–572
Native Son (Richard Wright), 399
Natural, The (Bernard Malamud), 432

Naturalism, naturalistic, 239, 299, 305, 364, 399–400, 433, 506, 603–604
"Neighbors" (Raymond Carver), 506, 507–510
New Testament, The, 40–41
Nightmares and Geezenstacks (Fredric Brown), 554
"Ninochka" (Anton Chekhov), 5–6, 14, 213–216
Nobel Prize, The, 256, 384, 396, 449, 566
Novella, novelle, nouvelle, 7, 43, 173, 604
Novels and Tales of Henry James, The (Henry James), 174

"O Youth and Beauty" (John Cheever), 416
Oak and the Calf, The (Aleksandr I. Solzhenitsyn), 450
Oates, Joyce Carol, 19, 510–511, 581
"Occurrence at Owl Creek Bridge, An" (Ambrose Bierce), 167–172
O'Connor, Flannery, 4, 16, 18, 409, 469–470
O'Connor, Frank, 5, 11, 80, 396
O'Faolain, Sean, 5, 8, 11, 461
Old Man and the Sea, The (Ernest Hemingway), 396
Old Testament, The, 1, 26–28
Olson, Lawrence, 484
Omniscience (point of view), 12, 240, 556–557, 571
Omoo (Herman Melville), 121
One Day in the Life of Ivan Denisovitch (Aleksandr I. Solzhenitsyn), 450
One Hundred Years of Solitude (Gabriel García Márquez), 575
One Time, One Place: Mississippi in the Depression (Eudora Welty), 410
"Open Boat, The" (Stephen Crane), 12, 19, 240–255
Opposites (Richard Wilbur), 458

Optimist's Daughter, The (Eudora Welty), 410
Oriental tale, 44
"Origin of Stories" (Seneca Indian myth), 31–34
"Overcoat, The" (Nikolai Gogol), 2, 6, 11, 16–18, 20, 21, 81–101
Ozick, Cynthia, 4, 498–499

Pagan Rabbi and Other Stories, The (Cynthia Ozick), 498
"Painful Case, A" (James Joyce), 9, 300–305
Paley, Grace, 461
Parable, 38–41, 72, 121, 604
Paradox Lost (Fredric Brown), 554
Pardoner's Tale, The (Geoffrey Chaucer), 38
"Parker's Back" (Flannery O'Connor), 470
Passage to India (E. M. Forster), 289, 290
Pater, Walter, 484
"Patriotism" (Yukio Mishima), 2, 12, 484–498
Perrault, Charles, 44
"Peter Pan" (Sir James Barrie), 44
"Petition" (John Barth), 3, 4, 16, 19, 581–588
Picaresque, 44
Pierre (Herman Melville), 121
Pinter, Harold, 535
"Playboy" (Richard Wilbur), 458
Plot, 16–17, 213, 305, 395, 409, 416, 432
Poe, Edgar Allan, 5, 9, 15, 71, 80, 101–102, 337, 409, 562
Poetic justice, 17
Point Counterpoint (Aldous Huxley), 337
Point of illumination, 8–10, 200
Point of view, 11–15, 240, 283, 556–557, 571
Polhemus, Robert, 535
Ponder Heart, The (Eudora Welty), 410

Portable Chekhov, The, 216
Porter, Katherine Anne, 13, 359, 409
Portrait of the Artist as a Young Man (James Joyce), 299
Prejudice (thematic topic), 600
Premios, Los (Julio Cortázar), 562
Pritchett, V. S., 9
Proust, Marcel, 256, 443

Rabbit is Rich (John Updike), 502
Rabbit, Run (John Updike), 502
Rahv, Philip, 25, 310
Rainbow, The (D. H. Lawrence), 317
Ransom, John Crowe, 409
"Raspberry Spring" (Ivan Turgenev), 18, 114
"Raymond's Run" (Toni Cade Bambara), 523–528
Rayuela (Julio Cortázar), 562
Realism, 3, 80, 144–145, 167, 239, 283, 298–299, 305–306, 364, 399–400, 432–433, 562–563, 604
Red Badge of Courage, The (Stephen Crane), 239
Redburn (Herman Melville), 121
Reflections in a Golden Eye (Carson McCullers), 444
Resnais, Alain, 572
Responses (Richard Wilbur), 458
"Revelation" (Flannery O'Connor), 16, 18, 470–483
Reyes, Los (Julio Cortázar), 562
"Right Hand, The" (Aleksandr I. Solzhenitsyn), 450–457
Rising action, 17
Rites of passage (thematic topic), 595
Robbe-Grillet, Alain, 3, 4, 15, 17, 571–572
Róheim, Géza, 24, 26
"Roman Fever" (Edith Wharton), 16, 231–239
Romance, romantic, romanticism, 43

Room With a View, A (E. M. Forster), 289
Runaway Horses (Yukio Mishima), 484

St. Gregory, 38, 41–42
St. Matthew, The Gospel According to, 40–41
Salammbô (Gustave Flaubert), 144
Salt Eaters, The (Toni Cade Bambara), 522
Sandburg, Carl, 283
Sargeant, Geoffrey, 484
Satire, 44, 166, 416, 566, 575, 604
Scarlet Letter, The (Nathaniel Hawthorne), 71
Scholes, Robert, 581
Schorer, Mark, 444
Schwartz, Delmore, 3, 4, 14, 15, 556–557
Science fiction (thematic topic), 604–605
Screaming Mimi, The (Fredric Brown), 554
Sea Birds Are Still Alive (Toni Cade Bambara), 522
Sea Gull, The (Anton Chekhov), 213
Sea of Fertility, The (Yukio Mishima), 484
Seidensticker, Edward G., 484
Seneca (Indian myth), 25
Sentimentality, 337, 410, 416
Setting, 18–19, 395–396
Sex, marriage, family, children (thematic topic), 598
Shakespeare, William, 213, 306, 530, 567
"Shawl, The" (Cynthia Ozick), 4, 23, 499–505
Shelley, Mary Wollstonecraft, 604
Ship of Fools (Katherine Anne Porter), 359
"Shore, The" (Alain Robbe-Grillet), 3, 4, 17, 572–574

Short Stories of John Cheever, The, 415
Short Story Proper, The: The First Age, 71–255
Showing and telling, 14, 19
"Silent Snow, Secret Snow" (Conrad Aiken), 348–359
"Simple Heart, A" (Gustave Flaubert), 20, 145–166
Simpletons and underdogs (thematic topic), 600
"Sin of Jesus, The" (Isaac Babel), 367–369
Situation, 17
"Sleeping Beauty, The," 44
Smoke (Ivan Turgenev), 114
Snapshots (Alain Robbe-Grillet), 572
Snow White (Donald Barthelme), 588–589
"Solipsist" (Fredric Brown), 4, 21, 555–556
Solotaroff, Theodore, 432
Solzhenitsyn, Aleksandr I., 11, 449–450
Sons and Lovers (D. H. Lawrence), 337
Sot-Weed Factor, The (John Barth), 580
Sound and the Fury, The (William Faulkner), 384
South, the, 359, 384, 409, 443, 469
"Southern Renascence, The," 409
Southey, Robert, 44
Space on My Hands (Fredric Brown), 555
Spring Snow (Yukio Mishima), 484
Stein, Gertrude, 396
Steiner, George, 3
Stephen Hero (James Joyce), 9
Stevick, Philip, 4, 10, 17
Stories and Texts for Nothing (Samuel Beckett), 535
Stories of Three Decades (Thomas Mann), 257
Story (*see* Plot)

Stowe, Harriet Beecher, 113
Stream-of-consciousness, 305, 409
Successful Love and Other Stories (Delmore Schwartz), 556
Suggestion, 7–8, 212–213
Sukenick, Ronald, 17
Summer Knowledge (Delmore Schwartz), 556
Sun Also Rises, The (Ernest Hemingway), 396
Surrealism, 3, 562, 605
Symbol, symbolic, symbolism, 8, 21–22, 71–72, 239, 306, 347, 396, 499, 503, 547, 566–567, 605

"Taboo" (Enrique Anderson Imbert), 4
Tales of Soldiers and Civilians (Ambrose Bierce), 166
Tanner, Tony, 588–589
Taras Bulba (Nikolai Gogol), 81
Tate, Allen, 144
Temple of Dawn, The (Yukio Mishima), 484
Tender is the Night (F. Scott Fitzgerald), 370
Tentation de Saint-Antoine, La (Gustave Flaubert), 144
"That Evening Sun" (William Faulkner), 23
them (Joyce Carol Oates), 510
Theme (and subject), 22–23, 347, 360, 370, 383–384, 395, 444, 450, 469–470, 499, 506, 535, 594–595, 598
Things of This World (Richard Wilbur), 458
Third person intimate (point of view), 14–15, 20, 173
This Side of Paradise (F. Scott Fitzgerald), 370
Three Sisters, The (Anton Chekhov), 213

"Tickets, Please" (D. H. Lawrence), 23, 329–336
Timid and the brave, the (thematic topic), 600
To the Lighthouse (Virginia Woolf), 305
Todd, Richard, 589
Tolstoy, Leo, 114, 450
Tone, 15–16, 19, 101, 359, 364, 395–396, 409, 416
Tonio Kröger (Thomas Mann), 257
Tragedy, 404, 432
Train was on Time, The (Heinrich Böll), 566
Traveller, If You Come to Spa (Heinrich Böll), 566
Trial, The (Franz Kafka), 311
Trilling, Lionel, 3
Triumph of the Egg, The (Sherwood Anderson), 283
Trois Contes (Gustave Flaubert), 145
Trust (Cynthia Ozick), 498
Turgenev, Ivan, 18, 80, 113–114, 200, 283
Twice-Told Tales (Nathaniel Hawthorne), 71
Two Cheers for Democracy (E. M. Forster), 289
Typee (Herman Melville), 121

Ultraísmo, 529
Ulysses (James Joyce), 299
Uncle Vanya (Anton Chekhov), 213
Unnamable, The (Samuel Beckett), 535
Unreliable witness, 14
Unspeakable Practices, Unnatural Acts (Donald Barthelme), 589
Updike, John, 3, 4, 8, 14, 38, 39, 502–503
Ushant (Conrad Aiken), 347

Vande Kieft, Ruth, 409
Vennewitz, Leila, 567

Vershiny, Peter Burgskie, 546
Voice, 13, 571
Voyage Out, The (Virginia Woolf), 305

"Waiting, The" (Jorge Luis Borges), 530–532
Waiting for Godot (Samuel Beckett), 535
Walking to Sleep (Richard Wilbur), 458
War and peace (thematic topic), 600
Warren, Robert Penn, 409
Waves, The (Virginia Woolf), 6, 305, 306
Way to Rainy Mountain, The (N. Scott Momaday), 29
Wells, H. G., 239, 305
Wellwarth, George, 535
Welty, Eudora, 4, 11, 21, 409–410
Wescott, Glenway, 370
Wharton, Edith, 16, 230–231
What I Believe (E. M. Forster), 289
What Mad Universe (Fredric Brown), 555
What We Talk About When We Talk About Love (Raymond Carver), 506
Where Angels Fear to Tread (E. M. Forster), 289
"Where Are You Going, Where Have You Been?" (Joyce Carol Oates), 19, 20, 511–522

White Jacket (Herman Melville), 121
Whoroscope (Samuel Beckett), 535
Wilbur, Richard, 38, 457–458
Wilde, Oscar, 484
Will You Please Be Quiet, Please? (Raymond Carver), 506
Wind in the Willows, The (Kenneth Grahame), 44
Winesburg, Ohio (Sherwood Anderson), 283
Wizard of Oz, The (L. Frank Baum), 44
Women in Love (D. H. Lawrence), 317, 337
Wood, Michael, 506
Woodruff, Stuart C., 166
Woolf, Virginia, 6*n*., 213, 305–306, 337
World is a Wedding, The (Delmore Schwartz), 556
"Worn Path, The" (Eudora Welty), 410–415
Wright, Richard, 22, 399–400
Writer's Diary, A (Virginia Woolf), 305

Yarmolinsky, Avrahm, 216
Yeats, John Butler, 556
Young, Wayland, 547

"Zakhar the Pouch" (Aleksandr I. Solzhenitsyn), 450
Zola, Emile, 200, 239